1997

HISTORIC
DOCUMENTS
OF
1997

1997

HISTORIC
DOCUMENTS
OF
1997

Cumulative Index, 1993–1997

Congressional Quarterly Inc.

Historic Documents of 1997

Editors: Marty Gottron, John Felton, Bruce Maxwell
Production and Associate Editor: Kerry V. Kern
Indexer: Victoria Agee

"Kids These Days: What Americans Really Think About the Next Generation," copyright 1997 by Public Agenda. Reprinted courtesy of Public Agenda, New York, N.Y.

"End-of-Life Care," *JAMA,* June 18, 1997; copyright 1997 by the American Medical Association. Reprinted courtesy of the American Medical Association, Chicago, Ill.

The Library of Congress cataloged the first issue of this title as follows:

Historic documents. 1972–
    Washington. Congressional Quarterly Inc.

    1. United States — Politics and government — 1945– — Yearbooks.
2. World politics — 1945– — Yearbooks. I. Congressional Quarterly Inc.

E839.5H57   917.3'03'9205   72-97888

ISBN 1-56802-385-5
ISSN 0892-080X

PREFACE

The tides of democratization and economic interdependence—two of the most important global trends of the 1990s—continued their seemingly unstoppable advance in 1997. Iran and South Korea, nations with long histories of authoritarian regimes, elected populist presidents. The new Korean president, Kim Dae-jung, had been one of the world's most durable opposition leaders for nearly three decades, having survived at least two government attempts to kill him. Iran's new president was a respected clergyman who appeared more willing than the nation's other Islamic leaders to improve relations with the West, particularly the United States.

In Africa, Zaire's dictatorial leader fell from power in a popularly supported rebellion that demonstrated the inevitable weakness of authoritarian regimes. Great Britain, one of the world's oldest democracies, celebrated its heritage with an election that turned the Conservative Party out of power after eighteen years in favor of a Labour Party leader who copied many pages from President Bill Clinton's political play book.

Of course there were exceptions to the trend. The fragile process of establishing democracy in war-torn Cambodia was blocked in July when one of two co-prime ministers ousted the other and then took only halting steps toward new elections. And there were no indications that the communist regime in China was getting ready to embrace democracy. Deng Xiaoping, China's paramount leader for more than fifteen years, died in February, leaving a legacy of astounding economic growth for his country but no progress toward an open political system. China's president, Jiang Zemin, traveled to Washington in October for a summit meeting with President Clinton. Jiang made some headway in repairing relations between the two powers, which had been deeply troubled since Beijing's brutal crackdown on student pro-democracy demonstrators in 1989.

Anyone who doubted the vital role of economics in international affairs received a rude awakening in the second half of the year, when a currency crisis that started in Thailand rippled across East Asia and eventually caused upheavals in financial markets worldwide. The crisis put an end—at least for the time being—to surging economic growth in a group of countries that had been known as "tigers," including Thailand, Indonesia, Malaysia, and South Korea. Even Hong Kong, one of the world's economic powerhouses, felt the

How to Use This Book

The documents are arranged in chronological order. If you know the approximate date of the report, speech, statement, court decision, or other document you are looking for, glance through the titles for that month in the table of contents.

If the table of contents does not lead you directly to the document you want, turn to the index at the end of the book. There you may find references not only to the particular document you seek but also to other entries on the same or a related subject. The index in this volume is a five-year cumulative index of *Historic Documents* covering the years 1993–1997. There is a separate volume, *Historic Documents Index, 1972–1995*, which may also be useful.

The introduction to each document is printed in italic type. The document itself, printed in roman type, follows the spelling, capitalization, and punctuation of the original or official copy. Where the full text is not given, omissions of material are indicated by the customary ellipsis points.

economic pain in October, just three months after it passed from British control to become once again a part of China.

The sudden dip in Asia, especially Hong Kong, led on October 27 to the biggest one-day fall in a decade in the U.S. stock markets. The markets later recovered but the United States was one of many countries having to put up billions of dollars in emergency loans to bail the Asian nations out of trouble.

An experiment in international cooperation with the potential for an enormous economic and environmental impact on the entire world got under way in Kyoto, Japan, in December. More than 150 nations signed a treaty intended to limit the emissions of "greenhouse gases," which many scientists said were gradually causing climate changes around the globe. If fully implemented—a prospect in great doubt at the end of the year—the treaty would force the United States and other industrialized nations to curtail their burning of coal and petroleum products. President Clinton and other proponents said the United States could live with the treaty's mandates, but opponents insisted the treaty would cause undue economic hardship and force Americans to reduce their standard of living.

Other treaties played an important role on the international scene. The U.S. Senate in April approved ratification of a United Nations treaty banning the production and use of chemical weapons. Some conservatives had opposed the treaty, and delayed its ratification in 1996, because of concerns that it infringed on U.S. sovereignty.

The Clinton administration stood aloof in December as 123 nations signed another treaty banning the production and use of antipersonnel land mines. Worldwide support for that treaty was built by nongovernmental organizations and the government of Canada. In refusing to sign it, Clinton bowed to the wishes of military leaders who hesitated to give up land mines in such places as the Korean peninsula, where nearly 40,000 U.S. troops were helping protect South Korea against the possibility of an attack by North Korea.

Two high-level panels issued warnings that U.S. national security faced new dangers in the post-cold war era. One committee appointed by Clinton said key elements of the nation's infrastructure—highways, telecommunications systems, and industrial plants—were increasingly vulnerable to attack by terrorists or the malicious. That panel recommended dozens of steps to strengthen security, especially of increasingly important computer networks. Another Defense Department panel, mandated by Congress, warned that the nation's military was ill-prepared to meet the challenges of terrorism and blackmail from rogue nations capable of deploying nuclear, chemical, or biological weapons against the United States. That panel urged an immediate review of Pentagon priorities to place more emphasis on nonconventional security threats.

Such reexaminations of national security issues came as yet another closing chapter was written in the history of the cold war. The North Atlantic Treaty Organization (NATO) in July formally extended membership to three nations that had been part of the Soviet bloc: Hungary, Poland, and the Czech Republic. This move eastward made NATO a next-door neighbor of Russia, a development that caused considerable consternation in Moscow, especially among ultranationalists who feared domination by the West.

Partly to placate the Russians, the world's most exclusive and powerful club—the leading industrialized nations known as the G-7—officially embraced Russia as the eighth member during a summit meeting in Denver. Russian membership in that economic fraternity consisted more of symbolism than substance. Despite its vast potential Russia remained a second- or even third-rate economic power that had little influence over the weighty matters pondered at the annual economic summits.

President Clinton had good news to offer his fellow summiteers in June: the U.S. economy continued its strong pattern of growth with low inflation and unemployment. His aides at that point were negotiating with congressional leaders on the details of an agreement for a balanced federal budget by 2002. A final agreement came in August, resolving, at least for the moment, what had been one of the most contentious issues in U.S. national affairs.

The temporarily mellow political atmosphere in Washington did not extend to other issues. For most of the year the capital was convulsed with allegations surrounding the Democratic Party's desperate rush to collect campaign dollars for the 1996 election. Two congressional committees, the Justice Department, and a sizable army of news reporters investigated alleged wrongdoing by the Democrats—with some attention given to the even more successful fund-raising efforts of the Republicans. Numerous lapses of judgment came to light, especially on the part of the Clinton White House, but little evidence emerged that any public official broke the nation's loosely written campaign finance laws.

Attorney General Janet Reno refused to ask for appointment of an independent counsel to investigate allegations that Clinton and Vice President Al Gore may have acted unethically or even illegally. To the fury of Republicans, Reno said "thousands of hours" of work by Justice Department investigators had uncovered no illegal actions by the president or vice president.

All the political noise generated about campaign finance produced a predictable result on Capitol Hill: Legislation to reform the system under which politicians raised money for federal campaigns went nowhere. The House refused to consider the matter, and a brief debate on a reform bill in the Senate was quashed by the Republican leadership.

Clinton's efforts to defer another political hot potato at least until after he left office came to naught, when the Supreme Court ruled that a sitting president could be sued for damages arising out of his personal conduct. That ruling cleared the way for the sexual harassment suit against the president brought by Paula Jones, who said the president forced unwanted sexual attentions upon her when he was governor of Arkansas and she was a state employee. The case subsequently was dismissed.

In another important decision, the Supreme Court left squarely in the political arena the question of whether doctors should be legally able to help the terminally ill commit suicide. In rulings upholding two state laws that barred physician-assisted suicide, the Court said individuals did not have a general constitutional right to such assistance but suggested this issue was one that the people should deal with through their elected representatives. In another decision that angered many members of Congress, the Court overturned a federal law aimed at strengthening freedom for religious practices. After the Court ruled that Congress, in enacting the law, had unconstitutionally encroached on the traditional rights of the states and the role of the judiciary, several members began to search for a way to accomplish the same goal without running afoul of the Constitution.

The U.S. government at several points during the year attempted to address citizens' concerns about its other failures. The army in September acknowledged that female soldiers had not always been treated with the greatest respect; in fact, an official army panel said, drill sergeants and others had used their positions of authority to intimidate women and demand sexual favors from them. Among the panel's recommendations was placing greater emphasis on traditional army values such as personal honor and integrity.

Yet another investigation, by the National Cancer Institute, confirmed that U.S. above-ground atomic tests in the late 1940s and early 1950s may have heightened the risk of thyroid cancer among thousands of Americans. The study, in the works for fourteen years, made no definitive statements, however, on how many people may have developed cancer because of the tests.

The nation's premier tax collection agency, the Internal Revenue Service (IRS), formally apologized to several taxpayers who told a Senate committee the agency had unjustly persecuted them. Congressional hearings on alleged abuses by the IRS gave Republicans a popular issue to use against the Clinton administration and the tax system in general.

Revelations about the IRS bolstered the cynicism about government that was increasingly evident among Americans in the late 1990s. A commission appointed by the president and congressional leaders said in March that the government was fostering that cynicism by keeping too many secrets too long. The panel said government agencies should sharply reduce the number of documents stamped "secret" and should be more systematic in declassifying documents once any justified need for secrecy had passed.

The government also acknowledged that key elements of the FBI's crime laboratory had not always adhered to the highest standards of scientific investigation. Some analysts at the laboratory had drawn unwarranted conclusions from evidence before them, used questionable techniques, and presented flawed testimony in dozens of cases, according to an internal Justice Department investigation.

Those revelations about the FBI came into play during the nation's most important criminal trial of the year. Defense lawyers representing Timothy McVeigh—accused of planting the bomb that destroyed the federal building in Oklahoma City in 1995, killing 168 and injuring hundreds—argued that the FBI's evaluation of evidence from the bombing scene could not be trusted. That argument, along with others presented by the defense, failed to sway the jury, which convicted McVeigh of conspiracy and murder and sentenced him to death. Another jury in December convicted McVeigh's codefendant, Terry Nichols, of the lesser charges of conspiracy and manslaughter. Nichols escaped the death penalty when the jury was unable to reach agreement on a sentence.

Another long legal saga came to an end in February when a jury in a civil trial in Los Angeles found former football star O.J. Simpson responsible for the 1994 death of his former wife Nicole Simpson and a friend. Simpson was ordered to pay $33.5 million in damages to the families of the victims. Another jury in 1995 had acquitted Simpson on criminal charges in the case.

The event of 1997 that most people were likely to remember, however, was the death of Diana, Princess of Wales, in a car accident in Paris at the end of August. Diana's life—from her marriage to Prince Charles, the heir to the British throne, to the births of her sons, to the tawdry accusations of infidelity and instability that preceded her divorce, to her liaison with playboy Dodi Fayed—seemed to hold endless fascination for the British public and much of the rest of the world. Her death brought forth an outpouring of public grief nearly unparalleled in modern history.

These are only some of the topics of national and international interest chosen by the editors for *Historic Documents of 1997*. This edition marks the twenty-sixth volume of a Congressional Quarterly project that began with *Historic Documents of 1972*. The purpose of the series is to give students, librarians, journalists, scholars, and others convenient access to documents on a wide range of topics that set forth some of the most important issues of the year. In our judgment, the official statements, news conferences, speeches, special studies, and court decisions presented here will be of lasting interest.

Each document is preceded by an introduction that provides context and background material and, when relevant, an account of continuing developments during the year. We believe these introductions will become increasingly useful as memories of current times fade.

John Felton and Marty Gottron

CONTENTS

January

February

March

April

May

June

July

August

September

October

CONTENTS

November

December

January

SPECIAL COUNSEL ON
GINGRICH ETHICS VIOLATIONS
January 17, 1997

Newt Gingrich, the firebrand partisan who taught conservative Republicans how to be political revolutionaries, nearly reaped the whirlwind of his teachings in 1997. Gingrich became the first sitting Speaker of the House ever to be reprimanded for ethics violations. Five months later, dissatisfied colleagues—including some of his most trusted lieutenants—briefly plotted to oust him from the Speakership.

Gingrich survived those challenges and even gained some temporary political strength within his House majority party. But at year's end he remained the most unpopular politician of national stature, a leader no longer able to command broad public support for his dramatic ideas to reshape American government.

The Gingrich Ethics Case

The Speaker's political troubles began in late 1995, when he overplayed his hand by forcing two prolonged shutdowns of much of the federal government during a budget confrontation with President Bill Clinton. Then in December 1996 a four-member subcommittee of the House Committee on Standards of Official Conduct (known as the ethics committee) wound up a two-year investigation into charges that Gingrich had improperly used two nonprofit foundations to advance his political causes. The panel ruled on December 21, 1996, that Gingrich had violated House rules—a ruling he accepted. (Budget dispute, Historic Documents of 1995, p. 737; Ethics case, Historic Documents of 1996, p. 838)

Despite the cloud of the ethics case, Gingrich won reelection as Speaker on January 7, after an all-out lobbying campaign by his aides quelled opposition within the Republican Party. Gingrich received 216 votes and minority leader Richard A. Gephardt of Missouri received 205 votes. In an unusual rebuke to a Speaker, five Republicans voted "present" rather than support Gingrich, and four others voted for someone else. Among the latter four was Jim Leach of Iowa, the respected chairman of the Banking and

Financial Services Committee, who had called for Gingrich to step down as Speaker.

Ten days later, on January 17, the full ethics committee held a six-hour hearing on the charges against Gingrich. At that hearing, special counsel James M. Cole, hired by the ethics subcommittee to investigate the Gingrich case, released a strongly worded 213-page report detailing the allegations against Gingrich. In the report and in his testimony before the ethics committee, Cole described how Gingrich had created a network of tax-exempt foundations to finance a nationally televised "town hall" and a college course, both of which were key elements of his partisan strategy to wrest control of Congress from the Democrats. The foundations received donations from loyal Republicans, who received federal tax deductions for their "charitable" gifts. That arrangement violated federal tax law, Cole said.

More important, from a political point of view, was Gingrich's response to the ethics committee investigation of these matters. Through his lawyers, Gingrich on October 4, 1994, December 8, 1994, and March 27, 1996, sent the ethics panel letters denying that his activities and those of his foundations were political. Both letters contained statements the committee later found to be false, incomplete, and misleading. Gingrich blamed his former lawyer, Jan Baran, for these lapses. But Cole and the committee noted that the Speaker reviewed the letters before they were sent and should have known that they contained inaccurate information.

Cole said he was convinced that Gingrich had lied to the ethics subcommittee in hopes of thwarting the inquiry. The committee itself was not willing to accept Cole's harsh conclusion. However, Cole said, the committee did conclude that Gingrich's actions were either "reckless" or an "intentional" violation of the law and House rules. In its report, the panel said Gingrich's responses to the investigation had "caused a controversy over the matter to arise, and last for a substantial period of time, it disrupted the operations of the House, and it cost the House a substantial amount of money in order to determine the facts."

After hearing Cole's testimony and a rebuttal by two lawyers for Gingrich, the committee voted 7–1 to accept its subcommittee's recommendation to reprimand Gingrich. The lone dissenter was Republican Lamar Smith of Texas, a staunch supporter of the Speaker. The committee also voted to require Gingrich to pay a $300,000 penalty, which was described as a reimbursement to the House for the expense of the investigation.

Accepting the committee recommendation, the full House on January 21 voted 395–28 to reprimand the Speaker and require him to pay the $300,000 penalty. Even Gingrich's most ardent Republican supporters acknowledged that he had made mistakes. Rep. Tom DeLay of Texas said: "What he's charged with today is, during the process, he happened to screw up." A much harsher assessment came from ethics committee member Nancy Pelosi, D-Calif., who said that Gingrich, "in his dealings with the committee, is not to be believed."

The action represented the only time the House had ever voted to impose an ethics penalty against a sitting Speaker. Jim Wright, a Texas Democrat, resigned as Speaker in 1989, thereby avoiding a vote by the full House on charges brought by the ethics committee. Wright's chief nemesis was a back-bench Republican named Newt Gingrich. (Wright investigation, Historic Documents of 1989, p. 239)

Gingrich announced April 17 that he would pay the penalty by borrowing the $300,000 from former Senate majority leader Bob Dole. Gingrich told the House that it was "the right thing to do" for him to pay the penalty personally, rather than from leftover campaign funds. He insisted the loan from Dole was a personal debt that he would repay. Dole and Gingrich had never been close political allies.

The Speaker's plan to use Bob Dole's money to pay the penalty failed to satisfy critics, who said Gingrich was seeking to delay, and possibly avoid altogether, any personal sacrifice as a result of his wrongdoing. In response to such criticism, Gingrich later negotiated a revised payment procedure with the ethics committee. Under that plan, Gingrich agreed to pay half the penalty himself, starting with a $50,000 check on May 15, with the remainder coming from the Dole loan, which carried a 10 percent interest rate.

A Failed "Coup"

In the weeks following the humiliation of a reprimand by his House colleagues, Gingrich showed few signs of having learned any lessons from the ethics controversy. Fellow conservatives complained that he was failing to establish and follow a serious legislative agenda. His often erratic actions—including threats and taunts against members of his own party—revived concerns about his political instincts and leadership abilities. In one incident, on March 20, Gingrich forced eleven conservative Republicans who had rebelled against the party on a procedural issue to stand before their colleagues, like naughty schoolboys, and explain themselves.

In mid-July one of the most extraordinary events in recent congressional history took place: a failed attempt by some of Gingrich's nominal allies to oust him as Speaker. The key events of the coup occurred on July 10, when three senior House Republicans—Majority Leader Dick Armey and Whip Tom DeLay, both of Texas, and Bill Paxon of New York, chairman of the party's leadership meetings—appeared to offer encouragement to a group of some twenty junior members who wanted to oust Gingrich as Speaker. Armey reportedly entertained thoughts of taking Gingrich's place. But Armey and some of the other leaders backed off the plot the next day, July 11, and the attempted coup failed. Within days, news reports gave details of the coup—who was involved and who took what position—bringing the House to a standstill. Paxon was the first victim of the inevitable second-guessing, forced by Gingrich to resign from his leadership position. By mid-August Gingrich had reorganized his leadership team to include several new faces, thus diluting the influence of Armey, DeLay, and others whose loyalty he now had reason to question.

In the immediate aftermath, there was a consensus that Gingrich emerged from the failed coup in a stronger position within his own party. Many Republicans saw the Speaker as the victim of devious plotting by traitorous subalterns. Even so, the incident was yet another reminder of Gingrich's failure to unite his party, much less the general public, behind his vision for America.

Following are excerpts from the report issued January 17, 1997, by James M. Cole, special counsel to the subcommittee of the House Committee on Standards of Official Conduct, summarizing its investigation into an ethics complaint against Speaker Newt Gingrich, R-Ga.:

C. Summary of the Subcommittee's Factual Findings

The Subcommittee found that in regard to two projects, Mr. Gingrich engaged in activity involving 501(c)(3) organizations that was substantially motivated by partisan, political goals. The Subcommittee also found that Mr. Gingrich provided the Committee with material information about one of those projects that was inaccurate, incomplete, and unreliable.

1. AOW/ACTV

The first project was a television program called the American Opportunities Workshop (AOW). It took place in May 1990. The idea for this project came from Mr. Gingrich and he was principally responsible for developing its message. AOW involved broadcasting a television program on the subject of various governmental issues. Mr. Gingrich hoped that this program would help create a "citizens' movement." Workshops were set up throughout the country where people could gather to watch the program and be recruited for the citizens' movement. While the program was educational, the citizens' movement was also considered a tool to recruit non-voters and people who were apolitical to the Republican Party. The program was deliberately free of any references to Republicans or partisan politics because Mr. Gingrich believed such references would dissuade the target audience of non-voters from becoming involved.

AOW started out as a project of GOPAC, a political action committee dedicated to, among other things, achieving Republican control of the United States House of Representatives.

Its methods for accomplishing this goal included the development and articulation of a political message and the dissemination of that message as widely as possible. One such avenue of dissemination was AOW. The program, however, consumed a substantial portion of GOPAC's revenues. Because of the expense, Mr. Gingrich and others at GOPAC decided to transfer the project to a 501(c)(3) organization in order to attract tax-deductible funding. The 501(c)(3) organization chosen was the Abraham Lincoln Opportunity Foundation (ALOF).

ALOF was dormant at the time and was revived to sponsor AOW's successor, American Citizens' Television (ACTV). ALOF operated out of GOPAC's offices. Virtually all its officers and employers were simultaneously GOPAC officers or employees. ACTV had the same educational aspects and partisan, political goals as AOW. The principal difference between the two was that ACTV used approximately $260,000 in tax-deductible contributions to fund its operations. ACTV broadcast three television programs in 1990 and then ceased operations. The last program was funded by a 501(c)(4) organization because the show's content was deemed to be too political for a 501(c)(3) organization.

2. Renewing American Civilization

The second project utilizing 501(c)(3) organizations involved a college course taught by Mr. Gingrich called Renewing American Civilization. Mr. Gingrich developed the course as a subset to and tool of a larger political and cultural movement also called Renewing American Civilization. The goal of this movement, as stated by Mr. Gingrich, was the replacement of the "welfare state" with an "opportunity society." A primary means of achieving this goal was the development of the movement's message and the dissemination of that message as widely as possible. Mr. Gingrich intended that a "Republican majority" would be the heart of the movement and that the movement would "professionalize" House Republicans. A method for achieving these goals was to use the movement's message to "attract voters, resources, and candidates." According to Mr. Gingrich, the course was, among other things, a primary and essential means to develop and disseminate the message of the movement.

The core message of the movement and the course was that the welfare state had failed, that it could not be repaired but had to be replaced, and that it had to be replaced with an opportunity society based on what Mr. Gingrich called the "Five Pillars of American Civilization." These were: 1) personal strength; 2) entrepreneurial free enterprise; 3) the spirit of invention; 4) quality as defined by Edwards Deming; and 5) the lessons of American history. The message also concentrated on three substantive areas. These were: 1) jobs and economic growth; 2) health; and 3) saving the inner city.

This message was also Mr. Gingrich's main campaign theme in 1993 and 1994 and Mr. Gingrich sought to have Republican candidates adopt the Renewing American Civilization message in their campaigns. In the context of political campaigns, Mr. Gingrich used the term "welfare state" as a negative label for Democrats and the term "opportunity society" as a positive label for Republicans.

As General Chairman of GOPAC, Mr. Gingrich decided that GOPAC would use Renewing American Civilization as its political message and theme during 1993–1994. GOPAC, however, was having financial difficulties and could not afford to disseminate its political messages as it had in past years. GOPAC had a number of roles in regard to the course. For example, GOPAC personnel helped develop, manage, promote, and raise funds for the course.

GOPAC Charter Members helped develop the idea to teach the course as a means for communicating GOPAC's message. GOPAC Charter Members at Charter Meetings helped develop the content of the course. GOPAC was "better off" as a result of the nationwide dissemination of the Renewing American Civilization message via the course in that the message GOPAC had adopted and determined to be the one that would help it achieve its goals was broadcast widely and at no cost to GOPAC.

The course was taught at Kennesaw State College (KSC) in 1993 and at Reinhardt College in 1994 and 1995. Each course consisted of ten lectures and each lecture consisted of approximately four hours of classroom instruction, for a total of forty hours. Mr. Gingrich taught twenty hours of each course and his co-teacher, or occasionally a guest lecturer, taught twenty hours. Students from each of the colleges as well as people who were not students attended the lectures. Mr. Gingrich's 20-hour portion of the course was taped and distributed to remote sites, referred to as "site hosts," via satellite, videotape and cable television. As with AOW/ACTV, Renewing American Civilization involved setting up workshops around the country where people could gather to watch the course. While the course was educational, Mr. Gingrich intended that the workshops would be, among other things, a recruiting tool for GOPAC and the Republican Party.

The major costs for the Renewing American Civilization course were for dissemination of the lectures. This expense was primarily paid for by tax-deductible contributions made to the 501(c)(3) organizations that sponsored the course. Over the three years the course was broadcast, approximately $1.2 million was spent on the project. The Kennesaw State College Foundation (KSCF) sponsored the course the first year. All funds raised were turned over to KSCF and dedicated exclusively for the use of the Renewing American Civilization course.

KSCF did not, however, manage the course and its role was limited to depositing donations into its bank account and paying bills from that account that were presented to it by the Dean of the KSC Business School. KSCF contracted with the Washington Policy Group, Inc. (WPG) to manage and raise funds for the course's development, production and distribution. Jeffrey Eisenach, GOPAC's Executive Director from June 1991 to June 1993 was the president and sole owner of WPG. WPG and Mr. Eisenach played similar roles with respect to AOW/ACTV.

When the contract between WPG and KSCF ended in the fall of 1993, the Progress and Freedom Foundation (PFF) assumed the role WPG had with the course at the same rate of compensation. Mr. Eisenach was PFF's founder and president. Shortly after PFF took over the management of the course, the Georgia Board of Regents passed a resolution prohibiting any elected official from teaching at a Georgia state educational institution. This was the culmination of a controversy that had arisen around the course at KSC. A group of KSC faculty had objected to the course being taught on the campus because of a belief that it was an effort to use the college to disseminate a political message. Because of the Board of Regents' decision and the controversy, it was decided that the course would be moved to a private college.

The course was moved to Reinhardt for the 1994 and 1995 sessions. While there, PFF assumed full responsibility for the course. PFF no longer received payments to run the course but, instead, took in all contributions to the course and paid all the bills, including paying Reinhardt for the use of the college's video production facilities. All funds for the course were raised by and expended by PFF under its tax-exempt status.

3. Failure to Seek Legal Advice

Under the Internal Revenue Code, a 501(c)(3) organization must be operated exclusively for exempt purposes. The presence of a single non-exempt purpose, if more than insubstantial in nature, will destroy the exemption regardless of the number or importance of truly exempt purposes. Conferring a benefit on private interests is a non-exempt purpose. Under the Internal Revenue Code, a 501(c)(3) organization is also prohibited from intervening in a political campaign or providing any support to a political action committee. These prohibitions reflect congressional concerns that taxpayer funds not be used to subsidize political activity.

During the Preliminary Inquiry, the Subcommittee consulted with an expert in the law of tax-exempt organizations and read materials on the subject. Mr. Gingrich's activities on behalf of AOW/ACTV and Renewing American Civilization, as well as the activities of others on behalf of those projects done with Mr. Gingrich's knowledge and approval, were reviewed by the expert. The expert concluded that those activities violated the status of the organizations under section 501(c)(3) in that, among other things, those activities were intended to confer more than insubstantial benefits on GOPAC, Mr. Gingrich, and Republican entities and candidates, and provided support to GOPAC.

At Mr. Gingrich's request, the Subcommittee also heard from tax counsel retained by Mr. Gingrich for the purposes of the Preliminary Inquiry. While that counsel is an experienced tax attorney with a sterling reputation, he has less experience in dealing with tax-exempt organizations law than does the expert retained by the Subcommittee. According to Mr. Gingrich's tax counsel, the type of activity involved in the AOW/ACTV and Renewing American Civilization projects would not violate the status of the relevant organizations under section 501(c)(3). He opined that once it was determined that an activity was "educational," as defined by the IRS, and did not have the effect of benefiting a private interest, it did not violate the private benefit prohibition. In the view of Mr. Gingrich's tax counsel, motivation on the part of an organization's principals and agents is irrelevant. Further, he opined that a 501(c)(3) organization does not violate the private benefit prohibition or political campaign prohibition through close association with or support of a political action committee unless it specifically calls for the election or defeat of an identifiable political candidate.

Both the Subcommittee's tax expert and Mr. Gingrich's tax counsel, how-ever, agreed that had Mr. Gingrich sought their advice before embarking on activities of the type involved in AOW/ACTV and the Renewing American Civ-ilization course, each of them would have advised Mr. Gingrich not to use a 501(c)(3) organization as he had in regard to those activities. The Subcom-mittee's tax expert said that doing so would violate 501(c)(3). During his appearance before the Subcommittee, Mr. Gingrich's tax counsel said that he would not have recommended the use of 501(c)(3) organizations to sponsor the course because the combination of politics and 501(c)(3) organizations is an "explosive mix" almost certain to draw the attention of the IRS.

Based on the evidence, it was clear that Mr. Gingrich intended that the AOW/ACTV and Renewing American Civilization projects have substantial partisan, political purposes. In addition, he was aware that political activi-ties in the context of 501(c)(3) organizations were problematic. Prior to embarking on these projects, Mr. Gingrich had been involved with another organization that had direct experience with the private benefit prohibition in a political context, the American Campaign Academy. In a 1989 Tax Court opinion issued less than a year before Mr. Gingrich set the AOW/ACTV pro-ject into motion, the Academy was denied its exemption under 501(c)(3) because, although educational, it conferred an impermissible private bene-fit on Republican candidates and entities. Close associates of Mr. Gingrich were principals in the American Campaign Academy, Mr. Gingrich taught at the Academy, and Mr. Gingrich had been briefed at the time on the tax controversy surrounding the Academy. In addition, Mr. Gingrich stated publicly that he was taking a very aggressive approach to the use of 501(c)(3) organizations in regard to, at least, the Renewing American Civi-lization course.

Taking into account Mr. Gingrich's background, experience, and sophisti-cation with respect to tax-exempt organizations, and his status as a Member of Congress obligated to maintain high ethical standards, the Subcommittee concluded that Mr. Gingrich should have known to seek appropriate legal advice to ensure that his conduct in regard to the AOW/ACTV and Renewing American Civilization projects was in compliance with 501(c)(3). Had he sought and followed such advice—after having set out all the relevant facts, circumstances, plans, and goals described above—501(c)(3) organizations would not have been used to sponsor Mr. Gingrich's ACTV and Renewing American Civilization projects.

4. Mr. Gingrich's Statements to the Committee

In responding to the complaints filed against him concerning the Renew-ing American Civilization course, Mr. Gingrich submitted several letters to the Committee. His first letter, dated October 4, 1994, did not address the tax issues raised in Mr. Jones' complaint, but rather responded to the part of the complaint concerning unofficial use of official resources.

In it Mr. Gingrich stated that GOPAC, among other organizations, paid peo-ple to work on the course. After this response, the Committee wrote Mr. Gingrich and asked him specifically to address issues related to whether the course had a partisan, political aspect to it and, if so, whether it was appropriate for a 501(c)(3) organization to be used to sponsor the course. The Committee also specifically asked whether GOPAC had any relationship to the course. Mr. Gingrich's letter in response, dated December 8, 1994, was prepared by his attorney, but it was read, approved, and signed by Mr. Gingrich. It stated that the course had no partisan, political aspects to it, that his motivation for teaching the course was not political, and that GOPAC neither was involved in nor received any benefit from any aspect of the course. In his testimony before the Subcommittee, Mr. Gingrich admitted that these statements were not true.

When the amended complaint was filed with the Committee in January 1995, Mr. Gingrich's attorney responded to the complaint on behalf of Mr. Gingrich in a letter dated March 27, 1995. His attorney addressed all the issues in the amended complaint, including the issues related to the Renewing American Civilization course. The letter was signed by Mr. Gingrich's attorney, but Mr. Gingrich reviewed and approved it prior to its being delivered to the Committee. In an interview with Mr. Cole, Mr. Gingrich stated that if he had seen anything inaccurate in the letter he would have instructed his attorney to correct it. Similar to the December 8, 1994 letter, the March 27, 1995 letter stated that the course had no partisan, political aspects to it, that Mr. Gingrich's motivation for teaching the course was not political, and that GOPAC had no involvement in nor received any benefit from any aspect of the course. In his testimony before the Subcommittee, Mr. Gingrich admitted that these statements were not true.

The goal of the letters was to have the complaints dismissed. Of the people involved in drafting or editing the letters, or reviewing them for accuracy, only Mr. Gingrich had personal knowledge of the facts contained in the letters regarding the course. The facts in the letters that were inaccurate, incomplete, and unreliable were material to the Committee's determination on how to proceed with the tax questions contained in the complaints.

D. Statement of Alleged Violation

On December 21, 1996, the Subcommittee issued a Statement of Alleged Violation (SAV) stating that Mr. Gingrich had engaged in conduct that did not reflect creditably on the House of Representatives in that by failing to seek and follow legal advice, Mr. Gingrich failed to take appropriate steps to ensure that activities with respect to the AOW/ACTV project and the Renewing American Civilization project were in accordance with section 501(c)(3); and that on or about December 8, 1994, and on or about March 27, 1995, information was transmitted to the Committee by and on behalf of Mr. Gingrich that was material to matters under consideration by the Committee, which information, as Mr. Gingrich should have known, was inaccurate, incomplete, and unreliable.

On December 21, 1996, Mr. Gingrich filed an answer with the Subcommittee admitting to this violation of House Rules.

IX. Analysis and Conclusion

A. Tax Issues

In reviewing the evidence concerning both the AOW/ACTV project and the Renewing American Civilization project, certain patterns became apparent. In both instances, GOPAC had initiated the use of the messages as part of its political program to build a Republican majority in Congress. In both instances there was an effort to have the material appear to be nonpartisan on its face, yet serve as a partisan, political message for the purpose of building the Republican Party.

Under the "methodology test" set out by the Internal Revenue Service, both projects qualified as educational. However, they both had substantial partisan, political aspects. Both were initiated as political projects and both were motivated, at least in part, by political goals.

The other striking similarity is that, in both situations, GOPAC was in need of a new source of funding for the projects and turned to a 501(c)(3) organization for that purpose.

Once the projects had been established at the 501(c)(3) organizations, however, the same people continued to manage it as had done so at GOPAC, the same message was used as when it was at GOPAC, and the dissemination of the message was directed toward the same goal as when the project was at GOPAC—building the Republican Party. The only significant difference was that the activity was funded by a 501(c)(3) organization.

This was not a situation where one entity develops a message through a course or a television program for purely educational purposes and then an entirely separate entity independently decides to adopt that message for partisan, political purposes. Rather, this was a coordinated effort to have the 501(c)(3) organization help in achieving a partisan, political goal. In both instances the idea to develop the message and disseminate it for partisan, political use came first. The use of the 501(c)(3) came second as a source of funding.

This factual analysis was accepted by all Members of the Subcommittee and the Special Counsel. However, there was a difference of opinion as to the result under 501(c)(3) when applying the law to these facts. Ms. Roady, the Subcommittee's tax expert, was of the opinion that the facts presented a clear violation of 501(c)(3) because the evidence showed that the activities were intended to benefit Mr. Gingrich, GOPAC, and other Republican candidates and entities. Mr. Holden, Mr. Gingrich's tax attorney, disagreed. He found that the course was non-partisan in its content, and even though he assumed that the motivation for disseminating it involved partisan, political goals, he did not find a sufficiently narrow targeting of the dissemination to conclude that it was a private benefit to anyone.

Some Members of the Subcommittee and the Special Counsel agreed with Ms. Roady and concluded that there was a clear violation of 501(c)(3) with respect to AOW/ACTV and Renewing American Civilization. Other Members of the Subcommittee were troubled by reaching this conclusion and believed that the facts of this case presented a unique situation that had not previously been addressed by the legal authorities.

As such, they did not feel comfortable supplanting the functions of the Internal Revenue Service or the Tax Court in rendering a ruling on what they believed to be an unsettled area of the law.

B. Statements Made to the Committee

The letters Mr. Gingrich submitted to the Committee concerning the Renewing American Civilization complaint were very troubling to the Subcommittee. They contained definitive statements about facts that went to the heart of the issues placed before the Committee. In the case of the December 8, 1994 letter, it was in response to a direct request from the Committee for specific information relating to the partisan, political nature of the course and GOPAC's involvement in it.

Both letters were efforts by Mr. Gingrich to have the Committee dismiss the complaints without further inquiry. In such situations, the Committee does and should place great reliance on the statements of Members. The letters were prepared by Mr. Gingrich's lawyers.

After the Subcommittee deposed the lawyers, the reasons for the statements being in the letters was not made any clearer. The lawyers did not conduct any independent factual research.

Looking at the information the lawyers used to write the letters, the Subcommittee was unable to find any factual basis for the inaccurate statements contained therein. A number of exhibits attached to the complaint were fax transmittal sheets from GOPAC.

While this did not on its face establish anything more than GOPAC's fax machine having been used for the project, it certainly should have put the attorneys on notice that there was some relationship between the course and GOPAC that should have been examined before saying that GOPAC had absolutely no involvement in the course.

The lawyers said they relied on Mr. Gingrich and his staff to ensure that the letters were accurate; however, none of Mr. Gingrich's staff had sufficient knowledge to be able to verify the accuracy of the facts. While Mr. Gaylord and Mr. Eisenach did have sufficient knowledge to verify many of the facts, they were not asked to do so. The only person who reviewed the letters for accuracy, with sufficient knowledge to verify those facts, was Mr. Gingrich.

The Subcommittee considered the relevance of the reference to GOPAC in Mr. Gingrich's first letter to the Committee dated October 4, 1994. In that letter he stated that GOPAC was one of the entities that paid people to work on the course. Some Members of the Subcommittee believed that this was evidence of lack of intent to deceive the Committee on Mr. Gingrich's part because if he had planned to hide GOPAC's involvement, he would not have made such an inconsistent statement in the subsequent letters. Other Members of the Subcommittee and the Special Counsel appreciated this point, but believed the first letter was of little value. The statement in that letter was only directed to establishing that Mr. Gingrich had not used congressional resources in developing the course.

The first letter made no attempt to address the tax issues, even though it was a prominent feature of the complaint. When the Committee specifically focused Mr. Gingrich's attention on that issue and questions concerning GOPAC's involvement in the course, his response was not accurate.

During his testimony before the Subcommittee, Mr. Gingrich stated that he did not intend to mislead the Committee and apologized for his conduct. This statement was a relevant consideration for some Members of the Subcommittee, but not for others.

The Subcommittee concluded that because these inaccurate statements were provided to the Committee, this matter was not resolved as expeditiously as it could have been. This caused a controversy over the matter to arise and last for a substantial period of time, it disrupted the operations of the House, and it cost the House a substantial amount of money in order to determine the facts.

C. Statement of Alleged Violation

Based on the information described above, the Special Counsel proposed a Statement of Alleged Violations (SAV) to the Subcommittee on December 12, 1996. The SAV contained three counts:

1) Mr. Gingrich's activities on behalf of ALOF in regard to AOW/ACTV, and the activities of others in that regard with his knowledge and approval, constituted a violation of ALOF's status under section 501(c)(3);

2) Mr. Gingrich's activities on behalf of Kennesaw State College Foundation, the Progress and Freedom Foundation, and Reinhardt College in regard to the Renewing American Civilization course, and the activities of others in that regard with his knowledge and approval, constituted a violation of those organizations' status under section 501(c)(3); and

3) Mr. Gingrich had provided information to the Committee, directly or through counsel, that was material to matters under consideration by the Committee, which Mr. Gingrich knew or should have known was inaccurate, incomplete, and unreliable.

1. Deliberations on the Tax Counts

There was a difference of opinion regarding whether to issue the SAV as drafted on the tax counts. Concern was expressed about deciding this tax issue in the context of an ethics proceeding. This led the discussion to the question of the appropriate focus for the Subcommittee. A consensus began to build around the view that the proper focus was on the conduct of the Member, rather than a resolution of issues of tax law. From the beginning of the Preliminary Inquiry, there was a desire on the part of each of the Members to find a way to reach a unanimous conclusion in this matter. The Members felt it was important to confirm the bipartisan nature of the ethics process.

The discussion turned to what steps Mr. Gingrich had taken in regard to these two projects to ensure they were done in accord with the provisions of 501(c)(3). In particular, the Subcommittee was concerned with the fact that:

1) Mr. Gingrich had been "very well aware" of the American Campaign Academy case prior to embarking [on this] project;

2) he had been involved with 501(c)(3) organizations to a sufficient degree to know that politics and tax-deductible contributions are, as his tax counsel said, an "explosive mix;"

3) he was clearly involved in a project that had significant partisan, political goals, and he had taken an aggressive approach to the tax laws in regard to both AOW/ACTV; and

4) Renewing American Civilization projects. Even Mr. Gingrich's own tax lawyer told the Subcommittee that if Mr. Gingrich had come to him before embarking on these projects, he would have advised him to not use a 501(c)(3) organization for the dissemination of AOW/ACTV or Renewing American Civilization.

Had Mr. Gingrich sought and followed this advice, he would not have used the 501(c)(3) organizations, would not have had his projects subsidized by taxpayer funds, and would not have created this controversy that has caused significant disruption to the House. The Subcommittee concluded that there were significant and substantial warning signals to Mr. Gingrich that he should have heeded prior to embarking on these projects. Despite these warnings, Mr. Gingrich did not seek any legal advice to ensure his conduct conformed with the provisions of 501(c)(3).

In looking at this conduct in light of all the facts and circumstances, the Subcommittee was faced with a disturbing choice. Either Mr. Gingrich did not seek legal advice because he was aware that it would not have permitted him to use a 501(c)(3) organization for his projects, or he was reckless in not taking care that, as a Member of Congress, he made sure that his conduct conformed with the law in an area where he had ample warning that his intended course of action was fraught with legal peril.

The Subcommittee decided that regardless of the resolution of the 501(c)(3) tax question, Mr. Gingrich's conduct in this regard was improper, did not reflect creditably on the House, and was deserving of sanction.

2. Deliberations Concerning the Letters

The Subcommittee's deliberation concerning the letters provided to the Committee centered on the question of whether Mr. Gingrich intentionally submitted inaccurate information. There was a belief that the record developed before the Subcommittee was not conclusive on this point. The Special Counsel suggested that a good argument could be made, based on the record, that Mr. Gingrich did act intentionally, however it would be difficult to establish that with a high degree of certainty.

The culmination of the evidence on this topic again left the Subcommittee with a disturbing choice. Either Mr. Gingrich intentionally made misrepresentations to the Committee, or he was again reckless in the way he provided information to the Committee concerning a very important matter.

The standard applicable to the Subcommittee's deliberations was whether there is reason to believe that Mr. Gingrich had acted as charged in this count of the SAV. All felt that this standard had been met in regard to the allegation that Mr. Gingrich "knew" that the information he provided to the Committee was inaccurate.

However, there was considerable discussion to the effect that if Mr. Gingrich wanted to admit to submitting information to the Committee that he "should have known" was inaccurate, the Subcommittee would consider deleting the allegation that he knew the information was inaccurate.

The Members were of the opinion that if there were to be a final adjudication of the matter, taking into account the higher standard of proof that is involved at that level, "should have known" was an appropriate framing of the charge in light of all the facts and circumstances.

3. Discussions with Mr. Gingrich's Counsel and Recommended Sanction

On December 13, 1996, the Subcommittee issued an SAV charging Mr. Gingrich with three counts of violations of House Rules. Two counts concerned the failure to seek legal advice in regard to the 501(c)(3) projects, and one count concerned providing the Committee with information which he knew or should have known was inaccurate.

At the time the Subcommittee voted this SAV, the Members discussed the matter among themselves and reached a consensus that it would be in the best interests of the House for the matter to be resolved without going through a disciplinary hearing. It was estimated that such a hearing could take up to three months to complete and would not begin for several months.

Because of this, it was anticipated that the House would have to deal with this matter for another six months. Even though the Subcommittee Members felt that it would be advantageous to the House to avoid a disciplinary hearing, they all were committed to the proposition that any resolution of the matter had to reflect adequately the seriousness of the offenses.

To this end, the Subcommittee Members discussed and agreed upon a recommended sanction that was fair in light of the conduct reflected in this matter, but explicitly recognized that the full Committee would make the ultimate decision as to the recommendation to the full House as to the appropriate sanction.

In determining what the appropriate sanction should be in this matter, the Subcommittee and Special Counsel considered the seriousness of the conduct, the level of care exercised by Mr. Gingrich, the disruption caused to the House by the conduct, the cost to the House in having to pay for an extensive investigation, and the repetitive nature of the conduct.

As is noted above, the Subcommittee was faced with troubling choices in each of the areas covered by the Statement of Alleged Violation. Either

Mr. Gingrich's conduct in regard to the $501(c)(3)$ organizations and the letters he submitted to the Committee was intentional or it was reckless. Neither choice reflects creditably on the House.

While the Subcommittee was not able to reach a comfortable conclusion on these issues, the fact that the choice was presented is a factor in determining the appropriate sanction. In addition, the violation does not represent only a single instance of reckless conduct.

Rather, over a number of years and in a number of situations, Mr. Gingrich showed a disregard and lack of respect for the standards of conduct that applied to his activities.

Under the Rules of the Committee, a reprimand is the appropriate sanction for a serious violation of House Rules and a censure is appropriate for a more serious violation of House Rules. Rule 20(g), Rules of the Committee on Standards of Official Conduct.

It was the opinion of the Subcommittee that this matter fell somewhere in between. Accordingly, the Subcommittee and the Special Counsel recommend that the appropriate sanction should be a reprimand and a payment reimbursing the House for some of the costs of the investigation in the amount of $300,000.

Mr. Gingrich has agreed that this is the appropriate sanction in this matter.

Beginning on December 15, 1996, Mr. Gingrich's counsel and the Special Counsel began discussions directed toward resolving the matter without a disciplinary hearing. The discussions lasted through December 20, 1996.

At that time an understanding was reached by both Mr. Gingrich and the Subcommittee concerning this matter. That understanding was put on the record on December 21, 1996 by Mr. Cole [as] follows:

Mr. Cole: The subcommittee has had an opportunity to review the facts in this case, and has had extensive discussion about the appropriate resolution of this matter.

Mr. Cardin: If I might just add here to your next understanding, the Members of the subcommittee, prior to the adoption of the Statement of Alleged Violation, were concerned that the nonpartisan deliberations of the subcommittee continue beyond the findings of the subcommittee. Considering the record of the full Ethics Committee in the 104th Congress and the partisan environment in the full House, the Members of the subcommittee felt that it was important to exercise bipartisan leadership beyond the workings of the subcommittee.

Mr. Cole: It was the opinion of the Members of the subcommittee and the Special Counsel, that based on the facts of this case as they are currently known, the appropriate sanction for the conduct described in the original Statement of Alleged Violations is a reprimand and the payment of $300,000 toward the cost of the preliminary inquiry.

In light of this opinion, the subcommittee Members and the Special Counsel intend to recommend to the full committee that this be the sanction recommended by the full committee to the House. The Members also intend to support this as the sanction in the committee and on the Floor of the House.

However, if new facts are developed or brought to the attention of the Members of the subcommittee, they are free to change their opinions.

The Subcommittee, through its counsel, has communicated this to Mr. Gingrich, through his counsel. Mr. Gingrich has agreed that if the subcommittee will amend the Statement of Alleged Violations to be one count, instead of three counts, however, still including all of the conduct described in the original Statement of Alleged Violations, and will allow the addition of some language which reflects aspects of the record in this matter concerning the involvement of Mr. Gingrich's counsel in the preparation of the letters described in the original Count 3 of the Statement of Alleged Violations, [note: these changes included the removal of the word "knew" from the original Count 3, making the charge read that Mr. Gingrich "should have known" the information was inaccurate] he will admit to the entire Statement of Alleged Violation and agree to the view of the subcommittee Members and the Special Counsel as to the appropriate sanction.

In light of Mr. Gingrich's admission to the Statement of Alleged Violation, the subcommittee is of the view that the rules of the committee will not require that an adjudicatory hearing take place; however, a sanction hearing will need to be held under the rules.

The subcommittee and Mr. Gingrich desire to have the sanction hearing concluded as expeditiously as possible, but it is understood that this will not take place at the expense of orderly procedure and a full and fair opportunity for the full committee to be informed of any information necessary for each Member of the full committee to be able to make a decision at the sanction hearing.

After the subcommittee has voted a new Statement of Alleged Violation, Mr. Gingrich will file his answer admitting to it. The subcommittee will seek the permission of the full committee to release the Statement of Alleged Violation, Mr. Gingrich's answer, and a brief press release which has been approved by Mr. Gingrich's counsel. At the same time, Mr. Gingrich will release a brief press release that has been approved by the subcommittee's Special Counsel.

Both the subcommittee and Mr. Gingrich agree that no public comment should be made about this matter while it is still pending. This includes having surrogates sent out to comment on the matter and attempt to mischaracterize it.

Accordingly, beyond the press statements described above, neither Mr. Gingrich nor any Member of the subcommittee may make any further public comment. Mr. Gingrich understands that if he violates this provision, the subcommittee will have the option of reinstating the original Statement of Alleged Violations and allowing Mr. Gingrich an opportunity to withdraw his answer.

And I should note that it is the intention of the subcommittee that "public comments" refers to press statements; that, obviously, we are free and Mr. Gingrich is free to have private conversations with Members of Congress about these matters. [Note: It was also agreed that in the private conversations Mr. Gingrich was not to disclose the terms of the agreement with the Subcommittee.]

After the Subcommittee voted to issue the substitute SAV, the Special Counsel called Mr. Gingrich's counsel and read to him what was put on the record concerning this matter. Mr. Gingrich's counsel then delivered to the Subcommittee Mr. Gingrich's answer admitting to the Statement of Alleged Violation.

D. Post-December 21, 1996 Activity

Following the release of this Statement of Alleged Violation, numerous press accounts appeared concerning this matter. In the opinion of the Subcommittee Members and the Special Counsel, a number of the press accounts indicated that Mr. Gingrich had violated the agreement concerning statements about the matter. Mr. Gingrich's counsel was notified of the Subcommittee's concerns and the Subcommittee met to consider what action to take in light of this apparent violation. The Subcommittee determined that it would not nullify the agreement.

While there was serious concern about whether Mr. Gingrich had complied with the agreement, the Subcommittee was of the opinion that the best interests of the House still lay in resolving the matter without a disciplinary hearing and with the recommended sanction that its Members had previously determined was appropriate. However, Mr. Gingrich's counsel was informed that the Subcommittee believed a violation of the agreement had occurred and retained the right to withdraw from the agreement with appropriate notice to Mr. Gingrich. To date no such notice has been given.

PRESIDENT CLINTON'S
SECOND INAUGURAL ADDRESS
January 20, 1997

William Jefferson Clinton took the oath of office January 20 to begin his second term as the forty-second president of the United States. The ceremony at the front of the Capitol was the fifty-third presidential inauguration in the nation's history, and the first in sixty years to mark the beginning of a second term for a president representing the Democratic Party. The inauguration also completed a generational transition: It was the first in which the president, the vice president, and the top four congressional leaders all came to adulthood following World War II.

The inauguration marked one of the most remarkable political comebacks in American history. Narrowly elected in 1992 over an incumbent Republican president, Clinton had seemed to endure, rather than preside over, a first term noted more for blunders than successes. The low point for him came in 1994, when the voters repudiated the president and his Democratic Party by putting Republicans in control of both houses of Congress for the first time in forty years. Most observers were inclined at the time to write Clinton off as a spent political force. But Clinton came back to win a second term in 1996, overcoming a Republican Party divided along deep factional and ideological lines.

Basking in his triumph and noting that his inauguration was the last of the twentieth century, Clinton sought to use the event as the opening of an inspirational crusade toward what he called a "land of new promise." He advocated racial and political harmony and called on Americans to imagine a better world where values of the past—family, community, self-reliance, and self-sacrifice—are coupled with technological advances of the future. Clinton was the latest in a long line of presidents hoping to inspire Americans to help others as well as themselves, but he was the first to tell them their lives could be made better by microchips and the Internet.

The president offered few policy prescriptions in his second inaugural speech. He avoided any mention of legislation pending before Congress and talked only in generalities about the broad issues the 104th Congress would face. On tough questions such as education, crime, and health care, the president said the government and its people can do better, but gave no specifics.

Unease Behind the Facade

Despite Clinton's appeals for harmony, numerous commentators noted the contrast between the temporary unity of Inauguration Day and the stark political divisions evident in Washington and the nation during the previous four years. Although Clinton received high marks in public opinion polls, there was little doubt that the public had an extraordinarily cynical view of politicians. The campaign leading up to the November 1996 election was widely viewed as one of the least inspiring in decades, one relying almost entirely on public relations imagery and in which neither Clinton nor his Republican rival, Bob Dole, offered substantive ideas or challenges to the electorate. Fewer than half of all eligible voters bothered to go to the polls. To pay for the campaign—by far the most expensive in history—both parties resorted to questionable fund-raising tactics, including some that may have been illegal. Both houses of Congress were preparing investigations that would focus on wrongdoing by the Clinton campaign. (Campaign finance, p. 822)

Clinton also was burdened by two separate scandals, either of which had the potential to cause him serious political or legal damage. The first was the ongoing investigation by independent counsel Kenneth W. Starr into the "Whitewater" real estate deal involving Clinton and his wife, Hillary Rodham Clinton, when he was governor of Arkansas. Starr had broadened his investigation to include other issues, such as the 1993 firing of officials in the White House travel office and a White House effort to obtain confidential FBI files on Republicans.

Clinton also faced the embarrassment of a sexual harassment suit filed against him by former Arkansas state employee Paula Jones. The Supreme Court in May rejected Clinton's claim that he should not be subject to civil law suits while sitting as president, thus allowing Jones to proceed with her case. (Jones case, p. 290)

Noting this backdrop, New York Times *commentator R. W. Apple wrote on Inauguration Day: "It is hard to find the high moral ground in Washington these days."*

In his speech Clinton addressed the public about politicians, noting that the people elected "a president of one party and a Congress of another." Then to hearty applause, as the sun broke through the clouds on an otherwise gray day, he said: "Surely they did not do this to advance the politics of petty bickering and extreme partisanship they plainly deplore." Reformulating a phrase from Isaiah 58:12 from the open Bible on which he placed his left hand as he swore his oath of office, Clinton added: "No, they call all of us instead to be repairers of the breach and to move on with America's mission. America demands and deserves big things from us, and nothing big ever came from being small."

The Racial Divide

If Clinton offered a big idea in his inaugural speech, it was one that he had pressed for many years, indeed one he lamented had eluded the nation since its inception: the idea of racial peace and harmony. Clinton began his inaugural day with a prayer breakfast at a predominantly black church in Washington, and he devoted a key section of his speech to the topic he said had been "America's constant curse," the divide of race.

"Each new wave of immigrants gives new targets to old prejudices," he said. And in what many saw as a veiled reference to the religious right, Clinton added: "Prejudice and contempt, cloaked in the pretense of religious or political conviction, are no different. They have nearly destroyed us in the past. They plague us still." The obsessions of racial hatred, he said, "cripple both those who are hated and, of course, those who hate, robbing both of what they might become."

Clinton was speaking on a double federal holiday: in addition to being Inauguration Day, January 20 was the annual celebration of Martin Luther King Jr. Day, commemorating the civil rights leader. Echoing King's words, Clinton rejected the "dark impulses" of hatred and said: "We shall overcome them, and we shall replace them with the generous spirit of a people who feel at home with one another."

Following is the text of inaugural address of President Bill Clinton on January 20, 1997:

My fellow citizens:

At this last presidential inauguration of the 20th century, let us lift our eyes toward the challenges that await us in the next century. It is our great good fortune that time and chance have put us not only at the edge of a new century, in a new millennium, but on the edge of a bright new prospect in human affairs—a moment that will define our course, and our character, for decades to come. We must keep our old democracy forever young. Guided by the ancient vision of a promised land, let us set our sights upon a land of new promise.

The promise of America was born in the 18th century out of the bold conviction that we are all created equal. It was extended and preserved in the 19th century, when our nation spread across the continent, saved the union, and abolished the awful scourge of slavery.

Then, in turmoil and triumph, that promise exploded onto the world stage to make this the American Century.

And what a century it has been. America became the world's mightiest industrial power; saved the world from tyranny in two world wars and a long cold war; and time and again, reached out across the globe to millions who, like us, longed for the blessings of liberty.

Along the way, Americans produced a great middle class and security in old age; built unrivaled centers of learning and opened public schools to all;

split the atom and explored the heavens; invented the computer and the microchip; and deepened the wellspring of justice by making a revolution in civil rights for African Americans and all minorities, and extending the circle of citizenship, opportunity and dignity to women.

Now, for the third time, a new century is upon us, and another time to choose. We began the 19th century with a choice, to spread our nation from coast to coast. We began the 20th century with a choice, to harness the Industrial Revolution to our values of free enterprise, conservation, and human decency. Those choices made all the difference. At the dawn of the 21st century a free people must now choose to shape the forces of the Information Age and the global society, to unleash the limitless potential of all our people, and, yes, to form a more perfect union.

When last we gathered, our march to this new future seemed less certain than it does today. We vowed then to set a clear course to renew our nation.

In these four years, we have been touched by tragedy, exhilarated by challenge, strengthened by achievement. America stands alone as the world's indispensable nation. Once again, our economy is the strongest on Earth. Once again, we are building stronger families, thriving communities, better educational opportunities, a cleaner environment. Problems that once seemed destined to deepen now bend to our efforts: our streets are safer and record numbers of our fellow citizens have moved from welfare to work.

And once again, we have resolved for our time a great debate over the role of government. Today we can declare: Government is not the problem, and government is not the solution. We—the American people—we are the solution. Our founders understood that well and gave us a democracy strong enough to endure for centuries, flexible enough to face our common challenges and advance our common dreams in each new day.

As times change, so government must change. We need a new government for a new century—humble enough not to try to solve all our problems for us, but strong enough to give us the tools to solve our problems for ourselves; a government that is smaller, lives within its means, and does more with less. Yet where it can stand up for our values and interests in the world, and where it can give Americans the power to make a real difference in their everyday lives, government should do more, not less. The preeminent mission of our new government is to give all Americans an opportunity—not a guarantee, but a real opportunity—to build better lives.

Beyond that, my fellow citizens, the future is up to us. Our founders taught us that the preservation of our liberty and our union depends upon responsible citizenship. And we need a new sense of responsibility for a new century. There is work to do, work that government alone cannot do: teaching children to read; hiring people off welfare rolls; coming out from behind locked doors and shuttered windows to help reclaim our streets from drugs and gangs and crime; taking time out of our own lives to serve others.

Each and every one of us, in our own way, must assume personal responsibility—not only for ourselves and our families, but for our neighbors and our nation. Our greatest responsibility is to embrace a new spirit of community for a new century. For any one of us to succeed, we must succeed as one America.

The challenge of our past remains the challenge of our future—will we be one nation, one people, with one common destiny, or not? Will we all come together, or come apart?

The divide of race has been America's constant curse. And each new wave of immigrants gives new targets to old prejudices. Prejudice and contempt, cloaked in the pretense of religious or political conviction are no different. These forces have nearly destroyed our nation in the past. They plague us still. They fuel the fanaticism of terror. And they torment the lives of millions in fractured nations all around the world.

These obsessions cripple both those who hate and, of course, those who are hated, robbing both of what they might become. We cannot, we will not, succumb to the dark impulses that lurk in the far regions of the soul everywhere. We shall overcome them. And we shall replace them with the generous spirit of a people who feel at home with one another.

Our rich texture of racial, religious and political diversity will be a Godsend in the 21st century. Great rewards will come to those who can live together, learn together, work together, forge new ties that bind together.

As this new era approaches we can already see its broad outlines. Ten years ago, the Internet was the mystical province of physicists; today, it is a commonplace encyclopedia for millions of schoolchildren. Scientists now are decoding the blueprint of human life. Cures for our most feared illnesses seem close at hand.

The world is no longer divided into two hostile camps. Instead, now we are building bonds with nations that once were our adversaries. Growing connections of commerce and culture give us a chance to lift the fortunes and spirits of people the world over. And for the very first time in all of history, more people on this planet live under democracy than dictatorship.

My fellow Americans, as we look back at this remarkable century, we may ask, can we hope not just to follow, but even to surpass the achievements of the 20th century in America and to avoid the awful bloodshed that stained its legacy? To that question, every American here and every American in our land today must answer a resounding "Yes."

This is the heart of our task. With a new vision of government, a new sense of responsibility, a new spirit of community, we will sustain America's journey. The promise we sought in a new land we will find again in a land of new promise.

In this new land, education will be every citizen's most prized possession. Our schools will have the highest standards in the world, igniting the spark of possibility in the eyes of every girl and every boy. And the doors of higher education will be open to all. The knowledge and power of the Information Age will be within reach not just of the few, but of every classroom, every library, every child. Parents and children will have time not only to work, but to read and play together. And the plans they make at their kitchen table will be those of a better home, a better job, the certain chance to go to college.

Our streets will echo again with the laughter of our children, because no one will try to shoot them or sell them drugs anymore. Everyone who can work, will work, with today's permanent under class part of tomorrow's growing middle class. New miracles of medicine at last will reach not only those who can claim care now, but the children and hardworking families too long denied.

We will stand mighty for peace and freedom, and maintain a strong defense against terror and destruction. Our children will sleep free from the threat of nuclear, chemical or biological weapons. Ports and airports, farms and factories will thrive with trade and innovation and ideas. And the world's greatest democracy will lead a whole world of democracies.

Our land of new promise will be a nation that meets its obligations—a nation that balances its budget, but never loses the balance of its values. A nation where our grandparents have secure retirement and health care, and their grandchildren know we have made the reforms necessary to sustain those benefits for their time. A nation that fortifies the world's most productive economy even as it protects the great natural bounty of our water, air, and majestic land.

And in this land of new promise, we will have reformed our politics so that the voice of the people will always speak louder than the din of narrow interests—regaining the participation and deserving the trust of all Americans.

Fellow citizens, let us build that America, a nation ever moving forward toward realizing the full potential of all its citizens. Prosperity and power— yes, they are important, and we must maintain them. But let us never forget: The greatest progress we have made, and the greatest progress we have yet to make, is in the human heart. In the end, all the world's wealth and a thousand armies are no match for the strength and decency of the human spirit.

Thirty-four years ago, the man whose life we celebrate today spoke to us down there, at the other end of this Mall, in words that moved the conscience of a nation. Like a prophet of old, he told of his dream that one day America would rise up and treat all its citizens as equals before the law and in the heart. Martin Luther King's dream was the American Dream. His quest is our quest: the ceaseless striving to live out our true creed. Our history has been built on such dreams and labors. And by our dreams and labors we will redeem the promise of America in the 21st century.

To that effort I pledge all my strength and every power of my office. I ask the members of Congress here to join in that pledge. The American people returned to office a President of one party and a Congress of another. Surely, they did not do this to advance the politics of petty bickering and extreme partisanship they plainly deplore. No, they call on us instead to be repairers of the breach, and to move on with America's mission.

America demands and deserves big things from us—and nothing big ever came from being small. Let us remember the timeless wisdom of Cardinal

Bernardin, when facing the end of his own life. He said: "It is wrong to waste the precious gift of time, on acrimony and division."

Fellow citizens, we must not waste the precious gift of this time. For all of us are on that same journey of our lives, and our journey, too, will come to an end. But the journey of our America must go on.

And so, my fellow Americans, we must be strong, for there is much to dare. The demands of our time are great and they are different. Let us meet them with faith and courage, with patience and a grateful and happy heart. Let us shape the hope of this day into the noblest chapter in our history. Yes, let us build our bridge. A bridge wide enough and strong enough for every American to cross over to a blessed land of new promise.

May those generations whose faces we cannot yet see, whose names we may never know, say of us here that we led our beloved land into a new century with the American Dream alive for all her children; with the American promise of a more perfect union a reality for all her people; with America's bright flame of freedom spreading throughout all the world.

From the height of this place and the summit of this century, let us go forth. May God strengthen our hands for the good work ahead—and always, always bless our America.

February

STATE OF THE UNION ADDRESS AND REPUBLICAN RESPONSE
February 4, 1997

President Bill Clinton laid out a modest agenda for action in the first State of the Union speech of his second term, calling for a renewed emphasis on education and for a bipartisan approach to balancing the budget and reforming campaign spending. The president's appeal February 4 bore modest fruit in the coming months, as he and Congress agreed on a balanced budget for fiscal year 1998 but they were unable to set aside differences on campaign finance or his education goals.

The president's annual speech to a joint session of Congress put some specifics behind the broad generalities Clinton had laid out just two weeks earlier in his second inaugural address. In both speeches the president used grand themes, such as combating racism and preparing to meet numerous challenges of the twenty-first century. The inaugural speech made no mention of a specific legislative agenda, but Clinton included a long list of items, both big and small, in his hour-long State of the Union address. (Inaugural speech, p. 20)

The Republican leadership of Congress gave Clinton a warm but not enthusiastic reception. GOP leaders praised his calls for bipartisanship but found fault with several of the specific points raised. Republicans focused much of their attention on Clinton's proposed education agenda, on which he put a $51 billion price tag for the forthcoming fiscal year. "Where is all this money going to come from?" asked Representative Robert L. Livingston, R-La., who chaired the House Appropriations Committee. Several Republicans expressed disappointment that Clinton did not repeat the marquee-line of his 1996 State of the Union speech, that "the era of big government is over."

Clinton's speech had to compete for public attention with a sensational news story. Shortly before Clinton arrived at the House chamber, the jury in the civil trial of former football star O. J. Simpson was preparing to deliver its verdict holding Simpson responsible for the death of his former wife. The Simpson case, which had dominated American headlines for months, clearly distracted attention from the speech. (Simpson case, p. 74)

A Plan for Education

Clinton announced that giving Americans "the best education in the world" would be his "number one priority" in his second term in office. He offered specific proposals to back up that grandiose goal, most notably a plan for national education standards and testing. Clinton called on all states to adopt a set of standards proposed in 1990 by a bipartisan commission. By 1999, he said, every state should test every fourth-grader in reading and every eighth-grader in math "to make sure those standards are being met." Other major proposals included establishing a system to enable 100,000 teachers to obtain certification as "master teachers," indicating that they had met certain standards of excellence, and creating a network of 1,000,000 volunteer tutors to help primary children learn to read. (Education standards, Historic Documents of 1990, p. 153)

"Raising standards will not be easy, and some of our children will not be able to meet them at first," Clinton told the Congress. "The point is not to put our children down, but to lift them up."

To make college more affordable, Clinton proposed a $1,500-a-year tax credit for two years of college tuition, along with up to $10,000 worth of tax deductions for all tuition after high school. The president put the first-year (fiscal year 1998) cost of all his education proposals at $51 billion—about a 20 percent increase over the fiscal 1997 level.

Members of both parties praised Clinton's focus on education, but Republicans challenged the cost and his emphasis on a federal role. The proposal for national education standards and testing also proved to be controversial, especially among states-rights advocates who saw it as an attack on the rights of states and localities to run public education. Congress in 1997 authorized initial preparatory steps for Clinton's testing program but delayed actual implementation for at least a year, thus guaranteeing another debate on the matter in 1998.

Balanced Budget and Campaign Finance

The president offered direct challenges to congressional Republicans on two of the most contentious issues of the day: the drive for a balanced budget and the dispute over how to clean up the system of federal election campaign finances. On the first issue, Clinton reiterated his flat opposition to a constitutional amendment mandating a balanced budget—the number one item on the stated wish list of many Republicans.

"Balancing the budget requires only your vote and my signature [on annual budget legislation]," Clinton told Congress. "It does not require us to rewrite our Constitution." A proposal for a constitutional requirement for a balanced budget died for 1997 when it fell one vote short in the Senate on a March 4 roll call. Democratic Senator Robert G. Torricelli of New Jer-

sey cast the deciding vote, switching positions to oppose the measure. The vote was 66–34, one vote short of the two-thirds necessary for constitutional amendments. The outcome was identical to a Senate vote in 1995. (Budget amendment, Historic Documents of 1995, p. 737)

The president also sought to usurp the high road on the matter of campaign finance reform. That was one issue on which his footing was unsure because of allegations that his 1996 reelection campaign had resorted to questionable, if not illegal, tactics in trying to match the Republicans' superior fund-raising ability. Clinton endorsed legislation crafted by Senators John McCain, an Arizona Republican, and Russell D. Feingold, a Democrat from Wisconsin. Their bill set limits on spending in federal campaigns and banned "soft money" contributions funneled through political parties. Saying that congressional delay "will mean the death of reform," Clinton called on Congress to enact the McCain-Feingold bill by July 4, "the day we celebrate the birth of our democracy." The Senate did take up the bill late in its session, but nearly solid Republican opposition kept it from a final vote. Under pressure from some members of his own party, Senate Majority Leader Trent Lott agreed to schedule a vote on the bill early in 1998. The issue did not reach the House floor in 1997. (Campaign finance issues, p. 822)

Republican Response

The official Republican response to Clinton's speech came from J. C. Watts, a thirty-nine-year-old second-term representative who was the first African American elected to Congress from Oklahoma since Reconstruction. Watts told his television audience after Clinton's speech that the answers to America's problems could be found in the heartland and in family homes, not in Washington, D.C. "The strength of America is not in Washington," he said. "The strength is at home, in lives well lived in the land of faith and family."

Watts's speech was overshadowed by news coverage of the Simpson case, and much of the attention paid to Watts's appearance on national television focused on two controversies. On the day of his speech, the Tulsa World *reported that Watts was using the event as a campaign fund-raiser; his aides had mailed supporters a preprinted card saying: "J. C., what a great speech! Here's some help to rebuild your campaign fund." On the same day, the* Washington Post *quoted Watts as denouncing "race-hustling poverty pimps," naming Mayor Marion Barry of Washington, D.C., and the Rev. Jesse Jackson as examples. Watts insisted he had not named Barry and Jackson, but the* Post *stood by its story.*

Following are the texts of President Bill Clinton's State of the Union address, delivered to a joint session of Congress on February 4, 1997, and the Republican response by Rep. J. C. Watts of Oklahoma:

STATE OF THE UNION ADDRESS

Mr. Speaker [Newt Gingrich], Mr. Vice President [Al Gore], members of the 105th Congress, distinguished guests, and my fellow Americans:

I think I should start by saying, thanks for inviting me back. I come before you tonight with a challenge as great as any in our peacetime history, and a plan of action to meet that challenge, to prepare our people for the bold new world of the 21st century.

We have much to be thankful for. With four years of growth, we have won back the basic strength of our economy. With crime and welfare rolls declining, we are winning back our optimism, the enduring faith that we can master any difficulty. With the Cold War receding and global commerce at record levels, we are helping to win unrivaled peace and prosperity all across the world.

My fellow Americans, the state of our union is strong. But now we must rise to the decisive moment, to make a nation and a world better than any we have ever known. The new promise of the global economy, the Information Age, unimagined new work, life-enhancing technology—all these are ours to seize. That is our honor and our challenge. We must be shapers of events, not observers. For if we do not act, the moment will pass—and we will lose the best possibilities of our future.

We face no imminent threat, but we do have an enemy—the enemy of our time is inaction. So, tonight, I issue a call to action—action by this Congress, action by our states, by our people, to prepare America for the 21st century. Action to keep our economy and our democracy strong and working for all our people; action to strengthen education and harness the forces of technology and science; action to build stronger families and stronger communities and a safer environment; action to keep America the world's strongest force for peace, freedom and prosperity. And above all, action to build a more perfect union here at home.

The spirit we bring to our work will make all the difference. We must be committed to the pursuit of opportunity for all Americans, responsibility from all Americans, in a community of all Americans. And we must be committed to a new kind of government—not to solve all our problems for us, but to give our people—all our people—the tools they need to make the most of their own lives.

And we must work together. The people of this nation elected us all. They want us to be partners, not partisans. They put us all right here in the same boat, they gave us all oars, and they told us to row. Now, here is the direction I believe we should take.

First, we must move quickly to complete the unfinished business of our country—to balance our budget, renew our democracy, and finish the job of welfare reform.

Over the last four years, we have brought new economic growth by investing in our people, expanding our exports, cutting our deficits, creating over 11 million new jobs, a four-year record. Now we must keep our economy the strongest in the world. We here tonight have an historic opportunity. Let this Congress be the Congress that finally balances the budget.

In two days, I will propose a detailed plan to balance the budget by 2002. This plan will balance the budget and invest in our people while protecting Medicare, Medicaid, education, and the environment. It will balance the budget and build on the Vice President's efforts to make our government work better, even as it costs less. It will balance the budget and provide middle class tax relief to pay for education and health care, to help to raise a child, to buy and sell a home.

Balancing the budget requires only your vote and my signature. It does not require us to rewrite our Constitution. I believe it is both unnecessary and unwise to adopt a balanced budget amendment that could cripple our country in time of crisis, and force unwanted results, such as judges halting Social Security checks or increasing taxes. Let us at least agree, we should not pass any measure—no measure should be passed that threatens Social Security. Whatever your view on that, we all must concede we don't need a constitutional amendment, we need action.

Whatever our differences, we should balance the budget now. And then, for the long-term health of our society, we must agree to a bipartisan process to preserve Social Security and reform Medicare for the long run, so that these fundamental programs will be as strong for our children as they are for our parents.

And let me say something that's not in my script tonight. I know this is not going to be easy. But I really believe one of the reasons the American people gave me a second term was to take the tough decisions in the next four years that will carry our country through the next fifty years. I know it is easier for me than for you to say or do. But another reason I was elected is to support all of you, without regard to party, to give you what is necessary to join in these decisions. We owe it to our country and to our future.

Our second piece of unfinished business requires us to commit ourselves tonight, before the eyes of America, to finally enacting bipartisan campaign finance reform.

Now, Senators [John] McCain [R-Ariz.] and [Russell] Feingold [D-Wis.], Representatives [Christopher] Shays [R-Conn.] and [Martin T.] Meehan [D-Mass.], have reached across party lines here to craft tough and fair reform. Their proposal would curb spending, reduce the role of special interests, create a level playing field between challengers and incumbents, and ban contributions from noncitizens, all corporate sources, and the other large soft money contributions that both parties receive.

You know and I know that this can be delayed. And you know and I know the delay will mean the death of reform. So let's set our own deadline. Let's work together to write bipartisan campaign finance reform into law and pass McCain-Feingold by the day we celebrate the birth of our democracy—July the 4th.

There is a third piece of unfinished business. Over the last four years, we moved a record 2.25 million people off the welfare rolls. Then last year,

Congress enacted landmark welfare reform legislation, demanding that all able-bodied recipients assume the responsibility of moving from welfare to work.

Now each and every one of us has to fulfill our responsibility—indeed, our moral obligation—to make sure that people who now must work, can work. Now we must act to meet a new goal: 2 million more people off the welfare rolls by the year 2000.

Here is my plan: Tax credits and other incentives for businesses that hire people off welfare; incentives for job placement firms and states to create more jobs for welfare recipients; training, transportation, and child care to help people go to work.

Now I challenge every state: Turn those welfare checks into private sector paychecks. I challenge every religious congregation, every community non-profit, every business to hire someone off welfare. And I'd like to say especially to every employer in our country who ever criticized the old welfare system, you can't blame that old system anymore, we have torn it down. Now do your part. Give someone on welfare the chance to go to work.

Tonight, I am pleased to announce that five major corporations—Sprint, Monsanto, UPS, Burger King and United Airlines—will be the first to join in a new national effort to marshal America's businesses, large and small, to create jobs so that people can move from welfare to work.

We passed welfare reform. All of you know I believe we were right to do it. But no one can walk out of this chamber with a clear conscience unless you are prepared to finish the job.

And we must join together to do something else, too—something both Republican and Democratic governors have asked us to do—to restore basic health and disability benefits when misfortune strikes immigrants who came to this country legally, who work hard, pay taxes and obey the law. To do otherwise is simply unworthy of a great nation of immigrants.

Now, looking ahead, the greatest step of all—the high threshold of the future we now must cross—and my number one priority for the next four years is to ensure that all Americans have the best education in the world.

Let's work together to meet these three goals: Every eight-year-old must be able to read; every twelve-year-old must be able to log on to the Internet; every eighteen-year-old must be able to go to college; and every adult American must be able to keep on learning for a lifetime.

My balanced budget makes an unprecedented commitment to these goals—$51 billion next year. But far more than money is required. I have a plan, a Call to Action for American Education, based on these ten principles.

First, a national crusade for education standards—not federal government standards, but national standards, representing what all our students must know to succeed in the knowledge economy of the 21st century. Every state and school must shape the curriculum to reflect these standards, and train teachers to lift students up to them. To help schools meet the standards and measure their progress, we will lead an effort over the next two years to develop national tests of student achievement in reading and math.

Tonight, I issue a challenge to the nation: Every state should adopt high national standards, and by 1999, every state should test every fourth grader in reading and every eighth grader in math to make sure these standards are met.

Raising standards will not be easy, and some of our children will not be able to meet them at first. The point is not to put our children down, but to lift them up. Good tests will show us who needs help, what changes in teaching to make, and which schools need to improve. They can help us to end social promotion. For no child should move from grade school to junior high, or junior high to high school until he or she is ready.

Last month, our Secretary of Education Dick Riley and I visited Northern Illinois, where eighth grade students from twenty school districts, in a project aptly called "First in the World," took the Third International Math and Science Study. That's a test that reflects the world-class standards our children must meet for the new era. And those students in Illinois tied for first in the world in science and came in second in math. Two of them, Kristin Tanner and Chris Getsla, are here tonight, along with their teacher, Sue Winski; they're up there with the First Lady. And they prove that when we aim high and challenge our students, they will be the best in the world. Let's give them a hand. Stand up, please.

Second, to have the best schools, we must have the best teachers. Most of us in this chamber would not be here tonight without the help of those teachers. I know that I wouldn't be here. For years, many of our educators, led by North Carolina's Governor Jim Hunt and the National Board for Professional Teaching Standards, have worked very hard to establish nationally accepted credentials for excellence in teaching. Just 500 of these teachers have been certified since 1995. My budget will enable 100,000 more to seek national certification as master teachers. We should reward and recognize our best teachers. And as we reward them, we should quickly and fairly remove those few who don't measure up, and we should challenge more of our finest young people to consider teaching as a career.

Third, we must do more to help all our children read. Forty percent—40 percent—of our eight-year-olds cannot read on their own. That's why we have just launched the America Reads initiative—to build a citizen army of one million volunteer tutors to make sure every child can read independently by the end of the third grade. We will use thousands of AmeriCorps volunteers to mobilize this citizen army. We want at least 100,000 college students to help. And tonight I am pleased that sixty college presidents have answered my call, pledging that thousands of their work-study students will serve for one year as reading tutors.

This is also a challenge to every teacher and every principal. You must use these tutors to help students read. And it is especially a challenge to our parents. You must read with your children every night.

This leads to the fourth principle: Learning begins in the first days of life. Scientists are now discovering how young children develop emotionally and intellectually from their very first days, and how important it is for parents to begin immediately talking, singing, even reading to their infants. The First

Lady has spent years writing about this issue, studying it. And she and I are going to convene a White House Conference on Early Learning and the Brain this spring, to explore how parents and educators can best use these startling new findings.

We already know we should start teaching children before they start school. That's why this balanced budget expands Head Start to one million children by 2002. And that is why the Vice President and Mrs. Gore will host their annual family conference this June on what we can do to make sure that parents are an active part of their children's learning all the way through school.

They've done a great deal to highlight the importance of family in our life, and now they're turning their attention to getting more parents involved in their children's learning all the way through school. And I thank you, Mr. Vice President, and I thank you especially, Tipper [Gore], for what you do.

Fifth, every state should give parents the power to choose the right public school for their children. Their right to choose will foster competition and innovation that can make public schools better. We should also make it possible for more parents and teachers to start charter schools, schools that set and meet the highest standards, and exist only as long as they do. Our plan will help America to create 3,000 of these charter schools by the next century—nearly seven times as there are in the country today—so that parents will have even more choices in sending their children to the best schools.

Sixth: Character education must be taught in our schools. We must teach our children to be good citizens. And we must continue to promote order and discipline, supporting communities that introduce school uniforms, impose curfews enforce truancy laws, remove disruptive students from the classroom, and have zero tolerance for guns and drugs in school.

Seventh: We cannot expect our children to raise themselves up in schools that are literally falling down. With the student population at an all-time high, and record numbers of school buildings falling into disrepair, this has now become a serious national concern. Therefore, my budget includes a new initiative—$5 billion to help communities finance $20 billion in school construction over the next four years.

Eighth: We must make the thirteenth and fourteenth years of education—at least two years of college—just as universal in America by the 21st century as a high school education is today, and we must open the doors of college to Americans.

To do that, I propose America's HOPE Scholarship, based on Georgia's pioneering program: two years of a $1,500 tax credit for college tuition, enough to pay for the typical community college. I also propose a tax deduction of up to $10,000 a year for all tuition after high school; an expanded IRA you can withdraw from tax free for education; and the largest increase in Pell Grant scholarships in twenty years. Now, this plan will give most families the ability to pay no taxes on money they save for college tuition. I ask you to pass it—and give every American who works hard the chance to go to college.

Ninth: In the 21st century, we must expand the frontiers of learning across a lifetime. All our people, of whatever age, must have a chance to learn new skills. Most Americans live near a community college. The roads that take them there can be paths to a better future. My G.I. Bill for America's Workers will transform the confusing tangle of federal training programs into a simple skill grant to go directly into eligible workers' hands. For too long, this bill has been sitting on that desk there without action—I ask you to pass it now. Let's give more of our workers the ability to learn and to earn for a lifetime.

Tenth: We must bring the power of the Information Age into all our schools. Last year, I challenged America to connect every classroom and library to the Internet by the year 2000, so that, for the first time in our history, children in the most isolated rural towns, the most comfortable suburbs, the poorest inner city schools, will have the same access to the same universe of knowledge. That is my plan—a Call to Action for American Education. Some may say that it is unusual for a President to pay this kind of attention to education. Some may say it is simply because the President and his wonderful wife have been obsessed with this subject for more years than they can recall. That is not what is driving these proposals.

We must understand the significance of this endeavor: One of the greatest sources of our strength throughout the Cold War was a bipartisan foreign policy; because our future was at stake, politics stopped at the water's edge. Now I ask you—and I ask all our nation's governors; I ask parents, teachers, and citizens all across America—for a new nonpartisan commitment to education—because education is a critical national security issue for our future, and politics must stop at the schoolhouse door.

To prepare America for the 21st century we must harness the powerful forces of science and technology to benefit all Americans. This is the first State of the Union carried live in video over the Internet. But we've only begun to spread the benefits of a technology revolution that should become the modern birthright of every citizen.

Our effort to connect every classroom is just the beginning. Now, we should connect every hospital to the Internet, so that doctors can instantly share data about their patients with the best specialists in the field. And I challenge the private sector tonight to start by connecting every children's hospital as soon as possible, so that a child in bed can stay in touch with school, family and friends. A sick child need no longer be a child alone.

We must build the second generation of the Internet so that our leading universities and national laboratories can communicate in speeds 1,000 times faster than today, to develop new medical treatments, new sources of energy, new ways of working together.

But we cannot stop there. As the Internet becomes our new town square, a computer in every home—a teacher of all subjects, a connection to all cultures—this will no longer be a dream, but a necessity. And over the next decade, that must be our goal.

We must continue to explore the heavens—pressing on with the Mars probes and the international space station, both of which will have practical applications for our everyday living.

We must speed the remarkable advances in medical science. The human genome project is now decoding the genetic mysteries of life. American scientists have discovered genes linked to breast cancer and ovarian cancer, and medication that stops a stroke in progress and begins to reverse its effect, and treatments that dramatically lengthen the lives of people with HIV and AIDS.

Since I took office, funding for AIDS research at the National Institutes of Health [NIH] has increased dramatically—to $1.5 billion. With new resources, NIH will now become the most powerful discovery engine for an AIDS vaccine, working with other scientists to finally end the threat of AIDS. Remember that every year—every year we move up the discovery of an AIDS vaccine will save millions of lives around the world. We must reinforce our commitment to medical science.

To prepare America for the 21st century, we must build stronger families. Over the past four years, the Family and Medical Leave law has helped millions of Americans to take time off to be with their families. With new pressures on people in the way they work and live, I believe we must expand family leave so that workers can take time off for teacher conferences and a child's medical checkup. We should pass flex-time, so workers can choose to be paid for overtime in income or trade it in for time off to be with their families.

We must continue—we must continue, step by step, to give more families access to affordable, quality health care. Forty million Americans still lack health insurance. Ten million children still lack health insurance—80 percent of them have working parents who pay taxes. That is wrong.

My balanced budget will extend health coverage to up to 5 million of those children. Since nearly half of all children who lose their insurance do so because their parents lose or change a job, my budget will also ensure that people who temporarily lose their jobs can still afford to keep their health insurance. No child should be without a doctor just because a parent is without a job.

My Medicare plan modernizes Medicare, increases the life of the trust fund to ten years, provides support for respite care for the many families with loved ones afflicted with Alzheimer's. And for the first time, it would fully pay for annual mammograms.

Just as we ended drive-through deliveries of babies last year, we must now end the dangerous and demeaning practice of forcing women home from the hospital only hours after a mastectomy. I ask your support for bipartisan legislation to guarantee that a woman can stay in the hospital for forty-eight hours after a mastectomy. With us tonight is Dr. Kristen Zarfos, a Connecticut surgeon whose outrage at this practice spurred a national movement and inspired this legislation. I'd like her to stand so we thank her for her efforts. Dr. Zarfos, thank you.

In the last four years, we have increased child support collections by 50 percent. Now we should go further and do better by making it a felony for any parent to cross a state line in an attempt to flee from this, his or her most sacred obligation.

Finally, we must also protect our children by standing firm in our determination to ban the advertising and marketing of cigarettes that endanger their lives.

To prepare America for the 21st century, we must build stronger communities. We should start with safe streets. Serious crime has dropped five years in a row. The key has been community policing. We must finish the job of putting 100,000 community police on the streets of the United States. We should pass the Victims Rights Amendment to the Constitution.

And I ask you to mount a full-scale assault on juvenile crime, with legislation that declares war on gangs, with new prosecutors and tougher penalties; extends the Brady Bill so violent teen criminals will not be able to buy handguns; requires child safety locks on handguns to prevent unauthorized use; and helps to keep our schools open after hours, on weekends, and in the summer, so our young people will have someplace to go and something to say yes to.

This balanced budget includes the largest antidrug effort ever: to stop drugs at their source, punish those who push them, and teach our young people that drugs are wrong, drugs are illegal, and drugs will kill them. I hope you will support it.

Our growing economy has helped to revive poor urban and rural neighborhoods. But we must do more to empower them to create the conditions in which all families can flourish and to create jobs through investment by business and loans by banks.

We should double the number of empowerment zones. They've already brought so much hope to communities like Detroit, where the unemployment rate has been cut in half in four years. We should restore contaminated urban land and buildings to productive use. We should expand the network of community development banks. And together we must pledge tonight that we will use this empowerment approach—including private sector tax incentives—to renew our Capital City, so that Washington is a great place to work and live, and once again the proud face America shows to world.

We must protect our environment in every community. In the last four years, we cleaned up 250 toxic waste sites, as many as in the previous twelve. Now, we should clean up 500 more, so that our children grow up next to parks, not poison. I urge you to pass my proposal to make big polluters live by a simple rule: If you pollute our environment, you should pay to clean it up.

In the last four years, we strengthened our nation's safe food and clean drinking water laws; we protected some of America's rarest, most beautiful land in Utah's Red Rocks region; created three new national parks in the California desert; and began to restore the Florida Everglades. Now we must be as vigilant with our rivers as we are with our lands. Tonight, I announce that this year I will designate ten American Heritage Rivers, to help communities alongside them revitalize their waterfronts and clean up pollution in the rivers, proving once again that we can grow the economy as we protect the environment.

We must also protect our global environment, working to ban the worst toxic chemicals and to reduce the greenhouse gases that challenge our health even as they change our climate.

Now, we all know that in all of our communities, some of our children simply don't have what they need to grow and learn in their own homes, or schools or neighborhoods. And that means the rest of us must do more, for they are our children, too. That's why President Bush, General Colin Powell, former housing secretary Henry Cisneros will join the vice president and me to lead the President's Summit of Service in Philadelphia in April.

Our national service program, AmeriCorps, has already helped 70,000 young people to work their way through college as they serve America. Now we intend to mobilize millions of Americans to serve in thousands of ways. Citizen service is an American responsibility which all Americans should embrace, and I ask your support for that endeavor.

I'd like to make just one last point about our national community. Our economy is measured in numbers and statistics, and it's very important. But the enduring worth of our nation lies in our shared values and our soaring spirit. So instead of cutting back on our modest efforts to support the arts and humanities, I believe we should stand by them and challenge our artists, musicians, and writers—challenge our museums, libraries and theaters— we should challenge all Americans in the arts and humanities to join with our fellow citizens to make the year 2000 a national celebration of the American spirit in every community—a celebration of our common culture in the century that has passed, and in the new one to come in a new millennium, so that we can remain the world's beacon not only of liberty, but of creativity, long after the fireworks have faded.

To prepare America for the 21st century we must master the forces of change in the world and keep American leadership strong and sure for an uncharted time.

Fifty years ago, a farsighted America led in creating the institutions that secured victory in the cold war and built a growing world economy. As a result, today more people than ever embrace our ideals and share our interests. Already, we have dismantled many of the blocs and barriers that divided our parents' world. For the first time, more people live under democracy than dictatorship, including every nation in our own hemisphere, but one—and its day, too, will come.

Now, we stand at another moment of change and choice—and another time to be farsighted, to bring America fifty more years of security and prosperity. In this endeavor, our first task is to help to build, for the first time, an undivided, democratic Europe. When Europe is stable, prosperous and at peace, America is more secure.

To that end, we must expand NATO by 1999, so that countries that were once our adversaries can become our allies. At the special NATO summit this summer, that is what we will begin to do. We must strengthen NATO's Partnership for Peace with nonmember allies. And we must build a stable partnership between NATO and a democratic Russia. An expanded NATO is good for America. And a Europe in which all democracies define their future not in terms of what they can do to each other, but in terms of what they can do together for the good of all—that kind of Europe is good for America.

Second, America must look to the East no less than to the West. Our security demands it. Americans fought three wars in Asia in this century. Our prosperity requires it. More than two million American jobs depend upon trade with Asia.

There, too, we are helping to shape an Asian Pacific community of cooperation, not conflict. Let our progress there not mask the peril that remains. Together with South Korea, we must advance peace talks with North Korea and bridge the Cold War's last divide. And I call on Congress to fund our share of the agreement under which North Korea must continue to freeze and then dismantle its nuclear weapons program.

We must pursue a deeper dialogue with China—for the sake of our interests and our ideals. An isolated China is not good for America. A China playing its proper role in the world is. I will go to China, and I have invited China's President to come here, not because we agree on everything, but because engaging China is the best way to work on our common challenges like ending nuclear testing, and to deal frankly with our fundamental differences like human rights.

The American people must prosper in the global economy. We've worked hard to tear down trade barriers abroad so that we can create good jobs at home. I am proud to say that today, America is once again the most competitive nation and the number one exporter in the world.

Now we must act to expand our exports, especially to Asia and Latin America—two of the fastest growing regions on Earth—or be left behind as these emerging economies forge new ties with other nations. That is why we need the authority now to conclude new trade agreements that open markets to our goods and services even as we preserve our values.

We need not shrink form the challenge of the global economy. After all, we have the best workers and the best products. In a truly open market, we can out-compete anyone, anywhere on Earth.

But this is about more than economics. By expanding trade, we can advance the cause of freedom and democracy around the world. There is no better example of this truth than Latin America where democracy and open markets are on the march together. That is why I will visit there in the spring to reinforce our important tie.

We should all be proud that America led the effort to rescue our neighbor, Mexico, from its economic crises. And we should all be proud that last month Mexico repaid the United States—three full years ahead of schedule—with half a billion dollar profit to us.

America must continue to be an unrelenting force for peace—from the Middle East to Haiti, from Northern Ireland to Africa. Taking reasonable risks for peace keeps us from being drawn into far more costly conflicts later.

With American leadership, the killing has stopped in Bosnia. Now the habits of peace must take hold. The new NATO force will allow reconstruction and reconciliation to accelerate. Tonight, I ask Congress to continue its strong support for our troops. They are doing a remarkable job there for America, and America must do right by them.

Fifth, we must move strongly against new threats to our security. In the past four years, we agreed to ban—we led the way to a worldwide agreement to ban nuclear testing. With Russia, we dramatically cut nuclear arsenals and we stopped targeting each others citizens. We are acting to prevent nuclear materials from falling into the wrong hands and to rid the world of land mines. We are working with other nations with renewed intensity to fight drug traffickers and to stop terrorists before they act, and hold them fully accountable if they do.

Now, we must rise to a new test of leadership: ratifying the Chemical Weapons Convention. Make no mistake about it, it will make our troops safer from chemical attack; it will help us to fight terrorism. We have no more important obligations—especially in the wake of what we now know about the Gulf War. This treaty has been bipartisan from the beginning—supported by Republican and Democratic administrations and Republican and Democratic members of Congress—and already approved by sixty-eight nations.

But if we do not act by April the 29th—when this Convention goes into force, with or without us—we will lose the chance to have Americans leading and enforcing this effort. Together we must make the Chemical Weapons Convention law, so that at last we can begin to outlaw poison gas from the Earth.

Finally, we must have the tools to meet all these challenges. We must maintain a strong and ready military. We must increase funding for weapons modernization by the year 2000, and we must take good care of our men and women in uniform. They are the world's finest.

We must also renew our commitment to America's diplomacy, and pay our debts and dues to international financial institutions like the World Bank, and to a reforming United Nations. Every dollar we devote to preventing conflicts, to promoting democracy, to stopping the spread of disease and starvation, brings a sure return in security and savings. Yet international affairs spending today is just 1 percent of the federal budget—a small fraction of what America invested in diplomacy to choose leadership over escapism at the start of the Cold War. If America is to continue to lead the world, we here who lead America simply must find the will to pay our way.

A farsighted America moved the world to a better place over these last fifty years. And so it can be for another fifty years. But a shortsighted America will soon find its words falling on deaf ears all around the world.

Almost exactly fifty years ago, in the first winter of the cold war, President Truman stood before a Republican Congress and called upon our country to meet its responsibilities of leadership. This was his warning—he said, "If we falter, we may endanger the peace of the world, and we shall surely endanger the welfare of this nation." That Congress, led by Republicans like Senator Arthur Vandenberg, answered President Truman's call. Together, they made the commitments that strengthened our country for fifty years.

Now let us do the same. Let us do what it takes to remain the indispensable nation—to keep America strong, secure and prosperous for another fifty years.

In the end, more than anything else, our world leadership grows out of the power of our example here at home, out of our ability to remain strong as one America.

All over the world, people are being torn asunder by racial, ethnic, and religious conflicts that fuel fanaticism and terror. We are the world's most diverse democracy, and the world looks to us to show that it is possible to live and advance together across those kinds of differences.

America has always been a nation of immigrants. From the start, a steady stream of people, in search of freedom and opportunity, have left their own lands to make this land their home. We started as an experiment in democracy fueled by Europeans. We have grown into an experiment in democratic diversity fueled by openness and promise.

My fellow Americans, we must never, ever believe that our diversity is a weakness—it is our greatest strength. Americans speak every language, know every county. People on every continent can look to us and see the reflection of their own great potential—and they always will, as long as we strive to give all of our citizens, whatever their background, an opportunity to achieve their own greatness.

We're not there yet. We still see evidence of abiding bigotry and intolerance, in ugly words and awful violence, in burned churches and bombed buildings. We must fight against this, in our country and in our hearts.

Just a few days before my second Inauguration, one of country's best known pastors, Reverend Robert Schuller, suggested that I read Isaiah 58:12. Here's what it says: "Thou shalt raise up the foundations of many generations, and thou shalt be called, the repairer of the breach, the restorer of paths to dwell in." I placed my hand on that verse when I took the oath of office, on behalf of all Americans. For no matter what our differences—in our faiths, our backgrounds, our politics—we must all be repairers of the breach.

I want to say a word about two other Americans who show us how. Congressman Frank Tejeda [D-Texas] was buried yesterday, a proud American whose family came from Mexico. He was only fifty-one years old. He was awarded the Silver Star, the Bronze Star and the Purple Heart, fighting for his country in Vietnam. And he went on to serve Texas and America fighting for our future in this chamber. We are grateful for his service and honored that his mother, Lillie Tejeda, and his sister, Mary Alice, have come from Texas to be with us here tonight. And we welcome you.

Gary Locke, the newly elected governor of Washington State, is the first Chinese-American governor in the history of our country. He's the proud son of two of the millions of Asian-American immigrants who have strengthened America with their hard work, family values and good citizenship. He represents the future we can all achieve. Thank you, Governor, for being here. Please stand up.

Reverend Schuller, Congressman Tejeda, Governor Locke, along with Kristin Tanner and Chris Getsla, Sue Winski and Dr. Kristen Zarfos—they're all Americans from different roots, whose lives reflect the best of what we can become when we are one America. We may not share a common past, but we surely do share a common future.

Building one America is our most important mission—"the foundation for many generations," of every other strength we must build for this new century. Money cannot buy it. Power cannot compel it. Technology cannot create it. It can only come from the human spirit.

America is far more than a place. It is an idea, the most powerful idea in the history of nations. And all of us in this chamber, we are now the bearers of that idea, leading a great people into a new world. A child born tonight will have almost no memory of the 20th century. Everything that child will know about America will be because of what we do now to build a new century.

We don't have a moment to waste. Tomorrow there will be just over 1,000 days until the year 2000. One thousand days to prepare our people. One thousand days to work together. One thousand days to build a bridge to a land of new promise. My fellow Americans, we have work to do. Let us seize those days and the century.

Thank you, God bless you and God bless America.

WATTS'S REPUBLICAN RESPONSE

Good evening.

My name is J. C. Watts Jr. I'm the Republican congressman from the 4th District of Oklahoma, and I've been asked to speak to the American people in response to the president's address this evening.

Before I get into my presentation, I want to send condolences to the [Rep. Frank] Tejeda [D-Texas] family on behalf of the 105th Congress. Frank was a friend, he was a wonderful spirit, and he will be surely missed.

I don't intend to take a lot of your time. It's late and there has been a lot of talk already this evening, but I want to tell you a little bit about where I'm from.

I grew up in Oklahoma. My district includes the towns of Midwest City, Norman, Lawton, Walters, Waurika and Duncan, just to name a few. We raise cattle back home, we grow some cotton and wheat, peanuts, and we drill for oil.

We've got Tinker and Altus Air Force bases nearby, and we have the Army post at Fort Sill. The University of Oklahoma is there. That's where I went to school. I played a little football and graduated with a degree in journalism. I tell you all this because I want you to know that the district I'm blessed to represent is as diverse as America itself.

It's the kind of place reporters usually call the heartland. And they're right. In so many ways it is America's heart.

I'm going to try to use my words tonight and my time not to confuse issues but to clarify them; not to obscure my philosophy and my party's, but to illuminate it, because the way I see it the purpose of politics is to lead, not to mislead.

Those of us who have been sent to Washington have a moral responsibility to offer more than poll-tested phrases and winning smiles. We must offer a serious vision. We must share our intentions. We must make our plans clear. That's my job tonight: to tell you what we believe, what the Republican Party believes, and what we will work for.

We believe first of all that the state of this union really isn't determined in Washington D.C. It never has been, and it never will be. But for a long time the federal government has been grabbing too much power and too much authority over all of the people. And it is those people, it is all of us, who decide the real state of the union.

Doc Benson in Oklahoma City decides the state of the union. He runs a nonprofit called the Education and Employment Ministry where he believes that you restore men and women by restoring their dreams and finding them a job.

Freddy Garcia is the state of the union also. Freddy was a drug addict in San Antonio, Texas. Now he has a ministry helping people get off drugs. His Victory Fellowship has success rates that the social scientists can only dream of.

I saw the state of the union last week in Marlow, Okla. A bunch of us met at the elementary school where we ate beef brisket and baked beans, and the Chamber of Commerce recognized the Farm Family of the Year. The McCarleys won, and their kids were oh, so proud.

The strength of America is not in Washington, the strength of America is at home in lives well lived in the land of faith and family. The strength of America is not on Wall Street but on Main Street, not in big business but in small businesses with local owners and workers. It's not in Congress, it's in the city hall. And I pray Republicans and Democrats both understand this. We shouldn't just say it, we should live it.

And so we have made it our mission to limit the claims and demands of Washington; to limit its call for more power, more authority and more taxes. Our mission is to return power to your home, to where mothers and fathers can exercise it according to their beliefs.

So let me tell you three actions the Republicans will take in the coming year.

Values First, we can help our country by bringing back the knowledge, the ancient wisdom, that we're nothing without our spiritual, traditional and family values. The Republicans will take action to give those values a bigger place in solving America's problems. After all, our values are more important to our future than any so-called bureaucratic breakthrough. Think about your life and how you built it.

I didn't get my values from Washington. I got my values from my parents, from Buddy and Helen Watts, in Eufaula, Okla. I got my values growing up in a poor black neighborhood on the east side of the railroad tracks, where money was scarce but dreams were plentiful and love was all around. I got my values from a strong family, a strong church and a strong neighborhood.

I wasn't raised to be Republican or Democrat. My parents just taught by example. They taught me and my brothers and sisters that, if you lived under their roof, you were going to work. They taught us, if you made a mistake, as we all do, you've got to own up to it, you call it what it is, and you try to turn it around. They taught us, if you spend more money than you make, you're on a sure road to disaster.

I was taught to respect everyone for the simple reason that we're all God's children. I was taught, in the words of Dr. Martin Luther King Jr., and from my uncle, Wade Watts, to judge a man not by the color of his skin, but by the content of his character. And I was taught that character does count, and that character is simply doing what's right when nobody's looking.

My parents also taught me I could do anything if I applied myself and understood sacrifice and commitment.

Now if you if you agree with those things my parents taught me and that I'm trying to teach my children, then, friends, we have common ground.

It is the Republican Party that has been trying to return these values to government, and it hasn't been easy, because for a long time the government has acted as if it didn't have any common sense.

Here's an example: For the past 30 years our nation's spent $5 trillion trying to erase poverty, and the result, as you know, is that we didn't get rid of it at all. In fact, we spread it. We destroyed the self-esteem of millions of people, grinding them down in a welfare system that penalizes moms for wanting to marry the father of their children, and penalizes mom for wanting to save money. Friends, that's not right.

Last year the Republican Congress moved to reform the welfare system, and for the first time in my lifetime, we're helping people climb the ladder of economic opportunity.

Let me tell you the next step.

A number of my colleagues and I, my Republican colleagues and I are working on a package called The American Community Renewal Act. It seeks to return government to the side of the institutions that hold communities together: faith, family, hard work, strong neighborhoods. This will help rebuild low income communities through their own moral renewal and giving them economic opportunity. It also recognizes that faith-based institutions contribute to the healing of our nation's problems.

So our first priority is to bring values back and give them pride of place in our moral and economic renewal. And in the next few weeks we will be visiting a number of communities to highlight the accomplishments of active faith-based organizations.

The second thing Republicans will do is face a problem that demands immediate attention. We must get our government's financial affairs in order. The biggest step in that direction is an amendment to the U.S. Constitution that demands that the federal government balance its books.

We are more than $5 trillion in debt. This year we will spend $330 billion on interest payments alone on the national debt. And you know what? Not one dime of that $330 billion will go to strengthen Medicare, Medicaid. Not one dime of it will go to find a cure for cancer or fight drugs and crime. And worse yet, not one dime will go toward learning, making the classrooms a centerpiece of our education.

Over $5 trillion worth of national debt is more than financially irresponsible. Friends, it's immoral, because someone is going to have to pay the piper. And you know who it's going to be? It's going to be our kids and our grandkids.

The American family is already overtaxed. Right now the average family spends about half of every dollar they earn in some type of government tax or government fee.

Consider a 5-year-old child today. If things continue as they are, by the time they're 25 they'll pay about 84 cents of every dollar they make in some government tax or government fee. Friends, that's more than a shame, it's a scandal.

The balanced budget amendment will force the government to change its ways permanently.

No longer will the president or Congress be able to spend money we don't have on benefits our children will never see.

In a few weeks, we will vote on that amendment. Republicans can't pass it on our own; it takes a two-thirds majority. So we need Democrat votes and we need your help. We need you to write or call your representative and senators and tell them to pass the balanced budget amendment now.

And here's the good news. A balanced budget will lower your house payment, lower your car payment, lower your student loan payments. The savings could be as much as $1,500 a year. Well, to some up here in Washington $1,500 may not be much, however, it's a new washer and dryer, it's a home computer, or money toward a much needed second car for a hard-working family.

And by the way, don't believe all those dire warnings about the amendment wrecking Social Security. That's just not true. I encourage all of us in Congress—Republicans and Democrats—to appeal to people's intelligence and not to their fears.

President Clinton was right on target tonight. He said people want bipartisanship. I believe they do. But they want the kind of bipartisanship that results in progress. They don't want phony compromise; they don't want the kind of weak, back-scratching, go-along-to-get-along bipartisanship that allows lawmakers to feel good but gets bad results.

There are some striking examples of cooperation this past year. When Republicans led the effort to reform welfare, President Clinton opposed it at first, but eventually, after we passed it, he bowed to the will of the people and signed it. We applaud the president's embrace of reform. And, Mr. President, from the bottom of my heart, we are pleased to continue this bipartisan effort.

And there was a promise of bipartisanship tonight when the president signaled his interest in tax relief.

Working Americans need real tax relief, not just targeted tax cuts to help one group at the expense of another. We all pay too much in taxes.

I hope the president shares this belief with us and works with us to bring desperately needed tax relief to America's working families. And we must work together—Democrats and Republicans—to win the twin wars against drugs and ignorance. The war on drugs can and will be won in large measure by making sure that every child in America can walk to school safely, sit in a classroom where the teacher can really help them learn.

Third and finally, I want to say a few words about the Republican vision of how we can continue to make this one nation under God, indivisible with liberty and justice for all.

You know, I'm just old enough to remember the Jim Crow brand of discrimination. I've seen issues of race hurt human beings and hurt our entire nation. Too often when we talk about racial healing, we make the old assumption that government can heal the racial divide.

In my lifetime there have been some great and good laws that took some evil and ignorant laws off the books, so legislation has its place. But friends, we're at a point now where we have to ask ourselves some questions, and I ask you—if legislation is answer to the racial divide in our nation, then why in God's name in our time has the division grown? Why is the healing we long for so far from reality? Why does it seem that the more laws we pass, the less love we have?

The fact is our problems can't be solved by legislation alone. Surely we have learned from our long, difficult journey a great truth: government can't ease all pain. We must deal with the heart of man.

Republicans and Democrats—red, yellow, black and white—have to understand that we must individually, all of us, accept our share of responsibility. We must decide as we stand on the edge of the new age if we will captive of the past. America must be a place where all of us—red, yellow, brown, black and white—in some way feel a part of the American Dream. It does not happen by dividing us into racial groups. It does not happen by trying to turn rich against poor or by using the politics of fear. It does not happen by reducing our values to the lowest common denominator. And, friends, it does not happen by asking Americans to accept what's immoral and wrong in the name of tolerance.

We must make our mark on the future as a people who care, care for our families, for one another, for our neighbors, for all the beautiful children. We must make our mark as people who share and help each other in need. We must be a people who dare, dare to take responsibility for our hatreds and fears and ask God to heal us from within.

And we must be a people of prayer, a people who pray as if the strength of our nation depended on it, because it does. When you come right down to it, that's our vision and our agenda.

All over the country I've often told the story of a boy and his father. The father was trying to get some work done, and the boy wanted the daddy's attention, but the father was busy at his desk with so much to do. To occupy the boy, this father gave his son a pencil and a paper and said, "Here, son, go draw the family." Two minutes later, he was back with a picture, all stick figures. So the dad, trying to buy some more time, said, "Here, go draw the dog." Two minutes later, he comes back with another stick figure.

Now the father was exasperated. He looked around, he saw a magazine, and he remembered that he had seen a picture of the world in this magazine. In what he thought was a stroke of genius, the father tore out the picture and tore it into 20 different pieces, and he said, "Here, son. Go put the world back together."

And you know what happened? Five minutes later the little Michelangelo was back, saying, "Daddy, look what I've done." The father looked, and he said, "Son, how did you do it so quickly? How did you put the world back together so quickly?" And the little boy answered, "Dad, it was easy. There was a picture of a man on the back of the map, on the back of the world. And once I put the man back together, the world fell into place."

And friends, this is our agenda: to put our men and women back together, to put ourselves back together, and, in that way, get our country back together.

I am reminded of the final words of President John Kennedy's inaugural address. He said this: "Let us go forth to lead the land we love, knowing that here on Earth, God's work truly must be our own." I say amen to that.

Thank you for your graciousness in listening to me so late in the evening. God bless you, and God bless our children. And thank you very much.

PRESIDENT'S ECONOMIC REPORT, ECONOMIC ADVISERS' REPORT
February 10, 1997

President Bill Clinton began his second term as president in the enviable position of presiding over a strong and apparently stable economy. Low inflation and unemployment rates combined with continued job and productivity growth to produce the "healthiest" American economy in three decades, according to the president's Council of Economic Advisers (CEA). That assessment of the nation's economic health was contained in the council's report, which accompanied the annual economic report of the president. Both reports were released February 10.

Between January 1993, when Clinton took office, and the end of 1996, the unemployment rate fell by a third, from 7.5 percent to 5.4 percent, and inflation averaged 2.8 percent. More than 11 million jobs were created, and business investment grew by more than 11 percent annually. At the same time, the poverty rate was falling and median family income, adjusted for inflation, was rising. "America's workers are back at work and our factories are humming," Clinton said in his brief report, urging a continuation of his economic program—deficit reduction, investment in education and training, expansion of free trade, and government reform.

The Effect of Declining Budget Deficits

In his report, the president noted that the federal budget deficit had fallen 63 percent, from $290 billion in fiscal 1992 to $107 billion in fiscal 1996. The CEA attributed the dramatic decline to a combination of federal budget legislation and the strong economy, which resulted in lower federal spending and higher tax revenues than the administration had anticipated. In October the administration announced that the deficit for fiscal 1997 had dropped to $23 billion, giving rise to speculation that the budget would be in balance several years before the legislated target date of fiscal 2002. (Budget agreement, p. 602; stock market streak, p. 721)

Although economists cannot isolate the precise effect deficit reduction has on the economy, the CEA said that without the Clinton budget policies, it was unlikely that the economy would have experienced such a healthy expansion. The Clinton administration's trade agreements were also instrumental in the expanding economy, the CEA said. Exports since 1993 had increased by more than a third and accounted for a third of all economic growth. Jobs in industries that export goods paid about 13 to 16 percent more than the average job in the United States.

Economic Expansion Likely to Continue

By the end of 1996 the economic expansion had lasted for sixty-nine months, the third-longest in postwar history, and many were asking how long it could continue. Some economists, among them Federal Reserve Chairman Alan Greenspan, had questioned how long unemployment could remain low without sparking inflation. In the past, economists have thought that when the jobless rate falls below a certain level, called a natural or nonaccelerating-inflation rate of unemployment, workers begin to demand higher wages, which in turn cause higher prices, leading to a cycle of rising inflation, higher interest rates, and slower economic growth.

For some years the natural rate of unemployment was thought to be somewhere around 6 percent. But between September 1994 and December 1996 the average jobless rate was 5.5 percent, and during that same period inflation fell from 3 percent to 2.6 percent. If the natural rate of unemployment were 6 percent, inflation should have gone up half a percentage point, the CEA said. Thus, they reasoned, the natural rate of unemployment must have declined.

According to the CEA, two main factors accounted for this decline. First, the baby boom generation was aging, leading to a more mature labor force with fewer teenagers and young adults—the age groups that traditionally had higher jobless rates. This demographic effect was likely to persist for some time, the CEA said. A second factor was what the CEA called "the wage aspiration effect," in which workers recognize that their demands for inflation-adjusted, or real, wage increases are limited by growth of real productivity. Since productivity began to slow in 1973, "workers have now had time to lower their aspirations for real wage growth to reflect the slower productivity growth," the advisers said.

The CEA acknowledged the difficulty of predicting how long workers would continue to delay their wage aspirations. Statistics showed some acceleration in wage levels in 1996, but the CEA said those increases were offset by a slowing of increases in employee benefits, particularly health benefits. Even if the reduction in the rise of employer-paid health premiums were temporary, the CEA said the wage increases alone were not high enough to put upward pressure on inflation.

Other factors were also working to hold down inflation, according to the CEA. High corporate profits were apparently acting as "a temporary buffer," allowing companies to absorb some increases in labor costs without raising prices. Increased competition, both domestically in deregulated markets and from overseas, was also helping to hold down prices. Overall, the CEA said, the risk of heightened inflation was minimal, and there was "no foreseeable reason" why the economic expansion should not continue.

Long-Term Economic Challenges

Despite the strong economy, the nation still faced several thorny economic challenges. A persistent problem for several years has been rising inequality between the richest and poorest Americans. Income statistics from 1993 to 1995 indicated that the twenty-year trend might be reversing, the CEA said. The decline in poverty, from 15.1 percent in 1993 to 13.8 percent in 1995, was the largest two-year reduction since 1973. Once the effects of the Earned Income Tax Credit were taken into account, the reduction in the poverty rate was even higher. Moreover, the CEA said, while household income increased across the board, income for the poorest fifth of the population increased at more than double the rate of income for the wealthiest two-fifths of the population. But cautioned CEA Chairman Joseph E. Stiglitz at a news briefing on February 10, "these reversals, while dramatic, do not come close to undoing the 20 years of increasing inequality. Also it seems rash to declare definitively an end to a 20-year trend based on two years of data."

Another major challenge was the aging of the population. As the baby boom generation begins to move into old age, Social Security spending was expected to grow from 4.7 percent of gross domestic product (GDP) in 1996 to 6.4 percent in 2030 and then stabilize. Projected outlays for Medicare and Medicaid were even higher, from 3.9 percent of GDP in 1996 to 13.0 percent in 2050. Without major reform, such high levels of spending would either swell the federal budget or crowd out other government spending on such important functions as education, infrastructure, and basic research and development. Determining how government allocates its resources between the aged and the rest of its citizens poses difficult issues that can best be addressed in a bipartisan fashion, the CEA said.

Following is the text of the Economic Report of the President and excerpts from chapter 1 of the Annual Report of the Council of Economic Advisers, both issued by the White House on February 10, 1997:

ECONOMIC REPORT OF THE PRESIDENT

To the Congress of the United States:

Four years ago, we began a journey to change the course of the American economy. We wanted this country to go into the 21st century as a Nation in which every American who was willing to work for it could have a chance— not a guarantee, but a real chance at the American dream. We have worked hard to achieve that goal, and today our economy is stronger than it has been in decades.

The Economic Record

The challenge we faced in January 1993 was to put the economy on a new course of fiscal responsibility while continuing to invest in our future. In the last 4 years, the unemployment rate has come down by nearly a third: from 7.5 percent to 5.4 percent. The economy has created 11.2 million new jobs, and over two-thirds of recent employment growth has been in industry/occupation groups paying above-median wages. Over the past 4 years inflation has averaged 2.8 percent, lower than in any Administration since John F. Kennedy was President. The combination of unemployment and inflation is the lowest it has been in three decades. And business investment has grown more than 11 percent per year—its fastest pace since the early 1960s.

As the economy has grown, the fruits of that growth are being shared more equitably among all Americans. Between 1993 and 1995 the poverty rate fell from 15.1 percent to 13.8 percent—the largest 2-year drop in over 20 years. Poverty rates among the elderly and among African-Americans are at the lowest level since these data were first collected in 1959. And real median family income has risen by $1,600—the largest growth rate since the Administration of President Johnson.

The Economic Agenda

Our comprehensive economic agenda has helped put America's economy back on the right track. This agenda includes:

- *Historic Deficit Reduction.* Since the 1992 fiscal year, the Federal budget deficit has been cut by 63 percent—from $290 billion to $107 billion in fiscal 1996. As a percentage of the Nation's gross domestic product, the deficit has fallen over the same period from 4.7 percent to 1.4 percent, and it is now the lowest it has been in more than 20 years. In 1992 the budget deficit for all levels of government was larger in relation to our plan that balances the budget by 2002, while protecting critical investments in America's future.

- *Investments in Education and Technology.* Deficit reduction remains a priority, but it is not an end in itself. Balancing the budget by cutting investments in education, or by failing to give adequate support to science and technology, could actually slow economic growth. To succeed in the new global economy, our children must receive a world-class education. Every child in America should be able to read by the age of 8, log onto the Internet by the age of 12, and receive at least 14 years of quality education: 2 years of college should become as universal as high school is today. And we must make sure that every child who wants to go to college has the resources to do so.

- *Expanding Markets.* We have aggressively sought to expand exports and open markets abroad. In the past 4 years we have achieved two major trade agreements: the North American Free Trade Agreement and the Uruguay Round accord of the General Agreement on Tariffs and Trade, which established the World Trade Organization. Members of the

53

Asia-Pacific Economic Cooperation forum and the proposed Free Trade Area of the Americas have committed to establishing free trade among themselves by 2020 and 2005, respectively. And we have opened new markets abroad by signing more than 200 other important trade agreements. As a result, U.S. exports have boomed, which means higher wages for American workers in export industries—often 13 to 16 percent higher than the rest of the workforce.

- *Reforming Government.* The strength of the American economy lies in the energy, creativity, and determination of our citizens. Over the past 4 years we have worked hard to create an environment in which business can flourish. And as the private sector has expanded, the Federal Government has improved its efficiency and cost-effectiveness. We have energetically reformed regulations in key sectors of the economy, including telecommunications, electricity, and banking, as well as environmental regulation. And we have reduced the size of the Federal Government as a percentage of the workforce to the smallest it has been since the 1930s.

Continuing to Create an Economy for the 21st Century

America's workers are back at work and our factories are humming. Once again, America leads the world in automobile manufacturing. Our high-technology industries are the most competitive in the world. Poverty is down and real wages are at last beginning to rise. And we have laid the foundations for future long-term economic growth by reducing the deficit and investing in education.

During the past 4 years, we have worked to prepare all Americans for the challenges and opportunities of the new global economy of the 21st century. We have worked to restore fiscal discipline in our government, to expand opportunities for education and training for our children and workers, to reform welfare and encourage work, and to expand the frontiers of free trade. But there is more work to be done. We must continue to provide our citizens with the tools to make the most of their own lives so that the American dream is within the reach of every American.

William J. Clinton
The White House
February 10, 1997

THE ANNUAL REPORT OF THE COUNCIL OF ECONOMIC ADVISERS

Growth and Opportunity: Creating a New Economic Order

The American economy today is the healthiest it has been in three decades. But just as important as the economy's current performance is the foundation being laid for its future health and strength. Like its predecessors, this Economic Report of the President, the last of this President's first Administration, summarizes the present state of the economy and the accomplishments of the past 4 years. But it also sets forth the economic legacy this Administration hopes to leave. That legacy includes a vibrant and evolving set of public institutions, investments that will provide the basis for continued growth, and an economic philosophy of government and markets that will help to guide these institutions and investments. Together these will constitute a bequest to future generations, contributing to rising living standards, expanded opportunities, and a greater sense of community.

The real measure of the success of any Administration's economic policies is not just today's economic statistics, but also the strength of the Nation's economy in 10 or 20 years' time. Today's economic policies will be judged favorably if, as a result, growth is stronger, the environment cleaner, and the number of children growing up in poverty fewer. History will pronounce these efforts a success if, a generation from now, opportunity has been expanded in our cities, tomorrow's senior citizens are at least as economically secure as today's, and all our citizens have the education they need not just to cope with but to profit from the challenges of a changing world. If we can look back upon a record of such accomplishments, we will know that the last years of the 20th century laid a solid foundation for the 21st.

No Administration starts with a clean slate: each must work with the assets and the liabilities it has inherited, and each Administration that follows will to some degree reshape and revise what this one has built. We are constrained and enabled not just by our physical and our fiscal inheritance, but also by our intellectual inheritance—by prevailing modes of thought and by the ways in which we and our contemporaries view and approach the world. Consequently, it is hard enough in the present to formulate the policies that will guide us toward a more prosperous future, harder still to assess today their impact decades hence.

For more than two decades America has faced several serious problems: productivity growth has been slower than in the past, income inequality has increased, and poverty has persisted. In addition, serious challenges loom for the future, such as the aging of the baby boom, which threatens to create severe fiscal strains in the next century. In the last 4 years the Administration has taken important steps to respond to these challenges. Only if we maintain and extend these initiatives will we leave a strong legacy for the future. . . .

An Economic Philosophy

At the center of the U.S. economy is the market: vibrant competition among profit-maximizing firms has enhanced economic efficiency and generated innovation, giving the United States one of the highest standards of living in the world. Within this market-based economy, government plays a limited, yet critical, role. It is essential to understand the proper role of government if the economy's strong performance is to continue and to improve.

In the past, two opposing visions of the American economy have vied for dominance. To put it starkly, one is a Panglossian view of an America of vigorous, self-sufficient individualism, the other of a world in which government is primarily responsible for our well-being. The first view is one of Horatio Algers making their way on their own, of self-reliant entrepreneurs creating wealth from which everyone eventually benefits. In this vision the main job of government is to keep out of the way, to do no harm. This economic world-view has its roots in the writings of Adam Smith, was refined into the classical liberalism of the 19th century, and has persisted into contemporary times in the rhetoric of the Reagan Presidency and its supporters.

The second vision is one that distrusts markets. At its extreme, this is a vision of an America full of monopolistic firms despoiling the environment and exploiting the masses of workers to earn huge profits for a handful of managers and shareholders. It sees pervasive market failures producing dire consequences, such as farmers and workers precluded from earning a decent living, and large parts of society—particularly in the inner cities and impoverished rural areas—simply left behind. The hero of this vision is government, endowed with both the omniscience and the omnipotence to cure these ills through active intervention in the market. The New Deal crystallized these currents into a new kind of liberalism, in some ways antithetical to the old.

The New Vision

Over the past 4 years, this Administration has promoted a third vision, one that synthesizes and transcends these two polar worldviews. This vision puts individuals at its center, but it emphasizes that individuals live within and draw strength from communities. It recognizes that many have been left behind by the changing economy and may need government assistance, but that the role for government is limited: it can and should promote opportunity, not dependence.

This new vision includes a renewed conception of government—one in which government recognizes both the market's efficiencies and its imperfections. The government can sometimes make markets work better, but it is seldom in a position to replace them. Government has its strengths and its limitations. We need to understand those limitations and, where possible, work to improve government's performance. The government cannot ignore the role of market forces in its own programs: it needs to take advantage of the power of incentives to accomplish its objectives.

Critics of government often pose a false dilemma: which can do the job better, the government or the market? Yet the question is seldom whether government should replace the market, but rather whether government can usefully complement the market. On this question a consensus holds that, in many particular circumstances, the answer is clearly yes. In the trough of the Great Depression, for example, one out of four workers was without a job—clearly the market was not performing well. It was that harrowing experience that led to enactment of the Employment Act of 1946 (the same legislation that established the Council of Economic Advisers), which assigned to the Federal Government the responsibility to "promote maximum employment, production, and purchasing power."

Over the years, economists have identified the various circumstances in which markets fail to produce desirable outcomes, and in which selective government intervention can complement markets. Competition may be imperfect, market participants may lack needed information, or markets may be missing. Would-be innovators and entrepreneurs may fail to capture enough of the benefits of their activity to justify their effort, or the users of resources, such as clean air and water, may escape the full costs of their use, degrading the resources for all. Although such problems may occur throughout the economy, it is important for the government to focus on those that are particularly severe. Like any successful enterprise, it must identify a core mission and pursue it.

Government's Core Economic Mission

Government's presence in the economy has become so pervasive that we can easily lose sight of its core mission. A few simple principles can serve as a guide to rediscovering that core mission.

The criterion for government involvement in any activity should not be how essential that activity is to the economy, or how many jobs it generates, or how much it contributes to the trade balance. In the overwhelming number of cases, the government cannot hope to surpass private firms at generating output, jobs, and exports. The proper question in circumstances where a choice between government and the market arises is whether any reason exists not to rely on markets. Is there—in the language of economists—a market failure?

The government should focus its attention on those areas in which markets will not perform adequately on their own, in which individual responsibility is insufficient to produce desirable results, and in which collective action through government is the most effective remedy. Americans are better off in a society in which individuals are encouraged to exercise as much responsibility as possible. But both economic theory and historical evidence indicate that, left to themselves, individuals and firms will produce too little of some goods like basic scientific research, and too much of others, such as pollution and toxic wastes. We also know that, without government assistance, many children from disadvantaged backgrounds may not be able to realize their full potential. Government social insurance programs have enabled individuals to make provision for risks that almost all individuals face and that, at the time the programs were launched, markets did not—and still largely do not—address effectively. Among them are programs that provide some insurance against unemployment, retirement benefits secured against the risk of inflation, and medical care for the aged.

It is essential to remember, whenever evaluating an existing government program or contemplating a new one, that the government cannot direct resources to someone without taking resources away from someone else. In a full-employment economy such as the Nation enjoys today and hopes to maintain, misguided subsidies pull resources away from more productive sectors and divert them toward less productive ones. Some individuals gain, but society as a whole suffers a net loss.

To prepare the economy, and the government, for the 21st century, we need to rethink and revitalize our policies to respond to the new challenges.

We also need to strip away outmoded programs that respond primarily to problems of the past.

An International Vision

In international just as in domestic economic policy, two fundamentally different visions have long dominated the debate. At one extreme, countries interact atomistically in an undifferentiated world of free trade abroad and free markets at home. In this view, international economic relations are just a matter of opening markets. The other perspective harks back to 18th-century mercantilism, often supplemented with metaphors from the Cold War. It replaces ideological competition with economic competition, and sees the gains on one side of the border coming at the expense of losses on the other. The trade deficit, in this view, replaces the missile gap as the measure of our national inadequacy.

Here, too, this Administration has sought to carve a new path. It recognizes the benefits of free trade, but also the existence of international public goods, not just in the trade arena but in other dimensions of international affairs as well. This new vision does not split the difference between these two views; rather, it recognizes that the vision of trade as war is profoundly wrong. Trade is not a zero-sum game. It does not merely create a winner for every loser: all countries can gain. As America's trading partners grow, they buy more U.S. goods and services. As the U.S. economy grows, we buy more of theirs, so that trade can play a catalytic role in a virtuous cycle of ever-higher levels of growth and living standards. The opposite is also true: attempts by many countries in the 1930s to escape from the Great Depression by pursuing beggar-thy-neighbor policies only made everyone worse off.

Defenders of free trade can do it a disservice by promoting it as a way to create more jobs or to reduce bilateral trade deficits. Jobs, the unemployment rate, and the overall balance of payments are ultimately a consequence of macroeconomic policies, not of trade barriers. The real objective of free trade is to raise living standards by ensuring that more Americans are working in areas where the United States is comparatively more productive than its trading partners. In a full-employment economy, trade has more impact on the distribution of jobs than on the quantity of jobs.

The new philosophy recognizes that unfettered global markets are not, by themselves, sufficient. Markets function best within an institutional environment that makes rules to promote free competition while facilitating the cooperation necessary for a stable world economy. What is required is general understanding of the issues and difficulties in international trade and mutual commitments, of the kind embodied in the General Agreement on Tariffs and Trade and the World Trade Organization (WTO), not to allow the pleadings of special interests to interfere with the gains that all enjoy from free international trade.

The new philosophy also recognizes that just as domestic public goods will be underprovided by free markets at home, so a decentralized trading system is insufficient to supply public goods that benefit people around the globe. An important example of an international public good is economic cooperation, including that essential to maintaining free trade. Basic research and a clean environment are other examples of international public goods in which cooperation can provide benefits to the United States, while also helping other countries. In making these international public goods available, we need to combine competition in the international marketplace with cooperation in establishing the rules of the game.

The Economic Record

In 1992, against a backdrop of an uncertain and jobless recovery and rising budget deficits, the then-Governor of Arkansas, campaigning for President, set two basic goals for economic performance in his first term: to establish an economic environment in which more than 8 million jobs would be created, and to cut the Federal budget deficit in half. Both these goals have been surpassed.

The Achievements

In 1992 the national unemployment rate averaged 7.5 percent. Almost 10 million people were looking for work. Over the last 4 years the unemployment rate has come down to 5.4 percent. Not only has the economy created more than 11 million new jobs, over 3 million more than promised, but the new jobs are mostly good jobs: two-thirds of recent employment growth has been in industry/occupation groups paying wages above the median.

Meanwhile underlying inflationary pressures have subsided. In 1992, inflation as measured by the core consumer price index (the core CPI excludes the volatile food and energy components) was 3.7 percent. In 1996 core inflation was only 2.7 percent. The combination of low unemployment and stable inflation has given the United States the lowest "misery index" since the 1960s. . . .

Economic growth has been strong and sustainable. The economic expansion has been marked by a healthy balance among the components of demand. Private, not public, demand has been the engine of growth. The Administration's initiative to reinvent government has slowed the growth of the public sector. Private sector demand, by contrast, has grown at a 3.2 percent annual rate since the beginning of this Administration, up from 2.4 percent over the previous 12 years. It is particularly heartening to note that investment and exports have led the expansion. Investment is booming: real spending on producers' durable equipment has grown a stunning 11 percent per year since 1993. Not only has investment been the strongest component of demand for the past 4 years, but the new structures and equipment that it represents will remain part of the Nation's capital stock, promoting growth and productivity for years to come. The second-strongest component of growth has been exports, which have increased by 7 percent per year since this Administration took office.

Just as important as today's conjuncture of growth, unemployment, and inflation is the question of whether the economy can continue to grow, with low unemployment and stable inflation. In terms of sustainability and sound fundamentals, this expansion is one of the strongest in recent memory. In contrast, much of the growth of the 1980s and early 1990s was fueled by large deficits and a quadrupling of the national debt. This path of growth fueled by government spending could not have continued indefinitely. No less important, over that period changes in the tax system created perverse incentives that led to overbuilding of commercial real estate and high vacancy rates. Although investment rates were high, much of this investment did not enhance the long-run productive potential of the economy. Another factor that bodes well for this expansion to continue is the health of the financial system, which has finally recovered from the debacle of the late 1980s, caused in part by lax regulatory oversight.

Not only has the economy grown rapidly and sustainably, but the fruits of that growth have begun to be shared more equitably. Between 1993 and 1995, the most recent year for which data are available, the poverty rate fell from 15.1 percent to 13.8 percent—the largest 2 year drop in over 20 years. Poverty rates for elderly and for black Americans reached their lowest levels since these data began to be collected in 1959. Not only have the incomes of every quintile of the income distribution increased, but the largest percentage increase has been seen by the poorest in American society. Median real household income rose 2.7 percent in 1995—and more if, as some believe, the CPI has been overstating actual inflation. . . .

The Reasons

Since 1993 this Administration has developed a comprehensive agenda that has contributed to the Nation's current economic health and strength. The key elements of this agenda are reducing the deficit, opening markets at home and abroad, and restoring prudence to macroeconomic management.

Reducing the Deficit

The Administration's most important economic policy accomplishment has been a substantial reduction in the Federal budget deficit. Since the 1992 fiscal year the deficit has been cut, not just in half as the President promised, but by 63 percent—from $290 billion in 1992 to $107 billion in fiscal 1996. . . . As a share of gross domestic product (GDP), the deficit has fallen over the same period from 4.7 percent to 1.4 percent—its lowest level in more than 20 years. . . .

The dramatic decline in the deficit over the past 4 years is the result of many factors. By far the most important are the fiscal policy changes adopted in the Omnibus Budget Reconciliation Act of 1993 (OBRA93) and the stronger economic performance to which it contributed. Under the policies in place when this Administration took office, the 1996 deficit was projected to rise to $298 billion, even though the projection assumed 5 years of robust expansion.

Lower spending and increased revenues resulting from OBRA93 and subsequent legislation were responsible for more than $100 billion of deficit reduction in the fiscal year that ended in September 1996. The remaining budget savings are due to a combination of higher-than-expected tax revenues and lower-than-expected spending, which resulted from the stronger economy and a variety of technical factors unrelated to legislative changes. Many of these economic and technical factors are also the product, although less directly, of the Administration's policies—including the policy of deficit reduction itself. Even though the Administration felt confident that its policies would significantly improve the economy, it continued to use conservative forecasts for budgetary purposes: growth in every year of this Administration has turned out to exceed these budgetary forecasts. . . .

In short, had the Administration not put deficit reduction at the top of its economic agenda, the Nation's debt would surely be much larger, and its economic future bleaker, than they are today. And it is unlikely that the economy would have experienced as healthy an expansion as it has.

Opening Markets at Home

Another cornerstone of the Administration's economic strategy has been an aggressive policy of reforming regulatory structures in key sectors of the economy, including telecommunications, electricity, and banking. In reforming electricity and telecommunications regulation, the Administration's belief was that the proper regulatory structure would enhance competition, which would lead to valuable new services and lower prices. Recent financial reforms have provided greater incentives for competition and innovation, in ways that have reduced the overall cost of regulation to both the government and the banking sector itself while preserving and enhancing the safety and soundness of the Nation's banks. On the environmental front, the Administration has shown that regulatory policies that recognize the importance of incentives can be both cheaper and more effective than traditional regulatory controls. Tradable permits for sulfur dioxide emissions are a prime example. The full import of these and other regulatory changes will not be felt for years to come.

Opening Markets Abroad

The third element of the Administration's economic policy has been an aggressive effort to increase exports through the opening of markets abroad. Two major trade agreements—the North American Free Trade Agreement (NAFTA) and the Uruguay Round accord of the General Agreement on Tariffs and Trade, which established the World Trade Organization—were enacted during the President's first term. The first major fruits of the WTO are now on the horizon, with the December 1996 agreement in Singapore to reduce tariffs on a wide variety of information technology products to zero. The United States will certainly gain, both as a major exporter of information technology and as an importer, as American industries take advantage of new foreign technologies that will lower their costs and increase their productivity. In addition, the value of NAFTA to U.S. exports was proved during Mexico's 1995 financial crisis. Despite Mexico's sharp economic contraction, NAFTA ensured that Mexico kept its markets open to U.S. products, in sharp contrast to the restrictive policies that had followed Mexico's 1982 financial crisis. As a result, U.S. exports were maintained, and by 1996 they had risen to new records. Mexico also benefited because NAFTA prevented any potential recourse to insular and protectionist policies; partly as a result, by the second half of 1995 the Mexican economy had started to recover.

Two other major regional groupings—our Pacific Rim trading partners in the Asia-Pacific Economic Cooperation forum and our Western Hemisphere neighbors engaged in talks toward a Free Trade Area of the Americas—have made commitments toward free trade among their members by 2020 and 2005, respectively. More than 200 other trade agreements have been completed since the beginning of this Administration.

As already noted, U.S. exports have boomed, especially in those areas where trade agreements have been reached. Increased trade allows the United States—and its trading partners—to exploit comparative advantage. These gains from trade are reflected in the fact that wages in jobs supported by goods exports are 13 to 16 percent higher than the national average. Some critics suggest that the growth in exports was simply a matter of exchange rates tilting in favor of the United States. Over the last 4 years, however, the trade-weighted exchange rate of the dollar (a standard measure of exchange rates with all of the United States' principal trading partners) changed by only about 2 percent.

Restoring Confidence in Economic Policymaking

Americans now have more confidence in their government's handling of the economy. Polls show that more Americans rated the conduct of economic policy favorably in November 1996 than at any time in the previous decade. This vote of confidence was the result of a number of factors. First, the government was putting into practice an economic philosophy that not only seemed to be working, but was in accord with the country's basic values. That economic philosophy, as enunciated above, understands both that neither the market nor the government can correct all the shortcomings in American society. Government has a place, but government has to know its place. The initiatives outlined above—from getting the deficit under control to securing the long-overdue passage of a new telecommunications bill—were proof that this philosophy could work.

Not only was the substance of economic policy viewed as a success; so was the process of policy development. The establishment of a National Economic Council (NEC) to oversee that process ensured that the economy would get the same attention within the White House that foreign affairs had gotten since the National Security Council was established nearly 50 years earlier. The NEC has effectively coordinated the inputs of the many Federal agencies, to ensure that the President receives the best options and advice, without setting agency against agency in wasteful internal turf battles. Also, the public differences between the Federal Reserve and the executive branch that had sometimes characterized earlier Administrations were replaced with a respect for the central bank's independence.

The Economic Agenda

The United States still faces major economic challenges. American technology, the economy, and society are all changing rapidly. Instead of ignoring or lamenting these changes, the Nation must embrace them, transforming problems into opportunities. We can do this only if we set a coherent economic agenda. This Administration has already accomplished much with the policies of the last 4 years. In the next 4 years the Administration will continue to build on those policies, holding fast to its new vision of the government's role in the economy as the basis for an agenda to promote growth, opportunity, and responsibility.

Growth

Productivity growth has been slow since the early 1970s. Since 1973, annual rises in productivity in nonfarm businesses have averaged 1.1 percent, a drastic decline from the 2.8 percent annual average that the Nation enjoyed between 1960 and 1973. . . . Slower productivity growth has the direct consequence of retarding increases in the Nation's standard of living. It also places obstacles in the way of solving some of the Nation's other challenges. Americans may be less supportive of freer trade when trade liberalization has been associated, however spuriously, with slower growth. It will be harder to balance the budget over the long term, especially while supporting a growing aged population, when productivity growth is slow. And workers are more reluctant to share their resources with those who are worse off when they feel that their own wages are stagnant.

The sources of economic growth can be grouped under three headings: increases in physical capital, improvements in human capital, and increases in the overall efficiency of the economy—the amount of output per unit of input. The Administration's economic agenda is based on strengthening each of these three pillars of economic growth.

Increasing Physical Capital

The first pillar of economic growth is increases in physical capital, which enable workers to produce more goods and services. Because it reduces the government's borrowing, deficit reduction will remain the key to how much of national saving is available for private investment in physical capital. The Nation has made great progress in bringing down the deficit in the last 4 years, but this ground will be lost unless we address the strains that some of the major entitlement programs will place on the budget over the long term. As the population ages, expenditures on Social Security are expected to grow from an estimated 4.7 percent of GDP in 1996 to around 6.4 percent in 2030, then stabilize. A much more serious challenge is posed by Medicare and Medicaid. If nothing is done to reform these programs, their outlays are projected to grow from an estimated 3.9 percent of GDP in 1996 to 13.0 percent in 2050. Their projected growth is due not just to the aging of the population, as in the case of Social Security, but also to the expectation that the volume and intensity of medical services consumed will continue their rapid rise. . . .

Assuming Federal tax revenues remain at their historically constant level of around 18 percent of GDP, the projected increase in entitlements, especially Medicare and Medicaid, will have one of two effects: either it will balloon the budget deficit, or it will all but crowd out other vital government expenditures, including those necessary to sustain long-term economic growth, such as education and research and development. The deficit reduction of the last 4 years, however, has put the Nation in a position to address these long-term issues in a manner that preserves the important achievements of Medicare, Medicaid, and Social Security.

When the government runs a smaller deficit, it absorbs less private saving and frees up resources for private sector investment. But public investments in infrastructure, such as roads, schools, and airports, are also important. It is false economy to release funds for investment in one area by cutting back in another where the need and the return are just as great. Entrepreneurs will be reluctant to build new factories, homes, and offices if the highways and bridges that link them are inadequate for the new traffic they generate.

To be sure, government must take pains to see that every dollar it invests, like every other government dollar, is well spent. We have to think hard about how to put into place incentives that make such outcomes more likely. And we have to think carefully about which public investments should be the responsibility of the Federal Government and which the responsibility of States and localities. But fear of misdirected investment should not lead to underinvestment, because too little investment is costly to future growth. In short, we should not create an infrastructure deficit while attempting to improve the budget deficit.

Improving Human Capital

The second pillar of economic growth is improvements in what economists call human capital: the knowledge, experience, and skills of the workforce. As the economy has changed, the demands imposed on the brainpower of the American workforce have increased enormously. . . . [T]he returns to education, as measured by the difference in incomes between college and high school graduates, have risen sharply in the last 20 years. Much of this difference probably reflects the increasing importance of computer skills in the workplace.

Many American schools do a superb job of human capital formation, but some are failing at the task. Standardized test scores reflect only part of the learning that goes on in schools, yet the fact that American children perform less well on standard science and mathematics tests than many of their foreign counterparts is a continuing source of concern. There is no easy answer.

Recognizing the challenge that these changes pose, the President has set ambitious goals for the Nation's education system: every 8-year-old should be able to read, every 12-year-old should be able to log onto the Internet, every 18-year-old should be able to go to college, and every classroom and library in America should be linked to the Internet.

An array of policies, current and proposed, are directed toward achieving these goals. The America Reads initiative, working through the National Service program, will call on thousands of people to mobilize an army of a million volunteer tutors, dedicated to ensuring that every child in America can read by the age of 8. A good education in the early years of a child's life is necessary, but hardly sufficient to endow that child with the skills that our technological society demands. Therefore, in addition to early-education programs, we need to promote technology in the classroom and encourage young people to take more years of college.

Although the returns to additional years of education are substantial—between 5 percent and 15 percent—without government involvement many students would find it difficult to borrow for college. Not only do they lack a credit history, but they cannot borrow against expected future earnings—human capital cannot be pledged as collateral. The result is a classic market failure: markets by themselves do not provide all the education for which the benefits exceed the costs, even when the benefits are measured only in narrow economic terms. Since the G.I. Bill was passed in the 1940s, the Federal Government has had an acknowledged role in making higher education more affordable. Policies already implemented by this Administration are bringing us much closer to the day when every American who wants to will be able to attend at least 2 years of college. Under the new direct student loan program, for example, individuals can borrow money for college directly from the Federal Government and tailor their repayments to suit their own financial circumstances. Seeking to build on the success of this program, the President has also proposed tuition tax credits, to support those seeking higher education, and penalty-free withdrawals from individual retirement accounts, to encourage them to save for it themselves.

Meanwhile the Technology and Literacy Challenge initiative is bringing advanced computer technology into every classroom in the Nation. It is making significant progress toward ensuring that all American students are computer literate, equipped with the skills they will need in the 21st century. Under this initiative, 20 percent of all the schools in California have already been wired to the Internet—a good example of government and the private sector complementing each other. The Federal Government served as entrepreneur for this initiative, but much of the work was done by 50,000 volunteers, with many of the Nation's leading high-technology firms donating equipment. The initiative also stresses the development of educational software and the training of teachers to harness the potential of these new technologies.

Other steps are important in preparing the Nation's educational system for the 21st century. Recent reports have documented the extent to which America's public schools have become dilapidated. Schools with leaky and collapsing roofs have had to be closed. Because students need a more conducive environment in which to learn, the President has proposed $5 billion in Federal funding to support a program, administered by the States, that would spend $20 billion for school construction and renovation. Additional efforts are focused on enhancing resources for those communities facing the hardest problems (e.g., those with disproportionate numbers of disadvantaged children), improving standards through the Goals 2000 program, and promoting new approaches through the charter school movement.

Education does not end with college. That is why this Administration has consistently emphasized lifelong learning and employability security, to boost economic growth and reduce the adjustment costs associated with a vibrant economy. Unfortunately, the legacy of past efforts in this sphere has left workers facing a complicated maze of dozens of government-assisted training programs, each with its own rules, regulations, and restrictions. The President has proposed replacing this complex system with a single choice-based system for adults. This system should use a market-oriented approach, relying on training vouchers or grants to empower people directly to seek the training that will help them the most.

Research and Development

The third pillar of growth is greater economic efficiency—learning to produce more output with fewer inputs. Additions to the Nation's technological arsenal through research and development are an important contributor to efficiency: private industry invests over $100 billion in research and development each year. This is a huge sum, but it may not be enough: history and economic theory suggest that, left to their own devices, private firms will not invest sufficiently in improving technology, because they themselves do not realize the full benefit therefrom. Even though the patent system encourages invention by guaranteeing that inventors retain property rights to their innovations, many very useful ideas developed in more basic scientific research cannot (and should not) be patented.

The Federal Government has long played a critical role in promoting research and development. It has financed growth in telecommunications, for instance, from that industry's inception, with the first Baltimore-to-Washington telegraph line, to its latest major development, the Internet. In agriculture, government-funded research provided the basis for enormous improvements in productivity that today allow less than 3 percent of the workforce to feed the entire Nation, and have made the United States one of the world's leading agricultural exporters.

Detractors of government support for research have often distorted the issue. Some have posed a false dichotomy between basic research, for which public support is almost universal, and technology, which they say should remain the province of the private sector. Yet many areas of technology have huge spillover benefits and therefore would be underprovided without government support. Critics have also accused government of trying to "pick winners"—of seeking to supplant the market at one of the things it does best. But government support of technology is not aimed at outguessing the market. Rather, it is focused on setting up partnerships and other structures to identify, together with the private sector, those areas in which large benefits to society are not likely to be produced by the market alone.

In the spirit of the Administration's new vision for the economy, the Federal Government has placed public-private partnerships at the center of its research and development policy. The Advanced Technology Program (ATP), expanded substantially under this Administration, is a good example. ATP awards matching funds to industry, on a competitive basis, to conduct research on cutting-edge technologies and processes that, despite their great economic potential, might otherwise not have been pursued. The firms themselves set much of the research agenda, but this pairing has been an effective way to leverage government funding into larger increases in research and development. The record shows that the success rate of this and similar programs is indeed formidable.

Increasing Competition

Improving the efficiency of the economy is not just a matter of improving technology. How the economy is organized plays just as important a role in creating incentives for firms to use their capital and labor as efficiently as possible. If the market economy is to deliver on its promise of growth and prosperity, markets have to be competitive, because it is competition that drives firms to be efficient and innovative. Firms, however, often find it easier to increase profits by reducing competition than by improving efficiency in response to competition. Monopolies and oligopolies not only can charge inefficiently high prices and restrict output, but may also have a diminished drive to innovate.

The traditional way to increase competition is to prevent the growth of monopoly power in the first place. This Administration has restored vigor to the enforcement of the antitrust laws, blocking anticompetitive mergers and, where warranted, prosecuting alleged violators. But competition is not viable in some industries, namely, those called natural monopolies. Antitrust enforcement may be of little help in these areas; instead government regulation can help to ensure that monopoly power is not abused.

The extent and the form of competition are constantly changing. Joseph Schumpeter, one of the 20th century's great economists, described capitalism as a process of creative destruction. New industries constantly come into existence as old industries are destroyed. The late 19th and early 20th centuries saw the transformation of the economy from a mostly agricultural to a mostly industrial one. Today services and information are assuming the lead position, while at the same time demand for U.S. goods is increasingly coming from abroad. Sometimes analysts focus on manufacturing as if it still represented the core of the economy. Manufacturing is important—it is the Nation's largest investor in research and development and its leading exporter—but manufacturing employment today represents only 15 percent of total employment, and service industries also produce many of our important exports, for example in telecommunications, financial services, and other intellectual property.

Today, new technologies have expanded the scope for competition in many sectors that have historically been highly regulated, such as telecommunications and electric power. Traditional regulatory structures, however, with their rigid categories of regulation versus deregulation, and competition versus monopoly, have become increasingly unhelpful in guiding policy in these areas. These new technologies do not call for wholesale deregulation because not all parts of these industries are adequately competitive. Instead they call for appropriate changes in regulatory structure to meet the new challenges. Such changes must recognize the existence of hybrid areas of the economy, some parts of which are more suited to competition, while others are more vulnerable to domination by a few. Market power in one part of a regulated industry cannot be allowed to maneuver itself into a stranglehold over other parts, or else economic efficiency may be severely compromised. The Administration's regulatory reforms in the telecommunications and electric power industries have attempted to achieve competitive balance.

Even as these changes have intensified competition in some parts of the economy, it remains limited in others. In particular, where goods and services are locally provided, and where transportation costs are high, consumers in some areas may have too little choice, even if providers in the country as a whole are numerous. In parts of the country, for example, a single hospital may be the only one serving a large rural area. In the health care sector, new guidelines for antitrust enforcement were recently issued in response to concerns such as these, and the Administration has resisted attempts to scale back antitrust enforcement in this area. The benefits of competition can be seen in our university system, where competition remains keen—and perhaps partly accounts for the dominant position American universities hold in the world of higher education.

Expanding Trade

The third source of increasing efficiency in the economy is more-open markets abroad. Like the freeing up of domestic markets, opening of foreign markets shifts resources into relatively more productive areas. The Administration will continue to pursue its outward-oriented, protrade agenda through multilateral, regional, and bilateral means, expanding on and bringing to fruition initiatives like the Asia-Pacific Economic Cooperation group and the proposed Free Trade Area of the Americas.

The global economy, like the domestic economy, is evolving, and its change brings with it new challenges. A clean environment, a safe workplace, and competitive markets are important to us internationally just as they are at home. Trade liberalization can complement these goals in many ways. Anticompetitive practices abroad, for example, frequently cohabit with restrictions on trade and may forestall entry of American firms into foreign markets. Liberalizing trade in agriculture can lead to a more environmentally sound international allocation of farming activity. The side agreements to NAFTA, on which the Administration conditioned its approval of the agreement, demonstrate that safeguarding a shared environment, promoting better working conditions, and liberalizing trade are not mutually exclusive goods to be traded off against each other. Pursuing these goals in the multilateral framework of the WTO will be increasingly important. At the same time, it is important that countries not allow domestic regulation to become a pretext for nontariff trade barriers whose real purpose is to restrict competition. . . .

Improving Public Sector Efficiency

The fourth and final way to increase the overall efficiency of the economy is by improving the efficiency with which the government itself does its job. By freeing up resources for potentially more productive uses in other sectors, and by reducing the cost of regulation, government reform can raise economy-wide productivity. The Vice President's reinventing government initiative has been doing just that. Thousands of pages of Federal regulations have been eliminated, and thousands more are being streamlined or improved in other ways. Hundreds of obsolete Federal programs have been eliminated, and red tape has been reduced dramatically. The Federal civilian workforce has been cut by more than 250,000, and as a percentage of the Nation's total employment it is now smaller than at any time since the early 1930s. . . .

Opportunity and Individual Responsibility

America cannot reach its full economic potential if any of its assets— including its human resources—do not live up to theirs. Just as the productivity slowdown since 1973 poses a challenge for growth, so the persistence of income inequality and the entrenchment of poverty of the past two decades make it more difficult to ensure that all Americans have the opportunity to make the most of their lives. . . .

Another major problem is the persistence in some areas of pockets of poverty. The nationwide poverty rate has hovered between 10 and 15 percent for the past 30 years, but the burdens of poverty have been spread very unevenly throughout American society. The poverty rate for blacks fell to its lowest level in 1995, yet over 40 percent of black children still grow up in poor homes. Poverty seems particularly entrenched—with poverty rates in some cases exceeding 50 percent—in the inner cities and in certain remote rural areas. The gap between rich and poor has a variety of origins. Changes in technology inevitably confer advantages on some parts of the country more than others, and citizens and governments in some places have more effectively seized upon the opportunities offered. Vestiges of discrimination, directed at the large share of minority members in many communities, may also have played a role in the geographic entrenchment of poverty.

Government programs have had much success in reducing inequality and poverty. Government cash transfers lifted over 21 million people out of poverty in 1995, lowering the poverty rate from 21.9 percent to 13.8 percent. If the effect of all taxes, the earned income tax credit (EITC), and the valuation of noncash transfers were included, the poverty rate would be still lower, at 10.3 percent. All told, more than half of all those who are reckoned poor on a before-tax-and-transfers basis escaped poverty with the help of government policies.

We must never allow the Nation's social safety net to become tattered, but it is also imperative to design policies in ways that will fully integrate our lagging communities into the American economy. The Administration's approach is based on four principles: providing people with opportunities to find work, making sure they have the right incentives to avail themselves of those opportunities, strengthening communities, and easing the transition between jobs for dislocated workers. Education, discussed above in the context of economic growth, also plays an important role in enhancing opportunities.

Work Opportunity

One of the most important contributions that any Administration can make to the Nation's economy is to ensure that every American seeking work can find it. The decline in the unemployment rate from over 7 percent in 1992 to below 5½ percent in 1996 was a major step forward not only for growth, but also for opportunity. But moving welfare recipients into jobs takes more than just creating job openings. Access to transportation, child care, and other infrastructure support will be needed. Many job seekers will also need to acquire the critical "soft skills"—a habit of punctuality, low absenteeism, and so forth—that will make them effective members of the labor force.

Jobs, skills, and infrastructure are all important, but discrimination and its legacy can still place obstacles in the way of some Americans. Some employers continue to deny employment or advancement on the basis of race or sex. This is illegal as well as economically irrational, and the Administration is committed to the vigorous enforcement of equal opportunity laws. But this may not be enough; affirmative action programs, based not on quotas but on principles of advancing opportunity, are also called for.

Incentives

Few individuals consciously choose a life of dependency, whether on public welfare or private charity. True, the environment into which a child is born, and the opportunities he or she is afforded, strongly influence whether that child matures into a productive member of society or becomes dependent on the state. But most economists believe that incentives also play a role in determining that outcome. When a worker earns little more from a minimum wage job than what he or she could get by going on welfare and accepting food stamps and free public housing, the incentive to work is not strong. In the past, the availability of welfare made the effective wage for many low-wage workers (i.e., the addition to income from an extra hour of work) not the advertised $4 or $5 an hour, but half of that or less.

Over the past 4 years this Administration has increased the returns to work relative to welfare in several ways. The expansion of the EITC and the recently legislated increases in the minimum wage have together increased the return to work for low-wage workers, to the point where a full-time, year-round minimum wage worker with two children will receive more income than ever before, even after adjusting for inflation. And the reforms of the welfare system, including the imposition of work requirements and time limits on benefits, may provide further incentives.

Incentives are not only important for individuals, but need to be designed with businesses in mind as well. The President has taken the first step in reforming welfare. As important as the public sector's role in creating opportunity is, however, the private sector must also participate if welfare reform is to result in better lives for those who have depended on support in the past. This Administration challenges the private sector to work with government to help welfare recipients move into the mainstream of work and opportunity. The welfare-to-work tax credit proposed by the President last summer is one example of how the government can help create the incentive for businesses to hire long-term welfare recipients.

Community

Many of the themes of this Administration's economic strategy are drawn together in policies that work not just with and for individuals, but with and for the communities in which they live. Part of any sensible economic strategy for reducing poverty involves concentrating on those areas where, as already noted, poverty is most entrenched. The Federal Government, however, cannot and should not be solely responsible for revitalizing these communities; rather, the most effective strategy is to provide local communities with the resources and tools they need to realize their full potential.

The Empowerment Zone/Enterprise Community initiative incorporates an entirely new approach to community revitalization. Rather than imposing restrictive Federal mandates on America's distressed central cities and rural areas, this effort begins from the premise that local residents know best how to solve their communities' problems. To be considered for an Empowerment Zone or Enterprise Community designation, communities have to meet eligibility criteria, be nominated by their State or local government, and submit a strategic plan that describes the community's vision for its future. This competition for designation provides an incentive for community leaders to develop innovative strategies to address their problems. The designated communities are then provided with access to a combination of flexible grants, tax incentives, and special assistance in removing bureaucratic red tape.

The Administration plans to expand the Empowerment Zone/Enterprise Community initiative. The Community Empowerment Act, which was introduced in the 104th Congress, embodies the Administration's proposal for a second round of zones and communities. This act would designate an additional 20 zones and 80 communities to receive, over 3 years, $1 billion in tax incentives and $1 billion in discretionary funds. The Administration will work with the 105th Congress in securing passage of this extension.

Dislocated Workers

It is a subject of some debate whether the pace of change today is such that individuals are more likely than in the past to lose their jobs. . . . But even if the risk of job loss is no greater than in the recent past, dislocation is still hard on workers and their families. The market does not provide insurance against job loss, which is understandably a source of anxiety for workers. Economists generally endorse the virtues of Schumpeter's creative destruction. But for individual workers and their families the costs of a changing economy are far more apparent than the broader benefits to society from an economy that is better able to adapt to changing technology and markets.

In a variety of ways, government can help individuals make the transition between jobs, and in the process help make the economy more supple, able to respond quickly to changes in markets and technology. Unemployment insurance has long been the most important system of support for dislocated workers. This Administration considers it one of its special responsibilities to help those in transition between jobs. One of the harshest ironies of an economy in which employers provide most health insurance is the fact workers typically lose their health benefits when they lose their jobs—precisely the time when they can least afford to purchase health insurance on their own. The Administration has proposed providing unemployed workers with 6 months of health insurance through the existing unemployment insurance system. At the same time, it is important to help the unemployed find new jobs through job retraining programs and "one-stop shopping" career centers to cushion and facilitate the transition for those hurt by economic change. Finally, the Administration has worked to make benefits more portable between jobs. For instance, the Health Insurance Portability and Accountability Act of 1996 (the Kassebaum-Kennedy bill) ensures that as many as 25 million workers will not be denied health insurance, including coverage of preexisting conditions, at their new jobs. Similarly, pension simplification and improved portability also make it easier to maintain crucial benefits when changing jobs.

Conclusion

The American economy is dynamic. This Administration's economic philosophy recognizes that American workers and enterprises, interacting through markets, are the source of that dynamism. The strength of this economy is its ability to adapt to change; at the same time, its dynamism sets further change in motion, ultimately enriching the lives and raising the living standards of all Americans.

Government has a limited but essential role in maintaining this dynamism. It creates an economic climate in which individuals and firms can flourish. It promotes competition. It seeks to ensure that all individuals have an opportunity to make the most of their talents. It protects our environment, our health, and our safety. . . .

Government must both adapt to and foster change. The past 4 years have demonstrated that the Federal Government is up to this challenge. And the private sector has more than amply demonstrated that it, too, can fulfill its part in this ever-evolving partnership.

The process is never-ending. Most of the challenges the Nation faces have deep roots in the past. Just as the productivity slowdown and the increase in inequality have no single, simple cause, neither do they have any single, simple solution. No magic policy wand can transport us back to the income distribution or the productivity growth America enjoyed in the 1960s. It takes time to respond effectively to, and even more time to reverse, trends that have been two decades in the making. To take just one example among myriad: the purely economic benefits of Head Start take 15 years or more to ripen—the time it takes for a Head Start child to grow up and join the labor force.

Our assessment of the success of government programs must therefore go beyond their impact on this year's or next year's GDP. Success will be measured by the kinds of lives that all Americans will live in the future. That success will be enhanced by the legacies we leave: not only investments in people, in the tools of production, and in technology that will increase our productivity, but also a philosophy of markets and of government that will guide us in the difficult choices we must make as we reach out toward the 21st century and beyond.

JURORS' REMARKS ON
O. J. SIMPSON'S CIVIL TRIAL
February 10, 1997

Sixteen months after being acquitted in a criminal trial of the brutal murders of his former wife and her companion, former football star O. J. Simpson was held responsible in a civil trial for causing the deaths and assessed a total of $33.5 million in punitive and compensatory damages. The outcome was a vindication for many of those who believed that Simpson's acquittal on the criminal charges in October 1995 was a miscarriage of justice. The families of Nicole Brown Simpson and her friend Ronald L. Goldman said they were relieved that justice had finally been served. "The money is not an issue. It never has been. It's holding the man who killed my son and Nicole responsible," Goldman's father, Fred, said February 10.

Nicole Simpson and Ronald Goldman were stabbed to death outside Nicole Simpson's Los Angeles home the night of June 12, 1994; five days later Simpson was charged with the murders. The criminal trial, which commentators likened to a soap opera and a circus, became a trial not only of Simpson's innocence or guilt, but also of whether a black man, even a wealthy black man, could get a fair hearing in Los Angeles. After Simpson's defense attorneys introduced evidence that Mark Fuhrman, one of the detectives investigating the murders, was a racist and had harassed blacks and made up evidence in the past, blacks both in the courtroom and in the public at large were confirmed in their views that blacks in general, and Simpson in particular, were the victims of a racist and unfair legal system. It took the predominantly black jury about four hours of deliberations to find Simpson not guilty of the murder charges. (Historic Documents of 1995, p. 611)

Because of the constitutional protection against double jeopardy, Simpson's acquittal meant that he could not be retried in a criminal proceeding. But California law permitted Simpson to be sued for monetary damages in civil court for causing the wrongful death of his former wife and her friend. The civil suit was actually three suits brought by Goldman's father, Fred, and his stepmother; Goldman's mother, Sharon Rufo; and Nicole Simpson's estate, filed by her father. The beneficiaries of that estate were Nicole and O. J. Simpson's two children; Simpson had been awarded full custody of the children on December 20, 1996. Goldman and Rufo sought both compensatory and punitive damages; Nicole Simpson's estate sought only punitive damages.

Many commentators said the different outcomes in the two trials were attributable to the composition of the two juries. The jury in the criminal trial, held in downtown Los Angeles, was predominantly black; in the civil trial, held in suburban Santa Monica, it was predominantly white. Most legal experts cited other differences, among them new evidence and different standards of proof, as important factors. "I believe the downtown verdict was correct. I also believe, that with a much lower burden of proof, the Santa Monica verdict was also correct," a prominent defense attorney told the Washington Post. *"I have no quarrel with the outcome in either case."*

Unlike the criminal trial, in which a unanimous jury had to find Simpson guilty "beyond a reasonable doubt" for a conviction, only nine of the twelve jurors in the civil suit had to agree that "a preponderance of the evidence" proved Simpson was responsible for the murders. While all twelve jurors found Simpson liable for the wrongful deaths, their comments at a news conference on February 10 indicated that they might not have agreed that the plaintiffs had proved their case beyond a reasonable doubt. One juror flatly said they had not.

Although it was not televised, the civil trial did not lack for drama. One such moment came when Simpson was forced to take the witness stand in his own defense. Another came at the conclusion of the trial, when Daniel Petrocelli in his closing remarks said, "There is a killer in this courtroom." The final drama came on February 4, when television networks interrupted the opening ceremonies of President Clinton's annual State of the Union address to a national television audience from the U.S. Capitol in Washington, D.C., with news that the jury had reached a decision. Throughout their coverage of the speech, television networks used a split screen to show footage of Simpson and the Brown and Goldman families arriving at the Santa Monica courtroom to hear the verdict. But overall the trial and its conduct did not generate the intense public interest nor cause the racial divide that had attended the first trial.

Differences in the Two Trials

Both trials followed the same general outlines, and much of the evidence was the same. Prosecuting attorneys in the criminal case and plaintiffs in the wrongful death case argued that blood identified as Simpson's found at the murder scene was also mingled with blood from the victims found in Simpson's home. Defense attorneys in both cases argued that the blood evidence had been handled carelessly and thus could not be trusted. Both also argued that corrupt police officers had planted some of the blood evidence to incriminate Simpson.

In the criminal trial, the defense was able to introduce the dramatic and highly damaging evidence regarding Fuhrman. According to interviews

*with jurors after the trial, these accusations of police racism were impor-
tant factors in Simpson's acquittal. But in the wrongful death suit, the
judge ruled early in the proceedings that the defense could not make race a
major issue, thus denying Simpson the "race card" that had been so crucial
in his criminal case.*

*Plaintiffs in the civil case also introduced evidence that had been
unavailable to prosecutors in the criminal case. New testimony, for example, revealed that Simpson had owned a dark sweatsuit similar to the one
the killer wore. Also allowed into evidence was an excerpt from Nicole
Simpson's diary, in which she wrote that Simpson had once beaten the
"holy hell" out of her and vowed to "get her." The most damaging new evidence was a series of more than thirty photographs of Simpson wearing the
same type of Bruno Magli shoes that experts said had left bloody footprints
at the scene of the murders.*

*The most damning evidence might have come from Simpson himself. He
chose not to testify at his criminal trial, but could not avoid being called
by plaintiff's attorneys in the civil proceeding. On the stand, Simpson
denied ever owning a dark sweatsuit or hitting his wife. When he was
shown the first picture of the shoes, he said he had never owned the shoes
and called the picture a fake. When he was shown the other photos, Simpson amended his statement to say that he did not remember owning such
shoes. Several of the jurors later said that much of Simpson's testimony
was not believable. "O. J. ruined his credibility so fast on that stand that
later on . . . we really didn't know what to believe and what not to believe,"
one juror said.*

*Other significant differences were also apparent in the conduct of the
two trials. In the criminal trial Judge Lance Ito was widely criticized for
ruling in favor of the defense on several key issues, and his decision to
allow the trial to be televised lead to much of the theatricality employed by
both teams of attorneys during the proceedings. Hiroshi Fujisaki, judge in
the civil suit, barred television cameras from his courtroom, severely limited the evidence he permitted the defense to introduce, and ran a much
tighter court than Ito had. The civil trial lasted four months; the criminal
trial ran more than twice as long. Legal analysts also said the defense
lawyers were better than the prosecutors in the criminal case and benefited
from the mistakes made in that trial; many have suggested that crucial
mistakes made by the prosecution may have cost them the guilty verdict.
These same experts gave high marks to the plaintiff's attorneys in the civil
case, particularly Petrocelli in his questioning of Simpson. "Simpson was
destroyed," one legal expert said.*

Damage Awards and Aftermath

*In the first phase of the trial, which concluded February 4, the jury held
Simpson liable for the deaths and awarded Fred Goldman and Rufo $8.5
million in compensatory damages. In the second phase of the trial, which
began immediately afterward and concluded February 10, the same jury*

awarded the Goldman family and the Nicole Simpson estate $12.5 million each in punitive damages, for a total of $33.5 million.

The damages were among the highest ever assessed an individual and were far higher than most observers had expected. "The jury obviously focused on the reprehensibility" of the murders, one attorney told the New York Times, *"particularly in view of the fact that he's not going to be punished anywhere else." During the punitive phase, plaintiffs' witnesses testified that Simpson was worth at least $15.7 million, primarily in current and future earnings. One witness said Simpson could earn between $2 million and $3 million each year for the rest of his life, estimated at twenty-five years, by marketing his name and trademark.*

Simpson had already filed six trademark applications for six different names and likenesses and for more than one hundred uses, but his attorneys claimed Simpson's net worth had been greatly exaggerated. They said Simpson was more than $9.3 million in debt, including the $8.5 million compensatory damage award, and that the outcome of the civil trial destroyed any chance Simpson had to earn money. Simpson could appeal the decision, but he was required to post bond equal to one and a half times the amount of the judgments to do so. The judgments could also be reduced as a result of posttrial motions. By the end of 1997 he had not appealed.

> *Following are excerpts from a news conference February 10, 1997, with several unidentified jurors from the civil trial in which O. J. Simpson was found responsible for the wrongful deaths of Nicole Brown Simpson and Ronald L. Goldman:*

Juror #11: I'd like to say that I'm very proud to have served on this jury. I went into this trial with my mind and heart open, and after I spent four months on the jury, finding O. J. Simpson liable of the murders and acting with oppression and malice was one of the easiest decisions I have ever had to make. I'm very grateful to have been a part of bringing justice to these families' lives, and I just hope it can bring them some peace. I'd just love to go home right now. If I can answer more questions later, I'll make myself available. Thank you. . . .

Question: You were one of the two who did not agree with the punitive damage award, and I'm wondering why.

Juror #294: I basically felt that the financial situation of O. J. Simpson was possibly not as high as the plaintiffs had said; so I would have gone slightly lower with the figure that the rest of the jury concurred with.

Question: . . . What impact did O. J. Simpson not being present during the punitive damages phase of his trial have on your deliberations, if anything?

Answer: None. . . .

Question: Yes, I'm wondering—much was made in the media that this trial turned on the credibility of O. J. Simpson, whether you guys believed him or not. Was that important?

Juror #294: Yes, that was very important.

Question: . . . What was it you didn't believe about what he said? His claims of never hitting his wife? His claims of never owning those shoes? What were the factors?

Juror #294: Everything as it related to the evidence.

Question: The shoes, the hitting?

Juror #5: The shoes, the hitting, where the gloves were, the sweatsuit.

Question: He was not a credible witness for you?

Juror #5: As it related to the evidence, it was not credible.

Question: It took you—you talk about how convincing the evidence was, and yet there was a period of three days with the previous juror, and then almost three days with this new jury panel, can you tell us a little bit about the deliberation process and why things were so clear, it took three days to come to the verdict.

Juror #290: We went through every single bit of evidence to make sure in our own minds the only people we have to answer to as jurors is ourselves. When we look into the mirror, we need to be able to have a clear and convincing presence—this is really, like, overwhelming having all the cameras in the face—And going through every single bit of evidence, going through a time frame, going through a possible intent, I mean, we had to break down everything and examine everything so we could have a clear conscience, because we're the ones who have to answer to you people.

Question: There's so much made in this case about the contrast between you folks and the jury in the criminal case, and I'm wondering, even though you didn't have to deal with the standard [of reasonable proof]. . . . Do you think the level of proof rose to beyond a reasonable doubt in this case, if you had to use that standard? I'm just wondering if we could survey you. Do you feel it rose to that high a level of beyond a reasonable doubt?

Juror #186: To myself—I didn't realize how much I didn't know about the first case until I found out the evidence in this case. I didn't realize there were two gloves. I didn't know there was a blood trail at Bundy. All this evidence I didn't realize existed. I don't know what the first jurors were given, but by this evidence, I think without a doubt in my mind, he's definitely guilty of the crime.

Question: What about the other ones? I'm just wondering if we could survey you.

Juror #27: Just as an example, and though I was an alternate, I've come to the conclusion that I'll never second guess another jury. I don't know what those people were given, I don't know what they heard. I know what I heard, and I know my own feelings. I will never second guess another jury. . . .

Juror #5: I was going to respond that for me, what I needed to be able to walk out of that room was not just beyond a reasonable doubt, but beyond a shadow of a doubt, and I was willing to stay there a month if that's what it took to answer all of the questions for myself.

Question: During the deliberation on the punitive award for the Brown estate, did you give any consideration to the discussion to the fact that that's essentially an award to the children against their father?

Juror #5: No. I don't think we discussed that.

Juror #294: I don't think we really talked about the children. . . .

Question: . . . On this question of the standard of proof, reasonable doubt, somebody said they thought it was well above. I'd like to know from each of you, do you think it was—were you right on the fence with 50 percent, 51 percent, or how do you feel?

Juror #5: I think we answered that question, that I needed for myself to feel beyond a shadow of a doubt, and I felt that that was proven to me.

Juror #294: Without putting a percentage on it, because I don't really know what my percentage would be, but I definitely think, like I said before, the plaintiffs proved the preponderance of evidence in this case, definitely. . . .

Question: Beyond a reasonable doubt?

Juror #294: No. I told you that before. No.

Juror #186: Yeah, I believe beyond a reasonable doubt. In fact 100 percent I believe that the evidence shows that there's just no way anybody could have planted all of that evidence. It just doesn't make sense. Who would have known those pictures would have showed up? Who knows that that DNA would match Simpson's? And the fact they don't even match his reference vial as far as degradation, things like that, there's just no way. And they called them incompetent. How could incompetent people plant all of this? It doesn't make sense?

Juror #400: Well, it was 100 percent for me. I really believe that Mr. Simpson was guilty. We—we just—we went by all of the evidence, and it had nothing to do with the color of Mr. Simpson's skin.

Juror #290: As I said earlier, we did go through all the evidence, and the only ones that we had to be clear with was ourselves, and I believed that the plaintiffs did prove their case beyond a reasonable doubt.

Question: We did not hear from Mr. Simpson in the criminal case. How credible, as a witness, was Mr. Simpson to you? What were your opinions of him on the stand? If I could hear from each of you.

Juror #27: Right. I'll just start because I was—I sat four to five feet from the man, and I had a lot of trouble really believing what he was telling me. I made it a point to—to just look at him and be as receptive as I can because this was not an easy thing to do sit here in judgment of this man. I had no feelings about Mr. Simpson before, but I respected him for what he'd achieved, he was a father, et cetera. This was not an easy thing to do to sit here and possibly, potentially accuse him of a double murder. But I have to tell you that his actions seemed very rehearsed. It seems like he was just waiting for the questions to get done so he could—he was just waiting to say that is undoubtedly false or whatever he was saying. But it just seemed like his head was ready to snap, and as soon as whatever question was being asked was done, he denied it. He did not seem credible.

Juror #290: I didn't believe in any credibility on Mr. Simpson's behalf. I did have problems with some of his testimony, in his denials of testimony in his absolute, that I have never wore these shoes, I would never own these shoes, I have never hit Nicole. He was very definite in certain aspects, and on other questions, he evaded them. So I did have problems with his credibility.

Juror #400: Yes, he would change his mind. First he said he cut his fingers, which were obviously fingernail gouges from the attacks, he said he received those from roughhousing with his young son. . . . Then he changed his mind and said he cut his hand when he was in Chicago in the hotel room. . . .

Juror #186: I was just going to say I find it hard to believe that someone cannot, the day after, remember a scar-producing cut on the finger. He can remember chipping golf balls, he can remember talking to Paula on a—the driveway on a cell phone, but for some reason, he can't remember a scar-producing cut. I thought Kato Kaelin was more credible.

Juror #295: For me, the inconsistencies between the interview that he had with the officers right the day after that the incident happened to the pre-trial testimony, to the criminal trial testimony, to this testimony, and how the plaintiff brought it all together and showed the inconsistencies throughout, as far as the finger, whether he was in the Bronco when he called Paula or wasn't in the Bronco when he called Paula, I mean, a number of things. He really should have gotten his story straight before he got up there.

Juror #5: He wasn't credible.

Question: Gentleman at the end?

Juror #206: O. J. ruined his credibility so fast on that stand that later on when he might answer some truth, we really didn't know what to believe and what not to believe him. He—he just—some obvious—some obvious things he was saying, it's not so. It—the guy was lying on the stand.

Question: When you first went back to deliberate, how soon did you poll yourselves on what you thought, and were you unanimous early on?

Juror #294: We had. . . .

Juror #400: We never polled till the end, the very last moment.

Question: Were you unanimous instantly?

Jurors: Yes.

Jurors: Mm-hmm. . . .

REPORT ON PREVENTING THE SPREAD OF AIDS
February 13, 1997

Deaths from AIDS (acquired immunodeficiency syndrome) declined dramatically in the United States in 1996, primarily because of the success of new drug therapies that appear to suppress HIV, the human immunodeficiency virus that causes the incurable disease. But health care officials stressed that thousands more lives could be saved every year if public policymakers and civic leaders would drop their opposition to implementation of proven interventions such as needle exchange programs for drug addicts and safe-sex education for teenagers. "Even as evidence rapidly accumulates on the success of these programs, however, legislation has been passed to make provision of these interventions extremely difficult," said a panel of experts in February. "There is no more urgent need than to remedy this dangerous chasm" between scientific knowledge and public policy.

Prevention was also the watchword among international organizations as new, more accurate estimates in Africa and Asia pushed the worldwide numbers of HIV infections up substantially. Experts warned that the epidemic could soon spread across China, India, and Eastern Europe unless prevention programs were quickly put into place.

According to the Centers for Disease Control and Prevention (CDC), the number of deaths from AIDS and associated illnesses declined from 50,140 in 1995 to 38,780 in 1996, a decrease of 23 percent. The number of new cases of AIDS in 1996 was estimated at 56,730, a 6 percent decrease from the previous year. The CDC said the estimates were consistent with reports showing that improved medical care for HIV-infected people, including combination drug therapies, were delaying or preventing the onset of AIDS. The most successful of these therapies was the "triple therapy," a combination of three antiviral drugs, one of which was usually a protease inhibitor. On June 19 the Department of Health and Human Services backed guidelines that urged aggressive use of the triple therapy for people with AIDS and for HIV patients with a high "viral load," even if they have no symptoms.

About 500,000 Americans had been diagnosed with HIV, and between 150,000 and 180,000 of those were taking triple therapy. But not all HIV-infected patients could avail themselves of the therapy. A course of treatment cost between $10,000 and $12,000 a year. Moreover, some patients could not physically tolerate the treatment, which involved taking as many as twenty pills a day, often on a rigid schedule. Some doctors were reluctant to prescribe the therapy. A further setback came in late September with new reports that the therapies were beginning to fail in about half the patients. In one of these reports, data from a large AIDS clinic operated by the University of California at San Francisco found that the HIV virus had dropped to undetectable levels in 136 patients after they began taking triple therapy in March 1996; since then, the virus had returned to detectable levels in slightly more than half those patients. The report confirmed similar findings elsewhere. (AIDS research, Historic Documents of 1996, p. 156)

Politics an Obstacle to Successful Prevention

Even with better medical care, AIDS was still the leading cause of death among both men and women aged twenty-five to forty-four, and an estimated 40,000 to 80,000 people were infected with the HIV virus each year. Gay men and intravenous drug users accounted for the largest number of cases, but the rate of increase was greater among women than among men. The epidemic appeared to be shifting to young people, particularly those who were gay or members of ethnic minorities. Many of these cases could be prevented, a panel of experts said February 13, if politicians would actively promote proven prevention practices rather than oppose them.

"AIDS is a preventable disease, and the behavior placing the public health at greatest risk may be occurring in legislative and other decision-making bodies," said panel chairman David Reiss, a doctor and the director of psychiatric research at George Washington University Medical Center. "Community and policy level changes made through government leadership in severely AIDS-stricken communities like Uganda and Thailand have set model examples of how government leaders can coordinate interventions that effectively reduce the numbers of new cases of HIV infection. It's not too late for the political leadership of the United States to follow their example."

Politicians and community leaders at all levels of government often objected to prevention programs such as needle exchanges for drug users and sex education for teenagers on the grounds that such programs would actually increase either drug use or sexual activity. To the contrary, the panel said, studies of needle exchange programs show up to an 80 percent reduction in risk behavior and at least a 30 percent reduction in the incidence of HIV among drug users. "Can the opposition to needle exchange programs in the United States be justified on scientific grounds?" the panel asked. "Our answer is simple and emphatic—no."

Rather than leading to an earlier onset of sexual activity or to promiscuity, the panel said, studies show that safe sexual education, including the *proper use of condoms, leads many young people to delay initiation of sexual intercourse or to limit their number of partners. The panel was especially critical of federal legislation that provided $50 million in block grants for programs to teach sexual abstinence to teenagers. Abstinence-only programs "cannot be justified" because they put "policy in direct conflict with science" by ignoring "overwhelming evidence that other programs are effective," the panel said.*

The independent panel of twelve health research experts was convened by the National Institutes of Health as part of its Consensus Development Program. The report, based on an extensive review of the scientific literature, presentations from other experts, and public testimony, was released at the end of a three-day conference on "Interventions to Prevent HIV Risk Behaviors."

Prevention Efforts Advocated Worldwide

The U.S. consensus panel's message was reinforced in November, when the World Bank released a far-ranging report that emphasized the benefits of AIDS prevention programs at any stage of the epidemic. The report stressed the need for governments to target prevention efforts at people with multiple sexual partners and those who inject drugs and share nonsterile needles because such prevention measures "will prevent the largest number of infections among all people—even among people who do not take risks," the report said.

According to the authors of the report, an estimated 10,000 HIV infections a year were prevented among clients of prostitutes, their spouses, and other sex partners by a program in Nairobi, Kenya, that treated 500 sex workers for sexually transmitted diseases and educated them on condom use. In contrast, if a group of 500 men chosen at random achieved the same level of condom use, about 80 HIV infections would have been prevented.

The earlier the intervention, the better, the report said, because HIV is more easily transmitted when a person's infection is relatively recent. HIV can spread quickly; the report cited data from the Ukraine, where the infection among injecting drug users who did not use sterile needles rose from under 2 percent to 57 percent in less than a year. The report said that Russia and other former Soviet republics, India, and China were on the brink of suffering large epidemics. Aggressive prevention strategies could not avert those epidemics, but would reduce their magnitude, the report said.

The bank, which has spent $800 million on HIV control in developing countries since 1986, said it was prepared to at least double that amount and outlined the "minimum set" of prevention activities that all countries, developed and developing, should engage in. "Political leaders and government officials must take the necessary step to confront the epidemic, even when these are politically controversial," Joseph E. Stiglitz, the bank's chief economist, said at a news conference November 4.

In a related development, the United Nations announced November 25 that it had revised its estimates of HIV infection upward as a result of new, more accurate estimates based on national rather than regional data. According to the new data, 30.6 million people worldwide were infected with HIV, and about 16,000 new infections occurred every day. A year earlier the estimate had been 22.6 million infected with HIV, with the daily rate at 8,200.

Following are excerpts from the National Institutes of Health Consensus Development Statement entitled "Interventions to Prevent HIV Risk Behaviors," released on February 13, 1997:

Introduction

One in 250 people in the United States is infected with the human immunodeficiency virus (HIV), which causes AIDS [acquired immunodeficiency syndrome]; AIDS is the leading cause of death among men and women between the ages of 25 and 44. Every year, an additional 40,000–80,000 Americans become infected with HIV, mostly through behaviors that are preventable. In the United States, unsafe sexual behavior among men who have sex with men and unsafe injection practices among drug users still account for the largest number of cases. However, the rate of increase is greater for women than men, and there have been larger annual increases from heterosexual HIV transmission than among men who have sex with men.

The purpose of this conference was to examine what is known about behavioral interventions that are effective with different populations in different settings for the two primary modes of transmission: unsafe sexual behavior and nonsterile injection practices. Experts also provided the international and National epidemiology of HIV and a review of AIDS prevention efforts.

An extensive body of research has led to significant information on how to help individuals change their HIV-related risk behaviors. The interventions studied were based on a variety of models of behavior change, including social learning theory and related health and substance abuse models. The interventions begin with HIV and substance abuse education, but also include skill acquisition, assertiveness training, and behavioral reinforcement components. Recent research leads to the conclusion that aggressive promotion of safer sexual behavior and prevention and treatment of substance abuse could avert tens of thousands of new HIV infections and potentially save millions of dollars in health care costs. To date, however, there has not been widespread agreement among health professionals as to which interventions are most effective, in which settings, and among which populations.

Because behavioral interventions are currently the only effective way of slowing the spread of HIV infection, recommendations coming from this conference have immediate implications for service delivery in health care and educational settings, including schools; substance abuse treatment programs; community-based organizations; sexually transmitted disease clinics; innercity health programs reaching disenfranchised high-risk women, men, and adolescents; rural health programs; and mental health programs that serve high-risk people with chronic mental illness. Knowing which behavior change interventions are most effective will assist public health personnel in allocating resources. . . .

1. How Can We Identify the Behaviors and Contexts That Place Individuals/Communities at Risk for HIV?

Major Behavioral Risks

Research to date has identified the key risk behaviors for HIV transmission to be unprotected anal and vaginal intercourse, having multiple sex partners, and using nonsterile drug injection equipment. . . .

Contexts That Influence Risk

Important social and biological contexts and cofactors increase or decrease the likelihood of risk behaviors. A major contextual influence is the prevalence of HIV itself in the local population, which greatly influences the impact of any risk behavior. Other contextual influences include: individual factors such as age and developmental stage, early initiation of sexual behavior, sexual identity, self-esteem, untreated sexually transmitted diseases, use of alcohol, and use of other drugs; interpersonal factors such as sex with a partner of unknown HIV status, partner commitment, and negotiation of safe sex; social norms and values such as cultural and religious beliefs, gender role norms, and social inclusion versus marginalization of gay men, ethnic minorities, people of color, sex workers, women, and drug users; and political, economic, and health policy factors such as laws and regulations, employment opportunities, poverty, sexism, racism, homophobia, and availability of basic public health tools for protective behavior, such as condoms and sterile injection equipment.

Although many of the behavioral risk factors are quite well known, the contextual risk factors are only beginning to be understood. For example, intervention programs with younger gay men need to address the fact that some of them consider HIV to be a threat mainly to older men. Negotiation about safe sex practices is much more difficult for women in populations where there are cultural barriers to doing so. Programs targeting sex workers have been highly efficacious in other countries, but in this country would encounter cultural and political barriers. The impact of poverty on seeking treatment for sexually transmitted diseases is much greater in countries without access to universal medical care. These contextual factors combine in dynamic ways to increase behavioral risk. . . .

Changing Trends in Specific Behaviors and Community Contexts That Produce Elevated Risk for HIV Infection

A number of established and several new and emerging behaviors and community contexts increase risk for HIV infection. In general, youth in school are showing an increase in condom use at last contact, but a trend for decreased condom use as they get older. Among gay men, the infection rate is increasing among African-American, Latino, and younger men. Injecting drug users are at increased risk because of conditions in their communities, including unavailability of sterile injecting equipment, dealer provision of infected needles, and social situations that encourage multiperson reuse of needles and other drug paraphernalia. Women, particularly women of color, recently increased dramatically as a risk group in the United States and constitute 50 percent of those infected worldwide. Much of the growth in their risk is caused by sexual contact with partners whose sexual or drug use behavior put the women at risk. Vertical transmission from infected mother to infant continues to be a source of high risk for the infant, even with the treatment for mothers and infants that is now available. In addition, a variety of other special settings and subpopulations at increased risk, including incarcerated youth and adults, and individuals with chronic mental illnesses, deserve greater attention.

2. What Individual-, Group-, or Community-Based Methods of Intervention Reduce Behavioral Risks? What Are the Benefits and Risks of These Procedures?

When we consider the available knowledge from the entire body of literature, we can reach a clear conclusion: Prevention programs significantly reduce HIV risk behaviors. This is true across a variety of risk behaviors and in a variety of populations at risk. . . .

Men Who Have Sex with Men

Considerable research has focused on risk reduction in men who have sex with men. Descriptive studies and nonrandomized studies with control groups show positive behavioral effects, as do randomized studies. The studies with random assignment to groups are clustered in two areas: individual interventions delivered in small group settings and programs aimed at changing community norms (e.g., using peer leaders in community settings to deliver programs). These intervention programs focus on information, skills building, self-management, problemsolving, and psychological factors such as self-efficacy and intentions. Studies with clearly defined interventions, retention of samples to allow followup periods as long as 18 months, and reasonable sample sizes show substantial effects for intervention over minimal intervention or control conditions. More intensive interventions (e.g., more sessions) boost efficacy.

Heterosexual Transmission

Adult Women at Risk from Sexual Transmission. Data from a variety of settings demonstrate the ability to prevent HIV risk behaviors in women. A randomized trial involving a cognitive behavioral intervention aimed at inner-city women with high risk of acquiring HIV through heterosexual contact provides some of the strongest evidence of impact. Three months after intervention, women in the intervention reported a doubling of condom use from 26 percent to 56 percent for all intercourse occasions; no such change occurred for women in the comparison group. A second randomized trial, targeted at pregnant women, shows similar results at a 6-month followup. Results from a third randomized study yet to be published show reductions in unprotected sex and sexually transmitted diseases. . . .

Couples. There is evidence that consistent and correct condom use reduces HIV seroconversion to nearly zero in both male and female heterosexual partners. Counseling of couples in a European study was associated with large increases in protected sexual behavior.

Adolescents. The strongest support for reductions in a broad array of risky sexual behaviors comes from rigorous studies. Five randomized controlled trials used cognitive and behavioral skills training and targeted male and female, African-American, Latino, and European-American adolescents in health clinics and inner-city schools. Studies varied in sample size, and followups were limited to 1 year or less, but results were consistently positive, with outcomes such as condom acquisition, condom use, and reduced number of partners.

Injecting Drug Users

Prevention for injecting drug users has involved drug abuse treatment in some cases, and outreach focused on both drug use and HIV risk behavior in others. Both approaches have been effective. Programs aimed specifically at treating drug abuse show positive effects on risk behavior and have the additional benefit of affecting drug use. These have shown minimal effects on high-risk sex. Community studies training outreach workers or using an educational media campaign to reduce the use of nonsterile needles show increased protected sexual behavior and slowing of seroconversion rates, along with impressive reductions in drug use.

Needle Exchange Programs

An impressive body of evidence suggests powerful effects from needle exchange programs. The number of studies showing beneficial effects on behaviors such as needle sharing greatly outnumber those showing no effects. There is no longer doubt that these programs work, yet there is a striking disjunction between what science dictates and what policy delivers. Data are available to address three central concerns:

1. Does needle exchange promote drug use? A preponderance of evidence shows either no change or decreased drug use. The scattered cases showing increased drug use should be investigated to discover the conditions under which negative effects might occur, but these can in no way detract from the importance of needle exchange programs. Additionally, individuals in areas with needle exchange programs have increased likelihood of entering drug treatment programs.

2. Do programs encourage non–drug users, particularly youth, to use drugs? On the basis of such measures as hospitalizations for drug overdoses, there is no evidence that community norms change in favor of

drug use or that more people begin using drugs. In Amsterdam and New Haven, for example, no increases in new drug users were reported after introduction of a needle exchange program.

3. Do programs increase the number of discarded needles in the community? In the majority of studies, there was no increase in used needles discarded in public places. There are just over 100 needle exchange programs in the United States, compared with more than 2,000 in Australia, a country with less than 10 percent of the U.S. population. Can the opposition to needle exchange programs in the United States be justified on scientific grounds? Our answer is simple and emphatic-no. Studies show reduction in risk behavior as high as 80 percent in injecting drug users, with estimates of a 30 percent or greater reduction of HIV. The cost of such programs is relatively low. Needle exchange programs should be implemented at once.

Policy and Large-Scale Interventions

As in other areas (e.g., smoking, injury control), policy interventions can remove barriers to protective behavior. In the United States and other countries, such interventions have resulted in dramatic reductions in risk behavior. In Connecticut, for example, a single legislative action legalizing over-the-counter purchase of sterile injection equipment led to an immediate and profound reduction in the sharing of nonsterile needles. A national campaign in Switzerland to promote the use of condoms dramatically reduced risky sexual behavior. Regulations on the use of condoms by sex workers in Thailand also led to fewer unprotected sex acts. The results thus far have been impressive. Given the potential benefit of policy changes, these should be implemented as local circumstances allow and, once implemented, should be evaluated as often and thoroughly as possible. . . .

Policy

Current evidence suggests that some of the most powerful positive effects on HIV risk behavior have been produced by legislative and regulatory changes. One need look no further than to the experience in Connecticut, where one legislative action permitting the purchase of sterile injection equipment had an immediate and pronounced effect on behavior. Here we see the potentially low cost and high effectiveness of intervention at the policy level. Policymaking can be conceptualized as behavior, and as such can and should be studied. Social policy, legal change, and community mobilization are powerful means of intervention and must be a legitimate area of inquiry at the National Institutes of Health and the Centers for Disease Control and Prevention. . . .

Of utmost importance is that HIV prevention policy be based, whenever possible, on scientific information. This occurs too little—the behavior placing the public health at greatest risk may be occurring in legislative and other decisionmaking bodies. The Federal ban on funding for needle exchange programs as well as restrictions on selling injection equipment are absolutely contraindicated and erect formidable barriers to implementing what is known to be effective. Many thousands of unnecessary deaths will occur as a result.

The single greatest increase in HIV prevention funding occurred with 1996 Federal legislation in the United States providing $50 million within block grant entitlements for programs teaching adolescents abstinence from sexual behavior. Among the criteria for programs funded through the block grant program are the following two requirements: (1) "has as its exclusive purpose, teaching the social psychological, and health gains to be realized by abstaining from sexual activity" and (2) "teaches that a mutually faithful monogamous relationship in the context of marriage is the expected standard of human sexual activity" (Public Health Service Act, Public Law 104-193, Sec. 912). Some programs based on an abstinence model propose that approaches such as the use of condoms are ineffective. This model places policy in direct conflict with science because it ignores overwhelming evidence that other programs are effective. Abstinence-only programs cannot be justified in the face of effective programs and given the fact that we face an international emergency in the AIDS epidemic.

Another instance of policy conflicting with knowledge is in providing treatment for drug abuse. Research shows that treatment of drug abusers with methadone maintenance, outpatient drug-free treatments, residential treatment, or detoxification not only decreases drug use but has a substantial effect on risk behaviors (use of shared needles and protected sex). At the same time that this knowledge has reached a critical mass, funding of drug treatment programs has been reduced in many localities. This tragic trend must be reversed.

Policy and legislative change can have rapid, powerful, and positive results. This key area of the field has been given little attention, a problem that needs remedy. A coordinated effort is needed, and the Government must take strong and immediate steps to protect its citizens. Drawing together legal and policy changes and program implementation occurring at international, National, and local levels offers great promise. Strong political leadership is necessary to direct this effort. The United States has much to learn from other countries where political leaders have taken this issue seriously and, by supporting vigorous prevention strategies, have prevented even more tragedy from occurring from AIDS. . . .

4. How Can Risk-Reduction Procedures Be Implemented Effectively?

Studies Ready for Implementation

A number of interventions have been evaluated in current research and are ready to be implemented within communities. Indeed, some are already being implemented by health departments and community-based organizations. Interventions at the individual level include the following:

- Outreach, needle exchange activities, treatment programs, and face-to-face counseling programs for substance-abusing populations
- Cognitive-behavioral small group, face-to-face counseling, and skills-building (proper condom use, negotiation, refusal) programs for men who have sex with men
- Cognitive-behavioral small group, face-to-face counseling, and skills building (i.e., proper condom use, negotiation, refusal) programs for women that pay special attention to their concerns (e.g., child care, transportation, and relationships with significant others)
- Condom distribution and testing and treatment for sexually transmitted diseases for sex workers and other sexually active individuals at high risk for sexually transmitted diseases
- Cognitive-behavioral educational and skills-building groups for youth and adolescents in various settings.

At the family or dyad level, interventions include counseling for couples . . . in both the United States and other countries. Within the community, interventions include changing community norms through community outreach and opinion leaders for men who have sex with men as well as injection drug-using networks.

At the policy level there are a number of strategies:

- Lifting government restrictions on needle exchange programs
- Providing increased government funding for drug and alcohol treatment programs, including methadone maintenance
- Support for sex education interventions that focus beyond abstinence
- Lifting constraints on condom availability (e.g., in correctional facilities).

Implementation Considerations

Several factors may influence implementation of HIV risk behavior interventions within the United States. First, compliance with interventions is improved when targeted individuals are involved at every phase of the process of conceptualization, development, and implementation of the programs. Input of these individuals is needed to help solve this health crisis.

Second, programs need to be culturally sensitive. This requires attention not only to ethnicity and language but also to other factors including social class, age, developmental stage, and sexual orientation.

Third, an appropriate intervention dosage must be selected for the population; this includes the number, length, and intensity of the intervention. Studies demonstrate that numerous intervention points over extended periods of time are more efficacious than once-only approaches for most populations. Almost all reported studies have short followup (3–18 months), which suggests that attention must be paid to maintenance efforts. It may be necessary to include additional, periodic intervention points for subsets of the population; longer-term followup would assist in determining this fact.

Fourth, when HIV risk behavior interventions are being introduced, it is important to address community myths. For example, scientifically derived results do not support assertions that needle exchange programs will lead to increased needle-injecting behavior among current users or an increase in the number of users. Nor do the data indicate that sex education programs result in earlier onset of sexual behavior or more sexual partners, or that condom distribution fosters more risky behavior. To the contrary, outcomes of these programs are quite consistent with the values of most communities. For example, behavioral interventions lead injecting drug users to inject less frequently, and the number of users in a community may decrease; after interventions, young people tend to delay initiation of intercourse or, if they are sexually active, have fewer partners; and adults, following intervention, engage in fewer incidents of risky sexual behavior. Armed with this knowledge, those who implement programs should confidently solicit the support and involvement of local government, educational, and religious leaders. . . .

5. What Research Is Most Urgently Needed?

The most urgently needed research is that which is essential for containing the HIV/AIDS epidemic. In particular, we need to track emerging behavioral risk factors and to aim preventive procedures at these risk factors with as much precision as possible. . . .

Young People

The epidemic in the United States is currently shifting to young people, particularly those who are gay, members of racial and ethnic minorities, and out-of-school adolescents. Because adolescents may be at risk for HIV infection in their early to mid teens, it is important to establish interventions for youth at an earlier age before the onset of risk behavior (sexual activity and drug use). Thus, the U.S. program of research must give highest priority to providing effective prevention programs for these subpopulations. Programs already shown to be effective for these subpopulations must be improved to ensure long-term maintenance of the reduction in risky behavior. Current interventions should be widely disseminated, and improved interventions, as they become available, should quickly replace those that have been less effective. Dissemination should include careful training of providers, monitoring to ensure fidelity of delivery, continuous evaluation of effectiveness, and modification where required by community and cultural needs and circumstances.

HIV-Positive Individuals

Effective interventions with people who are HIV positive can enable them to practice safer sex and safer needle use and thus help to contain the HIV epidemic. There is a startling paucity of well-developed interventions specifically designed for HIV-positive persons. Moreover, as biological treatment for those who are HIV-positive improves, the need for these preventive services will become even more pressing.

Women

It is essential to continue development of interventions to reduce heterosexual transmission of HIV to women as well as their risk of drug abuse behavior. These interventions should focus on the effect of community expectations of women and power differentials in their relationships with men. Moreover, additional research with female condoms and microbicides may facilitate preventive interventions that enhance women's control of exposure to HIV risk.

Linking Scientific Findings to Law and Policy

Most urgent is the need to rapidly bridge the serious gap that is widening between clear scientific results and the law and policies of the United States. As this statement has noted forcefully, there is clear scientific evidence supporting needle exchange programs, drug abuse treatment, and interventions with adolescents as essential components of our National program to contain the AIDS epidemic. Even as evidence rapidly accumulates on the success of these programs, however, legislation has been passed to make provision of these interventions extremely difficult. There is no more urgent need than to remedy this dangerous chasm. National leaders, legislators, scientists, and service providers must unite to understand fully this growing catastrophe. Why are voters unaware of these issues? What pressures and circumstances of government make it unresponsive to these compelling public health needs and effective programs? What are the limits in scientific communication that may obscure the legislative import of these scientific findings?

Conclusions and Recommendations

1. Preventive interventions are effective for reducing behavioral risk for HIV/AIDS and must be widely disseminated. Their application in practice settings may require careful training of personnel, close monitoring of the fidelity of procedures, and ongoing monitoring of effectiveness. Results of this evaluation must be reported; and where effectiveness in field settings is reduced, program modifications must be undertaken immediately.

Three approaches are particularly effective for risk in drug abuse behavior: needle exchange programs, drug abuse treatment, and outreach programs for drug abusers not enrolled in treatment. Several programs were deemed effective for risky sexual behavior. These programs include (1) information about HIV/AIDS and (2) building skills to use condoms and to negotiate the interpersonal challenges of safer sex. Effective safer sex programs have been developed for men who have sex with men, for women, and for adolescents.

2. The epidemic in the United States is shifting to young people, particularly those who are gay and who are members of ethnic minority groups. New research must focus on these emerging risk groups. Interventions must be developed and perfected, and special attention must be given to long-term maintenance of effects. In addition, AIDS is steadily increasing in women, and transmission of HIV virus to their children remains a major public health problem. Interventions focused on their special needs are essential.

3. Regional tracking of changes in behavioral risk will be necessary to identify settings, subpopulations, and geographical regions with special risk for seroconversion to HIV-positive status as the epidemic continues to change.

This effort, if properly coordinated with National tracking strategies, could play a critical part in a U.S. strategy to contain the spread of HIV.

4. Programs must be developed to help individuals already infected with HIV to avoid risky sexual and substance abuse behavior. This National priority will become more pressing as new biological treatments prolong life. Thus, prevention programs for HIV-positive people must have outcomes that can be maintained over long periods of time, in order to slow the spread of infection.

5. Legislative restriction on needle exchange programs must be lifted. Such legislation constitutes a major barrier to realizing the potential of a powerful approach and exposes millions of people to unnecessary risk.

6. Legislative barriers that discourage effective programs aimed at youth must be eliminated. Although sexual abstinence is a desirable objective, programs must include instruction in safe sex behavior, including condom use. The effectiveness of these programs is supported by strong scientific evidence. However, they are discouraged by welfare reform provisions, which support only programs using abstinence as the only goal.

7. The erosion of funding for drug and alcohol abuse treatment programs must be halted. Research data are clear that the programs reduce risky drug and alcohol abuse behavior and often eliminate drug abuse itself. Drug and alcohol abuse treatment is a central bulwark in the Nation's defense against HIV/AIDS.

8. The catastrophic breach between HIV/AIDS prevention science and the legislative process must be healed. Citizens, legislators, political leaders, service providers, and scientists must unite so that scientific data may properly inform legislative process. The study of policy development, the impact of policy, and policy change must be supported by Federal agencies.

CHINESE PRESIDENT ON
THE DEATH OF DENG XIAOPING
February 25, 1997

Chinese leader Deng Xiaoping, who opened his country's communist economy to the influence of capitalism but maintained a rigid political system, died on February 1 at age ninety-two. Deng's death ended an important era that saw China's economy become one of the fastest growing in the twentieth century. Deng also had ordered the 1989 military crackdown on prodemocracy protesters in Beijing's Tiananmen Square, a televised tragedy that reminded the world of the complexities and contradictions of modern China.

Although he had not held a senior government or Communist Party position since his retirement in 1989, Deng was still regarded as China's paramount leader, the man who set the tone for Chinese leaders at all levels and whose name was invoked when major policy changes were made. His death left the country in the hands of a cadre of party and government officials who lacked the prestige of Deng and other leaders from the revolutionary era, most importantly Mao Zedong. For years, these junior leaders had been jockeying for position in the post-Deng era.

At least for the moment, the man on top was Jiang Zemin, Deng's designated successor, who held the three top positions as president of the national government, general secretary of the Communist Party, and chairman of the Central Military Commission. At a memorial service for Deng, held on February 25 at the Great Hall of the People in Beijing, Jiang pledged to continue Deng's policies—especially the push for economic reform—but asserted that he was now in charge.

Deng did not live to see one event that had long been one of his most cherished goals: the British handover of Hong Kong to China on July 1. (Hong Kong, p. 501)

Six months after Deng's death, at the fifteenth Communist Party Congress, Jiang pushed through a plan for sharply reducing the government's role in the economy by selling most of the nation's 15,000 state-owned businesses. While most details of this plan remained to be worked out, the move was an implicit acknowledgment by the party that many aspects of communism needed to give way to free markets if economic growth was to continue.

The Deng Era

Deng Xiaoping was one of the most resilient leaders of the twentieth century. He was with Mao Zedong and other Communist leaders during the fabled "Long March" of 1934–1935, the battles against the Japanese occupation from 1937 to 1945, and then the violent revolution that overthrew the Western-backed Nationalist regime in 1949. Mao named Deng as general secretary of the Communist Party in 1954, and Deng served as one of Mao's foremost assistants for the next decade.

In 1966, at the outset of the decade-long "Cultural Revolution," Deng was purged from the party leadership, denounced as a public enemy, and forced to live for two years under house arrest and to work as a laborer in a tractor factory. Deng was rehabilitated politically in 1973, only to be purged again three years later as a consequence of demonstrations stemming from the death of Prime Minister Zhou Enlai. After Mao's death in 1976, Deng began another march back to political power, carefully maneuvering his way among various factions until he had consolidated control over the party, the government, and the military in 1978. Deng visited the United States in 1979, when President Jimmy Carter restored diplomatic relations with China. In one of the most famous scenes on that trip, the tiny Deng donned a ten-gallon cowboy hat at a Texas rodeo.

Deng launched a series of economic reforms, beginning with the dismantling of agricultural communes that controlled, and stifled, most of China's food production. Deng also opened areas of the southern coast to foreign investment; these "special economic zones" allowed overseas companies a share of ownership, along with the lure of low tax rates and low wages for employees.

Deng refused to allow political concessions along with the economic reforms. He ordered a crackdown on the "Democracy Wall" movement of 1978–1979, during which students and dissidents posted notices mildly critical of the government and party in public places. When thousands of students gathered in Beijing's Tiananmen Square in 1989 asking for more freedom and protesting official corruption, Deng worried about a return of the chaos that had gripped China in the 1920s and 1930s and again during the Cultural Revolution. His denunciation of the "turmoil" set in motion the bloody repression at Tiananmen Square on June 4, 1989, witnessed on television by millions of people around the world. (Chinese protests, Historic Documents of 1989, p. 275)

Deng formally retired in 1989 from his last major post as chairman of the Central Military Commission. Deng tapped Jiang Zemin, a former engineer, as China's next leader, but he remained the country's guiding figure and reportedly was consulted on major policy issues and personnel matters. Deng was last seen in public in 1994 when he was photographed inspecting a bridge in Shanghai; he was frail and barely able to walk, but

those around him gave him the deference due a man often called China's
"last emperor."

Jiang Carries On

Jiang wiped tears from his eyes as he delivered the opening lines of his
eulogy to Deng during a memorial service on February 25. Then he got
down to business, delivering a fifty-minute speech that paid tribute to Deng
and sought to align Jiang's own positions with those of his mentor. Jiang
declared that China would continue on the path of economic reform started
by Deng and would pursue good relations with the outside world, includ-
ing the United States.

Jiang offered solid evidence of his policies six months later, when the fif-
teenth Chinese Communist Party Congress convened in Beijing. In a
keynote speech to the Congress on September 13, Jiang announced that inef-
ficient state-owned businesses would be sold, unneeded workers would be
laid off, and private ownership of property would be allowed. Jiang said
none of those things directly; instead he resorted to the euphemisms and
contorted rhetoric that Chinese communists have used for decades to dis-
guise their actions. For example, Jiang spoke of putting thousands of state-
run factories and businesses under "public ownership"—meaning that the
government would sell its stock to members of the public.

Jiang solidified his stature on the world stage early in November when
he visited the United States and avoided rancorous public disputes on the
numerous issues confronting the two countries, most notably trade and
human rights. (Jiang visit, p. 728)

> *Following are excerpts from the eulogy to Deng Xiaoping deliv-*
> *ered February 25, 1997, at a memorial ceremony by Chinese*
> *president Jiang Zemin:*

Comrades and Friends:

Today, we are at the Great Hall of the People in the capital to hold a memorial meeting and mourn for our beloved Comrade Deng Xiaoping with profound grief. At this moment, the broad masses of the people at factories, the
countryside, shops, schools, army units, government institutions and urban
neighborhoods throughout our country's vast territory, are together with us to
cherish the memory of Comrade Deng Xiaoping's tremendous achievements
and outstanding qualities and to give expression of our grief.

For the past few days, people of all ethnic groups, including compatriots in
Hong Kong, Macao and Taiwan, and overseas Chinese, felt boundless grief for
China's loss of a great man in the passing of Deng Xiaoping. People all over
the world, leaders of other countries and international friends in various
fields have also expressed their heartfelt condolences over the world's loss of
a great man in the passing of Deng Xiaoping.

The Chinese people love Comrade Deng Xiaoping, thank Comrade Deng Xiaoping, mourn for Comrade Deng Xiaoping, and cherish the memory of Comrade Deng Xiaoping because he devoted his life-long energies to the Chinese people, performed immortal feats for the independence and liberation of the Chinese nation as well as for China's cause of socialist modernization.

His revolutionary career with magnificent sweeps in more than seven decades is closely associated with the founding and development of the Communist Party of China [CPC], with the founding and development of the Chinese people's army, and with the founding and development of the People's Republic of China [PRC]. He was among founders of the people's republic and after the founding of the PRC he became an important member of the Communist Party of China's first generation of the central collective leadership with Comrade Mao Zedong at the core. After the third plenum of the 11th CPC Central Committee, he became the core of the Communist Party of China's second generation of central collective leadership and led us to pioneer a new road of building socialism with Chinese characteristics. Following this path, China's national economy has developed rapidly, its comprehensive national strength has grown stronger day by day, the living standards of its people has gradually improved, and socialism has shown unprecedented vigor and vitality. Comrade Deng Xiaoping said that without Comrade Mao Zedong, we Chinese people would have to grope in the dark for at least a longer period of time. And likewise, we should say today that without Comrade Deng Xiaoping, the Chinese people would not live a new life like today's and there would not be today's new situation of reforms and opening-up and the bright prospects of the socialist modernization. . . .

The "Cultural Revolution" is a grave mistake in our Party's history during the socialist period. In this movement, Comrade Deng Xiaoping was wrongly criticized and denounced, and was stripped of all his posts, suffering another major setback in his political career.

After Lin Biao's plot of counter-revolutionary coup d'etat was smashed, Comrade Deng Xiaoping came out to work again, and served in 1975 as vice chairman of the CPC Central Committee, vice premier of the State Council, vice chairman of the Central Military Commission, and chief of the PLA General Staff, taking charge of the day-to-day affairs of the Party, the state, and the army.

He made vigorous efforts to turn the tide, urging boldness and decisiveness in action, and determination to carry out drastic rectification of the seriously chaotic situation caused by the "Cultural Revolution."

For the benefits of the Party and the people, he gave no thought to his own interests or safety, and, despite the risk of being overthrown again, waged a resolute struggle against the Gang of Four.

This rectification drive was, in essence, an experiment for the reforms afterwards. It reflected the aspirations of the cadres and the people, and represented the Party's correct leadership, leading to conspicuous successes within a short period of time.

Since the deepening of the rectification drive would surely lead to the systematic correction of the errors of the "Cultural Revolution," Comrade Deng Xiaoping was accused of whipping up "the right deviationist wind to reverse the previous verdicts," and he was again wrongly deprived of all his posts. This was the third serious setback in his political career.

However, the achievements in the rectification drive and his strength of character displayed in the rectification drive had helped him win the support of the Party, the army, and the people of the whole country. And this served as full popular preparations for smashing the Gang of Four.

Following the downfall of the Gang of Four and the end of the "Cultural Revolution," China was facing a critical historical moment, that is, whether China could change the grave situation caused by the ten-year "Cultural Revolution," and arise from amid difficulties to open a new road of developing socialism.

Under the urgent demand of the Party members and the people, Comrade Deng Xiaoping was restored to his former posts. At the Party Central Committee plenum that decided to restore him to his posts, he said: When I come out to work, there may be two kinds of attitudes. One is to act as a bureaucrat, the other is to work. I said to myself: Who asked you to be a Communist? Since you are a Communist, you can neither act as a bureaucrat nor have selfish considerations. You can not have other options.

With his great foresight, rich political experience, and superb art of leadership, Comrade Deng Xiaoping seized the decisive link from numerous events, and started the rectification drive from bringing the ideological line back onto the right track.

Stressing that seeking truth from facts is the essence of Mao Zedong Thought, he opposed the erroneous idea of "two Whatevers" ("We should firmly uphold whatever policy decisions Chairman Mao made, and unswervingly adhere to whatever instructions Chairman Mao gave.") . . .

Comrade Deng Xiaoping guided us in formulating the development strategy for the basic realization of modernization in three steps, and affirming the comprehensive plan for reform and opening up. He vigorously supported and promoted rural reform characterized mainly by the contract responsibility system with remuneration linked to the household, and warmly praised the rise of rural enterprises.

He was the first to put forth the idea that the market economy can be pushed under socialism, and promoted overall economic restructuring with focus in the cities, creating for us a new road of combining socialism with market economy to further liberate and develop productivity.

Comrade Deng Xiaoping proposed and promoted the establishment of special economic zones in coastal areas, the opening of coastal cities, the development and opening of the Pudong New Area in Shanghai. As a result, a pattern of overall opening to the outside world has gradually taken form.

He showed great concern for the economic development and people's life in central and western regions as well as poverty-stricken areas, demanding that solution of such problems be gradually elevated to a more important position. He put forth the new idea that science and technology are the primary productive force, called for respect for knowledge and talents, and stressed the development of education, science and culture.

He also repeatedly stressed that great importance should be attached and warm support be rendered to people's creativity in the course of reform and opening up, and their experience should be summarized conscientiously and spread energetically.

Under the leadership of the Party Central Committee with Comrade Deng Xiaoping at the core, our country went through in the new era the great historical process from rural reform to urban reform, from economic restructuring to restructuring in all other fields, from invigoration of the domestic economy to opening up to the outside world, a process of paying equal attention to economic development and ethical and cultural progress.

As a result, China's productivity has been upgraded by leaps and bounds, people's living standards have been considerably raised, and the face of the country has seen profound changes. All these have won heart-felt support from the people.

With political upheavals occurring both domestically and internationally at the end of the 1980s and the beginning of the 1990s, our Party faced another major historical juncture. Under the firm and strong support of Comrade Deng Xiaoping and other senior comrades, and relying on the people, the Party and the Government adhered to the four Cardinal Principles with a clear-cut stand, and safeguarded the independence, dignity, security and stability of the nation while unswervingly persisting in taking economic construction as the focus and in reform and opening up. . . .

Comrade Deng Xiaoping's most precious legacy to us is his theory of building socialism with Chinese characteristics and the Party's basic line for the initial stage of socialism which was formulated under the guidance of that theory.

Deng's theory of building socialism with Chinese characteristics took shape and developed gradually under the historical conditions of peace and development being the theme of the times, through the practice of China's reform, opening-up and socialist modernization drive, and on the basis of summing up the historical experiences of the triumphs and setbacks of China's socialist cause and the ups and downs of other socialist countries. . . .

The new situation and new achievements socialism has accomplished in China has enabled us to arrive at the conviction, which is based on historical comparison and international observation, that Deng Xiaoping's theory of building socialism with Chinese characteristics is correct. . . .

Reform is the inevitable road through which China will be able to achieve socialist modernization. Comrade Deng Xiaoping drew up a master plan for our all-round reforms. We must act in accordance with the teaching of Comrade Deng Xiaoping, taking the deepening of the reform as the key to eliminating barriers to the development of productive forces and further advancing our entire cause. The establishment of a socialist market economic structure on the basis of taking the socialist public ownership as the mainstay and the common development of multi-economic sectors is a great pioneering work that our predecessors have never undertaken. On the basis of the achievements which we have already scored, we must carry on the reform of the economic structure in depth. To meet the needs in this regard, we must persist in the restructuring in political and other fields.

Opening up to the outside world is an essential condition for China to achieve its socialist modernization. Comrade Deng Xiaoping emphasized repeatedly that the current world is an open one, that China's development is inseparable from the world and that it is imperative to pursue the policy of opening up to the outside world on the basis of persisting in self-reliance. We must act in accordance with the teaching of Comrade Deng Xiaoping, soberly assess the development of the world, courageously meet the severe challenge, adhere to the fundamental national policy of opening up, develop an all-directional and multi-layer pattern of opening up, strive to enhance the level of our opening up, extensively absorb and draw on all results of advanced civilization created by all countries in the world including developed capitalist countries, and actively participate in international economic and technological cooperation and competition.

The state power of the people's democratic dictatorship constitutes the political guarantee for the healthy development of our cause. Comrade Deng Xiaoping always paid close attention to the consolidation and development of the people's political power. . . .

The complete reunification of our motherland is the common aspiration of the entire Chinese nation. Using the form of "one country, two systems" to realize peaceful reunification is Comrade Deng Xiaoping's great creation. We must act in accordance with the teaching of Comrade Deng Xiaoping, striving to attain the objective to the motherland's reunification. In accordance with the Sino-British and Sino-Portuguese agreements, Hong Kong will return to the embrace of the motherland soon and Macao will return to the embrace of the motherland in 1999. The Taiwan question will be settled eventually and the complete reunification of the motherland will certainly be achieved.

Concentrating on the socialist modernization drive requires a peaceful international environment. Scientifically observing the changes in the international situation, Comrade Deng Xiaoping led us in re-determining our international strategy, readjusting China's relations with Japan, the United States and the former Soviet Union, and developing friendly relations with surrounding countries and the third world countries, thereby creating a new situation in China's external relations during the new period. . . .

Comrade Deng Xiaoping has parted from us forever. But, his name, deeds of merit, thoughts and outstanding qualities will go down the annals of history and remain immortal in the hearts of the people from generation to generation. Under the strong leadership by the Party Central Committee, the whole Party, the whole army and the people of various ethnic groups across the country will certainly carry forward his behest, and firmly and full of confidence, push forward the great cause of building socialism with Chinese characteristics pioneered by Comrade Deng Xiaoping and to build our country into a socialist and modernized country which is strong, prosperous, democratic, and civilized.

Eternal glory to Comrade Deng Xiaoping!

March

COMMISSION REPORT ON GOVERNMENT SECRECY

March 4, 1997

The federal government keeps too many secrets for too long and with too little reason, a bipartisan commission reported March 4. The commission recommended that Congress enact legislation regulating how secrets are made and kept. With few exceptions, the only authority for government officials to stamp documents "secret" came from presidential executive orders.

The Commission on Protecting and Reducing Government Secrecy was appointed by President Bill Clinton and congressional leaders in 1994, under authority created by the fiscal 1994–1995 State Department authorizations bill (PL 103-236). The commission's investigation was the first broad examination of government secrecy since the mid-1950s.

The commission was chaired by Sen. Daniel Patrick Moynihan, a New York Democrat and former chairman of the Senate Intelligence Committee. Rep. Larry Combest, a Texas Republican and former chairman of the House Intelligence Committee, served as commission vice-chairman. Among its other ten members were John M. Deutch, former director of central intelligence; Sen. Jesse Helms, R-N.C., chairman of the Senate Foreign Relations Committee; and Rep. Lee H. Hamilton, D-Ind., who formerly chaired the House Intelligence Committee and the House Foreign Affairs Committee.

The commission's report was unanimous, although some members— most notably Combest and Helms—expressed concerns about the prospect that government secrets might be declassified too rapidly. Such concerns, along with the natural resistance of government bureaucracies to change— made it likely that many commission recommendations would not be fully implemented for years, if ever.

Backlog of Secrets

While arguing that the government keeps too many secrets, the commission said it was impossible to determine just how many secret documents are stored in government bureaus and warehouses, or at the offices and plants of thousands of private contractors. The commission produced one astonishing figure: an estimate that in 1997 there were more than 1.5 billion pages of classified documents that were at least twenty-five years old. Some of those documents were still sensitive and should remain classified, the commission said, but most were no longer of any significance and should be declassified. In one of several examples cited by the commission, weather reports produced by an aide to General Dwight D. Eisenhower during World War II were still classified thirty years later.

As with the quantity of secrets, the commission said it could not report with any certainty how much it costs the taxpayers to make and keep all those documents secret. Citing surveys and other estimates made in 1994 and 1995, the commission concluded that the total cost of protecting secrets in government and national security-related industries (such as defense contractors) was at least $5.6 billion in 1995.

Along with the budgetary cost of maintaining all that paperwork, the commission said, excessive secrecy entailed political costs. Public cynicism about the government—especially secret or semisecret agencies such as the CIA and FBI—is fostered by the government's ability to hide embarrassing information. Conspiracy theories take root when the government keeps too much information from the public, the commission said. As an example, Senator Moynihan noted polls showing that a majority of the American public continues to believe that the CIA was somehow involved in the assassination of President John Kennedy.

The commission said excessive secrecy can hinder decision making within the government when information is deliberately or inadvertently kept from policymakers who might need it. The commission cited the "Verona" project following World War II, which cracked secret codes of the Soviet Union. FBI director J. Edgar Hoover kept information developed by the Verona project secret from President Harry Truman, his senior aides, and even the Central Intelligence Agency. Moynihan said Hoover used that information for political purposes, such as accusing government officials he disliked of being communists.

Far too often, members said, information is kept secret not because of any tangible danger to national security but to keep the government or some of its officials from suffering embarrassment. Senator Helms said government agencies have used secrecy to shield illegal activities and "indefensible" policies. Moynihan cited, as the classic demonstration of this maxim, the 1971 "Pentagon Papers" case, in which the Nixon administration unsuccessfully tried to block publication of a Pentagon-written history of the Vietnam War. Most experts subsequently concluded that disclosure of the Pentagon Papers strengthened the antiwar movement but revealed no true military or diplomatic secrets.

Keeping Fewer Secrets

The commission offered more than a dozen specific proposals to accomplish its general recommendations that the government should stamp fewer documents "secret" and should be more diligent in declassifying existing documents. At the core of the commission proposals was a call for Congress to enact a statute governing classification and declassification of secrets. Such a law would replace a series of presidential orders dating back to the Wilson administration that form the basis for nearly all existing secrecy classifications.

As a basic standard for secrecy, the commission recommended that information should be classified only "if there is a demonstrable need to protect the information in the interests of national security. . . ." Government officials would be required to justify their decisions to classify documents and to put their names on those documents.

The commission recommended establishing a "life cycle" for secrets, reflecting the seriousness of the information and the length of time it might be sensitive. In general, the commission said secrets should be declassified after ten years at most, unless the responsible agency determines that "current risk assessments" show a continuing need for secrecy. All information should be declassified after thirty years, the commission said, "unless it is shown that demonstrable harm to an individual or to ongoing government activities will result" from release of that information.

Other key recommendations of the commission included: putting a single executive branch agency in charge of classification policies; training officials about the rationale for secrecy and how to judge the risks and benefits of disclosing information; and creating a National Declassification Center, within an existing agency such as the National Archives, to declassify documents and coordinate this task across government agencies.

The commission's central recommendations were incorporated into legislation (S 712 and HR 1546) introduced May 7 by Moynihan, Helms, Combest, and Hamilton. Congress did not act on those bills or on any of the major recommendations during 1997.

> *Following are excerpts from the "Summary of Findings and Recommendations" in the Report of the Commission on Protecting and Reducing Government Secrecy, which was sent to President Clinton and congressional leaders March 3 and made public March 4, 1997:*

It is time for a new way of thinking about secrecy.

Secrecy is a form of government regulation. Americans are familiar with the tendency to overregulate in other areas. What is different with secrecy is that the public cannot know the extent or the content of the regulation.

Excessive secrecy has significant consequences for the national interest when, as a result, policymakers are not fully informed, government is not held accountable for its actions, and the public cannot engage in informed debate. This remains a dangerous world; some secrecy is vital to save lives, bring miscreants to justice, protect national security, and engage in effective diplomacy. Yet as Justice Potter Stewart noted in his opinion in the Pentagon

Papers case, when everything is secret, nothing is secret. Even as billions of dollars are spent each year on government secrecy, the classification and personnel security systems have not always succeeded at their core task of protecting those secrets most critical to the national security. The classification system, for example, is used too often to deny the public an understanding of the policymaking process, rather than for the necessary protection of intelligence activities and other highly sensitive matters.

The classification and personnel security systems are no longer trusted by many inside and outside the Government. It is now almost routine for American officials of unquestioned loyalty to reveal classified information as part of ongoing policy disputes—with one camp "leaking" information in support of a particular view, or to the detriment of another—or in support of settled administration policy. In the process, this degrades public service by giving a huge advantage to the least scrupulous players.

The best way to ensure that secrecy is respected, and that the most important secrets remain secret, is for secrecy to be returned to its limited but necessary role. Secrets can be protected more effectively if secrecy is reduced overall.

Benefits can flow from moving information that no longer needs protection out of the classification system and, in appropriate cases, from not classifying at all. We live in an information-rich society, one in which more than ever before open sources—rather than covert means of collection—can provide the information necessary to permit well-informed decisions. Too often, our secrecy system proceeds as if this information revolution has not happened, imposing costs by compartmentalizing information and limiting access.

Greater openness permits more public understanding of the Government's actions and also makes it more possible for the Government to respond to criticism and justify those actions. It makes free exchange of scientific information possible and encourages discoveries that foster economic growth. In addition, by allowing for a fuller understanding of the past, it provides opportunities to learn lessons from what has gone before—making it easier to resolve issues concerning the Government's past actions and helping prepare for the future.

This does not mean that we believe the public should be privy to all government information. Certain types of information—for example, the identity of sources whose exposure would jeopardize human life, signals or imagery intelligence the loss of which would profoundly hinder the capability to collect critical data, or information that could aid terrorists—must be assiduously protected. There must be zero tolerance for permitting such information to be released through unauthorized means, including through deliberate or inadvertent leaks. But when the business of government requires secrecy, it should be employed in a manner that takes risks into account and attempts to control costs.

It is time to reexamine the long-standing tension between secrecy and openness, and develop a new way of thinking about government secrecy as we move into the next century. It is to that end that we direct our recommendations.

Ours is the first analysis authorized by statute of the workings of secrecy in the United States Government in 40 years, and only the second ever. We started our work with the knowledge that many commissions and reports on government secrecy have preceded us, with little impact on the problems we still see and on the new ones we have found.

In undertaking our mission to look at government secrecy, we have observed when the secrecy system works well, and when it does not. We have looked at the consequences of the lack of adequate protection. We have sought to diagnose the current system, and to identify what works and ways the system can work better. Above all, we have sought to understand how best to achieve both better protection and greater openness.

That the secrecy system that evolved and grew over the course of the 20th century would remain essentially unchanged and unexamined by the public was predictable. It is to be expected of a regulatory system essentially hidden from view. Some two million Federal officials, civil and military, and another one million persons in industry, have the ability to classify information. Categories of administrative markings also have proliferated over time, and the secrecy system has become ever more complex. The system will perpetuate itself absent outside intervention, and in doing so maintain not only its many positive features, but also those elements that are detrimental to both our democracy and our security.

It is time for legislation. There needs to be some check on the unrestrained discretion to create secrets. There needs to be an effective mode of declassification.

To improve the functioning of the secrecy system and the implementation of established rules, we recommend a statute that sets forth the principles for what may be declared secret.

Apart from aspects of nuclear energy subject to the Atomic Energy Act, secrets in the Federal Government are whatever anyone with a stamp decides to stamp secret. There is no statutory base and never has been; classification and declassification have been governed for nearly five decades by a series of executive orders, but none has created a stable and reliable system that ensures we protect well what needs protecting but nothing more. What has been consistently lacking is the discipline of a legal framework to clearly define and enforce the proper uses of secrecy. Such a system inevitably degrades.

We therefore propose the following as the framework for a statute that establishes the principles on which classification and declassification should be based:

Sec. 1 Information shall be classified only if there is a demonstrable need to protect the information in the interests of national security, with the goal of ensuring that classification is kept to an absolute minimum consistent with these interests.

Sec. 2 The President shall, as needed, establish procedures and structures for classification of information. Procedures and structures shall be established and resources allocated for declassification as a parallel program to classification. Details of these programs and any revisions to them shall be published in the *Federal Register* and subject to notice and comment procedures.

Sec. 3 In establishing the standards and categories to apply in determining whether information should be or remain classified, such standards and categories shall include consideration of the benefit from public disclosure of the information and weigh it against the need for initial or continued protection under the classification system. If there is significant doubt whether information requires protection, it shall not be classified.

Sec. 4 Information shall remain classified for no longer than ten years, unless the agency specifically recertifies that the particular information requires continued protection based on current risk assessments. All information shall be declassified after 30 years, unless it is shown that demonstrable harm to an individual or to ongoing government activities will result from release. Systematic declassification schedules shall be established. Agencies shall submit annual reports on their classification and declassification programs to the Congress.

Sec. 5 This statute shall not be construed as authority to withhold information from the Congress.

Sec. 6 There shall be established a National Declassification Center to coordinate, implement, and oversee the declassification policies and practices of the Federal Government. The Center shall report annually to the Congress and the President on its activities and on the status of declassification practices by all Federal agencies that use, hold, or create classified information.

A statute will not change the current state of affairs overnight, but it will give officials grounds for saying No—and supervisors grounds for asking Why. Secrecy exists to protect national security, not government officials and agencies. There is not the least reason to think that our Government cannot make and then enforce this distinction.

A more stable foundation for the entire classification and declassification system, with more consistent application of established rules across all agencies that classify and less ability to "opt out" where there is disagreement with particular rules, is required. The tendency of individuals in a government agency to protect too much by erring on the side of secrecy will not change through mere exhortation, but only as a result of common principles that are grounded in statutory language. In short, a legislative basis for the classification system, establishing clear guiding principles while retaining broad authority within the Executive Branch to establish and administer the details of the system, offers a better and more predictable way to achieve meaningful changes.

To enhance the understanding of classification and declassification decisions, we suggest adopting the concept of a life cycle for secrets.

All information, classified and unclassified alike, has a life span in which decisions must be made with respect to its creation, management, and use.

But the management of classified material should also involve the important consideration of whether the information should be classified at all, and if so, for how long. Some information needs to be kept secret for a day; some for a year; some for a generation or more.

Thinking about even highly sensitive information in terms of its life cycle can help resolve the inconsistencies between the protection that different information requires and the protection it actually receives during different points in its life cycle. The current classification system, however, is notable for the absence of clear standards to gauge the need for and type of protection. . . .

To improve declassification procedures, we recommend establishing a national declassification center to coordinate how information that no longer needs to be secret will be made available to the public; among its roles would be to declassify information using guidance from the agencies that originate the information.

Declassification should be seen as a form of deregulation. Currently, there are over 1.5 billion pages of government records over 25 years old in government vaults that are unavailable to the public because they are still classified. Some of these are still highly sensitive and should remain secret, but others are at the end of their life cycle and should be moved out of the classification system.

The present regulatory system simply will not let go; it will not and cannot declassify enough material in a cost-effective way. The backlog of decades-old classified records exists in part because of the way the Federal Government is organized to provide access. Some systematic mode of deregulation needs to be established: declassification should not be a random procedure. However, because few agencies view this as a primary mission to which resources and expertise should be devoted, timely and cost-effective declassification of older government records of permanent historical value does not now occur. . . .

Investment in a Declassification Center would pay dividends over time in terms of savings in both financial and opportunity costs. At the same time, the Center would help build greater confidence in the Government's ability to distinguish between core secrets and information that may be made available at the end of its life cycle.

To promote greater accountability, we recommend establishing a single, independent Executive Branch office responsible for coordinating classification and declassification practice and enhancing incentives to improve such practice.

Any policy, including on classification and declassification, is only as good as its implementation. Accountability should be a hallmark of a well-functioning secrecy system. Those charged with creating and maintaining government secrets need to do it well, and they need to know that they will be expected to do so.

Unfortunately, the secrecy system has developed into one in which accountability barely exists. Confusion over the proper roles of existing oversight bodies in the Executive Branch, including the Information Security Oversight Office and the Security Policy Board, has hampered the development and oversight of sound classification policies and practices. The absence of adequate oversight across the Executive Branch and by the Congress has resulted in little accountability for decisions and little incentive to reduce the scope of government secrecy. We therefore recommend improving training and enhancing incentives so that classifying officials will consider more carefully the costs of secrecy and recognize that they will be accountable for their decisions.

The Commission recommends improving Executive Branch mechanisms by identifying a single office—independent of the agencies that classify and able to demand compliance—that would be responsible for coordinating oversight of classification and declassification practice. This office would make recommendations directly to the National Security Council for establishing classification and declassification policies. It also would ensure that classification and declassification are treated primarily as information management issues, not merely as extensions of security policy. The Commission also proposes improved oversight programs within individual agencies by enhancing positive incentives for officials to improve their handling of classified materials.

To ensure that classification is used more efficiently, we recommend improving the initial classification of information by requiring classifying officials to weigh the costs and benefits of secrecy and to consider additional factors in the decision to make or keep something secret.

The initial decision to classify is critical: it is the most important part of the life cycle of secrets, and the place where the entire regulatory process begins. The decision should be made sparingly, and then vigorously enforced.

Classification means that resources will be spent throughout the information's life cycle to protect, distribute, and limit access to it that would not be spent if the information were not classified. Classification means that those who need to use that information in the course of their work have to be investigated and the results of that investigation analyzed to determine whether access should be granted. Classification means that a document may have to be edited to remove certain sensitive details in order for the rest of the information to be more widely shared inside the Government. And classification means that some kind of review has to take place when the document containing that material is considered for declassification. . . .

We recommend that the national security question be weighed differently than heretofore. The issue for classifiers is not just to see if particular information can potentially fit within a category of material that is eligible for protection, but to analyze in the first instance whether information requires the protection afforded by the classification system. Absent a more thoughtful process for making initial decisions, we will continue to see classification by rote, without a careful analysis of whether there is a risk from release of the information that requires it to be protected through classification. . . .

To clarify the grounds for classifying intelligence information, we recommend that the Director of Central Intelligence issue a directive

concerning the appropriate scope of sources and methods protection as a rationale for secrecy.

Underlying the rationale of "sources and methods" as the reason that information is kept secret is not the content of the information itself, but instead the way it was obtained. Yet the public and historians generally do not care how the information was collected; they want to know how it was used and what decisions it informed. Too often, there is a tendency to use the sources and methods language contained in the National Security Act of 1947 to automatically classify virtually anything that is collected by an intelligence agency—including information collected from open sources.

A more thoughtful approach is needed to identify and protect the highly sensitive material that needs protection but not overload the system with information that does not require the expenditure of limited resources to protect it. Clarification through issuance of a directive by the Director of Central Intelligence of the scope of and reasons for sources and methods protection would still ensure that sensitive information stays secret. At the same time, such a directive explaining the appropriate scope of that protection would help prevent the automatic withholding of all information that might relate in any manner, however indirectly, to an intelligence source or method.

To promote the use of personnel security resources in a manner that ensures more effective and efficient protection, we recommend standardizing security clearance procedures and reallocating resources to those parts of the personnel security system that have proven most effective in determining who should or should not have access to classified information. . . .

The Commission recommends directing resources where they are most likely to be of value in determining who should, and who should not, have access to classified information. This means, for example, that those parts of the process—such as neighborhood investigations—shown, both in studies and through experience, not to yield helpful information should no longer be required as a matter of course in every investigation. . . .

To promote more awareness of the threats to automated information systems, we recommend steps to focus greater attention and promote increased cooperation on means for protecting such systems.

This is an era of extraordinary change not only in information technology, but also in the very way that individuals communicate with each other. Information vital to the security and continued prosperity of the United States resides on a series of increasingly interconnected classified and unclassified systems. Those responsible for the protection of national security information face new and increasingly difficult challenges presented by the widespread use of computer networks linked by telephone lines, cable, direct broadcast service, and wireless communications, and by the proliferation of personal computers. New and rapidly changing electronic information systems, on which both secret and open information travels and is stored, are threatened when their protection is not adequate to ensure the integrity of the content and meaning of that information.

This new environment requires a fundamental rethinking of traditional approaches to safeguarding national security information. Despite some recent efforts, however, there are no standards for protecting and managing automated information systems, nor is there any national forum designed to promote cooperation in this area. A more focused and directed approach to oversight of these issues on the part of both the Executive Branch and the Congress, and a reinvigorated and closer cooperation between government and industry, are key to developing and implementing effective and coordinated computer security measures.

In the future, better ways to disseminate threat information, improve public and government awareness of computer attacks and related incidents, and develop means for audit and intrusion detection all will be important to promoting greater awareness of the vulnerabilities to national information systems. The Commission sees it as vital that steps be taken in the near term to address these and other critical protection problems.

This report should be seen as a call for changes that may require years to accomplish and will not occur simply through new regulations or organizational restructuring. Many of the problems identified in the report developed and grew over generations and will not be fixed overnight. Key to ensuring that real change occurs will be the realization by senior government officials—whether career civil servants or political appointees—that it is in their own self-interest, as well as in the country's interest, to gain control over the secrecy system and, by so doing, to promote more effective protection of the information that should remain secret. . . .

GAO REPORT ON AVIATION SAFETY RECOMMENDATIONS
March 5, 1997

A high-level commission chaired by Vice President Al Gore on February 12 proposed billions of dollars worth of technological improvements to enhance the safety of the nation's civil aviation industry and to guard against terrorism. The government and airlines already had begun implementing many of the recommendations, which the Gore Commission had first presented to President Bill Clinton as an interim report in September 1996. But the most sweeping changes—including a total modernization of the air traffic control system—would be costly and would take years to put into effect.

In an analysis of the Gore Commission report, the General Accounting Office (GAO), the investigative arm of Congress, lauded the proposals as necessary and, in some cases, overdue. The GAO raised serious questions, however, about the ability of the Federal Aviation Administration (FAA) to oversee the changes in the airline industry and to make needed reforms in its own bureaucratic structure. The GAO had made many of the same observations and recommendations in congressional testimony on April 30, 1996, less than two weeks before a ValuJet plane crashed in the Florida Everglades, killing all 110 passengers. Critics had charged that the FAA had not adequately monitored ValuJet's safety procedures. (GAO report, Historic Documents of 1996, p. 237; Gore Commission interim report, Historic Documents of 1996, p. 662)

Gore Commission Report

The Gore Commission made dozens of recommendations on a wide range of issues involving the safety and security of the U.S. airline industry. Some proposals called for procedural changes in the way the government and the airline industry did business, such as tightening up security to ensure that unauthorized persons could not gain access to sensitive areas in airports. Other recommendations were more sweeping and involved enormous costs, including a proposal that the FAA speed up its plan to modernize the aging air traffic control system.

Much of the immediate attention on the commission report was focused on proposals that would directly affect the traveling public. The commission recommended, for example, that the FAA require that children under the age of two be assigned their own seats on aircraft, rather than being allowed to sit on a parent's lap. Intended to provide protection for very young children, this recommendation would be costly to the families who would have to purchase additional tickets.

Perhaps the most controversial commission recommendation was that the airlines establish a system of "profiling" passengers to provide an alert against potential terrorists. Under such a system—used for years by European airlines—information about passengers and their travel plans would be matched against characteristics fitting terrorists. For example, a passenger with no luggage who had purchased a last-minute ticket using cash might be singled out for interrogation before boarding a plane. Civil liberties groups and organizations representing Arab-Americans charged that such a system might unfairly target minority groups, especially people who appeared to be Arabic, and would be unconstitutional.

In accepting the Gore Commission report and saying the recommendations would be carried out, President Clinton made no mention of the controversial items. Clinton said the report would help ensure that air travel remains "our safest mode of transportation." Clinton noted that the government already had moved to implement some of the proposals Gore made in the September 1996 interim report, including installing fifty-four bomb detection machines in major airports and hiring three hundred new FAA agents to test airport security measures.

GAO Analysis of Gore Report

In a detailed review of the Gore Commission report, the GAO said most of the recommendations were sound but that carrying them out would be difficult, time-consuming, and expensive. That analysis came in testimony on March 5 by Gerald L. Dillingham, the GAO's associate director for transportation issues, before the aviation subcommittee of the Senate Committee on Commerce, Science, and Transportation.

Dillingham said many of the FAA's problems stemmed from an "organizational culture"—its bureaucratic ways of doing business that had grown up over the decades. Other reports by government and independent agencies had noted that the FAA was too dependent on paperwork, had a cumbersome decision-making process, and was too closely allied with the aviation industry it was supposed to oversee. The GAO noted that a lack of continuity in the FAA's top leadership also had fostered an organizational culture "that has tended to avoid accountability, focus on the short term, and resist fundamental improvements in the acquisitions process." Because of the FAA's past inability to reform its operations, the GAO predicted that the changes in FAA procedures recommended by the Gore panel "may require years of concerted effort by all parties concerned."

The Gore panel's recommendation for speeding up installation of a new air traffic control system was "commendable," the GAO said, but realisti-

cally "there is little evidence that this goal can be achieved." In particular, the GAO cited the FAA's historical problems in developing new air traffic control programs and the enormous technological challenges of updating the system with satellites, new computers, and other devices. The GAO noted that the FAA had said, in its own previous reports, that the agency tended to make "billion-dollar investment decisions without reliable information." Given such past failings, forcing it to spend money even faster on unproven technology "could increase the risk that FAA will make poor investment decisions," the GAO said.

The GAO noted that some of the Gore Commission recommendations on airline security already were being implemented. Even so, the GAO recalled that the FAA had been unable to meet its deadlines for previous airline security improvements—raising questions about the agency's ability to carry out the Gore Commission proposals for which it was responsible. The GAO also said the Gore Commission failed to recommend how the government and airlines should pay for security improvements, which would cost billions of dollars over the course of many years.

Inspections of Repair Stations

In a separate report issued in October, the GAO focused on the FAA's oversight of the 2,800 commercial aviation repair stations, which perform nearly half of all repairs and maintenance on the nation's airliners. The GAO said the FAA appeared to be meeting its goal of inspecting each repair station at least once a year. But, the report said, the aviation agency did not keep adequate records to enable it to determine whether repair stations had corrected violations found by FAA inspectors.

The issue of inspecting aircraft maintenance facilities came to public attention in 1996 after the FAA determined that the ValuJet crash was caused by a fire ignited by oxygen generators that had been improperly mounted at a repair station. The FAA then announced plans to upgrade its inspections of those stations. The October 24 GAO report commended the FAA plans but said the agency needed to improve its system of documenting the violations uncovered by its inspectors and the follow-up corrective steps.

> *Following is the text of testimony by Gerald L. Dillingham, associate director for transportation issues of the General Accounting Office, on March 5, 1997, before the aviation subcommittee of the Senate Committee on Commerce, Science, and Transportation, on the subject of "Challenges to Implementing the Recommendations of the White House Commission on Aviation Safety and Security":*

We appreciate the opportunity to share our views on the recommendations contained in the recently released report of the White House Commission on Aviation Safety and Security. The Commission's 57 recommendations broadly cover safety, security, air traffic control, and disaster response. As you know, 1996 was a bad year for aviation safety. Last year, 380 people died in air accidents involving large U.S. air carriers, the highest number in 11 years. The crashes of TWA Flight 800 off New York and ValuJet Flight 592 in Florida accounted for most of those deaths. Although the nation's air transportation system remains the safest in the world and the Federal Aviation Administration (FAA) the model for other nations, these tragic events have served to raise the Congress's, the administration's, the aviation industry's, and the flying public's consciousness of the need to continuously increase the existing margin of safety. . . .

We believe that the Commission's recommendations are a good start toward an evolutionary process of making real the Commission's vision of ensuring greater safety and security for passengers, restructuring the relationships between the government and the industry, and maintaining America's position of global leadership in aviation. However, key questions remain about how and when the recommendations will be implemented, how much it will cost to implement them, and who will pay the cost. Our message this morning focuses on the challenges that lie ahead in taking the next steps to convert the Commission's recommendations from concepts to realities.

Aviation Safety

The Commission made 14 recommendations in the general area of aviation safety. Foremost among these is establishing a national goal to reduce the fatal accident rate by 80 percent within 10 years. This is a very challenging goal, particularly in the light of the projected increases in the amount of air traffic in the coming decade.

We applaud the Commission's adopting such a goal for accident reduction and endorse many of its recommendations for improving safety. These recommendations include, for example, expanding FAA's inspection program to cover not only aging aircraft's structural integrity but also such areas as electrical wiring, fuel lines, and pumps. A number of these recommendations resonate with safety and efficiency improvements that we and others, including FAA, have suggested over the years. However, we believe that, as FAA tries to fundamentally reinvent itself as the Commission contemplates through some of its recommendations, FAA and the aviation industry will be challenged in three areas: (1) FAA's organizational culture and resource management, (2) FAA's partnerships with the airline industry, and (3) the costs of and sources of funding to implement the recommendations.

A number of recent studies and the FAA itself have pointed to the importance of culture in the agency's operations. Last year, our review of FAA's organizational culture found that it had been an underlying cause of the agency's persistent acquisition problems, including substantial cost overruns, lengthy schedule delays, and shortfalls in the performance of its air traffic control modernization program. Furthermore, the lack of continuity in FAA's top management, including the Administrator and some senior executive positions, has fostered an organizational culture that has tended to avoid accountability, focus on the short term, and resist fundamental improvements in the acquisitions process.

Similarly, a 1996 report issued by the Aviation Foundation and the Institute of Public Policy stated that the recent actions taken to reorganize FAA have done nothing to change the long-term structural problems that plague the organization. The study concluded that FAA does not have the characteristics to learn and that its culture does not recognize or serve any client other than itself.

As FAA's own 1996 report entitled *Challenge 2000* points out, it will take several years to overcome the many cultural barriers at FAA, determine the skill mix of the workforce of the 21st century, and recruit the necessary talent in a resource-constrained environment. In the light of these studies' results, we would caution that the organizational and cultural changes envisioned by the Commission may require years of concerted effort by all parties concerned.

In connection with resource management, FAA's fiscal year 1998 budget request reveals some difficult choices that may have to be made among safety-related programs. For example, FAA proposes increasing its safety inspection workforce by 273 persons while decreasing some programs for airport surface safety, including a program designed to reduce runway incursions. The National Transportation Safety Board has repeatedly included runway incursions on its annual lists of its "most wanted" critical safety recommendations. FAA's budget request includes a reduction in the Runway Incursion program from $6 million in fiscal year 1997 to less than $3 million in fiscal year 1998. Although FAA set a goal in 1993 to improve surface safety by reducing runway incursions by 80 percent by the year 2000 from the 1990 high of 281, the results have been uneven; there were 186 runway incursions in 1993 and 246 in 1995. As was shown by the November 1994 runway collision in St. Louis, Missouri, between a commercial carrier and a private plane, such incidents can have fatal consequences—2 people lost their lives. It is unclear what progress will be made in this area, given the proposed budget cuts.

Similarly, we have reported since 1987 that the availability of complete, accurate, and reliable FAA data is critical to expanding the margin of safety. However, funding for FAA's National Aviation Safety Data Analysis Center, a facility designed to enhance aviation safety by the rigorous analysis of integrated data from many aviation-related databases, is slated to be reduced from $3.7 million in fiscal year 1997 to $2 million in fiscal year 1998.

The Commission's report stresses that safety improvements cannot depend solely on FAA's hands-on inspections but must also rely on partnerships with the aviation industry in such areas as self-monitoring and certification. Several programs for the airlines' self-disclosure of safety problems have already contributed to identifying and resolving some of these types of problems. For example, one airline's program for reporting pilot events or observations—a joint effort by the airline, the pilot union, and FAA—has identified safety-related problems, the vast majority of which would not have been detected by relying solely on FAA surveillance. The discovery of these problems has resulted in safety improvements to aircraft, to the procedures followed by flight crews, and to air traffic patterns. As the Commission has recognized, however, such information will not be provided if its disclosure threatens jobs or results in punitive actions. However, FAA's role in some broader partnerships with industry has also raised some questions. For example, FAA's cooperative process working with Boeing on the 777 aircraft helped enable the manufacturer to meet the planned certification date, but FAA was also criticized by some FAA engineers and inspectors for providing inadequate testing of the aircraft's design.

In the case of self-disclosure programs, decisions will have to be made on which aviation entities are best suited to such partnership programs, how to monitor these programs and make effective use of the data they offer, how to balance the pressure for public disclosure against the need to protect such information, and how to standardize and share such information across the aviation industry. With broader cooperation between FAA and the aviation industry, the Congress and FAA need to be on guard that the movement toward partnerships does not compromise the agency's principal role as the industry's regulator.

Finally, it is important to point out that the costs associated with achieving the accident reduction goal and who should pay for these costs have not yet been determined. In accordance with the Commission's call for more government-industry partnerships, government, the industry, and the traveling public would likely share in these costs. For example, FAA's partnership programs involve significant costs for both the agency and the industry. In the case of equipping the cargo holds of passenger aircraft with smoke detectors, the cost would fall initially on the industry, while the costs associated with the recommendation that children under the age of 2 be required to have their own seats on airplanes would fall more directly on the traveling public.

Regardless of who bears the cost of the proposed improvements, the Commission has correctly recognized that additional safety improvements may sometimes be difficult to justify under the benefit-cost criteria applied to regulatory activities. The Commission recommended that cost not always be the determining factor or basis for deciding whether to put new aviation safety and security rules into effect. Specifically, the Commission notes that the potential reduction in the fatal accident rate merits a careful weighing of the options for improving safety in terms of the benefits that go beyond those traditionally considered in benefit-cost analyses. However, we also believe that it is important to recognize that the recommendation (1) represents a significant departure from traditional processes, (2) could result in significant cost increases for relatively modest increases in the safety margin, and (3) could rest on a limited empirical justification. In effect, this recommendation may increase the number of instances in which the primary factor determining whether or not to go forward with a safety or security improvement is what might be referred to as a public policy imperative rather than the result of a benefit-cost analysis. One instance of such a decision is the Commission's recommendation to eliminate the exemption in the Federal Aviation Regulations that allows children under 2 to travel without the benefit of an FAA-approved restraint.

Air Traffic Control Modernization

The Commission also reviewed the modernization of the air traffic control (ATC) system. FAA is in the midst of a $34 billion dollar, mission-critical capital investment program to modernize aging ATC equipment. This program includes over 100 projects involving new radars, automated data processing, and navigation, surveillance, and communications equipment. We believe this modernization is also important for attaining the next level of safety by replacing aging equipment and providing controllers and pilots with enhanced communication and better information.

Recognizing that new technology, such as satellite-based navigation and new computers in ATC facilities and in aircraft cockpits, offers tremendous advances in safety, efficiency, and cost-effectiveness for users of the ATC system and for FAA, the Commission recommended accelerating the deployment of this new technology. According to FAA's current plan, many of these elements would not be in place until the year 2012 and beyond. However, the Commission has recommended that these technologies be in place and operational by the year 2005—7 years ahead of FAA's planned schedule. The Commission's goal is commendable, but given FAA's past problems in developing new ATC technology and the technical challenges that lie ahead, there is little evidence that this goal can be achieved.

We have chronicled FAA's efforts to modernize the air traffic control system for the past decade. Because of the modernization effort's size, complexity, cost, and past problems, we designated it as a high-risk information technology initiative in 1995 and again in 1997. Many of FAA's modernization projects have been plagued by cost-overruns, schedule delays, and shortfalls in performance that have delayed important safety and efficiency benefits. We reported last year that the agency's culture was an underlying cause of FAA's acquisition problems. FAA's acquisitions were impaired because employees acted in ways that did not reflect a strong commitment to, among other things, the focus on and the accountability to the modernization mission. More recently, we have identified other important factors that have contributed to FAA's difficulty in modernizing the ATC system. For example, FAA's lack of effective cost-estimating and -accounting practices forces it to make billion-dollar investment decisions without reliable information. Also, the absence of a complete systems architecture, or overall blueprint, to guide the development and evolution of the many interrelated ATC systems forces FAA to spend time and money to overcome system incompatibilities.

We agree with the Commission's recommendations to integrate the airports' capacity needs into the ATC modernization effort and to enhance the accuracy, availability, and reliability of the Global Positioning System. However, we have two concerns about accelerating the entire modernization effort that focus on the complexities of the technology and the integrity of FAA's acquisition process. First, the complexity of developing and acquiring new ATC technology—both hardware and software—must be recognized. The Commission contends that new ATC technology to meet FAA's requirements is available "off-the-shelf." However, FAA has found that significant additional development efforts have been needed to meet the agency's requirements for virtually all major acquisitions over the past decade. More recently, two new major contracts for systems—the Standard Terminal Automation Replacement System and the Wide Area Augmentation System— called for considerable development efforts.

Second, requiring FAA to spend at an accelerated rate could prove to be inconsistent with the principles of the agency's new Acquisition Management System, established on April 1, 1996, in response to the legislation freeing it from most federal procurement laws and regulations. FAA's acquisition management system calls for FAA to go through a disciplined process of (1) defining its mission needs, (2) analyzing alternative technological and operational approaches to meeting those needs, and (3) selecting only the most cost-effective solutions. Until FAA goes through this analytical and decision-making process, it is premature to predict what new technology FAA should acquire. For example, FAA itself points out that while satellite communications that link the communication and navigation functions offer tremendous potential benefits, the technology is not yet mature enough for civil aviation—significant development is needed to determine the requirements and operational concepts of the technology. In this particular case, accelerating the ATC modernization too much could increase the risk that FAA will make poor investment decisions. Overall, our message in this area is one of caution—accelerating the entire modernization effort will have to overcome a long history of problems that FAA's new acquisition management system was designed to address and a number of obstacles.

Aviation Security

Aviation security is another component of ensuring the safety of passengers. It rests on a careful mix of intelligence information, procedures, technology, and security personnel. The Commission strongly presented aviation security as a national security priority and recommended that the federal government commit greater resources to improving it. Many of the Commission's 31 recommendations on security are similar to those that we have made in previous reports. For example, the Commission urged FAA to deploy commercially available systems for detecting explosives in checked baggage at U.S. airports while also continuing to develop, evaluate, and certify such equipment. Similarly, the Commission echoed our recommendation that the government and the industry focus their safety and security research on the human factors associated with using new devices, especially on how operators will work with new technology. The Committee's recommendations address a number of long-standing vulnerabilities in the nation's air transportation system, such as (1) the screening of checked and carry-on baggage, mail, and cargo and (2) unauthorized individuals gaining access to an airport's critical areas. Many of the 20 initial security recommendations that the Commission made on September 9, 1996, are already being implemented by the airlines or by government agencies.

We found, however, that in the past FAA has had difficulty in meeting some of the time frames for implementing the safety improvements recommended by GAO and the Department of Transportation (DOT) Inspector General. Similarly, in the security area, FAA has also had problems meeting the implementation time frames. For example, FAA is just beginning to purchase explosives-detection systems to deploy at U.S. airports, although the Aviation Security Improvement Act of 1990 set an ambitious goal for FAA to have such equipment in place by November 1993. This delay was due primarily to the technical problems slowing the development and approval of the explosives-detection devices. But we also found that FAA did not develop an implementation strategy to set milestones and realistic expectations or to identify the resources to guide the implementation efforts. It is important that FAA sustain the momentum generated by the Commission's report and move forward systematically to implement its recommendations.

Finally, although the Commission concluded that many of its proposals will require additional funding, it did not specifically recommend funding levels for new security initiatives over the long term. Instead, the Commission recommended that the federal government devote at least $100 million annually to meet security capital requirements—leaving the decision on how to fund the remaining security costs to the National Civil Aviation Review Commission. The National Civil Aviation Review Commission is charged with looking at FAA funding issues, and we do not want to preempt its report and recommendations. But, for example, the $144.2 million appropriated by the Congress in 1997 for new security technology represents a fraction of the estimated billions of dollars required to enhance the security of air travel. To improve aviation security, the Congress, the administration, and the aviation industry need to agree on what to do and who will pay for it—and then to take action.

In closing, Mr. Chairman, we face a turning point. The public's concern about aviation safety and security has been heightened. The Congress and the administration have a renewed commitment to addressing this urgent national concern. The Commission's work is a good start toward an evolutionary process of reaching agreement on the goals and steps to improve aviation safety and security. To guide the implementation of the Commission's recommendations, DOT and FAA will need a comprehensive strategy that includes (1) clear goals and objectives, (2) measurable performance criteria to assess how the goals and objectives are being met, and (3) a monitoring, evaluation, and reporting system to periodically evaluate the implementation. This strategy could serve as a mechanism to track progress and establish the basis for determining funding trade-offs and priorities. In addition, successful implementation will require strong, stable leadership at DOT and at FAA. Although several complex questions remain unanswered, we hope that the Commission's work can serve as a catalyst for change and a strengthened commitment to resolving these challenges to improving safety.

CULT'S PRESS RELEASE
ON OWN MASS SUICIDE
March 22, 1997

"By the time you read this, we suspect that the human bodies we were wearing have been found and that a flurry of fragmented reports have begun to hit the wire services." So read the opening statement of a press release posted on the World Wide Web March 22 by a religious cult shortly before thirty-nine of its members committed mass suicide in a mansion in Rancho Santa Fe, California. According to Internet messages and videos left behind, the members of "Heaven's Gate" apparently believed they were not dying, but shedding their "human vehicles" or "containers" and that their souls would be retrieved by a UFO following in the wake of the comet Hale-Bopp and taken to their true home in the "Level Above Human."

The initial reports on the suicide were indeed fragmented. The bodies of the twenty-one women and eighteen men, between the ages of twenty-six and seventy-two, were discovered on March 26, all dressed identically in black shirts, pants, and Nike sneakers, all laid out neatly in various rooms of the mansion, suitcases neatly packed nearby. All but two were covered with purple squares of cloth. Medical examiners and police in San Diego county surmised that the deaths had occurred in waves, with about fifteen dying on March 23, another fifteen on March 24, and the remaining members on March 25. The cult members all ate pudding or applesauce laced with phenobarbital and drank vodka, apparently to relax themselves. But most died from suffocation; investigators found at least twenty plastic bags neatly folded in the trash, and the last two to die still had plastic bags over their heads when they were found.

Among the dead was the group's leader, Marshall Herff Applewhite, a sixty-five year old charismatic personality who had founded the cult in the early 1970s with Bonnie Lu Trousdale Nettles. They sometimes called themselves, "The Two." After Nettles' death in 1985, Applewhite mixed together what one report called "a concoction of New Age spirituality, distorted Christianity, Internet computer technology, and space-age science fiction." Applewhite promised his followers that they would be transported to salvation in the "Level Above Human," but first they had to forswear their fam-

ilies, give up all personal possessions, and abstain from sex, alcohol, and drugs. Autopsies showed that Applewhite and several of his male followers had been surgically castrated. The cultists were so androgynous in appearance that the dead were first reported to be all men.

The deaths at Rancho Santa Fe were the latest in a string of mass suicides involving American cults. In November 1978, 914 followers of the Reverend Jim Jones, most of them American, died in Jonestown, Guyana. Most of them died from drinking a cyanide-laced fruit drink, but several were shot to death when they refused the drink. More recently, 75 members of the Branch Davidian sect, including its leader, David Koresh, died on April 19, 1993, when fire swept their armed compound in Waco, Texas. The fire broke as FBI agents in armored combat vehicles crashed through the walls of the compound and pumped tear gas inside in an effort to end a fifty-one day standoff between the cultists and the FBI. Investigators later concluded that the Davidians had set the fires in what appeared to be a mass suicide pact; several of the cultists, including Koresh, also suffered unexplained gunshot wounds. (Waco confrontation, Davidians, Historic Documents of 1993, pp. 293–301 and 819–840)

Evolution of a Doomsday Cult

By all accounts, Applewhite was a troubled man. The son of a Presbyterian minister in Texas, Applewhite in the 1960s left a wife and two children, and a job as a college professor of music at the University of Alabama, amid rumors that he was engaged in a homosexual affair. He moved to Houston, where he found another teaching job and sang several roles in the Houston Grand Opera. According to some reports he also took drugs and his homosexuality apparently troubled him greatly. In the early 1970s he met Nettles, a nurse and astrologer, apparently during a stay in a hospital. He told a relative he was being treated for a heart condition, but others variously reported that he had overdosed on drugs or was seeking a "cure" for his homosexuality. He and Nettles soon became soul mates, and she left her husband and four children to travel with Applewhite.

The pair opened a short-lived book store in Houston, called the Christian Arts Center, where they sold books on astrology, metaphysics, and other New Age materials. When the store closed, they set up a spiritual retreat where they explored their beliefs that they were emissaries from space sent to Earth to share with others their vision of apocalypse and salvation by spacecraft. Calling themselves Bo and Peep, a reference to shepherds guiding their flock, the pair traveled throughout the West and Midwest and by the mid-1970s had attracted several dozen people to their cause. In 1975 they received a great deal of media attention when they predicted that they would be assassinated and then rise from the dead and take their followers away in a space ship. That attention turned to scorn and mockery when the space ship failed to arrive at the appointed time, and Bo and Peep took their movement underground to escape the notoriety and intensifying scrutiny by federal authorities and cult watchers.

Although out of the public view, Applewhite and Nettles, now calling themselves Do and Ti in reference to the first and last notes on the musical scale, continued their nomadic existence, usually accompanied by a handful of believers and seeking more converts. After Nettles died of cancer in 1985, Applewhite elevated her in his theology, calling her "my Father." In 1992 he decided it was time for the cult to reemerge, and he took out an ad in USA Today *announcing "UFO Cult Resurfaces with Final Offer." The cult began to use the Internet to recruit new members—Applewhite is said to have focused particularly on sites that focused on suicide, depression, and substance abuse—and the Internet also became the medium Heaven's Gate used to communicate its warnings about impending doom for the planet and salvation for those willing to forgo material goods and other human pleasures. In 1996, when the cult moved to the mansion in Rancho Santa Fe, the Internet also became a source of income as cult members started a business, called the Higher Source Contract Enterprises, to design websites.*

The cult's final months appeared to be spent preparing for their departure. In a video made in October 1996, a transcript of which was posted on the Heaven's Gate website, Applewhite predicted that the Earth was now so corrupt it was "about to be refurbished, spaded under" and would have "another chance to serve as a garden for a future human civilization." Insinuating that he was Jesus Christ come to Earth again, Applewhite said he would lead those who had "overcome human flesh—the genetic vibrations, the lust of the flesh, the desire to reproduce, the desire to cling to offspring, or spouse, or parents, or house, or money, or fame, or job" to the "Evolutionary Level Above Human," where their spirits would inhabit a kind of body that was not mammalian, did not reproduce, and was neither male nor female and where they would travel in spacecrafts to be "effective servants" in "my Father's Kingdom."

Making Sense of the Message

Despite its dependence on spacecraft and other aspects of science fiction, the message espoused by Heaven's Gate shared many similarities with other cults and religions throughout the ages. Robert Ellwood, a professor at the University of Southern California who specialized in new American religions, noted likenesses to the beliefs of the early Gnostics, a group of Christians in the first century who thought they were privy to information about God and the universe that was not available to the uninitiated and who saw a sharp division between body and soul. "These people come from a 90's kind of culture, with all its hardware and world views. But they have hewed to the traditional apocalyptic scenario: that radical changes are imminent and foretold by signs in the heavens," Ellwood said. Catherine Wessinger, an associate professor at Loyola University, agreed: "Space aliens, UFOs are playing the role that angels, God, Satan used to play. They are unseen, superhuman powers who can hurt us or help us."

The comet Hale-Bopp, the brightest comet to appear in northern skies since 1976, seemed a natural choice as a signal that the end was near.

Comets and other celestial events have been construed as signs from super-human or spiritual beings throughout history. "The Star of Bethlehem was probably a comet or supernova," James T. Richardson, a professor at the University of Nevada in Reno, told the New York Times. *"But people imbued it with great meaning, meaning that dominates all of Western culture today."*

> *Following is a press release, entitled "Heaven's Gate 'Away Team' Returns to Level Above Human in Distant Space," posted on the Heaven's Gate website on the Internet on March 22, 1997, one day before the beginning of a mass suicide by thirty-nine cult members:*

RANCHO SANTO FE, CA—By the time you receive this, we'll be gone—several dozen of us. We came from the Level Above Human in distant space and we have now exited the bodies that we were wearing for our earthly task, to return to the world from whence we came—task completed. The distant space we refer to is what your religious literature would call the Kingdom of Heaven or the Kingdom of God.

We came for the purpose of offering a doorway to the Kingdom of God at the end of this civilization, the end of this age, the end of this millennium. We came from that Level, that time, that space, and entered this one. And in so doing, we had to enter human bodies—which we did, for the most part, in the mid-seventies. Now it was time for us to leave those bodies (vehicles)—bodies that we borrowed for the time we were here (by previous arrangement) for this specific task. The task was not only to bring in information about that Evolutionary Kingdom Level Above Human, but to give us the experience of working against the forces of what the human evolutionary level, at this time, has become. And while it was a good learning experience for us, it also gave all who ever received knowledge from that Kingdom an opportunity to recognize us and this information, and to even move out of the human level and into the Next Level or the Next Evolutionary Level, the "Kingdom of Heaven," the Kingdom of God.

The Kingdom of God, the Level Above Human, is a physical world, where they inhabit physical bodies. However, those bodies are merely containers, suits of clothes—the true identity (of the individual) is the soul or mind/spirit residing in that "vehicle." The body is merely a tool for that individual's use—when it wears out, he is issued a new one.

No one can enter the Kingdom of Heaven by trying to live a good life in this world, and then, thinking that when this world's life takes your body, you get to "go to heaven." The only time that Next Kingdom can be entered is when there is a Member or Members of that Kingdom who have come into the human kingdom, incarnated as we have, offering clarification of that information. To get into a discarnate condition just by disconnecting from your body doesn't mean that you are going to go anywhere, whether that loss of body is "premature" or not. When we step out of our "vehicle," we have to know where and who our "tour guide" (our Shepherd) is—for what's next. We have to know we can connect with a Shepherd whom we trust, and that we have decided, "If that Shepherd will have me, I want to continue to be a sheep—and I will do everything I can to please that Shepherd."

Periodically, that Next Level sends in a Representative—a Shepherd—and offers a graduation class, offers life, out of this evolutionary level into that Next Evolutionary Level, and we are at the end of one of those times. TI and DO were the names used by the Representatives of that Next Level, the Kingdom of God, sent to the "surface" of this planet to serve as our Teachers/ "Midwives" at this time.

During a brief window of time, some may wish to follow us. If they do, it will not be easy. The requirement is to not only believe who the Representatives are, but, to do as they and we did. You must leave everything of your humanness behind. This includes the ultimate sacrifice and demonstration of faith—that is, the shedding of your human body. If you should choose to do this, logistically it is preferred that you make this exit somewhere in the area of the West or Southwest of the United States—but if this is not possible—it is not required. You must call on the name of TI and DO to assist you. In so doing, you will engage a communication of sorts, alerting a spacecraft to your location where you will be picked up after shedding your vehicle, and taken to another world—by members of the Kingdom of Heaven.

Only a Member of the Next Level can give you Life—can take you out of "Death"—but it requires that you disconnect, separate, from the last element holding you to the human kingdom.

We know what we're saying—we know it requires a "leap of faith." But it's deliberate—designed for those who would rather take that leap than stay in this world.

We suggest that anyone serious about considering this go into their most quiet place and ask, scream, with all of their being, directing their asking to the Highest Source they can imagine (beyond Earth's atmosphere), to give them guidance. Only those "chosen" by that Next Kingdom will know that this is right for them, and will be given the courage required to act.

Some Relevant Scriptures

- Therefore doth my Father love me, because I lay down my life, that I might take it again. No man taketh it from me, but I lay it down of myself. I have power to lay it down, and I have power to take it again. This commandment have I received of my Father. *John 10:15–18*
- He that believeth on me, the works that I do shall he do also. *John 14:12*
- And except that the Lord shorten those days, none shall be saved: but for the elect's sake, whom He has chosen, He hath shortened the days. *Mark 13:20*
- He who loves his life will lose it, and he who hates his life in this world will keep it for eternal life. *John 12:25*
- Blessed are the dead who die in the Lord. *Revelation 14:13*

EMPLOYER GUIDELINES ON MENTAL DISABILITIES
March 25, 1997

The federal government on March 25 issued the first extensive guidelines telling employers how to avoid discriminating against current or prospective workers with mental illnesses. The guidelines were issued by the Equal Employment Opportunity Commission (EEOC) under the provisions of the Americans with Disabilities Act of 1990. That act prohibited discrimination against individuals with physical or mental handicaps; its workplace provisions applied to businesses with fifteen or more employees.

In the first years after Congress passed the disabilities act, most public attention was focused on provisions relating to physical handicaps. Millions of employers and public accommodations, such as restaurants, hotels, and government offices, were required to install access ramps and special bathrooms for the physically handicapped. But the act also applied to those with psychiatric impairments, and the EEOC said that during the previous four years it had received more than nine thousand complaints of alleged discrimination against those with mental illnesses.

Until the commission issued its guidelines, employers had little concrete information about how the disabilities law applied to workers with psychiatric problems. The law itself offered minimal guidance on how employers or employees were to deal with specific situations, such as a worker's contention that his chronic failure to show up for work on time was caused by a mental disorder.

The commission said its guidelines applied to persons whose ability to perform "major life activities," such as thinking and working, was impaired by chronic disabilities, including major depression, personality disorders, schizophrenia, bipolar disorder (manic depression), and anxiety disorders such as obsessive-compulsive behavior. In general, the commission said short-term disorders such as temporary depression following the breakup of a romance or personality traits such as irritability and poor judgment were not covered by the provisions of the disabilities act.

The Guidelines

The commission's guidelines consisted of general statements about how employers can avoid discriminating against individuals with psychiatric disorders and what employers must do to accommodate those individuals. The commission provided numerous examples to illustrate its general guidelines and to distinguish between discriminatory and nondiscriminatory behavior. On several specific issues, the commission said employers would have to act on a case-by-case basis, but always within the framework of nondiscrimination against those with mental illnesses.

The most fundamental guideline was that employers may not discriminate against otherwise qualified workers who suffer from mental illnesses, either in hiring practices or in daily work situations. During a job interview, an employer may not ask an applicant if he has a mental illness, the commission said. If a psychiatric disability shows up during otherwise routine testing of a prospective worker, the employer may not refuse to hire him because of that disability.

Much of the commission's guidance centered around the requirement, under the disability act, that employers provide "reasonable accommodation" for an otherwise qualified worker with a psychiatric disability. An employer could avoid this requirement only by demonstrating that providing special accommodations for such a worker would pose an "undue hardship."

As an example, the commission cited the case of a worker who asks for time off because he is "depressed and stressed." Such a request is a notification to the employer that the worker needs a "reasonable accommodation." The employer can ask the worker for "reasonable documentation" to back up his claim, such as a note from a doctor indicating that the worker suffers from a psychiatric illness, but the employer cannot demand that the worker submit all his medical records.

In other cases, the commission said, employers may have to offer special working conditions for employees with mental disabilities. For example, the guidelines said an employer should consider adjusting the hours of a worker who has trouble showing up for work in the morning because he must take medicine that makes him groggy, or an employer might have to install special partitions for a worker whose mental illness makes him uncomfortable around his coworkers. In some cases, the commission said an employer might have to reassign a worker to a different position if his mental illness precluded him from doing certain tasks.

The commission said it recognized that special accommodations for such employees might raise questions from other workers. Even so, an employer may not disclose medical information about an employee to his colleagues. The commission suggested that an employer tell inquiring workers that it was acting for "legitimate business reasons" or "in compliance with federal law."

The commission said there were limits to how far an employer must go to accommodate workers with mental illnesses. For example, the commis-

sion said a business could take disciplinary action against a mentally ill employee who threatened bodily harm to his coworkers or supervisors— provided that the employer would impose the same discipline on a worker without such a disability.

Reaction

For the most part, reaction to the commission's guidelines fell along predictable lines. Advocates for the mentally ill praised the guidelines as reasonable and humane, while representatives of some business groups insisted the measures were extreme and would impose excessive hardships, especially on smaller employers.

Ronald S. Honberg, director of legal affairs for the National Alliance for the Mentally Ill, told the New York Times that the guidelines "will be extremely helpful to people with severe mental illness, employers, judges," and officials responsible for investigating discrimination complaints. Honberg said the guidelines were clear enough to be understood by most employers.

Susan R Meisinger, senior vice president of the Society for Human Resource Management, which represents corporate personnel directors, disputed Honberg's optimistic view, saying the commission document "creates confusion for employers, especially small employers who don't have any special expertise" in handling such cases. Other advocates for business groups noted, for example, that the guidelines offered no specific definition of what types of special accommodations would constitute an "undue hardship" for employers.

Similar arguments were reflected in some newspaper editorials. For example, the Florida Times Union, in Jacksonville, called the guidelines "ridiculous" and predicted they would hurt, rather than help, the mentally disabled. "That's because large companies with better salaries and benefits are likely to shelter themselves against problems (including potential lawsuits) and costs of accommodating mental disabilities by relying on fee-charging employment agencies to screen job applicants," the newspaper said. "Great reliance on temporary staffing also is likely, giving employers an easy out if a new worker exhibits any kind of behavioral problem."

Following are excerpts from the "Enforcement Guidance on the Americans with Disabilities Act and Psychiatric Disabilities," issued on March 25, 1997, by the federal Equal Employment Opportunity Commission:

Introduction

The workforce includes many individuals with psychiatric disabilities who face employment discrimination because their disabilities are stigmatized or misunderstood. Congress intended Title I of the Americans with Disabilities Act (ADA) to combat such employment discrimination as well as the myths, fears, and stereotypes upon which it is based.

The Equal Employment Opportunity Commission ("EEOC" or "Commission") receives a large number of charges under the ADA alleging employment discrimination based on psychiatric disability. These charges raise a wide array of legal issues including, for example, whether an individual has a psychiatric disability as defined by the ADA and whether an employer may ask about an individual's psychiatric disability. People with psychiatric disabilities and employers also have posed numerous questions to the EEOC about this topic.

This guidance is designed to:

- facilitate the full enforcement of the ADA with respect to individuals alleging employment discrimination based on psychiatric disability;
- respond to questions and concerns expressed by individuals with psychiatric disabilities regarding the ADA; and
- answer questions posed by employers about how principles of ADA analysis apply in the context of psychiatric disabilities.

What Is a Psychiatric Disability Under the ADA?

Under the ADA, the term "disability" means: "(a) A physical or mental impairment that substantially limits one or more of the major life activities of [an] individual; (b) a record of such an impairment; or (c) being regarded as having such an impairment."

This guidance focuses on the first prong of the ADA's definition of "disability" because of the great number of questions about how it is applied in the context of psychiatric conditions.

Impairment

1. What is a "mental impairment" under the ADA?

The ADA rule defines "mental impairment" to include "[a]ny mental or psychological disorder, such as ... emotional or mental illness." Examples of "emotional or mental illness[es]" include major depression, bipolar disorder, anxiety disorders (which include panic disorder, obsessive compulsive disorder, and post-traumatic stress disorder), schizophrenia, and personality disorders. The current edition of the American Psychiatric Association's *Diagnostic and Statistical Manual of Mental Disorders* (now the fourth edition, DSM-IV) is relevant for identifying these disorders. The DSM-IV has been recognized as an important reference by courts and is widely used by American mental health professionals for diagnostic and insurance reimbursement purposes.

Not all conditions listed in the DSM-IV, however, are disabilities, or even impairments, for purposes of the ADA. For example, the DSM-IV lists several conditions that Congress expressly excluded from the ADA's definition of "disability." While DSM-IV covers conditions involving drug abuse, the ADA provides that the term "individual with a disability" does not include an individual who is currently engaging in the illegal use of drugs, when the covered entity acts on the basis of that use. The DSM-IV also includes conditions that are not mental disorders but for which people may seek treatment (for example, problems with a spouse or child). Because these conditions are not disorders, they are not impairments under the ADA.

Even if a condition is an impairment, it is not automatically a "disability." To rise to the level of a "disability," an impairment must "substantially limit" one or more major life activities of the individual.

2. Are traits or behaviors in themselves mental impairments?

No. Traits or behaviors are not, in themselves, mental impairments. For example, **stress,** in itself, is not automatically a mental impairment. Stress, however, may be shown to be related to a mental or physical impairment. Similarly, traits like **irritability, chronic lateness, and poor judgment** are not, in themselves, mental impairments, although they may be linked to mental impairments.

Major Life Activities

An impairment must substantially limit one or more **major life activities** to rise to the level of a "disability" under the ADA.

3. What major life activities are limited by mental impairments?

The major life activities limited by mental impairments **differ from person to person.** There is no exhaustive list of major life activities. For some people, mental impairments restrict major life activities such as learning, thinking, concentrating, interacting with others, caring for oneself, speaking, performing manual tasks, or working. Sleeping is also a major life activity that may be limited by mental impairments.

4. To establish a psychiatric disability, must an individual always show that s/he is substantially limited in working?

No. The first question is whether an individual is substantially limited in a major life activity **other than working** (*e.g.*, sleeping, concentrating, caring for oneself). *Working* should be analyzed only if *no other major life activity* is substantially limited by an impairment.

Substantial Limitation

Under the ADA, an impairment rises to the level of a disability if it substantially limits a major life activity. "Substantial limitation" is evaluated in terms of the **severity** of the limitation and the **length of time** it restricts a major life activity.

The determination that a particular individual has a substantially limiting impairment should be based on information about how the impairment affects that individual and not on generalizations about the condition. Relevant evidence for EEOC investigators includes descriptions of an individual's typical level of functioning at home, at work, and in other settings, as well as evidence showing that the individual's functional limitations are linked to his/her impairment. Expert testimony about substantial limitation is not necessarily required. Credible testimony from the individual with a disability and his/her family members, friends, or coworkers may suffice.

5. When is an impairment sufficiently severe to substantially limit a major life activity?

An impairment is sufficiently severe to substantially limit a major life activity if it **prevents** an individual from performing a major life activity or **significantly restricts the condition, manner, or duration** under which an individual can perform a major life activity, as compared to **the average person in the general population.** An impairment **does not significantly restrict** major life activities if it results in only mild limitations.

6. Should the corrective effects of medications be considered when deciding if an impairment is so severe that it substantially limits a major life activity?

No. The ADA legislative history unequivocally states that the extent to which an impairment limits performance of a major life activity is assessed without regard to mitigating measures, including medications. Thus, an individual who is taking medication for a mental impairment has an ADA disability if there is evidence that the mental impairment, when left untreated, substantially limits a major life activity. Relevant evidence for EEOC investigators includes, for example, a description of how an individual's condition changed when s/he went off medication or needed to have dosages adjusted, or a description of his/her condition before starting medication.

7. How long does a mental impairment have to last to be substantially limiting?

An impairment is substantially limiting if it lasts for more than several months and significantly restricts the performance of one or more major life activities during that time. It is not substantially limiting if it lasts for only a brief time or does not significantly restrict an individual's ability to perform a major life activity. Whether the impairment is substantially limiting is assessed without regard to mitigating measures such as medication.

> *Example A:* An employee has had major depression for almost a year. He has been intensely sad and socially withdrawn (except for going to work), has developed serious insomnia, and has had severe problems concentrating. This employee has an impairment (major depression) that significantly restricts his ability to interact with others, sleep, and concentrate. The effects of this impairment are severe and have lasted long enough to be substantially limiting.

In addition, some conditions may be long-term, or potentially long-term, in that their duration is indefinite and unknowable or is expected to be at least several months. Such conditions, if severe, may constitute disabilities. . . .

However, conditions that are temporary and have no permanent or long-term effects on an individual's major life activities are not substantially limiting. . . .

8. Can chronic, episodic disorders be substantially limiting?

Yes. Chronic, episodic conditions may constitute substantially limiting impairments if they are substantially limiting when active or have a high likelihood of recurrence in substantially limiting forms. For some individuals, psychiatric impairments such as bipolar disorder, major depression, and schizophrenia may remit and intensify, sometimes repeatedly, over the course of several months or several years. . . .

Disclosure of Disability

Individuals with psychiatric disabilities may have questions about whether and when they must disclose their disability to their employer under the ADA. They may have concerns about the potential negative consequences of disclosing a psychiatric disability in the workplace, and about the confidentiality of information that they do disclose.

13. May an employer ask questions on a job application about history of treatment of mental illness, hospitalization, or the existence of mental or emotional illness or psychiatric disability?

No. An employer may not ask questions that are likely to elicit information about a disability before making an offer of employment. Questions on a job application about psychiatric disability or mental or emotional illness or about treatment are likely to elicit information about a psychiatric disability and therefore are prohibited before an offer of employment is made.

14. When may an employer lawfully ask an individual about a psychiatric disability under the ADA?

An employer may ask for disability-related information, including information about psychiatric disability, only in the following limited circumstances:

- **Application Stage.** Employers are prohibited from asking disability-related questions before making an offer of employment. An exception, however, is if an applicant asks for **reasonable accommodation for the hiring process.** If the need for this accommodation is not obvious, an employer may ask an applicant for **reasonable** documentation about his/her disability. The employer may require the applicant to provide documentation from an appropriate professional concerning his/her disability and functional limitations. A variety of health professionals may provide such documentation regarding psychiatric disabilities including primary health care professionals, psychiatrists, psychologists, psychiatric nurses, and licensed mental health professionals such as licensed clinical social workers and licensed professional counselors.

    An employer should make clear to the applicant why it is requesting such information, i.e., to verify the existence of a disability and the need for an accommodation. Furthermore, the employer may request only information necessary to accomplish these limited purposes.

> *Example A:* An applicant for a secretarial job asks to take a typing test in a quiet location rather than in a busy reception area "because of a medical condition." The employer may make disability-related inquiries at this point because the applicant's need for reasonable accommodation under the ADA is not obvious based on the statement that an accommodation is needed "because of a medical condition." Specifically, the employer may ask the applicant to provide documentation showing that she has an impairment that substantially limits a major life activity and that she needs to take the typing test in a quiet location because of disability-related functional limitations.

Although an employer may not ask an applicant if s/he will need reasonable accommodation **for the job,** there is an exception if the employer could **reasonably believe,** before making a job offer, that the applicant will need accommodation to perform the functions of the job. For an individual with a non-visible disability, this may occur if the individual voluntarily discloses his/her disability or if s/he voluntarily tells the employer that s/he needs reasonable accommodation to perform the job. The employer may then ask certain limited questions, specifically: whether the applicant needs reasonable accommodation; and what type of reasonable accommodation would be needed to perform the functions of the job.

• **After making an offer of employment, if the employer requires a post-offer, preemployment medical examination or inquiry.** After an employer extends an offer of employment, the employer may require a medical examination (including a psychiatric examination) or ask questions related to disability (including questions about psychiatric disability) if the employer subjects all entering employees in the same job category to the same inquiries or examinations regardless of disability. The inquiries and examinations do not need to be related to the job.

• **During employment, when a disability-related inquiry or medical examination of an employee is "job-related and consistent with business necessity."** This requirement may be met when an employer has a reasonable belief, based on objective evidence, that: (1) an employee's ability to perform essential job functions will be impaired by a medical condition; or (2) an employee will pose a direct threat due to a medical condition. Thus, for example, inquiries or medical examinations are permitted if they follow-up on a request for reasonable accommodation when the need for accommodation is not obvious, or if they address reasonable concerns about whether an individual is fit to perform essential functions of his/her position. In addition, inquiries or examinations are permitted if they are required by another Federal law or regulation. In these situations, the inquiries or examinations **must not exceed the scope of the specific medical condition and its effect on the employee's ability, with or without reasonable accommodation, to perform essential job functions or to work without posing a direct threat. . . .**

15. Do ADA confidentiality requirements apply to information about a psychiatric disability disclosed to an employer?

Yes. Employers must keep all information concerning the medical condition or history of its applicants or employees, including information about psychiatric disability, confidential under the ADA. This includes medical information that an individual voluntarily tells his/her employer. Employers must collect and maintain such information on separate forms and in separate medical files, apart from the usual personnel files. There are limited exceptions to the ADA confidentiality requirements:

- supervisors and managers may be told about necessary restrictions on the work or duties of the employee and about necessary accommodations;
- first aid and safety personnel may be told if the disability might require emergency treatment; and
- government officials investigating compliance with the ADA must be given relevant information on request.

16. How can an employer respond when employees ask questions about a coworker who has a disability?

If employees ask questions about a coworker who has a disability, the employer must not disclose any medical information in response. Apart from the limited exceptions listed in Question 15, the ADA confidentiality provisions prohibit such disclosure.

An employer also may not tell employees whether it is providing a reasonable accommodation for a particular individual. A statement that an individual receives a reasonable accommodation discloses that the individual probably has a disability because only individuals with disabilities are entitled to reasonable accommodation under the ADA. In response to coworker questions, however, the employer may explain that it is acting for legitimate business reasons or in compliance with federal law. As background information for all employees, an employer may find it helpful to explain the requirements of the ADA, including the obligation to provide reasonable accommodation, in its employee handbook or in its employee orientation or training.

Requesting Reasonable Accommodation

An employer must provide a reasonable accommodation to the known physical or mental limitations of a qualified individual with a disability unless it can show that the accommodation would impose an undue hardship. An employee's decision about requesting reasonable accommodation may be influenced by his/her concerns about the potential negative consequences of disclosing a psychiatric disability at work. Employees and employers alike have posed numerous questions about what constitutes a request for reasonable accommodation.

17. When an individual decides to request reasonable accommodation, what must s/he say to make the request and start the reasonable accommodation process?

When an individual decides to request accommodation, the individual or his/her representative must let the employer know that s/he needs an adjustment or change at work for a reason related to a medical condition. To request accommodation, an individual may use "plain English" and need not mention the ADA or use the phrase "reasonable accommodation."

> *Example A:* An employee asks for time off because he is "depressed and stressed." The employee has communicated a request for a change at work (time off) for a reason related to a medical condition (being "depressed and stressed" may be "plain English" for a medical condition). This statement is sufficient to put the employer on notice that the employee is requesting reasonable accommodation. However, if the employee's need for accommodation is not obvious, the employer may ask for **reasonable** documentation concerning the employee's disability and functional limitations. . . .

18. May someone other than the employee request a reasonable accommodation on behalf of an individual with a disability?

Yes, a family member, friend, health professional, or other representative may request a reasonable accommodation on behalf of an individual with a disability. Of course, an employee may refuse to accept an accommodation that is not needed.

19. Do requests for reasonable accommodation need to be in writing?

No. Requests for reasonable accommodation do not need to be in writing. Employees may request accommodations in conversation or may use any other mode of communication.

20. When should an individual with a disability request a reasonable accommodation to do the job?

An individual with a disability is not required to request a reasonable accommodation at the beginning of employment. S/he may request a reasonable accommodation at any time during employment.

21. May an employer ask an employee for documentation when the employee requests reasonable accommodation for the job?

Yes. When the **need for accommodation is not obvious,** an employer may ask an employee for **reasonable** documentation about his/her disability and functional limitations. The employer is entitled to know that the employee has a covered disability for which s/he needs a reasonable accommodation. A variety of health professionals may provide such documentation with regard to psychiatric disabilities.

> *Example A:* An employee asks for time off because he is "depressed and stressed." Although this statement is sufficient to put the employer on notice that he is requesting accommodation, the employee's need for accommodation is not obvious based on this statement alone. Accordingly, the employer may require reasonable documentation that the employee has a disability within the meaning of the ADA and, if he has such a disability, that the functional limitations of the disability necessitate time off. . . .

22. May an employer require an employee to go to a health care professional of the employer's (rather than the employee's) choice for purposes of documenting need for accommodation and disability?

The ADA does not prevent an employer from requiring an employee to go to an appropriate health professional of the employer's choice if the employee initially provides insufficient information to substantiate that s/he has an ADA disability and needs a reasonable accommodation. Of course, any examination must be job-related and consistent with business necessity. If an employer requires an employee to go to a health professional of the employer's choice, the employer must pay all costs associated with the visit(s).

Selected Types of Reasonable Accommodation

Reasonable accommodations for individuals with disabilities must be determined on a case-by-case basis because workplaces and jobs vary, as do people with disabilities. Accommodations for individuals with psychiatric disabilities may involve changes to workplace policies, procedures, or practices. Physical changes to the workplace or extra equipment also may be effective reasonable accommodations for some people.

In some instances, the precise nature of an effective accommodation for an individual may not be immediately apparent. Mental health professionals, including psychiatric rehabilitation counselors, may be able to make suggestions about particular accommodations and, of equal importance, help employers and employees communicate effectively about reasonable accommodation. The questions below discuss selected types of reasonable accommodation that may be effective for certain individuals with psychiatric disabilities.

23. Does reasonable accommodation include giving an individual with a disability time off from work or a modified work schedule?

Yes. Permitting the use of accrued paid leave or providing additional unpaid leave for treatment or recovery related to a disability is a reasonable accommodation, unless (or until) the employee's absence imposes an undue hardship on the operation of the employer's business. This includes leaves of absence, occasional leave (e.g., a few hours at a time), and part-time scheduling.

A related reasonable accommodation is to allow an individual with a disability to change his/her regularly scheduled working hours, for example, to work 10 AM to 6 PM rather than 9 AM to 5 PM, barring undue hardship. Some medications taken for psychiatric disabilities cause extreme grogginess and lack of concentration in the morning. Depending on the job, a later schedule can enable the employee to perform essential job functions.

24. What types of physical changes to the workplace or equipment can serve as accommodations for people with psychiatric disabilities?

Simple physical changes to the workplace may be effective accommodations for some individuals with psychiatric disabilities. For example, room dividers, partitions, or other soundproofing or visual barriers between workspaces may accommodate individuals who have disability-related limitations in concentration. Moving an individual away from noisy machinery or reducing other workplace noise that can be adjusted (e.g., lowering the volume or pitch of telephones) are similar reasonable accommodations. Permitting an individual to wear headphones to block out noisy distractions also may be effective.

Some individuals who have disability-related limitations in concentration may benefit from access to equipment like a tape recorder for reviewing events such as training sessions or meetings.

25. Is it a reasonable accommodation to modify a workplace policy?

Yes. It is a reasonable accommodation to modify a workplace policy when necessitated by an individual's disability-related limitations, barring undue hardship. For example, it would be a reasonable accommodation to allow an individual with a disability, who has difficulty concentrating due to the disability, to take detailed notes during client presentations even though company policy discourages employees from taking extensive notes during such sessions. . . .

26. Is adjusting supervisory methods a form of reasonable accommodation?

Yes. Supervisors play a central role in achieving effective reasonable accommodations for their employees. In some circumstances, supervisors may be able to adjust their methods as a reasonable accommodation by, for example, communicating assignments, instructions, or training by the medium that is most effective for a particular individual (e.g., in writing, in conversation, or by electronic mail). Supervisors also may provide or arrange additional training or modified training materials.

Adjusting the level of supervision or structure sometimes may enable an otherwise qualified individual with a disability to perform essential job functions. For example, an otherwise qualified individual with a disability who experiences limitations in concentration may request more detailed day-to-day guidance, feedback, or structure in order to perform his job. . . .

27. Is it a reasonable accommodation to provide a job coach?

Yes. An employer may be required to provide a temporary job coach to assist in the training of a qualified individual with a disability as a reasonable accommodation, barring undue hardship. An employer also may be required to allow a job coach paid by a public or private social service agency to accompany the employee at the job site as a reasonable accommodation.

28. Is it a reasonable accommodation to make sure that an individual takes medication as prescribed?

No. Medication monitoring is not a reasonable accommodation. Employers have no obligation to monitor medication because doing so does not remove a barrier that is unique to the workplace. When people do not take medication as prescribed, it affects them on and off the job.

29. When is reassignment to a different position required as a reasonable accommodation?

In general, reassignment **must** be considered as a reasonable accommodation when accommodation in the present job would cause undue hardship or would not be possible. Reassignment **may** be considered if there are circumstances under which **both** the employer and employee **voluntarily agree** that it is preferable to accommodation in the present position.

Reassignment should be made to an equivalent position that is vacant or will become vacant within a reasonable amount of time. If an equivalent position is not available, the employer must look for a vacant position at a lower level for which the employee is qualified. Reassignment is not required if a vacant position at a lower level is also unavailable.

Conduct

Maintaining satisfactory conduct and performance typically is not a problem for individuals with psychiatric disabilities. Nonetheless, circumstances arise when employers need to discipline individuals with such disabilities for misconduct.

30. May an employer discipline an individual with a disability for violating a workplace conduct standard if the misconduct resulted from a disability?

Yes, provided that the workplace conduct standard is job-related for the position in question and is consistent with business necessity. For example, nothing in the ADA prevents an employer from maintaining a workplace free of violence or threats of violence, or from disciplining an employee who steals or destroys property. Thus, an employer may discipline an employee with a disability for engaging in such misconduct if it would impose the same discipline on an employee without a disability. Other conduct standards, however, may not be job-related for the position in question and consistent with business necessity. If they are not, imposing discipline under them could violate the ADA.

> *Example A:* An employee steals money from his employer. Even if he asserts that his misconduct was caused by a disability, the employer may discipline him consistent with its uniform disciplinary policies because the individual violated a conduct standard—a prohibition against employee theft—that is job-related for the position in question and consistent with business necessity. . . .

31. Must an employer make reasonable accommodation for an individual with a disability who violated a conduct rule that is job-related for the position in question and consistent with business necessity?

An employer must make reasonable accommodation to enable **an other-wise qualified individual with a disability** to meet such a conduct standard **in the future,** barring undue hardship. Because reasonable accommodation is always prospective, however, an employer is not required to excuse past misconduct. . . .

32. How should an employer deal with an employee with a disability who is engaging in misconduct because s/he is not taking his/her medication?

The employer should focus on the employee's conduct and explain to the employee the consequences of continued misconduct in terms of uniform disciplinary procedures. It is the **employee's** responsibility to decide about medication and to consider the consequences of not taking medication.

Direct Threat

Under the ADA, an employer may lawfully exclude an individual from employment for safety reasons only if the employer can show that employment of the individual would pose a "direct threat." Employers must apply the "direct threat" standard uniformly and may not use safety concerns to justify exclusion of persons with disabilities when persons without disabilities would not be excluded in similar circumstances.

The EEOC's ADA regulations explain that "direct threat" means "a significant risk of substantial harm to the health or safety of the individual or others that cannot be eliminated or reduced by reasonable accommodation." A "significant" risk is a high, and not just a slightly increased, risk. The determination that an individual poses a "direct threat" must be based on an individualized assessment of the individual's present ability to safely perform the functions of the job, considering a reasonable medical judgment relying on the most current medical knowledge and/or the best available objective evidence. With respect to the employment of individuals with psychiatric disabilities, the employer must identify the specific behavior that would pose a direct threat. An individual does not pose a "direct threat" simply by virtue of having a history of psychiatric disability or being treated for a psychiatric disability.

33. Does an individual pose a direct threat in operating machinery solely because s/he takes medication that may as a side effect diminish concentration and/or coordination for some people?

No. An individual does not pose a direct threat solely because s/he takes a medication that may diminish coordination or concentration for some people as a side effect. Whether such an individual poses a direct threat must be determined on a case-by-case basis, based on a reasonable medical judgment relying on the most current medical knowledge and/or on the best available objective evidence. Therefore, an employer must determine the nature and severity of this individual's side effects, how those side effects influence his/her ability to safely operate the machinery, and whether s/he has had safety problems in the past when operating the same or similar machinery while taking the medication. If a significant risk of substantial harm exists, then an employer must determine if there is a reasonable accommodation that will reduce or eliminate the risk. . . .

34. When can an employer refuse to hire someone based on his/her history of violence or threats of violence?

An employer may refuse to hire someone based on his/her history of violence or threats of violence if it can show that the individual poses a direct threat. A determination of "direct threat" must be based on an individualized assessment of the individual's present ability to safely perform the functions of the job, considering the most current medical knowledge and/or the best available objective evidence. To find that an individual with a psychiatric disability poses a direct threat, the employer must identify the specific behavior on the part of the individual that would pose the direct threat. This includes an assessment of the likelihood and imminence of future violence. . . .

35. Does an individual who has attempted suicide pose a direct threat when s/he seeks to return to work?

No, in most circumstances. As with other questions of direct threat, an employer must base its determination on an individualized assessment of the person's ability to safely perform job functions when s/he returns to work. Attempting suicide does not mean that an individual poses an imminent risk of harm to him/herself when s/he returns to work. In analyzing direct threat (including the likelihood and imminence of any potential harm), the employer must seek reasonable medical judgments relying on the most current medical knowledge and/or the best available factual evidence concerning the employee. . . .

Professional Licensing

Individuals may have difficulty obtaining state-issued professional licenses if they have, or have a record of, a psychiatric disability. When a psychiatric disability results in denial or delay of a professional license, people may lose employment opportunities.

36. Would an individual have grounds for filing an ADA charge if an employer refused to hire him/her (or revoked a job offer) because s/he did not have a professional license due to a psychiatric disability?

If an individual filed a charge on these grounds, EEOC would investigate to determine whether the professional license was required by law for the position at issue, and whether the employer in fact did not hire the individual because s/he lacked the license. If the employer did not hire the individual because s/he lacked a legally-required professional license, and the individual claims that the licensing process discriminates against individuals with psychiatric disabilities, EEOC would coordinate with the Department of Justice, Civil Rights Division, Disability Rights Section, which enforces Title II of the ADA covering state licensing requirements.

REPORT ON MAMMOGRAMS
FOR WOMEN IN THEIR FORTIES
March 27, 1997

Accepting the advice of an advisory board, the National Cancer Institute (NCI) on March 27 announced that all women in their forties should routinely have a mammogram every one or two years to screen for breast cancer. The controversial recommendation reversed the institute's previous position and directly contradicted the advice of another panel of experts that the NCI had convened earlier in the year. President Bill Clinton hailed the new guidelines. "Now, women in their forties will have clear guidance based on the best science and action to match it," the president said, adding that he would urge insurance companies to pay for the screenings.

Breast cancer was the second leading cause of cancer deaths, after lung cancer, among women in the United States. During the 1990s an estimated 1.8 million women were expected to be diagnosed with the cancer and 500,000 were likely to die from it. The NCI estimated that one in eight women would develop breast cancer in her lifetime, with the risk increasing with age. Breast x-rays, known as mammograms, were the most effective available technique for finding cancer. They could detect tumors as small as an eighth of an inch in diameter, whereas regular self-examination could not find tumors much smaller than half an inch. The earlier a tumor was detected, the more likely that treatment could prevent its spread and thus save the woman's life.

The effectiveness of routine mammograms for women aged fifty—the average age for the onset of menopause—and older has been widely accepted for several years. Studies showed that routine screening could reduce breast cancer deaths in this age group by 30 percent. That was due both to the increased incidence of cancer among older women—about 80 percent of all breast cancers are found in women over fifty—and to changes in the breast tissue of older women that make small tumors easier to detect. The medical profession also agreed that regular mammograms for most women under forty are not advisable, in part because so few breast cancers develop in younger women and because tumors are harder to detect in younger women.

*But the evidence for routine mammogram screening of women in their for-
ties was not so clear-cut, and for years cancer specialists and others had
been trying to determine whether the number of lives saved by routine mammograms in this age-group outweighed the risks incurred.*

Consensus Development Panel Recommendations

*The controversy over the value of mammograms for women in their for-
ties had been building since 1977, when the NCI recommended mammograms for that age group only if their mothers or sisters had breast cancer.
Ten years later, the NCI adopted working guidelines recommending that
women in their forties get a mammogram every one or two years. In 1993
the institute reversed that advice, saying there was "insufficient evidence
to make an informed decision" about the value of mammography for
women in their forties. Some twenty private and nonprofit organizations,
including the American Cancer Society, disagreed and continued to recommend routine annual or biennial screening for these women.*

*Since 1993, however, seven large-scale, randomized trials had been con-
ducted. Although several of them showed no significantly statistical benefits to routine screening for women in their forties, an analysis of the combined results of the trials indicated that mammograms might reduce breast
cancer deaths in this age group by as much as 17 percent. Largely as a
result of the new evidence, the NCI decided to convene a consensus development panel, a devise used by the National Institutes of Health to develop a
consensus on appropriate medical practices. Recommendations by consensus panels are influential not only in helping to set a standard of care
within the medical community for a particular disease, but in persuading
insurance companies to cover the costs.*

*The mammogram panel—thirteen medical experts and consumer repre-
sentatives—reviewed all the available data and then listened to testimony
from expert witnesses during a three-day conference in January 1997. At
the conclusion of the conference on January 23, the panel said there was
still not enough evidence to recommend routine screening for all women in
their forties. "Each woman should decide for herself whether to undergo
mammography," the panel said.*

*At best, the panel said, mammograms might save the lives of 10 women
in their forties out of every 10,000 that had annual screenings. That potential benefit had to be weighed against several recognized downsides to
mammograms. Mammograms failed to detect about 25 percent of cancers
in women in their forties, compared with a 10 percent failure rate in older
women. As many as 10 percent of all mammograms show abnormalities
that turn out not to be cancerous upon further examination. An estimated
30 percent of the women in their forties who get an annual mammogram
have a chance of getting one of these "false positive" readings, which can
cause anxiety and additional expense. Even early detection of a cancerous
tumor might not be sufficient if the tumor has already spread into other
parts of the body.*

The widespread use of mammograms has also markedly increased detection of abnormalities known as ductal carcinomas in situ (DCIS). Although experts were divided on whether these abnormalities were life-threatening, most women opt to have them removed. In about 40 percent of these operations, the entire breast is removed. Finally, the panel said, about 3 of every 10,000 women who had annual mammograms might develop breast cancer from the x-rays themselves.

The consensus panel's recommendation drew fire from many of the conference participants. One said that he feared the recommendation was "tantamount to a death sentence for thousands of women," while another called the panel's report "fraudulent" and urged that it be corrected before it was released to the public. The American Cancer Society said it was "disappointed" in the recommendation. NCI director Richard Klausner, who had asked that the panel be convened in the first place, told the New York Times *that he was "shocked" at the outcome and would ask the institute's advisory board to review the consensus panel conclusions.*

Reversal by the National Cancer Advisory Board

On March 27 the National Cancer Advisory Board reversed the consensus panel and recommended that most women in their forties get a mammogram every one or two years. The board's findings were based on the same data used by the consensus panel.

At a news conference the advisory board's chairperson, Barbara Rimer, acknowledged that there was honest disagreement among medical experts about the value of mammograms for this age group. "The data are complex and the evidence is not transparent," she said. "Well-trained, well-intentioned scientists have come to different conclusions because they hold different standards of evidence." Rimer went on to say that although the board accepted evidence that mammograms reduce breast cancer deaths by about 17 percent in women in their forties, that reduction "is hard to detect" and has a "high level of uncertainty."

Critics of the NCI's new position, which included some women's advocacy groups, said that the NCI had caved into political pressure from some members of Congress, radiologists, and some women's advocacy groups. Klausner and Rimer both acknowledged that the institute had been under some pressure to reverse the consensus panel's recommendation, but they denied that the pressure had any effect on their decision.

In addition to recommending regular exams for women in their forties, the advisory board also urged women at a higher risk of breast cancer to consult with a doctor about how often to have mammograms. High risk was defined as having had a previous breast cancer or other type of breast disease; having been tested positive for a specific genetic change that increases susceptibility to breast cancer; having a mother, sister, or daughter with a history of breast cancer; having two or more other close relatives, such as cousins, with a history of breast cancer; having a first child after age 30;

and having had so much dense breast tissue that a previous mammography was difficult to read.

Despite the advisory board's reversal, the NCI recommendation was still out of sync with that of the American Cancer Society, which only days before had urged women in their forties to get annual mammograms. Some groups said the different sets of recommendations and the reversal of NCI's position would only serve to confuse women about what they should do.

> *Following are excerpts of a news conference March 27, 1997, in which Richard Klausner, director of the National Cancer Institute, and Barbara Rimer, chairperson of the National Cancer Advisory Board, announced the board's recommendations on mammography screening for women in their forties:*

KLAUSNER: This year, over 180,000 women will be newly diagnosed with breast cancer. And this year over 40,000 American women will die of this disease. Over the decade of the 1980s, the incidence of breast cancer rose overwhelmingly due to the diagnosis of early or localized disease, generally attributable to the increased use of screening mammography.

Since 1990, the age-adjusted mortality rates of breast cancer have begun to fall, and this drop is most striking in younger women. Women under 50 now comprise about 18 percent of the newly diagnosed cases of breast cancer. We believe that the recent decline in the mortality is the result of better and more effective therapy as well as earlier diagnosis and perhaps other factors. In truth, the relative contribution of all of these to the dropping mortality rates are not known.

There is, however, no doubt—and we've known for quite some time—that screening mammography is capable of saving lives, of reducing mortality from breast cancer. The question that has been difficult to resolve is when women should begin regular screening mammography. All of us look to clinical trials for answers to such questions—answers based upon evidence.

In 1993, the National Cancer Institute [NCI] dropped its previous recommendation that all women over 40 have regular mammography on the basis of concern that clinical studies available at the time did not satisfactorily support evidence of benefit for women in their forties. Since that time, more evidence from clinical trials has accrued, leading us at the NCI about a year ago to begin a process which we laid out at the time and have not varied from at all in that year to reevaluate our recommendations.

We decided at that time that the presidentially appointed National Cancer Advisory Board [NCAB] representing the wide constituency of the NCI and peopled by experts in a wide area of those constituencies—and as the only board constituted to provide advice to and oversight of the NCI—that that board would propose recommendations for the Institute on this important issue.

Part of the process that we set in motion a year ago was to stimulate the updating and public presentation of data on the benefits and the limitations of mammography in women under the age of 50. This was primarily through a internationally attended conference held here at NIH [National Institutes of Health] in January.

This conference was extremely helpful in providing open discussion and updated data on which the NCAB could deliberate as was laid out in our process a year ago. . . .

So let me now introduce Barbara Rimer, . . . who was chair of the NCAB, who will report to you on the conclusions and recommendations of the board.

Dr. Rimer is director of Cancer Prevention, Detection and Control Research at the Duke Comprehensive Cancer Center at Duke University. And there she is professor of community and family medicine.

Dr. Rimer is a recognized expert in her field of research which is focused on cancer prevention and early detection and decisionmaking for mammography. Dr. Rimer.

RIMER: Thank you and good morning. I'd like to begin by reading several sections of the recommendations so that you can hear them in the board's own words. And I'd like to begin with the introduction.

The risk of developing breast cancer is not the same for all women. Several expert groups and professional organizations have examined the available data on mammography in women aged 40 to 49 and have reached different conclusions. Current mammography recommendations for women 40 to 49 are of necessity interim and subject to change as new data continue to be collected.

This statement reflects the perspective of the National Cancer Advisory Board and our advice to the National Cancer Institute.

Recommendations—To assist women ages 40 to 49 who seek definitive advice on mammography, the NCI should recommend regular screening mammograms between ages 40 and 49 for women at average risk. For women 40 to 49 years of age, it is prudent to have mammograms every one to two years.

Some women are at higher risk than others. Women at higher risk should seek medical advice about beginning mammography before age 40 and to determine their schedule in the 40s.

Mammography for women at higher risk is described later in this document and I'll get to that.

All women who do not meet the criteria for higher risk are assumed to be at average risk.

The NCI should continue to recommend regular mammograms for women in their 50s as advised by all professional organizations.

Benefits—the benefit of mammography is detection of cancer early, when it is more easily treated with a better outcome. Regular screening mammography in average risk women ages 40 to 49 reduces deaths from breast cancer by about 17 percent. By early detection of breast cancer, treatment is not only more effective, but potentially less disfiguring and toxic.

Women whose breast cancers are found by mammography may also be able to have surgery that spares the breast or part of the breast.

Limitations of mammography—no medical test is always 100 percent accurate. And mammography is no exception. Research is underway to improve the technology which will lead to better accuracy in screening with mammography.

While women 40 to 49 and older may benefit from having regular mammograms, some cancers will be missed by this test—as many as 25 percent in women 40 to 49. That is why it is important that a clinical breast exam be part of regular routine care.

Distinguishing early cancers from suspicious but not cancerous breast abnormalities found on a mammogram is more difficult in younger women. These false positive mammograms require careful attention, including breast biopsies to assure a woman that she does not have breast cancer.

It is estimated that if a woman in her 40s got mammograms every year between 40 and 49, she'd have about a 30 percent chance of having a false positive mammogram research—excuse me, result.

Who pays for mammograms? For women within the age and risk groups recommended to have mammograms, all third party payers should pay for mammography.

Mammograms for women at higher risk of breast cancer—women who have a higher risk of breast cancer or who suspect they may be prone to breast cancer should seek good medical advice about when and how often to have mammograms and should also practice other approaches, including examinations by health professionals.

Elevated risk of breast cancer is associated with the following. Having had a previous breast cancer, laboratory evidence that a woman is carrying a specific mutation or genetic change that increases susceptibility to breast cancer, having a mother, sister or daughter with a history of breast cancer or two or more close relatives with a history of breast cancer, having had a diagnosis of other types of breast disease, and having had so much breast, dense breast tissue on a previous mammographic examination that a clear reading is difficult and having a first birth after age 30 or older.

Women will need to consult a health professional to determine if some of these conditions are present.

The controversy over mammography for women age 40 to 49 is not new. In 1993 the NCI made the difficult decision to withdraw its previous recommendation for routine screening for women in their 40s. Since then, studies have found additional scientific evidence of a reduction in breast cancer mortality from screening mammography. Currently available data are from seven randomized studies in which women were assigned to either routine mammography or usual care and thereafter followed for cancer occurrence and mortality.

By combining available data from the seven randomized studies around the world, about a 17 percent reduction in cancer mortality was found for those who were invited for screening. To many but not all experts this is statistically significant. This level of mortality reduction appears impressive but it's actually difficult to detect with a high level of certainty because the seven studies differ with regard to study design, implementation, age of the participants, screening interval and other factors.

The currently observed beneficial effect of mammography might increase, decrease or disappear over time. There may [be] unexpected late beneficial or harmful effects of screening.

To improve the quality, analysis, interpretation and dissemination of data from the seven randomized studies, the NCAB recommends that the following actions be undertaken as soon as possible. The NCI professional, voluntary and public interest organizations should develop innovative methods to educate women, physicians and other health professionals about the benefits of screening mammography and the state of knowledge regarding screening.

The NCI should make every effort to encourage and assist all investigators conducting randomized trials of mammography, to provide primary data for combined analyses. And third, the NCI should convene an independent mammography data monitoring board to prospectively define the analytic procedures and regularly review and report on the progress of mammography trials to NCAB and the public.

I hope you will pay close attention to the statement about uncertainly. The reason the mammography issue has been so difficult to resolve is because the data are complex and the evidence is not transparent. Well trained, well intentioned scientists have come to different conclusions because they hold different standards of evidence.

As the recommendations read, we caution that although we accept that there is about 17 percent reduction in mortality, that difference is hard to detect[,] with a high level of uncertainty. Like it or not, this uncertainty is a fact of life.

I'd like to thank the members of NCAB and especially the working group for their hard work and willingness to transcend individual positions and differences to develop an NCAB statement that we believe is scientifically defensible but also useful. These people have worked countless hours without compensation over the last month because of their commitment to the National Cancer Institute and the American public.

The recommendations that we have made are not brought forth as tablets etched in stone but as dynamic, living and evolving. As the science base grows and evolves, the National Cancer Institute will share new information and adjust the advice when appropriate. . . .

The NCI is committed to providing women the information they need to make informed decisions. Thank you.

KLAUSNER: Thank you Dr. Rimer. I want to thank you and I want to thank all of the members of the National Cancer Advisory Board for all of their work, for indeed, they worked very seriously and very hard in formulating clear and useful guidance, guidance based upon their scientific and professional view of the evidence concerning screening mammography.

The NCI will implement the recommendations of its advisory board effective immediately. As a result, the NCI will recommend that women in their 40s be screened every one to two years, with mammography, that women aged 50 and older continue to follow the recommendations to be screened every one to two years, that women who are . . . at higher than average risk of breast cancer should seek expert medical advice about whether they should begin screening before the age of 40 as well as the frequency of screening.

The board also stated that because of mammography's limitations, it is important that a clinical breast exam by a health care provider be included as part of regular, routine health care. And the NCI will include that in its statements and its recommendations.

As recommended the NCI has begun to develop new educational and information materials for women and physicians aimed at communicating and explaining these recommendations concerning information about the risks and the limitations of mammography and concerning the risks of developing breast cancer.

We will continue to provide updated information for women and physicians concerning treatment options for women diagnosed with breast cancer. Let me re-emphasize what Dr. Rimer said. All practice recommendations and guidances change over time.

They change as we learn more and develop new and effective and hopefully more effective approaches to diseases such as breast cancer. Such changes in recommendations reflect progress. And we look forward to new and improved approaches to the ability to detect and to diagnose breast cancer than in fact we have today.

We hope that these new recommendations will help to clarify what has been a confusing issue for women in their forties. It is important, however, to recognize and to emphasize that too many women over fifty do not receive regular mammograms where the demonstrated benefit of screening is clearly greater than that reported for women under fifty.

We currently estimate that over 35 percent of women over fifty have not had a mammogram in the past two years. And finally, despite the benefits of mammography, despite its role in our attempt to reduce the morbidity and mortality from breast cancer, mammography is not nor will ever be a substitute for the desperate need to discover effective preventions and real cures. It is these that are central tasks of our nation's research program in breast cancer. . . .

GAO REPORT ON UNITED NATIONS PEACEKEEPING OPERATIONS
March 27, 1997

United Nations peacekeeping operations—frequently the subject of partisan political squabbles in Washington—faced sharp questioning in 1997 from a nonpartisan source: the General Accounting Office (GAO). The GAO issued two reports in March and April questioning the United Nations' ability to lead peacekeeping operations in such trouble spots as the Balkans and the Middle East. One report, issued March 27, said institutional limitations made it debatable whether the United Nations was the appropriate agency to mount and lead large-scale peacekeeping operations that had to use armed force to carry out their assignments. A second report, issued April 9, examined eight long-running UN peacekeeping missions and found that most were not fulfilling their stated mandates.

One UN peacekeeping operation came to an end in 1997: a three-year mission that was intended to stabilize the island nation of Haiti. The mandate of that force ended November 30, leaving Haiti in only slightly better shape than when the mission started—as a deeply troubled nation beset by political intrigue, corruption, drug trafficking, and economic stagnation.

The reports by the GAO, the investigative arm of Congress, came as Congress and the Clinton administration were engaged in the annual debate about the value of all UN operations, including the peacekeeping missions. The administration pushed Congress to begin paying the United Nations approximately $1 billion that Washington owed from previous years, most of it to pay for peacekeeping projects. For much of the year it appeared the administration would have some success. But the issue became snarled in last-minute partisan maneuvering as Congress wound up its session in November, and the money for UN arrearages fell by the wayside.

Can the United Nations Lead?

The GAO report released on March 27 examined seven UN-led peacekeeping missions that had to use some measure of military force to accomplish their missions. The UN Security Council explicitly authorized three missions to use military force: those in Bosnia, eastern Croatia (one of the republics of the former Yugoslavia), and Somalia. In four other cases—the Congo, Haiti, Lebanon, and Rwanda—the council did not specifically authorize the use of force but did establish mission objectives that had the same effect.

Only two of those peacekeeping operations were able to use force successfully to carry out their missions, the GAO said: those in Haiti and Eastern Slavonia. The United States led the Haiti mission and provided an adequate command structure for the use of force when it was required. Similarly, the mission in Eastern Slavonia was under the command of a Belgian general who had his own headquarters staff and could rely on support from NATO military forces.

The five other missions examined by the GAO each suffered from one or more institutional limitations resulting from the nature of UN-led military operations. First, the GAO said, the United Nations cannot order member nations to supply troops, equipment, and other resources for peacekeeping operations. The Rwanda mission, for example, went for months during a critical period of 1994 without adequate reinforcements. As a result, the GAO said, that mission "was not able to respond to the slaughter of hundreds of thousands of civilians" during tribal conflict. The GAO also noted that troop strength for the Bosnia mission fell far below what the UN secretary general said was needed, with the result that the mission could not protect so-called safe havens such as Gorazde, Bihac, Srebrenica, and Zepa. Serbian forces captured the latter two cities in 1995, reportedly executing thousands of Bosnian civilians and soldiers.

Similarly, the GAO said, commanders of UN peacekeeping missions cannot be certain that their orders will be carried out. This is particularly true in dangerous situations, the report said, when commanders of national contingents may second-guess orders from UN headquarters. The GAO noted that most nations, including the United States, allow UN peacekeeping commanders only a limited degree of responsibility over the troops they provide. The GAO cited several cases in which commanders of contingents from individual nations refused to follow orders from overall UN commanders. In one incident in Bosnia, for example, one troop contingent refused an order to move to the city of Mostar, where the civilian population needed—and did not receive—protection against heavy fighting.

A third issue cited by the GAO was the UN's insistence on respecting national sovereignty, meaning that the United Nations generally will not undertake a peacekeeping mission unless it has consent from all the parties to the conflict. In several cases cited by the GAO, UN operations were hamstrung by requirements for commanders to obtain permission for their operations from warring local factions. In Bosnia, Serbian authorities openly defied the UN mission, and at one point hundreds of peacekeepers and other personnel were taken hostage while the United Nations was debating its course of action.

Because of these limitations, the GAO concluded that the United Nations "may not be an appropriate vehicle for heading missions where force is required to restore peace and order if vital U.S. national interests are at stake, unless a nation or coalition with sufficient military capability and commitment leads the operation." The United Nations can successfully play a role in peacekeeping missions, even when the use of force is required, the report said, for example by providing humanitarian relief.

In commenting on the report, the State Department and the Defense Department generally concurred with the GAO's conclusions. The Pentagon, however, noted that the United Nations and member nations had learned lessons from mistakes of the past and had developed a "more effective approach" to peacekeeping operations.

In a related report, issued on April 9, the GAO examined eight UN-led peacekeeping missions that had operated for many years and had become "costly and open-ended commitments." Two of these missions dated from the late 1940s: the UN Truce Supervisory Organization, which monitored the truce that ended the 1948 war between Israel and its Arab neighbors and continued to monitor truces from subsequent wars; and the UN Military Observer Group in India and Pakistan, which since 1949 had monitored a cease-fire between those two countries in their dispute over the state of Kashmir.

The GAO said most of the eight missions had failed to carry out the mandates set for them by the UN Security Council. Most of the missions were supposed to create stable and secure environments so diplomats could try to settle the underlying conflicts, but most of the diplomatic efforts had stalled or even failed. Despite the lack of progress in most of the cases, U.S. policymakers continued to support the long-term peacekeeping operations because "they help to stabilize conflicts that could threaten U.S. foreign policy objectives," the GAO said.

Washington's UN Dues

The Clinton administration had hoped 1997 would be the year for resolving one of the most intense diplomatic disputes in the world: the one between Washington and the United Nations. Congress for years had refused to appropriate all the money that presidents requested for various UN programs. By 1997 the backlog of U.S. payments was at least $580 million (according to the Republican chairman of the House Appropriations Committee) or as much as $1.3 billion (according to the United Nations). Congressional critics said the UN bureaucracy was bloated and that the United States was being asked to underwrite too high a share of the world body's budget.

In hopes of shoring up congressional support for the United Nations, the Clinton administration in 1996 forced from office Secretary General Boutros Boutros-Ghali, an Egyptian diplomat who was widely disliked in Congress. Boutros-Ghali's replacement was Kofi Annan, a U.S.-educated native of Ghana who had spent most of his career working in the UN sys-

tem. Annan quickly established better relations with Congress and on March 17 announced a series of organizational reforms to streamline the United Nations. (Boutros-Ghali resignation, Historic Documents of 1996, p. 824)

In June the Clinton administration struck a deal with key congressional leaders to pay the United Nations $819 million in delinquent dues over three years—so long as the UN reforms were on track. The key congressional figure on the issue was Sen. Jesse Helms, the North Carolina Republican who chaired the Foreign Relations Committee and had long been a harsh critic of the United Nations. Despite Helms's approval of the plan, an appropriation of the UN dues fell victim to last-minute politics as Congress finished its session in November. A White House spokesman criticized Congress for its "boneheaded decision" and said Clinton would try again to get the money in 1998.

Following are excerpts from the report, "Limitations in Leading Missions Requiring Force to Restore Peace," sent to Congress March 27, 1997, by the General Accounting Office:

Background

According to U.N. reports and Security Council statements, peacekeeping missions are operations in the field using military and/or civilian personnel to help maintain international peace and security, but where the use of force is not authorized except in self-defense. Such missions require voluntary troop contributions from member states, since the United Nations has no troops of its own, and are generally considered to be authorized under chapter VI of the U.N. charter, although Security Council resolutions mandating peacekeeping missions frequently omit specific charter citations. According to the U.N. Secretary General, and based on nearly 50 years of experience, three core principles guide peacekeeping missions led by the United Nations: (1) obtaining the consent of the warring parties to the peacekeeping mission, (2) ensuring the peacekeepers remain neutral and impartial in their actions and do not interfere in the nation's internal affairs, and (3) using force only in self-defense. Although peace operations have been increasingly used to help resolve internal conflicts, these principles still apply.

In addition to peacekeeping missions conducted with the consent of the parties involved in the conflict, the U.N. Security Council can also authorize enforcement actions, under chapter VII of the U.N. charter, that call for the use of force to maintain or restore peace. Such operations can be large scale military efforts that obtain international sanction from the United Nations but are led by individual nations or coalitions, such as the actions in Korea (1950–53) and Iraq (1990–91). Or they can be smaller operations led by the United Nations, such as in Somalia. These operations are defined by the U.S. Joint Doctrine for Military Operations Other Than War as the application of military force, or the threat of its use, normally pursuant to international authorization, to compel compliance with resolutions or sanctions designed to maintain or restore international peace and order. Consent by the warring parties is not required in these operations and neutrality may not be relevant. Security Council resolutions mandating such operations usually cite chapter VII of the U.N. charter as their authority.

Although the United Nations has considerable experience in leading peacekeeping missions and an overall approach to conducting them, it has not worked out accepted core principles and an overall approach to guide operations calling for the use of force.

For this report, we use the term peace operation to refer to the entire spectrum of U.N. activities aimed at maintaining or restoring peace and security, ranging from traditional peacekeeping missions to chapter VII peace enforcement to operations falling somewhere in between.

Results in Brief

The U.N. Security Council has three precedents for mandating the United Nations to lead peace operations where the use of force was authorized under chapter VII of the U.N. charter—the missions in Somalia, Bosnia, and Eastern Slavonia. In four other U.N.-led operations, the Security Council established mission objectives that required some measure of force to be achieved, but did not explicitly authorize its use under chapter VII. In these operations—the Congo, Rwanda, Lebanon, and Haiti—the Security Council authorized the United Nations to lead missions and, respectively, to use the means necessary to apprehend, detain, and deport foreign forces; establish secure humanitarian zones; take measures to assure the effective restoration of Lebanese sovereignty; and help ensure a secure environment.

Although the United Nations has improved its capability to support peace operations, our study indicates there are, nonetheless, organizational limits of the United Nations that increase the risk of U.N.-led operations calling for the use of force. These limitations have been overcome when a nation with sufficient military prestige, credibility, and the commitment of military forces necessary to conduct operations has taken the lead role in the U.N. operation. The limitations stem from the U.N.'s structure as an organization of individual sovereign states, which provides the world forum for international diplomacy. Because the United Nations is an international political body, and as such, does not have the attributes of sovereignty, it cannot conscript troops and arms from member states. Similarly, because member states cannot or will not relinquish command over their own troops, U.N. force commanders cannot always be sure their orders will be carried out. This places the following three limitations on operations calling for the use of force that are led by the United Nations.

• First, the United Nations cannot ensure that troops and resources will be provided to carry out and reinforce operations as necessary, especially since such operations are risky and nations volunteering troops and arms may not have a national interest in the operation.

• Second, the U.N. force commander cannot be assured his orders will be carried out, particularly in dangerous situations where his authority over national contingents may be questioned or second-guessed by national authorities who do not relinquish command of their troops to the United Nations.

• Third, because of the U.N.'s core principle of respecting national sovereignty, it generally seeks the consent of all parties to the conflict in conducting a peace operation and thus has not developed an overall approach to guide operations calling for the use of force.

These three factors have limited the operational effectiveness of U.N.-led peace operations calling for the use of force. For example, despite Security Council approval, the United Nations was not able to obtain adequate troops, equipment, and reinforcements to carry out the operations in Rwanda (1993–96), Bosnia (1992–95), and Somalia (1992–95). Nations were unwilling to provide the necessary troops, reinforcements, and resources when requested. Limits on U.N. command and control during actions in the Congo (1960–64), Somalia (1992–95), Bosnia (1992–95), and Lebanon (1978 and ongoing) hindered U.N. commanders from effectively deploying U.N. peacekeepers to mission-critical locations. And the U.N.'s use of force in Somalia, Bosnia, and the Congo was uncertain at key points and lacked credibility as the U.N. operations relied heavily on the consent of the warring parties to conduct operations.

In contrast, the second phase of the U.N. mission in Haiti (UNMIH)—(1995–96) has been operationally effective, as has been the operation in Eastern Slavonia to date (1996 and ongoing). For the second phase of UNMIH, a nation with credible and respected military authority provided leadership and command and control structures. The United States acted as the lead nation for the second phase of UNMIH and (1) ensured adequate resources were available for planning; (2) provided the necessary information, troops, armament, and political influence; and (3) used its command and control structure and its doctrine for operations other than war to help guide operations. Under the U.S. doctrine, the core principle of obtaining the consent of the parties was not the predominant principle. In Eastern Slavonia, the operation is conducted as a variant of the lead nation concept. The force commander is Belgian and his Belgian military staff provide headquarters command and control and are assured support by the NATO force in Bosnia. . . .

Limits on U.N.-Led Use of Force

As discussed, the United Nations had little experience leading operations calling for the use of force prior to the end of the Cold War. Since then it has undertaken several, most of which have been less than fully successful. The United Nations and member states have studied these operations and developed a series of lessons learned which they intend to implement for future operations. They have also undertaken a broad range of initiatives to improve the operational support for peacekeeping.

Nonetheless, there remain three limitations on the U.N. effectively leading peace operations that call for the use of force. These are (1) the U.N.'s inability to ensure that sufficient troops, armaments, and reinforcements will be available to effectively use force in operations; (2) the uncertainty that orders of the U.N. commander will be carried out by national contingents in the field; and (3) the U.N.'s lack of an approach to guide the use of force. However, these limits have been effectively dealt with when a nation with sufficient credibility, prestige, and commitment has taken the lead.

Limitations When Armed Forces Are Needed

According to U.S. military doctrine, it is critical for missions to have sufficient armed forces when needed, especially in situations where force may be necessary. This not only provides a credible deterrent to opposition, but also ensures adequate troops and armament to conduct operations. However, U.N. operations, particularly those in which combat may take place, do not have assurance of timely and adequate troops and reinforcement. The United Nations must negotiate voluntary help from member states. This process involves obtaining

- authorization from the Security Council,
- voluntary force contributions from member states, and
- approval by the General Assembly for the operation's budget that is usually paid for by member nations in addition to their regular U.N. assessments.

Although the United Nations has been working on standby force arrangements to ensure the right troops and forces are available for missions, nations could still refuse to provide these forces. Several examples help illustrate that (1) the United Nations, as an organization could not ensure troops, arms, and reinforcements would be available when needed, particularly, in U.N.-led operations that called for the use of force; whereas (2) lead nations have provided the resources, command, and direction to make the U.N. force credible in carrying out operations calling for the use of force. . . .

Conclusion

The United Nations has successfully led peacekeeping missions as part of its mandate under the U.N. charter. However, its record in effectively carrying out operations requiring the use of force has been less noteworthy. This is due, in part, to several limitations of the organization: the United Nations must rely on sovereign member states to volunteer the means for carrying out missions; U.N. force commanders cannot always be sure that orders will be carried out; and the U.N.'s core principles of neutrality, impartiality, and seeking consent of warring parties have limited effective action to restore peace. In Somalia, the former Yugoslavia, Rwanda, Lebanon, and the Congo, U.N. missions had operational problems because they lacked the necessary resources, did not have an effective command and control structure, and did not have an approach appropriate to conducting operations calling for the use of force. However, in the cases of Haiti and Eastern Slavonia, the limitations were overcome. In these situations, the prestige and credibility of the nations' leading the operations and the assurance of adequate forces made it possible to conduct effective operations, with all parties assured that force would be used if necessary.

Given its limitations in leading operations requiring the use of force, the United Nations may not be an appropriate vehicle for heading missions where force is required to restore peace and order if vital U.S. national interests are at stake, unless a nation or coalition with sufficient military capability and commitment leads the operation. In missions that do not involve vital national interests but call for the use of force, the United Nations will most likely still confront fundamental limitations as an effective lead organization. Nonetheless, U.N. missions may still be an appropriate vehicle in such situations. They can assist in the provision of humanitarian relief, signal the international community's concern, and demonstrate a willingness to provide some level of support. . . .

GUIDELINES ON BENEFITS OF SPORTS FOR GIRLS
March 28, 1997

Several federal reports and scientific studies were released in 1997 high-lighting the health benefits of regular exercise and healthy diets. Perhaps the most conclusive of these was a report by the President's Council on Physical Fitness and Sports outlining the social and mental as well as physical benefits of sports and physical activity for girls. Another federal report found that the number of overweight Americans was steadily increasing, largely as a result of overeating and physical inactivity. Other studies suggested that regular exercise could lower the incidence of breast cancer and that the risk of heart disease in women might be more affected by the kind of fat they eat rather than how much.

Girls and Physical Activity

The fitness council's report, the first federal report to look at the effect of physical activity on all aspects of young girls' lives, listed a host of benefits girls receive from physical activity and sports. Not only did regular phys-ical activity reduce chances of developing obesity, heart conditions, and osteoporosis later in life, but it helped to reduce stress and depression and improve self-confidence and academic achievement.

More girls than ever before were participating in sports programs. According to the report about 37 percent of all high school athletes were girls. In 1971, the year before passage of Title IX, the federal legislation that required schools to offer girls the same opportunities to play sports as they offered boys, one in twenty-seven girls participated in high school athletics; by 1994 the ratio was one in three.

Still, the report said, girls encountered many barriers to participation, including traditional stereotypes about femininity, continued domination of sports programs by men, and poverty. "There are still too many people who think getting fit isn't feminine and not enough opportunities for girls to participate at every level. Young girls are still twice as likely to be inac-tive as young boys. And girls living in poverty—especially girls of color—

still face even greater obstacles," Donna E. Shalala, secretary of health and human services, said at a news conference March 28 in Cincinnati, Ohio, where only hours later the National Collegiate Athletic Association's women's "final four" basketball championships would take place.

Shalala, who was accompanied by several of the basketball players and their coaches, used the release of the report to publicize the department's "Girl Power!" campaign, a national public education campaign begun in November 1996 to give girls aged nine to fourteen the self-confidence to take control of their own lives and avoid such dangers as smoking, drugs, and teenage pregnancy. "Our 'Girl Power' campaign is about helping young adolescent girls reach their full potential, and today's report makes an important contribution to that effort," Shalala said. "It shows that sports and physical activity can help a girl across the full spectrum of her life."

Obesity Tied to Overeating, Inactivity

Inactivity, along with overeating, were found to be the two main contributors to the growing weight problem in the United States, according to a report issued March 6 by the federal Centers for Disease Control and Prevention (CDC). The CDC found that 35 percent of American adults were seriously overweight in 1994, up from 25 percent in 1980. Fourteen percent of children aged six to eleven and 12 percent of adolescents aged twelve to seventeen were considered overweight, nearly double the percentage in 1980.

Obesity, considered to be the second most preventable cause of death next to smoking, contributed to an estimated 300,000 deaths a year. Being overweight increased the risk of heart disease, diabetes, high blood pressure, respiratory disorders, and some cancers. According to one estimate, obesity cost Americans $68 billion a year in excess medical expenses and loss of income. Americans spent another $30 billion annually on diet foods and other weight-reducing products and programs. These diet efforts were apparently to little avail: between 1980 and 1994 the daily average calorie intake increased for both men and women. Moreover, 59 percent of women and 49 percent of men engaged in little if any physical activity.

Experts stressed that the trend toward obesity could be reversed with only modest modifications in diet and physical activity. Only a year earlier, in July 1996, the surgeon general recommended that even half an hour of moderate activity, such as walking or gardening, every day had substantial health benefits. (Surgeon general's report, Historic Documents of 1996, p. 418)

In a related development, the Centers for Disease Control and Prevention released guidelines March 13 to help schools and communities promote physical activity among young people, boys, and girls. Such activity would promote not only lifelong health benefits, but also lifelong habits of physical activity. The guidelines said physical activity programs were likely to be most effective if they emphasized "enjoyable participation," offered a diverse range of competitive and noncompetitive activities, developed the skills and confidence children need to participate in physical activity, and made facilities available to children outside of school hours. The report also said that schools should require daily physical education for all students in all grades, reduce or eliminate exemptions granted for physical education classes, and increase the amount of time students are active in physical education classes.

Other Findings on Diet and Health

Several other reports and studies on health and dietary habits were issued in 1997. Among these were:

- *New guidelines from the National Academy of Sciences recommending roughly a 50 percent increase in calcium intake for young adolescents and older adults. Calcium is essential to promoting bone formation in children and to slowing bone loss in the aging, particularly women. The recommendation, issued August 13, was the first in a planned series of changes to update the government's nutritional guidelines known as "recommended dietary allowances," or RDAs, which had not been updated since 1989. RDAs were first issued in 1941 and were designed primarily to prevent illnesses caused by nutritional deficiencies, such as scurvy and rickets. Once common, such diseases were now seldom seen in the United States, and the focus of the new RDAs was on helping to prevent chronic diseases such as heart disease, osteoporosis, and obesity. The recommendations on calcium were among those for the five bone-building nutrients, which also include vitamin D, phosphorus, magnesium, and fluoride.*

- *Results from a study of more than 25,000 Norwegian women indicated that regular physical exercise reduced the risk of developing breast cancer, compared with women who were inactive. Women who exercised at least four hours a week cut their risk by more than a third, the study said, and women who exercised more reduced their risk even further. Although the study was not definitive it confirmed the findings of several smaller studies that all found similar beneficial effects from exercise. The Norwegian study was published May 1 in the* New England Journal of Medicine.

- *The results of a fourteen-year study of 80,000 nurses suggested that it was not the total level of fat consumed but rather the type that most influenced the risk of heart disease. The harmful fats were saturated fat, which is found in meat and dairy products, and trans fats, found in most margarines and solid cooking fats, such as vegetable shortening. According to the study, increases in consumption of trans fats could raise the risk of heart attack by 50 percent. Confirming earlier research, the study also found that mono- and poly-unsaturated fats lowered the risk of heart attack below normal levels.*

The study fueled a debate among experts about dietary strategies to protect against heart disease. Many said people should continue to focus on reducing their total fat intake. High-fat diets have been implicated in colon, rectum, and prostate cancers and have also been linked to breast cancer. High-fat diets also contribute to obesity.

Following are excerpts from the summary and overview of the report released March 28, 1997, entitled "Physical Activity & Sport in the Lives of Girls," prepared under the direction of the Center for Research on Girls and Women in Sport at the University of Minnesota for the President's Council on Physical Fitness and Sports:

Summary

The President's Council on Physical Fitness and Sports (PCPFS) serves as a catalyst to promote, encourage and motivate the development of physical activity, fitness and sport participation for all Americans. This report expresses the PCPFS's mission to inform the general public of the importance of developing and maintaining physical activity and fitness in our daily lives, and to heighten awareness of the links that exist between regular physical activity and good health. In the past, involvement in sport and physical activity has been primarily associated with males. Over the past two decades, however, girls' and women's involvement in such activity has increased dramatically. This is in large part due to the impact of Title IX, federal legislation passed in 1972 designed to prohibit sex discrimination in educational settings. For example, prior to Title IX, 300,000 young women participated in interscholastic athletics nationwide; today, that figure has leaped to approximately 2.25 million participants. In the wake of this participation explosion, scholars and educators have begun to explore its impact on girls and women.

Physical Activity and Sport in the Lives of Girls: Physical and Mental Health Dimensions from an Interdisciplinary Approach was created in order to highlight relevant research and draw on expert opinion regarding girls' involvement in physical activity and sport. This is the first report that brings together research findings—and practical suggestions for implementing these findings—from three interdisciplinary bodies of knowledge: physiological, psychological and sociological. An additional section explores the relationships among physical activity, sport and the mental health of girls. The primary goal was to identify and discuss the beneficial ways that physical activity and sport influence girls' physical health, psychological well-being and overall social and educational development. An additional goal was to identify the problematic aspects of girls' involvement. These include, but are not limited to, eating disorders, gender stereotyping and institutional barriers such as lack of opportunity and access to various resources. Although this report examines some of the most current and cutting-edge issues, because of space limitations, the authors do not claim to include all relevant research and concerns surrounding girls' involvement with sport and physical activity.

The report focuses on girls and not boys (other than for comparison where appropriate) for several reasons. First, with respect to sport and physical activity, girls have been neglected by researchers in the biomedical sciences, education, physical education and the social sciences. Second, though girls and boys share common experiences, girls also exhibit unique physiological, emotional and social outcomes that merit special investigation. Next, scholars need to keep pace with the aforementioned explosion and diversification of girls' involvement with sport and physical activity in the wake of Title IX. And finally, researchers increasingly recognize that the social world of physical activity and sport is not a one-dimensional universe, but a highly complex set of institutions populated by two genders with diverse racial and ethnic backgrounds, cultural values, physical abilities and sexual orientations.

Public apathy about physical education, and the glitzy distractions of commercialized sports in mass media, sometimes hide the basic fact that physical activity is a public health resource for millions of American girls as well as their families and communities. In order to advance knowledge regarding the real and potential contributions of physical activity and sport in the lives of millions of girls, several areas for future research are highlighted by the authors at the end of each section. Finally, a set of policy recommendations is also included in order to encourage responsible action on the part of parents, coaches, educators, sport leaders and elected officials. With such a "teamwork" approach, we can make a difference in the lives of girls.

Key Research Findings

Some of the most important research findings documented and highlighted in this report suggest that:

- More girls are participating in a wider array of physical activities and sports than ever before in American history. . . .
- Regular physical activity in adolescence can reduce girls' risk for obesity and hyperlipidemia (i.e., high levels of fat in the blood) which, in turn, have been known to be associated with lower adult onset of coronary heart disease and certain cancers. Regular physical activity can also help girls build greater peak bone mass, thereby reducing adult risk for osteoporosis. . . .
- Exercise and sport participation can be used as a therapeutic and preventative intervention for enhancing the physical and mental health of adolescent females. . . .
- Exercise and sport participation can enhance mental health by offering adolescent girls positive feelings about body image, improved self-esteem, tangible experiences of competency and success and increased self-confidence. . . .
- Research suggests that physical activity is an effective tool for reducing the symptoms of stress and depression among girls. . . .
- Sports are an educational asset in girls' lives. Research findings show that many high-school female athletes report higher grades and standardized test scores and lower dropout rates, and are more likely to go on to college than their nonathletic counterparts. . . .

- Recognition of physical activity and sport as an effective and money-saving public health asset is growing among researchers and policy makers. . . .
- Poverty substantially limits many girls' access to physical activity and sport, especially girls of color who are overrepresented in lower socio-economic groups. . . .
- Excessive exercise and certain forms of athletic participation have been found to be associated with a higher prevalence of eating disorders. . . .
- The potential for some girls to derive positive experiences from physical activity and sport is marred by lack of opportunity, gender stereotypes and homophobia. . . .

Conclusions and Recommendations

A summary of some of the most important conclusions and practical recommendations discussed in this report suggest that:

- Girls should be encouraged to get involved in sport and physical activity at an early age because such involvement reduces the likelihood of developing a number of deleterious health-related conditions. For example, active girls' high caloric expenditure decreases their risk of becoming obese. . . .
- Specific mechanisms which enhance girls' opportunities to be physically active must be developed and supported. Recreational, school-based physical education and sport programs are ideal ways to facilitate both health-related fitness and the acquisition of fundamental motor skills for a lifetime of activity. . . .
- Involvement in sport and physical activity has tremendous potential to enhance a girl's sense of competence and control. Therefore, leaders should incorporate cooperative as well as competitive opportunities to learn physical skills in a nonthreatening environment. . . .
- Parents, coaches and teachers must be aware of girls' motives for participating in sport and physical activity. Girls participate not only for competitive reasons, but to get in shape, socialize, improve skills and have fun. All motives, not just those related to highly competitive activity, must be respected and validated. . . .
- Physical educators, exercise leaders and coaches are in a primary position to recognize disordered eating patterns among girls. These individuals must be knowledgeable about the physical and psychological signs and be able to make referrals to specialists as necessary. . . .
- Girls and boys need to work and play together, starting from an early age. It is often easier for both sexes to play together and learn in small, relaxed groups where children know each other well and have the prerequisite skills. . . .
- Coaches and physical educators should give girls equal access and attention. Girls as well as boys should play the important and interesting positions in a game and receive feedback to help improve their physical skills. . . .

- Professionals must actively intervene in the face of discrimination. When adults observe inequities or gender stereotyping on the playing field or in the physical education classroom, it is often best to openly confront issues of prejudice such as sexism. . . .
- Involvement in physical activity, exercise and sport promotes psychological well-being; the therapeutic use of physical activity and exercise for improving the mental health of adolescent girls goes beyond traditional treatment and mental health programs. . . .
- Physical activity and exercise have been shown to be a mood enhancer and an anxiety reducer, thereby acting as a natural, cost-effective intervention for the mental health of adolescent girls. . . .

Overview of the Report

When the President's Council on Physical Fitness and Sports was established by Executive Order in 1956, few Americans could have imagined the surge of participation in physical activity and sport among girls and women over the last two decades. Millions of girls now participate in a rapidly expanding variety of physical activities, and female athletes perform feats that once were deemed physiologically impossible. Despite the startling speed of these recent changes, however, the explosion of women's participation and ability is more accurately viewed as an acceleration of a centuries-long march toward greater physical freedom and athletic excellence.

During the nineteenth century, health reformers and educators included "female gymnastics," walking, riding and dancing as key components of young women's education. . . . In the countryside and towns, archery, tennis, bicycling, ice boating, roller skating, croquet, golf and dance became popular among girls and women. A "new model of able-bodied womanhood" emerged, which challenged traditional notions about female frailty and ladylike behavior . . . . The integration of exercise and athletic activity into school curricula expanded during the twentieth century. Recreational athletics for girls became popular in the form of "play days" between 1920 and 1950 and competitive varsity sports such as basketball and track and field multiplied after World War II . . . . The passage of Title IX in 1972 ushered in an era of coed physical education and greater opportunities for girls to play high school and college sports. The fitness revolution also grabbed the attention and allegiance of millions of girls and women during the 1970s and 1980s.

Physical Activity and Sport in the Lives of Girls: Physical and Mental Health Dimensions from an Interdisciplinary Approach presents an interdisciplinary portrayal of the connections among the physical, psychological, social and cultural aspects of physical activity and sport in girls' lives. When viewed collectively, the research findings discussed here show how physical activity and sport impact the "complete girl": that is, the many interrelated aspects of a girl's life ranging from musculoskeletal and cardiovascular functioning, to psychological well-being, gender identity, relationships with friends and family and performance in school. Physical activity and sport offer girls more than gateways to fun, competition or an elevated heart rate. While the authors of this report are aware that girls' experiences vary a great deal, the vision of the complete girl fosters a comprehensive awareness that exercise and sport are not just about physical movement but personal development, identity and values as well.

Participation, Opportunity and Barriers

American girls now participate in a wider range of physical activities and sports, and at more levels of competition, than ever before in our history. While Oregon girls learn to square their shoulders to the volleyball net, a group of girls play "four squares" in rural New Hampshire, an Arkansas teenager teaches hopscotch to her little sister, and Native American teenagers meet for lacrosse practice. As girls bounce and chatter through double-dutch jump rope in Bedford-Stuyvesant, in-line skaters glide through a Houston suburb. As an Ohio high school basketball team runs through drills, friends from DeKalb, Illinois, meet for an aerobics class. And women give gutsy performances while winning gold medals at the 1996 Summer Olympic Games in sports ranging from softball, soccer and basketball to gymnastics, track and field and swimming.

Females have become prime movers in the fitness realm. A recent nationwide survey conducted by the National Sporting Goods Association indicated that more women (55.4 million) than men (43.4 million) participate in several leading fitness activities—aerobic exercising, bicycling, exercising with equipment, exercise walking, running and swimming. A more specific breakdown reveals that an estimated 18.3 million women do aerobics, 26.5 million bike for exercise or mountain bike, 23.8 million exercise with weights, 45.2 million walk, 8.65 million run or jog and 32.6 million swim. . . .

Girls' participation in school athletic programs and community-based programs is also mushrooming. Girls now comprise about 37 percent of all high-school athletes, representing an increase from one in 27 girls who participated in 1971 to one in three girls in 1994. The ratio for boys during this timeframe remained constant at one in two. In 1994–1995, 2,240,000 girls participated in high-school sports, compared to 3,554,429 boys, 37 percent and 63 percent respectively. . . . In terms of some specific sports, an estimated eight million girls under age 17 played basketball in 1994 (compared to 12.5 million boys) while 6.7 million girls played soccer. As more girls developed athletic interests and physical skills at the grassroots levels of competition during the 1970s and 1980s, participation in college and Olympic sports also exploded. Women now comprise 33 percent of all college athletes and approximately 39 percent of United States Olympic team members. Reciprocally, as more female role models become available for young girls to emulate, their interest and involvement in fitness and athletic activities will continue to grow.

Despite these gains, it is important to realize that women's historical trek toward greater physical and athletic opportunity has been filled with barriers. In the past, various individuals have condemned exercise and sport as unladylike and eminent physicians warned women against overstrain and sterility. One of the authors of this report, sport sociologist Margaret Carlisle Duncan, points out that stereotypes associated with traditional notions of femininity and masculinity exalted boys' strength and athletic feats while equating girls' athletic talents with "tomboyism." Parents, coaches and teachers often encouraged boys to test their physical and emotional limits while ignoring or coddling girls.

Today, girls' achievements in physical activity and sport remain overshadowed by the cultural prominence of men's sports. In school and community-based programs, boys still receive a disproportionate share of opportunities to participate in exercise and sport. Male-dominated sports organizations remain mired in policies and beliefs that shortchange girls and women, and parents or advocates of girls are forced to wage expensive legal battles in the pursuit of gender equity. Indeed, it is unlikely that the large increase in girls' athletic participation and growing cultural acceptance of physically active and athletic females would have occurred without the passage of Title IX. . . . Pressured by the perceived threat of lawsuits or payment of legal fees, and pulled by increasing demands for greater opportunity for girls, Parent Teacher Associations and school administrators began to rethink traditional clichés like "girls just aren't as physical as boys" or "sports are more important for boys than for girls."

And finally, harsh economic conditions, prejudice and institutional barriers have limited the participation of many poor girls, girls of color and girls with disabilities. Ironically, where the real and potential health outcomes of physical activity and sport are probably most needed, participation rates and access to resources are most lacking. As the authors of this report repeatedly document, girls' increasing participation and interest in physical activity and sport bode well for their health. Yet these positive national trends are being undermined by the growing numbers of adolescents who are becoming sedentary and obese, the substantial numbers of girls who are dropping out of sports, and the persistence of social and economic barriers that limit girls' opportunities to develop physically active lifestyles.

Understanding the Complete Girl

Physical activity and sport are not simply things young girls do in addition to the rest of their lives, but rather, they comprise an interdependent set of physiological, psychological and social processes that can influence, and, in varying degrees, sustain girls' growth and development. The interdisciplinary approach that underpins this report is designed to make more visible some of the connections among physical activity, sport and the rest of girls' lives. Some examples of the broader linkages that are examined in the body of this report are highlighted below.

Psychological Well-Being

Within the traditional framework of psychoanalytic theory, nonconformity to traditional gender expectations was considered pathological. Hence, women's interest and involvement in business, science, sport or other "masculine" activities were clinically suspect. In contrast, the review of psychological research presented in this report shows that physical activity and sport are apt to strengthen rather than worsen the psychological health of girls. The authors document a combination of psychosocial benefits such as self-confidence, self-esteem, higher energy levels and positive body image. It is important to note that these gains appear to be influenced by interactions with parents, who can either encourage or dampen a daughter's interest and involvement. So, too, do persistent and narrow cultural prescriptions for appropriately "feminine" behavior erode the potential of physical activity and sport to enhance girls' mental health. On the other end of the interdisciplinary spectrum, some of the biological and chemical processes associated with health and fitness concerns are also highlighted. And finally, two of the authors of this report ... discuss the growing recognition among mental health professionals that exercise and sport can be effective treatment interventions for the significant number of girls who suffer from depression or anxiety disorders.

Obesity

The Surgeon General's report on nutrition and health . . . identified obesity as a major public health problem in the United States; subsequently, the Surgeon General's report on physical activity and health . . . identified physical inactivity as a serious public health problem nationwide. Aware of this concern, the authors of this report discuss a variety of factors associated with the rising rate of obesity among American adolescents. Social factors include the influence of television, dwindling requirements for physical education in the schools, and the steep sport dropout rate among adolescents. Related to physical health concerns, this report explores the physiological and epidemiological aspects of obesity such as the links between the development of hyperlipidemia, hypercholesterolemia, hypertension and diabetes, which in turn elevate risk for coronary heart disease. Finally, in her section on the psychological dimensions of participation, psychology of sport scholar Diane Wiese-Bjornstal stresses the need to help overweight or obese girls overcome social pressures and personal misgivings about physical activity so that they can become less sedentary.

The Female Athlete Triad

Several authors discuss the complex combination of psychological and physiological processes that operate in relation to the female athlete triad. In Section I, exercise physiologist Patty Freedson and psychology of sport scholar Linda Bunker document many physiological benefits of exercise and sport participation for girls such as potential gains in strength and aerobic power. It also appears promising that girls' involvement in sport and exercise could effect increased immune functioning and the prevention of certain cancers in adult life. They also express their concerns about the "female athlete triad," which refers to three interrelated health problems that are prevalent among some types of female athletes and some girls who engage in excessive exercise: eating disorders, exercise-induced amenorrhea and bone loss. Several authors demonstrate how these syndromes have complex psychological, physiological and social origins and profiles. For example, girls' perceptions of their bodies are partly shaped by unrealistic media images that create false connections between a lean body type or "washboard abs" and subsequent success, sex appeal and self-mastery. The obsession with thinness can also be fed by a coach who demands weight loss from the athlete, or the desire to be attractive to boys and accepted by one's peers. Because we are in the early stages of investigating this syndrome, the data we have are very limited. Female athletes most at risk should certainly be aware of the dangers, but we should not assume that the triad is limited to an athletic population. . . .

Sport and Academic Achievement

It is said that "the fish are the last ones to discover the ocean." In Section III, Margaret Carlisle Duncan illustrates how several research findings debunk the "dumb jock" stereotype that high school athletes perform poorly in the classroom. School administrators are often unaware of the positive interplay between high-school athletics and academic achievement as measured by grade point average, standardized achievement test scores, lowered risk for dropout and greater likelihood to attend college. On average, female athletes fare better academically than female nonathletes, though Caucasian and Hispanic female athletes are more apt to derive some direct educational gains than are their African-American counterparts. . . . Good physical and mental health are also correlates of academic performance and social adjustment. Hence, from an interdisciplinary perspective, it is likely that athletic participation is part of a mutually reinforcing array of physical, psychological and social processes that enhance the overall educational experiences and commitments of many girls.

In summary, understanding the role of physical activity and sport in the life of the "complete girl" is a dauntingly complex agenda. The mosaic of interdisciplinary findings and interpretations assembled in this report will deepen both insight and resolve in this regard.

Poverty, Race and Physical Ability

Girls from economically disadvantaged backgrounds, girls of color and girls with disabilities can face unique obstacles in relation to physical activity and sport. Poor families cannot afford to invest in health club memberships, exercise machines and equipment for their daughters. Families of color, who are disproportionately poor, often cannot pay user fees or transportation costs to bring daughters back and forth between home and school. Fitness and sport are often seen as unattainable luxuries rather than potential resources. Dual-worker parents or single parents (most often mothers) sometimes depend on older daughters to cook or care for smaller children after school, thus curbing their involvement with extracurricular activities. Poor or working-class girls often work part-time jobs to help families make ends meet, thereby reducing the amount of time and energy available for exercise or sports. Parental perceptions of the benefits of exercise and athletic participation for daughters also vary by race and class. For example, one national survey found that Caucasian parents more often mentioned health-related benefits, character benefits and social factors than did African-American parents. . . .

Many of the problems girls of color experience in relation to physical activity and sport grow out of the same soil—poverty. Epidemiological research shows that exposure to violence, family fragmentation, substance abuse, sexually transmitted diseases and greater risk for unwanted sexual activity often share the common causality of poverty. Lack of physical activity and athletic opportunity can be added to this list. Economically disadvantaged girls of color are more likely to suffer from an unsafe and unhealthy environment. The simple act of walking or jogging may be problematic in neighborhoods where crime flourishes. Poor girls often do not have access to athletic resources, effective coaching and expert training. There is a lack of basic information about exercise, diet and sport. They are less apt to receive quality physical education and athletic training at earlier ages which, in turn, erodes the foundation for subsequent motor development. Because school and community athletic programs depend on tax dollars to thrive, capital flight from many urban areas is undermining the provision of adequate exercise and athletic opportunities for both minority girls and boys. The rising cost of liability insurance is also making it difficult for school districts, especially poorer ones, to provide quality athletic and intramural programs.

Little is known about the dreams, interests and physical activities of girls of color. Although women of color are often more visible in sport media, and in certain sports like basketball and track and field, they are underrepresented in sports such as swimming and tennis. . . . During the early 1980s, African-American and Hispanic adolescent females comprised about 4.4 percent and 3.2 percent of high school athletes respectively, compared to 29.1 percent of their Caucasian counterparts. . . . There is also indirect evidence that African-American and other ethnic minority females are less physically active than Caucasian females. . . .

And finally, despite the accomplishments of the Special Olympics and Paralympics, few opportunities exist for emotionally or physically challenged adolescents to engage in exercise and sport. Differently-abled children are three times more likely to be sedentary than their able-bodied peers and the physical activity levels of children with disabilities drop precipitously during adolescence. . . . It should be noted that the authors of this report make only periodic references to socioeconomic status, race, ethnicity and physical disability. This is due not so much to choice, however, as to the fact that so little research has focused on these groups of girls.

What Researchers Don't Know Can Hurt Girls

This report is the first to assemble the bulk of existing research on girls' involvement with physical activity and sport. However, because of the lack of available data and analysis, the authors of this report were unable to address in any depth some key aspects of girls' experiences with physical activity and sport. Three emerging research concerns are briefly discussed below.

Unwanted Sexual Behavior and Adolescent Pregnancy

Adolescent pregnancy is a major social problem in the United States. Though the belief that sports can help many young girls avoid unwanted sexual behavior and pregnancy is widespread among coaches and athletes, precious little research has been done in this area.... Two recent studies shed some initial empirical light on the hypothesized connections among exercise, athletics and adolescent girls' sexual behavior. First, Brown, Ellis, Guerrina, Paxton and Poleno (1996) analyzed female adolescents' responses to the United States Department of Health and Human Services, Public Health Service, Centers for Disease Control and Prevention (1995) survey, "Health Risk Behavior for the Nation's Youth." The researchers found that the more days adolescent females exercised per week, the more likely they were to postpone their first experience with sexual intercourse. Second, preliminary analysis from a study of adolescents from western New York (an area with one of the highest rates of adolescent pregnancy in the United States) indicated that higher rates of athletic participation among adolescent females were significantly associated with lower rates of both sexual activity and pregnancy....

Sexual Harassment

Sexual harassment is experienced by approximately 31 percent of female high school students.... Sport scholars have recently begun to study the prevalence and social-psychological dynamics of sexual harassment in athletic settings.... Many key questions need to be addressed. For example, how do female athletes perceive and react to sexual harassment from boys and adults? Do higher self-esteem and physical prowess fostered by sports help females to be more assertive with inappropriately invasive males than their non-athletic counterparts? Additional research needs to be done on the ways that athletic participation may empower girls to more effectively cope with sexually hostile situations.

Exercise and Sport as a Family Asset

Regretfully, little research has focused on the ways that exercise and sport promote interaction and insight between parents and children. As is the case with sexual harassment, many important questions in this area remain unanswered. Do parents look to sport to provide after-school activities that keep daughters physically active, socially engaged and off the streets? To what extent do physical activity and sport help parents nurture moral development and values in their children? In what ways can parents effectively encourage their daughters' involvement with physical activity and sport? Clearly, more investigation of the interdependencies among physical activity, sport, families and schools is needed.

Conclusion: Expanding the Resource

This report will fuel the growing awareness that physical activity and sport are enormously important in the lives of girls. Perhaps this message is being sent by girls themselves who are, as the saying goes, "voting with their feet," and entering the realms of fitness and sport in vastly increasing numbers. In contrast to the nineteenth century naysayers who decried strenuous exercise and athletic participation for women as dangerous and unladylike, today, educators and public health advocates recognize the overall benefits for girls' physical health and emotional well-being. As health care costs continue to escalate, and pressures on the American health care system to provide quality care intensify, the logic of preventive health strategies that involve physical activity and sport becomes economically salient.

The overall vision that emerges from this report frames physical activity as a developmental aid and public health asset for girls and, by inference, for boys as well. Physical activity can serve as a social and cultural intersection where adolescents, parents and caring adults can come together in mutually supportive ways. The aerobics class, fitness run or basketball court are safety zones where young girls can hang out together, test and challenge themselves, learn about competition, develop physical fitness components such as cardiovascular endurance, strength and flexibility, and have fun all at the same time.

The real and potential benefits that physical activity and sport have to offer girls, their families and communities, however, continue to be stymied by several factors. Economic and cultural barriers block wider participation, especially for poor girls and girls of color. Despite increasing interest and participation rates, physical activity and sport remain underutilized resources for the many girls who are mired by sedentary lifestyles or dissuaded from getting involved because of gender stereotypes, discriminatory practices and lack of opportunity. There are also appreciable numbers of girls for whom athletic participation is associated with illness, injury and addiction to exercise rather than with physical and mental well-being. And finally, there needs to be more systematic research on the numerous ways that physical activity and sport influence girls' lives. Simply put, too little research has been done in an area where girls have too much to gain. For this reason, each of the authors has listed priorities for future research at the end of their respective sections.

This report concludes with a list of policy recommendations. The information and analyses gathered here hold implications for parents, educators, coaches, athletic administrators, public health officials and lawmakers. There is more at stake in the struggle to expand girls' physical abilities and athletic opportunities than learning to do jumping jacks or winning and losing games. Future policy decisions need to be grounded in the broader understanding that girls' involvement with physical activity and sport is just as much about physical vitality, emotional well-being, community health and educational opportunity as it is about who runs the farthest or scores the most points.

April

CENSUS BUREAU REPORT
ON IMMIGRATION
April 8, 1997

Official reports and studies issued during 1997 suggested that recent immigration—whether legal or illegal—was less of an economic burden to the United States than was widely perceived. A report by the Census Bureau on April 8 showed that nearly one in ten people in the United States was foreign-born and disputed popular assumptions that most immigrants live in poverty and exist off government handouts.

Other studies estimated the total number of illegal immigrants in the United States at about 5 million, and that an average of about 100,000 Mexicans migrated illegally to the United States each year—far less than the millions of Mexican migrants that some politicians have claimed enter the United States annually.

Taken together, the various studies showed that immigration remained a major factor in U.S. population growth. At the approach of the twenty-first century, immigrants and children born to them accounted for nearly two-thirds of the annual increase in U.S. population.

A bipartisan study panel, the U.S. Commission on Immigration Reform, issued a report October 10 calling for a broader effort to "Americanize" immigrants by educating them in English and the "common civic culture" of the United States. Among the commission's more controversial recommendations was a call for abolition of the Immigration and Naturalization Service, with its functions turned over to the Labor, Justice, and State departments.

Census Bureau Estimates

In a report based on survey estimates made in 1996, the Census Bureau said that about 24.5 million people living in the United States were "foreign-born," that is, they were born outside the United States or its possessions to parents who were not U.S. citizens. That figure represented 9.3 percent of the total U.S. population in 1996, the highest proportion since the 1930s. The estimated foreign-born population reached a high of 14.7 percent in 1910, then declined steadily to a low of 4.8 percent in 1970, and has since been on the rise.

Nearly half of the foreign-born came from Latin America and the Caribbean, the Census Bureau said: 27.2 percent from Mexico, 10.5 percent from the Caribbean, 7 percent from the rest of Central America, and 4.9 percent from South America. Another 26.7 percent came from Asia and 16.9 percent from Europe. Just 32 percent of all foreign-born had become naturalized citizens.

As could be expected, recent immigrants—those who entered the United States during the 1990s—tended to be poorer than the general population and those who had immigrated earlier. One-third of recent immigrants were classified as living in poverty, according to the Census Bureau. That was nearly three times the poverty rate for native-born Americans and nearly twice the rate for the foreign-born who had entered the United States during the 1970s.

Contrary to widely held views revealed in public opinion surveys, the study showed that recent immigrants were only slightly more reliant on welfare than the general public. According to the Census Bureau report, 6.1 percent of recent immigrants received some form of means-tested cash benefits (such as Aid to Families with Dependent Children or Supplementary Security Income). That compared with 5.8 percent of all immigrants and 4.6 percent of the total American population.

The report showed a sharp disparity in education levels among foreign-born residents. More than one-third of all foreign-born people who entered the United States since 1970 lacked a high school diploma—more than twice the comparable percentage of native-born. Nearly one-fourth of all foreign-born residents held college degrees, however, closely paralleling the rate for native-born Americans. Surprisingly, the rate of advanced education was higher for recent immigrants than for any other segment of society: Nearly one in eight recent immigrants had a graduate or professional degree, compared with one in thirteen people in the general population.

In a related survey released February 7, the Immigration and Naturalization Service estimated the number of illegal aliens in the United States—formally called "undocumented" immigrants—at 5 million. The Immigration service said that figure had been growing at a rate of about 275,000 annually. Mexicans accounted for 2.7 million of the total.

Mexican Immigration

A joint U.S.-Mexican panel on September 4 released the most comprehensive report to date on Mexican immigration to the United States and the impact of that population shift on both countries. The Binational Study on Migration, sponsored by the two governments, suggested that illegal immigration of Mexicans into the United States was not as extensive as many American politicians and citizens seemed to believe. The study estimated that there had been a net increase of 630,000 Mexicans living illegally in the United States between 1990 and 1996—an average of about 105,000 per year. That annual figure was far below the estimates of some politicians and commentators that hundreds of thousands or even millions of Mexicans flee across the U.S. border every year. The study estimated that 2.3 million to 2.4 million Mexicans were living illegally in the United States; that figure was slightly below the estimate of 2.7 million made by the Immigration and Naturalization Service.

The joint study detailed the costs and benefits to both countries of Mexican migration. It noted, for example, that the United States benefits from economic growth generated by the employment of Mexicans, even though low-wage and unemployed Mexican immigrants often pose a net cost to state and local governments in terms of welfare benefits and education. The study also noted that Mexico suffers because of the migration to the United States of working age people, many of whom are well educated and highly motivated to work. Overall, the study predicted that Mexican migration had reached a peak, following the country's severe economic crisis in 1995, and likely would taper off in the future.

Adjustments to 1996 Immigration Provisions

A year after enacting legislation cracking down on immigrants, Congress at the close of 1997 reversed itself and enacted two provisions allowing more than 1 million illegal immigrants to remain in the United States, at least temporarily. Congress acted as a result of public pressure that built up following enactment of its controversial 1996 legislation denying many welfare benefits to immigrants, including those who were in the United States legally. Among those protesting the 1996 legislation were immigrant groups in key states, such as California and Florida, whose political support had been sought by Republican leaders in Congress. (Welfare restrictions, Historic Documents of 1996, p. 450)

In one provision enacted at the close of the 1997 session, Congress agreed to allow an estimated 1 million illegal immigrants to remain in the United States while they applied for a permanent visa, known as a "green card." The 1996 legislation would have forced those people to leave the United States even as they sought their green cards—but also would have barred them from reentering the country once they left.

In another reversal, Congress exempted more than 400,000 immigrants from imminent deportation proceedings. An estimated 150,000 Nicaraguans and 5,000 Cubans were granted amnesty, essentially granting them permanent residency status. Another 200,000 Salvadorans, 50,000 Guatemalans, and an unknown number of people from Eastern Europe and the former Soviet bloc were allowed to apply for green cards under provisions making it likely they would receive them.

People in these groups had been in various degrees of legal limbo since their entrance into the United States, but all faced deportation as a result of new restrictions imposed by Congress in 1996. Again as a result of political pressure from representatives of these groups and their supporters (including business lobbies), Congress relented in 1997 and authorized the immigrants to apply for green cards.

Congress also acquiesced on one of its 1996 provisions barring welfare payments to immigrants. Under a deal negotiated between the Clinton administration and Congress, legal immigrants already in the United

177

States could continue receiving Supplementary Security Income payments despite a cutoff provision of the 1996 welfare act. This exemption was expected to cost about $10 billion over five years.

Following is the text of the report, "The Foreign Born Population: 1996," issued April 8, 1997, by the U.S. Census Bureau:

Great interest and public debate has been generated by the increase in the number of foreign born persons in the United States in recent years. To allow for informed discussion based on fact rather than uninformed opinion and anecdotal evidence, the Census Bureau has begun more frequent collection of data about the foreign-born population. Questions on country of birth, citizenship, and year of entry were added to the Current Population Survey (CPS) beginning in 1994. This report, based on data collected in March 1996, is the second using the March CPS data to compare the characteristics of natives and the foreign-born.

The foreign-born population in the United States is not homogeneous. There are great differences in their demographic, social, and economic characteristics, not only based on country of origin but also related to how long they have lived here and whether or not they have become citizens. For instance, recent arrivals among the foreign-born are more likely to be in poverty, to have lower incomes, and to have higher unemployment rates than the native born. But foreign-born people who have been here more than six years seem to have recovered from their initial economic hardship. In fact, those who arrived during the 1970's are doing as well as natives in terms of income in 1995.

Number and Percent Foreign-Born

In March 1996, 9.3 percent (24.6 million) of the U.S. population were foreign-born. During this century, the percentage who were foreign-born declined from a high of 14.7 percent in 1910, to a low of 4.8 percent in 1970. Since then, that percentage has increased steadily.

Year of Entry and Citizenship

More than one-quarter of the foreign-born population of the United States has come into this country since 1990 and another 34.3 percent entered during the 1980's. The remaining 38.9 percent of the foreign-born have been here more than 15 years.

The 1996 CPS shows that 32.2 percent of the foreign-born population in the United States are naturalized citizens. It is not known what percent of the remainder are only temporary residents or what percent intend to become citizens.

In the past, the rate of naturalization has increased with the length of residence. While only 22.9 percent of those who entered during the 1980's are naturalized citizens, the rate increases to 46.3 percent for those who came during the 1970's and to 71.6 percent for those who entered before 1970.

The citizenship rate for the most recent arrivals (5.0 percent) is low for several reasons. Some of these people are temporary residents such as college students and persons on temporary business visas who will return to their home country. Others have not been residents long enough to be eligible for naturalization or may have no intention of becoming U.S. citizens.

Country of Origin

In 1996, over half of all foreign-born persons living here were born in the western hemisphere. More than one-quarter (6.7 million) of the total were born in Mexico, 10.5 percent were born on one of the Caribbean islands, 7.0 percent in Central America, 4.9 percent in South America, and 2.7 percent in Canada.

More than twenty-five percent of the foreign-born population claim Asia as their birthplace, and 16.9 percent are from Europe. Only about 2.6 percent came from either Africa, Australia, or one of the Pacific Islands. The remaining 1.6 percent could not be categorized by country or continent.

Following Mexico, the Philippines is the second largest country of origin, with 1.2 million persons born there. . . .

State of Residence

The foreign-born population is not distributed evenly throughout the country. California has the largest foreign-born population in terms of both numbers (8 million) and percentage (one quarter of the State's population).

New York has the second highest number (3.2 million) of foreign born. Other States with at least a million foreign-born residents include Florida, Texas, New Jersey, and Illinois. The other States with at least 10 percent foreign-born persons are New York, Hawaii, Florida, New Jersey, Nevada, Texas, Arizona, and Rhode Island.

Age

Foreign-born persons are older on average than natives, with a median age of 37.4 years, compared to 33.4 years for natives. When the foreign-born population is divided into those who are naturalized citizens and those who are not, however, a different picture appears. Naturalized citizens are older on average (48.0 years) than natives, whereas the median age of foreign-born persons who are not citizens is about the same as natives—33.1 years.

Current age and year of entry have obvious connections. Not surprisingly, the most recently arrived foreign-born are younger, on average, than those who came to this country in earlier decades, but they are also younger than natives. Those who entered the United States in the 1990–1996 period have a median age of only 26.5 years, compared with 60.1 years for those who arrived before 1970.

Race and Hispanic Origin

The foreign-born population includes larger proportions of minorities than the native population. While two-thirds of the foreign-born population are

White (67.7 percent), about one-quarter are Asian or Pacific Islander (23.8 percent) and 8.1 percent are Black. The remainder reported their race as "American Indian, Eskimo, or Aleut". Over 40 percent of all foreign-born persons are of Hispanic origin. In comparison, 84.2 percent of natives are White, 13.3 percent are Black, and 1.6 percent are Asian or Pacific Islander. Only 7.4 percent of natives are of Hispanic origin.

Foreign-born Asian and Pacific Islanders have higher rates of naturalization than foreign-born Hispanics. At least two-thirds of each group have lived in the United States long enough to qualify for naturalization (they arrived before 1990). While 38.4 percent of the foreign-born Asian and Pacific Islanders are naturalized citizens, only 18.3 of foreign-born Hispanics have been naturalized. This lower rate of naturalization among Hispanics may result from their relatively low educational attainment compared with many Asian and Pacific Islanders, larger numbers being undocumented and afraid to apply for citizenship, or a desire among many to return "home" eventually.

Educational Attainment

Educational attainment of the foreign-born population is correlated with citizenship. Foreign-born persons 25 years and over are just as likely as natives to have a college degree (23.5 percent compared with 23.6 percent). But naturalized citizens are more likely to have college degrees (30.8 percent) than either foreign-born persons who are not citizens (19.1 percent) or natives. At the same time, foreign born persons as a group are also less likely to have graduated from high school than natives. Only 16.0 percent of natives over the age of 25 do not have a high school degree, compared with 35.6 percent of the foreign-born.

When educational attainment of the foreign-born is disaggregated by year of entry, the most recent arrivals (those who came to this country during the 1990's) have the highest percentage of persons with college degrees—28.9 percent. Many of them (11.6 percent of the recent arrivals) have graduate or professional degrees.

Labor Force Status

The foreign-born population as a whole had a higher unemployment rate in March 1996 than natives (4.9 percent compared with 3.8 percent). However, the unemployment rate of naturalized citizens (2.7 percent) was lower than that of natives, while the rate for foreign-born persons who are not citizens was higher (6.0 percent).

Foreign-born people who arrived before 1970 have a lower unemployment rate (2.4 percent) than more recent arrivals, but that may be more a reflection of their older age structure than a direct result of the length of time they have been in the United States. In addition to having a much lower unemployment rate than either natives or later arrivals, those who entered before 1970 also have a much higher percentage of persons not in the labor force—52.1 percent compared with 33.4 percent for natives.

Income in 1995

Foreign-born persons as a group had a lower median income in 1995 than natives ($14,772 compared with $17,835). However, there is no significant difference between the median incomes of foreign-born persons who came during the 1970's and natives. Recent arrivals have the lowest median income ($10,875) of the foreign-born groups.

Because foreign-born people who came to the United States before 1970 are, on average, older than the more recent arrivals, the former group includes larger numbers of retirees. As a result, the median income for those entering before 1970 ($15,795) is smaller than those of either natives ($17,835) or the foreign born who arrived during the 1970's ($17,403).

Poverty Status

The foreign-born as a whole have a much higher poverty rate than natives (22.2 compared with 12.9 percent), while the most recent arrivals have the highest rate (33.3 percent). Only persons who arrived prior to 1970 are less likely than natives to be in poverty (9.9 percent).

Public Assistance Income

Participation in programs for those with low incomes is another measure of how well or poorly a person or group is doing economically. The CPS includes data on the three major sources of means-tested cash benefits—Aid to Families with Dependent Children (AFDC), Supplemental Security Income (SSI), and general welfare. The total receiving means-tested cash assistance includes persons 16 years and over who received income from one or more of these three sources.

Foreign-born persons were more likely to receive one or more of these types of cash public assistance than natives (5.8 percent compared with 4.5 percent). However, the rates decline as length of residence increases. While 6.3 percent of the foreign-born who entered the United States after 1979 received some form of cash public assistance in 1995, the rates for foreign-born persons who have been here more than 15 years are no different from those of natives.

Non-Cash Benefits

The most widely received means-tested non-cash benefit is food stamps. While there is a slight difference in the percentages of all natives and foreign-born persons who receive this benefit, elderly foreign-born persons are much more likely to depend on food stamps than elderly natives.

While foreign-born persons as a whole are no more likely to be enrolled in Medicaid than are natives, foreign-born people over the age of 65 are more likely to participate. A likely explanation is that more of the elderly foreign-born have not worked in the United States long enough to be eligible for Medicare, which covers 99 percent of elderly natives.

There are two ways that the poor get direct assistance with housing costs—some live in public housing projects and others receive rent subsidies.

The foreign-born are no more likely to receive housing assistance than natives, and only very small percentages of either group receive it.

Home Ownership

Over two-thirds of natives live in owner-occupied housing units, compared with less than half of the foreign-born. However, home ownership among the foreign-born increases with length of residence. Persons who arrived before 1970 have higher home ownership rates than natives, while only 22.1 percent of the most recent arrivals are living in their own homes.

Source of the Data

In 1994, the Bureau of the Census began collecting nativity data on the Current Population Survey (CPS). Beginning in January 1994, all persons in sample were asked their country of birth and their parents' countries of birth. Persons born outside the United States were also asked their citizenship status and year of entry into the United States. In subsequent months, the nativity questions were only asked for persons in new sample households and for persons without data from the previous month. . . .

FEDERAL APPEALS PANEL ON AFFIRMATIVE ACTION BAN
April 8, 1997

The momentum in the battle over affirmative action appeared to swing toward its opponents, who won two significant victories in 1997. In April a three-judge federal appeals court panel lifted a temporary injunction imposed on enforcement of California's Proposition 209, saying that there was "no doubt" that the voter-approved ban on racial preferences in public hiring, contracting, and education was constitutional. The California ban became effective when both the full appeals court for the Ninth Circuit and the U.S. Supreme Court declined to review the case.

In November a coalition of civil rights groups was instrumental in set-tling a case pending before the U.S. Supreme Court in which a white teacher was challenging the Piscataway, New Jersey, school board's deci-sion to lay her off instead of an equally qualified black teacher in the inter-ests of maintaining racial diversity in the school system. The settlement was a tactical move by supporters of affirmative action programs who feared the Supreme Court might use the case as a vehicle to limit the use of racial preferences in all hiring programs, public and private. Opponents of affirmative action viewed the settlement as a victory because it left in place an appeals court ruling holding the layoff to be a violation of federal civil rights law. Opponents also said the settlement showcased the weakness of the supporters' position.

Affirmative action ranges from outreach programs expanding the par-ticipation of women and minorities to programs reserving a specific num-ber or percentage of contracts or admissions to a university for women and minorities. Taken together these programs, both public and private, had ensured access to opportunities formerly foreclosed to women and racial minorities. But the programs had been controversial since they began to be adopted in the 1960s and were frequently challenged in federal court. The Supreme Court's rulings on the issue have never been definitive; although it has upheld the use of racial preferences under certain circumstances, in recent years, it has been narrowing those circumstances. (Court on affir-mative action, Historic Documents of 1995, p. 307)

Proposition 209 Upheld

The controversy over affirmative action had also reached the political arena, where sentiment against it was thought to have been a major contributor to the Republican takeover of Congress in 1994. Although affirmative action did not play a major role in the 1996 presidential election, it took center stage in California. In November 1996, 54 percent of the state's voters opted for a ballot initiative barring the state from discriminating against or giving preferential treatment in public employment, education, or contracting to anyone on the basis of race, gender, or ethnicity. It was the first ban of its kind enacted in the United States. A suit challenging the constitutionality of Proposition 209 was immediately filed in federal district court, where Judge Thelton Henderson issued first a temporary restraining order and then a preliminary injunction against enforcing the initiative. (Proposition 209, Historic Documents of 1996, p. 759)

In overturning that preliminary injunction, the federal appeals panel said April 8 that a "system which permits one judge to block with the stroke of a pen what 4,736,180 state residents voted to enact as law tests the integrity of court constitutional democracy." The panel then went beyond that narrow question of whether Henderson had acted properly to examine the constitutionality of Proposition 209. "As a matter of 'conventional' equal protection analysis, there is no doubt that Proposition 209 is constitutional," the panel concluded. "The ultimate goal of the equal protection clause [of the Fourteenth Amendment of the Constitution] is to do away with all governmentally imposed discrimination based on race and gender. . . . When the government prefers individuals on account of their race or gender, it correspondingly disadvantages individuals who . . . belong to another race or the other gender."

Although the three judges—Diarmuid F. O'Scannlain, Edward Leavy, and Andrew J. Kleinfield—were considered to be more conservative on the issue of affirmative action than other judges on the appeals court, the full appeals court on August 26 voted not to reconsider the panel's decision. The full court also refused to stay implementation of the law until it could be appealed to the Supreme Court, and Proposition 209 went into effect on August 28. On September 4 the Supreme Court rejected arguments that the law should be suspended immediately pending appeal, and on November 3 the Court refused, without comment, to hear the case, which left the law in place.

Proponents of Proposition 209 were jubilant with the Supreme Court's decision not to hear arguments. "Today's ruling sends a green light to citizens of other states who can now act to end racial preferences," said Tom Wood, a cosponsor of the ban. But opponents noted that the Supreme Court did not rule on the constitutionality of Proposition 209 and predicted that the battle was not over. Mark Rosenbaum, legal director of the American Civil Liberties Union of Southern California, noted the near-certainty that some woman or minority would file suit claiming actual harm under the ban. "The question of the constitutionality of Proposition 209 and copycat measures must await another day for a definitive ruling from our highest court," he said.

Layoff in Piscataway

The California ban was challenged under the equal protection clause of the Constitution. The case in Piscataway challenged affirmative action programs under Title VII of the 1964 Civil Rights Act, which prohibited discrimination in employment on the basis of race or gender. The case began in 1989 when the Piscataway Township school district was forced for budget reasons to lay off one teacher in the high school's business education department. It chose to lay off Sharon Taxman, a white, and retain Debra Williams, a black. Although both women had equal seniority (they had been hired on the same day) and were equally qualified, the board said it wanted to retain Williams to promote racial diversity in the school system. Taxman filed a complaint with the federal Equal Employment Opportunity Commission, which was charged with enforcing Title VII.

The Justice Department under President George Bush entered the case on Taxman's side, bringing suit in 1991 alleging that the school board had discriminated on the basis of race. In 1994 the Justice Department, now under President Bill Clinton, switched its position, arguing that racial diversity in the workplace was a legitimate goal of a voluntary affirmative action plan. The United States Court of Appeals for the Third District rejected that argument in 1996, ruling not only that Taxman's layoff, solely for reasons of race, was a violation of Title VII, but also that Title VII permitted the use of affirmative action only to remedy specific incidents of past discrimination.

That ruling was worrisome to supporters of affirmative action who feared that, on appeal, the Supreme Court might adopt similarly broad language. To avert that outcome, a coalition of the leaders from a dozen major civil rights organizations began to look for ways to negotiate a settlement. On November 21 it was announced that a settlement had been reached, in which the Piscataway school board would pay $433,500, including $186,000 in back pay and interest to Taxman and $247,500 in attorneys' fees. The civil rights coalition agreed to pay about 70 percent of the settlement. A substantial portion of the coalition money was said to have come from corporations that have embraced affirmative action as a positive way to achieve racial diversity in the workplace.

The settlement was greeted with relief by many proponents of affirmative action, including Walter Dellinger, the acting solicitor general, who told the New York Times *that the Supreme Court's "near-certain rejection of the school board's action might well have produced an opinion that swept away other, more defensible uses of affirmative action." Sen. Orrin G. Hatch, R-Utah, chairman of the Senate Judiciary Committee, reflected the sentiments of many opponents of affirmative action when he said that the "extraordinary lengths to which liberal civil rights organizations have gone to prevent the Supreme court from ruling on the Piscataway case*

*plainly serves as an acknowledgment that racial preferences are presump-
tively unconstitutional under current case law."*

Declines in Minority Enrollment

*How were racial minorities and women likely to fare in the absence of
affirmative action programs? Not very well, supporters said, pointing to
declines in minority enrollments at the two state university law schools
where bans on racial preferences had already taken effect. Applications,
admissions, and enrollments in the law schools at both the University of
California and the University of Texas were down significantly from the
previous year. The California law school at Berkeley announced in late
June that only one African American, out of seventeen admitted, had
enrolled for the class beginning in the fall of 1997. The law school had
accepted seventy-five blacks for admission in 1996. At the University of
Texas law school, only three black and twenty Hispanics were set to begin
fall classes in 1997, down from thirty-one blacks and forty-two Hispanics
the previous year.*

*These figures were seen by some as proof that the ban on affirmative
action will narrow educational diversity and opportunity. "It's so stunning
it's almost unbelievable," said Marjorie Schultz, a Berkeley law professor
and proponent of affirmative action. "What do we think? The leading public university in the most diverse state and the most diverse educational
system is going to just withdraw behind some siege wall and be a white
institution? It's preposterous."*

*Supporters of the ban saw the decline as proof that racial preferences had
created two sets of standards, one for whites and another, lower, one for
minorities. They also said the decline showed how much still needed to be
done to raise minority, especially black, achievement. Ward Connerly, the
prime proponent of Proposition 209, said the decline in the application and
enrollment figures was "a bucket of cold water in the face. I am obviously
concerned. I am petrified at the fact that we have as far to go as we do. You
cannot look at the situation and come away from it with anything other
than dismay."*

> *Following are excerpts from the opinion filed April 8, 1997, in
> San Francisco by a three-judge panel of the U.S. Court of Appeals
> for the Ninth Circuit vacating the preliminary injunction pre-
> venting implementation of Proposition 209, which banned pref-
> erential treatment in public hiring, contracting, and educa-
> tional programs in California:*

O'SCANNLAIN, Circuit Judge:

We must decide whether a provision of the California Constitution prohibiting public race and gender preferences violates the Equal Protection
Clause of the United States Constitution.

I

A

On November 5, 1996, the people of the State of California adopted the California Civil Rights Initiative as an amendment to their Constitution. The initiative, which appeared on the ballot as Proposition 209, provides in relevant part that

> [t]he state shall not discriminate against, or grant preferential treatment to, any individual or group on the basis of race, sex, color, ethnicity, or national origin in the operation of public employment, public education, or public contracting. . . .

The California Legislative Analyst's Office portrayed Proposition 209 to the voters as a measure that would eliminate public race-based and gender-based affirmative action programs. . . .

Proposition 209 passed by a margin of 54 to 46 percent; of nearly 9 million Californians casting ballots, 4,736,180 voted in favor of the initiative and 3,986,196 voted against it.

B

On the day after the election, November 6, 1996, several individuals and groups ("plaintiffs") claiming to represent the interests of racial minorities and women filed a complaint in the Northern District of California against several officials and political subdivisions of the State of California ("the State"). The complaint, brought under 42 U.S.C. S 1983, alleges that Proposition 209, first, denies racial minorities and women the equal protection of the laws guaranteed by the Fourteenth Amendment, and, second, is void under the Supremacy Clause because it conflicts with Titles VI and VII of the Civil Rights Act of 1964, and Title IX of the Educational Amendments of 1972. As relief, plaintiffs seek a declaration that Proposition 209 is unconstitutional and a permanent injunction enjoining the State from implementing and enforcing it.

With their complaint, plaintiffs filed an application for a temporary restraining order ("TRO") and a preliminary injunction. The district court entered a TRO on November 27, 1996, and granted a preliminary injunction on December 23, 1996. The preliminary injunction enjoins the State, pending trial or final judgment, "from implementing or enforcing Proposition 209 insofar as said amendment to the Constitution of the State of California purports to prohibit or affect affirmative action programs in public employment, public education or public contracting." *Coalition for Econ. Equity v. Wilson*, (N.D. Cal. 1996).

The district court provided extensive findings of fact and conclusions of law in support of the injunction. This lawsuit, the court explained, challenges Proposition 209's prohibition against race and gender preferences, not its prohibition against discrimination. Plaintiffs' constitutional challenge is "only to that slice of the initiative that now prohibits governmental entities at every level from taking voluntary action to remediate past and present discrimination through the use of constitutionally permissible race- and gender-conscious affirmative action programs."

The elimination of such programs, the district court found, would reduce opportunities in public contracting and employment for women and minorities. It further would cause enrollment of African-American, Latino, and American Indian students in public colleges to fall, though enrollment of Asian-American students would increase. Finally, the court found that minorities and women, to reinstate race-based or gender-based preferential treatment, would have to re-amend the California Constitution by initiative.

From these findings of fact the district court concluded, first, that plaintiffs have demonstrated a likelihood of success on their equal protection claim. Proposition 209, the court reasoned, has a racial and gender focus which imposes a substantial political burden on the interests of women and minorities. The court held that *Hunter v. Erickson* (1969), and *Washington v. Seattle School District No. 1* (1982), prohibit such treatment of racial and gender issues in the political process.

The district court concluded, second, that plaintiffs have also demonstrated a likelihood of success on their pre-emption claims. Title VII, the court reasoned, preserves the discretion of public employers voluntarily to use race and gender preferences. To the extent that Proposition 209 bans such preferences statewide, the court held that Title VII pre-empts it under the Supremacy Clause.

The district court next explained that plaintiffs would suffer irreparable harm if Proposition 209 takes effect. If not enjoined, Proposition 209 immediately would ban existing preference programs in violation of plaintiffs' constitutional rights. The State, in contrast, the court concluded, would suffer little hardship from a preliminary injunction, which merely would suspend implementation of Proposition 209 pending trial.

Finally, the district court believed that a preliminary injunction would serve the public interest. Preserving the pre-election status quo would "harmonize" the public need for "clear guidance with respect to Proposition 209" with "the compelling interest in remedying discrimination that underlies existing constitutionally-permissible state-sponsored affirmative action programs threatened by Proposition 209." . . .

II

Before reaching the merits of the preliminary injunction, we pause to consider whether this case even belongs in federal court. No California state court has yet construed the meaning or effect of Proposition 209. Rather, plaintiffs ask a federal tribunal to enjoin flat-out this state constitutional amendment passed by a majority of the voters. The district court remarked that the issue in this case is not "whether one judge can thwart the will of the people; rather, the issue is whether the challenged enactment complies with our Constitution and Bill of Rights."

No doubt the district court is correct, at least in theory. Judges apply the law; they do not *sua sponte* thwart wills. If Proposition 209 affronts the federal Constitution—the Constitution which the people of the United States themselves ordained and established—the district judge merely reminds the people that they must govern themselves in accordance with principles of their own choosing. If, however, the district judge relies on an erroneous legal premise, the decision operates to thwart the will of the people in the most literal sense: What the people of California willed to do is frustrated on the basis of principles that the people of the United States neither ordained nor established. A system which permits one judge to block with the stroke of a pen what 4,736,180 state residents voted to enact as law tests the integrity of our constitutional democracy.

The Supreme Court recently reminded federal judges that we should not even undertake to review the constitutionality of a state law without first asking: "Is this conflict really necessary?" *Arizonans for Official English v. Arizona* (U.S. Mar. 3, 1997). As a general rule, federal courts "ought not to consider the Constitutionality of a state statute in the absence of a controlling interpretation of its meaning and effect by the state courts." Id. (quoting *Poe v. Ullman* [1961], Harlan, J., dissenting). Justice Ginsburg emphasized for a unanimous court that "[w]hen anticipatory relief is sought in federal court against a state statute, respect for the place of the States in our federal system calls for close consideration of that core question." "Warnings against premature adjudication of constitutional questions bear heightened attention when a federal court is asked to invalidate a State's law, for the federal tribunal risks friction-generating error when it endeavors to construe a novel state Act not yet reviewed by the State's highest court."

The ink on Proposition 209 was barely dry when plaintiffs filed this lawsuit. For this federal tribunal to tell the people of California that their one-day-old, never-applied-law violates the Constitution, we must have more than a vague inkling of what the law actually does. Plaintiffs challenge Proposition 209 to the extent that it eliminates "affirmative action." A California court that considered Proposition 209's pre-enactment ballot title and ballot label remarked that the term "affirmative action" is an "amorphous, value-laden term," "rarely defined so as to form a common base for intelligent discourse." *Lundgren v. Superior Court* (Ct. App. 1996) (internal ellipses and citation omitted). "Most definitions of the term would include not only the conduct which Proposition 209 would ban, i.e., discrimination and preferential treatment, but also other efforts such as outreach programs."

The district court properly limited its use of the term "affirmative action" to state programs that use race or gender classifications. It enjoined Proposition 209 only to the extent that it eliminates programs that grant preferential treatment to individuals on the basis of their race or gender. The court cited as examples programs that would prefer contractors of a certain race or gender in the evaluation of bids for public contracts, programs that would prefer prospective employees of a certain race or gender for public employment, and programs that would prefer prospective students of a certain race or gender for public education or financial aid. Unlike in *Arizonans*, the State does not dispute that Proposition 209 operates to eliminate such programs. Quite the contrary, the district court found that Defendant/Appellant Pete Wilson, Governor of California, issued an Executive Order on November 6, 1996, implementing Proposition 209 to do just that.

Without this factual basis, we would not hesitate to remand to the district court for reconsideration of the State's abstention motion in light of *Arizonans*. From the district court's findings, however, we are satisfied, to answer the Supreme Court's question, that "yes—this conflict really is necessary." We may now address the merits.

III

A preliminary injunction may issue "if the movant has shown either a likelihood of success on the merits and the possibility of irreparable injury, or that serious questions are raised and the balance of hardships tips sharply in the movant's favor." . . .

In granting the preliminary injunction, the district court first concluded that plaintiffs have demonstrated a likelihood of success on their claim that Proposition 209 violates the Equal Protection Clause of the Fourteenth Amendment. We must examine whether the district court's conclusion is based on an erroneous legal premise as a matter of "conventional" equal protection analysis, which looks to the substance of the law at issue, or as a matter of "political structure" equal protection analysis, which looks to the level of government at which the law was enacted. We shall apply each mode of analysis to Proposition 209 in turn.

IV

As a matter of "conventional" equal protection analysis, there is simply no doubt that Proposition 209 is constitutional. The Equal Protection Clause provides that "[n]o State shall . . . deny to any person within its jurisdiction the equal protection of the laws." U.S. Const. amend. XIV, S 1. The central purpose of the Equal Protection Clause "is the prevention of official conduct discriminating on the basis of race." *Washington v. Davis* (1976). The Fourteenth Amendment forbids such conduct on the principle that "[d]istinctions between citizens solely because of their ancestry are by their very nature odious to a free people whose institutions are founded upon the doctrine of equality." *Hirabayashi v. United States* (1943). Racial distinctions "threaten to stigmatize individuals by reason of their membership in a racial group and to incite racial hostility." *Shaw v. Reno* (1993) (citations omitted).

The ultimate goal of the Equal Protection Clause is "to do away with all governmentally imposed discrimination based on race." *Palmore v. Sidoti* (1984) (citation and footnote omitted). Therefore, "whenever the government treats any person unequally because of his or her race, that person has suffered an injury that falls squarely within the language and spirit of the Constitution's guarantee of equal protection." *Adarand Constructors v. Pena* (1995). The Equal Protection Clause also protects against classifications based on gender. . . .

The standard of review under the Equal Protection Clause does not depend on the race or gender of those burdened or benefited by a particular classification. *Richmond v. J. A. Croson Co.* (1989) (plurality opinion). When the government prefers individuals on account of their race or gender, it correspondingly disadvantages individuals who fortuitously belong to another race or to the other gender . . . Proposition 209 amends the California Constitution simply to prohibit state discrimination against or preferential treatment to any person on account of race or gender. Plaintiffs charge that this ban on unequal treatment denies members of certain races and one gender equal protection of the laws. If merely stating this alleged equal protection violation does not suffice to refute it, the central tenet of the Equal Protection Clause teeters on the brink of incoherence.

The Equal Protection Clause guarantees that the government will not classify individuals on the basis of impermissible criteria. Most laws, of course—perhaps all—classify individuals one way or another. Individuals receive, or correspondingly are denied, governmental benefits on the basis of income, disability, veteran status, age, occupation and countless other grounds. Legislative classifications as a general rule are presumptively valid under the Equal Protection Clause. *City of Cleburne v. Cleburne Living Ctr.* (1985). A legislative classification will deny equal protection only if it is not "rationally related to a legitimate state interest." Id. (citations omitted).

The general rule does not apply, however, when a law classifies individuals by race or gender. Any governmental action that classifies persons by race is presumptively unconstitutional and subject to the most exacting judicial scrutiny. *Adarand.* To be constitutional, a racial classification, regardless of its purported motivation, must be narrowly tailored to serve a compelling governmental interest, an extraordinary justification. See, e.g., *Wygant v. Jackson Bd. of Ed.* 277-78 (1986) (plurality opinion). When the government classifies by gender, it must demonstrate that the classification is substantially related to an important governmental interest, requiring an "exceedingly persuasive" justification. *Cleburne*; see *Virginia.*

The first step in determining whether a law violates the Equal Protection Clause is to identify the classification that it draws. Proposition 209 provides that the State of California shall not discriminate against, or grant preferential treatment to, any individual or group on the basis of race or gender. Rather than classifying individuals by race or gender, Proposition 209 prohibits the State from classifying individuals by race or gender. A law that prohibits the State from classifying individuals by race or gender a fortiori does not classify individuals by race or gender. Proposition 209's ban on race and gender preferences, as a matter of law and logic, does not violate the Equal Protection Clause in any conventional sense.

V

As a matter of "political structure" analysis, however, plaintiffs challenge the level of government at which the State of California has prohibited race and gender preferences. Plaintiffs contend, along with the United States as *amicus curiae*, that Proposition 209 imposes an unequal "political structure" that denies women and minorities a right to seek preferential treatment from the lowest level of government. The district court agreed, relying on the so-called "Hunter" doctrine.

A

In *Hunter v. Erickson*, the Supreme Court addressed the constitutionality of an amendment to the Charter of the City of Akron, Ohio. Before the charter amendment was enacted, the Akron City Council had authority to pass ordinances regulating the real estate market. *Hunter*. Most ordinances became effective thirty days after the Council passed them. The charter amendment operated to prevent the city council from enacting ordinances addressing racial discrimination in housing without majority approval of the Akron voters. The plaintiff, Nellie Hunter, who wanted a fair housing ordinance enforced, claimed that the amendment violated her right to equal protection of the laws.

The Supreme Court found in the charter amendment "an explicitly racial classification treating racial housing matters differently from other racial and housing matters." The law disadvantaged those who would benefit from laws barring racial discrimination in the real estate market as against those who would benefit from other regulations of the real estate market. Absent a compelling state interest, the state "may no more disadvantage any particular group by making it more difficult to enact legislation in its behalf than it may dilute any person's vote or give any group a smaller representation than another of comparable size." ...

The district court applied *Hunter* ... to invalidate Proposition 209. Proposition 209, the court found, effected a race and gender classification by singling out race and gender preferences for unique political burdens. The court concluded that race and gender preferences, like antidiscrimination laws and integrative busing, are of special interest to minorities and women. Before Proposition 209 was enacted, the court reasoned, women and minorities could petition local government for preferential treatment. To obtain preferential treatment now, the court concluded, women and minorities must appeal to the statewide electorate, a "new and remote level of government."

The district court next analyzed whether the classifications it gleaned from Proposition 209 withstood "heightened scrutiny." The court concluded that the classifications served no important government interest, let alone a compelling one, thus denying women and minorities equal protection of the laws.

B

... Plaintiffs challenge Proposition 209 not as an impediment to protection against unequal treatment but as an impediment to receiving preferential treatment. The controlling words, we must remember, are "equal" and "protection." Impediments to preferential treatment do not deny equal protection. It is one thing to say that individuals have equal protection rights against political obstructions to equal treatment; it is quite another to say that individuals have equal protection rights against political obstructions to preferential treatment. While the Constitution protects against obstructions to equal treatment, it erects obstructions to preferential treatment by its own terms.

The alleged "equal protection" burden that Proposition 209 imposes on those who would seek race and gender preferences is a burden that the Constitution itself imposes. The Equal Protection Clause, parked at our most "distant and remote" level of government, singles out racial preferences for severe political burdens—it prohibits them in all but the most compelling circumstances. It is well-settled that "all governmental action based on race—a group classification long recognized as in most circumstances irrelevant and therefore prohibited—should be subject to detailed judicial inquiry to ensure that the personal right to equal protection of the laws has not been infringed." *Adarand* (internal quotation marks and citation omitted). That is because "there is simply no way of determining what classifications are 'benign' or 'remedial' and what classifications are in fact motivated by illegitimate notions of racial inferiority or simple racial politics." (quoting *Croson* [1989, plurality]). Rather, "any person, of whatever race, has the right to demand that any governmental actor subject to the Constitution justify any racial classification subjecting that person to unequal treatment under the strictest judicial scrutiny." A governmental action that classifies persons on the basis of gender demands an "exceedingly persuasive justification" to survive constitutional scrutiny. *Virginia.*

That the Constitution permits the rare race-based or gender-based preference hardly implies that the state cannot ban them altogether. States are free to make or not make any constitutionally permissible legislative classification. Nothing in the Constitution suggests the anomalous and bizarre result that preferences based on the most suspect and presumptively unconstitutional classifications—race and gender—must be readily available at the lowest level of government while preferences based on any other presumptively legitimate classification—such as wealth, age or disability—are at the mercy of statewide referenda.

After all, the "goal" of the Fourteenth Amendment, "to which the Nation continues to aspire," is "a political system in which race no longer matters." *Shaw.* When the people enact a law that says race somehow matters, they must come forward with a compelling state interest to back it up. Plaintiffs would have us also require the people to come forward with a compelling state interest to justify a state law that says that race cannot matter in public contracting, employment, and education. Plaintiffs' counsel went even one step further at oral argument. He urged that "[t]he people of the State of California are not entitled to make a judgment as to whether compelling state interests have been vindicated. That is for the courts." Au contraire! That most certainly is for the people of California to decide, not the courts. Our authority in this area is limited to deciding whether the interests proffered by the people are sufficient to justify a law that classifies among individuals. If the federal courts were to decide what the interests of the people are in the first place, judicial power would trump self-government as the general rule of our constitutional democracy.

The Constitution permits the people to grant a narrowly tailored racial preference only if they come forward with a compelling interest to back it up. See, e.g., *Adarand*, "[I]n the context of a Fourteenth Amendment challenge, courts must bear in mind the difference between what the law permits, and what it requires." *Shaw*. To hold that a democratically enacted affirmative action program is constitutionally permissible because the people have demonstrated a compelling state interest is hardly to hold that the program is constitutionally required. The Fourteenth Amendment, lest we lose sight of the forest for the trees, does not require what it barely permits.

A state law that prohibits classifications based on race or gender is a law that addresses in neutral-fashion race-related and gender-related matters. As in *Crawford*, "[i]t would be paradoxical to conclude that by adopting the Equal Protection Clause of the Fourteenth Amendment, the voters of the State thereby had violated it." *Crawford*. For these reasons, we are persuaded that the district court relied on an erroneous legal premise when it concluded that plaintiffs have demonstrated a likelihood of success on their equal protection claim.

[VI omitted]

VII

With no likelihood of success on the merits of their equal protection or preemption claims, plaintiffs are not entitled to a preliminary injunction. The district court determined that plaintiffs had demonstrated irreparable harm because Proposition 209 threatened to inflict an immediate and ongoing constitutional injury upon them. That conclusion, for reasons we have explained, rests on an erroneous legal premise. . . . Assuming all facts alleged in the complaint and found by the district court to be true, and drawing all reasonable inferences in plaintiffs' favor, we must conclude that, as a matter of law, Proposition 209 does not violate the United States Constitution. With no constitutional injury on the merits as a matter of law, there is no threat of irreparable injury or hardship to tip the balance in plaintiffs' favor.

For the foregoing reasons, we vacate the preliminary injunction, deny the motion to stay the injunction as moot, and remand to district court for further proceedings consistent with this opinion.

Preliminary injunction VACATED; stay DENIED as moot; REMANDED.

SECRETARY OF STATE ON CHEMICAL WEAPONS TREATY
April 8, 1997

A United Nations treaty banning chemical weapons took effect on April 29, five days after the U.S. Senate approved U.S. participation in the accord. The treaty was the first in history to ban an entire class of weapons of mass destruction. Nations adhering to the treaty were required to stop producing chemical weapons and to dismantle existing stockpiles within ten years.

Conservative Republicans had delayed Senate approval of the treaty, insisting that it would open the United States to chemical weapon attacks by terrorists or by rogue nations that refused to abide by international norms of behavior. The Clinton administration—backed by the foreign policy establishment, including key officials from previous Republican administrations—lobbied aggressively for the treaty. Final approval came on a vote of 74–26, seven votes more than were required for approval of treaties. All forty-five Democrats voted for the treaty, as did twenty-nine Republicans, a narrow majority of that party's Senate membership.

Treaty with a Long History

The UN treaty was the second major effort in the twentieth century to curb the horrors of chemical weapons. The first was the 1925 Geneva Protocol, negotiated in response to the massive use of mustard gas during World War I. That treaty prohibited the use of chemical weapons, but its scope was limited and it contained no sanctions or verification procedures.

Negotiations toward a broader and stronger treaty began in 1968 and dragged on inconclusively for nearly twenty years. Work on the treaty took on a new urgency after reports circulated in 1988 that some 5,000 Kurds in northern Iraq had been killed by poisonous gas. It was never proven conclusively whether the gas was used by Iraq or Iran, although most commentators alleged that Iraq was responsible.

Diplomats concluded the new treaty near the end of 1992, and it was opened for signature on January 13, 1993. U.S. Secretary of State Lawrence

Eagleburger signed the treaty on behalf of the Bush administration, then in its final days in office. The treaty would still have to be ratified by the Senate. At that time the United States had a stockpile of about 60,000 tons of chemical weapons, by far the largest in the world. Russia, with a stockpile of about 40,000 tons, also signed the treaty. (Chemical weapons treaty, Historic Documents of 1993, p. 71)

Formally known as the Convention on the Prohibition of the Development, Production, Stockpiling, and Use of Chemical Weapons and on Their Destruction, the treaty reached a critical stage on October 31, 1996, when Hungary became the sixty-fifth nation to ratify it. That started a 180-day period before the treaty would take legal effect on April 29, 1997. (UN secretary on treaty, Historic Documents of 1996, p. 740)

Clinton Administration Pushes for Ratification

President Bill Clinton did little to secure Senate approval of the chemical weapons treaty until 1996, assuming that election-year pressures would help overcome any opposition. But the administration underestimated the determination of a small core of conservatives who insisted that the treaty posed a danger to U.S. security. Among the opponents was Sen. Jesse Helms, R-N.C., who used his position as chairman of the Foreign Relations Committee to delay action on the treaty. Former senator Robert Dole, the Republican presidential candidate, sealed the fate of the treaty in 1996 just two months before the elections, when he echoed the criticisms of treaty opponents. The opponents argued that intrusive inspections mandated by the treaty would compromise U.S. sovereignty and expose the country's military and trade secrets. Opponents also argued that the treaty would do little to block the acquisition and use of chemical weapons by nations such as Libya and Iraq.

Early in 1997, as the treaty was about to enter into force with or without U.S. participation, the Clinton administration mounted a more serious and sustained drive for approval in the Senate. Testifying before the Foreign Relations Committee on April 8, Secretary of State Madeleine K. Albright argued that, as the world's leading diplomatic and military power, the United States could not afford to step away from a major international treaty it had helped negotiate. By spurning the treaty, she said, "we will shed the cloak of leadership and leave it on the ground for others to pick up."

The heart of the administration's campaign was an effort to mollify key undecided senators. The most important of these was the Republican majority leader, Trent Lott of Mississippi, who had expressed serious concerns about the treaty but had not announced a formal position on it.

With administration backing, Joseph R. Biden Jr. of Delaware, the ranking Democrat on the Foreign Relations Committee, negotiated with Helms a series of twenty-eight "understandings," most of which were intended to reduce the treaty's appearance of infringement on U.S. sovereignty. Those agreements helped make the treaty more acceptable to some senators, although not to Helms, who never wavered in his opposition. To win Lott's support, Clinton on the morning of the Senate vote sent the majority leader a letter pledging that the United States would withdraw from the treaty if it compromised U.S. security or if it enabled unfriendly nations to acquire chemical weapons. Clinton's assurances also persuaded Dole to announce his support for the treaty at a White House news conference with the president on April 23.

With Clinton's letter in hand, Lott endorsed the treaty, although grudgingly. "The country is marginally better off with it than without it," he told the Senate. Lott joined many of his fellow Republicans in voting for four amendments that the administration opposed on the grounds that they would "kill" U.S. participation in the treaty. But the administration had enough votes to stifle all four amendments. Lott was thus able to demonstrate statesmanship, by enabling the treaty to win Senate approval, and to play to his conservative allies, by voting for hard-line positions that had no chance of becoming law. Even so, leaders of several conservative organizations bitterly denounced Lott.

With Senate approval, the United States became the seventy-fifth nation to ratify the treaty. After the treaty took effect April 29, a new UN agency, the Organization for the Prohibition of Chemical Weapons, began working at The Hague on the business of carrying out its provisions and verifying compliance with it.

Under the treaty, countries that had manufactured chemical weapons were required to stop production immediately, close their production facilities within ninety days, and begin eliminating chemical weapons stockpiles within two years. They were to dispose of all those weapons within ten years, unless they obtained a waiver from the Organization for the Prohibition of Chemical Weapons. No country could obtain an extension for more than five years.

Following are excerpts from testimony of Secretary of State Madeleine K. Albright to the Senate Foreign Relations Committee on April 8, 1997, in which she argued for approval of the Convention on the Prohibition of the Development, Production, Stockpiling and Use of Chemical Weapons and on Their Destruction:

. . . I begin with the imperative of American leadership. The United States is the only nation with the power, influence and respect to forge a strong global consensus against the spread of weapons of mass destruction. . . .

American leadership on arms control is not something we do as a favor to others. Our goal is to make the world safer for Americans and to protect our allies and friends. We have now another opportunity to exercise leadership for those ends. And once again, we look to this Committee for help.

The CWC [Chemical Weapons Convention] will enter into force on April 29. Our goal is to ratify the agreement before then so that America will be an original party. By so doing, as the President said last Friday, we "can help to shield our soldiers from one of the battlefield's deadliest killers . . . and we can bolster our leadership in the fight against terrorism and proliferation around the world."

Chemical weapons are inhumane. They kill horribly, massively, and—once deployed—are no more controllable than the wind. That is why the United States decided—under a law signed by President Reagan in 1985—to destroy the vast majority of our chemical weapons stockpiles by the year 2004. Thus, the CWC will not deprive us of any military option we would ever use against others; but it would help ensure that others never use chemical weapons against us.

In considering the value of this treaty, we must bear in mind that today, keeping and producing chemical weapons are legal.

The gas Saddam Hussein used to massacre Kurdish villagers in 1988 was produced legally. In most countries, terrorists can produce or procure chemical agents, such as sarin gas, legally.

Regimes such as Iran and Libya can build up their stockpiles of chemical weapons legally.

If we are ever to rid the world of these horrible weapons, we must begin by making not only their use, but also their development, production, acquisition and stockpiling illegal. This is fundamental. This is especially important now when America's comparative military might is so great that an attack by unconventional means may hold for some potential adversaries their only perceived hope of success. And making chemical weapons illegal is the purpose of the CWC.

The CWC sets the standard that it is wrong for any nation to build or possess a chemical weapon, and gives us strong and effective tools for enforcing that standard. This is not a magic wand. It will not eliminate all danger. It will not allow us to relax or cease to ensure the full preparedness of our armed forces against the threat of chemical weapons. What it will do is make chemical weapons harder for terrorists or outlaw states to buy, build or conceal.

Under the treaty, parties will be required to give up the chemical weapons they have, and to refrain from developing, producing or acquiring such weapons in the future. To enforce these requirements, the most comprehensive and intense inspection regime ever negotiated will be put in place. Parties will also be obliged to enact and enforce laws to punish violators within their jurisdictions.

Of course, no treaty is 100 percent verifiable, but this treaty provides us valuable tools for monitoring chemical weapons proliferation world-wide—a task we will have to do with or without the CWC.

CWC inspections and monitoring will help us learn more about chemical weapons programs. It will also enable us to act on the information we obtain. In the future, countries known to possess chemical weapons and who have joined the CWC will be forced to choose between compliance and sanctions. And countries outside the CWC will be subject to trade restrictions whether or not they are known to possess chemical arms.

These penalties would not exist without the treaty. They will make it more costly for any nation to have chemical weapons, and more difficult for rogue states or terrorists to acquire materials needed to produce them.

Over time, I believe that—if the United States joins the CWC—most other countries will, too. Consider that there are now 185 members of the Nuclear Nonproliferation Treaty, and only five outside. Most nations play by the rules and want the respect and benefits the world bestows upon those who do.

But the problem states will never accept a prohibition on chemical weapons if America stays out, keeps them company and gives them cover. We will not have the standing to mobilize our allies to support strong action against violators if we ourselves have refused to join the treaty being violated.

The core question here is who do we want to set the standards? Critics suggest that the CWC is flawed because we cannot assume early ratification and full compliance by the outlaw states. To me, that is like saying that because some people smuggle drugs, we should enact no law against drug smuggling. When it comes to the protection of Americans, the lowest common denominator is not good enough. Those who abide by the law, not those who break it, must establish the rules by which all should be judged.

Moreover, if we fail to ratify the agreement by the end of April:

- we would forfeit our seat on the treaty's Executive Council for at least one year, thereby costing us the chance to help draft the rules by which the Convention will be enforced;
- we would not be able to participate in the critical first sessions of the Organization for the Prohibition of Chemical Weapons, which monitors compliance;
- we would lose the right to help administer and conduct inspections; and
- because of the trade restrictions imposed on non-member states, our chemical manufacturers are concerned that they would risk serious economic loss.

According to a letter signed by the CEOs of more than fifty chemical manufacturing companies, the American chemical industry's "status as the world's preferred supplier . . . may be jeopardized if . . . the Senate does not vote in favor of the CWC."

According to those executives "we stand to lose hundreds of millions of dollars in overseas sales, putting at risk thousands of good-paying American jobs."

Eliminating chemical weapons has long been a bipartisan goal. The Convention itself is the product of years of effort by leaders from both parties. And the treaty has strong backing from our defense and military leaders.

I am aware, Mr. Chairman, that the Committee heard this morning from three former Secretaries of Defense who do not favor approval of this Convention. There is no question their arguments are sincerely held, and deserve consideration. I would point out, however, that other former Secretaries of Defense from both parties are on record in support of the treaty, and that every former chairman of the Joint Chiefs of Staff, going back to the Carter Administration, has endorsed it.

Just this past week, we received a letter of support signed by 17 former four star generals and admirals, including three of the former chairmen of the Joint Chiefs of Staff and five former service chiefs. In their words: "Each of us can point to decades of military experience in command positions. We have all trained and commanded troops to prepare for the wartime use of chemical weapons and for defenses against them. . . . Our focus is not on the treaty's limitations, but instead on its many strengths. The CWC destroys stockpiles that could threaten our troops; it significantly improves our intelligence capabilities; and it creates new international sanctions to punish those states who remain outside of the treaty. For these reasons, we strongly support the CWC."

I also note, Mr. Chairman, that the former officials who testified before the Committee this morning have not had the benefit of the intensive dialogue we have been conducting with Members of the Senate leadership, including yourself, the ranking Member and other key members of this Committee. We have attempted, in the course of this dialogue, to address the major issues the opponents of the treaty have raised, and to provide appropriate assurances in binding conditions to accompany the resolution of ratification.

For example, critics have asserted that the CWC obliges member states to exchange manufacturing technology that can be used to make chemical agents. This is untrue. The CWC prohibits members from providing any assistance that would contribute to chemical weapons proliferation.

Nothing in the CWC requires any weakening of our export controls. Further, the United States will continue to work through the Australia Group to maintain and make more effective internationally agreed controls on chemical and biological weapons technology. And, as I have said, the CWC establishes tough restrictions on the transfer of precursor chemicals and other materials that might help a nation or terrorist group to acquire chemical weapons.

Opponents also suggest that if we ratify the CWC, we will become complacent about the threat that chemical weapons pose. This, too, is false—and this body can help ensure it remains false. The President has requested an increase of almost $225 million over five years in our already robust program to equip and train our troops against chemical and biological attack. We are also proceeding with theater missile defense programs and intelligence efforts against the chemical threat.

Some critics of the treaty have expressed the fear that its inspection requirements could raise constitutional problems here in the United States. However, the CWC provides explicitly that inspections will be conducted according to each nation's constitutional processes.

Another issue that arose early in the debate was that the CWC could become a regulatory nightmare for small businesses here in the United States. But after reviewing the facts, the National Federation of Independent Business concluded that its members "will not be affected" by the treaty.

Finally, I have heard the argument that the Senate really need not act before April 29. But as I have said, there are real costs attached to any such delay. The treaty has already been before the Senate for more than 180 weeks. More than 1500 pages of testimony and reports have been provided and hundreds of questions have been answered. The Senate is always the arbiter of its own pace. But from where I sit, a decision prior to April 29 would be very much in the best interests of the United States.

Mr. Chairman, America is the world's leader in building a future of greater security and safety for us and for those who share our commitment to democracy and peace. The path to that future is through the maintenance of American readiness and the expansion of the rule of law. We are the center around which international consensus forms. We are the builder of coalitions, the designer of safeguards, the leader in separating acceptable international behavior from that which cannot be tolerated.

This leadership role for America may be viewed as a burden by some, but I think to most of our citizens, it is a source of great pride. It is also a source of continuing strength, for our influence is essential to protect our interests, which are global and increasing. If we turn our backs on the CWC, after so much effort by leaders from both parties, we will scar America with a grievous and self-inflicted wound. We will shed the cloak of leadership and leave it on the ground for others to pick up.

But if we heed the advice of wise diplomats such as James Baker and Brent Scowcroft, experienced military leaders such as Generals [Colin] Powell, [Carl] Mundy and [H. Norman] Schwartzkopf, and thoughtful public officials such as former Senators [Sam] Nunn, [David] Boren and [Nancy] Kassebaum-Baker, we will reinforce America's role in the world.

By ratifying the CWC, we will assume the lead in shaping a new and effective legal regime. We will be in a position to challenge those who refuse to give up these poisonous weapons. We will provide an added measure of security for the men and women of our armed forces. We will protect American industry and American jobs. And we will make our citizens safer than they would be in a world where chemical arms remain legal.

This treaty is about other people's weapons, not our own. It reflects existing American practices and advances enduring American interests. It is right and smart for America. It deserves the Senate's timely support.

NASA REPORT ON *GALILEO'S* INSPECTION OF JUPITER'S MOONS
April 9, 1997

New observations by the spacecraft Galileo *of four moons orbiting Jupiter offered tantalizing new evidence for the possibility of life outside the Earth.* Galileo *made several close inspections of Jupiter's four inner moons during 1997. The photographs and other information provided by* Galileo *led scientists to believe one of the moons—Europa—probably had some of the conditions necessary for the creation of primitive life.*

Galileo's *explorations followed by one year a sensational claim by the National Aeronautics and Space Administration (NASA) that a small meteorite found in Antarctica had originated on Mars and contained "evidence of primitive life" on the red planet. Some scientists disputed that claim, and the space agency agreed to have the meteorite examined by independent specialists. A NASA probe also roamed the Martian landscape in 1997, looking, among other things, for further clues to possible life there.* (Mars meteor, Historic Documents of 1996, p. 471; *Pathfinder* probe, p. 509)

Fire and Ice on Europa

Using his revolutionary telescope, the Italian scientist Galileo Galilei in 1610 discovered the four inner moons of Jupiter—Europa, Io, Callisto, and Ganymede. Galileo's discovery provided critical evidence for the then-controversial theory that the Sun, rather than the Earth, was the center of the solar system.

Several spacecraft, including the Voyager I *and* Voyager II *missions in 1979, provided a wealth of information about Jupiter and its sixteen moons. NASA launched the* Galileo *spacecraft in October 1989 with the mission of providing close-up views of Jupiter and the four inner moons.* Galileo *entered into an orbit around Jupiter in December 1995, and during 1996 and 1997 made several close passes by the moons.*

Some of the most intriguing observations were of Europa, which scientists long had suspected might be able to support life. With a diameter of

1,946 miles, Europa is slightly smaller than the Earth's moon. It is covered with a crust of brown and black ice.

Photographs and other observations sent back to Earth by Galileo showed that Europa's icy surface is etched with thousands of miles of ridges and grooves, interrupted by domes and giant chunks of ice similar to polar ice floes on Earth. Those features provided evidence, scientists said, that Europa's thin icy surface covers a huge ocean that might be liquid or slushy. Beneath that ocean most likely is a core of metal and rock that gives off enough heat—through radioactive decay and gravitational stresses caused by the pull of Jupiter—to melt the ocean periodically, causing the cracks, ridges, and floes in the surface ice.

Life in Extreme Conditions

These findings had special meaning to scientists because of recent discoveries on Earth. In the past two decades, oceanographers have found primitive organisms and even relatively advanced creatures such as clams and worms surviving along volcanic vents on deep ocean floors. Some scientists believe life on Earth may have begun in similar settings nearly four billion years ago.

If living organisms can survive in the most inhospitable places on Earth, NASA scientists reasoned, it is possible that life could have formed in similarly hostile climates on Europa. Galileo's observations appeared to demonstrate that Europa has both water and energy (in the form of heat), two of the three minimum necessary ingredients for life. NASA scientists announced in October that Galileo had detected the third ingredient— organic compounds—on Callisto and Ganymede, suggesting that Europa might have those compounds as well. However, scientists said it was unlikely that Callisto, Ganymede, or Io could sustain life because they did not appear to have water.

In their statements, NASA scientists emphasized that there was as yet no concrete evidence that life ever existed on Europa. Rather, the scientists said they were reporting that the conditions necessary for the creation of life appeared to be present on that moon.

The Galileo probe completed its primary mission of examining Jupiter and its inner moons on December 7. But, spurred by Galileo's findings, NASA extended the mission for two years, through the end of 1999. This extended mission was to include eight viewings of Europa from as close as two hundred miles. NASA also convened a panel of scientists to study proposals for follow-up missions to examine Europa with lasers, a radar system, and possibly even a probe that would burrow into the ice to determine the structure of the ocean beneath it.

Following is the text of an announcement issued April 9, 1997, by the Jet Propulsion Laboratory at the California Institute of Technology, which managed the Galileo inspection of Jupiter's moons on behalf of the National Aeronautics and Space Administration:

Chunky ice rafts and relatively smooth, crater-free patches on the surface of Jupiter's frozen moon Europa suggest a younger, thinner icy surface than previously believed, according to new images from *Galileo's* spacecraft released today.

The images were captured during *Galileo's* closest flyby of Europa on February 20, when the spacecraft came within 586 kilometers (363 miles) of the Jovian moon. These features, which lend credence to the idea of hidden, subsurface oceans, are also stirring up controversy among scientists who disagree about the age of Europa's surface.

Dr. Ronald Greeley, an Arizona State University geologist and *Galileo* imaging team member, said the ice rafts reveal that Europa had, and may still have, a very thin ice crust covering either liquid water or slush.

"We're intrigued by these blocks of ice, similar to those seen on Earth's polar seas during springtime thaws," Greeley said. "The size and geometry of these features lead us to believe there was a thin icy layer covering water or slushy ice, and that some motion caused these crustal plates to break up."

"These rafts appear to be floating and may, in fact, be comparable to icebergs here on Earth," said another *Galileo* imaging team member, Dr. Michael Carr, a geologist with the U.S. Geological Survey. "The puzzle is what causes the rafts to rotate. The implication is that they are being churned by convection."

The new images of Europa's surface have also sparked a lively debate among scientists. *Galileo* imaging team member Dr. Clark Chapman is among those who believe the smoother regions with few craters indicate Europa's surface is much younger than previously believed. In essence, Chapman, a planetary scientist at Southwest Research Institute, Boulder, CO, believes the fewer the craters, the younger the region. Chapman based his estimate on current knowledge about cratering rates, or the rate at which astronomical bodies are bombarded and scarred by hits from comets and asteroids.

"We're probably seeing areas a few million years old or less, which is about as young as we can measure on any planetary surface besides Earth," said Chapman. "Although we can't pinpoint exactly how many impacts occurred in a given period of time, these areas of Europa have so few craters that we have to think of its surface as young."

Chapman added, "Europa's extraordinary surface geology indicates an extreme youthfulness—a very alive world in a state of flux."

However, Carr sees things differently. He puts Europa's surface age at closer to one billion years old.

"There are just too many unknowns," Carr said. "Europa's relatively smooth regions are most likely caused by a different cratering rate for Jupiter and Earth. For example, we believe that both Earth's moon and the Jovian moon, Ganymede, have huge craters that are 3.8 billion years old. But when we compare the number of smaller craters superimposed on these large ones, Ganymede has far fewer than Earth's moon. This means the cratering rate at Jupiter is less than the cratering rate in the Earth-moon system."

Scientists hope to find answers to some of the questions surrounding Europa and its possible oceans as the *Galileo* spacecraft continues its journey through the Jovian system.

"We want to look for evidence of current activity on Europa, possibly some erupting geysers," Greeley said. "We also want to know whether Europa's surface has changed since the *Voyager* spacecraft flyby in 1979, or even during the time of the *Galileo* flybys."

The craft will return for another Europa flyby on November 6, 1997, the final encounter of *Galileo's* primary mission. However, eight more Europa flybys are planned as part of *Galileo's* two-year extended mission, which will also include encounters with two other Jovian moons, Callisto and Io.

The Jet Propulsion Laboratory manages the *Galileo* mission for NASA's Office of Space Science, Washington, DC.

CLINTON ON AGREEMENT
TO END SWEATSHOPS
April 14, 1997

Under prodding from the Clinton administration, leaders of the U.S. apparel industry agreed April 14 to a code of conduct prohibiting sweat-shop conditions in their factories, both overseas and in the United States. Firms adopting the code could put "No Sweat" labels on their products. Negotiations to put the code into effect bogged down in subsequent months, however, and by the end of 1997 disputes remained about how the code would be enforced and how much the public should be told when violations were discovered.

President Bill Clinton on August 2, 1996, appointed a task force to develop wage and working standards for the U.S.-based clothing and shoe industries. Clinton acted in response to numerous reports that factories producing items for leading brand-name companies were forcing employees to work eighty or more hours a week at wages as low as 25 cents an hour. Many of the worst abuses were reported in Third World countries, such as Vietnam and Pakistan, where giant companies had established factories to take advantage of low labor costs. Some of the most difficult issues faced by the task force involved working conditions in authoritarian countries, such as China, which banned collective bargaining and restricted workers' rights to form associations.

Clinton's panel included representatives from labor unions, consumer advocacy organizations, and human rights groups, as well as senior officials from such apparel firms as NIKE Inc., Phillips-Van Heusen Corp., Reebok International Ltd., LL Bean Inc., and Liz Claiborne, Inc. Senior administration officials participated in many of the panel's discussions.

An embarrassing setback for the industry came in December 1997, when New York State Attorney General Dennis Vacco said three factories in New York City were forcing Chinese immigrants to work sixty to eighty hours a week, in some cases at pay below the minimum wage or even with no pay at all. The factories produced clothing for a fashion line represented by television personality Kathie Lee Gifford, who was a member of Clinton's apparel industry task force and who had denouced sweatshop conditions in the fashion industry. A spokesman said Gifford had launched her own investigation into the factories and had stopped doing business with them as of October 1.

Terms of the Agreement

The agreement announced by Clinton April 14 was essentially an outline in which key leaders of the apparel industry agreed to abide by a code of conduct to be monitored independently, and in return they could place a "seal of approval" on their products. Most parties to the agreement—including key White House officials—acknowledged that it was a compromise that would not fully satisfy anyone. Even so, Gene Sperling, Clinton's chief economic adviser, called the accord "a breakthrough agreement. It is historic. It is unique."

Key components of the agreement covered wages, working hours, child labor, and working conditions at apparel industry factories, both in the United States and overseas, that were directly owned by, or under contract to, U.S.-based companies. The agreement would not require rigid uniformity on any of its standards but instead would rely on laws and prevailing standards within each country.

The provision on wages would require that each apparel factory pay its workers at least the legal minimum wage, or the prevailing industry wage, whichever was higher, for the country in which it was located. At the insistence of the representatives of unions and human rights groups, the accord added that pay should be linked with the "basic needs" of workers. Those representatives had said that the legal or prevailing minimum wages in many countries were far below what families needed to support themselves.

Similarly, the agreement established a complex formula for the maximum workweek, which was set at sixty hours. In general, the maximum regular workweek should be forty-eight hours or less. Workers could be required to put in no more than twelve hours of overtime a week, with overtime compensated at whatever the legal premium was in the country involved, or at least at the level of regular hourly pay. The agreement also required that workers be given at least one day off in every seven-day period.

In the United States, the agreement would result in a maximum workweek of fifty-two hours: the standard forty-hour workweek plus up to twelve hours of overtime. Sperling noted that the United States had no national legal limit on overtime hours.

To curtail the use of young children in factories, the agreement established a minimum working age of fifteen, except in countries that allowed employment of fourteen-year-old children. The agreement also left open the possibility for an even higher minimum age in countries where "the age for completing compulsory education" was greater than fifteen.

Another element of the code of conduct was aimed at offering workers some protection against harassment by their employers. The code stated that "no employee shall be subject to any physical, sexual, psychological or verbal harassment or abuse."

Much of the private negotiating that went into the agreement was devoted to the sensitive question of how to monitor industry compliance with the code of conduct. Many industry representatives wanted individual firms to be able to monitor their own compliance, while representatives of labor unions and human rights groups demanded monitoring by independent, outside observers. "In no way should employers be the only ones monitoring what they're doing," Jay Mazur, president of the Union of Needletrades, Industrial and Textile Employees told the New York Times in May.

The final agreement called for "independent reviews" by monitors who would visit factory sites, interview employers and supervisors, and examine production records to verify that individual companies had complied with the code. Apparel companies could hire outside accounting firms to monitor compliance, but the accountants would be required to consult with labor unions and human rights groups.

In announcing the agreement, Clinton said it "will improve the lives of millions of garment workers around the world." Clinton praised the willingness of the apparel industry leaders on his task force to curtail sweatshop practices and called on "every other company in America in their line of work" to follow their lead.

Even though representatives of key labor unions and human rights groups served on Clinton's panel, other antisweatshop activists harshly condemned the accord. Sweatshop Watch, a coalition of unions and rights groups, issued a strongly worded response on May 21 saying that, rather than improving working conditions, the accord "entrenches even more deeply the indecent wages, inhumane hours and lack of accountability that pervade the industry by lending its stamp of approval to the existing exploitative system." The Sweatshop Watch statement noted, for example, that prevailing minimum wages in many countries such as Haiti and Indonesia were below even the local poverty levels. By allowing companies to pay such wages, Sweatshop Watch said, the accord meant that "workers laboring long hours will still be unable to rise above poverty and starvation."

Follow-up Issues

The announcement of the code of conduct left some of the most contentious issues on the table, the most important of which were the makeup of a board that would oversee compliance with the code and the procedures for disclosing violations to the public. Clinton had said he expected the task force to settle those issues within six months, or by the middle of November 1997. The deadline came and went without an agreement, and the New York Times reported on November 21 that panel members remained "badly divided" on key issues.

The Times reported that panel members could not agree on how much the public should be told about any sweatshop violations uncovered by industry monitors. Representatives of labor unions and human rights groups *were demanding "broad disclosure" of violations, the newspaper said, while industry representatives wanted little information made public.*

An even more divisive issue, according to the newspaper, was control over the board that would approve the monitors who inspect apparel industry plants. Representatives of labor unions and human rights groups insisted that they should have a majority of members on the board to ensure that the monitors would be truly independent of the companies whose work they inspected. Industry representatives were holding out for a board evenly divided between industry officials on the one hand and the labor unions and human rights groups on the other. At year's end the two sides reportedly were still struggling to resolve their disputes on these issues.

Following is the text of an announcement by President Bill Clinton, at the White House April 14, 1997, of the "Apparel Industry Partnership Agreement," in which leading clothing and shoe manufacturers agreed to abide by a code of workplace conduct:

I would like to begin, first of all, by thanking all the members of this partnership—the cochairs, Paul Charron of Liz Claiborne; and Linda Golodner, the National Consumers League; Jay Mazur of UNITE.

I thank Kathy Lee Gifford, who has done so much to bring public attention to this issue. I thank the members of Congress who were here—Congressman George Miller [D-Calif.], Congressman Bernie Sanders [I-Vt.], Congressman Lane Evans [D-Ill.], Congressman Marty Martinez [D-Calif.]. And especially I thank my good friend, Senator Tom Harkin [D-Iowa], who first brought this issue to my attention a long time ago. Thank you very much, sir.

Thank all of you for your passion and concern.

I thank the former secretary of labor, Bob Reich; and acting secretary Cynthia Metzler; and secretary-designate Alexis Herman, who's here. And I thank Maria Echaveste and Gene Sperling for their work.

The announcement we make today will improve the lives of millions of garment workers around the world. As has now been painfully well-documented, some of the clothes and shoes we buy here in America are manufactured under working conditions which are deplorable and unacceptable, mostly overseas, but unbelievably, sometimes here at home as well.

In our system of enterprise, which I have done my best to promote and advance, we support the proposition that businesses are in business to make a profit. But in our society, which we believe to be good and want to be better, we know that human rights and labor rights must be a part of the basic framework within which all businesses honorably compete.

As important as the fabric apparel workers make for us is the fabric of their lives, which is a part of the fabric of our lives here at home and around the world. Their health and their safety, their ability to make a decent wage, their ability to bring children into this world and raise them with dignity and have their children see their parents working with dignity—that's an important part of the quality of our lives and will have a lot to do with the quality of our children's future.

Last August, when the vice president and I brought together the leaders of some of our nation's largest apparel and footwear companies, and representatives of labor, consumers, human rights and religious groups, I was genuinely moved at the shared outrage at sweatshop abuses and the shared determination to do something about it.

That led to this apparel industry partnership.

This partnership has reached an agreement, as already has been said, that will significantly reduce the use of sweatshop labor over the long run. It will give American consumers greater confidence in the products they buy.

And again, I say, they have done a remarkable thing. Paul Charron said it was just the beginning, because even though there's some very impressive and big companies represented on this stage, there are some which are not.

But I would like to ask all the members of the partnership here to stand. And I think we ought to express our appreciation to them for what they have done.

Now, here's what they agreed to do. First, a workplace code of conduct that companies will voluntarily adopt and require their contractors to adopt to dramatically improve the conditions under which goods are made.

The code will establish a maximum work week, a cap of twelve hours in the amount or overtime a company can require, require that employers pay at least the minimum or prevailing wage, respect basic labor rights.

It will require safe and healthy working conditions and freedom from abuse and harassment. Most important, it will crack down on child labor, prohibiting the employment of those under fifteen years of age in most countries.

It will also take steps to ensure that this code is enforced and that American consumers will know that the tenets of the agreement are being honored. The apparel industry has developed new standards for internal and external monitoring to make sure companies and contractors live up to that code of conduct.

It will also form an independent association to help implement the agreement and to develop an effective way to share this information with consumers, such as labels on clothing, seals of approval in advertising, or signs in stores to guarantee that no sweatshop labor was used on a given product line.

Of course, the agreement is just the beginning. We know sweatshop labor will not vanish overnight. We know that while this agreement is an historic step, our real measure of progress must be in the change that improved lives and livelihoods of apparel workers here at home and around the world. That is why we need more companies to join this crusade and follow its strict rules of conduct.

One of the association's most important tasks will be to expand participation to as many large and small companies as possible. And I urge all of America's apparel companies to become part of this effort.

If these people are willing to put their names, their necks, their reputations and their bottom lines on the bottom line of America, every other company in America in their line of work ought to be willing to do the very same thing.

We have spent a lot of time trying to find jobs for everybody in America who wants to work. And we have spent a lot of time saying that people who are able-bodied, who can work, should be required to work. Now, we are also reminding ourselves that no one anywhere should have to put their safety or their dignity on the line to support themselves or their children.

This is a great day for America, a great day for the cause of human rights, and I believe a great day for free enterprise. And I thank all of those who are here who made it possible.

I'm proud that this agreement was industry-led and wholly voluntary, like the TV industry's decision to rate its programming; like the new private-sector effort to help move people from welfare to work; like the high tech industry's efforts to wire our schools and our classrooms to the Internet, all of them by the year 2000, which we will continue this Saturday.

This is further evidence that we can solve our problems by working together in new and creative ways. The apparel industry understands that we all share a stake in preparing our country for the 21st century and preparing the world to be a good partner.

Reaching across lines that have too often divided us in the past, this new partnership will create more opportunity for working families. It will demand more responsibility for working conditions. It will build a stronger community here in America, and bind us to the community of people all around the world who believe in the value of work, but who also believe in the importance of its dignity and sanctity.

Thank you, and God bless you all.

GENETIC RESEARCHER ON THE CLONING OF "DOLLY"
April 15, 1997

Scientists at a genetic research institute in Scotland said on February 22, 1997, that they had succeeded in cloning an adult sheep. The offspring, named Dolly, was born in July 1996 at the Roslin Institute near Edinburgh and was growing to maturity. The announcement stunned the scientific world—which for many years had thought the cloning of adult mammals was impossible—and stirred deep passions in the public around the world. Scientists, religious leaders, ethicists, and politicians rushed to debate the moral and legal implications of the cloning of humans. President Bill Clinton imposed a moratorium on the use of federal funds for human cloning, and Congress debated the issue but took no action in 1997.

Addressing the National Press Club in Washington, D.C., on April 15, Ian Wilmut, the lead researcher in the Dolly experiment, called the idea of human cloning "unethical." But Wilmut, along with many other scientists, urged Congress and legislatures in other countries to act carefully in passing any anticloning legislation, so that beneficial research efforts would not be curtailed.

Leading Up to Dolly

For decades cloning had been a staple of science fiction, but since the 1950s scientists had been experimenting with various means of cloning animals, starting with frogs. The first successful cloning of a mammal was in 1984, when Steen M. Willadsen, a Danish embryologist working in Texas, bred a live sheep that was cloned from immature embryo cells. In later years, other researchers were able to duplicate this feat in cattle, goats, pigs, and monkeys. In 1994 at the University of Wisconsin researcher Neal First used more advanced embryo cells to clone cattle. These experiments left open the question of whether cells taken from an adult animal could be used to clone, or exactly reproduce, that adult.

The groundbreaking research to clone an adult sheep took place at the government-funded Roslin Institute. There, scientists were working with a private company, PPL Therapeutics P.L.C., to develop genetically engineered animals that produced proteins useful in making drugs to treat human diseases.

In 1996 two scientists working at the Roslin Institute, Wilmut and Keith Campbell, replicated First's cloning experiment in sheep, producing two lambs named Megan and Moran. In their experiment, Wilmut and Campbell added a procedure that led eventually to the Dolly cloning: they put the embryo cells into a state similar to hibernation before transferring their nuclei into the egg of a sheep. When used in the Dolly experiment, this technique enabled the scientists to implant the DNA from a live sheep onto an embryo before the embryo was transferred to a sheep's egg. This meant that Dolly was cloned from a live adult, rather than from an embryo that had never advanced to later stages.

Wilmut and Campbell in January 1996 fused the cell to the egg that eventually produced Dolly, and six days later planted it in a ewe. The live fetus was discovered about six weeks later, and Dolly was born, a vital and healthy lamb, on July 5, 1996. She was named for country-and-western singer Dolly Parton because mammary cells were used in the cloning.

The experiment was not easy or straightforward. The researchers fused 277 sheep eggs with genetically altered cells, and Dolly was the only lamb to develop into a live fetus that was carried to term. Wilmut acknowledged that he might have been lucky to succeed even at the 1-in-277 rate, although he predicted that the rate of success would improve in the future.

Five months later, in July, Wilmut and Campbell announced that they had created another live lamb—named Polly—that had a human gene in each of its cells. Scientists said animals genetically altered in this fashion could be used to produce hormones to treat human diseases, or even to produce internal organs that could be transplanted into humans.

Banning Human Cloning

The announcement of Dolly's birth set off a high profile and high decibel debate around the world about the implications for the cloning of human beings. The cloning of one mammal—a sheep—raised at least the theoretical possibility that humans could be cloned as well. Several countries, including Great Britain, Denmark, Spain, Australia, and Germany, already had laws banning human cloning. The United States, which banned federal funding of research on human embryos, did not bar human cloning or even privately funded research on human embryos.

On February 24, two days after the news of Dolly's birth first appeared in the British media, President Clinton asked the National Bioethics Advisory Commission to examine the policy implications raised by the Dolly experiment. Clinton followed up on March 4 by imposing a moratorium on federal funding of research that could lead to the cloning of humans; the president asked private agencies to observe such a moratorium, as well.

The advisory commission reported its recommendations to Clinton on June 9. The panel recommended putting Clinton's moratorium into law *and extending it to prohibit private organizations from attempting to clone humans. The panel said any anticloning law should be temporary, expiring in three to five years unless experts determined that the laws should remain in effect.*

In a letter to Clinton, the panel said the legal, scientific, and moral issues raised by the cloning controversy "can only be resolved, even temporarily, by a great deal more widespread deliberation and education." Commission members noted that a legal ban on cloning research would represent the first prohibition of a field of medical research in U.S. history. Commission members said they could not agree among themselves about the legal, moral, and other implications of Dolly's birth for human cloning. The only thing they could agree on, they said, was that it was not yet safe to allow human cloning, given the difficulty researchers had in producing Dolly.

Clinton accepted the commission recommendations and immediately sent Congress proposed legislation to put the anticloning moratorium into law. Clinton said he believed the commission's conclusions represented a "national consensus," and added that he personally believed "it is the right thing to do."

Congress considered Clinton's bill and several other proposals on the cloning issue in 1997, but only one (HR 922, barring federal funding for cloning a human or a human embryo) made it as far as approval by a full committee (the House Science Committee, in July). Representatives of pharmaceutical and biotechnology industries opposed the wording of some of the bills before Congress, saying that such proposals could impede legitimate scientific research in genetics and other areas.

While politicians debated the issue, scientists continued their research, and some began reassessing their initial reactions to the birth of Dolly. The New York Times *reported on December 2 that several leading scientists had changed their minds about the feasibility, or even desirability, of cloning humans. Some scientists, the newspaper reported, had concluded that cloning of humans was inevitable.*

> *Following are excerpts from an address by Ian Wilmut, of the Roslin Institute in Scotland, on April 15, 1997, to the National Press Club in Washington, D.C.:*

. . . [T]hank you very much for that very interesting introduction and also for the opportunity to come and talk to you about our research and its significance.

What I'd like you to do is to think of me as an ambassador for the group that's actually done this research. There's already been some mention of my colleague, Keith Campbell, but it is important to realize that a project like this depends upon a lot of skills.

Whereas I am an embryologist with experience of embryology and reproductive biology in farm animals, Keith has research experience in the mechanisms which control cells. What is it which ensures that a cell can grow and then divide, what we call cell cycle?

And to gain that experience, he worked with very different organisms. He worked with yeast and with a toad, experimental animals which have given us an awful lot of understanding about these basic mechanisms.

So whenever you think about this research, I hope that you will think of Wilmut and Campbell in just the same way that we are all accustomed to the idea of thinking about Watson and Crick, who were the people who together discovered the structure of the DNA code. This is very much a team effort.

In addition to Keith, we also need other people with experience of micro manipulation. Embryos are about a 250th of an inch across, a tenth of a millimeter. So that as well as specialist equipment, you also need a lot of patience and skill in order to micro manipulate, and my colleague Bill Richey has done most of the micro manipulation in the experiments which have been published.

But you need people who can grow cells, people who can recover embryos from sheep and then put new embryos back into the foster mothers. So I'm very much an ambassador for that group and grateful for the opportunity to be here and to represent us. . . .

One of the privileges of modern science is the opportunity to travel and not only to visit places, but also to have the excitement of new discoveries which are being reported to you by people in other laboratories.

And of course, we've built upon the research which has been carried out by other people. The first people to do a nuclear transfer in mice—in mammals, in other words—among the first, was Devor Sulter, working here in the United States.

Steen Willadsen, working in Cambridge in England, was the first to use nuclear transfer in a farm animal, and he then came across to the United States and worked in a company in College Station in Texas. . . .

Neal First in Wisconsin has contributed a lot to this area of research. So we really have had the opportunity to build upon the research which these people had already published and described.

One last general point before I explain to you the title of my talk and move into the really important part of the talk concerns the publicity which has already been mentioned.

I simply have no idea how many TV, radio, and newspaper interviews we've given. But I can tell you because computers count automatically, I can tell you that we've found over 600 e-mails in the roughly six weeks since this story broke.

Last week we were still getting something of the order of ten e-mails, half a dozen or so ordinary mail letters, and about four phone calls a day. And these were bringing in usually one of two invitations to speak or to take part in meetings.

So we have quite literally been overwhelmed. I only have a part-time secretary at the present time, so if you are among the people to whom we failed to offer a reply so far, I apologize for our discourtesy. I would ask you to be patient.

For those of you who are asking for interviews, I hope that you will now understand why it is that we are trying to politely decline them. You'll also remember perhaps that we have had trouble with our funding in recent weeks. And so it's very important to us to go back to our own work for a while to secure that funding to plan out the new research programs, to carry out the ones which are in progress, and to go back to the basic running of the science the labs.

But neither we, nor this subject are going to go away. In a few months time, there will be some new results from our lab. I'm sure there will be other labs now working in this area. And we will then be pleased to talk to you about our work and other people's work. So I just ask you to be patient.

Mention has already been made of the idea of using the technique of nucleic transfer to copy people. This is probably the aspect, the application which has written about most since the story was first publicized.

I expect by now that most of you have heard me say that as far as I'm concerned, I have still not heard an application for this technology which involves copying a person, which I find ethically unacceptable.

And there are two reasons for this: One is that in many cases I think that it's actually a misunderstanding—that the suggestion is based upon a misunderstanding. That what people are trying to do is to bring back a person who sadly has passed away—perhaps a child, perhaps a parent—much loved and sadly missed.

It is simply not possible to do that. If you use this technique to produce a new individual they might be born to a different mother. They would certainly be born in a different age. And I think most important of all I think they would be treated as a different individual. There would be no possibility that you could treat that little person, that child, in a normal way.

So I think it is a gross misunderstanding to think that you can use this technique for many of the applications that have been suggested. But I've already mentioned the main reason why I personally would find it unacceptable, and that is because I think that each one of us deserves to be treated as an individual.

And I would urge anybody who is thinking of using this technique to make a new person to ask themselves not the question can you really think, can you really believe that you would be able to treat that person as an individual? Because if you cannot I don't think you should do it. And I personally don't think you could treat them as an individual. They would be there as a copy and therefore not as an individual. And to me that is the reason why it would be unacceptable.

The title that I gave for the talk was My Dad and Dolly. And I would like now to explain why I gave that title. My father, my dad was a school teacher. He was little guy about five feet four inches tall and about 145, 150 pounds all of his life.

I'm obviously biased but he was actually a very, very good teacher. He had a lot of personality and was really effective at teaching. Even those people who did not enjoy mathematics. . . .

Now when he was a student in Cambridge in England he collapsed. Because he—it turned out that he was suffering from the disease we call diabetes mellitus. He became unconscious and if things had gone on he would have suffered all of the other symptoms which are associated with that disease.

Now fortunately for him by that time the cause of the disease and the means of treatment had been discovered by classic physiological research. Fortunately for me of course, as well. Because if that treatment hadn't been available then I wouldn't be here.

What I want to do is describe briefly the physiological research in the past—much of it a hundred, fifty to a hundred years ago—which lead to an understanding of diabetes which brought forward the treatment. And then indicate to you the way in which I think that the research which brought forward Dolly would be used to study in an exactly analogous way the role of particular genes.

The classic physiological research was to understand the functioning of particular organs and particular tissues. The analogous set of experiment would be to find out what is the product of a particular gene. What is the role of a particular gene? What's wrong under certain conditions where there is a genetic disease?

And I'm confident in the future that this will bring forward a number of new treatments.

So diabetes—its symptoms vary broadly. Despite the fact that they eat a lot, they lose weight, they waste away. Ultimately they become unconscious and they will die.

In their urine there is typically a very large amount of sugar. And the compounds which have the typical characteristic smell of acetone.

So it's been diagnosed for a long time.

In 1869, research with dogs identified the fact that if the pancreas—that's a small diffuse organ which sits between the stomach and the upper intestine—that if that particular tissue was removed, that the dogs developed some of the similar symptoms. The urine was changed. They began to waste away.

And so the classic interpretation, obviously, would be that there is some product from the pancreas which is controlling metabolism in the animal and that in patients like my father, absence of that product was leading to their death.

Now the classic physiological approach is that you take away an organ. You identify any defects and you then try and replace the functioning of that organ. So for a number of years, people extracted proteins from the organ and injected it, and obviously the expectation is that you would be able to delay the onset of symptoms.

Now for a long time, this failed to have any effect. This was despite the fact that if they took some of the tissue and put it into animals, that had a slight delaying effect which gave some encouragement to the idea that they were on the right lines.

Now hindsight, of course, is a wonderful thing. It gives you perfect vision. So we can now explain and understand why it is that there was a technical problem for these people.

If you look at the structure of the pancreas, you can see that there are two different types of cells. One type is made up of groups of cells, called islands, islets, and this is where ultimately the name insulin came from.

But the rest of the tissue is associated with tubes which lead into the digestive tract. And what we now know is that those cells were secreting an enzyme which is released into the digestive tract and which is partly responsible for the breakdown of food.

But what was happening to the people who were trying to extract the proteins was that the very enzymes which were there were causing breakdown of everything that was being extracted, and that's why it wasn't active. It wasn't until 1921, roughly 50 years later, that this idea occurred to people— Bunting and Bast are their names. Again, it's another duo.

And they developed a procedure of disrupting the function of the pancreas. It's often the case that if you ligate the tubes, there is, if you like, a sort of a build up. I think it's probably naive to think of it as pressure, but there is, as it were, a back effect on the secretory cells. And so the net result in this case is that the secretory cells stopped functioning.

And so in 1921, Bunting and Bast extracted protein, injected it into dogs, and yes, it caused the delay in the onset of the condition. It altered the level of sugar and the circulation of the urine. That must have been as exciting to them as Dolly and her predecessors were to us. It was a major breakthrough.

And it was subsequent to that that other people working in that same laboratory came up with procedures for isolating the protein. Usually, I think it's obtained from pig tissue. So my guess is that there's somebody in this room who's been injecting insulin daily, like my dad did, in order to control the level of sugar in their circulation.

More recently, of course, it's been made by molecular biology. It's human recombinant insulin. But for a long time I guess something like 60, 70 years it was extracted from pig tissue.

Now I chose the pancreas because of the involvement in my family. But you could have equally well have chosen the adrenal gland and cortical steroids. The thyroid and the hormones concerned with metabolism there.

The ovary, much, much more recently it first became possible to use the hormones obtained from the ovary for the contraceptive pill. It had long been known that the ovary was important for reproductive cycles for the maintenance of pregnancy. . . . If you put back the hormones you can maintain pregnancy.

It's the same structure as the classic physiological approach that you take out a tissue to see what happens. And you try and replace the functioning of that tissue by injecting extracts.

You also need to monitor the effects really carefully. The mere fact that you've gotten pregnant if you put in progesterones doesn't show you that it's the only hormone that's involved. You need to do a lot of studies.

Similar with insulin, it's quite clear that there are other interactions with hormones coming from the adrenal for example in maintaining normal metabolism.

But it's the classic approach of disrupting something. What's changed, how can we replace it.

So how is it that copying things is producing something that's the same? How is it that this nuclear transfer technology of ours can be used in analogous way to study the functioning of genes?

The whole point is that when you're doing nuclear transfer you have two cells. You have the unfertilized egg from which you remove all of the genetic material. And you have a donor cell; in the case of Dolly it was the mammary cell. And you use that to provide all of the genetic information.

Now this application of the technique will depend upon using well established procedures to target precise genetic changes in those donor cells before they're used for nuclear transfer. So that then the offspring would all be genetical to themselves. But they would have that one slight difference from the source of the cells. And so this is certainly one of the ways in which we think our research will be really important.

. . . There are a lot of other uses for this technique. But a big area can be grouped together as being basic research into the role of particular gene products and the mechanisms that regular their functioning.

To give you one specific example which has been quoted quite a lot. It concerns the genetic disease cystic fibrosis. This, if you remember, is the disease which in children is associated with congestion of the lungs. Particular susceptibility to infection.

The children have to be put over a parent's knee and patted on the back to cough up the mucus. It's known that this affliction arises because of one error in a particular gene.

It's possible to use mice in a different system which is unfortunately not available to us in any of the laboratory or farm animal to make that same genetic modification. But mice are really very difficult to study if you think about it, they're so small, to make repeated observations in them is really very difficult.

Physiologically they're very different from humans and it's been suggested to us by people who are studying this disease that the sheep would make a much better model. So we will collaborate with these people to introduce the same genetic difference into sheep and then to work with them to try to bring forward new pharmacological treatments, new drugs, to treat the affliction.

And also perhaps the development of techniques for gene therapy. For putting back into the patient a fully functioning gene. But cystic fibrosis is just one example and I'm quite clear that very few of us have really thought about this application much yet. There are probably people in labs all around the world who are beginning to think about it.

And we needn't restrict ourselves to sheep. It's almost certain that this technique will also work in rabbits, probably in rats and mice, and the other farm animals. So biologists will be able to choose the species which is most appropriate for the particular condition that they want to study, perhaps rabbits for cardiovascular diseases, to be able to make for the first time precise changes in either the product of the gene, or in those neighboring regions of DNA which regulate the functioning of the gene.

This is exactly analogous to the physiologists' experiments. What happens if we remove the product of this gene? If we show in effect what happens, how can we replace it? How can we replace it? Either by giving a drug or by transferring into that animal a different, but fully functional gene. . . .

It's very easy to be misrepresented with the best of intentions. But to try to put all of this into a broad summary, it seems to me quite clear that as far as human medicine is concerned, that application of this technique not only in sheep, pigs, but probably rabbits, and possibly rats, will offer a whole new range of opportunities for people wanting to study genetic diseases.

Now there are, of course, a number of genetic diseases with profound effects, probably quite a small number of diseases. But the geneticists estimate that all of us have what would probably be considered a much smaller genetic error.

Some of you have noticed that I tremble all the time, just a little bit. Why? It's probably a small, genetic error. Probably most of us, as they estimate, have got small errors in the DNA which makes up our chromosomal complement. And so over the years, people will begin to understand these mechanisms more and to be able to offer treatments for more and more of these conditions.

I think it's clear that this research will be long term. You will have noticed the two dates that I mentioned, 1869 and 1921. People like to think that things happen rather more quickly these days, and maybe they do. But I suspect that even so, the developments that I'm talking about are 25 years away, in many cases. So it's going to be long-term research.

I think that people can predict that there will be help for some conditions. It would be very surprising, as well as disappointing, if there isn't a benefit for, for example, cystic fibrosis. But sadly, I think that some conditions will be difficult to treat, so I think it would be folly to suggest that we will bring forward treatments for all genetic conditions.

And lastly, we only have identified, I guess, around 2,000 to 5,000 of all of the genes which are believed to make up the human complement. And there are estimated to be about 100,000.

So clearly, there are very many things which we haven't even begun to imagine, because we haven't yet identified the genes. We haven't even begun these studies.

So I'm confident . . . that in the future, you will be addressed here by people who have used this technique for basic research. I look forward to hearing about it myself. And I believe that this is the way in which this technique will contribute to human medicine.

Thank you again for the invitation.

JUSTICE DEPARTMENT REPORT
ON FBI CRIME LABORATORY
April 15, 1997

An internal investigation by the Justice Department found evidence that the FBI's famed crime laboratory had issued some reports that were seriously flawed and had allowed investigators to give inaccurate testimony in several dozen criminal cases. The laboratory's failings over nearly a decade resulted in the presentation of faulty evidence in such major cases as the 1993 bombing of the World Trade Center and the 1995 bombing of the federal office building in Oklahoma City, according to a report released April 15 by Michael R. Bromwich, the Justice Department's inspector general. (Oklahoma City trial, p. 623)

The Justice Department report seriously undermined the FBI lab's credibility among judges, lawyers, and law enforcement officials, according to many observers. The lab conducted more than 600,000 tests each year for federal, state, and local authorities. The report also caused political and public relations damage to the agency, already suffering from allegations that it botched the investigation of a suspect in the 1996 bombing of Olympic Centennial Park in Atlanta and had improperly given background files to aides in the Clinton White House. (Olympic bombing case, Historic Documents of 1996, p. 445)

The FBI said it accepted Bromwich's suggestions for reforms at the crime lab and had already moved to implement many of them. The agency in October hired a new director for the lab, Donald M. Kerr Jr., a former head of the Los Alamos National Laboratory, which conducts research on nuclear weapons. Although Kerr was a respected scientist and administrator, some FBI critics expressed dissatisfaction with the selection because he lacked expertise in forensic science.

Attorney General Janet Reno on April 15 said the Bromwich investigation turned up information on fifty-five cases in which the lab had committed mistakes that were serious enough to justify informing defense attorneys. She said information had already been turned over to defense lawyers in twenty-five cases; thirteen of those cases had gone to trial but "there has been no change in the outcome of the case" because of the new information, Reno said. Reports of the crime lab's failings appeared to have no serious impact on the World Trade Center and Oklahoma City bombing cases; defendants were convicted in both cases after the Bromwich report was made public.

Major Findings

Bromwich initiated the investigation largely in response to numerous allegations made by Frederic Whitehurst, a senior scientist at the FBI crime lab. Starting in 1989 Whitehurst had filed hundreds of complaints charging incompetence, recklessness, and even criminal behavior by some of his colleagues and supervisors at the lab. In his report, Bromwich said most of Whitehurst's allegations were not substantiated, including "his most inflammatory" charges that some lab employees had fabricated evidence and committed perjury. Other of Whitehurst's charges did turn out to be true, Bromwich said, as did allegations made during the investigation by other crime lab employees.

Although he said Whitehurst had made a "significant contribution" by bringing problems in the crime lab to light, Bromwich faulted Whitehurst for his "frequently overstated and incendiary way of criticizing laboratory personnel," many of whom were innocent of any wrongdoing. Calling Whitehurst a "complex person" and citing doubts about whether he "has the requisite common sense and judgment to serve as a forensic examiner," Bromwich recommended that the FBI transfer him to an assignment outside the crime lab. The agency already had placed Whitehurst on administrative leave with pay—an action he claimed was retaliation for his criticisms.

The eighteen-month investigation covered only three of the laboratory's twenty-five major units, but the three were among the busiest and had some of the most sensitive responsibilities in the entire lab. Bromwich investigated actions of the Explosives Unit, the Materials Analysis Unit, and the Chemistry-Toxicology Unit. Bromwich said his findings involving those units did not necessarily mean that other crime lab units had similar failings. He also praised the "superb work" of many laboratory employees who were "dedicated to the highest traditions of forensic science."

The Bromwich report cited several general problems in the crime lab, among them: testimony in criminal cases that was scientifically flawed, inaccurate, or beyond the expertise of the employee giving the testimony; improper preparation of laboratory reports; insufficient documentation of test results; scientifically flawed reports; and management failures, including inadequate records storage and a flawed staffing system in the Explosives Unit.

The report cited by name fourteen individuals who had worked at the laboratory, including several supervisors who allegedly failed to correct problems that were brought to their attention. Much of the report concerned the work of David Williams, an examiner in the Explosives Unit who ana-

lyzed evidence and offered testimony for the prosecutions in the World Trade Center and Oklahoma City bombing cases.

In the World Trade Center case, Whitehurst alleged in 1996 that Williams had misrepresented the truth, testified outside his area of expertise, and presented evidence that was biased in favor of the prosecution. After reviewing Whitehurst's allegations, Bromwich concluded that Williams had given "inaccurate and incomplete testimony" and had testified "to invalid opinions that appeared tailored to the most incriminating result." Bromwich said his investigation did not substantiate Whitehurst's "many other allegations" against Williams.

In particular, Bromwich cited Williams's testimony that the main explosive used in the World Trade Center bombing was approximately 1,200 pounds of urea nitrate and that the defendants had the capacity to manufacture that amount of the material. Bromwich reported that Williams had no scientific evidence or expertise to back up his conclusions, and so his testimony was merely "speculation" and was "deeply flawed." The World Trade Center case demonstrated the need for the Explosives Unit to have examiners with scientific expertise who understand their role as experts, as opposed to the role of criminal prosecutors, Bromwich said.

Williams committed many of the same errors in the Oklahoma City bombing case, for which he wrote the Explosive Unit's report in September 1995, Bromwich said. Most importantly, the investigation found that Williams once again "based some of his conclusions not on a valid scientific analysis but on speculation from the evidence associated with the defendants." In that case, Williams testified that the main explosive agent was ammonium nitrate fuel oil. Bromwich said Williams based his testimony on the fact that one of the defendants—Terry Nichols—allegedly had purchased the fuel oil, rather than on a scientific examination of evidence from the bombing scene. Bromwich concluded that Williams should be assigned a job outside the crime lab because "he lacks the objectivity, judgment and scientific knowledge that should be possessed by a laboratory examiner."

The report cited several other laboratory officials whose work was sloppy or who had exaggerated their findings or otherwise acted improperly. He also noted instances in which supervisors had failed to correct problems. In one case, former lab director John J. Hicks gave a bonus check—along with a mild verbal reprimand—to an analyst whose work had been found to be seriously flawed. Bromwich recommended that some of these employees be reassigned or given new responsibilities; in several other cases the employees already had left the FBI.

Bromwich made numerous recommendations for "organizational and cultural changes" in the FBI crime lab. Some suggestions represented basic management reforms, such as improving the management of case files. Other recommendations called for more sweeping changes, such as revamping the structure and methods of the Explosives Unit.

FBI Response

In a statement made April 15, FBI deputy director Bill Esposito acknowledged that the agency had allowed "very serious" problems to develop at the crime lab and had not moved quickly enough to resolve them. Acknowledging the political damage the FBI had suffered, he told reporters: "I guess a good day is when we're not in the paper."

Esposito said the agency disagreed with some details in the report but accepted that major changes had to be made. He said the agency had begun to implement the changes suggested by Bromwich's investigation and had invited the inspector general to reinspect the crime lab every six months "until both he and the FBI are satisfied that all issues have been resolved."

Esposito defended the FBI's decision to place Whitehurst on administrative leave, noting that the Bromwich report had questioned whether he "could usefully serve any role in the FBI." The agency had asked the Justice Department Management Division to review the Bromwich report and decide what action to take in the cases of Whitehurst and the other individuals cited by the inspector general.

Esposito also said the FBI had initiated the process to have the crime lab accredited by the American Society of Crime Laboratory Directors/Laboratory Accreditation Board. Bromwich said the FBI should have sought accreditation a decade previously and that the accreditation process "should enhance quality performance."

> *Following are excerpts from the executive summary of a report issued April 15, 1997, by Michael R. Bromwich, inspector general of the Justice Department, on his investigation of the FBI crime laboratory:*

This investigation by the Department of Justice Office of the Inspector General (OIG) concerned allegations of wrongdoing and improper practices within certain sections of the Federal Bureau of Investigation (FBI) Laboratory. Those allegations involved some of the most significant prosecutions in the recent history of the Department of Justice, including the World Trade Center bombing, the Oklahoma City bombing, and the mail bomb assassination of U.S. Circuit Judge Robert Vance (which was referred to within the FBI as the VANPAC case). The allegations implicated fundamental aspects of law enforcement: the reliability of the procedures employed by the FBI Laboratory to analyze evidence, the integrity of the persons engaging in that analysis, and the trustworthiness of the testimony by FBI Laboratory examiners. The allegations were brought to the OIG's attention by Supervisory Special Agent Frederic Whitehurst, a Ph.D. scientist employed in the FBI Laboratory. We also investigated problems that we ourselves identified in the course of our investigation, as well as information brought to our attention by other employees in the Laboratory.

The investigation spanned more than eighteen months and addressed a very large number of allegations. Most of Whitehurst's allegations were not substantiated; some important ones were. Our investigation identified policies and practices in need of substantial change. Since the allegations involved incidents that occurred over nearly a decade, some of those policies had already been changed by the FBI or were in the process of being changed before the draft report was completed. In a number of key instances, we found problems that Whitehurst had not raised. We also saw examples of superb work and encountered Laboratory personnel dedicated to the highest traditions of forensic science. But we also found some Laboratory supervisors and examiners whose performance merits critical comment, and raises serious questions about whether they should continue in their current roles within the Laboratory. Accordingly, in addition to general recommendations we made about Laboratory practices and procedures, we recommended that certain supervisors and examiners be reassigned from their current positions.

This investigation and our findings primarily concerned three units of the FBI Laboratory—the Explosives Unit (EU), the Materials Analysis Unit (MAU), and the Chemistry-Toxicology Unit (CTU), all of which were in the Scientific Analysis Section (SAS), one of five sections of the Laboratory. Our findings and conclusions regarding certain cases in those units should not be imputed to other cases within those units, nor to other units in the SAS or other sections of the Laboratory that we did not investigate. . . .

I. Principal Findings and Recommendations

A. Findings Regarding Alleged Misconduct And Performance Deficiencies

We did not substantiate the vast majority of the hundreds of allegations made by Whitehurst, including the many instances in which he alleged that Laboratory examiners had committed perjury or fabricated evidence. We found, however, significant instances of testimonial errors, substandard analytical work, and deficient practices. . . . The types of problems we found included:

- Scientifically Flawed Testimony [in four cases, including the World Trade Center bombing case].
- Inaccurate Testimony by an EU examiner in the World Trade Center case, by a former Laboratory examiner (who is still an FBI agent) in a hearing conducted by the judicial committee of the Judicial Council of the Eleventh Circuit regarding then-Judge Alcee Hastings, and by the CTU Chief [in another case].
- Testimony Beyond the Examiner's Expertise [in three cases, including the World Trade Center case].
- Improper Preparation of Laboratory Reports by three EU examiners who altered, omitted, or improperly supplemented some of Whitehurst's internal reports (dictations) as they were being compiled into an official

report of the Laboratory. A former EU Chief failed to substantively review all of the reports in his unit, authorized EU examiners to modify Whitehurst's dictations when incorporating them into EU reports, and fostered a permissive attitude toward changes to Whitehurst's dictations.

- Insufficient Documentation of Test Results by the examiner who had performed work on hundreds of cases . . .
- Scientifically Flawed Reports . . . [in several cases].
- Inadequate Record Management and Retention System by the Laboratory.
- Failures by Management to resolve serious and credible allegations of incompetence lodged against the examiner who worked on [one case]; to review properly the EU report in the Oklahoma City case; to resolve scientific disagreements among Laboratory examiners in three cases . . . ; to establish and enforce validated procedures and protocols that might have avoided problems in examiner reports in [two cases]; and to making a commitment to pursuing accreditation by the American Society of Crime Laboratory Directors/Laboratory Accreditation Board before 1994.
- A Flawed Staffing Structure of the Explosives Unit that should be reconfigured so that examiners possess requisite scientific qualifications.

B. Findings and Recommendations Concerning Individuals

The OIG investigation exonerated most of the persons named in Whitehurst's allegations. Regarding some personnel, however, we criticized certain practices and performances in particular cases and recommended reassignments from their current positions and other actions. Our principal recommendations included:

- Because we recommended that the EU be restructured so that its unit chief and examiners have scientific backgrounds, EU Chief J. Thomas Thurman and all non-scientist EU examiners should be reassigned outside the Laboratory when the restructuring is accomplished. In the interim, the FBI should assess whether Thurman should continue to hold a supervisory position.
- CTU Chief Roger Martz should not hold a supervisory position in the Laboratory, and the FBI should assess whether he should continue to serve as a Laboratory examiner.
- EU examiner David Williams, who worked on the World Trade Center and Oklahoma City cases, should be reassigned outside the Laboratory.
- The FBI should assess what disciplinary action is now appropriate for Michael Malone, the former Laboratory examiner who testified in the Hastings hearing.
- We concluded that Frederic Whitehurst cannot effectively function within the Laboratory and suggested that the FBI consider what role, if any, he can usefully serve in other components of the FBI. In making

that determination, the FBI and the Department of Justice must weigh the significant contribution he has made by raising issues that needed to be addressed within the Laboratory against (1) the harm he has caused to innocent persons by making many inflammatory but unsubstantiated allegations, and (2) the doubts that exist about whether he has the requisite common sense and judgment to serve as a forensic examiner.

C. Recommendations Concerning Policies and Procedures

To enhance the quality of the Laboratory's forensic work, we made recommendations in the following areas: (1) accreditation, (2) restructuring the EU, (3) the roles of Laboratory examiners and resolutions of disputes, (4) report preparation, (5) peer review, (6) case documentation, (7) record retention, (8) examiner training and qualification, (9) examiner testimony, (10) protocols, (11) evidence handling, and (12) the role of management. In response to a draft of this Report, the FBI accepted full responsibility for the failings we identified within the Laboratory. The FBI's response concurred with nearly all of the OIG's recommendations and stated that the Laboratory has implemented or is taking steps to implement them. The FBI's response to the draft report is contained in an Appendix, along with our reply to specific points raised in its response.

II. The OIG Investigation

The OIG investigation essentially occurred in two phases. The first phase, lasting from 1994 to the summer of 1995, was limited in scope. As is detailed in the Report, during that period, allegations by Whitehurst were the subject of various reviews by the FBI Office of General Counsel (FBI OGC), the FBI Office of Professional Responsibility (FBI OPR), and the FBI Laboratory itself until mid-1995. The OIG's investigation in that period focused on Whitehurst's contentions that his analytical reports had been substantively altered by an EU examiner.

By the summer of 1995, after other scientists in the Laboratory confirmed certain aspects of Whitehurst's allegations, it became clear that a more global, comprehensive investigation was warranted. With the agreement of FBI Director Louis Freeh, and the full cooperation of the FBI, the OIG undertook such an investigation and retained an international panel of five scientific experts to consult with the OIG. Those experts, whose combined experience exceeds 100 years of work in forensic and national laboratories, have been integrally involved in the process of interviewing witnesses, reviewing documents, and writing this report. Four experienced prosecutors from United States Attorneys' Offices and the Criminal Division were detailed to the OIG to lead the investigation, and have provided considerable investigative expertise in this matter.

From the autumn of 1995 to the present, the OIG team has conducted hundreds of interviews, including re-interviews of key witnesses, and reviewed more than 60,000 pages of documents and transcripts. Upon completion of a draft report on January 21, 1997, the OIG solicited comments from the FBI and from prosecutors (primarily in the United States Attorneys' Offices) and other lawyers who handled the cases at issue to ensure that no factual errors were inadvertently included. The responses themselves, as well as our replies, are contained in a separate Appendix. In evaluating those responses, the OIG made some revisions to the Report. After careful consideration, in most instances we did not agree with requests to change the language in the draft report or our findings, and have explained our reasoning either in the Report itself or in the Appendix.

One general point about the responses bears highlighting in this summary. As to cases in which we criticize the work of FBI Laboratory personnel . . . the FBI and U.S. Attorneys have responded by saying, in essence, that nothing in the Report should be read as affecting the outcome of those cases. Our purpose has not been to determine whether a defendant in any given case was improperly convicted of a crime; it was to ascertain whether the performance of the Laboratory personnel met general standards of conduct for forensic scientists and complied with policies in the FBI Laboratory in effect at the time the work was performed. Our findings of deficiencies in the work performed in cases should in no circumstance be read as expressing a view as to whether that case should have reached a different outcome. That role is properly performed by the prosecutors, defense counsel, and judges who can assess the work of the FBI Laboratory in the context of all of the evidence in the case. We, therefore, concluded that it would be inappropriate for us to make any judgments as to whether our findings will or should affect a particular case. . . .

VIII. Conclusion

The FBI's cooperation with the OIG investigation and acceptance of our systemic recommendations should be lauded. The process of managing necessary changes will be challenging in an environment in which scientific knowledge is expanding and forensic science is increasingly under scrutiny. We welcome the FBI's suggestion of our continued involvement in oversight to assist in ensuring that needed reforms are fully implemented. We will seek to perform that function in a manner consistent with the Laboratory's expeditious efforts to obtain ASCLD/LAB [American Society of Crime Laboratory Directors/Laboratory Accreditation Board] accreditation and its ongoing development of first-class examiners and standards. Although we have rejected the most inflammatory allegations made by Whitehurst, the FBI Laboratory must fully acknowledge past problems that have been identified as it continues its pursuit of excellence in forensic science.

CLINTON ON RELIEF EFFORTS FOR RED RIVER FLOOD
April 22, 1997

A once-in-a-century flood of the Red River of the North hit the upper Midwest in April, devastating the cities of Grand Forks, North Dakota, and East Grand Forks, Minnesota. Tens of thousands of people were made homeless—many of them for several months—and individuals and businesses suffered property damage totaling several hundred millions of dollars. Remarkably, the massive flood led to no immediate deaths.

Visiting the scene of the flood on April 22, President Bill Clinton praised the dogged spirit of people whose lives had been turned upside down. Clinton promised swift delivery of federal aid and said he would ask Congress for more money to help people in North and South Dakota and Minnesota rebuild their communities. Clinton kept his promise, but Congress took nearly two months to pass emergency aid legislation. The result was a bruising battle in Washington that resulted in a major political victory for the president at the expense of the Republican congressional leadership, which appeared weak, opportunistic, and divided.

Blizzards Then Flood

The genesis of the Red River flood was in a series of mammoth blizzards over the winter of 1996–1997 on the Great Plains of the upper Midwest. At some points, houses were buried in snow nearly to their rooftops. When the snow began melting in early spring, the water ran into the Red River of the North, which forms the border between North Dakota and Minnesota then flows into Lake Winnipeg in Canada.

As the river rose, it flowed swiftly over the surrounding flat-as-a-pancake countryside. Starting south of Fargo, North Dakota, in late March, the river rose to twice the normal flood stage then rose even more dramatically as it coursed north toward Grand Forks. Levees built to contain the river made the flood even worse downstream (north) by speeding up the flow of water. Once the flooded river reached frozen Lake Winnipeg, it backed up, worsening the flooding to the south.

The levees, massive sandbagging, and other emergency flood control measures held the river at bay in the Grand Forks area for a few weeks but ultimately failed as the torrent of water surged north. By April 18 an estimated 70 percent of the city of Grand Forks was covered with water, and the 50,000 residents were told to leave their homes. On Saturday, April 19, fire broke out in a five-story office building in downtown Grand Forks and quickly spread to other buildings as fire fighters struggled to reach the flooded scene. The spectacle of buildings on fire, surrounded by water, added a grim irony to the tragedy of Grand Forks. A half-dozen buildings were destroyed in the fire, giving part of downtown the appearance of a bombed-out city.

The Red River ultimately crested in Grand Forks on April 22 at fifty-four feet, nearly twice the twenty-eight-foot flood stage. More than 3,000 people took refuge in giant aircraft hangers at the U.S. air force base west of Grand Forks. The Minnesota town of East Grand Forks was almost entirely flooded, and its residents were forced to seek emergency shelter fifty or even one hundred miles away.

President Clinton arrived in Grand Forks as the flood crested on April 22. After touring the watery scene by helicopter for a half-hour, Clinton spoke to residents and relief workers at the air force base. Clinton praised the resilience and determination of those who had suffered. "We have hardly ever seen such a remarkable demonstration of courage and commitment and cooperation and basic human strength, and we are very impressed and proud to be Americans when we see what you have done in the face of this terrible disaster," he told the crowd. The president noted, for example, the local newspaper, the Grand Forks Herald, *which kept publishing even after its building was flooded. "How in the world they keep producing the newspaper for you is beyond me," he said. "And you ought to be very proud of them for doing that."*

Accompanied by several cabinet members and agency directors, Clinton promised a massive infusion of federal aid. He said he would ask Congress to approve an additional $200 million for the two Dakotas and Minnesota, bringing the total of both short-term and long-term aid to $488 million. The government, he said, will "be there with you every step of the way."

In another meeting with state and local officials, Clinton acknowledged that federal aid could not possibly wipe out the impact of the disaster on thousands of people. "I know that $488 million or $4 billion wouldn't make that go away," he said.

By November, when the water was long gone and cleanup had given way to fix-up, the Herald *reported that nearly 90 percent of the area's single-family homes had been damaged by the flood; an estimated 600 to 800 were no longer livable, and about one-third of all rentals units had been damaged. The Federal Emergency Management Agency had 3,500 applications for funding, the paper reported.*

Congress Stumbles on Aid

Clinton almost immediately made good on his promise, sending Congress catchall legislation asking for $5.6 billion for disaster aid to thirty-five states, including the Red River flood area. Disaster-aid bills normally represent must-pass legislation in Congress and often become vehicles to which lawmakers attach unrelated items that might not make it into law on their own merit.

In that spirit, the Republican leadership in Congress immediately seized on Clinton's request as an opportunity to apply political leverage on the president. Republicans attached to the aid legislation two politically sensitive items they knew the president would not otherwise accept. One would have prohibited the Census Bureau from using sampling techniques that were intended to improve the year 2000 census count of residents in urban areas; Republicans feared these techniques would boost the count of Democratic-leaning residents in inner cities. The other Republican-sponsored measure would have guaranteed that funding would flow at current levels to any federal agency whose regular appropriations bill had not become law by the October 1 start of the fiscal year. Republicans hoped this provision would avoid partial shutdowns of the federal government, such as the two that occurred in 1995 when Republicans went nose-to-nose with Clinton on budget issues. Most surveys showed that voters blamed Republicans for the 1995 government shutdowns, and so the Republicans were anxious to deny the political leverage that any future budget crisis might provide Clinton. (1995 budget battles, Historic Documents of 1995, p. 737)

Despite the political opportunities offered by the aid legislation, Congress moved slowly, not giving final approval until June 5. Even then, the Republican leadership delayed sending the bill to Clinton for several days. The bill finally reached the White House on the afternoon of June 9, when Clinton had a lengthy and hard-hitting veto message ready. White House aides claimed Clinton vetoed the bill and sent it back to Congress within nineteen minutes. Their bluff called, the congressional Republicans quickly folded and agreed to strip from the aid legislation the measures Clinton opposed. Congress cleared a new aid bill to the president's liking on June 12, and he signed it a few hours later. As he signed the bill, Clinton clenched his fist in the air. On Capitol Hill Republicans blamed each other for the political loss they had suffered from the watery disaster of the Red River of the North.

Following is the text of remarks made April 22, 1997, at the Grand Forks Air Force Base by President Bill Clinton to residents and relief workers in the area around the Red River of the North:

Let me begin by thanking everyone who is a part of the Grand Forks Air Force Base for what you do for our national security, and especially for what you have done to support the people of the Grand Forks community in these last few days. I'm very proud of you. Thank you.

As I think all of you know, I have just come from viewing the devastation of the floods as well at a very moving community meeting, presided over by Mayor Owens, attended by Mayor Stauss and other mayors, the entire congressional delegation from North Dakota and from South Dakota, Senator [Rod] Grams and Senator [Paul] Wellstone from Minnesota, Congressman Colin Peterson from Minnesota, and the Governors from North Dakota and Minnesota.

It has been a very moving experience for all of us. Five members of my Cabinet are here, the Secretaries of Agriculture, Health and Human Services, Housing and Urban Development, Transportation, and the Administrator of the Small Business Administration. The Secretary of the Army is here. We have all come, first of all, to see firsthand what it is you've been going through; secondly, to pledge to do our part to help make you whole; and thirdly, to tell you that we're for you.

We have hardly ever seen such a remarkable demonstration of courage and commitment and cooperation and basic human strength, and we are very impressed and proud to be Americans when we see what you have done in the face of this terrible disaster.

We know that this rebuilding is going to be a long-term prospect, and we also know that there are some very immediate and pressing human needs that many people have. Before I left this morning, I took some steps I wanted to tell you about. First, I authorized James Lee Witt and the Federal Emergency Management Agency [FEMA] to provide 100 percent of the direct federal assistance for all the emergency.

The second thing we did was to add to the counties already covered another 18 counties in Minnesota and 53 in South Dakota who need help.

The third thing I did was to ask Congress to approve another $200 million in emergency funds for North Dakota, South Dakota and Minnesota. These funds will be available for both short-term emergency response activities and for long-term efforts to help you rebuild. If approved, this action will bring to $488 million the total amount of disaster assistance that I have requested for the people of these three states.

Now, let me say there are—I say again, I know there are short-term and immediate concerns—people who need a place to sleep, people who don't know where their next check is coming from, even people who don't have access to basic sanitary facilities except here on the Air Base. We are working to restore those things with your local community folks. And we had some specific talks about what we could do to get proper housing available while you're rebuilding your communities.

So anyway, we'll have our folks here, and there will be lots of them. And let me just say, this is going to be—these next few days—our FEMA Director, James Lee Witt, and I have been working on these things a long time. He was my emergency director when I was Governor of Arkansas. I know what's going to happen. I've been through floods and tornadoes and terrible losses.

The next few days are going to be very, very hard on a lot of people. A lot of you who have been very, very brave and courageous, helped your friends and neighbors are going to—it's going to sink in on you what you have been through and what has been lost. And I want to encourage all of you to really look out for each other in the next few days and be sensitive to the enormous emotional pressures that some of you will feel, and also be good to yourselves. Understand you don't have to be ashamed if you're heartbroken. But it's going to be tough in the next few days.

But I also want you to feel very resolute about the long run. I have asked Director Witt to head an interagency task force to develop a long-term plan for what our responsibilities are to help you rebuild and be stronger and better than ever. And believe me, it may be hard to believe now, but you can rebuild stronger and better than ever. And we're going to help you do that. And we want you to keep your eyes on that future.

Let me also say, as I go back to Washington to ask the Congress to approve this emergency package, I will never forget what I have seen and heard here. Four of your community leaders who played various roles in the last several weeks—Ken Vein, Jim Shothorse, Randy Johnson and Curt Kruen—talked to me and to others in the meeting a few moments ago. I have seen the pictures of people battling the flames of the fire in the rising floods. I have seen rescue workers working around the clock even as they lost their own homes. I have seen people pitching in to rescue books from the University of North Dakota library.

I have read the last three days editions of this newspaper. How in the world they kept producing the newspaper for you is beyond me. And you ought to be very proud of them for doing that.

I read this morning that there's a message board right here that's covered with offers for free housing all around. And that's the kind of spirit that will get everyone through this.

With all the losses, I hope when this is bearing down on you in the next few days, you will remember the enormous courage and shared pride and values and support that all of you have given each other. You have shown that when we think of our duties to one another, our own lives are better; that we're all stronger when we try to make sure our friends and neighbors are safe and strong as well.

And no matter what you have lost in this terrible flood, what you have saved and strengthened and sharpened and shown to the world is infinitely better. And you should be very, very proud of that.

I saw something your Mayor said the other day that struck me in particular. She said, what makes a community a place to live in is not the buildings, it's the people—the spirit and faith that are in those people. Water cannot wash that away, and fire cannot burn that away, and a blizzard cannot freeze that away. And if you don't give it away, it will bring you back better than ever. And we'll be there with you every step of the way.

Thank you and God bless you.

JAPANESE PRIME MINISTER ON PERUVIAN HOSTAGE CRISIS
April 23, 1997

A hostage crisis that had threatened the political and economic stability of Peru came to an end April 22 with the dramatic rescue of six dozen diplomats, government officials, and businessmen who had been held by leftist guerrillas at the Japanese ambassador's residence in Lima. After four months of inconclusive efforts to resolve the crisis diplomatically, the Peruvian military stormed the building, safely rescuing all but one of the seventy-two hostages and killing all fourteen Marxist rebels who had held them.

At a press conference April 23, Japanese prime minister Ryutaro Hashimoto, whose government had worked hard to resolve the crisis, thanked Peru's president, Alberto K. Fujimori, for the successful rescue. Hashimoto noted, however, that his government had not been notified in advance of the rescue attempt, despite a promise by the Peruvian government to consult with Tokyo before taking any military action.

The rescue immediately boosted the popularity of Fujimori (himself of Japanese descent), whose strong-arm governing tactics had been under constant attack both at home and abroad. But in subsequent weeks Fujimori launched a new crackdown on his political opponents and the news media, driving his popularity to a new low. Critics accused him of trying to force his way into a third term as president in 1999.

Drawn-Out Crisis

The Peruvian crisis began December 17, 1996, when fourteen armed men from the Tupac Amaru Revolutionary Movement burst into the Japanese ambassador's residence in Lima during a cocktail party. More than 500 diplomats, Peruvian government officials, business leaders, and other dignitaries were taken hostage. The next day the guerrillas, representing a Marxist faction, threatened to kill the hostages systematically unless the government released other Tupac Amaru rebels who were in prison. Fujimori refused the demand and allowed the guerrillas' deadline to pass.

By New Years Day the guerrillas had released most of their captives, including ambassadors and other senior diplomats from a dozen countries. Under pressure from Tokyo to resolve the crisis swiftly and peacefully, Fujimori's government opened direct talks with the guerrillas on February 15. In the meantime, the Peruvian military trained special forces for a rescue attempt, and miners began digging tunnels under the residence. The government also launched an intense intelligence-gathering effort, placing microphones and cameras in the building to probe for weaknesses in the guerrillas' operation. A U.S. intelligence plane flew over the residence daily, taking aerial photographs and monitoring conversations in the building. The knowledge gathered from these devices enabled the military to learn the location of each hostage and the habits of the guerrillas.

Attempting to convince his people and the rest of the world—especially the Japanese government—that he was doing everything possible to resolve the crisis, Fujimori opened several diplomatic channels, including meeting in Washington with President Bill Clinton and in Canada with Prime Minister Hashimoto. In the most surprising move of all, Fujimori flew to Cuba on April 3 and secured an offer of asylum for the rebels from Fidel Castro.

In midafternoon April 22, as the guerrillas were relaxing, Peruvian commandos set off plastic explosives beneath the building, blowing holes in the floors and walls. The heavily armed commandos stormed the building, rescued the hostages, and killed all fourteen guerrillas, including their leader, Nestor Cerpa Cartolini. Only one hostage, Peruvian Supreme Court justice Carlos Guisti, died, from complications resulting from a gunshot wound to a leg. Two soldiers also were killed.

A triumphant Fujimori visited the residence shortly after the raid and told reporters "there was no other way out" of the hostage crisis. Fujimori said he mourned the deaths of Justice Guisti and the two soldiers, but he pointedly excluded mentioning any sympathy for the guerrillas.

In the days following the rescue, there were reports that the commandos killed and even mutilated some guerrillas after they had surrendered. Television footage taken immediately after the rescue appeared to show that the bodies of some guerrillas had been dismembered. The government refused to allow families to bury the dead guerrillas.

Fujimori Lashes out at Critics

The success of the hostage rescue temporarily strengthened Fujimori's domestic standing, but the president's critics noted that the raid further indebted him to the generals who planned and executed it. Opposition figures for years had charged that Fujimori's power was based on the support of army generals and the Peruvian intelligence services.

The widespread praise for Fujimori's handling of the hostage crisis faded in the following months as his government moved against his critics. In a series of actions, Fujimori forced from office three supreme court justices who had declared that it would be unconstitutional for him to seek a third term in 1999; his intelligence service placed wiretaps on telephones

of domestic and foreign journalists and prominent critics; and the govern-
ment revoked the citizenship of the Israeli-born owner of a television sta-
tion that exposed the wiretaps. In the public uproar over these incidents,
five cabinet members resigned, including the foreign minister, the defense
minister, and the justice minister.

Addressing the congress on July 28—Peru's independence day—Fuji-
mori acknowledged that the country was in a "confused political situation"
but denied rumors that he was being controlled by the military and the
intelligence services. In an apparent attempt to build public support and
assuage the concerns of domestic and overseas business interests, Fujimori
announced plans for several tax cuts, coupled with pay increases for pub-
lic employees. Critics said the measures would be of only marginal help to
a deeply troubled economy in which more than half the population lived
below the official poverty level.

> *Following is the text of a press conference April 23, 1997, by*
> *Japanese prime minister Ryutaro Hashimoto following the suc-*
> *cessful freeing of all but one of seventy-two hostages held at the*
> *residence of the Japanese ambassador to Peru:*

Special forces of the Peruvian military stormed the Japanese Ambassador's Residence in the Republic of Peru at 3:23 p.m. yesterday Peru time.

The Cabinet immediately called for a meeting of the Headquarters and
gathered information while keeping a close watch on the developments of the
situation at the Ambassador's Residence. At 6:43 this morning Japan time
Ambassador Aoki was able to speak directly with me on the phone after being
rescued. All of the Japanese hostages were safely rescued, and a few of them
have sustained light injuries. However, none of those are serious. Right now
we are in the process of confirming everyone, one-by-one, and determining
the degree of their injuries.

Unfortunately, Japan was not informed prior to the initiation of this rescue
operation.

While I must say that it is regrettable that Japan did not learn of the action
in advance, I would like once again to express my gratitude to President
Alberto Fujimori and the other members of the Government of Peru who
seized the opportunity and carried out this remarkable rescue operation.

Among the media reports that have come out, there are some reports that
some of the Peruvian military personnel involved have been killed and
wounded. My heart grieves for the dead and wounded and for their bereaved
families.

Ambassador Aoki, and Mrs. Aoki, whom I also spoke with on the phone,
were in extremely good spirits. It seems that Ambassador Aoki has a slight
injury to his elbow, but he sounded great and told me that "it is just a slight
scratch."

The Ambassador said that he intends personally to visit all of the hospitals where the injured are. At any rate, efforts to confirm the safety of all involved have already begun.

The Government of Japan has decided to dispatch Foreign Minister Ikeda to Lima today in order to take any measures which will be necessary following what has happened.

If the situation is as it seems to be, there probably is no need for the medical team which we prepared in advance. Still, considering that those hostages who were held for such a long time may be prone to fatigue after they are relieved, I have given instructions that preparations be made to dispatch the medical team as well. Also, I have instructed the Chairman of the National Public Safety Commission and the Director-General of the National Police Agency to prepare to send their staff members to Lima to investigate and confirm everything that has occurred since the incident broke out.

I have given you a report on the situation as it is and I am glad to be able to share with you the joyous news that the hostages are all right. Furthermore, although the reports are still not confirmed, if it is true that some of the members of the Peruvian military who participated in this rescue operation have been killed or injured, then I would like to express my heartfelt condolences and prayers that their injuries are light ones.

We will be reporting on the situation to the countries who have been so generous with assistance during this incident and to thank them. I would like to express my deep gratitude to the many individuals who, in this extremely difficult situation, showed their goodwill and gave us their cooperation. That is all that I have to tell you now.

Question: Earlier just now you said that there was no prior notification. How did you learn of the storming by the Peruvian military forces.

Hashimoto: As of 5:30 a.m., I had not yet heard, but I received a phone call immediately after the reports of the storming came through.

Question: Who called you?

Hashimoto: I received calls from several of my assistants and from the Headquarters. I will take only one more question.

Question: You stated that you hoped to see a peaceful solution. However, in fact the military forces stormed the residence. What are your thoughts on that?

Hashimoto: We truly hoped that this situation would end without incident and not through a forced storming of the Residence. Still, those were the thoughts of people in a location separated by 14 time zones from those who were there watching the situation. It is natural that there was a difference. I wonder if there is anyone who could criticize President Fujimori for the use of force now that the hostages have been safely rescued, whether or not there was prior notification.

CLINTON AND OTHER LEADERS
AT VOLUNTEERISM SUMMIT
April 28, 1997

President Bill Clinton, several of his predecessors, and a host of American political and civic leaders met in Philadelphia for three days in late April and pledged new volunteer efforts to help the nation's 15 million disadvantaged children. Formally called the Presidents' Summit for America's Future, the gathering was a high-profile attempt to spark new interest in voluntary charity by corporations, organizations, and individuals.

In the following months, several hundred corporations made commitments of time and money toward various programs intended to help at least 2 million youth. Sponsors of the summit said those commitments demonstrated that Americans still believe that private charitable works can make a difference in peoples' lives. Skeptics said the focus on volunteerism masked the fact that the federal government was cutting back its spending on social programs, and they insisted that some corporations were more interested in public relations bonuses than in helping poverty-stricken children.

The Philadelphia Summit

Former Michigan governor and Republican presidential aspirant George Romney conceived the idea of a national "summit" meeting to promote volunteerism. Romney died in 1995, but other national leaders carried through with his proposal. Among them was retired general Colin Powell, who served as chairman of the Joint Chiefs of Staff under Presidents George Bush and Clinton. Powell chaired the summit that convened in Philadelphia on April 27. In addition to Clinton, attendees included Vice President Al Gore and three former presidents: Gerald R. Ford, Jimmy Carter, and Bush. Nancy Reagan represented her ailing husband, former president Ronald Reagan. Thirty governors, more than one hundred mayors, and several thousand civic leaders also attended.

Clinton, Gore, Carter, Bush, Powell, and hundreds of others donned special T-shirts on April 27 to put action behind their words. Working in teams, they cleaned up garbage, renovated playgrounds, and painted over graffiti along an eight-mile stretch of Germantown Avenue that ran through rough neighborhoods of north Philadelphia. During the three days of the summit, delegates attended rallies and small-group meetings where they discussed the needs of disadvantaged youth and various ways of meeting those needs.

In the course of the meetings, the presidents appeared to have differing notions about the state of American society and the role of government. In statements and interviews, Carter painted a grim view of "two Americas"—one of "the rich people" holding good jobs and living in attractive neighborhoods and the other of poor people struggling against long odds to make ends meet. Although a dedicated volunteer himself for many years, Carter said volunteer efforts were not enough to help the downtrodden improve their lives. Bush, in comments echoed by some of the other summit leaders, seemed to focus more on promoting the benefits volunteers themselves could reap by "giving something back" to society.

Summit organizers, led by Powell, identified five general areas in which they said volunteers could help the nation's disadvantaged youth reach a better life: providing mentors, creating safe places for afterschool activities, promoting adequate health care, helping develop job skills, and giving youth the opportunity to help others through community service. Powell said the summit's goal was to help 2 million youth in all five categories by the year 2000.

Clinton and the former presidents (along with Nancy Reagan representing her husband) signed a "Summit Declaration" saying that the problems of children "require a special commitment of us all. People of all ages and from all walks of life must claim society's problems as their own, pulling together, leading by example, and lifting American lives."

Addressing a rally of 3,000 people at Independence Hall on April 28, Clinton proposed doubling the number of young adults serving in AmeriCorps, the domestic version of the Peace Corps, from 25,000 to 50,000. AmeriCorps provided scholarships and paid living expenses for young people performing community service. Clinton said the number of volunteers could be doubled if churches and other charitable groups paid for the living expenses of AmeriCorps volunteers.

Powell told the summit attendees that—while government, corporate, and organizational programs were vital—the efforts of individuals could make the most important contributions to the lives of disadvantaged children. "All of us can spare 30 minutes a week or an hour a week," he said. "All of us can give an extra dollar. All of us can touch someone who doesn't look like us, who doesn't speak like us, who may not dress like us, but, by God, needs us in their lives."

Follow-Through

Powell chaired a volunteer organization, "America's Promise: The Alliance for Youth," that coordinated volunteer pledges by states and local-

239

ities, corporations, and nonprofit organizations to follow through on the Philadelphia meeting. In a "Report to the Nation" dated November 25, 1997, Powell said the alliance had received more than 300 "national commitments" from major corporations, such as Oracle Corp. and Cisco Systems, and national voluntary organizations. Twelve states (Kentucky, Louisiana, Maryland, Massachusetts, Michigan, Mississippi, Oklahoma, Texas, Utah, West Virginia, Wisconsin, and Wyoming) had held statewide volunteerism summits, he said, as had forty-one communities. "America's Promise is this nation's best chance to improve our children's lives for the better," Powell's report said. "It is a unique opportunity to make compassion count."

News media reports showed that many of the volunteer commitments cited by Powell were, indeed, new ones spawned by the enthusiasm of the Philadelphia summit. But the New York Times *noted that some of the "commitments" cited by Powell's organization had originated well before the summit or were reformulations of volunteer programs that had been in effect for years. The* Times *noted, for example, that the accounting firm KPMG Peat Marwick gave 20,000 employees September 22 as a day off, called "World of Spirit Day," so they could volunteer in schools, hospitals, nursing homes, and other locations. The program was cited as one of the 300 new "commitments" stemming from the volunteer summit, but KPMG Peat Marwick had planned it more than a year before the summit, the* Times *reported. News media reports also quoted some academic experts as saying that much of the philanthropy touted by Powell was little more than corporate self-promotion with little lasting impact on those in need.*

Following is the text of the "Summit Declaration" signed on April 28, 1997, by President Bill Clinton and his living predecessors, followed by excerpts from speeches made by retired general Colin Powell and Clinton on April 28 in Philadelphia at the Presidents' Summit for America's Future:

SUMMIT DECLARATION

Two centuries ago, America was founded on the proposition that just as all people are endowed by their Creator with inalienable rights, citizenship entails undeniable responsibilities. As each of us has the right to Life, Liberty and the Pursuit of Happiness, each of us has an obligation to give something back to our country and community—a duty to take responsibility not just for ourselves and our families, but for one another. We owe a debt of service to fulfill the God-given promise of America and our children.

In this time of opportunity—at the down of a new century and a new millennium—the need for shared responsibility is self-evident.

The challenges of today, especially those that confront out children, require a special commitment of us all. People of all ages and from all walks of life must claim society's problems as their own, pulling together, leading by example, and lifting American lives.

Our obligation, distinct and unmistakable, is to assure that all young Americans have:

- Caring adults in their lives, as parents, mentors, tutors, coaches.
- Safe places with structured activities in which to learn and grow.
- A healthy start and healthy future.
- An effective education that equips them with marketable skills.
- An opportunity to give back to their communities through their own service.

As Americans and as presidents, we ask every caring citizen to pledge individual commitments of citizen service, voluntary action, the efforts of their organizations, or commitments to individual children in need By doing so, this nation pledges the fulfillment of America's promise for every American child.

THE PRESIDENTS OF THE UNITED STATES OF AMERICA
Gerald R. Ford
James Earl Carter
Ronald W. Reagan (by Mrs. Nancy Reagan)
George H. W. Bush
William Jefferson Clinton

REMARKS BY GENERAL POWELL

The great American poet, Langston Hughes, talked about a dream deferred, and he said, "What happens to a dream deferred? Does it dry up like a raisin in the sun, or fester like a sore and then run? Does it stink like rotten meat or crust and sugar over like a syrupy sweet? Maybe it just sags, like a heavy load. Or, does it explode?"

For too many young Americans, that dream deferred does sag like a heavy load that's pushing them down into the ground, and they wonder if they can rise up with that load. And as we see too often in our daily life, it does explode in violence, in youngsters falling dead, shot by other youngsters. It does explode, and it has the potential to explode our society.

So today, we gather here today to pledge that the dream must no longer be deferred and it will never, as long as we can do anything about it, become a dream denied. That is why we are here, my friends. We gather here to pledge that those of us who are more fortunate will not forsake those who are less fortunate. We are a compassionate and caring people. We are a generous people. We will reach down, we will reach back, we will reach across to help our brothers and sisters who are in need.

Above all, we pledge to reach out to the most vulnerable members of the American family, our children. As you've heard, up to 15 million young Americans today are at risk. They are at risk of growing up unskilled, unlearned or, even worse, unloved. They are at risk of growing up physically or psychologically abused. They are at risk of growing up addicted to the pathologies and poisons of the street. They are at risk of bringing up children into the world before they, themselves have grown up. They are at risk of never growing up at all. Fifteen million young lives are at risk, may not make it unless we care enough to do something about it.

In terms of numbers, the task may seem staggering. But if we look at the simple needs that these children have, then the task is manageable, the goal is achievable. We know what they need. They need an adult caring person in their life, a safe place to learn and grow, a healthy start, marketable skills and an opportunity to serve so that early in their lives they learn the virtue of service so that they can reach out then and touch another young American in need.

These are basic needs that we commit ourselves today, we promise today. We are making America's promise today to provide to those children in need. This is a grand alliance. It is an alliance between government and corporate America and nonprofit America, between our institutions of faith, but especially between individual Americans.

You heard the governors and the mayors, and you'll hear more in a little minute that says the real answer is for each and every one of us, not just here in Philadelphia, but across this land—for each and every one of us to reach out and touch someone in need.

All of us can spare 30 minutes a week or an hour a week. All of us can give an extra dollar. All of us can touch someone who doesn't look like us, who doesn't speak like us, who may not dress like us, but, by God, needs us in their lives. And that's what we all have to do to keep this going.

And so there's a spirit of Philadelphia here today. There's a spirit of Philadelphia that we saw yesterday in Germantown. There is a spirit of Philadelphia that will leave Philadelphia tomorrow afternoon and spread across this whole nation—30 governors will go back and spread it; over 100 mayors will go back and spread it, and hundreds of others, leaders around this country who are watching will go back and spread it. Corporate America will spread it, nonprofits will spread it. And each and every one of us will spread it because it has to be done, we have no choice. We cannot leave these children behind if we are going to meet the dreams of our founding fathers.

And so let us all join in this great crusade. Let us make sure that no child in America is left behind, no child in America has their dream deferred or denied. We can do it. We can do it because we are Americans. We are Americans who draw our strength from this place. We are Americans who believe to the depth of our hearts that this is not a land that was put here by historic accident, it is a land that was put here by Divine Providence who told us to be good stewards of the land, but especially to be good stewards of each other. Divine Providence gave us this land, blessed it and told us always to be proud to call it America.

And so we go forward. Let's go save our children. Thank you very much.

REMARKS BY PRESIDENT CLINTON

We cherish our citizen volunteers. There are already more than 90 million of us, and after this summit there will be more. Especially because General Powell, Ray Chambers and others have organized a follow-up to this. And the really important work of this summit will begin after my talk's over, when you go into the workshops and the meetings and make a commitment that in every community there will be a systematic, disciplined, comprehensive effort to deal with the five areas outlined as the challenges for our young people. That is what really matters here.

Young people, above all, however, have the time, the energy and the idealism for this kind of citizen service. Before they have their own families, the young can make a unique contribution to the family of America. In doing so, they can acquire the habit of service and get a deeper understanding of what it really means to be a citizen. That is the main reason, perhaps, we are here.

In Philadelphia, the Superintendent of Schools is working to make service the expected thing in elementary and middle schools. Maryland has required it in high school. And I challenge every state and every school in this country at least to offer in a disciplined, organized way every young person in school a chance to serve. A recent survey said if they were just asked, over 90 percent of them would do it. We ought to be ashamed of ourselves if we don't give them the chance to do that.

Let me also say, of course, that we need some of them to serve full-time. They do, you know, in the Peace Corps. And we have some former Peace Corps volunteers out there applauding. But we should all applaud them because they have helped to change the world for the better. And they do in AmeriCorps, the national service program that was started in our administration. The idea behind AmeriCorps was to instill an ethic of mutual responsibility in our children so that young people could improve their own lives in return for improving the life of America.

Since its creation, 50,000 young Americans have earned college tuition by serving their communities in many ways. And we know that the typical full-time community servant recruits at least a dozen more volunteers. I saw that in North Dakota when I went to see what the Red River had done to Grand Forks and to the rest of North Dakota and Minnesota. I saw our young AmeriCorps volunteers and I knew that because they were able to serve full-time they'd be there when the waters receded, the mess was there, the people had to put their lives back together and the cameras were gone. I saw it again yesterday when we were working on the streets and on the stadium and on the schools.

The will to serve has never been stronger and more of our young people want to serve full-time. But there's a limit to what we can do now. And, yet, there is a solution—ironically, one I came to right here in Philadelphia. For here in Philadelphia a minister who is a friend of mine, Reverend Tony Campolo, is helping to organize a movement among churches to get churches to sponsor 10,000 full-time youth volunteers to take a year off from college or defer a year from college under the sponsorship of their churches.

The churches will do what we do in AmeriCorps, helping to provide for the living expenses of the young people. But I think we ought to say to them, at the very least, it shouldn't cost you any money to serve. And so if you've got a college loan and you take a year off to serve under the sponsorship of a religious organization, I'm going to propose legislation to say during that year no interest should accrue on that college loan. It should not cost you any money to serve your country.

But we can do more. We can double the impact of AmeriCorps with the help of our religious and charitable institutions. I want to challenge every charity, every religious group, every community group and their business supporters to give young people the support they need to do a year of community service. If you do that, then in our budget now we will be able to give every one of them the scholarship that AmeriCorps volunteers get for their year of community service. Work with your churches, work with your community organizations, and we can provide that to young people.

Put them to work as mentors, as teachers, as organizers of other volunteers, and we can double the number of full-time youth volunteers by adding another 50,000. By the year 2000, that would mean that in eight years, more children will have served full-time on our streets than have worked in the entire history of the Peace Corps around the world. We can change America, folks, if we'll do it together, hand in hand, community by community.

The same thing is true of the police corps, which offers young people a chance to pay for their college education if they'll be police officers for four years. We can triple the number of young people who do that, and I intend to try. We need more young people going as teachers into our schools. And we must support them in that.

We have to understand that we need a balance between volunteers on a part-time basis, volunteers on a full-time basis, and there is no conflict between the two. We have to understand that we value America's free enterprise system, we know we need our government, but there will never be a time when we need citizen servants more than we need them today, because these children have got to be saved one by one.

And let me say to all of you, the most important people here today are not the Presidents or the General or the governors or the senators. The most important people are those who teach the student to read; who save the health of the infant; who give help to families when all help seems gone. The most important title today is not Senator, Vice President, General, Governor or President. It is, as Harry Truman reminded us so long ago, the most important title any of us will ever hold in this country is the title of citizen.

This is our republic. Let us keep it. Thank you.

SENTENCING COMMISSION ON MINIMUM COCAINE PENALTIES
April 29, 1997

Following the lead of the U.S. Sentencing Commission, the Clinton administration in 1997 recommended to Congress that it reduce the disparities in mandatory penalties for crack and powder cocaine but not eliminate them altogether. Under existing law, a person convicted of selling 5 grams of crack cocaine must be sentenced to a minimum of five years in prison; the trigger for powder cocaine was 500 grams.

The two forms of cocaine are chemically similar. Powder cocaine (cocaine hydrochloride), which is usually snorted or injected, is refined from alkaloids extracted from coca leaves. Crack (or base cocaine) is smoked and is manufactured from powder cocaine in a simple process that involves cooking it with water and baking soda. Crack first made its appearance on the drug scene in the early 1980s and, because it was cheaper than powder cocaine, was popular among young, disadvantaged drug users, often from inner cities. White drug users tended to use powder cocaine.

Congress approved the harsher penalties for crack in 1986, after a public outcry about the high levels of violence associated with crack, both among its users and among dealers trying to corner a share of the crack market. The higher penalties for crack soon raised questions of fairness and discrimination—nearly 90 percent of those convicted in 1993 of selling crack were black. The disparity also raised questions about allocation of scarce law-enforcement resources and about treating small drug dealers as harshly or more harshly than mid- and high-level drug traffickers.

Responding to these concerns, Congress in 1994 asked the U.S. Sentencing Commission to review the matter and report back with recommendations. The commission, which is charged with ensuring uniform sentencing in federal courts, recommended in May 1995 that the quantity trigger for crack be reduced and made the same as that for powder cocaine, with harsher sentences available for crack convictions to reflect the greater violence and other dangers associated with crack. Congress rejected those recommendations later in 1995, triggering outrage among civil rights groups and a week of unrest at a handful of federal prisons.

Sentencing Commission's Report

In rejecting the commission's recommendations, Congress asked the panel to try again, directing it in effect to maintain higher penalties for crack than for powder cocaine. In its second report, issued April 29, the commission said its members were "unanimous in reiterating" that "although research and public policy may support somewhat higher penalties for crack than for powder cocaine, a 100-to-1 quantity ratio cannot be justified." The commission then recommended that the quantity of crack cocaine triggering the minimum mandatory sentence be reduced to between 125 and 375 grams and that the quantity for powder cocaine be raised to between 25 and 75 grams. It further recommended that the penalty for simple possession (possession without the intent to sell) of crack cocaine be made the same as that for powder cocaine.

These recommendations, the commission said, would reflect the dangers caused by both forms of the drug, while easing the "perception of unfairness and inconsistency" associated with the existing disparity. The narrower gap between penalties for the two drugs would also refocus federal priorities on "curbing interstate and international drug trafficking and violent crime" while leaving enforcement of drug laws against low-level offenders caught with street-level amounts of crack with the states, where such cases could be handled more economically and effectively. "It is the view of the Sentencing Commission that current federal cocaine policy inappropriately targets limited federal resources by placing the quantity triggers for the five-year mandatory minimum penalty for crack cocaine too low," the panel said.

Administration Recommendation

After reviewing the commission's recommendations, Attorney General Janet Reno and the White House drug policy director, Gen. Barry R. McCaffrey, retired, recommended that the quantity triggers be set at 250 grams for crack and 25 grams for powder cocaine, narrowing the gap to a 10-to-1 ratio. President Bill Clinton accepted their recommendation on July 22.

In their letter to the president, dated July 3, Reno and McCaffrey said the penalty disparity "has become an important symbol of racial injustice in our criminal justice system. We cannot turn a blind eye to the corrosive effect this has had on respect for the law in certain communities and on the effective administration of justice." Reno and McCaffrey essentially agreed with the sentencing commission that federal law enforcement efforts had been diverted from going after serious drug offenders because it was so much easier to get long prison terms for low-level users and pushers of crack. They added that much of the violence associated with the crack drug trade had leveled off, eroding the original rationale for imposing harsher penalties.

The administration recommendations immediately drew fire from the Congressional Black Caucus, which said that the disparities should be erased altogether. "We believe that strong law enforcement is a must," Rep. Maxine Waters, D-Calif., the caucus chairwoman, said at a June 23 news conference. "But we believe that enforcement must be just and fair. There is no rationale for a disparity in what triggers a mandatory minimum sentence for cocaine possession." Congress had not acted on the recommendation by the end of the year.

Following are excerpts from the report entitled "Cocaine and Federal Sentencing Policy," released April 29, 1997, by the U.S. Sentencing Commission:

I. Introduction

Federal sentencing policy for cocaine offenses has come under extensive criticism during the past few years. Public officials, private citizens, criminal justice practitioners, researchers, and interest groups have all challenged the fairness and efficacy of the current approach to sentencing cocaine offenses. Critics have focused on the differences in federal penalty levels between the two principal forms of cocaine—powder (cocaine hydrochloride) and crack (cocaine base)—and on the disproportionate impact the more severe crack penalties have had on African American defendants.

In 1994, these concerns led Congress, in the Violent Crime Control and Law Enforcement Act of 1994, to direct the Sentencing Commission to issue a report and recommendations on cocaine and federal sentencing policy. On February 28, 1995, the Commission issued a comprehensive report to Congress in which it unanimously recommended that changes be made to the current cocaine sentencing scheme, including a reduction in the 100-to-1 quantity ratio between powder cocaine and crack cocaine. The report indicated that the Commission would investigate ways to account for the harms associated with cocaine offenses in the sentencing guidelines and would then recommend appropriate enhancements and adjustments in the quantity ratio.

On May 1, 1995, by a 4–3 vote, the Commission sent to Congress proposed changes to the sentencing guidelines for cocaine offenses. The changes proposed by the majority would have made the starting point for determining sentences for powder and crack offenders the same by adopting a 1-to-1 quantity ratio at the powder cocaine level and would have provided sentencing enhancements for violence and other harms disproportionately associated with crack cocaine. . . . The minority dissented based on an assessment that then recommended enhancements could not sufficiently account for the added harms associated with crack cocaine and thus did not warrant the total elimination of a differential between base sentences.

. . . Congress passed and the President signed legislation rejecting the Commission's proposed guideline changes. . . . In the legislation, Congress effectively returned the issue to the Commission for further consideration and directed the Commission to submit to Congress new recommendations regarding changes to the statutes and sentencing guidelines for the unlawful manufacturing, importing, exporting, and trafficking of cocaine. We submit this report in compliance with the 1995 congressional directive that "the sentence imposed for trafficking in a quantity of crack cocaine should generally exceed the sentence imposed for trafficking in a like quantity of powder cocaine."

In response to that directive, the Commission again has deliberated carefully over federal cocaine sentencing policy and has assessed the concerns raised by Congress, conducted new research, consulted with law enforcement and substance abuse experts, and reviewed all of the Commission's prior research and analysis. The Commission has accumulated a vast array of information about both powder and crack cocaine and about the changing markets for these drugs. Based on this work, the Commission is unanimous in reiterating its original core finding, outlined in its February 1995 report to Congress that, although research and public policy may support somewhat higher penalties for crack than for powder cocaine, a 100 to 1 quantity ratio cannot be justified. The Commission is firmly and unanimously in agreement that the current penalty differential for federal powder and crack cocaine cases should be reduced by changing the quantity levels that trigger mandatory minimum penalties for both powder and crack cocaine. Therefore, for powder cocaine, the Commission recommends that Congress reduce the current 500-gram trigger for the five-year mandatory minimum sentence to a level between 125 and 375 grams; and for crack cocaine, that Congress increase the current five gram trigger to between 25 and 75 grams. . . .

II. The Current Law

The current sentencing structure for cocaine offenses is primarily the result of the Anti-Drug Abuse Act of 1986. The Act established mandatory minimum penalties for persons convicted of trafficking in a variety of controlled substances. The 1986 Act pegged the mandatory minimums to specific quantities of drugs distributed (based on a mixture or substance containing a detectable amount of the drug). The quantities triggering the Act's mandatory minimum penalties differed for various drugs and in some cases for different forms of the same drug. The Act treated powder cocaine differently than crack cocaine by establishing what has come to be known as the 100-to-1 quantity ratio between the two forms of cocaine. In other words, it takes one hundred times as much powder cocaine as crack cocaine to trigger the same mandatory penalties. Thus, a person convicted of selling 500 grams of powder cocaine is subject to the same five-year mandatory minimum sentences as a person selling 5 grams of crack cocaine, while a person convicted of selling 5,000 grams (5 kilograms) of powder is subject to the same ten-year mandatory minimum sentence as a person who sells 50 grams of crack.

In 1987, the Sentencing Commission used the drug quantity levels designated by Congress—including the quantity levels for cocaine offenses based on the 100-to-1 quantity ratio—in developing sentencing guidelines for drug offenses. Using the mandatory minimum statutes, which list only the quantities corresponding to the five- and ten-year mandatory minimum sentences, the sentencing guidelines set proportionate sentences for the full range of other powder and crack cocaine quantities.

Congress also distinguished crack cocaine from both powder cocaine and other controlled substances in the Anti-Drug Abuse Act of 1988 by creating a mandatory minimum penalty for its simple possession. This is the only federal mandatory minimum for a first offense of simple possession of a controlled substance. Under this law, possession of more than five grams of crack cocaine is punishable by a minimum five years in prison. Simple possession (without the intent to distribute) of any quantity of powder cocaine by first-time offenders is a misdemeanor punishable by no more than one year in prison.

III. The Goals of Federal Drug Sentencing Policy

A. Sentences Should Be Commensurate with the Dangers Associated with a Given Drug

Regardless of the quantity of drug involved, distributing any of the primary domestic illegal drugs—heroin, cocaine (powder or crack), methamphetamine, PCP, LSD, or marijuana—is a serious crime. All of these drugs cause great harm to individuals and to society at large, and the stern punishments meted out under federal law for drug distribution reflect congressional, executive, and Sentencing Commission judgment about the gravity of these offenses and the menace caused by these drugs.

Congress and the Commission have also concluded, however, that some of these drugs have more attendant harms than others and that those who traffic in more dangerous drugs ought to be sentenced more severely than those who traffic in less dangerous drugs. . . .

The Commission's research, detailed at great length in its 1995 report, found significant dangers associated with both crack and powder cocaine trafficking and use. The Commission also found, however, that many of these dangers are associated to a greater degree with crack cocaine than with powder cocaine. For example, crack cocaine is more often associated with systemic crime—crime related to its marketing and distribution—particularly the type of violent street crime so often connected with gangs, guns, serious injury, and death. In addition, because it is easy to manufacture and use and relatively inexpensive, crack is more widely available on the street and is particularly appealing and accessible to the most vulnerable members of our society. Unfortunately, the purveyors of crack worked hard to design a method to distribute the drug at a cheap price, making it appealing to the most economically disadvantaged of our society. Finally, because crack is smoked rather than snorted, it produces more intense physiological and psychotropic effects than snorting powder cocaine, and so the crack user is more vulnerable to addiction than the typical powder user, though we note that injecting powder cocaine into the bloodstream produces effects similar to smoking crack and hence creates a similar vulnerability to addiction. Based

249

upon these findings, the Commission reiterates the conclusion from its 1995 report that federal sentencing policy must reflect the greater dangers associated with crack.

B. Five- and Ten-Year Mandatory Sentences Should Be Targeted at Serious Traffickers

Since 1986, federal drug sentencing policy has been based in part on the principle that the quantity of drug involved in an offense reflects both the harm to society as well as the offender's culpability. Accordingly, Congress countenanced in the Anti-Drug Abuse Act of 1986 that any drug trafficker accountable for a quantity of drug indicative of a "mid-level" or "serious" trafficker ought to receive, with very few exceptions, at least a five-year prison sentence. . . .

. . . [T]he Commission concludes that the five-gram trigger for crack cocaine is over inclusive because it reaches below the level of mid-level or serious traffickers who deserve the five-year statutory penalty.

Five grams of crack cocaine is indicative of a retail or street-level dealer rather than a mid-level dealer. Accordingly, the Commission concludes that the five-gram trigger should be increased to better target mid-level dealers. This is not to say that all street-level cocaine dealers should receive sentences of less than five-years imprisonment. If a street-level dealer possesses a gun, is involved in violence or other aggravating conduct, uses juveniles, or is involved in unusually large quantities of drugs, a more severe sentence would be warranted. Both the guidelines and other laws provide for such enhancements. But based solely on quantity, our analysis suggests that an appropriate trigger for the five-year mandatory sentence for crack offenses should be higher than five grams.

For powder cocaine, the information and data suggest that some decrease in the quantity trigger may be warranted. Because nearly all cocaine is initially distributed in powder form until some later time in the distribution chain when some is then converted to crack, the Commission believes that it is appropriate to increase penalty levels for trafficking in powder cocaine to partially reflect the greater harms associated with crack and to reduce unwarranted sentencing disparity between powder and crack cocaine traffickers. In addition, the ease with which powder cocaine is converted to crack cocaine also suggests that some increase in powder cocaine penalties may be appropriate. For these reasons, the Commission concludes that a more appropriate quantity trigger for the five-year mandatory sentence for powder cocaine would be less than 500 grams.

It is important to note that, although changes in the quantity triggers for crack and powder cocaine would change the starting point for determining sentences under the guidelines, ultimate sentences are based on more than simply drug quantity. In contrast to a penalty structure that relies exclusively or primarily on a quantity ratio to distinguish among offenders, the guidelines approach allows for the more refined and individualized sentencing that Congress envisioned under the Sentencing Reform Act as well as the most efficient and effective use of scarce federal prison resources. The Commission reiterates its 1995 conclusion that, when applicable, guideline enhancements should be used to account for harms related to crack and powder cocaine offenses with less reliance put on drug quantity. For example, any cocaine trafficker who possesses or uses a firearm or other dangerous weapon during a drug crime ought to receive a substantially enhanced sentence. Other factors—such as the use of juveniles in a drug trafficking offense, a defendant's prior drug trafficking convictions, a defendant's role in the offense, and the other factors listed in the 1995 congressional directive—are all important in determining an appropriate drug sentence. The enhancements in the guidelines system can account for these and other important factors related to a defendant's criminal culpability and should be relied on to the greatest extent possible.

C. Cocaine Sentencing Policy Should Advance the Federal Government's Role in the National Drug Control Effort and Rationalize Priorities for the Use of State and Federal Resources in Targeting Drug Use and Trafficking

The federal government and state governments share a common interest in developing an effective drug control policy that allocates responsibility for prosecution, adjudication, sentencing, and imprisonment in such a way that these functions are carried out in the most efficient, effective, and constitutionally appropriate manner. Sentencing policy plays an important role in the allocation of resources among federal, state, and local government entities. Thus, the Commission is increasingly convinced that federal sentencing policy must be designed in coordination with a larger national effort that recognizes and takes into account the appropriate allocation of drug enforcement and drug control efforts at all levels of government. . . .

To this end, it is our view that federal sentencing policy should reflect federal priorities by targeting the most serious offenders in order to curb interstate and international drug trafficking and violent crime. Consistent with general constitutional principles of interstate commerce and the appropriate roles of the federal government, it is our view that an effort to rationalize federal sentencing policy would attempt to identify those components of the criminal element in drug trafficking that are most appropriate for federal concern and reserve to the states those criminal activities and defendants that state resources could most effectively target and consider in their own sentencing schemes. Though most of the overlapping jurisdiction between the state and federal governments in national crime control policy may be authorized by the Constitution, it does not necessarily follow that such overlapping jurisdiction is either the most effective or the most efficient use of the combined resources of the federal and state governments. For example, it is clear in looking at state sentencing schemes that states have historically made a wide variety of choices about the sentencing of persons who are deemed low-level offenders or who are apprehended with street-level amounts of drugs. These choices reflect traditional state responsibility for addressing public health, safety, and welfare issues related to addicts, street-level crime, and persons low in local distribution chains. States may be able to address these issues more economically and with more locally-focused penal and social goals than can be achieved by the federal government.

Federal cocaine sentencing policy is an excellent example of a place to start rationalizing federal and state priorities with respect to drug control. It is the view of the Sentencing Commission that current federal cocaine policy inappropriately targets limited federal resources by placing the quantity triggers for the five-year mandatory minimum penalty for crack cocaine too low. The use of federal sentencing policy as the machine to drive enforcement, adjudication, and imprisonment choices does not reflect a thoughtful and considered choice about the most effective use of public resources at all levels. This debate about the proper role of the respective levels of government goes far beyond federal cocaine policy. We are convinced, however, that adjusting the powder and crack five-year quantity triggers to target serious dealers will begin the process of adjusting national drug policy in a way that effectively and efficiently directs resources at all levels.

D. Cocaine Sentencing Policy and Practice Must Be Perceived by the Public as Fair

One of the issues of greatest concern surrounding federal cocaine sentencing policy is the perception of disparate and unfair treatment for defendants convicted of either possession or distribution of crack cocaine. Critics argue that the 100-to-1 quantity ratio is not consistent with the policy, goal, and mission of federal sentencing—that is to be effective, uniform, and just. While there is no evidence of racial bias behind the promulgation of this federal sentencing law, nearly 90 percent of the offenders convicted in federal court for crack cocaine distribution are African-American. . . . Thus, sentences appear to be harsher and more severe for racial minorities than others as a result of this law. The current penalty structure results in a perception of unfairness and inconsistency.

Designing sentencing policy to properly focus federal resources on the most violent and dangerous offenders will also help alleviate concerns that have been raised with the Commission about prosecutorial and investigative sentencing manipulation. For example, because powder cocaine is easily converted into crack cocaine and because the penalties for crack cocaine offenses are significantly higher than for similar quantity powder cocaine offenses, law enforcement and prosecutorial decisions to wait until powder has been converted into crack can have a dramatic impact on a defendant's final sentence. To the extent that the differential is reduced, the potential for this practice will also diminish.

IV. Conclusions and Recommendations

A. Penalties for Cocaine Trafficking

In reassessing penalties for cocaine trafficking, the Commission has moved step-by-step through an evaluative process that examined all of the factors listed by Congress in the 1995 legislation and the goals set forth above. In arriving at recommended changes to current policy, the Commission has balanced conflicting goals. The Sentencing Commission shares congressional and public concern about the harms associated with both forms of cocaine—both to users and to the society as a whole—including the violence associated with its distribution, its use by juveniles, the involvement of juveniles in its distribution, and its addictive potential. However, as the Commission reported in 1995, we again conclude unanimously that congressional objectives can be achieved more effectively without relying on the current federal sentencing scheme for cocaine offenses that includes the 100-to-1 quantity ratio.

The Sentencing Commission thereby recommends that Congress revise the federal statutory penalty scheme for both crack and powder cocaine offenses. Selecting the appropriate threshold for triggering the five-year mandatory minimum penalties is not a precise undertaking, but based on the best available research and the goals detailed above, the Commission recommends for Congress's consideration a range of alternative quantity triggers for both powder and crack cocaine offenses. For powder cocaine, the Commission concludes that the current 500-gram trigger for the five-year mandatory minimum sentence should be reduced to a level between 125 and 375 grams, and for crack cocaine, the five-gram trigger should be increased to between 25 and 75 grams.

We urge Congress to adopt a ratio within the quantity ranges we have recommended to address the problem as soon as possible, as hundreds of people will continue to be sentenced each month under the current law. After Congress has evaluated our recommendations and expressed its views, the Commission will amend the guidelines to reflect congressional intent. Consistent with the principles of the Sentencing Reform Act of 1984, the Commission believes that better sentencing policy—for cocaine as well as for other offenses—is developed through Commission research and expertise together with regular and ongoing consultation with Congress and the Executive Branch. We intend to continue to work closely with Congress and senior administration officials as pertinent legislation is developed. By doing so, we believe a fairer and more effective cocaine sentencing policy—one that better targets serious and upper-level dealers and the most violent and dangerous drug offenders—can be created.

The Commission is mindful that these and other related sentencing changes could have a substantial impact on the federal prison population, thus changing the resources available for other drug control strategies. The President, the Attorney General, the Congress, and the Office of National Drug Control Strategy have repeatedly indicated that an effective drug control strategy requires a balanced approach of domestic and international law enforcement, interdiction, prevention, and treatment. The impact of policy changes on drug control resources must be considered seriously before making any substantial increase in drug sentences. The Commission is prepared to provide impact analysis and other expertise to both Congress and the Executive Branch at any time.

B. Penalties for the Simple Possession of Crack Cocaine

The Commission has also reassessed the penalties uniquely applicable to the simple possession of crack cocaine. Much of the rationale for reexamining the 100 to 1 quantity ratio applicable to cocaine trafficking offenses similarly applies to the penalties applicable to crack simple possession offenses. The Commission reiterates its unanimous finding that the penalty for simple possession of crack cocaine should be the same as for the simple possession of powder cocaine.

May

REPORT ON HOW "NEUTRALS" AIDED NAZI GERMANY
May 7, 1997

A series of investigations and historical studies released in 1997 severely tarnished the image of Switzerland as a benign neutral during World War II. Newly released documents confirmed what many scholars and Jewish groups had alleged for years: that Swiss banks and businesses, with the active support of their government, helped finance Adolph Hitler's military machine and provided weapons and other material essential to the German army's conquest of much of Europe and its fight against the Allies.

The most damning information came in a U.S. government report, issued May 7, which documented aid to Nazi Germany by neutral nations, most importantly Switzerland. The report contended that Switzerland used its neutrality to disguise business dealings with Germany that helped prolong the war. After years of insisting it had no obligation to the victims of German aggression, the Swiss government agreed during 1997 to provide funds to aid survivors of the Nazi holocaust, which killed an estimated 6 million Jews. But Swiss officials and many citizens appeared ambivalent about the charges of war-time complicity with the Nazis, insisting that war-time Switzerland was forced to do business with Hitler's regime.

Eisenstat Report

The U.S. study was the result of seven months of work by historians, archivists, and researchers from eleven government agencies, among them the CIA, the State Department, and the National Archives and Records Administration. President Bill Clinton ordered the study in 1996 at the request of Jewish groups, principally the World Jewish Congress, and following congressional disclosures of the role of Swiss banks in handling assets that had been looted by the Nazis. William Z. Slany, chief historian of the State Department, prepared the report under the direction of Stuart E. Eisenstat, undersecretary of commerce for international trade.

Labeled a "preliminary study," the report documented what it called "one of the greatest thefts by a government in history"—Germany's confiscation of *an estimated $579 million worth of gold (approximately $5.6 billion in 1997 values) from the central banks of eleven nations it had conquered. Germany transferred an estimated $400 million of the gold to Swiss banks. Swiss bankers knew the gold was stolen because they were aware that Germany had spent all its own gold reserves gearing up for the war, the report said.*

Germany also melted down and converted into gold bars vast quantities of rings, dinner plates, dental fillings, and other personal items from millions of Jews in concentration camps. The report said it uncovered no evidence that Swiss bankers knew the origin of this gold.

The U.S. report offered no estimate for the value of this "personal" gold. In December, however, a study by Swiss historians put an estimated value of $146 million in 1945 prices (or about $1.3 billion in 1997 prices) on gold stolen by Nazis from individuals.

Germany's theft of gold from other countries and from individuals was "no rogue operation," the report said. It was "essential to the financing of the German war machine."

A separate study by the World Jewish Congress estimated that Germany confiscated at least $8.5 billion worth of gold (in 1997 values) between 1933 and 1945. That study estimated that about two-thirds of the looted gold came from European central banks and the rest was stolen from private businesses and individuals.

Allied armies recovered millions of dollars worth of gold bars and valuable items that came from holocaust victims and nations overrun by the Germans. The gold bars were put into a pool, managed by the Tripartite Gold Commission, that was used to build the central bank reserves of those nations. Eisenstat said nearly $70 million remained in that pool, stored in New York and London, and "could be given to holocaust survivors."

Another report by the U.S. Federal Reserve Bank of New York, based on postwar documents, revealed that after the war the United States melted down gold personal items—such as coins, plates, buttons—that the Nazis probably had taken from their victims. The melted gold was made into more than 40 gold bars that were shipped to European central banks.

The Swiss Role

The report acknowledged the dangers of "making simplistic moral judgments about the conduct of neutral nations in wartime." Even so, the report said that neutrality "too often provided a pretext of avoiding moral considerations." Trade with Berlin by the neutral nations "had the clear effect of supporting and prolonging Nazi Germany's capacity to wage war," the report said. And after the war, several neutral nations—including Switzerland—resisted attempts by the Allies to return assets that had been looted by the Nazis.

Of all the neutrals, the report said, Switzerland played the most complex role during the war. On the one hand, Switzerland took in many European refugees and allowed the Allies to use its territory for intelligence-gathering operations. But, the report added, Switzerland also was "Nazi Germany's banker and financial facilitator, taking and transferring German gold—

most of it looted—and providing Germany with Swiss francs to purchase needed products." Switzerland also supplied Germany with key war materials, such as arms, ammunition, aluminum, machinery, and locomotives, according to the report. Other neutral nations that provided financial and logistical support to Germany included Argentina, Sweden, Turkey, Portugal, and Spain.

After the war, the study said, Switzerland attempted to hide from the Allies the full extent of its holdings of Nazi plunder. In 1946 Switzerland signed an agreement promising to liquidate millions of dollars worth of German-owned assets, with the money used to aid European reconstruction. Switzerland refused to abide by that agreement, leading U.S. officials to conclude by 1950 that Switzerland "had no intention of every implementing" the accord. Switzerland did honor another part of its agreement, to pay the equivalent of $58 million worth of gold (in 1946 dollars) to offset its wartime purchases of gold stolen by the Nazis.

The study accused the Truman administration of a weak response to Swiss intransigence in the years following World War II. Washington failed to demand a complete accounting from Switzerland of its relations with Nazi Germany or to inquire into the origin of Nazi gold.

In a formal response issued May 22, the Swiss Foreign Ministry called the U.S. report a "one-sided blanket judgment" that failed to take into account Switzerland's wartime predicament as a small country surrounded by the Nazi military machine. "Neutrality led to a difficult tightrope walk between adaptation and resistance," the statement said. "Today, we know that this also led to mistakes."

The Swiss statement acknowledged that the country's "fainthearted" policy of preventing thousands of Jewish refugees from entering the country to escape the Nazi's was "inexcusable." It said that Swiss business and financial interests made concessions to the Axis powers "which are very hard to comprehend today in view of the inner convictions of the [Swiss] population. . . ." But, the statement added, trading with the Axis, as well as the Allied, powers was "a question of national political and economic survival" for Switzerland.

Swiss president Arnold Koller on March 5 announced a plan to establish a fund, called the Swiss Foundation for Solidarity, valued at $4.7 billion. The interest on the fund, which would amount to several hundred million dollars annually, would be used to help victims of the holocaust and other disasters. Money for the fund would come from a revaluing of Swiss gold reserves, which had been deliberately understated by the government. This proposal was subject to a national referendum scheduled for early 1998. Fierce opposition to this proposal came from Christoph Blocher, a wealthy industrialist who led the Swiss Peoples Party, the smallest of four parties in the governing coalition.

In addition, the Swiss National Bank and the three largest Swiss private banks created a fund, valued at about $120 million, for short-term aid, such as medical care, for holocaust survivors. Three private banks (the Union Bank of Switzerland, Credit Suisse, and the Swiss Bank Corp.) had created the fund to head off charges by Jewish groups and heirs of holocaust

259

*victims that Swiss banks had refused to release assets from Jewish deposi-
tors who died during the holocaust.*

Swiss Bank Accounts

*A related issue that generated intense international interest in 1997
concerned secret Swiss bank accounts that may have belonged to holocaust
victims. Under pressure from international Jewish groups, Swiss banks in
1995 said they had found 775 accounts, containing about $32 million, that
were opened in the 1930s and early 1940s by Jews and others who hoped to
keep their money out of Nazi hands. That announcement came more than
thirty years after Swiss banks said they had turned over the last of their
unclaimed deposits from the World War II era.*

*In 1996 the Swiss Bankers Association, cooperating with the World Jew-
ish Congress and the World Jewish Restitution Organization, asked Paul A.
Volker, former chairman of the U.S. Federal Reserve Board, to form an independent commission to investigate the issue of unclaimed bank accounts. To facilitate the probe, the Swiss Parliament lifted the country's
stringent bank secrecy laws.*

*The Volker commission in 1997 began a series of test audits of dormant
accounts to determine how many had belonged to Jews and others fleeing
the Nazis. Just before the audits began, Swiss banks revealed that they had
discovered between 15,000 and 20,000 dormant accounts that had been
opened by Swiss nationals during the World War II era. Jewish leaders for
years had said that many European Jews turned their money over to Swiss
nationals for safekeeping. The bankers promised cooperation with the
Volker commission to determine whether any of those accounts were "for
the benefit of holocaust victims."*

*Starting in late July, the Swiss banks began publishing thousands of
names on bank accounts that had been dormant since 1945. The initial list
published by the bankers in July contained 1,756 names and had a total
value of about $42 million. Another list published in October included 3,687
accounts with non-Swiss names, with a total value of about $4 million, and
more than 10,000 Swiss-owned accounts, with a total value of about $8 mil-
lion. Both lists were available, in limited form, on the World Wide Web.*

> *Following are excerpts from the foreword of the report, "U.S. and
> Allied Efforts to Recover and Restore Gold and Other Assets
> Stolen or Hidden by Germany During World War II," prepared by
> U.S. government agencies and released May 7, 1997:*

Introduction

This report addresses a vital but relatively neglected dimension of the history of the Second World War and its aftermath, one that became the focus of
intense political, diplomatic and media attention over the last year. It is a
study of the past with implications for the future.

The report documents one of the greatest thefts by a government in history: the confiscation by Nazi Germany of an estimated $580 million of central bank gold around $5.6 billion in today's values—along with indeterminate amounts in other assets during World War II. These goods were stolen from governments and civilians in the countries Germany overran and from Jewish and non-Jewish victims of the Nazis alike, including Jews murdered in extermination camps, from whom everything was taken down to the gold fillings of their teeth.

Our mandate from the President in preparing this report was to describe, to the fullest extent possible, U.S. and Allied efforts to recover and restore this gold and other assets stolen by Nazi Germany, and to use other German assets for the reconstruction of postwar Europe. It also touches on the initially valiant, but ultimately inadequate, steps taken by the United States and the Allies to make assets available for assistance to stateless victims of Nazi atrocities.

It is in the context of this mandate that the report catalogues the role of neutral countries, whose acceptance of the stolen gold in exchange for critically important goods and raw materials helped sustain the Nazi regime and prolong its war effort. This role continued, despite several warnings by the Allies, even long past the time when these countries had any legitimate reason to fear German invasion.

Among the neutral countries, Switzerland receives the most attention in the report. We have no desire to single out a country that is a robust democracy, a generous contributor to humanitarian efforts, and a valued partner of the United States today. But Switzerland figures prominently in any history of the fate of Nazi gold and other assets during and after World War II because the Swiss were the principal bankers and financial brokers for the Nazis, handling vast sums of gold and hard currency.

Prepared by the chief Historian of the State Department, Dr. William Slany, the study is the product of an extraordinary seven-month effort on the part of eleven U.S. Government agencies, which I coordinated at President Clinton's request. All involved have worked tirelessly in beginning the process of reviewing 15 million pages of documentation in the National Archives. This represents the largest such effort ever undertaken using the Archives' records, and it has required the declassification and transfer of more documents at one time— between 800,000 and one million pages—than ever before in the history of that repository. Those documents are now available to researchers for the first time.

Nevertheless, this study is preliminary and therefore incomplete. Not every U.S. document related to looted Nazi assets could be located and analyzed in the very short time we had to conduct and complete the study. As we progressed, additional documents were constantly found. While we were compelled to rely mostly on U.S. documents, we are well aware that not until the documents of other countries are examined can a more complete picture be drawn.

This is a report by historians. It is a search for facts from the past. It seeks neither to defend nor offend any nation; it endeavors to shade no hard realities, obfuscate no issue. It focuses on the role of the U.S. Government and touches on the roles of countries who are now among our closest friends and allies—from our wartime Allies to the then-neutral countries of Argentina, Portugal, Spain, Sweden, Switzerland, and Turkey (which joined the Allied effort just before the end of the War).

The picture which emerges from these pages, particularly of the neutral nations, is often harsh and unflattering. Many profited handsomely from their economic cooperation with Nazi Germany, while the Allied nations were sacrificing blood and treasure to fight one of the most powerful forces of evil in the annals of history. At the same time, our team knew that if we were going to shine the bright light of history on other nations, we also had to look carefully at America's role, and the study does so.

Why the sudden surge of interest in these tragic events of five decades ago? There are a variety of explanations. The end of the Cold War gave us the chance to examine issues long pushed to the background. Some previously unavailable documents have been declassified, and made publicly available. As Holocaust survivors come to the end of their lives, they have an urgent desire to ensure that long-suppressed facts come to light and to see a greater degree of justice to assuage, however slightly, their sufferings. And a younger generation seeks a deeper understanding of one of the most profound events of the twentieth century as we enter the twenty-first.

But the most compelling reason is the extraordinary leadership and vision of a few people who have put this issue on the world's agenda: the leadership of the World Jewish Congress, Edgar Bronfman, Israel Singer and Elan Steinberg; a bipartisan group in the U.S. Congress, in particular, the early, tenacious and important role of Senator Alfonse D'Amato of New York; and President Bill Clinton, who has insisted on our establishing and publishing the facts. These leaders have stirred our conscience and stiffened our resolve to achieve justice, particularly for the surviving victims of the Holocaust and Nazi oppression.

Major Conclusions and Policy Implications

A number of major conclusions arise from the pages of this preliminary study, some of which have significant implications today.

First, the massive and systematic plundering of gold and other assets from conquered nations and Nazi victims was no rogue operation. It was essential to the financing of the German war machine. The Reichsbank itself—the central bank of the German state—was a knowing and integral participant. It was the Reichsbank that knowingly incorporated into its gold reserves looted monetary gold from the governments of countries occupied by the Nazis. Judging by German reserves at the beginning of the War, the majority of the gold was looted from central banks. It is also evident from the documents we have uncovered and reviewed that some amount was confiscated from individual civilians, including victims of Nazi atrocities, and incorporated into Reichsbank gold stocks. It was the Reichsbank that assisted in converting victim gold coins, jewelry and gold fillings into assets for the SS "Melmer" account. The Reichsbank organized the sale or pawning of this concentration camp loot, and the resmelting of a portion of this gold into gold ingots—with their origins often disguised and therefore indistinguishable by appearance from that looted from central banks.

As its trading partners began to refuse to accept the German Reichsmark, Germany increasingly had to turn to making payments in gold in exchange for foreign hard currency and for materials and goods vital to the German war effort. Between January 1939 and June 30, 1945, Germany transferred gold worth around $400 million ($3.9 billion in today's values) to the Swiss National Bank in Bern. Of this amount, the Swiss National Bank bought about three-quarters, worth $276 million ($2.7 billion today), and the remainder went directly to the accounts of other countries in payment for goods and raw materials.

Second, in the unique circumstances of World War II, neutrality collided with morality; too often being neutral provided a pretext for avoiding moral considerations. Historically a well established principle in international law, neutrality served through centuries of European wars as a legitimate means by which smaller nations preserved their political sovereignty and economic viability. But it is painfully clear that Argentina, Portugal, Spain, Sweden, Switzerland, Turkey and other neutral countries were slow to recognize and acknowledge that this was not just another war. Most never did. Nazi Germany was a mortal threat to Western civilization itself, and had it been victorious, to the survival of even the neutral countries themselves.

Of course, we must be cautious in making simplistic moral judgments about the conduct of neutral nations in wartime. None of these nations started World War II or caused the Holocaust; that responsibility rested squarely with Nazi Germany. No country, including the United States, did as much as it might have or should have to save innocent victims of Nazi persecution—Jews, Gypsies, political opponents, and others. America itself remained a nonbelligerent for over two years following the outbreak of the War in Europe. Restrictive U.S. immigration policies kept hundreds of thousands of refugees from finding safety in the United States, most tragically exemplified by our refusal to allow the St. Louis to dock with its cargo of refugees many of whom perished when the ship was forced to return to Europe. Nevertheless, the U.S. froze German assets in April 1940 (18 months before entering the War), conducted little trade and commerce with Nazi Germany, and generously assisted Britain, the Soviet Union and the anti-Nazi cause—despite fierce domestic opposition through programs like Lend-Lease.

Many of the neutrals had a rational fear that their own independence was only a Panzer division away from extinction. But if self-defense and fear were factors in that rationale for neutrality, so too were profit in all neutral countries and outright Nazi sympathy in some. The neutrals ignored repeated Allied entreaties to end their dealings with Nazi Germany. Whatever their motivation, the fact that they pursued vigorous trade with the Third Reich had the clear effect of supporting and prolonging Nazi Germany's capacity to wage war.

In considering the actions of the neutrals, three phases can be identified:

- During the first phase, from the outbreak of war in 1939 until the battle of Stalingrad in early 1943, German military prowess was such that there was a legitimate fear of imminent invasion.
- In the second phase, the tide of battle shifted in the Allies' favor and culminated in victory. Beginning in mid-1943 with the Allied invasion of Italy, the D-Day invasion in June, 1944 and the diversion of German forces to halt the Soviet Army's advance, the Nazi occupation of Europe was rolled back and the threat to the neutrals greatly diminished, although there were still fears of other forms of reprisal. Commerce with Germany, however, continued. German assets in neutral countries were not frozen, despite Allied requests and warnings. The neutrals continued to profit from their trading links with Germany and thus contributed to prolonging one of the bloodiest conflicts in history. During this period, the Allies suffered hundreds of thousands of casualties and millions of innocent civilians were killed.
- In the third phase, the immediate postwar period, the neutrals disputed the legality of the Allied request to control German assets; often denied they had any looted Nazi gold; defended their commercial interests; dragged out negotiations with the Allies; and eventually pressed their own claims for restitution against Germany. In contrast to the other wartime neutrals, Sweden was relatively forthcoming in terms of the extent and pace of its cooperation in transferring Nazi gold and other assets to the Allied powers. Spain, Portugal, Switzerland, Turkey and others continued to resist cooperation even though the War was over.

To varying degrees, each of the neutrals cooperated with Nazi Germany for their own economic benefit. Sweden was one of Nazi Germany's largest trading partners, supplying critically-needed iron ore and ball bearings, among other goods. Portugal supplied a variety of vital mineral resources for the Third Reich's war machine, including the ore for tungsten, a key additive used in the production of weapon-grade steel. Spain maintained an active trade in goods and raw materials. Turkey was Germany's source of very scarce chrome. Argentina's pro-Axis regime failed to control the transfer of German funds from Europe.

Third, of all the neutral nations, the one with the most complex roles in World War II, together with the deepest and most crucial economic relationship with Nazi Germany, was Switzerland. Switzerland's role was very mixed. It ended World War II as one of the wealthiest nations in Europe. It conducted trade with the Allied countries as well as with the Axis powers. The Swiss National Bank kept gold accounts for and received gold not only from Nazi Germany, but from the United States, Canada, and Great Britain as well. Switzerland served as a key base for U.S. intelligence-gathering. It was also a protecting power for the Allies, most critically for our POWs. But as the Swiss Government acknowledged as early as 1952 (and reiterated in recent months), there were shortcomings in Switzerland's refugee policies. Switzerland persuaded the Nazis to establish the "J" stamp which prevented tens of thousands of Jews from entering Switzerland or other potential sanctuaries. Like Canada and the United States, Switzerland tightened its immigration policies, and during the War it virtually closed its borders to Jews fleeing deportation from France and Belgium. As many as about 50,000 Jewish refugees were admitted from 1933 until the end of the War, of whom some 30,000 remained and survived the War in Switzerland. But Switzerland imposed on Jewish communities the burden of sustaining the Jews who were admitted after the outbreak of war (most of whom were interned in labor camps). In August and December 1944, Switzerland admitted an additional 1,700 concentration camp inmates from Bergen Belsen, and in February 1945 an additional 1,200 from Theresienstadt. Various Jewish communities were required to support these additional survivors. Switzerland also accepted well over 100,000 other refugees after 1940.

As late as the end of 1944, Secretary of State Stettinius and his State Department colleagues concluded that, on balance, Switzerland's neutrality had been more a positive than a negative for the Allies during the War. This relatively benign judgment was not shared by other agencies, from the War Department and Treasury Department to the Office of Strategic Services (OSS) and the Justice Department. These agencies noted that in addition to its critical banking role for the Nazis, Switzerland's industries engaged in direct production for the Axis and helped protect Axis investments; Swiss shipping lines also furnished Germany with a large number of boats for the transport of goods. Switzerland also allowed an unprecedented use of its railways to link Germany and Italy for the transport of coal and other goods. Switzerland provided Germany with arms, ammunition, aluminum, machinery and precision tools, as well as agricultural products. Swiss convoys carried products from Spain across France through Switzerland to Germany. Swiss banks serviced Nazi markets in Latin America. This conduct continued even as the Germans retreated and the threat of invasion evaporated. As late in the War as early 1945, Switzerland vitiated an agreement it had just reached with the United States to freeze German assets and to restrict purchases of gold from Germany.

The amount of Germany's gold reserves before the War was well known. Clearly, the evidence presented in this report is incontrovertible: the Swiss National Bank and private Swiss bankers knew, as the War progressed, that the Reichsbank's own coffers had been depleted, and that the Swiss were handling vast sums of looted gold. The Swiss were aware of the Nazi gold heists from France of Belgian gold as well as from other countries.

Switzerland's "business as usual" attitude persisted in the postwar negotiations, and it is this period which is most inexplicable. The Swiss team were obdurate negotiators, using legalistic positions to defend their every interest, regardless of the moral issues also at stake. Initially, for instance, they opposed returning any Nazi gold to those from whom it was stolen, and they denied having received any looted gold. The Swiss contended they had purchased it in good faith, that it was part of war booty obtained in accordance with international legal principles by the Third Reich during its victorious campaigns, and that there was no international legal principle which would entitle the Allies to recover and redistribute Nazi assets. Finally, after long, contentious and difficult bargaining, agreement was reached in the form of the 1946 Allied-Swiss Washington Accord. The Accord obligated Switzerland to transfer 250 million Swiss francs ($58.1 million) in gold to the Allies and to liquidate German assets transferring 50 percent of the proceeds from the assets to the Allies for the reconstruction of war-torn Europe, of which a portion would be directed to assistance of stateless victims. At the same time, the Swiss made a commitment in a side letter to identify dormant accounts which were heirless and could be used for the benefit of Nazi victims.

The $58 million in German-looted gold to be returned to the Allies was far less than the range of $185–$289 million in looted gold the State and Treasury Departments estimated was at the Swiss National Bank for its own account at the end of the War. An additional $120 million of German-looted gold was also estimated to be on account for other countries at that time. This $58 million in monetary gold was promptly paid to the Tripartite Gold Commission (TGC) for redistribution to the claimant countries.

But the other part of the Accord, the liquidation of hundreds of millions of dollars in German assets, was neither promptly nor ever fully implemented. The Swiss raised one objection after another, arguing over exchange rates, insisting that German debt settlements be included, and demanding that the U.S. unblock assets from German companies seized during the War but which the Bern government claimed were actually Swiss-owned. They refused to make an exemption for the assets of surviving Jews from Germany and heirless German Jewish assets, and continued to make them subject to liquidation. They refused to recognize any moral obligation to return looted Dutch gold when evidence became available after the conclusion of the 1946 negotiations. U.S. negotiators concluded by 1950 that the Swiss had no intention of ever implementing the 1946 Washington Accord. Secretary of State Dean Acheson remarked that if Sweden was an intransigent negotiator, then Switzerland was intransigence "cubed."

Over a six-year period, before the final 1952 settlement, the Swiss government had made only a token 20 million Swiss franc advance ($4.7 million then or $31 million today) for resettlement of stateless victims. Finally, in 1952, after a lengthy and frustrating effort, Switzerland and the Allies agreed to a total payment of only $28 million—far less than the agreed 50 percent of the value of German assets in their country. The amount of German assets in Switzerland after the War ranged between press accounts of $750 million, U.S. and Allied estimates of $250–$500 million, and Swiss estimates of around $250 million.

This 1952 accord, superseding the 1946 obligation, was concluded within days of the initialing of a Swiss-German debt agreement by which the German government satisfied its wartime debt to Switzerland. Clearly, Switzerland's delay was intended to keep German assets under its control as a guarantee for settlement of Swiss claims against the Nazi regime. Effectively, the German payment was used to fund Switzerland's own payment to the Allies.

It was not until 1962 that Switzerland began to comply with its 1946 side letter agreement to the Washington Accord "to look sympathetically" at using heirless assets for the benefit of Holocaust survivors. After long denying the possession of any heirless assets, some Swiss banks then found over $2 million in bank accounts, most of which was not transferred to Jewish and other relief organizations until the 1970s. In a renewed effort in 1996, they indicated they had located around $32 million in dormant accounts in various banks. Over the years, the inflexibility of the Swiss Bankers' Association and other Swiss banks made it extremely difficult for surviving family members of Nazi victims to successfully file claims to secure bank records and other assets. This overall pattern of apparent Swiss bankers' indifference to the needs of the victims of the Holocaust and their heirs persisted until the current international pressures came to bear and, for instance, the appointment of an Ombudsman in 1996.

The lack of attention to the letter and spirit of this side agreement was also evident in the separate 1949 agreement the Swiss concluded with Poland under which Switzerland agreed to transfer funds in heirless bank accounts from Polish Holocaust survivors and other Polish nationals to the then-Communist government of Poland. This was coupled with a Polish agreement to satisfy the claims of Swiss businesses for properties expropriated after the War. Although defensible under international law, (since the Poles committed themselves to restore these heirless assets to any surviving Polish claimants), there was no Swiss follow-through. Switzerland failed to provide Poland with the names of Polish heirless account holders until a few months ago. Switzerland also entered into a similar protocol with Hungary.

Negotiations with other neutrals also had mixed results. Sweden was the most cooperative in liquidating the German assets it held, although it was not until 1955 that Sweden resolved final questions on transferring monetary gold. Negotiations with Spain were lengthier and less successful, with many German assets in Spain virtually disappearing into the Spanish economy by the time negotiations were completed in 1948. A small amount of gold was returned and assets liquidated. Negotiations with Portugal were even more protracted, with gold discussions dragging on into the 1950s because of Portuguese resistance. It was not until 1960 that a small amount of cash and gold was turned over to the Allies. Turkey and Argentina paid nothing in gold or assets.

Fourth, the United States lent its military, material, and moral might to the free world's fight against Nazi tyranny and led the magnanimous effort to rebuild post-war Europe through the landmark Marshall Plan. It is fair to conclude that on the Nazi gold and assets issues addressed by this report, the role of the U.S. was also positive. The U.S. Government took the lead in economic warfare against the Axis by initiating the Safehaven program with our Allies. The U.S. scored significant successes in blocking German assets from leaving this country and in tracking the flow of Nazi assets, particularly looted gold, to prevent any Nazi resurgence after the War. The U.S. also led the effort, during and after the War, to obtain compensation for the nations and individuals victimized by the Third Reich. Although restrictive immigration policies remained in place until 1948, the U.S. was the most active in addressing the plight of the refugees, initiating the proposal in the Paris Reparation Conference to assure some share of reparations went to the victims of Nazism and proposing an early conference on assistance for refugees. The U.S. also provided substantial funds for displaced persons and for the resettlement and rehabilitation of refugees.

Nonetheless, the report raises serious questions about the U.S. role. American leadership at the time, while greater than that of our Allies, was limited. There was a demonstrable lack of senior-level support for a tough U.S. negotiating position with the neutrals. Moreover, there was an even greater lack of attention to ensuring implementation of negotiated agreements. Because, for instance, the U.S. Government decided to unblock frozen Swiss assets in the U.S. soon after the signing of the 1946 Accord, and, over the objections of the Treasury Department, decided not to pursue sanctions, most leverage was lost before Switzerland had met its obligations. Finally, neither the U.S. nor the Allies pressed the neutral countries hard enough to fulfill their moral obligation to help Holocaust survivors by redistributing heirless assets for their benefit.

These serious shortcomings in U.S. and Allied policy, coupled with stiff resistance on the part of the neutrals, had two negative consequences:

- With greater support and interest from Allied leadership, it might have been possible to strike a better bargain on the looted gold and other German assets with the neutral countries;
- Allied and interagency disagreements also made it easier for the neutrals to string out negotiations and thereby delay the transfer of needed funds to the Inter-Allied Reparations Agency (IARA) and to the International Refugee Organization (IRO).

The inadequacies of U.S. postwar policy were due to a number of factors which tied the hands of American negotiators, not the least of which was unrelenting opposition from the neutral countries. In addition to interagency disagreements over how tough to be with the neutrals, there were also splits within Allied ranks. The U.S. was the most aggressive in seeking compensation for the refugees, but was met by resistance, for example, from Britain (which according to the analysis of U.S. officials at the time, feared the policy of providing funds for resettlement of refugees would conflict with its restrictions on the number of Jewish refugees who could enter Palestine).

Most fundamentally, wartime objectives were replaced by the need to rebuild an integrated postwar Europe and then by new Cold War imperatives, including the creation of NATO in order to contain the Soviet threat so dramatically highlighted by the 1948 Berlin blockade. Putting a democratic West Germany on its feet and strengthening its economy took priority over denying it access to German assets in neutral countries—assets which could be applied to broader European recovery efforts. The Allies knew that German efforts to meet their obligation to the neutral countries would strain their economy. In the case of Portugal, the quest for access to the important Azores air base led negotiators to settle for a token payment. Security interests became paramount with Turkey, a key NATO ally. Switzerland, though neutral, was seen officially in a 1951 decision by President Truman as a democratic deterrent to Soviet expansionism.

Fifth, the report also deals with the hotly debated issue of whether some victim gold was sent to Switzerland and other neutral countries, and whether it was also included in the TGC Gold Pool. This was the Pool into which looted central bank gold was placed for redistribution by the TGC to the governments from which it was stolen during the War. This study concludes that both occurred. The Reichsbank or its agents smelted gold taken from concentration camp internees, persecutees and other civilians, and turned it into ingots. There is clear evidence that these ingots were incorporated into Germany's official gold reserves, along with the gold confiscated from central banks of the countries the Third Reich occupied. Although there is no evidence that Switzerland or other neutral countries knowingly accepted victim gold, the study provides clear evidence—on the basis of the pattern and practice of Reichsbank gold smelting, the co-mingling of monetary and non-monetary gold, gold transfers and an analysis of a shipment of looted Dutch gold that at least a small portion of the gold that entered Switzerland and Italy included non-monetary gold from individual civilians in occupied countries and from concentration camp victims or others killed before they even reached the camps.

It is also clear that some victim gold "tainted" the Gold Pool. There was great confusion and disagreement between the Allies and within the U.S. government over the definition of "monetary gold" (destined for the Gold Pool) and "non-monetary gold" (to be used for resettlement of stateless victims). In the end, the U.S. decided on a definition that was based on appearance rather than origin. As a result, gold taken by the Nazis from civilians in occupied countries and from individual victims of the Nazis in concentration camps and elsewhere was swept into the Gold Pool. In addition, the U.S. and Britain agreed that gold bars suspected to be from the Nazi's Terezin concentration camp in Czechoslovakia should be included in the Gold Pool, although no evidence has been uncovered yet that they were transferred to the TGC. Further research might determine how much was included.

Finally, one aspect of the study deserves immediate attention and action: the plight of those who were victims not only of war and the Holocaust, but of the sad combination of indifference on the part of the neutrals and inaction by the Allies. The decision by the 18 nations at the 1946 Paris Reparations Conference to leave assistance and reparations for individual victims to national governments and international relief organizations, while understandable at the time, in hindsight had unfortunate consequences:

- Serious inequities developed in the treatment of victims depending upon where they lived after the War. Those Holocaust victims who met the applicable definitions were assisted in resettlement, and if they emigrated to the West or to Israel, they have received pensions from the German government. But the "double victims," those trapped behind the Iron Curtain after the War, have essentially received nothing;

- Beyond initial emergency resettlement assistance, most governments did not have a long-term commitment to rehabilitation, to the search for heirs of abandoned assets, nor to distribution of heirless assets for appropriate causes. This meant that the burden of providing ongoing relief for surviving victims was left largely to private organizations.

For the victims, justice remains elusive. Their grievances must be seen as the appropriate responsibility of the entire international community on behalf of humanity.

Challenges for Action

The cumulative facts and conclusions contained in this report should evoke a sense of injustice and a determination to act. Now, half a century later, this generation's challenge is to complete the unfinished business of the Second World War to do justice while its surviving victims are still alive. To do justice is in part a financial task. But it is also a moral and political task that should compel each nation involved in these tragic events to come to terms with its own history and responsibility.

It is a time for reconciliation as well. A positive, healing process has already begun. Besides the pathbreaking September 1996 British Foreign Office report and this U.S. historical study, a growing number of countries have initiated reviews of their wartime roles—including their relationship to the Third Reich and the theft and disposition of valuables from their Jewish and non-Jewish citizens alike.

Among the neutral countries, Switzerland has taken the lead. It has established two separate commissions—the Volcker Commission to examine assets in dormant bank accounts in Swiss banks and the Bergier Commission to examine the entire historical relationship of Switzerland to Nazi Germany. Major Swiss banks and companies and the Swiss National Bank have established what is now a $180 million—and growing—fund for needy surviving victims of the Nazis or their heirs. The Government of Switzerland has proposed establishing an endowment to generate income for survivors and for other humanitarian causes. Private groups, including churches and high school students, have collected over 500,000 Swiss francs (about $350,000) for Holocaust survivors. The United States welcomes and applauds these significant gestures.

Many other important efforts are beginning. For example, Sweden, Spain, Portugal, France, Norway, the Netherlands, Belgium, Brazil, and Argentina have created historical commissions. Poland has published a report of its post-war agreement with Switzerland to settle property claims. The Czech Republic has searched its records and determined that no heirless accounts in Swiss banks were included in Swiss claims settlements. The Austrian Government has established a fund to compensate its Holocaust survivors. Shortly, the Government of Hungary will begin paying monthly compensation to over 20,000 Holocaust survivors living in that country. Several other countries in Central and Eastern Europe have also taken steps to restitute communally-owned Jewish and non-Jewish property (such as schools, churches, and synagogues) confiscated by the Nazis and/or the Communists, although often at a slow pace. These efforts should be accelerated.

To move this healing process forward, it is vital that all of the facts be made public. The Clinton Administration has made an extraordinary effort to declassify documents that may shed further light on these issues. In addition:

- The U.S. favors the immediate declassification of all of the TGC's documents that bear on the origin of the TGC gold pool.
- The U.S. will explore the idea of an international conference of historians and other experts to exchange information, insights, and documents about the flow of Nazi assets, relationships with the Third Reich during the war, and measures for finding surviving owners or disposing of heirless property. The U.S. and other concerned governments would then need to assess the results of these efforts. It will be important, for example, to have German Reichsbank records available so that we can all reach a more complete understanding of the origin and flows of looted assets.

The U.S. hopes that other governments continue to build on these hopeful beginnings. We all need to pursue unresolved issues, such as the disposition of heirless assets. We also need to create museums and educational curricula, and to find other ways to teach future generations the truth about the war years and their countries' relationship with Nazi Germany.

Most urgently, these actions should focus on providing justice for Holocaust survivors. That is why we are discussing with Britain and France final disposition of the Gold Pool. The report concludes that this Pool contained at least some individual gold that did not belong to the central banks of governments who have now received it from the TGC. Moreover, there is a moral dimension. The remaining amount, almost $70 million to be divided among the claimant countries—is small, but if a significant portion of this amount could be given to Holocaust survivors, it would help them live out their declining years in dignity. This is particularly important for those "double victims" in Central and Eastern Europe and the former Soviet Union who survived both Nazism and Communism, and have received little or no compensation from Germany. While we recognize that the final decision will need to be made in consultation with our TGC partners and the claimant countries, we favor a substantial portion of this remaining gold being made available for a fund for the benefit of surviving victims.

There are additional unresolved issues which are only briefly mentioned in this report. One which has arisen recently concerns the disposition of heirless assets in U.S. banks and, indeed, whether there may have been looted Nazi assets in U.S. banks—including the American affiliates of Swiss-owned banks. This is an important matter that requires further investigation by other institutions, including relevant state authorities. It is also important to pursue insurance claims by families of Holocaust victims whose policies were confiscated by the Nazis or whose claims were denied due to a variety of circumstances, including the lack of a death certificate.

Much work remains to be done, but this preliminary study is a major step forward. Ultimately, the United States, our Allies, and the neutral nations alike should be judged not so much by the actions or inactions of a previous generation, but more by our generation's willingness to face the past honestly, to help right the wrongs, and to deal with the injustices suffered by the victims of Nazi aggression. Our hope is that this study will advance that broader purpose.

IBM ON CHESS VICTORY BY "DEEP BLUE" COMPUTER
May 11, 1997

In a victory of machine over man—and a public relations bonanza for one of the world's largest companies—IBM Corporation's "Deep Blue" supercomputer on May 11 defeated the world's reigning chess champion, Garry Kasparov. It was the first time a computer had defeated a chess master, and it was the first loss of a multigame match ever for Kasparov.

Kasparov, who had been the world champion since 1985, maintained his title despite the loss to the computer. But he said he was ashamed of his playing in the final two games and demanded a rematch. The final count was 3½ for Deep Blue to 2½ for Kasparov.

The 1997 match was the second between Kasparov and Deep Blue. Kasparov prevailed 4 to 2 in the first match, in Philadelphia in February 1996. The machine's victory in the first game of that match stunned Kasparov, but he later said he learned enough about the computer's capabilities to aid his own game later.

Deep Blue was IBM's name for a specially-built mainframe computer technically known as the RS/6000 SP. The Kasparov-Deep Blue match generated intense international interest; more than 150 news organizations from around the world were represented at the match, which was open to the public.

Computers and Chess

Experts in computers and chess began teaching computers how to play games in the early 1950s, but it was not until the late 1980s that computers became powerful enough to have a realistic chance of competing against top chess champions. Computers can process information much more rapidly than any human; IBM said the 1997 version of Deep Blue could process 200 million chess moves a second, or 50 billion in the three-minute average for players to make a move in a tournament. But computers lack the inherent judgment for serious strategy: the ability to focus on the limited number of moves with a potential for advantage over the full course of a game rather than wasting time considering dead-end moves.

IBM began its Deep Blue project in 1989 and continually upgraded the machine's capabilities, both by adding new processing speed and by "teaching" it more about chess. In the year after the 1996 match, a five-person team of IBM computer scientists worked full-time with former U.S. chess champion Joel Benjamin to improve Deep Blue's chess skills. IBM officials said the training made the computer more efficient in looking for the most promising moves.

IBM officials rejected suggestions that their machine was "intelligent," that it was capable of acting on intuitive judgments or harboring emotional feelings. In a World Wide Web page devoted to the match, the Deep Blue team said the computer "is stunningly effective at solving chess problems, but it is less 'intelligent' than even the stupidest human."

Before the 1997 match, Kasparov told reporters he had sensed intelligence in the computer during the 1996 contest, based on the net result of its calculations, if not in the way it achieved those results. "I don't care how the machine gets there," he said. "It feels like thinking."

The 1997 Match

The 1997 rematch between Kasparov and Deep Blue began on May 3, in the New York office tower where the computer was housed. The match got off to a good start for Kasparov, who won the first game using the aggressive attacking techniques that had kept him as the world champion for twelve years.

Kasparov and several expert observers said the pivotal point in the entire match came the next day in the second game, when Deep Blue played much more skillfully than it ever had before. Some experts later said Kasparov might have been able to force Deep Blue into a draw in the game, but he failed to do so and was forced to resign after a contest of nearly four hours. Kasparov said after the match that the defeat in the second game hampered his ability to concentrate for the rest of the match.

Each of the intervening three games ended in a draw. Some experts said that in game five Kasparov appeared unnerved by the computer's ability to rebound from what appeared to be a losing position. Still shaken by the result of that game, Kasparov stumbled badly in the sixth game on May 11, making mistakes that a player of his ability and experience almost never makes. Deep Blue responded aggressively, forcing Kasparov to resign after only nineteen moves in the game.

Kasparov acknowledged that he was tired and dispirited at the opening of the sixth game and that his frame of mind led to him make uncharacteristic mistakes. "I had no real strength left to fight," he said. "And today's win by Deep Blue was justified."

Even so, Kasparov bitterly complained—as he had before the rematch—that the computer had an unfair advantage in addition to its enormous calculating power. Deep Blue's programmers, he said, were able to study all his previous matches and store them in the computer's memory banks. Kasparov said IBM refused to grant him comparable access to previous games

Deep Blue had played, so he had no opportunity to study his opponent's methods. Despite his complaints, Kasparov challenged Deep Blue to a rematch, saying "the competition has just started."

Members of Deep Blue's development team were elated. Team leader C. J. Tan and other IBM officials said the processing capabilities demonstrated by the computer could be helpful in many of the real-world applications that machines similar to Deep Blue were handling every day, such as air traffic control and the development of pharmaceutical products. "This will benefit everyone, from the audience to school children, to businesses everywhere, even to Garry Kasparov," Tan said.

Following is a report on Deep Blue's victory over chess champion Garry Kasparov, issued on IBM Corporation's "Deep Blue Home Page" on the World Wide Web, May 11, 1997:

In a shocking finale that lasted barely more than an hour, World Champion Garry Kasparov resigned 19 moves into Game 6, handing a historic victory to Deep Blue.

The win gave the IBM supercomputer a 3.5–2.5 victory in the six-game rematch. It was the first time a current world champion has lost a match to a computer opponent under tournament conditions.

"What we just witnessed was a landmark achievement in chess," said match commentator Yasser Seirawan. "All I can say is that I'm stunned. I absolutely didn't expect this to happen."

Kasparov, who afterward admitted he was in a poor frame of mind entering Game 6, fell into a well-known trap that has been established as a bad line to follow.

According to commentators covering the match, it was almost inconceivable that someone of Kasparov's ability could allow this to happen. It appeared that the pressure of the past five games had taken its toll on Kasparov. His disastrous mistake early in the game was certainly uncharacteristic of a man generally considered to be the greatest player in the history, and Kasparov's early resignation was a sign that he'd lost his will to fight. "For me, the match was over yesterday," he said. "I had no real strength left to fight. And today's win by Deep Blue was justified."

Game 6 began with a very quiet, positional-based opening, the Caro-Kann. Unlike in four of the previous five games, Kasparov, playing black, began with a "real" opening—one that wasn't specifically improvised to throw off Deep Blue—but he then developed it into a losing variation.

Based on this beginning, the commentators predicted a strategic battle. Said Seirawan, "This is also a very solid set up for black."

That forecast quickly went out the window after Kasparov's seventh move, when Deep Blue sacrificed a knight for a pawn, costing Kasparov the ability to castle. At this point, Kasparov's disposition changed dramatically. "Kasparov has a look of terror on his face," said Seirawan. "He's showing his disbelief by falling for a well-known opening trap." The error provided Deep Blue with a highly advantageous position and marked the beginning of the end for Kasparov.

After the game, Deep Blue development team leader C. J. Tan expressed satisfaction with the result. He also pointed out that there was more to Deep Blue's battle with Garry Kasparov than just a game of chess. "We are very proud to have played a role in this historic event," he said. "This will benefit everyone—from the audience to school children, to businesses everywhere, even to Garry Kasparov."

Kasparov, who on several occasions expressed unhappiness with the ground rules of the six-game rematch, challenged Deep Blue to a showdown under regular tournament conditions. "The match was lost by the world champion," he said, "but there are very good and very profound reasons for this. I think the competition has just started. This is just the beginning."

The Deep Blue development team took home the $700,000 first prize, while Kasparov received $400,000.

QUEEN ELIZABETH'S SPEECH TO THE BRITISH PARLIAMENT
May 14, 1997

British voters decided May 1 that eighteen consecutive years of Conservative Party rule was enough, turning the government over to a redesigned Labour Party headed by the charismatic Tony Blair. The son of a well-to-do attorney, Blair used sophisticated market research techniques to fashion a "New Labor" party that shed its socialist past and targeted young urban professionals while continuing to appeal to the working class. Blair easily swept aside the tired and divided Conservative Party, which had governed Britain for nearly two decades under the dynamic leadership of Margaret Thatcher and then the cautious guidance of John Major.

The Labour landslide victory was one of the most overwhelming in British history. Before the election, the Conservatives held a narrow 331-seat majority of the 659-seat House of Commons. The party lost half its seats on May 1, falling to a 165-seat minority, while Labour gained a comfortable 418-seat majority—compared to the 271 seats it had before the election. Labour's majority was larger even than the margin Thatcher enjoyed at the height of her political power in the early 1980s. The Liberal Democrats also gained at the expense of the Conservatives, more than doubling their number of seats to 46. The rout of the Conservatives was most striking in Scotland and Wales, where no member of the party held onto a seat. Among those defeated were Major's foreign secretary and defense minister.

The Conservative Legacy

Blair's trouncing of the Conservatives bore a few similarities to the beating that Margaret Thatcher's Conservative Party administered to the tired and divided Labour Party in May 1979. Thatcher became Britain's first female prime minister that year with a comfortable majority in Parliament, then won two more elections in 1983 and 1987 before she was dumped by her own restless colleagues in 1990. Major, her successor, won his own term as prime minister in 1992, although with a sharply diminished majority. (Resignation of Thatcher, Historic Documents of 1990, p. 747)

*Counting the eighteen Thatcher-Major years, the Conservatives had gov-
erned Britain for thirty-five of the previous fifty years. During many of the
Thatcher years, the Conservatives appeared invincible, in part because of
the weakness of Labour's leadership.*

*Thatcher transformed the politics and the economy of Britain, slashing
taxes and welfare spending and privatizing stated-owned businesses. The
overall economy steadily improved, as did the bottom lines of large corporations, transforming Britain into one of the economic engines of Europe.
But as factories closed and unemployment soared (to a high of nearly 13
percent in 1982), it became clear that Thatcherism was widening the economic divide in a society that long had been class conscious. Labour's
efforts to exploit working-class resentment of Thatcher's policies fell victim
to a broader fear of damaging the overall economic upswing. In the late
1980s Thatcher became less popular than her policies, especially within
her own party, which eased her out of power in 1990 in favor of the more
consensus-oriented John Major.*

*Major's bland leadership was at first a refreshing tonic for a country
used to the glaring, domineering figure of Margaret Thatcher. Public opinion polls showed that Britons liked and respected Major and gave his party
credit for the country's continuing economic rejuvenation. Major never
commanded intense loyalty within his own party, however, and as the
years wore on internal divisions became more evident.*

*The Conservative infighting was most serious on the touchstone issue of
Britain's role in a politically and economically united Europe. Major for
years had tried to hew to a middle-of-the-road stance, advocating more
British involvement in a greater Europe, but not at the expense of British
sovereignty or dignity.*

*The chief issue in 1997 was whether Britain would participate in the
single European currency, pushed by Germany and France, which was to
go into effect in 1999. Major took the position that Britain should wait
until the final details of the single currency plan were worked out, probably in 1998, and then base a decision on whether participation was, on balance, in the country's best interest. Although not a model of aggressive political leadership, this straddling position was aimed at alienating as few
voters as possible. Blair's Labour Party had taken a similar position, for
the same reason.*

*Major's control of his own party came into question just a few weeks
before the election when several dozen Conservative Members of Parliament,
including three of his own cabinet ministers, announced their outright
opposition to joining Europe's single currency. Major at first chastised the
dissenters, who called themselves "Euroskeptics," and appealed for party
unity. But just two weeks before the election, Major appeared to switch
sides, saying he had concluded that accepting planned rules for the Eurocur-
rency would be "quite unthinkable." The incident clearly revealed deep divisions in the party and bolstered public perceptions of Major as a weak general who could not command his own troops and instead had to join them.*

Blair's Winning Formula

Blair took over leadership of the Labour Party in 1994 and immediately began recasting its image by curtailing the influence of Britain's once-powerful trade unions and gradually dropping the use of the word "socialism" from the party manifesto. Blair insisted on referring to his party as "New Labor," to distinguish it from the left-leaning, trouble-prone assemblage that had lost four straight elections.

Blair proved to be an aggressive and dynamic leader capable of controlling a once-turbulent party and broadening its appeal. Critics, especially on the left, called him "Tony Blur"—a man able to take any side in a debate with apparent conviction—and said he was aping Bill Clinton's reshaping of the Democratic Party in the United States. But his youth, good looks, and ability to talk in broad, nonthreatening terms caught the public fancy—just as the public's dissatisfaction with the long-governing Conservatives was on the rise.

Blair's favorite word appeared to be "decent." He used it in nearly every campaign speech, often several times in the same sentence, promising to transform Britain into a "decent society" in which "decent people" could lead a "decent life." If Blair failed to define exactly what he meant by this vague rhetoric, the voters who gave him a majority in Parliament never seemed to mind.

In the 1997 campaign Labour strategists managed to defuse one issue that had been used against the party in the past: taxes. Despite predictions that it would win, Labour had lost the 1992 election in large part because Major said his opponents would raise taxes. Blair headed off the issue in 1997 by promising to live within the Conservative Party budget projections for at least two years, without raising taxes.

Labour also went after the Conservatives on one of the most politically sensitive issues in any postindustrialist society: old-age pensions. Using scare tactics similar to those employed successfully in the United States by Democrats against Republicans on the issue of Social Security, Labour charged that the Conservative policies ultimately would force cutbacks in pensions.

Once in office, Blair moved beyond the refashioning of a political party to the refurbishing of an entire country, at least in terms of marketing. He began promoting "New Britain," describing it as a forward-looking nation ready for the challenges of the twenty-first century. Some of Blair's changes were pure symbolism, such as updating British tourism promotions to emphasize London's trendy restaurants and boutiques rather than ancient British pomp and pageantry. Other changes had more substance, including Blair's successful promotion of referendums to give some political power to local assemblies in Scotland and Wales and proposals to curtail the influence of the House of Lords. Overall, Blair's main agenda items appeared to maintain steady economic growth while giving Britons more confidence in their ability to face a new century in which the glory of the British empire would be only a distant memory.

*Following is the text of the traditional speech to the opening ses-
sion of Parliament on May 14, 1997, delivered by Queen Elizabeth; the speech was written by the new government headed by
Prime Minister Tony Blair of the Labour Party:*

My Government intends to govern for the benefit of the whole nation.

The education of young people will be my Government's first priority. They
will work to raise standards in schools, colleges and universities and to promote lifelong learning at the workplace. They will cut class sizes using money
saved as a result of legislation phasing out the assisted places scheme. A further Bill will contain measures to raise educational standards, develop a new
role for local education authorities and parents, establish a new framework
for the decentralised and equitable organisation of schools, propose reforms
to the teaching profession, and respond positively to recommendations from
the National Committee of Inquiry into the future of higher education.

The central economic objectives of my Government are high and stable
levels of economic growth and employment, to be achieved by ensuring
opportunity for all. The essential platform for achieving these objectives is
economic stability.

To that end a Bill will be introduced to give the Bank of England operational responsibility for setting interest rates, in order to deliver price stability and support the Government's overall economic policy, within a framework of enhanced accountability. My Government will also ensure that public
borrowing is controlled through tough fiscal rules and that the burden of public debt is kept at a stable and prudent level. They will aim to deliver high and
sustainable levels of growth and employment by encouraging investment in
industry, skills, infrastructure and new technologies; by reducing long-term
unemployment, especially among young people; by promoting competition;
and by helping to create successful and profitable business. These policies
will enhance Britain's position as a leading industrial nation.

My Government has pledged to mount a fundamental attack upon youth
and long-term unemployment and will take early steps to implement a
welfare-to-work programme to tackle unemployment, financed by a levy on
the excess profits of the privatised utilities which will be brought forward in
an early Budget.

A new partnership with business will be at the heart of my Government's
plans to build a modern and dynamic economy to improve the competitiveness of British industry. They will bring forward legislation to reform and
strengthen competition law and introduce a statutory right to interest on late
payment of debts. My Government is committed to fairness at work and will
introduce a national minimum wage.

Legislation will be brought forward to amend criminal law and to combat
crime, including reform of the youth justice system and measures against
anti-social behaviour. A Bill will be introduced to prohibit the private possession of handguns.

My Government will improve the National Health Service [NHS], as a service providing care on the basis of need to the whole population. They will bring forward new arrangements for decentralisation and co-operation within the service and for ending the internal market. Legislation will be introduced to clarify the existing powers of NHS Trusts to enter into partnerships with the private sector. A White Paper will be published on measures to reduce tobacco consumption, including legislation to ban tobacco advertising.

My Government will contribute to the achievement of high standards of food safety and protection of public health throughout the food chain, will ensure openness and transparency of information to consumers, and will consult widely on recommendations for a Food Standards Agency.

A Bill will be introduced to ensure that as many people as possible have access to the benefits of the National Lottery including for health and education projects.

Measures will be introduced to enable capital receipts from the sale of council houses to be invested in housebuilding and renovation as part of my Government's determination to deal with homelessness and unemployment.

My Government is committed to open and transparent Government. They will introduce a Bill to strengthen data protection controls. They will enhance people's aspirations for better, more accessible and accountable public services, using Information Technology to the full. A White Paper will be published on proposals for a Freedom of Information Bill.

A Bill will be introduced to incorporate into United Kingdom law the main provisions of the European Convention on Human Rights.

Decentralisation is essential to my Government's vision of a modern nation. Legislation will be introduced to allow the people of Scotland and Wales to vote in referendums on my Government's proposals for a devolved Scottish Parliament and the establishment of a Welsh Assembly. If these proposals are approved in the referendums, my Government will bring forward legislation to implement them. Legislation will be introduced to provide for a referendum on a directly elected strategic authority and a directly elected mayor for London. A Bill will be brought forward to establish Regional Development Agencies in England outside London.

In Northern Ireland my Government will seek reconciliation and a political settlement which has broad support, working in co-operation with the Irish Government. They will work to build trust and confidence in Northern Ireland by bringing forward legislation to deal with terrorism and to reduce tension over parades, and other measures to protect human rights, combat discrimination in the workplace, increase confidence in policing and foster economic development.

Members of the House of Commons
Estimates for the public service will be laid before you.
My Lords and Members of the House of Commons
In the European Union, my Government will take a leading role. They will seek to promote employment, improve competitiveness, complete the Single Market and opt into the Social Chapter. They will seek further reform of the

Common Agricultural Policy to secure lower food prices for consumers and save money, support the rural economy and enhance the environment. They will seek changes to the Common Fisheries Policy to conserve fish stocks in the long-term interest of the UK fishing industry. They will play a full part in the debate about Economic and Monetary Union.

My Government will work for the early and successful enlargement of the European Union. They will pursue an outcome to the Intergovernmental Conference and use their Presidency in the first half of 1998 to strengthen European co-operation while advancing the United Kingdom's interests and to make the Union more open, democratic and efficient. A Bill will be introduced to amend the European Communities Act if necessary.

My Government will ensure a strong defence based on the North Atlantic Treaty Organisation, and promote international peace and security. They will play a major role in decisions to shape NATO's future, including enlargement, and to include Russia in a wider security framework. To ensure that the United Kingdom's defence capabilities are matched to the changing strategic setting, my Government will reassess our essential security interests and defence needs.

My Government will retain strong armed forces, including the nuclear deterrent. Preventing the proliferation of weapons of mass destruction will be a priority.

My Government will work for reforms to make the United Nations more effective and for an early resolution of its funding crisis. My Government will continue to support peace in Bosnia and Herzegovina. They will work for a settlement in Cyprus. They will promote efforts for a durable peace in the Middle East.

My Government will work on behalf of Hong Kong's people to achieve a successful transition which preserves their way of life and promotes their continued stability and prosperity.

Preparations will continue for the G7 Summit to be held in Birmingham and the second Asia-Europe Meeting in London in 1998. My Government will host the meeting of the Commonwealth Heads of Government in October 1997 and seize the opportunity to increase co-operation between the United Kingdom and other members of the Commonwealth.

My Government has established a Department for International Development. They will publish a White Paper setting out how, through more coherent policies, they will tackle global poverty and promote sustainable development. They will rejoin the United Nations Educational, Scientific and Cultural Organisation.

My Government will promote open markets around the world, while ensuring that the interests of developing countries and the global environment are fairly reflected.

The promotion of human rights worldwide will be a priority, as will the fight against terrorism, organised crime, money laundering and drug misuse and trafficking at home and abroad.

My Government will seek to restore confidence in the integrity of the nation's political system by upholding the highest standards of honesty and propriety in public life. They will consider how the funding of political parties should be regulated and reformed.

They will programme House of Commons business to ensure more effective scrutiny of Bills and better use of the time of Members of the House of Commons. During the course of the session, my Government will also publish in draft for public consultation a number of Bills, which it intends to introduce in subsequent sessions of this Parliament. They will propose the establishment of a new Select Committee of the House of Commons to look at ways of making Parliamentary procedure more effective and efficient.

Other measures will be laid before you.

My Lords and Members of the House of Commons

I pray that the blessing of Almighty God may rest upon your counsels.

KHATAMI ON HIS ELECTION
AS PRESIDENT OF IRAN
May 27, 1997

Mohammed Khatami, a relative moderate among the Iranian political and religious leadership, stunned the hard-line Islamic establishment in May by winning an overwhelming victory in the country's first truly contested presidential election. Khatami won 69 percent of the 29.1 million votes cast in the May 23 election, defeating a candidate chosen by the Islamic leadership.

Khatami took office in August and cautiously began pushing reforms in the domestic and foreign policies that had been in place with few changes since the 1979 revolution that ousted the shah, Mohammed Reza Pahlavi. Khatami in December took a first tentative step toward improving relations with the United States, long reviled by the Iranian mullahs (Islamic clergymen) as the "Great Satan." Khatami said he had "great respect" for the American people—if not their government—and called for a "thoughtful dialogue" with them.

Rising Through the Ranks

Khatami, fifty-four at the time of his election, was born in the south-western part of Iran, the son of a prominent ayatollah, Ruhollah Khatami. The younger Khatami undertook theological studies at key Islamic centers and earned undergraduate degrees in philosophy and education. Khatami got a job with the Militant Cleric's Association, a hotbed of opposition to the shah, and became acquainted with Ayatollah Ruhollah Khomeini, the spiritual leader of the Islamic opposition, through the ayatollah's son, Ahmed.

In 1978 Khatami was named to head the Islamic Center in Hamburg, Germany, where some exiled leaders of the Iranian opposition were based. After the revolution that ousted the shah in 1979, Khatami returned to Iran, was elected to parliament, and took over an institute that published progovernment newspapers.

Khatami was appointed in 1982 to head the Ministry of Culture and Islamic Guidance, which was responsible for reviewing and censoring films, newspapers, magazines, and books. In that position Khatami developed a reputation as a moderate through such actions as easing the government's restrictions on the types of publications (including foreign newspapers and books) that could be circulated and encouraging a more vibrant film industry in Iran. Khatami's actions as culture minister were highly controversial among more conservative clerics, who disputed many of his liberalizations and eventually forced him to resign in 1992. Apparently as consolation, he was named director of the national library, a post that enabled him extensive time for study and writing.

Friends and associates encouraged Khatami to run for president in 1997, especially after then-president Ali Akbar Hashemi Rafsanjani lost an attempt to overturn a ban on his seeking a third term in office. Even after Khatami agreed to run, most analysts gave him no chance to win, assuming that the hard-line mullahs would resort to fraud, if necessary, to keep a so-called moderate out of the presidency.

Despite—and possibly even because of—the hostility of many of his fellow clerics, Khatami's candidacy caught fire among younger voters and women, especially in urban areas. Nearly 70 percent of all Iranians in 1997 were under twenty-five years of age, and many young adults reportedly felt little connection with the ideological fervor of the 1979 revolution. Women were particularly attracted to Khatami's candidacy. Although Iranian women lived under less stringent restrictions than did women in many other Islamic societies, they were subject to official discrimination, including the requirement that they cover themselves in public.

The breadth of Khatami's election victory went beyond the young, women, and urbanites, however. Khatami won at least a majority in nearly every section of the country, apparently the result of a widespread yearning for change.

Up Against the Establishment

In his few statements immediately after his election victory, Khatami denied having any plans for sweeping reforms of Iranian government or society. Speaking to reporters at a May 27 news conference, Khatami took a cautious line, saying Iranians had voted for "stability" and had supported the system. Even if he did have plans for major changes, the structure of government created by the hard-line mullahs posed obstacles to any serious reform effort.

As president, Khatami appointed government ministers and had overall responsibility for the day-to-day operations of the national government. But Khatami had to maneuver among other power centers. The most important was the Council of Guardians, Iran's most senior religious body, which was responsible for protecting revolutionary and Islamic ideals. The council, with Iran's fiercely hard-line spiritual leader Ayatollah Ali Khamenei at its head, had approved Khatami's presidential candidacy, but that was generally seen as no guarantee that Khatami's policies would win a similar endorsement. Khatami also faced likely opposition within the parliament, which continued to be dominated by conservatives who had opposed his candidacy.

Government policies could be reviewed by the Expediency Council, which had authority to mediate disputes between the government and religious establishments. Khatami had a possible ally in former president Rafsanjani, who chaired the Expediency Council and who had given Khatami tacit support in the presidential campaign.

In his first months in office, Khatami moved cautiously and rarely spoke in public. Observers said Khatami appeared to be feeling his way through Iran's complex maze of political and religious power. Khatami scored a key victory August 21, when the parliament approved all twenty-two members of his new cabinet despite opposition from conservatives to some of his choices.

Iran and Khatami commanded world attention for several weeks before and during a global Islamic conference held in Iran in November. Addressing his first news conference as president, on December 14, Khatami took a modest step toward patching up relations with the United States, praising its people and expressing hope that U.S. political leaders would change their attitude toward Iran. "I would hope for a thoughtful dialogue with the American people and through this thoughtful dialogue we could get closer to peace and security and tranquillity," he told reporters.

The next day, President Bill Clinton welcomed Khatami's remarks, telling reporters at a photo session that he "would like nothing better than to have a dialogue with Iran." Clinton insisted, however, that he would not change the U.S. policy of attempting to isolate Iran internationally as long as that country sponsored terrorism and sought to develop weapons of mass destruction. Khatami's initiative toward the United States came just as the Clinton administration was debating how to respond to Iranian plans to develop it natural gas resources with the aid of private companies from Canada, France, Russia, and other countries. The administration had not announced any policy decisions on the matter by the end of 1997.

Following are excerpts from a news conference by Mohammed Khatami on May 27, 1997, as translated, six days after he had been elected president of Iran:

In the name of God, the compassionate and merciful, at the outset I would like to extend my greetings to the journalists that are representatives of the mass media, external and internal, from our country that are the ear, the tongue and the eye—the reliable ear, eye and tongue of the people for telling the stories of the realities to the people are harboring or do have such important duties upon.

And also I would like to welcome all the foreign journalists and the media representatives who have come to our country to witness one of the glorious stages of our determination of the destiny of our nation by themselves to witness the stability and the strength of our nation and also their active, happy presence in this stage of our country.

At first they have cast their votes in favor of the stability and the power of the country. And the second stage they have presented the manifestation of the freedom. And I do wish and I do wish them every success in transmitting the realities of this glorious presence of the people of Iran to their countries, as well as to the public opinion of the world.

Whatever that has occurred is a unique opportunity for all of us. Our nation has been able to regain its humiliated identity in the light of the revolution. And has established a system of the cultural religious values upon its religion, that people do have a major role in. And an example of that could be seen in the recent elections.

All these grandeurs of the presence of the people is definitely in the palm of the late Iman Khomeini and also the understanding and the awakened conscience of our people at this stage. And this great outcome which has been incarnated in the form of the Islamic Republic of Iran shall continue its way under the leadership of His Imminence Ayatollah Khamenei for years to come.

I am ready to answer to the questions of the journalists and the media. . . .

First of all, I do believe that people have cast their votes in favor of their system, the independence of their country. And as I have mentioned in my electioneering propogandas, that after 18 years of different stages of the Holy defense and also the construction of our country more than ever we have reached a stability of our system and our country.

And this is the best opportunity to stabilize a civil society within the framework of the civilized and the expansion and deepening of a civil life would be among the major objectives to be pursued. And also the stabilization of the Constitution would be to be pursued under the guidelines of the great imminent leaders by themselves. That with the participation of the people by itself and the outcomes that we have had thus far, moment by moment it is progressing. . . .

Question: Mr. President, 20 million people cast a vote for a change of course of direction in their revolution. You have spoken about civil liberties, civil rights and the rule of law.

What specifically do you plan to do to meet those demands? Are you surprised by the 20 million vote and what they said?

And one last question. Do you think the atmosphere will exist for better relations between Iran and the United States?

Khatami: Prior to being surprised from the number of the votes, I should say that I am—it is a matter of honor to me. And of course, to the same extent, I do feel a heavy-duty burden. And as I mentioned at the beginning, this vote has been casted as a confidence towards the system, the leadership and the revolution. And it is an indication of the presence of our people with vigilance at the stage of determining their destiny and the future.

And they are all living within a system that has been quite—it is quite dear to them and has been quite costly for them. And they would not easily get parted from. And of course, fortunately there is freedom and the right of choice in our system. And also one of the reasons for having the exciting stages of the revolution has been the right to compete.

That means the people interested in the system have been able to make a choice within the framework of the system. And naturally what they have chosen would be a matter of respect to everybody. While we do have due respect for the programs and the ideas of the other competitors or the rivals, and also there shall be chances of having debates and discussions between different points of view existing as well in future.

It would be quite natural that I would be committed to the programs that I have introduced and I do hope that I would be able to materialize them through the legal channels in coordination with the other organizations. And what I could say in one sentence was that all election was participation and the right of choice for the people and no opposition to the system. And God willing, that the grounds of the participation and the power of the choice of the people shall remain in place and it would be strengthened as well.

In regards to the relations with the United States of the America, I should say that the America is the source or the upspring of this problem.

We are sorry to say that the U.S. policies has always been directed or has been hostile toward our revolution, our system. The great outcome of our revolution is independence and we are not willing to give up on this valuable outcome that we have gained. The basis of our relation with the other countries is reliance upon the independence and the national interests of our country.

Until the day that the Americans are willing to bring any harm to this independence and the national interests of our country, there would be no ground for any relations. We cannot accept the domineering or injunction policies in general.

Any change in the relation with the United States is dependent upon the changes of the policies of the America towards the revolution and Iran. hand unfortunately, we do not see any sign of such change in the Americans' policy. . . .

Question: Mr. President, John Simpson from the BBC. You have spoken about the rule of law and just now you called the election result a manifestation of freedom.

Many people in Iran complain about the interference in their daily lives of unauthorized and unelected people. Will this now change under your presidency and will you reintroduce the greater degree of intellectual and cultural freedom that existed here when you were minister of culture?

Khatami: Of our honor is that in accordance with Islam, we are experiencing a system that man is of high spiritual value and its views as well. And of course should there be security prevailing in a society, all the freedom and liberties should be defined within a constant framework.

And in fact, we have been a revolution that just by passage of one year from the revolution we have been able to have our Constitution. And of course, it is quite clear that the freedoms have been defined within the framework of our society and there are articles regarding the freedom of the view, freedom of the life, freedom of the associations and freedom of the employment.

And the boundaries which have been observed for this freedom is not to have any intervention with the basic principles of the Islam and not serve as a disturbance to the public freedom. And of the top prioritized or important duties of the president is to act upon the Constitution, except for the areas that are related to the leadership.

Therefore, we are all thinking of a society which is legal and defending the right and the freedoms of the people within the framework of the Constitution and the expectations from the people to observe the boundaries and the frameworks which have been defined by the Constitution.

Therefore, we are hoping and looking forward to have a more legal system and also with the observance of the limitations the civil—the rights and the regulations that are well defined for the dear citizens of our country for further solidarity and also progress to be made. . . .

Question: Sir, the question of cultural—greater cultural freedom?

Khatami: Definitely, all the rights and the freedoms that are defined within the frameworks of the Constitution for our citizens should be observed. What is important is to bring about social and individual security within the framework of the Constitution.

This is within the framework of the Constitution, that we could defend the interest and the values of the country, as well as the civil rights and the freedoms of its citizens. Our slogan is to bring about an ever more legal system, a social system and this is an expectation that we should have from the president. . . .

Question: Will there be any woman minister appointed to your excellency's cabinet or not? I wanted to inquire into that.

Khatami: Fortunately, our women after the victory of the revolution have been able to gain in prominent status in our society and the distinguished foreign medias could observe for themselves that what great achievements have made upon the victory of the revolution for Iran, for our women as compared to the other similar countries.

And fortunately, wherever that our dear, great women have been able to gain equal opportunities, they have been able to prove their ability. And fortunately, there is no legal ban on the active presence of our women in different stages of the political, cultural, scientific, art and the other areas.

And of course, just having the rights would not be enough. And the possibilities also should be provided to the women in order to be able to utilize this opportunity. And this is the duty of our government to provide this equal opportunities for our valuable women.

So, while preserving the values and also the foundation of the family, they would be able to have the chance of active participation in different economic, cultural and political fields. I definitely do believe in the eligibility and the potentials of the Iranian woman.

And I don't see no impediment or obstacle toward their presence at the highest possible position in the system of our country. Therefore, the appointment of the responsibilities would be left with the potentiality and also the abilities—capabilities that would be shown, and not the gender. They could be. We are reviewing it. It is under review.

SUPREME COURT ON
PRESIDENTIAL IMMUNITY
May 27, 1997

In a ruling that cleared the way for Paula Corbin Jones to go forward with her sexual harassment suit against President Bill Clinton, the Supreme Court ruled unanimously May 27 that sitting presidents are not immune to civil suits for personal actions outside the official scope of their duties. "The Federal District Court has jurisdiction to decide this case," the Court said. "Like every other citizens . . . [Jones] has a right to an orderly disposition of her case." The ruling represented a major defeat for Clinton and his lawyers, who had hoped to be able to put off any trial in the case until after he left office in January 2001. It also set a historic precedent for future presidents.

In her suit Jones alleged that during an economic development conference in a Little Rock, Arkansas, hotel in 1991, Clinton had Jones invited to a hotel room where he exposed himself to her and asked her to perform oral sex. She allegedly refused and left the room; she said she told family and friends immediately afterwards that she had been humiliated by the overture and feared she might lose her job. At the time Clinton was governor of Arkansas and Jones was a state employee.

Jones did not file suit until May 1994, after an article in a conservative opinion magazine suggested that she had said she would be willing to be Clinton's "regular" girlfriend. Denying that she had ever said such a thing, Jones initially asked only for a public apology from Clinton, who by 1994 had been in the White House for a year and a half; later she asked for $700,000 in damages, which she said she would donate to charity.

Clinton's political advisers and his private lawyers downplayed the allegations, characterizing Jones as a gold digger seeking celebrity. The two sides reportedly came close to negotiating a settlement before Jones filed suit. But when James Carville, one of Clinton's top campaign strategists, referred publicly to Jones as "trailer trash," Jones and her family, angered and hurt by what they considered White House smears, decided to proceed. Clinton's attorneys, led by Washington superlawyer Robert S. Bennett, challenged Jones's right to sue a sitting president.

A federal district court in Arkansas ruled in December 1994 that a sitting president was not immune to a civil suit involving personal action but ordered any trial stayed until Clinton had left office. The district judge held that the public interest in avoiding litigation that might impede the president in the performance of his official duties outweighed the need for an immediate trial. Both sides appealed, and on January 9, 1996, only days before Clinton was due to be sworn in for a second term, a divided three-judge appeals court panel ruled in favor of Jones, holding that the president had no constitutional right to a delay in the civil suit. Clinton's attorneys appealed to the Supreme Court, arguing that the constitutional doctrine of separation of powers as well as respect for the office and nature of the presidency require the courts to postpone, in all but the most exceptional cases, any civil litigation against a president until after leaving office.

Request for Immunity

The unanimous Court rejected both arguments. Clinton's "effort to construct an immunity from suit for unofficial acts grounded purely in the identity of his office is unsupported by precedent," Justice John Paul Stevens wrote for the Court. Stevens noted that the Court in 1982 had granted former president Richard Nixon complete immunity from civil litigation for actions taken in his official capacity to avoid rendering the President "unduly cautious" in carrying out his official duties. "But," Stevens said, "we have never suggested that the President, or any other official, has an immunity that extends beyond the scope of any action taken in an unofficial capacity."

Rejecting Clinton's claims on separation of powers, Stevens said the Court had long held that it had the authority to determine whether official actions of the president were within the law. He cited in particular the Court's 1952 ruling that President Harry S. Truman had acted unconstitutionally when he tried to seize the steel industry to avert the effects of a steelworkers' strike. Stevens also cited the Court's 1974 ruling requiring President Nixon to comply with a subpoena to produce the now-infamous tape recordings of conversations with his aides. "If the Judiciary may severely burden the executive branch by reviewing the legality of the President's official conduct, and if it may direct appropriate process to the President himself, it must follow that the Federal courts have to the power to determine the legality of his unofficial conduct," Stevens wrote. "The burden on the President's time and energy that is a mere by-product of such review surely cannot be considered as onerous as the direct burden imposed by judicial review and the occasional invalidation of his official actions."

The Court also said that the case "if properly managed" should not take "any substantial amount" of Clinton's time. Moreover, Stevens wrote, the respect that "is owed of the office of the chief executive . . . should inform the conduct of the entire proceeding" against Clinton. "We assume that the testimony of the President, both for discovery and for use at trial, may be taken at the White House at a time that will accommodate his busy schedule." Stevens added that there would be no necessity for Clinton to attend his trial in person.

The Court also downplayed predictions that the ruling would lead to more civil suits against sitting presidents by people seeking to harm the president politically. "Only three sitting Presidents have been subjected to suits for their private actions," Stevens observed. "If the past is any indicator, it seems unlikely that a deluge of such litigation will ever engulf the Presidency." Although Justice Stephen G. Breyer agreed with the outcome of the case, he wrote a separate opinion saying he was more "skeptical" than the rest of the Court that the decision would not lead to more civil suits and that Clinton's conduct of his official duties would not be unduly hampered by the legal proceedings.

Preparation for Trial

Clinton "adamantly" denied Jones's allegations in his first formal legal response, filed July 3. In the papers, which asked the federal district judge in Little Rock to schedule the case for trial, Clinton said that "at no time" did he make "sexual advances toward the plaintiff, or otherwise act improperly in her presence. At no time did the president conspire to or sexually harass the plaintiff." The papers also alleged that Jones had deliberately "thrust herself into the public limelight . . . to maximize her potential to derive economic benefit and to harm the president politically."

Clinton's request for a trial date was an apparent reversal of his lawyers' earlier strategy to delay action in the case at least until the president won a second term in 1996. Once the Supreme Court ruled that he was not immune to the suit while he was in the White House, Clinton strategists apparently decided that the faster the incident could be put behind the president, the less it would mar his presidential legacy. "Part one was the election. Part two is his place in history," one adviser told the Washington Post. His strategists "don't want him to have this over his head for the next few years."

> Following are excerpts from the opinion, written by Justice John Paul Stevens, in which a unanimous Supreme Court ruled May 27, 1997, that a sitting president was not immune to civil suit arising from alleged personal actions taken before taking office:

No. 95-1853

William Jefferson Clinton, Petitioner	On writ of certiorari to the United
v.	States Court of Appeals for the
Paula Corbin Jones	Eighth Circuit

[May 27, 1997]

JUSTICE STEVENS delivered the opinion of the Court.

This case raises a constitutional and a prudential question concerning the Office of the President of the United States. Respondent, a private citizen, seeks to recover damages from the current occupant of that office based on actions allegedly taken before his term began. The President submits that in all but the most exceptional cases the Constitution requires federal courts to defer such litigation until his term ends and that, in any event, respect for the office warrants such a stay. Despite the force of the arguments supporting the President's submissions, we conclude that they must be rejected.

I

Petitioner, William Jefferson Clinton, was elected to the Presidency in 1992, and re-elected in 1996. His term of office expires on January 20, 2001. In 1991 he was the Governor of the State of Arkansas. Respondent, Paula Corbin Jones, is a resident of California. In 1991 she lived in Arkansas, and was an employee of the Arkansas Industrial Development Commission.

On May 6, 1994, she commenced this action in the United States District Court for the Eastern District of Arkansas by filing a complaint naming petitioner and Danny Ferguson, a former Arkansas State Police officer, as defendants. The complaint alleges two federal claims, and two state law claims over which the federal court has jurisdiction because of the diverse citizenship of the parties. As the case comes to us, we are required to assume the truth of the detailed—but as yet untested—factual allegations in the complaint.

Those allegations principally describe events that are said to have occurred on the afternoon of May 8, 1991, during an official conference held at the Excelsior Hotel in Little Rock, Arkansas. The Governor delivered a speech at the conference; respondent—working as a state employee—staffed the registration desk. She alleges that Ferguson persuaded her to leave her desk and to visit the Governor in a business suite at the hotel, where he made "abhorrent" [quoting from complaint] sexual advances that she vehemently rejected. She further claims that her superiors at work subsequently dealt with her in a hostile and rude manner, and changed her duties to punish her for rejecting those advances. Finally, she alleges that after petitioner was elected President, Ferguson defamed her by making a statement to a reporter that implied she had accepted petitioner's alleged overtures, and that various persons authorized to speak for the President publicly branded her a liar by denying that the incident had occurred. . . .

. . . With the exception of the last charge, which arguably may involve conduct within the outer perimeter of the President's official responsibilities, it is perfectly clear that the alleged misconduct of petitioner was unrelated to any of his official duties as President of the United States and, indeed, occurred before he was elected to that office.

II

In response to the complaint, petitioner promptly advised the District Court that he intended to file a motion to dismiss on grounds of Presidential immunity, and requested the court to defer all other pleadings and motions until after the immunity issue was resolved. Relying on our cases holding that immunity questions should be decided at the earliest possible stage of the litigation, our recognition of the " 'singular importance of the President's duties,' " (quoting *Nixon v. Fitzgerald* [1982]), and the fact that the question did not require any analysis of the allegations of the complaint, the court granted the request. [1994] Petitioner thereupon filed a motion "to dismiss . . . without prejudice and to toll any statutes of limitation [that may be applicable] until he is no longer President, at which time the plaintiff may refile the instant suit." Extensive submissions were made to the District Court by the parties and the Department of Justice.

The District Judge denied the motion to dismiss on immunity grounds and ruled that discovery in the case could go forward, but ordered any trial stayed until the end of petitioner's Presidency. (1994). . . .

Both parties appealed. A divided panel of the Court of Appeals affirmed the denial of the motion to dismiss, but because it regarded the order postponing the trial until the President leaves office as the "functional equivalent" of a grant of temporary immunity, it reversed that order. (1996). . . .

III

The President, represented by private counsel, filed a petition for certiorari. . . .

While our decision to grant the petition expressed no judgment concerning the merits of the case, it does reflect our appraisal of its importance. The representations made on behalf of the Executive Branch as to the potential impact of the precedent established by the Court of Appeals merit our respectful and deliberate consideration. . . .

IV

Petitioner's principal submission—that "in all but the most exceptional cases," the Constitution affords the President temporary immunity from civil damages litigation arising out of events that occurred before he took office—cannot be sustained on the basis of precedent.

Only three sitting Presidents have been defendants in civil litigation involving their actions prior to taking office. Complaints against Theodore Roosevelt and Harry Truman had been dismissed before they took office; the dismissals were affirmed after their respective inaugurations. Two companion cases arising out of an automobile accident were filed against John F. Kennedy in 1960 during the Presidential campaign. After taking office, he unsuccessfully argued that his status as Commander in Chief gave him a right to a stay under the Soldiers' and Sailors' Civil Relief Act of 1940. The motion for a stay was denied by the District Court, and the matter was settled out of court. Thus, none of those cases sheds any light on the constitutional issue before us.

The principal rationale for affording certain public servants immunity from suits for money damages arising out of their official acts is inapplicable to unofficial conduct. In cases involving prosecutors, legislators, and judges we have repeatedly explained that the immunity serves the public interest in enabling such officials to perform their designated functions effectively without fear that a particular decision may give rise to personal liability.... That rationale provided the principal basis for our holding that a former President of the United States was "entitled to absolute immunity from damages liability predicated on his official acts" [*Fitzgerald*]. Our central concern was to avoid rendering the President "unduly cautious in the discharge of his official duties."

This reasoning provides no support for an immunity for unofficial conduct. As we explained in *Fitzgerald*, "the sphere of protected action must be related closely to the immunity's justifying purposes." Because of the President's broad responsibilities, we recognized in that case an immunity from damages claims arising out of official acts extending to the "outer perimeter of his authority." But we have never suggested that the President, or any other official, has an immunity that extends beyond the scope of any action taken in an official capacity....

Moreover, when defining the scope of an immunity for acts clearly taken within an official capacity, we have applied a functional approach.... Hence, for example, a judge's absolute immunity does not extend to actions performed in a purely administrative capacity. As our opinions have made clear, immunities are grounded in "the nature of the function performed, not the identity of the actor who performed it."

Petitioner's effort to construct an immunity from suit for unofficial acts grounded purely in the identity of his office is unsupported by precedent.

V

We are also unpersuaded by the evidence from the historical record to which petitioner has called our attention. [Remainder of section omitted.]

VI

Petitioner's strongest argument supporting his immunity claim is based on the text and structure of the Constitution. He does not contend that the occupant of the Office of the President is "above the law," in the sense that his conduct is entirely immune from judicial scrutiny. The President argues merely for a postponement of the judicial proceedings that will determine whether he violated any law. His argument is grounded in the character of the office that was created by Article II of the Constitution, and relies on separation of powers principles that have structured our constitutional arrangement since the founding.

As a starting premise, petitioner contends that he occupies a unique office with powers and responsibilities so vast and important that the public interest demands that he devote his undivided time and attention to his public duties. He submits that—given the nature of the office—the doctrine of separation of powers places limits on the authority of the Federal Judiciary to interfere with the Executive Branch that would be transgressed by allowing this action to proceed.

We have no dispute with the initial premise of the argument....

It does not follow, however, that separation of powers principles would be violated by allowing this action to proceed. . . .

. . . [I]n this case there is no suggestion that the Federal Judiciary is being asked to perform any function that might in some way be described as "executive." Respondent is merely asking the courts to exercise their core Article III jurisdiction to decide cases and controversies. Whatever the outcome of this case, there is no possibility that the decision will curtail the scope of the official powers of the Executive Branch. The litigation of questions that relate entirely to the unofficial conduct of the individual who happens to be the President poses no perceptible risk of misallocation of either judicial power or executive power.

Rather than arguing that the decision of the case will produce either an aggrandizement of judicial power or a narrowing of executive power, petitioner contends that—as a by-product of an otherwise traditional exercise of judicial power—burdens will be placed on the President that will hamper the performance of his official duties. We have recognized that "[e]ven when a branch does not arrogate power to itself . . . the separation-of-powers doctrine requires that a branch not impair another in the performance of its constitutional duties." *Loving v. United States* (1996). As a factual matter, petitioner contends that this particular case—as well as the potential additional litigation that an affirmance of the Court of Appeals judgment might spawn—may impose an unacceptable burden on the President's time and energy, and thereby impair the effective performance of his office.

Petitioner's predictive judgment finds little support in either history or the relatively narrow compass of the issues raised in this particular case. As we have already noted, in the more than 200-year history of the Republic, only three sitting Presidents have been subjected to suits for their private actions. If the past is any indicator, it seems unlikely that a deluge of such litigation will ever engulf the Presidency. As for the case at hand, if properly managed by the District Court, it appears to us highly unlikely to occupy any substantial amount of petitioner's time.

Of greater significance, petitioner errs by presuming that interactions between the Judicial Branch and the Executive, even quite burdensome interactions, necessarily rise to the level of constitutionally forbidden impairment of the Executive's ability to perform its constitutionally mandated functions. . . . The fact that a federal court's exercise of its traditional Article III jurisdiction may significantly burden the time and attention of the Chief Executive is not sufficient to establish a violation of the Constitution. Two long-settled propositions . . . support that conclusion.

First, we have long held that when the President takes official action, the Court has the authority to determine whether he has acted within the law. . .

Second, it is also settled that the President is subject to judicial process in appropriate circumstances. Although Thomas Jefferson apparently thought otherwise, Chief Justice Marshall, when presiding in the treason trial of Aaron Burr, ruled that a subpoena *duces tecum* could be directed to the President. . . . We unequivocally and emphatically endorsed Marshall's position when we held that President Nixon was obligated to comply with a subpoena commanding him to produce certain tape recordings of his conversations with his aides. *United States v. Nixon* (1974). . . .

. . . If the Judiciary may severely burden the Executive Branch by reviewing the legality of the President's official conduct, and if it may direct appropriate process to the President himself, it must follow that the federal courts have power to determine the legality of his unofficial conduct. The burden on the President's time and energy that is a mere by-product of such review surely cannot be considered as onerous as the direct burden imposed by judicial review and the occasional invalidation of his official actions. We therefore hold that the doctrine of separation of powers does not require federal courts to stay all private actions against the President until he leaves office.

The reasons for rejecting such a categorical rule apply as well to a rule that would require a stay "in all but the most exceptional cases." Indeed, if the Framers of the Constitution had thought it necessary to protect the President from the burdens of private litigation, we think it far more likely that they would have adopted a categorical rule than a rule that required the President to litigate the question whether a specific case belonged in the "exceptional case" subcategory. In all events, the question whether a specific case should receive exceptional treatment is more appropriately the subject of the exercise of judicial discretion than an interpretation of the Constitution. Accordingly, we turn to the question whether the District Court's decision to stay the trial until after petitioner leaves office was an abuse of discretion.

VII

The Court of Appeals described the District Court's discretionary decision to stay the trial as the "functional equivalent" of a grant of temporary immunity. Concluding that petitioner was not constitutionally entitled to such an immunity, the court held that it was error to grant the stay. Although we ultimately conclude that the stay should not have been granted, we think the issue is more difficult than the opinion of the Court of Appeals suggests.

Strictly speaking the stay was not the functional equivalent of the constitutional immunity that petitioner claimed, because the District Court ordered discovery to proceed. Moreover, a stay of either the trial or discovery might be justified by considerations that do not require the recognition of any constitutional immunity. . . . Although we have rejected the argument that the potential burdens on the President violate separation of powers principles, those burdens are appropriate matters for the District Court to evaluate in its management of the case. The high respect that is owed to the office of the Chief Executive, though not justifying a rule of categorical immunity, is a matter that should inform the conduct of the entire proceeding, including the timing and scope of discovery.

Nevertheless, we are persuaded that it was an abuse of discretion for the District Court to defer the trial until after the President leaves office. Such a lengthy and categorical stay takes no account whatever of the respondent's interest in bringing the case to trial. The complaint was filed within the statutory limitations period—albeit near the end of that period—and delaying trial would increase the danger of prejudice resulting from the loss of evidence, including the inability of witnesses to recall specific facts, or the possible death of a party.

The decision to postpone the trial was, furthermore, premature. The proponent of a stay bears the burden of establishing its need. In this case, at the stage at which the District Court made its ruling, there was no way to assess whether a stay of trial after the completion of discovery would be warranted. Other than the fact that a trial may consume some of the President's time and attention, there is nothing in the record to enable a judge to assess the potential harm that may ensue from scheduling the trial promptly after discovery is concluded. We think the District Court may have given undue weight to the concern that a trial might generate unrelated civil actions that could conceivably hamper the President in conducting the duties of his office. If and when that should occur, the court's discretion would permit it to manage those actions in such fashion (including deferral of trial) that interference with the President's duties would not occur. But no such impingement upon the President's conduct of his office was shown here.

VIII

We add a final comment on two matters that are discussed at length in the briefs: the risk that our decision will generate a large volume of politically motivated harassing and frivolous litigation, and the danger that national security concerns might prevent the President from explaining a legitimate need for a continuance.

We are not persuaded that either of these risks is serious. Most frivolous and vexatious litigation is terminated at the pleading stage or on summary judgment, with little if any personal involvement by the defendant. Moreover, the availability of sanctions provides a significant deterrent to litigation directed at the President in his unofficial capacity for purposes of political gain or harassment. History indicates that the likelihood that a significant number of such cases will be filed is remote. Although scheduling problems may arise, there is no reason to assume that the District Courts will be either unable to accommodate the President's needs or unfaithful to the tradition—especially in matters involving national security—of giving "the utmost deference to Presidential responsibilities." . . . In short, we have confidence in the ability of our federal judges to deal with both of these concerns.

If Congress deems it appropriate to afford the President stronger protection, it may respond with appropriate legislation. . . . If the Constitution embodied the rule that the President advocates, Congress, of course, could not repeal it. But our holding today raises no barrier to a statutory response to these concerns.

The Federal District Court has jurisdiction to decide this case. Like every other citizen who properly invokes that jurisdiction, respondent has a right to an orderly disposition of her claims. Accordingly, the judgment of the Court of Appeals is affirmed.

It is so ordered.

June

FEDERAL TASK FORCE REPORT ON CHURCH ARSON CASES
June 6, 1997

A federal task force issued a preliminary report June 6, 1997, conclud-ing that there appeared to be no nationwide conspiracy involved in a rash of burnings and other attacks against churches in the mid-1990s. The task force said some of the attacks against synagogues and predominantly black churches were motivated by racism, but many other cases appeared to involve factors such as burglary and revenge.

After meeting with church leaders on June 10, Attorney General Janet Reno pledged to pursue vigorous investigations of church arson cases. Some church leaders asked the government to redouble its efforts to determine the motivations for attacks on churches, and they expressed concern that the news media and others would misinterpret the task force report as mini-mizing the extent of racial attacks.

An Upsurge of Attacks

Bombings and arson attacks on black churches in the South were com-mon and widely publicized during the civil rights movement of the 1960s. During the following decades, churches all over the country were burglar-ized, burned, or otherwise damaged in criminal attacks—but there ap-peared to be no common motive, as there had been during the civil rights years.

An apparent outbreak of attacks on churches, most noticeably on black churches around the time of the annual Martin Luther King Jr. holiday in January 1996, sparked nationwide concern. Congress held hearings on the matter and eventually passed legislation (the Church Arson Prevention Act of 1996, PL 104-155) broadening the federal jurisdiction over church arsons and increasing the maximum prison term for convictions in federal arson cases from ten to twenty years. In June 1996 President Bill Clinton ordered the Treasury and Justice Departments to form a joint task force to investigate church arson cases and help communities rebuild burned churches.

Task Force Report

In a "preliminary report" to Clinton dated June 6, Attorney General Reno and Treasury Secretary Robert E. Rubin described the first year's work of the National Church Arson Task Force, which included representatives of the FBI; the Bureau of Alcohol, Tobacco, and Firearms; the Justice Department; and other federal, state, and local agencies. Rubin and Reno said the task force would continue its work.

The task force said it had investigated 429 cases involving arsons, bombings, and other attacks on churches between January 1, 1995, and May 27, 1997. One hundred ninety-nine persons had been arrested in connection with 150 of those cases; of those arrested, 110 had been convicted in connection with 77 cases. The task force said the rate of arrests—35 percent of the total cases—was more than double the national average for arson cases in general. The task force report detailed the results of 83 incidents.

The task force said it found "a wide array" of motivations for the attacks on churches. Some cases involved "blatant racism" or religious hatred. In particular, the task force noted that twenty-five persons had been charged under federal civil rights or antiarson statutes in cases in six states; fourteen had been convicted as of the date of the report. For example, four former members of the Ku Klux Klan pled guilty to federal charges in connection with the burning of two black churches in South Carolina in June 1995. The task force report did not quantify the total number of cases in which racial motives appeared to be involved.

In many cases investigated by the task force, factors other than racism appeared to have motivated the attackers. The report said most persons charged with attacking churches had not been members of "hate groups" such as the Klan.

Burglars often set fire to churches in hopes of covering up evidence of their crimes. In some cases, attackers were seeking revenge for perceived slights, and in numerous cases juveniles (some of them as young as nine years of age) set fire to churches either accidentally or deliberately but with no clear motivations. The task force also found cases in which persons with satanic beliefs set fire to churches or wrote messages such as "Satan Lives" on church walls.

Despite these findings based on its first year of investigations, the task force said it was too early "to speak conclusively about the motivation behind many of the fires. . . ." The task force said it would continue to investigate and prosecute attacks "on all houses of worship, regardless of their denomination or racial composition."

The task force report appeared to reject theories that the sudden upsurge of attacks on churches early in 1996 was the result of a national conspiracy. Only a few of the cases were linked to common defendants, the report said, and those in which conspiracy charges were filed "tended to be confined to the small geographic areas where the arsons have occurred."

The task force report also detailed efforts by federal agencies to rebuild or repair churches that had been attacked. The 1996 antiarson law put the Department of Housing and Urban Development in charge of administer-

ing a $10 million fund to aid those churches. That department also had conducted workshops in local areas to give guidance to ministers, volunteers, and other agencies on how to deal with the problem.

Reaction of Church Leaders

Church leaders who met with Reno to discuss the task force report said they were pleased with the attention and resources the federal government was devoting to the matter. Even so, some leaders said they hoped the government would focus more attention on possible motivations. Reverend Vernon Reed, pastor of a Pentecostal church in Dallas that had been burned three times since 1994, told reporters: "I don't think they [the task force] zeroed in close enough on the cause of these fires. I really don't think that's been researched enough."

Appearing at the June 10 news conference with Reno, Joan Brown Campbell, secretary general of the National Council of Churches, expressed concern that news reports about the task force report would lead the public to believe that racial attacks on churches were no longer a problem. "We want to make very certain that the report is not understood to be saying that it was not a racial issue and that these fires were not driven by racial hostility," she said.

Following are excerpts from the "First Year Report for the President," dated June 6, 1997, from the National Church Arson Task Force, composed of representatives from agencies of the Justice and Treasury Departments:

Overview

In early 1996, federal officials detected a sharp rise in the number of reported attacks on our nation's houses of worship, especially African American churches in the South. This trend troubled communities, challenged law enforcement agencies, and stirred the nation's conscience.

In June 1996, President Clinton formed the National Church Arson Task Force ("NCATF" or "Task Force"), made the investigation of these fires a top priority of federal law enforcement, and called on all Americans to come together in a spirit of respect and reconciliation.

The President directed his Administration to implement a strategy to (1) identify and prosecute the arsonists; (2) help communities rebuild the burned houses of worship; and (3) offer assistance in preventing more fires. Working with state and local law enforcement and private groups, federal officials achieved great success on these fronts. Significantly, many Americans came together as a result of these arsons, often independent of the federal effort, to lend assistance in many ways.

Prosecutions

• 429 Investigations Launched—The NCATF has opened 429 investigations into arsons, bombings or attempted bombings that have occurred at houses of worship between January 1, 1995, and May 27, 1997.

- 199 Arrested—Federal, state and local authorities have arrested 199 suspects since January 1995, in connection with 150 of the 429 investigations.
- 35% Solved—The 35% rate of arrest in NCATF cases is more than double the 16% rate of arrest for arsons in general.
- 110 Convicted—Federal and state prosecutors have successfully convicted 110 individuals in connection with fires at 77 houses of worship.

Rebuilding

- The Department of Housing and Urban Development (HUD) is working closely with the National Council of Churches, the Congress of National Black Churches, Habitat for Humanity and other organizations in the rebuilding effort.
- As a result of this cooperation, 25 houses of worship have been rebuilt and 65 are undergoing construction.
- HUD is administering a $10 million Federal Loan Guarantee Fund—established by Congress as part of the 1996 Church Arson Prevention Act—to assist with the rebuilding effort.

Prevention

- Arson prevention efforts continue across the nation. The U.S. Department of Justice awarded $3 million in grants to counties in 13 states to intensify their enforcement and surveillance efforts around vulnerable houses of worship, and the Federal Emergency Management Agency (FEMA) awarded approximately $1.5 million in arson prevention and training grants.
- FEMA established a Clearinghouse for arson prevention resources that has received over 15,000 telephone inquiries from all 50 states and the District of Columbia.
- FEMA has distributed more than 500,000 arson prevention packets, including the NCATF Church Threat Assessment Guide.
- FEMA efforts also include a four-city pilot project in Nashville, TN, Charlotte, NC, Macon, GA, and Utica, NY, to develop grass-roots arson prevention programs. . . .

I. Prosecuting Defendants

A. Coordinating the Investigations

In 1996, following a series of fires around the time of the Martin Luther King Jr. holiday, federal authorities began to focus on the sharp increase in reports of attacks on churches, particularly African American churches in the South. These church fires led officials to take steps to improve the coordination within federal law enforcement and between federal, state and local law enforcement.

In June 1996, President Clinton established the National Church Arson Task Force to better coordinate the efforts of federal, state and local law enforcement. Shortly thereafter, Attorney General Janet Reno directed U.S. Attorneys to establish local task forces focusing on arsons at houses of worship or to join an existing local task force. These local task forces include state and local law enforcement and fire prevention officials, special agents of the ATF and FBI, mediators from the Community Relations Service, and victim/witness coordinators.

In addition to the local task forces, the NCATF established an operations team in Washington staffed by special agents of the ATF and the FBI, as well as seasoned prosecutors from the Justice Department's Civil Rights Division and U.S. Attorney's Offices around the country. Working with local task forces, the operations team continues to investigate incidents, identify potential connections and prosecute cases.

Since the formation of the Task Force, hundreds of ATF and FBI investigators have been deployed to work with more than 80 federal prosecutors and state and local authorities. It is one of the largest series of arson investigations in history and is currently the largest ongoing civil rights investigation.

B. Conducting the Investigations

For years, many arsons at houses of worship were handled by local authorities, and not reported to any federal agency. As a result, local law enforcement often did not benefit from the resources of the federal government in pursuing these incidents. Following the formation of the Task Force, local law enforcement and fire authorities began regularly reporting these incidents to federal authorities. As a result, they now are receiving additional assistance in these investigations.

From its inception, the NCATF developed a protocol for investigating and prosecuting suspected arsons. The protocol sets forth procedures for facilitating the exchange of information among Task Force agencies, developing an investigative plan for each incident, and ensuring that investigators pursue all lines of inquiry, including whether the crime was motivated by race or religion, and whether any one incident is connected to any other. To gain a more complete picture of the arson problem, the Task Force determined it would investigate arsons going back to January 1995.

Once an investigation is opened, the NCATF compiles statistical information about the case in a unified database. In addition, the databases and computer systems of the ATF and FBI are used to track and analyze evidence and to generate investigative leads.

In pursuing these investigations, the FBI calls upon its experience in conducting civil rights investigations, and the ATF relies on its experience in conducting arson and explosives investigations. The NCATF also engaged in training among its constituent agencies. ATF experts trained FBI agents and Department of Justice prosecutors regarding arson investigations. Civil Rights Division prosecutors and FBI experts trained ATF agents regarding civil rights investigations and prosecutions.

As the past year has proven, arson cases are among the most difficult criminal cases to solve. Forensic evidence is often destroyed in the fire, and there are often no eye witnesses to the incidents because some of the burned churches are located in isolated, rural areas. For these reasons, the arsons can often take years to solve. Moreover, as with many criminal acts, it is difficult to discern the motive for setting fire to a house of worship

C. Strengthening Laws and Adding Resources

Over the past year, Congress has provided tremendous support to the efforts of the Task Force, by strengthening federal laws and providing additional resources.

When the Task Force was formalized, federal prosecutors relied on several statutes to prosecute arson cases. Among others, they had authority under the Anti-Arson Act of 1982 to prosecute those who used fire to destroy property involved in interstate commerce (18 U.S.C. 844(i)). Under criminal civil rights statutes, they also had the authority to prosecute those who conspired to deprive persons of their civil rights or who desecrated religious property or a house of worship (18 U.S.C. 241 and 247).

On July 3, 1996, President Clinton signed the Church Arson Prevention Act of 1996, which granted federal prosecutors greater power in pursuing burnings and desecrations at houses of worship. Sponsored by Senator Edward M. Kennedy (D-MA), Senator Lauch Faircloth (R-NC), Congressman Henry J. Hyde (R-IL) and Congressman John Conyers, Jr. (D-MI), the statute was passed unanimously by both Houses of Congress.

The new law, which amended 18 U.S.C. 247, enables federal prosecutors to file charges in racially motivated arsons without having to demonstrate that the incident involved the use of interstate facilities and without showing that the resulting damage totaled $10,000 or more. Also, prosecutors can now seek sentences of up to 20 years imprisonment for arson.

In addition, in August 1996, Congress provided more than $12 million to support ATF's role in the Task Force, until the end of that fiscal year. The next month, Congress appropriated an additional $12 million for ATF's role in the following fiscal year. Additional funds for Task Force activities by the Justice Department and the FBI also were appropriated or reprogrammed.

D. Making Progress

1. Investigations

The NCATF has opened investigations into 429 arsons, bombings or attempted bombings that have occurred at houses of worship between January 1, 1995, and May 27, 1997. This number does not include vandalism and other desecration at houses of worship, which continue to be investigated and prosecuted by the FBI, the Justice Department's Civil Rights Division and U.S. Attorneys offices; nor does it include fires that the investigators have determined to be accidental.

Of these 429 incidents, 162 have involved African American churches—more than three quarters of which are located in the southern United States.....

The NCATF continues to launch a new investigation for every new suspicious fire. As of May 27, 1997, there were 279 investigations in which arrests had not yet been made. The Task Force remains committed to expending the necessary time, resources and effort to solving these crimes and prosecuting those who are responsible. To expand the sources of information available to investigators, the NCATF established a toll-free tip line for citizens to report information on arsons at houses of worship. . . .

To date, the NCATF has received more than 1500 calls through its tip line service. The ATF and FBI also are offering rewards for information in a number of arson cases. Private organizations, including Nationsbank and an insurance industry association, are also offering rewards.

2. Arrests

The partnership among various enforcement agencies has produced a significant number of state and federal arrests.

Since January 1995, federal, state and local authorities have arrested 199 suspects in connection with 150 of the 429 investigations that the Task Force has launched. This 35% rate of arrest is more than double the general arrest rate for arsons, which is approximately 16%, according to Justice Department statistics.

Of the 199 persons arrested, 160 are white, 34 are African American, and 5 are Hispanic. Eighty three people arrested were juveniles. Of the 81 suspects arrested for arsons at African American churches, 55 are white, 25 are African American and 1 is Hispanic. Of the 123 suspects arrested for arsons at non-African American houses of worship, 110 are white, 9 are African American, and 4 are Hispanic. Five of the white suspects were arrested for arsons at both African American and non-African American churches.

3. Convictions

Since January 1, 1995, 110 defendants have been convicted in federal and state prosecutions in connection with fires at 77 houses of worship. [See Appendix 2, for a list of incidents in which a conviction has been obtained.] These successes include the first convictions under provisions of the Church Arson Prevention Act of 1996. Of the 25 defendants who have been convicted of federal charges, 14 have been convicted of criminal civil rights charges.

Federal charges are also pending in a number of other cases, and grand jury investigations are ongoing as well. The Task Force has found that only a few of the fires are linked by common defendants. Conspiracy charges have been filed in a limited number of cases. These conspiracies, though, have tended to be confined to the small geographic areas where the arsons have occurred. Investigators continue to pursue the question of whether broader conspiracies were responsible for some of the fires, but to date the evidence has not established the existence of a national conspiracy.

In still other cases, state prosecutions have been initiated in consultation with federal prosecutors or investigators. The NCATF actively monitors these prosecutions to ensure that any federal interest is vindicated and to ensure that accurate information is compiled regarding law enforcement's response to attacks on houses of worship.

II. Helping to Rebuild

A. Coordinating the Rebuilding Effort

The Department of Housing and Urban Development has forged a coalition with the National Council of Churches, the Congress of National Black Churches, Habitat for Humanity, local financial institutions and other organizations to coordinate the rebuilding effort. Together they have assessed the overall arson damage and worked to target resources to affected houses of worship as quickly as possible.

Resources available through this rebuilding coalition include grants, low interest loans, materials and in-kind donations, pro-bono legal services, architectural design services, assistance with insurance, and volunteers.

The resources came from a wide array of participants who responded to the arsons. Volunteer and religious organizations, such as Habitat for Humanity, Christmas in April, Mennonite Disaster Services, United Methodist's Volunteers in Mission, and the Washington Quaker Workcamps, among others, organized construction volunteers; the American Institute of Architects provided volunteer architectural design services; the AFL-CIO and other unions organized union construction workers; the Lawyers Committee for Civil Rights Under Law organized private law firms to provide pro-bono legal services; and the Enterprise Foundation worked with a coalition of foundations to contribute financial resources to the rebuilding effort.

As a result of this cooperation, 25 houses of worship have been rebuilt and 65 more are currently being constructed.

B. Strengthening Resources to Help Rebuild

Working with President Clinton, Congress enacted legislation that authorized a HUD loan guarantee program that can be used for rebuilding houses of worship. The Church Arson Prevention Act of 1996 made HUD responsible for administering a $10 million Federal Loan Guarantee Fund to assist with the rebuilding of houses of worship and buildings of other non-profit organizations that have been damaged or destroyed by arson.

Through its work with local financial institutions, HUD is working actively with approximately 20% of the houses of worship identified as candidates for loan assistance.

In addition, the rebuilding coalition is awarding "rebuilding resource packages" to 79 churches in 18 states in the form of grants from the National Council of Churches, federally guaranteed loans, volunteer labor and in-kind materials. Of these 79 churches, 13 are eligible for a HUD loan, 20 have received or are eligible for a National Council of Churches grant, and 46 are eligible for a resource package including a grant and loan.

C. Reaching out to the Communities

The private-public partnership is continuing to identify other areas where help can be provided. The partnership conducts on-site visits and group workshops, at which technical advice and guidance is offered. HUD has organized regional workshops to bring together ministers from the burned churches with organizations and financial institutions, volunteers, and other grant-making agencies.

III. Preventing Arsons

A. Coordinating Prevention Efforts

The Federal Emergency Management Agency (FEMA) is coordinating the federal government's efforts to enhance local and state programs to prevent fires at houses of worship and to promote arson awareness generally. The National Arson Prevention Initiative, announced by President Clinton in June 1996, has focused on coordinating public and private sector resources to support community-based grass roots efforts to prevent arsons. FEMA Director James Lee Witt met with and enlisted the support of national fire and law enforcement organizations, and religious and volunteer groups in arson prevention activities.

In June 1996, FEMA established a Clearinghouse for arson prevention resources. The toll-free number for the Clearinghouse is: 1-888-603-3100.

To date, the Clearinghouse has received over 15,000 telephone inquiries from all 50 states and the District of Columbia, and has provided more than 500,000 packets of arson prevention materials. Included in those materials is the Church Threat Assessment Guide, prepared by the NCATF, that informs congregations about steps they can take to make their houses of worship safer, as well as steps to take after an incident has occurred.

In addition, following a meeting with Vice President Al Gore in June 1996, the insurance industry announced its plan to participate in the arson prevention initiative. Insurance representatives pledged to help find insurance for houses of worship destroyed by arson. The industry also established a toll-free insurance hotline and offered free site surveys to reduce the risk of arson for any interested house of worship.

B. Strengthening Prevention Resources

1. Grants

In an effort to help communities prevent future arsons, the federal government provided additional resources. For instance, with Congress' authorization, the Justice Department awarded $3 million in grants to counties from 13 states to intensify their enforcement and surveillance efforts around vulnerable houses of worship. The states were: Alabama, Florida, Georgia, Kentucky, Louisiana, Maryland, Mississippi, North Carolina, Oklahoma, South Carolina, Tennessee, Texas and Virginia.

In FY 1996, FEMA disbursed $774,000 in arson training grants to enhance state and local arson investigations and prevention capabilities. These grants have been used to deliver National Fire Academy courses by the state fire training organizations and also to support the training of state and regional arson task forces. In FY 1997, FEMA has disbursed an additional $635,000 to the states for arson awareness and prevention efforts.

2. Prevention Education

The NCATF updated and distributed a Church Threat Assessment Guide containing valuable information on the steps that may be taken to try to prevent fires at houses of worship and the steps to follow after an incident has occurred. Using this guide, special agents of ATF and FBI continue to conduct prevention outreach efforts in communities across the nation. Local and state fire and law enforcement leaders and members of the insurance industry have also successfully utilized the guide to conduct threat assessments of religious structures.

The NCATF is working closely with FEMA, the Bureau of Justice Assistance, the National Sheriffs' Association and Southern governors to develop a series of interdisciplinary training conferences and workshops on arson prevention that will be conducted in 13 targeted Southern states in 1997. An additional 4 regional conferences outside the Southern region are also planned.

Recognizing that arson is a local problem that must be addressed at the grassroots level, FEMA has developed a pilot community action program for arson prevention in four communities: Nashville, TN, Charlotte, NC, Macon, GA, and Utica, NY. A coalition of fire prevention personnel, law enforcement personnel and community, school and business leaders has been recruited to develop local arson prevention programs. These include: workshops on juvenile firesetters, arson risk assessment surveys, arson hot-lines, improved building and fire code enforcement and neighborhood watch programs. These demonstration programs will become the basis for a national grassroots arson prevention effort.

IV. Reconciliation

A. Reaching Out to the Affected Communities

Without the confidence and cooperation of the congregations whose houses of worship burned, many of these investigations, which were difficult at the outset, would have been destined to fail. Faced with criticism of law enforcement from some congregations, the NCATF took steps early on to ensure solid, working relationships between law enforcement and the affected communities.

Less than a week after being formalized, the NCATF met with FBI and ATF Special Agents in Charge and U.S. Attorneys from the Southeast region to discuss the perceptions within the affected communities and to emphasize the critical importance of pursuing the investigations with vigilance, determination and dispatch, as well as with sensitivity to the needs of the victims. Following these meetings, the agents and prosecutors, together with representatives from the CRS, worked to improve lines of communications with the affected communities and make their commitment to these investigations clear.

President Clinton, Vice President Gore, Secretary of the Treasury Robert Rubin and Attorney General Reno have helped reach out to the affected communities, by bringing the church arsons to the nation's attention, speaking out forcefully on the commitment of the federal government to solve these arsons and meeting with ministers from the burned churches.

In June 1996, President Clinton traveled to the site of a burned African American church in Greeleyville, SC, to help dedicate a new church. Later that month, he organized an interfaith breakfast where he called on leaders of all faiths to open discussions to resolve our nation's racial and religious divisions. In August, the President and Vice President and their families traveled to Fruitland, TN, to help rebuild a church that had been destroyed earlier.

The President also convened a meeting of governors from affected states, who have worked hard to marshal resources in their states to help investigate arsons, prevent future arsons, and rebuild burned houses of worship. He also acknowledged the work of many groups which responded to these incidents, including the National Council of Churches, the Anti-Defamation League, the Southern Christian Leadership Conference, the National Association of Evangelicals, and the NAACP.

In addition to meeting with representatives from these groups and the Congressional Black Caucus, Assistant Secretary Johnson, then-Assistant Attorney General Patrick, and current Acting Assistant Attorney General Pinzler, have visited churches in the South to reinforce the Task Force's commitment to these investigations and view the devastation these arsons have wrought.

CRS have worked in many communities across the country to identify and resolve racial conflicts and reduce racial tensions, to foster healthy relationships between law enforcement and minority communities and to facilitate communications among all parties.

The NCATF also developed, with the help of CRS, a "Best Practices" guide for conducting community outreach activities.

CRS plays an integral part in the Administration's response in local towns and cities, working with over 150 local communities in reducing racial polarization, bridging communication between law enforcement and minority communities, facilitating a biracial rebuilding effort, and training law enforcement on cultural diversity and race relations. Throughout the South, CRS convened a series of dialogues on race relations in an effort to reduce the likelihood of further church burnings.

B. Watching the Nation Respond

In addition to the efforts of Congress, federal agencies and the states, many private companies and organizations, as well as an untold number of Americans, pitched in to respond to the arsons.

Private companies offered funds and materials to help rebuild the burned churches. Transportation companies offered reduced fares for volunteers who traveled south to lend a hand.

And thousands of Americans donated time and money to support these efforts. Habitat for Humanity estimates that more than 15,000 individuals volunteered to help in the rebuilding process.

Seventy-three VISTA and AmeriCorps volunteers traveled to 18 rural communities in which church arsons have occurred and to over 70 other communities in Alabama, Georgia, Louisiana, Mississippi, North Carolina, South Carolina and Tennessee. In these communities, volunteers conducted community and church threat assessments, organized arson watch groups and town hall meetings on arson prevention, and engaged in community relations projects.

In the end, Americans of all walks of life refused to let these acts of destruction tear apart our communities or our nation.

V. Drawing Preliminary Conclusions

Although the investigations of most of the fires continue, the charges filed and the convictions obtained to date enable the Task Force to offer some preliminary conclusions. These conclusions are not based on cases that have not been completed or where evidence is not sufficient to support additional charges. As a result, the Task Force cannot answer all of the questions raised by the fires.

• **Damage.** Hundreds of houses of worship burned, congregations were temporarily displaced, and many people were left wondering how this could happen in the 1990's. These arsons destroyed rural wooden churches, ruined 100-year old Bibles, and caused tens of millions of dollars in damage. But those communities which suffered a burned house of worship came to realize that thousands of Americans really care. The arsonists may have sought to divide our communities by burning our houses of worship, but in the end they only helped bring them closer together.

• **Multiple Motives.** The arsons at African American churches raised significant fears about an increase in racially motivated crimes. As a result of our efforts to date, we have determined that the arsons—at both African American and other houses of worship—were motivated by a wide array of factors, including not only blatant racism or religious hatred, but also financial profit, burglary, and personal revenge. The Task Force continues to investigate many cases. When sufficient evidence of racial motive is developed, we will continue to seek and obtain criminal civil rights convictions, as we have against 14 of the 25 defendants convicted of federal charges in Alabama, Nevada, North Carolina, South Carolina, Tennessee and Texas.

• **National Conspiracy.** While the Task Force continues to explore the question whether there are connections between the fires across the nation, the cases closed to date and the charges that have been filed do not support the theory that these fires were the product of a nationwide conspiracy. For instance, the Task Force has found that only a few of the fires are linked by common defendants. Conspiracy charges have been filed in a limited number of cases. These conspiracies, though, have tended to be confined to the small geographic areas where the arsons have occurred.

• **Hate Group Involvement.** While there have been a handful of cases in which members and former members of hate groups, such as the Ku Klux Klan, have been convicted for arsons at houses of worship, most of the defendants were not found to be members of hate groups. Prosecutors need not show, however, that a defendant belongs to a particular hate group in order to gain a conviction.

- **Investigations Continue.** The Task Force continues to investigate and prosecute those responsible for burning our nation's houses of worship. It is, therefore, too soon for the task force to speak conclusively about the motivation behind many of the fires at churches and other houses of worship. While it was the number of fires at African American churches that brought these crimes to national attention, the NCATF will continue to investigate and prosecute attacks on all houses of worship, regardless of their denomination or racial composition.

Conclusion

We have seen how law enforcement working together can produce tremendous successes. We have seen how government agencies and private groups can work together to help rebuild a house of worship. And we have seen how all Americans from all walks of life can come together as one. We are committed to building on the progress that we have seen to date and to eliminating the divisions in our society. The federal effort continues to prosecute the arsonists, rebuild the burned houses of worship, and prevent more fires. There is more work to be done. We are committed to seeing the task completed. . . .

CLINTON SPEECH ON
IMPROVING RACE RELATIONS
June 14, 1997

President Bill Clinton sought to open a national dialogue about race relations in 1997. But by year's end the president's call for "a great and unprecedented conversation about race" was being criticized as unfocused and without direction. Civil rights leaders complained that Clinton's initiative was long on rhetoric and short on concrete proposals for improving the lot of minorities, while conservatives complained that people whose views on racial issues differed from Clinton's were being excluded from the conversation altogether.

Clinton formally launched his initiative on race in a commencement speech at the University of California at San Diego on June 14, where he introduced a presidential advisory panel, headed by the distinguished historian John Hope Franklin. The panel was charged with helping the president conduct a series of town meetings and other efforts to encourage Americans "to confront and work through" their feelings about race in all facets of American life. But by the end of the year the advisory board appeared to be struggling to translate the president's initiative into a concrete plan of action. Only one town meeting had been held, and an advisory board hearing on achieving racial diversity on college campuses drew fire when it failed to invite any speakers who opposed affirmative action.

Clinton faced other obstacles in moving his initiative forward. In the absence of a crisis in race relations, such as those that led to enactment of the Civil Rights Act of 1964 and the Voting Rights Act of 1965, it was unclear that Americans could be motivated to take any significant action. According to a Washington Post-*ABC News Poll conducted shortly before the president's speech, only one in ten said the country faced a racial crisis and only 3 percent cited race or civil rights as the most serious problem facing the country. The poll also showed that whites and blacks had very different perceptions about the racial climate in the United States. Three-fourths of white Americans believed that blacks in their community were treated the same as they were; only half the blacks thought they were. Even more dis-*

parate were the perceptions of discrimination. According to the poll, 44 percent of blacks but only 17 percent of whites believed that blacks faced "a lot" of discrimination in American society. A Gallup Poll conducted at about the same time found that 55 percent of blacks and whites believed that race relations would "always be a problem" in the United States.

Clinton's Speech

The initiative Clinton offered in June was the culmination of months of debate within the White House about how best to try to improve race relations. Clinton had spoken often in his first term of his belief in the country's need to come to grips with its racial divisions. He made a major speech on the subject in October 1995 when he implored Americans to "clean our house of racism." The initiative was seen as a way to help bring that about—and, if successful, to give some weight to Clinton's achievements as president. (Clinton plea to end racism, Historic Documents of 1995, p. 646)

In San Diego, Clinton sought to recast the debate from one that focused on two races to one that encompassed the many races and ethnicities that populate the United States. He noted that there was no majority race in Hawaii and soon would not be one in California and predicted that within fifty years no single race or ethnic group would be in a majority in the United States. "To be sure, there is old, unfinished business between black and white Americans," Clinton said, "but the classic American dilemma has now become many dilemmas of race and ethnicity." Clinton called on Americans to refrain from tarring an entire race or ethnic group with the misdeeds of a few. Condemn the act, he said, but not the race to which the perpetrator belongs.

Clinton repeated familiar themes of providing expanded opportunity for and demanding greater responsibility from all Americans. But he offered only one specific proposal—more funding for the Equal Employment Opportunity Commission. "It is imperative that Congress—especially those members who say they're for civil rights but against affirmative action—at least give us the money necessary" to enforce the civil rights laws already on the books.

Clinton also used his appearance in California to defend the use of affirmative action. In 1996 California voters adopted Proposition 209, an amendment to the state constitution prohibiting racial preferences in public programs. Clinton said he knew that the voters had not acted out of ill will but he nonetheless asked them to consider the results: minority enrollments in graduate schools were "plummeting for the first time in decades" and seemed likely to at undergraduate levels. "We must not resegregate higher education or leave it to private universities to do the public's work." Clinton directly challenged those who opposed affirmative action "to come up with an alternative." (Appeals panel on affirmative action ban, p. 183; Proposition 209 adopted, Historic Documents of 1996, p. 759)

In conclusion, Clinton returned to his appeal for a unified America strengthened, rather than divided, by the racial and ethnic differences of its

*people. "More than 30 years ago, at the high tide of the civil rights move-
ment, the Kerner Commission said we were becoming two Americas, one
white, one black, separate and unequal. Today, we face a different choice:
will we become not two, but many Americas, separate, unequal and isolated? Or will we draw strength from all our people and our ancient faith
in the quality of human dignity, to become the world's first truly multi-
racial democracy?" the president asked.*

*The immediate reaction to Clinton's speech and the initiative he pro-
posed was fairly predictable. For the most part, civil rights leaders applauded
the speech, but warned that the rhetoric would have to be replaced with
specific proposals. A few noted that while Clinton was no doubt sincere
in his desire to improve race relations, his endorsement of the welfare
reform enacted in 1996 and his failure to put more money toward education, housing, and other federal programs that could improve opportunity
for minorities undercut his rhetoric.*

*Opponents of affirmative action found much to criticize in the speech.
"This is not a dialogue," said Abigail Thernstrom, a senior fellow at the
Manhattan Institute. "This is an effort to shove his unpopular ideas down
America's throat." House Speaker Newt Gingrich of Georgia issued the
Republican's first formal response to the San Diego speech on June 18. "We
must make America a country with equal opportunity for all and special
privilege for none by treating all individuals as equals before the law and
doing away with quotas, preferences and set-asides in government contracts, hiring and university admissions," Gingrich said in a speech to the
Orphan Foundation of America. Gingrich then offered a ten-point program
aimed at achieving equality without using affirmative action programs.*

Goals of the Initiative

*As outlined by the president in his speech and by briefing papers from
the White House, the goals of the initiative were to help educate the nation
about the facts surrounding the issue of race, to promote a constructive dialogue on ways to narrow divisions between the races, to encourage leaders
at all levels to take steps to help close those divisions, and to find and implement solutions in critical areas such as education, employment opportunity, housing, health care, and criminal justice. Clinton himself was to
take an active role, participating in regional town meetings, meeting with
the advisory board on various issues, and showcasing promising reconciliation and community-building projects around the country. Clinton
promised to report to the American people in the summer of 1998, reviewing the year's work and detailing recommendations and solutions.*

*At the heart of the initiative was the seven-member advisory panel,
which was to assist Clinton with outreach efforts and consultations with
experts. In addition to Franklin, the author of* From Slavery to Freedom: A
History of African-Americans, *considered by many to be the definitive text
on the subject, the other members of the panel were former governors
William F. Winter of Mississippi and Thomas H. Kean of New Jersey;
Linda Chavez-Thompson, executive vice president of the AFL-CIO; Robert*

Thompson, president and chief executive officer of Nissan Motor Corp. USA; Angela E. Oh, an attorney and community leader in Los Angeles; and Suzan Johnson Cook, a minister from the Bronx, New York. The seven joined Clinton for his speech in San Diego.

Clinton took a few other public steps to further the dialogue in the remaining months of 1997. On September 25 he spoke from the steps of Little Rock Central High School on the fortieth anniversary of the integration of the school by nine black teenagers, who at that time had to be protected by federal troops. In remarks that his press secretary said were intended for white Americans, Clinton declared that "segregation is no longer the law, but too often separation is still the rule. . . . Far too many communities are all white, all black, all Latino, all Asian. Indeed, too many Americans of all races have actually begun to give up on the idea of integration and the search for common ground." Clinton also moderated the first of the initiative's town meetings, on December 3 in Akron, Ohio.

The advisory board was slow in getting organized. It took four months to hire staff, and in one of its first hearings—on ways to achieve diversity on college campuses—the panel opened itself to criticism by not inviting anyone opposed to affirmative action. One of those who complained was Ward Connerly, a chief sponsor of California's Proposition 209. "The people whom we did invite had something special to say about how to make universities more diverse than they are," Franklin said following the November 19 meeting. "The people in California that advocated Proposition 209, for example, are not addressing the subject of how to make the university more diverse. Consequently, I'm not certain what Mr. Connerly, for example, could contribute to this discussion." "I truly find it astounding," Connerly told the Washington Post, *"that the President's race panel believes they can have a national dialogue . . . without involving those of us who represent a point of view that is shared by probably 60 percent of the people of the nation."*

Following are excerpts from the commencement speech by President Bill Clinton, delivered June 14, 1997, at the University of California at San Diego, in which he called for a national dialogue to improve race relations:

Thank you very much. Thank you. . . .

Today we celebrate your achievements at a truly golden moment for America. The Cold War is over and freedom is now ascendant around the globe, with more than half of the people in this old world living under governments of their own choosing for the very first time.

Our economy is the healthiest in a generation and the strongest in the world. Our culture, our science, our technology promise unimagined advances and exciting new careers. Our social problems, from crime to poverty, are finally bending to our efforts.

Of course, there are still challenges for you out there. . . .

. . . I believe the greatest challenge we face . . . is also our greatest opportunity. Of all the questions of discrimination and prejudice that still exist in our society, the most perplexing one is the oldest, and in some ways today, the newest: the problem of race. Can we fulfill the promise of America by embracing all our citizens of all races, not just at a university where people have the benefit of enlightened teachers and the time to think and grow and get to know each other within the daily life of every American community. In short, can we become one America in the 21st century?

I know, and I've said before, that money cannot buy this goal, power cannot compel it, technology cannot create it. This is something that can come only from the human spirit—the spirit we saw when the choir of many races sang as a gospel choir.

Today, the state of Hawaii . . . has no majority racial or ethnic group. It is a wonderful place of exuberance and friendship and patriotism. Within the next three years, here in California no single race or ethnic group will make up a majority of the state's population. Already, five of our largest school districts draw students from over 100 different racial and ethnic groups. At this campus, 12 Nobel prize winners have taught or studied from nine different countries. A half-century from now, when your own grandchildren are in college, there will be no majority race in America.

Now, we know what we will look like, but what will we be like? Can we be one America respecting, even celebrating, our differences, but embracing even more what we have in common? Can we define what it means to be an American, not just in terms of the hyphen showing our ethnic origins but in terms of our primary allegiance to the values America stands for and values we really live by. Our hearts long to answer yes, but our history reminds us that it will be hard. The ideals that bind us together are as old as our nation, but so are the forces that pull us apart. Our founders sought to form a more perfect union; the humility and hope of that phrase is the story of America and it is our mission today.

Consider this: We were born with a Declaration of Independence which asserted that we were all created equal and a Constitution that enshrined slavery. We fought a bloody civil war to abolish slavery and preserve the union, but we remained a house divided and unequal by law for another century. We advanced across the continent in the name of freedom, yet in so doing we pushed Native Americans off their land, often crushing their culture and their livelihood. Our Statue of Liberty welcomes poor, tired, huddled masses of immigrants to our borders, but each new wave has felt the sting of discrimination.

In World War II, Japanese Americans fought valiantly for freedom in Europe, taking great casualties, while at home their families were herded into internment camps. The famed Tuskegee Airmen lost none of the bombers they guarded during the war, but their African American heritage cost them a lot of rights when they came back home in peace.

Though minorities have more opportunities than ever today, we still see evidence of bigotry—from the desecration of houses of worship, whether they be churches, synagogues or mosques, to demeaning talk in corporate suites. There is still much work to be done by you, members of the class of 1997. But those who say we cannot transform the problem of prejudice into the promise of unity forget how far we have come, and I cannot believe they have ever seen a crowd like you. . . .

To be sure, there is old, unfinished business between black and white Americans, but the classic American dilemma has now become many dilemmas of race and ethnicity. We see it in the tension between black and Hispanic customers and their Korean or Arab grocers; in a resurgent anti-Semitism even on some college campuses; in a hostility toward new immigrants from Asia to the Middle East to the former communist countries to Latin America and the Caribbean—even those whose hard work and strong families have brought them success in the American Way.

We see a disturbing tendency to wrongly attribute to entire groups, including the white majority, the objectionable conduct of a few members. If a black American commits a crime, condemn the act—but remember that most African Americans are hard-working, law-abiding citizens. If a Latino gang member deals drugs, condemn the act—but remember the vast majority of Hispanics are responsible citizens who also deplore the scourge of drugs in our life. If white teenagers beat a young African American boy almost to death just because of his race, for God's sakes condemn the act—but remember the overwhelming majority of white people will find it just as hateful. If an Asian merchant discriminates against her customers of another minority group, call her on it—but remember, too, that many, many Asians have borne the burden or prejudice and do not want anyone else to feel it.

Remember too, in spite of the persistence of prejudice, we are more integrated than ever. More of us share neighborhoods and work and school and social activities, religious life, even love and marriage across racial lines than ever before. More of us enjoy each other's company and distinctive cultures than ever before. And more than ever, we understand the benefits of our racial, linguistic, and cultural diversity in a global society, where networks of commerce and communications draw us closer and bring rich rewards to those who truly understand life beyond their nation's borders.

With just a twentieth of the world's population, but a fifth of the world's income, we in America simply have to sell to the other 95 percent of the world's consumers just to maintain our standard of living. Because we are drawn from every culture on earth, we are uniquely positioned to do it. Beyond commerce, the diverse backgrounds and talents of our citizens can help America to light the globe, showing nations deeply divided by race, religion and tribe that there is a better way.

Finally, as you have shown us today, our diversity will enrich our lives in non-material ways—deepening our understanding of human nature and human differences, making our communities more exciting, more enjoyable, more meaningful. That is why I have come here today to ask the American people to join me in a great national effort to perfect the promise of America for this new time as we seek to build our more perfect union.

Now, when there is more cause for hope than fear, when we are not driven to it by some emergency or social cataclysm, now is the time we should learn together, talk together and act together to build one America.

Let me say that I know that for many white Americans, this conversation may seem to exclude them or threaten them. That must not be so. I believe white Americans have just as much to gain as anybody else from being a part of this endeavor—much to gain from an America where we finally take responsibility for all our children so that they, at last, can be judged as Martin Luther King hoped, "Not by the color of their skin, but by the content of their character."

What is it that we must do? For four and a half years now, I have worked to prepare America for the 21st century with a strategy of opportunity for all, responsibility from all, and an American community of all our citizens. To succeed in each of these areas, we must deal with the realities and the perceptions affecting all racial groups in America.

First, we must continue to expand opportunity. Full participation in our strong and growing economy is the best antidote to envy, despair and racism. We must press forward to move millions more from poverty and welfare to work; to bring the spark of enterprise to inner cities; to redouble our efforts to reach those rural communities prosperity has passed by. And most important of all, we simply must give our young people the finest education in the world. There are no children who, because of their ethnic or racial background, who cannot meet the highest academic standards if we set them and measure our students against them, if we give them well-trained teachers and well-equipped classrooms, and if we continue to support reasoned reforms to achieve excellence, like the charter school movement.

At a time when college education means stability, a good job, a passport to the middle class, we must open the doors of college to all Americans and we must make at least two years of college as universal at the dawn of the next century as a high school diploma is today.

In our efforts to extend economic and educational opportunity to all our citizens, we must consider the role of affirmative action. I know affirmative action has not been perfect in America—that's why two years ago we began an effort to fix the things that are wrong with it—but when used in the right way, it has worked.

It has given us a whole generation of professionals in fields that used to be exclusive clubs—where people like me got the benefit of 100 percent affirmative action. There are now more women-owned businesses than ever before. There are more African American, Latino and Asian American lawyers and judges, scientists and engineers, accountants and executives than ever before.

But the best example of successful affirmative action is our military. Our armed forces are diverse from top to bottom—perhaps the most integrated institution in our society and certainly the most integrated military in the world. And, more important, no one questions that they are the best in the world. So much for the argument that excellence and diversity do not go hand in hand.

There are those who argue that scores on standardized tests should be the sole measure of qualification for admissions to colleges and universities. But many would not apply the same standard to the children of alumni or those with athletic ability.

I believe a student body that reflects the excellence and the diversity of the people we will live and work with has independent educational value. Look around this crowd today. Don't you think you have learned a lot more than you would have if everybody sitting around you looked just like you? I think you have.

And beyond the educational value to you, it has a public interest because you will learn to live and work in the world you will live in better. When young people sit side by side with people of many different backgrounds, they do learn something that they can take out into the world. And they will be more effective citizens.

Many affirmative action students excel. They work hard, they achieve, they go out and serve the communities that need them for their expertise and role model. If you close the door on them, we will weaken our greatest universities and it will be more difficult to build the society we need in the 21st century.

Let me say, I know that the people of California voted to repeal affirmative action without any ill motive. The vast majority of them simply did it with a conviction that discrimination and isolation are no longer barriers to achievement. But consider the results. Minority enrollments in law school and other graduate programs are plummeting for the first time in decades. Assuming the same will likely happen in undergraduate education. We must not resegregate higher education or leave it to the private universities to do the public's work.

At the very time when we need to do a better job of living and learning together, we should not stop trying to equalize economic opportunity. To those who oppose affirmative action, I ask you to come up with an alternative. I would embrace it if I could find a better way. And to those of us who still support it, I say we should continue to stand for it, we should reach out to those who disagree or are uncertain and talk about the practical impact of these issues, and we should never be thought unwilling to work with those who disagree with us to find new ways to lift people up and bring people together.

Beyond opportunity, we must demand responsibility from every American. Our strength as a society depends upon both—upon people taking responsibility for themselves and their families, teaching their children good values, working hard and obeying the law, and giving back to those around us. The new economy offers fewer guarantees, more risks, and more rewards. It calls upon all of us to take even greater responsibility for our education than ever before.

In the current economic boom, only one racial or ethnic group in America has actually experienced a decline in income—Hispanic Americans. One big reason is that Hispanic high school drop-out rates are well above—indeed, far above—those of whites and blacks. Some of the drop-outs actually reflect a strong commitment to work. We admire the legendary willingness to take the hard job at long hours for low pay. In the old economy, that was a responsible thing to do. But in the new economy, where education is the key, responsibility means staying in school.

No responsibility is more fundamental than obeying the law. It is not racist to insist that every American do so. The fight against crime and drugs is a fight for the freedom of all our people, including those—perhaps especially those—minorities living in our poorest neighborhoods. But respect for the law must run both ways. The shocking difference in perceptions of the fairness of our criminal justice system grows out of the real experiences that too many minorities have had with law enforcement officers. Part of the answer is to have all our citizens respect the law, but the basic rule must be that the law must respect all our citizens.

And that applies, too, to the enforcement of our civil rights laws. For example, the Equal Employment Opportunity Commission has a huge backlog of cases with discrimination claims—though we have reduced it by 25 percent over the last four years. We can do not much better without more resources. It is imperative that Congress—especially those members who say they're for civil rights but against affirmative action—at least give us the money necessary to enforce the law of the land and do it soon.

Our third imperative is perhaps the most difficult of all. We must build one American community based on respect for one another and our shared values. We must begin with a candid conversation on the state of race relations today and the implications of Americans of so many different races living and working together as we approach a new century. We must be honest with each other. We have talked at each other and about each other for a long time. It's high time we all began talking with each other.

Over the coming year I want to lead the American people in a great and unprecedented conversation about race. In community efforts from Lima, Ohio, to Billings, Montana, in remarkable experiments in cross-racial communications like the uniquely named ERACISM, I have seen what Americans can do if they let down their guards and reach out their hands.

I have asked one of America's greatest scholars, Dr. John Hope Franklin, to chair an advisory panel of seven distinguished Americans to help me in this endeavor. He will be joined by former Governors Thomas Kean of New Jersey and William Winter of Mississippi, both great champions of civil rights; by Linda Chavez-Thompson, the Executive Vice President of the AFL-CIO; by Reverend Suzan Johnson Cook, a minister from the Bronx and former White House Fellow; by Angela Oh, an attorney and Los Angeles community leader; and Robert Thompson, the CEO of Nissan U.S.A.—distinguished leaders, leaders in their community.

I want this panel to help educate Americans about the facts surrounding issues of race, to promote a dialogue in every community of the land to confront and work through these issues, to recruit and encourage leadership at all levels to help breach racial divides, and to find, develop and recommend how to implement concrete solutions to our problems—solutions that will involve all of us in government, business, communities, and as individual citizens.

I will make periodic reports to the American people about our findings and what actions we all have to take to move America forward. This board will seek out and listen to Americans from all races and all walks of life. They are performing a great citizen service, but in the cause of building one America all citizens must serve.

As I said at the President's Summit on Service in Philadelphia, in our new era such acts of service are basic acts of citizenship. Government must play its role, but much of the work must be done by the American people as citizen service. The very effort will strengthen us and bring us closer together.

In short, I want America to capture the feel and the spirit that you have given to all of us today. I'd like to ask the board to stand and be recognized. I want you to look at them, and I want you to feel free to talk to them over the next year or so. Dr. Franklin and members of the board.

Honest dialogue will not be easy at first. We'll all have to get past defensiveness and fear and political correctness and other barriers to honesty. Emotions may be rubbed raw, but we must begin.

What do I really hope we will achieve as a country? If we do nothing more than talk, it will be interesting but it won't be enough. If we do nothing more than propose disconnected acts of policy, it would be helpful, but it won't be enough.

But if ten years from now people can look back and see that this year of honest dialogue and concerted action helped to lift the heavy burden of race from our children's future, we will have given a precious gift to America.

I ask you all to remember just for a moment, as we have come through the difficult trial on the Oklahoma City bombing, remember that terrible day when we saw and wept for Americans and forgot for a moment that there were a lot of them from different races than we are.

Remember the many faces and races of the Americans who did not sleep and put their lives at risk to engage in the rescue, the helping and the healing. Remember how you have seen things like that in the natural disasters here in California. That is the face of the real America. That is the face I have seen over and over again. That is the America, somehow, some way we have to make real in daily American life.

Members of the graduating class, you will have a greater opportunity to live your dreams than any generation in our history, if we can make of our many different strands, one America—a nation at peace with itself bound together by shared values and aspirations and opportunities and real respect for our differences.

I am a Scotch-Irish Southern Baptist, and I'm proud of it. But my life has been immeasurably enriched by the power of the Torah, the beauty of the Koran, the piercing wisdom of the religions of East and South Asia— all embraced by my fellow Americans. I have felt indescribable joy and peace in black and Pentecostal churches. I have come to love the intensity and selflessness of my Hispanic fellow Americans toward la familia. As a Southerner, I grew up on country music and county fairs and I still like them. But I have also reveled in the festivals and the food, the music and the art and the culture of Native Americans and Americans from every region in the world.

In each land I have visited as your President, I have felt more at home because some of their people have found a home in America. For two centuries, wave upon wave of immigrants have come to our shores to build a new life drawn by the promise of freedom and a fair chance. Whatever else they found, even bigotry and violence, most of them never gave up on America. Even African American, the first of whom we brought here in chains, never gave up on America.

It is up to you to prove that their abiding faith was well-placed. Living in islands of isolation—some splendid and some sordid—is not the American way. Basing our self-esteem on the ability to look down on others is not the American way. Being satisfied if we have what we want and heedless of others who don't even have what they need and deserve is not the American way. We have torn down the barriers in our laws. Now we must break down the barriers in our lives, our minds and our hearts.

More than 30 years ago, at the high tide of the civil rights movement, the Kerner Commission said we were becoming two Americas, one white, one black, separate and unequal. Today, we face a different choice: will we become not two, but many Americas, separate, unequal and isolated? Or will we draw strength from all our people and our ancient faith in the quality of human dignity, to become the world's first truly multi-racial democracy. That is the unfinished work of our time, to lift the burden of race and redeem the promise of America. Class of 1997, I grew up in the shadows of a divided America, but I have seen glimpses of one America. You have shown me one today. That is the America you must make. It begins with your dreams, so dream large, live your dreams, challenge your parents and teach your children well.

God bless you and good luck.

DOCTORS REPORT ON END-OF-LIFE CARE

June 18, 1997

Two million Americans, most of them over age sixty-five, were expected to die in 1997, and too many of them were likely to suffer unnecessarily in their dying days. That was the primary conclusion of several major reports issued in 1997 on end-of-life, or palliative, care. The reports found that too many dying patients experienced severe pain, breathlessness, confusion, and other physical and emotional hardships that could be mitigated by better palliative care. Others were subjected to medical treatment that served only to protract their suffering without improving the quality of their lives. Virtually all the reports recommended that doctors and other health care personnel be given better training to deal more skillfully with death and the dying; that laws inhibiting doctors from prescribing pain-relieving drugs be reformed; and that the emphasis in care be shifted away from medical technology that often prolongs suffering to easing a dying patient's final days.

"People who are dying should be able to count on skillful and compassionate care that reflects their own wishes and those of their families. . . . Consistently good care is an urgent and attainable goal," said Christine Cassell, head of a committee that investigated the problem for the Institute of Medicine. "Professionals and the public are troubled by current patterns of inadequate care and are seeking improvements," wrote the authors of a report published in the Journal of the American Medical Association (JAMA). *"Almost every type of health care professional and organization treat dying patients, so responsibility is broad and myriad changes are needed."*

The reports were spurred in large part by the aging of the baby boom generation. "We baby boomers are aging, caring for our parents and watching our grandparents die," said Ira Byock of the University of Montana, director of a program to improve end-of-life care. "Many of us who had never lost anyone we loved, except maybe a pet, are now seeing colleagues die and have even cradled a dying child. And we're bringing the same healthy skepticism to dying that we brought to the experience of pregnancy and childbirth during our child-bearing years."

Another factor was the national debate on the legal and moral issues sur-rounding physician-assisted suicide. In June the Supreme Court ruled that individuals did not have a general constitutional right to physician-assisted suicide. That left the matter to each state and its voters to determine whether the terminally ill should be permitted to take their own lives with the aid of a doctor. Many, both in and out the medical profession, argued that much of the interest in physician-assisted suicide would disappear if end-of-life care were improved and the number of patients who spent their last days in pain were reduced. (Supreme Court on physician-assisted suicide, p. 459)

Yet a third factor in the growing interest in issues of death and dying was foundation support. Financier George Soros had pledged to spend at least $15 million on an effort to change American attitudes about death. Since the mid-1990s the Project on Death in America had funded a variety of research and demonstration projects and scholars in medical centers studying palliative care. The Robert Wood Johnson Foundation had earmarked $41 million for similar grants, including one to the American Medical Association of $1.54 million to educate practicing physicians about palliative care. "Death is finally coming out of the closet," Kathleen M. Foley, director of the Project on Death, told the New York Times.

How People Die

Several of the reports looked at how people die and found that the patients' preferences about care and hospitalization were often ignored or overlooked. In one study published January 15 in the Annals of Internal Medicine *researchers surveyed "surrogate decision-makers" of patients who died at five hospitals around the country. Based on those interviews, the study found that most people experience severe pain, breathlessness, confusion, or some other unpleasant symptom in their dying days, some of which could be relieved by medical treatment. More than half (56 percent) underwent one of three life-extending measures in their last three days of life—cardiopulmonary resuscitation (CPR), assisted breathing with a mechanical ventilator, or feeding through a tube. About 10 percent of the surrogates said the treatment was not what the patient wanted.*

A study by medical researchers at Dartmouth University, released in October, also found that patient preferences were not fulfilled. Based on an analysis of all Medicare patients who had died in 1994 and 1995, the study found significant variations in the treatment patients received from region to region. For example, people on the East Coast were twice as likely to die in hospitals as were people on the West Coast. These differences, said John E. Wennberg, the chief author of the report, reflected "the characteristics of the health care system and not what patients want or what is best for them." (About three-fourths of all Americans die in hospitals or nursing homes, although four out of five Americans say they prefer to die at home.)

That patient preferences are often disregarded was reinforced by three studies published in the April issue of the Journal of the American Geriatrics

Society, *which found that advance directives about medical care, such as living wills and other written proxies, have little effect on the care given to dying patients. For one thing, the studies found, only about one-fifth of patients actually write down their treatment preferences in a formal directive, and most of those do not discuss their preferences with their doctor, so only about one-third of the directives show up on patients' medical charts. Furthermore, many of the directives are worded so generally that they are of little help in guiding physicians in specific situations. The studies reviewed the medical charts for 4,804 dying patients in five hospitals. Only 688 had advance directives, and only 22 of those were specific enough to be of help to the patients' doctors. Living wills and health care proxies were "meant to be a way of stimulating conversation" between patients and doctors, said Joanne Lynn, director of the George Washington University's Center to Improve Care of the Dying. "But there's no evidence they've stimulated anything at all."*

JAMA *Report*

Lynn was a coauthor of an article published June 18 in JAMA, *surveying the efforts taken by the medical profession, philanthropic foundations, and others to stimulate interest in and improve palliative care. The authors also listed several obstacles to success, including lack of federal funding. "Federal funding to improve care of the dying through research or education is hard to discern, especially at the National Institutes of Health," wrote Lynn and Daniel P. Sulmasy of the Georgetown University Medical Center. "Current funding for health professionals' education does not require attention to end-of-life care."*

They also wrote that palliative care would probably not improve much without "major changes in financing and organization of care." Doctors and other health professionals specializing in the field need to be better compensated, and insurance reform was also required, they wrote. "Dying patients are undesirable to enroll or retain in capitated health plans since they incur major expenses without bringing additional income."

Institute of Medicine Report

Many of these same points were reiterated and amplified in a separate report, prepared by a panel of experts for the Institute of Medicine at the National Academy of Science. In its report, released June 4, the panel made several recommendations that it said would help the nation attain a humane care system. Foremost among them was better palliative care training for doctors, nurses, and other health personnel. In addition, the panel said, hospitals and other health care organizations need to provide patients and their families with better information about what the patient can expect in his or her final days and what services are available. The panel also urged that drug laws be reformed so that doctors can provide morphine and other pain-relieving drugs in adequate quantities. Although drug addiction among patients taking morphine or other addicting drugs for pain relief is extremely rare—occurring in between 1 in 1,000 to 1 in 10,000 cases—many states limit the dosages that doctors may prescribe and require an excessive amount of paperwork, the panel said.

Like the authors of the JAMA article, the panel expressed concern that fee-for-service care resulted in overuse of surgery, tests, and other procedures, while fixed enrollment fees used by health maintenance organizations discouraged them from enrolling or retaining people with serious chronic illnesses. The panel urged that more money be made available for physicians to visit patients at home or in nursing homes and that the disincentives for insuring sicker patients be removed.

"[P]eople have come both to fear a technologically overtreated and protracted death and to dread the prospect of abandonment and untreated physical and emotional distress," the panel wrote. The current system should be replaced with a humane care system, the experts said, one that "honors and protects those who are dying, conveys by word and action that dignity resides in people, not physical attributes, and helps people to preserve their integrity while coping with unavoidable physical insults and losses."

Following is the text of the article, "End-of-Life Care," by Daniel P. Sulmasy and Joanne Lynn that appeared in the June 18, 1997, issue of the Journal of the American Medical Association:

Hippocrates wrote that the art of medicine consisted of relieving the sufferings of the sick, lessening the violence of their diseases, and refraining from attempts at cure when patients were overmastered by disease. Physicians, unfortunately, seemed to interpret this as advice to avoid those who are dying. By 1505, Francis Bacon was urging physicians to treat patients' symptoms not only when they might recover, "but also when, all hope of recovery gone, it serves only to make a fair and easy passage from life." Five centuries later, the profession is beginning to address Bacon's challenge.

Professionals and the public are troubled by current patterns of inadequate care and are seeking improvements. Almost every type of health care professional and organization treat dying patients, so responsibility is broad and myriad changes are needed. Reform requires broad interdisciplinary collaboration and depends primarily on better use of existing therapeutic knowledge and continued expansion of the research base. Searching the Medical Subject Heading key word "terminal care" yielded 124 articles per year in the early 1970s. That figure for the last 3 years averages 543. The World Health Organization, the Agency for Health Care Policy and Research (AHCPR), and the American Pain Society have promulgated guidelines for treating cancer pain within the past few years.

Most of us now die of progressive chronic illness, mostly in old age (average age at death is 77 years) and mostly after a substantial period of disability. Thus, most people know someone whose dying seemed to go awry, whether through injudicious overtreatment or inadequate supportive care services. The limited data available support the pervasiveness of these anecdotes. The Study to Understand Prognoses and Preferences for Outcomes and Risks of Treatment (SUPPORT) found that half of conscious patients suffered severe pain near death. Serious chronic illness threatens almost everyone with impoverishment. Most oncologists report feeling unskilled at pain management and few care systems ensure continuity. Advance care planning remains the exception rather than the rule, even for predictable decisions like resuscitation.

In response, the Open Society Institute initiated the Project on Death in America, which is funding an array of research and demonstration projects and a few dozen scholars in medical centers. The biennial palliative care conference in Montreal (the International Congress on the Care of the Terminally Ill, September 7–11, 1996) and various hospice providers' meetings were joined this past year by 4 prominent meetings focused on reform agendas: The Robert Wood Johnson Foundation brought together public and professional organizations to share information and set agendas; the Center to Improve Care of the Dying convened policymakers; the American Medical Association convened professional society representatives to focus on education and practice reform; and the Milbank Memorial Fund convened professional society representatives to consider policy statements and practice guidelines. The American Medical Association's Council on Scientific Affairs called for improvements in education, research, and services for the dying.

Forty professional and lay organizations have signed a statement that advocates that health care organizations and clinicians be held accountable for quality of care at the end of life and presents a list of 10 areas that should be measured: symptoms, function, advance planning, aggressive life-extending treatments, satisfaction (patient and family), quality of life, family burden, survival time, provider continuity and skill, and bereavement support. A collaborative effort to develop measures of quality of care was initiated at a meeting of survey researchers in August (Toolkit Conference, Woods Hole, Mass, August 27–28, 1996).

The movement to legalize physician-assisted suicide has made legislative and judicial gains. As of January 1, 1997, Jack Kevorkian, MD, an unlicensed pathologist, has acknowledged assisting at least 44 patients with suicide, though several attempted prosecutions have failed. Oregon passed a statute legalizing physician-assisted suicide, but legal challenges have blocked implementation. In the spring of 1996, 2 US district courts declared state bans on assisted suicide to be unconstitutional, invoking the liberty/due process and the equal protection clauses of the Fourteenth Amendment. Both states appealed. The US Supreme Court heard oral arguments on January 8, 1997, and is likely to rule this summer. The American Medical Association and most established health care professional groups are opposed to constitutionalizing the question and to legalizing the practice, but the public and physicians are divided.

The suicide debate might galvanize medical and social forces to effect real improvement in the care of the dying. In Oregon, for example, most physicians have received continuing education on good care of the dying in the past 2 years, and the site of death is shifting from hospitals to nursing homes, hospices, and homes. Regardless of the Supreme Court decision, health care has a moral imperative and a political mandate to provide better care for the dying.

Federal funding to improve care of the dying through research or education is hard to discern, especially at the National Institutes of Health. Current funding for health professionals' education does not require attention to end-of-life care. The Agency for Health Care Policy and Research has sponsored an array of projects on advance care planning and now on the measurement of quality. The Robert Wood Johnson Foundation, which funded the SUPPORT project, is following up with a major public information campaign and a research and demonstration initiative. Congress required the US Department of Veterans Affairs to evaluate their hospice services, though this will be a very limited study.

Educators are also beginning to respond. Initiatives for medical students are under way at multiple medical schools, with 1 collaborative project being coordinated by the consumer group Choice in Dying in New York City. Representatives from several specialty boards recently met to incorporate curricular requirements into the reviews of the Residency Review Committees and to develop board examination questions. The American Board of Internal Medicine has produced an educational resource on care of the dying, and new recommendations of the Federated Council for Internal Medicine require classroom and hands-on clinical experiences.

Care at the end of life probably cannot improve dramatically without major changes in financing and organization of care. At present, supportive services and palliative care are inadequately compensated, especially in comparison with technological interventions. Incentives also discourage continuity. Dying patients are undesirable to enroll or retain in capitated health plans since they incur major expenses without bringing additional income. One small improvement may be the current experiment with an *International Classification of Diseases* code for palliative care. More fundamental reform is also gathering support. "MediCaring," for example, proposes hospicelike comprehensive service programs on a salary or capitation basis for those who are seriously ill with an eventually fatal illness, even if survival time is relatively unpredictable.

We are now poised to respond to Bacon's 500-year-old plea to make the care of the dying an integral part of medical research, teaching, and practice. The truism that all of us will die means that all of us have an interest in being confident that our suffering and pain will be compassionately addressed, and that we will find our time at the end of life conducive to the experiences of being loved and finding meaning. Clinicians will need improved skills and more appropriate care systems in order to improve care at the end of life.

PROPOSED SETTLEMENT OF TOBACCO CLAIMS
June 20, 1997

The tobacco industry and state attorneys general announced a proposed settlement June 20 in which the nation's four biggest cigarette makers agreed to accept strict federal controls on the way they make and market their products and to pay $368.5 billion to compensate the states and individuals for smoking-related health care costs. In return the companies were granted immunity from dozens of state and class action lawsuits that, had they been successful, could have ruined the industry financially. A statement released by the four tobacco companies described the settlement as "a bitter pill," but said that the "plan is preferable to the continuation of a decades-long controversy that has failed to produce a constructive outcome for anyone." The four companies were Philip Morris Companies; RJR Nabisco Holdings Corporation; B.A.T. Industries P.L.C., the British parent of the Brown & Williamson Tobacco Corporation; and the Loews Corporation, owner of the Lorillard Tobacco Company.

The proposed settlement represented the largest concessions the tobacco industry had ever agreed to make. In addition to the money, which would also be used to fund a national antismoking campaign, the tobacco companies agreed to admit that smoking was addictive and lethal. It further agreed to restrictions on marketing and advertising, committed itself to reducing smoking among minors, and agreed to drop its appeal of a federal district court ruling upholding the authority of the Food and Drug Administration (FDA) to regulate nicotine as a drug and cigarettes as drug delivery devices.

The agreement, however, was not the end of the matter. Because it affected federal regulatory authority and rights to sue, any final settlement had to be put into legislative form and approved by Congress and the president. Many members of Congress and the Clinton administration greeted the announced settlement with reservation, however. Speaking June 22, President Bill Clinton said he would withhold final judgment on the settlement until after his administration had reviewed all the fine print, but indicated he was concerned about how it would affect the FDA's regulatory authority. He also said he wanted to ensure "that those things which made the tobacco interests conclude that it was in their interest to make the agreement do not compromise or undermine our obligation and our opportunity to protect the public health." Several health organizations opposed the agreement, saying it was too lenient and did not go far enough in its efforts to prevent teenagers from smoking. The American Lung Association called the deal a "bailout" for an industry with "a dismal record of lies and bad faith." By year's end, several lawmakers in both chambers had offered their own legislative versions of the settlement, and both the tobacco industry and its opponents were mounting massive lobbying campaigns for the legislative battle anticipated in 1998.

Long Road to a Negotiated Settlement

Since the surgeon general warned in 1964 that smoking was linked to cancer and other diseases, the curbs on cigarettes and the industry have been steadily growing in number and severity. In 1970 Congress banned cigarette advertising on television and radio and strengthened cigarette pack label warnings that smoking is hazardous to health. Concerns about health problems from secondhand smoke led Arizona in 1973 to become the first state to restrict smoking in some public places. Since then many states and localities have taken steps to bar smoking in restaurants, bars, offices, and other public places. The federal government in 1990 barred smoking on all flights of six hours or less.

Meanwhile, scientists and other researchers were uncovering more and more evidence that smoking contributes to a variety of serious diseases. In 1967 the surgeon general reported that smoking was the leading cause of lung cancer. Smoking has also been linked to heart disease, other cancers, and low birthweights. Several individual and class action lawsuits were brought against tobacco companies seeking to hold them liable for various illnesses and deaths; none of these suits was successful. In the early 1990s individual states began to file class action suits against the tobacco industry seeking to recoup the costs of Medicaid payments made for smoking-related illnesses. These suits, eventually filed by at least forty states, led to the negotiations between the state attorneys general and the tobacco industry.

Meanwhile the health warnings and antismoking campaigns seemed to be having an effect. In 1989, twenty-five years after the first federal warning was issued, Surgeon General Everett C. Koop reported that half of all smoking adults had kicked the habit. But three of every ten adults still smoked, he said, and every day at least 3,000 teenagers began to smoke. Concern that tobacco companies were deliberately directing their advertising to youngsters mounted in 1991, when a study found that almost as many preschoolers recognized Joe Camel, the cartoon character prominent in R. J. Reynolds's ads, as recognized Mickey Mouse. (Smoking report, Historic Documents of 1989, p. 31)

Throughout these years, the tobacco companies insisted that smoking was not addictive and that it did not cause cancer or other health problems.

That facade began to crumble in the early 1990s with reports that the industry was well aware of the health hazards associated with smoking. These reports gained credence in 1993 when Jeffrey S. Wigand, then director of research at Brown & Williamson, blew the whistle, saying that the companies had long known that nicotine was addictive and that Brown & Williamson's chief executive had lied when he told a congressional committee otherwise. Wigand also charged that the company deliberately manipulated the nicotine levels in cigarettes, allegations that eventually led to several congressional and legal investigations of the cigarette makers. (Addictive nature of tobacco, Historic Documents of 1994, p. 205)

With public sentiment turning against the manufacturers, the Clinton administration in 1995 proposed new regulations that would allow the FDA to regulate nicotine as a drug and cigarettes as drug delivery devices. The regulations, which were finalized in 1996, would also impose restrictions on cigarette marketing and advertising aimed at minors. The tobacco companies immediately challenged the constitutionality of the regulations. On April 25, 1997, a federal district court judge in North Carolina upheld the FDA's authority to regulate nicotine as a drug, but said the FDA did not have the authority to regulate advertising directed at minors. The ruling did not directly foreclose the possibility that another federal agency, such as the Federal Trade Commission, might have such authority. (Proposed regulation, Historic Documents of 1995, p. 670; final regulations, Historic Documents of 1996, p. 589)

The ruling—in a tobacco-growing state by a conservative judge who as a private attorney had represented tobacco interests—was seen as a severe setback to the tobacco industry. Only a month earlier, the industry had suffered a major defection when the Liggett Group Inc. acknowledged that smoking is addictive and causes cancer and that tobacco industries had deliberately aimed some of their advertising at youngsters. The admission came as part of a settlement between Liggett, makers of Chesterfield and L&M brands among others, and twenty states suing to recoup the costs of smoking-related health care paid for by Medicaid. Liggett also agreed to turn over to the states internal documents, including confidential discussions among the five major cigarette companies, on marketing strategies.

Both the Liggett settlement and the unfavorable court ruling put additional pressure on the remaining four tobacco companies to reach settlement in the suits pending against them. The talks, which had gotten underway in February and which were closely monitored by the White House, eventually included the companies, state attorneys general, plaintiffs' attorneys, and public health advocates. In the end the participants produced a complex sixty-eight-page agreement that many said would serve only as a starting point for a final settlement.

Highlights of the Settlement

Apart from its liability provisions and those penalizing cigarette makers if underage smoking does not decline to specified levels, the agreement largely tracked the outlines of the FDA regulation finalized in 1996. Following are the highlights of the proposed settlement.

Liability. *The four companies would provide $368.5 billion to the states, lawsuit plaintiffs, and public health campaigns over twenty-five years. Pending lawsuits against the tobacco companies, including addiction-dependency claims, the cases brought by the forty states, and class action suits—would be legislatively settled and paid for out of the $368.5 billion. All future prosecutions of such claims would be barred. Individual plaintiffs involved in "past conduct" cases—those involving past actions of the tobacco companies—could claim damages for medical services and lost wages, but not punitive damages. Individuals could claim actual and punitive damages involving future conduct of the companies—conduct occurring after the settlement was in place. The amount the industry would have to pay in any one year was capped.*

Regulation. *For the first time the FDA would have authority to regulate the development and manufacturing of tobacco products. The FDA could require companies to reduce the amount of nicotine in cigarettes but could not ban nicotine outright for twelve years. The FDA would be required to evaluate all additives to tobacco products.*

Underage Smoking. *The agreement banned sale of tobacco products to anyone under the age of eighteen, and several provisions, including a ban on vending machines, were intended to make it difficult for minors to obtain tobacco products. The settlement required that underage smoking decline by 30 percent from estimated current levels within five years, by 50 percent in seven years, and by 60 percent in ten years. Failure to meet those goals could result in a surcharge on cigarette makers of $80 million for each percentage point by which the goal was missed, up to a total of $2 billion a year. States would also be subject to penalties for failing to enforce the prohibition on sales to minors.*

Advertising. *The settlement barred tobacco advertising on clothing and other merchandise not related to tobacco, on outdoor billboards, and on the Internet. Human and cartoon characters such as the Marlboro Man and Joe Camel were also banned. (R. J. Reynolds Tobacco Co. announced July 10 that it was ending its advertising campaign based on the Joe Camel character.) The tobacco companies also agreed to new warning labels, including one stating: "WARNING: Smoking can kill you."*

Battle Shifts to Capitol Hill

Once the settlement was announced, attention shifted to the White House and Congress, where legislation incorporating the agreement had to be drafted and approved before any of it could take effect. The first group to officially weigh in was a congressionally appointed advisory panel of health advocates, led by former surgeon general Koop and former FDA commissioner David A. Kessler, that found several key provisions unacceptable. One important concern was whether the proposed settlement contained procedural hurdles that would inhibit FDA's ability to regulate nicotine and tobacco products. The panel also questioned whether the incentives to reduce smoking among minors were strong enough to be effective, whether tobacco companies should be immune to future lawsuits, and whether the funding earmarked for various health programs was sufficient.

President Clinton did not formally respond to the settlement until September 17, when he outlined "five key elements" any final settlement should contain. Among these was a proposal to impose a combination of taxes and penalties on the cigarette companies that would increase the price of a pack of cigarettes by $1.50. This step had been advocated by Kessler, who argued that substantial increases in cigarette prices were the only proven means of reducing underage smoking. Clinton also said that any tobacco legislation must protect tobacco farmers, a subject that the proposed settlement did not touch upon. Other elements closely tracked the concerns raised by the advisory panel.

As the year ended, the tobacco industry and its opponents were preparing for a political battle on Capitol Hill in 1998 that was already making strange bedfellows. Legislators from tobacco-growing states who usually backed tobacco interests, for example, were displeased because the settlement contained no protections for tobacco farmers. The settlement also divided the antismoking forces, with some arguing that more comprehensive tobacco-control legislation needed to be enacted and others warning that such demands could kill the settlement altogether to the detriment of the public. "It will not serve the public health if we all go back to trench warfare," said Bill Novelli of the National Center for Tobacco-Free Kids.

While the tobacco industry may have lost favor with much of the American public, it still was able to mount a powerful lobbying organization. In an effort to increase its waning credibility in Congress, the tobacco industry hired several prominent Washington figures to conduct its lobbying campaign, including former Senate majority leaders George J. Mitchell, a Democrat from Maine, and Howard H. Baker, Jr., a Republican from Tennessee, as well as former Republican National Committee chairman Haley Barbour, who helped elect dozens of Republicans to the House in 1996. The industry also continued its tradition as a generous donor to political campaigns, giving at least $2.5 million to both Republicans and Democrats in the first half of 1997.

> *Following is the preamble of the proposed resolution of lawsuits brought by forty states against the four leading American cigarette manufacturers, released to the public June 20, 1997:*

This legislation would mandate a total reformation and restructuring of how tobacco products are manufactured, marketed and distributed in this country. The nation can thereby see real and swift progress in preventing underage use of tobacco, addressing the adverse health effects of tobacco use and changing the corporate culture of the tobacco industry.

The Food and Drug Administration ("FDA") and other public health authorities view the use of tobacco products by our nation's children as a "pediatric disease" of epic and worsening proportions that results in new generations of tobacco dependent children and adults. There is also a consensus within the scientific and medical communities that tobacco products are inherently dangerous and cause cancer, heart disease and other serious adverse health effects.

The FDA and other health authorities have concluded that virtually all new users of tobacco products are under legal age. President Clinton, the FDA, the Federal Trade Commission ("FTC"), state Attorneys General and public health authorities all believe that tobacco advertising and marketing contribute significantly to the use of nicotine-containing tobacco products by adolescents. These officials have concluded that because past efforts to restrict advertising and marketing have failed to curb adolescent tobacco use, sweeping new restrictions on the sale, promotion and distribution of such products are needed.

Until now, federal and state governments have lacked many of the legal means and resources they need to address the societal problems caused by the use of tobacco products. These officials have been armed only with crude regulatory tools which they view as inadequate to achieve the public health objectives with which they are charged.

This legislation greatly strengthens both the federal and state governments' regulatory arsenal and furnishes them with additional resources needed to address a public health problem that affects millions of Americans, including most importantly underage tobacco use. Further, it is contemplated that certain of the obligations of the tobacco companies will be implemented by a binding, enforceable contractual protocol.

The legislation reaffirms individuals' right of access to the courts, to civil trial by jury and to full compensatory damages. Resolution through the Act of potential punitive damages liability of the tobacco industry for past conduct is only made in the context of the comprehensive settlement proposed by the legislation. It is not intended to have precedential effect, nor does it express any position adverse to the imposition of punitive damages in general or as applied to any other specific industry, case, controversy or product and does not provide any authority whatsoever regarding the propriety of punitive damages.

Among other things, the new regime would:

- Confirm FDA's authority to regulate tobacco products under the Food, Drug and Cosmetic Act, making FDA not only the preeminent regulatory agency with respect to the manufacture, marketing and distribution of tobacco products but also requiring the tobacco industry to fund FDA's oversight out of ongoing payments by the manufacturers pursuant to the new regime ("Industry Payments").
- Go beyond FDA's current regulations to ban all outdoor tobacco advertising and to eliminate cartoon characters and human figures, such as Joe Camel and the Marlboro Man, two tobacco icons which the public

health community has long assailed as advertising appealing to our nation's youth.

- Impose and provide funding out of the Industry Payments for an aggressive federal enforcement program, including a State-administered retail licensing system, to stop minors from obtaining tobacco products, while in no way preventing the States from enacting additional measures.
- Ensure that the FDA and the States have the regulatory flexibility to address issues of particular concern to public health officials, such as youth tobacco usage and tobacco dependence.
- Subject the tobacco industry to severe financial surcharges in the event underage tobacco use does not decline radically over the next decade.
- Empower the federal government to set national standards controlling the manufacturing of tobacco products and the ingredients used in such products.
- Provide new and flexible regulatory enforcement powers to ensure that the tobacco industry works to develop and introduce less-hazardous tobacco products, including, among other things, vesting FDA with the power to regulate the levels of nicotine in tobacco products.
- Require the manufacturers of tobacco products to disclose all previously non-public internal laboratory research and all new internal laboratory research generated in the future relating to the health effects or safety of their products.
- Establish a minimum federal standard with tough restrictions on smoking in public places with enforcement funding from the Industry Payments, while preserving the authority of state and local governments to enact even more severe standards.
- Authorize and fund from Industry Payments a $500 million annual, national education-oriented counter-advertising and tobacco control campaign seeking to discourage the initiation of tobacco use by children and adolescents and to encourage current tobacco product users to quit use of the products.
- Authorize and fund from Industry Payments the annual payment to all States of significant, ongoing financial compensation to fund health benefits program expenditures and to establish and fund a tobacco products liability judgments and settlement fund.
- Authorize and fund from Industry Payments a nationwide program, administered through State governments and the private sector, of smoking cessation.

The sale of tobacco products to adults would remain legal but subject to restrictive measures to ensure that they are not sold to underage purchasers. These measures respond directly to concerns voiced by federal and state public health officials, the public health community and the public at large that the tobacco industry should be subject to the strictest scrutiny and regulatory oversight. This statute imposes regulatory controls, including civil and criminal penalties, equal to, and in many respects exceeding, those imposed on other regulated industries. Further, it imposes on tobacco manufacturers the obligation to provide funding from Industry Payments for an array of public health initiatives.

The sale, distribution, marketing, advertising and use of tobacco products are activities substantially affecting interstate commerce. Such products are sold, marketed, advertised and distributed in interstate commerce on a nationwide basis, and have a substantial effect on the nation's economy. The sale, distribution, marketing, advertising and use of such products are also activities substantially affecting interstate commerce by virtue of the health care and other costs that federal and State governmental authorities have attributed to usage of tobacco products.

Various civil actions are pending in state and federal courts arising from the use, marketing or sale of tobacco products. Among these actions are cases brought by some 40 state Attorneys General, cases brought by certain cities and counties, the Commonwealth of Puerto Rico, and other third-party payor cases seeking to recover monies spent treating tobacco-related diseases and for the protection of minors and consumers. Also pending in courts throughout the United States are various private putative class action lawsuits brought on behalf of individuals claiming to be dependent upon and injured by tobacco products. Additionally, a multitude of individual suits have been filed against the tobacco products manufacturers and/or their distributors, trade associations, law firms and consultants.

All of these civil actions are complex, slow-moving, expensive and burdensome, not only for the litigants but also for the nation's state and federal judiciaries. Moreover, none of those litigation's has to date resulted in the collection of any monies to compensate smokers or third-party payors. Only national legislation offers the prospect of a swift, fair, equitable and consistent result that would serve the public interest by (1) ensuring that a portion of the costs of treatment for diseases and adverse health effects linked to the use of tobacco products is borne by the manufacturers of these products, and (2) restricting nationwide the sale, distribution, marketing and advertising of tobacco products to persons of legal age. The unique position occupied by tobacco in the nation's history and economy, the magnitude of actual and potential tobacco-related litigation, the need to avoid the cost, expense, uncertainty and inconsistency associated with such protracted litigation, the need to limit the sale, distribution, marketing and advertising of tobacco products to persons of legal age, and the need to educate the public, especially young people, of the health effects of using tobacco products all dictate that it would be in the public interest to enact this legislation to facilitate a resolution of the matters described.

Public health authorities believe that the societal benefits of this legislation, in human and economic terms, would be vast. In particular, FDA has found that reducing underage tobacco use by 50% "would prevent well over 60,000 early deaths." FDA has estimated that the monetary value of its present regulations will be worth up to $43 billion per year in reduced medical costs, improved productivity and the benefit of avoiding the premature death of loved ones. This statute, which extends far beyond anything FDA has previously proposed or attempted, can be expected to produce human and economic benefits many times greater than such existing regulations.

As part of this settlement, the tobacco companies recognize the historic changes that will be occurring to their business. They will fully comply with increased federal regulation, focus intense efforts on dramatic reductions in youth access and youth tobacco usage, recognize that the regulatory scheme encourages the development of products with reduced risk and acknowledge the predominant public health positions associated with the use of tobacco products. . . .

FINAL STATEMENT OF THE "SUMMIT OF THE EIGHT"
June 22, 1997

*The leaders of the major industrial democracies took a significant sym-
bolic step in 1997 to bolster the cause of political and economic reform in
Russia by expanding the participation of President Boris Yeltsin in their
annual economic summit. Yeltsin was given the honor of making the opening speech at the summit, held June 20–22, in Denver, Colorado. In their
final communiqué, issued June 22, the leaders called themselves the "Group
of the Eight," adding Yeltsin to the world's most exclusive club that had been
known for two decades as the "G-7."*

*During their private negotiating sessions, the leaders sparred over a
wide range of issues and were unable to reach agreement on two of the most
contentious matters before them: specific reductions in so-called greenhouse gases that contribute to global warming, and how many nations
should be invited into an expansion of NATO. Both of those issues were
dealt with at international meetings later in 1997. (Global warming treaty,
p. 859; NATO expansion, p. 514)*

*As was customary for these summits, the leaders' final statement dealt
with dozens of items on the world agenda, ranging from the Middle East
peace process to caring for aging populations in industrialized societies.
The leaders resolved none of those matters but in some cases did agree on
specific directions their aides should pursue in later negotiations.*

Yeltsin Makes an Impression

*Former Soviet leader Mikhail Gorbachev attended a luncheon at the 1991
economic summit in London, just a few months before the Soviet Union collapsed. Yeltsin, who as president of Russia effectively succeeded Gorbachev,
was invited to attend some functions of the summits in succeeding years.
But neither Gorbachev nor Yeltsin were ever considered as true members of
the group representing the leading economic powers; their presence was
based more on Moscow's prowess as a nuclear power and its long-range economic potential.*

In 1996 and early 1997 the Clinton administration offered several car-rots to Yeltsin in exchange for his tacit acceptance of the eastward expan-sion of NATO—a prospect that alarmed political and military leaders in Moscow. One carrot was that Washington would urge its trading partners to speed up consideration of Russia for membership in the World Trade Organization, which established global trading regulations, and in the Paris Club, the group of major creditor countries responsible for renegoti-ating the debts of developing nations. Another carrot Clinton offered—over the muted diplomatic objections of Japan and France—was the expanded participation by Yeltsin in the G-7 summit.

At the Denver summit, Yeltsin appeared trimmer and in better health than in years. He had turned back a serious challenge by the leader of the Communist Party in the 1996 presidential elections but then fell seriously ill and underwent a quintuple heart bypass. He quickly grabbed the summit limelight, posing for numerous photographs with Clinton and the other lead-ers and making it clear he now considered himself a full member of the eco-nomic club. Clinton was effusive about the meaning of the event: "What you see here is a sweeping integration of Russia into the major decision-making institutions in the world in a way that is very positive for the rest of us."

Even before he arrived, Yeltsin received the news that negotiators repre-senting the Paris Club had reached an agreement in principle to extend membership to Russia. Although a debtor nation itself, Russia claimed bil-lions of dollars worth of loans made by the Soviet Union to countries in Africa and Asia. Moscow hoped that joining the Paris Club would give it more clout to collect at least a portion of those loans some day.

There was one important limit to Yeltsin's participation at the Denver summit. Recognizing Russia's still-feeble economy, the leaders did not include Yeltsin in their hour-long discussion of financial and monetary matters on June 21. At that session, the leaders agreed on a statement in which they encouraged each other to adopt policies at home promoting eco-nomic growth and free international trade.

The statement represented an artful skirting of sensitive differences in how the leaders viewed the world economic scene. Clinton and his aides, for example, held out U.S. fiscal and monetary policies as examples to be emu-lated because they had led to economic growth with low inflation and reduced unemployment. European leaders, including the conservative French president, Jacques Chirac, insisted there were limits to how far they could curtail their countries' extensive social welfare systems.

Other Issues

In working sessions throughout the summit, the leaders (including Yeltsin) and their aides debated a host of diplomatic, political, military, and environmental issues but came to few definitive conclusions. Among the items of agreement was united opposition to the cloning of human beings. The summit occurred just three months after researchers in Scot-land announced the successful cloning of an adult sheep. (Cloning, p. 212)

In addition to the disagreements over global warming and NATO expansion, the leaders failed to reach consensus on the question of how long to keep NATO peacekeepers in Bosnia, where they were monitoring the Dayton peace accord. Clinton had announced before the summit that he was sticking to an earlier plan to withdraw the remaining 8,000 U.S. troops from the peacekeeping mission by June 30, 1998. European leaders insisted that the NATO mission should be extended past that date because communal tensions in Bosnia remained high. In a separate statement on Bosnia, the leaders pledged that the international community will maintain "a long-term engagement" in Bosnia and in the Balkans generally. But, they said, "our commitment is not unconditional," adding that leaders in the region must fulfill their "responsibilities and obligations."

On December 18, Clinton announced that he planned to keep U.S. forces in Bosnia past the June 1998 deadline. Clinton said he had concluded that withdrawal of the peacekeeping forces should be tied to "concrete benchmarks" of progress in complying with the peace agreement rather than a deadline on the calendar. (Bosnia peace agreement, Historic Documents of 1995, p. 717; Historic Documents of 1996, p. 816)

Other leaders attending the summit were Prime Minister Tony Blair of Great Britain, Chancellor Helmut Kohl of Germany, Prime Ryutaro Hashimoto of Japan, Prime Minister Jean Chretien of Canada, Prime Minister Romano Prodi of Italy, and representatives of the European Union.

Following is the text of the final communiqué issued June 22, 1997, by the "Summit of the Eight" after three days of meetings in Denver, Colorado:

Introduction

1. We, the participants in the Denver Summit of the Eight, as major industrialized democracies, have discussed the steps necessary, both internationally and domestically, to shape the forces of integration to ensure prosperity and peace for our citizens and the entire world as we approach the twenty-first century. We have agreed to work- closely with all willing partners in fostering global partnership for peace, security, and sustainable development that includes strengthening democracy, and human rights, and helping prevent and resolve conflicts.

2. Continuing the important steps we have taken, the Denver Summit of the Eight marks a new and deeper participation by Russia in our efforts. Russia has taken bold measures to complete an historic transformation into a democratic state with a market economy. We are committed to continue the trend of increased Russian participation in the work of our officials between Summits and reiterate our shared commitment to the promotion of a fuller involvement of Russia in the Summit process. Cooperation to integrate Russia's economy into the global economic system represents one of our most important priorities. We welcome the understanding reached between Russia and the Chairman of the Paris Club on the basis for Russia's participation and

look forward to the Paris Club and Russia finalizing an agreement in the near future. We support the goal of early Russian accession to the WTO on the basis of conditions generally applicable to newly acceding members. We also look forward to continued Russian progress toward accession to the OECD using the potential of the recently created Liaison Committee between Russia and the OECD.

Economic and Social Issues

3. The process of globalization, a major factor underlying the growth of world prosperity in the last fifty years, is now advancing rapidly and broadly. Globalization encompasses the expansion of cross-border flows of ideas and information, goods and services, technology and capital. More openness and integration across the global economy create opportunities for increased prosperity as countries specialize in those economic activities which they do best, while also promoting increased competition and efficiency, and the rapid spread of technological innovations. Our task, as we enter the 21st Century, is to make the most of these opportunities.

4. At the same time, globalization may create new challenges. The increasing openness and interdependence of our economies, with deep trade linkages and ever greater flows of private capital, means that problems in one country can spill over more easily to affect the rest. We must cooperate to promote global growth and prosperity. We must also insure that all segments of society, and indeed all countries across the globe, have the opportunity to share in the prosperity made possible by global integration and technological innovations. It is particularly important that young adults see the path to a successful life, and be adequately prepared to follow that path.

5. Rapid technological change and demographic shifts are also having an important impact on the global economy. We must take advantage of the possibilities for growth to address unemployment and economic insecurity. Sound economic policies and the structural reforms necessary to allow markets to function properly are essential if we are to meet the many domestic and international challenges we all face. Measures that expand the availability of high quality education and training and increase the responsiveness of labor markets to economic conditions will aid the ability of our people to adjust to all types of structural changes. We look forward to the high-level conference on employment that takes place this fall in Japan, which is expected to contribute to the discussion on responses to structural changes. We also welcome the proposal by the United Kingdom to host a conference of ministers responsible for finance and social affairs early next year on growth, employability, and inclusion, to prepare for further discussion of these vital issues at our meeting next year.

The Opportunities and Challenges of Aging Populations

6. Increased life expectancy and improved health among our elderly are two major achievements of this century. In the next century, these successes will present us with both opportunities and challenges, as longer life expectancies and lower birth rates significantly raise the proportion of seniors in our

countries' populations. Prime Minister Hashimoto's "Initiative for a Caring World" has provided us the opportunity to focus on the implications of these developments.

7. We discussed the idea of "active aging"—the desire and ability of many older people to continue work or other socially productive activities well into their later years, and agreed that old stereotypes of seniors as dependent should be abandoned. We considered new evidence suggesting that disability rates among seniors have declined in some countries while recognizing the wide variation in the health of older people. We discussed how our nations can promote active aging of our older citizens with due regard to their individual choices and circumstances, including removing disincentives to labor force participation and lowering barriers to flexible and part-time employment that exist in some countries. In addition, we discussed the transition from work to retirement, life-long learning and ways to encourage volunteerism and to support family care-giving.

8. We examined the differing implications of population aging for our nations' pension, health and long-term care systems in the next century. Active aging strategies can be a useful way to advance structural reforms in the areas of health and social welfare. Some of our countries face major challenges in sustaining their public pension systems and would benefit from early action to restore balance. Different ways were suggested to address this issue, including increasing the labor force participation of seniors and raising national savings rates. Investing in human capital, including maximizing opportunities for life-long learning, were mentioned as ways to facilitate the continued work preparedness of mature adults. Some countries will be more affected by the demands of health care financing for seniors. We concluded that efficient and effective management of this challenge should help us to meet the needs of an aging society without overburdening younger generations.

9. We agreed that it is important to learn from one another how our policies and programs can promote active aging and advance structural reforms to preserve and strengthen our pension, health and long-term care systems. Our governments will work together, within the OECD and with other international organizations, to promote active aging through information exchanges and cross-national research. We encourage collaborative biomedical and behavioral research to improve active life expectancy and reduce disability, and have directed our officials to identify gaps in our knowledge and explore developing comparable data in our nations to improve our capacity to address the challenges of population aging into the 21st Century.

Small and Medium Enterprises

10. The contributions of small and medium-sized enterprises to employment and economic dynamism in our societies are widely recognized. Fostering a business setting conducive to the growth of dynamic young enterprises is a key to job creation. In our discussion, we surveyed the obstacles to such growth, including the unavailability of debt or equity capital at critical stages of a firm's growth, unnecessary regulation, difficulties adopting

existing innovative technologies, and the problems of smaller businesses in entering global markets. We stress the need to remove these obstacles. We also examined some exemplary practices within our countries to promote the growth of small and medium-sized companies, as well as vocational training and education within these companies, and considered how we might benefit from these successes. Best practices in our countries could also be useful examples for developing and transition-market economies, as development of small and medium-sized enterprises favors creation of jobs and social stability, disseminates entrepreneurial capacities and helps to promote and diversify exports. We will pursue our work in other areas.

Global Issues

11. Even as global integration and rapid advances in communications and transportation have spurred economic growth, these same trends have exposed us to complex problems that defy unilateral solutions. In recent years our Summits have devoted increasing attention to our cooperative efforts to confront these problems.

Environment

12. This is a pivotal year for efforts to promote sustainable development and protect the environment. We are determined to address the environmental challenges that will affect the quality of life of future generations and to enhance public awareness, especially among our youth, of the importance of advancing sustainable development goals.

UN General Assembly Special Session

13. We discussed the progress that has been made since the 1992 Rio Earth Summit in defining and promoting sustainable development, and we commit ourselves to taking action in areas critical to advancing this agenda. Sustainable development demands the full integration of environment, economic and social policies; should be based upon democratic governance and respect for human rights; and should have poverty eradication as one of its ultimate objectives. In this connection, we reaffirm the vital contribution of civil society. We urge the United Nations General Assembly, at its Special Session to be held next week, to reaffirm and give impetus to the Rio commitments, to take stock of implementation since Rio, and, most importantly, to develop a manageable list of priority issues to address in future work on sustainable development.

Climate Change

14. Overwhelming scientific evidence links the build-up of greenhouse gasses in the atmosphere to changes in the global climate system. If current trends continue into the next century, unacceptable impacts on human health and the global environment are likely. Reversing these trends will require a sustained global effort over several decades, with the involvement of all our citizens, and changes in our patterns of consumption and production.

15. We are determined to take the lead and show seriousness of purpose in strengthening international efforts to confront climate change. Our ultimate goal must be to stabilize atmospheric concentrations of greenhouse gasses at an acceptable level. This will require efficient and cost-effective policies and measures sufficient to lead to a significant reduction in emissions.

16. International cooperation will be essential. At the Third Conference of Parties to the UN Framework Convention on Climate Change in Kyoto we must forge a strong agreement that is consistent with the Berlin Mandate and that contains quantified and legally-binding emission targets. We intend to commit to meaningful, realistic and equitable targets that will result in reductions of greenhouse gas emissions by 2010. The agreement must ensure transparency and accountability and allow Participants flexibility in the manner in which they meet their targets.

17. Action by developed countries alone will not be sufficient to meet this goal. Developing countries must also take measurable steps, recognizing that their obligations will increase as their economies grow. We agree to work in partnership with them to that effect by implementing technological development and diffusion and supporting environmental education and capacity building.

18. We stress the importance of setting up an appropriate mechanism for monitoring and ensuring compliance among Parties. We also agree to work together to enhance international efforts to further develop global systems for monitoring climate change and other environmental trends.

Forests

19. Forests continue to be destroyed and degraded at alarming rates in many parts of the world. To reverse this trend, we call upon all countries to make a long-term political commitment to achieve sustainable forest management practices worldwide and to join us in the immediate implementation of proposals put forward by the UNCSD Intergovernmental Panel on Forests. We have discussed in Denver and have agreed to support a practical Action Program that includes implementing national programs and building capacity for sustainable forest management; establishing networks of protected areas; assessing the state of each nation's forests using agreed criteria and indicators; promoting private sector management of forests; and eliminating illegal logging. We ask that our officials meet early next year to assess progress in implementing this Action Program and call for a report at our next meeting.

20. At the Special Session of the United Nations, we will work with the active involvement of environmental groups to build consensus on an international agreement with appropriately high international standards to achieve these goals. We welcome the progress made in implementing the Brazil Pilot Program initiated in Houston, and see it as an example of practical international cooperation.

Freshwater

21. Many people throughout the world do not have access to safe water. Increased human, industrial and agricultural wastes can diminish water qual-

ity, with adverse effects for ecosystems and human health and safety, particularly for children. The Special Session of the UN General Assembly should encourage the CSD to develop a practical plan of action to address freshwater-related issues, including promotion of efficient water use, improvement of water quality and sanitation, technological development and capacity building, public awareness and institutional improvements. To achieve these objectives, we have also agreed to promote bilateral and regional cooperation on freshwater concerns, and to enhance coordination of our efforts in this area.

Oceans

22. We must strengthen our efforts to protect the world's oceans. We will work to ensure an effective and integrated effort to deal with key issues, including sustainable fishing, shipping, marine pollution from land-based and off-shore activities, and oil spill prevention and emergency response. In this connection, we will also enhance cooperation in monitoring the ecology in the Northern Pacific, as well as in forecasting earthquakes and tsunamis in this region.

Desertification

23. We welcome the entry into force of the "Convention to Combat Desertification," and urge the parties to develop concrete steps to implement the convention at the First Conference of the Parties this Fall in Rome.

Environmental Standards for Export Credit Agencies

24. Private sector financial flows from industrial nations have a significant impact on sustainable development worldwide. Governments should help promote sustainable practices by taking environmental factors into account when providing financing support for investment in infrastructure and equipment. We attach importance to the work on this in the OECD, and will review progress at our meeting next year.

Children's Environmental Health

25. Protecting the health of our children is a shared fundamental value. Children throughout the world face significant threats to their health from an array of environmental hazards, and we recognize particular vulnerabilities of children to environmental threats. Our governments will explicitly incorporate children into environmental risk assessments and standard setting and together will work to strengthen information exchange, provide for microbiologically safe drinking water, and reduce children's exposure to lead, environmental tobacco smoke and other air pollutants.

Institutions

26. Strong international institutions are essential to coordinating global efforts to protect the environment and to achieve sustainable development.

27. The UNGA Special Session should confirm the role of the UN Commission on Sustainable Development (CSD) as the strategic forum for integrating

the social, environmental and economic aspects of sustainable development. The CSD should develop action plans with concrete objectives and timetables to guide its work in the four agreed priority areas: freshwater; oceans; land resources, including forests; and sustainable energy use.

28. To ensure an effective response to urgent global environmental problems, we have supported the refocused mandate for the United Nations Environment Program (UNEP), the leading global environmental authority, as affirmed by the UNEP Governing Council in Nairobi this year. UNEP should promote the coherent implementation of environmental protection within the UN system and serve as an authoritative advocate for the global environment. The newly formed High-level Committee of Environment Ministers and Officials should consider the international environmental agenda and elaborate upon and advance the reforms needed to ensure UNEP's effectiveness, with a particular emphasis on greater policy, program and financial accountability. We look forward to a revitalized UNEP being able to attract the resources needed for its tasks.

29. Further efforts are necessary to ensure the long-term coherence and efficiency of the UN's work on the environment. We encourage the Secretary General to review the handling of environmental matters within the UN system and to explore possible means and structures to improve further the coordination among, and effectiveness of, the concerned institutions.

30. We reaffirm the importance of the Global Environmental Facility as the leading multilateral funding mechanism for the global environment. We will work to strengthen its finances and enhance its effectiveness. In this regard, we will each do our part to contribute to a successful replenishment of the Facility.

Infectious Diseases

31. Infectious diseases, including drug-resistant tuberculosis, malaria, and HIV/AIDS are responsible for a third of all deaths in the world. They pose significant challenges to the health, security and financial resources of the global community. In many parts of the world, infectious diseases and deaths from infectious disease have risen sharply in the last decade for a variety of reasons, including the emergence of drug-resistant microbes and the increased movement of people and products.

32. In the coming year, our governments will promote more effective coordination of international responses to outbreaks; promote development of a global surveillance network, building upon existing national and regional surveillance systems; and help to build public health capacity to prevent, detect and control infectious diseases globally including efforts to explore the use of regional stocks of essential vaccines, therapeutics, diagnostics and other materials. Central to this work will be strengthening and linking existing activities in and among each of our countries, with developing countries, and in other fora, especially the World Health Organization. We support the efforts of the WHO and the recent World Health Assembly resolutions regarding the quality of biological and pharmaceutical products.

33. Preventing the transmission of HIV infection and the development of AIDS is an urgent global public health imperative. While other prevention and treatment methods must be pursued, in the long term the development of safe, accessible, and effective vaccines against AIDS holds the best chance of limiting, and eventually eliminating, the threat of this disease. We will work to provide the resources necessary to accelerate AIDS vaccine research, and together will enhance international scientific cooperation and collaboration. Cooperation among scientists and governments in the developed and developing world and international agencies will be critical. We call on other states to join us in this endeavor.

34. The Joint United Nations Program on HIV/AIDS (UNAIDS) must help expand the scale and quality of the response to HIV/AIDS. As a group and with others, we will work to assure that it has resources adequate to fulfill its mandate.

Nuclear Safety

35. We reaffirm our commitments from the 1996 Moscow Summit on Nuclear Safety and Security to give an absolute priority to safety in the use of nuclear energy. We note that further substantial progress is still required in the countries of Central and Eastern Europe and in the Newly Independent States, especially by strengthening regulatory authorities, enhancing reactor safety and improving safety culture. We consider further joint efforts to this end a major priority. In this regard, we attach the greatest importance to the full implementation of the Nuclear Safety Account agreements.

36. We note with satisfaction the entry into force by the Nuclear Safety Convention and the preparations now underway for the first review meeting to be held in April 1999. We applaud the rapid progress made in developing the Joint Convention on the Safety of Spent Fuel Management and the Safety of Radioactive Waste Management and encourage finalization. We welcome the forthcoming adoption of the Protocol to amend the Vienna Convention on civil liability for nuclear damage and of a new Supplementary Funding Convention. These conventions will facilitate international safety cooperation and provide for increased compensation for victims in the event of a nuclear accident.

Global Energy Issues

37. We decided to convene a ministerial on energy issues in Moscow next year, and request our officials to start preparations for such a meeting. Its results will be discussed at our next Summit.

Transnational Organized Crime

38. Our efforts to combat transnational crime will be a priority of the group for the foreseeable future. Transnational criminal groups can often adapt to global change more swiftly and efficiently than our governments. International crime not only threatens our citizens, but also undermines young democracies and nations in transition.

39. Last year, we adopted the Lyon forty recommendations to combat transnational organized crime. We have substantially implemented those recommendations, taking action within our own borders and with one another. Together, we have strengthened cooperation bilaterally, multilaterally, and with other nations and groups to bring criminals to justice through mutual legal assistance and extradition, to promote cooperation among our law enforcement agencies, to strengthen document security and improve strategies to combat alien smuggling, and to prevent illegal trafficking in firearms.

40. We must intensify our efforts to implement the Lyon recommendations. In the coming year we will focus on two areas of critical concern: First, the investigation, prosecution, and punishment of high-tech criminals, such as those tampering with computer and telecommunications technology, across national borders; Second, a system to provide all governments the technical and legal capabilities to respond to high-tech crimes, regardless of where the criminals may be located.

41. We also will develop additional methods to secure our borders. Border security is central to all efforts to fight transnational crime, drug-trafficking and terrorism. To this end, we will combat illegal firearms trafficking, by considering a new international instrument. We will seek to adopt standard systems for firearms identification and a stronger international regime for import and export licensing of firearms. We will continue our work to strengthen document security, and improve strategies to combat alien smuggling, attacking the problem at the source and transit the destination countries. Our governments will also move further ahead with efforts to strengthen international legal regimes for extradition and mutual legal assistance, to ensure that no criminal receives safe haven anywhere in the world.

Illicit Drugs

42. We are determined to intensify our efforts to combat the production, trafficking and use of illicit drugs, which represent a global threat to the safety of our citizens, and the well-being of our societies and institutions. Reaffirming the common responsibility of all concerned States, we recognize that a successful strategy to combat illicit drugs requires effective action against both the supply and the demand for such drugs. We stress the importance of demand reduction. Together with strict enforcement of drug-related laws, programs aimed at treatment and rehabilitation, education and prevention are of major importance in our fight against drugs.

43. We have asked our appropriate government agencies to build on their established patterns of cooperation to address this common threat. In particular, we will study mechanisms that would assist in the development of healthy, drug-free economies in all States; support further efforts to share relevant information on money-laundering, chemical precursors, new synthetic drugs, trafficking patterns and methods, and other data; and will work together to strengthen the capabilities of law enforcement institutions to combat illicit drugs. Our governments will work together to develop the agenda for the UN General Assembly Special Session on Drugs in June 1998.

Terrorism

44. We reaffirm our determination to combat terrorism in all forms, irrespective of motive. We oppose concessions to terrorist demands and are determined to deny hostage-takers any benefits from their acts. We welcome the growing consensus on adopting effective and legitimate means of countering terrorism.

45. Last year, our Ministers adopted twenty-five recommendations to combat terrorism. We have received a positive response worldwide, in particular in the UN General Assembly. Together we have made substantial progress on many of these recommendations, including: drafting and negotiating a UN convention on terrorist bombing; promoting improved international standards for airport security, explosives detection, and vehicle identification; promoting stronger laws and export controls on the manufacture, trade and transport of explosives; initiating a directory of counter-terrorism competencies; inviting all States to promote the use of encryption which may allow, consistent with OECD guidelines, lawful government access to combat terrorism.

46. We have asked our Ministers to intensify diplomatic efforts to ensure that by the year 2000 all States join the international counterterrorism conventions specified in the 1996 UN resolution on measures to counter terrorism. We have instructed our officials to take additional steps: to strengthen the capability of hostage negotiation experts and counterterrorism response units; to exchange information on technologies to detect and deter the use of materials of mass destruction in terrorist attacks; to develop means to deter terrorist attacks on electronic and computer infrastructure; to strengthen maritime security; to exchange information on security practices for international special events; and to strengthen and expand international cooperation and consultation.

Human Cloning

47. We agree on the need for appropriate domestic measures and close international cooperation to prohibit the use of somatic cell nuclear transfer to create a child.

Space Station

48. We look forward to the signing of the Agreement to establishing an international space station. This is an excellent example of international cooperation in carrying out large and promising projects in the field of exploration and peaceful uses of outer space.

United Nations Reform

49. We reaffirm the crucial role of the United Nations in maintaining international peace and security and in fostering global partnership and sustainable development. We support thorough-going reform, with the goal of strengthening the UN. We welcome progress that has occurred in the economic and social fields since our meetings in Halifax and Lyon. In this regard,

we welcome Secretary General Kofi Annan's recent reform proposals and support their rapid implementation; we also look forward to the Secretary General's more extensive proposals next month. We remain committed to working with all UN members to realize these reforms.

50. In order for the UN to cope with the challenges of the 21st century, financial reform should proceed together with necessary reform measures in other areas. The UN system must be placed on a firm financial footing through full and timely payment of obligations, and development of a more logical and equitable scale of assessments. Budgets throughout the UN system should be scrutinized with emphasis on prioritization and maximum operating efficiency. We look forward to the Secretary General's specific proposals for reinvesting savings from improved cost-effectiveness in high priority development programs. Robust oversight mechanisms and sound personnel policies are essential for success.

51. The urgent challenges of economic and social development require the UN to coordinate more effectively the policies and activities of its various bodies including the specialized agencies. To this end, the UN's Economic and Social Council (ECOSOC), supported by the Under Secretary General for economic and social issues, should strengthen its policy and coordination role, in particular through streamlining its subsidiary bodies and improving its working relationship with international financial institutions and the WTO. We welcome the recent reforms in the governance of the funds and programs as well as in the various UN bodies, in particular at UNCTAD and in the regional commissions; these efforts should be sustained and expanded.

52. We call for a thorough and urgent review of the UN's funds and programs, as well as a system-wide review of the roles and mandates of specialized agencies and commissions. We welcome the Secretary General's recommendations for strengthened integration at the country level and better coordination at headquarters. In this context, we recommend the UN undertake performance evaluations of the coordination of its development activities in a range of representative countries. We expect the least developed countries to be the principal beneficiaries of improved efficiency in the UN's development work.

53. We reaffirm that the UN must further improve its ability to act quickly and effectively to address threats to international peace and security. We will continue to help develop the capacities of the UN in preventing and resolving conflicts. We support steps taken recently by the UN to strengthen its capacity for rapid reaction from the early warning stage to the stage of rapid deployment of new, approved, peacekeeping operations and urge continued improvements in these areas.

Africa: Partnership for Development

54. At Lyon, we initiated a New Global Partnership for Development, noting—both that developing countries have a fundamental responsibility for promoting their own development, and that developed countries must support these efforts. We paid particular attention to the problems of Sub-Saharan

African countries, many of which continue to face unusually severe challenges. This year, we aim to translate the principles of that Partnership into new concrete action to support the efforts of African countries to participate fully in the expansion of global prosperity and to spread the benefits throughout their societies. Our objective is not only to facilitate the progressive integration of African countries into the world economy, but also to foster the integration of poor populations into economic, social and political life of their countries.

55. We are encouraged by positive developments, including the adoption of democratic and economic reforms in many Sub-Saharan African countries. Since 1990, more than twenty African nations have held free and fair elections. Democratic governance and the rule of law, in Africa as elsewhere, lay the foundation for human rights, including the rights of women, and sustainable development. We commend those African countries that have set an example by undertaking democratic reforms, improving rule of law and administration of justice, avoiding unproductive expenditures (including excessive military expenditures), and strengthening public institutions and civil society. We will support African efforts to promote democracy and good governance, improve the integrity of public institutions, enhance the transparency of government spending, in particular of procurement, and develop national anti-bribery regulations.

56. Increased prosperity ultimately depends upon creating an environment for domestic capital formation, private sector-led growth and successful integration into global markets. We are encouraged by the increasing number of Sub-Saharan countries that have made progress toward financial sustainability through fiscal and financial practices and have adopted growth and market oriented economic policies, including trade liberalization and investment climate improvement. These initiatives have produced a welcome acceleration of growth since 1994. We expect the international financial institutions to play an important role in supporting reform in Sub-Saharan African countries. Their support should help to promote productive foreign direct investment and domestic capital formation. We look forward to the IFIs reporting on their efforts by the time of the Hong Kong World Bank/IMF meetings.

57. Access to our markets is a crucial tool for fostering economic growth in Sub-Saharan Africa. We each will continue to improve, through various means, access to our markets for African exports. We support the further integration of the least developed countries into the world trading system. In this regard, African countries will be major beneficiaries of efforts in the WTO on a plan of action to promote capacity building and to provide predictable and favorable market access conditions for least developed countries. We are committed to the effective implementation of this plan and intend to participate actively in the high-level WTO/UNCTAD/International Trade Center meeting later this year. Furthermore, trade liberalization by African countries will promote more efficient utilization of resources. We also welcome African initiatives for regional trade liberalization and economic cooperation.

58. We will consider ways to enhance opportunities for the Sub-Saharan African countries that need them most and are undertaking effective reform measures. We will review our own bilateral aid and trade promotion programs to ensure that they support climates conducive to economic growth and private investment, including by strengthening capacity.

59. Substantial flows of official development assistance will continue to play an essential role in building the capacity of Sub-Saharan African countries to achieve their sustainable development objectives. We are committed to a results-oriented approach to development policy, with the particular goal of combating extreme poverty. But development assistance alone cannot overcome inappropriate policies. We will work with African countries to ensure adequate and well-targeted assistance for those countries which have the greatest need and carry out the necessary broad-based reforms. This assistance will include support for democratic governance, respect for human rights, sound public administration, efficient legal and judicial systems, infrastructure development, rural development, food security, environmental protection and human resource development, including health and education of their people. In this regard, we will work to strengthen cooperation among concerned institutes to facilitate and coordinate capacity building efforts.

60. To maximize the effectiveness of our efforts, we will deepen the dialogue with African partners, work for greater local ownership of development strategies and encourage the participation of non-governmental actors. We will also strengthen donor coordination, including with emerging donors. We welcome and fully support the emerging trend of intraregional and interregional cooperation to further African development.

61. The United Nations plays a major role in development in Africa, and African countries will be major beneficiaries of reform of the UN economic and social development activities. We encourage the UN's development funds and programs and specialized agencies, to emphasize work in the field in Africa and to fully integrate and coordinate their efforts, both at the headquarters and at the country level. We are encouraged by the Economic Commission on Africa's efforts to energize and focus its activities. The UN Development Program's decision to allocate a portion of its resources based on program quality is a useful approach to assuring effectiveness, and we urge that it be adopted more broadly in the UN's work.

62. A number of African countries are making impressive efforts to harness the information revolution in support of democracy and sustainable development. We welcome the Africa Information Society Initiative. We support their efforts to establish information networks to link African countries with each other and to the rest of the world. In this regard, we welcome the Toronto Global Knowledge '97 Conference.

63. We applaud African leadership in developing effective local capacities in conflict prevention, peacekeeping and post-conflict reconciliation and recovery. We will support African peacebuilding initiatives at the regional, sub-regional and national levels, in particular by the Organization of African

Unity (OAU), taking into account the recent OECD Guidelines on Conflict, Peace, and Development Cooperation, and we will help to forge active partnerships with the United Nations and other donors. We encourage the UN Secretary General, as part of his reform efforts, to identify ways the international community can further strengthen Africa's initiatives. We also call for the expanded utilization of the existing UN Trust Fund for African peacekeeping and conflict prevention, as well as other relevant UN funds; and broader and substantial donor commitments to the OAU and to subregional bodies with specialized mechanisms for conflict mediation, as well as to the UN/OAU Special Envoy to the Great Lakes.

64. We express our support for long-term efforts to promote rapidly deployable African peacekeeping capacities. We welcome closer coordination among African troop-contributing countries, regional and subregional organizations, donors, and the UN in the development of training, joint exercises, common peacekeeping doctrine, and other efforts to ensure interoperability. We also welcome recent progress towards the establishment of an African Peacekeeping Support Group at the UN, and we urge interested countries to actively explore mechanisms for coordination of practical activities.

65. We express our grave concern at the recent attacks against refugees as well as against personnel of refugee and humanitarian organizations. We emphasize that host States must prevent such acts and prosecute the perpetrators.

66. We have requested that our officials report to us prior to next year's Summit about the efforts they have undertaken together to implement all aspects of this partnership.

Political Issues

67. Together, we are pursuing a strategy of global integration to create a more secure and stable international community. Already, we have used our political cooperation to broaden and deepen the community of open markets and open societies, and in the next year we will work together to build on these efforts. Our Partnership for Development is designed explicitly to support the economic and political development of nations which run the risk of being marginalized from the process of integration. We will focus our energies on strengthening adherence to the norms and principles of international cooperation, and will work together to take effective measures against those who threaten those objectives. We recognize our common interest and responsibility in helping bring an end to conflicts that threaten to disturb international peace and to undermine our deepened cooperation.

Democracy and Human Rights

68. Recent years have seen an unprecedented growth of democracy worldwide. Yet young democratic states can be fragile and short-lived. We have a responsibility and opportunity to further strengthen democratic values and fundamental freedoms where they have taken hold and extend their reach where they have not.

69. Human rights are at the heart of our concerns. Ensuring accountability for violations of human rights and international humanitarian law is essential to promote conflict resolution and peace. The new UN High Commissioner for Human Rights will have a crucial role to play. We will continue to give full support to the International Tribunals for the former Yugoslavia and Rwanda, and work to ensure that the international community and States concerned bring to justice through due process persons responsible for violations of human rights and international humanitarian law.

70. Recognizing that strengthening democracy is essential to strengthening peace and human rights, and looking to the 50th anniversary of the Universal Declaration of Human Rights in 1998, we will work together in the coming year to build on our governments' most effective democratic development, peacebuilding and human rights programs. Our efforts will focus on promoting good governance and the rule of law, strengthening civil society, expanding women's political participation, and boosting business and labor support for democracy, particularly in young democracies and societies in conflict. The protection of the most underrepresented or vulnerable is critical to broaden participation in the democratic process and prevent societal conflict. We will work to ensure adoption and ratification of international instruments designed to provide protection to these groups, in particular the speedy adoption of an International Labor Organization Convention on the eradication of intolerable forms of child labor. We will work through multilateral and regional organizations, particularly with the Development Assistance Committee of the OECD as well as in partnership with nongovernmental organizations and young democracies. We also will consider common efforts to promote democracy where it is not now established.

71. We have asked our Ministers to pursue these efforts and to make recommendations for consideration at our next Summit.

72. Democracy, economic growth and development cannot reach their full potential without good governance, in particular the accountability of political leaders and public servants, especially for corruption. We will actively work to eliminate corruption in aid-funded procurement. We will take prompt steps to criminalize, in an effective and coordinated manner, bribery of foreign public officials, and to implement previous undertakings on the tax-deductibility of such bribes. We call upon all other countries to do the same.

Non-Proliferation, Arms Control and Disarmament

73. Since the Moscow Summit on Nuclear Safety and Security, we have taken important steps to implement the agreed "Programme for Preventing and Combating Illicit Trafficking in Nuclear Materials." We will expand participation in this program to include countries in Central and Eastern Europe, and in Central Asia and the Caucasus.

74. Further regarding the safe and effective management of fissile material, with respect to such materials no longer required for defense purposes, we will continue our cooperation through concrete initiatives, in particular the French-German-Russian project to build a pilot plant in Russia to produce

MOX fuel from weapons plutonium, which is open to additional states, and the related U.S.-Russian cooperation on the conversion of weapons plutonium.

75. We have worked together to advance our common non-proliferation, arms control, and disarmament goals. The Comprehensive Test Ban Treaty is an historic milestone, and we call upon all States to sign and ratify it rapidly to ensure its early entry into force. We welcome the entry into force of the Chemical Weapons Convention. We advocate its full, effective and universal implementation, and look forward to the early ratification of the Convention by the States that have not yet done so. Recognizing that enhancing confidence in compliance would reinforce the Biological and Toxin Weapons Convention, we reaffirm our determination to complete as soon as possible through negotiation a legally-binding and effective verification mechanism.

76. We reaffirm our unwavering commitment to full implementation of the objectives set forth in the Non-Proliferation Treaty. To that end, we welcome the IAEA's recent adoption of a program on strengthening the effectiveness and improving the efficiency of the safeguards system. We urge all States to conclude additional protocols with the IAEA at the earliest possible date. We reaffirm our commitment to the immediate commencement and early conclusion of a convention banning the production of fissile material for nuclear weapons or other nuclear explosive devices.

77. We welcome the progress on strategic arms control made at Helsinki in March, and look forward to the early entry-into-force of the START II agreement and the initiation of START III negotiations. We reaffirm the key role of the Conventional Forces in Europe Treaty in strengthening European security, and welcome the decision to conclude its adaptation as expeditiously as possible. We welcome the recent agreement among Russia, Kazakstan, Kyrgystan, Tajikistan, and China on reduction of military forces along their borders and consider it an important contribution to the region's security.

78. We endorse unequivocally efforts by the UN Special Commission and the IAEA to eliminate weapons of mass destruction capabilities in Iraq and to monitor compliance. We reaffirm the importance of implementing the U.S.-DPRK Agreed Framework and full compliance by North Korea with its non-proliferation obligations. We therefore place great value on the continuing role of the IAEA in monitoring the freeze on North Korea's nuclear program, implementing safeguards, and helping preserve all information relating to the DPRK's past activity. We welcome the conclusion of negotiations for the EU [European Union] to participate in the Korean Peninsula Energy Development Organization (KEDO) and call for further international support for KEDO, including the provision of funds. We stress the importance of Four Party talks and the necessity of North-South dialogue. We call on North Korea to halt its development, deployment and export of ballistic missiles.

79. We welcome the emerging high-level dialogue between India and Pakistan. We encourage both countries to bring their activities into conformity with international non-proliferation norms. Consistent with our support for the CTBT's early entry into force, we encourage both countries to adhere to that treaty.

80. We recognize that global security and stability are strengthened by promoting international responsibility in the transfer of arms and sensitive technologies, and to that end reaffirm our support for the Wassenaar Arrangement. We welcome the steady achievements under the UN Register of Conventional Arms in promoting transparency in armaments. We encourage the work of the UN Panel of Governmental Experts on Small Arms to identify the ways and means to prevent and reduce the excessive and destabilizing transfer of small arms and light weapons and we will continue to work together to curb illegal trafficking in firearms.

Export Control Regimes

81. We underline our support for the arrangements that make up the international export control regimes. The Zangger Committee and the Nuclear Suppliers Group, the Missile Technology Control Regime, and, for those who are members, the Australia Group export control regime, all contribute critically to the global application and enforcement of international export control norms.

Anti-Personnel Landmines

82. Last year we committed ourselves to spare no effort in securing a global ban on antipersonnel landmines. To this end, we note the useful and complementary efforts in a variety of fora, including at the Conference on Disarmament and in formal negotiations to take place in Oslo in September through the Ottawa Process which has set the goal of achieving such a ban before the end of the year. We welcome the restrictions on anti-personnel landmines unilaterally declared by States, including by the members of the EU. We reaffirm the UN General Assembly resolution, approved overwhelmingly, calling for concluding an effective, legally-binding international agreement to ban anti-personnel landmines as soon as possible. All States should adhere to the strengthened Protocol on Mines, Booby Traps and Other Devices. We encourage the international community to develop technological solutions to mine detection and clearance, and to strengthen its support for humanitarian demining and assistance to mine victims.

Political Situations

Hong Kong

83. We recognize the historic nature of China's imminent resumption of sovereignty over Hong Kong. Considering our durable interests in this financial and economic center, we welcome and place weight on China's commitments, contained in the 1984 UK-PRC Joint Declaration and in the 1990 PRC Basic Law. These include ensuring Hong Kong's continued stability and prosperity and preserving its way of life, its high degree of autonomy—including an independent monetary and economic system—its fundamental freedoms and the rule of law. These will provide the essential underpinnings for Hong Kong's future economic success. We look forward to democratic elections in

Hong Kong for a new legislature as soon as possible. We take serious note of China's assurances in the Joint Declaration and Basic Law that the provisions of the International Covenant of Civil and Political Rights and the International Covenant on Economic, Social and Cultural Rights will continue to apply in Hong Kong.

Middle East

84. The Peace Process faces a crisis, and we are determined to reinject momentum into it. Restoring the sense of security and confidence among Israelis and Palestinians is essential.

We shall do our utmost to reinvigorate implementation of the Oslo Accords and to uphold the principles of Madrid, including the exchange of land for peace. All the problems need to be addressed peacefully through serious and credible negotiations. Both sides must refrain from actions that impede the peace process by preempting permanent status negotiations. We believe strongly in the importance of working with Israel, Syria and Lebanon to resume direct talks in order to achieve a comprehensive settlement in the region. We welcome the important role the Monitoring Group has played in strengthening the Understanding of April 26, 1996 and in reducing risks to civilians in southern Lebanon and in Israel. We affirm the importance of the activities within the multilateral framework of the peace process.

85. Economic growth and prosperity are critical to peace. We urge regional parties to pursue economic cooperation among themselves and integration into the global economy. We welcome all efforts to promote the region's development of viable and sustainable economies, including assistance to the Palestinians, and urge donors to fulfill pledges made.

86. We have noted with interest the results of the recent elections in Iran and renew our call upon the Government of Iran to play a constructive role in regional and world affairs. In this regard, while noting the role Iran played in inter-Tajik talks in conjunction with the United Nations and other regional parties, we call upon the Government of Iran to desist from material and political support for extremist groups that are seeking to destroy the Middle East peace process and to destabilize the region. We further call upon the Iranian Government to respect the human rights of all Iranian citizens and to renounce the use of terrorism, including against Iranian citizens living abroad, and, in that connection, to desist from endorsing the continued threat to the life of Mr. Salman Rushdie and other people associated with his work. We call on all States to avoid cooperation with Iran that might contribute to efforts to acquire nuclear weapons capabilities, or to enhance chemical, biological, or missile capabilities in violation of international conventions or arrangements.

87. We confirm our determination to obtain full compliance with all UN Security Council resolutions related to Iraq and Libya. Only full compliance with these resolutions could result in the lifting of sanctions. We are pleased to note that the distribution of food and medicine under UNSCR 986 is providing some humanitarian relief to the Iraqi people.

Cyprus

88. The Cyprus dispute has remained unresolved for far too long. We fully support the mission of good offices of the United Nations Secretary General on Cyprus aimed at engaging the two Cypriot communities in negotiations to achieve a comprehensive settlement in accordance with relevant UN Resolutions and high-level agreements. We strongly endorse the Secretary General's recent invitation to the leaders of both communities and call on them to approach negotiations constructively and in good faith. We call upon the governments of Turkey and Greece to do everything possible to contribute to a solution of the Cyprus problem and to work towards solving their bilateral disputes with regard to the Aegean through early meetings of "Wise Men."

Albania

89. Noting the situation in Albania and its implications for regional stability, we express our appreciation to those organizations and institutions, acting within the coordinating framework of the OSCE under the strong leadership of Franz Vranitzky—especially the EU as well as the WEU, UNHCR and Red Cross—that are working with the Government of National Reconciliation to restore normalcy in the country. We applaud the deployment of the Multinational Protection Force under Italian leadership and the authority of the UN Security Council. We underscore the need for the Albanian parties to work together to ensure that the elections reinforce democracy and thereafter work to reestablish order and public safety, pursue economic reform, and create a sound financial system.

Next Summit

90. We have accepted the invitation of the Prime Minister of the United Kingdom to meet in Birmingham on 15–17 May next year.

SUPREME COURT ON
PAROCHIAL SCHOOL AID
June 23, 1997

In a highly controversial decision, the Supreme Court overturned one of its own precedents on June 23 to rule that public school teachers could enter parochial schools to teach remedial courses to needy children. The decision sharply divided the Court, with the four dissenters questioning not only the substance of the majority opinion but the procedure the Court used to hear the case.

The case, Agostini v. Felton, *had its roots in Title I of federal education aid legislation enacted in 1965. Among other things, that title required public school systems to provide federally funded remedial instruction to all low-achieving poor students, including those attending religious schools. New York City tried several different ways to provide the remedial aid and finally settled on sending public school teachers into religious schools to offer the remedial courses during the regular school day. This approach appeared to reach the most children for the least cost, and the school board took care to try to ensure that the program operated in accord with religious neutrality—even removing all religious symbols from the classrooms in which the remedial courses were conducted.*

In 1978 a group of parents challenged this arrangement as a violation of the First Amendment's Establishment Clause, and in 1985 the Supreme Court agreed. In a 5–4 decision in the case of Aguilar v. Felton, *the Court said that New York's program was unconstitutional because it resulted in an "excessive entanglement of church and state in the administration of [Title I] benefits." In a companion case* (Grand Rapids School District v. Ball), *the court also barred a similar "shared time" program in Grand Rapids, Michigan, that provided remedial and enrichment classes to students at nonpublic schools during regular school hours or after the school day.* (Court on public-school teachers in parochial classes, Historic Documents of 1985, p. 433)

To comply with the Court ruling in Aguilar, *New York City typically leased mobile vans, which were parked on the public street outside religious* *schools during the day. Throughout the day students from the schools would leave their classrooms to receive remedial instruction from public school teachers in the vans. Each night the vans would be returned to city garages. New York eventually leased more than 100 vans at an annual cost of $15 million; the cost was covered by the federal government from funding that otherwise could have been spent on providing more remedial aid to needy students. Parents, teachers, school administrators, and even federal education officials lamented the situation, saying that it was a poor learning environment as well as a waste of money.*

Meanwhile, the Supreme Court appeared to be easing its rules on financial aid for religious parochial school students. In 1986 it unanimously approved the use of federal funds from an aid program for the handicapped to help a blind ministerial student (Witters v. Washington Department of Services for the Blind) *and in 1993 it allowed the use of public funds to pay for a sign-language interpreter for a deaf parochial school pupil* (Zobrest v. Catalina Foothills School District). (Court on public aid for deaf parochial student, Historic Documents of 1993, p. 399)

In 1994, with three justices in the majority on the Aguilar *case now gone from the Court, conservatives on the Court used an unrelated church-state case coming from New York* (Board of Education of Kiryas Joel School v. Grumet) *to signal their interest in reconsidering and possibly overturning the* Aguilar *decision. The problem, however, was that the Court had few options for rehearing a case.*

In 1995 the New York City school board hit on a solution to the rehearing problem—Rule 60(b) from the Federal Rules of Civil Procedure, which allowed a trial judge to lift a court order when changed circumstances no longer made it equitable. With support from the Clinton administration, the New York school board filed a motion asking for relief under the rule, citing as changed circumstances the costs of compliance, the change in the Supreme Court decisions, and the indications from a majority of the justices that Aguilar *was no longer good law.*

A Precedent Undermined

Writing for the majority Justice Sandra Day O'Connor said that neither the costs of compliance nor the comments of the justices in the 1994 case were enough to warrant a reconsideration of the Aguilar *case, but Rule 60(b) would be applicable if, as New York argued, later decisions undermined the precedent. And indeed they did, according to O'Connor. In reexamining the decisions handed down in 1986 and 1993, she found that they rejected "the notion" relied upon in* Aguilar *"that solely because of her presence on private school property, a public school employee will be presumed to inculcate religion in the students." The 1986 decision also undermined the* Aguilar *ruling by departing from the rule that "all government aid that directly aids the educational function of religious schools is invalid."*

With that issue disposed of, O'Connor turned to a reexamination of the original question in Aguilar—*whether New York's placement of public* school teachers in religious school classrooms in fulfillment of its Title I obligations improperly advanced religion and concluded that it did not. The program, she said, "does not result in governmental indoctrination; define its recipients by reference to religion; or create an 'excessive entanglement' between church and state." Aguilar was "no longer good law," O'Connor declared.

In maintaining that it was proper to reexamine Aguilar because later cases undermined its validity as a precedent, O'Connor warned that this was an exceptional case. "We do not acknowledge, and we do not hold, that other courts should conclude our more recent cases have, by implication, overruled an earlier precedent." Moreover, she said, the majority saw no reason why the Court should wait for a "better vehicle" for reviewing its Aguilar decision. "It would be particularly inequitable for us to bide our time waiting for another case to arise" while New York spends money on mobile vans that could be spent "to give economically disadvantaged children a better chance at success in life" through a program "perfectly consistent with the Establishment Clause." O'Connor was joined by Chief Justice William H. Rehnquist, and Justices Anthony M. Kennedy, Antonin Scalia, and Clarence Thomas.

The dissenters objected to the majority on both substantive and procedural grounds. In an opinion joined by Justices John Paul Stevens, Ruth Bader Ginsburg, and Stephen G. Breyer, Justice David H. Souter said that the decisions in the 1986 and 1993 cases involved instances of isolated aid to individuals within a school system and thus provided no authority for eroding the distinction the court had long maintained between direct and indirect aid to religious schools. "That principled line is being breached only here and now," he wrote.

In a separate dissenting opinion, Ginsburg, joined by the other three dissenters, said the decision established a procedure that trial courts could use to obtain an "'anytime' rehearing" by the Court. The result, she said, was an undermining of what she called the Court's "responsive, non-agenda-setting character."

Potential Implications of the Ruling

Federal and New York state officials hailed the decision. Secretary of Education Richard W. Riley called it "a step forward for American education," while New York City Mayor Rudolph W. Giuliani called it "very wise." Ted Staniecki, the principal of the School of the Incarnation probably spoke for many in the city when he said, "We finally got some common sense."

But there was more disagreement about the long-term implications of the ruling, particularly for voucher plans, several of which were currently being challenged in lower courts. Such plans, which allow parents to use public funds to pay their children's tuition at private and religious schools, had long been controversial precisely because they appear to violate the constitutional bar on state aid to religion. But the plans had gained in popularity as people searched for alternatives to what they considered to be a *failing public school system. Supporters saw the decision in* Agostini *as a signal that the Court might approve the controversial voucher plans. "This decision confirms that vouchers can be constitutional" so long as the plans are religiously neutral and apply equally to all parents, said Mark Chopko, general counsel of the United States Catholic Conference.*

Some opponents of vouchers also saw the ruling as a "green light" for such programs, but others were more cautious. "It's a very big leap from this [ruling] to vouchers," said Steven Shapiro, the national legal director for the American Civil Liberties Union, which opposes vouchers. "This case did not involve any religious indoctrination and did not transfer any funds to a parochial school. Vouchers are all about the transfer of funds to parochial schools for the purpose of religious indoctrination."

> *Following are excerpts from the majority and minority opinions in the case of* Agostini v. Felton, *in which the Supreme Court on June 23, 1997, announced that it was reversing its ruling in the 1985 case of* Aguilar v. Felton, *which barred public school teachers from entering religious schools to provide federally required remedial education programs to needy children:*

Nos. 96-552 and 96-553

Rachel Agostini, et al., Petitioners
v.
Betty-Louise Felton et al.

On writs of certiorari to the United States Court of Appeals for the Second Circuit

Chancellor, Board of Education of the City of New York, et al., Petitioners
v.
Betty-Louise Felton et al.

[June 23, 1997]

JUSTICE O'CONNOR delivered the opinion of the Court.

In *Aguilar v. Felton* (1985), this Court held that the Establishment Clause of the First Amendment barred the city of New York from sending public school teachers into parochial schools to provide remedial education to disadvantaged children pursuant to a congressionally mandated program. On remand, the District Court for the Eastern District of New York entered a permanent injunction reflecting our ruling. Twelve years later, petitioners—the parties bound by that injunction—seek relief from its operation. Petitioners maintain that Aguilar cannot be squared with our intervening Establishment Clause jurisprudence and ask that we explicitly recognize what our more recent cases already dictate: *Aguilar* is no longer good law. We agree with petitioners that *Aguilar* is not consistent with our subsequent Establishment Clause decisions and further conclude that, on the facts presented here, petitioners are entitled under Federal Rule of Civil Procedure 60(b)(5) to relief from the operation of the District Court's prospective injunction.

I

In 1965, Congress enacted Title I of the Elementary and Secondary Education Act of 1965 to "provid[e] full educational opportunity to every child regardless of economic background." Toward that end, Title I channels federal funds, through the States, to "local educational agencies" (LEA's). The LEA's spend these funds to provide remedial education, guidance, and job counseling to eligible students. . . . An eligible student is one (i) who resides within the attendance boundaries of a public school located in a low-income area and (ii) who is failing, or is at risk of failing, the State's student performance standards. Title I funds must be made available to all eligible children, regardless of whether they attend public schools, and the services provided to children attending private schools must be "equitable in comparison to services and other benefits for public schoolchildren."

An LEA providing services to children enrolled in private schools is subject to a number of constraints that are not imposed when it provides aid to public schools. Title I services may be provided only to those private school students eligible for aid, and cannot be used to provide services on a "schoolwide" basis. In addition, the LEA must retain complete control over Title I funds; retain title to all materials used to provide Title I services; and provide those services through public employees or other persons independent of the private school and any religious institution. The Title I services themselves must be "secular, neutral, and nonideological," and must "supplement, and in no case supplant, the level of services" already provided by the private school.

Petitioner Board of Education of the City of New York (Board), an LEA, first applied for Title I funds in 1966 and has grappled ever since with how to provide Title I services to the private school students within its jurisdiction. Approximately 10% of the total number of students eligible for Title I services are private school students. Recognizing that more than 90% of the private schools within the Board's jurisdiction are sectarian, the Board initially arranged to transport children to public schools for after-school Title I instruction. But this enterprise was largely unsuccessful. Attendance was poor, teachers and children were tired, and parents were concerned for the safety of their children. The Board then moved the after-school instruction onto private school campuses, as Congress had contemplated when it enacted Title I. After this program also yielded mixed results, the Board implemented the plan we evaluated in *Aguilar v. Felton.*

That plan called for the provision of Title I services on private school premises during school hours. Under the plan, only public employees could serve as Title I instructors and counselors. Assignments to private schools were made on a voluntary basis and without regard to the religious affiliation of the employee or the wishes of the private school. . . .

Before any public employee could provide Title I instruction at a private school, she would be given a detailed set of written and oral instructions emphasizing the secular purpose of Title I and setting out the rules to be followed to ensure that this purpose was not compromised. [Specification of instructions omitted.] To ensure compliance with these rules, a publicly employed field supervisor was to attempt to make at least one unannounced visit to each teacher's classroom every month.

In 1978, six federal taxpayers—respondents here—sued the Board in the District Court for the Eastern District of New York. Respondents sought declaratory and injunctive relief, claiming that the Board's Title I program violated the Establishment Clause. The District Court permitted the parents of a number of parochial school students who were receiving Title I services to intervene as codefendants. The District Court granted summary judgment for the Board, but the Court of Appeals for the Second Circuit reversed. While noting that the Board's Title I program had "done so much good and little, if any, detectable harm," the Court of Appeals nevertheless held that *Meek v. Pittenger* (1975) and *Wolman v. Walter* (1977) compelled it to declare the program unconstitutional. In a 5–4 decision, this Court affirmed on the ground that the Board's Title I program necessitated an "excessive entanglement of church and state in the administration of [Title I] benefits." On remand, the District Court permanently enjoined the Board

> "from using public funds for any plan or program under [Title I] to the extent that it requires, authorizes or permits public school teachers and guidance counselors to provide teaching and counseling services on the premises of sectarian schools within New York City."

The Board, like other LEA's across the United States, modified its Title I program so it could continue serving those students who attended private religious schools. Rather than offer Title I instruction to parochial school students at their schools, the Board reverted to its prior practice of providing instruction at public school sites, at leased sites, and in mobile instructional units (essentially vans converted into classrooms) parked near the sectarian school. The Board also offered computer-aided instruction, which could be provided "on premises" because it did not require public employees to be physically present on the premises of a religious school.

It is not disputed that the additional costs of complying with *Aguilar*'s mandate are significant. Since the 1986–1987 school year, the Board has spent over $100 million providing computer-aided instruction, leasing sites and mobile instructional units, and transporting students to those sites. Under the Secretary of Education's regulations, those costs "incurred as a result of implementing alternative delivery systems to comply with the requirements of *Aguilar v. Felton*" and not paid for with other state or federal funds are to be deducted from the federal grant before the Title I funds are distributed to any student. These "*Aguilar* costs" thus reduce the amount of Title I money an LEA has available for remedial education, and LEA's have had to cut back on the number of students who receive Title I benefits. From Title I funds available for New York City children between the 1986–1987 and the 1993–1994 school years, the Board had to deduct $7.9 million "off-the-top" for compliance with *Aguilar*. When *Aguilar* was handed down, it was estimated that some 20,000 economically disadvantaged children in the city of New York and some 183,000 children nationwide would experience a decline in Title I services. . . .

In October and December of 1995, petitioners—the Board and a new group of parents of parochial school students entitled to Title I services—filed motions in the District Court seeking relief under Federal Rule of Civil Procedure 60(b) from the permanent injunction entered by the District Court on remand from our decision in *Aguilar*. Petitioners argued that relief was proper under Rule 60(b)(5) and our decision in *Rufo v. Inmates of Suffolk County Jail* (1992), because the "decisional law [had] changed to make legal what the [injunction] was designed to prevent." Specifically, petitioners pointed to the statements of five Justices in *Board of Ed. of Kiryas Joel Village School Dist. v. Grumet* (1994) calling for the overruling of *Aguilar*. The District Court denied the motion. The District Court recognized that petitioners, "at bottom," sought "a procedurally sound vehicle to get the [propriety of the injunction] back before the Supreme Court," and concluded that the "the Board ha[d] properly proceeded under Rule 60(b) to seek relief from the injunction." Despite its observations that "the landscape of Establishment Clause decisions has changed," and that "[t]here may be good reason to conclude that *Aguilar*'s demise is imminent," the District Court denied the Rule 60(b) motion on the merits because *Aguilar*'s demise had "not yet occurred." The Court of Appeals for the Second Circuit "affirmed substantially for the reasons stated in" the District Court's opinion. We granted certiorari (1997) and now reverse.

II

The question we must answer is a simple one: Are petitioners entitled to relief from the District Court's permanent injunction under Rule 60(b)? Rule 60(b)(5), the subsection under which petitioners proceeded below, states:

> "On motion and upon such terms as are just, the court may relieve a party . . . from a final judgment [or] order . . . [when] it is no longer equitable that the judgment should have prospective application."

In *Rufo v. Inmates of Suffolk County Jail*, we held that it is appropriate to grant a Rule 60(b)(5) motion when the party seeking relief from an injunction or consent decree can show "a significant change either in factual conditions or in law." . . .

Petitioners point to three changes in the factual and legal landscape that they believe justify their claim for relief under Rule 60(b)(5). They first contend that the exorbitant costs of complying with the District Court's injunction constitute a significant factual development warranting modification of the injunction. Petitioners also argue that there have been two significant legal developments since *Aguilar* was decided: a majority of Justices have expressed their views that *Aguilar* should be reconsidered or overruled; and

Aguilar has in any event been undermined by subsequent Establishment Clause decisions, including *Witters v. Washington Dept. of Servs. for Blind* (1986), *Zobrest v. Catalina Foothills School Dist.* (1993), and *Rosenberger v. Rector and Visitors of Univ. of Va.* (1995).

Respondents counter that, because the costs of providing Title I services off-site were known at the time *Aguilar* was decided, and because the relevant case law has not changed, the District Court did not err in denying petitioners' motions. . . .

We agree with respondents that petitioners have failed to establish the significant change in factual conditions required by *Rufo*. Both petitioners and this Court were, at the time *Aguilar* was decided, aware that additional costs would be incurred if Title I services could not be provided in parochial school classrooms. . . . That these predictions of additional costs turned out to be accurate does not constitute a change in factual conditions warranting relief under Rule 60(b)(5). . . .

We also agree with respondents that the statements made by five Justices in *Kiryas Joel* do not, in themselves, furnish a basis for concluding that our Establishment Clause jurisprudence has changed. [Discussion of case omitted.] . . . [T]he question of *Aguilar*'s propriety was not before us. The views of five Justices that the case should be reconsidered or overruled cannot be said to have effected a change in Establishment Clause law.

In light of these conclusions, petitioners' ability to satisfy the prerequisites of Rule 60(b)(5) hinges on whether our later Establishment Clause cases have so undermined *Aguilar* that it is no longer good law. We now turn to that inquiry.

III

A

In order to evaluate whether *Aguilar* has been eroded by our subsequent Establishment Clause cases, it is necessary to understand the rationale upon which *Aguilar*, as well as its companion case, *School Dist. of Grand Rapids v. Ball* (1985), rested.

[Discussion of *Ball*, which struck down a "Shared Time" program for public school teachers to teach supplemental courses on the premises of church-affiliated schools, and further discussion of *Aguilar* omitted.]

Distilled to essentials, the Court's conclusion that the Shared Time program in *Ball* had the impermissible effect of advancing religion rested on three assumptions: (i) any public employee who works on the premises of a religious school is presumed to inculcate religion in her work; (ii) the presence of public employees on private school premises creates a symbolic union between church and state; and (iii) any and all public aid that directly aids the educational function of religious schools impermissibly finances religious indoctrination, even if the aid reaches such schools as a consequence of private decisionmaking. Additionally, in *Aguilar* there was a fourth assumption: that New York City's Title I program necessitated an excessive government entanglement with religion because public employees who teach on the premises of religious schools must be closely monitored to ensure that they do not inculcate religion.

B

Our more recent cases have undermined the assumptions upon which *Ball* and *Aguilar* relied. To be sure, the general principles we use to evaluate whether government aid violates the Establishment Clause have not changed since *Aguilar* was decided. For example, we continue to ask whether the government acted with the purpose of advancing or inhibiting religion, and the nature of that inquiry has remained largely unchanged. . . . Likewise, we continue to explore whether the aid has the "effect" of advancing or inhibiting religion. What has changed since we decided *Ball* and *Aguilar* is our understanding of the criteria used to assess whether aid to religion has an impermissible effect.

1

As we have repeatedly recognized, government inculcation of religious beliefs has the impermissible effect of advancing religion. Our cases subsequent to *Aguilar* have, however, modified in two significant respects the approach we use to assess indoctrination. First, we have abandoned the presumption erected in *Meek* and *Ball* that the placement of public employees on parochial school grounds inevitably results in the impermissible effect of state-sponsored indoctrination or constitutes a symbolic union between government and religion. In *Zobrest v. Catalina Foothills School Dist.* (1993), we examined whether the [Individuals with Disabilities Education Act (IDEA)] was constitutional as applied to a deaf student who sought to bring his state-employed sign-language interpreter with him to his Roman Catholic high school. We held that this was permissible, expressly disavowing the notion that "the Establishment Clause [laid] down [an] absolute bar to the placing of a public employee in a sectarian school." . . . We refused to presume that a publicly employed interpreter would be pressured by the pervasively sectarian surroundings to inculcate religion by "add[ing] to [or] subtract[ing] from" the lectures translated. . . . *Zobrest* therefore expressly rejected the notion—relied on in *Ball* and *Aguilar*—that, solely because of her presence on private school property, a public employee will be presumed to inculcate religion in the students. *Zobrest* also implicitly repudiated another assumption on which *Ball* and *Aguilar* turned: that the presence of a public employee on private school property creates an impermissible "symbolic link" between government and religion.

Second, we have departed from the rule relied on in *Ball* that all government aid that directly aids the educational function of religious schools is invalid. In *Witters v. Washington Dept. of Servs. for Blind* (1986), we held that the Establishment Clause did not bar a State from issuing a vocational tuition grant to a blind person who wished to use the grant to attend a Christian college and become a pastor, missionary, or youth director. Even though the grant recipient clearly would use the money to obtain religious education, we observed that the tuition grants were " 'made available generally without regard to the sectarian-nonsectarian, or public-nonpublic nature of the institution benefited.'" The grants were disbursed directly to students, who then used the money to pay for tuition at the educational institution of their choice. In our view, this transaction was no different from a State's issuing a paycheck to one of its employees, knowing that the employee would donate part or all of the check to a religious institution. In both situations, any money that ultimately went to religious institutions did so "only as a result of the genuinely independent and private choices of" individuals. The same logic applied in *Zobrest*, where we allowed the State to provide an interpreter, even though she would be a mouthpiece for religious instruction, because the IDEA's neutral eligibility criteria ensured that the interpreter's presence in a sectarian school was a "result of the private decision of individual parents" and "[could] not be attributed to state decisionmaking." (emphasis added). Because the private school would not have provided an interpreter on its own, we also concluded that the aid in *Zobrest* did not indirectly finance religious education by "reliev[ing] the sectarian schoo[l] of costs [it] otherwise would have borne in educating [its] students."

Zobrest and *Witters* make clear that, under current law, the Shared Time program in *Ball* and New York City's Title I program in *Aguilar* will not, as a matter of law, be deemed to have the effect of advancing religion through indoctrination. Indeed, each of the premises upon which we relied in *Ball* to reach a contrary conclusion is no longer valid. First, there is no reason to presume that, simply because she enters a parochial school classroom, a full-time public employee such as a Title I teacher will depart from her assigned duties and instructions and embark on religious indoctrination. . . .

As discussed above, *Zobrest* also repudiates *Ball*'s assumption that the presence of Title I teachers in parochial school classrooms will, without more, create the impression of a "symbolic union" between church and state. . . . We do not see any perceptible (let alone dispositive) difference in the degree of symbolic union between a student receiving remedial instruction in a classroom on his sectarian school's campus and one receiving instruction in a van parked just at the school's curb side. To draw this line based solely on the location of the public employee is neither "sensible" nor "sound," and the Court in *Zobrest* rejected it.

Nor under current law can we conclude that a program placing full-time public employees on parochial campuses to provide Title I instruction would impermissibly finance religious indoctrination. In all relevant respects, the provision of instructional services under Title I is indistinguishable from the provision of sign-language interpreters under the IDEA. Both programs make aid available only to eligible recipients. That aid is provided to students at whatever school they choose to attend. Although Title I instruction is provided to several students at once, whereas an interpreter provides translation to a single student, this distinction is not constitutionally significant. Moreover, as in *Zobrest*, Title I services are by law supplemental to the regular curricula. These services do not, therefore, "reliev[e] sectarian schools of costs they otherwise would have borne in educating their students." [Quoting *Zobrest.*] . . .

We are also not persuaded that Title I services supplant the remedial instruction and guidance counseling already provided in New York City's sectarian schools. . . . We are unwilling to speculate that all sectarian schools provide remedial instruction and guidance counseling to their students, and are unwilling to presume that the Board would violate Title I regulations by continuing to provide Title I services to students who attend a sectarian school that has curtailed its remedial instruction program in response to Title I. Nor are we willing to conclude that the constitutionality of an aid program depends on the number of sectarian school students who happen to receive the otherwise neutral aid. *Zobrest* did not turn on the fact that James Zobrest had, at the time of litigation, been the only child using a publicly funded sign-language interpreter to attend a parochial school. . . .

What is most fatal to the argument that New York City's Title I program directly subsidizes religion is that it applies with equal force when those services are provided off-campus, and *Aguilar* implied that providing the services off-campus is entirely consistent with the Establishment Clause. . . . [W]e find no logical basis upon which to conclude that Title I services are an impermissible subsidy of religion when offered on-campus, but not when offered off-campus. Accordingly, contrary to our conclusion in *Aguilar*, placing full-time employees on parochial school campuses does not as a matter of law have the impermissible effect of advancing religion through indoctrination.

2

Although we examined in *Witters* and *Zobrest* the criteria by which an aid program identifies its beneficiaries, we did so solely to assess whether any use of that aid to indoctrinate religion could be attributed to the State. A number of our Establishment Clause cases have found that the criteria used for identifying beneficiaries are relevant in a second respect, apart from enabling a court to evaluate whether the program subsidizes religion. Specifically, the criteria might themselves have the effect of advancing religion by creating a financial incentive to undertake religious indoctrination. . . . This incentive is not present, however, where the aid is allocated on the basis of neutral, secular criteria that neither favor nor disfavor religion, and is made available to both religious and secular beneficiaries on a nondiscriminatory basis. Under such circumstances, the aid is less likely to have the effect of advancing religion. . . .

In *Ball* and *Aguilar*, the Court gave this consideration no weight. Before and since those decisions, we have sustained programs that provided aid to all eligible children regardless of where they attended school. . . .

Applying this reasoning to New York City's Title I program, it is clear that Title I services are allocated on the basis of criteria that neither favor nor disfavor religion. The services are available to all children who meet the Act's eligibility requirements, no matter what their religious beliefs or where they go to school. The Board's program does not, therefore, give aid recipients any incentive to modify their religious beliefs or practices in order to obtain those services.

3

We turn now to *Aguilar*'s conclusion that New York City's Title I program resulted in an excessive entanglement between church and state. Whether a government aid program results in such an entanglement has consistently been an aspect of our Establishment Clause analysis. We have considered entanglement both in the course of assessing whether an aid program has an impermissible effect of advancing religion, *Walz v. Tax Comm'n of City of New York* (1970), and as a factor separate and apart from "effect," *Lemon v. Kurtzman* [1971]. Regardless of how we have characterized the issue, however, the factors we use to assess whether an entanglement is "excessive" are similar to the factors we use to examine "effect." That is, to assess entanglement, we have looked to "the character and purposes of the institutions that are benefited, the nature of the aid that the State provides, and the resulting relationship between the government and religious authority." [Quoting *Lemon*.] Similarly, we have assessed a law's "effect" by examining the character of the institutions benefited (e.g., whether the religious institutions were "predominantly religious"); and the nature of the aid that the State provided (e.g., whether it was neutral and nonideological). Indeed, in *Lemon* itself, the entanglement that the Court found "independently" to necessitate the program's invalidation also was found to have the effect of inhibiting religion. . . . Thus, it is simplest to recognize why entanglement is significant and treat it—as we did in *Walz*—as an aspect of the inquiry into a statute's effect.

Not all entanglements, of course, have the effect of advancing or inhibiting religion. Interaction between church and state is inevitable, and we have always tolerated some level of involvement between the two. Entanglement must be "excessive" before it runs afoul of the Establishment Clause. . . .

The pre-*Aguilar* Title I program does not result in an "excessive" entanglement that advances or inhibits religion. As discussed previously, the Court's finding of "excessive" entanglement in *Aguilar* rested on three grounds: (i) the program would require "pervasive monitoring by public authorities" to ensure that Title I employees did not inculcate religion; (ii) the program required "administrative cooperation" between the Board and parochial schools; and (iii) the program might increase the dangers of "political divisiveness." Under our current understanding of the Establishment Clause, the last two considerations are insufficient by themselves to create an "excessive" entanglement. They are present no matter where Title I services are offered, and no court has held that Title I services cannot be offered off-campus. [Citing lower court cases.] Further, the assumption underlying the first consideration has been undermined. In *Aguilar*, the Court presumed that full-time public employees on parochial school grounds would be tempted to inculcate religion, despite the ethical standards they were required to uphold. Because of this risk pervasive monitoring would be required. But after *Zobrest* we no longer presume that public employees will inculcate religion simply because they happen to be in a sectarian environment. Since we have abandoned the assumption that properly instructed public employees will fail to discharge their duties faithfully, we must also discard the assumption that pervasive monitoring of Title I teachers is required. There is no suggestion in the record before us that unannounced monthly visits of public supervisors are insufficient to prevent or to detect inculcation of religion by public employees. Moreover, we have not found excessive entanglement in cases in which States imposed far more onerous burdens on religious institutions than the monitoring system at issue here.

To summarize, New York City's Title I program does not run afoul of any of three primary criteria we currently use to evaluate whether government aid has the effect of advancing religion: it does not result in governmental indoctrination; define its recipients by reference to religion; or create an excessive entanglement. We therefore hold that a federally funded program providing supplemental, remedial instruction to disadvantaged children on a neutral basis is not invalid under the Establishment Clause when such instruction is given on the premises of sectarian schools by government employees pursuant to a program containing safeguards such as those present here. The same considerations that justify this holding require us to conclude that this carefully constrained program also cannot reasonably be viewed as an endorsement of religion. . . . Accordingly, we must acknowledge that *Aguilar*, as well as the portion of *Ball* addressing Grand Rapids' Shared Time program, are no longer good law.

C

The doctrine of *stare decisis* does not preclude us from recognizing the change in our law and overruling *Aguilar* and those portions of *Ball* inconsistent with our more recent decisions. As we have often noted, "[s]tare decisis is not an inexorable command," but instead reflects a policy judgment that "in most matters it is more important that the applicable rule of law be settled than that it be settled right. That policy is at its weakest when we interpret the Constitution because our interpretation can be altered only by constitutional amendment or by overruling our prior decisions. . . . Thus, we have held in several cases that *stare decisis* does not prevent us from overruling a previous decision where there has been a significant change in or subsequent development of our constitutional law. . . . As discussed above, our Establishment Clause jurisprudence has changed significantly since we decided *Ball* and *Aguilar*, so our decision to overturn those cases rests on far more than "a present doctrinal disposition to come out differently from the Court of [1985]." [Quoting *Planned Parenthood of Southeastern Pa. v. Casey* (1992).] We therefore overrule *Ball* and *Aguilar* to the extent those decisions are inconsistent with our current understanding of the Establishment Clause.

Nor does the "law of the case" doctrine place any additional constraints on our ability to overturn *Aguilar*. Under this doctrine, a court should not reopen issues decided in earlier stages of the same litigation. The doctrine does not apply if the court is "convinced that [its prior decision] is clearly erroneous and would work a manifest injustice." In light of our conclusion that *Aguilar* would be decided differently under our current Establishment Clause law, we think adherence to that decision would undoubtedly work a "manifest injustice," such that the law of the case doctrine does not apply. . . .

IV

We therefore conclude that our Establishment Clause law has "significant[ly] change[d]" since we decided *Aguilar*. We are only left to decide whether this change in law entitles petitioners to relief under Rule 60(b)(5). We conclude that it does. Our general practice is to apply the rule of law we announce in a case to the parties before us. *Rodriguez de Quijas v. Shearson/American Express, Inc.* (1989). . . .We adhere to this practice even when we overrule a case. . . .

We do not acknowledge, and we do not hold, that other courts should conclude our more recent cases have, by implication, overruled an earlier precedent. We reaffirm that "if a precedent of this Court has direct application in a case, yet appears to rest on reasons rejected in some other line of decisions, the Court of Appeals should follow the case which directly controls, leaving to this Court the prerogative of overruling its own decisions." [Quoting *Rodriguez de Quijas*.] Adherence to this teaching by the District Court and Court of Appeals in this case does not insulate a legal principle on which they relied from our review to determine its continued vitality. The trial court acted within its discretion in entertaining the motion with supporting allegations, but it was also correct to recognize that the motion had to be denied unless and until this Court reinterpreted the binding precedent.

Respondents and JUSTICE GINSBURG urge us to adopt a different analysis because we are reviewing the District Court's denial of petitioners' Rule 60(b)(5) motion for an abuse of discretion. It is true that the trial court has discretion, but the exercise of discretion cannot be permitted to stand if we find it rests upon a legal principle that can no longer be sustained. The standard of review we employ in this litigation does not therefore require us to depart from our general practice.

Respondents nevertheless contend that we should not grant Rule 60(b)(5) relief here, in spite of its propriety in other contexts. They contend that petitioners have used Rule 60(b)(5) in an unprecedented way—not as a means of recognizing changes in the law, but as a vehicle for effecting them. If we were to sanction this use of Rule 60(b)(5), respondents argue, we would encourage litigants to burden the federal courts with a deluge of Rule 60(b)(5) motions premised on nothing more than the claim that various judges or Justices have stated that the law has changed. . . . We think their fears are overstated. As we noted above, a judge's stated belief that a case should be overruled does not make it so.

Most importantly, our decision today is intimately tied to the context in which it arose. This litigation involves a party's request under Rule 60(b)(5) to vacate a continuing injunction entered some years ago in light of a bona fide, significant change in subsequent law. The clause of Rule 60(b)(5) that petitioners invoke applies by its terms only to "judgment[s] hav[ing] prospective application." Intervening developments in the law by themselves rarely constitute the extraordinary circumstances required for relief under Rule 60(b)(6), the only remaining avenue for relief on this basis from judgments lacking any prospective component. Our decision will have no effect outside the context of ordinary civil litigation where the propriety of continuing prospective relief is at issue. . . . Given that Rule 60(b)(5) specifically contemplates the grant of relief in the circumstances presented here, it can hardly be said that we have somehow warped the Rule into a means of "allowing an 'anytime' rehearing." [Quoting GINSBURG, J., dissenting].

Respondents further contend that "[p]etitioners' [p]roposed [u]se of Rule 60(b) [w]ill [e]rode the [i]nstitutional [i]ntegrity of the Court." Respondents do not explain how a proper application of Rule 60(b)(5) undermines our legitimacy. Instead, respondents focus on the harm occasioned if we were to overrule *Aguilar*. But as discussed above, we do no violence to the doctrine of *stare decisis* when we recognize bona fide changes in our decisional law. And in those circumstances, we do no violence to the legitimacy we derive from reliance on that doctrine.

As a final matter, we see no reason to wait for a "better vehicle" in which to evaluate the impact of subsequent cases on *Aguilar*'s continued vitality. To evaluate the Rule 60(b)(5) motion properly before us today in no way undermines "integrity in the interpretation of procedural rules" or signals any departure from "the responsive, non-agenda-setting character of this Court." (GINSBURG, J., dissenting). Indeed, under these circumstances, it would be particularly inequitable for us to bide our time waiting for another case to arise while the city of New York labors under a continuing injunction forcing it to spend millions of dollars on mobile instructional units and leased sites when it could instead be spending that money to give economically disadvantaged children a better chance at success in life by means of a program that is perfectly consistent with the Establishment Clause.

For these reasons, we reverse the judgment of the Court of Appeals and remand to the District Court with instructions to vacate its September 26, 1985, order.

It is so ordered.

JUSTICE SOUTER, with whom JUSTICE STEVENS and JUSTICE GINSBURG join, and with whom JUSTICE BREYER joins as to Part II, dissenting.

In this novel proceeding, petitioners seek relief from an injunction the District Court entered 12 years ago to implement our decision in *Aguilar v. Felton* (1985). For the reasons given by JUSTICE GINSBURG, the Court's holding that petitioners are entitled to relief under Rule 60(b) is seriously mistaken. The Court's misapplication of the rule is tied to its equally erroneous reading of our more recent Establishment Clause cases, which the Court describes as having rejected the underpinnings of *Aguilar* and portions of *Aguilar*'s companion case, *School Dist. of Grand Rapids v. Ball* (1985). The result is to repudiate the very reasonable line drawn in *Aguilar* and *Ball*, and to authorize direct state aid to religious institutions on an unparalleled scale, in violation of the Establishment Clause's central prohibition against religious subsidies by the government.

I respectfully dissent.

I

In both *Aguilar* and *Ball*, we held that supplemental instruction by public school teachers on the premises of religious schools during regular school hours violated the Establishment Clause. . . .

. . . I believe *Aguilar* was a correct and sensible decision, and my only reservation about its opinion is that the emphasis on the excessive entanglement produced by monitoring religious instructional content obscured those facts that independently called for the application of two central tenets of Establishment Clause jurisprudence. The State is forbidden to subsidize religion directly and is just as surely forbidden to act in any way that could reasonably be viewed as religious endorsement. . . .

. . . [T]he flat ban on subsidization antedates the Bill of Rights and has been an unwavering rule in Establishment Clause cases, qualified only by the conclusion two Terms ago that state exactions from college students are not the sort of public revenues subject to the ban. *Rosenberger v. Rector and Visitors of Univ. of Va.* (1995). The rule expresses the hard lesson learned over and over again in the American past and in the experiences of the countries from which we have come, that religions supported by governments are compromised just as surely as the religious freedom of dissenters is burdened when the government supports religion. . . . The ban against state endorsement of religion addresses the same historical lessons. Governmental approval of religion tends to reinforce the religious message (at least in the short run) and, by the same token, to carry a message of exclusion to those of less favored views. . . .

These principles were violated by the programs at issue in *Aguilar* and *Ball*, as a consequence of several significant features common to both Title I, as implemented in New York City before *Aguilar*, and the Grand Rapids Shared Time program: each provided classes on the premises of the religious schools, covering a wide range of subjects including some at the core of primary and secondary education, like reading and mathematics; while their services were termed "supplemental," the programs and their instructors necessarily assumed responsibility for teaching subjects that the religious schools would otherwise have been obligated to provide . . . ; the public employees carrying out the programs had broad responsibilities involving the exercise of considerable discretion . . . ; while the programs offered aid to nonpublic school students generally (and Title I went to public school students as well), participation by religious school students in each program was extensive . . . ; and, finally, aid under Title I and Shared Time flowed directly to the schools in the form of classes and programs, as distinct from indirect aid that reaches schools only as a result of independent private choice. . . .

What, therefore, was significant in *Aguilar* and *Ball* about the placement of state-paid teachers into the physical and social settings of the religious schools was not only the consequent temptation of some of those teachers to reflect the schools' religious missions in the rhetoric of their instruction, with a resulting need for monitoring and the certainty of entanglement. What was so remarkable was that the schemes in issue assumed a teaching responsibility indistinguishable from the responsibility of the schools themselves. The obligation of primary and secondary schools to teach reading necessarily extends to teaching those who are having a hard time at it, and the same is true of math. Calling some classes remedial does not distinguish their subjects from the schools' basic subjects, however inadequately the schools may have been addressing them.

What was true of the Title I scheme as struck down in *Aguilar* will be just as true when New York reverts to the old practices with the Court's approval after today. There is simply no line that can be drawn between the instruction paid for at taxpayers' expense and the instruction in any subject that is not identified as formally religious. While it would be an obvious sham, say, to channel cash to religious schools to be credited only against the expense of "secular" instruction, the line between "supplemental" and general education is likewise impossible to draw. If a State may constitutionally enter the schools to teach in the manner in question, it must in constitutional principle be free to assume, or assume payment for, the entire cost of instruction provided in any ostensibly secular subject in any religious school. . . .

In sum, if a line is to be drawn short of barring all state aid to religious schools for teaching standard subjects, the *Aguilar-Ball* line was a sensible one capable of principled adherence. It is no less sound, and no less necessary, today.

II

The Court today ignores this doctrine and claims that recent cases rejected the elemental assumptions underlying *Aguilar* and much of *Ball*. But the Court errs. Its holding that *Aguilar* and the portion of *Ball* addressing the Shared Time program are "no longer good law" rests on mistaken reading.

A

Zobrest v. Catalina Foothills School Dist. [1993] held that the Establishment Clause does not prevent a school district from providing a sign-language interpreter to a deaf student enrolled in a sectarian school. The Court today relies solely on *Zobrest* to support its contention that we have "abandoned the presumption erected in *Meek*, [*v. Pittenger* (1975)] and *Ball* that the placement of public employees on parochial school grounds inevitably results in the impermissible effect of state-sponsored indoctrination or constitutes a symbolic union between government and religion." *Zobrest*, however, is no such sanction for overruling *Aguilar* or any portion of *Ball*.

In *Zobrest* the Court did indeed recognize that the Establishment Clause lays down no absolute bar to placing public employees in a sectarian school, but the rejection of such a per se rule was hinged expressly on the nature of the employee's job, sign-language interpretation (or signing) and the circumscribed role of the signer. . . .

. . . The Court may disagree with *Ball*'s assertion that a publicly employed teacher working in a sectarian school is apt to reinforce the pervasive inculcation of religious beliefs, but its disagreement is fresh law.

The Court tries to press *Zobrest* into performing another service beyond its reach. The Court says that *Ball* and *Aguilar* assumed "that the presence of a public employee on private school property creates an impermissible 'symbolic link' between government and religion," and that *Zobrest* repudiated this assumption. First, *Ball* and *Aguilar* said nothing about the "mere presence" of public employees at religious schools. It was *Ball* that specifically addressed the point and held only that when teachers employed by public schools are placed in religious schools to provide instruction to students during the school day a symbolic union of church and state is created and will reasonably be seen by the students as endorsement; *Aguilar* adopted the same conclusion by reference. *Zobrest* did not, implicitly or otherwise, repudiate the view that the involvement of public teachers in the instruction provided within sectarian schools looks like a partnership or union and implies approval of the sectarian aim. On the subject of symbolic unions and the strength of their implications, the lesson of *Zobrest* is merely that less is less.

B

The Court next claims that *Ball* rested on the assumption that "any and all public aid that directly aids the educational function of religious schools impermissibly finances religious indoctrination, even if the aid reaches such schools as a consequence of private decisionmaking." . . .

Ball did not establish that "any and all" such aid to religious schools necessarily violates the Establishment Clause. It held that the Shared Time program subsidized the religious functions of the parochial schools by taking over a significant portion of their responsibility for teaching secular subjects. The Court . . . enquired whether the effect of the proffered aid was "direct and substantial" (and, so, unconstitutional) or merely "indirect and incidental," (and, so, permissible), emphasizing that the question "is one of degree." *Witters [v. Washington Dept. of Servs. for Blind* (1986)] and *Zobrest* did nothing to repudiate the principle, emphasizing rather the limited nature of the aid at issue in each case as well as the fact that religious institutions did not receive it directly from the State. . . .

It is accordingly puzzling to find the Court insisting that the aid scheme administered under Title I and considered in *Aguilar* was comparable to the programs in *Witters* and *Zobrest*. Instead of aiding isolated individuals within a school system, New York City's Title I program before *Aguilar* served about 22,000 private school students, all but 52 of whom attended religious schools. Instead of serving individual blind or deaf students, as such, Title I as administered in New York City before *Aguilar* (and as now to be revived) funded instruction in core subjects (remedial reading, reading skills, remedial mathematics, English as a second language) and provided guidance services. Instead of providing a service the school would not otherwise furnish, the Title I services necessarily relieved a religious school of "an expense that it otherwise would have assumed" and freed its funds for other, and sectarian uses.

Finally, instead of aid that comes to the religious school indirectly ... , a public educational agency distributes Title I aid in the form of programs and services directly to the religious schools. In *Zobrest* and *Witters*, it was fair to say that individual students were themselves applicants for individual benefits on a scale that could not amount to a systemic supplement. But under Title I, a local educational agency ... may receive federal funding by proposing programs approved to serve individual students who meet the criteria of need, which it then uses to provide such programs at the religious schools; students eligible for such programs may not apply directly for Title I funds. The aid, accordingly, is not even formally aid to the individual students (and even formally individual aid must be seen as aid to a school system when so many individuals receive it that it becomes a significant feature of the system).

In sum, nothing since *Ball* and *Aguilar* and before this case has eroded the distinction between "direct and substantial" and "indirect and incidental." That principled line is being breached only here and now.

C

The Court notes that aid programs providing benefits solely to religious groups may be constitutionally suspect, while aid allocated under neutral, secular criteria is less likely to have the effect of advancing religion. . . . [E]venhandedness is a necessary but not a sufficient condition for an aid program to satisfy constitutional scrutiny. . . . If a scheme of government aid results in support for religion in some substantial degree, or in endorsement of its value, the formal neutrality of the scheme does not render the Establishment Clause helpless or the holdings in *Aguilar* and *Ball* inapposite.

III

Finally, there is the issue of precedent. *Stare decisis* is no barrier in the Court's eyes because it reads *Aguilar* and *Ball* for exaggerated propositions that *Witters* and *Zobrest* are supposed to have limited to the point of abandoned doctrine. The Court's dispensation from *stare decisis* is, accordingly, no more convincing than its reading of those cases. . . .

The continuity of the law, indeed, is matched by the persistence of the facts. When *Aguilar* was decided everyone knew that providing Title I services off the premises of the religious schools would come at substantial cost in efficiency, convenience, and money. Title I had begun off the premises in New York, after all, and dissatisfaction with the arrangement was what led the City to put the public school teachers into the religious schools in the first place. When *Aguilar* required the end of that arrangement, conditions reverted to those of the past and they have remained unchanged: teaching conditions are often poor, it is difficult to move children around, and it costs a lot of money.

That is, the facts became once again what they were once before, as everyone including the Members of this Court knew they would be. . . .

That is not to deny that the facts just recited are regrettable; the object of Title I is worthy without doubt, and the cost of compliance is high. In the short run there is much that is genuinely unfortunate about the administration of the scheme under *Aguilar*'s rule. But constitutional lines have to be drawn, and on one side of every one of them is an otherwise sympathetic case that provokes impatience with the Constitution and with the line. But constitutional lines are the price of constitutional government.

JUSTICE GINSBURG, with whom JUSTICE STEVENS, JUSTICE SOUTER, and JUSTICE BREYER join, dissenting.

The Court today finds a way to rehear a legal question decided in respondents' favor in this very case some 12 years ago. Subsequent decisions, the majority says, have undermined *Aguilar* and justify our immediate reconsideration. This Court's Rules do not countenance the rehearing here granted. For good reason, a proper application of those rules and the Federal Rules of Civil Procedure would lead us to defer reconsideration of *Aguilar* until we are presented with the issue in another case.

We have a rule on rehearing, Rule 44, but it provides only for petitions filed within 25 days of the entry of the judgment in question. Although the Court or a Justice may "shorte[n] or exten[d]" this period, I am aware of no case in which we have extended the time for rehearing years beyond publication of our adjudication on the merits. . . . Moreover, nothing in our procedures allows us to grant rehearing, timely or not, "except . . . at the instance of a Justice who concurred in the judgment or decision." Petitioners have not been so bold (or so candid) as to style their plea as one for rehearing in this Court, and the Court has not taken up the petition at the instance of JUSTICE STEVENS, the only still-sitting member of the *Aguilar* majority.

Lacking any rule or practice allowing us to reconsider the *Aguilar* judgment directly, the majority accepts as a substitute a rule governing relief from judgments or orders of the federal trial courts. The service to which Rule 60(b) has been impressed is unprecedented, and neither the Court nor those urging reconsideration of *Aguilar* contend otherwise. . . . The Court makes clear, fortunately, that any future efforts to expand today's ruling will not be favored. I therefore anticipate that the extraordinary action taken in this case will remain aberrational.

Rule 60(b) provides, in relevant part:

> "On motion and upon such terms as are just, the [district] court may relieve a party or a party's legal representative from a final judgment, order, or proceeding for the following reasons: . . . (5) . . . it is no longer equitable that the judgment should have prospective application."

Under that rule, a district court may, in its discretion, grant relief from a final judgment with prospective effect if the party seeking modification can show "a significant change either in factual conditions or in law" that renders continued operation of the judgment inequitable. . . .

Appellate courts review denials of Rule 60(b) motions for abuse of discretion. . . . As we recognized in our unanimous opinion in *Browder* [*v. Director, Dept. of Corrections of Ill.* (1978)], "an appeal from denial of Rule 60(b) relief does not bring up the underlying judgment for review." . . .

In short, relitigation of the legal or factual claims underlying the original judgment is not permitted in a Rule 60(b) motion or an appeal therefrom. . . . Thus, under settled practice, the sole question legitimately presented on appeal of the District Court's decision denying petitioners' Rule 60(b)(5) motion to modify the *Aguilar* injunction would be: Did the District Court abuse its discretion when it concluded that neither the facts nor the law had so changed as to warrant alteration of the injunction?

The majority acknowledges that there has been no significant change in factual conditions. The majority also recognizes that *Aguilar* had not been overruled, but remained the governing Establishment Clause law, until this very day. Because *Aguilar* had not been overruled at the time the District Court acted, the law the District Court was bound to respect had not changed. The District Court therefore did not abuse its discretion in denying petitioners' Rule 60(b) motion. . . .

In an effort to make today's use of Rule 60(b) appear palatable, the Court describes its decision not as a determination of whether *Aguilar* should be overruled, but as an exploration whether *Aguilar* already has been "so undermined . . . that it is no longer good law." But nothing can disguise the reality that, until today, *Aguilar* had not been overruled. Good or bad, it was in fact the law.

Despite the problematic use of Rule 60(b), the Court "see[s] no reason to wait for a 'better vehicle.'" There are such vehicles in motion, and the Court does not say otherwise. [Citing pending cases.] . . .

Unlike the majority, I find just cause to await the arrival of [some other case] in which our review appropriately may be sought, before deciding whether *Aguilar* should remain the law of the land. That cause lies in the maintenance of integrity in the interpretation of procedural rules, preservation of the responsive, non-agenda-setting character of this Court, and avoidance of invitations to reconsider old cases based on "speculat[ions] on chances from changes in [the Court's membership].

SUPREME COURT ON
CONFINING SEX OFFENDERS
June 23, 1997

Upholding a Kansas state law designed to protect the state's citizens from sex offenders deemed likely to repeat their crimes, the Supreme Court ruled June 23 that states could confine violent sex offenders in mental hospitals even after they had served their full prison terms. Although the justices split 5–4, the two sides were not deeply divided, and the dissenters essentially spelled out how states could write their laws to avoid constitutional concerns.

The decision was widely applauded. Public demand for ways to keep sex offenders off the streets had reached a peak in the 1990s following a spate of particularly horrific sex crimes whose victims primarily were children. Five states—Arizona, California, Minnesota, Washington, and Wisconsin— already had laws similar to Kansas's on their books. Thirty-eight states and the District of Columbia had filed a brief supporting the Kansas law. "This law is going to spread like wildfire," said Lynn S. Branham, an Illinois attorney.

The confinement law was only one of several means that states were using in their efforts to curb sexual predators. Every state required sex offenders who had completed their prison sentences to register their whereabouts, and most states had also passed laws requiring communities to be notified when sex offenders who had served their jail time moved into the area. The best known of these laws—New Jersey's "Megan's Law"—was upheld by a three-judge federal appeals court panel on August 20. Officials in at least two states, California and Montana, had approved the use of hormones to reduce the sex drive in repeat offenders, and some had suggested chemical castration.

Civil Confinement and Due Process

Under the Kansas law, enacted in 1994, a person who had been convicted of a sexually violent crime could be confined to a mental hospital after completing his jail term if, at a civil hearing, the state could prove the indi-

vidual had a "mental abnormality" or "personality disorder" and was likely to repeat his sexually violent acts. Once confined, the person was entitled to an annual review to ensure that the confinement was still justified.

The first person committed to a mental hospital under the state law was Leroy Hendricks, who had a thirty-year history of sexually abusing children and who was serving a ten-year sentence for taking "indecent liberties" with two thirteen-year-old boys. At his civil confinement hearing, held shortly before he was scheduled to be released from prison, Hendricks acknowledged that he was not cured of his pedophilia, that he could not "control the urge to molest children," and that the only sure way he could stop molesting them was "to die." Hendricks challenged the law, stating that it denied him due process, that it punished him twice for the same crime, and that it was an ex post facto law, imposing a retroactive penalty on a crime already committed. The Kansas Supreme Court found in favor of Hendricks, ruling that a "mental abnormality" was not a mental illness as that term was legally understood and that the Kansas law thus violated the constitutional protection of due process.

In reversing that decision, the Supreme Court held that the state law did not violate due process. Writing for the majority, Justice Clarence Thomas noted that the Court had consistently upheld state laws that involuntarily confined people who are unable to control their behavior and who are thus a danger to others. A "finding of dangerousness, standing alone" was not enough to justify a civil confinement, Thomas said, but must be linked, as it was in Hendricks' case, with a finding of "a 'mental abnormality' or 'personality disorder' that makes it difficult, if not impossible, for the person to control his dangerous behavior. . . ." That the Kansas Legislature used the term mental abnormality *rather than* mental illness *was of little relevance, Thomas said, noting that the psychiatric profession regarded pedophilia as a serious mental disorder. Hendricks's "admitted lack of volitional control, coupled with a prediction of future dangerousness, adequately distinguishes [him] from other dangerous persons who are perhaps more properly dealt with exclusively through criminal proceedings."*

Thomas also dismissed Hendricks's arguments that the law violated the Constitution's ban on double jeopardy and on ex post facto laws. Civil commitment was not equivalent to criminal punishment, Thomas said, because it was meant neither as retribution nor as a deterrent, "the two primary objectives of criminal punishment." And because the law "did not criminalize conduct legal before its enactment, nor deprive Hendricks of any defense that was available to him at the time of the crimes," it did not violate the ban on ex post facto laws, Thomas said. Thomas was joined in his opinion by Chief Justice William H. Rehnquist and Justices Sandra Day O'Connor, Antonin Scalia, and Anthony M. Kennedy.

In a dissent Justice Stephen G. Breyer agreed with the majority that the Kansas law did not violate substantive due process. But, Breyer continued, "the Act did not provide Hendricks (or others like him) with any treatment until after his release date from prison and only inadequate treatment thereafter. These [facts] convince me that it was not simply an effort to commit Hendricks civilly, but rather an effort to inflict further punishment upon him. . . ." For that reason, Breyer said, the law violated the Constitution's ex post facto clause. States could, however, enact what Breyer called "dangerous sexual offender statutes" if they operated prospectively, and such laws could even be applied retroactively "if the confinement it imposes is not punishment. . . ." Justice John Paul Stevens and David H. Souter joined Breyer's opinion; Justice Ruth Ginsburg joined the part on the ex post facto clause, but she did not write a separate opinion giving her views on due process question.

State Laws Upheld by Lower Courts

With the favorable Supreme Court ruling in hand, several states quickly began to consider enacting similar civil confinement laws. New York state enacted its version of a confinement law just two days after the Court ruling. Advocates of tough restrictions on sex offenders were also pleased with two appeals court rulings in August. On August 20 a three-judge federal appeals court panel upheld New Jersey's "Megan's Law" against a challenge that it imposed additional punishment on convicted sexual predators. The New Jersey law required county officials to notify local residents and community groups when sex offenders deemed to be at high risk of repeating their crime moved into their neighborhood. It was enacted in October 1994 in response to public outrage over the rape and murder of seven-year-old Megan Kanka by a neighbor who had twice been convicted of sexual offenses. "The fundamental premise of Megan's Law is that registration and carefully tailored notification can enable law enforcement and those likely to encounter a sex offender to be aware of a potential danger and to stay vigilant against possible abuse," the panel from the Court of Appeals for the Third Circuit wrote. "That is not an unreasonable premise." The panel decision was split, 2–1. Two days later, on August 22, a three-judge panel from the Court of Appeals for the Second Circuit unanimously upheld a similar law in New York that called for the names and addresses of thousands of sex offenders to be made public.

Law enforcement officials and others said that such laws were necessary to prevent known offenders from repeating their crimes. "One of the points we've made from the beginning is that sex offenders are different," said Ernie Allen, the president of the National Center for Missing and Exploited Children, one of the primary advocates of state sexual offender laws. "Because of the nature of these offenses, because of the psychological element in their offense, because of the high risk of reoffending, because of the population they prey on, the government has an obligation to do more than say, 'Do your time and go forth and sin no more.' "

But civil rights groups and some public defenders warned that the laws were the result of a public hysteria. "The notion that these are the most dangerous people in the community and the most likely to repeat [their crimes] needs to be looked at a lot more dispassionately," said Fred Berlin, the founder of the John Hopkins Sexual Disorders Clinic in Baltimore. Others argued that the laws did in fact amount to additional punishment, exposing sex offenders who had already served their time to loss of privacy and a form of vigilantism. They cited incidences of sex offenders being forced to move after neighbors publicly protested their presence in the community.

Following are excerpts from the majority and dissenting opinions in the case of Kansas v. Hendricks, *in which the Supreme Court upheld June 23, 1997, the right of states to confine certain sexual predators in mental hospitals even after they had completed their prison sentences:*

Nos. 95-1649 & 95-9075

Kansas, Petitioner
v.
Leroy Hendricks

On writs of certiorari to the Supreme Court of Kansas

Leroy Hendricks, Petitioner
v.
Kansas

[June 23, 1997]

JUSTICE THOMAS delivered the opinion of the Court.

In 1994, Kansas enacted the Sexually Violent Predator Act, which establishes procedures for the civil commitment of persons who, due to a "mental abnormality" or a "personality disorder," are likely to engage in "predatory acts of sexual violence." The State invoked the Act for the first time to commit Leroy Hendricks, an inmate who had a long history of sexually molesting children, and who was scheduled for release from prison shortly after the Act became law. Hendricks challenged his commitment on, *inter alia,* "substantive" due process, double jeopardy, and *ex post facto* grounds. The Kansas Supreme Court invalidated the Act, holding that its pre-commitment condition of a "mental abnormality" did not satisfy what the court perceived to be the "substantive" due process requirement that involuntary civil commitment must be predicated on a finding of "mental illness." (1996). The State of Kansas petitioned for certiorari. Hendricks subsequently filed a cross-petition in which he reasserted his federal double jeopardy and *ex post facto* claims. We granted certiorari on both the petition and the cross-petition (1996) and now reverse the judgment below.

I
A

The Kansas Legislature enacted the Sexually Violent Predator Act (Act) in 1994 to grapple with the problem of managing repeat sexual offenders. Although Kansas already had a statute addressing the involuntary commitment of those defined as "mentally ill," the legislature determined that existing civil commitment procedures were inadequate to confront the risks presented by "sexually violent predators." . . .

As a result, the Legislature found it necessary to establish "a civil commitment procedure for the long-term care and treatment of the sexually violent predator." The Act defined a "sexually violent predator" as:

> "any person who has been convicted of or charged with a sexually violent offense and who suffers from a mental abnormality or personality disorder which makes the person likely to engage in the predatory acts of sexual violence."

A "mental abnormality" was defined, in turn, as a "congenital or acquired condition affecting the emotional or volitional capacity which predisposes the person to commit sexually violent offenses in a degree constituting such person a menace to the health and safety of others."

As originally structured, the Act's civil commitment procedures pertained to: (1) a presently confined person who, like Hendricks, "has been convicted of a sexually violent offense" and is scheduled for release; (2) a person who has been "charged with a sexually violent offense" but has been found incompetent to stand trial; (3) a person who has been found "not guilty by reason of insanity of a sexually violent offense"; and (4) a person found "not guilty" of a sexually violent offense because of a mental disease or defect.

The initial version of the Act, as applied to a currently confined person such as Hendricks, was designed to initiate a specific series of procedures. The custodial agency was required to notify the local prosecutor 60 days before the anticipated release of a person who might have met the Act's criteria. The prosecutor was then obligated, within 45 days, to decide whether to file a petition in state court seeking the person's involuntary commitment. If such a petition were filed, the court was to determine whether "probable cause" existed to support a finding that the person was a "sexually violent predator" and thus eligible for civil commitment. Upon such a determination, transfer of the individual to a secure facility for professional evaluation would occur. After that evaluation, a trial would be held to determine beyond a reasonable doubt whether the individual was a sexually violent predator. If that determination were made, the person would then be transferred to the custody of the Secretary of Social and Rehabilitation Services (Secretary) for "control, care and treatment until such time as the person's mental abnormality or personality disorder has so changed that the person is safe to be at large."

In addition to placing the burden of proof upon the State, the Act afforded the individual a number of other procedural safeguards. In the case of an indigent person, the State was required to provide, at public expense, the assistance of counsel and an examination by mental health care professionals. The individual also received the right to present and crossexamine witnesses, and the opportunity to review documentary evidence presented by the State.

Once an individual was confined, the Act required that "[t]he involuntary detention or commitment . . . shall conform to constitutional requirements for care and treatment." Confined persons were afforded three different avenues of review: First, the committing court was obligated to conduct an annual review to determine whether continued detention was warranted. Second, the Secretary was permitted, at any time, to decide that the confined individual's condition had so changed that release was appropriate, and could then authorize the person to petition for release. Finally, even without the Secretary's permission, the confined person could at any time file a release petition. If the court found that the State could no longer satisfy its burden under the initial commitment standard, the individual would be freed from confinement. . . .

II

A

Kansas argues that the Act's definition of "mental abnormality" satisfies "substantive" due process requirements. We agree. . . . States have in certain narrow circumstances provided for the forcible civil detainment of people who are unable to control their behavior and who thereby pose a danger to the public health and safety. . . . We have consistently upheld such involuntary commitment statutes provided the confinement takes place pursuant to proper procedures and evidentiary standards. It thus cannot be said that the involuntary civil confinement of a limited subclass of dangerous persons is contrary to our understanding of ordered liberty.

The challenged Act unambiguously requires a finding of dangerousness either to one's self or to others as a prerequisite to involuntary confinement. . . . The statute thus requires proof of more than a mere predisposition to violence; rather, it requires evidence of past sexually violent behavior and a present mental condition that creates a likelihood of such conduct in the future if the person is not incapacitated. . . .

A finding of dangerousness, standing alone, is ordinarily not a sufficient ground upon which to justify indefinite involuntary commitment. We have sustained civil commitment statutes when they have coupled proof of dangerousness with the proof of some additional factor, such as a "mental illness" or "mental abnormality." . . . The Kansas Act is plainly of a kind with these other civil commitment statutes: It requires a finding of future dangerousness, and then links that finding to the existence of a "mental abnormality" or "personality disorder" that makes it difficult, if not impossible, for the person to control his dangerous behavior. . . .

Hendricks nonetheless argues that our earlier cases dictate a finding of "mental illness" as a prerequisite for civil commitment. . . . He then asserts that a "mental abnormality" is not equivalent to a "mental illness" because it is a term coined by the Kansas Legislature, rather than by the psychiatric community. Contrary to Hendricks' assertion, the term "mental illness" is devoid of any talismanic significance. . . .

Indeed, we have never required State legislatures to adopt any particular nomenclature in drafting civil commitment statutes. Rather, we have traditionally left to legislators the task of defining terms of a medical nature that have legal significance. As a consequence, the States have, over the years, developed numerous specialized terms to define mental health concepts. Often, those definitions do not fit precisely with the definitions employed by the medical community. . . .

To the extent that the civil commitment statutes we have considered set forth criteria relating to an individual's inability to control his dangerousness, the Kansas Act sets forth comparable criteria and Hendricks' condition doubtless satisfies those criteria. The mental health professionals who evaluated Hendricks diagnosed him as suffering from pedophilia, a condition the psychiatric profession itself classifies as a serious mental disorder. [Citing 1 American Psychiatric Association, Treatments of Psychiatric Disorders, 617–633 (1989), among other sources.] Hendricks even conceded that, when he becomes "stressed out," he cannot "control the urge" to molest children. This admitted lack of volitional control, coupled with a prediction of future dangerousness, adequately distinguishes Hendricks from other dangerous persons who are perhaps more properly dealt with exclusively through criminal proceedings. Hendricks' diagnosis as a pedophile, which qualifies as a "mental abnormality" under the Act, thus plainly suffices for due process purposes.

B

We granted Hendricks' cross-petition to determine whether the Act violates the Constitution's double jeopardy prohibition or its ban on *ex post facto* lawmaking. The thrust of Hendricks' argument is that the Act establishes criminal proceedings; hence confinement under it necessarily constitutes punishment. . . . We are unpersuaded by Hendricks' argument that Kansas has established criminal proceedings.

The categorization of a particular proceeding as civil or criminal "is first of all a question of statutory construction." We must initially ascertain whether the legislature meant the statute to establish "civil" proceedings. If so, we ordinarily defer to the legislature's stated intent. Here, Kansas' objective to create a civil proceeding is evidenced by its placement of the Sexually Violent Predator Act within the Kansas probate code, instead of the criminal code, as well as its description of the Act as creating a *"civil commitment procedure"* (emphasis added). Nothing on the face of the statute suggests that the legislature sought to create anything other than a civil commitment scheme designed to protect the public from harm.

Although we recognize that a "civil label is not always dispositive," we will reject the legislature's manifest intent only where a party challenging the statute provides "the clearest proof" that "the statutory scheme [is] so punitive either in purpose or effect as to negate [the State's] intention" to deem it "civil." . . . Hendricks, however, has failed to satisfy this heavy burden.

As a threshold matter, commitment under the Act does not implicate either of the two primary objectives of criminal punishment: retribution or deterrence. The Act's purpose is not retributive because it does not affix culpability for prior criminal conduct. Instead, such conduct is used solely for evidentiary purposes, either to demonstrate that a "mental abnormality" exists or to support a finding of future dangerousness. . . . In addition, the Kansas Act does not make a criminal conviction a prerequisite for commitment—persons absolved of criminal responsibility may nonetheless be subject to confinement under the Act. . . .

Moreover, unlike a criminal statute, no finding of scienter is required to commit an individual who is found to be a sexually violent predator; instead, the commitment determination is made based on a "mental abnormality" or "personality disorder" rather than on one's criminal intent. . . .

Nor can it be said that the legislature intended the Act to function as a deterrent. Those persons committed under the Act are, by definition, suffering from a "mental abnormality" or a "personality disorder" that prevents them from exercising adequate control over their behavior. Such persons are therefore unlikely to be deterred by the threat of confinement. And the conditions surrounding that confinement do not suggest a punitive purpose on the State's part. The State has represented that an individual confined under the Act is not subject to the more restrictive conditions placed on state prisoners, but instead experiences essentially the same conditions as any involuntarily committed patient in the state mental institution. . . .

Hendricks focuses on his confinement's potentially indefinite duration as evidence of the State's punitive intent. That focus, however, is misplaced. Far from any punitive objective, the confinement's duration is instead linked to the stated purposes of the commitment, namely, to hold the person until his mental abnormality no longer causes him to be a threat to others. . . . If, at any time, the confined person is adjudged "safe to be at large," he is statutorily entitled to immediate release.

Furthermore, commitment under the Act is only *potentially* indefinite. The maximum amount of time an individual can be incapacitated pursuant to a single judicial proceeding is one year. If Kansas seeks to continue the detention beyond that year, a court must once again determine beyond a reasonable doubt that the detainee satisfies the same standards as required for the initial confinement. . . .

Hendricks next contends that the State's use of procedural safeguards traditionally found in criminal trials makes the proceedings here criminal rather than civil. . . . The numerous procedural and evidentiary protections afforded here demonstrate that the Kansas Legislature has taken great care to confine only a narrow class of particularly dangerous individuals, and then only after meeting the strictest procedural standards. That Kansas chose to afford such procedural protections does not transform a civil commitment proceeding into a criminal prosecution.

Finally, Hendricks argues that the Act is necessarily punitive because it fails to offer any legitimate "treatment." Without such treatment, Hendricks asserts, confinement under the Act amounts to little more than disguised punishment. Hendricks' argument assumes that treatment for his condition is available, but that the State has failed (or refused) to provide it. The Kansas Supreme Court, however, apparently rejected this assumption, explaining:

> "It is clear that the overriding concern of the legislature is to continue the segregation of sexually violent offenders from the public. Treatment with the goal of reintegrating them into society is incidental, at best. The record reflects that treatment for sexually violent predators is all but nonexistent. The legislature concedes that sexually violent predators are not amenable to treatment under [the existing Kansas involuntary commitment statute]. If there is nothing to treat under [that statute], then there is no mental illness. In that light, the provisions of the Act for treatment appear somewhat disingenuous."

It is possible to read this passage as a determination that Hendricks' condition was *untreatable* under the existing Kansas civil commitment statute, and thus the Act's sole purpose was incapacitation. . . .

Accepting the Kansas court's apparent determination that treatment is not possible for this category of individuals does not obligate us to adopt its legal conclusions. We have already observed that, under the appropriate circumstances and when accompanied by proper procedures, incapacitation may be a legitimate end of the civil law. Accordingly, the Kansas court's determination that the Act's "overriding concern" was the continued "segregation of sexually violent offenders" is consistent with our conclusion that the Act establishes civil proceedings. . . . [W]e have never held that the Constitution prevents a State from civilly detaining those for whom no treatment is available, but who nevertheless pose a danger to others. A State could hardly be seen as furthering a "punitive" purpose by involuntarily confining persons afflicted with an untreatable, highly contagious disease. . . . Similarly, it would be of little value to require treatment as a precondition for civil confinement of the dangerously insane when no acceptable treatment existed. To conclude otherwise would obligate a State to release certain confined individuals who were both mentally ill and dangerous simply because they could not be successfully treated for their afflictions. . . .

Alternatively, the Kansas Supreme Court's opinion can be read to conclude that Hendricks' condition is treatable, but that treatment was not the State's "overriding concern" and that no treatment was being provided (at least at the time Hendricks was committed). . . . Even if we accept this determination that the provision of treatment was not the Kansas Legislature's "overriding" or "primary" purpose in passing the Act, this does not rule out the possibility that an ancillary purpose of the Act was to provide treatment, and it does not require us to conclude that the Act is punitive. . . .

Although the treatment program initially offered Hendricks may have seemed somewhat meager, it must be remembered that he was the first person committed under the Act. That the State did not have all of its treatment procedures in place is thus not surprising. What is significant, however, is that Hendricks was placed under the supervision of the Kansas Department of Health and Social and Rehabilitative Services, housed in a unit segregated from the general prison population and operated not by employees of the Department of Corrections, but by other trained individuals. And, before this Court, Kansas declared "[a]bsolutely" that persons committed under the Act are now receiving in the neighborhood of "31.5 hours of treatment per week."

Where the State has "disavowed any punitive intent"; limited confinement to a small segment of particularly dangerous individuals; provided strict procedural safeguards; directed that confined persons be segregated from the general prison population and afforded the same status as others who have been civilly committed; recommended treatment if such is possible; and permitted immediate release upon a showing that the individual is no longer dangerous or mentally impaired, we cannot say that it acted with punitive intent. We therefore hold that the Act does not establish criminal proceedings and that involuntary confinement pursuant to the Act is not punitive. Our conclusion that the Act is nonpunitive thus removes an essential prerequisite for both Hendricks' double jeopardy and *ex post facto* claims.

1

The Double Jeopardy Clause provides: "[N]or shall any person be subject for the same offence to be twice put in jeopardy of life or limb." Although generally understood to preclude a second prosecution for the same offense, the Court has also interpreted this prohibition to prevent the State from "punishing twice, or attempting a second time to punish criminally, for the same offense." *Witte v. United States* (1995). Hendricks argues that, as applied to him, the Act violates double jeopardy principles because his confinement under the Act, imposed after a conviction and a term of incarceration, amounted to both a second prosecution and a second punishment for the same offense. We disagree.

Because we have determined that the Kansas Act is civil in nature, initiation of its commitment proceedings does not constitute a second prosecution. . . . Moreover, as commitment under the Act is not tantamount to "punishment," Hendricks' involuntary detention does not violate the Double Jeopardy Clause, even though that confinement may follow a prison term. . . . If an individual otherwise meets the requirements for involuntary civil commitment, the State is under no obligation to release that individual simply because the detention would follow a period of incarceration. . . .

2

Hendricks' *ex post facto* claim is similarly flawed. The *Ex Post Facto* Clause, which " 'forbids the application of any new punitive measure to a crime already consummated,' " has been interpreted to pertain exclusively to penal statutes. As we have previously determined, the Act does not impose punishment; thus, its application does not raise *ex post facto* concerns. Moreover, the Act clearly does not have retroactive effect. Rather, the Act permits involuntary confinement based upon a determination that the person currently both suffers from a "mental abnormality" or "personality disorder" and is likely to pose a future danger to the public. To the extent that past behavior is taken into account, it is used, as noted above, solely for evidentiary purposes. Because the Act does not criminalize conduct legal before its enactment, nor deprive Hendricks of any defense that was available to him at the time of his crimes, the Act does not violate the *Ex Post Facto* Clause.

III

We hold that the Kansas Sexually Violent Predator Act comports with due process requirements and neither runs afoul of double jeopardy principles nor constitutes an exercise in impermissible *ex post facto* lawmaking. Accordingly, the judgment of the Kansas Supreme Court is reversed.

It is so ordered.

JUSTICE BREYER, with whom JUSTICES STEVENS and SOUTER join, and with whom JUSTICE GINSBURG joins as to Parts II and III, dissenting.

I agree with the majority that the Kansas Act's "definition of 'mental abnormality' " satisfies the "substantive" requirements of the Due Process Clause. Kansas, however, concedes that Hendricks' condition is treatable; yet the Act did not provide Hendricks (or others like him) with any treatment until after his release date from prison and only inadequate treatment thereafter. These, and certain other, special features of the Act convince me that it was not simply an effort to commit Hendricks civilly, but rather an effort to inflict further punishment upon him. The *Ex Post Facto* Clause therefore prohibits the Act's application to Hendricks, who committed his crimes prior to its enactment.

[I omitted]
II

Kansas' 1994 Act violates the Federal Constitution's prohibition of "any . . . *ex post facto* Law" if it "inflicts" upon Hendricks "a greater punishment" than did the law "annexed to" his "crime[s]" when he "committed" those crimes in 1984. The majority . . . finds the Act is not "punitive." With respect to that basic question, I disagree with the majority.

Certain resemblances between the Act's "civil commitment" and traditional criminal punishments are obvious. Like criminal imprisonment, the Act's civil commitment amounts to "secure" confinement and "incarceration against one's will." . . . In addition, a basic objective of the Act is incapacitation. . . .

Moreover, the Act, like criminal punishment, imposes its confinement (or sanction) only upon an individual who has previously committed a criminal offense. . . . And the Act imposes that confinement through the use of persons (county prosecutors), procedural guarantees (trial by jury, assistance of counsel, psychiatric evaluations), and standards ("beyond a reasonable doubt") traditionally associated with the criminal law.

These obvious resemblances by themselves, however, are not legally sufficient to transform what the Act calls "civil commitment" into a criminal punishment. . . . Nor does the fact that criminal behavior triggers the Act make the critical difference. . . . Neither is the presence of criminal law-type procedures determinative. . . .

If these obvious similarities cannot by themselves prove that Kansas' "civil commitment" statute is criminal, neither can the word "civil" written into the statute by itself prove the contrary. . . . [W]hen a State believes that treatment does exist, and then couples that admission with a legislatively required delay of such treatment until a person is at the end of his jail term (so that further incapacitation is therefore necessary), such a legislative scheme begins to look punitive. . . .

Several important treatment-related factors—factors of a kind that led the five-member *Allen* [*v. Illinois* (1986)] majority to conclude that the Illinois' legislature's purpose was primarily civil, not punitive—in this case suggest precisely the opposite. First, the State Supreme Court here . . . has held that treatment is not a significant objective of the Act. The Kansas court wrote that the Act's purpose is "segregation of sexually violent offenders," with "treatment" a matter that was "incidental at best." . . .

The record provides support for the Kansas court's conclusion. The court found that, as of the time of Hendricks' commitment, the State had not funded treatment, it had not entered into treatment contracts, and it had little, if any, qualified treatment staff. . . .

Second, the Kansas statute insofar as it applies to previously convicted offenders, such as Hendricks, commits, confines, and treats those offenders after they have served virtually their entire criminal sentence. That time-related circumstance seems deliberate. The Act explicitly defers diagnosis, evaluation, and commitment proceedings until a few weeks prior to the "anticipated release" of a previously convicted offender from prison. But why, one might ask, does the Act not commit and require treatment of sex offenders sooner, say soon after they begin to serve their sentences? . . .

Third, the statute, at least as of the time Kansas applied it to Hendricks, did not require the committing authority to consider the possibility of using less restrictive alternatives, such as postrelease supervision, halfway houses, or other methods that *amici* supporting Kansas here have mentioned. The laws of many other States require such consideration. . . .

Fourth, the laws of other States confirm, through comparison, that Kansas' "civil commitment" objectives do not require the statutory features that indicate a punitive purpose. I have found 17 States with laws that seek to protect the public from mentally abnormal, sexually dangerous individuals through civil commitment or other mandatory treatment programs. Ten of those statutes, unlike the Kansas statute, begin treatment of an offender soon after he has been apprehended and charged with a serious sex offense. Only seven, like Kansas, delay "civil" commitment (and treatment) until the offender has served his criminal sentence (and this figure includes the Acts of Minnesota and New Jersey, both of which generally do not delay treatment). Of these seven, however, six (unlike Kansas) require consideration of less restrictive alternatives. [Citations omitted.] Only one State other than Kansas, namely

Iowa, both delays civil commitment (and consequent treatment) and does not explicitly consider less restrictive alternatives. But the law of that State applies prospectively only, thereby avoiding *ex post facto* problems. . . .

. . . [W]hen a State decides offenders can be treated and confines an offender to provide that treatment, but then refuses to provide it, the refusal to treat while a person is fully incapacitated begins to look punitive.

The majority suggests that this is the very case I say it is not, namely a case of a mentally ill person who is untreatable. . . . [The Kansas Supreme Court], however, did not find that Hendricks was untreatable; it found that he was untreated—quite a different matter. . . .

The majority suggests in the alternative that recent evidence shows that Kansas is now providing treatment. That evidence comes from two sources. First, a statement by the Kansas Attorney General at oral argument that those committed under the Act are now receiving treatment. And second, in a footnote, a Kansas trial judge's statement, in a state habeas proceeding nearly one year after Hendricks was committed, that Kansas is providing treatment. I do not see how either of these statements can be used to justify the validity of the Act's application to Hendricks at the time he filed suit. . . .

III

To find that the confinement the Act imposes upon Hendricks is "punishment" is to find a violation of the *Ex Post Facto* Clause. Kansas does not deny that the 1994 Act changed the legal consequences that attached to Hendricks' earlier crimes, and in a way that significantly "disadvantage[d] the offender."

To find a violation of that Clause here, however, is not to hold that the Clause prevents Kansas, or other States, from enacting dangerous sexual offender statutes. A statute that operates prospectively, for example, does not offend the *Ex Post Facto* Clause. Neither does it offend the *Ex Post Facto* Clause for a State to sentence offenders to the fully authorized sentence, to seek consecutive, rather than concurrent, sentences, or to invoke recidivism statutes to lengthen imprisonment. Moreover, a statute that operates retroactively, like Kansas' statute, nonetheless does not offend the Clause *if the confinement that it imposes is not punishment*—if, that is to say, the legislature does not simply add a later criminal punishment to an earlier one.

The statutory provisions before us do amount to punishment primarily because, as I have said, the legislature did not tailor the statute to fit the nonpunitive civil aim of treatment, which it concedes exists in Hendricks' case. The Clause in these circumstances does not stand as an obstacle to achieving important protections for the public's safety; rather it provides an assurance that, where so significant a restriction of an individual's basic freedoms is at issue, a State cannot cut corners. Rather, the legislature must hew to the Constitution's liberty-protecting line.

I therefore would affirm the judgment below.

AIR FORCE REPORT ON ROSWELL UFO CITINGS
June 24, 1997

The United States Air Force in 1997 made its second attempt in four years to shoot down reports that a flying saucer landed at an air base near Roswell, New Mexico, in July 1947. The supposed landing of an alien spaceship—along with other reports of unidentified flying objects (UFOs)—had become known collectively as the "Roswell Incident."

Just one week before the fiftieth anniversary of the Roswell Incident, the air force on June 24 released a paperbound 231-page document, "The Roswell Report: Case Closed," detailing and refuting the various claims that had been made about flying saucers and little gray men. The air force report failed to convince true believers who argued that the government simply was continuing to cover up the truth of what happened near Roswell in 1947. Thousands of UFO fans turned out for an anniversary celebration in the desert, complete with live entertainment and a giant replica of an alien figure.

The Roswell Incident helped spawn hundreds of stories about UFOs, some of which were turned into novels, movies, and television shows. The hit 1996 movie Independence Day *focused on the alleged air force conspiracy to hide an alien who landed at Roswell.*

The Roswell Incident

Two events in July 1947 formed the basis for the Roswell Incident. First, a local ranch foreman, W. W. Bazell, found pieces of an unusual shiny material in the desert near Roswell. Bazell turned the material over to the sheriff, who gave it to officials at the local base of what was then known as the U.S. Army Air Forces (and later became the U.S. Air Force. The air base issued a press release announcing the discovery of a "flying disk," resulting in a story in the Roswell Daily Record *reporting that the base had captured a "flying saucer." The air base quickly retracted its press release, saying the strange material actually was debris from a weather balloon that had crashed.*

Years later, W. Glenn Dennis, who said he worked at a Roswell funeral home, claimed that in July 1947 he had been called by air force officials asking where they could obtain child-size caskets. Dennis also said a nurse at the base claimed she had participated in the autopsy of an alien creature.

In subsequent years, others in the Roswell area insisted they had seen aliens—often with bulbous heads, slits for eyes, and only four fingers—or had witnessed landings of UFOs. These reports from Roswell became an integral part of the lore of those who believe in UFOs and advanced extraterrestrial life.

A revival of general public interest in UFOs during the 1980s prompted renewed attention to the Roswell Incident. Dennis and others who believed aliens had visited Roswell became more vocal in their insistence that the air force was perpetuating a cover-up. In response, the air force in 1994 produced a 1,000-page report on the original Roswell Incident. That report said the shiny objects found by Bazell actually were fragments of a giant balloon that had been part of a top-secret U.S. program, called "Project Mogul," to monitor nuclear test explosions by the Soviet Union.

The 1994 report failed to silence critics, and instead raised new questions with its implicit acknowledgment that the air force had given misleading information when it claimed in 1947 that the objects were part of a weather balloon. Captain James McAndrew, who wrote the 1994 report, continued to investigate the matter, and the 1997 report was the result of his further researches.

In the 1997 report McAndrew offered new details, including photographs and other documentary evidence, to bolster his findings that the material found by Bazell was part of a Project Mogul balloon. But McAndrew devoted most of the 1997 report to an analysis of various reports of aliens, dead or alive, who had visited the Roswell area. McAndrew said the descriptions of the supposed aliens closely matched anthropomorphic dummies that were dropped from high altitude balloons and airplanes over the New Mexico desert between 1953 and 1959. The air force used the dummies in tests of various methods of returning pilots and astronauts to earth.

The tests with dummies were followed by three high altitude parachute jumps by Captain Joseph W. Kittinger Jr., including a 1960 jump from an altitude of 102,800 feet (nearly 20 miles)—the highest such jump of all time. In the 1997 report McAndrew said Kittinger's desire for secrecy following a mishap involving one of his test jumps may have formed the basis for contentions that the air force was covering up a crash landing involving aliens.

In the conclusion to his report McAndrew said people who claimed to have witnessed UFO landings near Roswell or who later interpreted the statements of those witnesses were either "confused" about the details of the events or were "attempting to perpetuate a hoax, believing that no serious efforts would ever be taken to verify their stories." McAndrew said many of the supposed UFO sightings actually were important scientific experiments of which the air force should be proud.

McAndrew's report failed to satisfy UFO proponents, especially Dennis and other founders of the UFO Museum and Research Center in Roswell. Dennis, often described as the "star witness" of the Roswell Incident, told the Roswell Daily Record: *"The ones who wrote the report are the ones who are the dummies."*

CIA Admission on UFOs

Just six weeks after the air force made public its Roswell report, the CIA published a study acknowledging that the government gave misleading information to the public for more than four decades in hopes of hiding its fleet of sophisticated spy planes. The CIA study, "CIA's Role in the Study of UFOs, 1947–1990," by historian Gerald K. Haines, was published in the declassified 1997 edition of the agency's journal, Studies in Intelligence.

Haines reported that the air force and the CIA invented cover stories to account for thousands of sightings of UFOs. In most cases, Haines said, the agencies told the public that unusual objects in the sky were ice crystals, temperature inversions, and other atmospheric phenomena. In fact, according to Haines, many people who thought they saw unusual flying objects were right: They had glimpsed top secret U.S. spy planes such as the U-2 or the SR-71 "Blackbird," both of which flew at very high altitudes.

"Over half of all UFO reports from the late 1950s through the 1960s were accounted for by manned reconnaissance flights," Haines said. "This led the air force to make misleading and deceptive statements to the public in order to allay public fears and to protect an extraordinarily sensitive national security project."

Some government critics praised the CIA for admitting the past deceit but wondered why it took so long. The existence of U.S. spy planes had been public knowledge at least since 1960, when U-2 pilot Francis Gary Powers crashed over the Soviet Union and was put on trial by Soviet authorities. John E. Pike, an analyst for the American Federation of Scientists, told the Washington Post *that the Haines paper was "a nicely done study. It's just three decades late." Other critics said the report bolstered their contentions that the government routinely lied to the public, especially on the subject of UFOs.*

Following are excerpts from "The Roswell Report: Case Closed," written by Captain James McAndrew and published June 24, 1997, by the U.S. Air Force:

Introduction

In July 1994, the Office of the Secretary of the Air Force concluded an exhaustive search for records in response to a General Accounting Office (GAO) inquiry of an event popularly known as the "Roswell Incident." The focus of the GAO probe, initiated at the request of New Mexico Congressman Steven Schiff, was to determine if the U.S. Air Force, or any other U.S. government agency, possessed information on the alleged crash and recovery of an extraterrestrial vehicle and its alien occupants near Roswell, N.M. in July 1947.

Reports of flying saucers and alien bodies allegedly sighted in the Roswell area in 1947, have been the subject of intense domestic and international media attention. This attention has resulted in countless newspaper and magazine articles, books, a television series, a full-length motion picture, and even a film purported to be a U.S. government "alien autopsy."

The July 1994 Air Force report concluded that the predecessor to the U.S. Air Force, the U.S. Army Air Forces, did indeed recover material near Roswell in July 1947. This 1,000-page report methodically explains that what was recovered by the Army Air Forces was not the remnants of an extraterrestrial spacecraft and its alien crew, but debris from an Army Air Forces balloon-borne research project code named *Mogul*. Records located describing research carried out under the *Mogul* project, most of which were never classified (and publicly available) were collected, provided to GAO, and published in one volume for ease of access for the general public.

Although *Mogul* components clearly accounted for the claims of "flying saucer" debris recovered in 1947, lingering questions remained concerning anecdotal accounts that included descriptions of "alien" bodies. The issue of "bodies" was not discussed extensively in the 1994 report because there were not any bodies connected with events that occurred in 1947. The extensive Secretary of the Air Force-directed search of Army Air Forces and U.S. Air Force records from 1947 did not yield information that even suggested the 1947 "Roswell" events were anything other than the retrieval of the *Mogul* equipment.

Subsequent to the 1994 report, Air Force researchers discovered information that provided a rational explanation for the alleged observations of alien bodies associated with the "Roswell Incident." Pursuant to the discovery, research efforts compared documented Air Force activities to the incredible claims of "flying saucers," "aliens" and seemingly unusual Air Force involvement. This in-depth examination revealed that these accounts, in most instances, were of actual Air Force activities but were seriously flawed in several major areas, most notably: the Air Force operations that inspired reports of "bodies" (in addition to being earthly in origin) did not occur in 1947. It appears that UFO proponents have failed to establish the accurate dates for these "alien" observations (in some instances by more than a decade) and then erroneously linked them to the actual Project *Mogul* debris recovery.

This report discusses the results of this further research and identifies the likely sources of the claims of "alien" bodies. Contrary to allegations that the Air Force has engaged in a cover-up and possesses dark secrets involving the Roswell claims, some of the accounts appear to be descriptions of unclassified and widely publicized Air Force scientific achievements. Other descriptions of bodies appear to be descriptions of actual incidents in which Air Force members were killed or injured in the line of duty.

The conclusions of the additional research are:

- Air Force activities which occurred over a period of many years have been consolidated and are now represented to have occurred in two or three days in July 1947.
- "Aliens" observed in the New Mexico desert were probably anthropomorphic test dummies that were carried aloft by U.S. Air Force high altitude balloons for scientific research.
- The "unusual" military activities in the New Mexico desert were high altitude research balloon launch and recovery operations. The reports of military units that always seemed to arrive shortly after the crash of a flying saucer to retrieve the saucer and "crew," were actually accurate descriptions of Air Force personnel engaged in anthropomorphic dummy recovery operations.
- Claims of bodies at the Roswell Army Air Field hospital were most likely a combination of two separate incidents:
  1. a 1956 KC-97 aircraft accident in which 11 Air Force members lost their lives; and,
  2. a 1959 manned balloon mishap in which two Air Force pilots were injured.

This report is based on thoroughly documented research supported by official records, technical reports, film footage, photographs, and interviews with individuals who were involved in these events.

Flying Saucer Crashes and Alien Bodies

The most puzzling and intriguing element of the complex series of events now known as the Roswell Incident, are the alleged sightings of alien bodies. The bodies turned what, for many years, was just another flying saucer story, into what many UFO proponents claim is the best case for extraterrestrial visitation of Earth. The importance of bodies and the assumptions made as to their origin is illustrated in a passage from a popular Roswell book:

> Crashed saucers are one thing, and could well turn out to be futuristic American or even foreign aircraft or missiles. But alien bodies are another matter entirely, and hardly subject to misinterpretation.

The 1994 Air Force report determined that project *Mogul* was responsible for the 1947 events. *Mogul* was an experimental attempt to acoustically detect suspected Soviet nuclear weapon explosions and ballistic missile launches. *Mogul* utilized acoustical sensors, radar reflecting targets and other devices attached to a train of weather balloons over 600 feet long. Claims that the U.S. Army Air Forces recovered a "flying disc" in 1947, were based primarily on the lack of identification of the radar targets, an element of weather equipment used on the long *Mogul* balloon train. The oddly constructed radar targets were found by a New Mexico rancher during the height of the first U.S. flying saucer wave in 1947. The rancher brought the remnants of the balloons and radar targets to the local sheriff after he allegedly learned of the broadcasted reports of flying discs. However, following some initial confusion at

Roswell Army Air Field, the "flying disc" was soon identified by Army Air Forces officials as a standard radar target.

From 1947 until the late 1970s, the Roswell Incident was essentially a non-story. The reports that existed contain only descriptions of mundane materials that originated from the Project *Mogul* balloon train—"tinfoil, paper, tape, rubber, and sticks." The first claim of "bodies" appeared in the late 1970s, with additional claims made during the 1980s and 1990s. These claims were usually based on anecdotal accounts of second-and third-hand witnesses collected by UFO proponents as much as 40 years after the alleged incident. The same anecdotal accounts that referred to bodies also described massive field operations conducted by the U.S. military to recover crash debris from a supposed extraterrestrial spaceship.

A technique used by some UFO authors to collect anecdotal corroboration for their theories was to solicit cooperating witnesses through newspaper announcements. For example, one such solicitation appeared in the *Socorro (N.M.) Defensor Chieftan* on November 4, 1992, on behalf of Don Berliner and Stanton T. Friedman the authors of the book *Crash at Corona*. This request solicited persons to provide information about the supposed crashes of alien spacecraft in the Socorro area.

In response to the newspaper announcement, two scientists central to the actual explanation of the "Roswell" events, Professor Charles B. Moore, a former U.S. Army Air Forces contract engineer, and Bernard D. Gildenberg, retired Holloman AFB Balloon Branch Physical Science Administrator and Meteorologist, came forward with pertinent information. According to Moore and Gildenberg, when they met with the authors their explanations that some of the Air Force projects they participated in were most likely responsible for the incident, they were summarily dismissed. The authors even went so far as to suggest that these distinguished scientists were participants in a multifaceted government cover-up to conceal the truth about the Roswell Incident. . . .

The "Crash Sites"

From 1947 until the late 1970s, the Roswell Incident was confined to one alleged crash site. This site, located on the Foster Ranch approximately 75 miles northwest of the city of Roswell, was the actual landing site of a Project *Mogul* balloon train in June 1947. The *Mogul* landing site is referred to in popular Roswell literature as the "debris field."

In the 1970s, the 1980s and throughout the 1990s, additional witnesses came forward with claims and descriptions of two other alleged crash sites. One of these sites was supposedly north of Roswell, the other site was alleged to have been approximately 175 miles northwest of Roswell in an area of New Mexico known as the San Agustin Plains. What distinguished the two new crash sites from the original debris field were accounts of alien bodies. . . .

Common Threads

Careful examination of the testimony revealed that primary witnesses of the two "crashed saucer" locations contained descriptions common to both.

These areas of commonality contained both general and detailed characteristics. However, before continuing, the accounts were carefully examined to determine if the testimony related by individual witnesses were of their own experiences and not a recitation of information given by other persons. While many aspects of the remaining accounts were judged to be similar, other aspects were found to be significantly different. The accounts on which the analysis is based were determined, in all likelihood, to have been independently obtained or observed by the witnesses.

General Similarities

The testimony presented for both crash sites generally followed the same sequence of events. The witnesses were in a rural and isolated area of New Mexico. In the course of their travels in this area, they came upon a crashed aerial vehicle. The witnesses then proceeded to the area of the crash to investigate and at some distance they observed strange looking "beings" that appeared to be crewmembers of the vehicle. Soon thereafter, a convoy of military vehicles and soldiers arrived at the site. Military personnel allegedly instructed the civilians to leave the area and forget what they had seen. As the witnesses left the area, the military personnel commenced with a recovery operation of the crashed aerial vehicle and "crew."

Detailed Similarities

Along with general similarities in the testimonies, there also existed a substantial amount of similar detailed descriptions of the "aliens," and the military vehicles and procedures allegedly used to recover them.

The first obvious similarity was the descriptions of the aliens. Mr. Gerald Anderson, an alleged witness of events at the site 175 miles northwest of Roswell, recalled, "I thought they were plastic dolls." Mr. James Ragsdale, an alleged witness of the site north of Roswell, stated, "They were using dummies in those damned things." Another alleged witness to a "crash" north of Roswell, Frank J. Kaufman, recalled that there was "talk" that perhaps an "experimental plane with dummies in it" was the source of the claims.

Additional similarities were also noted. Mr. Vern Maltais, a secondhand witness of the site 175 miles northwest of Roswell, described the hands of the "aliens" as, "They had four fingers." Anderson characterized the hands as, "They didn't have a little finger." He also described the heads of the aliens as "completely bald" while Maltais described them as "hairless." The uniforms of the aliens were independently described by Anderson as "one-piece suits . . . a shiny silverish-gray color" and by Maltais as "one-piece and gray in color." The date of this event was also not precisely known. Maltais recalled that it may have occurred "around 1950" and another secondhand witness, Alice Knight stated, "I don't recall the date." . . .

The Research Profile

When the general and specific similarities were combined, a profile emerged describing the event or activity that might have been observed. The profile, which contains elements common to at least two, and in some cases, all of the accounts, established a set of criteria used to determine what the witnesses may have observed. The profile is as follows:

a. An activity that, if viewed from a distance, would appear unusual.
b. An activity of which the exact date is not known.
c. An activity that took place in two rural areas of New Mexico.
d. An activity that involved a type of aerial vehicle with dolls or dummies that had four fingers, were bald, and wore one-piece gray suits.
e. An activity that required recovery by numerous military personnel and an assortment of vehicles that included a wrecker, a six-by-six, and a weapons carrier.

Based on this profile, research was begun to identify events or activities with these characteristics. Due to the location of the sites, attention was focused on Roswell AAF (renamed Walker AFB in 1948), White Sands Missile Range and Holloman AFB, N.M. The aerial vehicles assigned or under development at these facilities were aircraft, missiles, remotely-piloted drones, and high altitude balloons. The operational characteristics and areas where these vehicles flew were researched to determine if they played a role in the events described by the witnesses. . . .

High Altitude Balloon Dummy Drops

From 1953 to 1959, anthropomorphic dummies were used by the U.S. Force Aero Medical Laboratory as part of the high altitude aircraft escape projects *High Dive* and *Excelsior*. The object of these studies was to devise a method to return a pilot or astronaut to earth by parachute, if forced to escape at extreme altitudes.

Anthropomorphic dummies were transported to altitudes up to 98,000 feet by high altitude balloons. The dummies were then released for a period of free-fall while body movements and escape equipment performance were recorded by a variety of instruments. Forty-three high altitude balloon flights carrying 67 anthropomorphic dummies were launched and recovered throughout New Mexico between June 1954 and February 1959. Due to prevailing wind conditions, operational factors and ruggedness of the terrain, the majority of dummies impacted outside the confines of military reservations in eastern New Mexico, near Roswell, and in areas surrounding the Tularosa Valley in south central New Mexico. Additionally, 30 dummies were dropped by aircraft over White Sands Proving Ground, N.M. in 1953. In 1959, 150 dummies were dropped by aircraft over Wright-Patterson AFB, Ohio (possibly accounting for alleged alien "sightings" at that location). . . .

A number of these launch and recovery locations were in the areas where the "crashed saucer" and "space aliens" were allegedly observed.

Following the series of dummy tests, a human subject, test pilot Capt. Joseph W. Kittinger, Jr., now a retired Colonel, made three parachute jumps from high altitude balloons. Since free-fall tests from these unprecedented altitudes were extremely hazardous, they could not be accomplished by a human until a rigorous testing program using anthropomorphic dummies was completed. . . .

Summary

When the claims offered by UFO theorists to prove that an extraterrestrial spaceship and crew crashed and were recovered by the U.S. Air Force are compared to documented Air Force activities, it is reasonable to conclude, with a high degree of certainty, that the two "crashes" were actually descriptions of a launch or recovery of a high altitude balloon and anthropomorphic dummies. This conclusion was based on the remarkable similarities and independent corroboration between the witnesses who described *both* of the "crash sites." Statements such as "they was using dummies in those damned things" and a characterization of the crashed vehicle as, "I thought it was a blimp" are two of the many similarities. The extensive detailed descriptions provided by the witnesses, too numerous to be coincidental, were of the equipment, vehicles, procedures, and personnel of the Air Force research organizations who conducted the scientific experiments *High Dive* and *Excelsior.*

Though it is clear anthropomorphic dummies were responsible for these accounts, the specific locations of the events described was difficult, if not impossible, to determine since the witnesses were not specific. A witness to the "crash site" north of Roswell, Mr. James Ragsdale, was not certain of the actual location as evidenced by a change in his sworn testimony that moved the site many miles from its original location.

However, since Ragsdale reportedly lived or worked in the Roswell, Artesia, and Carlsbad, N.M. areas during the period when the dummies were used, it is likely he described one or more of the nine documented dummy recoveries in areas near there.

Reports of the other crash site, allegedly 175 miles northwest of Roswell on the San Agustin Plains, is likely based on descriptions of more than one launch and recovery of anthropomorphic dummies. Since one witness, Gerald Anderson, described procedures consistent with the launch *and* recovery of high altitude balloons, it is likely that he witnessed both of these activities, with at least one that included an anthropomorphic dummy payload.

The two secondhand witnesses to this "crash," Vern Maltais and Alice Knight, could have related descriptions from any of the dummy launch or landing sites. However, Maltais and Knight repeatedly described the impact location of the flying saucer as on the San Agustin Plains. One possible explanation is that the witnesses, in the 30 or more years since they were told the story by the original eyewitness, Mr. Barney Barnett, a soil conservation engineer who reportedly traveled extensively throughout New Mexico, may have confused San Agustin Plains with San Agustin Pass or San Agustin Peak, an area in the San Agustin Mountains of New Mexico. These areas are just outside the boundary of the White Sands Missile Range and the adjacent Jornada Test Range. Numerous anthropomorphic dummy balloon flights terminated and were recovered in this area. Furthermore, if the civilians witnessed dummy landings on either the White Sands Missile Range or the Jornada Test Range, both test areas and restricted U.S. Government reservations, then this explains why they may have been told to leave the landing site. In the popular Roswell scenarios, witnesses were allegedly instructed by military personnel to leave the area because they witnessed something of a highly classified nature. This would be unlikely since the witnesses described projects that utilized anthropomorphic dummies which were unclassified. It is likely, however, that if the witnesses ventured onto one of these ranges they were instructed to leave, not because of classified activities, but for their own safety.

These conclusions are supported by official files, technical reports, extensive photographic documentation, and the recollections of numerous former and retired Air Force members and civilian employees who conducted Projects *High Dive* and *Excelsior.* The descriptions examined here, provided by UFO theorists themselves, were so remarkably—and redundantly—similar to these Air Force projects that the only reasonable conclusion can be that the witnesses described these activities. . . .

Conclusion

When critically examined, the claims that the U.S. Army Air Forces recovered a flying saucer and alien crew in 1947, were found to be a compilation of many verifiable events. For the most part, the descriptions collected by UFO theorists were of actual operations and tests carried out by the U.S. Air Force in the 1950s. Despite the usual unsavory accusations by UFO proponents of cover-up, conspiracy, intimidation, etc., documented research revealed that many of the activities were actually historic scientific achievements of which the Air Force is very proud. However, other descriptions are believed to be distorted references to Air Force members who were killed or injured in the line of duty. The incomplete and inaccurate intermingling of these actual events were grounded in just enough fact to weave a sensational story, but cannot withstand close scrutiny when compared to official records.

To analyze reports of alien bodies that at first appeared to be so offbeat as to not be remotely based in fact, it was necessary to evaluate a wide range of books, interviews, videos, etc., that a less objective review might have rejected out of hand. Only through an inclusive evaluation of these sources were Air Force researchers able to understand the interconnectivity of the widely separated events believed responsible for this "incident." And, in opposition to critics who believe Air Force research involving this subject is anything but objective, this research relied almost exclusively on the descriptions *provided by the UFO proponents themselves.* When collected and examined, the actual statements of the witnesses—not the extraterrestrial interpretations of UFO proponents—indicated that something was very wrong. When these descriptions were compared to documented Air Force activities, they were much too similar to be a coincidence. Soon, it became apparent that the witnesses or the UFO proponents who liberally interpreted their statements were either 1) confused, or 2) attempting to perpetrate a hoax, believing that no serious efforts would ever be taken to verify their stories.

In preparing this report, attempts were made not to only explain what conclusions were reached, but *how* they were reached. This undertaking was to try to de-mystify the research process by outlining the simple and logical research techniques that identified the underlying actual events. In regard to statements of witnesses that were clearly descriptions of Air Force activities, such as those that described anthropomorphic dummies, these could be generously viewed as situational misunderstandings or even honest mistakes. Other descriptions, particularly those believed to be thinly veiled references to deceased or injured Air Force members, are difficult to view as naive misunderstandings. Any attempt to misrepresent or capitalize on tragic incidents in which Air Force members died or were injured in service to their country significantly alters what would otherwise be viewed as simple misinterpretations or honest mistakes.

Finally, after reviewing this report, some persons may legitimately ask why the Air Force expended time and effort to respond to mythical, if not comedic, allegations of recoveries of "flying saucers" and "space aliens." The answer to those persons is:

- Initially the Air Force was required to respond to an official request from the General Accounting Office.
- High altitude balloon research, aircraft escape systems, and other technologies that were misrepresented as part of the Roswell Incident, accounted for significant contributions to the knowledge of the atmosphere, to the quest for space flight, and to the defense of this nation. The U.S. Air Force is exceedingly proud of these accomplishments. Distorted and incomplete descriptions of these activities do not pay tribute to these important exploits or to the individuals who, often at great personal risk, boldly carried them out.
- A sobering reality of the mission of the U.S. Air Force, as evidenced by the aircraft mishaps described in this report, is that defending this nation is a dangerous profession. On a daily basis, members of the U.S. Air Force perform hazardous missions in many locations throughout the world. Unfortunately, these missions sometimes result in injuries or deaths. It is the right—and indeed the duty—of the Air Force to challenge those who attempt to exploit these human tragedies wherever, and whenever, they are discovered.
- The misrepresentations of Air Force activities as an extraterrestrial "incident" is misleading to the public and is simply an affront to the truth.

This comprehensive further examination of the so-called "Roswell Incident" found no evidence whatsoever of flying saucers, space aliens, or sinister government cover-ups. But, even if unintentionally, it did serve to highlight a series of events that embody the proud history of the finest air force in the world—the U.S. Air Force. The actual events examined here, rich in human and scientific triumph, tempered by the stark realities of the dangers of the Air Force mission, are but one small portion of that history. The many Air Force activities cobbled together in the ever changing collage that has become the "Roswell Incident," when examined in the clear light of historical research, revealed a remarkable chapter of the Air Force story. In the final analysis, this examination simply illustrates once again, that fact is indeed stranger, and often much more fascinating, than fiction.

SUPREME COURT ON RELIGION AND CONGRESSIONAL POWERS
June 25, 1997

A conflict between a small church and a local zoning board erupted into a major legal battle pitting federal powers against states' rights and Congress against the Supreme Court. On June 25 the Supreme Court ruled in favor of the zoning board, the states, and its own authority. By a 6–3 vote, the Court struck down the Religious Freedom Restoration Act, or RFRA, a law Congress had enacted in 1993 to make it easier for religious organizations or individuals to win exemptions from laws that incidentally infringed on their religious practices. The majority said Congress had unconstitutionally intruded both on judicial powers and on the state's traditional powers.

The ruling provoked an immediate and largely negative reaction from national legislators and a broad coalition of civil rights and religious organizations that had backed enactment of RFRA. The House had passed the legislation unanimously, while only three senators voted against it. A few months after the Court ruling, the church settled its problem with the zoning board. But the larger issues that dispute had raised still seemed unsettled as members of Congress and religious leaders sought ways around the ruling that might pass constitutional muster.

A Complicated Case

The case, City of Boerne v. Flores, Archbishop of San Antonio, *actually began with a Supreme Court ruling in 1990 in which it changed the standard it used for reviewing some cases under the First Amendment's ban on laws that prohibit free exercise of religion. The former standard had allowed states to limit that exercise only if they could demonstrate a compelling reason to do so. In the 1990 case of* Employment Division v. Smith, *the Court took a different tack; a five-justice majority led by Antonin Scalia ruled that laws that applied generally to everyone and were not intended to limit free expression of religion did not in fact violate the constitutional guarantee of religious liberty. In that particular case, the ruling meant that*

Oregon's narcotics laws did not violate the free exercise of religion by a Native American church that used peyote, an illegal hallucinogen, in its religious rituals.

That ruling was opposed by liberals and conservative alike in Congress, in religious organizations, and in civil rights groups. Together, they pushed a bill through Congress restoring the stricter judicial scrutiny test, which made it harder for states to deny exemptions for religious liberty claims. Under RFRA, no state or local law could "substantially burden a person's exercise of religion" unless the government could demonstrate that the burden furthered "a compelling governmental interest" and was "the least restrictive means of furthering that interest."

The passage of RFRA spawned a raft of legal challenges to state and local laws. An Amish group in Wisconsin escaped fines when it refused to post orange safety triangles on the backs of its horse-drawn buggies. Jehovah's Witnesses in California were exempted from taking loyalty oaths as a condition for holding state jobs. Other claims were more frivolous; a prison inmate argued that he had a right to conjugal visits based on the biblical command "to be fruitful and multiply."

One of the claims came from a small Catholic church in Boerne, Texas, outside San Antonio, that wanted to enlarge to accommodate a growing congregation. When the Reverend Anthony Cummins of St. Peter's Church applied for a building permit, however, he was turned down, because the church was within a historic district and any construction in that district had to be approved by the Historic Landmark Commission. Cummins appealed to his Archbishop in San Antonio and, through him, to the federal courts, claiming that the city's action violated the church's religious liberty rights under the recently enacted federal law. Boerne officials countered that RFRA was an unconstitutional limitation on the prerogatives of state and local governments. A federal district court agreed, but an appeals court reversed that ruling. With support from state and local governments throughout the country, the city appealed to the Supreme Court.

A Congressional Intrusion

Ruling in favor of the city, the Supreme Court said that Congress had exceeded the reach of its own powers in enacting RFRA. In support of its action, Congress had invoked Section 5 of the Fourteenth Amendment, which gave it the authority "to enforce by appropriate legislation" the amendment's guarantees of due process and equal protection. This was the same authority Congress had relied on in the past to enact civil rights laws such as the Voting Rights Act of 1965. But in the case of RFRA, Justice Anthony M. Kennedy wrote for the majority, Congress had not enforced the Fourteenth Amendment when it enacted RFRA, but instead tried to interpret the substance of the amendment. "Congress does not enforce a constitutional right by changing what the right is," Kennedy wrote. "It has been given the power 'to enforce,' not the power to determine what constitutes a constitutional violation." That power remains in the judiciary, Kennedy said.

The Religious Freedom Restoration Act, Kennedy continued, "cannot be considered remedial, preventive legislation, if those terms are to have any meaning." RFRA was "so out of proportion to a supposed remedial or preventive object that it cannot be understood as responsive to, or designed to prevent, unconstitutional behavior. It appears, instead, to attempt a substantive change in constitutional protections." Moreover, Kennedy said, by "displacing laws and prohibiting official actions of almost every description and regardless of subject matter," RFRA placed burdens on the states that far exceeded any pattern or practice of discrimination against religion that had ever been demonstrated. By subjecting any state law or action that had the incidental effect of making it more difficult for some people to practice their religion, Kennedy said, Congress had intruded considerably "into the states' traditional prerogatives and general authority to regulate for the health and welfare of their citizens."

Chief Justice William H. Rehnquist and Justices John Paul Stevens, Clarence Thomas, and Ruth Bader Ginsburg joined all of Kennedy's opinion; Scalia joined all but a part on the legislative history of the Fourteenth Amendment. Stevens also wrote a brief concurring opinion in which he maintained that RFRA also amounted to an unconstitutional "governmental preference of religion."

In dissent were Justices Sandra Day O'Connor, Stephen G. Breyer, and David H. Souter. O'Connor agreed with the majority that Congress had overstepped its powers when it enacted RFRA, but she felt strongly that the Court's decision in Smith, *the 1990 case that RFRA sought to circumvent, was in error and that the Court should have used the Boerne case to reconsider the* Smith *ruling. "In light of both our precedent and our Nation's tradition of religious liberty,* Smith *is demonstrably wrong," she declared, emphasizing her point by reading parts of her dissent from the bench. O'Connor had dissented in the* Smith *case. Breyer, who joined most of O'Connor's dissent, and Souter, who wrote separately, also urged that* Smith *be reconsidered.*

Reaction to Ruling Largely Negative

State and local governments hailed the decision and said it did not undermine any of the constitutional protections for the exercise of religion. But others questioned that assessment, arguing that unintended discrimination could be just as stifling to free exercise of religion as blatant discrimination. "A Jewish schoolboy's right to wear a yarmulke is impaired as much by a rule banning all hats in school as by a rule that specifically prohibits yarmulkes," said Melissa Rogers, associate general counsel for the Baptist Joint Committee. "Every church and synagogue, every religious person in America is going to be hurt by this decision," warned Oliver Thomas, counsel on religious liberty for the National Council of Churches.

Federal lawmakers from all points on the political spectrum also expressed outrage. Senate Judiciary Committee Chairman Orrin Hatch, a conservative Utah Republican, said the Court had "once again acted to push religion to the fringes of society," while Rep. Charles Schumer, a liberal New York Democrat who had sponsored RFRA in the House, said the Court had "turned its back on America's proud history of religious freedom." They and other legislators began to explore new ways to overcome the Smith *decision. Options under discussion included state laws to protect free exercise claims, a more narrowly focused federal law, or a constitutional amendment, which most admitted was a long shot. Another option, voiced by Sen. Edward M. Kennedy, D-Mass., was to find a case pending in a lower federal court that could be used to challenge the* Smith *standard.*

Following are excerpts from the majority and minority opinions in the City of Boerne v. Flores, Archbishop of San Antonio, *in which the Supreme Court, in a 6–3 decision issued June 25, 1997, overturned the Religious Freedom Restoration Act of 1993, ruling that Congress had exceeded its constitutional authority in enacting the law:*

No. 95-2074

City of Boerne, Petitioner
v.
P. F. Flores, Archbishop of
San Antonio and United States

On writ of certiorari to the United States Court of Appeals for the Fifth Circuit

[June 25, 1997]

JUSTICE KENNEDY delivered the opinion of the Court. [JUSTICE SCALIA joins all but Part III-A-1 of this opinion.]

A decision by local zoning authorities to deny a church a building permit was challenged under the Religious Freedom Restoration Act of 1993 (RFRA). The case calls into question the authority of Congress to enact RFRA. We conclude the statute exceeds Congress' power.

I

Situated on a hill in the city of Boerne, Texas, some 28 miles northwest of San Antonio, is St. Peter Catholic Church. Built in 1923, the church's structure replicates the mission style of the region's earlier history. The church seats about 230 worshippers, a number too small for its growing parish. Some 40 to 60 parishioners cannot be accommodated at some Sunday masses. In order to meet the needs of the congregation the Archbishop of San Antonio gave permission to the parish to plan alterations to enlarge the building.

A few months later, the Boerne City Council passed an ordinance authorizing the city's Historic Landmark Commission to prepare a preservation plan with proposed historic landmarks and districts. Under the ordinance, the

Commission must preapprove construction affecting historic landmarks or buildings in a historic district.

Soon afterwards, the Archbishop applied for a building permit so construction to enlarge the church could proceed. City authorities, relying on the ordinance and the designation of a historic district (which, they argued, included the church), denied the application. The Archbishop brought this suit challenging the permit denial in the United States District Court for the Western District of Texas.

The complaint contained various claims, but to this point the litigation has centered on RFRA and the question of its constitutionality. The Archbishop relied upon RFRA as one basis for relief from the refusal to issue the permit. The District Court concluded that by enacting RFRA Congress exceeded the scope of its enforcement power under §5 of the Fourteenth Amendment. (1995). The court certified its order for interlocutory appeal and the Fifth Circuit reversed, finding RFRA to be constitutional. (1996). We granted certiorari (1996) and now reverse.

II

Congress enacted RFRA in direct response to the Court's decision in *Employment Div., Dept. of Human Resources of Ore. v. Smith* (1990). There we considered a Free Exercise Clause claim brought by members of the Native American Church who were denied unemployment benefits when they lost their jobs because they had used peyote. Their practice was to ingest peyote for sacramental purposes, and they challenged an Oregon statute of general applicability which made use of the drug criminal. In evaluating the claim, we declined to apply the balancing test set forth in *Sherbert v. Verner* (1963), under which we would have asked whether Oregon's prohibition substantially burdened a religious practice and, if it did, whether the burden was justified by a compelling government interest. . . . The application of the *Sherbert* test, the *Smith* decision explained, would have produced an anomaly in the law, a constitutional right to ignore neutral laws of general applicability. The anomaly would have been accentuated, the Court reasoned, by the difficulty of determining whether a particular practice was central to an individual's religion. . . .

Four Members of the Court disagreed. They argued the law placed a substantial burden on the Native American Church members so that it could be upheld only if the law served a compelling state interest and was narrowly tailored to achieve that end. JUSTICE O'CONNOR concluded Oregon had satisfied the test, while Justice Blackmun, joined by Justice Brennan and Justice Marshall, could see no compelling interest justifying the law's application to the members.

These points of constitutional interpretation were debated by Members of Congress in hearings and floor debates. Many criticized the Court's reasoning, and this disagreement resulted in the passage of RFRA. Congress announced:

> "(1) [T]he framers of the Constitution, recognizing free exercise of religion as an unalienable right, secured its protection in the First Amendment to the Constitution;

"(2) laws 'neutral' toward religion may burden religious exercise as surely as laws intended to interfere with religious exercise;

"(3) governments should not substantially burden religious exercise without compelling justification;

"(4) in *Employment Division v. Smith* (1990), the Supreme Court virtually eliminated the requirement that the government justify burdens on religious exercise imposed by laws neutral toward religion; and

"(5) the compelling interest test as set forth in prior Federal court rulings is a workable test for striking sensible balances between religious liberty and competing prior governmental interests."

The Act's stated purposes are:

"(1) to restore the compelling interest test as set forth in *Sherbert v. Verne* (1963) and *Wisconsin v. Yoder* (1972) and to guarantee its application in all cases where free exercise of religion is substantially burdened; and

"(2) to provide a claim or defense to persons whose religious exercise is substantially burdened by government."

RFRA prohibits "[g]overnment" from "substantially burden[ing]" a person's exercise of religion even if the burden results from a rule of general applicability unless the government can demonstrate the burden "(1) is in furtherance of a compelling governmental interest; and (2) is the least restrictive means of furthering that compelling governmental interest." The Act's mandate applies to any "branch, department, agency, instrumentality, and official (or other person acting under color of law) of the United States," as well as to any "State, or ... subdivision of a State." The Act's universal coverage is confirmed in [one section], under which RFRA "applies to all Federal and State law, and the implementation of that law, whether statutory or otherwise, and whether adopted before or after [RFRA's enactment]." In accordance with RFRA's usage of the term, we shall use "state law" to include local and municipal ordinances.

III

A

Under our Constitution, the Federal Government is one of enumerated powers. The judicial authority to determine the constitutionality of laws, in cases and controversies, is based on the premise that the "powers of the legislature are defined and limited; and that those limits may not be mistaken, or forgotten, the constitution is written."

Congress relied on its Fourteenth Amendment enforcement power in enacting the most far reaching and substantial of RFRA's provisions, those which impose its requirements on the States. The Fourteenth Amendment provides, in relevant part:

"Section 1. . . . No State shall make or enforce any law which shall abridge the privileges or immunities of citizens of the United States; nor shall any State deprive any person of life, liberty, or property, without due process of law; nor deny to any person within its jurisdiction the equal protection of the laws. . . .

"Section 5. The Congress shall have power to enforce, by appropriate legislation, the provisions of this article."

The parties disagree over whether RFRA is a proper exercise of Congress' §5 power "to enforce" by "appropriate legislation" the constitutional guarantee that no State shall deprive any person of "life, liberty, or property, without due process of law" nor deny any person "equal protection of the laws."

In defense of the Act respondent contends, with support from the United States as *amicus*, that RFRA is permissible enforcement legislation. Congress, it is said, is only protecting by legislation one of the liberties guaranteed by the Fourteenth Amendment's Due Process Clause, the free exercise of religion, beyond what is necessary under *Smith*. It is said the congressional decision to dispense with proof of deliberate or overt discrimination and instead concentrate on a law's effects accords with the settled understanding that §5 includes the power to enact legislation designed to prevent as well as remedy constitutional violations. It is further contended that Congress' §5 power is not limited to remedial or preventive legislation.

All must acknowledge that §5 is "a positive grant of legislative power" to Congress. . . . Legislation which deters or remedies constitutional violations can fall within the sweep of Congress' enforcement power even if in the process it prohibits conduct which is not itself unconstitutional and intrudes into "legislative spheres of autonomy previously reserved to the States." For example, the Court upheld a suspension of literacy tests and similar voting requirements under Congress' parallel power to enforce the provisions of the Fifteenth Amendment, see U. S. Const., Amdt. 15, §2, as a measure to combat racial discrimination in voting, *South Carolina v. Katzenbach* (1966), despite the facial constitutionality of the tests. . . . We have also concluded that other measures protecting voting rights are within Congress' power to enforce the Fourteenth and Fifteenth Amendments, despite the burdens those measures placed on the States. [Citations omitted.] . . .

Congress' power under §5, however, extends only to "enforc[ing]" the provisions of the Fourteenth Amendment. The Court has described this power as "remedial." The design of the Amendment and the text of §5 are inconsistent with the suggestion that Congress has the power to decree the substance of the Fourteenth Amendment's restrictions on the States. Legislation which alters the meaning of the Free Exercise Clause cannot be said to be enforcing the Clause. Congress does not enforce a constitutional right by changing what the right is. . . .

While the line between measures that remedy or prevent unconstitutional actions and measures that make a substantive change in the governing law is not easy to discern, and Congress must have wide latitude in determining where it lies, the distinction exists and must be observed. There must be a congruence and proportionality between the injury to be prevented or remedied and the means adopted to that end. Lacking such a connection, legislation may become substantive in operation and effect. History and our case law support drawing the distinction, one apparent from the text of the Amendment.

1

The Fourteenth Amendment's history confirms the remedial, rather than substantive, nature of the Enforcement Clause. . . . [In a lengthy historical section, Kennedy noted that the first draft of what was to become the Fourteenth Amendment would have given Congress sweeping powers "to make all laws which shall be necessary and proper to secure to the citizens of each State all privileges and immunities of citizens in the several States, and to all persons in the several States equal protection in the rights of life, liberty, and property." The final version, giving Congress "power, to enforce by appropriate legislation, the provisions of this article," was adopted following criticism that the original proposal would have given Congress too much power.]

. . . The design of the Fourteenth Amendment has proved significant also in maintaining the traditional separation of powers between Congress and the Judiciary. The first eight Amendments to the Constitution set forth self-executing prohibitions on governmental action, and this Court has had primary authority to interpret those prohibitions. . . .

As enacted, the Fourteenth Amendment confers substantive rights against the States which, like the provisions of the Bill of Rights, are self-executing. The power to interpret the Constitution in a case or controversy remains in the Judiciary.

2

The remedial and preventive nature of Congress' enforcement power, and the limitation inherent in the power, were confirmed in our earliest cases on the Fourteenth Amendment. [Discussion of cases omitted.]

Recent cases have continued to revolve around the question of whether §5 legislation can be considered remedial. In *South Carolina v. Katzenbach*, we emphasized that "[t]he constitutional propriety of [legislation adopted under the Enforcement Clause] must be judged with reference to the historical experience . . . it reflects." There we upheld various provisions of the Voting Rights Act of 1965, finding them to be "remedies aimed at areas where voting discrimination has been most flagrant," and necessary to "banish the blight of racial discrimination in voting, which has infected the electoral process in parts of our country for nearly a century." . . . After *South Carolina v. Katzenbach*, the Court continued to acknowledge the necessity of using strong remedial and preventive measures to respond to the widespread and persisting deprivation of constitutional rights resulting from this country's history of racial discrimination. . . .

3

Any suggestion that Congress has a substantive, nonremedial power under the Fourteenth Amendment is not supported by our case law. In *Oregon v. Mitchell* [1970], a majority of the Court concluded Congress had exceeded its enforcement powers by enacting legislation lowering the minimum age of voters from 21 to 18 in state and local elections. The five Members of the

413

Court who reached this conclusion explained that the legislation intruded into an area reserved by the Constitution to the States. . . . Four of these five were explicit in rejecting the position that §5 endowed Congress with the power to establish the meaning of constitutional provisions. Justice Black's rejection of this position might be inferred from his disagreement with Congress' interpretation of the Equal Protection Clause. . . .

If Congress could define its own powers by altering the Fourteenth Amendment's meaning, no longer would the Constitution be "superior paramount law, unchangeable by ordinary means." . . . Under this approach, it is difficult to conceive of a principle that would limit congressional power. Shifting legislative majorities could change the Constitution and effectively circumvent the difficult and detailed amendment process contained in Article V.

We now turn to consider whether RFRA can be considered enforcement legislation under §5 of the Fourteenth Amendment.

B

Respondent contends that RFRA is a proper exercise of Congress' remedial or preventive power. The Act, it is said, is a reasonable means of protecting the free exercise of religion as defined by *Smith*. It prevents and remedies laws which are enacted with the unconstitutional object of targeting religious beliefs and practices. . . . To avoid the difficulty of proving such violations, it is said, Congress can simply invalidate any law which imposes a substantial burden on a religious practice unless it is justified by a compelling interest and is the least restrictive means of accomplishing that interest. If Congress can prohibit laws with discriminatory effects in order to prevent racial discrimination in violation of the Equal Protection Clause, then it can do the same, respondent argues, to promote religious liberty.

While preventive rules are sometimes appropriate remedial measures, there must be a congruence between the means used and the ends to be achieved. The appropriateness of remedial measures must be considered in light of the evil presented. Strong measures appropriate to address one harm may be an unwarranted response to another, lesser one.

A comparison between RFRA and the Voting Rights Act is instructive. In contrast to the record which confronted Congress and the judiciary in the voting rights cases, RFRA's legislative record lacks examples of modern instances of generally applicable laws passed because of religious bigotry. The history of persecution in this country detailed in the hearings mentions no episodes occurring in the past 40 years. [Citing testimony.] . . . Rather, the emphasis of the hearings was on laws of general applicability which place incidental burdens on religion. Much of the discussion centered upon anecdotal evidence of autopsies performed on Jewish individuals and Hmong immigrants in violation of their religious beliefs . . . , and on zoning regulations and historic preservation laws (like the one at issue here), which as an incident of their normal operation, have adverse effects on churches and synagogues. It is difficult to maintain that they are examples of legislation enacted or enforced due to animus or hostility to the burdened religious practices or that they indicate some widespread pattern of religious discrimination in this country. Congress' concern was with the incidental burdens imposed, not the object or purpose of the legislation. This lack of support in the legislative record, however, is not RFRA's most serious shortcoming. Judicial deference, in most cases, is based not on the state of the legislative record Congress compiles but "on due regard for the decision of the body constitutionally appointed to decide." As a general matter, it is for Congress to determine the method by which it will reach a decision.

Regardless of the state of the legislative record, RFRA cannot be considered remedial, preventive legislation, if those terms are to have any meaning. RFRA is so out of proportion to a supposed remedial or preventive object that it cannot be understood as responsive to, or designed to prevent, unconstitutional behavior. It appears, instead, to attempt a substantive change in constitutional protections. Preventive measures prohibiting certain types of laws may be appropriate when there is reason to believe that many of the laws affected by the congressional enactment have a significant likelihood of being unconstitutional. . . . Remedial legislation under §5 "should be adapted to the mischief and wrong which the [Fourteenth] [A]mendment was intended to provide against."

RFRA is not so confined. Sweeping coverage ensures its intrusion at every level of government, displacing laws and prohibiting official actions of almost every description and regardless of subject matter. RFRA's restrictions apply to every agency and official of the Federal, State, and local Governments. RFRA applies to all federal and state law, statutory or otherwise, whether adopted before or after its enactment. RFRA has no termination date or termination mechanism. Any law is subject to challenge at any time by any individual who alleges a substantial burden on his or her free exercise of religion.

The reach and scope of RFRA distinguish it from other measures passed under Congress' enforcement power, even in the area of voting rights. In *South Carolina v. Katzenbach*, the challenged provisions were confined to those regions of the country where voting discrimination had been most flagrant and affected a discrete class of state laws, i.e., state voting laws. Furthermore, to ensure that the reach of the Voting Rights Act was limited to those cases in which constitutional violations were most likely (in order to reduce the possibility of overbreadth), the coverage under the Act would terminate "at the behest of States and political subdivisions in which the danger of substantial voting discrimination has not materialized during the preceding five years." The provisions restricting and banning literacy tests, upheld in *Katzenbach v. Morgan* (1966) and *Oregon v. Mitchell* (1970) attacked a particular type of voting qualification, one with a long history as a "notorious means to deny and abridge voting rights on racial grounds." . . .

The stringent test RFRA demands of state laws reflects a lack of proportionality or congruence between the means adopted and the legitimate end to be achieved. If an objector can show a substantial burden on his free exercise, the State must demonstrate a compelling governmental interest and show that the law is the least restrictive means of furthering its interest.

415

Claims that a law substantially burdens someone's exercise of religion will often be difficult to contest.... Requiring a State to demonstrate a compelling interest and show that it has adopted the least restrictive means of achieving that interest is the most demanding test known to constitutional law.... Laws valid under *Smith* would fall under RFRA without regard to whether they had the object of stifling or punishing free exercise. We make these observations not to reargue the position of the majority in *Smith* but to illustrate the substantive alteration of its holding attempted by RFRA. Even assuming RFRA would be interpreted in effect to mandate some lesser test, say one equivalent to intermediate scrutiny, the statute nevertheless would require searching judicial scrutiny of state law with the attendant likelihood of invalidation. This is a considerable congressional intrusion into the States' traditional prerogatives and general authority to regulate for the health and welfare of their citizens.

The substantial costs RFRA exacts, both in practical terms of imposing a heavy litigation burden on the States and in terms of curtailing their traditional general regulatory power, far exceed any pattern or practice of unconstitutional conduct under the Free Exercise Clause as interpreted in *Smith*. Simply put, RFRA is not designed to identify and counteract state laws likely to be unconstitutional because of their treatment of religion. In most cases, the state laws to which RFRA applies are not ones which will have been motivated by religious bigotry. If a state law disproportionately burdened a particular class of religious observers, this circumstance might be evidence of an impermissible legislative motive. RFRA's substantial burden test, however, is not even a discriminatory effects or disparate impact test. It is a reality of the modern regulatory state that numerous state laws, such as the zoning regulations at issue here, impose a substantial burden on a large class of individuals. When the exercise of religion has been burdened in an incidental way by a law of general application, it does not follow that the persons affected have been burdened any more than other citizens, let alone burdened because of their religious beliefs. In addition, the Act imposes in every case a least restrictive means requirement—a requirement that was not used in the pre-*Smith* jurisprudence RFRA purported to codify—which also indicates that the legislation is broader than is appropriate if the goal is to prevent and remedy constitutional violations.

When Congress acts within its sphere of power and responsibilities, it has not just the right but the duty to make its own informed judgment on the meaning and force of the Constitution. This has been clear from the early days of the Republic. In 1789, when a Member of the House of Representatives objected to a debate on the constitutionality of legislation based on the theory that "it would be officious" to consider the constitutionality of a measure that did not affect the House, James Madison explained that "it is incontrovertibly of as much importance to this branch of the Government as to any other, that the constitution should be preserved entire. It is our duty." Were it otherwise, we would not afford Congress the presumption of validity its enactments now enjoy.

Our national experience teaches that the Constitution is preserved best when each part of the government respects both the Constitution and the proper actions and determinations of the other branches. When the Court has interpreted the Constitution, it has acted within the province of the Judicial Branch, which embraces the duty to say what the law is. When the political branches of the Government act against the background of a judicial interpretation of the Constitution already issued, it must be understood that in later cases and controversies the Court will treat its precedents with the respect due them under settled principles, including *stare decisis*, and contrary expectations must be disappointed. RFRA was designed to control cases and controversies, such as the one before us; but as the provisions of the federal statute here invoked are beyond congressional authority, it is this Court's precedent, not RFRA, which must control.

* * *

It is for Congress in the first instance to "determin[e] whether and what legislation is needed to secure the guarantees of the Fourteenth Amendment," and its conclusions are entitled to much deference. Congress' discretion is not unlimited, however, and the courts retain the power, as they have since *Marbury v. Madison* [1803], to determine if Congress has exceeded its authority under the Constitution. Broad as the power of Congress is under the Enforcement Clause of the Fourteenth Amendment, RFRA contradicts vital principles necessary to maintain separation of powers and the federal balance. The judgment of the Court of Appeals sustaining the Act's constitutionality is reversed.

It is so ordered.

JUSTICE STEVENS, concurring.

In my opinion, the Religious Freedom Restoration Act of 1993 (RFRA) is a "law respecting an establishment of religion" that violates the First Amendment to the Constitution.

If the historic landmark on the hill in Boerne happened to be a museum or an art gallery owned by an atheist, it would not be eligible for an exemption from the city ordinances that forbid an enlargement of the structure. Because the landmark is owned by the Catholic Church, it is claimed that RFRA gives its owner a federal statutory entitlement to an exemption from a generally applicable, neutral civil law. Whether the Church would actually prevail under the statute or not, the statute has provided the Church with a legal weapon that no atheist or agnostic can obtain. This governmental preference for religion, as opposed to irreligion, is forbidden by the First Amendment.

[Justice Scalia's concurring opinion omitted]

JUSTICE O'CONNOR, with whom JUSTICE BREYER joins except as to a portion of Part I, dissenting.

I dissent from the Court's disposition of this case. I agree with the Court that the issue before us is whether the Religious Freedom Restoration Act (RFRA) is a proper exercise of Congress' power to enforce §5 of the Fourteenth Amendment. But as a yardstick for measuring the constitutionality of RFRA, the Court uses its holding in *Employment Div., Dept. of Human Resources of Ore. v. Smith* (1990), the decision that prompted Congress to enact RFRA as a means of more rigorously enforcing the Free Exercise Clause. I remain of the view that *Smith* was wrongly decided, and I would use this case to reexamine the Court's holding there. Therefore, I would direct the parties to brief the question whether *Smith* represents the correct understanding of the Free Exercise Clause and set the case for reargument. If the Court were to correct the misinterpretation of the Free Exercise Clause set forth in *Smith*, it would simultaneously put our First Amendment jurisprudence back on course and allay the legitimate concerns of a majority in Congress who believed that *Smith* improperly restricted religious liberty. We would then be in a position to review RFRA in light of a proper interpretation of the Free Exercise Clause.

I

I agree with much of the reasoning set forth in Part III-A of the Court's opinion. Indeed, if I agreed with the Court's standard in *Smith*, I would join the opinion. As the Court's careful and thorough historical analysis shows, Congress lacks the "power to decree the substance of the Fourteenth Amendment's restrictions on the States." Rather, its power under §5 of the Fourteenth Amendment extends only to enforcing the Amendment's provisions. In short, Congress lacks the ability independently to define or expand the scope of constitutional rights by statute. Accordingly, whether Congress has exceeded its §5 powers turns on whether there is a "congruence and proportionality between the injury to be prevented or remedied and the means adopted to that end." This recognition does not, of course, in any way diminish Congress' obligation to draw its own conclusions regarding the Constitution's meaning. Congress, no less than this Court, is called upon to consider the requirements of the Constitution and to act in accordance with its dictates. But when it enacts legislation in furtherance of its delegated powers, Congress must make its judgments consistent with this Court's exposition of the Constitution and with the limits placed on its legislative authority by provisions such as the Fourteenth Amendment.

The Court's analysis of whether RFRA is a constitutional exercise of Congress' §5 power, set forth in Part III-B of its opinion, is premised on the assumption that *Smith* correctly interprets the Free Exercise Clause. This is an assumption that I do not accept. I continue to believe that *Smith* adopted an improper standard for deciding free exercise claims. In *Smith*, five Members of this Court—without briefing or argument on the issue—interpreted the Free Exercise Clause to permit the government to prohibit, without justification, conduct mandated by an individual's religious beliefs, so long as the prohibition is generally applicable. Contrary to the Court's holding in that case, however, the Free Exercise Clause is not simply an antidiscrimination principle that protects only against those laws that single out religious practice for unfavorable treatment. Rather, the Clause is best understood as an affirmative guarantee of the right to participate in religious practices and conduct without impermissible governmental interference, even when such conduct conflicts with a neutral, generally applicable law. Before *Smith*, our free exercise cases were generally in keeping with this idea: where a law substantially burdened religiously motivated conduct—regardless whether it was specifically targeted at religion or applied generally—we required government to justify that law with a compelling state interest and to use means narrowly tailored to achieve that interest. [Citation of cases omitted.]

The Court's rejection of this principle in *Smith* is supported neither by precedent nor, as discussed below, by history. The decision has harmed religious liberty. For example, a Federal District Court, in reliance on *Smith*, ruled that the Free Exercise Clause was not implicated where Hmong natives objected on religious grounds to their son's autopsy, conducted pursuant to a generally applicable state law. The Court of Appeals for the Eighth Circuit held that application of a city's zoning laws to prevent a church from conducting services in an area zoned for commercial uses raised no free exercise concerns, even though the city permitted secular not-for-profit organizations in that area. [Citation of other cases omitted.] These cases demonstrate that lower courts applying *Smith* no longer find necessary a searching judicial inquiry into the possibility of reasonably accommodating religious practice.

Stare decisis concerns should not prevent us from revisiting our holding in *Smith*. . . . I believe that, in light of both our precedent and our Nation's tradition of religious liberty, *Smith* is demonstrably wrong. Moreover, it is a recent decision. As such, it has not engendered the kind of reliance on its continued application that would militate against overruling it.

Accordingly, I believe that we should reexamine our holding in *Smith*, and do so in this very case. In its place, I would return to a rule that requires government to justify any substantial burden on religiously motivated conduct by a compelling state interest and to impose that burden only by means narrowly tailored to achieve that interest.

II

I shall not restate what has been said in other opinions, which have demonstrated that *Smith* is gravely at odds with our earlier free exercise precedents. . . . Rather, I examine here the early American tradition of religious free exercise to gain insight into the original understanding of the Free Exercise Clause—an inquiry the Court in *Smith* did not undertake. We have previously recognized the importance of interpreting the Religion Clauses in light of their history. . . .

The historical evidence casts doubt on the Court's current interpretation of the Free Exercise Clause. The record instead reveals that its drafters and ratifiers more likely viewed the Free Exercise Clause as a guarantee that government may not unnecessarily hinder believers from freely practicing their religion, a position consistent with our pre-*Smith* jurisprudence.

[O'Connor marshaled evidence from the history of the adoption of the First Amendment, colonial charters and state constitutions, and the practices of the colonies and early states to contend that the principle of religious "free exercise" was understood to mean that "government should, when possible, accommodate religious practice." She concluded by quoting writings from some of the early leaders, including George Washington, Thomas Jefferson, and James Madison:]

. . . Obviously, since these thinkers approached the issue of religious freedom somewhat differently, it is not possible to distill their thoughts into one tidy formula. Nevertheless, a few general principles may be discerned. Foremost, these early leaders accorded religious exercise a special constitutional status. The right to free exercise was a substantive guarantee of individual liberty, no less important than the right to free speech or the right to just compensation for the taking of property. . . .

Second, all agreed that government interference in religious practice was not to be lightly countenanced. Finally, all shared the conviction that " 'true religion and good morals are the only solid foundation of public liberty and happiness.' " . . . To give meaning to these ideas—particularly in a society characterized by religious pluralism and pervasive regulation—there will be times when the Constitution requires government to accommodate the needs of those citizens whose religious practices conflict with generally applicable law.

III

The Religion Clauses of the Constitution represent a profound commitment to religious liberty. Our Nation's Founders conceived of a Republic receptive to voluntary religious expression, not of a secular society in which religious expression is tolerated only when it does not conflict with a generally applicable law. As the historical sources discussed above show, the Free Exercise Clause is properly understood as an affirmative guarantee of the right to participate in religious activities without impermissible governmental interference, even where a believer's conduct is in tension with a law of general application. Certainly, it is in no way anomalous to accord heightened protection to a right identified in the text of the First Amendment. For example, it has long been the Court's position that freedom of speech—a right enumerated only a few words after the right to free exercise—has special constitutional status. Given the centrality of freedom of speech and religion to the American concept of personal liberty, it is altogether reasonable to conclude that both should be treated with the highest degree of respect.

Although it may provide a bright line, the rule the Court declared in *Smith* does not faithfully serve the purpose of the Constitution. Accordingly, I believe that it is essential for the Court to reconsider its holding in *Smith*—and to do so in this very case. I would therefore direct the parties to brief this issue and set the case for reargument.

I respectfully dissent from the Court's disposition of this case.

JUSTICE SOUTER, dissenting.

To decide whether the Fourteenth Amendment gives Congress sufficient power to enact the Religious Freedom Restoration Act, the Court measures the legislation against the free-exercise standard of *Employment Div., Dept. of Human Resources of Ore. v. Smith* (1990). For the reasons stated in my opinion in *Church of Lukumi Babalu Aye, Inc. v. Hialeah* (1993) (opinion concurring in part and concurring in judgment), I have serious doubts about the precedential value of the *Smith* rule and its entitlement to adherence. These doubts are intensified today by the historical arguments going to the original understanding of the Free Exercise Clause presented in JUSTICE O'CONNOR's opinion. . . . But without briefing and argument on the merits of that rule (which this Court has never had in any case, including *Smith* itself), I am not now prepared to join JUSTICE O'CONNOR in rejecting it or the majority in assuming it to be correct. In order to provide full adversarial consideration, this case should be set down for reargument permitting plenary reexamination of the issue. Since the Court declines to follow that course, our free-exercise law remains marked by an "intolerable tension," and the constitutionality of the Act of Congress to enforce the free-exercise right cannot now be soundly decided. I would therefore dismiss the writ of certiorari as improvidently granted, and I accordingly dissent from the Court's disposition of this case.

[Justice Breyer's dissent omitted]

SURVEY OF ADULT ATTITUDES ABOUT CHILDREN AND TEENS
June 26, 1997

At a time when the well-being of children was not only the focus of great public interest but used to justify adoption of public programs, a major survey of adult attitudes about children uncovered an antagonism toward teenagers and younger children that went beyond the normal adult frustration with the antics of their offspring. The survey, conducted by the nonprofit research and education group Public Agenda, found that most Americans were troubled by the lack of character and values they see in children. When asked what first came to mind when they thought about today's teenagers, two-thirds of those surveyed voiced negative adjectives—"rude," "irresponsible," and "wild." These attitudes even extended to children aged five to twelve. More than half the adults surveyed characterized children this age as "undisciplined," "rude," and "spoiled." Only 37 percent of adults said that today's children would eventually make this a better country.

If they were of one mind about what was wrong with modern youth, the adults were also largely agreed on the causes of and potential solutions to the problems. Most Americans "refuse to give up on kids." According to the survey researchers, American adults "care deeply" about the well-being of children, which they said was "of paramount importance to our society."

Other studies released throughout the year reinforced various aspects of the Public Agenda survey. A nationwide survey conducted by the Harvard School of Public Health found that adults considered drugs, crime, and a breakdown in home life—all social ills—to be the most serious problems facing children. A major federal report on the well-being of the nation's children found positive trends in overall health and education even as specific trends, such as smoking and use of drugs, showed little improvement. Finally, a large survey of teenagers found that those who believed that they were loved and understood by their parents and teachers were more likely to avoid risky behavior than those adolescents who did not have such positive relationships.

"Kids These Days"

The Public Agenda survey, entitled "Kids These Days: What Americans Really Think About the Next Generation," was the initial phase of a multi-year research effort intended to find out how typical Americans defined the problems facing children and adolescents and what, if anything, could be done to resolve them. The results showed a sharp change from earlier surveys both in the degree of alarm adults expressed about teenage behavior and the extension of that alarm to the behavior of younger children. These feelings were reflected about equally among whites, African Americans, and Hispanics and between parents and nonparents. Adults applied their criticisms about equally to all children, regardless of whether they were poor, middle-class, or affluent. "Adults are not confused, and they're not ambivalent," said Deborah Wadsworth, the executive director of Public Agenda. "Instead, they're virtually riveted by the need to teach kids integrity, ethical behavior, respect, civility, compassion, all those characteristics without which these children will never become responsible adults and our society can't function."

Adults, including parents, held parents responsible for the decline in their children's behavior. They acknowledged the difficulty of rearing children in today's world where both parents often worked and where drugs, crime, sexual and violent scenes in the media, and poor public schools often undermined parental efforts. But they still laid most of the blame at parents' doorsteps, saying they failed to teach children right from wrong. Too often, parents had children before they were ready, spoiled them with presents rather than giving them guidance, and failed to discipline them, the survey found.

Despite their harsh criticisms, the adults indicated that they cared deeply about the well-being of children and were "stubbornly optimistic" about the chances of helping even the most troubled teenagers. Two-thirds of the adults said improving public schools would be an effective way to help young people; by "improvement" they meant that schools should teach standards of behavior and values as well as academic subjects. Eighty-three percent said schools should teach children to be responsible, on time, and disciplined; 78 percent said schools should instill the value of hard work; and 74 percent said schools should teach honesty and tolerance. Adults also said that more after-school programs, greater participation in organizations such as the Boy Scouts, more flexible work hours for parents, and curfews would also be effective ways to keep children busy and out of trouble.

What the adults did not think would be effective was more government programs. Most such programs were aimed at ensuring the physical and economic well-being of children, but those issues were not as important to the adults surveyed as the moral well-being of the children, which they thought government could do little about. "Even when it comes to low-income, at-risk kids," adults were doubtful that government interventions could help; about half said they thought that parents who could benefit from such programs failed to take advantage of them.

Wadsworth said these findings should serve as a warning to public and private policymakers. Adults were "focused like a laser beam on the question of character," she said, "and if the political leadership and policy initiatives don't reflect that, they're out of alignment with the concerns the public has."

The survey, which was released June 26, entailed two separate telephone surveys conducted in December 1996, the first a random selection of 2,000 adults, and the second a random selection of 600 twelve- to seventeen-year-olds. The study also included six focus groups around the country and dozens of follow-up telephone calls to people who had completed the survey. Ronald McDonald House Charities underwrote the survey, saying it expected to use the survey's findings to guide its $100 million commitment in giving to children's programs. The survey was also conducted on behalf of the Advertising Council, a nonprofit organization that sponsored public service advertising. The council said it would use the findings to help it develop a ten-year effort to mobilize volunteer campaigns to improve children's circumstances throughout the country.

Other Studies of Children's Well-Being

A survey of 90,000 adolescents, published September 10, confirmed the importance of parents in teenagers' lives. Results from that survey showed that teenagers who felt strong emotional attachments to their parents were less likely to engage in risky behaviors—such as smoking, drugs, or early sex—than teenagers who did not feel such attachments. Positive relationships with teachers were found to have similar effects. Time spent with parents helped reduce emotional distress among teenagers, but feeling understood and loved by their parents was a far more powerful antidote. The study also found that the presence of parents in the home at "key" times— meals, after school, and bedtime—reduced the likelihood that teens would smoke, drink, or use marijuana, while clear parental disapproval of sexual activity and contraception made teens less likely to become sexually active. The presence of a gun in the house, even if locked away, increased the likelihood that a teen would think about or attempt suicide or get involved in violent behavior. The findings, reported in the Journal of the American Medical Association, *were the first from the National Longitudinal Study of Adolescent Health, a $25 million federal study that surveyed teenagers in grades 7 through 12. The data were to be analyzed in more depth over several more years.*

Yet another survey appeared to lend some support to the Public Agenda finding that traditional concerns about child health care and economic wellbeing had been supplanted in the public's eye by concerns about morals and values. A Harvard School of Public Health survey, released in December, asked respondents to name the two or three most serious problems facing children. More than half (56 percent) listed drugs, followed by crime (24 percent), the breakdown of home life and related problems (22 percent), and poor quality education (17 percent). "Health care, poverty, alcohol and smoking didn't even make it onto the list," said Ruby P. Hearn, senior vice president of the Robert Wood Johnson Foundation, which funded the study. "The public agenda as revealed in this survey is much narrower than we think it needs to be." The researchers were particularly surprised that poverty was not mentioned more often; 20 percent of all children lived below the poverty line. They also were surprised that so few people expressed concern about health care at a time when the states were considering legislation to extend Medicaid to uninsured children. "What this means is that if a big push isn't made to increase public support for children's health care, any hope of extending coverage to the majority of the 11 million uninsured children could fizzle out at the state level," said Robert J. Blendon, a professor of health policy and political analysis and the director of the survey.

The Federal Interagency Forum on Child and Family Statistics on July 2 published a compilation of twenty-five key indicators on the well-being of children. These data showed overall improvements in health and education. Fewer children were going hungry, more parents were reading to their children, and child and infant mortality was declining. But the numbers of adolescents who used drugs, smoked, or drank alcohol appeared to be either holding steady or increasing. Most of the indicators had been published earlier in other formats, but this compilation represented the first time all of them had been pulled together in one place. "For the first time, the Federal government, paralleling to a degree the way it reports on the nation's economic status, is taking a composite look at how our nation's children are faring," said Duane Alexander, director of the National Institute of Child Health and Human Development. The report, "America's Children: Key National Indicators of Well-Being," was expected to be published annually and would provide "a valuable tool for tracking the condition of children" and helping to "inform policy decisions that will affect them," Alexander said.

Following are excerpts from "Kids These Days: What Americans Really Think About the Next Generation," a survey on adult attitudes about teenagers and children, published June 26, 1997 by Public Agenda:

Introduction

A recent survey by Princeton Survey Research Associates showed that almost three-quarters of the American people think that young people with a poor education, poor job prospects, and problematic values now pose a greater danger to the United States than any threat from abroad. Thankfully, the end of the Cold War has far reduced public fears of foreign enemies, so it is hardly surprising to find people focused so definitively on a domestic concern. But the image evoked by this finding is somehow disturbing. Are Americans *really* afraid of the next generation? Do they *really* see the country's young people—or some group of them at least—as "the enemy within?"

Plenty of Symptoms

Grousing about the next generation, of course, is a time-honored activity among older citizens, and surveys have captured public concern about teens gets in particular for decades. However, the complaints of adults are not the only sign that all is not well among the nation's young. Drug use is on the rise among adolescents. Teen suicide has increased. One in five of the nation's children live in poverty. About 1 in 3 American children do not live in an intact two-parent household. Half the country's public high school students say drugs and violence are serious problems where they go to school. Seven in ten say cheating on tests and assignments is commonplace.

There are many indicators that something is wrong. Political leaders, along with liberal and conservative advocates, have offered competing diagnoses and solutions. But how do typical Americans think about and define the problems facing the country's children and teens? What, if anything, do most Americans think can be done to improve the condition and prospects for the nation's youth?

The Public Agenda Study

To find out, Public Agenda, a nonprofit research and education group based in New York, conducted an in-depth study of the views of the general public, along with those of African American, Hispanic, and white parents. The study also included focus groups in New Jersey, Colorado, and California and a shorter survey of youngsters themselves—those between the ages of 12 and 17. . . . *Kids These Days* is our report on the major findings from this research.

To our knowledge, Public Agenda's research is the most wide-ranging and in-depth examination of Americans' views on this issue conducted in recent years. It was underwritten by Ronald McDonald House Charities and conducted on behalf of The Advertising Council, both organizations having committed themselves to ambitious and sustained efforts to improve the lives of children. Ronald McDonald House Charities will use findings from the Public Agenda study to guide its $100 million commitment in giving to children's programs. The Advertising Council will do likewise as it launches a decade-long effort to mobilize citizens to volunteer their own communities in efforts on behalf of children and teens.

A Specific and Clear Message

But the implications of this research are far broader. As we describe in detail in the following pages, the public has a quite specific analysis of what troubles the nation's youth and a surprisingly clear set of recommendations. The findings show a public that is anguished about our young people but not bereft of ideas about how to help them. Americans see the potential for solutions in the public schools, law enforcement, community groups, religious bodies, charitable activities, and—albeit much less hopefully—government and the media. What's more, there is a widely-shared—and strongly-felt—definition of the problem. Americans from around the country, from different walks of life, from different racial and ethnic groups, with children and without them, are in ample agreement on what could and should be done.

As an opinion research organization, Public Agenda is continually interested, even fascinated, by Americans' views on the challenges facing today's world. What Americans have to say about the nation's children and youth, we are convinced, is more than merely interesting. *Kids These Days* charts a course for designing public and private policies and programs for children that can win broad public support. More important, this study—if opinion leaders will listen carefully—offers the key to rebuilding Americans' confidence in the future.

FINDING ONE: The Moral Meltdown

Americans are convinced that today's adolescents face a crisis—not in their economic or physical well-being but in their values and morals. Most Americans look at today's teenagers with misgiving and trepidation, viewing them as undisciplined, disrespectful, and unfriendly.

Ask Americans to pick one overriding national concern, and the chances are good they will pick kids. More than half of Americans surveyed by Public Agenda (52%) think that helping youngsters get a good start in life ought to be society's most important goal, even considering such competing priorities as protecting citizens from crime (18%) and creating more jobs (16%).

The concern is not youngsters' health problems, safety, or poverty rates. Rather, Americans are deeply troubled by the character and values exhibited by young people today. More than 6 in 10 adults (61%) think that youngsters' failure to learn such values as honesty, respect, and responsibility is a very serious problem. And almost half (49%) believe the same about fewer families teaching their youngsters religious faith and values. . . .

Many children's advocates fear that an aging society, a society that prizes independence and self-sufficiency, has begun to care less about its young people. They point to high rates of youth poverty and other indicators of deprivation and call on Americans to back measures to improve youngsters' material well-being. This study shows—in finding after finding across all demographic groups—that Americans are intensely concerned about young people, but their concerns center directly on youngsters' moral well-being. Thus, even as advocates worry about children and teens growing up with physical and material deficits, Americans worry about deficits in character and values.

Rude, Irresponsible, and Wild

When asked what first comes to their minds when they think about today's teenagers, two-thirds of Americans (67%) immediately reach for negative adjectives such as "rude," "irresponsible," and "wild." Another 16% point to social problems teens face, such as lack of guidance. Only a handful (12%) describe teens positively, using terms such as "smart" or "helpful." These descriptions point to the automatic, almost invisible evaluations people commonly make about teenagers. Are they polite or rude? Conscientious or irresponsible? Are they behaving themselves or are they acting out? Are they neat or sloppy? Most people seem to have made up their minds, and the answers are not good . . . .

Idle Hands

These initial impressions are far more than thoughtless, top-of-the-head reactions. In question after question, Americans express dissatisfaction with the demeanor and behavior of teenagers. Half say it's very common for teens to get into trouble because they have too much free time. "Teenagers used to have chores to do, and they learned how to work," said an Illinois man. "Teens today aren't being taught how to work." Four in ten Americans (41%) say it's very common to find teenagers who have poor work habits and lack self-discipline.

For many adults, teen behavior is more than disappointing; it can be intimidating. Three in ten say teens who are "wild and disorderly in public" are very common. "I know older adults who are afraid when a teenager walks past them," said a woman from Washington state. . . .

To Know Them Is to Love Them?

These are harsh and sobering judgments. But are they really judgments, or just vague impressions casually gathered from watching television or walking past the local school? . . .

A closer look at the survey results shows that people who have regular contact with teens are as critical of them as everyone else, if not more so. Two-thirds (65%) of those with a lot of contact describe teenagers disapprovingly. More than half (54%) believe teens get into trouble because they have too much time on their hands—versus 49% among those with little or no teen contact. And those who have a lot of contact with teens are slightly more likely than others to think they have poor work habits (45% versus 38%).

Nor are people who have a lot of contact with teens more likely to think they treat others with respect—14% say so, versus 11% among those with little or no teen contact. Similarly, they're not more likely to view teens as friendly and helpful (14% versus 11%). Thus, even those who have extensive experience with teenagers are reluctant to sing their praises.

Even Parents Agree

One would expect the parents of teenagers to be most likely to view teens in a positive light, but their judgment is identical to that of everyone else. Forty-five percent of parents who have teens at home say teens get into trouble because they have too much time on their hands; 43% say teens have poor work habits; 3 in 10 say teens are wild and disorderly. Ask parents about positive traits and again their responses echo those of the general public. Only 12% say teens are friendly and helpful, and only 9% say teens treat people with respect. Parents probably—hopefully—have more sympathetic and complimentary views of their own teenagers, but they have little praise for the other teens they come across.

The Root-Cause: A Lack of Values

The public's widespread disappointment with the character of today's teens (including their work ethic, behavior, and sense of responsibility) has resulted in an intense focus—a virtual preoccupation—on morals and values.

Why is the public so preoccupied with the character and values of America's teenagers? First and foremost, this focus reflects an over-arching public concern that extends to society as a whole. Asked to choose between two causes for the problems facing society today, 51% say they mainly stem from a decline in moral values; only 37% attribute them to economic and financial pressures on the family.

Values and character are, for most people, the root cause explanation for why things go wrong or right throughout society. For the public, values and character explain why some people give in to drugs and others resist, why some people get stuck in welfare and others climb out, why some people commit crime and others lead productive lives. The public believes values are a vaccine: if you inoculate teens with them, they will be able to resist the world's many troubles and traps. "You have got to instill values in them now at home," said a New York mother. "So that when they go out in the street and somebody comes up to them and says, 'Hey, try some,' they say 'No, I know what that does to you.' " . . .

FINDING TWO: It's Not Just Teens

Public dissatisfaction and disapproval extend beyond the nation's teenagers. Even young children are viewed in a negative light. Many Americans think children are spoiled and out of control, not friendly, helpful, or engaging. And people apply these criticisms to children across a broad economic spectrum, to children from disadvantaged backgrounds as well as children from the middle and affluent classes.

This study would hardly break new ground if all it reported were adult concerns over teenage behavior. After all, complaints that young people are sullen, adrift, hard to understand, and unaccountably attracted to ugly music and even uglier styles of dress are hardly original with this generation. Does this bleak view of America's youth simply reflect every generation's "kids-these-days" complaint?

Seven Going on Twenty-One

Public criticism is not limited to teenage behavior. Americans have surprisingly harsh things to say even about younger children, defined in this study as those older than 5 but not yet in their teens. When asked the first thing that comes to mind when describing today's children, 53% offer negative descriptions, with many people characterizing them as lacking discipline and being rude or spoiled. Only 23% of the respondents had positive things to say about children—that they were curious or enthusiastic, for example. These top-of-mind negative responses are uncomfortably close to what people say about teens. . . .

Children Who Have Too Much

What is significant and perhaps surprising is that children today do not inspire an instinctively positive feeling from adults. Instead, adults express widespread, and often harsh, disapproval of children between 5 and 12 years old. For example, nearly half the public (48%) thinks it is very common for children to be spoiled and not appreciate what they have.

When Americans complain about spoiled kids, they seem to have two thoughts in mind. One is the notion that children have become mindlessly acquisitive, mini-consumers who demand—and get—electronic gadgets and designer clothes and sneakers, things they have come to expect as a matter of right. "With all the technology, kids always want more," remarked a weary father in Denver. "It's 'I want, I want, I want.'" Americans increasingly suspect that a consumer ethic among the middle class is driving a never-ending chase of "things" with the result that children are simply overindulged. People also worry that when much is available to children so easily, bad habits form and the wrong values are conveyed. Three in ten Americans say children who are lazy and do not apply themselves are very common. A non-parent from New Jersey complained: "They have no sense of values. I think that the more you give, the more they want."

Getting No Respect

Another major shortcoming adults see in today's children is how they behave in public and how they relate to adults. Only 12% find it very common for children to treat people with respect, while only 17% consider it usual for children to be friendly and helpful toward their neighbors. About 3 in 10 Americans (31%) say it's very common for children to be out of control in public areas such as restaurants or the movies. One frequently-expressed theme—particularly from parents in focus groups—was the need for adult authority, for setting limits and standards of behavior. "The problem today is that a lot of kids are not held accountable for what they do, and there are no consequences," said a Denver mother. "If you don't have any consequences for your behavior, then you don't learn anything."

The stakes are high, many adults believe, because if such problems are left to fester they will only become more serious. "You have to train the younger kids first," said a New Jersey man. "If you let them [get] out of control, as they get older, their problems get bigger." There was also the sense in the focus groups that children are growing up faster and that the age of innocence is shrinking. What's more, increased sophistication is not often seen as a good thing. . . .

Rich Kids, Poor Kids

The public's preoccupation with youngsters learning the wrong values is applied widely, and not at all targeted at children from the "wrong side of the tracks." Nine in 10 (91%) say the failure to learn values is widespread; only 8% say it mostly affects youngsters from disadvantaged backgrounds.

Speaking from Experience

As was the case with teenagers, these perceptions hold even among adults who have a lot of contact with children (47%). Half of the adults in this category say that spoiled children are very common, about the same percentage as those who have little or no contact with children (48%). People who have a lot of contact with children are slightly more likely to describe children as out of control (35% versus 28%). At the same time, they are also slightly more likely to describe children who are friendly and helpful to their neighbors as very common (20% versus 14%).

Nor are the parents of children aged 5 to 12, who presumably have the most contact with kids this age, noticeably upbeat. In fact, they are as likely as the general public to say that children this age are spoiled (44%), lazy (30%), or out of control (28%). And they are not substantially more positive than the general public about whether children treat people with respect (14%) or are friendly and helpful (22%).

And the World Will Be a Better Place?

The public's judgments are not entirely negative. For example, about 3 in 10 Americans (32%) think that bright and eager-to-learn children are very common in our society. When Americans look at our nation's children, however, they generally conclude that something is wrong with the values they display and the standards of behavior they exhibit.

Across history and across various cultures, people have often considered the next generation as the best hope for the future. But for Americans in the 1990s, this bedrock belief seems to have been shaken to the core. Doubts start with teenagers and carry over to children; they apply to middle class kids as well as the disadvantaged. It's no wonder that only 37% of Americans believe that when today's children grow up, they will make this country a better place; while almost 6 in 10 (58%) believe children won't make a difference, or will make it even worse. The traditional ideal of children as a source of renewal and hope has, for the majority of the American public, been seriously undermined.

FINDING THREE: Careless Parents

Americans believe that parents are fundamentally responsible for the disappointing state of today's youth. People say parents fail to teach youngsters right from wrong and pass on the values children need to learn in order to become productive members of society. Too often, people say, today's parents have children before they're ready; give them presents instead of guidance and attention; and fail to provide necessary discipline. Even parents themselves from all income, ethnic, and racial backgrounds agree. . . .

So Where Are the Parents?

If children and teens fail to learn right from wrong, are spoiled, or misbehave—which the data clearly show is what people believe—Americans look first to the parents. Many Americans think children and teens are troubled and out of control because too many parents fail to do their job. People accept the notion advanced by John Locke—that at birth humans are a blank slate who develop attitudes and character through education and experience. Children are not born with a good or bad mindset, people believe; they absorb it. . . .

Falling Down on the Job

Since the public believes parents are the key to how youngsters turn out, it is not surprising to find their complaints about children and teens echoed in their complaints about parents. Only about 1 in 5 Americans (22%) say it's very common to find parents who are good role models for their kids. Half complain that parents fail to provide discipline. More than half (55%) believe parents break up marriages too easily instead of trying to stay together [for] the sake of their children. More than 6 in 10 (63%) say it's very common for parents to have children before they are ready to take responsibility for them. "Parents need to be mature themselves before they have children," said an Iowa woman.

Those who believe today's children and teens are spoiled and materialistic attribute these same faults to their parents. Half of those surveyed find it very common for parents to equate buying things for children to caring for them. "The fact is that children are learning values now—everyday," said an Ohio man with derision. "They're being taught: 'Number one is me.' and 'Spend and buy things and accumulate things.' The fact that kids need to have $200 Nikes shouldn't surprise anyone." Virtually half the public (49%) believe it's very common for parents to spoil their kids. . . .

Spare the Love, Ruin the Child

Much of the public's criticisms of parents might be taken to be a call to return to an old-fashioned, paternalistic, severe mode of parenting. But people's belief that children need values and discipline does not mean people are ready to return to the austere childrearing practices of the past. To the contrary, people believe parents must talk with their children, show interest in their lives, give them love, and put their interests first. "Dr. Spock" norms have penetrated most Americans' consciousness and carry more than a faddish, feel-good appeal. People believe that love and guidance are needed to raise healthy children who will become responsible and caring adults. Indeed, one fear is that if the family fails to provide love and guidance, young people will seek it elsewhere. . . .

And here again is an area where the public feels parents often fall short. Half the public (51%) think that parents who don't know how to communicate with their kids are very common. "You have to spend quality time with the child," said a New York woman. "Just talk. 'What happened today? I am here for you. Whatever it is, now is the time, let's talk.' That does not happen anymore." Said a Utah man, "Just being with your kids as much as you can is important. Help them with their homework. Explain things to them."

Parents: We Can't Tell Them No

Interestingly, the very people closest to this issue—parents themselves—are as critical of parents as everyone else. About two-thirds of parents (65%) say it's common for parents to have children before they are ready to take responsibility for them. . . .

Half the parents surveyed think it's very common for parents not to do their job on discipline. Only 1 in 5 (19%) say it's very common for parents to be good role models and teach their kids right from wrong. . . .

About half (51%) of the parents surveyed believe it's very common for parents to think that buying things for kids means the same thing as caring for them.

Many parents also agree that parents are perhaps overly sensitive to criticisms or suggestions about their children: approximately 4 in 10 (42%) say parents who resent advice about their kids are very common. A California mother thought parents were defensive because of ". . . a sense of guilt. Parents are not around their kids as much . . . so they become more protective of their child. So if someone else tries to come in and even says something. . . . "

Parental Authority

Many parents acknowledge that far too many of their number fail to fulfill their responsibilities to their children. But many also complained that society has undermined their authority as parents, particularly with regard to discipline. In nearly every focus group, at least one respondent brought up the subject of corporal punishment as an example of how society second-guesses parents and looks over their shoulders. There is very little evidence in this study that most parents see spanking as the "be all and end all" of raising well-behaved children. But many spoke with some anguish about the more complicated nature of parental authority today.

Are Kids Priority One?

While some parents are ready to shift some of the blame to society, many Americans believe, in contrast, that too many parents put their own personal needs and challenges ahead of the needs of their children. Fifty-five percent of Americans say parents break up their marriages too easily, instead of trying to stay together for their kids. "There are a lot of single-parent homes, and children are alone all the time," said a New Jersey woman explaining why kids are in trouble. "I think the big problem is so many divorces and single mother families that are having a tough time," said a Utah man. By virtually identical numbers, parents themselves agree with all of these assessments.

And, finally, there is also a sense that parents take on too many activities that needlessly compete with their kids for attention. "I think kids are in real crisis, and parents just don't get it," said a woman from Georgia. "They're missing the point that you just can't do effective parenting when you are this spread out, involved in so many things. Quality time, one-on-one time—I think they're missing it."

Many parents, by their own report, seem tentative and uncertain in matters of discipline and authority, and many believe that society is increasingly likely to question their judgment in this area.

FINDING FOUR: Mitigating Circumstances

Americans acknowledge it is tougher to be a parent or a child in today's world. They recognize that more than ever, parents—and especially mothers—must work hard and sacrifice for their children. Americans also believe today's youngsters face threats from society that can undermine their parents' best efforts. People are extremely concerned about ubiquitous threats endangering all kids: drugs and crime; sex and violence in the media; and public schools that often fail to deliver education in a safe and orderly environment.

Many Americans have strong criticisms of the job parents are doing. But these criticisms coexist—simultaneously and side-by-side—with substantial levels of empathy and understanding for what people see as the enormously difficult and challenging undertaking that raising children has become. These coexisting viewpoints may appear to be contradictory, but ordinary citizens seem to recognize the complexity of the situation, and the sometimes tumultuous circumstances of modern life. Instead of choosing to simply condemn parents or to view them as totally helpless or blameless, Americans seem to simultaneously subscribe to two truths: These are tough times—maybe the toughest of times—to be a parent, but parents are not rising to meet the challenge.

Tough Times to Be a Parent

Americans recognize the many challenges and demands facing today's parents and families. They are profoundly conscious of fundamental changes that have made the job of parenting tougher than ever before. In fact, 4 in 5 Americans say it's much harder for parents to do their job these days, while only about 1 in 5 (19%) say it's easier or about the same as in the past.

Thus, the harsh judgments about parental failings described in Finding Three are coupled with—and at least partially mitigated by—an acknowledgment that parents often struggle and make financial sacrifices for their kids. Half of all Americans (51%) say that parents who sacrifice and work hard for their kids are very common. Forceful finger pointing at parents is inevitably linked with some recognition of the pressures they face, pressures that lead them to make compromises and take short-cuts in parenting.

They may not be happy about it, but the public knows that the *Leave It To Beaver* days are gone. "My father, as a single wage-earner, took care of five children," said an Ohio man. "I don't think that can be done now. So now mothers feel the need to go out and work so they can live to a certain standard."

The Pressure on Mothers

While people in the focus groups pointed to the absence of mothers in the home as a problem, Americans clearly believe that most mothers work because they have to, not because they've chosen self-fulfilling careers over the well-being of their kids. Specifically, 3 in 4 people believe it's very common for mothers to give up time with their kids to work and make ends meet; only 27% say it's very common for mothers to give up time with their kids so they can work for personal satisfaction. An Illinois woman with grown children spoke sympathetically about the plight of today's mothers: "For mothers who are working today, it's the stress of doing a full-time job, and then coming home and doing the things you need to do with your kids, and even to further your own education. That's a lot of stress."

New-Age Dads

What society expects from fathers has changed markedly, well beyond the legislative focus on getting "deadbeat dads" to fulfill their financial responsibilities. What do Americans expect from fathers who are with their families? "It's a confusing time," said an Ohio man. "There was a time for my father's generation when what it meant to be a father was a lot simpler, a lot clearer. It isn't today. There's the modern, new-age guy who's trying to figure out how to be a warm, loving, caring father—not domineering and traditional. And then there's the totally absent one that can't deal with it."

One change has been the notion that fathers can and should show affection and love to their children, while still being considered "men." But only about 1 in 5 (22%) Americans say that such fathers are very common. Fathers agree—only about 1 in 4 (27%) think that the affectionate, loving Dad is very common.

Another change has challenged the notion that a father has fulfilled his responsibility simply by putting "food on the table." As a California mother put it: "If he is just being there, wearing the pants, it is better if he is not there at all. If he is not going to be with these kids, and talk to these kids, it is better that he is not there." The image of fathers is better here: only 35% of the general public thinks it's very common for fathers to put their jobs ahead of their kids. Once again, fathers essentially agree (37%).

The Job That's Never Over

People can easily imagine moments where the pressures of life can get to the most devoted parents. By an almost 2-to-1 margin (63% to 32%), Americans believe that "most parents face times when they really need help raising their kids" instead of the alternate proposition that "most parents can handle the job of raising their kids without help." Indeed, people even give some benefit of the doubt to parents of youngsters who are struggling and getting into trouble. Only 11% of the public believes that such parents are irresponsible; people are more likely to believe that such parents are simply overwhelmed by their own personal problems (40%).

In fact, the extraordinary challenges people see for today's families led some non-parents to be openly thankful that they did not have children, a striking reversal from times past, when not having children was seen as cause for pity. "I consider it a real blessing that I don't have any children," said a woman from Iowa. "It is a job that is never over."

Environmental Hazards

People also recognize that today's kids—even those with parents who work hard to raise them properly—face a world of dangers and temptations that threaten their well-being. Not only must parents double their efforts to make ends meet, they also face the daunting task of raising respectful, helpful, morally-grounded children in a world fraught with hazards and decidedly mixed messages about what's right and wrong. "I don't like the world I am raising my kids in," said a Denver father. "Today's world, it stinks and I don't like it." Americans think these are uniquely difficult times for kids: more than 8 in 10 (83%) say it's harder to be a kid growing up in America these days: only 16% say it is easier or about the same. The survey asked people to rate the severity of problems children and teenagers face. Topping the public's list of the problems facing youngsters is drug and alcohol abuse, which 7 in 10 Americans (71%) consider a very serious problem. "Nowadays you get young kids—13, 14, 15 carrying guns and beepers, and they want to be little drug dealers on the corner," said a California woman. "I think it's harder [to be a kid] today. Because we didn't have AIDS, crack, all these drugs kids are exposed to," said a New York woman. Seven in 10 people (69%) also see excessive violence and sex on television and in the movies as a very serious problem. "They just show things they shouldn't be showing on the local TV channel," said a frustrated Denver mother. "There is semi-nudity on TV now. When I was growing up, I watched *I Love Lucy* and they never showed those people in bed together—they had two separate beds." Another mother in the same group responded in agreement: "Even if you are watching a decent show or a radio station you have chosen, then you get the commercials coming in and, 'Oh, I thought I was safe for 15 minutes.' " Parents particularly seem to feel that they have no place to hide, even when they seek to control the influences to which their kids are exposed.

Crime and gangs are another very serious threat to kids, according to 62% of the population. "The streets are so dangerous in certain communities," said a California man. "[You don't want kids] hanging out on the street with a bicycle—there might be a drive-by shooting."

Schools: No Longer a Safe Haven

And finally, there is also growing disappointment with the public schools, which half (49%) of those surveyed believe fail to give kids a good education. Prior Public Agenda studies have documented the roots of this disaffection—a sense that schools fail to teach the academic basics in a safe and orderly environment. Even as educators protest that the schools face the same societal problems identified above, the public adds the quality of education to the list of serious problems facing kids today. And not only do people blame the schools for failure to deliver on their educational mission, many believe they no longer offer the safe haven of structure and discipline that young people need in order to thrive. For example, 7 in 10 people say drugs and violence are problems in the public schools, and even youngsters see this as a problem. . . .

The Suburbs—and Beyond

Once again, the public overwhelmingly believes these problems threaten all of America's youth, not just the disadvantaged. Those who identified problems as very or somewhat serious were asked how widespread they are. Ninety-five percent believe that drug and alcohol abuse is a widespread problem, not one affecting only children from lower-income families. Nine in ten (91%) think the failure to teach kids such values as honesty, respect, and responsibility is widespread, with only 8% linking it only to lower-income children. The same is true for crime and education, areas where middle-class families are supposed to have an advantage: two-thirds (67%) view crime and gangs as widespread, while more than three-quarters (76%) consider failing public schools to be a widespread problem.

The Bottom Line: Raise Them Right

Whether the problems young people face result more from parents or from social pressures is a widely debated question, dividing American politicians, educators, and social commentators. The American people seem to share this division. When pressed to choose whether the difficulties facing kids today are mostly the result of irresponsible parents or social and economic pressures, people split about evenly—44% to 41%.

Still, even after they recognize that these are tough times for parents, teens, and young children, and that every parent can face occasions when they are pressed, people often return to the refrain: if you're going to have children, raise them right. "We all have personal problems," said a New Jersey man, "some greater than others. But whoever has children, you have to put those problems aside and you've got to do your best to try to raise your children right and set a good example for them." In the public's mind, no matter what the personal problems and social pressures are, parents are obligated to shoulder the responsibility for their children's upbringing.

FINDING FIVE: Never Give Up

Notwithstanding their extensive criticisms of young people, Americans refuse to give up on kids. They care deeply about their well-being and believe that tackling the issue is of paramount importance to our society. Most encouraging, they are stubbornly optimistic about the chances of reclaiming the lives of even the most troubled teens.

Despite their deep disappointment over how teens and children are turning out, Americans demonstrate surprisingly high levels of caring and sympathy toward young people. More importantly, they believe that confronting the challenges youngsters face—especially the moral ones—is a paramount and urgent national priority.

About 7 in 10 people (71%) say the statement "I am strongly moved when I see media stories about children suffering" comes very close to how they feel. They also recognize the importance of this issue for the nation's future. As noted earlier, slightly more than half of those surveyed (52%) say that helping kids get a good start in life is more important than creating more jobs, protecting citizens from crime, or helping the poor or homeless.

Redeemable, Retrievable

Americans display an extraordinary, almost stubborn, refusal to write young people off as unsalvageable. Almost three-quarters (72%) say that "given enough love and kindness, just about any kid can be reached." A Denver man's comment was typical: "All kids can be helped if you get to them early enough, if you spend time with them."

From the public's viewpoint, even the toughest youngsters—teenagers already in real trouble—can be redeemed, given the right kind of effort. Even when the survey presented them with a scenario about "the tough customers"—teenagers who are always getting into trouble at school and in their neighborhood—85% believe given enough attention and the right kind of guidance, almost all such teens can get back on track; only 11% say instead that many of these teens are beyond the point where they can be helped.

Almost All Can Learn

Nor are people willing to give up on a young person's potential to learn, achieve, and—with the right kind of help—contribute to society. The refusal to give up on kids, to practice triage on the tough cases, continues when it comes to schools and education. Given a choice between two views, 74% say that given enough help and attention, just about all youngsters can learn and succeed in school; only 21% say that some just won't learn or succeed, no matter how much help and attention they get.

Most people just do not believe that youngsters are "born bad," or that they are unreachable and not worth salvaging. In fact, people's comments often reveal an undertone of faith in the capacity of young people to transcend their surroundings or shaky beginnings. "Kids are resilient and they will survive," said a Nebraska woman. People recognize that some kids can be "a handful," that it might take supreme effort to invest affection in a tough child. But they still want society—and parents—to make that effort, to keep trying, because there is likely to be a pay-off at the end. "Strong-willed children are very tough to love unconditionally," said a Denver mother, "and all kids need unconditional love—especially from parents. But they are the ones that, if you can just let them know you love them no matter what, they are the ones who are going to be super achievers . . . the people who make the difference in the world."

By Virtue of Their Character

Is this insistence that it is never too late unrealistic, merely an example of Americans' instinctive optimism? Are people simply offering socially acceptable responses? Perhaps. But people consistently draw on personal experience to share examples of individuals able to surmount the roughest environments and most difficult personal challenges. In every part of the country, people in every walk of life relate stories about late-bloomers, people who managed to overcome harsh beginnings by virtue of their character, and kids who were failures in school but somehow as adults discovered latent talents.

What's more, many people acknowledge that they themselves were no angels growing up (and presumably believe they turned out all light). Slightly more than half (54%) say that they got into mischief as youngsters, at least on occasion. The notion that one might get into trouble, then straighten out, fits people's own experience and their recognition that the path to productive adulthood is seldom a straight line.

Americans stubbornly resist giving up on individual youngsters or abandoning an entire generation. But if people believe that kids can straighten out and develop the values and attitudes that will guide them into responsible adulthood, how do they think that can happen?

FINDING SIX: Solutions That Miss the Mark

Government programs aimed at improving the health and economic circumstances of young people miss the mark in three important ways as far as the public is concerned. First, Americans define the children's issue as predominantly moral in nature, not one of money or health. Second, people believe the crux of the problem is parents, not a lack of government programs. And third, welfare has left a legacy of skepticism about government intervention on behalf of the family. Even when it comes to low-income, at-risk kids, Americans doubt that such programs could help. They suspect that parents who need such programs will fail to take advantage of them.

In recent years the most visible and dominant governmental efforts to address the problems of young people have centered on measures to improve their physical well-being and economic circumstances. Yet such ideas fail to attract much enthusiasm from the general public or—even more puzzling to some children's advocates—from parents themselves. From the public's perspective, such efforts are beside the point for three reasons: people fundamentally view the children's issue as moral in nature—better values and character are what's needed, not necessarily more spending; people think parents are not doing their job when it comes to "raising kids right" and severely doubt government programs can take their place; and people harbor doubts that government programs to help the family can truly work given their perceptions of how welfare turned out.

The Real Problem: Morality, Values, and Character

The most fundamental reason efforts to improve nutrition and health care for children fail to resonate with the public is that people define the children's issue in terms of morality, values, and character. Since this is hardly the stuff of most government programs, it is not surprising that few Americans (27%) consider a shortage of such programs to be a very serious problem. In fact, when presented with a range of 10 possible problems facing young people today—from drugs to crime to a failure to learn values—a shortage of government programs ranks last on the list. Comparing this result to an earlier finding in which 61% think kids' failure to learn such values as honesty, respect, and responsibility is a very serious problem, makes clear where the public stands on this issue.

To the public, it may not be so much that health initiatives on behalf of children and teenagers are worthless. Indeed, there is an archive of survey findings suggesting at least some support for a variety of such proposals. The key point is they do not speak to the public's definition of the issue, and they are therefore seen as less relevant. In this study, only 34% say more government funding for child and health care programs would be a very effective way to help kids. If such initiatives languish during legislative log-rolling sessions without public outcry, it's probably because they fail to address the public's fundamental concerns.

Parents Remain the Key

As already noted, people believe that children thrive when their parents care for them and teach them right from wrong. They hold parents responsible when their children go astray. This frustrates many children's advocates who want to bring the children's issue into the public policy realm, much as some European nations do. While parents are responsible for their own children, advocates say, society as a whole must still assume some responsibility for the next generation for its own good, if for no other reason. But to the public, the fate of young people chiefly hinges upon how well parents care for them—and how and what they teach them day-in and day-out. This image is so strong in the public mind that efforts to move the focus of attention to what government does for children and teenagers would seem to hold little promise of success.

In the public's mind, government programs that aim to supply the health and financial needs of youngsters cannot remedy the most glaring failures of parents—the failure to be there for their children and to take responsibility for the development of their character. People are thinking: "We might succeed at immunizing children against a full range of diseases; but how will that improve the quality of parenting and teaching they get at home? How will that make their parents better parents?"

A Legacy of Government Failure

But what about parents who—for a variety of reasons—are just not up to the job of parenting? Should government take the lead in trying to help them? When asked, "When parents have serious trouble raising their kids properly, who is in a better position to step in with help—other than relatives or close friends?", only 11% opt for government agencies and programs; 79% would rely on private efforts such as volunteer organizations or neighbors and citizens who pull together.

The extreme reluctance to count on the government, even for the neediest, most troubled families, reflects grave doubts about the efficacy—and wisdom—of asking government programs to rescue families in trouble. "I don't think we should turn to the government for help," said a Denver woman. "I don't want them to come up with more ways for them to take our children and raise them."

A principle source of this reluctance is the legacy of government welfare programs, prompting people to define government as causing problems for the poor, not solving them. In a 1996 study, *The Values We Live By: What Americans Want from Welfare Reform*, Public Agenda found the public's repudiation of welfare was driven not by its costs but by a sense that welfare rewarded values and behaviors that are anathema to most Americans. The public concluded that a program motivated by good intentions had gone seriously awry and was perpetuating and exacerbating the very problems it was intended to fix. Why? For one thing, the program focused on caring for the material and financial needs of recipients without making any morally-based demands upon them—that they work in return for their benefits, for example, or that they continuously strive to climb out of dependency. For another, the public believed welfare undermined rather than supported the family . . .

Will They Come?

But how government goes about helping the poor is not the only source of public skepticism. People also harbor serious doubts about whether those who need such programs make good use of them. When asked to evaluate government programs to help low-income, at-risk kids and families, only 8% say such programs usually succeed. The vast majority (71%) say the results are mixed, while 19% say the programs usually fail. Most interesting is the public's explanation for why such programs usually fail or produce mixed results. Only 5% say the reason is a lack of money. Instead, nearly 4 in 10 (38%) believe the programs are poorly designed, while 51% believe it is because the parents who need these programs don't make good use of them. About half of the public thus believes that it is the failure of at-risk parents to use government programs that helps explain the lack of results.

FINDING SEVEN: Solutions That Show Promise

Because they define the problem as one of values, Americans gravitate toward solutions that help develop young people's character. People believe the schools should help teach kids discipline, honesty, and respectfulness toward themselves and others. They believe community centers and volunteer organizations like the Boy Scouts could be effective because they lend moral structure to youngsters' lives.

If people do not look to government for effective solutions, what do they think might help? People see a need for action in several arenas, and they are surprisingly pragmatic and clear-sighted about what they think will work.

Schools Should Reinforce Values

After parents, people look to public schools as society's most critical point of contact with young people. But just as the public voices dissatisfaction with parents' performance, people also believe that public schools have abandoned their traditional and essential role of reinforcing responsibility, integrity, and respect—along with teaching academics. (Recall that about half identified inadequate public education as a very serious problem.) People believe that if the schools do a better job, young people will turn out better. In fact, two-thirds (67%) say that improving the public schools would be a very effective way to help young people.

441

But people's definition of what a good education includes goes beyond conveying academic skills. Studies by Public Agenda have shown repeatedly that the public overwhelmingly believes schools should teach values along with academics. "Schools have a social role as well," pointed out a Denver woman. "I think that is eminently important, equally as important as teaching them the basics of academics."

The values people want schools to teach are straightforward—and not likely to generate much controversy. Basically, people want schools to teach the values and standards of behavior that will stand kids in good stead out in the real world—being responsible, on time, and disciplined (83%); the value of hard work (78%); and honesty and tolerance of others (74%).

Educators sometimes complain that instilling strong character traits and teaching acceptable social behavior are tasks that more properly belong to parents. But the public wants the schools to *supplement* and reinforce the values parents should provide. They do not expect schools to replace parents. "You can model good behavior at school, but youngsters don't spend the bulk of their time in school," said an Illinois woman. "So if you're going to educate them with a value system, it's going to have to come from home." And many parents are quick to point out that from their perspective, the social environment tolerated at public schools—the behavior that is overlooked or allowed to go unpunished—undermines, rather than reinforces, what they try so hard to teach at home.

Keep Kids Busy

Since people believe that leaving young people with nothing to do is asking for trouble, one attractive solution is more after-school programs—seen by 6 in 10 Americans as a very effective way to help kids. "When my daughters were pre-school age, there were many things they could do," noted a Denver mother. "But now at the ages of 10 and 13, there are very, very few things, and what there are cost a lot. And now is when they really need it." The public doubly values such programs, since they not only take kids off the streets and give them constructive things to do, but also provide them with the structure and adult guidance they believe are missing from youngsters' daily lives.

For the same reasons, more than half of those surveyed (53%) also believe that greater reliance on volunteer organizations like the Boy Scouts would be a very effective way to help kids. In fact, the Scout Law is a promise to be trustworthy, loyal, helpful, friendly, courteous and more—a fairly neat summation of what Americans want young people everywhere to learn.

Help Parents Have More Time

Since parents are the key to good kids, and because people do recognize the stress that the workplace puts on parents' ability to do their job, more than half those surveyed (55%) think more flexible work schedules would be very effective to help young people. "Usually now, both mothers and fathers are working," said a Utah man, "and they can't get home before the kids are out of school. That's where the big problem is." The public sees so many families under such pressure and rushing to meet their many obligations that they want to help parents better juggle their responsibilities. By contrast, only 37% think holding parents legally responsible when their kids get into trouble would be very effective—another indication that the public considers the issue as more complicated than simple parental malfeasance.

The Problem Without a Solution: The Media

Given the intense complaints about the media, it is somewhat surprising that only half of those surveyed (49%) think pressuring the entertainment industry to produce movies and music with less violence and sex will be a very effective way to help kids. Perhaps people doubt that the industry will be responsive to public pressure, or wonder just how much influence they as individuals can bring to bear. Only 37% believe that protesting violence or sex *in* the media would help a lot. People may also question whether it is really possible to return to the days when most media content was at the G or PG level.

When To Get Firm . . . and How

Whatever else happens, many people say it is critical to keep kids off the streets where they can easily get into, or cause, trouble. Fifty-three percent of those participating in the survey consider nighttime curfews for kids to be a very effective way to help them. "Their parents are letting them out until midnight when they are in the sixth grade," complained a New Jersey man. People are thinking: if parents are not keeping their kids off the streets late at night, the law should force them to do so.

Half of the public (48%) believe that an effective measure to help youngsters is tougher punishment for those who commit crime. Public Agenda's research on attitudes toward crime indicates that people place great stock in how the criminal justice system responds to a young offender's first brush with the law. The worst lesson to transmit to such youngsters, people believe, is that they can commit a crime—no matter how petty—and just get away with it. People believe that the proverbial slap on the wrist only invites further, and ever worsening, violations. At the same time, people also are loath to put juvenile offenders who have not committed violent crimes in prison, fearing that the experience will only make them worse. The public's list of preferred sanctions is therefore very instructive: boot camp, community service, or restitution with intense supervision. All of these sanctions are intended to teach young offenders discipline, hard work, and responsibility. The consistent recurrence of these themes across different studies—from education, to welfare, to crime—is quite striking.

SUPREME COURT ON
INTERNET FREE SPEECH
June 26, 1997

The Supreme Court on June 26 offered the sweeping protection of the First Amendment's free-speech clause to the Internet, the world-wide computer network of ideas, documents, e-mail, and graphics—some of it pornographic. Striking down an attempt by Congress to protect children against pornography on the Internet, the Court ruled that speech in cyberspace has the same constitutional protection as speech in books, magazines, and newspapers.

The broad ruling by a unanimous Supreme Court in Reno v. American Civil Liberties Union *appeared to leave virtually no legal route for the government to regulate content on the Internet. Writing the court's main opinion for himself and six colleagues, Justice John Paul Stevens said the goal of protecting children from pornography was laudable, but overall "the interest of encouraging freedom of expression in a democratic society outweighs any theoretical but unproven benefit of censorship" of the Internet.*

The Clinton administration, which had supported Congress's attempt to curb pornography on the Internet, immediately encouraged major on-line computer services, such as America Online, to place voluntary restrictions on indecent material. The administration and private groups also encouraged parents to exercise their own control over what their children viewed on the Internet, in part by buying software intended to block access to Internet sites containing pornographic material.

The "Decency" Act

With little debate or serious review of the alternatives, Congress in 1996 added the Communications Decency Act to a massive bill (PL 104-104) revising federal telecommunications regulations. Based on legislation formulated by the Senate in 1995, the Decency Act made it a federal criminal offense to "make available" indecent material on computer networks, where it might be seen by minors. The law defined indecency as "any comment, request, suggestion, proposal, image or other communication that, in context, depicts or describes, in terms patently offensive as measured by contemporary community standards, sexual or excretory activities or organs."

The provision applied to anyone displaying such material, as well as to those who knowingly permitted their telecommunications facilities to be used for such purposes. Penalties for violations included prison terms of up to two years and fines of up to $250,000 for individuals or $500,000 for corporations. (Decency Act background, Historic Documents of 1996, p. 353)

Acknowledging questions about the constitutionality of the act, its sponsors inserted a provision allowing expedited consideration by a three-judge federal panel of any challenge to it. The challenge came quickly, from a coalition of civil liberties groups, booksellers, computer industry groups, and librarians. A federal judicial panel considered the issue in the spring of 1996 and on June 11 issued a unanimous ruling declaring the act unconstitutional and blocking its enforcement. The Supreme Court in December agreed to review the ruling during its 1996–1997 term.

The high court heard arguments on the case March 19. In questioning attorneys on both sides of the issue, the justices expressed skepticism about the practicality, as well as the constitutionality, of the law, and some justices acknowledged their own unfamiliarity with the technology of the Internet.

Upholding Free Speech

In striking down the law June 26, the justices issued two opinions. The Stevens opinion—endorsed by Justices Stephen G. Breyer, Ruth Bader Ginsburg, Anthony M. Kennedy, Antonin Scalia, David H. Souter, and Clarence Thomas—was unequivocal in rejecting the Decency Act as unconstitutional. A second opinion, written by Justice Sandra Day O'Connor and signed by Chief Justice William H. Rehnquist, also declared the act unconstitutional but held out a limited possibility that a much more narrowly drawn Internet restriction might pass constitutional muster.

The Stevens opinion took the Decency Act apart piece by piece, declaring it flawed in nearly every important respect. First, Stevens declared the act's definition of "indecency" to be vague, creating uncertainty about its application. "Could a speaker [on the Internet] confidently assume that a serious discussion about birth control practices, homosexuality, the First Amendment issues [of a previous landmark ruling by the Court on obscenity], or the consequences of prison rape would not violate" the law, Stevens asked. The severity of the criminal penalties provided by the law, he added, "may well cause speakers to remain silent rather than communicate even arguably unlawful words, ideas, and images."

In attempting to protect children against pornography, Stevens wrote, the act placed unconstitutional limitations on what adults might access on the Internet. Further, Stevens argued that the law, as written, opened parents to prosecution for allowing their children to view pornography over the Internet.

Stevens was particularly harsh in his criticism of one argument offered by the Clinton administration in its defense of the law. The Justice Department told the court that the presence of pornography was stifling the growth of the Internet as a communications medium because potential users feared exposing themselves or their children to that type of material. Curb-

ing pornography was therefore essential to the future growth of the Internet, the government argued.

"We find this argument singularly unpersuasive," Stevens wrote, noting that the growth of the Internet "has been and continues to be phenomenal." The Court traditionally had held a view directly opposite that stated by government lawyers, he said, presuming that "governmental regulation of the content of speech is more likely to interfere with the free exchange of ideas than to encourage it."

In her opinion generally concurring with Stevens, Justice O'Connor argued that the Decency Act attempted to create "adult zones" on the Internet, just as local communities had been permitted to create zones for adult book stores. The flaw in the Decency Act, she wrote, was that it prohibited access to pornographic material on the Internet by both adults and children—and the court had ruled repeatedly that it was unconstitutional to try to prevent adults from viewing that type of material. O'Connor compared the Decency Act to a law "that makes it a crime for a bookstore owner to sell pornographic magazines to anyone once a minor enters his store."

Even so, O'Connor held out the theoretical possibility of crafting a restriction on Internet pornography under a few narrow circumstances. For example, she wrote that a law could be constitutional if it could prohibit the sending of pornography over the Internet in situations "where the party initiating the communication knows that all of the recipients are minors."

> *Following are excerpts from the majority and concurring opinions in the case of* Reno v. American Civil Liberties Union, *in which the Supreme Court struck down as unconstitutional the Communications Decency Act of 1996, which imposed criminal penalties for the transmission of "indecent" material to minors over the Internet:*

No. 96-511

Janet Reno, Attorney General of the
United States, et al., Appellants
v.
American Civil Liberties Union
et al.

On appeal from the United States District Court for the Eastern District of Pennsylvania

[June 26, 1997]

JUSTICE STEVENS delivered the opinion of the Court.

At issue is the constitutionality of two statutory provisions enacted to protect minors from "indecent" and "patently offensive" communications on the Internet. Notwithstanding the legitimacy and importance of the congressional goal of protecting children from harmful materials, we agree with the three-judge District Court that the statute abridges "the freedom of speech" protected by the First Amendment.

[Sections I and II omitted, in which Stevens reviewed the development of the Internet and the legislative enactment of the Communications Decency Act of 1996 (CDA)]

III

On February 8, 1996, immediately after the President signed the statute, 20 plaintiffs filed suit against the Attorney General of the United States and the Department of Justice challenging the constitutionality of §223(a)(1) and 223(d). A week later, based on his conclusion that the term "indecent" was too vague to provide the basis for a criminal prosecution, District Judge Buckwalter entered a temporary restraining order against enforcement of §223(a)(1)(B)(ii) insofar as it applies to indecent communications. A second suit was then filed by 27 additional plaintiffs, the two cases were consolidated, and a three-judge District Court was convened pursuant to §561 of the Act. After an evidentiary hearing, that Court entered a preliminary injunction against enforcement of both of the challenged provisions. Each of the three judges wrote a separate opinion, but their judgment was unanimous. [Summary of opinions omitted.]

The judgment of the District Court enjoins the Government from enforcing the prohibitions in §223(a)(1)(B) insofar as they relate to "indecent" communications, but expressly preserves the Government's right to investigate and prosecute the obscenity or child pornography activities prohibited therein. The injunction against enforcement of §§223(d)(1) and (2) is unqualified because those provisions contain no separate reference to obscenity or child pornography.

The Government appealed under the Act's special review provisions, §561, and we noted probable jurisdiction (1996). In its appeal, the Government argues that the District Court erred in holding that the CDA violated both the First Amendment because it is overbroad and the Fifth Amendment because it is vague. While we discuss the vagueness of the CDA because of its relevance to the First Amendment overbreadth inquiry, we conclude that the judgment should be affirmed without reaching the Fifth Amendment issue. We begin our analysis by reviewing the principal authorities on which the Government relies. Then, after describing the overbreadth of the CDA, we consider the Government's specific contentions, including its submission that we save portions of the statute either by severance or by fashioning judicial limitations on the scope of its coverage.

IV

In arguing for reversal, the Government contends that the CDA is plainly constitutional under three of our prior decisions: (1) *Ginsberg v. New York* (1968); (2) *FCC v. Pacifica Foundation* (1978); and (3) *Renton v. Playtime*

Theatres, Inc. (1986). A close look at these cases, however, raises—rather than relieves—doubts concerning the constitutionality of the CDA.

[Stevens summarized and analyzed the three decisions. In *Ginsberg*, he said, the Court upheld the constitutionality of a New York statute that prohibited selling to minors under 17 years of age material that was considered obscene as to them even if not obscene as to adults. Stevens said the New York law was narrower than the CDA in four respects: it did not bar parents from purchasing the materials for their children if they wished; it applied only to commercial transactions; it applied only to material that was "utterly without redeeming social importance for minors;" and it applied only to persons under the age of seventeen, not eighteen, as the CDA provides.

[In *Pacifica*, Stevens continued, the Court upheld a declaratory order of the Federal Communications Commission, holding that the broadcast of a recording of a 12-minute monologue entitled "Filthy Words" that had previously been delivered to a live audience "could have been the subject of administrative sanctions." He noted several distinctions between that order and the CDA—including the facts that the CDA is "punitive," permitting a criminal prosecution; and that broadcasting had traditionally received "the most limited First Amendment protection."

[Finally, Stevens said that in *Renton* the Court upheld a zoning ordinance that kept adult movie theatres out of residential neighborhoods because of the "secondary effects," such as crime and deteriorating property values. By contrast, he said, the CDA "applies broadly to the entire universe of cyberspace." And the purpose of the CDA, he added, was to "protect children from the primary effects of 'indecent' and 'patently offensive' speech, rather than any 'secondary' effect of such speech."]

These precedents, then, surely do not require us to uphold the CDA and are fully consistent with the application of the most stringent review of its provisions.

V

... [S]ome of our cases have recognized special justifications for regulation of the broadcast media that are not applicable to other speakers. In these cases, the Court relied on the history of extensive government regulation of the broadcast medium; the scarcity of available frequencies at its inception; and its "invasive" nature.

Those factors are not present in cyberspace. Neither before nor after the enactment of the CDA have the vast democratic fora of the Internet been subject to the type of government supervision and regulation that has attended the broadcast industry. Moreover, the Internet is not as "invasive" as radio or television. The District Court specifically found that "[c]ommunications over the Internet do not 'invade' an individual's home or appear on one's computer screen unbidden. Users seldom encounter content 'by accident.'" It also found that "[a]lmost all sexually explicit images are preceded by warnings as to the content," and cited testimony that "'odds are slim' that a user would come across a sexually explicit sight by accident." ...

Finally, unlike the conditions that prevailed when Congress first authorized regulation of the broadcast spectrum, the Internet can hardly be considered a "scarce" expressive commodity. It provides relatively unlimited, low-cost capacity for communication of all kinds. The Government estimates that "[a]s many as 40 million people use the Internet today, and that figure is expected to grow to 200 million by 1999." This dynamic, multifaceted category of communication includes not only traditional print and news services, but also audio, video, and still images, as well as interactive, real-time dialogue. Through the use of chat rooms, any person with a phone line can become a town crier with a voice that resonates farther than it could from any soapbox. Through the use of Web pages, mail exploders, and newsgroups, the same individual can become a pamphleteer. As the District Court found, "the content on the Internet is as diverse as human thought." We agree with its conclusion that our cases provide no basis for qualifying the level of First Amendment scrutiny that should be applied to this medium.

VI

Regardless of whether the CDA is so vague that it violates the Fifth Amendment, the many ambiguities concerning the scope of its coverage render it problematic for purposes of the First Amendment. For instance, each of the two parts of the CDA uses a different linguistic form. The first uses the word "indecent," 47 U. S. C. A. §223(a), while the second speaks of material that "in context, depicts or describes, in terms patently offensive as measured by contemporary community standards, sexual or excretory activities or organs," §223(d). Given the absence of a definition of either term, this difference in language will provoke uncertainty among speakers about how the two standards relate to each other and just what they mean. Could a speaker confidently assume that a serious discussion about birth control practices, homosexuality, the First Amendment issues raised by the Appendix to our *Pacifica* opinion, or the consequences of prison rape would not violate the CDA? This uncertainty undermines the likelihood that the CDA has been carefully tailored to the congressional goal of protecting minors from potentially harmful materials.

The vagueness of the CDA is a matter of special concern for two reasons. First, the CDA is a content-based regulation of speech. The vagueness of such a regulation raises special First Amendment concerns because of its obvious chilling effect on free speech. Second, the CDA is a criminal statute. In addition to the opprobrium and stigma of a criminal conviction, the CDA threatens violators with penalties including up to two years in prison for each act of violation. The severity of criminal sanctions may well cause speakers to remain silent rather than communicate even arguably unlawful words, ideas, and images. . . .

The Government argues that the statute is no more vague than the obscenity standard this Court established in *Miller v. California* (1973). But that is not so. [Stevens stated and analyzed the three-part definition of obscenity established in *Miller:* a work, taken as a whole, appeals to the prurient interest; depicts sexual conduct in a patently offensive way; and lacks "serious literary, artistic, political, or scientific value." Stevens said the CDA provision was broader, in particular because it did not include the "societal value" requirement.]

In contrast to *Miller* and our other previous cases, the CDA . . . presents a greater threat of censoring speech that, in fact, falls outside the statute's scope. Given the vague contours of the coverage of the statute, it unquestionably silences some speakers whose messages would be entitled to constitutional protection. That danger provides further reason for insisting that the statute not be overly broad. The CDA's burden on protected speech cannot be justified if it could be avoided by a more carefully drafted statute.

VII

We are persuaded that the CDA lacks the precision that the First Amendment requires when a statute regulates the content of speech. In order to deny minors access to potentially harmful speech, the CDA effectively suppresses a large amount of speech that adults have a constitutional right to receive and to address to one another. That burden on adult speech is unacceptable if less restrictive alternatives would be at least as effective in achieving the legitimate purpose that the statute was enacted to serve.

In evaluating the free speech rights of adults, we have made it perfectly clear that "[s]exual expression which is indecent but not obscene is protected by the First Amendment." *Sable [Communications of Cal., Inc. v. FCC* (1989)]. . . .

It is true that we have repeatedly recognized the governmental interest in protecting children from harmful materials. But that interest does not justify an unnecessarily broad suppression of speech addressed to adults. . . .

The District Court was correct to conclude that the CDA effectively resembles the ban on "dial-a-porn" invalidated in *Sable*. In *Sable*, this Court rejected the argument that we should defer to the congressional judgment that nothing less than a total ban would be effective in preventing enterprising youngsters from gaining access to indecent communications. *Sable* thus made clear that the mere fact that a statutory regulation of speech was enacted for the important purpose of protecting children from exposure to sexually explicit material does not foreclose inquiry into its validity. . . .

In arguing that the CDA does not so diminish adult communication, the Government relies on the incorrect factual premise that prohibiting a transmission whenever it is known that one of its recipients is a minor would not interfere with adult-to-adult communication. The findings of the District Court make clear that this premise is untenable. Given the size of the potential audience for most messages, in the absence of a viable age verification process, the sender must be charged with knowing that one or more minors will likely view it. Knowledge that, for instance, one or more members of a 100-person chat group will be minor—and therefore that it would be a crime to send the group an indecent message—would surely burden communication among adults.

The District Court found that at the time of trial existing technology did not include any effective method for a sender to prevent minors from obtaining access to its communications on the Internet without also denying access to adults. The Court found no effective way to determine the age of a user who is accessing material through e-mail, mail exploders, newsgroups, or chat rooms. As a practical matter, the Court also found that it would be prohibitively expensive for noncommercial—as well as some commercial— speakers who have Web sites to verify that their users are adults. These limitations must inevitably curtail a significant amount of adult communication on the Internet. By contrast, the District Court found that "[d]espite its limitations, currently available *user-based* software suggests that a reasonably effective method by which *parents* can prevent their children from accessing sexually explicit and other material which *parents* may believe is inappropriate for their children will soon be widely available" (emphases added).

The breadth of the CDA's coverage is wholly unprecedented. Unlike the regulations upheld in *Ginsberg* and *Pacifica*, the scope of the CDA is not limited to commercial speech or commercial entities. Its open-ended prohibitions embrace all nonprofit entities and individuals posting indecent messages or displaying them on their own computers in the presence of minors. The general, undefined terms "indecent" and "patently offensive" cover large amounts of nonpornographic material with serious educational or other value. Moreover, the "community standards" criterion as applied to the Internet means that any communication available to a nation-wide audience will be judged by the standards of the community most likely to be offended by the message. The regulated subject matter includes any of the seven "dirty words" used in the Pacifica monologue, the use of which the Government's expert acknowledged could constitute a felony. It may also extend to discussions about prison rape or safe sexual practices, artistic images that include nude subjects, and arguably the card catalogue of the Carnegie Library.

For the purposes of our decision, we need neither accept nor reject the Government's submission that the First Amendment does not forbid a blanket prohibition on all "indecent" and "patently offensive" messages communicated to a 17-year old—no matter how much value the message may contain and regardless of parental approval. It is at least clear that the strength of the Government's interest in protecting minors is not equally strong throughout the coverage of this broad statute. Under the CDA, a parent allowing her 17-year-old to use the family computer to obtain information on the Internet that she, in her parental judgment, deems appropriate could face a lengthy prison term. Similarly, a parent who sent his 17-year-old college freshman information on birth control via e-mail could be incarcerated even though neither he, his child, nor anyone in their home community, found the material "indecent" or "patently offensive," if the college town's community thought otherwise.

The breadth of this content-based restriction of speech imposes an especially heavy burden on the Government to explain why a less restrictive provision would not be as effective as the CDA. It has not done so. The arguments in this Court have referred to possible alternatives such as requiring that indecent material be "tagged" in a way that facilitates parental control of material coming into their homes, making exceptions for messages with artistic or educational value, providing some tolerance for parental choice, and regulating some portions of the Internet—such as commercial web sites—differently than others, such as chat rooms. Particularly in the light of the absence of any detailed findings by the Congress, or even hearings addressing the special problems of the CDA, we are persuaded that the CDA is not narrowly tailored if that requirement has any meaning at all.

VIII

In an attempt to curtail the CDA's facial overbreadth, the Government advances three additional arguments for sustaining the Act's affirmative prohibitions: (1) that the CDA is constitutional because it leaves open ample "alternative channels" of communication; (2) that the plain meaning of the Act's "knowledge" and "specific person" requirement significantly restricts its permissible applications; and (3) that the Act's prohibitions are "almost always" limited to material lacking redeeming social value.

[Stevens rejected all three arguments. He said the government's argument about alternative channels of communication was "immaterial," saying it was "equivalent to arguing that a statute could ban leaflets on certain subjects as long as individuals are free to publish books." The government's argument that the "knowledge" requirement and "specific child" element would limit the scope of the act was "untenable," Stevens continued. "This argument ignores the fact that most Internet fora—including chat rooms, newsgroups, mail exploders, and the Web—are open to all comers," he wrote. Finally, Stevens said there was "no textual support" for the government's argument that the law would not apply to works with redeeming social value.]

IX

The Government's three remaining arguments focus on the defenses provided in §223(e)(5). First, relying on the "good faith, reasonable, effective, and appropriate actions" provision, the Government suggests that "tagging" provides a defense that saves the constitutionality of the Act. The suggestion assumes that transmitters may encode their indecent communications in a way that would indicate their contents, thus permitting recipients to block their reception with appropriate software. It is the requirement that the good faith action must be "effective" that makes this defense illusory. The Government recognizes that its proposed screening software does not currently exist. Even if it did, there is no way to know whether a potential recipient will actually block the encoded material. Without the impossible knowledge that every guardian in America is screening for the "tag," the transmitter could not reasonably rely on its action to be "effective."

For its second and third arguments concerning defenses—which we can consider together—the Government relies on the latter half of §223(e)(5), which applies when the transmitter has restricted access by requiring use of a verified credit card or adult identification. Such verification is not only technologically available but actually is used by commercial providers of sexually explicit material. These providers, therefore, would be protected by the defense. Under the findings of the District Court, however, it is not economically feasible for most noncommercial speakers to employ such verification. Accordingly, this defense would not significantly narrow the statute's burden on noncommercial speech. Even with respect to the commercial pornographers that would be protected by the defense, the Government failed to adduce any evidence that these verification techniques actually preclude minors from posing as adults. . . . The Government thus failed to prove that the proffered defense would significantly reduce the heavy burden on adult speech produced by the prohibition on offensive displays.

We agree with the District Court's conclusion that the CDA places an unacceptably heavy burden on protected speech, and that the defenses do not constitute the sort of "narrow tailoring" that will save an otherwise patently invalid unconstitutional provision. In Sable, we remarked that the speech restriction at issue there amounted to " 'burn[ing] the house to roast the pig.' " The CDA, casting a far darker shadow over free speech, threatens to torch a large segment of the Internet community.

X

At oral argument, the Government relied heavily on its ultimate fall-back position: If this Court should conclude that the CDA is insufficiently tailored, it urged, we should save the statute's constitutionality by honoring the severability clause and construing nonseverable terms narrowly. In only one respect is this argument acceptable.

. . . The "indecency" provision applies to "any comment, request, suggestion, proposal, image, or other communication which is obscene or indecent" (emphasis added.) Appellees do not challenge the application of the statute to obscene speech, which, they acknowledge, can be banned totally because it enjoys no First Amendment protection. . . . Therefore, we will sever the term "or indecent" from the statute, leaving the rest of §223(a) standing. In no other respect, however, can §223(a) or §223(d) be saved by such a textual surgery. . . .

XI

In this Court, though not in the District Court, the Government asserts that—in addition to its interest in protecting children—its "[e]qually significant" interest in fostering the growth of the Internet provides an independent basis for upholding the constitutionality of the CDA. The Government apparently assumes that the unregulated availability of "indecent" and "patently offensive" material on the Internet is driving countless citizens away from the medium because of the risk of exposing themselves or their children to harmful material.

We find this argument singularly unpersuasive. The dramatic expansion of this new marketplace of ideas contradicts the factual basis of this contention. The record demonstrates that the growth of the Internet has been and continues to be phenomenal. As a matter of constitutional tradition, in the absence of evidence to the contrary, we presume that governmental regulation of the content of speech is more likely to interfere with the free exchange of ideas than to encourage it. The interest in encouraging freedom of expression in a democratic society outweighs any theoretical but unproven benefit of censorship.

For the foregoing reasons, the judgment of the district court is affirmed.

It is so ordered.

JUSTICE O'CONNOR, with whom THE CHIEF JUSTICE joins, concurring in the judgment in part and dissenting in part.

I write separately to explain why I view the Communications Decency Act of 1996 (CDA) as little more than an attempt by Congress to create "adult zones" on the Internet. Our precedent indicates that the creation of such zones can be constitutionally sound. Despite the soundness of its purpose, however, portions of the CDA are unconstitutional because they stray from the blueprint our prior cases have developed for constructing a "zoning law" that passes constitutional muster. . . .

I

Our cases make clear that a "zoning" law is valid only if adults are still able to obtain the regulated speech. If they cannot, the law does more than simply keep children away from speech they have no right to obtain—it interferes with the rights of adults to obtain constitutionally protected speech and effectively "reduce[s] the adult population . . . to reading only what is fit for children." *Butler v. Michigan* (1957). The First Amendment does not tolerate such interference. . . .

The Court in *Ginsberg [v. New York* (1968)] concluded that the New York law created a constitutionally adequate adult zone simply because, on its face, it denied access only to minors. The Court did not question—and therefore necessarily assumed—that an adult zone, once created, would succeed in preserving adults' access while denying minors' access to the regulated speech. Before today, there was no reason to question this assumption, for the Court has previously only considered laws that operated in the physical world, a world with two characteristics that make it possible to create "adult zones": geography and identity. A minor can see an adult dance show only if he enters an establishment that provides such entertainment. And should he attempt to do so, the minor will not be able to conceal completely his identity (or, consequently, his age). Thus, the twin characteristics of geography and identity enable the establishment's proprietor to prevent children from entering the establishment, but to let adults inside.

The electronic world is fundamentally different. Because it is no more than the interconnection of electronic pathways, cyberspace allows speakers and listeners to mask their identities. Cyberspace undeniably reflects some form of geography; chat rooms and Web sites, for example, exist at fixed "locations" on the Internet. Since users can transmit and receive messages on the

Internet without revealing anything about their identities or ages, however, it is not currently possible to exclude persons from accessing certain messages on the basis of their identity.

Cyberspace differs from the physical world in another basic way: Cyberspace is malleable. Thus, it is possible to construct barriers in cyberspace and use them to screen for identity, making cyberspace more like the physical world and, consequently, more amenable to zoning laws. This transformation of cyberspace is already underway. . . . Internet speakers (users who post material on the Internet) have begun to zone cyberspace itself through the use of "gateway" technology. Such technology requires Internet users to enter information about themselves—perhaps an adult identification number or a credit card number—before they can access certain areas of cyberspace, much like a bouncer checks a person's driver's license before admitting him to a nightclub. Internet users who access information have not attempted to zone cyberspace itself, but have tried to limit their own power to access information in cyberspace, much as a parent controls what her children watch on television by installing a lock box. This user-based zoning is accomplished through the use of screening software (such as Cyber Patrol or SurfWatch) or browsers with screening capabilities, both of which search addresses and text for keywords that are associated with "adult" sites and, if the user wishes, blocks access to such sites. The Platform for Internet Content Selection (PICS) project is designed to facilitate user-based zoning by encouraging Internet speakers to rate the content of their speech using codes recognized by all screening programs.

Despite this progress, the transformation of cyberspace is not complete. Although gateway technology has been available on the World Wide Web for some time now, it is not available to all Web speakers and is just now becoming technologically feasible for chat rooms and USENET newsgroups. Gateway technology is not ubiquitous in cyberspace, and because without it "there is no means of age verification," cyberspace still remains largely unzoned—and unzoneable. User-based zoning is also in its infancy. For it to be effective, (i) an agreed-upon code (or "tag") would have to exist; (ii) screening software or browsers with screening capabilities would have to be able to recognize the "tag"; and (iii) those programs would have to be widely available—and widely used—by Internet users. At present, none of these conditions is true. Screening software "is not in wide use today" and "only a handful of browsers have screening capabilities." There is, moreover, no agreed-upon "tag" for those programs to recognize.

Although the prospects for the eventual zoning of the Internet appear promising, I agree with the Court that we must evaluate the constitutionality of the CDA as it applies to the Internet as it exists today. Given the present state of cyberspace, I agree with the Court that the "display" provision cannot pass muster. Until gateway technology is available throughout cyberspace, and it is not in 1997, a speaker cannot be reasonably assured that the speech he displays will reach only adults because it is impossible to confine speech to an "adult zone." Thus, the only way for a speaker to avoid liability under the CDA is to refrain completely from using indecent speech. But this forced silence impinges on the First Amendment right of adults to make and obtain this speech. . . .

The "indecency transmission" and "specific person" provisions present a closer issue, for they are not unconstitutional in all of their applications. . . . [T]he "indecency transmission" provision makes it a crime to transmit knowingly an indecent message to a person the sender knows is under 18 years of age. The "specific person" provision proscribes the same conduct, although it does not as explicitly require the sender to know that the intended recipient of his indecent message is a minor. Appellant urges the Court to construe the provision to impose such a knowledge requirement, and I would do so. . . .

So construed, both provisions are constitutional as applied to a conversation involving only an adult and one or more minors—e.g., when an adult speaker sends an e-mail knowing the addressee is a minor, or when an adult and minor converse by themselves or with other minors in a chat room. In this context, these provisions are no different from the law we sustained in *Ginsberg.* Restricting what the adult may say to the minors in no way restricts the adult's ability to communicate with other adults. He is not prevented from speaking indecently to other adults in a chat room (because there are no other adults participating in the conversation) and he remains free to send indecent e-mails to other adults. The relevant universe contains only one adult, and the adult in that universe has the power to refrain from using indecent speech and consequently to keep all such speech within the room in an "adult" zone.

The analogy to *Ginsberg* breaks down, however, when more than one adult is a party to the conversation. If a minor enters a chat room otherwise occupied by adults, the CDA effectively requires the adults in the room to stop using indecent speech. If they did not, they could be prosecuted under the "indecency transmission" and "specific person" provisions for any indecent statements they make to the group, since they would be transmitting an indecent message to specific persons, one of whom is a minor. The CDA is therefore akin to a law that makes it a crime for a bookstore owner to sell pornographic magazines to anyone once a minor enters his store. Even assuming such a law might be constitutional in the physical world as a reasonable alternative to excluding minors completely from the store, the absence of any means of excluding minors from chat rooms in cyberspace restricts the rights of adults to engage in indecent speech in those rooms. The "indecency transmission" and "specific person" provisions share this defect.

But these two provisions do not infringe on adults' speech in all situations. And as discussed below, I do not find that the provisions are overbroad in the sense that they restrict minors' access to a substantial amount of speech that minors have the right to read and view. Accordingly, the CDA can be applied constitutionally in some situations. Normally, this fact would require the Court to reject a direct facial challenge. . . . Appellees' claim arises under the First Amendment, however, and they argue that the CDA is facially invalid because it is "substantially overbroad." . . . I agree with the Court that the provisions are overbroad in that they cover any and all communications between adults and minors, regardless of how many adults might be part of the audience to the communication.

This conclusion does not end the matter, however. . . . There is no question that Congress intended to prohibit certain communications between one adult and one or more minors. . . . There is also no question that Congress would have enacted a narrower version of these provisions had it known a broader version would be declared unconstitutional. . . . I would therefore sustain the "indecency transmission" and "specific person" provisions to the extent they apply to the transmission of Internet communications where the party initiating the communication knows that all of the recipients are minors.

II

Whether the CDA substantially interferes with the First Amendment rights of minors, and thereby runs afoul of the second characteristic of valid zoning laws, presents a closer question. In *Ginsberg*, the New York law we sustained prohibited the sale to minors of magazines that were "harmful to minors." Under that law, a magazine was "harmful to minors" only if it was obscene as to minors. . . .

The Court neither "accept[s] nor reject[s]" the argument that the CDA is facially overbroad because it substantially interferes with the First Amendment rights of minors. I would reject it. *Ginsberg* established that minors may constitutionally be denied access to material that is obscene as to minors. As *Ginsberg* explained, material is obscene as to minors if it (i) is "patently offensive to prevailing standards in the adult community as a whole with respect to what is suitable . . . for minors"; (ii) appeals to the prurient interest of minors; and (iii) is "utterly without redeeming social importance for minors." Because the CDA denies minors the right to obtain material that is "patently offensive"—even if it has some redeeming value for minors and even if it does not appeal to their prurient interests—Congress' rejection of the *Ginsberg* "harmful to minors" standard means that the CDA could ban some speech that is "indecent" (i.e., "patently offensive") but that is not obscene as to minors.

I do not deny this possibility, but to prevail in a facial challenge, it is not enough for a plaintiff to show "some" overbreadth. Our cases require a proof of "real" and "substantial" overbreadth, and appellees have not carried their burden in this case. In my view, the universe of speech constitutionally protected as to minors but banned by the CDA—*i.e.*, the universe of material that is "patently offensive," but which nonetheless has some redeeming value for minors or does not appeal to their prurient interest—is a very small one. Appellees cite no examples of speech falling within this universe and do not attempt to explain why that universe is substantial "in relation to the statute's plainly legitimate sweep." That the CDA might deny minors the right to obtain material that has some "value" is largely beside the point. While discussions about prison rape or nude art may have some redeeming education value for *adults*, they do not necessarily have any such value *for minors*. . . . There is also no evidence in the record to support the contention that "many [e]-mail transmissions from an adult to a minor are conversations between family members," and no support for the legal proposition that such speech is absolutely immune from regulation. Accordingly, in my view, the CDA does not burden a substantial amount of minors' constitutionally protected speech.

Thus, the constitutionality of the CDA as a zoning law hinges on the extent to which it substantially interferes with the First Amendment rights of adults. Because the rights of adults are infringed only by the "display" provision and by the "indecency transmission" and "specific person" provisions as applied to communications involving more than one adult, I would invalidate the CDA only to that extent. Insofar as the "indecency transmission" and "specific person" provisions prohibit the use of indecent speech in communications between an adult and one or more minors, however, they can and should be sustained. The Court reaches a contrary conclusion, and from that holding I respectfully dissent.

SUPREME COURT ON
PHYSICIAN-ASSISTED SUICIDE
June 26, 1997

The national debate over whether doctors should be permitted to help the terminally ill commit suicide remained unsettled in 1997 despite—or perhaps because of—two key developments. On June 26, in a pair of cases from Washington and New York, the Supreme Court ruled that terminally ill patients did not have a general constitutional right to commit suicide with the assistance of a physician. The court's judgment was unanimous, but five justices wrote separate concurring opinions that suggested a majority of the court might find such a right to be constitutional under certain circumstances.

Even before the Court issued its ruling, however, the drama was shifting to Oregon, where a campaign was underway to persuade the state's voters to repeal the law they had adopted in 1994 legalizing physician-assisted suicide. On November 5, the day after 60 percent of the voters—more than had supported the original measure—opted to retain the law, the federal Drug Enforcement Administration warned doctors in the state that they could be violating the federal Controlled Substances Act if they prescribed drugs to help anyone commit suicide. The warning, which had been prompted by two members of Congress opposed to physician-assisted suicide, angered many in the state, including opponents of the law, who said that the federal government was meddling in the state's business. (Oregon's physician-assisted suicide measure, Historic Documents of 1994, p. 501)

The debate on physician-assisted suicide, which many observers likened to the abortion debate, raised difficult legal, moral, and ethical issues about the quality of life in its final months and about who should control the way a person died. Modern technology, which offered prolonged life to some while prolonging suffering for others, only contributed to the intensity of the debate. Medical experts said, and polls confirmed, that many doctors complied with patients' requests to help ease their dying by prescribing drugs, usually pain-killers, in doses large enough to induce death. That practice, however, was in conflict both with the Hippocratic Oath, which said physicians should not "give a deadly drug" to anybody if asked for it, and with the American Medical Association, which reaffirmed as late as 1996 that doctor-assisted suicide was "fundamentally incompatible with the physician's role as healer." (Reports on how Americans die, p. 325)

Legally, all but five states made physician-assisted suicide a crime, either by express statute or by implication as a matter of common law. The status was unclear in four states (Hawaii, Nevada, Utah, and Wyoming); only Oregon had legalized the practice, in a statewide referendum in 1994. Until 1997 the closest the Supreme Court had come to discussing the issue was in a 1990 case, in which it held, 4–5, that a person has a constitutional right to refuse unwanted life-sustaining medical treatment.

Most legislators and medical and legal experts saw a distinction between the passive action of withdrawing life support from a terminally ill patient and the active step of a doctor actually providing medication to cause a patient's deliberate death. The lawsuits in Washington and New York, which were filed by several doctors and their patients in 1994, challenged that distinction. They argued that the states' laws prohibiting physician-assisted suicide violated the constitutional guarantee of equal protection because it allowed some terminal patients to die by withdrawing their life-support system, while denying a similar choice to the terminally ill who were not on life-support systems. They also argued that the laws violated substantive due process by denying individuals their fundamental right to control the manner of their death.

Lower courts divided in the two cases, and both were appealed to federal appeals courts, which sided with the doctors. In the Washington case, the Ninth U.S. Circuit Court of Appeals ruled March 6, 1996, that the state's ban was an unconstitutional violation of due process. On April 2 the Second U.S. Circuit Court of Appeals rejected the due process argument, but agreed that the New York state law was a violation of equal protection. New York and Washington appealed to the Supreme Court. More than sixty briefs were filed in support of one side or the other. The states drew support from the Clinton administration, the American Medical Association, Catholic and other religious groups, right-to-life organizations, and disability rights groups. The American Civil Liberties Union and Americans for Death with Dignity were the main advocates for legalizing physician-assisted suicide.

The Supreme Court: Weighing Competing Interests

Chief Justice William H. Rehnquist wrote for the Court in both cases. In the Washington case (Washington v. Glucksberg), *Rehnquist said that the right to physician-assisted suicide was "not a fundamental liberty interest protected by the Due Process Clause." Moreover, the state had "unquestionably important and legitimate interests" in banning assisted suicide, including preserving life; protecting the integrity and ethics of the medical profession; protecting vulnerable groups, such as the poor, the disabled, and the elderly, from abuse, neglect, or mistakes; and avoiding "the path to vol-*

untary and perhaps even involuntary euthanasia." In footnote, Rehnquist noted Justice John Paul Stevens's concurring opinion, in which he argued that the Court's ruling in Glucksberg *did not preclude a successful claim "in a more particularized challenge." "Our opinion does not absolutely fore-close such a claim," Rehnquist wrote, but "such a claim would have to be quite different from the ones advanced" here. In the New York case (*Vacco, Attorney General of New York v. Quill*), Rehnquist maintained that the distinction between actively assisting suicide and passively withdrawing life-support equipment was "important and logical" and "certainly rational."*

Four justices joined Rehnquist's opinions in both cases: Sandra Day O'Connor, Antonin Scalia, Anthony M. Kennedy, and Clarence Thomas. In an important concurring opinion, however, O'Connor appeared to qualify her support. She emphasized that neither state barred a terminally ill patient suffering great pain from obtaining pain-relieving medication from a doctor to alleviate that pain "even to the point of causing uncon-sciousness and hastening death." O'Connor then said there was "no reason to think the democratic process will not strike the proper balance" between the interests of the terminally ill who want to end their suffering and the interests of the state in "protecting those who might seek to end life mis-takenly or under pressure."

The remaining four justices concurred in the judgment of the Court but not in Rehnquist's opinions. Justices Ruth Bader Ginsburg and Steven G. Breyer both joined O'Connor's opinion, and in a separate opinion Breyer underscored his belief in the legality of providing terminally ill patients with pain-relieving medications. If the law prevented "palliative care," he wrote, "the Court might have to revisit its conclusions in these cases." Jus-tices Stevens and David H. Souter each wrote separate opinions in which they indicated they might support a right to assisted suicide under differ-ent circumstances. Souter also encouraged experimentation by state legis-latures in finding the proper balance between the competing rights of the terminally ill and the states. Souter said such experimentation was not only "entirely proper" but "highly desirable."

Oregon: An Initial Experiment

The one state that had expressed an interest in experimenting with legal-ized assisted suicide was Oregon. In November 1994, 51 percent of the state's voters approved Measure 16 in a ballot referendum. The law allowed a patient expected to live six months or less to request a prescription for a lethal drug dose. To curb possible abuses, the law required that the patient make the request three times, both orally and in writing, with a fifteen-day waiting period after the first request. Two doctors had to agree that the patient was likely to die within six months, witnesses had to attest that the patient's request was made voluntarily, and a psychologist had to be con-sulted if the patient seemed depressed or incompetent. The patient, not the doctor, was required to self-administer the lethal dosage, and lethal injec-tions were prohibited.

Oregon Right to Life, with help from the National Right to Life organization, sued to keep the law from taking effect. A federal district court judge ruled in favor of Oregon Right to Life, but in February 1997 the Federal Court of Appeals for the Ninth Circuit ruled that Oregon Right to Life had no standing to sue, and on October 14 the Supreme Court refused, without comment, to hear an appeal from that ruling. Meanwhile in June the Oregon legislature voted to send the law back to the voters for possible repeal.

The repeal campaign drew national intention, as well as support and funding from interest groups. Repeal supporters outspent the law's advocates $4 million to $1 million. A substantial proportion of the $4 million came from Catholic dioceses around the country, while billionaire investor George Soros was a key contributor to those campaigning in behalf of the law. In one of the largest turnouts in several decades, 60 percent of the voters opted to retain the law. "This is a turning point for the death with dignity movement," said Barbara Combs Lee, the head of Compassion in Dying, one of the key groups working to preserve the law. "Not because we won, but because we proved the citizens of the state can band together and overcome the political machinery of those who oppose choice."

The vote in Oregon did not settle the matter, however. In a letter to Sen. Orrin G. Hatch, R-Utah, and Rep. Henry J. Hyde, R-Ill., dated November 5, DEA administrator Thomas A. Constantine warned that any doctor "delivering, dispensing or prescribing" a lethal dosage of narcotics "with the intent of assisting a suicide" would be violating the federal Controlled Substances Act, which did not recognize assisted suicide as a legitimate use of narcotic drugs. The two Republican legislators, both opponents of assisted suicide, had earlier asked the DEA for its opinion on the matter.

The DEA action was reminiscent of the Clinton administration's attempt to intervene in California after voters there approved a ballot initiative in November 1996 that allowed cultivation and possession of marijuana for medical use under the recommendation of a doctor. Barry R. McCaffrey, director of the Office of National Drug Control Policy, issued similar warnings, but the administration backed off after a group of physicians sued the government and a federal district judge issued a temporary restraining order in April 1997 barring federal prosecution of licensing action against California doctors who recommended using marijuana for medical purposes. (Medical use of marijuana, Historic Documents of 1996, p. 755)

The DEA letter on assisted suicide had two immediate effects. First, it apparently fulfilled its intended purpose of discouraging doctors from prescribing drugs for suicides for fear they would lose their license to prescribe any medicine. The Oregon Medical Association recommended that its 5,700 member physicians not take any actions under the Oregon Death with Dignity law until the issue with DEA was settled. Second, it outraged Oregonians, who said the federal government had no business trying to block a law that the people of the state had twice voted to enact. Several of those protesting the DEA action were, like Sen. Ron Wyden, D-Ore., opposed to assisted suicide. "We were told by the Supreme Court that this was a matter for the states to decide," Wyden said. "Now after Oregonians have made that deci-

sion, for the Federal Government to come after us with a weak, flimsy case is just wrong and a misreading of the law." Wyden and Oregon governor John Kitzhaber, a physician, took the DEA letter to Attorney General Janet Reno, who said that the DEA, an agency of the Justice Department, had acted without her consent and that Oregon law was under review. The results of that review had not been announced by the end of the year.

Following are excerpts from the opinions in the case of Vacco, Attorney General of New York v. Quill *and* Washington v. Glucksberg, *in which the Supreme Court on June 26, 1997, ruled that terminally ill individuals did not have a general constitutional right to a physician's assistance in helping them commit suicide; the ruling upheld laws in New York and Washington prohibiting physician-assisted suicides:*

No. 96-110

Washington, et al., Petitioners *v.* Harold Glucksberg et al.	On writ of certiorari to the United States Court of Appeals for the Ninth Circuit

[June 26, 1997]

CHIEF JUSTICE REHNQUIST delivered the opinion of the Court.

The question presented in this case is whether Washington's prohibition against "caus[ing]" or "aid[ing]" a suicide offends the Fourteenth Amendment to the United States Constitution. We hold that it does not. . . .

I

We begin, as we do in all due-process cases, by examining our Nation's history, legal traditions, and practices. . . .

. . . [F]or over 700 years, the Anglo-American common-law tradition has punished or otherwise disapproved of both suicide and assisting suicide. . . .

For the most part, the early American colonies adopted the common-law approach. . . .

Over time, however, the American colonies abolished . . . harsh common-law penalties. . . . [T]he movement away from the common law's harsh sanctions did not represent an acceptance of suicide; rather, . . . this change reflected the growing consensus that it was unfair to punish the suicide's family for his wrongdoing. . . .

That suicide remained a grievous, though nonfelonious, wrong is confirmed by the fact that colonial and early state legislatures and courts did not retreat from prohibiting assisting suicide. . . .

Though deeply rooted, the States' assisted-suicide bans have in recent years been reexamined and, generally, reaffirmed. Because of advances in medicine and technology, Americans today are increasingly likely to die in institutions, from chronic illnesses. Public concern and democratic action are therefore sharply focused on how best to protect dignity and independence at the end of life, with the result that there have been many significant changes in state laws and in the attitudes these laws reflect. Many States, for example, now permit "living wills," surrogate health-care decisionmaking, and the withdrawal or refusal of life-sustaining medical treatment. At the same time, however, voters and legislators continue for the most part to reaffirm their States' prohibitions on assisting suicide.

The Washington statute at issue in this case, Wash. Rev. Code §9A.36.060 (1994), was enacted in 1975 as part of a revision of that State's criminal code. Four years later, Washington passed its Natural Death Act, which specifically stated that the "withholding or withdrawal of life-sustaining treatment . . . shall not, for any purpose, constitute a suicide" and that "[n]othing in this chapter shall be construed to condone, authorize, or approve mercy killing. . . ." In 1991, Washington voters rejected a ballot initiative which, had it passed, would have permitted a form of physician-assisted suicide. Washington then added a provision to the Natural Death Act expressly excluding physician-assisted suicide.

California voters rejected an assisted-suicide initiative similar to Washington's in 1992. On the other hand, in 1994, voters in Oregon enacted, also through ballot initiative, that State's "Death With Dignity Act," which legalized physician-assisted suicide for competent, terminally ill adults. Since the Oregon vote, many proposals to legalize assisted-suicide have been and continue to be introduced in the States' legislatures, but none has been enacted. And just last year, Iowa and Rhode Island joined the overwhelming majority of States explicitly prohibiting assisted suicide.

Thus, the States are currently engaged in serious, thoughtful examinations of physician-assisted suicide and other similar issues. For example, New York State's Task Force on Life and the Law—an ongoing, blue-ribbon commission composed of doctors, ethicists, lawyers, religious leaders, and interested laymen—was convened in 1984 and commissioned with "a broad mandate to recommend public policy on issues raised by medical advances. . . . After studying physician-assisted suicide . . . , the Task Force unanimously concluded that "[l]egalizing assisted suicide and euthanasia would pose profound risks to many individuals who are ill and vulnerable. . . . [T]he potential dangers of this dramatic change in public policy would outweigh any benefit that might be achieved."

Attitudes toward suicide itself have changed . . . , but our laws have consistently condemned, and continue to prohibit, assisting suicide. Despite changes in medical technology and notwithstanding an increased emphasis on the importance of end-of-life decision-making, we have not retreated from this prohibition. Against this backdrop of history, tradition, and practice, we now turn to respondents' constitutional claim.

II

The Due Process Clause guarantees more than fair process, and the "liberty" it protects includes more than the absence of physical restraint. . . . The

Clause also provides heightened protection against government interference with certain fundamental rights and liberty interests. [Listing of cases omitted.] We have also assumed, and strongly suggested, that the Due Process Clause protects the traditional right to refuse unwanted lifesaving medical treatment. *Cruzan v. Director, Missouri Dept. of Health (1990)*.

But we "ha[ve] always been reluctant to expand the concept of substantive due process because guideposts for responsible decisionmaking in this unchartered area are scarce and open-ended." By extending constitutional protection to an asserted right or liberty interest, we, to a great extent, place the matter outside the arena of public debate and legislative action. We must therefore "exercise the utmost care whenever we are asked to break new ground in this field," lest the liberty protected by the Due Process Clause be subtly transformed into the policy preferences of the members of this Court....

Turning to the claim at issue here, the Court of Appeals stated that "[p]roperly analyzed, the first issue to be resolved is whether there is a liberty interest in determining the time and manner of one's death," or, in other words, "[i]s there a right to die?" Similarly, respondents assert a "liberty to choose how to die" and a right to "control of one's final days," and describe the asserted liberty as "the right to choose a humane, dignified death" and "the liberty to shape death." ... The Washington statute at issue in this case prohibits "aid[ing] another person to attempt suicide," and, thus, the question before us is whether the "liberty" specially protected by the Due Process Clause includes a right to commit suicide which itself includes a right to assistance in doing so.

We now inquire whether this asserted right has any place in our Nation's traditions. Here, ... we are confronted with a consistent and almost universal tradition that has long rejected the asserted right, and continues explicitly to reject it today, even for terminally ill, mentally competent adults. To hold for respondents, we would have to reverse centuries of legal doctrine and practice, and strike down the considered policy choice of almost every State....

Respondents contend, however, that the liberty interest they assert is consistent with this Court's substantive due-process line of cases, if not with this Nation's history and practice. Pointing to *Planned Parenthood v. Casey* (1992) and *Cruzan*, respondents read our jurisprudence in this area as reflecting a general tradition of "self-sovereignty," and as teaching that the "liberty" protected by the Due Process Clause includes "basic and intimate exercises of personal autonomy." ... According to respondents, our liberty jurisprudence, and the broad, individualistic principles it reflects, protects the "liberty of competent, terminally ill adults to make end-of-life decisions free of undue government interference." The question presented in this case, however, is whether the protections of the Due Process Clause include a right to commit suicide with another's assistance. With this "careful description" of respondents' claim in mind, we turn to *Casey* and *Cruzan*.

[In summarizing the two decisions, Rehnquist said that *Cruzan*'s recognition of a right to refuse life-sustaining medical treatment stemmed from "a long line of relevant state cases" holding that patients may reject unwanted medical treatment. As for the right to abortion recognized in *Casey*, Rehnquist said the ruling followed the Court's "tradition" of interpreting the Due Process Clause to protect "personal decisions relating to marriage, procreation, contraception, family relationships, child rearing, and education. . . ." Neither of those decisions, he said, "warrant the sweeping conclusion that any and all important, intimate, and personal decisions are so protected."]

The history of the law's treatment of assisted suicide in this country has been and continues to be one of the rejection of nearly all efforts to permit it. That being the case, our decisions lead us to conclude that the asserted "right" to assistance in committing suicide is not a fundamental liberty interest protected by the Due Process Clause. The Constitution also requires, however, that Washington's assisted-suicide ban be rationally related to legitimate government interests. This requirement is unquestionably met here. As the court below recognized, Washington's assisted-suicide ban implicates a number of state interests.

First, Washington has an "unqualified interest in the preservation of human life." The State's prohibition on assisted suicide, like all homicide laws, both reflects and advances its commitment to this interest. . . .

Respondents admit that "[t]he State has a real interest in preserving the lives of those who can still contribute to society and enjoy life." The Court of Appeals also recognized Washington's interest in protecting life, but held that the "weight" of this interest depends on the "medical condition and the wishes of the person whose life is at stake." Washington, however, has rejected this sliding-scale approach and, through its assisted-suicide ban, insists that all persons' lives, from beginning to end, regardless of physical or mental condition, are under the full protection of the law. . . .

Relatedly, all admit that suicide is a serious public-health problem, especially among persons in otherwise vulnerable groups. . . . The State has an interest in preventing suicide, and in studying, identifying, and treating its causes. . . .

Those who attempt suicide—terminally ill or not—often suffer from depression or other mental disorders. . . . Research indicates, however, that many people who request physician-assisted suicide withdraw that request if their depression and pain are treated. . . . The New York Task Force, however, expressed its concern that, because depression is difficult to diagnose, physicians and medical professionals often fail to respond adequately to seriously ill patients' needs. Thus, legal physician-assisted suicide could make it more difficult for the State to protect depressed or mentally ill persons, or those who are suffering from untreated pain, from suicidal impulses.

The State also has an interest in protecting the integrity and ethics of the medical profession. In contrast to the Court of Appeals' conclusion that "the integrity of the medical profession would [not] be threatened in any way by [physician-assisted suicide]," the American Medical Association, like many other medical and physicians' groups, has concluded that "[p]hysician-assisted suicide is fundamentally incompatible with the physician's role as healer." American Medical Association, Code of Ethics §2.211 (1994). . . . And physician-assisted suicide could, it is argued, undermine the trust that is essential to the doctor-patient relationship by blurring the time-honored line between healing and harming. . . .

Next, the State has an interest in protecting vulnerable groups—including the poor, the elderly, and disabled persons—from abuse, neglect, and mistakes. The Court of Appeals dismissed the State's concern that disadvantaged persons might be pressured into physician-assisted suicide as "ludicrous on its face." We have recognized, however, the real risk of subtle coercion and undue influence in end-of-life situations. [Citing *Cruzan.*] Similarly, the New York Task Force warned that "[l]egalizing physician-assisted suicide would pose profound risks to many individuals who are ill and vulnerable. . . . The risk of harm is greatest for the many individuals in our society whose autonomy and well-being are already compromised by poverty, lack of access to good medical care, advanced age, or membership in a stigmatized social group." . . . If physician-assisted suicide were permitted, many might resort to it to spare their families the substantial financial burden of end-of-life health-care costs.

The State's interest here goes beyond protecting the vulnerable from coercion; it extends to protecting disabled and terminally ill people from prejudice, negative and inaccurate stereotypes, and "societal indifference." The State's assisted-suicide ban reflects and reinforces its policy that the lives of terminally ill, disabled, and elderly people must be no less valued than the lives of the young and healthy, and that a seriously disabled person's suicidal impulses should be interpreted and treated the same way as anyone else's. . . .

Finally, the State may fear that permitting assisted suicide will start it down the path to voluntary and perhaps even involuntary euthanasia. The Court of Appeals struck down Washington's assisted-suicide ban only "as applied to competent, terminally ill adults who wish to hasten their deaths by obtaining medication prescribed by their doctors." Washington insists, however, that the impact of the court's decision will not and cannot be so limited. If suicide is protected as a matter of constitutional right, it is argued, "every man and woman in the United States must enjoy it." The Court of Appeals' decision, and its expansive reasoning, provide ample support for the State's concerns. . . . Thus, it turns out that what is couched as a limited right to "physician-assisted suicide" is likely, in effect, a much broader license, which could prove extremely difficult to police and contain. Washington's ban on assisting suicide prevents such erosion.

This concern is further supported by evidence about the practice of euthanasia in the Netherlands. The Dutch government's own study revealed that in 1990, there were 2,300 cases of voluntary euthanasia (defined as "the deliberate termination of another's life at his request"), 400 cases of assisted suicide, and more than 1,000 cases of euthanasia without an explicit request. In addition to these latter 1,000 cases, the study found an additional 4,941 cases where physicians administered lethal morphine overdoses without the patients' explicit consent. This study suggests that, despite the existence of various reporting procedures, euthanasia in the Netherlands has not been limited to competent, terminally ill adults who are enduring physical suffering, and that regulation of the practice may not have prevented abuses in cases involving vulnerable persons, including severely disabled neonates and elderly persons suffering from dementia. . . . The New York Task Force, citing the Dutch experience, observed that "assisted suicide and euthanasia are closely linked," and concluded that the "risk of . . . abuse is neither speculative nor distant." Washington, like most other States, reasonably ensures against this risk by banning, rather than regulating, assisting suicide. . . .

We need not weigh exactingly the relative strengths of these various interests. They are unquestionably important and legitimate, and Washington's ban on assisted suicide is at least reasonably related to their promotion and protection. We therefore hold that Wash. Rev. Code §9A.36.060(1) does not violate the Fourteenth Amendment, either on its face or "as applied to competent, terminally ill adults who wish to hasten their deaths by obtaining medication prescribed by their doctors."

[Rehnquist added this significant footnote: " . . . We emphasize that we today reject the Court of Appeals' specific holding that the statute is unconstitutional 'as applied' to a particular class. JUSTICE STEVENS agrees with this holding, but would not 'foreclose the possibility that an individual plaintiff seeking to hasten her death, or a doctor whose assistance was sought, could prevail in a more particularized challenge.' Our opinion does not absolutely foreclose such a claim. However, given our holding that the Due Process Clause of the Fourteenth Amendment does not provide heightened protection to the asserted liberty interest in ending one's life with a physician's assistance, such a claim would have to be quite different from the ones advanced by respondents here."]

* * *

Throughout the Nation, Americans are engaged in an earnest and profound debate about the morality, legality, and practicality of physician-assisted suicide. Our holding permits this debate to continue, as it should in a democratic society. The decision of the en banc Court of Appeals is reversed, and the case is remanded for further proceedings consistent with this opinion.

It is so ordered.

No. 95-1858

| Dennis C. Vacco, Attorney General of New York, et al., Petitioners
v.
Timothy E. Quill et al. | On writ of certiorari to the United States Court of Appeals for the Second Circuit |

[June 26, 1997]

CHIEF JUSTICE REHNQUIST delivered the opinion of the Court.

In New York, as in most States, it is a crime to aid another to commit or attempt suicide, but patients may refuse even lifesaving medical treatment. The question presented by this case is whether New York's prohibition on assisting suicide therefore violates the Equal Protection Clause of the Fourteenth Amendment. We hold that it does not.

Petitioners are various New York public officials. Respondents Timothy E. Quill, Samuel C. Klagsbrun, and Howard A. Grossman are physicians who practice in New York. They assert that although it would be "consistent with the standards of [their] medical practice[s]" to prescribe lethal medication for "mentally competent, terminally ill patients" who are suffering great pain and desire a doctor's help in taking their own lives, they are deterred from doing so by New York's ban on assisting suicide. Respondents, and three gravely ill patients who have since died, sued the State's Attorney General in the United States District Court. They urged that because New York permits a competent person to refuse life-sustaining medical treatment, and because the refusal of such treatment is "essentially the same thing" as physician-assisted suicide, New York's assisted-suicide ban violates the Equal Protection Clause. (1994).

The District Court disagreed: "[I]t is hardly unreasonable or irrational for the State to recognize a difference between allowing nature to take its course, even in the most severe situations, and intentionally using an artificial death-producing device." . . .

The Court of Appeals for the Second Circuit reversed. (1996). The court determined that, despite the assisted-suicide ban's apparent general applicability, "New York law does not treat equally all competent persons who are in the final stages of fatal illness and wish to hasten their deaths," because "those in the final stages of terminal illness who are on life-support systems are allowed to hasten their deaths by directing the removal of such systems; but those who are similarly situated, except for the previous attachment of life-sustaining equipment, are not allowed to hasten death by self-administering prescribed drugs." In the court's view, "[t]he ending of life by [the withdrawal of life-support systems] is *nothing more nor less than assisted suicide*." (emphasis added) The Court of Appeals then examined whether this supposed unequal treatment was rationally related to any legitimate state interests, and concluded that "to the extent that [New York's statutes] prohibit a physician from prescribing medications to be self-administered by a mentally competent, terminally-ill person in the final stages of his terminal illness, they are not rationally related to any legitimate state interest." We granted certiorari (1996) and now reverse.

The Equal Protection Clause commands that no State shall "deny to any person within its jurisdiction the equal protection of the laws." This provision creates no substantive rights. Instead, it embodies a general rule that States must treat like cases alike but may treat unlike cases accordingly. . . .

New York's statutes outlawing assisting suicide affect and address matters of profound significance to all New Yorkers alike. They neither infringe fundamental rights nor involve suspect classifications. . . . These laws are therefore entitled to a "strong presumption of validity."

On their faces, neither New York's ban on assisting suicide nor its statutes permitting patients to refuse medical treatment treat anyone differently than anyone else or draw any distinctions between persons. Everyone, regardless of physical condition, is entitled, if competent, to refuse unwanted lifesaving medical treatment; no one is permitted to assist a suicide. Generally speaking, laws that apply evenhandedly to all "unquestionably comply" with the Equal Protection Clause. . . .

The Court of Appeals, however, concluded that some terminally ill people—those who are on life-support systems—are treated differently than those who are not, in that the former may "hasten death" by ending treatment, but the latter may not "hasten death" through physician-assisted suicide. This conclusion depends on the submission that ending or refusing lifesaving medical treatment "is nothing more nor less than assisted suicide." Unlike the Court of Appeals, we think the distinction between assisting suicide and withdrawing life-sustaining treatment, a distinction widely recognized and endorsed in the medical profession and in our legal traditions, is both important and logical; it is certainly rational.

The distinction comports with fundamental legal principles of causation and intent. First, when a patient refuses life-sustaining medical treatment, he dies from an underlying fatal disease or pathology; but if a patient ingests lethal medication prescribed by a physician, he is killed by that medication. . . .

Furthermore, a physician who withdraws, or honors a patient's refusal to begin, life-sustaining medical treatment purposefully intends, or may so intend, only to respect his patient's wishes and "to cease doing useless and futile or degrading things to the patient when [the patient] no longer stands to benefit from them." [Quoting testimony of Dr. Leon R. Kass, before House Judiciary Subcommittee on the Constitution, 1996.] The same is true when a doctor provides aggressive palliative care; in some cases, painkilling drugs may hasten a patient's death, but the physician's purpose and intent is, or may be, only to ease his patient's pain. A doctor who assists a suicide, however, "must, necessarily and indubitably, intend primarily that the patient be made dead." Similarly, a patient who commits suicide with a doctor's aid necessarily has the specific intent to end his or her own life, while a patient who refuses or discontinues treatment might not. . . .

The law has long used actors' intent or purpose to distinguish between two acts that may have the same result. . . . Put differently, the law distinguishes actions taken "because of" a given end from actions taken "in spite of" their unintended but foreseen consequences. . . .

Given these general principles, it is not surprising that many courts, including New York courts, have carefully distinguished refusing life-sustaining treatment from suicide. [Citations omitted.] In fact, the first state-court decision explicitly to authorize withdrawing lifesaving treatment noted the "real distinction between the self-infliction of deadly harm and a self-determination against artificial life support." *In re Quinlan* [New Jersey Supreme

Court, 1976]. And recently, the Michigan Supreme Court also rejected the argument that the distinction "between acts that artificially sustain life and acts that artificially curtail life" is merely a "distinction without constitutional significance—a meaningless exercise in semantic gymnastics," insisting that "the *Cruzan* majority disagreed and so do we." [*People v.*] *Kevorkian* [1994].

Similarly, the overwhelming majority of state legislatures have drawn a clear line between assisting suicide and withdrawing or permitting the refusal of unwanted lifesaving medical treatment by prohibiting the former and permitting the latter. And "nearly all states expressly disapprove of suicide and assisted suicide either in statutes dealing with durable powers of attorney in health-care situations, or in 'living will' statutes." [Quoting from *Kevorkian*.] Thus, even as the States move to protect and promote patients' dignity at the end of life, they remain opposed to physician-assisted suicide.

New York is a case in point. The State enacted its current assisted-suicide statutes in 1965. Since then, New York has acted several times to protect patients' common-law right to refuse treatment. [Citing laws passed in 1987, 1990, and 1994, permitting "Do Not Resuscitate Orders" and authorizing appointment of "Health Care Agents and Proxies".] In so doing, however, the State has neither endorsed a general right to "hasten death" nor approved physician-assisted suicide. Quite the opposite: The State has reaffirmed the line between "killing" and "letting die." . . . More recently, the New York State Task Force on Life and the Law studied assisted suicide and euthanasia and, in 1994, unanimously recommended against legalization. . . .

This Court has also recognized, at least implicitly, the distinction between letting a patient die and making that patient die. In *Cruzan v. Director, Mo. Dept. of Health* (1990), we concluded that "[t]he principle that a competent person has a constitutionally protected liberty interest in refusing unwanted medical treatment may be inferred from our prior decisions," and we assumed the existence of such a right for purposes of that case. But our assumption of a right to refuse treatment was grounded not, as the Court of Appeals supposed, on the proposition that patients have a general and abstract "right to hasten death," but on well established, traditional rights to bodily integrity and freedom from unwanted touching. . . . *Cruzan* therefore provides no support for the notion that refusing life-sustaining medical treatment is "nothing more nor less than suicide." For all these reasons, we disagree with respondents' claim that the distinction between refusing lifesaving medical treatment and assisted suicide is "arbitrary" and "irrational." Granted, in some cases, the line between the two may not be clear, but certainty is not required, even were it possible. Logic and contemporary practice support New York's judgment that the two acts are different, and New York may therefore, consistent with the Constitution, treat them differently. By permitting everyone to refuse unwanted medical treatment while prohibiting anyone from assisting a suicide, New York law follows a longstanding and rational distinction.

New York's reasons for recognizing and acting on this distinction—including prohibiting intentional killing and preserving life; preventing suicide;

maintaining physicians' role as their patients' healers; protecting vulnerable people from indifference, prejudice, and psychological and financial pressure to end their lives; and avoiding a possible slide towards euthanasia—are discussed in greater detail in our opinion in [*Washington v.*] *Glucksberg* [1997]. These valid and important public interests easily satisfy the constitutional requirement that a legislative classification bear a rational relation to some legitimate end.

The judgment of the Court of Appeals is reversed.

It is so ordered.

JUSTICE O'CONNOR, concurring.

[JUSTICE GINSBURG concurs in the Court's judgments substantially for the reasons stated in this opinion. JUSTICE BREYER joins this opinion except insofar as it joins the opinions of the Court.]

Death will be different for each of us. For many, the last days will be spent in physical pain and perhaps the despair that accompanies physical deterioration and a loss of control of basic bodily and mental functions. Some will seek medication to alleviate that pain and other symptoms.

The Court frames the issue in this case as whether the Due Process Clause of the Constitution protects a "right to commit suicide which itself includes a right to assistance in doing so," and concludes that our Nation's history, legal traditions, and practices do not support the existence of such a right. I join the Court's opinions because I agree that there is no generalized right to "commit suicide." But respondents urge us to address the narrower question whether a mentally competent person who is experiencing great suffering has a constitutionally cognizable interest in controlling the circumstances of his or her imminent death. I see no need to reach that question in the context of the facial challenges to the New York and Washington laws at issue here. . . . The parties and *amici* agree that in these States a patient who is suffering from a terminal illness and who is experiencing great pain has no legal barriers to obtaining medication, from qualified physicians, to alleviate that suffering, even to the point of causing unconsciousness and hastening death. In this light, even assuming that we would recognize such an interest, I agree that the State's interests in protecting those who are not truly competent or facing imminent death, or those whose decisions to hasten death would not truly be voluntary, are sufficiently weighty to justify a prohibition against physician-assisted suicide.

Every one of us at some point may be affected by our own or a family member's terminal illness. There is no reason to think the democratic process will not strike the proper balance between the interests of terminally ill, mentally competent individuals who would seek to end their suffering and the State's interests in protecting those who might seek to end life mistakenly or under pressure. As the Court recognizes, States are presently undertaking extensive and serious evaluation of physician-assisted suicide and other related issues. In such circumstances, "the . . . challenging task of crafting appropriate procedures for safeguarding . . . liberty interests is entrusted to the 'laboratory' of the States . . . in the first instance." *Cruzan v. Director, Mo. Dept. of Health* (1990) (O'CONNOR, J., concurring).

In sum, there is no need to address the question whether suffering patients have a constitutionally cognizable interest in obtaining relief from the suffering that they may experience in the last days of their lives. There is no dispute that dying patients in Washington and New York can obtain palliative care, even when doing so would hasten their deaths. The difficulty in defining terminal illness and the risk that a dying patient's request for assistance in ending his or her life might not be truly voluntary justifies the prohibitions on assisted suicide we uphold here.

JUSTICE STEVENS, concurring in the judgments.

The Court ends its opinion with the important observation that our holding today is fully consistent with a continuation of the vigorous debate about the "morality, legality, and practicality of physician-assisted suicide" in a democratic society. I write separately to make it clear that there is also room for further debate about the limits that the Constitution places on the power of the States to punish the practice.

[I, II omitted]
III

The state interests supporting a general rule banning the practice of physician-assisted suicide do not have the same force in all cases. First and foremost of these interests is the " 'unqualified interest in the preservation of human life,' " which is equated with " 'the sanctity of life.' " That interest not only justifies—it commands—maximum protection of every individual's interest in remaining alive, which in turn commands the same protection for decisions about whether to commence or to terminate life-support systems or to administer pain medication that may hasten death. Properly viewed, however, this interest is not a collective interest that should always outweigh the interests of a person who because of pain, incapacity, or sedation finds her life intolerable, but rather, an aspect of individual freedom.

Many terminally ill people find their lives meaningful even if filled with pain or dependence on others. Some find value in living through suffering; some have an abiding desire to witness particular events in their families' lives; many believe it a sin to hasten death. Individuals of different religious faiths make different judgments and choices about whether to live on under such circumstances. There are those who will want to continue aggressive treatment; those who would prefer terminal sedation; and those who will seek withdrawal from life-support systems and death by gradual starvation and dehydration. Although as a general matter the State's interest in the contributions each person may make to society outweighs the person's interest in ending her life, this interest does not have the same force for a terminally ill patient faced not with the choice of whether to live, only of how to die. Allowing the individual, rather than the State, to make judgments " 'about the "quality" of life that a particular individual may enjoy' " does not mean that the lives of terminally-ill, disabled people have less value than the lives of those who are healthy. Rather, it gives proper recognition to the individual's interest in choosing a final chapter that accords with her life story, rather than one that demeans her values and poisons memories of her. . . .

Similarly, the State's legitimate interests in preventing suicide, protecting the vulnerable from coercion and abuse, and preventing euthanasia are less significant in this context. I agree that the State has a compelling interest in preventing persons from committing suicide because of depression, or coercion by third parties. But the State's legitimate interest in preventing abuse does not apply to an individual who is not victimized by abuse, who is not suffering from depression, and who makes a rational and voluntary decision to seek assistance in dying. . . .

Relatedly, the State and *amici* express the concern that patients whose physical pain is inadequately treated will be more likely to request assisted suicide. Encouraging the development and ensuring the availability of adequate pain treatment is of utmost importance; palliative care, however, cannot alleviate all pain and suffering. . . . An individual adequately informed of the care alternatives thus might make a rational choice for assisted suicide. For such an individual, the State's interest in preventing potential abuse and mistake is only minimally implicated.

The final major interest asserted by the State is its interest in preserving the traditional integrity of the medical profession. The fear is that a rule permitting physicians to assist in suicide is inconsistent with the perception that they serve their patients solely as healers. But for some patients, it would be a physician's refusal to dispense medication to ease their suffering and make their death tolerable and dignified that would be inconsistent with the healing role. . . . For doctors who have long-standing relationships with their patients, who have given their patients advice on alternative treatments, who are attentive to their patient's individualized needs, and who are knowledgeable about pain symptom management and palliative care options, heeding a patient's desire to assist in her suicide would not serve to harm the physician-patient relationship. Furthermore, because physicians are already involved in making decisions that hasten the death of terminally ill patients—through termination of life support, withholding of medical treatment, and terminal sedation—there is in fact significant tension between the traditional view of the physician's role and the actual practice in a growing number of cases.

As the New York State Task Force on Life and the Law recognized, a State's prohibition of assisted suicide is justified by the fact that the " 'ideal' " case in which "patients would be screened for depression and offered treatment, effective pain medication would be available, and all patients would have a supportive committed family and doctor" is not the usual case. Although, as the Court concludes today, these potential harms are sufficient to support the State's general public policy against assisted suicide, they will not always outweigh the individual liberty interest of a particular patient. Unlike the Court of Appeals, I would not say as a categorical matter that these state interests are invalid as to the entire class of terminally ill, mentally competent patients.

I do not, however, foreclose the possibility that an individual plaintiff seeking to hasten her death, or a doctor whose assistance was sought, could prevail in a more particularized challenge. Future cases will determine whether such a challenge may succeed.

IV

In New York, a doctor must respect a competent person's decision to refuse or to discontinue medical treatment even though death will thereby ensue, but the same doctor would be guilty of a felony if she provided her patient assistance in committing suicide. Today we hold that the Equal Protection Clause is not violated by the resulting disparate treatment of two classes of terminally ill people who may have the same interest in hastening death. I agree that the distinction between permitting death to ensue from an underlying fatal disease and causing it to occur by the administration of medication or other means provides a constitutionally sufficient basis for the State's classification. Unlike the Court, however, I am not persuaded that in all cases there will in fact be a significant difference between the intent of the physicians, the patients or the families in the two situations.

There may be little distinction between the intent of a terminally-ill patient who decides to remove her life-support and one who seeks the assistance of a doctor in ending her life; in both situations, the patient is seeking to hasten a certain, impending death. The doctor's intent might also be the same in prescribing lethal medication as it is in terminating life support. A doctor who fails to administer medical treatment to one who is dying from a disease could be doing so with an intent to harm or kill that patient. Conversely, a doctor who prescribes lethal medication does not necessarily intend the patient's death—rather that doctor may seek simply to ease the patient's suffering and to comply with her wishes. The illusory character of any differences in intent or causation is confirmed by the fact that the American Medical Association unequivocally endorses the practice of terminal sedation—the administration of sufficient dosages of pain-killing medication to terminally ill patients to protect them from excruciating pain even when it is clear that the time of death will be advanced. The purpose of terminal sedation is to ease the suffering of the patient and comply with her wishes, and the actual cause of death is the administration of heavy doses of lethal sedatives. This same intent and causation may exist when a doctor complies with a patient's request for lethal medication to hasten her death.

Thus, although the differences the majority notes in causation and intent between terminating life-support and assisting in suicide support the Court's rejection of the respondents' facial challenge, these distinctions may be inapplicable to particular terminally ill patients and their doctors. Our holding today in *Vacco v. Quill* that the Equal Protection Clause is not violated by New York's classification, just like our holding in *Washington v. Glucksberg* that the Washington statute is not invalid on its face, does not foreclose the possibility that some applications of the New York statute may impose an intolerable intrusion on the patient's freedom.

There remains room for vigorous debate about the outcome of particular cases that are not necessarily resolved by the opinions announced today. How such cases may be decided will depend on their specific facts. In my judgment, however, it is clear that the so-called "unqualified interest in the preservation of human life" is not itself sufficient to outweigh the interest in liberty that may justify the only possible means of preserving a dying patient's dignity and alleviating her intolerable suffering.

JUSTICE SOUTER, concurring in the judgment [in *Washington v. Glucksberg*].

Three terminally ill individuals and four physicians who sometimes treat terminally ill patients brought this challenge to the Washington statute making it a crime "knowingly . . . [to] ai[d] another person to attempt suicide," claiming on behalf of both patients and physicians that it would violate substantive due process to enforce the statute against a doctor who acceded to a dying patient's request for a drug to be taken by the patient to commit suicide. The question is whether the statute sets up one of those "arbitrary impositions" or "purposeless restraints" at odds with the Due Process Clause of the Fourteenth Amendment. [Quoting from dissenting opinion by Justice Harlan from ruling in *Poe v. Ullman* (1961), declining to rule on challenge to state law banning married couples from using contraceptives.] I conclude that the statute's application to the doctors has not been shown to be unconstitutional, but I write separately to give my reasons for analyzing the substantive due process claims as I do, and for rejecting this one.

[I, II, III omitted]
IV

. . . I take it that the basic concept of judicial review with its possible displacement of legislative judgment bars any finding that a legislature has acted arbitrarily when the following conditions are met: there is a serious factual controversy over the feasibility of recognizing the claimed right without at the same time making it impossible for the State to engage in an undoubtedly legitimate exercise of power; facts necessary to resolve the controversy are not readily ascertainable through the judicial process; but they are more readily subject to discovery through legislative factfinding and experimentation. It is assumed in this case, and must be, that a State's interest in protecting those unable to make responsible decisions and those who make no decisions at all entitles the State to bar aid to any but a knowing and responsible person intending suicide, and to prohibit euthanasia. How, and how far, a State should act in that interest are judgments for the State, but the legitimacy of its action to deny a physician the option to aid any but the knowing and responsible is beyond question.

The capacity of the State to protect the others if respondents were to prevail is, however, subject to some genuine question, underscored by the responsible disagreement over the basic facts of the Dutch experience. . . . Since there is little experience directly bearing on the issue, the most that can be said is that whichever way the Court might rule today, events could overtake its assumptions, as experimentation in some jurisdictions confirmed or discredited the concerns about progression from assisted suicide to euthanasia.

Legislatures, on the other hand, have superior opportunities to obtain the facts necessary for a judgment about the present controversy. Not only do they have more flexible mechanisms for factfinding than the Judiciary, but their mechanisms include the power to experiment, moving forward and pulling back as facts emerge within their own jurisdictions. There is, indeed, good reason to suppose that in the absence of a judgment for respondents here, just such experimentation will be attempted in some of the States.

I do not decide here what the significance might be of legislative foot-dragging in ascertaining the facts going to the State's argument that the right in question could not be confined as claimed. Sometimes a court may be bound to act regardless of the institutional preferability of the political branches as forums for addressing constitutional claims. Now, it is enough to say that our examination of legislative reasonableness should consider the fact that the Legislature of the State of Washington is no more obviously at fault than this Court is in being uncertain about what would happen if respondents prevailed today. We therefore have a clear question about which institution, a legislature or a court, is relatively more competent to deal with an emerging issue as to which facts currently unknown could be dispositive. The answer has to be, for the reasons already stated, that the legislative process is to be preferred. There is a closely related further reason as well.

One must bear in mind that the nature of the right claimed, if recognized as one constitutionally required, would differ in no essential way from other constitutional rights guaranteed by enumeration or derived from some more definite textual source than "due process." An unenumerated right should not therefore be recognized, with the effect of displacing the legislative ordering of things, without the assurance that its recognition would prove as durable as the recognition of those other rights differently derived. To recognize a right of lesser promise would simply create a constitutional regime too uncertain to bring with it the expectation of finality that is one of this Court's central obligations in making constitutional decisions.

Legislatures, however, are not so constrained. The experimentation that should be out of the question in constitutional adjudication displacing legislative judgments is entirely proper, as well as highly desirable, when the legislative power addresses an emerging issue like assisted suicide. The Court should accordingly stay its hand to allow reasonable legislative consideration. While I do not decide for all time that respondents' claim should not be recognized, I acknowledge the legislative institutional competence as the better one to deal with that claim at this time.

[Souter wrote a brief, separate opinion in *Vacco v. Quill*, also concurring in the judgment: " . . . The reasons that lead me to conclude in *Glucksberg* that the prohibition on assisted suicide is not arbitrary under the due process standard also support the distinction between assistance to suicide, which is banned, and practices such as termination of artificial life support and death-hastening pain medication, which are permitted. I accordingly concur in the judgment of the Court."]

JUSTICE GINSBURG, concurring in the judgments.

I concur in the Court's judgments in these cases substantially for the reasons stated by JUSTICE O'CONNOR in her concurring opinion.

JUSTICE BREYER, concurring in the judgments.

I believe that JUSTICE O'CONNOR's views, which I share, have greater legal significance than the Court's opinion suggests. I join her separate opinion, except insofar as it joins the majority. And I concur in the judgments. I shall briefly explain how I differ from the Court.

I agree with the Court in *Vacco v. Quill* that the articulated state interests justify the distinction drawn between physician assisted suicide and withdrawal of life-support. I also agree with the Court that the critical question in both of the cases before us is whether "the 'liberty' specially protected by the Due Process Clause includes a right" of the sort that the respondents assert. I do not agree, however, with the Court's formulation of that claimed "liberty" interest. The Court describes it as a "right to commit suicide with another's assistance." But I would not reject the respondents' claim without considering a different formulation, for which our legal tradition may provide greater support. That formulation would use words roughly like a "right to die with dignity." But irrespective of the exact words used, at its core would lie personal control over the manner of death, professional medical assistance, and the avoidance of unnecessary and severe physical suffering—combined.

. . . The respondents here . . . argue that one can find a "right to die with dignity" by examining the protection the law has provided for . . . interests relating to personal dignity, medical treatment, and freedom from state-inflicted pain. . . .

I do not believe, however, that this Court need or now should decide whether or a not such a right is "fundamental." That is because, in my view, the avoidance of severe physical pain (connected with death) would have to comprise an essential part of any successful claim and because, as JUSTICE O'CONNOR points out, the laws before us do not force a dying person to undergo that kind of pain. Rather, the laws of New York and of Washington do not prohibit doctors from providing patients with drugs sufficient to control pain despite the risk that those drugs themselves will kill. And under these circumstances the laws of New York and Washington would overcome any remaining significant interests and would be justified, regardless.

Medical technology, we are repeatedly told, makes the administration of pain-relieving drugs sufficient, except for a very few individuals for whom the ineffectiveness of pain control medicines can mean, not pain, but the need for sedation which can end in a coma. We are also told that there are many instances in which patients do not receive the palliative care that, in principle, is available, but that is so for institutional reasons or inadequacies or obstacles, which would seem possible to overcome, and which do *not* include *a prohibitive set of laws.* . . .

This legal circumstance means that the state laws before us do not infringe directly upon the (assumed) central interest (what I have called the core of the interest in dying with dignity). . . .

Were the legal circumstances different—for example, were state law to prevent the provision of palliative care, including the administration of drugs as needed to avoid pain at the end of life—then the law's impact upon serious and otherwise unavoidable physical pain (accompanying death) would be more directly at issue. And as JUSTICE O'CONNOR suggests, the Court might have to revisit its conclusions in these cases.

REVIEW OF UNITED NATIONS "EARTH SUMMIT"
June 27, 1997

A conflict of priorities between developing and industrialized nations prevented the second United Nations "Earth summit" in five years from reaching any major agreements on how to halt deterioration of the planet's environment. Delegates at a five-day meeting of representatives from 179 countries, held at UN headquarters in New York City, acknowledged the need for action on such environmental issues as conserving fresh water supplies and forests, but they adopted few specific plans to achieve those goals. In fact, the United States blocked progress on a treaty to cut emissions of "greenhouse" gases that cause global warming.

The New York summit was called to review progress since a UN environmental conclave held in 1992 in Rio de Janeiro, Brazil. The United Nations officially called the 1997 meeting "Earth Summit Plus 5." Noting the lack of agreement on concrete actions, however, some environmentalists derided the meeting as "Earth Summit Minus 5." (Rio summit, Historic Documents of 1992, p. 499)

A Replay of Rio

In some ways the New York meeting was a replay of the Rio summit. At both meetings, representatives of developing countries demanded that the United States and other industrialized nations take the first steps to curb practices that damage the environment, such as burning of fossil fuels, which produced carbon dioxide and other greenhouse gases. Also at both summits developing nations demanded more aid from the industrialized world to help them make their economies grow with minimal damage to the environment. Under budget pressures at home, leaders from the wealthy countries were reluctant to commit to huge increases in aid—and they demanded that the developing world avoid the environmental mistakes they had made in developing their economies over the previous two hundred years.

As the world's biggest economy, and by far the world's biggest polluter, the United States was at the center of these disputes at both summits. In Rio President George Bush, resolving a disagreement among his key environ-

mental aides, refused to authorize a U.S. signature on a "biodiversity treaty" designed to protect rare plant and wildlife species. The United States was the only nation attending that summit to refuse to sign the treaty. Some of Bush's aides insisted the treaty would hamper the work of U.S. biotechnology companies.

Addressing the New York meeting on June 26, President Bill Clinton disappointed environmentalists by refusing to commit the United States to specific reductions in emissions of greenhouse gases. Many scientists said such gases caused a global warming that over the next century could melt glaciers, causing the oceans to rise and flood millions of lowlands acres around the world.

Clinton acknowledged the dangers of global warming and the fact that the United States, with only 4 percent of the world's population, produced 20 percent of its greenhouse gases. "Here in the United States, we must do better," he said. But Clinton said he still needed to convince the American people and Congress that "the climate change problem is real and imminent," adding that he was not prepared to recommend a specific course of action until a global warming conference scheduled for December in Kyoto, Japan. At the Kyoto conference, the United States did accept new restrictions on greenhouse gas production. (Kyoto conference, p. 859)

Industry representatives praised Clinton for acknowledging the damage to industrialized economies that could result from the sudden curtailing of consumption of petroleum and coal. Environmentalists expressed disappointment, however, and contrasted Clinton's caution with a bold speech three days earlier by the new British prime minister, Tony Blair, pledging that his country would cut its greenhouse gas emissions even more than other European countries had promised. Implicitly criticizing the United States, Blair said: "We are all in this together. No country can opt out of global warming or fence in its own private climate."

North-South Divide

As at the Rio summit, much of the debate in New York centered around the age-old dispute between rich, industrialized countries (primarily in the northern hemisphere) and poorer, developing countries (primarily in the southern hemisphere).

This North-South cleavage was a prominent feature of nearly all global assemblies sponsored by the United Nations and had been at the center of most disagreements at the Rio summit. Echoing much of the rhetoric from the Rio summit, representatives from countries in Africa and Asia insisted that they were not receiving enough aid from the United States, Japan, and other wealthy nations. The developing nations said they could hardly be expected to curb damaging environmental practices—such as cutting down forests and polluting waterways—unless they received offsetting aid to help develop their economies.

The final declaration adopted June 27 by the UN General Assembly called on the wealthy nations to meet a target of spending 0.7 percent of their gross national products on economic aid to the developing world. But the *declaration set no specific dates for this target to be met, only that each country should do so "as soon as possible."*

Summing up the conference, Razali Ismail of Malaysia, president of the UN General Assembly, criticized his fellow representatives for lacking the political will to make tough decisions in the global interest. Razali said he was particularly disappointed that the enthusiasm for new environmental policies demonstrated at the Rio summit had vanished in the succeeding five years. "Since then many other things have come our way which have distracted our attention from that," he said. "Since then a sense of parochialism has spread over much of the developed world—a parochialism that affected the willingness of those countries to make available funds or resources, all kinds of things, technology transfer . . ." to the developing world.

Following are excerpts from the document, "Overall Review and Appraisal of the Implementation of Agenda 21," adopted June 27, 1997, by the United Nations General Assembly at the conclusion of a five-day special session on the environment and sustainable economic development:

I. Statement of Commitment

1. At the nineteenth special session of the United Nations General Assembly, we—heads of State or Government and other heads of delegations, together with our partners from international institutions and non-governmental organizations—have gathered to review progress achieved over the five years that have passed since the United Nations Conference on Environment and Development and to re-energize our commitment to further action on goals and objectives set out by the Rio Earth Summit.

2. The United Nations Conference on Environment and Development was a landmark event. At that Conference, we launched a new global partnership for sustainable development—a partnership that respects the indivisibility of environmental protection and the development process. It is founded on a global consensus and political commitment at the highest level. Agenda 21, adopted at Rio, addresses the pressing environment and development problems of today and also aims at preparing the world for the challenges of the next century in order to attain the long-term goals of sustainable development.

3. Our focus at this special session has been to accelerate the implementation of Agenda 21 in a comprehensive manner and not to renegotiate its provisions or to be selective in its implementation. We reaffirm that Agenda 21 remains the fundamental programme of action for achieving sustainable development. We reaffirm all the principles contained in the Rio Declaration on Environment and Development and the Forest Principles. We are convinced that the achievement of sustainable development requires the integration of its economic, environmental and social components. We recommit to working together—in the spirit of global partnership—to reinforce our joint efforts to meet equitably the needs of present and future generations.

4. We acknowledge that a number of positive results have been achieved, but we are deeply concerned that the overall trends with respect to sustainable development are worse today than they were in 1992. We emphasize that the implementation of Agenda 21 in a comprehensive manner remains vitally important and is more urgent now than ever.

5. Time is of the essence in meeting the challenges of sustainable development as set out in the Rio Declaration and Agenda 21. To this end, we recommit ourselves to the global partnership established at the United Nations Conference on Environment and Development and to the continuous dialogue and action inspired by the need to achieve a more efficient and equitable world economy, as a means to provide a supportive international climate for achieving environment and development goals. We therefore, pledge to continue to work together, in good faith and in the spirit of partnership, to accelerate the implementation of Agenda 21. We invite everyone throughout the world to join us in our common cause.

6. We commit ourselves to ensuring that the next comprehensive review of Agenda 21 in the year 2002 demonstrates greater measurable progress in achieving sustainable development. The present Programme for the Further Implementation of Agenda 21 is our vehicle for achieving that goal. We commit ourselves to fully implementing this programme.

II. Assessment of Progress Made Since the United Nations Conference on Environment and Development

7. The five years that have elapsed since the United Nations Conference on Environment and Development have been characterized by the accelerated globalization of interactions among countries in the areas of world trade, foreign direct investment and capital markets. Globalization presents new opportunities and challenges. It is important that national and international environmental and social policies be implemented and strengthened in order to ensure that globalization trends have a positive impact on sustainable development, especially in developing countries. The impact of recent trends in globalization on developing countries has been uneven. A limited number of developing countries have been able to take advantage of those trends, attracting large inflows of external private capital and experiencing significant export-led growth and acceleration of growth in per capita gross domestic product (GDP). Many other countries, however, in particular African countries and the least developed countries, have shown slow or negative growth and continue to be marginalized. As a result, they generally experienced stagnating or falling per capita GDP through 1995. In these and in some other developing countries, the problems of poverty, low levels of social development, inadequate infrastructure and lack of capital have prevented them from benefiting from globalization. While continuing their efforts to achieve sustainable development and to attract new investments, these countries still require international assistance in their efforts directed towards sustainable development. In particular the least developed countries continue to be heavily dependent on a declining volume of official development

assistance (ODA) for the capacity-building and infrastructure development required to provide for basic needs and more effective participation in the globalizing world economy. In an increasingly interdependent world economy, the responsible conduct of monetary and other macroeconomic policies requires that their potential impact on other countries be taken into account. Since the United Nations Conference on Environment and Development, the countries with economies in transition have achieved significant progress in implementing the principles of sustainable development. However, the need for full integration of these countries into the world economy remains one of the crucial problems on their way towards sustainable development. The international community should continue to support these countries in their efforts to accelerate the transition to a market economy and to achieve sustainable development.

8. Although economic growth—reinforced by globalization—has allowed some countries to reduce the proportion of people in poverty, for others marginalization has increased. Too many countries have seen economic conditions worsen and public services deteriorate; the total number of people in the world living in poverty has increased. Income inequality has increased among countries and also within them, unemployment has worsened in many countries, and the gap between the least developed countries and other countries has grown rapidly in recent years. On a more positive note, population growth rates have been declining globally, largely as a result of expanded basic education and health care. That trend is projected to lead to a stable world population in the middle of the twenty-first century. There has also been progress in social services, with expanding access to education, declining infant mortality and increasing life expectancy in most countries. However, many people, particularly in the least developed countries, still do not have access to adequate food and basic social services or to clean water and sanitation. Reducing current inequities in the distribution of wealth and access to resources, both within and among countries, is one of the most serious challenges facing humankind.

9. Five years after the United Nations Conference on Environment and Development, the state of the global environment has continued to deteriorate, as noted in the Global Environment Outlook of the United Nations Environment Programme (UNEP), and significant environmental problems remain deeply embedded in the socio-economic fabric of countries in all regions. Some progress has been made in terms of institutional development, international consensus-building, public participation and private sector actions and, as a result, a number of countries have succeeded in curbing pollution and slowing the rate of resource degradation. Overall, however, trends are worsening. Many polluting emissions, notably of toxic substances, greenhouse gases and waste volumes are continuing to increase although in some industrialized countries emissions are decreasing. Marginal progress has been made in addressing unsustainable production and consumption patterns. Insufficient progress has also been identified in the field of environmentally sound management and adequate control of transboundary move-

ments of hazardous and radioactive wastes. Many countries undergoing rapid economic growth and urbanization are also experiencing increasing levels of air and water pollution, with accumulating impacts on human health. Acid rain and transboundary air pollution, once considered a problem only in the industrialized countries, are increasingly becoming a problem in many developing regions. In many poorer regions of the world, persistent poverty is contributing to accelerated degradation of natural resources and desertification has spread. In countries seriously affected by drought and/or desertification, especially those in Africa, their agricultural productivity, among other things, is uncertain and continues to decline, thereby hampering their efforts to achieve sustainable development. Inadequate and unsafe water supplies are affecting an increasing number of people worldwide, aggravating problems of ill health and food insecurity among the poor. Conditions in natural habitats and fragile ecosystems, including mountain ecosystems, are still deteriorating in all regions of the world, resulting in diminishing biological diversity. At the global level, renewable resources, in particular fresh water, forests, topsoil and marine fish stocks, continue to be used at rates beyond their viable rates of regeneration; without improved management, this situation is clearly unsustainable.

10. While there has been progress in material and energy efficiency, particularly with reference to non-renewable resources, overall trends remain unsustainable. As a result, increasing levels of pollution threaten to exceed the capacity of the global environment to absorb them, increasing the potential obstacles to economic and social development in developing countries.

11. Since the United Nations Conference on Environment and Development, extensive efforts have been made by Governments and international organizations to integrate environmental, economic and social objectives into decision-making by elaborating new policies and strategies for sustainable development or by adapting existing policies and plans. As many as 150 countries have responded to the commitments established at the United Nations Conference on Environment and Development through national-level commissions or coordinating mechanisms designed to develop an integrated approach to sustainable development.

12. The major groups have demonstrated what can be achieved by taking committed action, sharing resources and building consensus, reflecting grassroots concern and involvement. The efforts of local authorities are making Agenda 21 and the pursuit of sustainable development a reality at the local level through the implementation of "Local Agenda 21s" and other sustainable development programmes. Non-governmental organizations, educational institutions, the scientific community and the media have increased public awareness and discussion of the relations between environment and development in all countries. The involvement, role and responsibilities of business and industry, including transnational corporations, are important.

Hundreds of small and large businesses have made "green business" a new operating mode. Workers and trade unions have established partnerships with employers and communities to encourage sustainable development in the workplace. Farmer-led initiatives have resulted in improved agricultural practices contributing to sound resource management. Indigenous people have played an increasing role in addressing issues affecting their interests and particularly concerning their traditional knowledge and practices. Young people and women around the world have played a prominent role in galvanizing communities into recognizing their responsibilities to future generations. Nevertheless, more opportunities should be created for women to participate effectively in economic, social and political development as equal partners in all sectors of the economy.

13. Among the achievements since the United Nations Conference on Environment and Development have been the entry into force of the United Nations Framework Convention on Climate Change, the Convention on Biological Diversity and the United Nations Convention to Combat Desertification in Those Countries Experiencing Serious Drought and/or Desertification, particularly in Africa; the conclusion of an agreement on the conservation and management of straddling and migratory fish stocks; the adoption of the Programme of Action for the Sustainable Development of Small Island Developing States; the elaboration of the Global Programme of Action for the Protection of the Marine Environment from Land-based Activities; and the entry into force of the United Nations Convention on the Law of the Sea. Implementation of these important commitments and of others adopted before the United Nations Conference on Environment and Development by all the parties to them, remains however, to be carried out, and in many cases further strengthening of their provisions is required as well as the mechanisms for putting them into effect. The establishment, restructuring, funding and replenishment of the Global Environment Facility (GEF) were a major achievement. However, its levels of funding and replenishment have not been sufficient fully to meet its objectives.

14. Progress has been made in incorporating the principles contained in the Rio Declaration on Environment and Development—including the principle of common but differentiated responsibilities, which embodies the important concept of and basis for international partnership; the precautionary principle; the polluter pays principle; and the environmental impact assessment principle—in a variety of international and national legal instruments. While some progress has been made in implementing United Nations Conference on Environment and Development commitments through a variety of international legal instruments, much remains to be done to embody the Rio principles more firmly in law and practice.

15. A number of major United Nations conferences have advanced international commitment for the achievement of long-term goals and objectives directed towards sustainable development.

16. Organizations and programmes of the United Nations system have played an important role in the progress made in the implementation of Agenda 21. The Commission on Sustainable Development was established to review progress achieved in the implementation of Agenda 21, advance global dialogue and foster partnerships for sustainable development. The Commis-

sion has catalysed new action and commitments and has contributed to the deliberations on sustainable development among a wide variety of partners within and outside the United Nations system. Although much remains to be done, progress has also been made at the national, regional and international levels in implementing the United Nations Conference on Environment and Development Forest Principles, including through the Commission's Ad Hoc Intergovernmental Panel on Forests.

17. Provision of adequate and predictable financial resources and the transfer of environmentally sound technologies to developing countries are critical elements for the implementation of Agenda 21. However, while some progress has been made, much remains to be done to activate the means of implementation set out in Agenda 21, in particular in the areas of finance and technology transfer, technical assistance and capacity-building.

18. Most developed countries have still not reached the United Nations target, reaffirmed by most countries at the United Nations Conference on Environment and Development, of committing 0.7 per cent of their gross national product (GNP) to ODA or the United Nations target, as agreed, of committing 0.15 per cent of GNP as ODA to the least developed countries. Regrettably, on average, ODA as a percentage of the GNP of developed countries has drastically declined in the post-United Nations Conference on Environment and Development period, from 0.34 per cent in 1992 to 0.27 per cent in 1995, but ODA has taken more account of the need for an integrated approach to sustainable development.

19. In other areas, results have been encouraging since the United Nations Conference on Environment and Development. There has been a sizeable expansion of private flows of financial resources from developed to a limited number of developing countries and, in a number of countries, efforts have been made in support of domestic resource mobilization, including the increasing use of economic instruments to promote sustainable development.

20. In many developing countries, the debt situation remains a major constraint on achieving sustainable development. Although the debt situation of some middle-income countries has improved, there is a need to continue to address the debt problems of the heavily indebted poor countries, which continue to face unsustainable external debt burdens. The recent World Bank/International Monetary Fund (IMF) Heavily Indebted Poor Countries Initiative could help to address that issue with the cooperation of all creditor countries. Further efforts by the international community are still required to remove debt as an impediment to sustainable development.

21. Similarly, technology transfer and technology-related investment from public and private sources, which are particularly important to developing countries, have not been realized as outlined in Agenda 21. Although increased private flows have led to investments in industry and technology in some developing countries and economies in transition, many other countries have been left behind. Conditions in some of these countries have been less attractive to private sector investment and technological change has been slower, thus limiting their ability to meet their commitments to Agenda

21 and other international agreements. The technology gap between developed countries and, in particular, the least developed countries has widened.

III. Implementation in Areas Requiring Urgent Action

22. Agenda 21 and the principles contained in the Rio Declaration on Environment and Development established a comprehensive approach to the achievement of sustainable development. While it is the primary responsibility of national Governments to achieve the economic, social and environmental objectives of Agenda 21, it is essential that international cooperation be reactivated and intensified, recognizing, inter alia, the principle of common but differentiated responsibilities as set forth in principle 7 of the Rio Declaration. This requires the mobilization of stronger political will and the invigoration of a genuine new global partnership, taking into account the special needs and priorities of developing countries. Such an approach remains as relevant and as urgently needed as ever. It is clear from the assessment above that, although progress has been made in some areas, a major new effort will be required to achieve the goals established at the United Nations Conference on Environment and Development, particularly in areas of cross-sectoral matters where implementation has yet to be achieved. . . .

SECRETARY OF STATE ON
U.S. CONSULATE IN VIETNAM
June 28, 1997

*The United States and Vietnam—two long-time foes who had been mov-
ing gradually toward closer relations—added substance in 1997 to their
reconciliation. In May U.S. and Vietnamese ambassadors arrived in each
other's capitals. A month later Secretary of State Madeleine K. Albright laid
the first brick for a new U.S. consulate building in Ho Chi Minh City, formerly Saigon, the capital of the South Vietnamese regime overthrown by
North Vietnam in 1975. The two sides also worked on agreements allowing
expanded economic ties between them.*

*Albright's visit marked one of the most important turning points in U.S.-
Vietnam relations since April 30, 1975, when Graham Martin, Washington's last ambassador to South Vietnam, boarded a helicopter and fled
Saigon. Hours later North Vietnamese forces captured the presidential
palace, ending a war that had killed 55,000 Americans and hundreds of
thousands of Vietnamese.*

*In response to Vietnam's cooperation in returning the remains of ser-
vicemen missing from the war and Hanoi's moves toward a market economy "with socialist characteristics," President Bill Clinton in 1994 lifted
U.S. sanctions against Vietnam. A year later the two countries agreed to
establish full diplomatic relations for the first time. Clinton in 1996 nominated Rep. Douglas "Pete" Peterson, a Florida Democrat who had been held
as a prisoner of war in Hanoi for nearly seven years, as the first U.S.
ambassador to a united Vietnam. Peterson's confirmation was delayed in
the Senate for several months as part of an overall battle between Congress
and the White House over nominations.* (Diplomatic relations, Historic Documents of 1995, p. 472)

*Peterson arrived in Hanoi to begin his diplomatic career on May 9.
"This is a historical event and the beginning of a new era of constructive
relations between Vietnam and the United States," he said upon his arrival.
On the same day Le Van Bang arrived in Washington as Hanoi's first
ambassador to the United States.*

Rubin Visit

A month earlier, Treasury Secretary Robert E. Rubin visited Vietnam and signed an accord under which the Hanoi government agreed to assume some of the debts to the United States of the former government of South Vietnam. Hanoi agreed to pay the United States $8.5 million in back interest immediately, but was given until 2019 to repay $146 million worth of debt from the Saigon regime. In effect, that agreement required one of the world's poorest countries—with an average per capita annual income of less than $250—to pay the world's richest country debts from a war the two fought against each other.

U.S. law barred aid to countries in arrears on official debt to the United States, and Washington had long demanded that Vietnam honor the debts as a condition for the opening of full trade relations between the two countries. A bilateral trade agreement also was under negotiation during 1997.

Rubin lectured the Vietnamese on necessary steps to build a free-market economy that could compete in the global marketplace. He stressed the importance of Vietnam opening itself to trade, investment, and open contact with the rest of the world. "Any economy that tries to shut itself off, that tries to build walls around itself, cannot succeed," he told one group of Vietnamese. "The only way to succeed is to become competitive in the world economy."

Later in April Vietnam initialed an agreement promising to honor U.S. copyrights on books, software, and other intellectual property. That agreement was another essential step toward the opening of expanded trade between the two countries. Albright formally signed the agreement during her visit in June.

Albright and the Consulate

The new consulate was built in the courtyard of the old U.S. embassy in Saigon—a building the Vietnamese had left empty since Martin's departure in 1975. Funding for the new building had been blocked in Congress and was released less than two weeks before Albright's scheduled visit to Vietnam.

In a ceremony fraught with emotional and political significance, Albright laid the first brick for the new consulate. In addition to symbolizing the reestablishment of U.S. diplomatic relations in the former South Vietnamese capital, the brick laid by Albright had personal significance for Ambassador Peterson and hundreds of other former American prisoners of war; it came from the famous "Hanoi Hilton" prison where they were kept during the war.

Albright said she expected that the consulate, when completed in 1999, would be one of the busiest ones in Asia, processing between 16,000 and 20,000 immigrant visa applications and 75,000 nonimmigrant visa applications annually. The United States rented space in Hanoi for its embassy. In addition to its embassy in Washington, Vietnam established a consulate in San Francisco.

During her visit to Vietnam, Albright met with senior Vietnamese officials and members of the small but growing U.S. business community there. In Ho Chi Minh City she also visited a clinic that provided prosthetic devices and wheelchairs to Vietnamese who were crippled during the war or since then by land mines or disease. The United States provided about $3 million each year for such programs.

"What has really moved me so deeply here is that it's so very hard to get away from the past," Albright said while visiting the clinic. "We all, whether American or Vietnamese, are never going to be fully able to put the past behind us. But I've been deeply moved by the desire of people to look toward the future."

One item from the past that was not fully resolved in 1997—and probably never would be—was the fate of nearly 1,600 American personnel still missing in action from the Vietnam war. The United States was spending nearly $10 million annually on various efforts to locate the missing military service personnel. By 1997 the search had narrowed to the cases of four dozen men who were alive when last seen by another American. Even so, U.S. officials said they had "no compelling evidence" that any American remained in captivity in Vietnam or any other country in Southeast Asia.

Albright said that obtaining a full accounting for the missing in action was "America's highest priority" in Vietnam. She defended the U.S. focus on it as a "deeply emotional issue for the American people."

Following is the text of an address June 28, 1997, by Secretary of State Madeleine K. Albright on the occasion of the groundbreaking ceremony for a new U.S. consulate building in Ho Chi Minh City, Vietnam:

Thank you very much. Ambassador Peterson, our distinguished friends from Vietnam, members of the diplomatic community, friends and guests, I really am delighted to be here this morning. As some of you know, I have had a little experience lately with opening days. This is, however, the first time at any ceremony that I have been asked to throw out the first brick. More accurately, I am honored to lay in the first brick of what will become the symbol and substance of America's first official diplomatic presence in a quarter century here in dynamic southern Vietnam.

The establishment of this Consulate, and its sister Consulate in San Francisco is another significant mile post in the development of U.S.-Vietnam relations. I want to express my special appreciation and thanks to the authorities here in Ho Chi Minh City who have been of enormous help in preparing the way for this new and magnificent facility.

We stand here in a historical spot and this Consulate-to-be reflects, in particular, the increasing multifaceted nature of our bilateral relationship. U.S.-Vietnamese ties have broadened steadily as we have been able to deal more and more successfully with the legacy of the past and thereby been able to focus more and more of our attention on the promise of the future. And it will be a very, very busy future. When this Consulate General is fully up and running, it will be one of our busiest visa issuing posts. We expect the Consulate to process between 16,000 to 20,000 immigrant visa applications and about 75,000 non-immigrant applications per year.

It will provide needed services to the more than 3,000 Americans who live in the area and the tens of thousands annually who visit. It will improve our ability to monitor the effort to achieve our highest priority in Vietnam which is to obtain the fullest possible accounting of Americans still missing or otherwise unaccounted for from the war in Southeast Asia.

It will enhance our capacity to pursue concerns on human rights. It will assist the American business community which is concentrated here in the south and it will accelerate refugee re-processing which has been an important humanitarian goal.

For Ambassador Peterson, a brick from the building in which he was once imprisoned has become a symbolic cornerstone of rebuilding in Vietnam— rebuilding not prisons, but businesses and hospital and schools. Rebuilding, as well, a structure of cooperation between two peoples on a shared journey from tragic conflict to deepening mutual respect.

It is in the same spirit that I will lay in a brick as a symbol of America's renewed diplomatic presence, and of America's commitment to continued progress towards full reconciliation and normalization between our people and the people of Vietnam.

And now the task.

GAO REPORT ON GULF WAR WEAPONS EFFECTIVENESS
June 30, 1997

The Persian Gulf War against Iraq may have lasted only a little more than a month in 1991, but its effects were still being felt in Washington in 1997. Overcoming Pentagon objections, the General Accounting Office (GAO), the investigative arm of Congress, in June released an unclassified version of a detailed report questioning the effectiveness of high-technology weapons during the Gulf war.

The GAO in 1996 had issued a heavily censored version of its critique of so-called smart weapons. The report said that the Pentagon and weapons manufacturers, during and after the war, had exaggerated the effectiveness of such high tech weapons as the F-117 Stealth bomber and the Tomahawk cruise missile. (Initial GAO report, Historic Documents of 1996, p. 403)

The Pentagon at first offered a mild response to the GAO report but insisted that the full report remain classified. Apparently with Congress on its side, the GAO succeeded in winning declassification for most of the report, and a public version was released on June 30.

GAO's Detailed Findings

The GAO called its report "Operation Desert Storm: Evaluation of the Air Campaign." The censored version released in 1996 concluded that expensive, high-technology airplanes and munitions did not necessarily perform better during the Gulf War than older, "dumb" weapons lacking the latest technological innovations. The report said that high-tech weapons faced many of the same limitations as the older weapons, and to achieve peak performance, some of the newer weapons needed ideal conditions (such as good weather) that were unlikely in wartime.

The declassified version released in 1997 made public many of the details on which the GAO had based its earlier conclusions. The agency said that approximately 85 percent of the material that had originally been stamped "secret" was made public in the 1997 version. The GAO study was based on an extensive review of information provided by the Pentagon, such as bomb damage assessments.

493

The GAO's underlying finding remained the same: High-tech weapons may have performed well during the Gulf War but in many cases not nearly as well as the military or defense contractors claimed, and in some cases older weapons were nearly as effective. For example, the GAO said precision-guided bombs dropped by the F-117 Stealth fighter appeared to hit their targets between 41 and 60 percent of the time. That was a "highly effective" rate, the GAO said, but was well below the 80 percent success rate claimed by the Pentagon and Lockheed Corp., the primary contractor for the plane. Similarly, the GAO disputed claims by the military and contractors that Tomahawk cruise missiles successfully hit their targets 85 to 98 percent of the time. Those claims could not be verified, the GAO said. The Pentagon censored the GAO's reporting of the Tomahawk's actual success rate.

The GAO report included the text of a response, dated March 28, 1996, from Frederick Frostic, deputy assistant secretary of defense for requirements and plans, in which the Pentagon "partially" concurred with the report's conclusions. Frostic insisted, however, that high-tech weapons were highly effective in the Gulf War and any deficiencies in them were being corrected.

But on July 1, the day after the unclassified GAO report was released, the Pentagon issued a sterner response denouncing the general thrust of the GAO criticisms. At a news conference, Kenneth H. Bacon, assistant secretary of defense for public affairs, called the report "the analytical equivalent of a dumb bomb—it's off target and loud." Bacon said the GAO made numerous false comparisons between older "dumb" weapons and the newer "smart" weapons, without acknowledging that the military had used the newer weapons against tougher targets. "It's like comparing a .350 hitter in the National League with a .350 hitter in high school and saying they're both the same because they both hit .350 without taking account of the different pitching conditions they encounter," Bacon said.

Private contractors and military officials may "have overdramatized" the effectiveness of high-tech weapons during the Gulf War, Bacon acknowledged. "It doesn't diminish the fact that they are significantly more effective than non-precision-guided munitions." Despite the GAO criticisms, he added: "We are not going to turn the clock back to an increased reliance on dumb bombs."

Analysis of Baghdad Bombing

A separate study of the air war against Iraq concluded that the use of high-tech, precision-guided weapons—at least when used against Baghdad—may have had an effect opposite to what U.S. officials intended. Writing in the Spring 1997 issue of Airpower, *an Air Force journal, William M. Arkin said that precision munitions were indeed effective in destroying or rendering unusable specific targets such as Iraq's defense ministry building and key communications links. But the pinpoint attacks did not destroy Iraq's overall communications network, enabling the Iraqi military leadership to maintain command of units in the field until the very end of the war, Arkin said.*

Further, Arkin argued that the allies never came close to killing Saddam and his top aides because the Iraqi leaders changed locations repeatedly, often several times in the same day. "There is no concrete evidence that any Baghdad leadership target was actually in use at the time of attack," Arkin said.

Arkin also disputed the widely held view that Baghdad was subjected to a massive bombing campaign similar to U.S. attacks during World War II on key cities in Japan and Germany. During the forty-three days of the war, he said, allied planes delivered "a mere" 330 weapons (laser-guided bombs and Tomahawk cruise missiles) against Baghdad, a much less intense bombing than enemy cities suffered in World War II. Arkin said news media reports—based largely on overly enthusiastic statements by some U.S. military officials and the claims of Iraqis—led to false impressions about the extent of damage in Baghdad.

Overall, Arkin said, some U.S. military officials and the public in general appeared to have drawn the false conclusion that wars can be won simply by bombing a nation's capital and targeting its leadership. "[T]he air attacks against Baghdad do not offer the operational experience for such postwar conventional wisdom," he said. "Nor is it proven that a combination of early attacks by stealth and precision guided weapons can defeat adversaries quickly and with a minimum of casualties."

Following are the summary sections of three key appendices to the declassified version of the report, "Operation Desert Storm: Evaluation of the Air Campaign," issued on June 30, 1997, by the General Accounting Office; items marked [DELETED] were portions that remained classified:

APPENDIX II: The Use of Aircraft and Munitions in the Air Campaign

Summary

In this appendix, we addressed questions concerning pre-Desert Storm claims made for air-to-ground aircraft, munitions, and target sensor systems versus how they were actually used in Desert Storm. In addition, we examined trends in aircraft and munition use, with particular emphasis on the F-117, and aircraft survivability, including the factors suggested by Desert Storm data that are most likely to account for aircraft casualties.

We first examined the operating environment of Desert Storm to provide the relevant context. The coalition faced a well-understood threat and had considerable lead time to prepare and actually practice for the eventual conflict. This provided coalition forces with an edge that should not be discounted in evaluations of the outcomes of the Persian Gulf War. The coalition had 6 months to plan for the war, deploy the necessary assets to the theater, practice strikes and deceptions, gather intelligence on targets, and become highly familiar with the operating environment. The fact that the coalition knew which IADS [Integrated Air Defense System] nodes to hit to inflict the most damage, the most quickly, was critical to its rapid degradation, and to the achievement of a form of air supremacy—elimination of an integrated, coordinated air defense. Without this supremacy, the air campaign might have proceeded at a much slower pace and perhaps with more losses. Further, the United States had the advantage of facing a highly isolated adversary, essentially unable to be reinforced by air, sea, or ground. The unique and often cooperative conditions of Desert Storm also severely limit the lessons of the war that can be reasonably applied to potential future contingencies.

We next compared planned aircraft and munitions use to actual Desert Storm use, along with patterns of aircraft and munition weight of effort against sets of strategic targets. While there were few notable discrepancies between original aircraft or munitions design and actual use of either in the conflict, two that are related did stand out: the survivability decision to bar munitions deliveries from below 12,000 feet after day 2 and the corresponding fact that most unguided munitions tactics, before the war, planned for low-altitude deliveries. The switch to medium- to high-altitude deliveries meant that the accuracy of unguided munitions was greatly reduced. This trade-off was feasible in Desert Storm as a way to reduce attrition—in fact, to almost eliminate it. But since 95 percent of the bombs and 92 percent of the total tonnage were unguided, there may have been a severe reduction in the accuracy of that ordnance.

In less than half of the strategic target categories, there was a clear preference for a particular type of air-to-ground platform. Preferences were evidenced for F-117s, F-15Es, A-6Es, and F/A-18s against C3 [command and control], GVC [government centers], NBC [nuclear, biological and chemical weapons] (F-117), NAV [naval] (A-6E and F/A-18), and SCU [scud missiles] (F-15E) targets. Nonetheless, considering all target categories and selected platforms, most aircraft were assigned to multiple targets across multiple target categories.

The combination of the ban on low-altitude tactics after day two, the degradation of radar SAMs and the IADS in the early days of the war, and the fact that a high proportion of strikes were flown at night—which constituted another form of aircraft sanctuary—almost certainly was responsible for a coalition aircraft attrition rate well below what planners expected and below historical precedent in the Middle East.

The Desert Storm air campaign was not accomplished by the efforts of strike aircraft alone. Aerial refueling tankers, airborne intelligence-gathering aircraft, reconnaissance aircraft, and strike support aircraft like F-4Gs, F-15Cs, and EF-111s were vital ingredients in the successful execution of the air campaign.

While many factors about the operating environment in Desert Storm were highly favorable to the coalition's air effort, aircraft targeting capabilities and precision munitions were put to the test by some periods of adverse weather as well as adverse conditions like smoke from oil fires or dust from bombing. Even mild weather conditions, including humidity, rendered precision bombing sensors (such as IR [infrared] target detection systems and laser target designation systems) either degraded or unable to work at all. Moreover, even in clear weather, pilots sometimes found it difficult to locate or identify valid targets from medium and high altitudes. In sum, our research and analysis found that official DOD [Department of Defense] descriptions of aircraft targeting capabilities were overstated based on the Desert Storm experience.

Finally, we addressed the role of the F-117 in the Desert Storm air campaign and examined some of the significant controversies about its use and contribution. Contrary to their "Lone Ranger" image, F-117s certainly required tanking as well as radar jamming support, while support from air-to-air fighter aircraft is less clear. The claim that F-117s—often, but not always— achieved tactical surprise, as defined by the absence of AAA until bombs made impact, was matched by the experience of other aircraft. The gains provided by stealthiness also required substantial trade-offs in terms of capabilities and flexibility, including [DELETED]. No F-117s were reported lost or damaged in Desert Storm, but they operated exclusively at night and at medium altitudes. This operational context was clearly less likely to result in aircraft casualties than low-level attacks or attacks at any level in daylight. Moreover, like the F-117s, some other nonstealth attack aircraft experienced no losses operating in the high-threat areas of Baghdad and operating at night at medium altitude. . . .

APPENDIX III: Aircraft and Munition Effectiveness in Desert Storm

Summary

Many claims of Desert Storm effectiveness show a pattern of overstatement. In this appendix, we addressed the effectiveness of different types of aircraft and munitions used in Desert Storm and the overall effectiveness of the air campaign in achieving its objectives. The Desert Storm input and BDA [bomb damage assessment] data did not permit a comprehensive aircraft-by-aircraft or munition-by-munition comparison of effectiveness; however, we were able to combine input and outcome data to (1) reveal associations of greater and lesser success against targets between types of aircraft and munitions and (2) examine the effects of *selected* types of munitions and aircraft where they were used in similar ways. Thus, we were able to work within the data constraints to examine several aspects of aircraft, munition, and campaign effectiveness.

While the available Desert Storm input and outcome data did not allow direct effectiveness comparisons between all aircraft types, they did indicate that overall effectiveness varied somewhat by type of aircraft and more so by type of target category attacked. The data also revealed patterns of greater and lesser success against targets, both between types of aircraft and munitions over the course of the campaign and with respect to individual target categories.

There was no consistent pattern indicating that the key to success in target outcomes was the use of either guided or unguided munitions. On average, targets where objectives were successfully achieved received more guided and fewer unguided munitions than targets where objectives were not determined to have been fully achieved. But in several target categories, the reverse was true. Nor were there major differences in the apparent effect of platform type on strike performance. When attacking the same targets with LGBs [laser-guided bombs], the F-111Fs reported achieving only a slightly greater target hit rate than the F-117s. Similarly, there was little difference in the rates of success achieved by F/A-18s and F-16s when delivering the MK-84 unguided munition.

The results of our analyses did not support the claim for LGB effectiveness summarized by "one target, one bomb." Moreover, planners apparently ordered restrikes either because BDA revealed that one bomb did not achieve target objectives or they did not believe that "one target, one bomb" was being achieved.

Desert Storm data also do not clearly support a number of major DOD claims for the F-117. For example, according to some, the accuracy of the F-117 in combat may have been unprecedented; our estimates of the bomb hit rate for the F-117 show that it was between 55 and 80 percent. Of equal importance, the rate of weapon release for the F-117 during Desert Storm was only 75 percent—largely because of a weather abort rate far higher than for other strike aircraft. Thus, the effectiveness of scheduled F-117 strikes was between 41 and 60 percent. And the accuracy and effectiveness of the TLAM [Tomahawk land attack "cruise" missile] was less than generally perceived.

Our analysis of manufacturers' claims revealed the same pattern of overstatement. All the manufacturers whose weapon systems we reviewed made public statements about the performance of their products in Desert Storm that the data do not fully support. And while the manufacturers' claims were often inaccurate, their assertions were not significantly different from, nor appreciably less accurate than, many of the statements of DOD officials and DOD reports about the same systems' performance in Desert Storm.

Finally, we found that the available quantitative and qualitative data indicate that damage to several major sets of targets was less complete than DOD's title V report to the Congress made clear and, therefore, that the objectives related to these target sets were only partially met. The gap between what has been claimed for air power in Desert Storm and what actually occurred was sometimes substantial. In effect, even under the generally favorable tactical and environmental conditions prevalent during Desert Storm, the effectiveness of air power was more limited than initially expected or subsequently claimed.

In light of the favorable conditions under which the air campaign was pursued and the technological and numerical advantages enjoyed by the coalition, it would not have been surprising if the effectiveness of the individual aircraft and munitions had been quite high. However, the commander of the U.S. air forces clearly stated at the onset of the war that his top priority in the air campaign was survivability. Conducting the war from medium and high altitudes precluded some systems from being used in ways that would probably have maximized their effectiveness. At the same time, the basically flat terrain, the attainment of air supremacy, and the dearth of Iraqi countermeasures provided favorable delivery conditions. Aircraft, munitions, and campaign effectiveness, to the extent that they can be measured, should be extrapolated only with care to another enemy in another contingency. . . .

APPENDIX IV: Cost and Performance of the Aircraft and Munitions in Desert Storm

Summary

In this appendix we found that each type of aircraft and munition under review demonstrated both significant strengths and weaknesses. There was no consistent pattern indicating that either high-cost or low-cost aircraft or munitions performed better or were more effective in Desert Storm.

The limited data do not show that multirole aircraft were either more or less effective in the air-to-ground capacity than more specialized, single-role aircraft. However, air-to-air missions were predominantly performed by single-role, air-to-air aircraft, and while multirole aircraft did perform some air-defense escort and some support missions, their use did not eliminate the need for single-role, air-to-air, and other support aircraft. The evidence from Desert Storm would seem to suggest the usefulness of single-role aircraft in their respective missions and the usefulness of multirole aircraft most predominantly in the air-to-ground mission.

The high-cost F-117 stealth bomber has significant operating limitations that affect when, where, and how it can be used; its target hit rate appears to have been matched by the F-111F against similar targets. Although the F-117 was often, but certainly not always, tasked against different targets, on certain performance dimensions—such as sortie rate, operations in weather, and tonnage delivered—it did not match the performance of several moderate- and even low-cost aircraft.

Guided munitions are many times more costly that unguided munitions, and their employment was constrained by poor weather, clouds, heavy smoke, dust, fog, haze, and even humidity. However, guided munitions were less affected by winds and, unlike unguided munitions, they were more consistently accurate from medium-to-high altitude. Although quite inexpensive and less restricted by low visibility, unguided munitions cannot reliably be employed against point targets from the medium and high altitudes predominantly used in Desert Storm.

Both guided and unguided munitions have important implications for aircraft survivability. To be accurate, unguided munitions need low-altitude delivery, which in Desert Storm was found to be associated with too many casualties. While guided munitions can be accurate from high altitude, their standoff capability does not necessarily protect them from defenses not at the target. [DELETED]

While guided munitions are clearly more accurate from medium and high altitudes, their high unit cost means that they may not be the least expensive way to attack certain targets, sometimes by a considerable margin, compared to unguided bombs. There was no apparent pattern indicating that guided munitions were, overall, more effective than unguided munitions in successfully destroying targets or that the difference between targets that were successfully destroyed and that were not successfully destroyed was simply that the latter were not attacked as often as the former by either guided or unguided munitions.

The TLAM cruise missile demonstrated a high-cost sortie rate, low survivability, and severe employment limitations. Its accuracy was substantially less than claimed; however, unlike any aircraft, its use does not risk an aircraft or, more importantly, its pilot.

BRITAIN, CHINA ON THE
TRANSFER OF HONG KONG
June 30, 1997

At the stroke of midnight on June 30, Britain handed control of Hong Kong, its fabulously successful crown colony on the southeast coast of China, over to the communist government in Beijing. Britain had ruled Hong Kong for 156 years, and under an 1899 treaty was obliged to return most of the tiny territory to China in 1997.

Under a 1984 agreement with Britain, China promised not to change Hong Kong's free-market economy for fifty years. Beijing's leaders invented the slogan, "one country, two systems" to describe how the mainland, with 1.2 billion people, would remain under communism, while Hong Kong, with 6.3 million residents, would remain capitalist.

Beijing's pledge did not extend to political freedoms, however, and in the months before the handover, the Chinese government unnerved many Hong Kong citizens and angered British officials. First, Beijing announced that it would replace Hong Kong's elected legislature with an appointed "provisional legislature" subservient to the Chinese government. In April, Tung Chee-hwa, appointed by Beijing as the new chief executive in Hong Kong, announced that the new legislature had approved regulations sharply curbing the right of public protest and allowing the government to ban organizations it deemed unacceptable. The new regulations had the potential to reverse many of the political liberalizations introduced by Britain in the early 1990s.

Then, on June 27, China announced that it would send some 500 armed troops into Hong Kong just before the handover and another 4,000 on July 1. Chinese officials said the troops would be needed to maintain public security after Britain withdrew the last of its 1,000 troops stationed in the territory. But Chris Patten, the last British governor of Hong Kong, said of the Chinese troop movement: "It doesn't sound to me the right sort of signal to send to the international community, and above all I think it is a most appalling signal to send to the people of Hong Kong."

The Handover Ceremony

Britain ended its rule of Hong Kong with all the pomp and ceremony of its past years of glory as the world's reigning empire. Marching bands, soldiers outfitted in splendid costumes, and a twenty-one-gun salute from the HMS Chatham *anchored in the harbor were among the royal trappings that marked the end of an era. In many ways, the loss of Hong Kong also ended any true semblance of the once-powerful British empire. The territory was by far the most important of the enclaves remaining from London's far-flung domain; without it, Britons still proud of their royal colonies had to be satisfied with a handful of holdings such as Bermuda, Gibraltar, and the Falkland Islands.*

To mark the handover, Britain's Prince Charles and Prime Minister Tony Blair were on hand, along with former prime minister Margaret Thatcher, who was in office in 1984 when Britain and China agreed on terms of the transfer of power. Patten, who in his five years as governor symbolized Britain's belated determination to turn Hong Kong into a democracy, rode from the driveway of his official residence, Government House, grimly holding a folded Union Jack in his lap.

The British were the hosts at the official handover ceremony, held at a new harborside convention center complex. As midnight approached, Prince Charles paid tribute to the people of Hong Kong, saying their success "demands—and deserves—to be maintained." Addressing Hong Kong's residents, Prince Charles said: "We shall not forget you, and we shall watch with the closest interest as you embark on this new era in your remarkable history."

After Prince Charles finished his remarks, a band played "God Save the Queen" and British soldiers lowered a giant Union Jack. As the flag reached the bottom of the flag pole at midnight, a Chinese flag was hoisted to the top of another flag pole, with the band playing the Chinese national anthem.

Chinese president Jiang Zemin then read a short speech pledging to maintain Hong Kong's "socio-economic system and way of life." Hong Kong would gradually develop a democratic system "that suits Hong Kong's reality," he said.

The transition was greeted with flag-waving celebrations over much of China, and Hong Kong residents had a three-day holiday. In an early test of China's willingness to tolerate dissent, the new government of Hong Kong allowed prodemocracy demonstrations that included many members of the disbanded elected legislature. "Why is it our leaders in China cannot give us more democracy?" Martin Lee, head of the Democratic Party asked supporters at one rally. "Why do they take away the democracy we fought so hard to win?" Representing the United States at the handover ceremonies, Secretary of State Madeleine K. Albright pointedly skipped the swearing-in of Hong Kong's new leadership to protest the disbanding of the old legislature.

Hong Kong's Future

The question of whether China would keep its promise of autonomy for Hong Kong was foremost in the minds of many in the territory and around the world, even though most observers assumed it would be years, even decades, before it would be answered. As an historical example, some pessimists looked to the nearby port city of Weihai, which Britain controlled from 1898 until 1930, when it returned the city to Chinese control after receiving assurances that Weihai would have special autonomy. The Chinese government then in power, and its communist successor, did not keep those promises, and Weihai soon became just another grim, economically backward Chinese city.

Other observers argued that the important question was not whether China would change Hong Kong, but how much and how fast Hong Kong would change China. Despite its tiny size, Hong Kong was one of the world's economic powerhouses, exceeding in global influence the giant nation to which it now belonged. Hong Kong's economy was the world's fourth-largest source of international investment capital—much of which went into capitalist enterprises in communist China.

Many observers predicted that Hong Kong's vast economic influence inevitably would help speed up the transformation of China to a mixed economy dominated more by free-market realities than by communist principles. These observers noted that it was the success of Hong Kong, as much as anything else, that convinced Chinese leaders such as Deng Xiaoping of the need to embrace foreign investment and, with it, elements of a free market economy. A parallel argument was that over the years the Chinese people would demand the same freedoms and advantages of their compatriots in Hong Kong, in effect making it impossible for leaders in Beijing to straddle the "one country, two systems" fence.

China in Control

Those who had been pessimistic about China's appetite for democracy in Hong Kong received some evidence for their concerns in September, when the provisional legislature set plans for elections in May 1998. The plan rejected universal suffrage and instead allowed all voters in Hong Kong to elect only twenty of the sixty legislative seats under a system of proportional representation. Another thirty seats would be filled by so-called constituency elections, in which corporations, professional groups, workers associations, and other sectors would vote. Only 180,000 votes would be cast for these seats, in contrast to the 2.7 million votes allowed under the constituency balloting supervised by Britain in 1995. The remaining ten seats would be filled by an 800-member council composed of representatives from business and other elements considered beholden to Beijing.

Despite this move, the new Hong Kong government appeared able in its early months to foster a general feeling of goodwill among most of the territory's residents. News reports said people in Hong Kong were reassured that little had changed and that predictions of a communist tyranny descending on their city had, so far, proven unfounded.

> *Following are statements by Charles, the Prince of Wales, and Chinese president Jiang Zemin, at a ceremony at midnight on June 30–July 1, 1997, marking the handover of control of Hong Kong from the United Kingdom to the Peoples Republic of China:*

STATEMENT BY CHARLES, PRINCE OF WALES

President Jiang Zemin, Premier Li Peng, Distinguished Guests, Ladies and Gentlemen.

This important and special ceremony marks a moment of both change and continuity in Hong Kong's history.

It marks, first of all, the restoration of Hong Kong to the People's Republic of China, under the terms of the Sino-British Joint Declaration of 1984, after more than 150 years of British administration.

This ceremony also celebrates continuity because, by that same treaty and the many subsequent agreements which have been made to implement its provisions, the Hong Kong Special Administrative Region will have its own government, and retain its own society, its own economy and its own way of life.

I should like to pay tribute this evening to those who turned the concept of 'one country, two systems' into the Joint Declaration, and to the dedication and commitment of those who have worked so hard over the last thirteen years to negotiate the details of the Joint Declaration's implementation.

But most of all I should like to pay tribute to the people of Hong Kong themselves for all that they have achieved in the last century and a half. The triumphant success of Hong Kong demands—and deserves—to be maintained.

Hong Kong has shown the world how dynamism and stability can be defining characteristics of a successful society. These have together created a great economy which is the envy of the world. Hong Kong has shown the world how East and West can live and work together. As a flourishing commercial and cultural cross-roads, it has brought us together and enriched all our lives.

Thirteen years ago the governments of the United Kingdom and the People's Republic of China recognised in the Joint Declaration that these special elements which had created the crucial conditions for Hong Kong's success should continue. They agreed that, in order to maintain that success, Hong Kong should have its own separate trading and financial systems, enjoy autonomy and an elected legislature, maintain its laws and liberties, and be run by the people of Hong Kong and be accountable to them.

Those special elements have served Hong Kong well over the past two decades. Hong Kong has coped with the challenges of great economic, social and political transition with almost none of the disturbance and dislocation which in other parts of the world have so often accompanied change on such a scale.

The United Kingdom has been proud and privileged to have had responsibility for the people of Hong Kong, to have provided a framework of opportunity in which Hong Kong has so conspicuously succeeded, and to have been part of the success which the people of Hong Kong have made of their opportunities.

In a few moments, the United Kingdom's responsibilities will pass to the People's Republic of China. Hong Kong will thereby be restored to China and, within the framework of 'one country, two systems,' it will continue to have a strong identity of its own and be an important international partner for many countries in the world.

Ladies and Gentlemen, China will tonight take responsibility for a place and a people which matter greatly to us all. The solemn pledges made before the world in the 1984 Joint Declaration guarantee the continuity of Hong Kong's way of life. For its part, the United Kingdom will maintain its unwavering support for the Joint Declaration. Our commitment and our strong links to Hong Kong will continue, and will, I am confident, flourish, as Hong Kong and its people themselves continue to flourish.

Distinguished guests, Ladies and Gentlemen, I should like on behalf of Her Majesty The Queen and of the entire British people to express our thanks, admiration, affection and good wishes to all the people of Hong Kong, who have been such staunch and special friends over so many generations. We shall not forget you, and we shall watch with the closest interest as you embark on this new era of your remarkable history.

STATEMENT BY CHINESE PRESIDENT ZEMIN

Your Royal Highness Prince Charles, Prime Minister Tony Blair, Distinguished Guests, Ladies and Gentlemen:

The national flag of the People's Republic of China and the regional flag of the Hong Kong Special Administrative Region of the People's Republic of China have now solemnly risen over this land. At this moment, people of all countries in the world are casting their eyes on Hong Kong. In accordance with the Sino-British Joint Declaration on the question of Hong Kong, the two governments have held on schedule the handover ceremony to mark China's resumption of the exercise of sovereignty over Hong Kong and the official establishment of the Hong Kong Special Administrative Region of the People's Republic of China. This is both a festival for the Chinese nation and a victory for the universal cause of peace and justice.

Thus, July 1, 1997 will go down in the annals of history as a day that merits eternal memory. The return of Hong Kong to the motherland after going through more than one century of vicissitudes indicates that from now on,

Hong Kong compatriots have become true masters of this Chinese land and that Hong Kong has now entered a new era of development.

History will remember Mr. Deng Xiaoping for his creative concept of "one country, two systems." It is precisely along the course envisaged by this great concept that we have successfully resolved the Hong Kong question through diplomatic negotiations and finally achieved Hong Kong's return to the motherland.

On this solemn occasion, I wish to express thanks to all the personages in both China and Britain who have contributed to the settlement of the Hong Kong question and to all those in the world who have cared for and supported Hong Kong's return to the motherland.

On this solemn occasion, I wish to extend cordial greetings and best wishes to more than six million Hong Kong compatriots who have now returned to the embrace of the motherland.

After the return of Hong Kong, the Chinese Government will unswervingly implement the basic policies of "one country, two systems," "Hong Kong people administering Hong Kong" and "a high degree of autonomy" and keep Hong Kong's previous socio-economic system and way of life of Hong Kong unchanged and its previous laws basically unchanged.

After the return of Hong Kong, the Central People's Government shall be responsible for foreign affairs relating to Hong Kong and the defense of Hong Kong. The Hong Kong Special Administrative Region shall be vested, in accordance with the Basic Law, with executive power, legislative power and independent judicial power, including that of final adjudication. Hong Kong people shall enjoy various rights and freedoms according to law. The Hong Kong Special Administrative Region shall gradually develop a democratic system that suits Hong Kong's reality.

After the return, Hong Kong will retain its status of a free port, continue to function as an international financial, trade and shipping center and maintain and develop its economic and cultural ties with other countries, regions, and relevant international organizations. The legitimate economic interests of all countries and regions in Hong Kong will be protected by law.

I hope that all the countries and regions that have investment and trade interests here will continue to work for the prosperity and stability of Hong Kong.

Hong Kong compatriots have a glorious patriotic tradition. Hong Kong's prosperity today, in the final analysis, has been built by Hong Kong compatriots. It is also inseparable from the development and support of the mainland. I am confident that, with the strong backing of the entire Chinese people, the Government of the Hong Kong Special Administrative Region and Hong Kong compatriots will be able to manage Hong Kong well, build it up and maintain its long-term prosperity and stability, thereby ensuring Hong Kong a splendid future.

Thank you.

July

NASA REPORT ON *PATHFINDER* MISSION TO MARS
July 4, 1997

Rocks named Barnacle Bill and Yogi, a skateboard-like object named So-journer, *and NASA scientists in California suddenly became as famous as world-class athletes and pop singers for a few weeks in the summer of 1997. The rocks were part of the Martian landscape, on which* Sojourner *was roaming in a new series of NASA missions to learn more about Mars. The NASA scientists became television commentators, describing the findings of their mechanical crew on Mars.*

Riding aboard a landing craft named Pathfinder, Sojourner *arrived on Mars on July 4 after a seven-month journey from Earth. Until early October, when their solar-powered batteries ran down,* Pathfinder *and* Sojourner *took thousands of photographs and scientific measurements of an area of the northern hemisphere of Mars called the Ares Vallis—once the site of massive floods.*

Pathfinder *(later renamed by NASA the* Sagan Memorial Station *in honor of astronomer/writer Carl Sagan) was the first U.S. mission to land on Mars since two* Viking *missions in 1976. David Baltimore, president of the California Institute of Technology, home of the Jet Propulsion Laboratory that managed the* Pathfinder *mission for NASA, said the findings had "advanced our knowledge of Mars tremendously."*

Worldwide interest in Pathfinder's *observations was enhanced by the continuing scientific debate about NASA's claim in 1996 that a meteorite from Mars contained evidence of life on the red planet. Independent research teams were examining evidence from the meteorite in 1997. At a conference on the subject in March, a research group affiliated with NASA said it had found evidence tending to corroborate claims that the meteorite contained evidence of organic material from Mars. Other researchers said it was too early to draw any conclusions from their studies.* (Martian meteorite, Historic Documents of 1996, p. 471)

NASA'S New Missions to Mars

Pathfinder *was part of a new ten-year NASA program of Martian explorations using relatively low-cost missions, each with a specific focus. The missions were to be launched every twenty-six months, just as the Earth and Mars were closest to each other in their respective orbits. The culmination was to be a mission launched in 2005, during which a robot would collect samples of Martian soil and rocks to be brought back to Earth.*

As the Pathfinder *mission wound down in September, the* Mars Global Surveyor *began orbiting the planet. Starting in March 1998,* Surveyor *was to map and examine the entire planet through photography, weather observations, and spectral analysis—providing the basis for decisions about where future landing missions should be directed. The* Surveyor *mission was similar to that of the ill-fated* Mars Observer, *which spun out of control in 1993 as it began maneuvering to enter the Martian orbit. The failure of the $1 billion* Observer *was a major setback for NASA, one that helped lead the agency to develop its new series of budget-minded missions.*

In justifying the missions, NASA officials cited the attraction of Mars as the one place in the universe where life seems most possible. "Mars has an unbelievable pull on people's imagination in America and around the world," NASA Administrator Daniel S. Goldin said the day before Pathfinder *landed.*

Of all the planets in the solar system, Mars is closest to having some of the features that made life possible on Earth. It has large amounts of frozen water, both on polar ice caps and in permafrost, and evidence (such as volcanic mountains) of a hot interior necessary for the energy to sustain life. Scientists said massive floods once scoured the Martian surface. The site of the Pathfinder *landing, for example, once was covered by a flood much greater than the gigantic Amazon River basin in Brazil. Because the climate on Mars had gone through enormous changes—as had the Earth's climate—scientists said the Martian past might even hold clues to how the Earth's climate might evolve.*

Another NASA probe in 1997 examined the moons of Jupiter and found conditions that might foster the development of life there. (Jupiter explorations, p. 202)

The Pathfinder *Mission*

The Pathfinder *mission was launched December 4, 1996, and entered the Martian atmosphere July 4, 1997. After a brief series of maneuvers,* Pathfinder *parachuted to the Martian surface, its actual landing cushioned by a cocoon of airbags.* Pathfinder *bounced around the surface upon impact, then landed upright in a near-perfect position. Once the airbags were deflated and other adjustments made, NASA scientists directed* Pathfinder *to take photographs and other observations of the surface. The first grainy images sent back to Earth showed that* Pathfinder *had landed in a rock-strewn valley with two hills (dubbed by NASA the "twin peaks") in the near distance.*

The next day, July 5, after a brief communications interruption, NASA ordered Pathfinder *to deploy two ramps to the Martian surface. Down those ramps rolled* Sojourner—*a roving vehicle two feet long by one foot high, traveling on six metal wheels and carrying three adapted Kodak cameras and an x-ray spectrometer.* Sojourner *began its observations July 6, testing the chemical composition of the Martian soil and taking pictures of nearby rocks, the soil, and the general neighborhood NASA scientists called the "rock garden."*

Sojourner's *adventures during the next several days captivated much of the world. Its first encounter was with a dark, pitted rock scientists dubbed Barnacle Bill. The first chemical analyses sent back to Earth showed the rock was composed of quartz, feldspar, and an igneous material called orthopyroxene. Scientists said the rock was similar to a common volcanic rock found on Earth.*

Sojourner *next examined a larger rock scientists called Yogi because of its purported resemblance to a sleeping bear ("Yogi Bear" was a popular cartoon figure back on Earth). At one point* Sojourner *got a little too close to Yogi and wound up with one of its wheels temporarily tilted against the surface of the rock. After that minor but well-publicized Martian traffic mishap,* Sojourner *kept on its rounds, examining several residents of the rock garden and sending photographs and chemical observations back to Earth.* Sojourner's *last examination, before NASA lost communications with it in early October, was of a rock scientists called Chimp.*

NASA officials had planned Sojourner's *observations to last only a week, although they hoped the vehicle would have a longer life span. During the nearly three months* Sojourner *functioned, it sent back 550 photographs and 15 chemical analyses of rocks.* Sojourner's *mothership*—Pathfinder—*sent back 2.6 billion bits of information, including 16,000 photographs, before it stopped communicating on September 27, NASA said.*

In a statement on November 4 summing up the mission's accomplishments, NASA said Pathfinder *and* Sojourner *had generated "a tremendous amount of new information" about Mars. This included the composition of some of the planet's rocks, dust, and soil, as well as weather observations showing rapid fluctuations in wind and temperature. Some information collected during the* Pathfinder *mission confirmed observations made by the* Viking *probes in 1976 and the NASA's Hubble telescope; other findings were different, suggesting areas for examination in future missions.*

Scientists working on the Pathfinder *mission published a study in the December 5, 1997, issue of the journal* Science *saying that life on Mars might have been possible—at least a few billion years ago. Matthew Golombek, chief project scientist for* Pathfinder, *and his colleagues detailed* Pathfinder's *findings that Mars was much warmer and wetter in ancient times than it is today, conditions more closely resembling those on Earth and more likely to foster the development of life.*

> *Following are three announcements from NASA on July 4, 1997, the day the* Pathfinder *mission reached Mars and sent its landing vehicle to the Martian surface:*

MISSION STATUS 7:30 A.M.

Mars Pathfinder is right on course for a landing in Ares Vallis, an ancient outflow channel in the northern hemisphere of Mars, at 10:07 a.m. Pacific Daylight Time [PDT] today.

The navigation team reported that the final trajectory correction maneuver, which could have been performed either 12 hours or six hours prior to *Pathfinder's* entry into the upper atmosphere, was not necessary. An early morning orbital update indicated that *Pathfinder* was heading straight for the center of its 60-mile-by-120-mile landing ellipse and was expected to enter the upper atmosphere at a 13.9-degree angle, just three-quarters of a degree off its original entry angle of 14.2 degrees. Pieter Kallemeyn, navigation team chief, estimated that the spacecraft would touch down at 19.0 degrees north latitude, 326.3 degrees east longitude.

"To give you an idea of the accuracy that we have achieved here, this is the equivalent of playing a round of golf in which the hole is in Houston, Texas, and the tee-off is in Pasadena, California," Kallemeyn said. "We're basically hitting a hole in one here."

Spacecraft events prior to landing will include release of the cruise stage at about 9:32 a.m. PDT; entry into the upper atmosphere at about 10:02 a.m. PDT; and landing 4.5 minutes later.

The spacecraft is currently about 198,000 kilometers (123,000 miles) from Mars, traveling at a velocity of about 24,500 kilometers per hour (15,277 miles per hour) with respect to Mars.

The flight team expects to receive the first low-gain signal from the spacecraft at about 2:07 p.m. PDT. Contained in that transmission will be information about the spacecraft's entry, descent and landing, atmospheric science data and details on the health of the lander and rover.

MISSION STATUS 4 P.M.

Mars Pathfinder successfully landed on the surface of Mars at 10:07:25 a.m. Pacific time, marking NASA's historic return to the red planet after more than 20 years.

The *Pathfinder* flight team received nearly instantaneous confirmation that the spacecraft had landed from an independent antenna mounted on one of the spacecraft's petals. Detection of the very weak signal, which came as a surprise, also indicated that the craft had landed on its base petal, thus eliminating the spacecraft's next task: to stand itself upright before deploying its petals.

Approximately 90 minutes after landing, engineering data indicated that *Pathfinder* had fully deployed its petals and was awaiting sunrise on Mars to power up. The flight team reported that the lander came to rest about 12 miles southwest of its targeted landing spot and was resting on the surface at a very slight tilt of about 2.5 degrees.

Pathfinder's first low-gain antenna transmission was received right on time at 2:07 p.m. PDT. The transmission contained preliminary information about the health of the spacecraft and rover, the spacecraft's orientation on the surface, data about its entry, descent and landing, and a first look at the density and temperatures of the Martian atmosphere.

Preliminary data from the atmospheric science instrument indicated that temperatures are somewhat warmer than they were in the Viking days of the mid-1970s. Dr. Timothy Schofield, principal investigator of the atmospheric science team, said early data suggested it was about minus 220 degrees Kelvin (minus 64 degrees Fahrenheit) at the landing site.

MISSION STATUS 9:15 P.M.

The *Mars Pathfinder* imaging team tonight unveiled the first photograph of Ares Vallis, an ancient water channel that at one time in Mars' early history carried more than 1,000 times the amount of flowing water carried by the Amazon River today. The color panorama, which drew enthusiastic applause at a 6:30 p.m. press briefing, was taken by the lander's Imager for Mars Pathfinder camera—called the "IMP"—before the camera was deployed on its mast. The photograph revealed a rocky desert scape with numerous large boulders and mountains on the horizon.

The images were transmitted during *Pathfinder's* first high-gain antenna transmission, which began at 4:28 p.m. PDT today. Totaling about 120, the postage stamp-sized black-and-white frames also included close-up photographs of the lander petals with the rover sitting in its stowed position in the foreground. Closer examination showed that one of the airbags did not fully retract and had become draped slightly over the edge of the rover's petal.

The *Pathfinder* flight and rover teams decided to test a new command sequence that would pull the obstructed petal up about 45 degrees, further retract the airbag, then lay the petal down again. The team tested this command sequence before uplinking it to the spacecraft starting at about 7:08 p.m. PDT. Return images from that transmission will be used by the rover team to determine if the "petal move" sequence cleared the petal enough to allow for safe deployment of the rover ramps. Some of the images were not received during the next downlink session due to a problem with the Deep Space Network tracking station. The remaining images were scheduled to be retransmitted during the last transmission of the day, which was to begin at 10 p.m. PDT.

If ramp deployment is postponed, the flight team will perform this activity Saturday morning. The rover would then be ready to roll off its ramp and onto the surface of Mars by about 5 p.m. PDT July 5.

NATO SUMMIT MEETING
STATEMENT ON EXPANSION
July 8, 1997

Just two years shy of reaching the half-century mark as one of the most successful military and diplomatic alliances in history, NATO in 1997 found a new reason for its existence. The alliance invited in three new members—Hungary, Poland, and the Czech Republic—all of which had once been in the enemy camp, the Warsaw Pact. To provide a measure of reassurance to Russia, which was not invited in, NATO signed a "charter" giving Moscow a voice, but not a veto, in the alliance's future.

Founded in the wake of World War II to protect Europe against potential attack by the Soviet Union, the North Atlantic Treaty Organization by the mid-1990s seemed to be an institution that had accomplished its job and needed either to declare victory and go out of business or find another line of work. The Soviet Union had collapsed; Russia, its successor state, was economically weak and militarily disorganized; and the cold war was over.

Most NATO members argued that the alliance was more than just a buffer against the Soviets. For one thing, it served as a unifying force in Europe, historically a continent of some of the most contentious nations on the planet. For another, NATO was the link that kept the United States actively involved in Europe, an involvement the Europeans often resented even as they counted on it. Lord Ismay, NATO's first secretary general, was quoted as saying Europe needed NATO "to keep the Russians out, the Americans in, and the Germans down."

In the mid-1990s, NATO members began talking about expanding the alliance membership eastward, to accommodate some of the aspiring democracies that once were part of the Soviet bloc and, not incidentally, to keep the alliance itself vital. Twelve countries applied for membership. By 1997 alliance members had narrowed the number of potential candidates to five and were ready to extend invitations. But, first, there was the question of what to do about Russia.

NATO Charter with Russia

From the outset of talk within NATO about expansion, there was never a serious chance that Russia would be invited to join, at least anytime soon. Despite Boris Yeltsin's reelection as president in 1996—a stunning victory over a resurgent Communist Party—Russia remained too unstable, too weak economically, and too threatening militarily for NATO members to feel comfortable with it as a formal ally. Under the NATO treaty, an attack on any member was considered an attack on all members. Few NATO members wanted to bring a turbulent Russia, beset by disagreements with several neighboring states, under NATO's "all for one" umbrella. (Yeltsin reelection, Historic Documents of 1996, p. 430)

With Yeltsin and his key aides muttering veiled, and sometimes not-so-veiled, threats against NATO expansion, allied leaders began looking for ways to calm fears in Moscow while moving ahead with their expansion plans. Secretary of State Warren Christopher in September 1996 announced Washington's solution: Offer Russia a "charter" promising cooperation and consultation between the alliance and Moscow, but without actual Russian membership in NATO. (Christopher proposal, Historic Documents of 1996, p. 655)

Transforming that proposal into reality took months of intense diplomatic negotiation, culminating in an announcement in Moscow on May 14, 1997, that Russia would sign such a document. The actual signing took place May 27, at the presidential Elysee Place in Paris. With French president Jacques Chirac heralding the event as ending "the last vestiges of the Cold War," Yelstin signed a document called the "Founding Act on Mutual Relations, Cooperation and Security Between NATO and the Russian Federation."

The charter described numerous levels of diplomatic, political, and military cooperation between NATO and Russia. The fundamental importance of all these appeared to be summarized in its second sentence, one that could never have appeared in an official NATO document during the cold war: "NATO and Russia do not consider each other as adversaries."

Despite the warm rhetoric accompanying the charter, Yeltsin made clear Russia's continuing unhappiness with NATO's drive eastward. "Russia still views negatively the expansion plans for NATO," he said. At the same time, Yeltsin threw momentary confusion into the Paris meeting by announcing that nuclear weapons pointed at NATO allies "are going to have their warheads removed." After a series of meetings to clarify the meaning of Yeltsin's apparently impromptu remarks, President Clinton's national security advisor, Samuel R. Berger, told reporters that Yeltsin was promising not to target NATO allies with Russian nuclear missiles. Berger described that promise as a "significant" expansion over Russia's previous pledge not to aim its nuclear weapons at the United States.

NATO Expansion Details

Having gotten Russia's tacit, if grudging, agreement to cooperate, the NATO allies turned to the last major question facing their expansion plans: how many nations to invite into the NATO fold. It was clear that Hungary, Poland, and the Czech Republic would be on the list; nine of the sixteen NATO members favored admitting Romania and Slovenia as well. France was the staunchest advocate for adding Romania; Italy had sponsored Slovenia's candidacy.

The Clinton administration for months had hinted that it wanted to invite only three new members: Hungary, Poland, and the Czech Republic. The administration made that position formal on June 12, when Secretary of Defense William S. Cohen met with his fellow NATO defense ministers, and the White House said the U.S. was "firm" in wanting only those three in the first round. U.S. officials said those three countries were close to being ready for NATO membership, both militarily and economically, while Romania and Slovenia were not.

Later in June, French and Italian officials raised the issue again at the "Group of Eight" economic summit in Denver, only to be told by Clinton that he would not change his mind. With the U.S. position fixed on such a fundamental question, and with Britain offering Washington support, the other Europeans had little choice but to back down, which they eventually did. As a fallback, the leaders agreed to put Romania and Slovenia at the head of the list for consideration at the April 1999 summit marking NATO's fiftieth anniversary. (Denver summit, p. 340)

The formal invitation to the three new members came at the NATO summit held July 8 in Madrid, issued in the Madrid Declaration on Euro-Atlantic Security and Cooperation. Clinton described the invitation as "a giant stride in our efforts to create a Europe that is undivided, democratic, and at peace literally for the first time since the rise of the nation-state on the European continent." Leaders of the three invited nations were on hand to express their satisfaction. Czech president Vaclav Havel, the former playwright who had symbolized dissent against the Soviet empire, declared: "This is an historic decision paving the way to a more stable and secure Europe."

NATO officials said they expected the three countries would be ready for actual membership by the 1999 summit. In the meantime, each country would have to upgrade its military to bring it into line with NATO standards.

Once again the grand statements of agreement and compromise disguised significant disputes among NATO members, and not just on the issue of how many new countries to invite in. Chirac used the occasion to voice long-standing French grievances—shared to a lesser extent by some other European nations—over Washington's domination of the alliance. For decades France had refused to participate in NATO's military command structure, sharply limiting its overall participation in the alliance.

Cost Issues

Inviting new members into NATO was the easy part. Agreeing on how to pay for an expansion of the alliance was another, more complicated issue. The task of estimating the cost of NATO expansion was a source of tension between the United States and some of its European allies.

In the months before and after the Madrid summit, Washington's military planners argued that the new members would have to undertake costly modernization programs to meet NATO standards. And, they said, existing NATO members would need to boost the communications, maintenance, and supply capabilities of their forces so they could respond to any threats to the new members. In February the Clinton administration estimated the total additional cost of NATO expansion at $27 billion to $35 billion over the following decade, including an average annual cost to the United States of less than $1 billion. A congressional estimate put the total potential cost for all NATO members at $125 billion.

Most European planners said the U.S. estimates were much too high, arguing that Washington's plans for modernization were too ambitious for the post-cold war era. After reviewing conflicting cost claims, the U.S.-led NATO staff prepared its own study in November estimating the total additional burden on NATO members would be less than $2 billion over the following decade.

The cost issue was expected to be one of several making NATO expansion a divisive issue when it reached Congress. As a revision to the original NATO treaty, the expansion needed approval of the Senate, and the full Congress would have to approve additional spending for NATO. Senate leaders initially said they expected the expansion would gain the necessary two-thirds majority, with advocates such as Indiana Republican Richard G. Lugar, a respected member of the Foreign Relations Committee, leading the charge for it.

When the committee began its debate on the matter October 7, critics of NATO expansion emerged from across the political spectrum. Some argued that the risk of antagonizing Russia was not worth the gain of expanding NATO's protection to Moscow's former client states. Others said the United States ultimately would have to foot much of the bill for modernizing the armies of the new members, at a cost the critics said would be too high. At least in the early stages of their debate, senators could find little guidance by turning to their constituencies; early polls showed that most Americans favored expanding NATO but few could remember anything about the matter.

> *Following is the text of the Madrid Declaration on Euro-Atlantic Security and Cooperation, issued July 8, 1997, by the heads of state and government attending the NATO summit meeting in Madrid, Spain:*

1. We, the Heads of State and Government of the member countries of the North Atlantic Alliance, have come together in Madrid to give shape to the new NATO as we move towards the 21st century. Substantial progress has been achieved in the internal adaptation of the Alliance. As a significant step in the evolutionary process of opening the Alliance, we have invited three countries to begin accession talks. We have substantially strengthened our relationship with Partners through the new Euro-Atlantic Partnership Council and enhancement of the Partnership for Peace. The signature on 27th May of the NATO-Russia Founding Act and the Charter we will sign tomorrow with Ukraine bear witness to our commitment to an undivided Europe. We are also enhancing our Mediterranean dialogue. Our aim is to reinforce peace and stability in the Euro-Atlantic area.

A new Europe is emerging, a Europe of greater integration and cooperation. An inclusive European security architecture is evolving to which we are contributing, along with other European organisations. Our Alliance will continue to be a driving force in this process.

2. We are moving towards the realisation of our vision of a just and lasting order of peace for Europe as a whole, based on human rights, freedom and democracy. In looking forward to the 50th anniversary of the North Atlantic Treaty, we reaffirm our commitment to a strong, dynamic partnership between the European and North American Allies, which has been, and will continue to be, the bedrock of the Alliance and of a free and prosperous Europe. The vitality of the transatlantic link will benefit from the development of a true, balanced partnership in which Europe is taking on greater responsibility. In this spirit, we are building a European Security and Defence Identity within NATO. The Alliance and the European Union [EU] share common strategic interests. We welcome the agreements reached at the European Council in Amsterdam. NATO will remain the essential forum for consultation among its members and the venue for agreement on policies bearing on the security and defence commitments of Allies under the Washington Treaty.

3. While maintaining our core function of collective defence, we have adapted our political and military structures to improve our ability to meet the new challenges of regional crisis and conflict management. NATO's continued contribution to peace in Bosnia and Herzegovina, and the unprecedented scale of cooperation with other countries and international organisations there, reflect the cooperative approach which is key to building our common security. A new NATO is developing: a new NATO for a new and undivided Europe.

4. The security of NATO's members is inseparably linked to that of the whole of Europe. Improving the security and stability environment for nations in the Euro-Atlantic area where peace is fragile and instability currently prevails remains a major Alliance interest. The consolidation of democratic and free societies on the entire continent, in accordance with OSCE principles, is therefore of direct and material concern to the Alliance. NATO's policy is to build effective cooperation through its outreach activities, including the Euro-Atlantic Partnership Council [EAPC], with free nations which share

the values of the Alliance, including members of the European Union as well as candidates for EU membership.

5. At our last meeting in Brussels, we said that we would expect and would welcome the accession of new members, as part of an evolutionary process, taking into account political and security developments in the whole of Europe. Twelve European countries have so far requested to join the Alliance. We welcome the aspirations and efforts of these nations. The time has come to start a new phase of this process. The Study on NATO Enlargement—which stated, inter alia, that NATO's military effectiveness should be sustained as the Alliance enlarges—the results of the intensified dialogue with interested Partners, and the analyses of relevant factors associated with the admission of new members have provided a basis on which to assess the current state of preparations of the twelve countries aspiring to Alliance membership.

6. Today, we invite the Czech Republic, Hungary and Poland to begin accession talks with NATO. Our goal is to sign the Protocol of Accession at the time of the Ministerial meetings in December 1997 and to see the ratification process completed in time for membership to become effective by the 50th anniversary of the Washington Treaty in April 1999. During the period leading to accession, the Alliance will involve invited countries, to the greatest extent possible and where appropriate, in Alliance activities, to ensure that they are best prepared to undertake the responsibilities and obligations of membership in an enlarged Alliance. We direct the Council in Permanent Session to develop appropriate arrangements for this purpose.

7. Admitting new members will entail resource implications for the Alliance. It will involve the Alliance providing the resources which enlargement will necessarily require. We direct the Council in Permanent Session to bring to an early conclusion the concrete analysis of the resource implications of the forthcoming enlargement, drawing on the continuing work on military implications. We are confident that, in line with the security environment of the Europe of today, Alliance costs associated with the integration of new members will be manageable and that the resources necessary to meet those costs will be provided.

8. We reaffirm that NATO remains open to new members under Article 10 of the North Atlantic Treaty. The Alliance will continue to welcome new members in a position to further the principles of the Treaty and contribute to security in the Euro-Atlantic area. The Alliance expects to extend further invitations in coming years to nations willing and able to assume the responsibilities and obligations of membership, and as NATO determines that the inclusion of these nations would serve the overall political and strategic interests of the Alliance and that the inclusion would enhance overall European security and stability. To give substance to this commitment, NATO will maintain an active relationship with those nations that have expressed an interest in NATO membership as well as those who may wish to seek membership in the future. Those nations that have previously expressed an interest in becoming NATO members but that were not invited to begin accession talks today will remain under consideration for future membership. The consider-

ations set forth in our 1995 Study on NATO Enlargement will continue to apply with regard to future aspirants, regardless of their geographic location. No European democratic country whose admission would fulfil the objectives of the Treaty will be excluded from consideration. Furthermore, in order to enhance overall security and stability in Europe, further steps in the ongoing enlargement process of the Alliance should balance the security concerns of all Allies.

To support this process, we strongly encourage the active participation by aspiring members in the Euro-Atlantic Partnership Council and the Partnership for Peace, which will further deepen their political and military involvement in the work of the Alliance. We also intend to continue the Alliance's intensified dialogues with those nations that aspire to NATO membership or that otherwise wish to pursue a dialogue with NATO on membership questions. To this end, these intensified dialogues will cover the full range of political, military, financial and security issues relating to possible NATO membership, without prejudice to any eventual Alliance decision. They will include meeting within the EAPC as well as periodic meetings with the North Atlantic Council in Permanent Session and the NATO International Staff and with other NATO bodies as appropriate. In keeping with our pledge to maintain an open door to the admission of additional Alliance members in the future, we also direct that NATO Foreign Ministers keep that process under continual review and report to us.

We will review the process at our next meeting in 1999. With regard to the aspiring members, we recognise with great interest and take account of the positive developments towards democracy and the rule of law in a number of southeastern European countries, especially Romania and Slovenia.

The Alliance recognises the need to build greater stability, security and regional cooperation in the countries of southeast Europe, and in promoting their increasing integration into the Euro-Atlantic community. At the same time, we recognise the progress achieved towards greater stability and cooperation by the states in the Baltic region which are also aspiring members. As we look to the future of the Alliance, progress towards these objectives will be important for our overall goal of a free, prosperous and undivided Europe at peace.

9. The establishment of the Euro-Atlantic Partnership Council in Sintra constitutes a new dimension in the relations with our Partners. We look forward to tomorrow's meeting with Heads of State and Government under the aegis of the EAPC.

The EAPC will be an essential element in our common endeavour to enhance security and stability in the Euro-Atlantic region. Building on the successful experience with the North Atlantic Cooperation Council and with Partnership for Peace, it will provide the overarching framework for all aspects of our wide-ranging cooperation and raise it to a qualitatively new level. It will deepen and give more focus to our multilateral political and security-related discussions, enhance the scope and substance of our practical cooperation, and increase transparency and confidence in security matters among all EAPC member states. The expanded political dimension of consultation and cooperation which the EAPC will offer will allow Partners, if they wish, to develop a direct political relationship individually or in smaller groups with the Alliance. The EAPC will increase the scope for consultation and cooperation on regional matters and activities.

10. The Partnership for Peace [PfP] has become the focal point of our efforts to build new patterns of practical cooperation in the security realm. Without PfP, we would not have been able to put together and deploy so effectively and efficiently the Implementation and Stabilisation Forces in Bosnia and Herzegovina with the participation of so many of our Partners.

We welcome and endorse the decision taken in Sintra to enhance the Partnership for Peace by strengthening the political consultation element, increasing the role Partners play in PfP decision-making and planning, and by making PfP more operational. Partners will, in future, be able to involve themselves more closely in PfP programme issues as well as PfP operations, Partner staff elements will be established at various levels of the military structure of the Alliance, and the Planning and Review Process will become more like the NATO force planning process. On the basis of the principles of inclusiveness and self-differentiation, Partner countries will thus be able to draw closer to the Alliance. We invite all Partner countries to take full advantage of the new possibilities which the enhanced PfP will offer.

With the expanded range of opportunities comes also the need for adequate political and military representation at NATO Headquarters in Brussels. We have therefore created the possibility for Partners to establish diplomatic missions to NATO under the Brussels Agreement which entered into force on 28th March 1997. We invite and encourage Partner countries to take advantage of this opportunity.

11. The Founding Act on Mutual Relations, Cooperation and Security between NATO and the Russian Federation, signed on 27th May 1997 in Paris, is a historic achievement. It opens a new era in European security relations, an era of cooperation between NATO and Russia. The Founding Act reflects our shared commitment to build together a lasting and inclusive peace in the Euro-Atlantic area on the principles of democracy and cooperative security. Its provisions contribute to NATO's underlying objective of enhancing the security of all European states, which is reinforced also through our actions here in Madrid. It provides NATO and Russia a framework through which we intend to create a strong, stable and enduring partnership. We are committed to working with Russia to make full use of the provisions of the Founding Act.

Through the new forum created under the Founding Act, the NATO-Russia Permanent Joint Council, NATO and Russia will consult, cooperate and, where appropriate, act together to address challenges to security in Europe. The activities of the Council will build upon the principles of reciprocity and transparency. The cooperation between Russian and NATO troops in Bosnia and Herzegovina and between the staffs at SHAPE demonstrate what is possible when we work together. We will build on this experience, including through PfP, to develop genuine cooperation between NATO and Russia. We look forward to consulting regularly with Russia on a broad range of topics, and to forging closer cooperation, including military-to-military, through the Permanent Joint Council, which will begin work soon.

12. We attach great importance to tomorrow's signing of the Charter on a Distinctive Partnership between NATO and Ukraine. The NATO-Ukraine Charter will move NATO-Ukraine cooperation onto a more substantive level, offer new potential for strengthening our relationship, and enhance security in the region more widely. We are convinced that Ukraine's independence, territorial integrity and sovereignty are a key factor for ensuring stability in Europe. We continue to support the reform process in Ukraine as it develops as a democratic nation with a market economy. We want to build on steps taken to date in developing a strong and enduring relationship between NATO and Ukraine. We welcome the practical cooperation achieved with the Alliance through Ukraine's participation within IFOR and SFOR, as well as the recent opening of the NATO Information Office in Kyiv, as important contributions in this regard. We look forward to the early and active implementation of the Charter.

13. The Mediterranean region merits great attention since security in the whole of Europe is closely linked with security and stability in the Mediterranean. We are pleased with the development of the Mediterranean initiative that was launched following our last meeting in Brussels. The dialogue we have established between NATO and a number of Mediterranean countries is developing progressively and successfully, contributes to confidence-building and cooperation in the region, and complements other international efforts. We endorse the measures agreed by NATO Foreign Ministers in Sintra on the widening of the scope and the enhancement of the dialogue and, on the basis of their recommendation, have decided today to establish under the authority of the North Atlantic Council a new committee, the Mediterranean Cooperation Group, which will have the overall responsibility for the Mediterranean dialogue.

14. We welcome the progress made on the Alliance's internal adaptation. Its fundamental objectives are to maintain the Alliance's military effectiveness and its ability to react to a wide range of contingencies, to preserve the transatlantic link, and develop the European Security and Defence Identity (ESDI) within the Alliance. We recognise the substantive work which has been carried out on the development of a new command structure for the Alliance; the implementation of the Combined Joint Task Forces (CJTF) concept; and the building of ESDI within NATO. We attach great importance to an early and successful completion of this process. Building on the earlier reductions and restructuring of the Alliance's military forces, it will provide the Alliance with the full range of capabilities needed to meet the challenges of the future.

15. We welcome the substantial progress made on the development of a new command structure which will enable the Alliance to carry out the whole range of its missions more effectively and flexibly, support our enhanced relationship with Partners and the admission of new members, and provide, as part of the development of ESDI within NATO, for European command arrangements able to prepare, support, command and conduct WEU-led operations.

We note that essential elements of the new command structure have been identified and will form the basis for further work. We must maintain the momentum of this work. We have, accordingly, directed the Council in Permanent Session, with the advice of the Military Committee, to work on the resolution of outstanding issues with the aim of reaching agreement on NATO's future command structure by the time of the Council Ministerial meetings in December.

16. Against this background, the members of the Alliance's integrated military structure warmly welcome today's announcement by Spain of its readiness to participate fully in the Alliance's new command structure, once agreement has been reached upon it. Spain's full participation will enhance its overall contribution to the security of the Alliance, help develop the European Security and Defence Identity within NATO and strengthen the transatlantic link.

17. We are pleased with the progress made in implementing the CJTF concept, including the initial designation of parent headquarters, and look forward to the forthcoming trials. This concept will enhance our ability to command and control multinational and multiservice forces, generated and deployed at short notice, which are capable of conducting a wide range of military operations. Combined Joint Task Forces will also facilitate the possible participation of non-NATO nations in operations and, by enabling the conduct of WEU-led CJTF operations, will contribute to the development of ESDI within the Alliance.

18. We reaffirm, as stated in our 1994 Brussels Declaration, our full support for the development of the European Security and Defence Identity by making available NATO assets and capabilities for WEU operations. With this in mind, the Alliance is building ESDI, grounded on solid military principles and supported by appropriate military planning and permitting the creation of militarily coherent and effective forces capable of operating under the political control and strategic direction of the WEU. We endorse the decisions taken at last year's Ministerial meeting in Berlin in this regard which serve the interests of the Alliance as well as of the WEU.

We further endorse the considerable progress made in implementing these decisions and in developing ESDI within the Alliance. In this context we endorse the decisions taken with regard to European command arrangements within NATO to prepare, support, command and conduct WEU-led operations using NATO assets and capabilities (including provisional terms of reference for Deputy SACEUR covering his ESDI-related responsibilities both permanent and during crises and operations), the arrangements for the identification of NATO assets and capabilities that could support WEU-led operations, and arrangements for NATO-WEU consultation in the context of such operations. We welcome inclusion of the support for the conduct of WEU-led operations in the context of the ongoing implementation of the revised Alliance defence planning process for all Alliance missions. We also welcome the progress made on work regarding the planning and future exercising of WEU-led operations, and in developing the necessary practical arrangements for release, monitoring and return of NATO assets and the exchange of information between NATO and WEU within the framework of the NATO-WEU Security Agreement. We note with satisfaction that the building of ESDI within the Alliance has much benefitted from the recent agreement in the WEU on the participation of all European Allies, if they were so to choose, in WEU-led operations using NATO assets and capabilities, as well as in planning and preparing for such operations. We also note the desire on Canada's part to participate in such operations when its interests make it desirable and under modalities to be developed. We direct the Council in Permanent Session to complete expeditiously its work on developing ESDI within NATO, in cooperation with the WEU.

19. The Alliance Strategic Concept, which we adopted at our meeting in Rome in 1991, sets out the principal aims and objectives of the Alliance. Recognising that the strategic environment has changed since then, we have decided to examine the Strategic Concept to ensure that it is fully consistent with Europe's new security situation and challenges. As recommended by our Foreign Ministers in Sintra, we have decided to direct the Council in Permanent Session to develop terms of reference for this examination, and an update as necessary, for endorsement at the Autumn Ministerial meetings. This work will confirm our commitment to the core function of Alliance collective defence and the indispensable transatlantic link.

20. We reiterate our commitment to full transparency between NATO and WEU in crisis management, including as necessary through joint consultations on how to address contingencies. In this context, we are determined to strengthen the institutional cooperation between the two organisations. We welcome the fact that the WEU has recently undertaken to improve its capacity to plan and conduct crisis management and peacekeeping operations (the Petersberg tasks), including through setting the groundwork for possible WEU-led operations with the support of NATO assets and capabilities, and accepted the Alliance's invitation to contribute to NATO's Ministerial Guidance for defence planning. We will therefore continue to develop the arrangements and procedures necessary for the planning, preparation, conduct and exercise of WEU-led operations using NATO assets and capabilities.

21. We reaffirm our commitment to further strengthening the OSCE as a regional organisation according to Chapter VIII of the Charter of the United Nations and as a primary instrument for preventing conflict, enhancing cooperative security and advancing democracy and human rights. The OSCE, as the most inclusive European-wide security organisation, plays an essential role in securing peace, stability and security in Europe. The principles and commitments adopted by the OSCE provide a foundation for the development of a comprehensive and cooperative European security architecture. Our goal is to create in Europe, through the widest possible cooperation among OSCE states, a common space of security and stability, without dividing lines or spheres of influence limiting the sovereignty of particular states.

We continue to support the OSCE's work on a Common and Comprehensive Security Model for Europe for the Twenty-First Century, in accordance with the decisions of the 1996 Lisbon Summit, including consideration of developing a Charter on European Security.

22. We welcome the successful holding of elections in Albania as a vital first step in providing the basis for greater stability, democratic government and law and order in the country. We stress, in this context, the importance of a firm commitment by all political forces to continue the process of national reconciliation. We also welcome the crucial role of the Italian-led Multinational Protection Force, with the participation of several Allies and Partners, in helping to create a secure environment for the re-establishment of peace and order. We value the efforts of the OSCE as the coordinating framework for international assistance in Albania, together with the important contributions made by the EU, WEU and the Council of Europe. We are following closely events in Albania and are considering measures through the Partnership for Peace to assist, as soon as the situation permits, in the reconstruction of the armed forces of Albania as an important element of the reform process. Continued international support will be essential in helping to restore stability in Albania.

23. We continue to attach greatest importance to further the means of non-proliferation, arms control and disarmament.

We welcome the progress made since the Brussels Summit, as an integral part of NATO's adaptation, to intensify and expand Alliance political and defence efforts aimed at preventing proliferation and safeguarding NATO's strategic unity and freedom of action despite the risks posed by nuclear, biological and chemical (NBC) weapons and their means of delivery. We attach the utmost importance to these efforts, welcome the Alliance's substantial achievements, and direct that work continue.

We call on all states which have not yet done so to sign and ratify the Chemical Weapons Convention. Recognising that enhancing confidence in compliance would reinforce the Biological and Toxin Weapons Convention, we reaffirm our determination to complete as soon as possible through negotiation a legally binding and effective verification mechanism. We urge the Russian Federation to ratify the START II Treaty without delay so that negotiation of START III may begin.

We support the vigorous pursuit of an effective, legally binding international agreement to ban world-wide the use, stockpiling, production and transfer of anti-personnel mines. We note the positive developments in the Conference on Disarmament. We further note the progress made by the Ottawa Process with its goal of achieving a ban by the end of the year.

24. We continue to attach utmost importance to the CFE Treaty and its integrity. In this context, we welcome the entry into force of the CFE Flank Agreement on 15th May 1997 and underline its importance for regional stability. We share the commitment of all thirty States Parties to continue full implementation of the CFE Treaty, its associated documents, and the Flank Agreement. We confirm our readiness to work cooperatively with other States Parties to achieve, as expeditiously as possible, an adapted CFE Treaty that takes account of the changed political and military circumstances in Europe,

continues to serve as a cornerstone of stability, and provides undiminished security for all. NATO has advanced a comprehensive proposal for adaptation of the CFE Treaty on the basis of a revised Treaty structure of national and territorial ceilings. The Allies have already stated their intention to reduce significantly their future aggregate national ceilings for Treaty-Limited Equipment. We look forward to working with other States Parties on the early completion of a Framework Agreement on CFE adaptation.

25. We reaffirm the importance of arrangements in the Alliance for consultation on threats of a wider nature, including those linked to illegal arms trade and acts of terrorism, which affect Alliance security interests. We continue to condemn all acts of international terrorism. They constitute flagrant violations of human dignity and rights and are a threat to the conduct of normal international relations. In accordance with our national legislation, we stress the need for the most effective cooperation possible to prevent and suppress this scourge.

26. The steps we have taken today, and tomorrow's meeting with our Partners under the aegis of the EAPC, bring us closer to our goal of building cooperative security in Europe. We remain committed to a free and undivided Euro-Atlantic community in which all can enjoy peace and prosperity. Renewed in structure and approach, strengthened in purpose and resolve, and with a growing membership, NATO will continue to play its part in achieving this goal and in meeting the security challenges in the times ahead.

27. We express our deep appreciation for the gracious hospitality extended to us by the Government of Spain. We are looking forward to meeting again on the occasion of the 50th anniversary of the North Atlantic Treaty in April 1999.

VICE PRESIDENT GORE ON NEW TELEVISION RATING SYSTEM
July 10, 1997

Political pressure from Congress and public interest groups forced the broadcast industry in 1997 to revise its much-criticized system for rating television shows. Just a few months after saying they would not cave into political pressure, broadcast and cable television executives announced July 10 that they would add several categories to a rating system intended to help parents decide what shows their children should watch. The revised ratings went into effect October 1. NBC was the only major holdout in not adopting them; that network continued to use the age-based ratings that had been put into effect in January.

The Federal Communications Commission (FCC) approved the new rating system. The commission also initiated a rulemaking process to require television sets sold in the United States to be equipped with so-called V-chips that allow parents to block programs with certain ratings. Congress had mandated installation of V-chips as part of a massive telecommunications bill (PL 104-104) enacted in 1996. An FCC rule requiring local television stations to air at least three hours of educational programming for children each week went into effect September 1, 1997. President Bill Clinton had negotiated the three-hour requirement with television industry representatives in 1996. (Ratings system and programming issues, Historic Documents of 1996, p. 831)

TV Ratings

Hoping to avoid adoption of legislation requiring ratings, the television industry in December 1996 agreed to a voluntary system of ratings to give parents help in deciding what their children should be allowed to watch. Based on the type of content appropriate for various age groups, the system was similar to motion picture industry codes used for nearly thirty years.

All programs, except news and sports, would be given one of six ratings. Two ratings were for shows intended for children: TV-Y, for programs considered appropriate for all children; and TV-Y7, for programs appropri-

ate for children age seven and above. The four remaining ratings were applied to programs intended for general audiences: TV-G, for programs most parents would find suitable for all ages; TV-PG, for programs containing material parents might consider unsuitable for young children; TV-14, for programs containing material parents might consider unsuitable for children under age fourteen; and TV-M, for programs that might be unsuitable for children under age seventeen.

Six broadcast networks (ABC, CBS, NBC, Fox, UPN, and WB) and some cable networks began using the new ratings in January 1997. Two networks did not adopt the system: the Public Broadcasting System (PBS), which was the industry leader in providing educational programming for children, and the Black Entertainment Network. Program producers and distributors rated their own shows because industry executives said no single entity could possibly rate all 2,000 hours of programming shown on U.S. television networks each day. Citing the success of motion picture ratings, television industry officials said the age-based system would be the simplest and most effective way to give parents guidance on what shows their children should watch.

Industry critics expressed dissatisfaction with the system, which they said did not give parents enough information about the actual content of television shows. "It's a bit like offering a weather forecast that says 'Warning: severe weather approaching' without telling you whether to expect rain, snow, wind or fog," said Dale Kunkel, a communications professor at the University of California-Santa Barbara. Some of the critics said the ratings system needed to tell parents whether shows contained potentially objectionable material such as violence, sexually suggestive scenes, or foul language. Among groups critical of the industry system were the National PTA, Children Now, and the Traditional Values Coalition.

Similar criticism came from many members of Congress who threatened legislation mandating content-based ratings. Faced with the criticism and the threat of new legislation, industry executives agreed in June to negotiate with their critics toward a new system. After three weeks of private talks, the two sides announced an agreement July 10 at a White House ceremony hosted by Vice President Al Gore.

Adding New Rating Symbols

The new system negotiated by the industry and its critics added five new symbols to the existing ratings adopted by the industry in 1996. The new ratings indicated the type of potentially objectionable material that might be found in a program: violence (V), sexual situations (S), coarse language (L), or suggestive or indecent dialogue (D). In addition, children's programs containing intense or combative fantasy violence would be labeled FV. These ratings would be added to the age-based ratings, so that a program could have several ratings symbols, such as "TV-14-DS," for a program intended for children over age fourteen that contained intensely suggestive dialogue and sexual situations. The symbols were to be posted in large letters on the upper left hand of the screen at the start of each program.

NBC was the major commercial network refusing to join other networks in adopting the new ratings. In a statement, the company said it feared industry critics were attempting to "dictate program content."

A major factor leading to the July 10 agreement was a willingness by key members of Congress to halt the drive for stronger legislation if the industry accepted new ratings. Sen. John McCain, the Arizona Republican who chaired the Commerce Committee, released a letter he and eight other senators (including Majority Leader Trent Lott, R-Miss.) had signed promising that Congress for "several years" would not enact legislation regulating "television ratings, program content or scheduling." Rep. Edward Markey, D-Mass., another critic of the television industry, signed a similar letter pledging a three-year moratorium on such legislation.

Proponents of ratings said they would be especially useful to parents once the V-chip became available. That was a device enabling parents to configure their television sets to block rated programs they did not want their children to watch. Congress in 1996 mandated that new televisions be equipped with V-chips starting in 1998. On September 25, 1997, the FCC announced its intent to require that half of all new televisions sold in the United States be equipped with the V-chip as of July 1, 1998. By July 19, 1999, all television sets would be required to contain a V-chip. Several companies were planning to market devices providing V-chip technology on existing television sets.

Following are excerpts from a statement by Vice President Al Gore at the White House July 10, 1997, announcing an agreement between the television industry and several children's advocacy groups to adopt a new ratings system for programs, along with excerpts from the text of the agreement itself:

STATEMENT BY VICE PRESIDENT GORE

Ladies and gentlemen, thank you very much for joining us today for this very, very welcome announcement. I would like to acknowledge the presence here along with me of Senator John McCain [R-Ariz.] and Congressman Ed Markey [D-Mass.]. And among those who have worked right along beside them, and beside the president on this issue are Senator Dan Coats [R-Ind.], right here, and Congressman Jim Moran [D-Va.]. And there are others who could not be present with us, and I want to thank them as well.

I want to acknowledge Lois Jean White, president of the National PTA; Katherine Montgomery, president of the Center for Media Education; and John Nelson, member of the Board of Trustees of the American Medical Association; and Caroline Breedlove, with the National Education Association;

and the others who have joined us here today. Welcome to the White House to all of you. . . .

Now, two years ago at the annual Family Policy Conference that my wife, Tipper, and I host in Nashville, President Clinton and I challenged Congress and the television industry. We asked them to give parents new tools to help them screen out television programs that are not fit for their children.

Incidentally, Congressman Ed Markey, who was the original sponsor of the V-chip legislation in the Congress, attended that conference and played a key role.

Last year, the president signed legislation and gave parents the V-chip, harnessing new technologies in the service of our oldest values. And immediately after that, the television industry did their part. They came to the table and committed themselves to developing a voluntary ratings system.

When that system was established last December, we urged parents to tell us how it was working, to tell us where it was succeeding, and to tell us where it could be improved. And in the announcement of the agreement in December, we made it clear that we anticipated that as we gained experience with the system, we anticipated that there would be modifications and changes along the way.

I want to compliment Senator John McCain, who became chairman of the Senate Commerce Committee in January and who has played a key role, especially on the Senate side, in helping to move these negotiations forward, and helping the parties come to a resolution.

Today I'm extremely please to announce that leaders in the television industry have worked with advocacy groups and have agreed to assign new ratings to their programs. Today America's parents have won back their living rooms. I recently met with some parent groups and I wasn't surprise with what they told me.

Age-based ratings were very helpful, but were not enough. Parents needed to know more. They need to know about the television images their children will see, and they need to know about the language and the dialogue that their children will hear.

So the new system that we announced today builds on the system that the industry put in place last December by adding letter ratings—S, V, L, and D for dialogue; S for sexual content; V for violence; L for coarse language; and D for mature dialogue.

This agreement puts the V back in the V-chip, and it will also give parents the information they need to know when cartoons or fantasy programs contain violence. While no agreement is perfect, this agreement is a major step forward. As I said a few weeks ago, it is time that we really give parents the tools that they need, and this agreement will do just that.

I do want to thank both John and Ed, and I want to thank their colleagues on both sides of the aisle who've worked so hard to make this possible. They deserve a tremendous amount of credit for helping to make this happen. This has been a bipartisan effort, it's historic, it is extremely important. And let me also say that I know that a lot of attention has been paid to the fact that some in the industry have not yet agreed to this new system. I would like to urge them to see how it works and reconsider.

This is very much in the interest of America's families.

You know, when you have a mass medium, and you have working parents—and working parents with lower incomes especially, where the television set is by far the highest value for entertainment—then it's just impractical to imagine that parents can be present and monitor every single program that the child in the home watches. It's impossible.

And it's also impractical to expect parents to pull the plug and throw the television out of the house. A few will do that, and I could make a strong case for that, but we haven't done that in my house, and most houses don't do that.

We need a third way to empower parents to use this V-chip to say directly to the television set through this V-chip, don't show my child material I don't think my child is ready to see. This new system makes that system possible.

And I hope that those who have not yet agreed to it will reflect on their tentative decision, and come back and join this American consensus that has such broad bipartisan support all across the United States of America.

The main credit, and others have made this point too, the main credit for this achievement goes to the parent groups, because they've really hung in there. They've been tireless, they've been determined, and they have expressed the heartfelt concerns of America's families.

Leaders in the television industry understood that they, too, had to be good citizens, good corporate citizens, and respond to this legitimate request. This transcends party lines, and it shows that we go a lot farther when we travel on common ground.

We look forward to working with the parents' groups and with industry and Congress, to ensure that this agreement is implemented in a meaningful way. And we hope that the television industry in its entirety will do the right thing and adopt this system.

So thanks to all who have made this possible.

AGREEMENT ON MODIFICATIONS

1. Content Information: The following content information, where appropriate, will be added to all non-exempt programming to supplement the existing TV Parental Guidelines: in the TV-Y7 category—FV for fantasy violence; in the TV-PG, TV-14 and TV-MA categories—V for violence, S for sexual situations, L for language, and D for dialogue.

2. Descriptions of the Guidelines: Modifications will be made to the category descriptions as specified in Attachment 1.

3. Monitoring Board: Five non-industry members, drawn from the advocacy community and selected by the Chairman, will be appointed to the Monitoring Board as full voting members. Recommendations for appointment to the Board will be offered by advocacy groups and Monitoring Board members.

4. V-chip: The industry and advocacy groups will recommend to the FCC that the MPAA movie rating system and the universal television rating system be the only systems mandated for inclusion on the V-chip.

5. Icons: Larger icons will appear on-screen for 15 seconds at the beginning of all rated programming and through use of a display button thereafter.

6. Assurances: Attachment 2 reflects the agreement reached between the industry and advocacy groups on treatment of the relevant proceedings at the FCC and pending and future legislation.

7. Research and Evaluation: Independent, scientific research and evaluation will be undertaken once the V-chip has been in the marketplace.

8. Effective Date: Networks will begin to rate programming using the new universal television rating system by October 1, 1997. The industry agrees to encode and transmit the rating information in Line 21 of the vertical blanking interval within 180 days of the date of this agreement.

The following categories apply to programs designed solely for children:

TV-Y All Children. *This program is designed to be appropriate for all children.* Whether animated or live-action, the themes and elements in this program are specifically designed for a very young audience, including children from ages 2–6. This program is not expected to frighten younger children.

TV-Y7 Directed to Older Children. *This program is designed for children age 7 and above.* It may be more appropriate for children who have acquired the developmental skills needed to distinguish between make-believe and reality. Themes and elements in this program may include mild fantasy violence or comedic violence, or may frighten children under the age of 7. Therefore, parents may wish to consider the suitability of this program for their very young children. Note: For those programs where fantasy violence may be more intense or more combative than other programs in this category, such programs will be designated TV-Y7-FV.

The following categories apply to programs designed for the entire audience:

TV-G General Audience. *Most parents would find this program suitable for all ages.* Although this rating does not signify a program designed specifically for children, most parents may let younger children watch this program unattended. It contains little or no violence, no strong language and little or no sexual dialogue or situations.

TV-PG Parental Guidance Suggested. *This program contains material that parents may find unsuitable for younger children.* Many parents may want to watch it with their younger children. The theme itself may call for parental guidance and/or the program contains one or more of the following: moderate violence (V), some sexual situations (S), infrequent coarse language (L), or some suggestive dialogue (D).

TV-14 Parents Strongly Cautioned. *This program contains some material that many parents would find unsuitable for children under 14 years* *of age.* Parents are strongly urged to exercise greater care in monitoring this program and are cautioned against letting children under the age of 14 watch unattended. This program contains one or more of the following: intense violence (V), intense sexual situations (S), strong coarse language (L), or intensely suggestive dialogue (D).

TV-MA Mature Audience Only. *This program is specifically designed to be viewed by adults and therefore may be unsuitable for children under 17.* This program contains one or more of the following: graphic violence (V), explicit sexual activity (S), or crude indecent language (L).

The attached modifications of the TV Parental Guideline System have been developed collaboratively by members of the industry and the advocacy community. We find this combined age and content based system to be acceptable and believe that it should be designated as the mandated system on the V-chip and used to rate all television programming, except for news and sports, which are exempt, and unedited movies with an MPAA rating aired on premium cable channels. We urge the FCC to so rule as expeditiously as possible.

We further believe that the system deserves a fair chance to work in the marketplace to allow parents an opportunity to understand and use the system. Accordingly, the undersigned organizations will work to: educate the public and parents about the V-chip and the TV Parental Guideline System; encourage publishers of TV periodicals, newspapers and journals to include the ratings with their program listings; and evaluate the system. Therefore, we urge governmental leaders to allow this process to proceed unimpeded by pending or new legislation that would undermine the intent of this agreement or disrupt the harmony and good faith of this process.

Motion Picture Association of America
National Association of Broadcasters
National Cable Television Association

American Medical Association
American Academy of Pediatrics
American Psychological
   Association
Center for Media Education
Children's Defense Fund
Children Now
National Association of
   Elementary School Principals
National Education Association
National PTA

GAO REPORT ON YEAR 2000 COMPUTER CONVERSION
July 10, 1997

A simple date change—from December 31, 1999, to January 1, 2000—was estimated to cost businesses and government agencies around the world billions of dollars and plenty of headaches. In the 1990s computer users realized that many of their machines might stop working or begin spitting out useless data on the first day of the year 2000. That was because many computers were programmed to recognize only the last two digits of the year and, unless fixed, these computers could not differentiate between 2000 and 1900, or any other year ending in 00.

The problem was especially severe at U.S. government agencies and businesses using large mainframe computer systems that were ten to thirty years old, run by customized software programs written in out-of-date languages. One study, by Howard A. Rubin, a professor of computer science at Hunter College in New York, estimated that U.S. business and government would need at least 500,000 more programmers to help fix the problem before 2000. Another study by the Gartner Group, a technology consulting firm, put the total worldwide cost of fixing computers to deal with 2000 at between $300 billion and $600 billion.

The impact on individuals could be as minor as not being able to record a television show on a videocassette recorder, or as serious as having a loan declared in default because the bank's computer thought a payment was 100 years late. Many individual owners of personal computers also had to figure out how to deal with favorite software programs written before the 2000 problem was widely recognized.

There never was any secret that the year 2000 was on the horizon, or that many computers would have to be adjusted to account for a year ending in 00. But numerous reports in the mid- and late-1990s indicated that top executives in business and government had not focused on the amount of work to be done, or the cost, in fixing their computer systems.

Michael P. Huerta, acting chief information officer for the Department of Transportation, told a House of Representatives subcommittee in February

1997 that he "didn't even know there was such a thing as a year 2000 problem until August" 1996. Others in government and business said they had assumed that somebody would produce a technological "quick fix," a simple software program that would solve the problem easily and inexpensively.

By 1997 it was evident that there would be no easy or cheap solutions. But it also appeared that doomsday predictions of nuclear missiles shooting wildly around the globe, satellites falling from the sky, and a collapse of the world's financial markets were just as inflated as hopes that the problem would simply go away.

GAO Warnings

The General Accounting Office (GAO), the investigative arm of Congress, issued a series of warnings in 1997 that many U.S. government agencies were not moving fast enough to fix or replace their computer systems. To help government executives and computer specialists deal with what it called the "year 2000 computing crisis," the GAO issued a thirty-four-page "assessment guide" detailing a chain of necessary steps, starting with recognizing the extent of the problem and ending with making double sure that any corrections actually worked.

Testifying on February 24 before the Management and Information subcommittee of the House Government Reform and Oversight Committee, Joel C. Willemssen, director of information resources management for the GAO, said computers at some government agencies might stop working on January 1, 2000. "There's a high probability there will be some failures," he said.

The Office of Management and Budget (OMB) early in 1997 estimated the total cost of fixing U.S. government computers at $2.3 billion, then in September boosted its estimate to nearly $3.8 billion and warned that even that estimate was likely to be low. Applying pressure on government officials to take the problem more seriously, the OMB in September said it was barring four agencies—the Agriculture, Education, and Transportation Departments, and the Agency for International Development—from buying new computer systems until they had made more progress in fixing the 2000 problem on their current systems.

For many Americans, the foremost concern was whether the Internal Revenue Service (IRS) would be able to fix its creaky computer systems in time to avoid a surge of millions of "past due" notices in 2000. Collecting taxes and processing returns required more than fifty computer systems using some 19,000 applications at the IRS. One agency official estimated dealing with the 2000 problem would cost the IRS—and the taxpayers—at least $150 million.

Other agencies with especially sensitive problems included the Federal Aviation Administration, which ran the government's air-traffic control system, and the Defense Department, which had more than 9,000 computer systems handling tasks ranging from paying the troops to aiming nuclear missiles.

Private Industry

The problems in dealing with the year change for private businesses were not as well publicized as in the government, but most business leaders were beginning to take the matter seriously by 1997. In one study, the Gartner Group said small companies were slower than big companies in facing and dealing with the problem. The study noted that the failure of small firms to cope with the year 2000 computer glitches could have a broad impact on the economy; for example, a computer-driven slowdown at a small but important parts supplier could damage production at a much bigger firm, such as an automaker.

Many businesses were hiring retired computer programmers to work on updating their mainframe systems. In some cases, companies were paying large bonuses to former employees who had been forced to retire just a few years earlier because their skills were no longer needed. The older workers found themselves suddenly in demand because they knew the languages, such as COBOL and FORTRAN, used in mainframe systems built in the 1960s through the 1980s; most younger computer specialists had never learned those languages.

Enterprising computer consultants also were doing a booming, if short-term business, helping companies deal with the year 2000 problem. Others were looking to cash in on the inevitable failures: Attorneys were ready to file lawsuits to recover damages caused by year 2000-inflicted computer glitches, and insurance companies were writing policies to cover those damages.

Following are excerpts from testimony given July 10, 1997, to a joint hearing of the Subcommittee on Government Management, Information and Technology of the House Committee on Government Reform and Oversight, and the Subcommittee on Technology of the House Science Committee, by Joel C. Willemssen, director of information resources management for the General Accounting Office:

During the past 12 months, the year 2000 computing problem has received increased attention—and deservedly so—in large part thanks to the efforts of your Subcommittees. Much has happened since the initial congressional hearings on this matter were held just over a year ago on whether computer systems that support federal programs will be equipped to handle dates later than 1999. At that time, most federal agencies were just beginning to be aware of the year 2000 issue and its importance, and few had prepared plans for addressing it.

Now, agencies report to the Office of Management and Budget (OMB) that they are in a much better position to resolve the year 2000 challenge before the actual change of millennium. However, while agencies have certainly made progress over the last year, we believe that the pace needs to be significantly accelerated if widespread systems problems are to be avoided as the year 2000 approaches.

Our testimony today will describe the federal government's strategy for addressing the year 2000 problem, and agencies' reported status in resolving the issue. In addition, we will provide observations on federal efforts to date based on work we have completed at certain agencies and on our review of OMB's implementation of the federal strategy, including year 2000 reports submitted by 24 federal agencies.

Readiness for the Year 2000: The Federal Strategy

The federal strategy for resolving the year 2000 computing crisis is detailed in a document OMB submitted on February 6 of this year to three House Committees: Government Reform and Oversight, Science, and Appropriations. The strategy is predicated on three assumptions: (1) senior agency managers will take whatever action is necessary to address the problem once they are aware of its potential consequences; (2) a single solution to the problem does not exist, and solving it requires modification or replacement of agency information systems; and (3) given the limited amount of time available, emphasis will be placed on mission-critical systems.

At the department and agency level, this strategy relies on the recently established chief information officers, or CIOs, to direct year 2000 actions. To complement individual agency efforts, OMB is (1) requesting that departments and agencies submit quarterly reports on their progress, and (2) sharing management and technical expertise through its CIO Council and the Council's Subcommittee on the Year 2000.

In addition, OMB has set as the standard that agency year 2000 activities should adhere to industry best practices for the five delineated phases of an effective year 2000 program: awareness, assessment, renovation, validation, and implementation. In consonance with these phases, we have developed and disseminated an assessment guide to help agencies plan, manage, and evaluate their year 2000 programs. The guide provides information on the scope of the challenge and offers a structured approach for agencies to use. We are following the approach outlined in the guide for our reviews at selected agencies, and are encouraging others to use it as well. To date, we have received over 16,000 requests for copies. . . .

Status of Agencies' Year 2000 Programs

On June 23, 1997, OMB transmitted its first quarterly report, dated May 15, 1997, to selected congressional committees on the progress of federal agencies in correcting the year 2000 problem. This report is based on the quarterly reports submitted by the individual departments and agencies, which address questions of organizational responsibility, program status, cost, and mission-critical systems that are behind schedule.

In its report, based on May 1997 agency estimates, OMB noted that agencies expect to spend about $2.75 billion correcting systems to be what is called year 2000 compliant. This is an increase of nearly $500 million, or about 20 percent, over the February 1997 estimate. OMB noted in its summary report that its next quarterly report will likely provide a higher cost estimate as more agencies complete the assessment phase.

While acknowledging that much work remains, OMB—on the basis of the agency reports—expressed its belief that agencies had made a good start in addressing the problem. OMB further summarized that most agencies had completed or would shortly complete their assessments of the problem, many had begun systems renovation, and no mission-critical systems were reported to be behind schedule.

The OMB report includes agency-specific schedules for completing the assessment, renovation, validation, and implementation phases of the year 2000 effort. Our accompanying chart, which appears at the end of this statement, summarizes those schedules.

. . . 18 of 24 departments and agencies reported that they would complete the assessment phase as of last month, the deadline in OMB's governmentwide schedule. Six reported that they would not meet the assessment phase deadline: Defense, Transportation, Treasury, Veterans Affairs, the Agency for International Development (AID), and the Nuclear Regulatory Commission (NRC). The current estimated cost for achieving year 2000 compliance for these 6 entities is about $1.9 billion, or about 70 percent of the total for the 24 agencies.

To complete the assessment phase, an agency needs to undertake a variety of activities. In our view these should include, at a minimum, (1) assessing the severity and timing of the impact of year 2000-induced failures; (2) developing a thorough inventory of all of its systems; (3) establishing priorities and schedules as to whether—and which—systems should be converted, replaced, or eliminated; (4) developing validation strategies and test plans; (5) addressing interface and data exchange issues; and (6) developing contingency plans for critical systems in the event of failure.

Our evaluations of year 2000 readiness at component agencies of both the Department of Veterans Affairs—one of the six reporting to OMB that its assessment was still underway—and of Health and Human Services—which reported that this phase would be completed in June 1997—show that assessment activities have not yet been completed.

For example, we recently testified that key readiness assessment processes at the Veterans Benefits Administration—including determining the potential severity of impact of the year 2000 on agency operations, inventorying information systems and their components, and developing contingency plans—had not been completed. The Department has indicated that it will complete its assessment next January.

We also reported and testified this past May that the Health Care Financing Administration (HCFA)—a major component agency within the Department of Health and Human Services (HHS)—had not completed numerous critical assessment activities for the systems run by its contractors to process approximately $200 billion annually in Medicare claims. Specifically, HCFA had not required systems contractors to submit year 2000 plans for approval, and lacked contracts or other legal agreements detailing how or when the year 2000 problem would be corrected, or indeed whether contractors would even certify that they would correct the problem. We made several recommendations to HCFA to address its shortcomings in this area, including regular reporting to HHS on its progress. HHS reported in May that it expected to complete the assessment phase last month.

Urgent Need to Accelerate Agency Year 2000 Programs

As we have pointed out in earlier testimony, if systems that millions of Americans have come to rely on for regular benefits malfunction, the ensuing delays could be disastrous.

OMB's perspective that agencies have made a good start and that no mission-critical systems were reported to be behind schedule would seem to imply that there is no cause for alarm. On the contrary, we believe ample evidence exists that OMB and key federal agencies need to heighten their levels of concern and move with more urgency. A closer look reveals why.

First, the agencies' reported schedules show that most are leaving essentially no margin of error for unanticipated schedule delays; 15 of 24 expect to complete implementation in either November or December of 1999. This leaves only a matter of weeks, at most, if something should require more work before January 1, 2000. According to their own reports, six agencies, including four large departments, have already missed OMB's June 1997 deadline for completion of assessment. Where assessments of mission criticality have not been completed, it is logical to assume that schedules for correcting those systems have not been made final. Given these factors, it is essential that OMB continue to monitor agency schedules to identify delays so that necessary action can be taken to enable programs to finish in time.

Second, OMB's perspective is based on agency self-reporting, which has not been independently validated. Indications are that agency reports may not be accurate; those saying that assessment has been completed include HHS which, as I have highlighted today, still has much to do.

Third, entities may have interpreted mission-critical in various ways—even within departments. For example, the Department of the Army reports that 7 percent of its systems are mission-critical, yet the Defense Information Systems Agency, a Defense Department support agency, considers all of its systems—100 percent—to be mission-critical. A further look within Defense shows that almost two-thirds of over 2,750 "mission-critical" systems slated for repair are still in the assessment phase. And this excludes over 11,000 lower priority systems that are in varying stages of assessment.

Fourth, OMB, in its governmentwide schedule, has established only 1 month—from December 1998 to January 1999—to complete validation. The validation phase is critical for thorough testing of all converted or replaced system components to (1) uncover any errors introduced during conversion or renovation, (2) validate year 2000 compliance, and (3) verify operational readiness. Without adequate testing, agencies can have no assurance that their solutions will actually work. According to the Gartner Group, a private research firm acknowledged for its expertise in year 2000 issues, activities such as unit and system testing could consume up to 40 percent of the time and resources dedicated to an entire year 2000 program. OMB's timeline does not convey this message. Accordingly, agencies may perceive that OMB does not view testing and validation activities as especially critical, and that OMB may approve overly optimistic schedules.

Other Critical Readiness Issues That Demand High-Priority Attention

Beyond the major areas covered in agency reports to OMB and, in turn, in OMB's report to Committees of the Congress, other issues surrounding year 2000 readiness are quickly emerging that will be of major importance as agencies move farther along in their year 2000 programs. These include data interfaces and exchanges, systems prioritization, and contingency planning. Our recent reports on year 2000 programs at the Veterans Benefits Administration and the Health Care Financing Administration include several recommendations to address these issues.

Data exchange. Many agencies exchange data with hundreds if not thousands of external entities. Unless both parties to any exchange are year 2000 compliant, information systems and databases may easily be contaminated by coding embedded in noncompliant systems. To combat this, agencies must inventory and assess all internal and external data exchanges, make appropriate notifications and, if necessary, develop appropriate bridges or filters to maintain the integrity of replaced or converted systems and the data within them.

Systems prioritization. It is becoming increasingly clear that agencies will likely be unable to correct all noncompliant systems before 2000. Accordingly, it is imperative that agencies set priorities, on the basis of mission needs and the timing and expected impact of year 2000-induced failures. Identification of mission-critical systems is not enough; each department's and agency's most important business activities must be given top priority to ensure their continued, uninterrupted operation.

Contingency planning. Because the cost of systems failure—in terms beyond just the monetary—can be very high, contingency plans must be prepared so that core business functions will continue to be performed even if systems have not been made year 2000 compliant.

We consider it essential that OMB emphasize in its ongoing oversight and monitoring these issues that we expect to grow in significance in the next 2 years.

In closing, as we have reiterated previously, preparing for the year 2000 is much more of a management challenge than a technical one. Managers—in the agencies and in OMB—must ensure that the technical solutions are implemented on time. It can be done, and the public is depending on us to do it. Continuing congressional oversight, such as this hearing, will be an important catalyst to effective, timely actions to ensure that information systems are prepared for the year 2000.

CLINTON ON IMPACT OF NAFTA AFTER THREE YEARS

July 11, 1997

The Clinton administration and its critics on free-trade issues engaged in a war of statistics during 1997 on the impact of the first three years of the North American Free Trade Agreement (NAFTA), which broke down barriers to trade among the United States, Canada, and Mexico. The dispute was part of a broader ideological and political struggle over free trade that lead to a major setback for the administration.

President Bill Clinton asked Congress to renew his broad authority to negotiate further trade agreements, including a possible extension of NAFTA to other countries in the Western Hemisphere. The administration failed to round up the required majority in both chambers, largely because of opposition within the president's own Democratic Party. Clinton was forced to withdraw his request November 11, even before a single vote had been cast on Capitol Hill. The humiliating defeat was the first suffered by a president on a free trade issue in more than half a century.

White House Report

Congress had approved NAFTA in 1993 after a bruising political fight. The treaty, which took effect January 1, 1994, lowered tariffs and other trade barriers between the United States and Mexico, extending the concept of free trade already in effect between the United States and Canada. The administration claimed the treaty would boost the U.S. economy by lowering Mexico's high tariffs on U.S. imports, thus opening Mexican markets to products and services from north of the border. (NAFTA, Historic Documents of 1993, p. 953)

Opposition to the treaty in 1993 centered among labor unions, environmental groups, and representatives of several industries. All expressed fear that Mexico would flood the United States with cheap goods and agricultural products made by low-wage, nonunion workers under unsafe and environmentally hazardous conditions.

In approving the treaty, Congress asked the administration to report on its impact by July 1997. Clinton's report on July 11 fulfilled that obligation and also attempted to frame the debate for congressional consideration of the president's later request for broad authority to negotiate new trade agreements.

The 139-page report stressed the positive contributions of NAFTA to the U.S. economy but made no sweeping claims of success. Perhaps the key sentences in the report were these, summarizing the economic impact of NAFTA: "Several studies conclude that NAFTA contributed to America's economic expansion. NAFTA had a modest positive effect on U.S. net exports, income, investments and jobs supported by exports."

The report attempted to back up that assertion with voluminous detail from studies done by the administration or commissioned by it. The report acknowledged that it was difficult to isolate the impact of NAFTA, noting that other factors also affected the U.S. economy and trade between the United States and Mexico, including the severe economic crisis in Mexico and the sharp devaluation of the peso in 1995. Many of the figures in the report were based on what might have happened if the Mexican financial crisis had not intervened. In addition, the United States reduced its tariffs during that same period as part of the international Uruguay Round trade agreement. (Uruguay Round agreement, Historic Documents of 1993, p. 997)

The low-key tone of the July 11 report was a deliberately sharp contrast to claims the administration had made for the treaty during the 1993 congressional debate. In 1993 administration officials insisted the treaty would help create hundreds of thousands of new high-paying jobs in the United States and would ensure the future of Mexico as a stable democracy. The Mexican economic crisis dashed those hopes, regardless of whether they had been realistic in the first place. By 1997 some officials acknowledged that they had oversold NAFTA, undermining administration credibility on trade issues. The 1997 report focused on positive elements and predicted that NAFTA would produce further benefits in the future, but it made no sweeping claims of success.

An Anti-NAFTA Report

Hoping to steal the president's thunder, a coalition of anti-NAFTA groups issued its own report June 26, calling the treaty a failure that "should be repealed or significantly restructured." Groups issuing that report were the Economic Policy Institute, the Institute for Policy Studies, the International Labor Rights Fund, Public Citizen's Global Trade Watch, the Sierra Club, and the U.S. Business and Industrial Council Educational Foundation.

The report said that while NAFTA had benefited some sectors of the three North American economies, it had failed to generate broad benefits and had actually caused more damage than good. NAFTA had widened the U.S. trade deficit with both Canada and Mexico and had been responsible for the loss of 420,000 jobs in the United States, the report argued. None of the social policy benefits claimed for NAFTA had materialized, the report said, including increased enforcement of environmental regulations in Mexico.

GAO Report

In a report to Congress, the General Accounting Office (GAO), the investigative arm of Congress, threw doubt on the claims of both NAFTA supporters and opponents. Testifying on September 11 before the House Ways and Means Trade Subcommittee, JayEtta Z. Hecker, GAO associate director for international relations and trade issues, said it was difficult, if not impossible, to document the actual impact of NAFTA on the U.S., Canadian, and Mexican economies.

Some sectors of the economies in each of the three countries probably had benefited as a result of the treaty, while other sectors had suffered, Hecker said. After just three years, she added, it was too early to draw conclusions about NAFTA's long-term impact on any areas of the economies in the three countries.

The GAO said neither side in the NAFTA dispute could document its claims about the number of jobs in the United States that had been lost or gained because of the treaty. Hecker cited "widely divergent" estimates of the impact on jobs, ranging from gains of 160,000 jobs to losses of 420,000 jobs. "We believe neither of these are reliable estimates of actual labor effects due to methodological limitations" of the studies, she said. Other factors such as macroeconomic policy and demographic conditions were certain to have a greater impact on U.S. employment levels than trade agreements such as NAFTA, she said.

Clinton Trade Setback

With the dispute over NAFTA very much in the forefront, Clinton in September began a drive for congressional approval of his authority to negotiate future trade agreements under a so-called fast track. Since Gerald Ford in the mid-1970s, every U.S. president had been able to negotiate trade agreements with the assurance that Congress would vote up or down on the agreement as a whole, without considering amendments on individual issues.

Presidents had said that without this authority it would be difficult to negotiate complex trade matters because other countries would fear that Congress might subject any agreement to endless renegotiations. Starting in 1998 the administration faced major negotiations within the World Trade Organization on tariffs and other trade issues involving intellectual property, agriculture, and services. In addition, Clinton had wanted to extend NAFTA to Chile as the first step toward a free trade agreement covering most of the Western Hemisphere.

The staunchest supporters of Clinton's fast-track request were his staunchest critics on Capitol Hill: conservative Republican leaders in both chambers, particularly in the House. Heading the opposition were key Democrats, including House Minority Leader Richard A. Gephardt of Missouri, who had long been skeptical of free trade agreements.

Clinton and his aides worked aggressively to secure support from waver-
ing members, extending numerous promises in exchange for votes. In the
House, where the crucial vote was to be held, the administration secured a
solid majority of Republicans but was able to win support from only about
forty Democrats—far from enough to win passage of the president's request.

Although many members had genuine concerns about issues directly
related to Clinton's fast-track request, much of the opposition appeared to
reflect a more generalized dissatisfaction with the president on Capitol
Hill, especially among Democrats. Clinton had never courted members of
Congress, even those in his own party, to the extent that members felt he
should. Some Democrats even argued that Clinton, in his zeal for biparti-
san support during the 1996 presidential campaign, had run against them
as much as against the Republicans. As a result, Clinton had a shallow well
of support to draw from on an issue as contentious as trade had become.
Clinton also damaged his cause with several impolitic remarks, such as an
off-hand comment that the issue should be a "no-brainer."

The immediate impact of Clinton's setback was that the United States
would be in a weakened position entering into international trade talks
starting in 1998. Any chance for an early extension of NAFTA to other
countries was considered dead. But many observers said the long-term
impact on U.S. trade relations—assuming Clinton or his successors failed
to regain fast-track negotiating authority—might not be felt for years.

Following is the text of President Bill Clinton's letter to Congress
July 11, 1997, transmitting a report on the first three years of
the North American Free Trade Agreement, along with the exec-
utive summary of the report:

CLINTON'S LETTER TO CONGRESS

I am pleased to transmit the Study on the Operation and Effect of the
North American Free Trade Agreement (NAFTA), as required by section 512
of the NAFTA Implementation Act (Public Law 103-182; 107 Stat. 2155; 19
U.S.C. 3462). The Congress and the administration are right to be proud of
this historic agreement. This report provides solid evidence that NAFTA has
already proved its worth to the United States during the 3 years it has been in
effect. We can look forward to realizing NAFTA's full benefits in the years
ahead.

NAFTA has also contributed to the prosperity and stability of our closest
neighbors and two of our most important trading partners. NAFTA aided
Mexico's rapid recovery from a severe economic recession, even as that country carried forward a democratic transformation of historic proportions.

NAFTA is an integral part of a-broader growth strategy that has produced
the strongest U.S. economy in a generation. This strategy rests on three mutu-

ally supportive pillars: deficit reduction, investing in our people through education and training, and opening foreign markets to allow America to compete in the global economy. The success of that strategy can be seen in the strength of the American economy, which continues to experience strong investment, low unemployment, healthy job creation, and subdued inflation.

Export growth has been central to America's economic expansion. NAFTA, together with the Uruguay Round Agreement, the Information Technology Agreement, the WTO Telecommunications Agreement, 22 sectoral trade agreements with Japan. and over 170 other trade agreements, has contributed to overall U.S. real export growth of 37 percent since 1993. Exports have contributed nearly one-third of our economic growth—and have grown three times faster than overall income.

Workers, business executives, small business owners, and farmers across America have contributed to the resurgence in American competitiveness. The ability and determination of working people across America to rise to the challenges of rapidly changing technologies and global economic competition is a great source of strength for this Nation.

Cooperation between the Administration and the Congress on a bipartisan basis has been critical in our efforts to reduce the deficit, to conclude trade agreements that level the global playing field for America, to secure peace and prosperity along America's borders, and to help prepare all Americans to benefit from expanded economic opportunities. I hope we can continue working together to advance these vital goals in the years to come.

EXECUTIVE SUMMARY OF NAFTA REPORT

Purpose of the Report

The North American Free Trade Agreement (NAFTA) entered into force on January 1, 1994. In accordance with Section 512 of the NAFTA Implementation Act, this Study provides a comprehensive assessment of the operation and effects of the NAFTA, including the economic effects in aggregate and in selected manufacturing sectors and agriculture, and the implementation of the NAFTA environmental and labor agreements. This Study reviews the findings from a variety of outside studies and analyzes Mexican and U.S. data, attempting wherever possible to isolate the effects of the NAFTA from other factors, as stipulated in the statute.

Trade in North America

U.S. trade with Canada and Mexico is much larger relative to the size of these economies than with any other trading partners, in large part reflecting shared land borders and geographical proximity.

- In 1996, nearly one-third of U.S. two-way trade in goods with the world was with Canada and Mexico ($421 billion). Two-way trade with our NAFTA partners has grown 44 percent since the NAFTA was signed, compared with 33 percent for the rest of the world. Mexico and Canada accounted for 53 percent of the growth in total U.S. exports in the first four months of 1997.

- Canada was in 1993—and remains today—our largest trading partner, accounting for $290 billion in two-way trade in 1996. Between 1993 and 1996, U.S. goods exports to Canada were up by 33.6 percent to $134.2 billion.
- U.S. exports to Mexico grew by 36.5 percent (or $15.2 billion) from 1993 to a record high in 1996, despite a 3.3 percent contraction in Mexican domestic demand over the same period.
- Exports to Canada and Mexico supported an estimated 2.3 million jobs in 1996; this represents an increase of 311,000 jobs since 1993, 189,000 supported by exports to Canada and 122,000 by exports to Mexico.
- Exports to Mexico were up by 54.5 percent in the first four months of 1997 relative to the same period in 1993. In the first four months of 1997, U.S. exports to Mexico virtually equaled U.S. exports to Japan, our second largest market—even though Mexico's economy is one twelfth the size of Japan's.

NAFTA's Effect on Trade Barriers

Under NAFTA, Mexico has reduced its trade barriers on U.S. exports significantly and dismantled a variety of protectionist rules and regulations, while the United States—which started with much lower tariffs—has made only slight reductions.

- Before NAFTA was signed, Mexican applied tariffs on U.S. goods averaged percent. U.S. tariffs on Mexican imports averaged 2.07 percent, and over half of Mexican imports entered the United States duty-free.
- Since NAFTA was signed, Mexico has reduced its average applied tariffs on U.S. imports by 7.1 percentage points, compared with a reduction of 1.4 percentage points in the United States. The United States would have made some of these tariff reductions under the Uruguay Round even in the absence of NAFTA.

NAFTA's Effects on the U.S. Economy

Several studies conclude that NAFTA contributed to America's economic expansion. NAFTA had a modest positive effect on U.S. net exports, income, investment and jobs supported by exports.

- It is challenging to isolate NAFTA's effects on the U.S. economy, since NAFTA has only been in effect for three years, and events such as the severe recession in Mexico, the depreciation of the Mexican peso, and U.S. tariff reductions under the Uruguay Round have taken place during the same period.
- Nonetheless, several outside studies conclude that NAFTA has resulted in a modest increase in U.S. net exports, controlling for other factors. A new study by DRI estimates that NAFTA boosted real exports to Mexico by $12 billion in 1996, compared to a smaller real increase in imports of

$5 billion, controlling for Mexico's financial crisis. An earlier study by the Dallas Federal Reserve finds that NAFTA raised exports by roughly $7 billion and imports by roughly $4 billion. The relatively greater effect on exports partly reflects the fact that under NAFTA Mexico reduced its tariffs roughly 5 times more than the United States.

- DRI estimates that NAFTA contributed $13 billion to U.S. real income and $5 billion to business investment in 1996, controlling for Mexico's financial crisis.
- These estimates suggest that NAFTA has boosted jobs associated with exports to Mexico between roughly 90,000 and 160,000. The Department of Commerce estimates that the jobs supported by exports generally pay 13 to 16 percent more than the national average for nonsupervisory production positions.

NAFTA's Effects on the Mexican Economy

In 1995, Mexico experienced its most severe economic recession since the 1930s. Comparing Mexico's recovery in 1996 with Mexico's recovery from its last financial crisis in 1982, when NAFTA was not in effect, reveals that both the Mexican economy and American exports recovered more rapidly following the 1995 crisis than the 1982 crisis, in part because of the economic reforms locked in by NAFTA. Mexico's strong economic adjustment program and bilateral and multilateral financial support were also important.

- Following Mexico's 1982 financial crisis, Mexican output drifted down for nearly two years before rising again and did not recover to pre-crisis levels for five years. Although Mexican economic output dropped more quickly in 1995, it also rebounded more quickly, reaching pre-crisis peaks by the end of 1996. Similarly, following the 1982 crisis, it took Mexico 7 years to return to international capital markets, while in 1995, it took 7 months.
- Following Mexico's 1982 financial crisis, Mexico raised tariffs by 100 percent, and American exports to Mexico fell by half and did not recover for seven years. In 1995, Mexico continued to implement its NAFTA obligations even as it raised tariffs on imports from other countries. As a result, American exports recovered in 18 months and were up nearly 37 percent by the end of 1996 relative to pre-NAFTA levels, even though Mexican consumption was down 3.3 percent.

NAFTA's Effects in Key Sectors

U.S. suppliers hold dominant shares of Mexico's import markets and in many sectors have expanded their shares significantly under NAFTA, at the expense of suppliers from other countries. In almost all sectors, Mexico has made large reductions in tariff barriers. Imports under NAFTA, compared with only slight U.S. reductions.

- Increases in the U.S. share of Mexico's import market are indicative of NAFTA's effects, since they control for factors that affect all foreign suppliers similarly, such as Mexico's recession. Since NAFTA went into effect, U.S. suppliers have seen their share of Mexico's import market grow from 69.3 percent to 75.5 percent, reflecting a 10 percentage point average tariff advantage over foreign suppliers. Mexico's share of American imports has risen from 6.9 percent to 9.3 percent.

- Reductions in Mexican barriers in sectors have led to U.S. share gains in Mexican import markets. Since NAFTA was signed, the U.S. share of Mexican imports is up 17.2 percentage points to 86.4 percent in the textiles sector, where Mexico has cut tariffs by 10.7 percentage points under NAFTA. The U.S. share is up 19.2 percentage points to 83.1 percent in the transport equipment sector, where Mexico has cut tariffs 10.2 percentage points under NAFTA. And the U.S. share is up 5.7 percentage points to 74.3 percent in the electronic goods and appliances sector, where Mexico has cut tariffs by 9.0 percentage points under NAFTA.
- Under NAFTA, Mexican tariff reductions of 9.0 percentage points on electronic goods and appliances are more than 4 times greater than U.S. reductions; Mexican tariff reductions on transport equipment of 10.2 percentage points are more than 9 times greater than U.S. reductions; and Mexican tariff reductions of 6.2 percentage points in the chemicals industry are more than 10 times greater than U.S. reductions.
- Since NAFTA was signed, U.S. exports to Mexico have made significant gains in several sectors, despite the severe Mexican recession. However, analysis by the International Trade Commission (ITC) shows that data inadequacies at the sectoral level make it difficult to isolate the effects of NAFTA on absolute trade flows.
- In industries such as autos, chemicals, textiles and electronics, NAFTA is permitting American companies to achieve synergies across the North American market, improving their strategic positions abroad and contributing to strong growth in employment, production, and investment at home.
- In several industries that have experienced strong import growth from Mexico, Mexican imports have largely displaced imports from other regions, which have lower U.S. domestic content. In the apparel industry, the share of U.S. imports supplied by Mexico rose from 4.4 percent in 1993 to 9.6 percent in 1996, while the share of U.S. imports from China, Hong Kong, Taiwan and Korea fell from 39 percent in 1993 to 30 percent in 1996. Close to 2/3 of the value of Mexican apparel imports in 1996 was comprised of U.S. content.

Labor Protection

The North American Agreement on Labor Cooperation (NAALC) established by the NAFTA has, for the first time, created North American cooperation on fundamental labor issues and has enhanced oversight and enforcement of labor laws.

- The NAALC submission process subjects member governments to public and international attention for alleged violations of labor laws. The submission process has resulted in such outcomes as recognition of a union previously denied recognition and permitting secret union ballots at two companies where union votes previously were not secret.

- Between 1993 and 1996, Mexico's Secretariat of Labor and Social Welfare increased funding for enforcement of labor laws by almost 250 percent.
- Mexico reports a 30 percent reduction in the number of workplace injuries and illnesses since the NAFTA was signed.
- Under the NAALC, the Canadian, Mexican, and U.S. governments have initiated cooperative efforts on a variety of labor issues, including occupational safety and health, employment and training, industrial relations, worker rights and child labor and gender issues.

Environmental Protection

NAFTA includes mechanisms to address environmental problems that have long challenged communities along the 2000-mile shared border with Mexico. NAFTA's environmental agreements are also encouraging regional cooperation on broader environmental issues and improved enforcement of Mexican environmental laws.

- Environmental institutions established under NAFTA are certifying and financing infrastructure projects designed to improve the environment along the U.S.-Mexico border. To date, 16 projects have been certified with a combined cost of nearly $230 million. Construction has already begun on seven projects, including a water treatment facility in Brawley, California and a water supply project in Mercedes, Texas. The NADBank will be able to leverage its capital into $2 to $3 billion in lending.
- The NAFTA Commission for Environmental Cooperation (CEC) has strengthened trilateral cooperation on a broad range of environmental issues, including illegal trade in hazardous wastes, endangered wildlife, and the elimination of certain toxic chemicals and pesticides.
- Through the CEC, Mexico has agreed to join the United States and Canada in banning the pesticides DDT and chlordane, ensuring that these long-lived, toxic substances no longer cross our border.
- The United States and Mexico have launched a Border XXI program establishing five-year objectives for achieving a clean border environment and a blueprint for meeting these objectives. U.S. and Mexican officials are now working to abate emissions from vehicles at border crossings, tracking transboundary shipments of hazardous wastes, and operating a U.S.-Mexico Joint Response Team to minimize the risk of chemical accidents, to name just a few activities.
- Mexico has established a voluntary environmental auditing program, which has completed audits of 617 facilities to date. Of these, 404 have signed environmental compliance Action Plans representing more than $800 million in environmental investments in Mexico.
- Mexico reports a 72 percent reduction in serious environmental violations in the maquiladora industry since the NAFTA was signed, and a 43 percent increase in the number of maquiladora facilities in complete compliance.

SAFETY ADMINISTRATOR ON AGGRESSIVE DRIVING
July 17, 1997

Greater traffic congestion and the stresses of modern life were among the factors leading to aggressive driving behavior that killed thousands of Americans every year, federal officials and traffic experts said in 1997. "Road rage" appeared to be an increasingly common occurrence on the nation's highways, joining drunk driving as the major traffic-related law enforcement problem.

Ricardo Martinez, administrator of the National Highway Safety Traffic Administration, told a House subcommittee on July 17 that one-third of all auto crashes (which injured three million Americans in 1996) and two-thirds of all highway fatalities "can be attributed to behavior associated with aggressive driving." Martinez and other officials said government agencies at all levels needed to pay more attention to the problem and devote more resources to combating it.

More Cars, More Frustration

Overall, federal officials said that highway travel was safer in 1996 than it was thirty years previously. They cited a decline since 1966 in total annual fatalities (from 50,984 to 31,907) and declines in several related accident statistics. Even so, the number of fatalities had increased in each of the previous four years (1992 through 1996), and aggressive driving was a significant reason, he said.

Increasingly common types of behavior on the nation's roadways included speeding, running red lights and stop signs, making illegal lane changes, passing on the right, and using offensive hand gestures. In extreme cases angry drivers rammed into other cars, tried to force others off the road, or even shot at other drivers. Seated in their cars, drivers could feel anonymous, even free to engage in types of behavior they would never consider in face-to-face encounters with other people.

Martinez acknowledged that numerous factors were responsible for the overall increase in aggressive driving, including the stresses of modern life and societal problems that led to uncivil or violent forms of behavior generally. But Martinez said three particular factors could be linked directly to aggressive driving:

- *A lack of responsible driving behavior. Increasingly, Martinez said, drivers had a "me-first" attitude rather than thinking of "our responsibilities to others with whom we share the road." Through driver education, people must be taught that "driving is a cooperative venture, not a competitive sport," he said.*
- *Reduced traffic enforcement. Martinez said many local jurisdictions were curtailing traffic enforcement because of budget cuts, when instead they should be increasing the number and visibility of police on the road. Laws also need to be adjusted to impose tougher penalties for aggressive driving, he said.*
- *Increased traffic congestion. Drivers frustrated by clogged streets and roads often become angry drivers, Martinez said. He noted that in the decade between 1987 and 1997, the number of miles of roads in the United States increased by just 1 percent, while the number of vehicle miles driven increased by 35 percent. One explanation for the increase in traffic was the increase in the number of cars. During the same decade, Americans acquired 27 percent more cars, while the number of Americans increased by just 10 percent.*

David K. Willis, president and chief executive officer of the American Automobile Association's Foundation for Traffic Safety reported the findings of a study conducted for his office by Mizell & Co., a consulting firm specializing in analyzing crime and terrorism issues. The Mizell study analyzed newspaper and police reports of 10,037 incidents of "violent aggressive driving" between January 1990 and August 1996. The overwhelming majority—96 percent—of the aggressors in those incidents were male, and the majority of them were men aged eighteen to twenty-six.

In 35 percent of the 10,037 incidents studied by Mizell, an automobile was used as a weapon; 37 percent of the incidents involved the use of a firearm as a weapon. Willis said the growing use of firearms in such incidents was "especially alarming" because of the rising popularity of laws enabling citizens to obtain permits for carrying concealed weapons. Enraged drivers also attacked others with pepper sprays, mace, and other "ostensibly defensive weapons," he said.

Combating Aggressive Driving

Federal officials and other experts cited numerous steps that could be taken to battle aggressive driving behavior. These steps fell into several broad categories, including establishing tougher traffic laws and enforcing those laws more consistently, reducing traffic congestion by building more roads and improving existing roads, designing roadways that will "calm" traffic flow rather than speed it up, updating traffic control devices to make traffic flow more smoothly, building more and better mass transportation

systems and bikeways to encourage drivers to get out of their cars, adopt-
ing driver awareness campaigns to alert the public to the dangers of aggres-
sive behavior on the road, and improving the content of driver education
courses.

Ultimately, Martinez said, it would be up to individual drivers to make
sure they did not become part of the aggressive driving problem. By wear-
ing seat belts, driving defensively, and reporting cases of aggressive dri-
ving to the authorities, he said, individuals can "take responsibility for not
contributing to this problem."

> *Following are excerpts from testimony given July 17, 1997, by*
> *Ricardo Martinez, administrator of the National Highway*
> *Traffic Safety Administration, to the Subcommittee on Surface*
> *Transportation of the House Committee on Transportation and*
> *Infrastructure:*

Mr. Chairman and Members of the Subcommittee. I am pleased to appear
before you today representing the U.S. Department of Transportation to discuss the problem of aggressive driving. I am particularly pleased to appear
with the witnesses you have brought together this morning. Everyone here
works with us to solve the problem of aggressive driving. . . .

The Highway Safety Picture

To place the problem of aggressive driving into context, let me begin by
mentioning several facts about the nation's highway safety picture.

Highway fatalities have decreased from 50,984 in 1966 to 41,907 in 1996,
despite an enormous increase in travel. The fatality rate—fatalities per mile
of travel—decreased by 69 percent during this period, from 5.5 fatalities per
hundred million miles traveled to 1.7, an all-time low. Alcohol involvement
in fatal crashes has dropped from 57 percent to 41 percent over this same
15-year period. Seat belt use has grown from 11 percent in 1982 to 68 percent
in 1996. Truck-related fatalities continue to decrease despite an increase in
truck travel and a 170-percent increase in the number of drivers holding commercial driver licenses. Rail-highway grade crossing fatalities at public crossings have also decreased by 31 percent over the last seven years (1990–1996).

The Department, in implementing the highway safety programs this Committee was so instrumental in developing, has contributed to this progress.
The number and costs of fatalities and injuries would be significantly higher
if not for our programs. Since 1992, seat belts, child safety seats, motorcycle
helmets, and the age-21 minimum drinking age laws have saved over 40,000
lives. Elimination of highway roadway hazards has saved an estimated 6,200
lives; an additional 1,700 lives have been saved through the rail-highway crossing improvement programs.

Despite these advances, recent statistics show there is no room for complacency. After years of steady decline, the total number of highway deaths

increased slightly in each of the last four years. In 1996, 41,907 people died and over 3 million more were injured in police-reported crashes. Though our fatality rate remains at an all-time low, these highway crashes still cost the Nation $150.5 billion a year. *We estimate that about one-third of these crashes and about two-thirds of the resulting fatalities can be attributed to behavior associated with aggressive driving.*

Aggressive Driving

For years the highway safety spotlight has been focused on the impaired driver, the speeding driver, and the unbelted drive and passengers. Today we must add the aggressive driver to the list of those contributing to the problems on our nation's roads and highways.

Everyone has seen examples of aggressive driving, and many of us, at some time, have driven aggressively ourselves. Let me begin with a definition of what we are talking about. The Department defines aggressive driving as "driving behavior that endangers or is likely to endanger people or property." This definition includes a broad spectrum of driving behaviors, ranging from risky driving and escalating to dueling and violence on the road.

Aggressive drivers are *more likely* to:

- Speed, tailgate, fail to yield, weave in-and-out of traffic, pass on the right, make improper and unsafe lane changes, run stop signs and red lights, make hand and facial gestures, scream, honk, and flash their lights
- Climb into the anonymity of an automobile and take out their frustrations on others at any time
- Allow high frustration levels to diminish any concern for fellow motorists
- Be impaired by alcohol or drugs, and drive unbelted or take other unsafe actions

Aggressive driving incidents are reported in newspapers throughout the country every day. Last year, on Virginia's George Washington Memorial Parkway, a dispute over a lane change led to a high-speed race that ended when both drivers lost control and crossed the median. Two people died. Horror stories like this one are now commonplace. Aggressive driving is taking its toll on America's highways, and these drivers must be stopped.

What Causes Aggressive Driving?

The causes of aggressive driving are complex; no one has all of the answers. Some psychiatrists point to deep-rooted personal causes such as stress disorders that lead to impaired judgment. Social scientists have tended to see a connection between societal problems and uncivil or violent forms of driving behavior.

What we do know is that three factors in particular are linked to aggressive driving: (1) lack of responsible driving behavior; (2) reduced levels of traffic enforcement; and (3) increased congestion and travel in our urban areas.

Lack of Responsible Driving Behavior. The problem of reducing aggressive driving begins with the individual driver. Driving is a privilege that demands responsibility. On the road, the focus is often on individual rights and freedom—a "me first" philosophy—not on our responsibility to others with whom we share the road. Each driver must accept responsibility for his or her actions on the road.

We must raise the level of responsible driving behavior. For example, greater attention must be given to the fact that all drivers are part of a system that includes other drivers, passengers, and pedestrians. As part of this system, we have to follow basic rules to make the system work. Driving is a cooperative venture, not a competitive sport; and cooperation really is the main way to achieve safety for all. Without cooperation we revert to the laws of the jungle, not of the road. All drivers, and new drivers in particular, beginning in driver's education classes, need to be made aware of more than just the "rules of the road." They must be taught that the consequences of aggressive driving lead to tragedy and that, in addition to being illegal, aggressive driving is often clearly criminal.

Reduced Levels of Traffic Enforcement. We also need vigorous enforcement of traffic laws. The perceived risk of being apprehended for a traffic violation is directly related to the level of traffic enforcement. The fewer the enforcement actions that are taken, the more frequent the aggressive behavior. Simply put, people tend to respect what the police inspect.

Unfortunately, some jurisdictions are cutting back on police traffic enforcement in this period of shrinking budgets. It is important to remember, however, that more Americans die by the violence of motor vehicle crashes than any another source of violence. As I mentioned earlier, last year 41,907 people died in traffic crashes. The number of these tragedies should help us realize that we need more police on our roads, not less. In short, more must be done to adjust law enforcement resources to address the heightened need of traffic enforcement.

We also need strong laws that are well enforced. Sound laws not only benefit the driving public and law enforcement officers, they also aid the judicial system. Aggressive driving is a serious offense, but it will not be treated as a serious offense if our courts are not given the ability to provide appropriate punishments. Strong penalties send strong messages that this form of behavior will not be tolerated.

Increased Congestion and Travel, Especially in Our Urban Areas. Traffic congestion is one condition frequently associated with aggressive driving. Since 1987, the number of miles of roads in the United States has increased by only 1 percent while the number of vehicle miles driven has increased by 35 percent. More cars and more drivers are also on the road. In the past decade, the number of cars grew 17 percent faster than the population, which grew at 10 percent.

When driver expectations are unmet, anger and aggression can be unleashed. For example, if a driver expects a trip to take 10 minutes and it takes more than 30 minutes, frustration grows. Many drivers respond to this frustration by acting and driving aggressively, sometimes even after the gridlock ends. New roads or added lanes should be considered; however, expansion is often not the answer, or even a viable option. In short, we cannot always "build" our way out of the problem. We will have to turn to improved traffic operations and technology to accommodate these increased traffic demands. Reauthorization of the Intermodal Surface Transportation Efficiency Act of 1991 (ISTEA) which the Congress is now working on, is a critical component to the solution of the aggressive driving. I will discuss this element in an additional detail later in my testimony.

In 1996, as part of the Capital Beltway Safety Initiative begun by Secretary [Rodney] Slater when he was FHWA Administrator, the Department undertook a study on the crash problem on the Capital Beltway—among the worst traffic-congested areas in the country. We found that congestion during peak hours is a frequent and primary factor for crashes. About 10 percent of these crashes were followed by subsequent crashes—and of course more congestion.

Aggressive Driving Countermeasures

The Department's activities to combat aggressive driving are focused on the 3 E's: education, enforcement, and engineering countermeasures.

Education. Last year, NHTSA distributed public information and education materials on aggressive driving to the 23 major media markets. In addition, NHTSA's Deputy Administrator Phil Recht and I have taken advantage of every opportunity for television and radio interviews to discuss this problem. We appeared on *Good Morning America*, *Oprah Winfrey*, *Dateline*, and a variety of other television shows. I also taped several inserts for airing on the *Real Stories of the Highway Patrol* series, and did a lengthy interview for the Law Enforcement Television Network. In addition to these media appearances, I spoke to a number of national organizations about the many issues related to aggressive driving.

One of our main information and education activities includes providing tips to motorists on how to avoid conflicts with aggressive drivers. We are sending this information to 50,000 highway safety professionals and advocates.

NHTSA and FHWA are working with the States and their law enforcement communities to establish a uniform, nationwide cell phone number for motorists to report aggressive drivers to State or local police. The agency's tips on how to avoid conflicts with aggressive drivers will be included in the bills sent to 20 million cell phone subscribers.

FHWA has initiated a program on the problem of running red lights—a common violation of aggressive drivers—and has developed an outreach campaign that incorporates vigorous enforcement. To date, over $600,000 has been awarded to 32 communities across the country to raise public awareness of this particular type of aggressive driving behavior. The City of Milwaukee recently received $25,000 to kick off their campaign on this problem.

The preliminary results of these campaigns show up to a 24 percent reduction in crashes.

Another of the Department's major programs that is making great strides in combating aggressive driving and increasing safety awareness on the highways is FHWA's Share-the-Road, or "No-Zone" Campaign. In its fourth year, the No-Zone campaign has been very successful in educating the public and increasing their awareness about sharing the road with commercial drivers in order to reduce traffic crashes. Through a host of strategic outreach tools, the campaign highlights the dangers of driving or "lingering" in the "blind spot" or "no-zone" areas of commercial motor vehicles.

Enforcement. Aggressive drivers must be held accountable for their actions. One of the best countermeasures to aggressive driving is the cop in the rear view mirror. The vigorous enforcement of traffic laws and the knowledge that there will be swift and sure penalties for their violation works better than anything else. Aggressive drivers must get the message that their behavior will not be tolerated, and that they will be prosecuted.

Delaware, Pennsylvania, New Jersey, and New Mexico recently initiated special, regional highway patrols targeting aggressive drivers.

In April, Secretary Slater announced a $100,000 grant to Washington area law enforcement agencies for their joint efforts in conducting the "Smooth Operator" program. "Smooth Operator" is a regional public awareness and enforcement effort targeting aggressive drivers on the Capital Beltway. In addition to routine traffic enforcement activities, State and local jurisdictions around the nation's capital currently are conducting enforcement "waves" throughout the summer. These enforcement "waves" are high profile operations with law enforcement officers targeting and issuing citations to aggressive drivers. We believe that the unprecedented effort of the "Smooth Operator" program—which will be discussed in detail shortly by a representative of Virginia—will show how effective law enforcement can be in combating aggressive driving.

Also, new technology is being used in the Capital Beltway Initiative to deter aggressive driving. Conventional law enforcement patrol tactics have been proven to have limited effectiveness in reaching a significant number of violators in the congested and hazardous operational environment of the Beltway. Instead, the Beltway project will use advanced technologies to detect and record traffic violations. Technologies to be used include laser imaging or video speed detection devices and high resolution digital traffic cameras. The imaging evidence will be used to support traffic enforcement actions and an associated public information campaign to reduce aggressive driving behavior associated with trucks, buses and other vehicles on the Beltway.

NHTSA strongly supports graduated licensing programs for young drivers, which we address under our Section 402 State and community highway safety program. It really is too easy to obtain a driver's license in many jurisdictions. Thirteen States now have graduated licensing programs in some form. These programs strengthen the licensing process by providing a provisional period for the novice driver during which certain restrictions are imposed, such as no driving between the hours of midnight and 5 a.m. This allows young drivers to develop safety conscious attitudes and behaviors in addition to the skills needed for safe driving.

Another of NHTSA's major efforts in this area is a demonstration project on aggressive driving enforcement. We will award a contract this year to one of the 27 highest traffic-congested metropolitan areas. The project's purpose will be to identify effective, innovative enforcement techniques, possible applications for new enforcement technology, legislative needs, prosecutorial or judicial needs, and the role, if any, that alcohol or drugs may play in this problem. Our results will be published and distributed nationally to law enforcement and other members of the criminal justice system. Any techniques that are proven effective in combating the aggressive driver will be tested in two other locations to validate the results.

Commercial vehicles are often mentioned as an area of particular concern. If a truck driver is an aggressive driver, he or she is particularly dangerous to the other drivers who share the road. (Most fatalities in fatal truck crashes are occupants of the other vehicle, not the truck's occupants!). FHWA's Motor Carrier Safety Assistance Program (MCSAP) and Pennsylvania law enforcement have teamed up to catch aggressive truck drivers using a high tech approach that includes using photo laser imaging or radar at high crash locations where excessive truck speed previously has been identified as a crash factor. If a truck driver is identified as driving too fast, the image is forwarded downstream using cellular technology. The vehicle is then pulled over for a commercial motor vehicle examination and the driver is charged with speeding. This concept has tremendous promise since it targets violators, and it serves as a "general deterrence" as the word spreads among commercial vehicle drivers and carriers on Pennsylvania highways.

FHWA has also worked with a group of 21 States to develop a new, national public information campaign on work zone safety. Work zones are a necessary stage of rebuilding our highways, but they contribute to traffic congestion and associated driver aggression. Every day, there are two deaths associated with work zone crashes in the United States. The campaign will be made available to all States later this year.

NHTSA and FHWA have jointly developed and continue to implement a Speed Management Plan combining research, enforcement, roadway engineering and public education. Speeding is frequently a significant aspect of the aggressive driving, and often precedes tailgating and sudden lane changes. In 1995, speeding was a factor in 31 percent of all fatal highway crashes, at a cost to society and the economy of more than $29 billion.

Traffic enforcement not only makes our roads safer, but can have a substantial effect on other criminal activity. Most criminals drive to and from their illegal activities, and therefore, when traffic enforcement increases, more criminals are detected and crime decreases. Perhaps the most famous example is Timothy McVeigh, the convicted Oklahoma City bomber, who was arrested at a routine traffic stop. A 1995 study in Grand Prairie, Texas, showed that 37 percent of all criminal arrests came from traffic stops. About one-half of the arrests in Grand Prairie were for non-traffic offenses, such as drug offenses, stolen vehicles, illegal weapons, and outstanding warrants for burglary, robbery, and violent crimes. Increased traffic enforcement in Modesto and San Bernadino, California, and Peoria, Illinois, resulted in reduced criminal activity as well as in increased traffic safety.

The court system has an important role to play, as well. Just as law enforcement must take traffic offenses seriously, so must the courts. The courts now recognize that drunk driving is not something to laugh at but is a serious crime that can injure or kill innocent bystanders. Other aggressive driving actions must be treated equally seriously.

Prosecutors must vigorously prosecute aggressive driving cases. Charges must not be reduced. When appropriate, the charges should be substantial, including vehicular homicide or reckless endangerment. Judges must treat these cases seriously and sentence offenders with appropriate severity. The courts must send a consistent message to the driving public that aggressive driving behavior will not be tolerated.

Engineering and Operations. The techniques our engineers use to design roads affect the safety of motorists. These countermeasures involve design and operational changes and often are focused to reduce speeding. Through engineering changes, we can reduce the likelihood of stress and reduce the likelihood of speeding.

Engineering approaches offer two basic types of countermeasures against the aggressive driver: highway design and traffic operations. With highway design, we can redesign the road to add capacity or accommodate increased traffic thruput. Highway design can also ameliorate the injury consequences for motorists who come into contact with aggressive drivers. Some examples are clear recovery zones, break way sign posts, and divided medians.

Traffic operations offer a way to accommodate increased traffic flow or at least get it under control, without building new roads. Intelligent Transportation Systems (ITS) applications offer great promise in this area. Three examples using smart traffic signal controls follow:

- In Lexington, KY, coordinated traffic signals reduced "stop and go" traffic delays by 40 percent and reduced crashes by 31 percent between 1985 and 1994.
- Minnesota's ramp metering management program increased peak period speeds by 35 percent and reduced crashes by 15–50 percent while peak period demand increased 32 percent.
- In Seattle, ramp metering along Interstate 5 kept traffic moving and cut crash rates by more than 38 percent over a six-year period despite a 10 to 100 percent increase in traffic along various interstate segments.

Freeway management systems are especially valuable in decreasing driver frustrations fueled by gridlock and slow traffic. ITS state-of-the-art freeway management systems can decrease travel time by 20–48 percent, increase capacity by 16–25 percent, and help create a cleaner atmosphere by cutting down fuel consumption used by vehicles while standing still in congestion.

This approach will be especially helpful in urban areas, where new road capacity is not likely to be possible.

A study of the 50 largest urbanized areas found that the roadway capacity needed to accommodate the next generation of drivers could be provided for 35 percent less cost than if only traditional lane-widening techniques were used. These savings would come from a combination of ITS technology and an expansion of capacity.

DOT's NEXTEA Proposal Provides
Resources for Countermeasures

The Department's proposed "National Economic Crossroads Transportation Efficiency Act of 1997" (NEXTEA) contains several provisions that can be used to develop comprehensive State and community programs aimed at combating aggressive driving.

The keystone of NHTSA's efforts in highway safety, jointly administered with FHWA, is the State and community highway safety grant program, known by its U.S. Code provision as the "Section 402" program.

The Section 402 program provides funds to every State to address their critical highway safety issues, and thus includes aggressive driving counter-measures. For example, Virginia, Maryland, and the District of Columbia are using their current Section 402 funds to implement innovative programs, such as Smooth Operator, and programs to curb aggressive drivers. In New Jersey, the New Jersey State Police, Division of Highway Safety, and municipal police departments in six counties used Section 402 funds to launch a program combining aggressive enforcement and public information efforts with a state-wide toll-free cellular phone number for motorists to report aggressive driving. By reauthorizing the Section 402 program, Congress can enable these States to continue funding such programs, and provide additional States will have the assistance they need to implement new aggressive driving programs throughout the country.

NEXTEA's Integrated Safety Fund, as proposed in NEXTEA, would reward States that have good integrated safety plans, by giving them new funds they could use on any or all of the following programs: Infrastructure Safety Program, Section 402 Highway Safety Programs (mainly the behavioral programs), and the Motor Carrier Safety Assistance Program. With these funds, States and local communities can develop a multi-faceted plan to address the problem of aggressive drivers. For example, a community could use Integrated Safety Funds to increase law enforcement on roadways where aggressive drivers are particularly prevalent, finance public information campaigns to make aggressive driving socially unacceptable, increase inspections to ensure truck drivers are not falsifying their travel logs (and driving longer than permitted), and install median barriers to ensure that if aggressive drivers do lose control of their vehicles, they will not cross over into on-coming traffic.

Our NEXTEA proposal also would increase the flexibility of the Surface Transportation Program (STP) to authorize the use of these funds to develop anti-aggressive driving initiatives. Under this proposal, States that have good integrated highway safety plans would be allowed to transfer STP funds to any of the three highway safety programs mentioned above.

NEXTEA also would sustain the Federal commitment to Intelligent Transportation Systems (ITS), mentioned earlier, and provide funds for using highway design features to counteract the effects of aggressive driving.

The Department's "Surface Transportation Safety Act of 1997," introduced as H.R. 1720, includes several significant safety initiatives—particularly an aggressive strategy to increase safety belt use through "primary" seat belt laws, which allow police to ticket motorists solely for failure to use a seat belt.

Our message is simple: seat belts are the best defense *against* aggressive driving! Seat belts are now saving 9,500 lives annually. A person is twice as likely to die or sustain a serious injury in a crash if unbelted. The experience of the 11 States that already have primary seat belt use laws has shown that these laws are one of the most effective strategies for increasing seat belt use—and for saving lives.

What Each Of Us Can Do Now

Finally, I want to stress what each of us can do *right now* about the aggressive driver. We can deal with this person on two levels: personal and societal.

On the *personal level*, seat belts are our best defense *against* aggressive driving, and each of us must ensure that we—

- Don't become part of the problem
- Don't personalize or challenge
- Report aggressive driving behavior

We also have to examine our own behavior to be sure that we are not doing something that another driver perceives as an insult. A certain percentage of our population always will retaliate to an insult. With this in mind, we need to be sure there is enough room to merge in front of another car, and we need to let another car merge in front of us in a fair way. Each of us needs to take responsibility for not contributing to the problem.

As a society, we have to send a clear message that driving is a privilege that demands responsibility. That message—which we are delivering with the help of our partners in highway safety—must increase public awareness that our communities support highly visible, aggressive enforcement. On the *social level*, each of us must ensure that we—

- Increase awareness of consequences and send strong social messages on responsible driving
- Support strengthened licensing systems (such as graduated licensing which ensure that the people who drive on the highways do so safely through solid driver training)
- Support strong, well-enforced laws (the answer to aggressive driving is aggressive enforcement)
- Support appropriate punishment from the judicial system (strong penalties send strong messages)

- Support improved highway management and operations (increase motorist information and capacity)

The good news is that we are beginning to see an increased nationwide awareness of the consequences of aggressive driving. A few recent cases have even charged aggressive drivers with negligent homicide.

Conclusion

Finally, I want to stress that motor vehicle crashes are not inevitable, they are avoidable. We are not helpless. We all have the power to make things better. We should use that power—and remember to Buckle Up on Every Trip!

STATE DEPARTMENT REPORT ON RELIGIOUS PERSECUTION
July 22, 1997

Complying with a congressional directive, the Clinton administration in 1997 issued the government's first comprehensive report on persecution of religious minorities—especially Christians—in foreign countries. The State Department on July 22 sent Congress a report detailing practices in countries such as China and the Sudan that curbed religious freedom and, in many cases, led to imprisonment and even death for religious leaders.

The Clinton administration also launched a high visibility campaign against legislation in Russia establishing the Orthodox Church as the country's preferred religious establishment. Despite intense lobbying by President Bill Clinton, Vice President Al Gore, and others, the Russian parliament approved the legislation twice, and President Boris Yeltsin signed it into law in September. The issue represented one of the first major tests of Washington's influence on human rights issues in the new Russian democracy.

Growing Concern about Religious Persecution

Ever since the presidency of Jimmy Carter, when human rights first rose to the top of the U.S. foreign policy agenda, Congress and successive administrations had paid some attention to how foreign countries treated religions, particularly religious minorities. The State Department's annual reports to Congress on human rights practices abroad routinely contained sections cataloging the degree to which other countries respected religious freedom.

In public discussions of human rights issues, religious persecution often lagged well behind such matters as abuses of political dissidents and ethnic minorities. Starting in the mid-1990s conservative religious groups in the United States demanded more attention to the issue, insisting that the Clinton administration and liberal human rights groups gave the matter short shrift. Michael Horowitz, a former Reagan administration official who launched a personal crusade to draw attention to persecution of Chris-

tians, accused such groups as Human Rights Watch of practicing a "double standard" of being less concerned about religious minorities than political minorities. Human Rights Watch vigorously disputed the charge, noting that for years it had drawn attention to abuses committed against religious minorities in countries such as China.

Both houses of Congress in 1996 passed nonbinding resolutions condemning persecution of Christians in communist and Islamic countries. Congress also required the State Department to submit a report in 1997 detailing how other countries treated Christians. Congress in 1997 considered, but did not enact, legislation to impose limited economic sanctions against countries that practice religious persecution.

State Department Report

In its report to Congress, the State Department's Bureau of Democracy, Human Rights and Labor Affairs detailed practices in nearly seventy countries that had the effect of curtailing religious freedom. The report discussed acts against non-Christians in Tibet, Iran, and a handful of other countries, but in keeping with the congressional mandate most of the focus was on how Christians of various denominations were treated.

Secretary of State Madeleine K. Albright said in a foreword to the report that the United States was "working actively to promote tolerance of legitimate religious expression for adherents of every faith." Implicitly disputing the contention of some conservative critics, she said that U.S. officials "have not hesitated to speak out when governments persecute Christians or fail to ensure the safety of any religious group." The report listed U.S. actions in recent years to put the issue of religious freedom before the international community.

As with most other U.S. reports on human rights issues since the Carter years, China came under the harshest criticism. Despite its economic liberalization starting in the 1980s, the Chinese communist regime remained one of most authoritarian in the world, one with little interest in what it considered western bourgeois sermons on human rights.

The State Department report noted that China's restrictions on religious practices were applied unevenly, allowing religious groups to grow rapidly since 1980 in some areas of the country. Since 1994 religious groups had been required to register with the government and to submit to the supervision of government-approved religious organizations. Many groups refused to comply with the requirement and as a result operated in secret.

The Chinese government in October 1996 launched a crackdown on "unauthorized" religious organizations, raiding and closing hundreds of so-called house church groups operating in private homes or other small facilities. China tolerated a few official religious organizations, including a 4 million-member Catholic Church that did not recognize the authority of the Vatican. The unofficial Catholic Church affiliated with the Vatican claimed many more members.

In Russia, the report said, the overall climate for religious freedom had "improved dramatically" since the collapse of the Soviet Union. The result was a "large influx" of foreign missionaries, including those representing small sects. The sudden competition unnerved leaders of the once-suppressed Russian Orthodox Church, who sought government protection.

In 1997 the Russian parliament passed legislation requiring religious groups to register with the government and prohibiting "non-traditional" groups from obtaining full legal status for fifteen years. President Yeltsin at first rejected the legislation as unconstitutional. When the parliament approved it again, the Clinton administration launched a sustained campaign—including an appeal by Vice President Gore during a Moscow visit—to convince Yeltsin to veto it again. Yeltsin brushed the advice aside and signed the bill into law September 26.

Most other countries singled out for sharp criticism in the State Department report were run by authoritarian regimes unfriendly to the United States. Among them were Cuba, which had eased some of its restrictions on religious groups but continued to harass Christian evangelical organizations; Iraq, which had routinely repressed all religious groups except for the established Sunni branch of Islam; Iran, which persecuted members of the Baha'i sect; North Korea, which discouraged all religious activity unless it supported government interests; and the Sudan, which repressed Christians in the rebellious southern part of the country and those holding traditional animist beliefs.

A few U.S. allies and friends also were noted in the report, including Mexico, where local authorities, especially in the highlands of Chiapas, had persecuted evangelical Christians; Pakistan, where Islamic extremists had attacked members of religious minorities; and Saudi Arabia, which made no pretense of tolerating religious freedom and required all citizens to be Muslims. In addition, the report noted that several U.S. allies (among them France, Germany, and Israel) hindered religious groups such as the Jehovah's Witnesses.

Following are excerpts from the State Department report, "United States Policies in Support of Religious Freedom: Focus on Christians," delivered to Congress July 22, 1997:

Overview

The United States Government upholds the principle that the freedom of religion, conscience, and belief is an inalienable and fundamental human right. Religious persecution is an intolerable invasion of an individual's basic human rights, and promoting freedom of religion and combating religious persecution are high priorities for the U.S. Government. President Clinton declared in his proclamation of Religious Freedom Day on January 16, 1997: "America's commitment to religious tolerance has empowered us to achieve an atmosphere of understanding, trust, and respect in a society of diverse cultures and religious traditions. And today, much of the world still looks to the United States as the champion of religious liberty."

Religious tolerance and respect for those who hold different beliefs are central elements of the American experience and our nation's core values. Indeed, the search for freedom of religion was a key factor in the settlement of colonial America. Today, these values go hand-in-hand with our interest in assisting the evolution of stable, democratic governments in all parts of the world. If people lack freedom of conscience and are unable to practice their faith, it is likely that other human rights will be restricted and that intolerance and violence will be more prevalent. Lack of these rights also impedes efforts to establish societies that promote liberty and justice. Accordingly, the U.S. Government actively works to integrate the promotion of freedom of conscience and religion, the support of religious tolerance, and the elimination of persecution as central elements of our global diplomacy.

Unfortunately, both governments and members of different communities in many parts of the world continue to persecute religious groups. In some instances, religious persecution is due to governments that do not tolerate independent thought, belief systems, or freedom of association. In other instances, political leaders have exploited religious and ethnic differences for self-serving and sometimes violent political ends. At times, political rhetoric and manipulation have exacerbated disputes between members of different religions—or between members of different groups within the same religion.

At the same time, many religious communities are actively engaged in promoting tolerance and religious freedom and in trying to resolve conflicts among groups. Such efforts are testimony to the strength of the human spirit, and complement government efforts to ensure that all persons are able to practice their faith as they choose.

The U.S. Government is concerned about incidents in which any individuals or groups are persecuted because of their religion or belief. This Administration has intensified efforts to address the issue of freedom of religion and to promote religious freedom in a number of ways. On a global scale, we have urged adherence to international human rights instruments, such as the Universal Declaration of Human Rights which provides for the right of all persons to freedom of thought, conscience, and religion. This right includes freedom to change one's religion or belief, and freedom—either alone or in community with others, and either in public or private—to manifest one's religion or belief in teaching, practice, worship, and observance.

We have highlighted and condemned religious persecution in our multilateral and bilateral diplomacy. Through private diplomatic efforts and public condemnation the U.S. Government has secured the release of and improvement in the treatment of individuals of various religions and beliefs who have faced incarceration, harassment, or other forms of abuse. At international fora, U.S. delegations have emphasized the importance of religious tolerance and reconciliation, and the need for multilateral opposition to the persecution of persons on the basis of their religious beliefs or practices. The White House, the Department of State and other agencies of the U.S. Government have issued official statements to spotlight incidents of religious persecution on a regular basis, and the U.S. Government provides a detailed summary of such abuses each year in the annual Country Reports on Human Rights Practices. We are also intensifying efforts to improve the review process for asylum and refugee applications.

An important step in highlighting religious freedom was the establishment of the Advisory Committee on Religious Freedom Abroad in 1996 by Secretary of State Warren Christopher. The White House announced the formation of the Committee and the members met with President Clinton and First Lady Hillary Rodham Clinton prior to their first official meeting. The significance of the Committee's work was emphasized by Secretary of State Madeleine Albright, who addressed the inaugural meeting in February 1997. The twenty leaders of religious, academic, and advocacy communities who are members of the Committee are formulating recommendations to the U.S. Government on means of advancing religious freedom throughout the world, with a focus on eliminating religious persecution and supporting the promotion of human rights and conflict resolution. The Committee will submit its final report to the Secretary of State and the President. The Committee convened its second official meeting in July and has held working group sessions in various parts of the country.

Our human rights objectives are also advanced through U.S. assistance programs to organizations that monitor and promote human rights, facilitate cultural and educational exchanges, and strengthen the rule of law, justice, civil society and good governance. The U.S. Government encourages other sectors of society, including the U.S. business community and the labor movement, to help advance human rights. And we support international broadcasting programs that disseminate human rights information throughout the world, including in countries where individual liberty and freedom are restricted.

The approaches used to promote religious freedom and combat violations of this right differ depending on the situation in each country. In some instances, the U.S. Government is able to raise problems of religious persecution directly with foreign governments. In other instances, such as where we do not have formal diplomatic relations, the U.S. Government's ability to press for redress is limited to acts in multilateral fora or to coordinated efforts with other governments that do have diplomatic relations with the country in question. In cases of inter-communal tension and strife, or action by individuals, in which foreign governments are not direct participants, the U.S. Government's ability to intervene is limited.

This report summarizes U.S. Government actions to promote religious freedom and to counter religious intolerance, discrimination, and persecution, with a focus on the protection of Christians from persecution, as requested by Congress. It is not an exhaustive list of all U.S. Government activities in this area. An annex to the report provides a summary of the current situation and bilateral initiatives in a number of countries. In some instances, there are no reports of religious persecution, but policies exist that could impact Christians and members of other religious and belief communities. In addition, the omission of a country from this report does not imply that incidents of discrimination, intolerance, or persecution against Christians or members of other faith communities does not occur. The report draws from the State Department's Country Reports on Human Rights Practices and information gathered in recent months, both officially and unofficially; every effort was made to verify the accuracy of the information contained in this report. In accordance with the congressional request, the emphasis in the annex is on the situation Christians face and actions taken by the U.S. Government. . . .

Burma

Current situation: The Government imposes several severe restrictions on fundamental freedoms. Adherents of all religions that are duly registered with the authorities generally enjoy freedom to worship as they choose. However, religious publications, like secular ones, remain subject to control and censorship. Christian Bibles translated into indigenous languages cannot legally be imported or printed. It remains extremely difficult for Christian and Muslim groups to obtain permission to build new churches and mosques, and there were credible reports of incidents in which the Government removed cemeteries in constructing infrastructure projects in urban areas. Buddhists constitute the vast majority of citizens. Buddhist organizations are also subject to government monitoring and interference. In December 1996, the Government ordered the removal of Christian, Chinese, and Buddhist graves from the Kyandaw Cemetery in Rangoon to make way for a planned real estate development.

Religious groups have established links with co-religionists in other countries, although these activities are reportedly monitored by the Government. Foreign religious representatives are usually allowed visas only for short stays, but in some cases have been permitted to preach to congregations. Permanent foreign missionary establishments have not been permitted since the 1960's, but seven Catholic nuns and four priests working in Burma since before independence in January 1948 continue their work.

The Government monitors the activities of members of all religions, in part because such members have, in the past, become politically active. The Muslim and Christian religious minorities continued to be regarded with suspicion by the authorities. In particular, there is a concentration of Christians among the ethnic minorities against whom the army has fought for decades, such as the Karen. In recent months there have been increased reports that thousands of Burmese soldiers have swept through Karen areas along the Burma-Thailand border, raping women and forcing men to act as porters for the military.

The DKBA—a government-supported faction of Buddhist Karen—has conducted cross-border raids into Thailand, attacking Karen refugee camps, killing and kidnapping Christian Karen National Union leaders and members, killing Thai police and soldiers, and burning two camps in late January 1997.

U.S. Government actions: The U.S. Embassy monitors restrictions on religious freedom, as well as other human rights problems, and repeatedly raises strong concerns and particular cases of persecution in meetings with government officials. The overall human rights situation in Burma deteriorated significantly in 1996, and, in response to the Government's dismal human rights record and a continuing pattern of severe repression, the President in April 1997 imposed a ban on new U.S. investment in Burma.

The U.S. Government has also applied a number of other measures against Burma, including suspension of all U.S. assistance, imposition of an arms embargo, and opposition to assistance for Burma from international financial institutions. As a sign of official concern, the United States is represented at the charge level in Burma, rather than by an ambassador. In October 1996, the President imposed a ban on visas for senior Burmese government officials and their families. These sanctions are intended to increase the pressure on the military-led government in Burma to move in the direction of dialogue with the democratic opposition and leaders of ethnic minority groups, as well as to respect fundamental human rights and religious freedom. . . .

China

Current situation: The constitution states that citizens "enjoy freedom of religious belief." Nonetheless, the Government of China has sought to restrict all actual religious practice to government-authorized religious organizations and registered places of worship. In practice, this effort has been implemented unevenly and in some areas unauthorized groups have flourished. Since 1980, and particularly in recent years, religious groups—both registered and unregistered—have grown rapidly, however, despite government attempts to assert control over religion. State Council regulations signed in 1994 require all religious groups to register with government religious affairs bureaus and come under the supervision of official religious organizations.

Some religious groups have registered, while others were refused registration, and others have not applied. Many groups have been reluctant to comply due to principled opposition to state control of religion, unwillingness to limit their activities, or refusal to compromise their position on matters such as abortion. They fear adverse consequences if they reveal, as required, the names and addresses of members and details about leadership activities, finances, and contacts in China or abroad.

Guided by a central policy directive of October 1996 that launched a national campaign to suppress unauthorized religious groups and social organizations, Chinese authorities in some areas made strong efforts to crack down on the activities of unregistered Catholic and Protestant movements in 1996–1997. They raided and closed several hundred "house church" groups, many with significant memberships, properties, and financial resources. Local authorities used threats, demolition of property, extortion of "fines," interrogation, detention, and reform-through-education sentences in carrying out this campaign. Some leaders of such groups were detained for lengthy investigation, and some were beaten. There were reports that unofficial groups were particularly hard hit in Beijing and the nearby provinces of Henan (where there are rapidly growing numbers of Protestants), and Hebei, a center of unregistered Catholics. At present, four Catholic underground bishops are among the many Christians who remain imprisoned or detained, or whose whereabouts are unknown. Catholic priests, Bishop Joseph Fan Zhongliang and Rev. Zen Caijun, were subjected to searches and seizures of religious articles and other property in 1997.

The unregistered Vatican-affiliated Catholic Church claims a membership far larger than the 4 million persons registered with the official Catholic Church (which does not recognize the authority of the Pope), although no precise figures are available. Government officials estimate that there are about 15 million Protestant worshipers in China; other estimates indicate that approximately 10 million people belong to the official church, while perhaps as many as three to seven times more worship in house churches that are independent of government control.

While officially-registered groups offer a growing range of services to their members and their communities, they are subject to government guidance, and have limits on their doctrinal teachings and activities. Bibles are printed in increasing numbers—three million in 1996, up from one million in 1995— and are distributed by official organizations in cooperation with foreign groups. Social services, including those that benefit from foreign cooperation, are permitted through designated quasi-official charitable organizations, as well as through some individual churches.

Communist Party officials state that party membership and religious belief are incompatible. This places a serious limitation on religious believers, since party membership is required for almost all high-level positions in government and state-owned businesses. This requirement is enforced unevenly; according to a 1995 government survey, 20 percent of Communist Party members engage in some form of religious activity.

The 1994 regulations also codified many existing rules involving foreigners, including a ban on proselytizing by foreigners. However, the regulations allow foreign nationals to preach to foreigners, bring in religious materials for their own use, and preach to Chinese at churches, mosques, and temples at the invitation of registered religious organizations.

The Government exercises control over the education of Christian and other religious clergy. According to the Government, there are now 68,000 religious sites in China and 48 religious colleges. Government-sanctioned religious organizations administer more than a dozen Catholic and Protestant seminaries and a limited number of institutes to train scholars of other religions. Students who attend these institutes must demonstrate "political reliability," and pass an examination on their political knowledge to qualify for the clergy. The Government is permitting growing numbers of religious leaders to go abroad for religious studies and allowing foreign organizations to provide training and materials in China. Unofficial churches, however, have significant problems training clergy. Hebei's underground church seminary was closed down in 1996. The Government bars the Vatican from designating bishops and appoints them directly instead.

Increased government concern about the potential impact of ethnic separatist movements has also led to restriction on the religious freedom of other believers. In Tibet, for example, the authorities tightened restrictions on the practice of Tibetan Buddhism, including public expression of reverence for the Dalai Lama. In the predominantly Muslim Xinjiang Autonomous Region, the government tightened control of religious activities in response to a separatist bombing campaign. A number of mosques have been closed or destroyed, unsanctioned religious classes have been canceled, and some local officials have been dismissed.

U.S. Government actions: The United States has made freedom of religion a major focus of its human rights policy toward China and has raised the issue frequently in bilateral discussions with Chinese officials. President Clinton raised human rights issues with President Jiang Zemin at the November 1996 Asian Pacific Economic Conference. Vice President Gore discussed U.S. concerns about restrictions on freedom of religion with senior government officials during his March 1997 trip to Beijing. Secretary Albright, during her visit to Beijing in February 1997, discussed U.S. concerns about restrictions on freedom of religion with senior government officials.

In January 1997, a U.S. Government delegation underscored the importance that the United States attaches to fundamental freedoms, including freedom of religion, and specifically expressed concern about the persecution of Christians in China. The United States also has raised specific cases of Christians with the Chinese Government, expressing our view that all those incarcerated for the peaceful expression of their religious (or political) views should be released immediately. For example, after Pastor Xu Yongze was arrested in March 1997 and reports circulated of his possible execution, the U.S. Embassy in Beijing raised his case with Chinese officials, who responded by providing information regarding Xu's activities and assurances that he would not be executed.

During Secretary Christopher's November 1996 trip to China, both he and Assistant Secretary Shattuck raised with senior Chinese leaders a range of human rights concerns and called for the release of political prisoners incarcerated for the peaceful expression of their religious, political, or social views. Secretary Christopher also emphasized that our relationship with China will not realize its fullest potential without significant progress in China's human rights situation. In addition, Secretary Christopher extensively discussed these problems with his counterpart, China's Vice Premier Qian Qichen, in their four meetings in April, July, September, and November 1996.

With regard to Tibet, the Administration has strongly encouraged dialogue between the Chinese Government and the Dalai Lama. During their April 1997 meeting with the Dalai Lama, President Clinton and Vice President Gore expressed their continuing concern for the situation of the Tibetan people, including the need to preserve the religious freedom of Tibetan Buddhists. Secretary Albright and members of her Advisory Committee on Religious Freedom Abroad reemphasized these in their meeting with the Dalai Lama.

The United States has continued its efforts to address the issue of freedom of religion in its public diplomacy. The Department of State has issued official statements on the issue of religious persecution on a regular basis.

We have also actively promoted human rights in multilateral fora. We co-sponsored a resolution on China's human rights situation at the UNHRC in Geneva in April that included the issue of religious freedom. We also delivered a statement on religious freedom at the Commission, which contained references to China.

In 1997 the first annual Best Global Practices Award was given to a company recognized for its aggressive advocacy before the business community and the Chinese public in encouraging respect for human rights, including interventions on behalf of religious prisoners. conflict that ensures that all human rights are respected. . . .

Cuba

Current situation: Although the Government of Cuba has eased the harsher aspects of its repression of religious freedom in recent years, religious persecution continues. In 1996 there were several instances of persecution of Christians in Cuba.

In December 1995, the Cuban Government issued a resolution preventing any Cuban or joint enterprise from selling computers, fax machines, photocopiers, or other equipment to any church. A December 1, 1995 decree signed by Politburo member Jose Ramon Machado Ventura prohibited Christmas trees and decorations in public buildings, except those related to the tourist or foreign commercial sector, and completely prohibited Nativity scenes. The Government ended official recognition of all religious holidays in 1961.

In February 1996, the Union of Communist Youth (UJC) affiliate within the lawyers' collective in the town of Palma Soriano, expelled attorney Cesar Antonio Martinez Melero from his long-standing membership in the UJC because of his active involvement in the Roman Catholic Church. In April 1996 a disciplinary board of the Julio Mella Polytechnic Institute suspended Raul Leyva Ameran's student stipend for 6 months for refusing on religious grounds to participate in a February 27 rally in support of the Government's February 24 shootdown of two civilian U.S. aircraft. Leyva had said that as a Catholic, he "did not support the violent death of anyone and for reasons of conscience (he) could not go to the rally."

Government restrictions on religious activities include limitations on access to the media, establishment of schools, and sponsorship of social activities. Government harassment of private houses of worship continued throughout 1996, with evangelical denominations reporting evictions from, and bulldozing of, houses used for these purposes. In the province of Las Tunas, neighbors of one private house of worship tried to provoke fights with parishioners, blared music during religious services, and tried to pour boiling water through the windows during a religious service. In the western mining town of Moa, a group of evangelical leaders submitted a written appeal to the local Communist Party to stop the harassment of church members and the demolition of houses of worship, and to lift the prohibition on the construction, expansion, or remodeling of churches. The authorities warned religious leaders in Havana that they would impose fines ranging from 10,000 to 50,000 pesos ($500 to $2,500), imprison leaders, and withdraw official recognition from the religious denomination itself, unless the private houses of worship were closed.

The Cuban Government, however, relaxed restrictions on members of Jehovah's Witnesses, whom it has considered "active religious enemies of the revolution" for their refusal to accept obligatory military service or participate in state organizations. The Government authorized small assemblies of Jehovah's Witnesses, the opening of a Havana central office, and the publishing of the group's "Watchtower" magazine and other religious tracts.

The Castro regime authorized a public mass for the first time since 1961 on June 29. This unprecedented outdoor event outside Havana's Cathedral celebrated the 19th anniversary of Pope John Paul II's election as Pope and served to kick off preparations for the Pope's January 1998 visit to Cuba. Jaime Cardinal Ortega celebrated mass for about 4,000 persons, while the regime provided polite yet pervasive security, drinking water, and sanitary facilities, and covered the mass in both televised and print reports.

U.S. Government actions: U.S. policy toward Cuba is to promote peaceful, democratic change and respect for human rights, including religious freedom. The United States does not have diplomatic relations with Cuba, and the U.S. Interests Section in Havana is unable to intervene formally regarding cases of religious discrimination and harassment in Cuba. However, the Interests Section reports on such cases, maintains regular contact with religious leaders of all faiths throughout the country, and supports non-governmental organization initiatives that aid religious groups. The U.S. Government continuously marshals international pressure on the Cuban Government to cease its repressive practices. . . .

Iran

Current situation: The Iranian constitution declares that Islam is the "official religion" of Iran and that "the sect followed is Ja'fari Shi'ism." The Government restricts freedom of religion both for other Muslim sects and other religious minorities, including Christians. The constitution states that other Islamic denominations "shall enjoy complete respect," and also recognizes Christianity, Judaism, and Zoroastrianism. Members of these religions elect representatives to reserved parliamentary seats. They may practice their religion and instruct their children, but the Government interferes with the administration of their schools and harassment by government officials is common. The law also stipulates penalties for government workers who do not observe "Islamic principles and rules."

Non-Muslims may not proselytize Muslims. Muslims who convert to another faith are considered apostates and may be subject to the death penalty. Four Baha'is remain in prison under death sentences, convicted on charges of apostasy in 1996. There have been no reports in recent years of Christians convicted on apostasy charges.

Official oppression of evangelical Christians increased in 1996. In early July 1996, a Muslim convert to Christianity, Shahram Sepehri-Fard, was arrested on charges of having "sensitive information." He has been denied visitors since shortly after his arrest, and his condition is unknown. In late September 1996, another Muslim convert to evangelical Christianity, Pastor Mohammed Yussefi (also known as Ravanbaksh), was found dead in a public park. He is widely believed to have been murdered by Iranian authorities. Yussefi had been imprisoned by the Government on several occasions prior to his death. Three members of an opposition movement, Mojahadin-e-Khaleq (MEK), Farohnaz Anami, Betoul Vaferi Kalateh, and Maryam Shahbazpoor, are currently in prison for the 1994 murder of Reverend Tatavous Michaelian, an evangelical Protestant pastor. The three women claim that two other Christian pastors murdered in 1994, Reverend Mehdi Dibaj and Reverend Haik Hovsepian Mehr, were also killed by the MEK. However, many observers believe that it is more likely that the Government is responsible for these deaths.

In January 1997, two Christian evangelists, Daniel Baumann and Stuart Timm, were arrested and detained under suspicion of espionage, a charge which is often levied against persons who proselytize in Iran. Baumann is a Swiss/American dual national and Timm holds South African citizenship. Both eventually were released without having been charged.

U.S. Government actions: The United States does not have diplomatic relations with Iran and is therefore unable to directly monitor the serious problems of religious persecution that exist in the country.

In coordination with the Swiss Embassy in Tehran, the United States worked to obtain the release of Daniel Baumann, who was freed in March. Stuart Timm was released in February.

In 1996 the U.S. Government publicly condemned Iran's persecution of Christians, Baha'is, and other religious minorities on a number of occasions at international fora, in policy statements, and through radio broadcasts.

At the UNHRC, the UNGA, and the International Labor Organization, the United States strongly supported resolutions condemning human rights violations in Iran, including the persecution of Christians. The United States also called for extending the mandates of the U.N. Special Representative for Iran, the U.N. Special Rapporteur on Religious Intolerance, and the U.N. Special Rapporteur on Freedom of Opinion and Expression, each of whom visited Iran in 1995 to ascertain details about conditions there. The U.N. Special Representative on Iran is awaiting an invitation from the Government and has been unable to visit the country.

The State Department spokesman has issued statements on the mistreatment of Baha'is and Christians in Iran and several Voice of America editorials have focused on this problem.

Iraq

Current situation: The provisional constitution of 1968 states that "Islam is the religion of the State," but the Government of Iraq severely limits freedom of religion. Ethnic and religious communities, including the majority Shi'a population and the Kurds in northern Iraq, not associated with the ruling clique have suffered massive repression for decades.

The U.N. Special Rapporteur on Iraq and others report that the Iraqi Government has engaged in various abuses against the country's 350,000 Assyrian Christians. Most Assyrians traditionally live in the northern governorates, and the Government often has suspected them of "collaborating" with Kurds. Assyrians are an ethnic group as well as a Christian community. They speak a distinct language—Syriac—which is banned de facto in public. The U.N. Special Rapporteur reported continued discrimination and persecution against Assyrians throughout 1996. Other sources also report that the Government continued in 1996 to harass and kill Assyrian Christians throughout the country, using forced relocations, terror, and artillery bombardments.

U.S. Government actions: The United States does not have diplomatic relations with Iraq and thus does not have bilateral channels in which to raise human rights issues. However, the United States has vigorously led the international community's condemnation of human rights violations in Iraq. At the UNGA, the U.S. led successful efforts to adopt a resolution condemning Iraq's human rights record. The U.S. Government has also strongly supported the U.N. Special Rapporteur on Iraq and assisted his staff in their interviews of refugees from northern Iraq, including Assyrian Christians, who were in Guam awaiting resettlement in the United States.

Israel

Current situation: The law provides for freedom of religion, and the Government respects this right. The Jewish, Christian, and Muslim communities each have legal authority over their members in matters of marriage and divorce, although Christians have the choice of religious or civil courts in some matters. In civic areas where religion is a determining criterion, such as the religious courts and centers of education, non-Jewish institutions receive less state support than their Jewish counterparts.

The status of a number of Christian organizations with representation in Israel has heretofore been defined by a collection of ad hoc arrangements with various government agencies. Several of these organizations are negotiating with the Government in an attempt to formalize their status. Attempts to establish meaningful negotiations are ongoing.

Missionaries are allowed to proselytize, although Mormons are specifically prohibited from doing so by mutual agreement between the Church of Jesus Christ of Latter-Day Saints and the Government. A 1977 anti-proselytizing law prohibits anyone from offering or receiving material benefits as an inducement to conversion.

In the spring of 1997, a private member's bill was introduced in the Israeli Knesset (parliament) to restrict proselytizing, apparently in reaction to an evangelical Christian group's mass mailing of brochures to thousands of Israelis. If passed in its current form, this bill would amend the current anti-proselytization law, and prohibit the production, import, or dissemination of religious materials "in which there is an inducement to religious conversion," and would provide for confiscation of the materials and one-year prison sentence.

Local civil rights activists and legal scholars strongly oppose the bill, which they state contravenes freedom of expression and freedom of religion provided for in Israel's basic laws. They note that the bill's sweeping language theoretically could prohibit even the ownership of a New Testament. Prime Minister Binyamin Netanyahu has publicly stated his government's opposition to the bill, which is still under preliminary consideration in the Knesset.

The small community of Jehovah's Witnesses has faced harassment and occasional violent attacks by private citizens opposed to religious prosyletization. On March 8, 1997, a mob of over 250 Haredim (ultra-conservative Orthodox Jews) attacked the Lod meeting hall, broke into the building, destroyed the interior, and burned religious literature, books, and furnishings. The police stated that they were notified by bystanders too late to intervene.

Members of Jehovah's Witnesses have reported being followed, and have also reported death threats. Police have occasionally evinced indifference to complaints, sometimes alleging that members of Jehovah's Witnesses proselytize without a permit (although there is no requirement or provision under Israeli law for such a permit). Police have warned that they would act to uphold the law if there was any further interference with anyone's right to worship.

U.S. Government actions: In March, after the attack on the Lod meeting hall, the U.S. Embassy raised the issue of police protection for Jehovah's Witnesses with the head of the Foreign Liaison Division of the Israeli National Police. The head of the division assured the Embassy that police patrols would be stepped up while the facility was being rebuilt, and that the police had already advised communities of Jehovah's Witnesses to notify them of any planned meetings so that adequate security could be provided. The Embassy inquired whether the Lod police had made any arrests or had filed charges against suspected perpetrators of the March 8 attack on the Lod meeting hall, and was informed that individuals had been detained, questioned, and warned, but that no charges had been brought. The Embassy emphasized that while assurances of police protection in the future for Jehovah's Witnesses were welcome, since the identity of those involved in the March 8 attack was apparently known, we expected active prosecution of those who had violated the law. . . .

Nigeria

Current situation: The Government generally respects freedom of religious belief, practice, and education, while taking measures to lessen the prospects for religious tension. State and local governments are prohibited from adopting a state religion. A 1987 ban on religious organizations in primary schools remains in effect, although individual students retain the right to practice their religion in recognized places of worship. Distribution of religious publications is generally unrestricted, although there is a lightly enforced ban on published religious advertisements, and religious programming remains closely controlled on television and radio. The Government discourages proselytizing, while not outlawing the practice. The Government bans open-air religious services away from places of worship. Christian and Muslim organizations accuse the government of restricting the entry of certain religious practitioners, particularly persons suspected of proselytizing.

In Kwara state in March 1996, state authorities ordered the closing of Christian schools that refused to teach Islamic studies. These schools supposedly had reacted to Islamic schools that were not required to teach Christian studies. After the transfer of the military administrator for the state, the schools were reopened. Also in Kwara state, in March 1997, soldiers beat and whipped members of the Christian Association of Nigeria during their annual Palm Sunday procession in Ilorin. An army captain had parked his car along the route, blocking the procession, and when asked to move it, the captain enlisted several soldiers stationed nearby to attack the procession. Several of the Christian Association members were detained for 2 days.

U.S. Government actions: The U.S. Embassy encourages and advocates a broad-based democratic system with respect for human rights, including the free expression of religious values. Through many means (State Department press releases, testimony at hearings, public statements, Voice of America editorials, embassy demarches, visa restrictions and other sanctions, etc.) the U.S. Government has made clear U.S. opposition to the present regime's oppressive human rights policies.

Pakistan

Current situation: Pakistan's constitution establishes Islam as the state religion. Since 1986, Section 295(c) of the Penal Code has stipulated the death penalty for blaspheming the Prophet Mohammed. According to the Human Rights Commission of Pakistan, police opened one case against a Christian, Ayub Masih, under Section 295(c) in 1996. This blasphemy provision contributes to inter-religious tension, intimidation, fear, and violence.

The Government permits Muslims to convert to other faiths, but proselytizing among Muslims is illegal. Islamic extremists have assaulted, raped, and even murdered members of religious minorities. In many cases, police fail to take necessary precautions or investigate or prosecute those responsible.

This failure has contributed to a feeling of insecurity in many minority religious communities. In October 1996, in one well-publicized case, 14 (some say 19) Christian families fled the Punjab village Number 35 Eb Arfiwala following the arrest of one member of their community for alleged blasphemy. The families reportedly feared attack by Muslim neighbors angered by the alleged incident. By December, the families had not returned to their homes in the village.

In February 1997, Muslim mobs destroyed homes and churches belonging to Christians in the Khanewal area. Local police failed to take adequate steps to control the mobs and thousands of people were rendered homeless. Following the attack, Prime Minister Nawaz Sharif and other officials visited the affected area, promised reparations for the victims, and publicly voiced support for minority rights. Discriminatory religious legislation has led to acts of violence directed at Ahmadis, Christians, Hindus, and Zakris. Although the constitution prohibits discrimination in government employment, religious minorities are reportedly underrepresented at all levels of government service, especially in the senior ranks.

U.S. Government actions: The U.S. Government has repeatedly urged Pakistan to repeal the blasphemy law. The issue has been raised with Pakistani officials on several occasions in recent years. Although Pakistan has responded by adopting administrative procedures to soften the effect of the law, the problem remains a matter of concern and the U.S. Government continues to press the issue. The U.S. Government has also expressed concern to the Pakistani Prime Minister and other officials over the February 1997 Khanewal riot, and urged equal legal protection for religious minorities.

U.S. Embassy and Consulate officials monitor individual cases of persecution and intervene with Pakistani government agencies when appropriate. In addition, U.S. Embassy officers meet regularly with leaders of religious communities, including Christians. . . .

Russia

Current situation: Russia's new constitution and a 1990 Soviet law on religion still in force provide for religious freedom and a strict separation of church and state. Since the breakup of the Soviet Union, the overall climate for religious freedom in Russia has improved dramatically, and made possible a large increase in the activities of foreign missionaries. This has troubled some sectors of Russian society, particularly nationalists and factions of the Russian Orthodox Church. During 1996 and 1997, the Russian Orthodox Church used its political influence to promote official actions that discriminate against religious groups and sects.

Most notably, the Duma and Federation Council recently passed legislation which, if enacted, would replace the 1990 law and introduce significantly more government regulation over religious organizations. While the law is not directed against Russia's established major faiths (Orthodoxy, Judaism, Islam, and Buddhism), it would impose registration requirements on religious groups, provide significant official discretion in decisions on registration, and would restrict the activities of foreign missionaries, as well as confessions, sects or religions, that are relatively new to Russia or that have relatively small numbers of adherents. These groups would have to wait up to 15 years before attaining full legal status, making it impossible for them to own property or have a bank account during this period. The draft legislation enjoys broad public support, but will not become law unless and until President Yeltsin signs it. (President Yeltsin previously rejected a similar proposal as unconstitutional.)

Some regional officials also have sought at times to limit the activities of foreign missionaries, many of whom are Christians. About one-fourth of Russia's 89 regional governments have passed restrictive laws and decrees that violate the 1990 law on religion by limiting or restricting the activities of religious groups, or by requiring registration. Enforcement is uneven, but there are reports that local governments have prevented religious gatherings. As a result, denominations that do not have their own property were denied the opportunity to practice their faith in large groups or to hold prayer meetings. In 1996 the Constitutional Court refused to consider a challenge to the constitutionality of one such law on procedural grounds.

There have been numerous instances in which local authorities have refused to register the passports (a requirement under Russia's visa laws) of foreign missionaries, effectively denying them the ability to function in some regions. Non-Orthodox faiths, including the Catholic Church, have also had difficulties recovering properties that were confiscated during the Soviet era, although some progress was made in 1996.

U.S. Government actions: The United States has acted consistently to encourage Russia to fulfill completely its constitution and pledges of religious tolerance. In June 1997, President Clinton expressed concern to President Boris Yeltsin about the restrictive law on religion then pending in the Duma. Assistant Secretary of State Shattuck also voiced concern about the draft law and local restrictions on religious freedom to his Russian counterpart during bilateral consultations on human rights in May. President Clinton expressed concern about Aleksandr Lebed's inflammatory statements on missionary activities of the Church of Jesus Christ of Latter-Day Saints when he met with Prime Minister Viktor Chernomyrdin at the G-7 Summit in Lyon in June 1996. Vice President Gore reiterated those U.S. concerns the following month at a session of the Gore-Chernomyrdin Commission.

The U.S. Embassy in Moscow and U.S. consulates have also been active in emphasizing the importance of freedom of conscience and religion. U.S. officials have voiced concern about initiatives by local and provincial governments to restrict the activities of missionary groups, and urged parliamentary deputies considering the new draft law on religion to uphold the principles of tolerance and separation of church and state embodied in the constitution and in the 1990 law.

The Embassy has frequently objected to attempts by the Russian authorities to administer visa regulations in a manner that restricts the freedom of movement of U.S. citizens, including missionaries, inside Russia.

Saudi Arabia

Current situation: Freedom of religion does not exist in Saudi Arabia. Islam is the official religion, and all citizens must be Muslims. The Government of Saudi Arabia believes that it has a unique position as guardian of the two holiest shrines of Islam, so it prohibits the public and private practice of other religions. Persons wearing religious symbols risk confrontation with the Mutawwa'in (religious police). The U.S. Embassy in Riyadh reports that both citizens and foreigners are targets of harassment by members of the Mutawwa'in and by religious vigilantes acting independently. Non-Muslim worshipers risk arrest, lashing, and deportation for engaging in any religious activity that attracts official attention. There are isolated reports of harassment and arrest of foreign workers conducting clandestine worship services, but precise numbers of such incidents can not be determined. However, most non-Muslim religious services are conducted without any interference.

U.S. Government actions: The United States has repeatedly raised human rights concerns with the Saudi Arabian Government. The U.S. Ambassador and other embassy officers have recently raised the issue of religious freedom with high government officials.

The U.S. Government regularly protests incidents in which U.S. citizens are improperly accosted by the Mutawwa'in. In 1996 the U.S. Consul General in Jeddah called on the governor of Medina region, and pressed him to curtail Mutawwa'in harassment in the region. The Consul General also discussed this issue with American community leaders, the Director of the Royal Commission in Yanbu, the chief of investment promotion, the Board of the Chamber of Commerce, and Mutawwa'in officials. The U.S. Government strongly protested an incident in late 1993, in which Mutawwa'in violently broke up a children's winter concert at the Yanbu International School. Soon after, the Saudi Arabian Government formally notified the U.S. Government that it neither approved nor agreed with such behavior by members of the Mutawwa'n, and that necessary measures had been taken to ensure that there would be no repetitions.

Privately-run religious services, attended by both U.S. Government employees and private Americans, are held regularly on the grounds of at least one U.S. diplomatic facility in Saudi Arabia. In instances where religious services are not presently held at U.S. diplomatic facilities, religious services take place at other locations locally. . . .

CABINET SECRETARY ON
MEDICAL RECORD PRIVACY
July 31, 1997

A national research panel, the Department of Health and Human Services, the U.S. Congress, and dozens of health care providers began to examine the issue of medical record privacy—or the lack of it—in 1997. By the end of the year, most agreed that actions were needed at the national level to improve the security of the population's health records, but there was little agreement on exactly what those steps should be.

Medical record security was largely a problem of the computer age. Until relatively recently, most people's medical records were stored in locked file drawers at their doctor's office or at the local hospital, and access to those records was limited. Now, however, most records were computerized and shared among a broader group of care providers—doctors, hospitals, insurers, pharmacies, government health agencies, researchers, employers, and law enforcement officials. Computerization had significant benefits, helping doctors and hospitals coordinate care and ensure minimum standards of care, speeding insurance reimbursements, and providing researchers with data that could help them identify public health problems and find cures for diseases more rapidly than they could in the past.

With so many people having access to personal medical records, the potential for invasion of privacy—and for abuse—was magnified. People with access to medical records could look at the records of friends, relatives, employers, celebrities, and others—records that they had no valid reason to see. An employer with access to medical records might use that information to deny a job offer or promotion. Extremely sensitive medical conditions, such as venereal disease or a mental or emotional disorder, might be leaked. Computer hackers could break into computerized information systems and steal, tamper, or even destroy medical records. Patients often did not know who had access to their files, let alone have an opportunity to give their consent.

"Every day, our private health information is being shared. It's being collected, it's being analyzed, and it's being stored with fewer federal safeguards than our video store records," Donna E. Shalala, the secretary of Health and Human Services, told the National Press Club on July 31. "In *fact, my video card and the record of what videos I rent are protected by federal laws, as [are] my credit card purchases and my credit record, as well as my motor vehicle record, but not my health information."*

No federal law specifically protected the confidentiality of health information, and the state laws that did exist were too narrowly focused to provide much protection. Although there were individual examples of misuse—a medical student who copied records at night and sold them to medical malpractice attorneys, for example—most experts agreed that abuses were not yet widespread. But they also urged that steps be taken soon to ensure privacy. In 1996 Congress put itself under some pressure to do just that when it passed the Health Insurance Portability and Accountability Act. That act called for "universal patient identifiers," or codes, that would enable all of a patient's files to be linked and gave Congress until August 1999 to set standards for protecting computerized medical records. If Congress did not act, the executive branch could put standards into effect on its own authority.

National Research Council Report

"Solutions are available to make electronic records even more secure than paper records," Paul Clayton, chairman of a panel of experts that studied the problem for the National Research Council, said at a news conference March 5 releasing the report. People who had a legitimate need for medical record information should be given computer passwords, remote access should be monitored, and sensitive data transmitted through public networks should be coded or encrypted, the panel said, noting that all these techniques were currently available. "Audit trails," logs of who used what records, should be kept. Practices such as leaving a person's medical record open on a computer screen should be punished, the panel said.

In its report, entitled "For the Record: Protecting Electronic Health Information," the expert panel also expressed concern about the concept of universal patient codes. Although it acknowledged the benefits of being able to link patient records from many health care organizations, it also said the "ability to link health information with other types of information such as employment, education, driving record, credit history, previous arrests and convictions, purchasing habits, telephone conversations, and e-mail exchanges . . . is more contentious." For example, the panel said, pharmaceutical companies might be able to use such links to market new drugs and medical therapies directly to individuals. Any system of universal patients codes should set out explicit linkages that would violate patient privacy and impose legal penalties on anyone who violated them, the panel said. To the extent possible, the linked records should be handled in such a way that the patient's identity could not be "easily deduced."

Administration Recommendations

Shalala's speech to the National Press Club previewed the administration's initial recommendations, which she formally presented in an eighty-one-page report to the Senate Labor Committee on September 11. The rec-

ommendations, which many observers viewed as a benchmark for future legislation, would:

- *Permit patients to obtain a copy of their medical records and propose corrections to mistakes.*
- *Require organizations that provide and pay for health care to give patients a clear, written explanation of how medical information about them will be used, kept, and disclosed. Those covered by this recommendation included not only doctors' offices and hospitals, but insurance companies, workplaces, claims administrators, and pharmacies.*
- *Allow patients to designate who may have access to information that may be linked to them, and who may not. Violators would be subject to civil and criminal penalties. "Information should not be used or given out unless either the patient authorizes it or there is a clear legal basis for doing so," Shalala told the committee. A legal basis for using medical information without proper authorization might be to prevent a threat to public health, such as an epidemic, she said.*

One aspect of the administration's proposal that drew immediate criticism was its recommendation that law enforcement agencies be allowed access to medical records without obtaining patient authorization. Law enforcement officers currently had broad access to such records, and the administration recommendations would do little to tighten that access. Police, the FBI, and the Justice Department all said that law enforcement agencies needed quick and unhindered access to the records to catch criminals. They were particularly concerned about fraud in the health care field—a crime that had been growing. The number of FBI investigations into health care fraud tripled in five years to more than 2,200 in 1996. In a letter to the White House, the Justice Department said there had been "no documented history" suggesting that law enforcement officials had abused their access to medical records, and nothing to indicate that existing federal and state laws were "inadequate to guard against such a danger."

Deirdre K. Mulligan of the Center for Democracy and Technology, a civil rights group that worked on privacy issues, scoffed at that claim. "It's easy to claim that there have been no violations because there are few laws to violate," she told the New York Times. *"There's no procedural requirement to inform patients that law enforcement agents are getting access to their records."*

If the law-enforcement exemption were enacted, A. G. Breitenstein, director of the JRI Health Law Institute in Boston, told the Senate Labor Committee, "doctors might as well warn patients as they perform an exam that 'Anything you say can and will be used against you in a court of law.'" Two senators, both of whom had introduced their own legislation protecting medical record privacy, also opposed the law enforcement exemption. That exemption would permit "any police officer to walk into a doctor's office and demand to see the medical records of their patients," Sen. Patrick J.

Leahy, D-Vt., said. Sen. Robert F. Bennett, R-Utah, said it was "critical" that law enforcement officers be required to obtain a subpoena or warrant before obtaining access to medical records, adding that police should have to specify what they were looking for and how the information was to be used. A presidential advisory commission, of which Shalala was the co-chair, subsequently recommended that law enforcement officials be allowed to obtain medical records without permission only in pursuit of suspected health care fraud. (Health care bill of rights, p. 787)

At another Senate Labor Committee hearing on October 28, patient and provider groups, as well as coalitions representing insurers, employers, and other business interests all said that medical records should be protected. "In order for physicians to provide the best and most appropriate medical care, patients must feel that they can disclose to their physicians personal facts and information that they would not want others to know," said a member of the American Medical Association's board of trustees. "Without such assurances, patients may not provide the information necessary for proper diagnosis and treatment."

The witnesses agreed on little else. Hospitals and insurers said they did not want to be required to obtain a patient's authorization every time they needed access to medical data. Allowing patients to designate which information was available and who got to see it would "impede the free flow of information that is necessary to deliver the best health care possible," said a spokesman for the American Hospital Association. A witness speaking on behalf of the American Association of Health Plans said that such requirements could make it difficult for health plans to take steps that not only would benefit their individual members but also enable them to "demonstrate their accountability."

> *Following are excerpts from a speech on protecting the privacy of medical records, given July 31, 1997, by Donna E. Shalala, secretary of health and human services, to the National Press Club in Washington, D.C.:*

... I've returned to the National Press Club to talk about what I believe is one of the most serious issues facing our health care system, something that affects every single American and every single one of you. That's the privacy of our most cherished and personal information, our medical records. They are, in fact, our family secrets.

Until recently, a Boston-based HMO [health maintenance organization]—in that Boston-based HMO, every single clinical employee could tap into patients' computer records and see detailed notes from psychotherapy sessions. In Colorado, a medical student copies countless health records at night and sells them to medical malpractice attorneys looking to win easy cases.

And in a major American city, a local newspaper publishes information about a Congresswoman's attempted suicide, information that she thought was safe and private at a local hospital. She was wrong. What about the rest of us?

When we give a physician or a health insurance company precious information about our mood or our motherhood, about our medications, what happens to it? As it zips from computer to computer, from doctors to insurance companies to hospitals, who can see it? Who protects it? What happens if they don't? It all depends on what state you live in. Every day, our private health information is being shared.

It's being collected, it's being analyzed, and it's being stored with fewer federal safeguards than our video store records. In fact, my video card and the record of what videos I rent are protected by federal laws, as is my credit card purchases and my credit record, as well as my motor vehicle record, but not my health information.

And that's the point.

Let me be very frank. The way in which we protect the privacy of our medical records right now is very erratic and it's dangerous. What I want to argue today is that, to eliminate this clear and present danger to our citizens and to our health care system, we have to act now with national legislation, with a national educational discussion, a national conversation. . . .

Nations in the European Union recently enacted a privacy directive that will require them to protect personal data and only exchange it with other nations that have the same high standards. . . .

Twenty-five years ago, our health care privacy was protected by our family doctor. He or she kept handwritten notes about us sealed away in the big file cabinet. I remember my doctor's file cabinet. We trusted our physicians to keep their file cabinets locked and their mouths shut. We trusted them not only because of the Hippocratic oath and the fundamental ethics of medicine, but because we knew them. They took care of our entire families. We asked their advice about our personal problems. We went to school with their kids. We shopped in the same stores. They came over for dinner, and they made house calls.

Today, the revolution in our health care delivery system means that, instead of Marcus Welby, we have to place our trust in entire networks of insurers and health care professionals, both public and private.

The computer revolution means that our deepest and darkest secrets no longer exist in one place and can no longer be protected by simply locking up the office doors every night. And revolutions in biology mean that a whole new world of genetic tests have the potential to either help prevent disease or reveal our family's most personal secrets. Because without safeguards that assure us as citizens that getting tested won't expose our family's privacy or their health insurance or their jobs, we could in turn endanger one of the most promising areas of research that this country has ever seen.

We are at a decision point. Depending on what we do over the next month, these revolutions in health care, in communications and biology could bring us great promise or even greater peril. The choice is ours. We must ask ourselves: Will we harness these revolutions to improve, not impede, our health care?

Will we harness them to safeguard, not sacrifice, our privacy? And will we harness these revolutions to strengthen, not strain, the very life blood of our health care system, the bond of trust between a patient and a doctor? For example, will health care information flow safely to improve care, to cut fraud, to ensure quality, to foster research and to reach citizens in undeserved areas, or will it flow recklessly into the wrong hands? Will it be used to deny our citizens health insurance, jobs and the confidentiality they expect and deserve? It really is up to us.

The Institute of Medicine has said that electronic health records should be the wave of the future, and the Congress has asked us to develop standards to make it happen.

Will they be used to help an emergency room doctor learn more about an unconscious patient, like what disease she has and which medication she's allergic to? Will it be used as it can be now to tell parents which immunizations their kids have and which ones they still need, or will a pharmaceutical company use it to market the newest antidepressant to someone with a family history of depression? Will a political group use it to embarrass a rival they believe once had an abortion or a child with a drug problem?

The fundamental question before us is: Will our health records be used to heal us or to reveal us? The American people want to know, and as a nation, we must decide.

Today, almost 75 percent of our people say they are at least somewhat concerned that computerized medical records will have a negative effect on their privacy.

In one survey, one-fourth of adolescents said they would not seek medical care unless their privacy and confidentiality were protected. . . .

Health care privacy can be safeguarded. To do that, we must first and foremost enact bipartisan, national legislation to protect the privacy of our medical records, and we must do it now. . . .

. . . Our [legislative] recommendations, . . . which we will send to Congress next month, will be guided by five key principles.

First, the principle of boundaries—with very few exceptions, a health care consumer's personal information should be disclosed for health care and health care only. Our goal is to make it easier to use information for health care purposes and very tough to use it for any other purpose. For example, we will recommend that a hospital be able to use personal health information to teach, to train and conduct research, provide care and ensure quality. But on the other hand, employers who get health care information to pay claims cannot use it for non-health purposes like hiring and firing and promotions.

And what about third parties, those who more and more often are hired to do billing and other kinds of services? They must be bound by the same tough standards. Even if they don't collect it, they have to protect it.

Second, the principle of security. When Americans give out their personal health care information, they should feel like they're leaving it in good, safe hands. With information traveling from doctors to hospitals to insurers, at every juncture there exists the potential for greater care and graver privacy violations. Think about all of the ways in which private information like your genetic tests could become public. People who are allowed to see it, like those at the lab, can misuse it or either carelessly or unintentionally let it loose. And people who shouldn't be seeing it, like the marketers, can find a way to do so anyway, either because an organization doesn't have private safeguards, or they find an easy way around them.

If we're going to block this leakage, Congress must pass a law that requires those who legally receive health information [to] take real steps to safeguard it.

Third, is the principle of consumer control. No one should have to trade in their privacy rights to get quality health care. We will recommend that Americans have the power to find out who's looking in their records, what's in them, how to get them and what they can do to change incorrect information, the same kind of protections that I actually have on my credit information. . . .

Fourth, the principle of accountability. If you're using information improperly, you should be severely punished, and we will be making recommendations to ensure that you are. . . . We need to enforce our messages with real criminal penalties for abuse.

And that brings me to my fifth and final principle, the principle of public responsibility. Just like our free speech rights, privacy rights can never be absolute. We have to balance our protections of privacy with our public responsibility to support national priorities, priorities like public health and research and quality care and our fight against health care fraud and abuse.

For example, public health agencies use health records to warn us of outbreaks of emerging infectious diseases. Our inspector general uses health records to zero in on kickbacks on over payments and on other kinds of fraud so we can bring perpetrators to justice and the money back to the taxpayers. Researchers have used health records to help us fight things like childhood leukemia and uncover the link between DES and reproductive cancers. In these cases, it's not always possible to ask for permission, and in many cases, doing so would create major obstacles in our efforts to fight crime and protect the public health. But that doesn't give us a free pass. . . .

But national standards alone will not inspire trust in one's rights or commitment to one's responsibilities. To protect health care privacy and instill trust from the American people, we need a major commitment to education, which is my second point. Every single health care professional, every insurance agent, every researcher, every member of an IRB [institutional review board], every public health official, every pharmacist and, yes, every member of the press, every single person who comes in contact with health care records must understand why it's important to keep them safe, how they can keep them safe and what will happen to them if they don't. And we need to enlist their help, your help in educating all consumers not just about the privacy risks in this new health care world, but also about the rewards. We need to help them understand not just their privacy rights, but also their responsibilities to ask questions and demand answers, to become active participants in their own health care.

And that's what the president's Advisory Commission on Quality and Consumer Protection, which I co-chair, has identified as privacy and confidentiality. That's why we've identified those things as key priorities as we draft a consumer's bill of rights.

We need an informed public because, as the National Research Council recently pointed out, we need an informed public debate, a national conversation to ask very tough questions, which is my third and final point. Take the issue of law enforcement. Should auditors be able to peek through your private medical records looking for fraud committed by your doctor? Most people would say yes. Should law enforcement officers be able to search through emergency room records looking for someone who has just fled the scene of a crime? Most people would say yes.

But what happens if law enforcement officers are looking through insurance records for fraud and stumble upon information almost totally unrelated to the fraud crime, say drug usage?

What then? Or for that matter, what happens if researchers stumble upon information about someone who may have been exposed or exposed you to HIV? Is it—is their obligation to your safety or to the other person's privacy? What happens if drug companies know you suffer from heart disease and send you information about their new treatment? Is that help? Is that helpful, or is it offensive? Does that change if the disease is depression? What about venereal disease? These questions will sometimes be extraordinarily difficult. They will always be changing, but they are not going to go away. We can't expect to solve this problem all at once. We need to be flexible. We need to change course if our strategy isn't working and meet very new challenges as they arise. . . .

Will we have boundaries to ensure that, with very few exceptions, our health care information is used only for health care? Will we have assurances that our information is secure? Will we have control over what happens to it? Will those who violate our privacy be held accountable, and will we be able to safeguard our privacy rights while still protecting our core public responsibilities like research and public health? In short, will we harness this revolution in biology and communications and health care to breathe new life into the trust between our patients and their doctors, between our citizens and their government, between our past and our future?

I believe we can. I believe we must, and if we act today, we will.

Thank you very much.

August

NCI REPORT ON NUCLEAR TESTING FALLOUT
August 1, 1997

A massive government scientific study that took more than fourteen years concluded that fallout from U.S. above-ground nuclear testing in the 1950s may have led to thousands of cases of thyroid cancer among Americans—or it was possible that the fallout caused few additional cancers.

In a summary of its study, released August 1, the National Cancer Institute (NCI) said it was impossible to determine the exact risk that early nuclear tests posed to Americans. In part, that was because there was no conclusive evidence that the relatively low levels of radiation generated by the tests actually caused cancer of the thyroid gland. The institute said it was possible that between 10,000 and 75,000 Americans might develop thyroid cancer because of the tests. An estimated 420,000 Americans alive during the 1950s were expected to develop the disease because of other causes.

The study was widely publicized, with some news reports making the findings appear more definitive than the authors of the study were willing to claim. A headline in the August 2 editions of the New York Times, *for example, declared: "Thousands Have Thyroid Cancer from Atomic Tests." The study itself made no such statement.*

Some public health experts and political leaders expressed concern about the study's findings and sharply criticized the NCI for taking so long to finish the report. If citizens had know earlier about the potential dangers, some critics said, they could have gotten regular thyroid examinations that might have detected cancers earlier. Republican Senator Larry Craig, whose state of Idaho may have received some of the heaviest radiation fallout, said he felt a "sense of urgency" to obtain more answers about the potential dangers.

Clark Heath, a spokesman for the American Cancer Society, told the Washington Post *that the findings should not cause severe public anxiety. He told the* Post *that no one had yet proven that relatively small doses of radiation actually caused thyroid cancer. The NCI study said evidence to date was "suggestive but not conclusive" that radioactive iodine-131, produced by the nuclear tests, was linked to thyroid cancer.*

To obtain more answers on that issue, the National Cancer Institute said it was asking for a study by the Institute of Medicine at the National Academy of Science. That study would examine the actual risk of thyroid cancer from low doses of radiation and make recommendations on how physicians could identify and treat people who might be at risk. In the meantime, Bruce Walchholz, an author of the report, said people who had been children during the 1950s, especially those who lived in western states upwind of the test site, should ask their physicians to check their thyroid glands during their regular physical examinations.

The NCI had planned to publish its study in the fall of 1997 but was forced to release a summary on August 1 after news reports gave many of the highlights. The full text of the study, including more than 100,000 pages of scientific data, was released in October.

A Complex Study

Congress in 1982 ordered the Department of Health and Human Services to study the possible effects of radiation from the nuclear tests in southern Nevada. As undertaken by the National Cancer Institute, the study became one of the most complex scientific inquiries ever conducted by a government agency. Institute researchers dug into thousands of decades-old records to determine weather patterns, fallout rates, and even where cattle were grazed during the periods when ninety nuclear tests were conducted above ground between 1952 and 1961. After the U.S.-Soviet test ban treaty of 1963, all U.S. nuclear tests were conducted underground.

The study found that fallout reached all the lower forty-eight states, and so all the 160 million Americans alive during the 1950s were exposed to at least some radiation. The highest levels of radioactive iodine appeared to be in twenty-four counties in Utah, Idaho, Montana, South Dakota, and Colorado—all downwind of the test site in southern Nevada. Pacific Coast states, upwind of the site, received little of the fallout.

Using mathematical models based on medical, meteorological, and other records, the study estimated that the ninety tests combined subjected Americans to an average dose of radioactive iodine-131 (I-131) of about two rads (rads is a measurement of how much radiation is absorbed by the body). In comparison, the NCI noted that routine thyroid examinations given children during the 1950s delivered 200 to 300 rads of I-131. Children also were treated with I-131 during the 1950s for acne, ringworm, and tonsillitis. Such exposures were among the reasons the institute gave for explaining why it was difficult to "disentangle" the effects from nuclear tests.

Effect on Children

Scientists were primarily concerned about the risk to people who were children during the testing years. That was because children drink more milk than adults, and milk could become contaminated with radiation because cows grazed in pastures where radiation fell when mixed with dust or rain. Radioactive iodine-131 accumulates in the thyroid gland, and because a child's thyroid is smaller than an adult's even a relatively small dose of radioactive iodine might cause damage to a child's thyroid, leading to cancer. For these reasons, the study estimated that children aged three months to five years probably received about three to seven times the average dose of radiation.

Thyroid cancer is relatively rare, affecting only about 3 in every 100,000 people. The NCI said that in 1997 an estimated 16,000 Americans would be diagnosed with the disease, and 1,230 would die from it. Women were twice as likely to be affected as men. Thyroid cancer is easy to detect and one of the most treatable cancers, with an estimated 95 percent of all victims living at least five years after diagnosis, the institute said.

Two other studies were under way to examine the relationship between radioactive fallout and thyroid cancer. In one study, National Cancer Institute researchers were working with international scientists studying children in Ukraine and Belarus who had been exposed to fallout from the 1986 Chernobyl nuclear accident. Another study sponsored by the Centers for Disease Control and Prevention was investigating the health effects on area residents of radiation released from the nuclear weapons plant in Hanford, Washington, during the 1940s and 1950s. Results of the latter study were to be released in 1998.

Protecting Film

In a related development, an environmental watchdog group uncovered documents showing that the government warned the Eastman Kodak Company and other film manufacturers about upcoming nuclear tests during the 1950s. Kodak in 1951 had discovered damage to photographic film packaged in material made from corn husks that had been contaminated by radioactive fallout. The government at the time did not warn the general public about the possible health hazards of its nuclear tests.

The revelation of government warnings to Kodak produced an outcry on Capitol Hill. Iowa Senator Tom Harkin, a Democrat who said he suffered from thyroid problems and whose brother died of thyroid cancer, said: "The government protected rolls of film, but not lives of people."

Following is a statement from the National Cancer Institute accompanying the release August 1, 1997, of a summary of a study on radioactive fallout from nuclear tests during the 1950s, and sixteen questions and answers on the issue, also prepared by the institute:

The National Cancer Institute (NCI) today released summary results from a study to assess Americans' exposures to radioactive iodine-131 fallout from atmospheric nuclear bomb tests carried out at the Nevada Test Site in the 1950s and 1960s. A full report is to follow. Depending on their age at the time of the tests, where they lived, and what foods they consumed, particularly milk, Americans were exposed to varying levels of I-131 for about two months following each of the 90 tests. Because I-131 accumulates in the thyroid gland, concerns have been raised that the fallout could cause thyroid cancer in people who were exposed to it as children.

The average cumulative thyroid dose to the approximately 160 million people in the country at the time was about 2 rads. (By comparison, a routine I-131 diagnostic thyroid scan of a child in the 1950s gave approximately 200 to 300 rads to the thyroid. Today, a thyroid scan would give about 0.4 to 4 rads to the thyroid, depending on the radionuclide used.)

NCI urges caution in interpreting the results, particularly because the study does not directly address the question of cancer risk from the fallout. NCI and the Department of Health and Human Services have enlisted the help of the foremost radiation experts in the country to fully evaluate the risk and develop an appropriate public health response.

The Department has requested that the National Academy of Sciences' Institute of Medicine (IOM) review the data to assess whether risks can be determined, and to recommend to physicians how to identify, evaluate, and treat persons who might be at risk of disease because of their exposure to radioactive iodine. In the meantime, persons concerned about fallout exposure should consult a health professional.

The IOM review—which will be comprehensive and public as are all IOM studies—is expected to take about six months after final arrangements are made. IOM is expected to establish a diverse expert panel. In addition, the administration will establish an interdepartmental group to look at broader policy issues.

Persons living in heavy fallout areas, children, and persons who drank large quantities of milk might have received higher doses. In general, those living in Western states to the north and east of the test site had the highest doses. Most children aged 3 months to 5 years probably received three to seven times the average dose for the population in their county, because in general they drank more milk than adults, and because their thyroids were smaller. By contrast, most adults probably received two to four times less than the average county dose . . .

In 1982, Congress passed legislation calling for the Department of Health and Human Services to develop methods to estimate I-131 exposure, to assess thyroid doses of I-131 received by individuals across the country from the Nevada tests, and to assess risks for thyroid cancer from these exposures. The fallout report fulfills the first two of these three requirements.

The report was not intended to fulfill the third requirement, risk assessment. To estimate thyroid cancer risk, the results of the report will be linked with findings from relevant epidemiological studies, including some currently in progress.

The limited data on persons exposed as children to I-131 from the nuclear test fallout have provided suggestive but not conclusive evidence that it is linked to thyroid cancer. The radiation doses received by young children who lived in areas with high fallout levels, particularly those who drank a great deal of milk, may well have increased the risk of thyroid cancer. The level of increased risk is highly uncertain.

To provide more accurate information on the risk of thyroid cancer from radioactive fallout, NCI investigators are collaborating with other U.S. government agencies, international organizations, and governments and scientists in Belarus and Ukraine to study thyroid cancer among persons exposed to fallout from the Chernobyl nuclear accident in 1986. A clear increase in thyroid cancer has been seen in this population.

In 1997, an estimated 16,100 Americans will be diagnosed with thyroid cancer and 1,230 will die from the disease. The incidence rate for women is more than twice as high as that for men. Thyroid cancer is highly curable: The 5-year survival rate is about 95 percent.

Questions and Answers on the NCI Fallout Report

1. What is the NCI Fallout Report?

The National Cancer Institute (NCI) report contains an assessment of radioactive Iodine-131 (I-131) fallout exposure from the nuclear bomb tests that were carried out at the Nevada Test Site in the 1950s and 1960s. In 1982, Congress passed legislation calling for the Department of Health and Human Services to develop methods to estimate I-131 exposure to the American people, to assess thyroid doses from I-131 received by individuals across the country from the Nevada tests, and to assess risks for thyroid cancer from these exposures. The fallout report fulfills the first two of these three requirements.

The report includes county-by-county estimates of average I-131 doses to the thyroid for persons living or born in the contiguous 48 states during the period when the bomb tests were carried out, mostly in the 1950s. Estimates of thyroid dose have been made for people by age category, sex, and amount and source of milk consumed (see Question 11). Doses have been estimated for each of the 90 tests that together released nearly 99 percent of the I-131 produced during the bomb testing program, and summed over test series and for all the tests combined.

2. What does the report show?

The report shows that everyone living in the contiguous 48 states was exposed to I-131 at some level. The average cumulative thyroid dose to the approximately 160 million people in the country at the time was about 2 rads. (By comparison, a routine I-131 diagnostic thyroid scan of a child in the 1950s gave approximately 200 to 300 rads to the thyroid. Today, a thyroid scan would give about 0.4 to 4 rads to the thyroid, depending on the radionuclide used. A rad is a unit of measurement that stands for radiation absorbed dose, the amount of radiation that is absorbed by the tissues in the body. Scientists now measure radiation dosage in grays: One gray equals 100 rads.)

Children and persons who drank large quantities of milk, or who drank milk from goats or family-owned cows, are estimated to have received higher doses. (Goat's milk concentrates I-131 more than cow's milk. Estimates of

I-131 doses in milk consumed soon after it was taken from a family-owned cow are usually higher than for store-bought milk because store-bought milk takes time to process and ship, allowing more time for the radioactivity in I-131 to diminish.) Most children aged 3 months to 5 years probably received about three to seven times the average dose for each test, because in general they drank more milk than adults did, and because their thyroids were smaller. Most adults, by contrast, probably received doses two to four times lower than the average estimated dose.

Doses varied widely according to geographic area. In general, persons living in Western states to the north and east of the test site had higher doses than those living in West Coast, Southern, and Eastern states. In the 24 counties with the highest exposures, estimated average cumulative doses ranged from 9 to 16 rads.

3. Does radiation cause thyroid cancer?
Does I-131 cause cancer?

The risk of thyroid cancer from childhood exposure to external radiation such as X-rays has been known for some time. Increased risk of thyroid cancer has continued for many years after the atomic bombings in Hiroshima and Nagasaki, and after childhood X-ray exposures to treat conditions of the head and neck, such as acne and tonsillitis. A combined analysis of seven studies of persons exposed to a wide variety of external radiation sources—including atomic bombs and treatment for cancer, tinea capitis (ringworm), and enlarged tonsils or thymus glands—found that on average, persons exposed as young children to 100 rads (1 gray) had a 7.7 times higher risk of thyroid cancer compared with persons not exposed to radiation. But the overwhelming majority of thyroid cancers are not related to X-ray treatments.

The limited data on persons exposed as children to I-131 from the nuclear test fallout have provided suggestive but not conclusive evidence that it is linked to thyroid cancer. I-131 is thought to be no more likely to cause thyroid cancer than the same dose of external radiation, and it may be as little as one-fifth as hazardous. However, the radiation doses received by young children, especially those who lived in areas with high fallout levels, and particularly those who drank a great deal of milk, may well have increased the risk of thyroid cancer. The level of increased risk can be estimated but it is highly uncertain.

4. How many cases of thyroid cancer have been or will be caused by the fallout?

Based on the average doses calculated by country for different age groups, NCI estimates that between 10,000 and 75,000 exposed persons might develop fallout-associated thyroid cancer during their lifetime. Nearly all of these persons were under 15 years of age at the time of exposure, and about 75 percent were under age 5. It is estimated that about 30 percent of fallout-related thyroid cancers have been diagnosed already. (About 95 million Americans were under age 20 at some time during 1951 to 1962, the period of above ground tests at the Nevada Test Site. According to current cancer rates, about

420,000 thyroid cancers would be expected to occur in a population of that size during their lifetimes.)

This estimate is based on studies of persons exposed to external radiation sources, such as medical treatments that were used in the past. Within the range of 10,000 to 75,000 cases, the estimate depends on what assumption is made about the cancer-causing potential of I-131 compared with external radiation (see Question 3). Uncertainties about the relationship of these risk factors make more precise examination difficult.

5. What has NCI done to assess the risk of thyroid cancer from the fallout? What further studies are planned?

In 1993, researchers at the University of Utah, Salt Lake City, published results of an NCI-sponsored study of children living in parts of Utah and Nevada that had high I-131 fallout levels, and a comparable number living in parts of Arizona that had relatively little fallout. The average dose for children in the study was estimated at about 10 rads. The researchers found a statistically significant association between I-131 exposure and all thyroid neoplasms combined (including cancer and benign tumors). They found some evidence of an association between estimated dose and thyroid cancer, but this was not statistically significant. The level of uncertainty was high because the number of cancer cases involved was very small. Reflecting this uncertainty, the researchers estimated that between zero and six of the eight observed thyroid cancers might have been caused by the fallout. The risks observed in the study were consistent with reported risks from external radiation (X-rays).

To provide more accurate information on the risk of thyroid cancer from radioactive fallout, NCI investigators are collaborating with other U.S. government agencies, international organizations, and governments and scientists in Belarus and Ukraine to study thyroid cancer among persons in those countries who were exposed during childhood to fallout from the Chernobyl nuclear accident in 1986. The tens of thousands of children exposed to the fallout received radiation doses to the thyroid that ranged from comparatively small doses to doses ten times higher than U.S. residents received from the Nevada tests, and a clear increase in thyroid cancer has been seen in this population. The dose to each person in the study group will be reconstructed based on thyroid measurements made within about two months of the accident, residential and dietary histories, and other environmental measurements. Because of the wide range of exposures, the large numbers of persons exposed, and the large number of thyroid cancer cases observed, information from the Chernobyl studies is expected to be relevant to the assessment of the impact of the U.S. exposures.

Researchers sponsored by the Centers for Disease Control and Prevention are studying the health effects of the radioactive iodine released from the Hanford, Wash., nuclear weapons plant in the 1940s and 1950s. Results are expected in 1998.

The new fallout data from NCI could be used to correlate fallout levels with thyroid cancer rates in specific geographic areas; however, such studies will encounter difficulties. Thyroid cancer is an uncommon disease, particularly among children. The small number of cases in any one geographic area—particularly in sparsely populated areas—makes it difficult to determine with confidence whether rates are significantly elevated. And while some states have registries with historical data on all cancer cases in the state, most do not. In addition, many children in the 1950s were exposed to medical X-rays at levels known to increase risk for thyroid cancer, and it is difficult to disentangle these effects from those of fallout exposure.

6. What is the U.S. government doing in light of this report?

The Department of Health and Human Services has requested that the National Academy of Sciences' Institute of Medicine (IOM) review the data to assess the risks to individuals, and to recommend to physicians how to treat persons who might be at risk of disease because of their exposure to radioactive iodine.

This review—which will be comprehensive and public as are all IOM studies—is expected to take about six months after final arrangements are made with IOM. IOM is expected to establish a diverse expert panel including epidemiologists, public health authorities, risk communication experts, specialists in thyroid disease and its treatment, family physicians, public interest groups, and citizen representatives. In the meantime, persons concerned about fallout exposure should consult a health professional.

The administration will establish an interdepartmental group to look at broader policy issues.

7. Is there danger of exposure to I-131 fallout now?

No. The I-131 that was released from the tests is no longer present in the environment. I-131 has a radioactive half-life of about eight days, meaning that its radioactivity decreases by half every eight days. This means that nearly all the exposures took place primarily within two months following each test.

8. Why did the study take 14 years to complete?

The study involved the identification, collection, synthesis, and analysis of an enormous amount of data from many sources, including the Department of Energy, the National Oceanic and Atmospheric Administration, the Department of Agriculture, the Department of Commerce, agencies in each state, county agencies, the American Dairy Herd Improvement Association, the dairy industry, and numerous private individuals knowledgeable in some aspect of the study.

Early in the study an advisory committee was established to guide and assist in the study's conduct. From 1985 until 1993, it provided guidance regarding what data existed and where, which data might be useful and how, the retrieval and compilation of data (much of which was not in computerized form), the analysis of data, the methodologies to be used in reconstructing fallout deposition levels, milk concentration of I-131, and in the calculation of dose estimates by test, county, age, and dietary assumptions. During

1994 and 1995, the study report of approximately 1,000 pages was redrafted several times. Since that time, efforts have been made to review, organize, and summarize the results (about 100,000 pages) in an understandable format, and to revise and improve the clarity of the text.

9. When will the report be released?

The executive summary and technical summary, along with a list of the 24 counties that were most highly exposed to the fallout, are being released Aug. 1, along with a list of all U.S. counties with their estimated average thyroid dose levels. The complete report, about 1,000 pages long, is scheduled to be published by Oct. 1, as well as the full data set with annexes and subannexes totaling about 100,000 pages.

The complete report will include a description of the study methods, the most important measurement results, and summary information on estimated I-131 doses to individuals. The full data set—to be released on CD-ROM and the Internet—will include tabulated results of all the dose information by county, by age, and by milk consumption. It will include the amount of I-131 fallout in each county after each test, and the amount of I-131 that got into the food supply. Users of the data set will be able to group and present data by county, by test, by test series, and for all tests. Maps displaying the tabulated data will also be available.

10. What is radioactive fallout? What is iodine-131?

Radioactive fallout refers to a variety of airborne radioactive particles that fall to the ground during and following nuclear weapons tests. People and animals may ingest these particles in their food or inhale them from the air. Iodine-131 is a radioactive isotope of iodine—an altered form of the element that is chemically the same as the naturally occurring element but is radioactive. I-131 is found in fallout from atmospheric nuclear bomb explosions along with a variety of other radionuclides such as strontium-90. I-131 has been the focus of most concern because it concentrates in the thyroid, particularly in children, and may increase the risk for thyroid cancer. There appears to be little risk of thyroid cancer for persons exposed to radiation as adults. Because iodine concentrates in the thyroid, high doses of I-131 are used to treat some types of benign thyroid disease and thyroid cancer.

11. How were people exposed to I-131?

For most people, the greatest I-131 exposure came from drinking contaminated milk. I-131 fell on pasture lands, and the vegetation was eaten by cows, contaminating their milk. Smaller amounts came from breathing contaminated air and eating other contaminated dairy products, eggs, and leafy vegetables.

12. How was the study conducted?

To assess the thyroid doses of I-131 received by persons residing in different areas of the country, researchers had to estimate the amount of I-131 deposited on soil and vegetation after each bomb test, the amount of contaminated vegetation consumed by dairy cows, the amount and source of milk (and to a lesser extent, other foods) that people consumed, and the proportion of I-131 accumulating in the thyroid.

For most of the bomb tests, passive fallout collection devices were placed in up to 100 locations across the United States in an attempt to measure the fallout. But these devices measured only overall radioactivity, not specific radionuclides such as I-131. To estimate the amount of I-131 that fell in each county following each test, the NCI researchers used a reanalysis of the original data collected at the time of the tests, along with meteorological records on wind and rainfall patterns at the time, plus mathematical models. (In Western states most I-131 fell to the ground in dry form, while in Eastern states most was associated with rainfall.)

To determine the amount of I-131 consumed by cows, the researchers used other mathematical models to estimate what proportion of I-131 fell on vegetation, and combined these estimates with data on whether cows were on pasture in numerous regions of the country at the time of the tests, how much fresh pasture grass was eaten by cows in each state, and how much of the I-131 ingested by cows gets into their milk. The researchers then used records of milk production and distribution within each state and in the entire United States during the time of the tests to estimate how much I-131 was in the milk consumed by the populations of each county. Finally, data on average milk consumption levels for persons of different ages and in different regions of the country were combined with data from the analyses described above to derive estimates of average I-131 thyroid doses following each test for persons residing in each U.S. county.

The data will be reported for 13 age categories (including four fetal age groups, four age groups for infants, four age groups for children, plus adults as a single group, with men and women reported separately). Within each of these age categories, four scenarios for milk consumption are being calculated: persons who drank average quantities of milk with average I-131 contamination levels for the county, persons who drank higher-than-average levels of the most highly contaminated milk available in the county, persons who drank milk from family-owned "backyard" cows (see Question 2), and persons who drank no milk. Much less detailed analyses are being done for exposures from foods other than milk, and for exposure through inhalation, because these exposure pathways are much less important than drinking milk.

13. How reliable are the study's estimates of I-131 exposure?

There are large uncertainties in the estimated thyroid doses that will be given in the report because it is impossible to know all the information needed to determine exact doses. To evaluate the validity of the mathematical models used in the study, results obtained from the model were compared with the limited data collected at the time of the tests. The comparisons also provide an estimate of the uncertainty attached to the calculated doses.

These comparisons show a relatively good agreement between actual data and predictions made by the mathematical models. For example, independent analysis of urine samples volunteered by soldiers at Army bases throughout the United States following one of the test series showed iodine-131 dose levels consistent with or lower than the doses predicted. However, it should be noted that the comparison between measured and predicted values required the use of several assumptions, and there is no assurance that the samples measured were representative of county averages.

14. Can an individual person calculate his or her own thyroid radiation dose?

Because of the large number of variables involved in calculating individual dose estimates, it would likely be difficult for an individual to estimate his or her own thyroid dose. However, detailed information will be provided in the full report so that individual cumulative doses can be estimated. This information is expected to be most useful to state or county health departments and epidemiologists who wish to assess the impact of the fallout on specific populations.

In general, the uncertainty of the thyroid dose from iodine-131 fallout for a representative individual included in the study is about a factor of 3. For example, if the thyroid dose estimate for an individual is 3 rads—based on county of residence, age and assumed milk consumption at the time of the tests—the true dose will likely lie between 1 and 9 rads. However, the uncertainty attached to the thyroid dose for an actual, specific person is larger, because of uncertainties about the dietary habits and the metabolism of any individual.

15. How common is thyroid cancer? How treatable is it?

Thyroid cancer is relatively uncommon compared with other forms of cancer, accounting for about 1 percent of all cancers diagnosed in the United States. An estimated 16,100 U.S. cases will be diagnosed in 1997. The number of new cases is about 10 times higher than the number of deaths, estimated at 1,230 in the United States in 1997. Thyroid cancer occurs more than twice as often in women as in men. Incidence rates for 1994—the most recent year available—were 7.6 per 100,000 U.S. women of all ages combined, and 2.8 per 100,000 U.S. men. Thyroid cancer mortality rates for that year were 0.3 per 100,000 for both men and women. Lifetime risk for thyroid cancer is estimated at 0.66 percent for women (about 1 in 152) and 0.27 percent for men (about 1 in 370). Thyroid cancer is highly curable: The 5-year survival rate is about 95 percent.

16. What should people do who are concerned about cancer risk from fallout exposure?

Anyone who is concerned about cancer risk from fallout should request a thyroid examination as part of their next visit to a physician.

CLINTON AND GINGRICH ON
BALANCED BUDGET AGREEMENT
August 5, 1997

President Bill Clinton and his Republican foes in Congress reached a series of agreements in 1997 providing for a balanced budget by 2002. The agreements were made possible by old-fashioned compromise, born of political necessity on both sides and aided by an expanding economy that made budget-balancing much easier than it had been for a generation.

Clinton and the Republicans agreed on the broad outlines of a balanced budget in May, then worked out final details, which Congress approved at the end of July and Clinton signed into law August 5. If carried out, the agreement would result in the first balanced budget for the federal government since fiscal 1969. The annual deficit had reached a high of $290 billion in fiscal 1992.

Because of budget-cutting and, more important, the growing economy, fiscal year 1997 ended September 30, 1997, with a deficit of $22.6 billion— the lowest in nominal dollar terms since 1974, when it was $6.1 billion. The sharp drop in the deficit stirred talk that the budget might be balanced much earlier than 2002. Naturally, there also was speculation about how Washington might try to spend any surplus.

Despite the political celebrations, some skeptics noted that the agreement did little to change the basic nature of federal spending, especially on entitlement programs such as Medicare and Social Security. The agreement also cut taxes that might be needed to help pay for those programs in the early decades of the twenty-first century. "Generally, spending cuts are never as large as they are predicted to be and tax cuts are larger," said Robert D. Reischauer, a senior fellow at the Brookings Institution and a former director of the Congressional Budget Office.

The agreement was the first significant budget deal since 1990 between a president of one party and a Congress led by the other party. Then, President George Bush negotiated a budget compromise with congressional Democrats, only to have it torpedoed in a nasty confrontation on the House floor. The odd-couple alliance against that agreement was led by liberal

Democrats and conservative Republicans, including Newt Gingrich. Later, as Speaker of the House, Gingrich first fought with, then negotiated with, President Clinton. (Historic Documents of 1990, p. 409)

A Convergence of Interests

As with any deal between political antagonists, numerous factors made the 1997 agreement possible. By far the most important was the fact that an expanding economy was generating more tax revenues for the government, thus reducing the pain of cutting spending. Both sides also wanted a political victory that would divert public attention from their respective scandals. House Republicans were anxious and divided in 1997 as the result of a reprimand of Gingrich for ethical lapses. The Clinton administration was beset with a host of complaints about unethical behavior, including charges of campaign finance abuses and an investigation into the president's involvement in a failed Arkansas land deal in the 1970s. (Gingrich ethics case, p. 3)

Another factor was that Republicans had discovered in 1995 and 1996 that they could not win a political battle with Clinton on budget issues— especially because party members were themselves divided over many of those issues. Starting in late 1995 Republicans embarked on a high-stakes strategy of forcing repeated closings of large parts of the federal government in an effort to force Clinton to accede to their budget demands. The move backfired: Polls showed that the public blamed the Republicans, not Clinton, for the inconvenience, cost, and embarrassment of shutting down the government. Republicans abandoned the tactic early in 1996 in favor of serious, behind-the-scenes negotiations with the administration. The ultimate outcome of those talks was that Clinton in 1996 agreed to the concept of balancing the budget by 2002, with details to be negotiated later. (Budget battles, Historic Documents of 1995, p. 737; Historic Documents of 1996, p. 147)

May Agreement

Budget negotiations in 1997 took place in the context of one overriding factor: Clinton had won reelection in 1996, after stealing Republicans' thunder on budget cutting, and Republicans were still in control of Congress. After the president submitted his fiscal 1998 budget in January, Republicans faced a choice between negotiating with him or crafting their own budget package and trying to muscle it through Congress and then force the president to accept it. Given their internal divisions and the overall political situation, the Republicans chose to deal.

Starting in April, administration officials and House Republicans engaged in intense negotiations that periodically came close to breaking off. The clincher was a revised estimate by the Congressional Budget Office boosting revenue projections by $45 billion annually, for a total of $225 billion in additional revenues over five years. Negotiators moved quickly to "spend" that extra money, scrapping several controversial budget-cutting proposals that had blocked an agreement. Clinton and the Republicans *announced May 2 the broad outlines of an agreement to balance the budget by 2002. Each side hailed the agreement as a political victory.*

In general terms, the May accord called for $135 billion in gross tax cuts over five years, to be offset by $50 billion worth of revenue raisers (most if it in an extension of airline ticket taxes, totaling $30 billion). On the spending side, the deal called for saving $115 billion over five years from Medicare and at least $15 billion from Medicaid; allocating $60 billion to $70 billion above a freeze, at current spending levels, for discretionary spending programs; allowing $34 billion over five years for new initiatives, including programs for education and health care for children; and restoring a total of about $11 billion that had been cut in 1996 from disability and medical benefits programs for legal immigrants and food stamps for the working poor.

During the negotiations leading to that agreement, Clinton angered many congressional Democrats who felt they had been excluded. When both chambers adopted elements of the budget plan by overwhelming margins on May 20–23, opposition was strongest in the House where 99 of the 206 Democrats voted no. The chief critic was Minority Leader Richard A. Gephardt of Missouri, who had not been involved in most of the budget talks and who criticized the intended tax cuts as subsidies for the rich.

Follow-up Negotiations

The May agreement covered the general issues; Congress and the administration then needed to write budget resolutions and so-called reconciliation bills filling in details and locking the agreement in place. Negotiations on those matters consumed the early part of the summer.

Despite the warm afterglow from the agreement in May, the summertime negotiations proved contentious at times, with Republicans and the White House clashing over the specifics of cutting entitlement programs and Republicans often arguing among themselves on both spending and tax matters. In the early stages, negotiations involved dozens of members of Congress meeting in thirteen "subconference" committees. Four men resolved the tough final issues, however: Gingrich, Senate Majority Leader Trent Lott of Mississippi, White House Chief of Staff Erskine Bowles, and Office of Management and Budget Director Franklin D. Raines.

Racing to meet an August recess deadline, the two sides produced an agreement July 28, which the House adopted July 30 and the Senate cleared for the president July 31. Clinton signed the agreement into law (PL 105-33) at an extraordinary White House ceremony on August 5, during which both he and the Republicans set aside, at least temporarily, the harsh personal and political rhetoric that so often had characterized battles over the budget.

Compromises by Both Sides

In both the May 2 agreement and the more detailed agreement signed by Clinton August 5, Republicans gave in on some of the most cherished aspects of their platform. Some of the elements were ones that Republicans previ-

ously had described as nonnegotiable requirements. The plan did not cap federal spending on Medicare or force the states to handle Medicaid on their own; the plan did not make radical cuts in nondefense discretionary spending; and the plan violated a previously agreed cap on spending outlays for fiscal 1998, something Republicans had vowed they would never allow.

Over the long term, Republicans also surrendered the budget as an issue with which they could clobber Democrats. For nearly a generation, since Ronald Reagan won the presidency in 1980, Republicans had derided Democrats as "tax and spend liberals." The rhetoric skirted the fact that it was under Reagan and his successor George Bush that the deficit ballooned to historic proportions. Even so, the attacks struck home and helped Republicans win elections. Now with an agreement to kill the deficit dragon, Republicans had lost their most potent political weapon.

The president also made concessions, most notably in accepting tax cuts for wealthy Americans that he had previously rejected. And while Clinton won some extra funding for his priorities, such as education and health care for children, he and his fellow Democrats on Capitol Hill were forced to accept a long-term squeeze on other domestic social programs that for decades had been at the heart of the Democratic party's agenda.

Following are excerpts from remarks August 5, 1997, by President Bill Clinton and House Speaker Newt Gingrich, during a ceremony at the White House for the signing of legislation calling for a balanced budget by fiscal year 2002:

CLINTON STATEMENT

Thank you very much. We come here today—Democrats and Republicans, Congress and president, Americans of goodwill from all points of view and all walks of life—to celebrate a true milestone for our nation. In a few moments, I will sign into law the first balanced budget in a generation—a balanced budget that honors our values, puts our fiscal house in order, expands vistas of opportunity for all our people, and fashions a new government to lead in a new era.

Like every generation of Americans before us, we have been called upon to renew our nation and to restore its promise.

For too long, huge, persistent and growing budget deficits threatened the choke the opportunity that should be every American's birthright.

For too long, it seemed as if America would not be ready for the new century, that we would be too divided, too wedded to old arrangements and ideas.

It's hard to believe now that it wasn't so very long ago that some people looked at our nation and saw a setting sun.

When I became president, I determined that we must believe and make sure that America's best days were still ahead.

After years in which the deficit drained our economy and dampened our spirit, in which our ability to lead the world was diminished by our inability to put our own house in order, after years in which too many people doubted whether our nation would ever come together again to address this problem, we set off on a new economic course—to cut the deficit to create the conditions in which business could thrive, to open more foreign markets to our goods and services, to invest in our people so that all Americans would have the tools they need to make the most of their lives.

Today our budget deficit has been cut by more than 80 percent. It is now among the smallest in the industrialized world as a percentage of our economy. Our businesses once again lead in world markets, now made more open, more free, more fair than ever before through our efforts. Our workers are clearly the most competitive on earth, and we have recast our old government so that a new one can take shape that does give our people the tools to make the most of their God-given abilities.

This year we, Democrats and Republicans alike, were given the opportunity and the responsibility to finish the job of balancing the budget for the first time in almost 30 years. And to do it in a way that prepares Americans to enter the next century stronger than ever. By large, bipartisan majorities in both houses, we have risen to that challenge.

The balanced budget I signed into law today will continue our successful economic strategy. It reflects the most fundamental values that brought us together. It will spur growth and spread opportunity. Even after we pay for tax cuts penny by penny, there will still be $900 billion in savings, including half a trillion dollars in entitlement savings over the next 10 years.

It opens the doors of college to a new generation with the largest investment in higher education since the G.I. Bill 50 years ago.

It makes it possible for the 13th and 14th years of college to become as universal as high school is today.

It strengthens our families with the largest expansion in health care for children since the Medicaid program 32 years ago. It modernizes Medicare and extends the life of the trust fund for a decade. It helps our communities to rebuild, to move a million more people from welfare to work, to bring the spark of private enterprise back to our most isolated inner city neighborhoods.

It provides the largest tax relief to help families raise their children, save for the future, and pass on their home and a dream to the next generation. These tax cuts are the equivalent of $1,000 raise in take home pay for the average family with two children.

For so many Americans, what goes on here in Washington often seems abstract and remote, unrelated to their daily concerns. Well, this balanced budget deals with the big issues of the deficit and long term economic growth in ways that respond to the practical challenges ordinary American citizens face every single day.

Because we have acted, millions of children all across this country will be able to get medicine and have their sight and hearing tested, and see dentists and doctors for the first time. Millions of young Americans will be able to go on to college. Millions of Americans not so young will be able to go back to school to get the education and training they need to succeed in life.

Millions of families will have more to spend on their own children's needs and upbringing. This budget is an investment in their future, and in America's.

Today, it should be clear to all of us without regard to our party or our differences that in common, we were able to transform this era of challenge into an era of unparalleled possibility for the American people.

I hope we can tap this spirit of cooperation and use it to meet and master the many challenges that remain before us.

I want to thank, in closing, the many people whose work made this day possible.

I want to thank Speaker [Newt] Gingrich [R-Ga.] and Senator [Trent] Lott [R-Miss.], Mr. [Dick] Armey [R-Texas] and the other members of the House and Senate leadership, especially Senator [Pete] Domenici [R-N.M.] and Congressman [John] Kasich [R-Ohio], and let me thank Chairman [Bill] Archer [R-Texas] and Chairman [William] Roth [R-Del.] and the other leaders of the House and Senate committees. They were dedicated partners. They fought hard for their priorities.

I want to thank Senator [Tom] Daschle [D-S.D.] and Congressman [David] Bonior [D-Mich.] and Congressman [Vic] Fazio [D-Calif.] and Congressman [Steny] Hoyer [D-Md.] and the other members of the House Democratic leadership who worked with us.

I want to thank especially Congressman [John] Spratt [D-S.C.] and Senator [Frank] Lautenberg [D-N.J.], Congressman [Charles] Rangel [D-N.Y.], and the other members of the House and Senate Democratic minority leaders in the committees for the work that they did. I thank all the members of the Congress who are here present, and the many whom they represent who are already back home who could not be.

All of them deserve our thanks and I would like to ask the members of the Congress who are here today to stand and be recognized and appreciated by the crowd.

I'd like to thank the members of our budget team—Erskine Bowles, [Treasury] Secretary [Robert] Rubin, John Hilley, OMB Director [Franklin] Raines, Gene Sperling, Janet Yellen, Rahm Emmanuel, Jack Lew, Larry Summers, Chris Jennings and many others—especially those who work in our legislative shop, too numerous to mention—for the enormous work that they did on this agreement.

I would like to thank the first lady, Mrs. Gore, the vice president for their concern for the health of our children, for the mental health of the American people, and the vice president especially, who led the fight to protect our urban initiatives and our environmental program and the interests of legal immigrants in America.

We owe to them a great deal.

Again, I say to all—I thank you. I believe that together we have fulfilled the responsibility of our generation to guarantee opportunity to the next generation, the responsibility of our generation to take America into a new century, where there is opportunity for all who are responsible enough to work for it, where we have a chance to come together across all of our differences as a great American community, where we will be able to continue to lead the world toward peace and freedom and prosperity.

That is worthy work and you have all contributed doing it.

We can say with pride and certainty that those who saw the sun setting on America were wrong. The sun is rising on America again, and I thank you all.

GINGRICH STATEMENT

Thank you all very much. Let me start by picking up where the president ended. And that is, saying thank you to an awful lot of people. This has been a long time coming. It has been a difficult process. But in that process we have proven together that the American constitutional system works, that slowly, over time, we listen to the will of the American people, that we reach beyond parties, we reach beyond institutions, and we find ways to get things done.

I want to start by thanking the president and Mrs. Clinton, the vice president and Mrs. Gore, because their willingness this year, coming off their victory, to reach out a hand and say let's work together, was the key from which everything else grew.

And the sincerity of their efforts over the last eight months has made an enormous difference in our capacity to make this system work, and I thank the four of you for your involvement.

There are many, many people on the president's staff, just as there are many, many members of the congressional staffs who are here today who put in extraordinarily long hours, who missed their families for weekends at a time, who worked seven days a week all through the spring and summer. But in particular, I want to join the president in thanking three people: Erskine Bowles, John Hilley and Secretary Bob Rubin, because again of the commitment they made from the very beginning that this would be a successful process. And I thank the three of you for serving your country.

I also want to thank the budget director Franklin Raines, not just for the budget, but for his special effort, working with [Rep.] Tom Davis [R-Va.] and [Delegate] Eleanor Holmes Norton [D-D.C.] and others, to do something special for the District of Columbia.

No bill ever passed by the U.S. Congress provides more opportunity for the rebirth and the renewal of the District of Columbia than the bills that will be signed today. They represent a major bipartisan effort to get resources and reform to the people of D.C., and to make this truly the finest capital city in the world. And I thank you, Frank, for the work you did to make that possible.

In the Congress the truth is that almost everybody had a major role. Senator Lott, who, without whom nothing would have happened in the Senate; Senator Domenici, who had spent over 20 years of his career working to get to a balanced budget, and who really was the big brother, if you will, the senior partner with John Kasich, whose courage and energy and drive inspired all of this. And without John's work, we would never have gotten to a balanced budget on the House side.

Majority Leader Dick Armey, Minority Leader Tom Daschle in the Senate, Chairman Roth and Archer on taxes, Chairman [Thomas] Bliley [R-Va.], who helped so much on so many different topics. Key members of the minority: Congressman Spratt and Senator Lautenberg, who really carried so much on the budget committees, and Congressman Rangel and Senator [Daniel Patrick] Moynihan [D-N.Y.], who were so integral on the tax side. And they stood for member after member who truly wanted to get the job done, who wanted to put aside partisanship, who wanted to reach beyond past enmities, and who wanted to do the job.

But all of us in Washington if we're sincere about will admit that the ultimate driving force of this bill was the will of the American people. It is the American people who have said to all of us, we want to balance the budget for our children and grandchildren. It is the American people who said our tax burden is too high, and we need lower taxes. And it is the American people who said, Medicare is so important, you must put aside your differences to save it.

And in that sense, all of us today stand here as servants of the American people.

And it is they who deserve the ultimate tribute, because it is their work in the economy that is producing the revenues to narrow the deficit, it was their political will that brought the two parties together, and we in our constitutional system serve them.

Because of these two extraordinary bills the president will sign in just a moment, we will get to a balanced budget by 2002, a commitment we had made on January 4, 1995, and which we worked closely in a bipartisan way to make real.

We will meet the moral integrity test in peace time of not spending our children and grandchildren's money. And we will as the markets come to realize we're sincere and bipartisan, see interest rates continue to come down, and continue to improve economic growth.

We'll see real tax cuts for the first time in 16 years. Families with children will get their $500, and through a long bipartisan tussle that will effect every family below $110,000 income. If you're working and you have a tax liability, you're going to get a tax cut, and I commend the president for leading that effort. And we, together, have done it.

No longer will there be a cliff as you leave welfare and have a sudden rise in your tax burden. If you have children, your country wants to encourage you to work, and it wants to encourage you to take care of your children.

The educational tax credits are going to help those children when they get ready to go to college or to vocational technical school. And then there will be incentives to save, to improve their lives. If they buy a house, there will be no capital gains tax if they have to sell it.

There will be incentives to create more jobs, small business will be relieved of the burden of AMT [Alternative Minimum Tax], and a big step towards simplification for small businesses.

And families will face the prospect that if your parents or grandparents have saved all their lives, you won't be punished nearly as much by the government in taxes when you die. And that's a first step in the right direction on eliminating the tax when people die.

On Medicare, we came together and we saved the system for at least a decade. But equally important with the president's leadership, we working as a team have established a commission to come right back here in 1999 with an obligation to save the Medicare system for our children and grandchildren, and to save it for the baby boom generation.

And as you look up here, you'll notice we have a deep, personal incentive to make sure we save it for the baby boom generation. And I pledge right here, working with the president, that we will work on a bipartisan basis not just to appoint of good commission, but to enact in 1999 the right savings and the rights steps to reform the system for the baby boomers and their children.

Finally, let me just close by echoing what the president said at the end, because he's so right. We have the chance over the next 3.5 years to work together through our very complex constitutional process of a legislative branch and executive branch guarded by the judiciary.

We have a chance to work together to accomplish a lot, to have a truly drug free America, to have every child learning at their best rate, to help children be born or adopted into families that can truly nurture and raise them. We have a chance to continue this economic incentives and growth that has led over the last five or six years to such remarkable progress.

And we have a chance to establish a firm understanding of the challenge America faces in the world, for we are the only country capable of providing leadership in the next generation in a calm, consistent and coherent manner. And that can only come if there's a bipartisan consensus on how America must shoulder its obligations as the leading country in the world.

Marianne and I came back today to be here to say that we pledge to work with the president and with our friends in the Congress on the Democratic side, that together we can make bipartisan progress at home, and we can provide bipartisan leadership across the planet. And that is our duty for our generation and to our children. Thank you very much.

CLINTON ON HIS FIRST USE
OF THE LINE-ITEM VETO
August 11, 1997

President Bill Clinton in 1997 was able to do what many of his prede-cessors had yearned to accomplish: strike out individual items in appro-priations bills sent him by Congress without having to veto the bills in their entirety. Clinton became the first president to exercise a form of "line-item veto" that gave him the power to reject congressional spending items he did not want. The veto authority had the potential both to curb the congres-sional appetite for pet spending projects and to give all presidents a sig-nificant political advantage over Congress in future budget battles.

Presidents since Ulysses S. Grant had asked for a line-item veto power similar to the authority most of the nation's governors had enjoyed for many years. Congressional Republicans began pushing for the veto in the 1980s, hoping to aid a Republican president, such as Ronald Reagan or George Bush, confronting a Democratic-controlled Congress. Congress finally acted in 1996. In a quirk of history, Clinton, a Democrat, was the first to use the power—when Congress was controlled by Republicans. In another irony, Clinton first used the veto against a handful of obscure provisions in an his-toric budget-balancing bill he and Republican leaders had celebrated less than a week earlier. (Budget accord, p. 602)

Clinton used the new veto power three times in 1997. The first time was August 11, when he rejected more than $600 million worth of special-inter-est tax breaks and entitlement spending programs. Overall, he vetoed eighty-two items that had carried a potential cost of $1.9 billion over five years. Congress moved to override Clinton's veto of thirty-eight military construc-tion projects but had not completed its action on the issue by the end of 1997.

Clinton had said he would use the power sparingly, and some line-item veto supporters said he was too timid. "I'd like to see far more items line-item vetoed," Sen. John McCain, R-Ariz., said. But some members of Con-gress whose pet projects succumbed to the veto knife felt differently, as did a handful of leaders who had opposed the veto as surrendering Congress's constitutional power of the purse.

Supreme Court Action

The line-item veto power that Congress gave to Clinton, effective in 1997, was not the traditional tool that most governors exercised, allowing them to veto individual spending items unless overruled by a supermajority of their legislatures. Enacting such a procedure on the federal level would have required a constitutional amendment, an uncertain and time-consuming process. Congress instead crafted a cumbersome procedure called "enhanced rescissions," under which the president could "cancel" specific spending items or narrow tax breaks. The president's action would take effect unless Congress passed a bill to reverse it, which the president also would have a chance to veto.

Led by Sen. Robert C. Byrd, D-W.Va., several members of Congress filed suit against the new veto, arguing that it undermined their constitutional role as legislators. Byrd and his colleagues won the first round in April when U.S. District Judge Thomas P. Jackson declared the line-item veto unconstitutional. But when the case (Byrd v. Raines) reached the Supreme Court, the veto opponents lost on a technicality. On a 7–2 decision, the high court ruled that because the president had not yet exercised the veto, Byrd and his colleagues had not suffered any injury under the law and therefore lacked the legal standing to sue. Justices John Paul Stevens and Stephen G. Breyer dissented; Stevens said he would have found the veto law unconstitutional; Breyer said Byrd and the other plaintiffs did have the proper legal standing, but he expressed no views on the constitutionality of the law.

While leaving the veto power intact for the time being, the Supreme Court decision left open the possibility that it could be challenged successfully in the future. Several groups and local jurisdictions affected by Clinton's initial vetoes filed suit in 1997; their cases were combined into one suit, City of New York v. Clinton, *in the federal district court for the District of Columbia.*

Clinton's Vetoes

In the political glow of Clinton's budget agreement with Congress early in August, some of the president's advisors urged caution in his use of the line-item veto. They reportedly argued that using the veto aggressively might damage the bipartisan spirit generated by the budget accord. These aides expressed particular concern about the impact a veto might have on what was expected to be the most contentious issue in the closing weeks of Congress: Clinton's request for an extension of his "fast track" authority to negotiate trade agreements. Other aides suggested that the president needed to demonstrate political strength by using the veto, regardless of the consequences on other issues. (Trade issues, p. 543)

Clinton chose a middle ground, using the veto sparingly at his first opportunity. The legislation involved was the bill implementing the balanced budget agreement he had signed August 5. The bill contained seventy-nine tax breaks or other concessions that benefited a limited number of taxpayers or entities.

Clinton selected three of those items to veto: a deferral of taxes on the sale of food processing facilities sold to farmer cooperatives; a provision allowing banks and other financial services firms to defer taxes on interest income produced by overseas subsidiaries and that also was subject to host-country taxation; and a special exemption allowing the state of New York (and no other state) to match federal contributions to the Medicaid program with taxes and other assessments collected from health care providers. White House officials said vetoing those three items would save taxpayers $615 million over five years.

In signing the vetoes, Clinton expressed the hope that Congress would get the message that he was serious about curbing special-interest items and so-called pork barrel spending projects. "It may be that the use of the line-item veto here will mean that it won't have to be used as much in the appropriations process, and that would please me greatly," he said. Clinton's action sparked outcries from some members of Congress and from officials in New York, including Gov. George E. Pataki, who said the Medicaid-related veto would endanger needy children and families.

The president acted again in October, first vetoing thirty-eight military construction projects, totaling $287 million, then thirteen other projects totaling $144 million that members of Congress had inserted into a Defense Department spending bill. In the latter case, Clinton said his veto was "responsible and quite restrained," considering the fact that Congress had added 750 defense projects totaling more than $11 billion that the administration had not requested.

The vetoes prompted some members of Congress who had originally supported the veto power to reconsider the issue now that spending for projects in their districts was being cut. Those members banded together with those who opposed the veto power and passed legislation—called a "disapproval" bill—to restore funding for the thirty-eight military construction projects Clinton had vetoed.

Clinton vetoed the disapproval bill on November 13, just before Congress recessed for the year. Both chambers had passed the bill by more than the two-thirds majority needed for an override, so it was anticipated that Congress would have the final say on that issue when it reconvened in 1998. The House also passed a bill to restore the two special tax breaks Clinton had vetoed on August 11, but the legislation stalled in the Senate.

Following is the text of President Bill Clinton's statement August 11, 1997, marking his first use of a line-item veto authority, followed by excerpts from his answers to reporters' questions on the matter:

Last week we took historic action to put America's economic house in order when I signed into law the first balanced budget in a generation, one that honors our values, invests in our people, prepares our nation for the 21st century.

It includes the largest increase in college aid since the G.I. Bill, largest increase in children's health since the creation of Medicaid over 30 years ago, tax cuts that are the equivalent of a $1,000 raise in take-home pay for the average family with two children—and much more that is good for America.

The new balanced budget law also offers the first opportunity to use a powerful new tool to protect taxpayers—the line item veto; a tool designed to fight against waste and unjustifiable expenditures, to ensure government works for the public interests, not the private interests.

In the past, good legislation could be cluttered up with unjustifiable or wasteful spending or tax provisions, leaving the President no choice but to sign or veto the overall legislation. With the line item veto, the President can sign an overall bill into law that cancelled a particular spending project or a particular tax break that benefits only a handful of individuals or companies.

Forty-three governors throughout our nation already have the line item veto power. Last year I signed the federal line item veto into law. Last month the United States Supreme Court, on procedural grounds, rejected a challenge to this authority. Today, for the first time in the history of our country, the President will use the line item veto to protect taxpayers and to ensure that national interests prevail over narrow interests.

In reaching agreement with Congress on how to balance the budget, we worked very hard to be fair to all Americans and to avoid wasting our citizens' tax dollars. For the same reason, I've asked the members of my administration to work carefully over the final legislation to identify any specific spending or tax provisions that I should consider cancelling. Here's what I told the budget team.

First, any provision I cancel must be one that was not included—and let me emphasize—not included—as a part of the balanced budget agreement process with Congress. Our agreement was entered into in good faith, and I will keep it. Second, any provision I cancel must be one that benefits just a few individuals, corporations or states at the expense of the general interest. Finally, any provision I cancel must be one that is inconsistent with good public policy. Just because something benefits a small number of people doesn't necessarily mean that it hurts the public interest or the American people at large.

After careful scrutiny and numerous meetings with my staff and Cabinet members, we have found three provisions that meet those criteria. In a few moments I will use the power of the line item veto to cancel a provision that would allow financial service companies to shelter income in foreign tax havens to avoid all U.S. taxation.

I will also cancel a provision that singles out New York by allowing it to tap into the federal Treasury to reduce its state expenditures through the use of health provider tax to match federal Medicaid dollars that are impermissible in every other state in the country and actually in existence now in several other states. No other state in the nation would be given this provision, and it is unfair to the rest of our nation's taxpayers to ask them to subsidize it.

Finally, I will cancel a provision that, though well-intended, is poorly designed. This provision would have allowed a very limited number of agribusinesses to avoid paying capital gains taxes possibly forever on the sales of certain assets to farmers' cooperatives. And it could have benefited not only traditional farm co-ops, but giant organizations which do not need and should not trigger the law's benefits.

Because I strongly support family farmers, farm cooperatives, and the acquisition of production facilities by co-ops, this was a very difficult decision for me. And I intend to work with Congressman [Charles] Stenholm [D-Texas] and [Kenny] Hulshof [R-Mo.] and Senators [Tom] Daschle [D-S.D.], [Byron] Dorgan [D-N.D.], and [Kent] Conrad [D-N.D.] and other interested members of the Congress to redesign this effort so that it is better targeted and not susceptible to abuse.

The actions I take today will save the American people hundreds of millions of dollars over the next 10 years, and send a signal that the Washington rules have changed for good—and for the good of the American people. From now on, Presidents will be able to say no to wasteful spending or tax loopholes, even as they say yes to vital legislation. Special interests will not be able to play the old game of slipping a provision into a massive bill in the hope that no one will notice.

For the first time, the President is exercising the power to prevent that from happening. The first balanced budget in a generation is now also the first budget in American history to be strengthened by the line item veto. And that will strengthen our country.

And now I want to go and sign these provisions.

Question: Mr. President, is that the only pork you can find in that budget?

The President: I think that my staff is going to brief you about it, but let me say that they have—the relevant Cabinet and staff members have gone over this quite extensively. Keep in mind, the primary use of the line item veto overwhelmingly was meant to be in the appropriations process, which is not even started yet. I don't have the first appropriations bill.

There are only a few spending items in this balanced budget that are part of the so-called entitlements process, so that, for example, you had the New York Medicaid provision there on provider taxes. With regard to the taxes, there were 79 items certified to me, but that was only because of their size—that is, the number of people affected by it. Of those 79, 30 or more were actually recommendations by the Treasury Department to fix flaws in the present laws or to ease the transitions in the tax laws. And another dozen or more were put in by Congress by agreement with the Treasury Department to fix procedural problems in the law. Then there were a number of others that I agreed were good policy.

So these are the ones that I think—and then there were several others that I might have line-item-vetoed, but they were plainly part of the understandings reached with Congress as a part of the budget process. So these seemed to me to be the ones, after being briefed by my staff, that both involved significant amounts of money and met the three criteria that I mentioned. And I believe it was the appropriate thing to do.

Question: May I ask another way, sir, the last question another way? Were these the most glaring examples of why you were given this power and, therefore, they might hold up better in a court challenge?

The President: Well, I wouldn't say that. I expect the most glaring examples to come up in the appropriations process, at least if the past is any prologue. Now, it may be that the use of the line item veto here will mean that it won't have to be used as much in the appropriations process, and that would please me greatly. But I think it's important that the American people understand that when the line item veto was given to the President, the primary assumption was that it would take out special projects that were typically funded in big bills, and those are those big appropriations bills, none of which have come to me yet.

But I do believe that this should withstand court challenge because the process by which the matters were reviewed at least was a very careful, exhaustive process, and I received input from people all over the country that had interests in it—through of my Cabinet and staff members. But we worked very hard on this. . . .

CLINTON ON WELFARE REFORM
August 12, 1997

The federal government's six-decade-old welfare program came to an end July 1, replaced by a patchwork of programs in the fifty states that were financed, in part, by block grants from Washington. Congress in 1996 had passed, and President Bill Clinton had signed into law, a massive revision of federal welfare policy, turning most responsibility for welfare over to the states. (Welfare reform, Historic Documents of 1996, p. 450)

The new system was based on work requirements, which varied by state; with few exceptions, adults could receive welfare payments for just two consecutive years. The official transformation of the federal system followed in the wake of major shifts already underway in the states. By 1997 the Clinton administration had approved a variety of experiments with welfare programs in forty-three states. Several states, such as Michigan and Wisconsin, had adopted tough work requirements on which much of the new federal system was modeled.

Shrinking Welfare Caseload

The number of people on the welfare rolls had been falling even before the new federal system took effect. According to White House figures, the number of people on welfare fell from 14.1 million in January 1993 (an all-time high) to 10.7 million in May 1997. That decrease of 24 percent put the nation's welfare caseload at its lowest point since 1970. About two-thirds of welfare recipients were children; 90 percent of the adults were single, divorced, or separated mothers.

The president's Council of Economic Advisers in May released a study concluding that economic growth was the most important factor in the decline. Slightly more than 44 percent of those who left the welfare rolls starting in 1993 did so because of economic expansion and falling unemployment, the council said. An estimated 31 percent of the decline was the result of experimental welfare policies in the states, such as work requirements and time limits on benefits. The remaining 25 percent of the decline resulted from other factors, such as increased state and federal spending on child care programs, which offered an alternative to welfare for single mothers. The report, which used mathematical models based on information provided by the states, offered no conclusions on what happened to former recipients after they left the welfare rolls.

The New Welfare System

The heart of the 1996 welfare reform law was abolition of the sixty-two-year-old system called Aid to Families with Dependent Children, which guaranteed cash payments to needy children and their parents. The new law created a program called Temporary Assistance to Needy Families, with the emphasis placed on the word temporary. *This program provided grants to the states, which would use the money for programs they created within general guidelines set by the federal government. The most important guidelines were that adult recipients were required to find jobs within two years and could receive welfare payments for no more than five years over a lifetime. Individual states could set even tougher limits but also could exempt up to 20 percent of recipients from the five-year maximum.*

The new law also had provisions intended to give welfare recipients positive incentives to find work, including a $14 billion federal fund to subsidize child care for mothers who left welfare for work. States were encouraged to find innovative ways to help low-income working families pay child care and transportation expenses. The law also guaranteed that mothers would continue to be eligible for health care insurance, including Medicaid, for at least one year after leaving welfare for work.

Other provisions required tougher enforcement of child-support laws. The law established uniform laws for handling interstate child-support cases and allowed states to take such steps as seizing assets and revoking drivers licenses of parents delinquent on their payments.

Several surveys of welfare policies at the state level showed that many state legislatures had provided relatively generous funding for child care, transportation, job placement, and other services for welfare recipients who found work—or even for low-income working families in general. Illinois, for example, created a $100 million fund to subsidize child care for any family earning less than $22,000 annually, regardless of whether the family had been on welfare. Some states also were offering transportation subsidies, such as mass transit vouchers, for former welfare recipients. Among other incentives offered by states were subsidies for employers who hired welfare recipients and creation of community service jobs for people who could not find work in the private sector.

Still unclear in the early stages of welfare reform was what would happen to those adults, and their families, who could not find any work. The new law allowed states to exempt up to 20 percent of recipients from the five-year total limit on welfare, but some experts were estimating that a much greater portion of those receiving welfare would be unable to find a job, and hold onto it, before their benefits ran out.

Clinton Reacts to Welfare Reform

Clinton had agonized in August 1996 about whether to sign the welfare reform law that was written by conservative Republicans in Congress and passed over the opposition of most Democrats. In the end, he decided his first priority was to keep his 1992 campaign promise to "end welfare as we know it." He said he would work to reverse several provisions he found objectionable, including a ban on most forms of welfare for immigrants, including those in the country legally.

In the year after Clinton signed the bill into law, his administration claimed much of the credit for changes under way in the welfare system, including the sharp drop in caseloads and the experimental programs in the states. Bruce Reed, Clinton's domestic policy advisor, called the decrease "a stunning success, totally unprecedented in the history of welfare." Speaking in St. Louis on August 12, a little more than a month after the new system was put in place, Clinton said that "welfare reform works." As evidence, he cited the 24 percent drop in welfare rolls, all of which occurred before the new law took effect.

Clinton appealed to private business to hire people off the welfare rolls. He gave a toll-free telephone number employers could call for information; the number was for the Welfare to Work Partnership, a private coalition of corporations that had pledged to find jobs for welfare recipients.

Following is the text of a speech by President Bill Clinton to business leaders, job trainees, and others in St. Louis, Missouri, on August 12, 1997, in which he discussed the new welfare reform law:

It's great to be back in St. Louis, even on a hot August day. This city is very much alive. You can see it in the revived area and your record job growth, your commitment to education reform, and now to welfare reform. And I want to talk about finishing the job of welfare reform, moving people from welfare to work.

If we expect to be the country we want to be in the next century, we have to provide opportunity for everyone who's willing to work for it, we have to require responsibility from everyone who's capable of providing it, and we have to find a way to come together across all the lines that divide us to make one America.

Fixing our broken welfare system is an important part of that because it means more opportunity, more responsibility and a stronger, more united community. It's been a priority of my presidency. You've heard others mention—I think the Governor [Mel Carnahan] talked about it—that shortly after I took office we began giving people waivers from federal rules that undermined their reform experiments so they could try new and innovative ways that would work perhaps in one community but not another, perhaps in one state but not another, to facilitate the movement of people from welfare to work.

Then a year ago next week, I signed the welfare reform legislation which really did end welfare as we know it. It was designed to make welfare a second chance, not a way of life. It gave the states far more responsibilities and opportunities to create new programs to move people from welfare to work. It guaranteed children their nutritional and health care benefits and provided several billion dollars more money to pay for child care for parents who otherwise could not afford to take jobs at entry levels if those were the only jobs they could get.

Now, a lot of people said that welfare reform would never work because the private economy wouldn't do its part or the government wouldn't do its part or we couldn't figure out how to get people from welfare to work or— you know, I heard all the reasons that people said it wouldn't work. But a year later, I think it's fair to say the debate is over. We know now that welfare reform works.

Today I am proud to announce that just since I signed the law a year ago, there are now 1.4 million fewer people on welfare in the last year alone. In the four years and seven months or so, almost eight now, since I took office, the welfare rolls have declined by 3.4 million, 24 percent, the biggest decline in history. We now have the smallest percentage of Americans living on public assistance we have had since 1970. We can make this work if we all work together.

I come here to St. Louis and to this fine place and to these programs—and let me again thank all of you who are part of all these programs—to say that the job is not over. And the law requires us to do more, because the law says that able-bodied people, people who are able physically and mentally to do work, should be on welfare continuously no more than two years, and no more than five years in a lifetime. Now, if you say that to someone and you don't want to be cruel to them or their children, then you must acknowledge that we, the rest of us, have a moral obligation to make sure there is a job there, and that if they need training that they have the training they need for the job.

The national government is determined to do its part. Last week when I signed the first balanced budget law in a generation into law, we had two provisions that I want to especially emphasize: one, $3 billion in a welfare-to-work challenge fund to help communities with higher unemployment rates move long-term welfare recipients into the work force; and two, an expanded and carefully targeted work opportunity tax credit which gives a significant incentive to private employers, including small business people who need to be brought into this equation, to move people from welfare to work.

And in that connection, let me say that we are committed to doing everything we can. As evidence of that, I would like to acknowledge the presence here today of the Secretary of Health and Human Services, Donna Shalala; the Secretary of Labor, Alexis Herman; the Administrator of the Small Business Administration, Aida Alvarez. They're here working with St. Louis, working with Missouri. We're going to do this with every major community in every state in our community. We want to do our part to help you meet the goals of the welfare reform law. And I thank you all for being here.

I have also asked the Vice President to head two other initiatives for me— one, to bring civic and business groups together to mentor new employees. I had a friend from the Midwest call me the other day, and he said, you know, I just want you to know I really am trying to do what you asked me to do—I run a small business—and we've been friends for many years. And he said, I'm trying to hire people from welfare to work, but because the economy is going so well, most of the people who can easily move into the work force already have, and the people I'm trying to hire, they're really having a hard time because they've actually never had to do this before. They've never even had to show up before at the same time. They don't understand how to find— how to handle conflict in the work force. If they run up against something they can't do, they're uncomfortable asking how to do it.

We forget that if we're going to go all the way we have a lot of work to do to make some of these folks believe in their own capacities and understand them and understand that, hey, we all mess up at work. You know that, read my polls, right? I mean, sometimes we all mess up at work. And we've got a lot of work to do to get people in the right frame of mind to understand that having a job and keeping a job is a continuous learning and growth experience. So we know we need to do that. We're trying to do our part with that.

And, finally, the Vice President is leading our effort to have the federal government, even in a time when we've downsized the overall government, fill as many new openings as possible with welfare recipients until we hire 10,000 welfare recipients on our part over the next couple of years.

Now, we know that the states, the communities, the private sector also have to do an awful lot. Believe it or not, 48 of the 50 states have seen their caseloads decline dramatically. Missouri has done better than the national average, at 27 percent decline in the last four years. Thirty-five states have now followed Missouri's lead. Missouri asked for one of these welfare waivers, so that in certain parts of the state you could authorize employers to receive the welfare check as a hiring and training supplement for a period of time—which I thought was a great idea, a legitimate idea, particularly with people who are harder to place—to give employers a premium to really work with those employees and train them and help them become full-time volunteers.

Since I came here, first in 1994 to Missouri to announce welfare reform efforts, then in 1996 to talk about getting the private sector involved, you might be interested to know that now 35 other states have allowed Missouri to show them that this is a good reform, and they are also doing it. I help all the rest of them will, too.

The most important thing we can do is get the private sector to hire people. That's why Barry and Chairman Shapiro are so important to us, because we've got to have the private sector hiring people. That's why the AmeriCorps project that I just visited downstairs, training young people for private sector jobs, is so important.

And last year when I came to Missouri, we announced that there would be a national effort involving in the beginning a number of Missouri corporations, and five corporations nationally to organize businesses of all sizes to commit to hire people from welfare to work. Since Monsanto and Sprint and Burger King and UPS and United Airlines agreed to start that effort, the Welfare to Work Partnership, which was founded by my good friend Eli Segal—who also, by the way, was the first head of our national service program, AmeriCorps, which has done a fabulous job, I believe, for young people in our country—but since we started, we now have over 800 companies of all sized signed up to promise to hire people from welfare to work. What you should be proud of is that 300 of them have locations here in St. Louis. And you should be very proud of that.

Now, I want to challenge every employer in America to join this crusade. And we have a toll-free number, it's 1-888-Usa-Job1—1-888-Usa-Job1. I want the employers in this country who get this number to call it and help a welfare recipient find a job. And, again, I'd like to thank Sprint for donating this number. This is quite a considerable financial investment to help people move from welfare to work, and I appreciate they're doing it. Remember that. I feel like I'm hawking something on one of those channels on television—1-888-Usa-Job1—I can do this.

Let me close by putting a personal face on this. There's a woman on stage with us today who is an example of what someone who once was on welfare with serious obstacles to overcome can do to become a valuable and successful employee. Felicia Booker's success took courage, responsibility and a dream that she could make a better life for her young children, ages two and six. It also took an employer, A. G. Edwards, willing to take a chance on her, and people along the way who wanted to help her realize that dream. Felicia Booker has been working at A. G. Edwards for nearly a year and a half now. She's a computer programmer and she's already been promoted once. I'd like for her to stand and be recognized. Felicia?

Again, let me say, if this is really going to be a country where everyone has an opportunity, then we have to prove that the young women I just met in that job-training program downstairs are going to be given the opportunity to make the most of their own lives. Ultimately, that's what welfare reform is about. It's not primarily about saving the government money—we're going to balance the budget regardless. It's about empowering every single person in this country to be a part of this country in a new century, in a new era.

Thank you. And God bless you all.

McVEIGH ON HIS SENTENCING
FOR OKLAHOMA CITY BOMBING
August 14, 1997

*In separate trials in 1997, juries convicted the two men accused of plan-
ning and carrying out the bombing April 19, 1995, of the Alfred P. Murrah
Federal Building in Oklahoma City. The bombing, which killed 168 people
and injured several hundred more, was the worst act of domestic terrorism
in American history. Although much of the evidence against him was circumstantial, a jury found Timothy J. McVeigh, 29, the apparent instigator
of the plot, guilty of eleven counts of conspiracy and murder and sentenced
him to death. A second jury convicted McVeigh's friend Terry L. Nichols, 42,
of conspiracy and involuntary manslaughter, but not murder. The jury had
not completed its deliberation on a sentence for Nichols by the end of the
year.*

*"Justice prevails," Joseph H. Hartzler, the lead prosecutor against
McVeigh, said after the jury returned its death sentence. "The verdict doesn't
diminish the great sadness that occurred in Oklahoma City two years ago.
Our only hope is that the verdict will go some way to preventing such a terrible, drastic crime from ever occurring again." Americans were horrified
by the bombing, which rocked their sense of security as few other incidents
had. Initially most people assumed the explosion was the work
of foreign terrorists, and their horror was magnified when the suspects
turned out to be American. A former soldier who had won a Bronze Star
during the Persian Gulf War, McVeigh had left the army in 1991 and spent
the next several years drifting around the country. Terry Nichols, a friend
of McVeigh's in the army, seemed to fail at every endeavor he tried.*

*Neither McVeigh nor Nichols testified at their trials, but from evidence
presented to the juries, it appeared that the two men were right-wing radi-
cals with a deep-seated hatred of the federal government. The federal building in Oklahoma was bombed on the second anniversary of the disaster in
Waco, Texas, when seventy-eight members of the Branch Davidians, an
armed religious cult, died in a raging fire that swept through their compound while it was under siege by government agents. Like others with an*

extreme distrust of the federal government, McVeigh and Nichols appar- ently saw the Waco disaster as evidence that the federal government was willing to use whatever force was necessary to suppress those whose views did not follow the mainstream. (Waco disaster, Historic Documents of 1993, p. 293)

Aided by good luck, law enforcement agents had McVeigh and Nichols in custody within two days of the bombing. The quick discovery of a vehicle identification number on a piece of the truck that carried the bomb allowed FBI agents to trace the truck to a Ryder rental agency in Junction City, Kansas. The clerk at the rental agency was able to describe the two men who had rented the truck, and agents soon tracked one of them to a motel where he had used his real name, Timothy McVeigh. Ironically, McVeigh had been arrested in Perry, Oklahoma, about ninety minutes after the bombing. A state trooper stopped McVeigh for driving without a license plate and then arrested him after discovering he had a knife and a loaded semiautomatic handgun. McVeigh was about to be released on bail April 21, when the FBI agents discovered where he was. Nichols surrendered to federal officials later that same day after the FBI declared him to be a suspect. (Oklahoma City bombing, Historic Documents of 1995, p. 176)

McVeigh and Nichols were indicted August 10, 1995, by a federal grand jury in Oklahoma City on eleven counts of conspiring to use a weapon of mass destruction (the 4,000 pound bomb made of ammonium nitrate fer- tilizer and fuel oil), destroying federal property, using a truck bomb to kill people, and murdering eight federal law enforcement officials (who were in their offices in the federal building). In December of that year, a federal appeals court removed U.S. District Judge Wayne Alley from the trial be- cause his office and courtroom were damaged by the bomb and assigned the trial to U.S. Federal Judge Richard P. Matsch of Denver. On February 20, 1996, Matsch moved the trial from Oklahoma City to Denver, saying that it was unlikely either man could get a fair trail in Oklahoma. He later ordered that the two be tried separately to avoid compromising the rights of either in a joint trial.

McVeigh Trial

The first phase of McVeigh's trial began April 24 and ended with his con- viction just five weeks later on June 2. Altogether the prosecution presented 137 witnesses in eighteen days, interspersing dramatic accounts from sur- vivors and families of bombing victims with the drier details linking McVeigh to the bombing through physical evidence. This evidence included findings that the ammonium nitrate found in the Ryder truck was also the same as that found on McVeigh's clothing and in some earplugs he had with him when he was arrested. Prosecutors also presented an array of evi- dence, including receipts, telephone records, and fingerprint evidence to tie McVeigh and Nichols together and both to the bomb. But the most damning evidence against McVeigh may have come from two friends, Lori and Michael J. Fortier, and his sister Jennifer.

Lori Fortier, whose husband, Michael, was McVeigh's roommate in the army and who had been granted immunity for her testimony, said McVeigh had told her in October 1994 that he planned to blow up the Murrah building because "it was an easy target, and it housed some of the [federal agents] involved in the Waco raid." Fortier also testified that she helped McVeigh make a false driver's license in the name of Robert Kling, the same name later used by the man renting the Ryder truck.

By all accounts Jennifer McVeigh was close to her brother and testified with reluctance for the prosecution under grant of immunity. She told of a letter she received from her brother saying that "something big is going to happen" in April or May. He was never more specific, she said, and she did not ask him exactly what he meant. She also told the jurors that McVeigh had given her a computer file labeled "ATF READ," referring to the Bureau of Alcohol, Tobacco and Firearms, a federal agency that had been involved in the Waco raid. The file read, "All you tyrannical [expletive] will swing in the wind one day for your treasonous actions against the Constitution and the United States. . . . Die, you spineless, cowardice bastards."

Michael Fortier told the jury that he had known for months about McVeigh's plans to bomb the Murrah building and had even driven around the building with McVeigh as McVeigh told him of his various scenarios for exploding the bomb. At one point, according to Fortier, McVeigh said "that if he had to, he was going to drive the truck down the stairs and crash it through the front doors." Fortier, who had already pleaded guilty to four charges relating to the bombing plot, said McVeigh wanted to blow up the building "to cause a general uprising" against the federal government. Fortier reported that McVeigh told him he considered all the people in the Murrah building "as if they were storm troopers in the movie Star Wars. *They may be individually innocent, but because they are part of the evil empire they were guilty by association."*

McVeigh's defense was brief—twenty-five witnesses were called in three days. The defense had hoped to divert attention away from McVeigh by suggesting alternative scenarios, including the suggestion that the bombing was the work of a larger conspiracy. But with no firm evidence and operating under tight constraints imposed by the judge, the most the defense could do along the conspiracy line was to suggest that a leg that experts had never been able to identify might in fact have belonged to the real bomber who died in blast. McVeigh's attorneys tried to undermine the testimony of the Fortiers, portraying them as drug users, liars, and opportunists who had changed their stories about McVeigh to escape further prosecution. McVeigh's attorneys sought to cast doubt on the credibility of the FBI's examination of the physical evidence. They called Frederic Whitehurst, a chemist who had prompted an investigation of the FBI's crime lab with allegations that the FBI's procedures for handling evidence were so sloppy and haphazard that the evidence might have been contaminated. On cross-examination, however, Whitehurst conceded that he did not know whether contamination of the evidence in the McVeigh case had occurred. Although

McVeigh's attorneys made much of the prosecution's failure to turn up a witness who had actually seen McVeigh at the Murrah building before the bomb exploded, the defense never offered the jury an alibi for him. (Investigation of FBI crime lab, p. 221)

After the jury reached its guilty verdict June 2, the trial entered the penalty phase, in which the prosecution and the defense offered arguments for and against the death penalty. The jury needed little time to make its decision, handing down a verdict of death on June 13. In interviews with news media after the sentencing, the jurors—seven men and five women—indicated they had little doubt about either McVeigh's guilt or the death sentence. Only one vote was taken on each issue. "It was unanimous from the get-go," James Osgood, the jury foreman, told Newsweek. *McVeigh showed little emotion or remorse throughout his trial, making it harder for his defense to portray him as something other than a calculating killer, and he remained calm when the jury announced June 13 that it had agreed on the death sentence. At his formal sentencing on August 14, McVeigh's only comment was to quote Supreme Court Justice Louis D. Brandeis: "Our government is the hope, the omnipresent teacher, for good or for ill. It teaches people by its example." McVeigh was the fourteenth person sentenced to death since the federal death penalty was reinstated in 1988. No federal prisoner had been executed since 1963. McVeigh would be killed by lethal injection if the appeals he was expected to file did not overturn his conviction. Both McVeigh and Nichols could still stand trial in Oklahoma for the murders of the 160 people who were not included in the federal indictment; that indictment covered only the deaths of eight law enforcement officials who were in the Murrah building on the morning it was bombed.*

The Nichols Trial

At Nichols's trial, which began in October, prosecutors presented much of the same physical and circumstantial evidence that had been used in the McVeigh trial to tie Nichols both to McVeigh and to the bombing. According to the prosecution, Nichols's involvement began when he bought a ton of ammonium nitrate fertilizer on September 30, 1994, under an assumed name. Over the next few months, the prosecution said, Nichols bought or stole more components for making a bomb. To finance their activities, he and McVeigh robbed a gun dealer in Arkansas of about $60,000 worth of guns, coins, and jade; some of that booty was later found in Nichols's home. Moreover, Nichols was lying, prosecutors said, when he denied having seen McVeigh in the days before the bombing. A receipt with both men's fingerprints indicated that they had been together on April 15. In fact, prosecutors said, Nichols helped McVeigh build the bomb in the Ryder truck in a Kansas state park.

But the case against Nichols was not as strong as was the case against McVeigh. He was not in Oklahoma City at the time of the bombing, but at his home in Herington, Kansas. Nor was there any physical evidence linking Nichols directly to the bomb, such as the ammonium nitrate crystals that were found in McVeigh's clothing. Defense attorneys challenged the prosecution's version of events, offering alternative possibilities to explain much of the damaging evidence introduced by the prosecution and undermining the credibility of some of the key witnesses, such as Michael Fortier. The defense acknowledged that Nichols had been involved with McVeigh in the early planning but maintained that had pulled back from the bomb plot and loosened his ties to McVeigh in the months leading up to the bombing. Nichols, the defense said, was trying to "build a life, not a bomb."

The jury apparently agreed with the defense that Nichols was not as culpable as McVeigh. After forty-one hours of deliberations over six days, the jury on December 23 found Nichols guilty of conspiracy to use a weapon of mass destruction (the bomb) and of eight counts of involuntary manslaughter in the deaths of the eight federal law enforcement officials. He was acquitted of the charges of using a weapon of mass destruction, of destroying federal property, and of first- or second-degree murder in connection with the eight law enforcement agents. The jury began its deliberations on a sentence on December 29 but did not complete them before the end of the year.

(On January 7, 1998, jurors in the Nichols trial said they were unable to reach an agreement on a sentence. The judge dismissed the jury and said he would impose sentence. But because federal law stipulated that only a jury could impose the death sentence, the most severe punishment Nichols could receive from the judge was life imprisonment. By press time the judge had not announced his decision.)

Following is the text of the statement made August 14, 1997, by Timothy J. McVeigh upon being sentenced to death for his role in the bombing of the Alfred P. Murrah Federal Building in Oklahoma City:

To use the words of Justice Brandeis—"Our government is the hope, the omnipresent teacher, for good or for ill. It teaches people by its example."

That is all I have, Your Honor.

TEAMSTERS AND UPS OFFICIALS ON END OF STRIKE
August 19, 1997

The most important strike by an American labor union in nearly two decades ended August 19 with a clear victory for the Teamsters union, which represented 185,000 workers at the United Parcel Service (UPS). The Teamsters victory in the fifteen-day strike gave a major psychological boost to the labor movement, which had been on the decline for more than a generation.

Success was short-lived for Teamsters President Ron Carey, however. Just three months later, Carey was forced to step aside as union president because of charges that he diverted union money to his reelection campaign in 1996. Carey had won the Teamsters presidency in 1991 on a pledge to clean up the country's most corrupt labor union. He delivered on many of his promises but, according to federal investigators, resorted to corrupt means to win reelection against James P. Hoffa—son of Jimmy Hoffa, the Teamsters president who for many years was the most visible symbol of labor union corruption in the United States.

A Winning Strategy

The Teamsters strike against UPS was an important one on many fronts. In terms of numbers of workers involved, it was the biggest strike in the United States for more than two decades. Because UPS was the nation's large commercial carrier of parcel packages, the strike had a widespread impact on the economy, affecting tens of thousands of businesses. Finally, the strike came at a time of uncertainty for the labor movement, which in 1997 represented only 15 percent of the work force, less than half its representation during the peak of unionism in the 1950s. Business trends in the 1990s—including corporate "downsizing," the transfer of industrial production jobs to low-wage countries in Asia and Latin America, and a widespread move by business to replace permanent full-time workers with part-time and temporary employees—had combined to make it more difficult for unions to recruit new members.

Other elements conspired to make 1997 a good time for the Teamsters to take on UPS. A strong economy, with low inflation and unemployment, gave UPS employees some confidence that the company needed them and would not be able to replace them quickly with tens of thousands of temporary workers willing to cross a picket line. The Teamsters had begun organizing for a possible strike against UPS months before their contract expired July 31, so their members were prepared for a walkout and its consequences. From the union's point of view, UPS was an inviting target; because its stock was not publicly traded, the company's managers did not face the usual pressure from stockholders to maximize profits at the expense of all other factors, including the needs of workers. Finally, the Teamsters rallied around an issue that won them sympathy among the general public: a demand that the company convert at least 10,000 of its 110,000 part-time jobs to full-time status. Public support on that issue most likely was a factor in the Clinton administration's rejection of an appeal by UPS for a temporary halt to the strike under the Taft-Hartley Act; such an intervention by the White House would have undercut the Teamsters' position.

Teamsters and UPS officials began negotiations toward a new contract on March 11 in Washington, but as the July 31 deadline for an agreement approached, the two sides were still far apart on the key issues. Among those issues were: the Teamsters' demand for creation of 10,000 new full-time jobs over a four-year period; the Teamsters' demand for wage increases totaling $3.60 an hour over four years for part-time workers and $2.60 an hour for full-time workers; UPS's insistence on pulling out of the union's multiemployer pension plan, in favor of a company-controlled plan; the company's desire to increase the amount of work subcontracted to other firms; and the company's desire for a five-year contract, as opposed to the union's push for a three-year contract.

UPS on July 30 presented its "final offer," which the union rejected. The July 31 deadline came and went, but the two sides agreed to continue negotiations under the guidance of John Calhoun Wells, director of the Federal Mediation and Conciliation Service. Those talks produced some movement, but not enough for Carey, who walked out August 3 and called a strike for 12:01 a.m. August 4. Company officials later said the union was intent on a strike all along—a charge union leaders rejected.

The strike caused massive disruptions in delivery services nationwide, especially for small- and medium-size firms that had relied on UPS and had been unable to make contingency arrangements with Federal Express and other commercial carriers. The U.S. Postal Service, which for years had been losing market share to commercial firms, suddenly was swamped with packages marked for "priority" or "express" delivery.

Both UPS and the union insisted they were prepared for a long strike, and for more than a week there was little activity at the bargaining table. Each side launched a public relations campaign, aimed in part at winning enough public support to force the Clinton administration to weigh in on its side. UPS asked its business customers to send letters to President Clin-

ton, demanding that he use his executive powers to halt the strike. The White House received some letters, but public support for the Teamsters, as shown in opinion polls, outweighed the mail.

Clinton intervened on August 11, dispatching Labor Secretary Alexis Herman to meet separately with both sides. Face-to-face negotiations resumed August 14 in Washington, and extended bargaining sessions over the next several days produced new concessions from both the company and the union that made an agreement possible late on August 18. UPS accepted the union's demand for 10,000 new full-time jobs, withdrew its proposal to pull out of the union pension plan, and agreed to phase out its use of subcontracts except for peak holiday periods. In return, the union compromised on its wage demands and accepted a five-year contract.

Carey declared the agreement a union victory that "shows what working people can accomplish when they all stick together." His claim was backed by John J. Sweeney, president of the AFL-CIO, which had supported the Teamsters even though the union did not belong to the federation. The Teamsters' battle with UPS, Sweeney said, "addresses the country's need for jobs. It was a fight over issues that workers all across the country related to: part-time work, outsourcing, protecting pensions, and health insurance. It was a wake-up call to employers who want to downsize and continue doing all these negative things."

UPS officials rejected the Teamsters' characterization of the settlement as total union victory. They noted that the company won five years of labor peace, and they pointed to clauses in the contract under which the union agreed to give the company more control over job assignments and work rules. The contract also allowed the company to back out of its pledge for 10,000 new full-time jobs if UPS sales volume declined.

Many outside experts on the labor movement said that the Teamsters' success did not necessarily mean that other unions could win similar victories against other companies. Experts noted that UPS was more willing than many other firms to make concessions to buy labor peace, and that the Teamsters had developed an extraordinarily well-organized approach to its negotiations. Some observers said other labor-intensive firms might also offer their workers concessions on wages and other issues in hopes of pre-empting union demands.

Carey Ousted

Carey had only a short while to savor his triumph. Even as the strike was underway, federal investigators were continuing a probe of charges that three Carey aides had diverted an estimated $735,000 from the union treasury to support his reelection battle against Hoffa in 1996. Shortly after the strike settlement, Barbara Zack Quindel, a federal monitor, cited illegal donations in declaring the 1996 Teamsters election invalid and ordering a rerun. Quindel later was forced to recuse herself because of reports that the Teamsters had donated to a political organization in which her husband was involved.

On November 17 another federal court-appointed union monitor, former U.S. District Court judge Kenneth Conboy, reported that Carey himself had been involved in the illegal campaign financing scheme. Conboy disqualified Carey from seeking reelection in the rerun ordered by Quindel. Conboy also implicated senior officials of other labor organizations in the Teamsters' election financing arrangement, including AFL-CIO Secretary-Treasurer Richard Trumka, and Gerald McEntee, president of the American Federation of State, County, and Municipal Employees.

Carey vigorously denied that he had been involved in illegal fund raising. But a week later, on November 25, he announced that he was stepping aside as union president indefinitely "in the best interest of the membership and the [Teamsters] reform movement." Carey acted just hours before a federal oversight panel, the Independent Review Board, formally accused him of diverting union funds to his election. Carey and the Teamsters also were facing an investigation into the 1996 union election by a federal grand jury in New York City.

Following are excerpts from two news conferences, by Ron Carey, president of the Teamsters, and James Kelly, UPS chief executive officer, held August 19, 1997, announcing an agreement between the Teamsters Union and the United Parcel Service:

STATEMENT BY TEAMSTERS PRESIDENT

Good afternoon. As you know, many events around the country have been planned for the Action Day for Good Jobs. And most of those locations in most areas, those events will continue, but with a little different focus. People will be celebrating our victory over corporate greed.

What's more than that, people will be showing their support for other workers, for standing up for the great American Dream. Non-union workers will be talking about how this victory as it inspires them to fight for the future, just as UPS workers did.

It's no accident that workers from FedEx walked the picket lines with us, with many UPS strikers in places like Indianapolis, New York, Philadelphia. The FedEx workers know our plight is there plight.

If your company comes to you and says they want to ship your job to part-time, temporary or sub-contract it to low-wage firms overseas, you have to be organized. You have to have leverage in order to do something about it.

UPS was subcontracting work, which meant that workers who made the company a success were losing opportunities for promotions to better jobs.

But because UPS workers are organized, we stop that subcontracting. And we made sure that as UPS grows, so do the jobs grow. At companies like FedEx, Continental Airlines, subcontracting is a serious problem.

And that's why nearly 5,000 Continental mechanics voted last month to become Teamsters. And that's why FedEx workers are organizing as well.

Before the FedEx workers started organizing to become Teamsters, the company said to them there would never be another general wage increase, only performance bonuses.

But after we got involved in the organizing and it started to click together, FedEx suddenly announced a wage increase. The same thing happened at Overnight, one of the largest non-union trucking companies in this country, where more than 3,000 workers have organized to become Teamsters.

Some of you may have seen this article in this morning's *New York Times*. It is about our efforts on the apple campaign. It tells about the largest union organizing drive in the nation, our drive to organize 15,000 Apple warehouse workers in Washington State. As the headlines says, we are coordinating the drive with the United Farm Workers Union, who are organizing the orchard workers as well.

A new commitment, new approaches to organizing have stopped our union's decline that had been going on in 16 years.

This fight with UPS shows what working people can accomplish when they all stick together. The UPS workers stood up to throw-away worker approach and the nation's working people stood behind us.

And now we're going to go out there to other workers who want to fight for that great American dream. In a few weeks Congress will decide whether to give the president fast track authority to expand the NAFTA trade deal to other countries. It's all the same fight, because what NAFTA really does is help corporations subcontract, not just to other countries, but to other companies as well.

It's all a part of the same throw-away worker concept. Throw away the jobs of American workers, exploit workers in countries like Mexico for $4 a day, and then if they start to get organized, move from one place to another. It's got to stop, and stopping fast track will be the kind of thing we need to do, and the things in terms of unity for working people that they have showed during the past two weeks.

And now I'll be happy to answer any questions that you may have, or of Ken Hall.

Question: Ron, would you mention three to four factors you think are the most important in achieving what you and labor regards as victory?

Carey: The creation of good full time jobs, bringing up the wage rates, increasing the pension programs, ending the subcontracting—those were the areas that were vital and those were the areas that were of deep concern.

Question: Also what were the factors that enabled you to win that victory?

Carey: They were out there in the street. That's what it was all about. You can sit at the table with 10 or 20 people. You can sit there for two or three weeks, but what gets the job done is the unity that's on the picket line, the membership, their involvement, getting out into the community, talking to the customers, building the kind of support and leverage that we need so we can get that job done at the bargaining table. . . .

Question: Mr. Kelly said that this isn't a victory for anyone. The company lost money. The strikers were out for 2 1/2 weeks, and then they're going to lose business in the future and have to cut back.

Carey: First, we are the folks that—I was a package car driver, and I can tell you that I can influence that customer when I go there. If I have a pleasing personality—and most of our members are very loyal to this company. If I get in there, I can work that customer. I can make sure that that air package goes out UPS as opposed to FedEx, which is non-union.

So I have a lot of influence. That work will come back.

Now I guess if I was in Mr. Kelly's shoes, I would be saying what he is saying.

And that is that there was no victory on either side.

You folks saw the August 2nd union proposal. That was before the strike. You have now, or will see—and I've explained a good portion of it to you— what we have achieved as a result of our membership, as a result of the communities, as a result of people all over this country reassuring us. There is a vast difference between Mr. Kelly's proposal and between our August 2nd proposal which we won. . . .

Question: Mr. Carey, as you look at the—we've seen union membership across a lot of America workers who are afraid to strike, partly because unemployment isn't as secure as it used to be.

What would you say to the workers who may face a situation that is similar to that of the Teamsters, but just don't have the guts to go on strike to get what they want?

Carey: Well, first, you have to be organized. You have to have something that brings you together. When you all organize, you have—you then create the leverage you need.

You've got to get involved. You can't let George do it. That's the problem in this country. Working people depend upon other people doing the job. They've all got to get involved.

What we saw on the picket lines, the carriages and children, and our folks going out there talking in the community, that's what it takes. It takes commitment. It takes hard work.

But that message is getting through. Part-time America just won't work. . . .

Question: . . . What I'm really trying to ask is, is your victory going to have essentially a negative effect. Is it going to create a tighter labor market. Is it going to be harder to get a job because wages go up, and therefore, businesses or employers wouldn't want to pay those wages and not hire those people?

Carey: I think what it does is it gets to heart of the corporate greed. It gets money out of there. That's what this is all about. It is about making sure that working people have decent jobs. If that reflects upon the bonuses, the CEO compensation and the rest, it ought to, it ought to.

That's one of the problems in this country—the separation between people who work for a living. And the millionaires, I think, are turning over every single day—I don't know what the numbers are—I think that's wrong. I don't think workers today, that big companies look at workers today, they don't think about loyalty, dedication, hard work. Today, you're just a number.

They don't think about whether or not they'll be money down the road to purchase their goods. You cannot do it on part-time wages.

STATEMENT BY UPS SPOKESMAN

Good morning. I am relieved that after two difficult weeks, we have something positive to talk about this morning and to look forward to. As you know, we have agreed upon a tentative proposal last night with the Teamsters Union.

We are comfortable that this contract will allow UPS to remain competitive. It represents the first ever five-year contract signed with the union, and it stays with the financial parameters we set prior to the negotiations.

There's been a lot of hype these last few weeks about different issues. I can assure you there was no one single issue that was more important than the dozens of others issues that existed during these negotiations.

The bottom line is that we have a contract that is good for our people, gets us back in business, and will keep us competitive in the coming years. Of course, we regret the disruption and the pain this unnecessary strikes has caused our people and our customers. We firmly believe that this agreement in its present form could have been achieved without a strike. But it's now time to look ahead together.

We turn our attention to the task of winning back the confidence of our customers and of our business. I know that all of us at UPS are looking forward to getting back to work, rolling up our sleeves, and continuing the great tradition of service that has defined UPS for the last 90 years. . . .

Question: Sir, given the inconvenience to your customers, given the strong impact on American business that this strike has had, given the high losses to your company, which you described to us as being something in excess of $600 million, and given the fact that the Teamsters seem to have gotten exactly what they wanted, what was the point of the exercise. Why didn't you just agree with them?

Kelly: I don't know if the Teamsters got everything they wanted. We certainly have achieved the contract that we think is well within the parameters allowing us to be competitive. It is a five-year agreement. It's a fair one for our people. There were dozens of issues, and there was compromise on both sides on all of those dozens of issues. . . .

Question: Can you tell us specifically, what did you get that you wouldn't have gotten 15 days ago. Where did they concede on certain issues?

Kelly: Well, there was concessions on—certainly on all the monetary and economic issues, on all the work rule issues. We were oceans apart 15 days ago, because virtually very little, if any, negotiations actually occurred prior to the strike. So we were very far apart on all of the issues and resolved it in the last few weeks. . . .

Question: Last week, you said that you could lose as many as 15,500 employees had the strike ended last week. Can you tell us how much this strike has hurt the company, and how many employees will not have their jobs back once the details are worked out?

Kelly: Well, it's hurt us a great deal. You know, the strike doesn't help anyone. It's hurt us, it's our employees, and it's hurt our customers. And we have lost business. We've had customers that tell us they will not be back. We're going to work as hard as we can to get every customers back and every packages back, and provide all the jobs that we had. But the reality is that they're not all coming back, and we will have fewer jobs. . . .

Question: Ron Carey has already declared this a victory for the union and for working families in America. Is it?

Kelly: This wasn't about working families in America. This was about UPS employees, and I don't know what broader agenda the Teamster Union had regarding working families in America. But we have provided great full-time and part-time jobs at the United Parcel Service, and we improved them. we improved them to the extent that we anticipated we have to improve them going into these negotiations. It is about a three percent improvement for our full-time employees and something greater than that for our part-time employees in terms of wage increases. . . .

Question: Don't you think there were some landmark issues here that would really set a precedent for labor relations and negotiations?

Kelly: No, I don't, no. I mean, we've always had great part-time jobs, and we continue to. The temporary jobs they were talking about, the low-paying jobs without benefits never existed at UPS, OK, and don't continue to exist at UPS. The pension issue is something we've been doing for 40 or 50 years. We think it should have been change. We weren't able to change it. But are those watershed issues that are going to change the history of labor relations? I don't believe so, no.

Question: The part-time job issues certainly seemed to strike a chord with some of the American public. A lot of people were astounded that you would have 10-year workers here who are still part-time. Does that bother that you have people working that long, that reliably, who are still considered part-time?

Kelly: Again, the overwhelming majority of our part-time folks want to work part-time. Almost half of them are students, and a great deal more want to work part-time. Those who want full-time jobs—there were 13,000 opportunities for them to do that in the last agreement. We created 8,000 full-time jobs during in the last agreement. UPS is one of the few places that has been growing jobs and creating jobs, rather than out-sourcing down-sizing. We're very proud of the opportunities we've created for our part-time people, and I hope we can get a whole lot of business back and create a whole lot more opportunities for those people.

September

U.S. STATE DEPARTMENT ON CAMBODIAN COUP
September 4, 1997

An attempt by the international community to bring democracy to the troubled country of Cambodia came to an end in 1997. Hun Sen, the leader of one of two factions that had jointly governed Cambodia since 1993, forced his coalition partner out of power in July and took total control of the government. The ousted leader, Prince Norodom Ranariddh, fled the country and was forced to watch the destruction of his political party from afar.

The collapse of Cambodia's fragile democracy represented a serious setback for the United Nations. The UN in 1991 had negotiated a settlement of the country's long-running civil war and then in 1993 had financed and managed the first contested elections in Cambodian history.

United States policy and prestige also were at stake; Washington had been the principal broker of the 1991 peace agreement and was a major source of foreign aid for Cambodia's struggling economy. The Clinton administration found itself conflicted by the year's developments. On the one hand, the administration had no choice but to curtail foreign aid and take other diplomatic steps to oppose Hun Sen's strong-arm tactics. At the same time, the administration recognized that there was little chance of restoring what had proven to be an unworkable coalition.

An Alliance Collapses

The ill-fated coalition between Hun Sen and Prince Ranariddh was a result of the UN-supervised elections in 1993. Ranariddh, whose royalist political party went by the French acronym FUNCINPEC, narrowly won the elections. But Hun Sen, who had been the country's de facto leader for several years in a variety of alliances, refused to accept the results. Faced with a potential stalemate, the United Nations bowed to Hun Sen's demands and agreed to a power-sharing arrangement with Prince Ranariddh as first prime minister and Hun Sen as second prime minister.

The two leaders cooperated for a brief period but soon allowed their bitter rivalry to interfere with the process of running the country. By early

1997, according to U.S. officials, the two Cambodian leaders were no longer speaking to each other, and their government had become paralyzed. The military was split into two factions, each loyal to one of the leaders, and each leader had recruited an independent paramilitary force of heavily armed "bodyguards."

On March 30 nineteen people were killed in a grenade attack on a political rally in Phnom Penh. The rally was led by an ally of Ranariddh's, and most observers held forces loyal to Hun Sen responsible for the attack. Relations between the two prime ministers deteriorated further in May, when Ranariddh moved to gain support from factions of the Khmer Rouge, the communist guerrilla force that had brutally ruled Cambodia in the late 1970s before being ousted in an invasion by Vietnam. Hun Sen, who had been a mid-level functionary in the Khmer Rouge regime, angrily denounced Ranariddh's courting of his one-time allies.

Tension between the two Cambodian factions erupted into a furious battle in the streets of Phnom Penh for several hours late on June 17. On July 4 Ranariddh flew to France, where he had a summer home. At the time, he said he was taking a vacation. He later said he had fled when aides told him Hun Sen's forces were trying to capture and possibly assassinate him.

The next day, July 5, Hun Sen's bodyguards attacked forces loyal to Ranariddh, setting off a two-day battle that ended only when the Hun Sen forces occupied Ranariddh's compound. More than fifty people died in the fighting. In the days after the battle, Hun Sen's forces rounded up many Ranariddh allies and effectively dismantled his political party. A UN team sent to investigate the situation reported in September that the Hun Sen paramilitary had executed more than forty military officers and others loyal to Ranariddh.

International Reaction

The disintegration of the political situation in Cambodia had been obvious for some time, but the outbreak of violence and retribution in July caught many observers by surprise and presented the international community with difficult choices. The United States, considered by many the key foreign power in Cambodia, hesitated for several days and then denounced the actions of Hun Sen and those loyal to him. The Clinton administration declared "completely unacceptable" Hun Sen's declarations that Ranariddh was no longer first prime minister and that the international community should stay out of Cambodian affairs. The administration also suspended about $25 million in U.S. aid to the Cambodian government (although it maintained aid to nongovernment organizations) and organized a similar suspension by the World Bank and International Monetary Fund.

The UN General Assembly in September declared Cambodia's seat vacant, and the Association of Southeast Asian Nations withdrew a membership invitation to Cambodia. Despite these moves, most countries with influence in Cambodia seemed prepared to accept Hun Sen's coup as a fait accompli. Some foreign aid donors, including Japan, rebuffed Washing-

ton's suggestion that they cut off their aid programs to Cambodia. France, the former colonial power in Phnom Penh, announced in September that it would not interfere in Cambodian affairs—a position that effectively gave France's blessing to the coup.

One explanation for the lack of international hand-wringing was that most observers held both Hun Sen and Ranariddh, as well as those aligned with them, responsible for the Cambodian dispute. The New York Times *in July quoted a European diplomat in Phnom Penh as saying: "You have to ask the question: Did either of them really care about the people as they proceeded with their grandstanding and sniping at each other and jostling for position?"*

As the end of 1997 approached, international diplomats placed their emphasis on a demand that Hun Sen allow free and fair elections in May 1998, as required by the constitution. Hoping to contest those elections, Ranariddh formed an alliance with two other parties, but it was uncertain whether he could safely return to Cambodia and even more uncertain whether Hun Sen would allow his one-time coalition partner to contest him in a free election.

Following are excerpts from testimony September 4, 1997, by Stanley O. Roth, assistant secretary of state for East Asian and Pacific Affairs to the Senate Foreign Relations Subcommittee on East Asian and Pacific Affairs:

Mr. Chairman, thank you and the other members of the Committee for the opportunity to review with you the situation in Cambodia and the Administration's response to the seizure of power by Hun Sen. I welcome this opportunity to share with you the Administration's assessment of the challenges that lie ahead, and to consult with the Committee about some of the difficult questions before us, including future disbursements of U.S. assistance.

I would like to commend the strong messages conveyed by the Congress about the events of July 5–6, messages which have sent an important signal to all key players in Cambodia that the Congress and the Executive Branch are united in their determination not to return to business as usual in Cambodia without a restoration of the Paris Peace Accords framework.

Mr. Chairman, like you and your colleagues in the Congress, the Administration was appalled by the political violence and extra-constitutional action against First Prime Minister Ranariddh on July 5–6—actions we condemned swiftly and vigorously. The Administration firmly opposes Hun Sen's overturning the results of the 1993 elections conducted by the United Nations with extensive contributions from the international community. Those elections were won by FUNCINPEC. That was true before July 5, and it remains true today. Until there is a restoration of the Paris Peace Accords, and free and fair elections are held, the United States will not conduct business as usual with Hun Sen.

From the beginning of this crisis, the core principles guiding our policy have remained constant:

1. The violence that overturned the results of the 1993 elections is unacceptable; fighting must stop immediately.
2. All political parties, including FUNCINPEC, must be allowed to operate freely in Cambodia.
3. There must be free and fair elections in 1998.
4. There should be no political role for the leaders of the Khmer Rouge; those responsible for crimes against humanity should be brought to justice.
5. The framework of the 1991 Paris Accords on Cambodia, which paved the way for UN-conducted elections in 1993, must be reinstated.

The Administration has focused its energies on answering the central question of how we and the international community can achieve genuine implementation of these core principles. Our strategy is based on strong support for ASEAN's Cambodia initiative as Secretary Albright emphasized during the July ASEAN meetings. In support of this initiative, the Secretary dispatched two Special Envoys, Stephen Solarz and Desaix Anderson, to begin the process of engaging all the Cambodian parties including King Sihanouk, our ASEAN partners and others in the region in an effort to identify common ground for an eventual negotiated settlement of Cambodia's crisis.

In addition, the Administration has consulted closely with signatories of the Paris Peace Accords, donor nations and prospective members of a "Friends of Cambodia" group, which the Secretary proposed in July to support ASEAN diplomatic efforts. A summary of these and additional actions is detailed in an attachment to my testimony for the record.

As a result of all this diplomatic activity, there is an emerging consensus, in principle, both among the parties in Cambodia and among key outside players, that the following elements would help to create confidence in the electoral process:

- Cessation by all parties of the use of force to resolve disputes;
- Renunciation of support for and links to the Khmer Rouge;
- Cessation of acts of political intimidation within Cambodia;
- Guaranteed freedom of the media;
- Establishment of an independent judiciary;
- Return and guaranteed safety of exiled political parties and personalities;
- Depoliticization of the military, which could include separating the military from political parties, the possible cantonment of certain units during elections, abolishing the rural militia prior to elections and confiscating their weapons.

With respect to the conduct of the elections themselves, our envoys have identified a number of specific steps that could be taken to create the basis for free and fair elections in 1998 including:

- Passage of election and political party laws;
- Establishment of the constitutional and magistracy councils;
- Establishment of the independent election commission;
- Timely registration of voters;
- Freedom for all political parties and personalities to conduct campaigns for elections; and,
- Invitation to international observers, ensuring adequate independent observation.

Challenges Ahead: ASEAN's Initiative and Next Steps

Frankly, implementing all of the steps I have just enunciated will be difficult. There is a great deal of uncertainty over whether it will be possible to create the conditions for a free and fair election as early as May 1998. The climate of intimidation and fear ushered in by the events of July 5–6 continues to exist in Phnom Penh and throughout the country. We know this from our own embassy and from concerned NGOs [nongovernmental organizations] such as Human Rights Watch, IRI and NDI. The U.S. government joins with those voices in urging that a full accounting of all those killed, arrested or missing be provided by the Cambodian government. The Administration remains disturbed and concerned by reports, some detailed by the Human Rights Watch, of continued killings and intimidation of FUNCINPEC officials. Administration officials have raised these concerns repeatedly with top Cambodian officials, most recently this week, and we will continue to do so.

As I have indicated earlier in my testimony, the Administration's strategy for implementing the goals which we share with the Congress—restoring the principles of the Paris Peace Accords and creating the conditions for free and fair elections in 1998—is closely tied to ASEAN's initiative. It is important to highlight the positive and unprecedented high-profile engagement of ASEAN in helping to restore political stability to Cambodia.

For example, despite the hopes ASEAN had for moving toward an "Southeast Asia Ten" with the planned admission of Cambodia (along with Burma and Laos) in July, the ASEAN Foreign Ministers took the difficult step of putting off Cambodia's entry in response to Hun Sen's actions on July 5–6. We continue to believe that the leverage of eventual membership in ASEAN is a powerful incentive for restoration of political stability in Cambodia.

The Administration strongly supports ASEAN's decision—reflected in its statement on August 11—to remain engaged in Cambodia. The Administration issued a strong public statement of support the following day and encouraged other nations to do so as well. The ASEAN Ministers' statement stressed the importance of holding free and fair elections in Cambodia as scheduled in May 1998 and reaffirmed the necessity for all political parties in Cambodia to participate fully in the elections.

We have made clear that a climate free of fear for personal safety and fear of political intimidation is a critical component of democratic elections. Exiled parliamentarians, ideally including Prince Ranariddh, should be allowed to return to Cambodia safely and participate freely in the upcoming electoral campaign. It is hard to imagine a free and fair election taking place without open participation.

Exiled opposition politicians rightly demand concrete steps by the Cambodian government to guarantee their safety and security so that they can return to participate in the elections. The Administration fully supports this basic position. We repeatedly have urged the Cambodian government to restore security in order to permit the safe return of the exiled opposition leaders. As one concrete step to help achieve this objective, the Administration is now exploring ways to strengthen the capability of the UN Center for Human Rights in Phnom Penh to assist in this area. The Administration believes that the Center's staff should be increased to enable it to monitor security guarantees and promote a return to a climate of political confidence and security in the period leading up to the elections.

What More Can We Do?

In further support of ASEAN's efforts to negotiate an overall political settlement, Secretary Albright has taken the lead in proposing the establishment of a "Friends of Cambodia" group bringing together a wide range of interested countries, including but not limited to aid donors. Efforts are underway now to prepare for consultations between ASEAN and the Friends of Cambodia both before and during the upcoming UNGA sessions.

During these meetings, the Administration hopes to reach a common view on both the political elements and technical steps needed to create a free and fair electoral process in Cambodia. An important issue for discussion is the extent to which international aid in support of Cambodia's elections preparations should be provided. International aid for elections preparations provides considerable leverage for the international community to press the Cambodian government to permit genuinely free and fair elections.

In addition to action by ASEAN and the Friends of Cambodia, there are several other important developments that hopefully will contribute to a political resolution of the conflict. In particular, King Sihanouk has returned to Cambodia and has offered to mediate talks as he explores ways to help restore political stability to his country. While it remains to be seen if the King's initiative will be embraced by the parties and lead to actual negotiations, it is certainly a welcome step. I will be discussing the King's role in the current situation in some detail, when I travel to Indonesia, the Philippines and Japan later this week, to see how his efforts can be coordinated with ASEAN and with the Friends of Cambodia.

It is also worth noting that China has issued positive statements in support of Cambodian elections and the Paris Peace Accords framework, and Vietnam has joined in the ASEAN initiative to mediate a settlement. The U.S. encourages positive engagement of this kind from the many nations that share a stake in Cambodian stability, whether because of geographic proximity or by virtue of their support for the Paris Accords and UNTAC [UN Transitional Authority in Cambodia].

U.S. Assistance Policy

The Administration has stopped all direct assistance to the Cambodian government. We continue to provide humanitarian assistance and are providing human rights and limited amounts of democracy assistance through Cambodian NGOs. Based on our FY 97 obligations, our total assistance for Cambodia remains cut by two-thirds from what it was before the events of July 5–6. There may be some adjustments for obligated funds currently in the pipeline, and the Administration will consult closely with the Congress on any changes in our overall assistance levels.

The Administration is mindful that in our policy approach we must do our utmost to ensure that the Cambodian people do not pay the price for the acts of their government leaders. Our decision to suspend aid to the Royal Cambodian Government explicitly permits continued support to Cambodian NGOs engaged in humanitarian and democracy building programs. While most of our pre-July 5 aid remains suspended, important work in support of Cambodian civil society has not ceased. Humanitarian programs—such as Doctors Without Borders and several others in support of child health care, basic rural health services, aid for war and mine victims, and rule of law—continue as well.

We believe it is important at this time to maintain our suspension of assistance that benefits directly the Cambodian government. At the same time, we have made every effort to maintain key humanitarian programs that benefit directly the Cambodian people.

We will apply the same policy principle in voting for any loans by international financial institutions for Cambodia. We will not support any loans, for example, for large infrastructure projects, the benefits of which flow primarily to the Cambodian government. We will also urge other major donors to adopt a similar approach.

In the context of our support for the ASEAN initiative, we will be looking carefully at the possibility of providing election assistance above and beyond the modest programs currently in place. Carefully calibrated technical assistance can be an important confidence-building mechanism as Cambodia prepares for free and fair elections. We do not intend, however, to provide support for an undemocratic process.

Actions to Protect Amcits and Cambodians

The protection of American citizens is our first priority in situations of crisis. Our embassies also stand ready to assist individuals—in this case, Cambodians—who find themselves at risk in such crises. The Administration was very concerned, therefore, about allegations that the embassy in Phnom Penh had not taken these responsibilities seriously. We have looked into these allegations carefully. So far, they appear to be unfounded.

To date, all of the evidence we have clearly shows that Ambassador Quinn and his embassy officers took quick and decisive action to safeguard the lives of U.S. citizens and to provide assistance to all Cambodians who requested our help. Under difficult and dangerous conditions, our embassy helped over 600 American citizens leave the country and then proceeded with an ordered drawdown of its own staff. The Ambassador and his staff personally provided safe escort to numerous Cambodians seeking to leave the country. The summary of U.S. government actions attached to this statement includes details of measures taken by the Ambassador personally and by his embassy to assure the safety of Cambodians who asked for help.

To date, the Administration has not received any information which corroborates specific allegations that the embassy turned away individuals seeking safehaven. Throughout the violence, beginning on the evening of July 5 and for ten days thereafter, the State Department monitored events in Cambodia on a 24-hour basis through a special task force that kept in constant telephone contact with the embassy. There was never any mention of turning Cambodians away; to the contrary, the embassy kept us informed of their energetic efforts to help.

Our embassy immediately set up a command center and safehaven at the Cambodiana Hotel, which was accessible and afforded more protection than the embassy compound itself which was cut off by roadblocks and violence. All those seeking the embassy's help received it, either at the compound or at the Cambodiana. On several occasions, the Ambassador ventured out into the city at great personal risk in search of fearful FUNCINPEC members, and made high-level representations to the government authorities on their behalf. To the best of my knowledge, no one who sought the embassy's help—American or Cambodian—suffered any harm.

The State Department has tried to track down the sources of the allegations against the embassy. In one case, an opposition politician who left the country on his own and came to the United States on special parole with our help was quoted as saying that the embassy in Phnom Penh had failed to help him. When this individual, who is safe, was subsequently asked whether he had made such statements, he acknowledged to us that he had never asked the U.S. Embassy for assistance.

Ambassador Quinn will be available to brief Members in more detail when he returns to Washington later this month. In the meantime, the State Department will continue to work with the Committee to clarify any additional questions that Committee members may have on this subject.

Conclusion

We have initiated a robust approach that signals to Hun Sen, in our direct contacts with him and through our friends in the region, that he has destroyed the framework of the international settlement we all agreed to in Paris six years ago. Until that framework is restored, we will not agree to business as usual with Cambodia. We will maintain pressure in the coming months to obtain assurances that exiles can return, election preparations can go forward, and free and fair elections can take place.

I leave tomorrow for a number of countries in Asia, where I will discuss these objectives and a common strategy with these countries. Cambodian issues will also be a major topic during our meetings at the UN General Assembly. The entire international community has a stake in Cambodia, and we intend to do our best to reach a satisfactory outcome.

STATEMENTS ON THE DEATH OF DIANA, PRINCESS OF WALES
September 5 and 6, 1997

Diana, Princess of Wales, the divorced wife of the heir to the British throne and one of the most recognized figures in the world, died August 31 in an early morning car crash in Paris. She was thirty-six years old. The accident also claimed the life of her lover, Emad "Dodi" Fayed, and the car's driver. A fourth person, Trevor Rees-Jones, a bodyguard, survived the crash but was unable to remember anything about the accident for several months. Initial reports suggested that the crash had been caused by "paparazzi" chasing the car on motorcycles to get photographs of the princess and Fayed. Several of the photographers were arrested after the accident. It later was found that the driver, Henri Paul, an employee of Fayed's father, had three times the legal limit of alcohol in his blood.

The news of Diana's death, which was confirmed at about 4:30 a.m., stunned millions in Great Britain and elsewhere who had been fascinated by the princess since her fairy-tale wedding to Prince Charles in August 1981. In an early morning statement, British prime minister Tony Blair said he was "utterly devastated. . . . The whole of our country, all of us, will be in state of shock and mourning." Prince Charles and his mother, Queen Elizabeth, were informed of the deaths at Balmoral Castle in Scotland where they were vacationing. Charles reportedly told his two sons, William, fifteen, and Harry, twelve, of their mother's death before flying to Paris with Diana's sisters to accompany her body back to London. Charles then returned to Balmoral Castle, where the family remained secluded.

If anything, Blair's remarks might have been an understatement. British citizens began bringing flowers to Kensington Palace, Diana's principal residence, within an hour after her death was announced. By the time of her funeral on Saturday, September 6, layers of flower bouquets filled the open spaces outside London's three main royal palaces, the Place de l'Alma near the site of the accident in Paris, and outside British embassies throughout the world. During the week newspapers and airwaves were filled with details of Diana's life and death. So pervasive were the stories about Diana that the death on September 5 of Mother Theresa, the nun and Nobel Peace laureate best known for her work with the poor in Calcutta, received limited coverage.

Grief was tempered by anger at the press and particularly the paparazzi, who had never seemed to let Diana out of the sight of their lenses. One of those expressing such anger was Diana's younger brother, Earl Spencer. "I always believed that the press would kill her in the end," he said from his Cape Town, South Africa, home after being told about the accident. But, he said, "not even I could imagine that they would take such a direct hand in the death, as seems to be the case."

As the week wore on, the British public and press also began to express their anger with the royal family, charging that by its silence it was dishonoring Diana and showing its insensitivity to the outpouring of public grief. Stung by those criticisms, Queen Elizabeth made an unprecedented personal statement in a rare television address, in which she said she "admired and respected" her former daughter-in law.

A Fairy Tale Turned Soap Opera

When she married Prince Charles, twelve years her senior, on July 29, 1981, Lady Diana Frances Spencer was living the dream of many young girls. The "wedding of the century" was quickly followed by the birth of two sons—"the heir and the spare"—in 1982 and 1984. For the first few years of their marriage Charles and Diana offered an admiring public a picture of a happy royal family. Tensions between the two mounted, however, exacerbated by infidelities; Charles apparently resumed his prewedding affair with Camilla Parker Bowles, while Diana engaged in an affair with a cavalry officer who later publicized the romance in a "kiss and tell" book. By 1989 the couple had separated, a situation that was formalized in 1992. (Royal family problems, Historic Documents of 1992, p. 1059)

In the next few years Charles and Diana traded public accusations about each other that embarrassed both of them and the royal family. Charles admitted in a television interview that he had been unfaithful and in an authorized biography said that he had never loved Diana and was pressured into the marriage by his father, Prince Philip. Friends of the prince portrayed Diana as mentally unstable, pointing to her admitted bouts with bulimia and flirtations with suicide. In response, Diana questioned whether Charles was fit to be king. At that point the marriage seemed irretrievable, and the pair began negotiations over a divorce, which was finalized in August 1996. Under its terms, Diana and Charles shared custody of their sons and she received a $26 million lump sum payment, as well an annual payments of $600,000 to maintain her office staff and residence in Kensington Palace. Diana could no longer be called "Her Royal Highness," although she retained her title as Princess of Wales.

The Princess and the Camera

Throughout this public break-up, Diana remained the darling of the public and the media. The most photographed woman in the world, she exhibited a naturalness on camera that drew people to her. Diana welcomed the cameras when the coverage focused public attention on the charitable causes she championed—the homeless, AIDS patients, cancer-stricken children, and land mine victims. She was skillful in using the press to gain public sympathy in her battles with her husband and his family. Diana was depicted as the beautiful young mother of two, familiar with the world of privilege but also in touch with a world where people suffered illness and poverty. In contrast, the royal family often appeared remote, out of touch, and unfeeling.

At the same time, Diana often criticized the press, and particularly the aggressive paparazzi, for constantly invading her privacy. She complained that the British press had "an obsessive interest in me and the children." Not long before her death, she told the Paris paper Le Monde that the pressure was so great that "any sane person would have left [England] long ago. But I cannot. I have my sons."

In the last months of her life, Diana spent more and more time with Fayed, the playboy son of Mohamed Al Fayed, a wealthy Egyptian who owned Harrods in London and the Ritz Hotel in Paris, among other things. Speculation about Diana and Dodi ran rampant in the tabloids, accompanied by photographs of the couple from several vacation spots in the Mediterranean. Photographers used boats, even helicopters to get near enough to shoot pictures of the two. On Friday, August 30, the two returned to Paris from Sardinia in a private jet and eventually had dinner in a private suite at the Ritz. Paparazzi attended their every public move and were waiting for them as they left the hotel a little after midnight.

Accident in a Paris Tunnel

The crash occurred in an expressway tunnel under the Place de l'Alma on the right bank of the Seine. Fayed and Paul, the chauffeur, were killed immediately. Diana was reportedly still conscious when emergency doctors reached the scene within five minutes of the accident, but her heart stopped beating in the ambulance, and doctors were unable to save her.

Initially the police and others blamed the motorcycle photographers who, they said, recklessly chased the car into the tunnel at speeds as high as 90 miles an hour, when the driver lost control. Subsequent blood tests revealed that Paul had been legally drunk, with enough alcohol in his bloodstream to seriously impair his driving ability. Police were also looking for a white Fiat that they said may have been in front of the Mercedes and moving at a much slower speed. Piecing together witness accounts and physical evidence, the police speculated that Paul braked to avoid the Fiat, then sped up to pass it, possibly sideswiping it, before losing control and crashing in to the tunnel's median pillars. By year's end, however, the car had not been found, nor had Rees-Jones, the bodyguard, been able to remember any of the details of the accident. It appeared possible that no one would ever know precisely what happened.

A Nation Bereft

Accusations and anger directed at the paparazzi and the driver were overwhelmed by the public mourning that steadily mounted for the "people's princess," as Prime Minister Blair had called her. The royal family re-

turned to London September 5, where they greeted mourners outside Buckingham Palace. Later in the day Queen Elizabeth in an extraordinary television appearance sought to soften the image of an uncaring royal family. The queen said it was "not easy to express a sense of loss" and that the family had spent the week "trying to help William and Harry to come to terms with devastating loss that they and the rest of us have suffered." Saying that she was speaking from her heart, the queen went on to praise Diana as "an exceptional and gifted human being" whom she "admired and respected," particularly for her devotion to her sons. "In good times and bad," the queen said, pointedly referring to the bitter rift between Diana and the royal family, Diana "never lost her capacity to smile and laugh, nor to inspire others with her warmth and kindness."

On the morning of the funeral, more than a million people thronged the streets of central London, the largest gathering of people in that city since the end of World War II. The crowd was almost eerily silent as Diana's coffin proceeded on a horse-drawn gun carriage from Kensington Palace to St. James Palace. There Diana's sons; their father, Prince Charles; grandfather, Prince Philip; and her brother, the Earl Spencer, joined the procession, walking behind the casket, for the last mile to Westminster Abbey. Like much else that attended the week's events, the funeral ceremony did not follow royal tradition although it had many of the royal trappings. Diana's sisters gave readings, Blair read from First Corinthians, and the Archbishop of Canterbury led the assembled audience of royals and celebrities in prayer.

The emotional highlight of the ceremony was Elton John's rendition of "A Candle in the Wind," with lyrics rewritten expressly in memory of Diana. Many in the cathedral, including Diana's sons, as well as thousands outside, were openly crying as John finished the song. Diana's brother then delivered a eulogy in which he bitterly condemned the press for hounding Diana to her death and made only thinly veiled references to the bad blood between Diana and the royal family. Diana, he said was a woman "with a natural nobility who was classless, who proved in the last year that she needed no royal title to continue to generate her particular brand of magic." Following a minute of silence at the end of the ceremony, Diana's casket was placed in a hearse and driven to Althorp, the Spencer family estate in Northamptonshire, northwest of London, where she was buried in a private ceremony on an island in a lake.

Following are two tributes to Diana, Princess of Wales—a statement by Queen Elizabeth, televised to the nation September 5, and the eulogy delivered by her brother, the Earl Spencer at her funeral service in Westminster Abbey September 6, 1997:

STATEMENT BY QUEEN ELIZABETH

Since last Sunday's dreadful news we have seen, throughout Britain and around the world, an overwhelming expression of sadness at Diana's death.

We have all been trying in our different ways to cope. It is not easy to express a sense of loss, since the initial shock is often succeeded by a mixture of other feelings: disbelief, incomprehension, anger—and concern for those who remain.

We have all felt those emotions in these last few days.

So what I say to you now, as your Queen and as a grandmother, I say from my heart.

First, I want to pay tribute to Diana myself. She was an exceptional and gifted human being. In good times and bad, she never lost her capacity to smile and laugh, nor to inspire others with her warmth and kindness.

I admired and respected her—for her energy and commitment to others, and especially for her devotion to her two boys.

This week at Balmoral, we have all been trying to help William and Harry to come to terms with the devastating loss that they and the rest of us have suffered.

No one who knew Diana will ever forgot her. Millions of others who never met her, but felt they knew her, will remember her.

I for one believe that there are lessons to be drawn from her life and from the extraordinary and moving reaction to her death.

I share in your determination to cherish her memory.

This is also an opportunity for me, on behalf of my family, and especially Prince Charles and William and Harry, to thank all of you who have brought flowers, sent messages and paid your respects in so many ways to a remarkable person.

These acts of kindness have been a huge source of help and comfort.

Our thoughts are also with Diana's family and the families of those who died with her. I know that they too have drawn strength from what has happened since last weekend, as they seek to heal their sorrow and then to face the future without a loved one.

I hope that tomorrow we can all, wherever we are, join in expressing our grief at Diana's loss, and gratitude for her all-too-short life.

It is a chance to show to the whole world the British nation united in grief and respect.

May those who died rest in peace and may we, each and every one of us, thank God for someone who made many, many people happy.

EARL SPENCER'S FUNERAL ORATION

I stand before you today the representative of a family in grief, in a country in mourning before a world in shock.

We are all united not only in our desire to pay our respects to Diana but rather in our need to do so. For such was her extraordinary appeal that the tens of millions of people taking part in this service all over the world via television and radio who never actually met her, feel that they too lost someone close to them in the early hours of Sunday morning. It is a more remarkable tribute to Diana than I can ever hope to offer her today.

Diana was the very essence of compassion, of duty, of style, of beauty. All over the world she was a symbol of selfless humanity. All over the world, a standard bearer for the rights of the truly downtrodden, a very British girl who transcended nationality. Someone with a natural nobility who was classless and who proved in the last year that she needed no royal title to continue to generate her particular brand of magic.

Today is our chance to say thank you for the way you brightened our lives, even though God granted you but half a life. We will all feel cheated always that you were taken from us so young and yet we must learn to be grateful that you came along at all. Only now that you are gone do we truly appreciate what we are now without and we want you to know that life without you is very, very difficult.

We have all despaired at our loss over the past week and only the strength of the message you gave us through your years of giving has afforded us the strength to move forward.

There is a temptation to rush to canonise your memory, there is no need to do so. You stand tall enough as a human being of unique qualities not to need to be seen as a saint. Indeed to sanctify your memory would be to miss out on the very core of your being, your wonderfully mischievous sense of humour with a laugh that bent you double.

Your joy for life transmitted where ever you took your smile and the sparkle in those unforgettable eyes. Your boundless energy which you could barely contain.

But your greatest gift was your intuition and it was a gift you used wisely. This is what underpinned all your other wonderful attributes and if we look to analyse what it was about you that had such a wide appeal we find it in your instinctive feel for what was really important in all our lives.

Without your God-given sensitivity we would be immersed in greater ignorance at the anguish of Aids and HIV sufferers, the plight of the homeless, the isolation of lepers, the random destruction of landmines.

Diana explained to me once that it was her innermost feelings of suffering that made it possible for her to connect with her constituency of the rejected.

And here we come to another truth about her. For all the status, the glamour, the applause, Diana remained throughout a very insecure person at heart, almost childlike in her desire to do good for others so she could release herself from deep feelings of unworthiness of which her eating disorders were merely a symptom.

The world sensed this part of her character and cherished her for her vulnerability whilst admiring her for her honesty.

The last time I saw Diana was on July 1, her birthday in London, when typically she was not taking time to celebrate her special day with friends but was guest of honour at a special charity fundraising evening. She sparkled of course, but I would rather cherish the days I spent with her in March when she came to visit me and my children in our home in South Africa. I am proud of the fact apart from when she was on display meeting President Mandela we managed to contrive to stop the ever-present paparazzi from getting a single picture of her—that meant a lot to her.

These were days I will always treasure. It was as if we had been transported back to our childhood when we spent such an enormous amount of time together—the two youngest in the family.

Fundamentally she had not changed at all from the big sister who mothered me as a baby, fought with me at school and endured those long train journeys between our parents' homes with me at weekends.

It is a tribute to her level-headedness and strength that despite the most bizarre-like life imaginable after her childhood, she remained intact, true to herself.

There is no doubt that she was looking for a new direction in her life at this time. She talked endlessly of getting away from England, mainly because of the treatment that she received at the hands of the newspapers. I don't think she ever understood why her genuinely good intentions were sneered at by the media, why there appeared to be a permanent quest on their behalf to bring her down. It is baffling.

My own and only explanation is that genuine goodness is threatening to those at the opposite end of the moral spectrum. It is a point to remember that of all the ironies about Diana, perhaps the greatest was this—a girl given the name of the ancient goddess of hunting was, in the end, the most hunted person of the modern age.

She would want us today to pledge ourselves to protecting her beloved boys William and Harry from a similar fate and I do this here Diana on your behalf. We will not allow them to suffer the anguish that used regularly to drive you to tearful despair.

And beyond that, on behalf of your mother and sisters, I pledge that we, your blood family, will do all we can to continue the imaginative way in which you were steering these two exceptional young men so that their souls are not simply immersed by duty and tradition but can sing openly as you planned.

We fully respect the heritage into which they have both been born and will always respect and encourage them in their royal role but we, like you, recognise the need for them to experience as many different aspects of life as possible to arm them spiritually and emotionally for the years ahead. I know you would have expected nothing less from us.

William and Harry, we all cared desperately for you today. We are all chewed up with the sadness at the loss of a woman who was not even our mother. How great your suffering is, we cannot even imagine.

I would like to end by thanking God for the small mercies he has shown us at this dreadful time. For taking Diana at her most beautiful and radiant and when she had joy in her private life. Above all we give thanks for the life of a woman I am so proud to be able to call my sister, the unique, the complex, the extraordinary and irreplaceable Diana whose beauty, both internal and external, will never be extinguished from our minds.

ARMY REPORT ON SEXUAL HARASSMENT IN THE MILITARY
September 11, 1997

The U.S. military was forced repeatedly during 1997 to confront the reality that recruiting women was much easier than ensuring that they were treated well. Allegations of sexual harassment, discrimination, misconduct, and marital infidelity plagued and embarrassed the military throughout the year. In highly publicized episodes, a candidate for the nation's top military post was forced to withdraw, the army's senior enlisted man faced a court-martial, and the first female pilot of a B-52 bomber accepted a general discharge from the air force—all because of alleged sexual misconduct.

The army on September 11 released the findings of two investigations of sexual harassment and discrimination. The reports found that the problems were systemic and that the army's leadership at all levels had allowed them to develop.

Army Report

The army released two reports September 11. One, by the seven-member Senior Review Panel on Sexual Harassment, was based on visits to fifty-nine army installations in the United States and overseas, along with a survey of 30,000 personnel. That panel was headed by retired major general Richard S. Siegfried. Another report, called "Special Inspection of Entry Training Equal Opportunity/Sexual Harassment Policies and Procedures," came from a task force formed by the army inspector general.

Army Secretary Togo D. West Jr. ordered the investigations in November 1996 in the wake of reports of serious incidents of sexual harassment of female recruits at the Aberdeen Proving Ground in Maryland. Several women said they felt compelled to have sex with drill instructors, and some said they had been raped. The army filed criminal charges, including sexual misconduct and obstruction of justice, against eleven noncommissioned officers and one captain who had served at Aberdeen. In September the army reprimanded the former commander of Aberdeen, Major General

Robert D. Shadley, saying he should have known about the sexual abuses at the base.

Announcing the results of the investigations, West insisted that criminal abuse, such as the incidents at Aberdeen, were an "aberration" in the army and were "not endemic" throughout the service. "Sexual harassment, however, continues to be a problem," he acknowledged.

The report of the special review panel said sexual harassment was more than simply a problem. Harassment "exists throughout the Army, crossing gender, rank, and racial lines," the panel said.

As could be expected, the survey of 30,000 army personnel found that women were much more likely than men to feel that they had been harassed because of their sex. Forty-seven percent of army women in the survey said they had experienced "unwanted sexual attention" (such as touching or fondling); 15 percent said they had been subjected to "sexual coercion" (defined as being told that job benefits depend on sexual cooperation); and 7 percent said they had been victims of "sexual assault" (including attempted or actual rape). Thirty percent of army men said they had experienced "unwanted sexual attention" and 8 percent said they had been subjected to "sexual coercion."

Much of the report dealt with job discrimination based on sex, which the panel said was much more pervasive in the army than sexual harassment. In the survey, 51 percent of the women and 22 percent of the men said they had faced job discrimination because of their sex. The panel said the concept of equal opportunity "has been marginalized, under-resourced and dismissed as a distraction" rather than as a useful tool for the army.

In a finding with serious implications for the army beyond the issues of sexual harassment and discrimination, the Senior Review Panel said many personnel did not trust their superiors. According to the survey, 40 percent of the women and 37 percent of the men agreed with a statement that their superior officers were more interested in their careers than in the well-being of the troops. "Unfair treatment, double standards, and a lack of discipline" were problems that soldiers raised during the investigation, the panel said. "Such a negative view of leaders is counterproductive to the objectives of EO [equal opportunity], unit cohesion, and combat readiness."

A major reason for the lack of trust, the panel said, was that the army was not receptive to complaints, especially complaints about harassment and job discrimination. In effect, the report said, the army's system "revictimized" those who filed complaints by making them feel like troublemakers who brought on misconduct in the first place. As a result, enlisted personnel, especially females, were reluctant to report abuses committed against them.

In response to the findings, the army developed what it called a "Human Relations Action Plan." The plan included organizational changes to give more top-level attention to the issues of sexual harassment and discrimination and changes in training procedures to emphasize the army's "core values" such as honor, duty, integrity, and respect for others. Among the latter changes was a new system of screening (including psychological testing) of drill sergeants and other instructors who dealt with new female recruits; those women were presumed to be the most vulnerable to sexual misconduct.

The army's report was welcomed by Defense Secretary William S. Cohen, who said it showed that "there is no room for sexual abuse, harassment or discrimination in today's military." Members of Congress who had taken the lead in addressing the issue also expressed satisfaction with the report. Sen. Olympia J. Snowe, R-Maine, a member of the Armed Services Committee, praised the report as "a scathing indictment of the climate and leadership that permits sexual harassment to permeate at all levels in the Army."

Ralston, Flinn, McKinney Cases

Several individual cases of sexual misconduct made it into the headlines during the year, heightening public concern about an apparent breakdown of morality in the military. The scandals reached to the top of the military when Air Force General Joseph W. Ralston, nominated by President Bill Clinton to be chairman of the Joint Chiefs of Staff, faced reports that he had had an affair in 1984–1985 while separated from his wife. There was widespread support for Ralston, a respected officer who had been confirmed repeatedly by the Senate for other military posts. But his nomination came at a time when the military was facing intense scrutiny over the issue of sexual misconduct. Several senators told Ralston he probably would be confirmed as Joint Chiefs chairman—but only after going through a bruising battle on Capitol Hill. Faced with that prospect, Ralston announced June 9 that he had asked to have his name removed from consideration for the post. Clinton later named, and the Senate easily confirmed, Army General Henry Shelton to the post.

One of the reasons that Ralston's decade-old adulterous affair attracted so much attention was that the air force had just dealt with another well-publicized case of adultery. At the center of that case was Lieutenant Kelly Flinn, the first (and as of 1997, only) female pilot of a B-52 bomber. The air force had charged Flinn with adultery (stemming from an affair with a married man), disobeying an order to cease her adulterous relationship, lying in a sworn statement about that relationship, and fraternization with an airman.

Facing a court martial on those charges, Flinn appealed for an honorable discharge from the air force. Her case was widely featured in the news media, including sympathetic profiles in the New York Times *and the* Washington Post *and two interviews on the CBS program,* 60 Minutes. *Under intense media scrutiny and political pressure, Air Force Secretary Sheila Widnall announced May 22 that Flinn was being given—and had accepted—a general discharge from the service. Such a discharge was given when "significant negative aspects" of a service member's conduct made an honorable discharge impossible.*

Also in 1997 the army court-martialed its senior enlisted man, Sergeant Major of the Army Gene C. McKinney, on charges of adultery and proposi-

tioning female servicewomen. McKinney, who was married, denied the charges and said the army had targeted him because he was black and most of the women involved were white. McKinney had been chosen to serve on the Special Review Panel investigating sexual abuses in the army, but he was pulled off the panel when women filed complaints against him. McKinney, whose Pentagon office was across the hall from the chairman of the Joint Chief of Staff, was suspended from his duties in February. His court-martial was scheduled for 1998.

The Kassebaum Baker Committee

In the wake of the military's troubles with sexual misconduct, a committee appointed by Defense Secretary Cohen recommended December 16 that the air force, army, and navy retreat on their policies of integrating men and women during basic and advanced training programs. The committee, chaired by former senator Nancy Kassebaum Baker, visited seventeen military bases and interviewed officers, noncommissioned officers, and enlisted personnel.

The air force began integrating men and women in basic training in the mid-1970s; the army experimented with integrated training in the 1980s and adopted it as policy in 1993; the navy followed suit in 1994. In each of the services, men and women trained and ate together; they often slept in the same buildings, although not in the same rooms. The U.S. Marine Corps was the only service maintaining a strict segregation of the sexes during basic training.

In its report the committee said integrated training had positive features but led to disciplinary problems that distracted service members at all levels. Rather than fully integrated training, the committee suggested that the services segregate the sexes at the "core unit" level: army platoons, air force flights, and navy divisions. Men and women would still train together much of the time under this procedure, but the committee said the opportunities for misbehavior would be reduced.

Cohen neither endorsed nor rejected the committee's recommendations and instead sent them to each of the military services for review and action. Several of Kassebaum Baker's former colleagues on Capitol Hill criticized the recommendations. Senator Snowe said the committee report "sends the wrong message about the direction we need to take in the military. Why create this separateness, this barrier almost from the outset?"

Following is the executive summary from the report of the Secretary of the Army's Senior Review Panel on Sexual Harassment, made public September 11, 1997:

General

The Senior Review Panel's mission was to review the human relations environment in the Army with particular emphasis on sexual harassment issues.

Our assessment took us to Army locations worldwide. The Panel visited units forward deployed, in garrison, at training sites, and in classrooms. We saw America's soldiers in every conceivable location, performing every type of mission. The Panel delved deeply into the human relations environment, identified shortcomings, and has recommended changes. While there are definitely shortcomings that need to be addressed and are discussed within this report, it is important to state that the Panel also saw a trained and ready Army—the best Army that the Panel members have seen in over 200 years collective experience with the Army. Our soldiers are ready to perform any mission assigned, effectively and efficiently, anywhere in the world. America's sons and daughters who are today's soldiers are better trained and better equipped than any Army before and they are rightfully proud to be called soldiers.

Purpose

The Secretary of the Army has said, "The Army is based on trust." In the fall of 1996, the trust between leaders and soldiers was called into question by serious allegations of sexual impropriety at several Army installations. Investigation indicated that breakdowns in good order and discipline had occurred and that some leaders had abused the authority and power vested in them. Accordingly, the Secretary of the Army directed that a Senior Review Panel on Sexual Harassment be established to undertake the following missions:

- Conduct a systems review of the Army's policies on sexual harassment and of the processes currently in place.
- Recommend changes needed to improve the human relations environment in which our soldiers live and work, with the specific goal of eradicating sexual harassment.
- Examine how Army leaders throughout the chain of command view and exercise their responsibility to prevent sexual harassment, specifically addressing behaviors that fail to acknowledge the dignity and respect to which every soldier is entitled.

Scope and Methodology

The focus of the Panel's assessment has been the human relations environment in which our soldiers live and work, measured in terms of the dignity and respect we extend to one another as an Army. Panel members, supported by a working group of over 40 military and civilian personnel, conducted an extensive policy review, collected data at 59 Army installations worldwide, and completed exhaustive analysis of the data collected. We used four methods of inquiry to collect the data: surveys, focus groups, personal interviews, and observation. Before leaving a unit or installation, Panel members outbriefed senior leaders on their observations. This allowed leaders to immediately begin addressing issues raised at their installations. This has been a very positive aspect of the Panel's efforts—teaching and advising, not just the gathering of data. In all, the effort took eight months with results based on information provided by over 30,000 Army respondents.

Findings

Our findings center on four main areas: the Army equal opportunity (EO) program, the extent of sexual harassment in the Army, leadership, and Initial Entry Training (IET). We found that:

- The Army lacks institutional commitment to the EO program and soldiers distrust the EO complaint system.
- Sexual harassment exists throughout the Army, crossing gender, rank, and racial lines; sex discrimination is more common than is sexual harassment.
- Army leaders are the critical factor in creating, maintaining, and enforcing an environment of respect and dignity in the Army; too many leaders have failed to gain the trust of their soldiers.
- The overwhelming majority of drill sergeants and instructors perform competently and well, but respect as an Army core value is not well institutionalized in the IET process.

Conclusions and Recommendations

The Panel concludes that the human relations environment of the Army is not conducive to engendering dignity and respect among us. We are firmly convinced that leadership is the fundamental issue. Passive leadership has allowed sexual harassment to persist; active leadership can bring about change to eradicate it.

Our recommendations are broad based and cover a wide variety of Army processes, including: leader development, EO policy and procedures, IET soldierization, unit and institutional training, command climate, and oversight. Key recommendations follow:

- Assign to one Department of the Army (DA) staff agency the primary responsibility for leadership, leader development, and human relations for the Army.
- Incorporate the human dimension of warfare into Army operational doctrine.
- Conduct a critical review of the staffing and organization of the DA elements responsible for human relations problems and issues and of the resourcing of those agencies responsible for assisting commanders in implementing and executing human relations policy.
- Embed human relations training in the Army training system as a doctrinal imperative.
- Re-engineer the EO program from top to bottom to make it responsive to leaders and soldiers, to protect those who use it, and to ensure that those working in it are not stigmatized.
- Mandate the conduct of a command climate assessment down to company-sized units at least annually; establish a mechanism to hold commanders accountable for their unit's command climate.
- Publish Army Regulation (AR) 600-20, *Army Command Policy*, immediately and publish interim changes in a timely manner.

- Increase the length of IET to allow for more intense, rigorous soldierization and the inculcation of Army values; design new training to inculcate Army values, appropriate behavior, and team building in IET.
- Improve IET cadre and recruiter training to include tools and techniques for addressing inappropriate behaviors in units; incorporate ethics and human relations training in recruiting and IET cadre courses, to include professionally facilitated sensitivity training.
- Implement a renewed Advanced Individual Training (AIT) approach that focuses on the continuation of the soldierization process begun in Basic Combat Training (BCT), as well as tactical, technical, and soldier skills and attitudes.
- Ensure that professionals and leaders (e.g., commanders, inspectors general, health care practitioners, criminal investigators, chaplains) who are expected to deal with soldiers reporting incidents of inappropriate sexual behavior are trained and qualified.

The Panel very strongly believes that we must ensure that we maintain a positive human relations environment in the Army. Personnel readiness relies on a positive human relations environment. It is the vital base upon which we build our Army, and the combat effectiveness of our most important weapon system—the soldier.

ACTING COMMISSIONER ON
IRS MISTAKES AND ABUSES
September 25, 1997

A few years after faulting the Internal Revenue Service (IRS) for failing to collect enough taxes, members of Congress discovered a more inviting subject for criticism in 1997: the agency's overzealousness in collecting taxes from a beleaguered public. Congressional committees in September held widely publicized hearings into IRS abuses, forcing the agency's acting commissioner to issue an unusual public apology. The hearings galvanized public opinion against the IRS, giving impetus to legislation mandating changes at the agency. In November the House overwhelmingly passed legislation establishing citizen oversight of the tax agency and giving taxpayers more recourse in their disputes with the IRS.

The political uproar left some tax experts shaking their heads. "I was rather dismayed at what happened last week" in the hearings, said Pamela F. Olson, vice chairman of committee operations for the American Bar Association's section on taxation. "It got out of hand." Others said they worried that IRS-bashing in Congress could embolden tax protesters and scofflaws—ultimately hurting honest taxpayers who would have to make up for what the cheaters refused to pay.

IRS Hearings

The Republican campaign against the IRS centered on hearings in September by the two tax-writing committees: House Ways and Means and Senate Finance. Most public attention was focused on a three-day set of hearings by the Senate panel, chaired by William V. Roth, R-Del. The first day featured comments by members of Congress and tax experts, including accountants and others who help taxpayers prepare their returns. Then came a series of witnesses with powerful testimony against the IRS: four taxpayers who said they had been victimized by IRS wrongdoing. Among them was Katherine Hicks, a California woman who said the IRS badgered her for fourteen years because of a mistake in her file, ultimately driving her into poverty and leading her to divorce her husband; and Msgr. Lawrence F.

Bailweg, a retired New York priest who said the IRS demanded that he pay $18,000 in taxes and penalties on a charitable trust established by his deceased mother. The taxpayers were followed by six IRS agents, wearing black hoods and speaking through voice boxes to disguise their identities. All described tactics by the agency of bullying and terrorizing taxpayers.

Aides said the committees deliberately focused on cases in which the IRS targeted middle-income taxpayers because there would have been little public sympathy for giant corporations or millionaires caught in the tax agency's net. In 1996 the IRS audited just under 3 million tax returns, representing about 1.4 percent of all returns. The vast majority of the audits involved businesses and upper-income taxpayers.

In the wake of the sensational allegations against the IRS, the agency's acting commissioner, Michael P. Dolan, stepped before the Finance Committee on September 25 and apologized. The four taxpayers who had described their ordeals were "legitimately frustrated" by actions of the IRS, Dolan said. "These taxpayers didn't receive the treatment that they deserved. And while each of these cases was different, the end result was indisputable. We were wrong in the way we handled many aspects of the cases."

Dolan said he was ordering IRS officials to review each of the four cases to determine what went wrong and would take a similar step for any other cases the committee brought to his attention. Dolan said he would report back to the committee on the results of those inquires. Dolan also told the committee he was ordering institutional reforms to end some of the abuses described by earlier witnesses.

Under one such reform, Dolan said, the agency would no longer rank its thirty-three district offices according to the amount of taxes, including penalties, they collected. Several observers had said the regional rankings had fostered competition within the agency, leading to abuses. Ironically, the use of tax collection figures and other criteria in measuring performance was an IRS attempt to comply with a 1993 law, the Government Performance and Results Act, sponsored by Senator Roth. That was one of several pieces of legislation intended to improve the functioning of government bureaucracies—including the IRS, which was criticized at the time for failing to collect all taxes owed by Americans.

The hearings generated intense media coverage, nearly all of it focusing on the handful of incidents the committees chose to highlight. Newsweek magazine headlined its article in the October 13 issue: "Infernal Revenue Disservice." The Finance Committee said it received more than 2,000 telephone calls, faxes, and e-mail messages from taxpayers in response to the hearings.

The IRS on December 12 released the results of an internal investigation into various abuses in the Oklahoma and Arkansas region—the region featured in the October 13 Newsweek article. The investigation found irregularities in twenty-three of sixty-seven cases in which that regional office seized property in lieu of taxes. The twenty-three seizures were legal, the investigation found, but either IRS procedures were not followed or the taxpayers were treated in an inappropriate manner.

IRS Reform Bill

Aside from generating a wave of public resentment against the IRS, the Senate hearings had one immediate tangible effect: They convinced the Clinton administration to abandon its opposition to legislation reforming the tax collection agency. Sen. Bob Kerrey, D-Neb., and Rep. Rob Portman, R-Ohio, had submitted legislation overhauling IRS procedures. Their legislation followed the recommendations of the National Commission on Restructuring the Internal Revenue Service, which they cochaired. The administration had opposed the legislation for numerous technical and policy reasons. But after the September hearings the White House decided that it made more sense politically to participate in the IRS reform movement than to be run over trying to stand in the way.

In October Treasury Secretary Robert E. Rubin negotiated several changes in the legislation that made it acceptable to the White House. The House passed IRS reform legislation (HR 2676) on November 5 by a 426–4 vote. The bill established an IRS supervisory board dominated by private sector tax and management experts; shifted the burden of proof of wrongdoing from the taxpayer to the IRS during tax court proceedings (although not during tax audits); and established new taxpayer rights, including the right to sue the IRS for damages if negligence could be shown.

As often happens on Capitol Hill, a legislative rush by the House was derailed in the Senate. Finance Committee Chairman Roth said he wanted changes in the bill and would call hearings on the matter in 1998. Roth's stance meant that Congress would be dealing with the politically hot IRS reform issue during an election year.

GOP Tax Strategy

House Republicans acknowledged that their attacks on the IRS were part of a much broader agenda to stoke public anger over taxes to the point that legislation scrapping the entire income tax code would be unstoppable. "Mark my words," said House Ways and Means Committee Chairman Bill Archer, R-Texas, as the House passed the IRS reform legislation. "We're just warming up."

That strategy faced several hurdles, however. Perhaps most important was the fact that key Republican leaders disagreed over a new tax system to replace the existing graduated income tax. Some wanted a national sales tax, while others wanted a "flat" income tax, with all taxpayers paying the same rate. The eagerness for change also was much stronger in the House than in the Senate. Furthermore, none of the new systems touted by Republicans would generate enough money to keep the federal government in business, even at the reduced rate mandated by a balanced budget agreement between the Republicans and Clinton. Finally, millions of Americans had vested interests in the system as it existed, including homeowners who treasured their mortgage interest deductions and businesses that had won countless special breaks in the tax code.

Members of Congress for years had talked about simplifying the tax code, but as recently as August 1997 Congress had enacted a new tax law that made matters worse. The centerpiece of the law was a tax credit for families with children and college-age dependents. To make those changes, Congress wrote into the law 315 pages of deductions, credits, and other tax provisions—further complicating a tax code that members claimed they wanted to make easier to understand.

Following are excerpts from testimony September 25, 1997, to the Senate Finance Committee by Michael P. Dolan, acting commissioner of the Internal Revenue Service:

[What] I hope to do this afternoon is offer some perspective on how it is I think that certainly we in the Service and maybe we collectively have the capability of getting at some of the issues that have been identified this week.

I also, I guess I have to tell you that as somebody who has spent his career in public service and specifically in the IRS, these have been a very painful three days, painful because it distresses me greatly to see the mistakes we've made, to see the impacts of those mistakes and perhaps more distressed is to sit and watch this morning's testimony where men and women, my colleagues, sat before the committee and even where I might not understand the facts as they do, or where I might have a perspective different than I do, I couldn't help but be taken by the seriousness of their comments, the genuineness of their willingness to come forward, and so my accounting of the facts almost becomes immaterial to the extent that they've got that concern.

And one of the things that concern me is in the questioning that the members did this morning, there seemed to be a reluctance on whether or not there would be a process by which those people could come forward and perhaps share more insight into things that they thought needed addressing. And, Mr. Chairman, with your permission, I'd like to work with you and the staff to find some way, either through the intervention of the Treasury inspector general or some other means by which we can invite those employees and other employees that have been in contact with the committee to come forward with the things that we should hear and we must hear.

What I'd like to do at the beginning, though, is stipulate that in the course of the week, you heard from taxpayers whose cases we handled very badly. You, and for that, I have said earlier, and I say today, I am extraordinarily sorry. As I listen to the statements that both the members of this committee made and witnesses during the week made, it struck me that there were three basic themes that we sounded in the course of the week's hearings. The first one is clearly, as I said, individual cases were identified that were handled badly. They caused the affected taxpayers to suffer in ways they should not have.

We were part of disrupting their lives. And this is wrong. No excuse for it. It's not acceptable.

The second theme that I think I heard this week has to do about IRS culture. . . .

And as I've, at least, listened to the week's witnesses and tried to glean from what you've heard, it strikes me that those who have asked you to concentrate on the culture prompt the question of whether the IRS culture indeed causes us to deal with taxpayers in a callous form, an overaggressive form, or perhaps a form of even more seriousness.

The third witness—the third issue that strikes me that came out in the course of the week was one where I would lump two kinds of concerns I heard.

One was on the basic fairness. And that got manifest in the form of several concerns about whether smaller taxpayers as contrasted with larger taxpayers were focused on disproportionately.

And the second part of that fairness issue, I think, had to do, Mr. Chairman, with something you mentioned in your opening. The business of quotas and goals.

And so, you probably could stack the week's testimony differently, but those are the three themes that I believe, at least from my listening, were ones that summarized some of the more crucial points. And that are the ones I would to address as I can this afternoon.

Maybe before I do that, I'll tell you something that I think you probably both know. In preparation for these hearings it's been real clear to me that both [Treasury] Secretary Rubin and Deputy Secretary Summers are vitally interested, not only in the hearings, but the issues that underlie the committee's attention.

They have had some considerable interest in the last several years with improving our customer service capacity, and treated it, actually, as one of their central priorities.

Upon the close of this hearing, I will clearly share with them both the assessments we've made of how cases got bollixed and, in addition, will talk to them about, on a forward-going basis, the things that need to be done.

With respect to the specific cases, you've heard from four taxpayers that were legitimately frustrated by the way the IRS dealt with them. These taxpayers didn't receive the treatment that they deserved. And while each of the cases was different, the end result was indisputable.

We were wrong in the way we handled many aspects of the cases. And I appreciate that, at this stage in their ordeal, an apology does little to correct the frustration they felt. But I would hope that, perhaps, in apologizing for them they may take some solace in the fact that we will deal with their cases—that the outcomes of their cases in a way that will hopefully result in others being kept from that same experience.

You said something, though, Mr. Chairman, at the beginning. And I think others have repeated it. I think, in all fairness to the work force of the IRS who succeed in doing a very complex job well, these hearings have to be placed ultimately in a larger context.

The context of the millions—the millions of successful taxpayer interactions that IRS has each year.

And many of you urged that in your statements. And I know I appreciate it, and I know my colleagues appreciate it.

Notwithstanding that fact, I think there are a number of actions we've got to take immediately to try to preclude the kind of case incidents that you saw before this committee earlier this week.

And in preparing to come before you, a series of us have spent a lot of time with these cases. Perhaps not as much time as some of your staff, but a lot of time. And in so doing, we've, I think, gotten a very graphic sense for some of the frustration that taxpayers experienced in these instances.

And one of the things I think incumbent on me is to demonstrate, in some visible way, what the impacts of this frustration have been to the rest of our organization. So that the organization doesn't treat this as a set of three days of hearings and four taxpayers, but as a device by which find out how to do things differently. Find out how to not cause these problems to recur.

As a consequence, I am in the process of doing several things related directly to what this hearing has brought to bear.

In the first instance, what I am doing is asking each of the regional commissioners under whose jurisdiction those four cases reside to take a transcript of this hearing, to take the witnesses testimony, to take the case files we assembled and to take that back to the individual office in which this case originally arose. And to the extent that there was more than one office as there was in several of the cases, to take it, break the case down, understand from the first moment, what happened in the case, understand where the errors were made, and perhaps more importantly, identify the places at which somebody could have fixed it. Because, as I look at these cases, as objectionable in many instance as the original error was, perhaps more troubling was the opportunity that people had along the way to recognize something off the track or to recognize that there was the capability to fix it.

The second thing we're going to do in connection with that and I make this kind of an invitation to you Mr. Chairman, I know you've said on several occasions when you made your announcement last year, you had a lot of people pick up the phone, fax you, write you, you said even in the course of these hearings. I would like to make to you the offer, any one of those cases or any number of those cases that the committee staff feels like they want to turn over this—I will put together a special task force under one of the best project managers I can find and we will work those cases to conclusion. And while they're in our custody, and while we're working to solve them, I'll make a report back to the committee every 30 days on the status of them and we won't quit until we're done.

The third issue is what I've asked, in asking this afternoon. Our 33 district directors and our 10 service center directors to do, is to take the last several months of correspondence into their office. Not necessarily the correspondence that found its way to the problem resolution office or found its way, but take and look at the correspondence that's come in the last several months and look for the cases, look for the evidence that things are off track, look for the indicia that something, some taxpayer, some practitioner, some senator or congressman for that matter, has registered something that may well not be getting the attention. I think out of that we'll do two things, hopefully we'll identify some cases that we can put under control and solve.

And secondly, I think it'll create an even higher energy level at the most senior levels of the organization and to be attentive day in and day out for the cases that in some early stage, are ones that we can take and do something about. By these actions, I think we'll not only take the lessons such as they are from the four cases that you all examined earlier in the week, but also think that we'll dramatize back to the organization that we're serious, not about four cases behind us, but serious about doing some things that will help us prevent these kind of four cases from occurring, and hopefully avoid some of the frustration and stress that was evident in each of the taxpayers that you brought before your committee.

The second area is this area of culture, and to me that's a far more complex issue. . . .

The culture issue is one that even if you look at—let me start again. When you look at a culture, I think again, it's a matter of putting, as you said your first day, putting things in perspective. If you think of our system as a whole, the vast majority of Americans meet their tax obligations. In most cases, there was some discussion I heard this morning between Senator Moynihan positing the difference in compliance rates. But roughly speaking, we think there's an 83, 85 percent level of compliance which means, an awfully lot of people are meeting regularly, their tax obligation.

For those millions of people, their normal interaction with the Internal Revenue Service is the act of filing, paying, getting a refund that goes on millions of times a year. And for those people, what the Internal Revenue Service has been trying to do, particularly in the last several years is make it easier. Those are folks for whom the burden of staying compliant, for whom the burden of operating effectively within the tax system ought to be a priority.

And we have tried increasingly to make that a priority in the Internal Revenue Service system, make it easier to file. And you see such instances as the kinds of progress we've been able to make. And one of the senators mentioned the other day, in our electronic filing. And the capability of allowing next year 25, 26 million Americans to satisfy their tax filing obligation with a 10-minute pushbutton telephone interaction. We've looked for ways to put the forms, the publications, the information that you used to have to go to a bank, a post office, to one of our offices. They're out on the [Internet] now. 117 million times during the filing season last year, people came there and got what they needed.

We've looked to beef up our ability to handle things over the telephone. Last year we got in excess of 100 million telephone calls. I believe we'll get many more this year with the introduction of a major piece of tax legislation. That's going to create a tremendous interest in how those benefits extend to me, how those obligations extend to me. My point is not necessarily to overdramatize that, but to suggest that some part of this culture that people have commented upon, I believe if you look at it in the context of the last couple of years, evidence is that the IRS has tried very hard to make a priority out of serving the taxpayer that is compliant, out of serving the taxpayer that is wrestling day in and day out to meet their obligations.

Now, on the other side of that, for taxpayers who do not file, I've heard again, almost every one of the members of this body, Senator Gramm, you said the other day quite eloquently that you don't stand for the proposition of people who ought to pay not paying, and I don't think anybody in this committee does or in the Congress does.

In those cases, we clearly I think are compelled to use the enforcement tools that you have given us, in almost out of fairness to the people who do comply. Now the question I think that's been before this committee is are those tools used as you want them to be used? Are they used with the sensitivity and with the care and with the precision the Congress authorized us to use them?

I think there have been some very valid questions raised in the course of the many people you've heard from about whether in each and every case they are. I think that's a very serious issue. And it's an issue that either in the context of this oversight, certainly in the context of the IRS' overall responsibility, that we need to pay absolutely care, absolute care, that those kind of tools are used with not only the utmost of precision, but with respect for the individual taxpayers.

One of the things I think that may have bothered me the most, both in this morning's discussion and some others, has been the notion that wrongdoing exists, and the wrongdoing doesn't get surfaced, doesn't get dealt with or some climate exists where it's not desired to be dealt with. That's not my experience. And it's also I don't think the culture of the Internal Revenue Service. Our rules of conduct are fairly explicit, are very explicit. The rule of conduct, and I quote, says, any employee who has information indicating that another employee engaged in any criminal conduct or violated any of the rules of the standards of conduct shall promptly convey such information to the inspector general or to the IRS Inspection Service.

One of the things I heard this morning were some questions about did those valves work as they should? Were people as comfortable as they should? And I think that's a fair question and one that I certainly will walk away from this morning's discussion wanting to know more about and wanting to look more about. But I say to you also, it does work to some extent. In the last three years, 475 employees have been disciplined as a result principally of the kind of referrals that come through those devices. The 475 employees in the area of some form of taxpayer mistreatment. Now, I can't tell you that that's the universe. I can't tell you that every one of those was handled exactly like I might handle it in retrospect, but I think the culture in place suggests it's an obligation to make those violations known, and the culture suggests that once known, the Inspection Service does take them and investigate them, and the culture is that once those investigations come back to management, action is taken when those kind of transgressions occur.

I don't put this before you as a perfect chapter in a perfect book, but I put it before you as evidence of a part of the culture that I do believe leads us in the direction that both you and we would have us go. . . .

REPORT ON THE SHORTAGE OF TECHNOLOGY WORKERS
September 29, 1997

A shortage of computer programmers, engineers, and other technical specialists was threatening the growth of high-technology industries in the United States and worldwide, a study by the U.S. Commerce Department reported September 30. The study said U.S. colleges and universities were graduating only about one-fourth as many computer specialists as were needed annually in business and industry.

In the early 1990s many major corporations had "downsized" their workforces by laying off tens of thousands of workers—many of them highly skilled and with years of experience. By 1997 the economy was booming and some of the same corporations were raiding each others' staffs and offering special bonuses to workers with sought-after technical and management skills.

Attempting to draw public attention to the issue, the Information Technology Association of America on February 25 released a survey of its members estimating a shortage of at least 190,000 technical specialists in mid-to-large size U.S. companies. Of the 2,000 firms responding to the survey, 82 percent said they expected to hire more technical workers, but two-thirds said the shortage of those workers was a barrier to the growth of their companies. The association represented software developers, computer service firms, and other companies in the computer industry.

Some critics said industry leaders—with support from the Clinton administration—were exaggerating the shortages of workers in hopes of persuading Congress to ease restrictions on immigration of skilled workers from overseas and to devote more federal money to computer science education. "This report [by the Commerce Department] is a tool of the special interests," Norm Matloff, a professor of computer science at the University of California at Davis told the Washington Post.

Commerce Study

The Commerce Department study released in September was a more comprehensive examination of the factors leading to the shortage of technology workers and various options for dealing with the problem. Even so, the report acknowledged that it was "at best, a snapshot of a rapidly changing phenomenon." The report said assessing the need for technology workers was made difficult by differing definitions among various industries; for example, it said there was no standard definition of an "information technology" worker—the general type of worker studied in the report. The term could be applied to computer scientists with advanced college degrees and also to lesser-skilled workers who enter information into computers, such as auto mechanics who use computer diagnostic equipment.

To provide an overall view of the shortage, the report cited an estimate by the Labor Department that U.S. business, industry, and government would need an average of 95,000 additional computer scientists, systems analysts, and programmers each year between 1994 and 2005. About four-fifths of those workers would be needed for newly created jobs; the remainder would be needed to replace workers who retired or left the field for other reasons. The demand was expected to be greatest for systems analysts—people with a broad range of technical, analytical, and managerial skills who developed computer systems to meet specific needs. The report projected that business and industry would need nearly twice as many systems analysts in 2005 as were available in 1994.

In 1994 U.S. colleges and universities awarded bachelor's degrees in computer-related fields to only 24,553 students—slightly more than one-fourth of the average annual requirement. Even more worrisome, according to the report, was that enrollment in computer-related fields at the college level had been on the decline for many years; the number of degrees awarded in those fields had fallen more than 40 percent between 1986 and 1994. In addition, many computer science students, especially those seeking advanced degrees, were foreigners, and a substantial portion of them could be expected to take their new skills back home. Not all technology workers needed to have college degrees in computer science, the report acknowledged, but other sources of education and training could not be expected to fill in the gap.

Because computer-based information systems had become "indispensable" in the workplace, the shortage of technology workers was having an impact on both the private and public sectors of the economy, the report said. Without enough workers, business and industry would not be able to develop and implement systems to improve performance and control costs. The report cited a survey by Deloitte & Touche Consulting showing that many companies already were delaying information technology projects because they could not find enough workers.

Hoping to attract new technology workers and hold onto their current workers, companies were prepared to pay premium salaries. The report cited several studies showing that average salaries in various computer-related fields had risen 10 to 20 percent annually in the mid-1990s, many times the overall inflation rate.

Factors such as delays in starting new technology projects and escalating labor costs were endangering the U.S. position in the global marketplace, the report said. "Shortages of IT [information technology] workers could inhibit the nation's ability to develop leading-edge products and services, and raise their costs, which, in turn, would reduce U.S. competitiveness and constrain economic growth."

Reasons for the Shortage

The study offered several explanations for the declining supply of technology workers relative to the demand. The shrinking enrollment in college-level computer fields could be explained by numerous factors, the report said: fewer than half of all high school graduates completed algebra II or chemistry, both of which were prerequisites for college mathematics and science courses; corporate downsizing and defense industry cutbacks gave many students "the impression" that there were fewer job opportunities in computer fields; and on-the-job training was taking the place of four-year college degrees in some aspects of computer science.

In addition, the report said, many students did not believe that universities taught marketable skills, especially in software development. Employers also found that students with computer science degrees might be "superb computer theorists," but they often lacked important job attributes such as real world experience and an ability to function well in business and industrial settings.

Another factor affecting the availability of technology workers was the rapidly changing pace of the computer industry, where new products entered the market daily and often became obsolete in a matter of months. The report noted, for example, that as recently as the late 1980s the Internet was primarily a tool for a few thousand academic researchers. By 1997, it said, the Internet and the World Wide Web were "information tools for the masses, which has driven up demand for skills needed to create and support on-line information services." The report cited an estimate that 760,000 people were working at Internet-related companies in 1997.

Other labor shortage factors cited in the report were the constant need to retrain workers in new skills, the relatively low number of women and minorities enrolled in computer science study at the college level, and the strict limit of 65,000 professional workers from overseas who could enter the United States each year under the sponsorship of U.S. employers.

Finding Solutions

The report said there had been no comprehensive study of how U.S. firms were attracting technology workers, and so most of the available information was "anecdotal." Hoping to attract and keep such workers, many companies were offering generous salaries, stock options, signing bonuses, and noncash incentives such as flexible work hours, telecommuting, day care centers, and on-site health clubs.

Companies also were providing their own worker education programs beyond simple on-the-job training, the report said. For example, some companies were hiring college graduates with degrees in other disciplines and then training them in computer skills, or were retraining existing employees who had little or no background with computer technology. Firms that once recruited only from the most exclusive colleges were broadening their searches to less prominent schools and were offering jobs and internships to students well before they graduated.

The report noted that many technology companies were turning to foreign sources, either for workers or for completed products, such as software. India, with more than 200,000 computer programmers, had become one of the world's largest exporters of software, much of it shipped to the United States. Some U.S. firms were trying to hire computer specialists from India, as well as Russia, South Africa, and countries in Eastern Europe and East Asia. In seeking foreign sources for workers and products, U.S. firms had to compete with other industrialized countries that also were experiencing worker shortages.

Following are excerpts from the report "America's New Deficit: The Shortage of Information Technology Workers," released September 29, 1997, by the U.S. Commerce Department:

I. Introduction

The sweep of digital technologies and the transformation to a knowledge-based economy have created robust demand for workers highly skilled in the use of information technology. In the past ten years alone, employment in the U.S. computer and software industries has almost tripled. The demand for workers who can create, apply and use information technology goes beyond these industries, cutting across manufacturing and services, transportation, health care, education and government.

Having led the world into the Information Age, there is substantial evidence that the United States is having trouble keeping up with the demand for new information technology workers. A recent survey of mid- and large-size U.S. companies by the Information Technology Association of America (ITAA) concluded that there are about 190,000 unfilled information technology (IT) jobs in the United States today due to a shortage of qualified workers. In another study, conducted by Coopers and Lybrand, nearly half the CEOs of America's fastest growing companies reported that they had inadequate numbers of information technology workers to staff their operations?

Evidence suggests that job growth in information technology fields now exceeds the production of talent. Between 1994 and 2005, more than a million new computer scientists and engineers, systems analysts, and computer programmers will be required in the United States—an average of 95,000 per year. One difficulty is that the formal, four-year education system is producing a small proportion of the workers required. Only 24,553 U.S. students earned bachelor's degrees in computer information sciences in 1994. While many IT workers acquire the needed skills through less formal training paths, it is difficult to determine whether such training can be adequately expanded to meet the demand for IT skills.

This shortage of IT workers is not confined within the borders of the United States. Other studies, including work by the Stanford Computer Industry Project, document that there is a world wide shortage of IT workers. That industries in other nations are facing similar problems exacerbates the U.S. problem since the geographic location of such workers is of decreasing importance to the conduct of the work. U.S. employers will face tough competition from employers around the world in a tight global IT labor pool. Thus, the United States cannot expect to meet its long-term needs through increased immigration or foreign outsourcing, and must rely on retaining and updating the skills of today's IT workers as well as educating and training new ones.

Since information technology is an enabling technology that affects the entire economy, our failure to meet the growing demand for IT professionals could have severe consequences for America's competitiveness, economic growth, and job creation. . . .

II. The Demand for Workers in the Information Technology-Driven Economy

The Office of Technology Policy analyzed Bureau of Labor Statistics' growth projections for the three core occupational classifications of IT workers computer scientists and engineers, systems analysts, and computer programmers—to assess future U.S. demand. BLS projections for occupational growth are given in three bands—low, moderate, and high. The following analysis uses the moderate growth figures.

BLS projections indicate that between 1994 and 2005, the United States will require more than one million new IT workers in these three occupations to fill newly created jobs (820,000) and to replace workers who are leaving these fields (227,000) as a result of retirement, change of professions, or other reasons.

Of the three occupations, the largest job growth is accounted for by systems analysts, which are projected to increase from 483,000 in 1994 to 928,000 in 2005, a 92 percent jump. This compares to a projected increase of 14.5 percent for all occupations. The number of computer engineers and scientists is expected to grow by 90 percent, from 345,000 to 655,000 over the same period, while the number of computer programmer positions is expected to grow at a much slower 12 percent rate, from 537,000 in 1994 to 601,000 in 2005. However, while only 65,000 new computer programmer jobs are projected to be created during this period, 163,000 new programmers will be required to replace those exiting the occupation

The service sector (not including transportation, communications, finance, insurance, real estate, and wholesale and retail trade) is expected to absorb the lion's share of all increases in these core information technology occupations. By 2005, the service sector is expected to increase its employment of computer scientists and engineers by 142 percent, systems analysts by 158 percent, and computer programmers by 37 percent. In contrast, the number of computer scientists and engineers and systems analysts in the manufacturing sector is expected to grow much more slowly (approximately 26 percent and 48 percent, respectively), while the number of computer programmers is expected to decrease by about 26 percent.

Rapid technological change and the growing complexity of information technologies and their applications are accelerating the trend toward outsourcing some computer-functions. Companies recognize the need to rely on outside experts to keep up with the technologies and to assemble multidisciplinary teams to meet the unique needs of each company. This is contributing to the growth of IT workers in services.

Certain industries are more IT worker intensive than others and thus, would be more severely affected by serious shortages of these workers. And these industries are only growing in their IT worker intensity. In the most IT worker intensive industry computer and data processing services—it is projected that, by 2005, 43 percent of the industry's employees will be computer programmers, systems analysts, and computer scientists and engineers.

However, IT worker intensity does not tell the whole story. The size of an industry's IT work force is an important consideration. For example, while the Federal government is projected to be less IT worker-intensive in 2005 than many other industries, the sheer size of its IT work force would make shortages of computer programmers, systems analysts, and computer scientists and engineers a troubling problem. When IT worker intensity and size of IT work force are taken together, a picture emerges as to which industries' competitive performance would be most adversely affected by severe IT worker shortages. The computer and data processing services industry stands out starkly as an industry with much at stake in the supply of IT workers.

III. Is There an Adequate Supply of IT Workers?

Current statistical frameworks and mechanisms for measuring labor supply do not allow for precise identification of IT workers shortages. However, evidence does suggest a problem may be emerging.

Upward Pressure on Salaries

The strongest evidence that a shortage exists is upward pressure on salaries. The competition for skilled IT workers has contributed to substantial salary increases in many IT professions. A compensation survey conducted by William M. Mercer showed that average hourly compensation for operating systems/software architects and consultants rose nearly 20 percent from 1995 to 1996. A survey conducted by the Deloitte & Touche Consulting Group revealed that salaries for computer network professionals rose an average of 7.4 percent from 1996 to 1997. Computerworld's annual survey found that in 11 of 26 positions tracked, average salaries increased more than 10 percent from 1996 to 1997. For example, systems analysts' salaries were up

15 percent, programmer/analysts' salaries were up 11 percent, and directors of systems development received an average increase of 10 percent. Starting salaries for graduates with bachelor's degrees in computer science have nudged up to an average of $36,666, while experienced programmers can command salaries ranging from $45,000–$75,000.

ITAA Survey

A recent survey of mid- and large-size companies, both information technology-related and non-information technology-related, conducted by the Information Technology Association of America found approximately 190,000 unfilled information technology jobs in the United States due to a shortage of qualified workers. According to this survey, shortages are likely to worsen. ITAA found that 82 percent of the information technology companies responding to the survey expect to increase their IT staffing in the coming year, while more than half of the non-information technology companies planned IT staff increases.

The Education Pipeline for IT Workers

Over the last ten years, there has been a decline in the number of students receiving university degrees in computer science. These graduates come from four-year degree-granting universities which focus on computer theory; that is, operating systems, languages, distributed systems, computer architecture and compilers. According to the U.S. Department of Education, the number of bachelor-level computer science degrees awarded by U.S. universities declined more than 40 percent between 1986 and 1994, from 42,195 to 24,553. The significant decline in bachelor-level computer science degrees is, however, an imperfect indicator of declining labor supply, given that many IT workers acquire their skills through alternative education and training paths. While there have been some increases in the award of computer science masters and doctoral degrees, overall computer science degrees awarded have dropped from a high of 50,000 in 1986 to 36,000 in 1994.

In addition, students make up a significant share of U.S. computer science graduates. Of the 36,000 individuals awarded graduate and undergraduate computer science degrees in 1994, about 18 percent were foreign nationals. For advanced degrees, the proportion of foreign nationals increases, reaching more than 50 percent for doctorates. The Computer Research Association estimates that foreign nationals comprise nearly 50 percent of computer engineering students in the United States? The high proportion of foreign nationals in the graduate population would indicate that American industry cannot count on capturing all new IT workers also obtain their skills from training providers other than four-year degree-granting universities. These include:

- two-year associate-degree-granting community colleges which provide grounding in applications (especially in new computer programs and hot areas such as "the year 2000" problem) as well as basic theory, and vocational technical education programs

- special university/community college one-year programs designed to upgrade the skills of IT workers already in the work force (new applications) or those with backgrounds in other technical fields who are looking for a fast track entry into the IT profession
- private-sector computer learning centers which typically offer courses to people with little or no computer background who are interested in discovering whether they have the aptitude to make it in the computer-related professions
- in-house company training to upgrade employee skills (e.g. client/server-based tools and architectures, C++ and Visual Basic) or to assist in the transition from one skill set (e.g. computer hardware engineers) to another (e.g. computer software engineers)
- computer user groups, Internet forums, and company-sponsored help sites also offer knowledge that can help expand or update computer skills

In addition to those earning four-year degrees in computer and information sciences, in 1994, 15,187 degrees and awards in computer and information sciences below the bachelors level were earned.

Offshore Sourcing and Recruiting

Some companies are drawing upon talent pools outside the United States to meet their demands for IT workers. India, with more than 200,000 programmers, in conjunction with predominantly U.S. partners, has developed into one of the world's largest exporters of software. In 1996–97, outsourced software development accounted for 41 percent of India's software exports. Companies are also searching for IT workers in foreign labor markets—in Russia, Eastern Europe, East Asia, and South Africa—using direct recruiting efforts, Internet techniques, and international recruiting agencies.

IV. Competitiveness Issues

Information technologies are the most important enabling technologies in the economy today. They affect every sector and industry in the United States, in terms of digitally-based products, services, and production and work processes. Thus, severe shortages of workers who can apply and use information technologies could undermine U.S. innovation, productivity, and competitiveness in world markets.

Productivity and the Cost of Doing Business

Competitive pressures have driven businesses to adopt a wide range of computer systems to improve productivity, manage production, improve both internal and external communications and to offer customers new services. Private sector investment in enterprise-wide applications alone was estimated to be $42 billion in 1996. The service sector, now representing 70 percent of U.S. GDP, is increasingly information technology intensive. Manufacturing also relies heavily on information technology from computer aided design and computer numerically controlled machine tools to computer-based systems for inventory control, production planning, and statistical process control. In short, computer-based information systems have become an indispensable part of managing information, workflow, and transactions in both the public and private sector. Therefore, a shortage of IT workers affects directly the ability to develop and implement systems that a wide variety of users need to enhance their performance and control costs. A recent survey by Deloitte & Touche Consulting reported that worker shortages are causing many companies to delay information technology projects.

As competition for IT workers heats up, rising salary levels increase the cost of doing business. For example, Electronic Data Systems Corp. (EDS) recently reported that IT worker shortages have contributed to pushing workers' compensation up by 15 to 20 percent annually. The company reported in April 1997 that it may reduce its work force by thousands to cut labor costs and maintain profits. Many computer companies faced with rising labor costs have passed those increases along to their customers. However, EDS and similar companies rely on long-term fixed contracts to develop and manage large computer systems and have less flexibility to pass increased costs to customers.

Shortage-driven increases in salaries for both skilled IT managers and IT workers also increase the amount of venture capital investment required by start-up companies in information technology-related businesses. For example, new software technology start-ups—which have benefited substantially from private venture capital and are IT worker-intensive—could require greater venture capital investment in the future to cover salary costs. These rising labor costs could result in venture capital seeking growth opportunities elsewhere, constraining the emergence and growth of many promising new companies.

Government and non-profit organizations may increasingly be squeezed out of the competition for IT talent. For example, while average starting salaries for graduates with bachelor's degrees in computer engineering grew to more than $34,000 in 1995, the Federal government's entry level salary for computer professionals with bachelor's degrees ranged from about $18,700 to $23,200 that year. The Department of Defense is already having difficulty retaining IT employees; it appears industry is offering them more attractive compensation packages. The U.S. Air Force Communications Agency reports a loss rate of 42 to 45 percent of systems administrators from 1993–1995.

Industry Growth

High-tech industries, particularly leading-edge electronics and information technology industries, are driving economic growth not only in the United States but around the world. According to industry estimates, the markets for computer and communications hardware and services, and for software have grown to one trillion dollars. With the current annual growth rate estimated at 10 percent, the global market for these products and services may be growing by $100 billion annually. These industries are IT worker intensive and shortages of critical skills would inhibit their performance and growth potential.

In the ITAA survey, 50 percent of the information technology company executives cited lack of skilled/trained workers as "the most significant barrier" to their companies' growth during the next year-a problem viewed as significantly greater than economic conditions, profitability, lack of capital investment, taxes, or regulation. An additional 20 percent of the IT company executives identified the shortage of these workers as "a barrier" to their companies' growth during the next year.

Innovation

The United States is a leader in the development of new products and services, and many important consumer and industrial innovations—from computers, consumer electronic products, and telecommunications services to automotive electronics, aerospace products, and advanced industrial systems—have been made possible by information technologies. Information technologies are expected to continue to form the basis of many of the most important products, services, and processes of the future. For example, it is expected that in less than a decade, electronics will account for about one-fifth of an automobile's value. Shortages of IT workers could inhibit the nation's ability to develop leading-edge products and services, and raise their costs which, in turn, would reduce U.S. competitiveness and constrain economic growth.

Trade

The shortage of IT workers could undermine U.S. performance in global markets. The global market for computer software and computer services reached $277 billion in 1994. The United States is both the predominant supplier of and the primary consumer for these goods and services. Ranked in terms of global market share in 1994, eight of the world's top ten applications software vendors and seven of the top ten systems software vendors are U.S. firms. Both of these markets are growing rapidly, with the computer software market growing 12 percent annually, and the computer services market growing 11 percent annually, reaching $420 billion by 1998, a 50 percent increase just between 1994 and 1998. Aerospace, another IT worker intensive industry is also a global market leader for the United States, and is the Nation's leading net exporter of manufactured goods. An adequate supply of IT workers is essential to America's continued strength in these markets.

High-Wage Jobs

A shortage of qualified IT workers could also prevent the United States from taking full advantage of high-wage job creation. Many information technology jobs are high-wage jobs. Workers in the software industry earn more than twice the national average. A William M. Mercer compensation study shows that the average hourly compensation in 1996 for an intermediate customer support technician was $40.80; software development architect, $77.70; operating systems software architect/consultant, $85.60, and operating systems/software programming analyst manager, $92.20. Even if shortages ease and upward pressure on salaries is reduced, the IT professions have traditionally been high-wage jobs.

October

FBI REPORT ON CRIME
October 4, 1997

The number and rate of serious crimes declined in 1996 for the fifth year in a row, according to the Federal Bureau of Investigation's annual report, "Crime in the United States." The most striking decline was in the murder rate, which fell to 7.4 per 100,000 population, its lowest level since 1969. Burglaries also fell to their lowest levels in two decades. Overall, violent crime dropped 6 percent from its level in 1995, while property crimes dropped 2 percent.

The FBI report was based on arrest statistics. Another report, which focused on the victims of crime, corroborated the FBI report, finding that the rate of violent crime had dropped 10 percent in 1996, while property crime fell 8 percent. The declines reflected in the FBI report and the National Crime Victimization Survey meant that "we can now have more confidence that we are in the midst of a trend, not simply a short-term or random fluctuation," Jeffrey Fagan, director of the Center for Violence Research and Prevention at Columbia University told the New York Times *in November.*

Reasons for the declining crime rate included aggressive and innovative police tactics, sometimes referred to as community policing; neighborhood volunteer efforts to change juvenile behavior; and higher rates of imprisonment for people convicted of crimes. Other reasons included an improving economy, tougher federal gun controls laws, stabilization of the crack cocaine trade, and a decline in the teenage and young adult population— the prime age groups for committing crime.

Crime in the United States

Overall, 13.5 million serious crimes were committed in 1996, 3 percent fewer than in 1995 and virtually the same number as in 1987. The crime rate—5,079 offenses for every 100,000 people—was the lowest it had been since 1984. While the crime rate was highest in the South (5,727 offenses per 100,000 population) and lowest in the Northeast (3,899), all regions showed a decline from 1995.

The number of violent crimes was the lowest total reported to law enforcement agencies since 1989. There were 19,645 murders reported in 1996, 9 percent fewer than in 1995. Three-fourths of the victims were men, and the number of victims was divided evenly between blacks and whites. Ninety percent of those arrested for murder were men; 52 percent of the offenders were black and 45 percent were white. More than half the murder victims knew their assailants. Thirty percent of the female murder victims in 1996 were killed by husbands or boyfriends. Other categories of violent crime were also down in 1996. Forcible rape dropped to its lowest level since 1989. Robberies declined 7 percent from their 1995 levels, and aggravated assaults were down 6 percent.

All categories of property crime—burglary, larceny, auto theft, and arson—also decreased. Burglary rates had dropped 44 percent since 1980. The decline in burglary "is unprecedented in magnitude compared to any other fluctuation in crime rates over the last century," said Scott Decker, a criminologist at the University of Missouri at St. Louis. Several experts attributed some of the decline in burglaries—breaking and entering in commission of a theft—to the shift from the use of heroin to crack cocaine among street criminals. Because the high produced by crack was so short, users needed ready cash to constantly replenish their supply, but burglary required time and planning and the stolen goods procured still had to be converted to money.

Reasons for Declining Crime

If the use of crack was seen as a significant factor in the decline in the number of burglaries, the ebbing of the crack cocaine epidemic was seen by many as an explanation for the decrease in the number of murders and other violent crimes. Since its appearance in the mid-1980s crack had been associated with heightened violence. Some experts argued that the violence resulted, in part, because the high produced by the drug often induced paranoia and, in part, because the way crack was marketed led to high levels of competition among street sellers, many of whom were armed and willing to use their guns to protect their turf. As the use of crack began to slow in the early 1990s, the rate of violent crime began to decline, and several studies found a strong relationship between the two events.

Others attributed much of the decline in violent crime to aggressive police tactics. In New York and other cities, the police put in practice the "broken windows" theory offered by criminologists James Q. Wilson and George L. Kelling in a 1982 Atlantic Monthly article. Their theory, in essence, held that broken windows in a neighborhood conveyed a message that no one was in charge and invited more broken windows. Soon residents abandoned the streets, which led to more serious crime. By cracking down on so-called quality-of-life crimes, such as aggressive panhandling and public drinking, the initial signal would be reversed, according to the theory, and the opportunity for serious crime diminished. New York City did just that in the early 1990s, with spectacular results; the number of murders in the city was halved between 1993 and 1996, and several other crime indicators also fell dramatically.

But even one of the formulators of the broken windows theory was reluctant to attribute the decline wholly to the police tactics. "Crime is down in cities with lots of cops being more aggressive, but there are other cities [where crime is] down where community policing is barely getting off the ground," Wilson, a professor of management at the University of California at Los Angeles, told the New York Times. *He pointed to Los Angeles as an example. The number of homicides in that city fell from 849 in 1995 to 709 in 1996, he said, yet "the L.A. police have become one of the least aggressive departments. They are doing less and making fewer arrests because they don't want to get into trouble."*

Still others maintained that the primary factor in the falling crime rate was demographic—a decline in the number of older teenagers and young adults, the age group most prone to commit crimes. With the number of children reaching their teens projected to increase by 1 percent a year for the next decade, however, some experts were not ready to say that the United States had won the war on crime. Alfred Blumstein, a professor of criminology at Carnegie-Mellon University, noted that the incidence of larceny had dropped only 1 percent in 1996, the smallest decrease of the eight categories of crime measured. Because it included relatively minor crimes such as shoplifting and pickpocketing, Blumstein said larceny was often the "entry level" crime for juveniles and was thus a "leading indicator" for crime trends. The smaller decline in larceny could be interpreted as a warning signal that juvenile crime might be trending upward. "Crime is down but not out," said James Alan Fox, dean of the college of criminal justice at Northeastern University in Boston.

Related Reports

Several other reports on crime were released throughout the year. These included the following findings:

• *After several years of acceleration, the growth in the incarceration rate slowed. Between June 1995 and June 1996, the number of people in federal and state prisons and local jails increased 4.4 percent, compared to an average annual rate of 7.8 percent in the previous ten years, according to a report released January 19 by the Bureau of Justice Statistics. Experts cautioned that the numbers might be just a normal fluctuation. Blumstein added that the slowing growth rate was "good news; it could be an early reflection in the incarceration rate of the drop in crime over the last five years."*

• *Emergency rooms were treating an estimated 1.3 million people a year for injuries caused by violent attacks—two and a half times more than had previously been estimated. According to the report, released August 24 by the Bureau of Justice Statistics, the higher estimates were not surprising because the previous estimates were based on the National Crime Victimization Survey, which focused only on attacks that the victims regarded as criminal. "Many of the victims, including those of long-term abuse, are unable or unwilling, because of fear or embarrassment, to report such abuse to authorities or to programs that measure these victimizations," the report said. The more recent survey, based on emergency room visits in 1994 to a sample of thirty-one hospitals that provided around-the-clock emergency treatment, counted all injuries "regardless of whether the victim perceived the event to have been criminal in nature."*

Sixty percent of the victims were men and 40 percent were women. Nearly 37 percent of the women but only 4.5 percent of the men were attacked by a spouse, former spouse, boyfriend, or girlfriend. But more men (29 percent) than women (14 percent) were the victims of strangers. (The relationship between the attacker and the victim was not recorded in nearly one-third of the cases.) Nearly half of the victims were under age twenty-five, and a disproportionate share were black. Blacks accounted for 13 percent of the population but nearly 25 percent of all those treated for injuries, the report said.

Weapons were used in only about 40 percent of the injuries; the other injuries were caused primarily by punches or kicks. About 5 percent of the victims were treated for gunshot wounds (the survey did not count fatal or self-inflicted injuries, or those caused by police "in the line of duty"). Almost all of the patients were released after they were treated; only about 7 percent had to be hospitalized.

• The United States had the highest rates of childhood homicide, suicide, and gun-related deaths of any of the world's twenty-six richest nations, according to a report released February 6 by the Centers for Disease Control and Prevention. The suicide rate alone for children age fourteen and under was twice that of the rest of the industrialized world, the report said. Experts attributed the high rates of violent death among children in the United States to the high numbers of working women, the high divorce rate, the social acceptability of violence in American society, poverty, and racism. Organizations that lobbied for gun control attributed much of it to the presence of handguns in American homes. About half of all American families owned firearms, many of which were handguns and many of which were kept loaded. Groups that lobbied in behalf of gun owners' rights contended that the problem was not the availability of guns, but the failure to regulate and discipline.

• Some of the most popular crime prevention techniques, such as boot camps and drug education classes, appeared to have little positive effect on reducing crime, according to a study done for Congress by a team of criminologists from the University of Maryland. The study, which was made public in August, also said that it was difficult to assess federal crime prevention programs because not much scientific evaluation of them had been

conducted. But the report said it was clear that instead of concentrating crime-fighting money in areas of high crime where it would do the most good, Congress too often spread the money to areas with less crime so that legislators could show their constituents that they were working to stop crime. "We need to put the money where the crime is, not just where the votes are," said the lead author of the report.

Popular programs, such as D.A.R.E. (Drug Abuse Resistance Education) and neighborhood crime watches tended to have only short-term effects that did not change fundamental behaviors and attitudes, the report said. Programs that did seem to have a positive effect, the report said, were stepped-up police patrols in high-crime areas, drug treatment programs for prison inmates, and home care for infants in troubled families.

> *Following is a press release issued October 4, 1997, by the Federal Bureau of Investigation that accompanied the release of its annual report "Crime in the United States" and summarized the data for 1996:*

The Federal Bureau of Investigation announced today that serious reported crime in the United States declined 3 percent in 1996, the fifth consecutive annual reduction.

Violent crime dropped 6 percent and property crime was down 2 percent from 1995 levels, the FBI said in releasing final Uniform Crime Reporting (UCR) Program statistics for last year.

For violent crimes, the reductions in 1996 from 1995 totals were murder, 9 percent; forcible rape, 2 percent; robbery, 7 percent; and aggravated assault, 6 percent.

For property crimes, the reductions were burglary, 4 percent; larceny-theft, 1 percent; motor vehicle theft, 5 percent; and arson, 3 percent.

In 1996, the South had 40 percent of reported serious crime; the West, 24 percent; the Midwest, 21 percent; and the Northeast, 15 percent. Crime was down 8 percent in the West, 7 percent in the Northeast, 1 percent in the Midwest; it was up 1 percent in the South.

Serious crime dropped 5 percent last year in the Nation's 64 largest cities those with populations of 250,000 or more and violent crime was down 7 percent.

The 1996 total of nearly 13.5 million serious crimes is 7 percent below 1992 figures. The number of violent crimes in 1996 was 13 percent below the 1992 level and was the lowest total since 1989 but remained 13 percent above the 1987 level. The number of rapes was the lowest since 1989 and the number of burglaries the lowest in more than 20 years.

The UCR is based on reports submitted by more than 16,000 city, county, and state law enforcement agencies. The 1996 data are published in Crime in the United States, the FBI's annual report which was released today.

Highlights from the 1996 edition include:

Crime Volume. The 1996 Crime Index total of approximately 13.5 million offenses represents a 3-percent decline from the 1995 total. Five- and 10-year comparisons show the 1996 national total has dropped 7 percent since 1992 and is virtually the same as in 1987.

Crime Rate. The Crime Index rate of 5,079 offenses per 100,000 United States inhabitants was 4 percent lower than the 1995 rate. The 1996 rate was the lowest since 1984; it was 10 percent below the 1992 rate; and 8 percent lower than the 1987 figure.

Regionally, the Crime Index rate in the South was 5,727 offenses per 100,000 inhabitants; 5,528 in the West; 4,664 in the Midwest; and 3,899 in the Northeast. All regions reported rate declines from 1995 levels.

The Nation's Metropolitan Statistical Areas (MSAs) also experienced a decrease in the Crime Index rate 5,512 reported offenses per 100,000 population in 1996, compared with 5,761 in 1995.

Violent Crime. The number of violent crimes reported to the Nation's law enforcement agencies during 1996 was the lowest total recorded since 1989. The rate of 634 violent crimes for every 100,000 inhabitants was the lowest since 1987.

All individual violent crimes showed declines in volume and rate from 1995 to 1996.

Data collected in 1996 on weapons used in connection with murder, robbery, and aggravated assault show that personal weapons (hands, fists, feet) were used in 30 percent of the offenses and that firearms were used in 29 percent.

Property Crime. The estimated property crime total 11.8 million offenses was down 2 percent from the 1995 total.

The property crime rate was 4,445 offenses per 100,000 population, 3 percent lower than the 1995 figure.

All property crime categories declined in volume and rate.

The dollar value of property stolen in connection with property crimes in 1996 was estimated at more than $15 billion an average loss per offense of $1,274.

Hate Crime. Crime in the United States 1996 includes data on bias crimes, i.e., criminal offenses committed against persons, property, or society motivated by the offender's bias against a race, religion, ethnic/national origin group, or sexual-orientation group.

The UCR Program began collecting hate crime data in 1992. That year, 6,181 law enforcement agencies covering 129.2 million U.S. inhabitants participated. In 1996, 11,355 agencies covering 223.7 million of the population reported to the Program.

Crimes against persons comprised 69 percent of the 10,702 offenses reported. Among the crimes against persons, intimidation accounted for approximately 56 percent; simple assault and aggravated assault accounted for approximately 24 percent and 20 percent, respectively; murder and rape each accounted for less than 1 percent.

Of all offenses reported, 6,768 were motivated by racial bias; 1,497 by religious bias; 1,258 by sexual-orientation bias; and 1,179 by ethnic bias.

Crime Clearances. Law enforcement agencies nationwide recorded a 22-percent Crime Index clearance rate in 1996. The clearance rate for violent crimes was 47 percent; for property crimes, 18 percent.

Among the Crime Index offenses, the clearance rate was highest for murder, 67 percent, and lowest for burglary and motor vehicle theft, 14 percent each.

Offenses involving only juvenile offenders (under 18 years of age) accounted for 21 percent of the Crime Index offenses cleared; 13 percent of the violent crime clearances; and 23 percent of the property crime clearances.

Arrests. Excluding traffic violations, law enforcement agencies made an estimated 15.2 million arrests for all criminal infractions in 1996, an increase of 1 percent over the previous year's figure. The highest arrest counts were for larceny-theft, drug abuse violations, and driving under the influence, each at 1.5 million. Arrests for simple assaults followed at 1.3 million. Relating the number of arrests to the total U.S. population, the rate was 5,838 arrests per 100,000 population.

For the 2-year period 1995–1996, juvenile arrests rose 3 percent while adult arrests showed virtually no change. Violent crime arrests of juveniles decreased 6 percent and those of adults, 3 percent.

Of all persons arrested in 1996, 45 percent were under the age of 25, 79 percent were male, and 67 percent were white.

Females and juveniles were most often arrested for the offense of larceny-theft. Males were most often arrested for drug abuse violations and driving under the influence.

Murder. The murder count for 1996 totaled 19,645, 9 percent lower than the 1995 total and 17 percent lower than the number reported in 1992. The murder rate was 7.4 offenses per 100,000 inhabitants.

Based on supplemental data received for 15,848 of the reported murders, 77 percent of murder victims in 1996 were males and 87 percent were persons 18 years or older. The percentage of white and black murder victims was equal at 49 percent.

Data based on a total of 18,108 murder offenders show that 90 percent of the assailants were male, and 86 percent were 18 years of age or older. Fifty-two percent of the offenders were black and 45 percent were white.

Over 50 percent of murder victims knew their assailants. Among all female murder victims in 1996, 30 percent were slain by husbands or boyfriends, while 3 percent of the male victims were slain by wives or girlfriends.

Arguments led to 31 percent of the murders, and 19 percent resulted from felonious activities such as robbery, arson, and other crimes.

As in previous years, firearms were the weapons used in approximately 7 out of every 10 murders reported.

Forcible Rape. The total of 95,769 forcible rapes reported to law enforcement during 1996 was the lowest total since 1989. The 1996 count was 2 percent lower than in 1995.

In the Uniform Crime Reporting Program, the victims of forcible rape are always female. In 1996, an estimated 71 of every 100,000 females in the country were reported rape victims, a rate that is 1 percent lower than the 1995 rate.

Robbery. The 1996 estimated robbery total was 537,050 or 202 robberies per 100,000 population nationwide. Robberies declined 7 percent in 1996 as compared to 1995 levels.

Monetary loss attributed to property stolen in connection with this offense was estimated at nearly $500 million. Bank robberies resulted in the highest average loss, $4,207 per offense; gas station robberies the lowest, $487.

Robberies on streets or highways accounted for 51 percent of the offenses in this category.

In 1996, robberies committed with firearms accounted for 41 percent of the total. Robberies committed with the use of strong-arm tactics accounted for 39 percent.

Aggravated Assault. Over 1 million aggravated assaults were reported to law enforcement in 1996, down 6 percent from the 1995 total.

Thirty-four percent of aggravated assaults in 1996 were committed with blunt objects or other dangerous weapons. Personal weapons such as hands, fists, and feet were used in 26 percent of reported incidents; firearms in 22 percent; and knives or cutting instruments in 18 percent.

Burglary. The estimated total of 2.5 million burglaries in 1996 represented the lowest figure in more than 20 years.

As in previous years, residences were the target of 2 of every 3 burglaries. Sixty-six percent of all burglaries involved forcible entry, and 51 percent occurred during daylight hours. The average loss for residential offenses was $1,350.

Larceny-theft. Larceny-theft, with an estimated total of 7.9 million offenses, comprised 67 percent of the property crime total for the year.

The total dollar loss to victims nationwide was over $4 billion during 1996. The average value of property stolen was $532 per incident.

Thefts of motor vehicle parts, accessories, and contents made up the largest portion of reported larcenies 36 percent.

Motor Vehicle Theft. A lower number of motor vehicles were reported stolen last year than in any year since 1987 under 1.4 million. From the 1995 number, the decrease in both the Nation and in cities was 5 percent.

The estimated average value of stolen motor vehicles at the time of theft was $5,372 per vehicle. The estimated total value of vehicles stolen nationwide was nearly $7.5 billion.

Arson. A total of 88,887 arson offenses was reported in 1996.

As in previous years, structures were the most frequent targets of arsonists in 1996 48 percent of the reported incidents. Residential property was involved in 59 percent of the structural arsons during the year; 40 percent of the arsons were directed at single-family dwellings.

In 1996, the monetary value of property damaged due to reported arsons averaged $10,280 per offense.

Of the arsons cleared by law enforcement during 1996, 45 percent involved only people under the age of 18, a higher percentage of juvenile involvement than for any other Index crime.

Law Enforcement Employees. A total of 13,025 city, county, and state police agencies submitting Uniform Crime Reporting data reported collectively employing 595,170 officers and 234,668 civilians in 1996. Reporting agencies provided law enforcement services to nearly 249 million U.S. inhabitants.

The average rate of 2.4 full-time officers for every 1,000 inhabitants across the country was unchanged from the 1995 rate.

Geographically, the highest rate of sworn officers to population was recorded in the Northeastern States, with 2.8 officers per 1,000 inhabitants.

AGRICULTURE SECRETARY ON FOOD SAFETY INITIATIVE
October 8, 1997

Following the recall in August of 25 million pounds of meat from a pro-cessing plant in Nebraska—the largest recall ever of meat produced at a U.S. plant—the Clinton administration was spurred to ask Congress for additional powers to enforce food safety standards. Despite heightened public interest in the issue, Congress did not act on the administration's request during 1997.

In 1996 the Clinton administration announced that both the Agriculture Department and the Food and Drug Administration (FDA) would move to a new inspection system that placed the burden on food processors to pre-vent contamination. Under the new system, called Hazard Analysis and Critical Control Points (HACCP), each food processing plant was required to develop its own plan for countering the greatest risks of food contami-nation. Federal inspectors would then concentrate on reviewing those plans and ensuring that the processors adhered to them. The Agriculture Depart-ment began phasing in its new system in 1997, with all meat and poultry plants to be complying by 2000. The FDA's new system for seafood process-ing plants took effect in December 1997. The FDA in 1997 also was consid-ering whether to implement HACCP systems for the processing of fruit and vegetable juices and fresh fruit and vegetables. (New food inspection regu-lations, Historic Documents of 1996, p. 414)

Contaminated Hamburger

The meat recall stemmed from several incidents during July in which sixteen residents of Colorado became seriously ill after eating hamburger patties contaminated with E coli O157:H7, one of the most dangerous food-borne bacteria. Investigations by state and federal authorities traced the contaminated meat to a state-of-the-art beef processing plant in Columbus, Nebraska, owned by the Hudson Foods Company of Rogers, Arkansas. The Agriculture Department, responsible for inspecting meat and poultry pro-cessing plants, demanded that Hudson recall most of its recent beef pro-

duction—a demand the company at first resisted. Under intense federal pressure, Hudson agreed in mid-August to recall 1.2 million pounds of beef, and then on August 21 to recall all the beef it had processed since early June, a total of 25 million pounds.

The Agriculture Department had no authority to force the recall, but it could have effectively shut down the Columbus plant by withdrawing federal inspectors. After the recall, Hudson closed the plant indefinitely. Federal officials later said their investigations at the plant had uncovered inadequate record-keeping systems, weak quality-control standards, and improper procedures, such as mixing leftover meat with new batches. The officials were unable to explain why federal inspectors—present at the plant on a daily basis—had not uncovered these lapses previously.

The incident caused nationwide anxiety about the safety of meat. Burger King, one of Hudson's biggest customers, temporarily stopped serving its most important product, hamburgers.

Request for New Authority

A week after the massive recall at the Hudson Plant, the Clinton administration said it was renewing a request to Congress for expanded enforcement powers at U.S. food processing plants. Agriculture Secretary Dan Glickman and Michael Friedman, acting commissioner of the FDA, said their agencies were asking for powers to order food recalls when plants were unwilling to take such steps on their own and to impose fines of up to $100,000 a day on food producers for serious safety violations.

Glickman, a former member of the House of Representatives, acknowledged that the administration had requested similar powers in the past but had been turned down by Congress, which was responding to lobbying by the food industry. "I think the dynamics of the debate have changed a bit in light of recent events," Glickman told reporters. "My sense is that the vast majority of people had no idea that industry, and not federal food safety experts, ultimately decide whether food is recalled when the public safety is involved."

Defending the request in an October 8 appearance before the Senate Committee on Agriculture, Nutrition, and Forestry, Glickman noted that government agencies had the authority to order recalls of unsafe toys, cars, insecticides, and infant formula "but not unsafe food." Glickman conceded that he could, in effect, force a recall of meat by threatening to withdraw his inspectors from a processing plant. But such a threat was a blunt instrument to be used only in extreme cases, he said. Instead, the department needed simple authority to order a recall, along with a system of civil fines against food processors who failed to address safety problems.

Glickman noted that his department had the authority to fine people who abused circus elephants or marketed undersize potatoes. But, just as it could not order recalls of food products, the department lacked the power to fine those who produced unsafe food. "At a certain point it becomes fairly evident who's being protected here," he said. "I think we need to come down a little more strongly on the side of the consumer."

Glickman also asked for regulations requiring food processing companies to tell the government immediately when they had reason to believe any of their products might cause a public food safety problem. He noted one case in which a food processor had notified a restaurant chain forty-eight hours "before it got around to telling USDA that there might be contaminated food in the marketplace."

The administration's request for expanded powers received the same reception in Washington as similar requests in previous years: fierce opposition from major elements of the food industry (the American Meat Institute, the National Food Processors Association, and the Grocery Manufacturers of America), and a resulting lack of action in Congress. A typical reaction on Capitol Hill came from Sen. Chuck Hagel, R-Neb., where the Hudson plant was located: "We have a pretty good system out there. Anytime anybody in the federal government says, 'I need more power,' I say, 'Wait a minute. I want to take a good look.'"

Inspecting Imported Food

Just as the recall of contaminated meat gave the administration incentive to seek broader powers over domestic food producers, several outbreaks of illness from imported food prompted a move for more regulation of fruits and vegetables from overseas.

President Bill Clinton announced October 2 that he would ask Congress in 1998 for additional funding for the FDA to increase its inspections of food from foreign sources and also to investigate agricultural methods in countries that exported to the United States. Countries that refused such inspections would be barred from exporting to the United States.

"At the time when Americans are eating more and more food from around the globe, we must spare no effort to insure the safety of our food supply from whatever source," Clinton said in announcing his request. Clinton acted in the wake of several cases of illnesses caused by foreign foods, including fresh raspberries from Guatemala, cantaloupes from Mexico, and canned coconut milk from Thailand. Clinton said he was also asking administration officials to work with food producers to develop new scientific standards for inspecting fruits and vegetables at all stages along the food chain—whether produced in the United States or imported from overseas.

U.S. imports of food from other countries had risen sharply during the 1980s and 1990s. By 1997 more than one-third of all fruit consumed in the United States and 12 percent of all vegetables came from other countries. During the same period FDA inspections of imported food had fallen sharply because of lack of agency personnel.

It was unclear how Congress would react to Clinton's request for expanded powers over food imports. More certain was that U.S. trading partners would resist the move as an infringement on free trade.

GAO Proposal for Food Safety Agency

The General Accounting Agency (GAO), the investigative arm of Congress, long had been critical of what it called the "fragmented" approach to food safety by federal agencies. The GAO repeated those criticisms in reports and testimony to Congress during 1997.

Testifying before the Senate Agriculture Committee on October 8, Robert A. Robinson, the GAO's director for food and agriculture issues, said the existing federal food safety system was "characterized by a maze of often inconsistent legal and regulatory requirements implemented by twelve different federal agencies." How often a food processing plant was inspected and what was done to enforce food safety standards were determined not by potential risks to public health but by the legislation governing the responsible federal agency, Robinson said.

He noted that the Agriculture Department was required to examine every one of the estimated 7 billion meat and poultry carcasses processed commercially in the United States each year. The Agriculture Department's 7,000 inspectors also were required to visit every meat plant at least once during every operating shift. But because of budget cutbacks and different regularity requirements, the FDA was able to inspect plants processing fruits and vegetables on average only once every ten years. As of 1997 the FDA had only 700 inspectors and laboratory personnel to monitor 53,000 food processing plants in the United States, plus food imported from other countries.

Periodic crises, such as the meat recall at the Hudson plant in 1997, had led the government to react with "a patch here and a band-aid there" to the food inspection system, Robinson said. What was needed instead, he argued, was a "uniform, risk-based inspection system under a single food safety agency." Having one agency in charge of inspecting all food on the basis of the potential risk to public health—rather than on the basis of which agency had jurisdiction over which food type—would allow for "more effective use of resources and ensure a safer food supply," he said.

Following are excerpts from testimony October 8, 1997, by Agriculture Secretary Dan Glickman to the Senate Committee on Agriculture, Nutrition and Forestry:

Mr. Chairman, amid the national fervor for less government, it is the nearly unanimous sentiment of the American people that government should do more to ensure food safety. In fact, a recent *Newsweek* poll indicated that two out of three people even feel that government should spend more in this arena. These sentiments should not surprise us. Today's consumers are well-educated. They grasp the complexity of food safety challenges in the modern world, and they look to us for peace of mind. Before anything else, I believe that people look to their government to protect them in ways that they cannot protect themselves—whether it's national security, the safety of airplane engines, the solvency of our banks or the safety of our food.

Ensuring consumers this security requires constant vigilance. More to the point of today's discussion, it also requires the ability to quickly adapt to changing circumstances.

Mr. Chairman, members of this committee, our most fundamental responsibility is ensuring that Americans have the safest food possible. The Clinton Administration and Congress have worked together in a fairly nonpartisan way to make progress on a number of food safety fronts. I am hopeful that we can do so again on behalf of the Food Safety Enforcement Enhancement Act.

We are working today in a food safety environment that is vastly different from just a decade ago. With the food industry changing so dramatically all around us, government's means of ensuring food safety have got to change, too.

That's the sentiment underlying the Administration's initiative on fruits and vegetables. We're recognizing that as we eat more food from around the world, our consumers still deserve one high level of safety, no matter where their food comes from.

Behind me, you see a chart that lists some of USDA's food safety accomplishments—from the safe-food-handling instructions that are on every meat and poultry product you buy at the grocery store to our modernized inspection system.

I show you this, not to boast, but to give you the context surrounding our request for enhanced enforcement tools. This legislation does not come in a vacuum. We are moving forward with a broad-based, sophisticated food safety strategy that includes: cutting-edge research into the root causes of contamination, stepped-up consumer education, expanded nationwide monitoring to more quickly control outbreaks, efforts to improve international food safety as well as a new meat and poultry inspection system.

In every way, this Administration is shifting America's food safety efforts toward a science-based preventive approach that's best exemplified by what we call HACCP, which is short for Hazard Analysis and Critical Control Points.

This new system will revolutionize meat and poultry safety. But for HACCP to live up to its full promise, government must be able to effectively enforce its higher standards. Simply put, we need new tools for our new rules.

Before HACCP, our meat and poultry inspection system went largely unchanged for 90 years. For most of this century, our inspections have been touch-sight-and-smell examinations aimed at catching contamination after the fact. Based on what we knew about food safety in the early 1900s, this system served the American people fairly well.

Now we know that there is one critical flaw: Even the most eagle-eyed inspector cannot detect invisible food safety threats—such as E. coli 0157:H7 and salmonella—which pose the greatest danger to people's health. These pathogens cause thousands of deaths and millions of illnesses each year, not to mention up to $3 billion in medical costs and productivity losses.

HACCP harnesses state-of-the-art technology to cut down dramatically on food-borne illness. For the first time, there will be regular tests for E. coli and salmonella. For the first time, plants will be required to draw up safety plans that don't just catch contamination, but close the safety gaps that invite it in the first place. For the first time, the focus is on prevention.

Beginning in January 1998 and continuing through January 2000, all meat and poultry plants will be required to put in place a HACCP safety plan that's tailored to their operations. That, too, is a major shift. No longer is government dictating a one-size-fits-all approach. Rather, we're giving each company the freedom to look at their operation, and craft a plan that works for them. Government only cares about results—the safety of the food—which we will confirm through audits' of pathogen tests, examination of company records, and rigorous on-site inspections.

In this way, HACCP represents a major shift in the relationship between government and industry because it clearly assigns industry the responsibility for producing safe food. USDA inspectors are there to confirm that companies live up to this new duty.

Obviously, producing safe food is a responsibility most in the industry already take very seriously. This legislation provides incentives for every company to rise to the new level of responsibility. The major provisions are: civil penalties for companies that fail to meet food safety standards, mandatory government notice when unsafe food may be on the market, mandatory recall authority when a voluntary effort fails, and clarification of our existing authority to refuse or withdraw inspection for willful or repeated violations of food safety laws or regulations.

Historical Perspective

I know that these proposals don't win many popularity contests with industry. I want to make clear that the vast majority of the industry has really stepped up to the plate on food safety. From consumer education, to research, to supporting HACCP, they have been allies. Unfortunately, we have always had our differences when it comes to government enforcement powers.

Back in 1907, the public outcry over Upton Sinclair's graphic depiction of unsanitary conditions in meat packing plants led to the first federal meat inspection law. It was one of America's first consumer protection laws, and industry stood firmly against it. One Chicago meat packer vigorously protested what he described as putting "our business in the hands of theorists, chemists, sociologists, and so forth." But Congress did the right thing, and consumers won an historic victory.

Sensory inspections worked fairly well back then when the major public health concerns were the transmission of diseases from sick animals to humans and unsanitary conditions for animal slaughter and processing. Enforcement authorities were limited to withdrawal of inspectors if a plant refused to destroy condemned product and criminal penalties for people who sold food that was unfit for human consumption. Radical ideas in their time, they're no-brainers today.

Just to illustrate how much things have changed: During the first year of mandatory inspections, USDA had inspectors at 163 plants in 58 cities examining about 42 million animals. Today, federal inspectors work in 6,496 plants in thousands of cities, inspecting about 137 million head of livestock and almost 8 billion poultry per year. That's a lot of meat.

In the 60s, as the volume and complexity of meat and poultry production increased, Congress gave USDA authority over allied industries—such as renderers, animal food manufacturers, transporters and retail operations—recognizing that they, too, play a role in food safety. Congress also gave USDA the power to detain and seize suspect product, conduct investigations, and request a court to issue an injunction.

HACCP: A Preventive Strategy

These are aggressive actions that come into play only after there is considerable evidence that the public health has been put at risk. Today, we are asking for more flexible powers aimed largely at prevention.

Take the case for civil penalties. Most folks correct minor safety slips on a warning, but some do need a stronger nudge. Civil penalties provide that, but more broadly they serve as deterrents—giving every company a powerful incentive to fix minor problems before they turn into major public health incidents. Why should government wait until people are sick and a massive recall and shutdown are necessary? Why do that when a fine may prevent things from getting out of hand in the first place?

For those who say government does not need these powers, that we've got plenty already, I've got to tell you: that really misses the whole point of HACCP. It is not enough that we catch most unsafe food and unsafe practices. It is not enough that we get outbreaks more quickly under control. We must take the next step. We must focus on preventing contamination in the first place. To do that, every plant and processor must be required to be self-vigilant.

That's not to say that federal inspectors just walk away. Their role will be even more important under the new system. What I'm saying is that it is no longer acceptable for a plant to rely solely on USDA inspectors to cry "gotcha." Given the volume of food we're dealing with today, industry has to be more directly responsible for producing safe food.

Civil Penalties

That's the preventive HACCP approach. I'll give you an example that illustrates the distinction. In a plant that generally does a good job, USDA inspectors kept finding contamination. Each time, they seized product and slowed down the line until the problem disappeared. Some say that's all the authority we need. But this approach never fixed the root cause of the problem. As a result, the contamination kept coming back, and inspectors were simply expected to keep catching it as carcass after carcass whizzed by. HACCP tells plants: You're responsible, too. Find the safety gap and close it. Most companies willingly rise to this responsibility. But in talking about enforcement, we're talking about how we deal with the few who don't.

Civil penalties will ensure results. They can also be tailored to fit the offense. The way the system's set up now, it's a fairly all-or-nothing approach. It would be like replacing our entire criminal justice system and its grades of punishment—from fines, to parole, to hard time—with one choice: Execution or acquittal. Eventually, bad actors figure out that they can get away with minor misdeeds. With degrees of penalties, we can keep everyone focused on exceeding the higher bar of safety. And, the penalties are kept fair. Poor record keeping, in most cases, is not the same as shoddy practices, but both need to be corrected.

I should add that civil penalties are not a new idea. This Administration has proposed them twice before, and 18 state meat and poultry inspection programs use them. North of the border, where 42% of our imported meat and poultry comes from, the Canadian government has civil penalty authority and the power to order mandatory recalls. That, too, is essential in today's world.

Mandatory Notification and Recall

The fact is, while HACCP will dramatically improve food safety, there is no 100% guarantee. We're working hard on the research front, and to ensure safe food from farm to table. But we do not yet have a silver bullet. This act better protects consumers from unsafe food by strengthening USDA's ability to pull all the suspect meat and poultry quickly from the marketplace.

Our ability to do that requires 2 authorities that we currently do not have: Mandatory notification. Government and industry cannot move to protect people until we know there is a problem. We had a plant that notified a top customer—a restaurant chain—48 hours before it got around to telling USDA that there might be contaminated food in the marketplace. That's two days before public health experts and everyone else—grocery stores, other restaurants—even had a chance to act. Two days when people could have become ill or worse.

It's easily avoided: When a company has reason to believe there's a public food safety problem, government should get the call first.

When necessary, government should also have the authority to order a mandatory recall. What we have to remember today is that even when everyone acts in good faith, the sheer volume of a recall can be overwhelming. It's not uncommon that a day's work in one plant involves a million pounds of product that's quickly shipped nationwide. Even well-intentioned plants cannot reach every corner store and restaurant to ensure a rapid response to a recall. Yet consumers expect government to ensure that every link in the commercial food chain responds promptly. Most do. That's why a voluntary recall will always be our first line of action.

Unfortunately, while most companies are run by good people who understand that safe food sells, in the food industry—as in any industry—there are bad actors who drag their feet. In those cases, government needs the power to step in and order the unsafe food recalled—wherever it remains in the food distribution chain. This authority is important. Sure, we can threaten to withdraw inspectors from a plant. But the fact is there are no inspectors to withdraw from a restaurant or a warehouse or a supermarket.

Mandatory recall is our back-up. It's consumers' insurance policy that in the event a voluntary recall falls short, their government can move quickly to complete it and protect them.

Food Is Provided Less Protection Than Other Products

Almost all consumer protection laws have been enacted since the end of World War II, and many provide for mandatory recalls of dangerous products. As the chart behind me shows, government can recall unsafe toys, cars, insecticides, and infant formula, but not unsafe food. I should add that the Consumer Product Safety Commission also regularly fines companies that distribute unsafe products, and the Federal Aviation Administration levels civil penalties against airlines with lax safety procedures. Why treat unsafe food any differently?

This enforcement gap gets downright absurd in comparison with powers USDA already has. As the third chart indicates: USDA can fine people who mistreat animals in violation of the Animal Welfare Act. We can use fines to protect farmers and ranchers from unfair trading practices. Abuse a circus elephant, sell a cat without a license, market a potato that's too small, keep bad records on your watermelons, fail to report to the onion committee—fine, fine, fine, fine, fine.

Yet if you produce unsafe food—the only one of these items that puts people's lives at stake—there is no civil penalty. At a certain point, it becomes fairly evident who's being protected here. I think we can come down a little more strongly on the side of the consumer.

Mr. Chairman, protecting the safety of America's food is a fundamental responsibility of government. I am here today to say that we can do more. The Food Safety Enforcement Enhancement Act is not the last step, but it is an essential next step. The bottom line is: Times have changed since 1907. We have new rules that promise a revolution in food safety, but they require modern, flexible, effective enforcement tools. This legislation will bring us up to speed. . . .

NEA ON THE FUTURE OF
THE NONPROFIT ARTS
October 13, 1998

Two studies of the nonprofit arts scene in the United States concluded that supporters of the arts—including artists themselves—urgently needed to demonstrate to the general public the value of culture in society. The reports said the arts, from folk singing in Appalachia to opera and modern dance in the big cities, were in danger of being overwhelmed by commercial entertainment and ultimately forgotten by a society more concerned with personal and financial health than with its cultural legacy.

One report, "Creative America: A Report to the President," was issued February 25 by the President's Committee on the Arts and Humanities. It called for an expansion of financial support for the arts by both the federal government and the private sector.

A second report, "American Canvas," was issued October 13 by the National Endowment for the Arts (NEA). The result of a series of six public seminars around the country, that report offered a pessimistic assessment of the state of public support for and interest in the arts. It warned that the country's rich cultural traditions could be diminished, or even lost altogether over time, unless a broad public movement developed to promote interest in the arts.

Both reports dealt with the nonprofit world of the arts, not the commercial world of entertainment dominated by television, the movies, massselling recordings, and emerging computer technologies. Even as they concluded that commercial entertainment had the potential to drive the nonprofit arts into extinction, both reports called on the leaders of commercial entertainment to provide more financial support for their nonprofit arts cousins.

These reports on the long-term future of the arts came during the third consecutive year in which the short-term future of the NEA was brought into question on Capitol Hill. Conservatives in the House of Representatives tried to kill the agency, a small but symbolically important provider of federal tax dollars to the arts. Senate backers of the agency managed to preserve a $98 million appropriation for it.

The President's Committee

President Bill Clinton in September 1994 appointed a committee to examine the status of arts and humanities in the United States. The committee had thirty-two private members (including corporate leaders, directors of foundations, and artists such as violinist Isaac Stern) and representatives of thirteen federal agencies with cultural programs. The chairman was John Brademus, retired president of New York University and a former Democratic leader in the U.S. House of Representatives.

In its report the committee presented the traditional view of the artistic community that culture was important to society in ways that were often intangible and not obvious. Brademus in an introduction said that "cultural life is vital to a democratic society." The committee said the United States had a rich cultural heritage of which all citizens should be proud.

Even so, the committee warned that declining funding from foundations, the government, and private donors was endangering theater, dance, music, painting, and other forms of art that "do not survive in the marketplace alone." The committee called on the president to lead a national initiative to renew philanthropic support for the arts. Attempting to counter the move in Congress to abolish the National Endowment for the Arts, the committee also proposed that funding for the NEA, its sister agency the National Endowment for the Humanities, and other grant-making organizations be increased to the equivalent of $2 a person by the year 2000—or more than $500 million annually.

NEA Report

The report issued October 13 by the National Endowment for the Arts was the last under the leadership of actress Jane Alexander, who had been the agency's chairman since October 1993. In an introduction Alexander called the report and the forums on which it was based part of a "national discussion" on the future of the arts.

The report outlined a paradox for the nonprofit arts. On the one hand, the previous three decades had seen a rapid expansion of the number of institutions offering all types of culture to the public. For example, between 1965 and 1994 the number of professional opera companies had grown from 27 to 120, professional orchestras from 100 to 230, dance companies from 37 to 400, and theatrical companies from 56 to 425. Between 1970 and 1990 the number of people defined by the Census Bureau as "artists in the workforce" more than doubled, from 720,000 to nearly 1.7 million. The report attributed these trends to such efforts as start-up grants provided to hundreds of groups by the Ford Foundation and the NEA's grants to state and local arts councils. Attendance at some cultural venues, especially museums, was at an all-time high.

On the other hand, the report said public and private support for the arts appeared to be in decline, according to such measurements as congressional appropriations for the NEA and grants to arts organizations from private foundations. The report cited other factors as well, including the rapid decline in the previous two decades of arts education in the public schools and the near total disappearance of serious cultural programming from commercial television and radio.

The report listed a number of reasons for the vulnerable state of the nonprofit arts, such as competition for attention and dollars within the arts community, competition from commercial entertainment, and societal changes that made it more difficult for busy families to enjoy or partici-pate in the arts. Many groups in the nonprofit arts sector also had an elit-ist attitude, the report said, leading some people to view the arts "as be-longing to someone else." Art in any of its manifestations had little or no role in the daily lives of most Americans, the report said, and so the absence of public concern about the financial travails of orchestras and dance com-panies should not be surprising.

Much of the news coverage of the report described its tone as "gloomy" be-cause of its focus on how the arts community was out of touch with the gen-eral public. But the report also recommended a series of actions that those in the arts community could take to strengthen public support. Some of the recommendations were general in nature, such as urging "new ways in which artists and arts organizations can bring art to the people, interact-ing with the public outside of the concert hall and museum." Other recom-mendations were more specific, including a series of suggestions that arts organizations shed their traditional isolation and develop mutually bene-ficial alliances with other community organizations. The report said the arts community should look to the environmental movement for lessons in how to build coalitions that broaden the base of public participation and, ultimately, financial support.

Following are excerpts from the report, "American Canvas," re-leased October 13, 1997, by the National Endowment for the Arts:

Among the more important lessons of the American Canvas is the recog-nition that the administrative and fiscal practices that served the nonprofit arts so well during their ascendancy over the past three decades will not nec-essarily prove as effective in the new century. If nothing else had changed, the sheer increase in the size of the arts community since the establishment of the Arts Endowment in 1965 would have made for a much different, much more competitive environment. And when ever-more-pressing social prob-lems, from AIDS to homelessness to drug abuse to race relations, are factored into the equation, each demanding attention in a context of deficit reduction at the federal level and balanced budgets in many states, it is little wonder that the soaring growth curves that the arts achieved in years past have proved impossible to sustain.

So, too, have the many new opportunities that have arisen in recent years added to the complexity of the cultural landscape. From the belated recognition of Americas cultural diversity to breakthroughs in technology, the variety of new options for cultural programming has contributed to the rapidly changing context of the arts in America. The closing years of the 20th century present an opportunity for the reexamination of the structural underpinnings of the nonprofit arts and for speculation on the development of a new support system: *one based less on traditional charitable practices and more on the exchange of goods and services.* American artists and arts organizations can make valuable contributions—from addressing social issues to enhancing education to providing "content" for the new information superhighway—to American society.

As the new century dawns, artists and arts organizations can "make the year 2000 a national celebration of the American spirit in every community," as President Clinton has suggested. But the real challenge, and the reason why a reexamination of the nonprofit arts infrastructure is so important, is an even greater one: to offer an alternative to conglomerate culture, to make those millennial celebrations look less like the half-time show of the Super Bowl, a triumph of American marketing, and more reflective of the true depth and variety of our culture, a triumph of American creativity. . . .

Sad to say, many American citizens fail to recognize the direct relevance of art to their lives. The product of an educational system that at best enshrined the arts as the province of elite cultures and at worst ignored the arts altogether, some people understandably view the arts as belonging to someone else. "Most . . . people," as William Wilson of Brigham Young University expressed it in the Salt Lake City forum, "if you talk to them about art, they're going to say, 'Art belongs out there. That's not part of my life.' " Failing to acknowledge their own expressive activities as part of the full spectrum of the arts, many of these Americans are apt to look with suspicion at an "arts world" that seems alternately intimidating, incomprehensible, expensive, alien, and, thanks to the generally poor job that the mass media have done in covering the arts, often disreputable. "We need to make people aware of how the arts fill their lives if we want their support," suggested glass artist Kate Vogel at the American Canvas forum in Charlotte. . . .

Culture and Community

Just as the arts loom large in the lives of many individual Americans, so can they exert an equally profound influence on our communities. The sense that art is firmly entrenched at the margins of many American communities is the result of a variety of factors. The arts community itself bears a measure of responsibility for the marginalization of the nonprofit culture. In the course of its justifiable concern with professionalization, institution-building, and experimentation during the 60s and 70s, for example, the arts community neglected those aspects of participation, democratization, and popularization that might have helped sustain the arts when the political climate turned sour. Some civic leaders view cultural activities as *amenities* engaged solely in aesthetic pursuits, rather than *necessities* to the health of community life.

Fortunately, the American Canvas forums offered an abundance of evidence from both the cultural and civic sectors suggesting that the arts can indeed play a central role in the lives of our communities. The legacy of the future may have a more common, if no less valued, profile. Included will be the art that is woven through the social fabric, that contributes to the quality of life, fosters civic pride and participation, stimulates the economy and attracts tourists, revitalizes neighborhoods and addresses social problems. Great works of the past won't be excluded from this tapestry—the $60 million in revenues generated by the Cezanne exhibition at the Philadelphia Museum of Art last year is evidence of the power of past masters—but the new cloth of culture will be much more of a quilt, joining a vast array of new patterns that range from folk, vernacular, and popular expressions, to social, political, and experimental works.

Some will bewail, no doubt, the alleged lowering of standards that permits these new forms to enter the "inner circle" of culture. Others will look askance at the utilitarian aspects of art—the "culture of therapeutics," as critic Robert Hughes puts it—that is expected to solve social problems, stimulate the economy, improve the young, and otherwise serve the common good. But in 1997, it hardly seems necessary to debate this point. In a perfect world, to be sure, we might expect the arts to justify their claim on the public purse and the private largesse on the basis of their intrinsic worth. Such justification, after all, is more a matter of translation than of transformation, expressing the value of the arts in terms that civic and corporate leaders—and the average citizen, for that matter—can more readily understand. But a Bill T. Jones who addresses social issues in his work is no less a choreographer, nor Henry Louis Gates any less a historian for tending to the present as well as to the past, and all of us, in fact, are the beneficiaries of their extraordinary efforts.

Calls to Action

The following Calls to Action, which were endorsed by the full American Canvas committee on 30 January 1997, were written by the American Canvas Steering Committee as a result of the discussions that took place in the several regional Forums.

Columbus

The American Canvas calls on civic and community leaders to join together in recognizing America's place among the great cultures of the world through artistic and cultural celebration at the turn of the century.

Los Angeles

The American Canvas calls on all artists and arts organizations nationwide (commercial, non-profit and volunteer) to work together, share resources, and broaden citizen exposure to the arts in order to strengthen, revitalize and promote communities.

Salt Lake City

The American Canvas calls on educators, parents and artists to work together to ensure that the arts are an integral part of their education system by recognizing the unique role of the arts as a resource for engaging students and developing skills necessary to compete in the information age that will expand in the 21st century.

Rock Hill/Charlotte

The American Canvas calls on business, civic and arts leaders to work collaboratively in designing community development plans which recognize the competitive and cultural advantages that the arts bring to the economic, social, and imaginative life of communities and their citizens.

San Antonio

The American Canvas calls on all departments of government (Federal, state and local) to develop partnerships within government and with the private and non-profit sectors that enhance the quality of the lives of all Americans by integrating arts and cultural opportunities into their decision-making and services.

Miami

The American Canvas calls on government, the private sector and arts organizations to support and develop broad reaching policy and services that ensure greater access to the arts and cultural heritage for all Americans.

General Actions

1. The American Canvas calls on artists, arts organizations, civic, business and religious leaders to recognize the unique opportunities that the arts provide America's communities and take responsibility For making the arts part of developing solutions in response to community needs.
2. The American Canvas calls on artists and arts organizations, elected officials, business, civic, and religious leaders to expand the description of the arts to be more inclusive of the broad array of cultural activities that the American public experiences and appreciates.
3. The American Canvas calls on individuals who appreciate the importance of the arts to mobilize at the local, state, regional and national levels to express the value of the arts to society and to ensure an arts legacy For future generations.
4. The American Canvas calls on the American public and government leaders to support the vital part of government in ensuring that the arts play an increasing role in the lives and education of our citizens and the strengthening of America's communities.

[The Challenge to Art]

As this century draws to a close, and as the National Endowment for the Arts enters its fourth decade, the arts community finds itself at a crossroads. Faced both with shrinking resources and with increased competition for funds, it needs to re-evaluate the nature of the nonprofit arts infrastructure, to clarify and underscore its relation to other social and economic concerns, and to determine the best means of ensuring that the full range of Americas cultural riches will be passed on to future generations. The larger community, beyond the nonprofit arts sector itself, must address the challenges and opportunities listed below. We need to acknowledge, in short, that our "cultural legacy" is not simply a concern for the continued health of the arts, but is in fact a primary factor in the strength and vitality of American society itself.

1. Redefining American Culture

Again and again at the American Canvas forums, the issue of the ways in which we define the arts in America was raised. The narrow, professional, institutional definition that we've used in the past must now be replaced with a more expansive view that includes a range of activities—avocational and ethnic, participatory and popular—within its sweep. The health of America's culture depends more on active citizen involvement in the arts than on mere spectatorship, for those who participate in the arts tend to go to cultural events. Just as our fascination with spectator sports is rooted in early participation in amateur athletics, so can a larger, more committed audience for the arts be developed out of a nation of avocational singers, dancers, painters, and musicians.

The challenge is to reach out to the majority of Americans who currently have no direct involvement with the professional, nonprofit arts, to expand the nations cultural palette to include a full range of participatory activities, without losing sight of the standards of professional excellence that still have a role in providing benchmarks of achievement. The opportunity is to build a much larger, more inclusive base of support for the arts, one that gives all Americans a stake in the preservation and transmission of our cultural legacy.

What artists and communities can do:

Take stock of the cultural resources that already exist, paying particular attention to those pockets of creativity—in the community center, the senior-citizen home, places of worship and the like—that might have been overlooked in previous inventories. In what ways are Americans already participating in the arts, and how can this involvement be increased? Find ways to provide forums for some of the newer voices in the community. What are the barriers to access and involvement in the arts, and how can they be overcome?

Make an effort to balance the needs of the professional arts sector with efforts to involve citizens more directly in the arts, through a range of outreach, educational, and participatory activities. How can cultural services be delivered in the same way that other community needs—health care, education, and public safety, for example—are met?

Instead of simply inviting citizens to attend the arts, find new ways in which artists and arts organizations can bring art to the people, interacting with the public outside of the concert hail and museum.

2. Supporting the Nonprofit Arts

Much of what we know about the nonprofit arts economy—in particular the delicate balance of public and private support, earned and contributed income—is rooted in older models largely unrelated to the realities of the present, with the sharp declines in public-sector support and increased competition for private funding. The statistical basis of our knowledge is woefully thin, and what we do know about cultural production in this country is skewed heavily toward the commercial end of the spectrum, anchored by the considerable economic clout of the film, television, and recording industries.

The American Canvas forums represent a significant first step in learning more about the current status of the arts infrastructure in this country—both how (and at what costs to the human capital involved) arts organizations currently operate within their communities, and how the most successful of them have established a network of community support beyond the traditional philanthropic models. The challenge is to communicate more effectively the nature of this infrastructure to a public that is only vaguely aware of the distinction between the nonprofit and the commercial, and between arts and entertainment. The opportunity is to achieve for the arts that same mantle of indispensability that other nonprofit institutions—schools and libraries, churches and hospitals—have long enjoyed.

What artists and communities can do:

Assess how the local arts infrastructure has changed in recent years, and what further changes might lie ahead. What new organizations have appeared (both arts producers/presenters as well as funders)? Which of the existing institutions are struggling financially? What are the primary sources of support and how have they changed? What facilities exist for the presentation of the arts in the community, and how effectively are they shared?

Identify new revenue streams that might be developed in the public sector. Does a designated local arts agency exist (either private, nonprofit or public)? Does the community have a cultural plan? Is there a percent-for-art program in place? A united arts campaign? Hotel-motel tax? Convention and Visitors Bureau support?

Convince the business community of the importance of including cultural activities within their philanthropic programs or their advertising and marketing budgets.

Work with a community foundation (there are now over 400 of them across the country, devoting nearly 17 percent of their funding—more than $40 million—to the arts every year) to develop a more systematic, community-wide support structure for the arts. Determine how other foundations might be collectively approached, to begin to address arts funding needs on a community or regional basis rather than in the standard context of head-to-head competition for funding.

Provide a forum in which both the economic needs of the arts, as well as the cultural and other services that the arts can provide to a community, can be discussed.

Help to open the lines of communication between the nonprofit and commercial sectors, developing the kinds of partnerships that will bolster the nonprofit arts economy.

Foster a "new philanthropy" in the community, with increased emphasis on the exchange of goods and services and less dependence on cash contributions, encouraging arts organizations to bring both their processes and their products to a wide range of community activities.

Work with the local media to begin providing more substantive and inclusive coverage of the community's cultural resources.

3. Working Together

American Canvas participants were unanimous in their agreement that the Future of the arts will depend far more on coalition-building and collaborative strategies, both within the arts community itself as well as among arts and nonarts organizations and agencies. The challenge is making that difficult transition from theory to practice, implementing and maintaining the kinds of alliances that depend on resource sharing, information exchange, and occasionally on the subordination of individual interests to the collective good. The opportunity is to derive in the nonprofit sector the same kind of economies of scale and strength in numbers that the corporate sector has used so effectively in recent years—not through "acquisitions and mergers," however, but through a shared vision and a shared commitment to serving the community.

What artists and communities can do:

Determine the kinds of partnerships and collaborations that will be most effective, both in meeting the cultural and other needs of the community as well as in protecting and sustaining the cultural legacy.

Find ways, using both public and private resources, to reward the formation of such partnerships, in a manner that genuinely benefits all participants. What can local governments do to foster alliances among arts and non-arts organizations, taking into account their differing goals, expectations, and operating procedures? What can the arts community itself do to ensure that collaborative strategies become the rule rather than the exception in organizational behavior?

Foster partnerships between arts and non-arts organizations in the business, political, social-service, religious, and educational sectors, taking into account the particular needs of the community. Those alliances should include municipal organizations (social services, economic development, housing, law enforcement, etc.), neighborhood/community organizations, school districts, public libraries, convention and visitors bureaus, and chambers of commerce.

Develop strategies to ensure that these partnerships will be sustained beyond the original activity or event that may have initiated their formation.

4. Meeting Community Needs

Perhaps more than any other American Canvas theme, the contributions that the arts can make to a wide variety of civic and community needs were seen as absolutely crucial to the future health of the arts. Arts organizations and artists alike need to become more directly involved in civic and community affairs, bringing their talents to bear on a full range of municipal activities: social services, education, youth programs, urban planning, public housing, law enforcement, economic development, and parks and recreation.

The challenge is to "translate" the value of the arts into terms that will be more readily understood in the political and business sectors. The opportunity is to transform the arts in the civic context from their present status as amenities that are added once the necessities are taken care of, into one of the primary means of addressing those necessities in the first place.

What artists and communities can do:

Move beyond the traditional role of the arts, in their formal performance and exhibition functions, to recognize the ways in which the arts bring people together, the opportunities they afford for participation in civic life, and the many contributions they can make to municipal affairs.

Highlight the ways that the arts contribute significantly to the economic vitality of our cites: *as* a source of cultural tourism, as a stimulus of ancillary spending (on parking, meals, lodging, and the like), and *as* a key factor in the location decisions of companies seeking the most attractive environment for their employees.

Recognize the two other significant economic contributions of the arts, both as a source of employment and as a key ingredient in the development of vital job skills.

Assist artists and arts organizations to bring the creative process to civic affairs, helping to address the problems that all communities must confront. Make a stronger case for the inclusion of the arts in such basic civic activities as urban planning, social services, and economic development.

5. Educating the Young

Education in the arts, both in developing the audience of the future as well as in shaping an electorate—and their leaders—who will recognize the values of arts to society, continues as a priority. Equally prominent, though, was a belief in the importance of the arts to education. The arts should become a basic part of the K-12 curriculum, not simply for their intrinsic value as a course of study—to help all children and young adults to interpret their world, better understand history and one another, and effectively communicate their most profound ideas—but also for their contribution to students' mastery of other basic areas of the curriculum.

For this to happen, however, a persuasive rationale for ensuring that the arts are made a basic part of a comprehensive elementary and secondary education should be promulgated. The challenge is to overcome the budgetary constraints, time pressures, and other social and political impediments that threaten to reduce the arts to mere extra-curricular activities, available to the fortunate few but beyond the reach of the vast majority of children. The opportunity is to ensure the arts' place in the classroom for all students, not as an occasional treat, but in a sequential, curriculum-based, systematic program that is on par with other core subjects. The results, at a minimum, will be a generation of students who can create and perform the arts, understand the role and importance of the arts in culture and history, and perceive and respond to the qualities of the arts.

What artists and communities can do:

Examine the Goals 2000 legislation and the Improving Americas Schools Act and begin working to implement their recommendations for the inclusion of the arts among the core subjects in the basic K-12 curriculum.

Build partnerships among schools, arts organizations, and teacher-training institutes in the interest of developing and sustaining arts education.

Determine which local organizations are affiliated with the national organizations that are a part of the Goals 2000 Arts Education Partnership, and work with these organizations in furthering the interests of arts education locally.

Encourage local school boards to adopt an arts education plan that takes into account child and adolescent development and the multiple ways in which students learn.

Make certain that local schools have well-trained and qualified teachers of the arts as well as artists in the schools who have a command of an arts discipline and/or a deep understanding of its forms, principles and methods and its history and tradition.

Assess the proficiencies of students in dance, music, theater, and the visual arts, using the standards developed for the National Assessment of Educational Progress.

Develop a network of education, arts, and cultural organizations and institutions that are committed to arts education.

6. Entering the Information Age

Perhaps more than any other aspect of contemporary life, the communications landscape—the various ways in which we transmit and receive a wide range of information and entertainment—is undergoing a fundamental change. Both in the conversion from analog to digital, and in the gradual convergence of the telephone, publishing, entertainment, and computer industries, the communications infrastructure of the next century will differ significantly from the existing patchwork quilt of mutually exclusive technologies. While the implications for the nonprofit sector of all of these changes are not immediately clear, the arts are potentially well positioned to take advantage of the rapidly evolving telecommunications landscape. As the producers of vast quantities of "content," artists and arts organizations can contribute significantly to the new system. Already, the arts community has benefited from the enhanced employment prospects of the "Information Economy"—more than 80,000 new jobs in the digital arts over the past two years alone, according to industry estimates—and the future promises to be even brighter. The challenge will be in overcoming the traditional barriers that have separated the nonprofit and commercial sectors, eliminating the distribution bottlenecks that keep most nonprofit fare—in music, the media arts, and publishing especially—out of the commercial marketplace. The opportunity is that of reaching vast new audiences electronically, converting the scattered, niche markets that have traditionally supported the arts into a critical mass, and using the new information systems to attract new audiences online. Nor should the live arts experience have to suffer in this new environment. For just as Americans today who enjoy the arts on radio and television are twice as likely to attend live arts events, so should the new media prove useful as an audience-building tool.

What artists and communities can do:

Work with public libraries and public broadcasters, many of which are already involved in developing the new computer technologies, to incorporate more arts programming within their online offerings.

Form partnerships with local arts organizations to enable them to adapt more quickly to the new communications environment, joining classrooms and libraries, hospitals and clinics as key nonprofit members of the online community.

Insist that those at the forefront of developing new online enterprises—including broadcasters, cable franchises, telephone companies, and newspapers—provide room on their systems for noncommercial, public-interest programming, including the offerings of local artists and arts organizations. The same kinds of "public spaces" that have long been the province of the arts in the "real world," in other words, must be replicated in the "virtual world" that is rapidly taking shape.

Just as the American Canvas Calls to Action have elicited a wide variety of public- and private-sector initiatives, there are any number of ways that communities can respond to the challenges and opportunities listed here. If we are to build a citizens' coalition to create and sustain a climate encouraging the arts, we each have responsibilities. Our artists must stay engaged in community life, for everyone who receives the benefits of society is obliged to repay that debt. Our country, as well, is obliged to preserve and protect its cultural resources. As the 21st century approaches, let us make certain that all of the varied cultural achievements of this century are carried safely into the next, and that American artists and arts organizations, and the communities in which they reside, continue to find new ways to mutually support one another. For this, we must take a page from the conservation movement, organize for action, and take care of our cultural legacy.

PRESIDENTIAL COMMISSION ON PROTECTING INFRASTRUCTURE
October 20, 1997

The nation's infrastructure—roads, bridges, factories, computer systems, and other essential elements of everyday life—was becoming increasingly vulnerable to attacks by terrorists, spies, and mischief-makers, a presidential commission warned October 20. In a report to President Bill Clinton, the commission said government and private business needed to cooperate to develop protections against threats to the infrastructure that could cripple the economy and damage national security.

After studying the issue for more than a year, the President's Commission on Critical Infrastructure Protection concluded that there was little immediate threat of a massive attack on the nation's physical and electronic lifelines. Nevertheless, the commission said the prospect of serious damage was increasing rapidly, and more planning to head off such threats was urgently needed.

The White House issued a statement October 22 praising the report and saying Clinton believed "it is important to act now to ensure that America's economic prosperity and national security" were protected against potential threats. The statement said the National Security Council would review the report and make recommendations to the president.

The General Accounting Office (GAO), the investigative arm of Congress, issued a separate, detailed report September 26 analyzing the efforts of more than forty federal agencies to combat terrorism. The report made no recommendations.

President's Commission

Clinton appointed the infrastructure commission in July 1996, partly in response to several incidents in which computer "hackers" had gained access to and damaged computer systems of several government agencies, including the Defense Department. John M. Deutch, then director of the Central Intelligence Agency, told a Senate subcommittee in June 1996 that he considered attacks on computer security the second most serious na-

tional security threat facing the country, after the worldwide proliferation of nuclear, chemical, and biological weapons. (Computer security issues, Historic Documents of 1996, p. 312)

The infrastructure commission included representatives of key government agencies and the private sector. Robert T. Marsh, the chairman, was a retired air force general who had led the Air Force Systems Command. The commission held five public hearings on the matter and said it consulted with approximately 6,000 representatives from the government, military, industry, academia, and other fields.

In speeches and congressional testimony before and after release of the report, Marsh emphasized that both the government and the private sector faced terrorist and other threats. Marsh told a Senate subcommittee November 5 that some commission members had started their work with the assumption that "this was an easy problem that government alone could solve in a few easy steps." But the review showed that combating threats to the infrastructure was a complex task requiring close cooperation between the government and the private sector. "Our national and economic security has become a shared responsibility—one that will require a new kind of partnership between government and industry—one which encourages information sharing and one which requires the government to lead by example," he said.

In contrast to many such high-level study groups, the infrastructure panel did not refer to the situation it studied as a "crisis" and did not call for a massive government program to deal with it. Instead, the commission said the most urgent need it found was to heighten public awareness of potential threats to the nation's infrastructure. The commission called for more coordination among government agencies and more cooperation between the government and the private sector—and it proposed more government research on ways to combat threats to the infrastructure.

In its report, the commission focused much of its attention on what it called "cyber threats" to computer systems that were becoming increasingly essential to every aspect of modern life. As the role of those systems grew, the nation's vulnerability to attack also grew, the commission said.

In the past, Americans were protected by the oceans and the country's overwhelming military power. By 1997, the commission said, "the right command sent over a network to a power generation station's control computer could be just as effective as a backpack full of explosives, and the perpetrator would be harder to identify and apprehend." The danger was heightened by the fact that millions of people possessed the computer skills and knowledge to attack infrastructure systems; even those who did not have the knowledge could obtain it readily by accessing "hacker tools" libraries posted on the Internet.

Lack of Awareness

The commission said it found that the general public was "unaware" of the vulnerability of everyday services such as telephones and electricity to attacks by terrorists or computer hackers. Even among decision-makers in government and the private sector, awareness of these threats was "limited," the commission said. To heighten awareness, the commission called on the White House to sponsor a series of conferences with national leaders and urged other government agencies to work with the private sector on ways to combat the threats. The commission also suggested education programs, for kindergarten through college-level, offering "ethical guidance regarding computer usage."

The commission suggested three main steps by the government to combat infrastructure threats. First, it said that the National Institute of Standards and Technology and the National Security Agency should jointly develop standards and practices for security of information systems. These standards and practices would be shared with all levels of government and private industry, and all federal agencies should be required to comply with them. Second, the commission called for more coordination of infrastructure protection among government agencies, with policies established by a White House Office of National Infrastructure Assurance working with the president's National Security Council and National Economic Council. Third, the commission called for federal spending on research and development projects for protecting national infrastructure to be doubled to $500 million in fiscal year 1999, with a 20 percent increase in each of the following five years.

One potentially controversial commission recommendation was that law enforcement officials be given expanded authority to investigate crimes committed by or against computer systems. Over the opposition of some civil liberties groups and many computer industry representatives, the Clinton administration had sought the authority to regulate "encryption" technology that enabled computer users to protect the privacy of information sent over telecommunications systems. Siding with the administration, the commission said Congress should consider legislation enabling law enforcement agencies, when investigating criminal activities, to obtain court orders allowing them to decode computerized communications.

> *Following is an excerpt from the summary of the report, "Critical Foundations: Protecting America's Infrastructures," issued October 20, 1997, by the President's Commission on Critical Infrastructure Protection:*

Introduction

The United States is in the midst of a tremendous cultural change—a change that affects every aspect of our lives. The cyber dimension promotes accelerating reliance on our infrastructures and offers access to them from all over the world, blurring traditional boundaries and jurisdictions. National defense is not just about government anymore, and economic security is not just about business. The critical infrastructures are central to our national defense and our economic power, and we must lay the foundations for their future security on a new form of cooperation between the private sector and the federal government.

The federal government has an important role to play in defense against cyber threats—collecting information about tools that can do harm, conducting research into defensive technologies, and sharing defensive techniques and best practices. Government also must lead and energize its own protection efforts, and engage the private sector by offering expertise to facilitate protection of privately owned infrastructures.

In the private sector, the defenses and responsibilities naturally encouraged and expected as prudent business practice for owners and operators of our infrastructures are the very same measures needed to protect against the cyber tools available to terrorists and other threats to national security. . . .

Venues for Change

Terrorist bombings of US forces in Saudi Arabia, the World Trade Center in New York City, and the federal building in Oklahoma City remind us that the end of the Cold War has not eliminated threats of hostile action against the United States.

In recognition of comparable threats to our national infrastructures, President Clinton signed Executive Order 13010 on July 15, 1996, establishing the President's Commission on Critical Infrastructure Protection. The Commission was chartered to conduct a comprehensive review and recommend a national policy for protecting critical infrastructures and assuring their continued operation. . . .

We Found

Increasing Dependence on Critical Infrastructures

The development of the computer and its astonishingly rapid improvements have ushered in the Information Age that affects almost all aspects of American commerce and society. Our security, economy, way of life, and perhaps even survival, are now dependent on the interrelated trio of electrical energy, communications, and computers.

Increasing Vulnerabilities

Classical physical disruptions

A satchel of dynamite or a truckload of fertilizer and diesel fuel have been frequent terrorist tools. The explosion and the damage are so certain to draw attention that these kinds of attacks continue to be among the probable threats to our infrastructures.

New, cyber threats

Today, the right command sent over a network to a power generating station's control computer could be just as effective as a backpack full of explosives, and the perpetrator would be harder to identify and apprehend.

The rapid growth of a computer-literate population ensures that increasing millions of people possess the skills necessary to consider such an attack. The wide adoption of public protocols for system interconnection and the availability of "hacker tool" libraries make their task easier.

While the resources needed to conduct a physical attack have not changed much recently, the resources necessary to conduct a cyber attack are now commonplace. A personal computer and a simple telephone connection to an Internet Service Provider anywhere in the world are enough to cause a great deal of harm.

System complexities and interdependencies

The energy and communications infrastructures especially are growing in complexity and operating closer to their designed capacity. This creates an increased possibility of cascading effects that begin with a rather minor and routine disturbance and end only after a large regional outage. Because of their technical complexity, some of these dependencies may be unrecognized until a major failure occurs.

A Wide Spectrum of Threats

Of the many people with the necessary skills and resources, some may have the motivation to cause substantial disruption in services or destruction of the equipment used to provide the service.

This list of the kinds of threats we considered shows the scope of activity with potentially adverse consequences for the infrastructures, and the diversity of people who might engage in that activity. It may not be possible to categorize the threat until the perpetrator is identified—for example, we may not be able to distinguish industrial espionage from national intelligence collection.

Natural events and accidents

Storm-driven wind and water regularly cause service outages, but the effects are well known, the providers are experienced in dealing with these situations, and the effects are limited in time and geography.

Accidental physical damage to facilities is known to cause a large fraction of system incidents. Common examples are fires and floods at central facilities and the ubiquitous backhoe that unintentionally severs pipes or cables.

Blunders, errors, and omissions

By most accounts, incompetent, inquisitive, or unintentional human actions (or omissions) cause a large fraction of the system incidents that are not explained by natural events and accidents. Since these usually only affect local areas, service is quickly restored; but there is potential for a nationally significant event.

Insiders

Normal operation demands that a large number of people have authorized access to the facilities or to the associated information and communications systems. If motivated by a perception of unfair treatment by management, or if suborned by an outsider, an "insider" could use authorized access for unauthorized disruptive purposes.

Recreational hackers

For an unknown number of people, gaining unauthorized electronic access to information and communication systems is a most fascinating and challenging game. Often they deliberately arrange for their activities to be noticed even while hiding their specific identities. While their motivations do not include actual disruption of service, the tools and techniques they perfect among their community are available to those with hostile intent.

Criminal activity

Some are interested in personal financial gain through manipulation of financial or credit accounts or stealing services. In contrast to some hackers, these criminals typically hope their activities will never be noticed, much less attributed to them. Organized crime groups may be interested in direct financial gain, or in covering their activity in other areas.

Industrial espionage

Some firms can find reasons to discover the proprietary activities of their competitors, by open means if possible or by criminal means if necessary. Often these are international activities conducted on a global scale.

Terrorism

A variety of groups around the world would like to influence US policy and are willing to use disruptive tactics if they think that will help.

National intelligence

Most, if not all, nations have at least some interest in discovering what would otherwise be secrets of other nations for a variety of economic, political, or military purposes.

Information warfare

Both physical and cyber attacks on our infrastructures could be part of a broad, orchestrated attempt to disrupt a major US military operation or a significant economic activity.

Lack of Awareness

We have observed that the general public seems unaware of the extent of the vulnerabilities in the services that we all take for granted, and that within government and among industry decision-makers, awareness is limited. Several have told us that there has not yet been a cause for concern sufficient to demand action.

We do acknowledge that this situation seems to be changing for the better. The public news media seem to be carrying relevant articles more frequently;

attendance at conferences of security professionals is up; and vendors are actively introducing new security products.

The Commission believes that the actions recommended in this report will increase sensitivity to these problems and reduce our vulnerabilities at all levels.

No National Focus

Related to the lack of awareness is the need for a national focus or advocate for infrastructure protection. Following up on our report to the President, we need to build a framework of effective deterrence and prevention.

This is not simply the usual study group's lament that "no one is in charge." These infrastructures are so varied, and form such a large part of this nation's economic activity, that no one person or organization can be in charge. We do not need, and probably could not stand, the appointment of a Director of Infrastructures. We do need, and recommend, several more modest ways to create and maintain a national focus on the issues.

Protection of our infrastructures will not be accomplished by a big federal project. It will require continuous attention and incremental improvement for the foreseeable future.

We Concluded

Life on the information superhighway isn't much different from life on the streets; the good guys have to hustle to keep the bad guys from getting ahead.

Rules Change in Cyberspace—New Thinking is Required

It is not surprising that infrastructures have always been attractive targets for those who would do us harm. In the past we have been protected from hostile attacks on the infrastructures by broad oceans and friendly neighbors. Today, the evolution of cyber threats has changed the situation dramatically. In cyberspace, national borders are no longer relevant. Electrons don't stop to show passports.

Potentially serious cyber attacks can be conceived and planned without detectable logistic preparation. They can be invisibly reconnoitered, clandestinely rehearsed, and then mounted in a matter of minutes or even seconds without revealing the identity and location of the attacker.

Formulas that carefully divide responsibility between foreign defense and domestic law enforcement no longer apply as clearly as they used to. "With the existing rules, you may have to solve the crime before you can decide who has the authority to investigate it."

We Should Act Now to Protect our Future

The Commission has not discovered an imminent attack or a credible threat sufficient to warrant a sense of immediate national crisis. However, we are quite convinced that our vulnerabilities are increasing steadily while the costs associated with an effective attack continue to drop. What is more, the investments required to improve the situation are still relatively modest, but will rise if we procrastinate.

We should attend to our critical foundations before the storm arrives, not after: Waiting for disaster will prove as expensive as it is irresponsible.

Infrastructure Assurance is a Shared Responsibility

National security requires much more than military strength. Our world position, our ability to influence others, our standard of living, and our own self-image depend on economic prosperity and public confidence. Clear distinctions between foreign and domestic policy no longer serve our interests well.

At the same time, the effective operation of our military forces depends more and more on the continuous availability of infrastructures, especially communications and transportation, that are not dedicated to military use.

While no nation state is likely to attack our territory or our armed forces, we are inevitably the target of ill will and hostility from some quarters. Disruption of the services on which our economy and well-being depend could have significant effects, and if repeated frequently could seriously harm public confidence. Because our military and private infrastructures are becoming less and less separate, because the threats are harder to differentiate as from local criminals or foreign powers, and because the techniques of protection, mitigation, and restoration are largely the same, we conclude that responsibility for infrastructure protection and assurance can no longer be delegated on the basis of who the attacker is or where the attack originates. Rather, the responsibility should be shared cooperatively among all of the players.

We Recommend

A Broad Program of Awareness and Education

Because of our finding that the public in general and many industry and government leaders are insufficiently aware of the vulnerabilities, we have recommended a broad and continuous program of awareness and education to cover all possible audiences. We include White House conferences, National Academy studies, presentations at industry associations and professional societies, development and promulgation of elementary and secondary curricula, and sponsorship of graduate studies and programs.

Infrastructure Protection through Industry Cooperation and Information Sharing

We believe the quickest and most effective way to achieve a much higher level of protection from cyber threats is to raise the level of existing protection through application of "best practices." We have accordingly recommended a sector-by-sector cooperation and information sharing strategy. In general, these sector structures should be partnerships among the owners and operators, and appropriate government agencies, which will identify and communicate best practices. We have especially asked the National Institute of Standards and Technology (NIST) and the National Security Agency (NSA) to provide technical skills and expertise required to identify and evaluate vulnerabilities in the associated information networks and control systems.

One very effective practice is a quantitative risk-management process, addressing physical attacks, cyber attacks that could corrupt essential information or deny service, the possibility of cascading effects, and new levels of interdependency.

The first focus of sector cooperation should be to share information and techniques related to risk management assessments. This should include development and deployment of ways to prevent attacks, mitigate damage, quickly recover services, and eventually reconstitute the infrastructure

We suggest consideration of these immediate actions prior to the completion of a formal risk assessment: (1) Isolate critical control systems from insecure networks by disconnection or adequate firewalls; (2) Adopt best practices for password control and protection, or install more modern authentication mechanisms; (3) Provide for individual accountability through protected action logs or the equivalent.

The sector cooperation and information sharing needed to improve risk assessments and to protect against probable attacks may naturally develop into sharing of information on current status. This would permit assessing whether one of the infrastructures is under a coordinated attack—physical, cyber, or combined. As this process develops, the national center for analysis of such information should be in place and ready to cooperate.

Reconsideration of Laws Related to Infrastructure Protection

Law has failed to keep pace with technology. Some laws capable of promoting assurance are not as clear or effective as they could be. Still others can operate in ways that may be unfriendly to security concerns. Sorting them all out will be a lengthy and massive undertaking, involving efforts at local, state, federal, and international levels. Recognizing the dynamic nature of legal reform, we attempted to lay a foundation through various studies, papers, and a legal authorities database that can aid eventual implementation of our recommendations and assist owners, operators, and government at all levels.

We also offered a number of preliminary legal recommendations intended to jump-start this process of reform. We identified existing laws that could help the government take the lead and serve as a model of standards and practices for the private sector. We identified other areas of law which, with careful attention, can enable infrastructure owners and operators to take precautions proportionate to the threat. We identified still other areas of law that should be molded to enable a greater degree of government-industry partnership in areas such as information sharing.

A Revised Program of Research and Development

The Commission believes that some of the basic technology needed to improve infrastructure protection already exists, but needs to be widely deployed. In other areas, additional research effort is needed.

At the same time the Commission recognizes that we are not now able to deploy several capabilities that we need. We have, therefore, recommended a program of research and development focused on those future capabilities.

Among them are new capabilities for detection and identification of intrusion and improved simulation and modeling capability to understand the effects of interconnected and fully interdependent infrastructures.

A National Organization Structure

In order to be effective, recommendations must discuss not only what is to be done, but how it will get done and who will do it. We have recommended the following partnering organizations be established to be responsible for specific parts of our vision:

Sector Coordinators to provide the focus for industry cooperation and information sharing, and to represent the sector in matters of national cooperation and policy;

Lead Agencies, designated within the federal government, to serve as a conduit from the government into each sector and to facilitate the creation of sector coordinators, if needed;

National Infrastructure Assurance Council of industry CEOs, Cabinet Secretaries, and representatives of state and local government to provide policy advice and implementation commitment;

Information Sharing and Analysis Center to begin the step-by-step process of establishing a realistic understanding of what is going on in our infrastructures—of distinguishing actual attack from coincidental events;

Infrastructure Assurance Support Office to house the bulk of the national staff which is responsible for continuous management and follow-through of our recommendations; and

Office of National Infrastructure Assurance as the top-level policy making office connected closely to the National Security Council and the National Economic Council.

Conclusion

It is clear to us that infrastructure assurance must be a high priority for the nation in the Information Age. With escalating dependence on information and telecommunications, our infrastructures no longer enjoy the protection of oceans and military forces. They are vulnerable in new ways. We must protect them in new ways. And that is what we recommend in this report.

The public and private sectors share responsibility for infrastructure protection. Our recommendations seek to provide structures for the partnership needed to assure our future security. Further, they seek to define new ways for approaching infrastructure assurance—ways that recognize the new thinking required in the Information Age, the new international security environment emerging from our victory in the Cold War and both the promise and danger of technology moving at breakneck speed.

We do not so much offer solutions as directions—compass headings that will help navigate through a new geography and ensure the continuity of the infrastructures that underpin America's economic, military, and social strength.

FEDERAL RESERVE CHAIRMAN ON STOCK MARKET VOLATILITY
October 29, 1997

Continued economic growth in the United States, featuring low unem-ployment and even lower inflation, kept Wall Street's long-lived "bull market" alive through 1997 despite some serious scares along the way. The biggest scare came October 27, when the Dow Jones Industrial Average plunged more than 7 percent, the biggest one-day drop in more than a decade. The market rebounded in the following weeks, however, and the Dow Jones aver-age ended the year at 7908.25, a 22.6 percent rise for the year. It was a record third-straight year of a stock market boost of more than 20 percent.

Economic turmoil in Asia—coupled with a feeling in many quarters that the bull market had about run its six-year course—contributed to stock market volatility, especially in the second half of the year. But the nation's underlying economic strength and continued healthy corporate profits ap-peared to be the key factors that kept the stock market on a generally up-ward course. (Economic Report of the President, p. 50; Asian financial crisis, p. 832)

Just two days after the October 27 market slump, Federal Reserve Board Chairman Alan Greenspan predicted that the massive sell-off might be seen in a few years as a "salutary event" for the economy. Although Greenspan's words provided cold comfort to investors who had lost thousands or even millions of dollars in the one-day tumble, the market's later rallies seemed to indicate that his crystal ball was working well.

Prelude to a Fall

Despite the usual dips and spirals, the U.S. stock market was generally on an upswing for the first seven months of the year. Corporate profits con-tinued to rise and individual investors had confidence in the market. The Federal Reserve Board never sniffed enough inflation in the air to cause it to raise interest rates, although Greenspan warned repeatedly that a tight labor market might set off a cycle of wage and price inflation, eventually forcing the board's hand on interest rates.

A currency crisis that started in Thailand and spread through much of Asia caused concern in the United States during late summer and early fall and fueled predictions by some pessimists that the stock market was ready for a tumble. The Asian economic turmoil hit Hong Kong in mid-October. That development was especially worrisome because most analysts had assumed that Hong Kong—which along with Japan was the investment engine for most of Asia—was in a much stronger economic position than its neighbors. In the week before Wall Street's plunge, Hong Kong stocks fell in value by one-third.

At the opening bell on October 27, the Dow Jones average stood at 7715.41. An early sell-off led to a brief rally, then was followed by a sharp slide until shortly after 2:30 p.m., when a 350-point drop in the Dow caused New York Stock Exchange officials to halt trading for thirty minutes. When trading resumed, the market plunged even more steeply, leading to an early halt in trading at 3:30 p.m. At the final bell, the Dow Jones average had lost 554.26 points, a drop of 7.18 percent for the day—the twelfth steepest one-day decline in stock market history. Other measures of U.S. markets also were off: the broader Standard & Poors 500 index was down by 6.9 percent, and the New York Stock Exchange composite index was down by 6.5 percent. Asian and European financial markets also declined for the day, although generally by lesser margins.

The market plunge sheared billions of dollars off the value of corporate equities and frightened many investors who had become accustomed to the longest bull market in history. Even so, many stock traders and analysts expressed a sense of relief; a market "correction" was inevitable, they said, and better to have it when the economy was robust than when there were signs of economic weakness.

Some economists said a downturn in the stock market might be beneficial in cooling off the economy, which had been growing at a pace Greenspan said was "unsustainable." In the wake of the October 27 stock market tumble, key economists lowered their predictions for economic growth in the fourth quarter of the year.

A Rebound

Investors both large and small seemed not at all deterred by the October 27 plunge. On October 28 they started buying stocks and, except for an hour in mid-morning, they bought all day. They traded nearly 1.2 billion shares on the New York Stock Exchange—about twice the previous record. The Dow Jones average climbed 337.17 points, regaining more than half of what it had lost the day before. Other U.S. stock indices were up by a range of 4 percent to 6 percent. Most markets in Asia also were up, although European markets continued to sag in response to the earlier plunges in Asia and on Wall Street.

Brokerage houses around the country reported that they were overwhelmed with "buy" orders, many of them from individual investors who might have been expected to avoid the market in the wake of the previous day's tumble. Brokers and economists said individual investors—whether corporate executives, factory workers, or senior citizens—appeared to have developed a stronger stomach for the ups and downs of Wall Street than was generally recognized.

The market posted other gains in the following days and by early November had recovered all the ground lost in the October 27 sell-off. By year's end the Dow Jones average was up nearly 200 points over its position before the October 27 sell-off.

Greenspan Testimony

On October 27 and the following day, Clinton administration officials tried to reassure the public about the underlying health of the nation's economy. Such assurances may have helped calm the markets, but most investors were looking for word from Chairman Greenspan of the Federal Reserve.

Appearing before the Joint Economic Committee of Congress on October 29, Greenspan also adopted a reassuring stance, saying that the nation's "foundation for good business performance remains solid." Specifically, Greenspan noted estimates that growth in productivity was on the rise—a factor he said was the basis for eventual increases in corporate earnings.

Even so, Greenspan said the financial markets had been ripe for what he called a "re-evaluation" in the financial markets. The financial turmoil in Asia probably contributed to nervousness on Wall Street, he said, but did not entirely explain the October 27 sell-off. If the Asian crisis had not happened, "something else" probably would have caused the stock market downturn.

Following is the text of testimony delivered October 29, 1997, by Alan Greenspan, chairman of the Federal Reserve Board, to the Joint Economic Committee of Congress:

We meet against the background of considerable turbulence in world financial markets, and I shall address the bulk of my remarks to those circumstances.

We need to assess these developments against the backdrop of a continuing impressive performance of the American economy in recent months. Growth appears to have remained robust and inflation low, and even falling, despite an ever tightening labor market. Our economy has enjoyed a lengthy period of good economic growth, linked, not coincidentally, to damped inflation. The Federal Reserve is dedicated to contributing as best it can to prolonging this performance, and we will be watching economic and financial market developments closely and evaluating their implications.

Even after the sharp rebound around the world in the past twenty-four hours, declines in stock markets in the United States and elsewhere have left investors less wealthy than they were a week ago and businesses facing higher equity cost of capital. Yet, provided the decline in financial markets does not cumulate, it is quite conceivable that a few years hence we will look back at this episode, as we now look back at the 1987 crash, as a salutary event in terms of its implications for the macroeconomy.

The 1987 crash occurred at a time when the American economy was operating with a significant degree of inflationary excess that the fall in market values arguably neutralized. Today's economy, as I have been suggesting of late, has been drawing down unused labor resources at an unsustainable pace, spurred, in part, by a substantial wealth effect on demand. The market's net retrenchment of recent days will tend to damp that impetus, a development that should help to prolong our six-and-a-half-year business expansion.

As I have testified previously, much of the stock price gain since early 1995 seems to have reflected upward revisions of long-term earnings expectations, which were implying a continuing indefinite rise in profit margins from already high levels. I suspect we are experiencing some scaling back of the projected gains in foreign affiliate earnings, and investors probably also are revisiting expectations of domestic earnings growth. Still, the foundation for good business performance remains solid. Indeed, data on our national economy in recent months are beginning to support the notion that productivity growth, the basis for increases in earnings, is beginning to pick up.

I also suspect earnings expectations and equity prices in the United States were primed to adjust. The currency crises in Southeast Asia and the declines in equity prices there and elsewhere do have some direct effects on U.S. corporate earnings, but not enough to explain the recent behavior of our financial markets. If it was not developments in Southeast Asia, something else would have been the proximate cause for a re-evaluation.

While productivity growth does appear to have picked up in the last six months, as I have pointed out in the past, it likely is overly optimistic to assume that the dimension of any acceleration in productivity will be great enough and persistent enough to close, by itself, the gap between an excess of long-term demand for labor and its supply. It will take some time to judge the extent of a lasting improvement.

Regrettably, over the last year the argument for the so-called new paradigm has slowly shifted from the not unreasonable notion that productivity is in the process of accelerating, to a less than credible view, often implied rather than stated, that we need no longer be concerned about the risk that inflation can rise again. The Federal Reserve cannot afford to take such a complacent view of our price prospects. There is much that is encouraging in the recent performance of the American economy, but, as I have often mentioned before, fundamental change comes slowly and we need to evaluate the prospective balance of supply and demand for various productive resources in deciding policy.

Recent developments in equity markets have highlighted growing interactions among national financial markets. The underlying technology-based structure of the international financial system has enabled us to improve materially the efficiency of the flows of capital and payment systems. That improvement, however, has also enhanced the ability of the financial system to transmit problems in one part of the globe to another quite rapidly. The recent turmoil is a case in point. I believe there is much to be learned from the recent experience in Asia that can be applied to better the workings of the international financial system and its support of international trade that has done so much to enhance living standards worldwide.

While each of the Asian economies differs in many important respects, the sources of their spectacular growth in recent years, in some cases decades, and the problems that have recently emerged are relevant to a greater or lesser extent to nearly all of them.

Following the early post World War II period, policies generally fostering low levels of inflation and openness of their economies coupled with high savings and investment rates contributed to a sustained period of rapid growth, in some cases starting in 1960s and 1970s. By the 1980s most economies in the region were expanding vigorously. Foreign net capital inflows grew, but until recent years were relatively modest. The World Bank estimates that net inflows of long-term debt, foreign direct investment, and equity purchases to the Asia Pacific region were only about $25 billion in 1990, but exploded to more than $110 billion by 1996.

A major impetus behind this rapid expansion was the global stock market boom of the 1990s. As that boom progressed, investors in many industrial countries found themselves more heavily concentrated in the recently higher valued securities of companies in the developed world, whose rates of return, in many instances, had fallen to levels perceived as uncompetitive with the earnings potential in emerging economies, especially in Asia. The resultant diversification induced a sharp increase in capital flows into those economies. To a large extent, they came from investors in the United States and Western Europe. A substantial amount came from Japan, as well, owing more to a search for higher yields than to rising stock prices and capital gains in that country. The rising yen through mid-1995 also encouraged a substantial increase in direct investment inflows from Japan. In retrospect, it is clear that more investment monies flowed into these economies than could be profitably employed at modest risk.

I suspect that it was inevitable in those conditions of low inflation, rapid growth and ample liquidity that much investment moved into the real estate sector, with an emphasis by both the public and private sectors on conspicuous construction projects. This is an experience, of course, not unknown in the United States on occasion. These real estate assets, in turn, ended up as collateral for a significant proportion of the assets of domestic financial systems. In many instances, those financial systems were less than robust, beset with problems of lax lending standards, weak supervisory regimes, and inadequate capital.

Moreover, in most cases, the currencies of these economies were closely tied to the U.S. dollar, and the dollar's substantial recovery since mid-1995, especially relative to the yen, made their exports less competitive. In addition, in some cases, the glut of semiconductors in 1996 suppressed export growth, exerting further pressures on highly leveraged businesses.

However, overall GDP growth rates generally edged off only slightly, and imports, fostered by rising real exchange rates, continued to expand, contributing to what became unsustainable current account deficits in a number of these economies. Moreover, with exchange rates seeming to be solidly tied to the dollar, and with dollar and yen interest rates lower than domestic currency rates, a significant part of the enlarged capital inflows, into these economies, in particular short-term flows, was denominated by the ultimate borrowers in foreign currencies. This put additional pressure on companies to earn foreign exchange through exports.

The pressures on fixed exchange rate regimes mounted as foreign investors slowed the pace of new capital inflows, and domestic businesses sought increasingly to convert domestic currencies into foreign currencies, or, equivalently, slowed the conversion of export earnings into domestic currencies. The shifts in perceived future investment risks led to sharp declines in stock markets across Asia, often on top of earlier declines or lackluster performances.

To date, the direct impact of these developments on the American economy has been modest, but it can be expected not to be negligible. U.S. exports to Thailand, the Philippines, Indonesia, and Malaysia (the four countries initially affected) were about four percent of total U.S. exports in 1996. However, an additional 12 percent went to Hong Kong, Korea, Singapore and Taiwan (economies that have been affected more recently). Thus, depending on the extent of the inevitable slowdown in growth in this area of the world, the growth of our exports will tend to be muted. Our direct foreign investment in, and foreign affiliate earnings reported from, the economies in this region as a whole have been a smaller share of the respective totals than their share of our exports. The share is, nonetheless, large enough to expect some drop-off in those earnings in the period ahead. In addition, there may be indirect effects on the U.S. real economy from countries such as Japan that compete even more extensively with the economies in the Asian region.

Particularly troublesome over the past several months has been the so-called contagion effect of weakness in one economy spreading to others as investors perceive, rightly or wrongly, similar vulnerabilities. Even economies, such as Hong Kong, with formidable stocks of international reserves, balanced external accounts and relatively robust financial systems, have experienced severe pressures in recent days. One can debate whether the recent turbulence in Latin American asset values reflect contagion effects from Asia, the influence of developments in U.S. financial markets, or home-grown causes. Whatever the answer, and the answer may be all of the above, this phenomenon illustrates the interdependencies in today's world economy and financial system.

Perhaps it was inevitable that the impressive and rapid growth experienced by the economies in the Asian region would run into a temporary slowdown or pause. But there is no reason that above-average growth in countries that are still in a position to gain from catching up with the prevailing technology cannot persist for a very long time. Nevertheless, rapidly developing, free-market economies periodically can be expected to run into difficulties because investment mistakes are inevitable in any dynamic economy. Private capital flows may temporarily turn adverse. In these circumstances, companies should be allowed to default, private investors should take their losses, and government policies should be directed toward laying the macroeconomic and structural foundations for renewed expansion; new growth opportunities must be allowed to emerge. Similarly, in providing any international financial assistance, we need to be mindful of the desirability of minimizing the impression that international authorities stand ready to guarantee the liabilities of failed domestic businesses. To do otherwise could lead to distorted investments and could ultimately unbalance the world financial system.

The recent experience in Asia underscores the importance of financially sound domestic banking and other associated financial institutions. While the current turmoil has significant interaction with the international financial system, the recent crises would arguably have been better contained if long-maturity property loans had not accentuated the usual mismatch between maturities of assets and liabilities of domestic financial systems that were far from robust to begin with. Our unlamented savings and loan crises come to mind.

These are trying days for economic policymakers in Asia. They must fend off domestic pressures that seek disengagement from the world trading and financial system. The authorities in these countries are working hard, in some cases with substantial assistance from the IMF, and the World Bank, and the Asian Development Bank, to stabilize their financial systems and economies.

The financial disturbances that have afflicted a number of currencies in Asia do not at this point, as I indicated earlier, threaten prosperity in this country, but we need to work closely with their leaders and the international financial community to assure that their situations stabilize. It is in the interest of the United States and other nations around the world to encourage appropriate policy adjustments, and where required, provide temporary financial assistance.

CLINTON AND JIANG ON
U.S.-CHINA RELATIONS
October 29, 1998

A summit meeting between President Bill Clinton and Chinese President Jiang Zemin focused new attention on what had become the most difficult bilateral relationship for the United States in the immediate post-Cold War era. Jiang spent eight days in the United States in late October and early November, attempting to improve relations between the two countries and, not incidentally, demonstrating his political standing back home eight months after the death of Deng Xiaoping. (Death of Deng, p. 94)

For Clinton, Jiang's visit was an opportunity to showcase his policy of "constructive engagement" with the Chinese. That policy called for cordial diplomatic and economic relations with China, even while Washington was gently pressing Beijing's leaders to open up their repressive political system. The policy used some of the same terminology and techniques that the Reagan and Bush administrations had applied toward the white minority regime in South Africa during the 1980s.

The Clinton policy bore some fruit in 1997: new trade deals, China's agreement to stop exporting nuclear technology to Iran, and the release from prison of the most prominent Chinese dissident. Even so, relations between Washington and Beijing remained frosty, characterized more by mutual suspicion than trust. Most of the substantive communication between Chinese and Americans was by business representatives rather than by diplomats.

Clinton-Jiang Press Conference

Although Clinton and Jiang had met four times previously, their October 29 Washington meeting was the first one-on-one "summit" between U.S. and Chinese leaders since President George Bush visited China in 1989. The four previous Clinton-Jiang encounters had taken place during larger gatherings of world leaders. Clinton agreed to visit China in 1998.

In formal remarks at a news conference following their meeting at the White House, neither president directly mentioned the 1989 massacre at

Tiananmen Square—an event that remained at the heart of U.S.-China relations even eight years later. As the leaders spoke, demonstrators were directly across the street, in Lafayette Park, loudly denouncing Chinese human rights abuses. When asked about the issue by an American reporter, both leaders quickly responded in direct and forceful terms that were highly unusual for such diplomatic occasions. (Tiananmen Square massacre, Historic Documents of 1989, p. 275)

Jiang responded first, saying China had taken "necessary measures" to deal with a "political disturbance" that had "seriously disrupted social stability and jeopardized state security." If a country with more than 1.2 billion people does not have social and political stability, he said, "it cannot possibly have the situation of reform and opening up that we are having today."

Clinton responded that the United States had "a very different view" of the matter, arguing that China's continuing repression of political dissents had undermined its support around the world. Over the long term, he said, countries survive best when they achieve stability "from their differences" because people are loyal to their country "when everyone has their say." On the issue of human rights, Clinton said, China was "on the wrong side of history." To make it clear where he thought Washington stood in historical terms, Clinton reminded Jiang that the United States was the only country still imposing economic sanctions against China because of Tiananmen Square.

As was often the case when political leaders met in such formats, many of the comments appeared to be intended more for each president's domestic audience than for each other. The comments on Tiananmen Square fell into this pattern: Clinton clearly was attempting to demonstrate that he had not forsaken U.S. interest in human rights, and Jiang was signaling to colleagues back home that he was not swayed by U.S. rhetoric on that issue.

Commercial Agreements

During their meeting, Clinton agreed to lift a ban on the sale to China of American-made nuclear technology, a step that enabled U.S. firms to compete for an expected $60 billion worth of business as China expanded its nuclear facilities to provide energy for civilian uses. In return, the Chinese gave Clinton written promises to halt all nuclear cooperation with Iran. A Chinese program of providing older nuclear technology to Iran had generated protests from the Clinton administration, which feared Iran was trying to develop nuclear weapons. Clinton called the nuclear deal with China a "win, win, win" arrangement for the United States.

On other business fronts, the White House summit produced an agreement allowing the Boeing Corporation to sell China fifty airliners with a total value of about $3 billion. China agreed to eliminate unusually high tariffs that had slowed U.S. exports of computers and telecommunications equipment. Clinton also agreed to allow the sale of U.S. air pollution control technology to Chinese factories.

Clinton, however, refused a request that the United States push for Chinese entry into the World Trade Organization in 1998. That organization supervised worldwide trade under the General Agreement on Tariffs and Trade. Washington had objected to China's subsidies for state-owned industries, giving them advantage over U.S. businesses seeking to enter the Chinese market.

Visiting American History and Business

The day after his meetings with Clinton, Jiang traveled to Capitol Hill, long a hotbed of U.S. distrust of Communist China. There, House Speaker Newt Gingrich and Senate Majority Leader Trent Lott, both conservative Republicans with impeccable anticommunist credentials, led Jiang on a tour of the Capitol and lectured him about human rights, forced abortion, and other contentious issues. Other members gave Jiang lists of political and religious dissidents languishing in Chinese prisons and demanded their release.

Later that day, Jiang flew to Philadelphia, where his keen interest in American history led him to visit Independence Hall. City leaders also made him an honorary member of the Philadelphia Flyers hockey team, presenting him with a team jersey with his name on the back. Visiting New York on October 31, Jiang toured the New York Stock Exchange, just four days after one of the steepest declines in stock prices in history. (Stock market, p. 721)

From the center of American capitalism, Jiang went to the most prestigious spot in American education, Harvard University, which he praised as the first U.S. university to accept Chinese students in the 1800s. Jiang spoke to an audience of Asian scholars, journalists, and Harvard faculty and students chosen by lottery. There were silent protests in the Sanders Theater, where he spoke; outside, noisy demonstrators, some supporting Jiang and others protesting his visit, competed for attention. Jiang repeated themes from earlier in his visit, focusing on China's economic progress.

Responding to a question about Tiananmen Square, Jiang took a somewhat milder line than in previous remarks on the subject. Instead of repeating his emphasis on the need for political stability, Jiang insisted his government was open to criticisms and suggestions. "It goes without saying that, naturally, we may have shortcomings and even make some mistakes in our work," he said, an ambiguous remark that was open to wildly divergent interpretations.

Jiang concluded his U.S. visit November 2 with a series of meetings with political and business leaders in Los Angeles. Jiang's reception there was the warmest he encountered on his trip, possibly reflecting the fact that China had became a major trading partner with California

Release of Wei Jingsheng

In the wake of Jiang's U.S. visit, Clinton was widely criticized for failing to persuade the Chinese leader to release any of the hundreds of political and religious dissidents held in Chinese prisons. Two weeks later, the Beijing authorities released the country's most prominent dissident, prodemocracy writer Wei Jingsheng, who had been imprisoned for sixteen years.

Wei was flown to Detroit, where he was treated for high blood pressure and other medical conditions resulting from his years in prison. After recovering, Wei embarked on a tour of the United States to promote the cause of human rights and democracy in China. He said he planned to write a book about his experiences in prison.

U.S. officials said Clinton had pressed Jiang to release Wei, along with other political prisoners, but they denied that Clinton struck any deals that led to Wei's freedom. Some analysts said the Chinese authorities may have calculated that releasing Wei might ease some of the U.S. pressure on human rights issues without posing any danger to China's political structure. It was clear that Wei would not be welcome back in China, and the government for years had barred official news organizations from mentioning his name.

Most Favored Nation Status

The annual congressional debate over according most favored nation trading status to China ended the same way in 1997 as all such debates since 1980. Congress turned back an attempt to reject the trading status—which offered low tariffs on Chinese imports into the United States—but opponents vowed to make a better showing the following year. (Most favored nation issue, Historic Documents of 1994, p. 73)

The 1997 debate on Capitol Hill, conducting in May and June, featured a coalition of liberals and conservatives with varying complaints about China. Some focused on human rights abuses, others on the alleged use of slave labor, others on forced abortions, and still others on unfair trading practices. Supporters of the trading status said the United States could not, by itself, isolate China from the rest of the world, and they argued that trade with China bolstered the U.S. economy.

As in most previous years, the key vote took place in the House and was lopsided. A resolution to deny the trading status for China failed 173–259. However, opponents of the trading status had gained thirty-two votes since the 1996 debate.

Following are excerpts from a joint news conference at the White House October 29, 1997, by President Bill Clinton and Chinese president Jiang Zemin:

President Clinton: Mr. President, let me again say how pleased we are to welcome the leader of a great people with a remarkable civilization, history and culture—a people now with its focus on the future. Your visit gives us the opportunity and the responsibility to build a future that is more secure, more peaceful, more prosperous for both our people.

To that end, I am pleased that we have agreed to regular summit meetings. I look forward to visiting China next year. We also have agreed to high-level dialogues between our Cabinet officials on the full range of security matters, and we will connect a presidential hotline to make it easier to confer at a moment's notice.

China and the United States share a profound interest in a stable, prosperous, open Asia. We've worked well together in convincing North Korea to end its dangerous nuclear program. Today, President Jiang and I agreed we will urge Pyongyang to take part in four-party peace talks with South Korea.

We also agreed to strengthen contacts between our militaries, including through a maritime agreement to decrease the chances of miscalculation and increase America's ties to a new generation of China's military leaders.

A key to Asia's stability is a peaceful and prosperous relationship between the People's Republic of China and Taiwan. I reiterated America's longstanding commitment to a one China policy. It has allowed democracy to flourish in Taiwan and provides a framework in which all three relationships can prosper—between the United States and the PRC, the United States and Taiwan, and Taiwan and the People's Republic of China.

I told President Jiang that we hope the People's Republic and Taiwan would resume a constructive cross-strait dialogue and expand cross-strait exchanges. Ultimately, the relationship between the PRC and Taiwan is for the Chinese themselves to determine—peacefully.

President Jiang and I agreed that the United States and China share a strong interest in stopping the spread of weapons of mass destruction and other sophisticated weaponry in unstable regions and rogue states—notably, Iran. I welcome the steps China has taken and the clear assurances it has given today to help prevent the proliferation of nuclear weapons and related technology.

On the basis of these steps and assurances, I agreed to move ahead with the U.S.-China agreement for cooperation concerning the peaceful uses of nuclear energy. It will allow our companies to apply for licenses to sell equipment to Chinese nuclear power plants, subject to U.S. monitoring. This agreement is a win-win-win. It serves America's national security, environmental and economic interests.

President Jiang and I agreed to increase the cooperations between our countries in fighting international organized crime, drug trafficking and alien smuggling. Our law enforcement officials will share information and consult regularly. And starting next year, we will station drug enforcement administration officers in Bejing.

I'm also pleased that we will expand our cooperation on rule of law programs. Through them, we'll help China to train judges and lawyers, increase our exchanges of legal experts and materials, strengthen commercial law and arbitration in China, and share ideas on issue such as legal aide and administrative reform.

In both China and the United States, trade has been a critical catalyst for growth. China's the fastest growing market in the world for our goods and services. Tomorrow, Boeing will sign a contract for the largest sale of air-planes to China in history—50 jets, valued at $3 billion. This contract will support tens of thousands of America jobs and provide China with a modern fleet of passenger planes.

Still, access to China's market remains restricted for many America goods and services. Just as China can compete freely and fairly in America, so our good and services should be able to compete freely and fairly in China. The United States will do everything possible to bring China into the World Trade Organization as soon as possible, provided China improves access to its market. China's decision today to join the information technology agreement, which cuts to zero tariffs on computers, semiconductors and telecommunications equipment, is a strong step in the right direction.

As we pursue growth, we almost protect our shared environment. Already, pollution has made respiratory illness the leading health problem in China. Today our countries agreed to a joint initiative that will help China reduce air pollution and increase clean energy production, including through the use of American technology. The initiative builds upon the work begun by the Vice President in Bejing this spring.

I also discussed with President Jiang the special responsibility our nations bear as the top two emitters of greenhouse gases to lead in finding a global solution to the global problem of climate change. This is a broad agenda in which China and the United States share important interests that we can best advance by working together.

But we also have fundamental differences, especially concerning human rights and religious freedom. I'm convinced the best way to address them is directly and personally, as we did yesterday and today, and as we will continue to do until this issue is no longer before us, when there is full room for debate, dissent and freedom to worship as part of the fabric of a truly free Chinese society.

Mr. President, I am very pleased that tomorrow you will visit Independence Hall and the Liberty Bell in Philadelphia, for it was there that our founders set forth the beliefs that define and inspire our nation to this very day. We believe all individuals, as a condition of their humanity, have the right to life, liberty, and the pursuit of happiness. We believe liberty includes freedom of religion, freedom of speech, freedom of association. We believe governments must protect those rights. These ideas grew out of the European Enlightenment, but today they are enshrined in the Universal Declaration of Human Rights, not as a birthright of Americans or Westerners, but of people everywhere.

I welcome China's decision to invite a delegation of distinguished American religious leaders to China to pursue a dialogue on religious freedom. I'm pleased we have recommitted to discuss our differences over human rights at both governmental and non-governmental levels.

Mr. President, China has known more millennia than America has known centuries. But for more than 220 years, we have been conducting our great experiment in democracy. We still struggle to make it work every day, and we know it requires struggle every day. The American people greatly admire

China's extraordinary economic transformation, and we understand the importance that your own experiences and your present challenges lead you to place upon maintaining stability. We also appreciate the fact that human rights have been advanced in China by greater freedom from want, freedom of movement in career choice, and widely-held local elections. But we also believe that China will enjoy more growth and more stability as it embraces more fully the political, as well as the economic aspirations of all your people.

In the Information Age, the true wealth of nations lies in people's ability to create, to communicate, to innovate. Fully developing these resources requires people who feel free to speak, to publish, to associate, to worship without fear of reprisal. It is China's extraordinary human resources that will lift it to its rightful destiny of leadership and widely-held prosperity in the 21st century.

As we look ahead, the United States welcomes China's emergence as a full and constructive partner in the community of nations—a great nation that joins its strength and influence to our own to advance peace and prosperity, freedom and security.

Mr. President, thank you for coming to the United States. We look forward to building on the good work of this day so that the best days for all our people are yet to come.

President Jiang: Ladies and gentlemen, a while ago I had an in-depth exchange of views with President Clinton on China-U.S. relations and on international and regional issues of mutual interest. The meeting was constructive and fruitful.

President Clinton and I have agreed on identifying the goal for the development of a China-U.S. relationship oriented toward the 21st century. The two sides believe that efforts to realize this goal will promote the fundamental interests of the two peoples and the noble cause of world peace and development.

We both agree that our two countries share extensive common interests in important matters bearing on the survival and development of mankind, such as peace and development, economic cooperation and trade, the prevention of the proliferation of weapons of mass destruction, and environment protection.

Both sides are of the view that it is imperative to handle China-U.S. relations and promptly address our differences in accordance with the principles of mutual respect, non-interference in each other's internal affairs, equality and mutual benefit, and seeking common ground while putting aside differences.

President Clinton and I have also reached broad agreement on the establishment of a mechanism of regular summit meetings, the opening of a hotline between the two heads of state, the establishment of a mechanism of meetings and consultations between the two foreign ministers and other officials, an increase in exchanges between the armed forces of the two countries, and exchanges and cooperation between our two countries in economic, scientific, and technological, cultural, educational and law enforcement fields.

My visit will achieve the purpose of enhancing mutual understanding, broadening common ground, developing cooperation, and building a future together, and bring China-U.S. relations into a new stage of development.

President Clinton and I share the view that China and the United States enjoy a high degree of complementarity and a huge potential for cooperation in the economic and trade feuds. To step up our economic cooperation and trade not only benefits our two peoples, but also contributes to economic development and prosperity of the world.

And I would also like to take this opportunity to thank you, Mr. President, for the kind reception accorded to me.

Now, questions are welcome.

President Clinton: Let a Chinese go first.

Question: I have a question which I would like to ask of President Jiang. President Jiang, for the past few years you have reiterated once and again that we need to take a long-term perspective and we should view China-U.S. relations from the perspective of the 21st century. Therefore, Mr. President, what measures will the Chinese government make and how can a sound and stable relationship between China and the United States be brought into the 21st century.

President Jiang: And your question recalled of me of the first meeting that President Clinton and I had in Seattle when we agreed that we need to work to bring a world of prosperity, stability, and peace into the 21st century. The meeting that I had with President Clinton during my current trip to the United States was the fifth one that we had with one another. However, my visit is the first by a Chinese head of state to the United States in 12 years.

And this shows that both sides are working together and taking many specific measures to achieve this goal, and, to put it more specifically, I believe it is very important for the two peoples of China and the United States to enhance mutual understanding. And I'm also coming here to the United States for the purpose of deepening mutual understanding between our two peoples.

There are a lot of works from ancient Chinese literature and culture describing the view that one should scale a great height in order to have a grander sight. And the development of modern science and technology also told us that if you have a greater height you can see farther into the long distance.

I do not want to take much of the time, so I would like to leave more time to President Clinton.

Question: Sir, we're told that you have asked, even last night, for the release of some political dissidents. And the Chinese have not done so. Is it acceptable for China to refuse even such a modest gesture?

President Clinton: Well, first of all, we had a long discussion about human rights; we discussed a lot of issues related to human rights, every conceivable aspect of it. And we have profound disagreements there. But that does not mean that this visit should not have occurred or that we don't have a big interest in continuing to work together. After all, this interest that we have in working with China relates to the fact that we have common values and common interest related to preserving peace, to growing the economy, to stopping the spread of dangerous weapons. We have an agreement to fight narco trafficking. We have an agreement to work together on the terrific environmental challenges we face—right across the board. So I think that you have to see this meeting in the context of that. But you shouldn't in any way minimize the steep differences that still remain between us over that issue.

Question: I have a question for Your Excellency, President Jiang Zemin. Why is the Taiwan issue, the core issue in China-U.S. relations?

President Jiang: The three Sino-U.S. joint communiqués all covered the question of Taiwan, because this question is involving the sovereignty of the People's Republic of China. The late Mr. Deng Xiaoping proposed the system of one country-two systems for the settlement of the Taiwan question and for the accomplishment of peaceful reunification of China, and this is the only correct policy.

However, we also say that we do not commit to renounce the use of force, that this is not directed at the compatriots in Taiwan, but rather at the external forces attempting to interfere in China's internal affairs and at those who are attempting to achieve separation of the country or the independence of Taiwan.

I'm very happy that I discussed this issue in clear-cut terms with President Clinton during my current trip as we have done in our previous meetings, and I believe the joint statement that the two sides are going to release will also carry explicit explanations on the Taiwan issue. Thank you.

Question: Mr. President—a question, actually, for both Presidents—the shootings in Tiananmen Square were a turning point in U.S.-Chinese relations and cause many Americans to view China as an oppressive country that crushes human rights. President Jiang, do you have any regrets about Tiananmen? And, President Clinton, are you prepared to lift any of the Tiananmen sanctions, and if not, why not?

President Jiang: The political disturbance that occurred at the turn of spring and summer in 1989 seriously disrupted social stability and jeopardized state security. Therefore, the Chinese government had to take necessary measures, according to law, to quickly resolve the matter to ensure that our country enjoys stability and that our reform and opening up proceeds smoothly.

The communist party of China and the Chinese government have long drawn the correct conclusion on this political disturbance, and facts have also proved that if a country with an over 1.2 billion population does not enjoy social and political stability, it cannot possibly have the situation of reform and opening up that we are having today. Thank you.

President Clinton: To answer your question, first, on the general point, I think it should be obvious to everyone that we have a very different view of the meaning events at Tiananmen Square. I believe that what happened and the aftermath and the continuing reluctance to tolerate political dissent has kept China from politically developing the level of support in the rest of the world that otherwise would have been developed. I also believe, as I said in my opening statement, that over the long run the societies of the 21st century that will do best will be those that are drawing their stability from their differences; that out of this whole harmony of different views, there is a coherence of loyalty to the nation because everyone has their say. It enables people to accept, for example, the results of the elections that they don't agree with. So we have a different view.

The depth of the view in the United States I think is nowhere better exemplified than in the so-called Tiananmen sanctions. We are the only nation in the world, as far as I know, that still has sanctions on the books as a result of the events of eight years ago.

Now, you asked a specific question. Our agreement on the nuclear proliferation issues allows me to lift the sanction on peaceful nuclear cooperation. It is the right thing to do for America. This is a good agreement. It furthers our national security interests. China is to be complimented for participating in it and the decision is the right one.

The other sanctions which cover a range of issues from OPIC loans to crime control equipment and many things in between under our law have to reviewed on a case-by-case basis. So as a result of our meeting today, the only Tiananmen Square sanction which is being lifted is the one on peaceful nuclear cooperation, and it is a good thing for America and China. And I applaud the Chinese side for the work they have done with us on this specific nuclear issue. It is a substantial step forward for us.

President Jiang: I would like to speak a few words in addition to this question. Our two countries have different geographical locations, and we are also thousands of miles apart geographically. We also have different historic and cultural tradition, different levels of economic development, and different values. Therefore, I believe it is just natural for our two countries to hold different views on some issues.

Now, people in the world are standing at the turn of the century when we're going to bring in the 21st century, and science and technology have developed significantly as compared with, for instance, the period when Newton lived. And I also believe the that world we are living in is a rich and diverse one, and, therefore, the concepts on democracy and human rights and on freedoms are relative and specific ones, and they are to be determined by the specific national situation of different countries.

And I am also strongly of the view that on such issues as the human rights issue, discussions can be held on the basis of non-interference in the internal affairs of a country. And it goes without saying that as for the general rules universally abided by in the world, China also abides these rules. My stay here in the United States is rather a brief one. There is the fact that since I came here I have been immersed in the atmosphere of friendship from the American people and I was also accorded a warm reception from President Clinton and Vice President Gore. However, sometimes noises came into my ears.

According to Chinese philosophy, Confucius say, isn't it a pleasure to have friends coming from afar. And, naturally, I am also aware that in the United

States different views can be expressed and this is a reflection of democracy. And, therefore, I would like to quote a Chinese saying, which goes, "Seeing it once is better than hearing about it a hundred times." I've also got my real understanding about this during my current trip. However, I don't believe this will have any negative impact on our effort to approach each other.

President Clinton: Let me—I just have to say one other thing. First of all, the United States recognizes that on so many issues China is on the right side of history, and we welcome it. But on this issue we believe the policy of the government is on the wrong side of history. There is, after all, now a Universal Declaration of Human Rights.

The second point I'd like to make is that I can only speak from our experience. And America has problems of its own, which I have frankly acknowledged. But in our country I think it would amaze many of our Chinese guests to see some of the things that have been written and said about me, my family, our government, our policies. And, yet, after all this time, I'm still standing here and our country is stronger than it was before those words were uttered six years ago.

Excuse me, before those words began to be said six years ago—they're still being said every day.

Question: Mr. President, I have a question for both President Jiang and President Clinton. President Clinton, you stated your position with regard to Taiwan that this is a question for the Chinese people to resolve. But we all understand you have brokered peace in Bosnia, in the Middle East. Do you see any role for the United States to play in the securing of a permanent peaceful environment in the Taiwan Strait?

And for President Jiang, about the cross-strait dialogue. President Clinton said that he has urged President Jiang to resume the interrupted dialogue. I wonder if President Jiang will respond positively and take some measures to resume the dialogue as soon as possible.

President Clinton: First of all, I think the most important thing the United States can do to facilitate a peaceful resolution of the differences is to adhere strictly to the one China policy we have agreed on, to make it clear that within the context of that one China policy, as articulated in the communiqués and our own laws, we will maintain friendly, open relations with the people of Taiwan and China; but that we understand that this issue has to be resolved and resolved peacefully, and that if it is resolved in a satisfactory way, consistent with statements made in the past, then Asia will be stronger and more stable and more prosperous. That is good for the United States. And our own relations with China will move on to another stage of success.

I think the more we can encourage that, the better off we are. But I think in the end, since so much investment and contact has gone on in the last few years between Taiwan and China, I think the Chinese people know how to resolve this when the time is right, and we just have to keep saying we hope the time will be right as soon as possible. Sooner is better than later.

President Jiang: To answer your question in rather brief terms, all in all, our policy is one of peaceful reunification and one country-two systems. And as for more details, elaboration on that—a few years ago I made my eight-point proposal along that line and at the just concluded 15th National Congress of the Chinese Communist Party, I also delivered a report which gave a rather comprehensive elaboration on this. Therefore, I will not repeat them here. . . .

Question: My question is for President Clinton. In China, sometimes we are confused by American different policy to China. We know when you—there are factions in Congress which aren't friendly to China. So as President, how do you coordinate the unbalance to have a unified policy to China? Is there any elements to damage an effective Sino-U.S. relationship?

President Clinton: Well, let me say—make a general point first. It is very important that we understand each other so that if we have a difference, it's a real difference and not a misunderstanding. Therefore, in dealing with the United States, unless there is some clear signal to the contrary, you should assume that a statement by the President, the Vice President, the Secretary of State, the Secretary of Defense, the Secretary of the Treasury, the National Security Advisor, the Trade Ambassador, the people in our direct line of authority—they represent our policy.

We need the support of important people in Congress, and much of the leadership does support this administration's China policy. But I think it would be a mistake to think that the United States has no unified China policy because individuals or groups in the Congress disagree with it. We do have a lot of disagreement. We have had for eight years now, ever since 1989. Until we resolve all these issues, in that sense, our relations will never be fully normal. But we have to keep pushing forward. . . .

Question: For President Jiang—sir, officials in your delegation have suggested that the protestors who have protested Chinese policies in Tibet are, in many cases, young people, students who have been misguided, misinformed by a Hollywood-led campaign. Sir, if that is so, and if we take to heart your old Chinese saying that seeing once is worth hearing a hundred times, would you be willing to invite either a delegation, a senior delegation from the United States Congress or a group of international journalists to travel to Tibet and to see for themselves? Thank you.

President Jiang: I do, indeed, would like to welcome more people to go to Tibet and see with their own eyes.

President Clinton: Let me just, following up on that, make it clear again that the United States has no political objective in pressing the cause of Tibetans, the Tibetan Buddhists, the Dalai Lama. We have only asked for the resumption of a constructive dialogue based on a commitment that there would be no attempt to sever Tibet from China, but instead an attempt to reconcile the peoples so that all freedom of religious expression and unique cultures could be preserved.

PRESIDENTIAL PANEL ON
GULF WAR ILLNESSES
October 31, 1997

Six years after the Persian Gulf War, veterans groups, members of Congress, and a presidential committee continued to criticize the government for its failure to address adequately the possibility that thousands of soldiers were poisoned by Iraqi chemical weapons and other toxic materials. Gulf War veterans for years had been reporting mysterious illnesses and wondering whether they might have been exposed to some of the chemical weapons the Iraqi military was known to possess. Only in June 1996 did the Pentagon acknowledge that some troops might have been exposed to chemical weapons when an Iraqi ammunition dump was demolished.

Several scientific panels had studied chronic illnesses collectively known as "Gulf War syndrome" and had come to varying conclusions. Some researchers said Gulf War veterans may have suffered damage from exposure to chemical weapons agents, smoke from oil well fires, or other toxic substances; other researchers said soldiers more likely were suffering from the lingering effects of combat stress.

A panel of scientists, medical specialists, and others appointed by President Bill Clinton to review the matter made three reports: one in February 1996, one at the end of 1996, and a third on October 31, 1997. The reports by the Presidential Advisory Committee on Gulf War Veterans' Illnesses offered no definitive explanations for the illnesses reported by Gulf War veterans and said the government generally had "acted in good faith" to address health concerns of veterans.

However, all three of the committee's reports criticized important aspects of the government's handling of the issue. The October 31 report contained the strongest criticism, singling out the Defense Department for special censure. That report said the Pentagon should be stripped of responsibility for supervising further investigations into whether Iraqi chemical or biological weapons might have been a cause of the veterans' illnesses. In response, Clinton named a five-member panel to oversee future investigations by U.S. agencies of Gulf War illnesses; that panel was chaired by retired senator Warren B. Rudman.

Similar criticism of the Pentagon came from the House Committee on Governmental Reform and Oversight, which released an extensive report November 7. That report said both the Pentagon and the Department of Veterans Affairs had mishandled the Gulf War veterans illness issue. The committee also recommended that another agency be given responsibility for further investigations, and it recommended congressional legislation on the matter if President Clinton failed to act.

Yet another report, by the General Accounting Office (GAO), the investigative arm of Congress, found "substantial evidence" that exposure to Iraqi chemical weapons was among the causes of Gulf War Syndrome. The GAO report, dated June 23, also faulted the Pentagon and the Department of Veterans Affairs for failing to take seriously the possibility that soldiers had indeed suffered from exposure to chemical weapons or other toxic substances.

Defense Secretary William S. Cohen acknowledged in September that the Pentagon had not handled the matter well in the past. He insisted, however, that his department was "fully capable" of supervising further investigations and should not be stripped of its responsibility.

Criticisms of the Pentagon

The Defense Department had long claimed that there was no credible evidence that chemical warfare agents had been present during the 1991 Gulf War. Only in June 1996 did the Pentagon acknowledge that chemical weapons were present at the Khamisiyah weapons dump in southern Iraq, which the U.S. military demolished just after the war, in March 1991. The Pentagon at first said approximately 20,000 American troops in the area may have been exposed to low levels of the nerve gas sarin when the dump was destroyed. The Pentagon in July 1997 raised its estimate to nearly 99,000 troops, although it said only a few were exposed to more than "trace amounts" of chemical weapons.

Also in July 1997 the Pentagon said as many as 6,000 mustard gas shells had been present at Ukhaydir in southern Iraq. This revelation came only after the United Nations weapons inspections team in Iraq had "called attention" to the site, the presidential committee said.

"Time after time over the past ten months, the committee has battled with DOD [the Department of Defense] about its fact finding and interpretations related to possible CW [chemical weapon] agent incidents—an approach we believe serves to exacerbate DOD's credibility problems," the panel said. The committee cited incidents in which it said the Pentagon had failed to follow through on information provided to it, concluding that the "DOD cannot itself lead an investigation on possible CW or BW [biological weapon] agent exposures that will be viewed as credible." The panel suggested the President's Foreign Intelligence Advisory Board or the National Academy of Science as possible alternative agencies to oversee further investigations of the issue.

The committee also challenged the standards the Pentagon planned to use for determining the likely effect of chemical weapons in the war zones. The military at first failed to set any standard, then in March 1997 said it would adopt a rule using "preponderance of the evidence." When the committee objected to using "courtroom standards" in such cases, the Pentagon switched to what it called a "common sense" approach, asking whether the available facts would lead a "reasonable person" to conclude whether chemical weapons were present. The committee harshly criticized that standard as well, saying it was "not appropriate" on such a controversial public policy issue. The committee called instead for an "objective" standard against which all information could be measured. In cases where the information was ambiguous, the government should make decisions based on a presumption ensuring veterans access to "information and/or benefits," the committee said.

The committee called on the administration and Congress to develop legislation providing specific benefits for veterans suffering from Gulf War illnesses. The panel suggested the legislation could require the Veterans Affairs Department to contract with an agency such as the National Academy of Sciences to review the available scientific evidence of the relationship between specific illnesses and service during the war.

In a related development, the Central Intelligence Agency said it had given the military "multiple warnings" that poison gas might be present at the Khamisiyah weapons depot. The CIA released an unclassified report on April 9 saying the agency had received information in the 1980s indicating that the depot contained chemical weapons, and information about these weapons was passed to U.S. military officials before the depot was destroyed in March 1991. The officer in charge of demolishing the depot, then-colonel Robert B. Flowers, and retired general Colin L. Powell, the chairman of the Joint Chiefs of Staff during the war, both said they had not been told about the likely presence of chemical weapons at that depot.

House Committee Report

The report issued by the Subcommittee on Human Resources of the House Government Reform and Investigations Committee offered many of the same criticisms of the Pentagon as the presidential committee. The House panel also extended its criticisms to the Department of Veterans Affairs, the Central Intelligence Agency, and the Food and Drug Administration. The panel said the government efforts had been "plagued by arrogant incuriosity and pervasive myopia that sees a lack of evidence as proof." The Defense and Veterans Affairs Departments, in particular, suffered from "institutional biases and constraints" that prevented them from analyzing the Gulf War veterans illness issue properly, the committee said.

The House panel said it had concluded that some of the illnesses reported by Gulf War veterans were caused by exposure to Iraqi chemical weapons, pesticides, smoke from fires the Iraqis set to oil wells, and other hazards. The committee thus came down on one side of a scientific debate that had been raging for several years. Some specialists pointed to Iraqi chemical weapons and other poisons as the probable causes for neurological and digestive tract illnesses reported by many Gulf War veterans, while others said other factors, particular lingering stress from combat, were more likely explanations.

One of the hazards may have been inflicted by the U.S. military, according to various reports. Thousands of troops were given pills containing the drug pyridostigmine bromide to protect them against the Iraqi nerve gas; later medical research suggested those pills could cause health problems when taken under stress or in combination with some other drugs.

Following are excerpts from the "Special Report" issued October 31, 1997, by the Presidential Advisory Committee on Gulf War Veterans' Illnesses:

Summary

In our December 1996 *Final Report*, the Presidential Advisory Committee on Gulf War Veterans' Illnesses reported the government largely had acted in good faith in handling Gulf War veterans' health concerns in comparison to the post-Vietnam War era. We took strong exception, however, to the Department of Defense's [DOD's] inquiries related to chemical and biological warfare agent investigations. We found DOD's actions had produced an atmosphere of mistrust surrounding every aspect of Gulf War veterans' illnesses.

President Clinton extended the Committee's tenure in January 1997, with a new charge to review the government's implementation of our previous recommendations and to continue our assessment of the government's investigations into possible chemical and biological warfare agent exposures. This Special Report assesses these issues. Based on our oversight activities, it also reports our analysis of the broader issue of the public's perception of the government's commitment to address Gulf War veterans' health concerns.

Ten months after the Committee concluded the government had a significant amount of ground to recover with the American public, we note the government's credibility on Gulf War veterans' illnesses continues to be challenged. The government's efforts have yielded and will continue to yield improved services and new knowledge. For example, we hope recently funded research on health effects of subclinical exposures to nerve agents and of interactions of multiple risk factors can address uncertainties surrounding Gulf War veterans' illnesses. Progress, however, is gradual. Regrettably, it now appears incremental advances will not address the pervasive perception of government neglect in handling Gulf War veterans' illnesses.

To address this perception, the Committee recommends that the Executive Branch work with Congress to establish a permanent program for Gulf War veterans' illnesses. We envision legislation that directs the Department of Veterans Affairs to contract with an appropriate organization for a periodic review—for benefits and future research purposes—of the available scientific evidence regarding associations between illnesses and service in the Gulf War. The Committee hopes a partnership among all concerned parties can establish this program. The legacy of the Gulf War should be a recognition by all Americans that the government acknowledges and honors its obligation to care for Gulf War veterans, not the perception the government cannot be trusted to candidly address their health concerns. . . .

Credibility and Commitment

Public distrust of government and large institutions has been on the rise since the mid-1970s. Such skepticism is not, of course, limited to issues raised by Gulf War health issues, but this spreading atmosphere of suspicion has fueled speculation about cover-ups and conspiracies surrounding governmental actions related to Gulf War veterans' illnesses—especially with respect to CW [chemical weapons] agent matters. Addressing the systemic nature of increased public misgivings about government falls beyond our scope. The Committee's oversight of investigations of possible CW agent exposures leads us, however, to believe the government must reinforce and renew its commitment to Gulf War veterans in order to begin erasing the perception of governmental inattention to them.

In the *Final Report*, the Committee reported that, for the most part, the government has largely acted in good faith and improved its handling of Gulf War veterans' health concerns in comparison to the post-Vietnam War era. We took strong exception, however, to DOD's inquiries into possible chemical and biological warfare agent incidents.

We noted DOD's denials, delays, and actions had strained public trust and that, understandably, an atmosphere of government mistrust surrounded every aspect of Gulf War veterans' illnesses. The Committee emphasized full public accountability would be essential in trying to restore public confidence in the government's, not just DOD's, commitment to Gulf War veterans.

Ten months after making this assessment, the government's credibility in addressing the health concerns of Gulf War veterans continues to be challenged. To be sure, room for improvement exists. The government's efforts have yielded significant improvements in services and essential, new knowledge—but, still, progress is gradual. Unfortunately, however, such progress now often is viewed skeptically, at best. There remains a widespread and deeply held view that the government is failing to adequately address the health concerns of Gulf War veterans. In fact, the Committee perceives public mistrust about the government's handling of Gulf War veterans' illnesses not only has endured, but has expanded since the *Final Report*. This persistent atmosphere of distrust ill serves the Nation.

The Committee concludes the credibility gap between the public's views of the government's efforts to address concerns about Gulf War veterans' illnesses and the reality of its initiatives cannot be bridged without bold policy action. Incremental policy refinements are, and have been to date, important. Regrettably, it now appears they will not address the pervasive belief of government neglect or wrongdoing in handling Gulf War veterans' illnesses. At the same time, the primary focus of the government's efforts needs to shift from investigations to the nth degree of individual incidents, to a process that will ensure that research data and clinical improvements with a direct impact on veterans' lives can be regularly accounted for and integrated into VA's disability compensation and medical benefits programs. As a policy mechanism, advisory committees like our effort are not well-suited for such tasks. We recommend:

- The White House and VA should work with Congress to establish a permanent, statutory program for Gulf War veterans' illnesses. The Committee envisions legislation that directs VA to contract with an organization with the appropriate scientific expertise—e.g., the National Academy of Sciences—for a periodic review, for benefits and future research purposes, of the available scientific evidence regarding associations between illnesses and Gulf War service. The object of such an analysis would be to determine statistical associations between service in the Gulf War and morbidity and mortality, while also considering whether a plausible biological mechanism exists, whether research results are capable of replication and of clinical significance, and whether the data withstand peer review. Based on the external evaluation, the Secretary of Veterans Affairs would make a presumption of service connection for positive associations or publish reasons for not doing so. We believe specific details of such a program—e.g., risk factors exposure; the timing, length, and location of an individual's service; frequency of the scientific review—are best left to the department and legislators.

We recognize our charge is not to advise Congress; our recommendation centers on urging the Executive Branch to work with Congress. We hope a partnership among all concerned parties can implement this recommendation. The Committee notes, however, that the burden of action ultimately rests with Congress, which must address this recommendation via legislation.

The legacy of the Gulf War should not be the perception the government cannot be trusted to candidly address legitimate concerns that veterans have raised—and often have been borne out—about their experiences during Operations Desert Shield/Desert Storm. Rather, the legacy should be a recognition by all Americans that the government acknowledges and honors its obligation to care for the men and women who served in the Gulf War. This Committee has appreciated the opportunity to serve Gulf War veterans, their families, and President Clinton.

November

FEDERAL HEALTH PANEL
STATEMENT ON ACUPUNCTURE
November 5, 1997

The Chinese art of acupuncture is an effective treatment for certain kinds of pain and nausea and could prove useful in several other areas, a federally sponsored panel said November 5. "There is sufficient evidence of acupuncture's value to expand its use into conventional medicine and to encourage further studies of its physiology and clinical value," the panel said. It was the first time that the federal government had endorsed a form of alternative medicine.

The panel said there was "clear evidence" that needle acupuncture was effective for treating the nausea and vomiting that often accompanied surgical operations and chemotherapy treatments, "morning sickness" nausea associated with pregnancy, and postoperative dental pain. The panel said additional scientific studies would have to be conducted to confirm acupuncture's effectiveness in treating several other conditions, including headache, menstrual cramps, tennis elbow, lower back pain, carpal tunnel syndrome, asthma, stroke rehabilitation, and some addictions.

"I view this as a beginning to a better integration of acupuncture into traditional Western medicine and to start to take it seriously," said David J. Ramsey, the president of University of Maryland, Baltimore, who chaired the consensus panel. Although the panel's conclusions were not binding on the medical profession or insurers, they gave acupuncture a legitimacy within the medical establishment that was likely to increase both the number of patients receiving the treatments and the number of insurers who covered the practice.

Acupuncture, which had been practiced in China for at least 2,000 years, typically involved inserting very fine metallic needles into specific points of the body, twirling them in specific ways, and leaving them in place for several minutes. The treatment was virtually unknown in the United States until 1972, when a well-known New York Times *reporter, James Reston, underwent emergency surgery for appendicitis in Beijing while accompanying President Richard Nixon on his historic trip to renew U.S. relations* *with China. Reston subsequently wrote about the acupuncture that Chinese doctors used to treat his postoperative pain and nausea. Since then, an estimated 15 million Americans have tried acupuncture at least once. In 1993 the Food and Drug Administration (FDA) estimated that more than 1 million people were spending about $500 million each year on acupuncture. Treatments generally cost about $100. According to the World Health Organization, there were about 10,000 acupuncture specialists in the United States, and about 3,000 of them were physicians who had integrated acupuncture into their traditional therapies. About 1,000 drug treatment facilities offered acupuncture as part of their treatment program. A few insurance companies covered the practice in certain circumstances.*

Despite the popularity of acupuncture and the growing body of evidence attesting to its efficacy, the practice still had its detractors. "What the proponents [of acupuncture] present as evidence is in fact delusion, and if the reviewing body is incapable of separating the two, then shame on them," said Victor Herbert, a professor of medicine at Mount Sinai School of Medicine. A longtime opponent of alternative medicine, Herbert called the practice "quackupuncture" and said any relief it offered patients was largely a matter of hypnotic suggestion.

The continuing controversy over the efficacy of acupuncture prompted the National Institutes of Health (NIH) to convene a national consensus panel on the issue. These panels were a devise that NIH used to develop a consensus on controversial medical technology and practices. The twelve members of the acupuncture consensus panel studied the scientific literature on the practice and then heard several presentations on the scientific evidence relating to acupuncture at a three-day conference held November 3–5. issuing a sixteen-page report summarizing their conclusions at the end of the conference.

Need for More Data

Eastern and Western approaches to medicine were almost diametrically opposed, with Eastern health care focused on the whole body and Western health care focused on specific treatments for specific diseases. The practice of acupuncture, for example, was premised on ancient Chinese theory which held that an energy force, called Qi (pronounced "chee"), encompassing all life activities—spiritual, emotional, mental, and physical—flowed through the body along paths called meridians. When disrupted by illness or injury, the flow could be restored to balance by piercing the body with extremely fine needles at specific points.

Traditional Western medicine was slow to accept acupuncture in large part because its beneficial effects and underlying theory were unproved by rigorous scientific data. The panel noted a "paucity of high-quality research" evaluating acupuncture in controlled scientific settings; most of the biomedical literature relied on case studies and other anecdotal evidence.

Nonetheless, the panel said that data from well-designed studies that supported acupuncture were "as strong as those for many accepted Western medical therapies" and often had the advantage of having fewer adverse side effects. For example, the panel said, painful conditions such as tennis elbow and fibromyalgia were often treated with anti-inflammatories such as aspirin or ibuprofen or with steroid injections, all of which could have serious side effects. Yet, the panel said, "the evidence supporting these therapies is no better than that for acupuncture."

Moreover, the report said, many studies showed that acupuncture could cause biological responses, primarily by activating pain-relieving substances within the body as well as hormones and other chemicals that could affect the brain's perception of pain. There was also some evidence that acupuncture affected the immune system. Nonetheless, the panel said, some of the "key traditional Eastern medical concepts" such as the circulation of Qi were "difficult to reconcile with contemporary biomedical information."

To evaluate more fully and scientifically the efficacy of acupuncture as a therapy for various conditions, the panel suggested several directions for future research. These included collecting better information about who currently used acupuncture for what conditions and conducting more high-quality, controlled trials to demonstrate the actual effects of acupuncture. The panel also encouraged researchers to approach the study of acupuncture from two standpoints—the Western approach of using biochemical and physiologic mechanisms to explain the effects of acupuncture and the Eastern approach of dealing with energy system of the whole body. One research question the panel suggested might be: "Does an organized energetic system exist in the human body that has clinical applications?"

Integrating Acupuncture into Western Health Care

The panel made several recommendations to ensure the smooth integration of acupuncture into traditional Western health care. Education and licensing requirements should be standardized and extended to all the states, the panel said. Thirty-four states currently required acupuncture specialists to register or have a license. All practitioners should follow FDA regulations, including use of sterile, single-use needles, to avoid transmission of disease. All patients seeking acupuncture should be informed of their treatment options, the likely prognosis, and potential risks. Patients should let their regular doctor and acupuncturist each know that they are being treated by both so that important medical problems will not be overlooked. The panel also encouraged insurers, including Medicare and Medicaid programs, to cover "appropriate" acupuncture services.

Following are excerpts from the revised draft of the National Institutes of Health Consensus Development Statement on Acupuncture, prepared by a panel of experts and released November 5, 1997:

Introduction

Acupuncture is a component of the health care system of China that can be traced back for at least 2,500 years. The general theory of acupuncture is based on the premise that there are patterns of energy flow (Qi) through the body that are essential for health. Disruptions of this flow are believed to be responsible for disease. The acupuncturist can correct imbalances of flow at identifiable points close to the skin. The practice of acupuncture to treat identifiable pathophysiological conditions in American medicine was rare until the visit of President [Richard] Nixon to China in 1972. Since that time, there has been an explosion of interest in the United States and Europe in the application of the technique of acupuncture to Western medicine.

Acupuncture describes a family of procedures involving stimulation of anatomical locations on the skin by a variety of techniques. The most studied mechanism of stimulation of acupuncture points employs penetration of the skin by thin, solid, metallic needles, which are manipulated manually or by electrical stimulation. The majority of comments in this report are based on data that came from such studies. Stimulation of these areas by moxibustion, pressure, heat, and lasers is used in acupuncture practice, but due to the paucity of studies, these techniques are more difficult to evaluate. Thus, there are a variety of approaches to diagnosis and treatment in American acupuncture that incorporate medical traditions from China, Japan, Korea, and other countries.

Acupuncture has been used by millions of American patients and performed by thousands of physicians, dentists, acupuncturists, and other practitioners for relief or prevention of pain and for a variety of health conditions. After reviewing the existing body of knowledge, the U.S. Food and Drug Administration [FDA] recently removed acupuncture needles from the category of "experimental medical devices" and now regulates them just as it does other devices, such as surgical scalpels and hypodermic syringes, under good manufacturing practices and single-use standards of sterility.

Over the years, the National Institutes of Health (NIH) has funded a variety of research projects on acupuncture, including studies on the mechanisms by which acupuncture may have its effects, as well as clinical trials and other studies. There is also a considerable body of international literature on the risks and benefits of acupuncture, and the World Health Organization lists a variety of medical conditions that may benefit from the use of acupuncture or moxibustion. Such applications include prevention and treatment of nausea and vomiting; treatment of pain and addictions to alcohol, tobacco, and other drugs; treatment of pulmonary problems such as asthma and bronchitis; and rehabilitation from neurological damage such as that caused by stroke.

To address important issues regarding acupuncture, the NIH Office of Alternative Medicine and the NIH Office of Medical Applications of Research organized a 2½-day conference to evaluate the scientific and medical data on the uses, risks, and benefits of acupuncture procedures for a variety of conditions. . . .The conference brought together national and international experts in the fields of acupuncture, pain, psychology, psychiatry, physical medicine and rehabilitation, drug abuse, family practice, internal medicine, health policy, epidemiology, statistics, physiology, and biophysics, as well as representatives from the public.

After 1½ days of available presentations and audience discussion, an independent, non-Federal consensus panel weighed the scientific evidence and wrote a draft statement that was presented to the audience on the third day. . . .

1. What is the efficacy of acupuncture, compared with placebo or sham acupuncture, in the conditions for which sufficient data are available to evaluate?

Acupuncture is a complex intervention that may vary for different patients with similar chief complaints. The number and length of treatments and the specific points used may vary among individuals and during the course of treatment. Given this reality, it is perhaps encouraging that there exist a number of studies of sufficient quality to assess the efficacy of acupuncture for certain conditions.

According to contemporary research standards, there is a paucity of high-quality research assessing efficacy of acupuncture compared with placebo or sham acupuncture. The vast majority of papers studying acupuncture in the biomedical literature consist of case reports, case series, or intervention studies with designs inadequate to assess efficacy.

This discussion of efficacy refers to needle acupuncture (manual or electroacupuncture) because the published research is primarily on needle acupuncture and often does not encompass the full breadth of acupuncture techniques and practices. The controlled trials usually have only involved adults and did not involve long-term (i.e., years) acupuncture treatment.

Efficacy of a treatment assesses the differential effect of a treatment when compared with placebo or another treatment modality using a double-blind controlled trial and a rigidly defined protocol. Papers should describe enrollment procedures, eligibility criteria, description of the clinical characteristics of the subjects, methods for diagnosis, and a description of the protocol (i.e., randomization method, specific definition of treatment, and control conditions, including length of treatment, and number of acupuncture sessions). Optimal trials should also use standardized outcomes and appropriate statistical analyses. This assessment of efficacy focuses on high-quality trials comparing acupuncture with sham acupuncture or placebo.

Response Rate. As with other interventions, some individuals are poor responders to specific acupuncture protocols. Both animal and human laboratory and clinical experience suggest that the majority of subjects respond to acupuncture, with a minority not responding. Some of the clinical research outcomes, however, suggest that a larger percentage may not respond. The reason for this paradox is unclear and may reflect the current state of the research.

Efficacy for Specific Disorders. There is clear evidence that needle acupuncture is efficacious for adult post-operative and chemotherapy nausea and vomiting and probably for the nausea of pregnancy.

Much of the research is on various pain problems. There is evidence of efficacy for postoperative dental pain. There are reasonable studies (although sometimes only single studies) showing relief of pain with acupuncture on diverse pain conditions such as menstrual cramps, tennis elbow, and fibromyalgia. This suggests that acupuncture may have a more general effect on pain. However, there are also studies that do not find efficacy for acupuncture in pain.

There is evidence that acupuncture does not demonstrate efficacy for cessation of smoking and may not be efficacious for some other conditions.

While many other conditions have received some attention in the literature and, in fact, the research suggests some exciting potential areas for the use of acupuncture, the quality or quantity of the research evidence is not sufficient to provide firm evidence of efficacy at this time.

Sham Acupuncture. A commonly used control group is sham acupuncture, using techniques that are not intended to stimulate known acupuncture points. However, there is disagreement on correct needle placement. Also, particularly in the studies on pain, sham acupuncture often seems to have either intermediate effects between the placebo and Öreal' acupuncture points or effects similar to those of the Öreal' acupuncture points.

Placement of a needle in any position elicits a biological response that complicates the interpretation of studies involving sham acupuncture. Thus, there is substantial controversy over the use of sham acupuncture as control groups. This may be less of a problem in studies not involving pain.

2. What is the place of acupuncture in the treatment of various conditions for which sufficient data are available, in comparison with or in combination with other interventions (including no intervention)?

Assessing the usefulness of a medical intervention in practice differs from assessing formal efficacy. In conventional practice, clinicians make decisions based on the characteristics of the patient, clinical experience, potential for harm, and information from colleagues and the medical literature. In addition, when more than one treatment is possible, the clinician may make the choice taking into account the patient's preferences. While it is often thought that there is substantial research evidence to support conventional medical practices; this is frequently not that case. This does not mean that these treatments are ineffective. The data in support of acupuncture are as strong as those for many accepted Western medical therapies.

One of the advantages of acupuncture is that the incidence of adverse effects is substantially lower than that of many drugs or other accepted medical procedures used for the same conditions. As an example, musculoskeletal conditions, such as fibromyalgia, myofascial pain, and "tennis elbow," or epicondylitis, are conditions for which acupuncture may be beneficial. These painful conditions are often treated with, among other things, anti-inflammatory medications (aspirin, ibuprofen, etc.) or with steroid injections. Both medical interventions have a potential for deleterious side effects, but are still widely used, and are considered acceptable treatment. The evidence supporting these therapies is no better than that for acupuncture.

In addition, ample clinical experience, supported by some research data, suggests that acupuncture may be a reasonable option for a number of clinical conditions. Examples are postoperative pain and myofascial and low back pain. Examples of disorders for which the research evidence is less convincing but for which there are some positive clinical reports include addiction, stroke rehabilitation, carpal tunnel syndrome, osteoarthritis, and headache. Acupuncture treatment for many conditions such as asthma, addiction, or smoking cessation should be part of a comprehensive management program.

Many other conditions have been treated by acupuncture; the World Health Organization, for example, has listed more than 40 for which the technique may be indicated.

3. What is known about the biological effects of acupuncture that helps us understand how it works?

Many studies in animals and humans have demonstrated that acupuncture can cause multiple biological responses. These responses can occur locally, i.e., at or close to the site of application, or at a distance, mediated mainly by sensory neurons to many structures within the central nervous system. This can lead to activation of pathways affecting various physiological systems in the brain as well as in the periphery. A focus of attention has been the role of endogenous opioids in acupuncture analgesia. Considerable evidence supports the claim that opioid peptides are released during acupuncture and that the analgesic effects of acupuncture are at least partially explained by their actions. That opioid antagonists such as naloxone reverse the analgesic effects of acupuncture further strengthens this hypothesis. Stimulation by acupuncture may also activate the hypothalamus and the pituitary gland, resulting in a broad spectrum of systemic effects. Alteration in the secretion of neurotransmitters and neurohormones and changes in the regulation of blood flow, both centrally and peripherally, have been documented. There is also evidence that there are alterations in immune functions produced by acupuncture. Which of these and other physiological changes mediate clinical effects is at present unclear.

Despite considerable efforts to understand the anatomy and physiology of the "acupuncture points," the definition and characterization of these points remains controversial. Even more elusive is the scientific basis of some of the key traditional Eastern medical concepts such as the circulation of Qi, the meridian system, and the five phases theory, which are difficult to reconcile with contemporary biomedical information but continue to play an important role in the evaluation of patients and the formulation of treatment in acupuncture.

Some of the biological effects of acupuncture have also been observed when "sham" acupuncture points are stimulated, highlighting the importance of defining appropriate control groups in assessing biological changes purported to be due to acupuncture. Such findings raise questions regarding the specificity of these biological changes. In addition, similar biological alterations including the release of endogenous opioids and changes in blood pressure have been observed after painful stimuli, vigorous exercise, and/or relaxation training; it is at present unclear to what extent acupuncture shares similar biological mechanisms.

It should be noted also that for any therapeutic intervention, including acupuncture, the so-called "non-specific" effects account for a substantial proportion of its effectiveness, and thus should not be casually discounted. Many factors may profoundly determine therapeutic outcome including the quality of the relationship between the clinician and the patient, the degree of trust, the expectations of the patient, the compatibility of the backgrounds and belief systems of the clinician and the patient, as well as a myriad of factors that together define the therapeutic milieu.

Although much remains unknown regarding the mechanism(s) that might mediate the therapeutic effect of acupuncture, the panel is encouraged that a number of significant acupuncture-related biological changes can be identified and carefully delineated. Further research in this direction not only is important for elucidating the phenomena associated with acupuncture, but also has the potential for exploring new pathways in human physiology not previously examined in a systematic manner.

4. What issues need to be addressed so that acupuncture may be appropriately incorporated into today's health care system?

The integration of acupuncture into today's health care system will be facilitated by a better understanding among providers of the language and practices of both the Eastern and Western health care communities. Acupuncture focuses on a holistic, energy-based approach to the patient rather than a disease-oriented diagnostic and treatment model.

An important factor for the integration of acupuncture into the health care system is the training and credentialing of acupuncture practitioners by the appropriate state agencies. This is necessary to allow the public and other health practitioners to identify qualified acupuncture practitioners. The acupuncture educational community has made substantial progress in this area and is encouraged to continue along this path. Educational standards have been established for training of physician and non-physician acupuncturists. Many acupuncture educational programs are accredited by an agency that is recognized by the U.S. Department of Education. A national credentialing agency exists that is recognized by some of the major professional acupuncture organizations and provides examinations for entry-level competency in the field.

A majority of States provide licensure or registration for acupuncture practitioners. Because some acupuncture practitioners have limited English proficiency, credentialing and licensing examinations should be provided in languages other than English where necessary. There is variation in the titles that are conferred through these processes, and the requirements to obtain licensure vary widely. The scope of practice allowed under these State requirements varies as well. While States have the individual prerogative to set standards for licensing professions, harmonization in these areas will provide greater confidence in the qualifications of acupuncture practitioners. For example, not all States recognize the same credentialing examination, thus making reciprocity difficult.

The occurrence of adverse events in the practice of acupuncture has been documented to be extremely low. However, these events have occurred in rare occasions, some of which are life threatening (e.g., pneumothorax).

Therefore, appropriate safeguards for the protection of patients and consumers need to be in place. Patients should be fully informed of their treatment options, expected prognosis, relative risk, and safety practices to minimize these risks prior to their receipt of acupuncture. This information must be provided in a manner that is linguistically and culturally appropriate to the patient. Use of acupuncture needles should always follow FDA regulations, including use of sterile, single-use needles. It is noted that these practices are already being done by many acupuncture practitioners; however, these practices should be uniform. Recourse for patient grievance and professional censure are provided through credentialing and licensing procedures and are available through appropriate State jurisdictions.

It has been reported that more than 1 million Americans currently receive acupuncture each year. Continued access to qualified acupuncture professionals for appropriate conditions should be ensured. Because many individuals seek health care treatment from both acupuncturists and physicians, communication between these providers should be strengthened and improved. If a patient is under the care of an acupuncturist and a physician, both practitioners should be informed. Care should be taken so that important medical problems are not overlooked. Patients and providers have a responsibility to facilitate this communication.

There is evidence that some patients have limited access to acupuncture services because of inability to pay. Insurance companies can decrease or remove financial barriers to access depending on their willingness to provide coverage for appropriate acupuncture services. An increasing number of insurance companies are either considering this possibility or now provide coverage for acupuncture services. Where there are State health insurance plans, and for populations served by Medicare or Medicaid, expansion of coverage to include appropriate acupuncture services would also help remove financial barriers to access.

As acupuncture is incorporated into today's health care system, and further research clarifies the role of acupuncture for various health conditions, it is expected that dissemination of this information to health care practitioners, insurance providers, policymakers, and the general public will lead to more informed decisions in regard to the appropriate use of acupuncture.

5. What are the directions for future research?

The incorporation of any new clinical intervention into accepted practice faces more scrutiny now than ever before. The demands of evidence-based medicine, outcomes research, managed care systems of health care delivery, and a plethora of therapeutic choices makes the acceptance of new treatments an arduous process. The difficulties are accentuated when the treatment is based on theories unfamiliar to Western medicine and its practitioners. It is important, therefore, that the evaluation of acupuncture for the treatment of specific conditions be carried out carefully, using designs which can withstand rigorous scrutiny. In order to further the evaluation of the role of acupuncture in the management of various conditions, the following general areas for future research are suggested.

What are the demographics and patterns of use of acupuncture in the U.S. and other countries?

There is currently limited information on basic questions such as who uses acupuncture, for what indications is acupuncture most commonly sought, what variations in experience and techniques used exist among acupuncture practitioners, and whether there are differences in these patterns by geography or ethnic group. Descriptive epidemiologic studies can provide insight into these and other questions. This information can in turn be used to guide future research and to identify areas of greatest public health concern.

Can the efficacy of acupuncture for various conditions for which it is used or for which it shows promise be demonstrated?

Relatively few high-quality, randomized, controlled trials have been published on the effects of acupuncture. Such studies should be designed in a rigorous manner to allow evaluation of the effectiveness of acupuncture. Such studies should include experienced acupuncture practitioners in order to design and deliver appropriate interventions. Emphasis should be placed on studies that examine acupuncture as used in clinical practice, and that respect the theoretical basis for acupuncture therapy.

Although randomized controlled trials provide a strong basis for inferring causality, other study designs such as used in clinical epidemiology or outcomes research can also provide important insights regarding the usefulness of acupuncture for various conditions. There have been few such studies in the acupuncture literature.

Do different theoretical bases for acupuncture result in different treatment outcomes?

Competing theoretical orientations (e.g., Chinese, Japanese, French) currently exist that might predict divergent therapeutic approaches (i.e., the use of different acupuncture points). Research projects should be designed to assess the relative merit of these divergent approaches, as well to compare these systems with treatment programs using fixed acupuncture points.

In order to fully assess the efficacy of acupuncture, studies should be designed to examine not only fixed acupuncture points, but also the Eastern medical systems that provide the foundation for acupuncture therapy, including the choice of points. In addition to assessing the effect of acupuncture in context, this would also provide the opportunity to determine if Eastern medical theories predict more effective acupuncture points, as well as to examine the relative utility of competing systems (e.g., Chinese vs. Japanese vs. French) for such purposes.

What areas of public policy research can provide guidance for the integration of acupuncture into today's health care system?

The incorporation of acupuncture as a treatment raises numerous questions of public policy. These include issues of access, cost-effectiveness, reimbursement by state, federal, and private payors, and training, licensure, and accreditation. These public policy issues must be founded on quality epidemiologic and demographic data and effectiveness research.

Can further insight into the biological basis for acupuncture be gained?

Mechanisms which provide a Western scientific explanation for some of the effects of acupuncture are beginning to emerge. This is encouraging, and may provide novel insights into neural, endocrine and other physiological processes. Research should be supported to provide a better understanding of the mechanisms involved, and such research may lead to improvements in treatment.

Does an organized energetic system exist in the human body that has clinical applications?

Although biochemical and physiologic studies have provided insight into some of the biologic effects of acupuncture, acupuncture practice is based on a very different model of energy balance. This theory may provide new insights to medical research that may further elucidate the basis for acupuncture.

How do the approaches and answers to these questions differ among populations that have used acupuncture as a part of its healing tradition for centuries, compared to populations that have only recently begun to incorporate acupuncture into health care?

Conclusions and Recommendations

Acupuncture as a therapeutic intervention is widely practiced in the United States. There have been many studies of its potential usefulness. However, many of these studies provide equivocal results because of design, sample size, and other factors. The issue is further complicated by inherent difficulties in the use of appropriate controls, such as placebo and sham acupuncture groups.

However, promising results have emerged, for example, efficacy of acupuncture in adult post-operative and chemotherapy nausea and vomiting and in post-operative dental pain. There are other situations such as addiction, stroke rehabilitation, headache, menstrual cramps, tennis elbow, fibromyalgia myofascial pain, osteoarthritis, low back pain, carpal tunnel syndrome, and asthma where acupuncture may be useful as an adjunct treatment or an acceptable alternative or be included in a comprehensive management program. Further research is likely to uncover additional areas where acupuncture interventions will be useful.

Findings from basic research have begun to elucidate the mechanisms of action of acupuncture, including the release of opioids and other peptides in the central nervous system and the periphery and changes in neuroendocrine function. Although much needs to be accomplished, the emergence of plausible mechanisms for the therapeutic effects of acupuncture is encouraging.

The introduction of acupuncture into the choice of treatment modalities that are readily available to the public is in its early stages. Issues of training, licensure, and reimbursement remain to be clarified. There is sufficient evidence, however, of acupuncture's value to expand its use into conventional medicine and to encourage further studies of its physiology and clinical value.

CLINTON ON GAY RIGHTS
November 8, 1997

President Bill Clinton became the first sitting president to address a gay rights organization when he delivered a speech November 8 to the Human Rights Campaign in Washington, D.C. The 1,500 guests who attended the $250-a-plate fund-raising dinner warmly applauded the president's speech, in particular his calls for equal treatment and his pledge to work for a federal ban on discrimination against gays and lesbians in the workplace. But the evening was notable not so much for what the president said—he was simply repeating what he had already said in other public speeches—as for the forum in which he said it. "It's a big deal," Kenneth Sherrill, chairman of the political science department at Hunter College, told the Washington Post *before the dinner. "In a way, what Clinton is doing is saying to the larger political community, 'There's nothing to be embarrassed about here.'"*

Although the president had deeply disappointed the gay rights community on some issues, most notably his failure to integrate gays and lesbians into the military and his decision to sign legislation discouraging same-sex marriages, his endorsement of many of their causes throughout his presidency gave the gay community a political legitimacy it might not have achieved so quickly otherwise. "What the president has done is change the atmosphere in this country, in terms of putting gay issues on the radar screen of America," Elizabeth Birch, the executive director of the Human Rights Campaign, said before the speech.

In return Clinton won the political support of a wide segment of the gay community. The Human Rights Campaign, which claimed 200,000 members, ran one of the largest gay political action committees in the United States. It estimated that gay donors gave $3.2 million to Democrats in 1996. An independent exit poll found that about two-thirds of those voters who said they were gay or lesbian voted for Clinton in 1996, accounting for 7 percent of his total votes.

Clinton's appearance at the fund-raising dinner was a payback for that support, but the White House also took pains to downplay its significance. In the days leading up to the speech, aides portrayed the event as just one

more of the president's efforts to bring his message of the need for reconcil-
iation and "one America" to as many different groups as possible. "The
president has done literally dozens of community outreach events this year,"
Michael D. McCurry, the White House press secretary said the day before
the speech. "He was just at the National Italian American Foundation din-
ner last week."

At the dinner, Clinton made no mention in his speech of Ellen DeGeneres,
the star of the television show Ellen, *who had created an uproar in the*
spring when both she and her character announced they were lesbians. The
Human Rights Campaign was honoring DeGeneres at the dinner, but Clin-
ton left before the award was given. Earlier in the fall, Vice President Al
Gore had riled conservatives when he praised DeGeneres for "coming out"
on national television.

A Mixed Record

In his run for the presidency in 1992, Clinton courted the gay and les-
bian vote, promising to let homosexuals serve openly in the military if he
was elected president. The promise drew only minor attention during the
campaign, but as his inauguration drew near, military and congressional
leaders began to voice strong objections. The controversy grew so heated
that it threatened to swamp economic concerns that had been at the fore-
front of Clinton's campaign and the new administration's political agenda.
Eventually Clinton agreed to a compromise under which the military
would no longer quiz recruits about their sexual orientation but would still
be permitted to discharge openly gay personnel—the so-called don't ask,
don't tell policy. (Clinton plan to remove military homosexual ban, Historic
Documents of 1993, p. 153)

Gay rights activists were upset that Clinton was unable to fulfill his
campaign promise. Over the next few years Clinton was able to repair some
of the damage by increasing funding for AIDS research, hiring openly ho-
mosexual personnel in the executive branch, and ending a decades-old
practice of prohibiting homosexual civilian and military personnel from
having access to classified information solely on the basis of their sexual
orientation. (Gay rights and security clearances, Historic Documents of 1995,
p. 532)

In September 1996, just weeks before the November election, President
Clinton signed into law—late at night and without ceremony—a bill stip-
ulating that no state need recognize the validity of another state's law al-
lowing same-sex marriages. Clinton said he had "long opposed govern-
mental recognition of same-gender marriages." In his signing statement he
urged Congress to approve legislation that would extend job discrimination
protections to gay and lesbian workers. The Senate earlier in the month had
defeated such legislation by a single vote. Many in the gay community ex-
pressed disappointment that Clinton had not taken their side on the issue
of same-sex marriages; they nonetheless supported his reelection bid in No-
vember. (Clinton on same-sex marriages, Historic Documents of 1996, p. 687)

"Equality for All Americans"

In introducing the president at the Human Rights Campaign dinner, executive director Birch chose to downplay the differences between Clinton and the gay community. "Because our needs were almost as great as our expectations, it was inevitable that we—you and this community—would experience both shared disappointment and some disagreement," she said. "But Mr. President, you have played a brave and powerful and indispensable role in the march toward justice for us."

In his remarks Clinton equated the struggle for gay rights with that for civil rights, noting that fifty years earlier, in June 1947, Harry Truman had become the first sitting president to address the NAACP. In that speech at the Lincoln Memorial, Clinton said, Truman pledged to work for freedom and equality for all Americans, adding, "When I say all Americans, I mean all Americans." "Well, my friends," Clinton said, "all Americans still means all Americans."

Clinton once again called on Congress to enact the Employment Nondiscrimination Act, which would prohibit discrimination against homosexuals in the workplace. "Being gay, the last time I thought about it," the president said, "seemed to have nothing to do with the ability to read a balance book, fix a broken bone, or change a spark plug." Discriminating against someone because of sexual bias was not different than discriminating against someone because of race or religion, Clinton said. "It is wrong. And it should be illegal."

Not everyone was happy with Clinton's decision to address the gay rights group. A handful of dinner guests heckled the president, accusing him of not spending enough to find a cure for AIDS. Outside the Grand Hyatt Hotel were small groups of protesters, some with signs that read "God hates fags," and others with signs reading "Ellen can change." A spokesperson for the Family Research Council called Clinton's appearance a "tragedy" and said his use of "the bully pulpit of the Presidential office to endorse homosexuality will lead more kids into the lifestyle and make it harder for other people to leave homosexuality for a better life."

> *Following are excerpts from a speech that President Bill Clinton delivered November 8, 1997, to a fund-raising dinner for the Human Rights Campaign, a gay rights organization:*

I'm delighted to be here. I thank the members of Congress who are here. I congratulate your honorees. I know that a number of my recent appointees are here, including Virginia Apuzzo, our new Assistant for Management and Administration. Fred Hochberg, John Berry, Jim Hormel. Where's Jim Hormel? He's here. Jesse White. Hal Creal. . . .

We have a lot of people here from the White House as well. I want to thank Richard Socarides, Marsha Scott, Karen Tramantano, Sean Maloney, Tom Shea, and our AIDS czar, Sandy Thurman for all their work.

And because it's dark here, I would like to ask everyone who works for this administration in any department of the federal government or who has an appointment in any way to please stand, including the White House. Thank you.

A little more than six years ago, I had this crazy idea that I ought to run for President. Only my mother thought I could win. And at the time, I was so obsessed with what I thought had to be done I thought winning would take care of itself. What bothered me was that our country seemed to be drifting and divided as we moved into a new and exciting and challenging area where we were living differently, working differently, relating to each other and the rest of the world in very different ways on the edge of a new century.

And I sat down alone before I decided to do this and asked myself, what is it that you want America to look like when you're done if you win? My vision for the 21st century, now, I have said hundreds and hundreds of times, but I still think about it every day—I want this to be a country where every child and every person who is responsible enough to work for it can live the American dream. I want this country to embrace the wider world and continue to be the strongest force for peace and freedom and prosperity, and I want us to come together across all our lines of difference into one America.

That is my vision. It drives me every day. I think if we really could create a society where there is opportunity for all and responsibility from all and we believed in a community of all Americans, we could truly meet every problem we have and seize every opportunity we have.

For more than two centuries now, our country has had to meet challenge after challenge after challenge. We have had to continue to lift ourselves beyond what we thought America meant. Our ideals were never meant to be frozen in stone or time. Keep in mind, when we started out with Thomas Jefferson's credo that all of us are created equal by God, what that really meant in civic political terms was that you had to be white, you had to be male, and that wasn't enough—you had to own property, which would have left my crowd out when I was a boy.

Over time, we have had to redefine the words that we started with, not because there was anything wrong with them and their universal power and strength of liberty and justice, but because we were limited in our imaginations about how we could live and what we were capable of and how we should live. Indeed, the story of how we kept going higher and higher and higher to new and higher definitions—and more meaningful definitions—of equality and dignity and freedom is in its essence the fundamental story of our country.

Fifty years ago, President Truman stood at a new frontier in our defining struggle on civil rights. Slavery had ended a long time before, but segregation remained. Harry Truman stood before the Lincoln Memorial and said, "It is more important today than ever to ensure that all Americans enjoy the rights (of freedom and equality). When I say all Americans, I mean all Americans."

Well, my friends, all Americans still means all Americans. We all know that it is an ideal and not perfectly real now. We all know that some of the old kinds of discrimination we have sought to rid ourselves of by law and purge our spirits of still exist in America today. We all know that there is continuing discrimination against gays and lesbians. But we also know that if we're ever going to build one America, then all Americans—including you and those whom you represent—have got to be a part of it.

To be sure, no President can grant rights. Our ideals and our history hold that they are inalienable, embedded in our Constitution, amplified over time by our courts and legislature. I cannot grant them—but I am bound by my oath of office and the burden of history to reaffirm them.

All America loses if we let prejudice and discrimination stifle the hopes or deny the potential of a single American. All America loses when any person is denied or forced out of a job because of sexual orientation. Being gay, the last time I thought about it, seemed to have nothing to do with the ability to read a balance book, fix a broken bone, or change a spark plug.

For generations, the American Dream has represented a fundamental compact among our people. If you take responsibility and work hard, you have the right to achieve a better life for yourself and a better future for your family. Equal opportunity for all, special privileges for none—a fate shared by Americans regardless of political views. We believe—or we all say we believe—that all citizens should have the chance to rise as far as their God-given talents will take them. What counts is energy and honesty and talent. No arbitrary distinctions should bar the way.

So when we deny opportunity because of ancestry or religion, race or gender, disability or sexual orientation, we break the compact. It is wrong. And it should be illegal. Once again I call upon Congress to honor our most cherished principles and make the Employment Non-Discrimination Act the law of the land.

I also come here tonight to ask you for another favor. Protecting the civil rights of all Americans—

Audience Member: People with AIDS are dying.

Audience: Sit down.

Clinton: Wait, wait, wait. I would have been disappointed if you hadn't been here tonight. I'm kind of used to this. People with AIDS are dying. But since I've become President we're spending 10 times as much per fatality on people with AIDS as people with breast cancer or prostate cancer. And the drugs are being approved more quickly. And a lot of people are living normal lives. We just have to keep working on it.

I thank you, but this, too, is part of what makes America great. We all have our say, and nobody has to be afraid when he or she screams at the President. That's a good thing. That's a good thing. And at a time when so many people feel their voices will never be heard, that's a good thing.

What is not a good thing, however, is when people believe their free speech rights trump yours. That's not good. That's not.

Now, I want to ask you for a favor. You want us to pass the Employment Non-Discrimination Act. You know when we do—and I believe it will pass—you know when we do it will have to be enforced. The law on the books only works if it is also a law in the life of America.

Let me say, I thank you very much for your support of my nominee for the Office of Civil Rights, Bill Lee. I thank you for that. But he, too, comes from a family that has known discrimination and now he is being discriminated against, not because there is anything wrong with his qualifications, not because anybody believes he is not even-tempered, but because some members of the Senate disagree with his views on affirmative action.

Now, if I have to appoint a head of the office of civil rights who is against affirmative action—it's going to be vacant a long time. That office is not there to advocate or promote—primarily to advocate or promote the policies of the government when it comes to affirmative action; it's there to enforce the existing laws against discrimination. You hope someday you will have one of those existing laws. We need somebody to enforce the laws, and Bill Lee should be confirmed, and I ask you to help me to get him confirmed.

I'd like to say just one more word. There are some people who aren't in this room tonight who aren't comfortable yet with you and won't be comfortable with me for being here.

Audience Member: We love you, Bill.

Clinton: Wait a minute. This is serious. On issue after issue involving gays and lesbians, survey after survey shows that the most important determinant of people's attitudes is whether they are aware—whether they knowingly have had a family or a friendship or a work relation with a gay person.

Now, I hope that we will embrace good people who are trying to overcome their fears. After all, all of us can look back in history and see what the right thing to do was. It is quite another thing to look ahead and light the way. Most people are preoccupied with the burdens of daily living. Most of us, as we grow older, become—whether we like it or not—somewhat more limited in our imaginations. So I think one of the greatest things we have to do still is just to increase the ability of Americans who do not yet know that gays and lesbians are their fellow Americans in every sense of the word to feel that way. I think it's very important.

When I say, "I believe all Americans means all Americans," I see the faces of the friends of 35 years. When I say, "all Americans means all Americans," I see the faces of the people who stood up when I asked the people who are part of our administration to stand tonight. When I say, "all Americans means all Americans," I see kind, unbelievably generous, giving people back in my home state who helped my family and my friends when they were in need. It is a different story when you know what you are seeing.

So I say to you tonight, should we change the law? You bet. Should we keep fighting discrimination? Absolutely. Is this Hate Crimes Conference important? It is terribly important. But we have to broaden the imagination of America. We are redefining, in practical terms, the immutable ideals that have guided us from the beginning. Again I say, we have to make sure that for every single person in our country, all Americans means all Americans.

After experiencing the horrors of the Civil War and witnessing the transformation of the previous century, Walt Whitman said that our greatest strength was that we are an embracing nation. In his words, a "Union, holding all, fusing, absorbing, tolerating all." Let us move forward in the spirit of that one America. Let us realize that this is a good obligation that has been imposed upon our generation, and a grand opportunity once again to lift America to a higher level of unity, once again to redefine and to strengthen and to ensure one America for a new century and a new generation of our precious children.

Thank you and God bless you.

UN SECURITY COUNCIL ON
WEAPONS INSPECTIONS IN IRAQ
November 12, 1997

Apparently testing the resolve of the United Nations, Iraq twice in late 1997 precipitated crises over the work of a UN commission attempting to locate and destroy Iraq's weapons of mass destruction. The first standoff between Iraq and the UN, which started at the end of October, had just been settled when Iraq threw another hurdle in the path of the UN commission. At year's end the confrontation was escalating, with a serious prospect that the United States and its allies might again use massive military force against Iraq.

After the Persian Gulf War in 1991, Iraq was forced to agree to allow a UN special commission, known as UNSCOM, to locate, dismantle, and destroy all the country's long-range ballistic missiles and nuclear, chemical, and biological weapons. A general UN trade embargo against Iraq was to remain in place until the commission certified that all of Baghdad's facilities capable of producing such weapons had been destroyed. (Sanctions against Iraq, Historic Documents of 1991, pp. 165, 191; Historic Documents of 1995, p. 355)

Despite forced pledges of cooperation, Iraq repeatedly tried to block the work of the commission by hiding weapons production sites and materiel, denying the existence of weapons programs, and destroying important documents, according to commission reports. Iraq in 1994 moved troops near its border with Kuwait and threatened to stop any cooperation with the commission but backed down under the threat of force from the United States. (Clinton on Iraqi troop build-up, Historic Documents of 1994, p. 431)

In moving against the UN commission again in 1997, Iraqi president Saddam Hussein seemed to be counting on divisions within the UN Security Council and the alliance that had fought him in the Gulf War. Three of the five permanent members of the Security Council—Russia, China, and France—appeared willing at various points to accept Iraq's assurances that it was cooperating with the weapons inspections, and thus complying with UN resolutions. Russia and France were eager to resume commercial rela-

tions with Iraq, and China long had opposed what it viewed as UN "interference" in the affairs of UN member nations. Those three nations made it difficult for Washington to enforce its hard-line approach against Baghdad.

On the other hand, the United States had significant leverage with its military might and its veto power over any move to lift the UN's sanctions against Iraq. The problem for Washington was that any threats to use military force could succeed only to a point, primarily as backup leverage for diplomacy. Saddam clearly would not be intimidated by a token military strike, such as a U.S. attack using forty-four "cruise" missiles in 1996. Even a massive military attack, comparable to the 1991 Gulf War, was not certain to obliterate the remaining weapons that Iraq was hiding. (U.S. strike against Iraq, Historic Documents of 1996, p. 680)

Focus on Biological Weapons

By 1997 the UN commission had succeeded in locating and destroying most of Iraq's ballistic missiles, along with known research and production facilities for that country's nuclear weapons program. The commission was devoting most of its attention to finding a huge arsenal of chemical and biological weapons that Iraq was believed to possess.

Iraq had denied, until 1995, that it had even attempted to develop biological weapons. Thereafter the Iraqis revealed information about its biological weapons program only when forced to do so by the UN inspectors. Under UN pressure Iraq had acknowledged producing thousands of gallons of two of the deadliest biological agents, botulinum toxin and anthrax— enough to wipe out the world's population several times over if deployed properly. UNSCOM also uncovered evidence in 1995 that Iraq had acquired the necessary materials to produce enormous quantities of an especially lethal nerve gas known as VX. The Washington Post *reported that the UN inspectors were particularly interested in locating twenty-five warheads, said to contain biological warfare agents, that had escaped destruction during the Gulf War and had been kept hidden by the Iraqi military.*

In an October 6 report, UNSCOM detailed numerous Iraqi evasions, including the destruction of records and repeated refusals to allow inspectors into sensitive areas. The report concluded that Iraq had been "insistent on blocking" all attempts by the commission to obtain facts about the biological weapons program. Several U.S. and UN officials said they suspected Iraq had used humans in testing biological weapons and had hoped to keep those experiments secret.

U.S. officials revealed in November that Iraqi authorities had been able to gain access to the secret planning of the UN inspection teams, most likely through electronic eavesdropping. As a result, U.S. officials said, the Iraqis often knew where and when the UN inspectors would go for their "surprise" visits and were able to hide suspected weapons components.

Barring U.S. Inspectors

The late-1997 standoff began October 27 when UNSCOM executive chairman Richard Butler sent a letter to Tariq Aziz, the Iraqi deputy prime minister, saying the inspectors planned to visit top secret sites controlled by the Republican Guards, Saddam's elite security force. The sites were among those that inspectors believed Iraq used to hide biological weapons agents.

Two days later, Iraq moved against the weapons inspections on two fronts: demanding a halt to flights of American U-2 spy planes that were on missions for the UN commission, and threatening to expel ten American members of UN inspection teams. Iraq followed through on the expulsion threat on November 13, and threatened to shoot down any U-2 planes over its territory. UN officials declared both Iraqi moves unacceptable and withdrew the rest of the 100-member UN team from Iraq, the first time such a step had been taken since inspections began in 1991.

Negotiations between UN representatives and Iraq led nowhere until Russian foreign minister Yevgeny M. Primakov stepped in to mediate the standoff. Primakov negotiated an arrangement for all the UN weapons inspectors, including the Americans, to return to their posts, which they did November 22. UN officials said Primakov made no promises to Iraq concerning the lifting of sanctions or any other issue in return for allowing the inspectors to return.

In the first week after resuming work, the UN inspectors visited eighty-three sites in Iraq, checking and resetting cameras and other monitoring equipment that they had left behind. But on November 27 Iraq told the UN commission that it could not inspect so-called presidential and sovereign sites, including several palaces and other buildings said to be used by Saddam and his key aides. Butler, the commission chairman, said December 8 that Iraq had further expanded the number of sites it was declaring off-limits to the inspectors.

Butler called the latest Iraqi action "unacceptable," and at year's end the Security Council once again was debating how to respond to an attempt by Iraq to thwart the work of its weapons inspectors. The council issued a statement December 22 demanding that Iraq allow "immediate and unconditional access to any and all areas, facilities, equipment, records and means of transportation" that UNSCOM wanted to inspect.

Divisions in the Alliance

Clinton administration officials had been concerned about Russian intervention in the 1997 standoff because Moscow appeared to be much more willing than Washington to give Iraq the benefit of the doubt on compliance with UN resolutions. Iraq had been a key Middle East ally of the Soviet Union during the cold war and had purchased billions of dollars worth of armaments from Moscow, much of which had not been paid for when the Soviet Union collapsed at the end of 1991. Russia took over the old Soviet accounts and badly needed the money still owed by Iraq. Lifting economic sanctions would allow Iraq to resume full oil production and thus give Russia a reasonable hope of receiving payment on the Iraqi debts. Similarly, French companies were eager to resume business in Iraq and had pressured their government on the sanctions issue.

Russia and France were among the countries that had persuaded Iraq in 1997 to accept a UN offer allowing limited exports of oil, with the proceeds dedicated to purchases of food and medicines for the civilian population. Iraq for several years had resisted the offer, saying that it constituted undue interference.

U.S. officials said the resumption of limited oil production apparently gave Baghdad an incentive to test the UN's determination to keep broader economic sanctions in place. Apparently hoping to foreclose any drive for the lifting of sanctions, Secretary of State Madeleine K. Albright said March 26 that the United States insisted that the sanctions remain in place until Iraq had complied with all UN Security Council resolutions. She strongly implied that such an outcome was not possible as long as Saddam remained in power because "the evidence is overwhelming that Saddam's intentions will never be peaceful."

Following is the text of UN Security Council Resolution 1137, issued November 12, 1997, demanding that Iraq cooperate with the UN special commission conducting weapons inspections in Iraq:

The Security Council,

Recalling all its previous relevant resolutions, and in particular its resolutions 687 (1991) of 3 April 1991, 707 (1991) of 15 August 1991, 715 (1991) of 11 October 1991, 1060 (1996) of 12 June 1996, 1115 (1997) of 21 June 1997, and 1134 (1997) of 23 October 1997,

Taking note with grave concern of the letter of 29 October 1997 from the Deputy Prime Minister of Iraq to the President of the Security Council (S/1997/829) conveying the unacceptable decision of the Government of Iraq to seek to impose conditions on its cooperation with the Special Commission, of the letter of 2 November 1997 from the Permanent Representative of Iraq to the United Nations to the Executive Chairman of the Special Commission (S/1997/837, annex) which reiterated the unacceptable demand that the reconnaissance aircraft operating on behalf of the Special Commission be withdrawn from use and which implicitly threatened the safety of such aircraft, and of the letter of 6 November 1997 from the Minister of Foreign Affairs of Iraq to the President of the Security Council (S/1997/855) admitting that Iraq has moved dual-capable equipment which is subject to monitoring by the Special Commission,

Also taking note with grave concern of the letters of 30 October 1997 (S/1997/830) and 2 November 1997 (S/1997/836) from the Executive Chairman of the Special Commission to the President of the Security Council advising that the Government of Iraq had denied entry to Iraq to two Special Commission officials on 30 October 1997 and 2 November 1997 on the grounds of their nationality, and of the letters of 3 November 1997 (S/1997/837), 4 November 1997 (S/1997/843), 5 November 1997 (S/1997/851) and 7 November 1997

(S/1997/864) from the Executive Chairman of the Special Commission to the President of the Security Council advising that the Government of Iraq had denied entry to sites designated for inspection by the Special Commission on 3, 4, 5, 6 and 7 November 1997 to Special Commission inspectors on the grounds of their nationality, and of the additional information in the Executive Chairman's letter of 5 November 1997 to the President of the Security Council (S/1997/851) that the Government of Iraq has moved significant pieces of dual-capable equipment subject to monitoring by the Special Commission, and that monitoring cameras appear to have been tampered with or covered,

Welcoming the diplomatic initiatives, including that of the high-level mission of the Secretary-General, which have taken place in an effort to ensure that Iraq complies unconditionally with its obligations under the relevant resolutions,

Deeply concerned at the report of the high-level mission of the Secretary-General on the results of its meetings with the highest levels of the Government of Iraq,

Recalling that its resolution 1115 (1997) expressed its firm intention, unless the Special Commission advised the Council that Iraq is in substantial compliance with paragraphs 2 and 3 of that resolution, to impose additional measures on those categories of Iraqi officials responsible for the non-compliance,

Recalling also that its resolution 1134 (1997) reaffirmed its firm intention, if *inter alia* the Special Commission reports that Iraq is not in compliance with paragraphs 2 and 3 of resolution 1115 (1997), to adopt measures which would oblige States to refuse the entry into or transit through their territories of all Iraqi officials and members of the Iraqi armed forces who are responsible for or participate in instances of non-compliance with paragraphs 2 and 3 of resolution 1115 (1997),

Recalling further the Statement of its President of 29 October 1997 (S/PRST/1997/49) in which the Council condemned the decision of the Government of Iraq to try to dictate the terms of its compliance with its obligation to cooperate with the Special Commission, and warned of the serious consequences of Iraq's failure to comply immediately and fully and without conditions or restrictions with its obligations under the relevant resolutions,

Reiterating the commitment of all Member States to the sovereignty, territorial integrity and political independence of Kuwait and Iraq,

Determined to ensure immediate and full compliance without conditions or restrictions by Iraq with its obligations under the relevant resolutions,

Determining that this situation continues to constitute a threat to international peace and security,

Acting under Chapter VII of the Charter,

1. *Condemns* the continued violations by Iraq of its obligations under the relevant resolutions to cooperate fully and unconditionally with the Special Commission in the fulfilment of its mandate, including its unacceptable decision of 29 October 1997 to seek to impose conditions on cooperation with the Special Commission, its refusal on 30 October 1997 and 2 November 1997 to

allow entry to Iraq to two Special Commission officials on the grounds of their nationality, its denial of entry on 3, 4, 5, 6 and 7 November 1997 to sites designated by the Special Commission for inspection to Special Commission inspectors on the grounds of their nationality, its implicit threat to the safety of the reconnaissance aircraft operating on behalf of the Special Commission, its removal of significant pieces of dual-use equipment from their previous sites, and its tampering with monitoring cameras of the Special Commission;

2. *Demands that* the Government of Iraq rescind immediately its decision of 29 October 1997;

3. *Demands also* that Iraq cooperate fully and immediately and without conditions or restrictions with the Special Commission in accordance with the relevant resolutions, which constitute the governing standard of Iraqi compliance;

4. *Decides*, in accordance with paragraph 6 of resolution 1134 (1997), that States shall without delay prevent the entry into or transit through their territories of all Iraqi officials and members of the Iraqi armed forces who were responsible for or participated in the instances of non-compliance detailed in paragraph 1 above, provided that the entry of a person into a particular State on a specified date may be authorized by the Committee established by resolution 661 (1990) of 6 August 1990, and provided that nothing in this paragraph shall oblige a State to refuse entry into its own territory to its own nationals, or to persons carrying out bona fide diplomatic assignments, or missions approved by the Committee established by resolution 661 (1990);

5. *Decides also*, in accordance with paragraph 7 of resolution 1134 (1997), to designate in consultation with the Special Commission a list of individuals whose entry or transit will be prevented under the provisions of paragraph 4 above, and requests the Committee established by resolution 661 (1990) to develop guidelines and procedures as appropriate for the implementation of the measures set out in paragraph 4 above, and to transmit copies of these guidelines and procedures, as well as a list of the individuals designated, to all Member States;

6. *Decides* that the provisions of paragraphs 4 and 5 above shall terminate one day after the Executive Chairman of the Special Commission reports to the Council that Iraq is allowing the Special Commission inspection teams immediate, unconditional and unrestricted access to any and all areas, facilities, equipment, records and means of transportation which they wish to inspect in accordance with the mandate of the Special Commission, as well as to officials and other persons under the authority of the Iraqi Government whom the Special Commission wishes to interview so that the Special Commission may fully discharge its mandate;

7. *Decides* that the reviews provided for in paragraphs 21 and 28 of resolution 687 (1991) shall resume in April 1998 in accordance with paragraph 8 of resolution 1134 (1997), provided that the Government of Iraq shall have complied with paragraph 2 above;

8. *Expresses* the firm intention to take further measures as may be required for the implementation of this resolution;

9. *Reaffirms* the responsibility of the Government of Iraq under the relevant resolutions to ensure the safety and security of the personnel and equipment of the Special Commission and its inspection teams;

10. *Reaffirms also* its full support for the authority of the Special Commission under its Executive Chairman to ensure the implementation of its mandate under the relevant resolutions of the Council;

11. *Decides* to remain seized of the matter.

TRANSPORTATION DEPARTMENT ON AIR BAG REGULATIONS
November 18, 1997

For the second year in a row, the Clinton administration attempted in 1997 to deal with public concern about the safety of air bags in automobiles. The administration in 1996 mandated that warning labels be placed on all air bags and allowed automobile owners to have the devices deactivated under certain circumstances. Responding to continuing unease about the devices—even among from some government officials—the administration decided in 1997 to allow owners to install switches enabling them to turn air bags on and off. (Airbag proposal, Historic Documents of 1996, p. 801)

Congress in 1991 mandated installation of air bags on all cars and light trucks by the late 1990s. Consumer demand for the devices was so strong that by 1996 virtually all new cars and trucks came equipped with air bags on both the driver and passenger sides.

Research studies showed that air bags had saved between 1,700 and 2,600 lives since they were introduced in 1986. But because they exploded at a rate of up to two hundred miles an hour, air bags also posed a hazard to children, small adults, and passengers who were not wearing seat belts. According to federal statistics, eighty-seven people—forty-nine of them children—had been killed by air bags between 1986 and late 1997.

Federal officials said most injuries caused by exploding air bags could have been avoided—by putting children in the rear seat, by using seat belts, and by pushing the front seat as far back as possible. Even so, some people, such as small adults who had to sit close to the steering wheel, would always be "at risk" from air bag injuries.

Reviewing the Options

Responding to public concerns about the safety of air bags, the National Transportation Safety Board held four days of public hearings in mid-March and heard testimony from citizens, federal officials, researchers, and automobile company representatives. Ricardo Martinez, administrator of the National Highway Traffic Safety Administration, acknowledged at the opening session March 17 that air bags had killed some adults and

*children because "the dose is too big." The solution, he said, was develop-
ment of "smart" air bags that could adjust their impact to the size of the occupant of each seat.*

*Others testifying at the hearings suggested that the government needed
to rethink the purpose of air bags. Existing federal regulations assumed
that air bags needed to be powerful enough to protect passengers who were
not wearing seat belts—the very type of passenger most likely to be injured
by an exploding air bag. An alternative, some witnesses told the safety
board, was to think of an air bag as a supplement to the seat belt, rather
than as a replacement for it.*

*Reviewing that testimony a month later before a Senate committee,
safety board chairman James Hall said the "one size fits all" type of air bag
"is obsolete." More sophisticated air bags capable of protecting "all people in
a variety of crash situations" would have to be developed over a period of
several years, he said. In the meantime, the government needed to step up
its campaign to convince parents to put all children under the age of twelve
in the rear seat and all occupants to wear seat belts.*

Deactivating Air Bags

*Despite increasing complaints from the public about the potential risk of
air bags, the government had been reluctant to allow exemptions to the requirement that all cars and light trucks be equipped with the devices on
both the driver and passenger sides. The National Highway Traffic Safety
Administration, which had jurisdiction on the matter, authorized the first
major exemption in 1995 when it allowed automakers to install on-off
switches for air bags on cars and light trucks that had no rear seats or rear
seats that were too small to accommodate a child's safety seat. In 1996 the
administration took a further step, allowing owners to have air bags deactivated by a dealer or mechanic if they had "reasonable concerns" about the
potential danger. Because deactivation was an all-or-nothing step, officials
believed that few owners would take this approach.*

*Reviewing the issue again in 1997, the safety administration in March
allowed automakers to install "reduced power" air bags that deployed at a
rate 20 percent to 35 percent below that of conventional air bags. Then, on
November 18, the safety administration announced new rules allowing auto
owners in certain "risk" categories to have on-off switches installed on their
seat belts, starting in January 1998. The four risk categories were: those
who cannot avoid placing rear-facing infant seats in the front passenger
seat; those with a medical condition that places them at a specific risk from
air bags; those who cannot adjust the driver's seat position to keep back at
least ten inches from the steering wheel; and those who cannot avoid situations (such as a car pool) in which a child under the age of twelve must
ride in the front seat.*

*To have an air bag on-off switch installed, an owner would have to fill
out a form available from dealerships or auto repair shops, certify on the
form that he or she was in one of the four "at risk" categories, certify that
he or she had read an information brochure provided by the safety admin-*

istration, and return the form to the administration. Once the safety administration gave its permission, the owner could have the switch installed by an authorized dealer or mechanic. The switches would cost $150 to $200 in most cases, officials said.

Federal officials said they expected that permission would be granted automatically to nearly all who applied. However, they said they anticipated that only a small percentage of auto owners would ask permission to have on-off switches installed. Transportation Secretary Rodney E. Slater called the new rule "a practical solution that allows you to turn off the air bag for someone at risk and turn it back on to preserve the lifesaving benefits for everyone else."

The safety administration said it was launching a nationwide education campaign to make auto drivers and passengers aware of the safety benefits—and also the risks—or air bags and seat belts. As part of the campaign, the administration said it would distribute "millions" of copies of an information brochure.

The safety administration also said it hoped to issue proposals early in 1998 on the development of "smart" air bags. New technology, the administration said, could "eliminate risks to all vehicle passengers."

Following is the executive summary of the "Final Rule" on new air bag regulations issued November 18, 1997, by the National Highway Traffic Safety Administration:

A. Final Rule

This final rule seeks to preserve the benefits of air bags, while providing a means for reducing the risks that some current air bag designs pose to discrete groups of people due to their extreme proximity to air bags. This final rule exempts motor vehicle dealers and repair businesses from the statutory prohibition against making federally-required safety equipment inoperative so that, beginning January 19, 1998, they may install, subject to certain conditions, retrofit manual on-off switches for the air bags of vehicle owners whose request is approved by NHTSA [National Highway Traffic Safety Administration]. To obtain approval, vehicle owners must submit a request form to NHTSA on which they have certified that they have read an agency information brochure about air bag benefits and risks and that they or a user of their vehicle is a member of one of the risk groups identified by the agency. The agency will begin processing and granting requests on December 18, 1997.

Air bags have saved the lives of about 2,620 drivers and passengers, primarily in moderate and high speed crashes, as of November 1, 1997. However, air bags have also caused fatal injuries, primarily in relatively low speed crashes, to a small but growing number of children, and on rare occasion to adults. These deaths were not random. They occurred when people were too close to their air bag when it began to inflate. The vast majority of these fatalities could have been avoided by preventive steps such as using seat belts, moving the front seats back as much as possible, and putting children in the back seat. Nevertheless, a relatively small number of people may still be at risk, even after taking these steps, because they will be more likely than the general population to be too close to their air bags. Although advanced air bags are the ultimate answer and manufacturers are beginning to install air bags with some advanced attributes, an interim solution is needed for those identifiable groups of persons for whom current air bags in existing vehicles may pose a risk of serious or fatal injury.

Under the exemption, vehicle owners may request a retrofit on-off switch, based on informed decisionmaking and their certification of their membership or the membership of another user of their vehicle in one of the risk groups identified by the agency. After reading the agency information brochure, owners can fill out and sign an agency request form and submit it to NHTSA. The information brochure, which provides guidance about which groups of people may be at risk from air bags and about appropriate use of on-off switches, is intended to inform consumers about which people are at risk from air bags and to promote informed decisionmaking by consumers about whether to request an on-off switch for those persons. To increase the likelihood that the decisions are, in fact, informed, owners requesting a retrofit on-off switch must certify on the request form that they have read the information brochure. To limit the availability of on-off switches to persons at risk of serious air bag injury, the owners must also certify that they or a user of their vehicle is a member of one or more of the risk groups described on the information brochure and listed on the request form. The particular risk group in which membership is claimed must be identified. Since the risk groups for driver air bags are different from those for passenger air bags, a separate certification must be made for each air bag to be equipped with an on-off switch.

To reinforce the importance of taking great care in accurately certifying risk group membership, the agency is requiring owners to submit their requests to the agency. The agency expects that owners will accurately and honestly make the necessary certifications and statements on their request forms, but reserves the right to investigate. The prior approval procedure will also enable the agency to monitor, from the very beginning, the volume of requests and patterns in switch requests and risk group certifications. The computerization of the process of preparing authorization letters will minimize the time needed by the agency to process and respond to the requests. The precise amount of time will depend in large measure on the volume of requests.

The agency strongly urges caution in obtaining and using on-off switches. As noted above, on-off switches are not needed for the vast majority of people since they are not at risk. Most people can take steps that will eliminate or significantly reduce their risk without turning off their air bag and losing its protective value. If they take those steps, they will be safer than if they did not take those steps and simply turned off their air bag. The most important steps are using seat belts and other restraints and moving back from the air bag. More important, people who are not at risk will be less safe if they turn off their air bag.

This exemption is subject to certain conditions to promote the safe and careful use of on-off switches. For example, the on-off switches installed pursuant to this exemption must meet certain performance criteria, such as being operable by a key and being accompanied by a telltale to alert vehicle occupants whether the air bag is "on" or "off." In addition, to provide a reminder about the proper use of on-off switches, vehicle dealers and repair businesses must give vehicle owners an owner's manual insert describing the operation of the on-off switch, listing the risk groups, stating that the on-off switch should be used to turn off an air bag for risk group members only, and stating the vehicle specific safety consequences of using the on-off switch for a person who is not in any risk group. Those consequences will include the effect of any energy managing features, e.g., load limiters, on seat belt performance.

In response to comments indicating that the definition of "advanced air bag" was too vague and that dealers could not reasonably ascertain whether a vehicle was equipped with such air bags, the agency has deferred adoption of that aspect of its proposal which would have prohibited installation of on-off switches for advanced air bags. NHTSA expects to adopt such a prohibition after it develops a more complete definition of "advanced air bags" that applies to driver as well as passenger air bags. This deferral should have no practical significance. Although the vehicle manufacturers are beginning to introduce air bags with advanced attributes, the agency does not expect the installation of significant numbers of advanced air bags before it is ready to establish a better definition.

The agency has selected January 19, 1998, as the beginning date for the installation of retrofit on-off switches under this rule. This date allows time for completion of the design, production and distribution of on-off switches and the training of installation personnel. It also allows time for the public education campaign of the agency and other interested parties (e.g., the Air Bag Safety Campaign (ABSC), American Automobile Association (AAA), Centers for Disease Control and Prevention (CDC), Insurance Institute for Highway Safety (IIHS), motor vehicle dealers, and state motor vehicle departments) to effectively reach a substantial percentage of the public before the installation of on-off switches begins. Until on-off switches become available from the vehicle manufacturer for a given vehicle make and model, NHTSA will continue to exercise its prosecutorial discretion to grant requests for deactivating the air bags in that make and model. In view of the relative inflexibility and permanence of deactivation, the discretion will be exercised on a case-by-case basis in the same limited set of circumstances in which the requests are currently granted, e.g., in cases in which unusual medical conditions suggest that deactivation is appropriate, and in cases in which infants must be carried in the front seat of vehicles lacking a rear seat capable of accommodating a rear-facing infant seat.

B. Comparison of NPRM [Notice of Proposed Rulemaking] and Final Rule

The final rule being issued today follows, in several important respects, the agency's January 1997 proposal. Most important, the rule makes a means of turning off air bags available to vehicle owners. It simplifies the current process of obtaining a means of turning off air bags. Instead of having to compose an original request letter and type or write the letter out in longhand, as they must to obtain authorization from the agency for deactivation, vehicle owners will be able to fill out an agency request form. To promote informed decisionmaking, this rule requires owners to certify on the request form that they have read an air bag information brochure prepared by NHTSA so that owners can separate fact from fiction about who is really at risk and therefore may need an on-off switch.

However, the final rule differs from the proposal in several other important respects. First, the sole means authorized for turning off air bags is a retrofit on-off switch. Deactivation (i.e., modifying the air bag so that it will not deploy for anyone under any circumstance) is not allowed under the exemption. Although the agency recognized in January 1997 that retrofit on-off switches offered some advantages, the agency proposed deactivation because the apparent unavailability of retrofit on-off switches in the near term made them impracticable. When the deactivation proposal was issued, there were indications from the vehicle manufacturers that they would not be able to provide retrofit on-off switches for existing vehicles in a timely manner. Subsequent to the January 1997 proposal, a number of major vehicle manufacturers began reassessing the practicability of on-off switches and making statements to the agency and the media that they were able to provide retrofit on-off switches for existing vehicles, and for future vehicles. The change to on-off switches in this final rule will enhance safety because the on-off switches are a more focused, flexible means of turning off air bags. They enable consumers to leave air bags on for people who are not at risk and thus will benefit from their protection, and turn them off for people at risk.

Second, vehicle owners must certify that they are a member of one of several specified risk groups or that their vehicle will be driven or occupied by a person who is a member of such a group. The agency proposed to allow any person to choose to have his or her air bags deactivated, without having to demonstrate or state a particular safety need. Under the proposal, applicants would simply have had to fill out an agency form on which they indicated that they had received and read an information brochure explaining the safety consequences of having an air bag deactivated. For the final rule, the agency has devised a new form on which owners desiring an on-off switch for either a driver or passenger air bag not only must certify that they have read the brochure, but also that they or one of the users of their vehicle fall into an identifiable risk group for that air bag. Use of the revised form will help provide reasonable assurance that the exemption is implemented in a manner consistent with safety.

Third, the agency is requiring owners to submit their filled-out forms to the agency for approval. Together with the requirement for certification of risk group membership, the necessity for obtaining agency approval will help limit the installation and use of on-off switches to people who are at risk from air bags and give the agency information about the volume of requests and patterns in switch requests and risk group certifications

FBI, NATIONAL SAFETY BOARD ON TWA 800 CRASH
November 18, 1997

An intense sixteen-month investigation by federal agencies failed to pin-point the exact cause of the explosion that blew TWA Flight 800 from the sky near Long Island, New York, on July 17, 1996, killing all 230 passengers and crew members. But the Federal Bureau of Investigation (FBI) con-cluded that the explosion was not caused by a bomb, missile, or any type of criminal action. Safety experts said the explosion forced them to look for new ways to make fuel tanks on airliners more resistant to explosions.

Federal officials at first suspected that flight 800 had been attacked by terrorists, possibly as part of a broad assault on U.S. targets. The crash of the Boeing 747 occurred just nine days before a bomb exploded during the 1996 summer Olympics in Atlanta, killing two persons and injuring more than one hundred. Numerous witnesses to the downing of the TWA airliner reported seeing rising lights just before an explosion—lending credence to a theory that the plane had been attacked by a missile. Conspiracy theories abounded, given weight by the claim of Pierre Salinger, a journalist who had served as President John Kennedy's press secretary, that he had evi-dence the plane had been hit by a U.S. military missile. (Atlanta bombing, Historic Documents of 1996, p. 445)

FBI Investigation

Immediately after the TWA crash, the FBI launched a criminal investi-gation to test the theory that the explosion had been caused by a bomb, mis-sile, or some other device. With help from the Central Intelligence Agency (CIA), the National Transportation Safety Board (NTSB), the Federal Avi-ation Administration (FAA), and other agencies, the FBI examined nearly one million pieces of evidence—including wreckage from the plane, nearly all of which was retrieved from the Atlantic Ocean south of Long Island. In-vestigators also interviewed about 7,000 people in the United States and several foreign countries, among them 244 witnesses who had seen the plane explode. The investigation was one of the most comprehensive in U.S.

history, including such steps as examining 371 boats that had been in the vicinity during the weeks before and after the crash.

At a news conference November 18, James Kallstrom, head of the FBI New York office, announced that he was suspending the investigation. Kallstrom said that "no evidence has been found which would indicate that a criminal act was the cause" of the explosion that downed flight 800. The investigative team, he said, "has done everything humanly possible, has pursued every lead, has looked at every theory and has left no stone unturned" in looking for an explanation.

Kallstrom said he had initially believed—along with most other people—that the explosion was caused by terrorists. Forensic experts examined more than 1,400 holes in recovered pieces from the plane, but none showed any sign of having been caused by a bomb, missile, or similar object, he said. Eventually, Kallstrom said, investigators looking for a criminal cause for the explosion "ran out of things to do," and so that aspect of the investigation was halted. Kallstrom said the FBI portion of the investigation cost at least $14 million, and NTSB chairman James Hall said his agency had spent about $30 million.

Kallstrom showed a video created by the CIA illustrating a computerized reconstruction of the short journey of flight 800. The video was based on examination of the plane's wreckage, an analysis of statements by witnesses, and information from such electronic sources as the plane's cockpit data recorder and infrared images from an overhead satellite.

The video showed the following course of events starting about twelve minutes after take-off from New York's Kennedy airport and lasting just forty-nine seconds: an explosion in the huge center fuel tank under the fuselage of the Boeing 747; the front third of the plane breaking off, causing the remainder to climb at least 1,000 feet before exploding and starting to fall; the left wing of the plane shearing off, releasing jet fuel, which exploded into a cascade of flame; and finally the burning wreckage of the plane plunging into the ocean. According to later testimony from medical experts, most of the 230 people aboard the plane had died immediately after the main explosion or had been knocked unconscious.

According to the video, the lights that witnesses had seen approaching the plane actually occurred after the plane exploded. "What these witnesses saw was, in fact, the Boeing 747 in various stages of crippled flight," the video narration said.

Kallstrom acknowledged that use of such a dramatic device as the video was "unprecedented" for the FBI. But he said the downing of the flight "was such an immense tragedy, with so many ramifications" that the agency needed to provide as much information as possible to families of the victims and to the general public.

The results of the FBI investigation appeared to satisfy most representatives of the victims' families. Many family members had been unhappy with the slow pace of the recovery of bodies from the ocean in the days after the explosion, but most said they appreciated the extent of the government's investigation into the cause. Even so, some people said they still believed that the plane was downed by a deliberate action of some kind, possibly even an attack by the government itself.

Safety Board Probe

The National Transportation Safety Board, which had conducted most technical aspects of the investigation into the TWA crash, held five days of public hearings on the matter the week of December 8 in Baltimore. Witnesses included government investigators, airline safety experts from outside the government, and representatives of the aviation industry, including Boeing Corporation.

The board focused much of its attention on ways to prevent explosions in the center fuel tanks of aircraft such as the Boeing 747. By the time of the December hearings, board investigators said they had concluded that the nearly empty fuel tank exploded because vapors in the tank had been heated to a flammable state by discharges from the plane's air conditioning system as it waited for departure at Kennedy Airport on a hot July evening. They could not determine, however, whether a spark from faulty wiring or something else caused the vapors to explode.

On December 9, the second day of the board's hearings, Boeing officials said they had concluded that changes were needed to prevent vapors in fuel tanks from developing to a flammable state. The Boeing officials said they were still analyzing the kinds of changes that might be necessary.

Daniel Cheney, a propulsion expert for the FAA, told the safety board that the TWA explosion had focused new attention on dangers posed by nearly empty fuel tanks. "It has become clear to us throughout this investigation that tank maintenance hasn't been a high priority issue fleetwide," Cheney said. Other experts said they had found that a very small amount of energy—such as that generated by dropping a dime on a metal surface—potentially could set off an explosion in a fuel tank filled with warm jet fuel vapors.

The safety board for months had been pressing the FAA to tighten safety requirements for fuel tanks but had met resistance from the FAA and from the aviation industry. The board in July sent the FAA a letter describing as "unacceptable" the FAA's delay in acting on the issue.

The FAA said it was premature to order changes until the exact cause of the TWA explosion was found. FAA administrator Jane E. Garvey in December said the agency had created a technical panel to make recommendations within six months for improvements in the safety of aviation fuel tanks.

Industry officials expressed concern about the potential cost of making changes to the thousands of planes they owned and flew every day. Aviation representatives also said the government should address specific problems discovered during the TWA investigation and not impose costly mandates that had nothing to do with those problems.

Following are excerpts from a news conference held November 18, 1997, by James Kallstrom, special agent in charge of the New York office of the Federal Bureau of Investigation, and James Hall, chairman of the National Transportation Safety Board, to discuss the investigation into the crash of TWA flight 800 in July 1996:

James Kallstrom, FBI assistant director: . . . The mission of the law enforcement team was to determine whether a criminal act was responsible for this disaster. The time has arrived to report to the American people, and certainly to the victims' families—a few of which we have here today, and we're honored that they're here—the results of that effort.

Following 16 months of unprecedented investigation, the effort which extended from the shores of Long Island to several countries abroad—an investigation where hundreds of investigators conducted thousands of interviews, an investigation which was confronted with the obstacles of having the most critical pieces of evidence lying in 130 feet of water at the bottom of the Atlantic Ocean—we must now report that no evidence has been found which would indicate that a criminal act was the cause of the tragedy of TWA Flight 800. We do know one thing, however: The law enforcement team has done everything humanly possible, has pursued every lead, has looked at every theory and has left no stone unturned. Now I'd like to outline for you the investigation. It will take some time.

As we know, TWA Flight 800 was on the tarmac at the John F. Kennedy International Airport for approximately three hours and 48 minutes prior to departure. The outside temperature was 81 degrees. The flight arrived from Athens at 4:31 p.m. and lifted off the ground at 8:19 p.m. At approximately 8:31 p.m., the flight experienced the tragic midair explosion. . . .

To summarize the forensic investigation, the team of FBI, NTSB [National Transportation Safety Board], ATF [Alcohol, Tobacco, and Firearms Bureau] and other government agencies found nothing consistent with a bomb, a missile, or an explosive device. In particular, the combined FBI-ATF laboratory conclusion was that, one, there was no evidence of high explosive damage. Two, there was no evidence of explosion of a missile warhead. Three, there was no evidence of missile impact. Likewise, the other experts and the independent consultants concluded: one, there was no evidence of a high explosive damage anywhere. There was no evidence of explosion of a missile warhead. There was no evidence of missile impact.

The metallurgy examiner's conclusions, scientists were that the damage was consistent with, one, the overpressurization of the center fuel tank, the breakup of the aircraft, the fire, and the impact of the aircraft into the ocean. Concerning the issue of friendly fire, I talked earlier that we looked at that from the beginning. The team conducted a total and thorough investigation. Of course, we asked the military the tough question—did you do this? And of course, the answer was no. We looked behind that. We had no reason to doubt what they said, but we looked behind that.

We looked at all the overhead resources of this country and other countries who cooperated. We looked at all the radar. We identified all the military assets within 200 nautical miles of this tragedy. We documented all training exercises. We accounted for all armaments capable of reaching flight 800. . . .

The investigation was not limited to strictly terrorist motives. All avenues of potential criminality were explored. The public was great and responded to our 800 number and our e-mail address. I know you all got sick of hearing that during the press conferences. Of the thousands and thousands of communications we had from the public, over 3,000 leads were developed and generated through the public contact. And I thank everyone in the public, certainly all the witness that we dealt with, all 244 of you, and everyone that took the time to call, to write and to write thoughtful responses and try to be helpful. That's what this is all about, working together. In total, there are over 7,000 interviews conducted by the team in this investigation. . . .

Let me say, it's essential that the public and the media and the victims' families fully understand that the FBI's and the law enforcement's team disengagement at this time from the TWA investigation is based solely on the overwhelming absence of evidence indicating a crime, and the lack of any leads that could bear on the issue. In fact, we ran out of things to do.

The investigation I have just described to you was done primarily by the men and women of the Terrorist Task Force here in New York, augmented by many FBI agents from around the country and many others from this office, in other segments of the law enforcement community of the United States and by law enforcement investigators, professionals, from all the law enforcement agencies. They are professionals and take great pride in their thoroughness in their investigations. Aside from the families of the victims of TWA Flight 800, no other group of people were more eager to find the answer to this tragedy. And no other group of people are more eager to continue—I include NTSB in this statement—to find the answer to this tragedy.

As the law enforcement team steps from this investigation, I want to emphasize that we'll maintain our lines of communication with the National Transportation Safety Board. We'll maintain our ability to gear up our criminal investigation should any information ever come to light, which would indicate that a criminal act was committed. . . .

Jim Hall, NTSB chairman: I'd just like to comment that I believe that a debt of gratitude is owed to the FBI for their enormous effort in trying to find out what happened to TWA Flight 800.

Given the circumstances of the crash and the nature of today's world, a thorough examination by the FBI into the possibility of sabotage was the right thing to do. The scope and thoroughness of the FBI investigation is indicative of their role as our nation's premier criminal investigation agency. I am very appreciative of the good working relationship that developed between the FBI and the NTSB, both strong agencies, staffed with highly motivated personnel.

In the pressurized aftermath of a tragedy such as TWA 800, operational or procedural questions inevitably arise. But do in no small measure to the leadership of Director Freeh and Jim Kallstrom, the level of our cooperation between our two agencies was excellent. We were able to work together effectively because we shared the goal of getting to the truth of what happened to TWA 800. . . .

The National Transportation Safety Board's investigation continues. Next month, we will hold a week-long hearing on TWA 800 that will demonstrate the extraordinary effort being made to conduct an objective and far-reaching examination of all aspects of the Flight 800 tragedy. Let me assure you and the American people that the National Transportation Safety Board will continue to spare no effort to find the cause of the TWA explosion. We owe it to the American people we serve, and we owe it to the cause that we work for, transportation safety.

Last year, we made a number of safety recommendations we believe would help prevent similar accidents. I trust our hearing next month will further our understanding of the circumstances of this tragedy. . . .

Question: Mr. Kallstrom, the FBI has come under some criticism for perhaps staying in this investigation longer than it should have. Could you address that?

Kallstrom: I think we stayed as long as we needed to. I mean, imagine the notion of us looking for the obvious things in an investigation, not finding them and sort of vacating the scene. I mean, we're the Federal Bureau of "total" Investigation. We try to be. I try to be, not the federal bureau of the obvious. I mean, we have to look at everything possible. We have to look—I mean, we got 230 people that died here. We have got whole families, children. We have to look at every dark crack and crevice of this investigation.

We did the right thing. We didn't have the mark-up until not that many months ago. We wanted to do the analysis of all the holes in relationship to each other. We want to bring in another metallurgist to look at all the holes and agree with the prior metallurgist. These are reasonable things to do. To do any less would be unprofessional and we'll not be forced to do something like that just to satisfy some talking head on some television show. It would never happen. . . .

Question: With no disrespect intended to the agency that worked great lengths here, you're trying to reassure the American public, and one of the things the American public has heard about in recent years is some questions of the FBI's forensic capabilities vis-à-vis years past of the glory days. There's even been change of personnel over there. If there are lingering doubts of that aspect of it because you did numerous exhaustive tests and—what would you say to the American people?

Kallstrom: I feel extremely confident in the test results. I feel extremely competent and confident of our laboratory personnel that did the testing that was also looked at by ATF labs, that was also looked at by independent consultants. I think we have a multilayered position on that. We didn't take the word of one particular person.

The FBI laboratory does millions of examinations every year. They do it brilliantly. You know we're all human beings. We make mistakes from time to time. That's why we built in redundant eyes. That's why we built in redundant procedures so that we wouldn't let something like that fall through the cracks. I have nothing but the highest regard for the people that were there that worked 20-hour days that did great things. It's a good question, though, I understand.

Question: Is there any reason to believe that any of the parts of the plane that have not been recovered would have caused any further step to be taken in the criminal investigation, or could shed light in the criminal investigation?

Kallstrom: There were parts that were not recovered. We feel that even if recovered, the parts, that we don't think they'd advance the criminal investigation any. We think we have enough of the plane to make the determination we made. Certainly we'd accept any parts, if there's any fisherman out there, obviously, I don't say this kiddingly, if you bring up a piece of this aircraft while you're out there scraping the bottom for clams or oysters or whatever you're doing you know, we want that piece of the plane and I am sure NTSB would want any other thing we could find. Certainly the fuel pump is missing. . . .

ADVISORY COMMISSION ON HEALTH CARE BILL OF RIGHTS
November 20, 1997

A brewing controversy over regulating managed health care plans heated up late in the year when President Bill Clinton endorsed minimum coverage standards embodied in a consumers' health care "bill of rights." Proposed by a presidential advisory commission on November 20, the bill of rights would guarantee consumers access to appropriate health care, including emergency and specialist services, access to information about treatment options, and procedures to appeal denials of coverage. In accepting the recommendations of the thirty-four member commission that he had appointed earlier in the year, Clinton called on Congress to enact federal standards where necessary. He urged private health insurers to adopt the bill of rights voluntarily, and he directed executive departments to implement those portions of the protections that did not require federal legislation.

Once hailed as the way for the health care industry to get a grip on soaring costs, health maintenance organizations (HMOs) and other types of managed care plans spread across the country like wildfire in the late 1980s and early 1990s, replacing the traditional fee-for-service plans that had grown so costly that many Americans could no longer afford them. In 1995, 149 million Americans were enrolled in either HMOs or preferred provider organizations, and that number represented a 15 percent increase over 1994. But dissatisfaction with managed care spread nearly as fast, as consumers realized that HMOs saved money by restricting patients' access to medical specialists, limiting their choice of physicians, reducing the length and frequency of their hospital stays, and requiring patients and doctors to get approval for coverage of expensive diagnostic tests and treatments. Consumers began to complain that managed care plans cared more about their bottom lines than about the health needs of their patients.

Stories about hospitals discharging new mothers within hours of giving birth, about payment denied for emergency room visits when a patient's chest pain that he thought was signaling a heart attack turned out to be indigestion, and about doctors' refusal to refer gravely ill patients to special-

ists all contributed to a growing mistrust of managed care plans. A survey released in November 1997 found that consumers were more distrustful of managed care plans than other forms of insurance. Less than half of those in managed-care plans (44 percent) thought it was "very likely" that their treatment would be covered if they became seriously ill, compared with more than two-thirds of those in "fee-for-service" plans (69 percent). Three-fifths of the people surveyed said doctors spent less time with their patients under managed care plans and that it was harder for patients to get specialized care. Three-fourths thought that any money saved by managed care plans was used to increase company profits rather than to make health care more affordable. "People are worried managed care companies care more about costs than about them" said Drew E. Altman, president of the Kaiser Family Foundation, which sponsored the study with Harvard University.

As horror story followed horror story into the public consciousness, legislators at the state and federal levels began to take actions. States traditionally regulated insurance, and individual states began to adopt laws requiring managed care plans to provide certain minimum levels of care if they wanted to do business in the state. But millions of people covered by managed care plans did not fall under state regulation because health care plans offered by self-insured companies were exempt from state regulation. Nearly three-fourths of all workers who received health care coverage through their employer were members of HMOs or other managed care programs, and many of those plans were self-funded by the employer and thus exempt from state regulation.

In recent years Congress tried to fill in some of the gaps, requiring all insurance companies to pay for at least two days in the hospital after childbirth, for example. Several other mandatory coverage bills had been introduced. But many legislators questioned the piecemeal approach to regulation—describing it as setting national health policy "body part by body part." They began to explore the possibility of writing comprehensive federal standards, a move that was opposed by the Republican leadership and most managed care plans. Administrators of managed care plans argued that regulations would only increase the costs of health care, pushing up premiums and forcing even more employers to abandon health care benefits for their employees. Even more people might go without adequate health care coverage, they warned. Nearly 41 million Americans did not have health insurance; some 10 million of them were children.

The Health Care "Bill of Rights"

It was in this context that President Clinton on March 26 named the Presidential Advisory Commission on Consumer Protection and Quality in the Health Care Industry. Chaired by Secretary of Health and Human Services Donna E. Shalala and Labor Secretary Alexis Herman, the commission was charged with drafting a consumer bill of rights and assessing the need for federal standards. The other thirty-two members of the commission represented consumers, business, labor, health care providers, in-

surers, and health care experts. On November 20, the commission issued an eight-part bill of rights, which the commission said could "help to establish a stronger relationship of trust" among consumers and the various elements of the health care industry. The commission recommended that consumers have the following rights:

- *The right to receive accurate and easily understood information about health care plans and the doctors and hospitals participating in the plan.*
- *The right to a choice of providers to ensure appropriate and high quality care. This right to access included the right for women to choose a gynecologist or other appropriate doctor to provide routine women's health care services and for patients with serious medical conditions to have direct access to a qualified specialist.*
- *The right to emergency services under the "prudent layperson" rule. This rule would require plans to pay for emergency services when a consumer comes to an emergency room with "symptoms of sufficient severity—including severe pain—such that a 'prudent layperson' could reasonably expect" that lack of treatment would result in severe harm to the person's health.*
- *The right to participate in treatment decisions and to be told about all possible options for treatment. This right would essentially bar the use of "gag clauses," which prohibited doctors from telling patients about treatment options that were not covered by their health plan. (A report released September 24 by the General Accounting Office said an examination of 1,150 contracts used by 529 HMOs failed to uncover any explicit "gag clauses." Some contract language might have a "chilling effect" on what doctors tell patients, the report said, but added that few doctors read their contract provisions and so were unlikely to be intimidated by such language. Moreover, laws in two-thirds of the states barred "gag clauses," the report said, and many doctors were more fearful of being sued for malpractice if they did not discuss all possible alternatives than they were of possible sanction by their HMO.)*
- *The right to be treated with respect. Health care plans must not discriminate against consumers on the basis of race, ethnicity, national origin, religion, sex, age, physical or mental disability, sexual orientation, genetic information, or source of payment either in marketing to and enrolling consumers in the plan or in providing health care to them.*
- *The right to privacy. The commission recommended that individually identifiable medical information be used without the patients' consent only for health purposes, medical research, public health reporting, and investigating health care fraud. This provision tightened an earlier administration proposal to permit identifiable medical records to be used without consent by law enforcement officials pursuing other sorts of investigations.* (Medical record privacy, p. 580)

- *The right to a timely and efficient process for resolving consumer complaints when a plan denied, reduced, or terminated services or refused payment for services. The commission recommended that an external appeals system be provided for consumers to use after all internal appeals had been exhausted. Only a handful of states had such a strong appeals process.*

Consumers also had responsibilities under the bill of rights, including cooperating with doctors and their insurers in decisions about care, being knowledgeable about the plan's coverage, being respectful of health care workers, and paying premiums and bills on time. The commission also said people should not knowingly spread disease and should adopt healthy habits, such as exercising, eating healthy diets, and not smoking.

The commission did not say how the bill of rights should be implemented or enforced, and noted that its provisions could be adopted voluntarily or mandated by federal or state legislation or regulation. But in accepting the commission's report, President Clinton made clear that he would seek federal standards wherever necessary. "These protections . . . are long overdue, and now we have to act to make them real for all Americans," Clinton said November 20. "Some will require federal standards to be implemented. Where they do, I challenge Congress to make them the law of the land." In directing executive branch departments and agencies to adopt the health care bill of rights, Clinton said all Medicare and Medicaid beneficiaries and all federal employees would receive better quality health care as a result. And he called upon all health care insurers to adopt the bill of rights voluntarily.

Battle Lines Drawn

Even before Clinton made clear that he would seek federal regulation, many insurers and business groups were already lobbying against such a move. Not only would federal regulation increase the costs of health care, to everyone's detriment, these groups argued, but it would interfere with the evolution of managed care, which, in addition to reducing costs, also provided a more coordinated approach to providing health care. These groups said the industry would respond to consumer complaints voluntarily because it realized that federal regulation would result if they did not.

Any hopes the industry might have had of presenting a uniform argument to Congress were dashed in late September, when three nonprofit HMOs and two consumer groups joined together to urge that all health care plans be subject to "legally enforceable national standards." The three companies—Kaiser Permanente; HIP Health Insurance Plans, based in New York; and the Group Health Cooperative of Puget Sound—had a combined membership of 10 million. The two consumer groups were Families USA and the American Association of Retired Persons, which itself had more than 33 million members. The group recommended eighteen standards that it said would guarantee patients more complete services, more information about their health care plans, and more ways to settle complaints. HMOs "have really failed to convince the public of our commitment to excellence in quality. That is the crisis we face today," said Daniel McGowan, president of HIP Health Plan of New York. But the standards must be applied to all health plans; if they are not, "it would put us at a disadvantage competitively," according to David M. Lawrence, the chairman of Kaiser Permanente.

Republican leaders in Congress also opposed federal standards, arguing that they were simply a backdoor route for enacting much of Clinton's health care reform plan that collapsed in 1994. "We do not want Clinton health care 'light.' The answer is not government controls," Senate Majority Leader Trent Lott said in November. The "practical result" of federal regulations will be the same as the earlier legislation, House Majority Leader Dick Armey wrote in a policy memo, "Washington bureaucrats defining people's health care choices." (Clinton health care reform proposal, Historic Documents of 1993, p. 781; Historic Documents of 1994, p. 463)

With legislators facing mid-term elections in November 1998, there was widespread speculation that those arguments might not be as persuasive as voters' complaints about managed care. By November 20, when the administration's bill of rights was released, eighty-nine Republicans in the House had already cosponsored legislation that would enact federal standards in several areas, including grievance procedures, access to providers, and emergency services. That legislation would also permit individuals to sue health plans for damages under state medical malpractice laws.

Following are excerpts from the "Consumer Bill of Rights and Responsibilities," issued November 20, 1997, by the Presidential Advisory Commission on Consumer Protection and Quality in the Health Care Industry:

EXECUTIVE SUMMARY

Consumer Bill of Rights and Responsibilities

The Advisory Commission on Consumer Protection and Quality in the Health Care Industry was appointed by President Clinton on March 26, 1997, to "advise the President on changes occurring in the health care system and recommend measures as may be necessary to promote and assure health care quality and value, and protect consumers and workers in the health care system." As part of its work, the President asked the Commission to draft a "consumer bill of rights."

The Commission includes 34 members and is co-chaired by The Honorable Alexis M. Herman, Secretary of Labor, and The Honorable Donna E. Shalala, Secretary of Health and Human Services. Its members include individuals from a wide variety of backgrounds including consumers, business, labor, health care providers, health plans, State and local governments, and health care quality experts. The Commission has four Subcommittees: Consumer Rights, Protections, and Responsibilities; Quality Measurement; Creating a Quality Improvement Environment; and Roles and Responsibilities of Public and Private Purchasers and Quality Oversight Organizations. The Commission and its Subcommittees meet monthly in public.

Following is a summary of the eight areas of consumer rights and responsibilities adopted by the President's Advisory Commission on Consumer Protection and Quality in the Health Care Industry:

I. Information Disclosure

Consumers have the right to receive accurate, easily understood information and some require assistance in making informed health care decisions about their health plans, professionals, and facilities. [The term "health plans" is used throughout this report and refers broadly to indemnity insurers, managed care organizations (including health maintenance organizations and preferred provider organizations), self-funded employer-sponsored plans, Taft-Hartley trusts, church plans, association plans, State and local government employee programs, and public insurance programs (i.e., Medicare and Medicaid).]

This information should include:

- **Health plans:** Covered benefits, cost-sharing, and procedures for resolving complaints; licensure, certification, and accreditation status; comparable measures of quality and consumer satisfaction; provider network composition; the procedures that govern access to specialists and emergency services; and care management information.
- **Health professionals:** Education and board certification and recertification; years of practice; experience performing certain procedures; and comparable measures of quality and consumer satisfaction.
- **Health care facilities:** Experience in performing certain procedures and services; accreditation status; comparable measures of quality and worker and consumer satisfaction; procedures for resolving complaints; and community benefits provided.

Consumer assistance programs must be carefully structured to promote consumer confidence and to work cooperatively with health plans, providers, payers and regulators. Sponsorship that assures accountability to the interests of consumers and stable, adequate funding are desirable characteristics of such programs.

II. Choice of Providers and Plans

Consumers have the right to a choice of health care providers that is sufficient to ensure access to appropriate high-quality health care.

To ensure such choice, health plans should provide the following:

Provider Network Adequacy: All health plan networks should provide access to sufficient numbers and types of providers to assure that all covered services will be accessible without unreasonable delay—including access to emergency services 24 hours a day and seven days a week. If a health plan has an insufficient number or type of providers to provide a covered benefit with the appropriate degree of specialization, the plan should ensure that the consumer obtains the benefit outside the network at no greater cost than if the benefit were obtained from participating providers. Plans also should establish and maintain adequate arrangements to ensure reasonable proximity of providers to the business or personal residence of their members.

Access to Qualified Specialists for Women's Health Services: Women should be able to choose a qualified provider offered by a plan—such as gynecologists, certified nurse midwives, and other qualified health care providers—for the provision of covered care necessary to provide routine and preventative women's health care services.

Access to Specialists: Consumers with complex or serious medical conditions who require frequent specialty care should have direct access to a qualified specialist of their choice within a plan's network of providers. Authorizations, when required, should be for an adequate number of direct access visits under an approved treatment plan.

Transitional Care: Consumers who are undergoing a course of treatment for a chronic or disabling condition (or who are in the second or third trimester of a pregnancy) at the time they involuntarily change health plans or at a time when a provider is terminated by a plan for other than cause should be able to continue seeing their current specialty providers for up to 90 days (or through completion of postpartum care) to allow for transition of care. Providers who continue to treat such patients must accept the plan's rates as payment in full, provide all necessary information to the plan for quality assurance purposes, and promptly transfer all medical records with patient authorization during the transition period.

Public and private group purchasers should, wherever feasible, offer consumers a choice of high-quality health insurance products. Small employers should be provided with greater assistance in offering their workers and their families a choice of health plans and products.

III. Access to Emergency Services

Consumers have the right to access emergency health care services when and where the need arises. Health plans should provide payment when a consumer presents to an emergency department with acute symptoms of sufficient severity—including severe pain—such that a "prudent layperson" could reasonably expect the absence of medical attention to result in placing that consumer's health in serious jeopardy, serious impairment to bodily functions, or serious dysfunction of any bodily organ or part.

To ensure this right:

- Health plans should educate their members about the availability, location, and appropriate use of emergency and other medical services; cost-sharing provisions for emergency services; and the availability of care outside an emergency department.

- Health plans using a defined network of providers should cover emergency department screening and stabilization services both in network and out of network without prior authorization for use consistent with the prudent layperson standard. Non-network providers and facilities should not bill patients for any charges in excess of health plans' routine payment arrangements.
- Emergency department personnel should contact a patient's primary care provider or health plan, as appropriate, as quickly as possible to discuss follow-up and post-stabilization care and promote continuity of care.

IV. Participation in Treatment Decisions

Consumers have the right and responsibility to fully participate in all decisions related to their health care. Consumers who are unable to fully participate in treatment decisions have the right to be represented by parents, guardians, family members, or other conservators.

In order to ensure consumers' right and ability to participate in treatment decisions, health care professionals should:

- Provide patients with easily understood information and opportunity to decide among treatment options consistent with the informed consent process. Specifically,
  - Discuss all treatment options with a patient in a culturally competent manner, including the option of no treatment at all.
  - Ensure that persons with disabilities have effective communications with members of the health system in making such decisions.
  - Discuss all current treatments a consumer may be undergoing, including those alternative treatments that are self-administered.
  - Discuss all risks, benefits, and consequences to treatment or non-treatment.
  - Give patients the opportunity to refuse treatment and to express references about future treatment decisions.
- Discuss the use of advance directives—both living wills and durable powers of attorney for health care—with patients and their designated family members.
- Abide by the decisions made by their patients and/or their designated representatives consistent with the informed consent process.

To facilitate greater communication between patients and providers, health care providers, facilities, and plans should:

- Disclose to consumers factors—such as methods of compensation, ownership of or interest in health care facilities, or matters of conscience—that could influence advice or treatment decisions.
- Ensure that provider contracts do not contain any so-called "gag clauses" or other contractual mechanisms that restrict health care providers' ability to communicate with and advise patients about medically necessary treatment options.

- Be prohibited from penalizing or seeking retribution against health care professionals or other health workers for advocating on behalf of their patients.

V. Respect and Nondiscrimination

Consumers have the right to considerate, respectful care from all members of the health care system at all times and under all circumstances. An environment of mutual respect is essential to maintain a quality health care system.

Consumers must not be discriminated against in the delivery of health care services consistent with the benefits covered in their policy or as required by law based on race, ethnicity, national origin, religion, sex, age, mental or physical disability, sexual orientation, genetic information, or source of payment.

Consumers who are eligible for coverage under the terms and conditions of a health plan or program or as required by law must not be discriminated against in marketing and enrollment practices based on race, ethnicity, national origin, religion, sex, age, mental or physical disability, sexual orientation, genetic information, or source of payment.

VI. Confidentiality of Health Information

Consumers have the right to communicate with health care providers in confidence and to have the confidentiality of their individually identifiable health care information protected. Consumers also have the right to review and copy their own medical records and request amendments to their records.

In order to ensure this right:

- With very few exceptions, individually identifiable health care information can be used without written consent for health purposes only, including the provision of health care, payment for services, peer review, health promotion, disease management, and quality assurance.
- In addition, disclosure of individually identifiable health care information without written consent should be permitted in very limited circumstances where there is a clear legal basis for doing so. Such reasons include: medical or health care research for which a institutional review board has determined anonymous records will not suffice, investigation of health care fraud, and public health reporting.
- To the maximum feasible extent in all situations, nonidentifiable health care information should be used unless the individual has consented to the disclosure of individually identifiable information. When disclosure is required, no greater amount of information should be disclosed than is necessary to achieve the specific purpose of the disclosure.

VII. Complaints and Appeals

All consumers have the right to a fair and efficient process for resolving differences with their health plans, health care providers, and

the institutions that serve them, including a rigorous system of internal review and an independent system of external review.

Internal appeals systems should include:

- Timely written notification of a decision to deny, reduce, or terminate services or deny payment for services. Such notification should include an explanation of the reasons for the decisions and the procedures available for appealing them.
- Resolution of all appeals in a timely manner with expedited consideration for decisions involving emergency or urgent care consistent with time frames consistent with those required by Medicare (i.e., 72 hours).
- A claim review process conducted by health care professionals who are appropriately credentialed with respect to the treatment involved. Reviews should be conducted by individuals who were not involved in the initial decision.
- Written notification of the final determination by the plan of an internal appeal that includes information on the reason for the determination and how a consumer can appeal that decision to an external entity.
- Reasonable processes for resolving consumer complaints about such issues as waiting times, operating hours, the demeanor of health care personnel, and the adequacy of facilities.

External appeals systems should:

- Be available only after consumers have exhausted all internal processes (except in cases of urgently needed care).
- Apply to any decision by a health plan to deny, reduce, or terminate coverage or deny payment for services based on a determination that the treatment is either experimental or investigational in nature; apply when such a decision is based on a determination that such services are not medically necessary and the amount exceeds a significant threshold or the patient's life or health is jeopardized. [The right to external appeals does not apply to denials, reductions, or terminations of coverage or denials of payment for services that are specifically excluded from the consumer's coverage as established by contract.]
- Be conducted by health care professionals who are appropriately credentialed with respect to the treatment involved and subject to conflict-of-interest prohibitions. Reviews should be conducted by individuals who were not involved in the initial decision.
- Follow a standard of review that promotes evidence-based decision-making and relies on objective evidence.
- Resolve all appeals in a timely manner with expedited consideration for decisions involving emergency or urgent care consistent with time frames consistent with those required by Medicare (i.e., 72 hours).

VIII. Consumer Responsibilities

In a health care system that protects consumers' rights, it is reasonable to expect and encourage consumers to assume reasonable responsibilities. Greater individual involvement by consumers in their

care increases the likelihood of achieving the best outcomes and helps support a quality improvement, cost-conscious environment. Such responsibilities include:

- Take responsibility for maximizing healthy habits, such as exercising, not smoking, and eating a healthy diet.
- Become involved in specific health care decisions.
- Work collaboratively with health care providers in developing and carrying out agreed-upon treatment plans.
- Disclose relevant information and clearly communicate wants and needs.
- Use the health plan's internal complaint and appeal processes to address concerns that may arise.
- Avoid knowingly spreading disease.
- Recognize the reality of risks and limits of the science of medical care and the human fallibility of the health care professional.
- Be aware of a health care provider's obligation to be reasonably efficient and equitable in providing care to other patients and the community.
- Become knowledgeable about his or her health plan coverage and health plan options (when available) including all covered benefits, limitations, and exclusions, rules regarding use of network providers, coverage and referral rules, appropriate processes to secure additional information, and the process to appeal coverage decisions.
- Show respect for other patients and health workers.
- Make a good-faith effort to meet financial obligations.
- Abide by administrative and operational procedures of health plans, health care providers, and Government health benefit programs.
- Report wrongdoing and fraud to appropriate resources or legal authorities.

PREAMBLE

Consumer Bill of Rights and Responsibilities

American consumers and their families are experiencing an historic transition of the U.S. system of health care financing and delivery. In establishing the Advisory Commission on Consumer Protection and Quality in the Health Care Industry, President Clinton asked that it advise him "on changes occurring in the health care system and recommend such measures as may be necessary to promote and assure health care quality and value, and protect consumers and workers in the health care system." As part of that effort, the President has asked the Commission to draft a Consumer Bill of Rights and Responsibilities. . . .

Objectives of a Consumer Bill of Rights and Responsibilities

The Consumer Bill of Rights and Responsibilities is intended to accomplish three major goals.

First, to strengthen consumer confidence by assuring the health care system is fair and responsive to consumers' needs, provides consumers with credible and effective mechanisms to address their concerns, and encourages consumers to take an active role in improving and assuring their health.

Second, to reaffirm the importance of a strong relationship between patients and their health care professionals.

Third, to reaffirm the critical role consumers play in safeguarding their own health by establishing both rights and responsibilities for all participants in improving health status.

Guiding Principles for the Consumer Bill of Rights and Responsibilities

The work of the Commission was guided by the following principles:

All consumers are created equal. The work of this Commission in establishing a Bill of Rights and Responsibilities must apply to all consumers. This includes all beneficiaries of such public programs as Medicare, Medicaid, the Department of Veterans Affairs, and the Department of Defense, as well as Federal, State, and local government employees. It also includes all those who have private insurance, including those who purchase their own insurance, those who work for companies that have self-funded health plans, and those who work for companies that purchase insurance for their employees and dependents. And, finally, to the extent possible, these rights should be accorded to those who have no health insurance but use the health care system.

Quality comes first. The first question we asked ourselves in each circumstance was: Will this improve the quality of care and of the system that delivers that care? Sometimes this led us to reject policy options that we believe could hinder the progress our Nation has made toward a health care system that is focused on improving quality through accountable organized systems.

Preserve what works. There are elements of managed care and of indemnity coverage that must be changed to protect the rights of consumers. But there also are elements of each system that have improved quality and expanded access. We have tried to make sure that we preserve what works while we address areas that can and should be improved.

Costs matter. Although a comprehensive cost-analysis was not performed for this Bill of Rights and Responsibilities, the Commission has sought to balance the need for stronger consumer rights with the need to keep coverage affordable. We recognize that, in some circumstances, rights may create additional costs for employers; health plans; Federal, State, and local governments; and consumers. We also recognize that ultimately consumers can bear these costs in the form of lower wages, higher prices, higher taxes, or reduced benefits in other areas. The Commission believes some components of the Bill of Rights may also enhance the efficiency and effectiveness of the health care marketplace. While these efficiencies cannot be well calculated, they may help to offset some cost increases. The Commission has attempted to weigh these factors carefully and support recommendations that may prompt additional spending in cases where such spending may represent an investment in higher quality health care and better health outcomes....

The Commission does not, in this report, speak to the issues of implementation or enforcement of the Consumer Bill of Rights and Responsibilities. The rights enumerated in this report can be achieved in several ways including voluntary actions by health plans, purchasers, facilities, and providers; the effects of market forces; accreditation processes; as well as State or Federal legislation or regulation. In its final report to the President, the Commission intends to speak to the optimal methods for implementing and enforcing these rights through one or more of these approaches.

Finally, the Commission believes that the American people should have access to health care that is of high quality, evidence-based, safe, free of errors, and is available to all Americans regardless of ability to pay. Progress, over time, will require changes that must be made prudently, realistically, and with due regard to the needs of all stakeholders in the system. This Consumer Bill of Rights and Responsibilities specifies improvements that we believe are achievable now and in the next several years. It acquires even more meaning in the context of a broader overarching commitment to ensure that full access to high-quality health care will eventually be available to all Americans.

OECD TREATY ON COMBATING BRIBERY OF PUBLIC OFFICIALS
November 20, 1997

Thirty-four countries, accounting for the bulk of international trade, agreed on November 20 to outlaw bribery of public officials by businesses seeking to gain government contracts. Agreement on the treaty was a diplomatic, and potential commercial, victory for the United States, which had banned bribery by American corporations in 1977. Bribery was a common and even accepted way of doing business in much of the world—especially in Asia. U.S. firms for years had complained that they were at a disadvantage compared with foreign competitors who routinely bribed officials to win lucrative business deals.

Complex Negotiations

The United States had pressed its key trading partners for an antibribery treaty ever since Congress passed the Foreign Corrupt Practices Act in 1977. That law prohibited U.S. firms from bribing public officials overseas. Although enforcement of the law was uneven, according to some observers, the law reportedly did curb bribery by U.S. firms—if only by making them think twice about the consequences of engaging in the practice.

At the urging of U.S. officials, discussion toward such a treaty began in 1993 among the twenty-nine member nations of the Organization for Economic Cooperation and Development (OECD), headquartered in Paris. In addition to the United States, the OECD represented most of the world's leading economic powers, including Germany, Japan, France, and Great Britain. Serious negotiations toward an antibribery treaty began in 1995, resulting in general support for the outline of an agreement on May 23, 1997. The agreement called on member nations to take "effective measures" to deter bribery, including enacting and enforcing laws making bribery of public officials illegal, punishable by "effective, proportionate, and dissuasive criminal penalties."

A key development leading toward eventual adoption of the treaty was support from several large European firms, including German automaker

Daimler-Benz and Italian tiremaker Pirelli. U.S. officials said many multinational firms had tired of having to bribe their way into business contracts.

The principal nongovernment organization lobbying for the treaty was Transparency International, based in Berlin and financed by multinational corporations. The organization's chairman, Peter Eigen, praised the treaty as a positive step but said the most important question was whether individual countries would take it seriously and enforce it. "We are afraid that countries will say they have agreed to the criminal measures and then leave the matter at that," Eigen told the New York Times.

In a statement issued November 21, State Department deputy spokesman James B. Foley called the treaty "a bold and historic step" in the fight against international bribery. The statement urged other OECD countries to ratify the treaty quickly and to adopt national legislation making bribery a criminal offense.

Final Negotiations

Meeting in Frankfurt in mid-November, negotiators worked to resolve several contentious issues on which the United States wanted a stronger position than some other nations were willing to adopt. Those issues were:

- *Bribing leaders of political parties. U.S. negotiators lobbied for a provision requiring each country to make it illegal for businesses to pay bribes to leaders of political parties who were not formal officials of the government. In some countries party leaders were just as important as—and often more important than—many government officials in setting official policy. Washington wanted to include political leaders under the definition of officials barred from accepting bribes, but several countries blocked the move by objecting to including any nongovernmental officials under treaty provisions. As approved, the treaty would not outlaw bribes to political party leaders or to government officials made indirectly through political parties. Washington's position was weakened by the controversy in the United States over allegedly illegal campaign contributions to political parties in the 1996 elections. Negotiators from other countries said that dispute in the United States demonstrated the difficulty of criminalizing payments to political parties.*
- *Bribing national legislators and officials of state-run businesses. Similarly, Washington pushed for the criminalization of bribes to members of parliaments and other national legislators, and to officials of businesses (such as airlines and postal services) owned or controlled by governments. Austria, Finland, and Germany objected to banning bribes of legislators, saying that laws in those countries permitted some payments to such officials that could be construed as bribes. With minor exceptions, the U.S. position eventually prevailed on both questions.*

- *The definition of bribery. Negotiators could not agree on specific language that would prohibit corporations from disguising bribes as "commissions" or "business fees." The treaty left it up to each country to establish definitions and accounting standards that would distinguish a bribe from an acceptable payment and prohibit companies from handling bribes "off-the-books."*
- *Tax deductions for bribes. Many European countries allowed domestic corporations to take tax deductions for bribes of foreign public officials, a practice the United States wanted outlawed as contradicting the underlying premise of the antibribery treaty. European negotiators refused to budge on the issue, however, and the treaty made no mention of curbing tax deductions for bribes.*

As approved, the treaty did not establish specific penalties for public officials who took bribes. Most countries represented in the negotiations wanted to leave that question to their own national legislatures. Another issue concerned an effective date, with some countries fearing they would ratify the treaty but others would not, thus giving competitors a business advantage. That issue was resolved with a formula: The treaty would take effect sixty days after five of the ten largest OECD members had ratified it, provided that those five countries represented at least 60 percent of the combined exports of the ten largest countries. The treaty called on, but did not require, member nations to submit the treaty to their legislatures by April 1998 and to seek ratification and enactment of antibribery laws by the end of 1998.

Because the OECD had no enforcement mechanism of its own, the treaty left it up to each member country to monitor its own compliance. Officials said real enforcement would come through countries checking on the activities of their trading competitors and calling attention to violations.

In addition to the twenty-nine member nations of the OECD, five non-members pledged to accept the treaty. They were Argentina, Brazil, Bulgaria, Chile, and the Slovak Republic. Among major trading countries not belonging to the OECD, and thus not agreeing to the treaty, were China, India, Indonesia, Russia, Singapore, and Taiwan.

Following is the text of the Convention on Combating Bribery of Foreign Public Officials in International Business Transactions, as adopted November 20, 1997, by negotiators representing the member nations of the Organization for Economic Cooperation and Development:

Preamble

The Parties,

Considering that bribery is a widespread phenomenon in international business transactions, including trade and investment, which raises serious moral and political concerns, undermines good governance and economic development, and distorts international competitive conditions;

Considering that all countries share a responsibility to combat bribery in international business transactions;

Having regard to the Revised Recommendation on Combating Bribery in International Business Transactions, adopted by the Council of the Organisation for Economic Co-operation and Development (OECD) on 23 May 1997, C(97)123/FINAL, which, *inter alia*, called for effective measures to deter, prevent and combat the bribery of foreign public officials in connection with international business transactions, in particular, the prompt criminalisation of such bribery in an effective and co-ordinated manner and in conformity with the agreed common elements set out in that Recommendation and with the jurisdictional and other basic legal principles of each country;

Welcoming other recent developments which further advance international understanding and co-operation in combating bribery of public officials, including actions of the United Nations, the World Bank, the International Monetary Fund, the World Trade Organisation, the Organisation of American States, the Council of Europe and the European Union;

Welcoming the efforts of companies, business organisations, trade unions as well as other non-governmental organisations to combat bribery;

Recognising the role of governments in the prevention of solicitation of bribes from individuals and enterprises in international business transactions;

Recognising that achieving progress in this field requires not only efforts on a national level but also multilateral co-operation, monitoring and follow-up;

Recognising that achieving equivalence among the measures to be taken by the Parties is an essential object and purpose of the Convention, which requires that the Convention be ratified without derogations affecting this equivalence.

Have agreed as follows:

Article 1—The Offence of Bribery of Foreign Public Officials

1. Each Party shall take such measures as may be necessary to establish that it is a criminal offence under its law for any person intentionally to offer, promise or give any undue pecuniary or other advantage, whether directly or through intermediaries, to a foreign public official, for that official or for a third party, in order that the official act or refrain from acting in relation to the performance of official duties, in order to obtain or retain business or other improper advantage in the conduct of international business.

2. Each Party shall take any measures necessary to establish that complicity in, including incitement, aiding and abetting, or authorisation of an act of bribery of a foreign public official shall be a criminal offence. Attempt and conspiracy to bribe a foreign public official shall be crimi-

nal offences to the same extent as attempt and conspiracy to bribe a public official of that Party.

3. The offences set out in paragraphs 1 and 2 above are hereinafter referred to as "bribery of a foreign public official".

4. For the purpose of this Convention:

   a. "foreign public official" means any person holding a legislative, administrative or judicial office of a foreign country, whether appointed or elected; any person exercising a public function for a foreign country, including for a public agency or public enterprise; and any official or agent of a public international organisation;

   b. "foreign country" includes all levels and subdivisions of government, from national to local;

   c. "act or refrain from acting in relation to the performance of official duties" includes any use of the public official's position, whether or not within the official's authorised competence.

Article 2—Responsibility of Legal Persons

Each party shall take such measures as may be necessary, in accordance with its legal principles, to establish the liability of legal persons for the bribery of a foreign public official.

Article 3—Sanctions

1. The bribery of a foreign public official shall be punishable by effective, proportionate and dissuasive criminal penalties. The range of penalties shall be comparable to those applicable to the bribery of the Party's own public officials and shall, in the case of natural persons, include deprivation of liberty sufficient to enable effective mutual legal assistance and extradition.

2. In the event that, under the legal system of a Party, criminal responsibility is not applicable to legal persons, that Party shall ensure that legal persons shall be subject to effective, proportionate and dissuasive non-criminal sanctions, including monetary sanctions, for bribery of foreign public officials.

3. Each Party shall take such measures as may be necessary to provide that the bribe and the proceeds of the bribery of a foreign public official, or property the value of which corresponds to that of such proceeds, are subject to seizure and confiscation or that monetary sanctions of comparable effect are applicable.

4. Each Party shall consider the imposition of additional civil or administrative sanctions upon a person subject to sanctions for the bribery of a foreign public official.

Article 4—Jurisdiction

1. Each Party shall take such measures as may be necessary to establish its jurisdiction over the bribery of a foreign public official when the offence is committed in whole or in part in its territory.

2. Each Party which has jurisdiction to prosecute its nationals for offences committed abroad shall take such measures as may be necessary to establish its jurisdiction to do so in respect of the bribery of a foreign public official, according to the same principles.
3. When more than one Party has jurisdiction over an alleged offence described in this Convention, the Parties involved shall, at the request of one of them, consult with a view to determining the most appropriate jurisdiction for prosecution.
4. Each Party shall review whether its current basis for jurisdiction is effective in the fight against the bribery of foreign public officials and, if it is not, shall take remedial steps.

Article 5—Enforcement

Investigation and prosecution of the bribery of a foreign public official shall be subject to the applicable rules and principles of each Party. They shall not be influenced by considerations of national economic interest, the potential effect upon relations with another State or the identity of the natural persons or legal entities involved.

Article 6—Statute of Limitations

Any statute of limitations applicable to the offence of bribery of a foreign public official shall allow an adequate period of time for the investigation and prosecution of this offence.

Article 7—Money Laundering

Each Party which has made bribery of its own public official a predicate offence for the purpose of the application of its money laundering legislation shall do so on the same terms for the bribery of a foreign public official, without regard to the place where the bribery occurred.

Article 8—Accounting

1. In order to combat bribery of foreign public officials effectively, each Party shall take such measures as may be necessary, within the framework of its laws and regulations regarding the maintenance of books and records, financial statement disclosures, and accounting and auditing standards, to prohibit the establishment of off-the-books accounts, the making of off-the-books or inadequately identified transactions, the recording of non-existent expenditures, the entry of liabilities with incorrect identification of their object, as well as the use of false documents, by companies subject to those laws and regulations, for the purpose of bribing foreign public officials or of hiding such bribery.
2. Each Party shall provide effective, proportionate and dissuasive civil, administrative or criminal penalties for such omissions and falsifications in respect of the books, records, accounts and financial statements of such companies.

Article 9—Mutual Legal Assistance

1. Each Party shall, to the fullest extent possible under its laws and relevant treaties and arrangements, provide prompt and effective legal assistance to another Party for the purpose of criminal investigations and proceedings brought by a Party concerning offences within the scope of this Convention and for non-criminal proceedings within the scope of this Convention brought by a Party against a legal person. The requested Party shall inform the requesting Party, without delay, of any additional information or documents needed to support the request for assistance and, where requested, of the status and outcome of the request for assistance.
2. Where a Party makes mutual legal assistance conditional upon the existence of dual criminality, dual criminality shall be deemed to exist if the offence for which the assistance is sought is within the scope of this Convention.
3. A Party shall not decline to render mutual legal assistance for criminal matters within the scope of this Convention on the ground of bank secrecy.

Article 10—Extradition

1. Bribery of a foreign public official shall be deemed to be included as an extraditable offence under the laws of the Parties and the extradition treaties between them.
2. If a Party which makes extradition conditional on the existence of an extradition treaty receives a request for extradition from another Party with which it has no extradition treaty, it may consider this Convention to be the legal basis for extradition in respect of the offence of bribery of a foreign public official.
3. Each Party shall take any measures necessary to assure either that it can extradite its nationals or that it can prosecute its nationals for the offence of bribery of a foreign public official. A Party which declines a request to extradite a person for bribery of a foreign public official solely on the ground that the person is its national shall submit the case to its competent authorities for the purpose of prosecution.
4. Extradition for bribery of a foreign public official is subject to the conditions set out in the domestic law and applicable treaties and arrangements of each Party. Where a Party makes extradition conditional upon the existence of dual criminality, that condition shall be deemed to be fulfilled if the offence for which extradition is sought is within the scope of Article 1 of this Convention.

Article 11—Responsible Authorities

For the purposes of Article 4, paragraph 3, consultation, Article 9, mutual legal assistance, and Article 10, extradition, each Party shall notify to the Secretary-General of the OECD, an authority or authorities, responsible for making and receiving requests, which shall serve as channel of communication for these matters for that Party, without prejudice to other arrangements between Parties.

Article 12—Monitoring and Follow-up

The Parties shall co-operate in carrying out a programme of systematic follow-up to monitor and promote the full implementation of this Convention. Unless otherwise decided by a consensus of the Parties, this shall be done in the framework of the OECD Working Group on Bribery in International Business Transactions and according to its terms of reference, or within the framework and terms of reference of any successor to its functions, and Parties shall bear the costs of the programme in accordance with the rules applicable to that body.

Article 13—Signature and Accession

1. Until its entry into force, this Convention shall be open for signature by OECD members and by non-members which have become or have been invited to become full participants in its Working Group on Bribery in International Business Transactions.
2. Subsequent to its entry into force, this Convention shall be open to accession by any non-signatory which is a member of or has become a full participant in the Working Group on Bribery in International Business Transactions or any successor to its functions.

Article 14—Ratification and Depositary

1. This Convention is subject to acceptance, approval or ratification by the Signatories, in accordance with their respective laws.
2. Instruments of acceptance, approval, ratification or accession shall be deposited with the Secretary-General of the OECD, who shall serve as Depositary of this Convention.

Article 15—Entry into Force

1. This convention shall enter into force on the sixtieth day following the date upon which five of the countries which have the ten largest export shares set out in document XXX, and which represent by themselves at least sixty per cent of the combined total exports of those ten countries, have deposited their instruments of acceptance, approval, or ratification. For each state depositing its instrument after such entry into force, the Convention shall enter into force on the sixtieth day after deposit of its instrument.
2. If, by 31 December 1998, the Convention has not entered into force under paragraph 1 above, any state which has deposited its instrument of ratification may declare to the depositary its readiness to accept entry into force of this convention under this paragraph 2. The Convention shall enter into force for such a state on the sixtieth day following the date upon which such declarations have been deposited by at least

two states. For each state depositing its declaration after such entry into force, the Convention shall enter into force on the sixtieth day following the date of deposit.

Article 16—Amendment

Any Party may propose the amendment of this Convention. A proposed amendment shall be submitted to the Depositary which shall communicate it to the other Parties at least sixty days before convening a meeting of the Parties to consider the proposed amendment. An amendment adopted by consensus of the parties, or by such other means as the Parties may determine by consensus, shall enter into force sixty days after the deposit of an instrument of ratification, acceptance or approval by all of the Parties, or in such other circumstances as may be specified by the Parties at the time of adoption of the amendment.

Article 17—Withdrawal

A Party may withdraw from this Convention by submitting written notification to the Depositary. Such withdrawal shall be effective one year after the date of the receipt of the notification. After withdrawal, co-operation shall continue between the Parties and the State which has withdrawn on all requests for assistance and extradition made before the effective date of withdrawal which remain pending.

December

DEFENSE PANEL ON FUTURE
NATIONAL SECURITY NEEDS
December 1, 1997

A half-century after the United States reshaped its national security structure to confront the cold war, and a half-decade after the end of the cold war, U.S. officials in 1997 accelerated their military planning for the first few decades of the post-cold war era. The Pentagon announced a series of steps to reduce its operating overhead so more emphasis could be placed on updating weapons systems and other high-priority programs. President Bill Clinton signed a top-secret directive revising, for the first time in sixteen years, U.S. nuclear strategy in the event of war. A high-level study panel, mandated by Congress, urged a fundamental "transformation" of the entire U.S. military so it could better deter and defend against threats such as the proliferation of nuclear, chemical, and biological weapons.

These efforts to look toward the future came on the fiftieth anniversary of the National Security Act of 1947, which merged the armed services under the Department of Defense and created the Central Intelligence Agency and the National Security Council. That law transformed the U.S. national security system to meet the challenges of the post-World War II era. By most accounts, the law and the structures it created served the United States reasonably well through the Korean War, the Vietnam War, the Persian Gulf War, and the cold war standoff between the Soviet Union and the U.S.-led western alliance.

Looking to the post-cold war era in the twenty-first century, U.S. officials appeared to agree during the late 1990s that changing threats overseas and new budget realities at home would force revisions in the national security apparatus as significant as those of a half-century before. The Clinton administration began planning for the changes; subsequent administrations would shoulder the burden of persuading Congress and the military services to march in step.

Cutting Pentagon Overhead

Even in an era of peace, with no adversary posing a near-term threat to U.S. domestic security, the Pentagon remained an enormous bureaucracy

*with an annual budget of nearly $270 billion. One of the Clinton adminis-
tration's priorities was to make that bureaucracy more efficient, and that
meant cutting overhead and costs.*

*Secretary of Defense William S. Cohen announced November 10 a series
of proposals to streamline the Defense Department by simplifying its purchasing, closing superfluous bases, and turning some functions over to private contractors. Because they affected the civilian economy as well as the
military, nearly all of Cohen's proposals were certain to prove controversial
as Congress reviewed them in 1998 and beyond.*

*By far the most contentious was Cohen's plan for two more rounds of
base closings in 2001 and 2005. Congress had reluctantly agreed to four series of base closings between 1988 and 1995. Most observers for years had
argued that the military services had too many bases, both in the United
States and overseas, absorbing too much of the Pentagon budget. Proposals
to close bases always were unpopular in Congress because military spending helped boost local economies.* (Base closings, Historic Documents of
1995, p. 407)

*Earlier in 1997 Congress blocked Cohen's request for authorization to
initiate rounds of base closings in 1999 and 2001. With his November 10
proposal Cohen obviously was hoping that Congress would be more receptive to cutbacks in later years, after local communities had more time to
prepare for the loss of jobs at military bases. Cohen estimated additional
base closings would save about $2.8 billion annually.*

*Cohen outlined a series of other measures intended to make the Penta-
gon run more smoothly at less cost. Potentially the most controversial of
those proposals was allowing private companies to bid against Pentagon
agencies for such services as payroll management, personnel services,
leased property management, and drug testing. Cohen estimated that turning these functions over to private contractors could save $2.5 billion an-
nually. Unions representing federal civilian employees strongly opposed
contracting with private employers.*

*Another set of cost-cutting measures Cohen said the military would im-
plement included adopting a paper-free procurement system for major
weapons contracts by 2000; using government credit cards, rather than formal contracts, for most purchases of less than $2,500; using private firms
to build and manage housing for military families; and eliminating
30,000 out of 141,000 military and civilian jobs in administrative and
headquarters operations.*

Transforming the Military

*A nine-member panel of retired military offices and civilian defense ex-
perts on December 1 offered the nation a critical analysis of where the U.S.
national security system—including the armed forces and intelligence services—should be headed in the post-cold war era. Congress in 1996 mandated the creation of a National Defense Panel to examine future options
for the military. Cohen appointed the nine members in February 1997,
with Philip A. Odeen as chairman.*

The panel suggested a serious rethinking of the entire spectrum of national security issues, ranging from the deployment of forces overseas to the use of such technology as spy satellites and so-called smart bombs. In calling for a "transformation strategy," the panel said the greatest danger faced by the United States would be "an unwillingness or an inability to change our security posture in time to meet the challenges of the next century."

For the immediate future, the panel said the United States needed to shift the underlying focus of its military forces. During the cold war, the U.S. military structure was based on the need to counter a conventional and nuclear threat from the Soviet Union, as well as the prospect of fighting two major regional wars at the same time. The collapse of the Soviet Union left the threat from Moscow greatly diminished (although still possible). And while the United States might again be drawn into conflicts in such regions as the Middle East or the Korean peninsula, the panel said the danger of two simultaneous regional wars had become a "low probability scenario." Over time, the military had used the two-front prospect "as a means of justifying current forces."

An alternative was to focus more attention and resources on countering threats to the "homeland," such as attacks on computer systems or on urban areas by terrorists armed with low-technology chemical or biological weapons. The Pentagon also needed to develop smaller, more flexible military units able to deploy quickly in the case of overseas crises. It was unlikely, the panel said, that the U.S. military would again have six months to prepare for a regional war, as it did in advance of the Persian Gulf War in 1991. (Gulf War preparations, Historic Documents of 1991, p. 15; Threats to U.S. infrastructure, p. 711)

The panel sharply questioned existing plans by all the military services for procurement of several major weapons systems. The military's plans were "focused primarily on current systems and do not adequately support the central thrust" of the services' future needs, the panel said. Specifically, the panel said it questioned such multibillion-dollar projects as upgrading the army's M-1A1 tank, the navy's priorities for shipbuilding, and the development of new tactical warplanes by both the navy and air force.

Overall, the panel said key elements of the U.S. national security structure—the military, the intelligence community, and the diplomatic service—needed to change their methods of operations in the wake of the end of the cold war. In a broad critique, the panel said that U.S. policymaking institutions "are largely reactive, highly compartmentalized, inwardly focused on their own missions, and only loosely connected to one another." Those institutions were still operating as they had for the previous fifty years and had failed to deal with new challenges or take advantage of new technology.

The panel said the military services needed to work more closely together in the future than in the past, setting aside service rivalries that had led to costly overlapping of manpower and weapons systems. In addition to closing unneeded bases, the Pentagon should consolidate functions in military bases for more than one armed service and should develop more high-level commands that brought the services together.

By cutting unnecessary and duplicated expenses, the panel said, the military would have more money to develop new weapons and technology to meet threats in the future. The panel suggested a budget of $5 billion to $10 billion annually for experimental programs in intelligence-gathering, space defense, urban warfare, and other fields.

The panel sought to infuse a sense of urgency in its recommendations, saying that by refusing to change the current military system soon "we could be fundamentally unprepared for the future, and put at risk the safety of future generations of Americans." As of 1997 the country had the opportunity and the time to make needed changes, the panel said, but added: "We must not equivocate. We must begin now."

New Strategic Doctrine

President Clinton in November signed a directive discarding key elements of the U.S. nuclear strategy in place for the latter part of the cold war. Clinton's directive, classified top secret, reportedly dropped a plan for the United States to conduct a nuclear war until it had been "won," regardless of the amount of devastation that would be caused. Instead, according to a senior White House official quoted by the Washington Post, *Clinton's directive placed an emphasis on deterring nuclear war by threatening opponents with a response that would be "overwhelming and devastating."*

During most of the cold war, U.S. nuclear policy was based on a doctrine popularly known as "mutually-assured destruction" (or MAD), which held that nuclear war between the United States and the Soviet Union was unlikely so long as both sides were certain to be destroyed in a prolonged nuclear war. President Ronald Reagan in 1981 reportedly signed a secret directive that went a step further by declaring that U.S. policy was to prevail over the Soviet Union in any nuclear war.

Outlining Clinton's new policy in general terms, Robert G. Bell, senior director for defense policy of the National Security Council, said nuclear weapons were still necessary to deter "aggression and coercion." But Clinton had removed "all previous references to being able to wage a nuclear war successfully or to prevail in a nuclear war," Bell said. Clinton had not abandoned the "first-use" option, under which the United States might be the first to use nuclear weapons if necessary, Bell said.

> *Following is the executive summary of the report, "Transforming Defense: National Security in the 21st Century," released December 1, 1997, by the National Defense Panel, chaired by Philip A. Odeen:*

The United States enters the new millennium as the preeminent political, economic, and military power in the world. Today we are in a relatively secure interlude following an era of intense international confrontation. But we must anticipate that future adversaries will learn from the past and confront us in very different ways. Thus we must be willing to change as well or risk having forces ill-suited to protect our security twenty years in the future. Only one thing is certain: the greatest danger lies in an unwillingness or an inability to change our security posture in time to meet the challenges of the next century.

The United States needs to launch a transformation strategy now that will enable it to meet a range of security challenges in 2010 to 2020. Yet we must do this without taking undue risk in the interim. This transformation promises to be complex. We cannot know the full extent and nature of future challenges. Yet, we must make critical decisions and choices entailing significant investments of resources and energies.

The Future Operational Environment

We can safely assume that future adversaries will have learned from the Gulf War. It is likely that they will find new ways to challenge our interests, our forces and our citizens. They will seek to disable the underlying structures that enable our military operations. Forward bases and forward-deployed forces will likely be challenged and coalition partners coerced. Critical nodes that enable communications, transportation, deployment, and other means of power projection will be vulnerable.

Our domestic communities and key infrastructures may also be vulnerable. Transnational threats may increase. As recently stated by [Defense] Secretary [William S.] Cohen, the proliferation of nuclear, chemical, and biological weapons and their delivery means will pose a serious threat to our homeland and our forces overseas. Information systems, the vital arteries of the modern political, economic, and social infrastructures, will undoubtedly be targets as well. The increasing commercialization of space makes it feasible for state and nonstate actors alike to acquire reconnaissance and surveillance services.

In short, we can expect those opposed to our interests to confront us at home and abroad—possibly in both places at once—with asymmetrical responses to our traditional strengths.

Near-term Implications

Defense choices invariably entail risk; the only question is where we take the risk. A significant share of today's Defense Department's resources is focused on the unlikely contingency that two major wars will occur at almost the same time. The Panel views this two-military-theater-of-war construct as, in reality, a force-sizing function. We are concerned that, for some, this has become a means of justifying current forces. This approach focuses significant resources on a low-probability scenario, which consumes funds that could be used to reduce risk to our long-term security. The Panel believes priority must go to the future. We recognize that, in the near term, the United States cannot ignore the threats posed by Iran and Iraq in the Persian Gulf and North Korea in Northeast Asia. However, our current forces, with the support of allies, should be capable of dealing with both contingencies.

The Range of Challenges

The types of missions our military and related security structures will be required to perform in 2010–2020 remain largely unchanged but the emphasis is likely to change. Maintaining regional stability is probably foremost among them, for the best way to forestall military challenges to the United States is to foster a stable international system. This demands full interaction with regional partners and alliances through diplomatic efforts as well as the full integration of U.S. diplomatic, economic, and military activities.

We must be able to project military power and conduct combat operations into areas where we may not have forward-deployed forces or forward bases. In particular, we must have the ability to put capable, agile, and highly effective shore-based land and air forces in place with a vastly decreased logistics footprint. Smaller force structures will be the norm, an evolution that must parallel the development of new operational concepts. Regular deployments to far-flung areas of the globe, from open deserts to confining urban terrain, therefore, are something we should expect. These deployments must not be viewed as a detraction from our traditional missions, but as a central element of the responsibilities of the future.

Just as deployments abroad are key to a stable international environment, an adequate defensive structure at home is crucial to the safety of our citizens and well-being of our communities. One of the salient features of U.S. security in 2010–2020 will be a much larger role for homeland defense than exists today.

Effective deterrence of potential nuclear adversaries can be maintained at the reduced levels envisioned by START III and beyond. Over time, the focus of our efforts to deter nuclear attacks against the United States, its allies, and interests may change substantially from that of today. Deterrence of attack as the central focus of nuclear policy already is being supplanted by the need to manage—identify, account for, and safeguard against—the proliferation and possible use of nuclear and other weapons of mass destruction. Traditional U.S. nuclear policies may not be sufficient to deter nuclear, chemical, or biological attacks by a rogue state against U.S. allies and coalition partners.

In regard to maintaining U.S. information superiority, we will need to integrate existing and new information systems while exploiting commercial technology. We must also have effective defensive and offensive information capabilities. We will need to recognize that the U.S. lead in space will not go unchallenged. We must coordinate the civil, commercial, and national security aspects of space, as use of space is a major element of national power.

Force Capabilities

Our military is superbly equipped, led, and trained and is blessed with magnificent men and women. We must never forget that our people in uniform have been the core of our strength in the past. They, more than any hardware system, form the real defense capability of today and tomorrow. Under no circumstances should we reduce the quality or training of our people. The technology revolution and advanced weapons we seek to embrace will be for naught if we take our military and civilian work force for granted.

It is clear, however, that in the 2010–2020 time frame our military forces will need capabilities very different from those they currently possess. We are on the cusp of a military revolution stimulated by rapid advances in information and information-related technologies. This implies a growing potential to detect, identify, and track far greater numbers of targets over a larger area for a longer time than ever before, and to provide this information much more quickly and effectively than heretofore possible. Those who can exploit these opportunities—and thereby dissipate the "fog of war"—stand to gain significant advantages.

Current force structures and information architectures extrapolated to the future may not suffice to meet successfully the conditions of future battle. Automation and systems architectures capable of disseminating information to widely dispersed and dissimilar units and integrating their actions will be key. We will need greater mobility, precision, speed, stealth, and strike ranges while we sharply reduce our logistics footprint. All operations will be increasingly joint, combined, and interagency. Furthermore, the reserve components will need to be fully integrated with active forces.

Legacy systems procured today will be at risk in 2010–2020. We must carefully scrutinize their utility for future conflicts as well as for peacetime military operations. Joint Vision 2010 and the visions of the services contain many of the capabilities we need in the future. However, the procurement budgets of the services are focused primarily on current systems and do not adequately support the central thrust of their visions. In light of these factors, the Panel questions the procurement plans for Army equipment, Navy ships, and tactical aircraft of all services.

Reserve and Guard units must be prepared and resourced for use in a variety of ongoing worldwide operations. They will play an increasing role in a variety of these by relieving active units and reducing the operational and personnel tempos of frequent and lengthy deployments.

While the other services have successfully integrated their active and reserve forces, the Army has suffered from a destructive disunity among its components, specifically between the active Army and the National Guard. This rift serves neither the Army nor the country well. The Panel strongly believes the rift must be healed and makes a series of recommendations toward that end.

A fully integrated total force requires a common culture to engender unity of thought and action. Shared operational and training experiences, common educational opportunities, and frequent exchange of leaders among active and reserve components, the different services, coalition partners, and national and international agencies will serve to deepen mutual respect and reinforce a common ethic.

Transformation Strategy

Transforming the armed forces into a very different kind of military from that which exists today, while supporting U.S. near-term efforts, presents a significant challenge. Beyond Defense, we must also transform the manner in which we conduct foreign affairs, foster regional stability, and enable projection of military power.

It is important to begin the transformation process now, since decisions made in the short term will influence the shape of the military over the long term. The Defense Department should accord the highest priority to executing a transformation strategy. Taking the wrong transformation course (or failing to transform) opens the nation to both strategic and technological surprise.

Transformation will take dedication and commitment—and a willingness to put talented people, money, resources, and structure behind a process designed to foster change. Greater emphasis should be placed on experimenting with a variety of military systems, operational concepts, and force structures. The goal is to identify the means to meet the emerging challenges, exploit the opportunities, and terminate those approaches that do not succeed. It will take wisdom to walk the delicate line that avoids premature decisions and unintended "lock-in" with equipment purchases, operational concepts, and related systems whose effectiveness may quickly erode in a rapidly changing environment.

At the core of this effort should be a much greater emphasis on jointness, building upon the legacy of Goldwater-Nichols. However, competition among the services can assist in determining how best to exploit new capabilities or solve emerging challenges. It takes a considerable amount of time, a decade or two, to play out an effective transformation. Indeed, even those military systems that are placed on a "fast track" for development and fielding often take ten years or more to reach forces in the field. Time also is required to determine how best to employ new military systems, and to make the appropriate adjustments in the force structure.

We must look beyond the challenges for defense and assess the relevance of the National Security Act of 1947 for the next millennium. This framework served us well during the Cold War, but we must objectively reexamine our national security structure if we intend to remain a world leader. Interagency processes, both international and domestic, must be reviewed and refined to provide the National Command Authority and the American people with an effective, integrated, and proactive organization.

We must also look closely at our alliances to ensure they are adjusting to the changing environment. As we work hard to establish mutual trust and commitment with our allies, we must be willing to sacrifice for common goals. Alliances have been and will continue to be a two-way street.

Our intelligence structure faces immensely more complicated tasks than during the Cold War. Asymmetric threats pose particular difficulties. Information technologies are a two-edged sword of both tremendous opportunities and vulnerabilities. The various facets of the intelligence community must merge their efforts and information, handle highly complicated technical challenges, ensure all parts of the intelligence gathering apparatus are robust, and work to ensure their products are easily accessible and meet the needs of the warfighter.

The Panel has identified areas in the Unified Command Plan where seams might hinder the effectiveness of our forces. We recommend that an Americas Command be created to address the challenges of homeland defense as well as those of the Western Hemisphere. A Joint Forces Command would be the force provider to the geographic CINCs, address standardization among the various Unified commands, oversee joint training and experimentation, and coordinate and integrate among the networked service battle labs. A Logistics Command would merge necessary support functions that are now divided among various agencies. Space Command would expand to absorb the domain of information.

Infrastructure

Fundamental reform of the Defense Department's support infrastructure is key to an effective transformation strategy for the years 2010–2020. Today, the Department of Defense is burdened by a far-flung support infrastructure that is ponderous, bureaucratic, and unaffordable. Unless its costs are cut sharply, the Department will be unable to invest adequately for the future. The Panel supports the initiatives put forward by the recent Defense Reform Initiative. However, the Panel believes even more can and should be done.

Meaningful reform of the support infrastructure is not possible unless the Department establishes a more effective and business-like approach to resource management. To that end, the Panel recommends that the Department continue its efforts to reform the acquisition process as well as to rethink the Planning, Programming, and Budgeting System (PPBS) to make it less burdensome and more receptive to innovation and change.

Accurate cost information is also a prerequisite for cost-effective resource management decisions. Without good cost data, Defense managers have difficulty identifying inefficient practices and unwittingly make suboptimal resource allocation decisions. In addition, the Department must work with Congress to relax "color of money" restrictions.

The Defense Reform Initiative recommends competing 150,000 positions across Defense. We endorse this plan, but recommend expanding it to the 600,000 military and civilian personnel who perform commercially oriented support tasks.

Industrial Base

In coming decades, the United States can only preserve its current technological advantage through time-based competition. The Department of Defense needs to provide industry with incentives to innovate so that we may maintain a qualitative technology and systems edge so that the United States will continue to be preeminent in military technology. Rather than being reactive, we should make our military acquisition process proactive. The Department must work with Congress to devise new rules and procedures that encourage technology development, rather than large production quantities, in order to recover cost and profit. This may create unit cost "sticker shock" unless we shorten the development cycle to lower development costs. But reduced production quantities will reduce total program cost, the real measure of the cost to the nation.

A close examination must be made of industrial mobilization programs. Much of the existing requirements and structures are predicated upon maintaining or overseeing an industrial and manpower mobilization base for a Cold-War era contingency. This approach and associated overhead is clearly inappropriate to the relatively short wars we expect in the future. Further, this mobilization approach is clearly inappropriate, given the short technological life-cycles we experience today and certainly will experience in 2010–2020.

Installations

The Panel strongly endorses the infrastructure recommendations within the Defense Reform Initiative, which stated that there is sufficient surplus capacity for two additional BRAC rounds. Indeed, we believe there may be even more excess capacity that could be identified, should a review be done from a joint-base perspective. Therefore, the Panel strongly recommends that two BRAC rounds be conducted earlier than the current 2001, 2005 Department proposal. The object is to transform the base structure from an impediment to a cost-effective enabler of readiness and modernization

The services should also reconsider the traditional concept of the military base. Rather than using on-base housing, commissaries, and other support services, military personnel would receive additional compensation. This shift would allow the services to reduce their on-base infrastructure, while increasing the benefit received.

The Cost

The issue of how to fund this transformation in this fiscally constrained environment is no small challenge. The Panel estimates an annual budget wedge of $5 to 10 billion will be needed to support a true transformation. This money would fund initiatives in intelligence, space, urban warfare, joint experimentation, and information operations. In the absence of additional defense funding, the transformation could best be funded by infrastructure and acquisition reform. If these reforms are not forthcoming, it will be necessary to reduce Operations Tempo (OPTEMPO), cancel acquisition programs, or reduce force structure and end strength. There will be no easy answers, and difficult choices must be made.

Conclusion

In the increasingly complex world that we foresee, the Department of Defense and its armed services cannot preserve U.S. interests alone. Defense is but one element of a broader national security structure. If we are to be successful in meeting the challenges of the future, the entire U.S. national security apparatus must adapt and become more integrated, coherent, and proactive.

Implementing the transformation described in this Report promises to be complex and will require careful balance to preserve our current security interests. It is our belief, however, that if we refuse to change in a timely manner we could be fundamentally unprepared for the future, and put at risk the safety of future generations of Americans. We have the time and the opportunity to adjust. But we cannot equivocate. We must begin now.

ATTORNEY GENERAL ON
CAMPAIGN FINANCE PROBE
December 2, 1997

Campaign finance, often seen by civic activists as the Achilles' heel of the American political system but generally ignored by the public, became a heated political issue in 1997. Republicans charged that President Bill Clinton, Vice President Al Gore, and their Democratic aides were so eager to get money for the 1996 elections that they engaged in improper or even illegal practices, including soliciting contributions at the White House.

Two Republican-led congressional committees held hearings on the issue, turning up embarrassing information about the Democrats but nothing that could lead to criminal indictments. Attorney General Janet Reno on December 2, 1997, rejected a call by Republicans to appoint an independent counsel to investigate alleged campaign finance irregularities by the Democrats, including Clinton and Gore. Reno said a thorough Justice Department investigation failed to turn up evidence that the president and vice president had violated an 1883 federal law barring campaign solicitations on federal property.

Many of the Democratic activities that brought criticism had also been standard fare for Republicans over the years. Clinton's Republican predecessors—indeed virtually every president in modern times—had hosted campaign contributors at the White House and given them special favors. Members of Congress of both parties routinely solicited campaign contributions from lobbyists and others seeking to influence the government. Both parties had made use of so-called soft money—unregulated contributions that supported candidates with "party building" or "issue campaigns" but never went directly to them.

The Clinton administration was vulnerable to criticism because the Democratic Party appeared to be so desperate for money that it failed to exercise any caution in how it solicited contributions. Some of the Democrats' money may have been raised illegally, including from foreign sources. Summarizing Senate hearings on the matter, the Washington Post *said the Clinton administration had been shown to be "a modern model of campaign excesses."*

Clinton defended his practices, and those of his party, as necessary to keep pace with the Republicans, who had long been much more successful in raising cash for political expenditures. "We had to work hard within the law to raise a lot of money, to be competitive," he said in a March 7 news conference. "We did work hard, and I'm glad we did, because the stakes were high" in the elections. Clinton said that despite his party's efforts, they raised $200 million less in 1996 than the Republicans.

Although Clinton, Gore, and top Democrats escaped—at least for 1997— any legal complications stemming from the campaign finance scandal, it seemed likely that Gore's prospects for the presidential race in 2000 would be hindered. Throughout his long political career, Gore had a reputation for rectitude that was the envy of many politicians. His involvement in questionable fund-raising schemes marked the first time he had ever been challenged on legal or ethical grounds. Political experts said the damage to his reputation could be long-lasting, noting that Gore's ratings in the public opinion polls routinely lagged behind Clinton's.

Reno's Decision

The allegations most directly involving Clinton and Gore concerned telephone calls they made from the White House to potential Democratic Party contributors. Soliciting campaign contributions from the White House could be seen as violating the 1883 Pendelton Act, which barred campaign fund-raising on federal property. The Justice Department opened an investigation of the fund-raising calls in September, after a request from the House Judiciary Committee.

Gore on March 3 had acknowledged making such calls but insisted he had done nothing wrong or illegal. He noted, for example, that he had charged long-distance calls to Democratic National Committee credit card.

Clinton at first said he did not remember making such calls. The Justice Department investigation then uncovered two cases in which Clinton had called donors to thank them for their contributions and one case, in October 1994, in which he had placed calls asking for donations.

Reno announced December 2 that an exhaustive investigation had turned up no credible evidence that Clinton or Gore had violated the law. Reno said the law did not apply to the calls made by Clinton and Gore because they telephoned from residential areas—not business areas—of the White House or had not directly asked for specific contributions.

Reno said she had made the decision entirely on her own, with no pressure from the White House. She said the Justice Department would continue to investigate "all allegations of illegal activity" involving campaign fund-raising.

Critics challenged Reno's decision on two counts. First, they said she had relied on a very narrow reading of the law authorizing appointment of independent counsels. Reno said the allegations against Clinton and Gore did not meet minimal tests of the independent counsel law, including that the alleged wrongdoing involve a crime the Justice Department commonly prosecutes. She noted that the government had never prosecuted anyone for making phone calls from a federal office building to solicit campaign donations.

Republicans did not dispute Reno's reading of the law, especially of the Pendelton Act. After all, many members of Congress routinely solicited campaign contributions from their offices. Rather, they said that in focusing on narrow legal questions she missed the bigger picture of whether an independent investigation was needed into Democratic campaign irregularities in general. That led to the second criticism.

Critics also said Reno was ignoring the purpose of an independent counsel: to relieve the Justice Department of the awkward responsibility of investigating senior officials within the administration. "This matter all boils down to a loud and clear conflict of interest between the attorney general's duty to the public to enforce the law and her personal loyalty to the president," said Rep. Henry J. Hyde, R-Ill., who chaired the House Judiciary Committee.

Newspapers that had been especially critical of Clinton's fund-raising efforts also denounced Reno. The New York Times, *in a December 7 editorial, chastised Reno on a wide front, accusing her of allowing "anarchy and mismanagement" in the Justice Department and offering excuses for the Democratic Party.*

Reno had overruled several top aides, including FBI Director Louis J. Freeh, who had argued for appointment of an independent counsel. Republicans had cited Freeh's position as evidence that the administration was divided on the need for an independent counsel's investigation. Despite their disagreement, Reno and Freeh appeared together at a House committee hearing December 9 and jointly refused to give the committee an internal memo written by Freeh on the matter. Freeh minimized his differences with Reno and refused to say why he had supported appointment of an independent counsel.

In her December 2 news conference Reno also said she had found no evidence of wrongdoing by former energy secretary Hazel R. O'Leary in a case that had become linked with the campaign finance scandals.

Other White House Activities

In addition to the Clinton and Gore telephone calls, critics suggested that the administration improperly used the White House for other fund-raising purposes. The administration had hosted more than 100 informal events called "coffees," where Clinton and other officials discussed current events with contributors. Those attending such events contributed an estimated $27 million to the Clinton-Gore campaign.

The Clintons also had invited 983 people to stay overnight at the White House between the 1994 and 1996 elections. Some were long-time personal friends of the Clintons and others were campaign contributors and celebrities, including entertainers Barbra Streisand and Tom Hanks. Many of the guests stayed in the Lincoln bedroom, prompting derisive news coverage, such as a banner headline in one New York tabloid newspaper describing that historic site as "Bill's B&B." Clinton defended the practice, however, saying at a February 25 news conference: "The Lincoln bedroom was never sold" for campaign contributions.

The Asian Connections

Some of the most explosive charges concerned Republican allegations that the Chinese government had attempted to influence U.S. policy by making campaign contributions to the Democratic Party. U.S. law prohibited contributions by foreign nationals. The FBI in June 1996 warned two mid-level officials of the National Security Council and six congressional aides that China was attempting to influence congressional races. China denied having any such intention, and Clinton said neither he nor senior White House aides were told about the FBI warning.

Two key figures were Asian-Americans who had known Clinton since his days as governor of Arkansas. John Huang, a vice chairman of the Democratic National Committee, raised money among Asian-Americans and reportedly from several foreign nationals as well. He had been a mid-level official in the Commerce Department and worked for the Lippo Bank, part of an Indonesian conglomerate owned by the Riady family, which reportedly had close ties with China.

Another central figure was Johnny Chung, a California businessman who visited the White House frequently. In 1995 he gave a $50,000 campaign check to Mrs. Clinton's chief of staff, which was then turned over to the Democratic Party. Also in 1995 he brought a group of Chinese officials to the White House to watch a taping of the president's weekly radio address; one of the officials reportedly was Huang Jichun, vice president of a Chinese weapons conglomerate.

Chung played a role in a case involving former energy secretary O'Leary. Chung in 1995 donated $25,000 to Africare, a relief organization that was one of O'Leary's favorite charities, in the expectation that she would agree to meet with a senior official of the Chinese petrochemical industry. In her December 2 news conference, Reno said an investigation had found "no evidence whatsoever" that O'Leary had been aware of the $25,000 donation or that there was any connection between the money and the meeting with the Chinese official. Reno said the Justice Department was continuing to investigate actions by O'Leary's aides.

For Gore, potentially the most damaging revelation concerned his attendance in April 1996 at an event at the Hsi Lai Buddhist Temple in Hacienda Heights, California. Gore at first said he had attended only a "community event" at the temple. Later, after evidence surfaced that the party had raised $140,000 at the event, Gore admitted he had known that party fund-raisers had been present.

Congressional Hearings

Two congressional panels conducted investigations into campaign finance issues in 1997. Republican leaders of both panels had hoped their probes would uncover extensive wrongdoing by the Democrats, possibly even enough to force Clinton from office. House Speaker Newt Gingrich said in March that the investigations would show that Democrats had engaged in conspiracies "even bigger than Watergate."

Republican expectations along that line were reinforced by the fact that the Senate hearings were chaired by Fred Thompson of Tennessee, who had been a key aide in the Senate Watergate hearings. Thompson himself raised expectations on the opening day of the hearings, speaking of plans to unveil a Chinese plot "to pour illegal money into American political campaigns." Thompson never followed through, however, and the hearings barely delved into the alleged Chinese plot.

The House Committee on Government Reform and Oversight spent $3 million on its investigations but held only one public hearing. Thompson's Governmental Affairs Committee spent $2.2 million and held thirty-two hearings, many of which were nationally televised—although to sparse audiences.

Despite the buildup by Republicans, the Senate hearings produced little drama and virtually no information that had not been previously publicized in news reports. Thompson announced October 31 that he was suspending the hearings and that the committee would issue a report in 1998. The House committee considered holding hearings in December but did not do so.

For many observers, the highlight of the Senate hearings was an appearance by Roger E. Tamraz, a flamboyant financier who had sought U.S. help for a pipeline project to ship oil from the Caspian Sea. Tamraz had visited the White House six times despite warnings from a National Security Council aide that he was a security risk, in part because he was sought by Lebanese authorities on embezzling charges. Tamraz told the committee he had paid the Democratic National Committee $300,000 solely to gain access to the president and his aides.

Other witnesses included three Buddhist nuns who had donated money to the Democratic Party after Gore's visit to the Buddhist temple in California. Former Clinton aides also testified, defending their fund-raising practices and insisting that the campaign finance system was the real culprit.

Democrats produced evidence that Republicans also had engaged in campaign finance irregularities, including soliciting funds from overseas. They focused attention on the National Policy Forum, a creation of former Republican National Committee chairman Haley Barbour. The forum obtained a $2.1 million loan guarantee from a wealthy Hong Kong businessman just before the 1994 elections, using it to bolster Republican campaign spending. The forum later defaulted on the loan and went out of business. Democrats had just begun their inquiry into Republican fund-raising tactics when Thompson decided to end the committee hearings.

Finance Reform

The administration attempted to shift the focus of attention to the campaign finance system, which Clinton said was "out of whack" and in need of major reform. With modest support from the administration, Sen. John

McCain, R-Ariz., and Sen. Russell D. Feingold, D-Wis., put together a coali-tion supporting a bill banning "soft money" contributions to political par-ties and limiting independent issue-oriented advertising intended to pro-mote specific candidates. The year's controversy over campaign finance generated enough interest to force Senate leaders to allow debate on the bill.

Despite its broad support from many political groups, the campaign fi-nance bill never generated much public enthusiasm—in part because it involved technical issues that were not easy to explain on television news programs. Numerous polls also showed that citizens had come to expect campaign funding abuses and found little new or surprising in the latest round of scandals.

Given political leeway by the lack of public pressure, the Republican leadership mounted a filibuster, which supporters of the bill were unable to cut off. The dearth of public interest also enabled Senate Majority Leader Trent Lott and other Republican leaders to say, with some confidence, that they would not suffer a political backlash because of their opposition to the reform bill.

Perhaps the best indication of Washington's seriousness—or lack of it— about campaign finance reform was that both parties continued to raise money as fast as possible in 1997. According to a study by Common Cause, the two parties raised a combined $34.3 million in "soft money" during the first half of the year, a record amount. As usual, Republicans led the fund-raising marathon by a two-to-one margin.

> *Following are excerpts from a news conference December 2, 1997, in which Attorney General Janet Reno announced that a Justice Department investigation of campaign fund-raising telephone calls by President Bill Clinton and Vice President Al Gore had not found sufficient evidence to justify appointment of an independent counsel:*

More than a year ago, the Justice Department assembled a task force of ex-perienced attorneys and FBI agents to investigate allegations of criminal wrongdoing surrounding the 1996 elections.

No criminal case in this department has more resources. The task force now numbers more than 120. More than a million pages of documents have been obtained. Hundreds of interviews have been conducted, and agents have been dispatched across the country and around the world to track down leads.

Numerous allegations have been made against high government officials. We have reviewed every one of them to see if there is specific and credible in-formation that a crime may have been committed by a covered person or someone for whom it would be a conflict of interest for the Justice Depart-ment to investigate.

When these allegations have been specific and credible, we have com-menced a preliminary investigation.

That is what the law demands, and we have implemented it faithfully.

Since I have been attorney general, I have referred matters to independent counsels no fewer than six times. Today, following the law's letter, I have decided that the allegations against President Clinton, Vice President Gore and former Energy Secretary Hazel O'Leary do not at this time warrant the appointment of an independent counsel.

This decision was mine, and it was based on the facts and the law—not pressure, politics or any other factor.

Before I discuss these decisions, I want to make one point clear. Any decision not to ask for an independent counsel does not mean that a person has been exonerated or that the work of the campaign finance task force is ended. These decisions do not end our work.

We will continue to vigorously investigate all allegations of illegal activity.

On October the 14th of this year, we began a preliminary investigation into allegations that President Clinton may have violated federal law by making fund-raising calls from his office.

Documents obtained by investigators identified 68 potential donors who might have been solicited by the president. Sixty-four of them were interviewed, and the other four gave statements through their attorneys. Investigators also interviewed White House and DNC [Democratic National Committee] personnel who might reasonably have been aware of any fund-raising calls made by the president.

President Clinton was interviewed. Investigators also thoroughly reviewed other records, including telephone toll records, White House operator diaries, scheduling requests and the president's schedule.

We have taken every reasonable step to investigate these allegations.

The investigation uncovered three occasions when the president made telephone calls from the White House relating to fund raising. In two of these instances, the president was calling to thank a contributor or fund-raisers and did not solicit contributions.

On the third occasion, on October the 18th, 1994, the president placed a number of fund-raising calls to potential contributors. Telephone records, investigative interviews and the president's schedule all established that these calls were made from the White House residence, not from the Oval Office or any other official White House space. The criminal law prohibiting solicitation on federal property does not encompass fund raising in residential areas of the White House, a position on record at the Justice Department since 1979.

Moreover, all donations were deposited into DNC soft money accounts, which means that they do not fall under the scope of the law which plainly prohibits only the solicitation of hard money.

On September 3rd of this year, we began a preliminary investigation into allegations that President Gore—Vice President Gore may have violated federal law by making fund-raising telephone calls from his office in the White House.

Investigators interviewed or obtained affidavits from approximately 250 witnesses, including the vice president and members of his staff, White

House, DNC and campaign officials and more than 200 individuals whom the DNC proposed that the vice president called to solicit donations.

Investigators also obtained numerous documents from many employees of the White House, the DNC and the Clinton-Gore re-election campaign, as well as persons whom the vice president called.

The evidence gathered by the task force suggests that the vice president made calls to his office to approximately 45 people between the fall of 1995 and the spring of 1996 to raise money for the Democratic National Committee.

However, evidence found by the investigators shows that the vice president solicited only soft money in these calls, not hard money. For example, no donor said the president, vice president solicited hard money.

Donors were given follow-up instructions on donating to DNC soft money accounts, and the amount solicited exceeded hard-money limits. Sometime after the 1994 elections, the DNC began to split large checks into soft and hard money accounts without the donors intent, including several of the donations solicited by the vice president.

However, investigators uncovered no evidence that the vice president was aware of the DNC's practice or in any way knew that donations he solicited would make their way into hard-money accounts.

We are, however, continuing to investigate whether the DNC's practices violate any criminal laws.

Finally, even if it were to assume that the vice president had violated 18 USC, Section 607, the independent counsel statute prohibits me from asking for an independent counsel to investigate allegations that the Justice Department would not prosecute under its existing standards.

Congress inserted this provision into the law so that government officials would not be subject to a different application of the law than other citizens.

In this case, the department's clear, longstanding policy is not to prosecute under 18 USC, Section 607, unless certain aggravating factors are present, such as coercion, knowing disregard of the law, a substantial number of violations or a significant disruption of government functions.

The investigation uncovered no evidence of any of these aggravating factors.

With respect to Secretary O'Leary, on September 19 of this year, we began a preliminary investigation into former Energy Secretary Hazel O'Leary. Allegations had been made that she may have violated federal laws by soliciting a $25,000 contribution for a charitable organization in return for an official meeting with the visiting delegation of Chinese petrochemical officials.

After an extensive review of the documents and more than 40 interviews, including an interview of Johnny Chung, investigators developed no evidence that she had anything to do with the solicitation of the charitable donation.

However, the Justice Department will continue to review whether anyone else may have broken the law in connection with the solicitation and payment of the $25,000 AfriCare donation.

These decisions were arrived at after thousands of hours of investigation and discussion with investigators, attorneys and senior officials at the Justice

Department and the FBI. I am proud of their work. That includes Director [Louis] Freeh, whose counsel I have regularly sought and whose advice I value highly. We may not always agree, but I believe that he and the FBI have done an outstanding investigative job.

However, the decision to ask for an independent counsel is mine, and I alone am responsible for it under the law.

I also want to make clear to everyone that I am not imposing any constraints on the task force ability to pursue the matters they are investigating. I have repeatedly told them to pursue every lead, explore every avenue, interview witnesses and ask any question that is relevant to the matters they are investigating.

If and when there is sufficient grounds to investigate whether a covered may have committed a crime, that is specific and credible information; we will again commence a preliminary investigation under the act as I am required to do.

I urge everyone to study the documents that we have filed with the court. They show how searching our inquiry is, how complex these matters can be and how hard we have worked to do the right thing.

A year is a long time. But it is not long enough to judge the progress of the Justice Department's largest criminal investigation. Many independent counsels and other Justice Department investigations have taken far longer to pursue far fewer and far simpler allegations.

Today's decisions represent if you will a snapshot, not an ending. Our investigation continues, and no allegation will go unexamined. I have referred matters to independent counsels no fewer than six times, and I will not hesitate to do so again if the facts and the law justify it.

In almost two decades as a prosecutor, I have learned that you cannot judge an investigation by what you read in the newspapers. In the end, a prosecutor's work, a prosecutor's success is not measured by headlines or by sound bites, but by diligence, thoroughness and a constant eye on the final result, even when it takes time to do it right.

They should know that we have worked as hard as we can to do the right thing, and now, I'll be happy to answer your questions.

Question: Ms. Reno, what did you tell Mr. Freeh when you rejected his recommendation, and what did he tell you?

Reno: Director Freeh and I have had long and wide-ranging discussions about this and many other matters. I think it is important that people feel free to talk to me, and so I don't think I should discuss my conversations with them.

Question: Is there any chance he offered his resignation?

Reno: Director Freeh, when I met with him today, we talked about this and we talked about a number of other matters that are of concern to both the department and the FBI. And we talked about the future and we talked about what we had to do.

Question: General Reno, do you think it is appropriate for Director Freeh to voice his—to publicly voice his disagreements with you on this issue? . . .

Reno: I think Director Freeh has been very professional in all his conduct with me, and I don't think that he has voiced anything publicly. I think he has given me the benefit of his best advice and counsel, and I value that a very great deal.

Question: Ms. Reno, your Republican critics claim that the outcome today was pre-ordained because the parameters of this investigation were too narrow by being confined to just the question of phone calls.

I'm sure you've been hearing the ruckus about that. And what is your response to their charge that this was simply too narrow of a look, and what went wrong?

Reno: As I have indicated today, we are going to continue to pursue every lead in a wide-ranging investigation.

If there is specific and credible information concerning a covered person, I will invoke the processes of the independent counsel statute.

But this is what I have. This is the evidence I have. I've applied the law respecting the independent counsel, and these are my decisions.

Question: It's been reported that Director Freeh, and certainly many of your critics on Capitol Hill believe, that you have an inherent conflict of interest in deciding—making the decision whether to go forward with an investigation against the person who hired you. Can you explain in layman's terms why you think you do not have such a conflict?

Reno: The Congress, as it passed the independent counsel statute, determined that there were a number of people who were automatically presumed to have a conflict. They said it would be the president, the vice president and Cabinet officials included—and others are included.

They said that before I triggered the independent counsel statute, I had to have specific and credible information that one of these covered persons, whether it be the president or anybody else, may have committed a violation of federal law.

They did that based on my understanding of the statute, to make sure that people didn't trigger an independent counsel at the drop of a hat and to make sure that there was a solid basis for proceeding.

They provided time for a preliminary investigation, which we have just completed in these three instances. Again, it was to make sure that there was a proper review of all the information then available before we went to the court to ask for the appointment of the independent counsel.

And so my response to all people who say there is an inherent conflict is that Congress has recognized and has presumed a conflict, but has said that there has got to be a threshold of information before you can trigger that conflict.

Question: Others are saying you're saying that the investigation will be continuing and ongoing. How extensive will it be? Will all 120 people remain? . . .

Reno: I am committed to putting in whatever resources are necessary in.

And so for the moment, the 120 will remain, and if more are necessary, we will provide them. I want to make sure that as I have indicated, I pursue every lead to make sure that we pursue the evidence to where it takes us and that we make a decision based on the evidence and the law about what we should do after we find where the evidence takes us.

IMF DIRECTOR ON
ASIAN FINANCIAL CRISIS
December 2, 1997

More than a decade of stunning economic growth in East Asia came to a crashing halt in 1997. A currency crisis that began in Thailand in the spring spread through much of the region by the fall, driving down stock prices and endangering economies that had been growing at such a rapid pace that many were known as "tigers." Along with Thailand the hardest hit were Indonesia, Malaysia, the Philippines, and Hong Kong.

The effects of the Asian financial crisis rippled worldwide. Interest rates and unemployment soared in many developing economies, particularly in Latin America and countries of the former Soviet bloc. Stock markets in the industrialized world plunged in late October, including the biggest one-day tumble in the U.S. stock market in a decade. Economists predicted that the weakening of Asia's economies would curb demand in that region for foreign services and technology, moderating what had been robust growth in the U.S. economy.

In a December analysis, the International Monetary Fund (IMF) predicted that the Asian economies would remain in a slump through much of 1998 but would begin picking up again in 1999—if the countries adopted the austere economic and fiscal policies the IMF had prescribed. If those countries did not take corrective action, the IMF said, "the crisis of confidence may persist and spread to other emerging market countries."

During the early months of the crisis, the Clinton administration refused to take a leading role in bailing out the Asian economies. Treasury Secretary Robert Rubin and others in Washington argued that Asia needed to resolve its own problems and that a U.S.-led financial rescue would reduce the incentive for the troubled countries to undertake needed economic reforms. But as the crisis spread and the so-called contagion effect reached worldwide, the administration agreed to participate in rescue programs put together by the IMF.

By year's end the world's economic powers, acting through the IMF, had assembled programs to bail out the troubled Asian economies. The initial price tag was more than $100 billion.

The crisis produced widespread resentment in Asia toward the United States, the IMF, and other representatives of the industrialized world. Some Asian leaders suggested that currency traders—"speculators" in their view— deliberately manipulated the crisis to weaken Asian competition against the West. Malaysia's prime minister, Mahathir Mohamad, told an international financial conference in Hong Kong in September that currency trading was "immoral" and should be illegal.

Many Asians, from the leadership to workers suddenly thrown out of what they had believed were lifetime jobs, angrily denounced outside interference in their economies. IMF managing director Michel Camdessus repeatedly reminded Asian leaders that foreign investment had financed the region's economic boom, and that accepting outside financing meant having to accept the risks of the global marketplace.

Causes of the Crisis

As with any event of the magnitude of the Asian financial crisis, there were many causes. Some, such as the determination of international currency traders to protect their investments, were short-term in nature. Others, including the tendency of most Asian economies to operate with a high degree of corruption, extended back many decades.

Many Asian economies began to stumble in 1996 due to such factors as a strengthening of the U.S. dollar, which made investments in those countries less attractive. Many Asian countries were forced to borrow more heavily, increasing the vulnerability of their economies to the whims of international markets.

As the currency crisis spread throughout Asia, problems that had developed over a period of years came to light. One common thread was the high proportion of bad debt held by Asian banks, many of which had made excessive loans to corporations based on personal or political influence, rather than sound business judgment. Banks also had heavy exposures in inflated real estate markets.

Other long-term economic problems in some or all of the countries included protectionist trade restrictions, government-supported monopolies (in some cases run by family members of high government officials), government subsidies and tax exemptions for inefficient industries, inadequate banking regulations, and a general tolerance of corruption of public officials in exchange for commercial favors. In nearly all cases, the IMF said, these structural problems in the region's economies had been ignored for years or hidden from public view—making them appear doubly serious when they were exposed.

A Rapidly Accelerating Crisis

The first public indications of serious financial instability in Asia came in mid-May when investors began selling off Thailand's currency, the baht, *which—like many Asian currencies—was pegged to the U.S. dollar. Internal economic problems in Thailand, including high short-term debt, the col-*

lapse of an overheated real estate market, competition with China, and a weak banking system had made investors wary of Thailand for some time. When pressure on the baht intensified, the Thai central bank reacted by spending heavily to shore up the currency and introducing exchange controls. Those steps put the country even further in debt.

Thailand on July 2 allowed the baht to float at market rates, and instead it sank as investors noticed that the government was failing to address the country's broader economic problems. Thailand's move, the IMF later said, "immediately raised doubts about the viability of exchange rate arrangements in neighboring countries." At the same time, according to the IMF, fiscal problems in several other countries in the region and as far away as the Czech and Slovak republics made currency investors more skittish about all emerging economies.

The doubts soon turned to action, as investors pulled their money out of Asian currencies: first the Philippines, then Malaysia, then Indonesia. Taiwan, which had not faced the speculative pressure, in mid-October acted on its own to devalue its currency to make its exports more competitive with its neighbors.

The currencies of all those countries plunged steeply, and with little hesitation, through the end of the year. The collapse of the baht was the most severe; by December it had fallen about 60 percent in value against the dollar, according to the IMF. Although some Asian leaders blamed foreign speculators, IMF officials said most of the currency decline was caused by local individuals and corporations seeking the safety of foreign exchange.

By October the crisis had reached Hong Kong, long considered to have one of the most stable economies in the world, in part because its banks had provided much of the investment money that powered Asia's remarkable economic boom. In mid-October, after the Hong Kong dollar began to fall, the Hong Kong stock market suffered a gigantic sell-off in which stocks lost more than 30 percent of their value in a week. The turmoil in Hong Kong generated a stampede in equity markets around the world, including a plunge of nearly 7 percent in the New York Stock Exchange on October 27. The stock market quickly recovered the following week, however. (Stock market, p. 721)

South Korea was the next to suffer, with stock prices and the currency, the won, both falling sharply. For many observers, the developments in South Korea were among the most disturbing of any in Asia. The Korean economies for years had one of the strongest and seemingly most stable in Asia. Some serious problems had been evident, most notably the extreme concentration of business ownership in a few huge conglomerates (called chaebol). Corruption also was institutionalized in Korea, as demonstrated by the fact that two Korean presidents who served during the 1980s each admitted accepting hundreds of millions of dollars in bribes in return for government business deals. But from the public's point of view, there had been little reason to doubt that Korean economic growth could continue indefinitely.

Instability in Thailand and other countries forced overseas investors to take a closer look at Korea. They saw the systemic problems that neither the government nor the private sector were addressing in any serious way. According to the IMF, Korean banks were holding incredibly high levels of bad debt, reaching at least 70 percent of equity in some cases. Much of the debt was owed by Korea's overextended chaebol, which were increasingly unable to meet their debt payments. Several of the chaebol declared bankruptcy in 1997, weakening the nation's financial system and severely undermining the confidence of foreign investors and lenders.

In December, as economic turbulence was at its height in Korea, the country held presidential elections. The three leading presidential candidates at first opposed austerity moves demanded by the IMF in return for a bailout package. But under outside pressure from President Clinton, among others, all three agreed to accept IMF-mandated reforms if elected. The winner was Kim Dae-jung, the most prominent opponent of a succession of military-based authoritarian regimes. (Korean election, p. 892)

Reactions to the Crisis

In addition to causing at least short-term dives in stock markets around the world, the Asian financial crisis had an immediate and dramatic impact on the economies of many countries worldwide. By late summer investors began pulling out of currencies in Latin America (including Argentina, Brazil, and Mexico) and the former Soviet bloc (especially Russia and Ukraine), forcing officials in those countries to raise interest rates and take other steps to defend their currencies. Russia's troubled economy was among the hardest hit: a steep plunge in the stock market in late October undermined the ruble and forced the government to raise interest rates sharply in both November an December. International banks virtually halted their lending to all of those countries through late 1997.

In its December report, the IMF predicted the financial effects on so-called emerging economies could be "relatively transitory" if the Asian crisis was stemmed. But if the Asian financial tumble continued, the damage to the ability of those countries to obtain investment capital "will be more far reaching."

Japan, still struggling to recover from a recession earlier in the 1990s, suddenly found its economy undermined by a crisis in countries that had been among the biggest borrowers from Japanese banks. Japan's fourth-largest brokerage firm folded November 24, sharply undermining confidence in the Japanese financial system and sparking yet another round of selling in Asian stock markets.

Noting the worldwide impact of Asia's troubles, the IMF's Camdessus said in a December 2 speech to Asian business leaders that the crisis demonstrated "that whether a country follows prudent policies is not simply a matter of national concern." The spillover effects of one country's problems "can be so rapid and so costly to countries with basically sound policies that every country has a strong interest in seeing that its neighbors manage their economies well," he said.

IMF Prescriptions

At the urging of the IMF, most of the troubled Asian countries took immediate steps to deal with their short-term problems in hopes of restoring investor confidence. These steps included closing insolvent banks, raising interest rates, allowing currencies to float against the world market, and cutting government expenditures. In most cases these actions partly stemmed the economic slide and gave the countries involved breathing room to deal with longer-term issues.

The suffering countries all appealed to the IMF for emergency bailout programs. Thailand was the first to ask for and receive a rescue package. The IMF, the World Bank, and a group of Asian nations led by Japan agreed August 12 to loan Thailand $16 billion to bolster its foreign reserves to pay for imports and pay off some of its overseas debt. At the time, that package was the second-largest in history, behind the $50 billion rescue of the Mexican economy in 1994–1995.

The bailout package for Thailand was followed by major IMF rescue packages of nearly $40 billion for Indonesia and $57 billion for South Korea. Japan and other economic powers contributed to the packages. The United States, dropping its earlier reluctance to bail out the Asian countries, was among the contributors.

The IMF, as usual, imposed strict conditions that in many cases would force the countries to alter drastically their ways of doing business. Korean firms were forced to lay off thousands of workers, an act with immense social and economic ramifications in a country where most people had believed their jobs were guaranteed for life. The IMF austerity package for Indonesia, if fully implemented, would force President Suharto to strip his family members and friends of business arrangements, including government-sanctioned monopolies, that had made them extremely wealthy.

In his December 2 speech, Camdessus lectured Asian leaders on the necessity of "openness and transparency" in their economic systems. When a government's economic policies are known to the public, he said, "policymakers have more incentive to pursue sound policies." As an example to be avoided, he cited the Thai central bank's secret accumulation of huge short-term liabilities. If the public had been aware of the situation, he said, authorities would have been forced to confront the country's dwindling reserves much sooner and "most likely they would have taken corrective action before reserve losses became so large." Openness also limits the opportunities for corruption, he said, which ultimately weakens any financial system.

The IMF's call for openness was not a welcome one in Asia. Many Asian countries had treated economic information—including the actions of central banks and other policymaking institutions—as state secrets.

Although few in the West disagreed with the IMF on the question of publishing economic data, some critics said IMF prescriptions for austerity (budget cuts and interest-rate hikes) would further weaken the Asian economies, rather than giving them strength to recover. In Washington, some congressional leaders questioned the wisdom of "bailing out" Asian countries that had taken thousands of industrial jobs from the United States and the international bankers who had invested in those economies. Congress was expected to address those issues in 1998 when it considered a Clinton administration request for additional U.S. financing of the IMF.

> *Following is the text of a speech, "Rebuilding Confidence in Asia," delivered by Michel Camdessus, managing director of the International Monetary Fund, on December 2, 1997, to Asian business leaders in Kuala Lumpur, Malaysia:*

I am very pleased to have this opportunity to speak to you, the business leaders of southeast Asia, at this critical moment in the region's economy. The crisis that began in Thailand has now shaken a number of other economies in the region, and its aftershocks have been felt as far away as Latin America and eastern Europe. Countries that have been accustomed to, in some cases, decades of high growth now face the prospect of a marked slowdown in economic activity. This has prompted some observers to suggest that perhaps the so-called "Asian miracle" was only a "mirage."

I do not hold that view. In my opinion, the region's economic success over the last couple of decades can be described in many ways—as outstanding, superlative, and certainly admirable. But it was no "miracle." Rather, it was the result of good policies that fostered saving and investment, including in human development; encouraged innovation and entrepreneurship and a quick response to market signals; and promoted trade. Recent developments have not wiped out past achievements. On the contrary, the region's longer term fundamentals—including its high domestic savings rates, strong fiscal positions, dynamic private sectors, and competitiveness—remain favorable. Moreover, most Asian countries still have a long way to go to catch up with advanced economies. Thus, to all the prophets of gloom and doom I would reply that with a lucid diagnosis of the problems, without complacency, and with appropriate economic adjustments now and sound policies in the future, these countries will be able to rekindle—in a more sustainable way—high rates of growth in the coming years.

In a situation, like the current one, that is evolving quickly, it is difficult to step back and take a longer view. But indeed that is what is required to get to the root of the region's problems and find appropriate solutions. In this spirit, I would like to talk very candidly with you about the causes of the current crisis and what they suggest about the requirements for rebuilding confidence in this dynamic region.

Causes of the Crisis

Let me start with the question that so many have asked: how could events in southeast Asia unfold this way, after so many years of outstanding economic performance?

In the case of Thailand, the answer is fairly clear. To begin with, standard economic indicators revealed large macroeconomic imbalances: the real exchange rate had appreciated considerably; export growth had slowed markedly; the current account deficit was persistently large and was financed increasingly by short-term inflows; and external debt was rising quickly. These problems, in turn, exposed other weaknesses in the economy, including substantial, unhedged foreign borrowing by the private sector, an inflated property market, and a weak and over-exposed banking system.

Markets pointed to the unsustainability of Thailand's policies: equity prices declined, and the exchange rate came under increasing pressure. The IMF [International Monetary Fund] stressed these problems and pressed for urgent action in a continuous dialogue with the Thai authorities during the 18 months leading up to the floating of the baht last July. But after so many years of outstanding macroeconomic performance, it was difficult for the authorities in Thailand—as in other countries—to recognize that severe underlying problems could seriously jeopardize their track record. And this "denial syndrome" contributed to the delay in taking corrective measures. Finally, in the absence of convincing action, the crisis broke.

We all have been troubled by developments in the Thai economy, both because they have been so costly for Thailand and its neighbors and because they were so preventable. But at least the origins of Thailand's problems are, by and large, clear. The more vexing question is why the crisis spread to other countries, such as Indonesia, Malaysia, the Philippines, and Korea.

Part of the explanation has to do with the fact that developments in the Thai economy undermined conditions in neighboring countries. For example, the depreciation of the baht was expected to erode the competitiveness of Thailand's trading partners, and that, in turn, put pressure on their currencies.

But beyond that, developments in Thailand prompted market participants—especially those who had initially underestimated the problems in Thailand—to take a much closer look at the risks in other countries. And what they saw—to different degrees in different economies—were many of the same problems affecting the Thai economy, including overvalued real estate markets, weak and over-extended banking sectors, poor prudential supervision, and substantial private short-term borrowing in foreign currency. Moreover, after Thailand, markets began to look more critically at weaknesses they had previously considered minor, or at least manageable, given time. In other words, markets became less forgiving.

Market doubts were compounded by a general lack of transparency—about the extent of government and central bank liabilities; about the underlying health of the financial sectors and about the links between banks, industry, and government and their possible impact on economic policy. In the absence of adequate information, markets tended to fear the worst and to doubt the capacity of governments to take timely corrective action. The imposition of controls on market activity—and the threat of future controls—not only made investments riskier, but tended to reinforce the view that governments were addressing the symptoms, rather than the causes, of their problems. This sent investors fleeing to safer havens and set back other efforts to restore confidence.

But perhaps the most important factor in the depreciation of exchange rates was the rush by domestic corporations to buy foreign exchange. Expecting that exchange rates would remain stable indefinitely, and in the context of inefficient banking systems, domestic firms had borrowed heavily in foreign currencies in order to take advantage of lower interest rates available in other markets. Once they recognized that the peg might not hold and that their debt service costs might rise, perhaps dramatically, they hastened to sell domestic currency, extending the currency slide.

Finally, in some cases, the contagion can be traced in part to the "denial syndrome" that I referred to earlier—to the conviction that "it couldn't happen to us."

Questions have also arisen about the role of hedge funds [managed by currency investors]. At the request of the NAB countries, the IMF has been looking into this question, talking to market participants and central banks about how hedge funds are set up and regulated, and what role they may have played in the crisis. But from what we know so far, it would be a mistake to blame hedge funds or other market participants for the turmoil in Asia. Turbulence in the market is only a symptom of more serious underlying problems, which are now being addressed seriously in many countries. Nevertheless, there are things that can be done to promote a more orderly working of the markets. For instance, consideration could be given to strengthening large trader reporting requirements; limiting position taking by requiring bankers and brokers to raise collateral and margin requirements so as to limit the use of leverage by hedge funds and other large investors; and other efforts to discourage herd behavior and avoid one-way bets, such as providing better information to markets on government policies and the condition of domestic financial institutions, to encourage investors to trade on fundamentals rather than to run with the herd.

So what does all of this imply about the way in which governments should manage their economies and approach the markets?

The first implication is the most obvious one: the necessity of taking early action to correct macroeconomic imbalances before they precipitate a crisis. This did not happen in Thailand, despite timely and vigorous warnings. Instead, policymakers attacked the symptom of the crisis—the pressure on the baht—and accumulated large reserve losses and forward foreign exchange liabilities in the process. This, together with delays in addressing Thailand's severe financial sector problems and lingering political uncertainties, clearly contributed to a deepening of the crisis and its spread to other economies in the region.

Second, countries may find that they are more vulnerable to crises in other markets than their own economic fundamentals would suggest. Consequently, they may need to take preemptive action to strengthen their policies. Several suggestions come to mind as to where such action might be needed:

- one, maintaining an appropriate exchange rate and exchange rate regime. Clearly, there is no single "right" choice, but more flexible exchange rates can help provide early and visible signals of the need for policy adjustments and are less likely to invite reckless behavior on the part of borrowers and lenders. But regardless of the exchange rate arrangement chosen, appropriate macroeconomic policies are essential to ensure its success;
- two, maintaining an appropriate macroeconomic policy mix to ensure that fiscal positions do not lead to unduly high domestic interest rates, which, in many cases, have contributed to excessive amounts of short-term capital inflows;
- three, strengthening structural policies—especially the policies and institutions, such as prudential supervision, needed to underpin a sound financial system. In particular, it is important that fragilities in the financial system are not allowed to become so acute that the authorities are unwilling to use the interest rate instrument in times of international financial instability;
- and four, carrying out other supporting reforms—what we call "second generation" reforms—to promote domestic competition, increase transparency and accountability, improve governance, help ensure that the benefits of future growth are widely shared, and otherwise strengthen the foundations for future growth.

Developments have shown that whether a country follows prudent policies is not simply a matter of national concern. As we have seen in this region, spillover and contagion effects can be so rapid and so costly to countries with basically sound policies that every country has a strong interest in seeing that its neighbors manage their economies well. Experience shows that there is considerable scope for improving policies when neighboring countries get together on a regular basis to encourage one another—and, at times, to exert some peer pressure on one another—to pursue sound policies. For this reason, it is very encouraging to see the efforts under way to develop a mechanism for more intensive surveillance and dialogue among participating finance ministries and central banks of the Pacific rim to complement the IMF's global surveillance over its members' policies and performance. Of course, to be effective, regional surveillance has to be based on sound economic analysis. In this connection, the IMF stands ready to contribute to regional surveillance in Asia, as requested in the recent Manila meeting and Vancouver Summit meetings, and as it already does in the G-7 and other fora.

Developments in southeast Asia also offer some insight into how governments should approach markets. Perhaps the best place to start would be by giving credit where credit is due: the capital provided by global markets has been a key factor in southeast Asia's exceptional growth rates and its ability to lift so many out of poverty. Certainly, there are risks in tapping global markets. But markets also provide tremendous opportunities to accelerate growth and development, as southeast Asia itself so vividly shows. The key is to approach markets in a responsible manner—with strong macroeconomic fundamentals and sound structural policies that give markets confidence and therefore encourage long-term investment; with respect for the signals that markets provide; and with transparent and market-friendly policies that allow markets to allocate resources efficiently.

Let me say a few more words about the benefits of openness and transparency. When economic policies are transparent, policymakers have more incentive to pursue sound policies. If I may cite one pointed example among many, would the Central Bank of Thailand have accumulated such large forward liabilities if the public had had regular access to information on central bank operations? On the contrary, the authorities would have had to face the problem of Thailand's dwindling reserves much sooner; and most likely, they would have taken corrective action before reserve losses became so large.

Likewise, when timely, accurate, and comprehensive data are readily available, markets adjust more smoothly. Thus, countries are less vulnerable to adverse market reactions when problems eventually come to light, as indeed they always do. Especially when governments are trying to rebuild confidence, a free flow of information allows markets to assess the extent of underlying problems and the seriousness of efforts to correct them. Of course, transparency also limits the opportunities for corruption, which can otherwise distort resource allocation, undermine investor confidence, and inhibit growth. For all of these reasons, openness and transparency can make a substantial contribution to better policies, more stable markets, and hence, more sustainable growth.

Ultimately, the crisis in Asia underlines the need of an orderly liberalization of capital flows to ensure that a greater number of countries can benefit from access to international capital markets, while reducing risks. This does not mean a return to antiquated methods of capital controls, nor does it mean a mad rush to immediate, full liberalization regardless of the risks. Thus, we are working toward an amendment of our Articles of Agreement to include the liberalization of capital flows as a mandate of the IMF and to broaden the institution's jurisdiction to include capital movements, so as to ensure orderly liberalization and proper sequencing and that other requirements to reduce the risks and maximize the benefits of tapping global markets are in place.

As developments have shown, confidence, once lost, is hard to regain. Restoring confidence takes a strong commitment to economic adjustment and reform demonstrated by the implementation of what are often painful measures. It also takes openness and transparency. And, of course, it takes time.

That process is now under way in southeast Asia. The first step has been to design effective strategies to reinforce macroeconomic policies, as needed, strengthen financial systems, and lay the basis for robust growth to resume. With the support of the IMF, Japan, and others in the region, Thailand's new government has recommitted itself to a courageous and comprehensive program that addresses the problems of large external deficits and troubled financial institutions. As a result, the budget is moving back into surplus and a comprehensive restructuring of the financial sector is getting under way. The

Philippines has extended its program with the IMF under which a substantial amount of economic adjustment and reform had already taken place. Indonesia has embarked on a major Fund-supported program to strengthen monetary and fiscal policies, restructure the financial sector, and deregulate the economy. South Korea is now working closely with the IMF to design a similar program that we expect will be worthy of broad international support.

Now comes the more difficult task: implementation. This is the task of the national authorities, and it takes leadership. One aspect of this leadership is to take responsibility for the programs being implemented, explain to citizens why adjustment is needed, and enlist their support. Too often citizens have the impression that the programs their governments are attempting to carry out have been imposed from outside. To authorities who have to carry out painful measures, this may seem convenient; but it is counterproductive because it undermines public support for their efforts. The IMF works very closely with the country authorities to design effective programs. We give our views on the pros and cons of various adjustment measures and on which combinations of measures are likely to work. Needless to say, we do not support programs we think will be ineffective. But ultimately, it is the authorities' decision what the program consists of. Our requirements are: one, that the program be well designed; and two, that it have the authorities' full support.

That being said, the IMF is there to help the countries of this region pull through this difficult period. The staff and management of the IMF are in constant dialogue with the authorities in the region. The programs we are supporting with our financial resources are bold, but realistic, and go to the heart of these economies' problems. In the case of Thailand, Indonesia, and soon Korea, IMF support has helped mobilize additional resources from other bilateral and multilateral resources. Along with the World Bank, the Asian Development Bank, and others, we are also providing a considerable amount of technical assistance, especially on financial sector issues.

Looking ahead, growth can be expected to rebound strongly after a relatively short, but sharp, weakening of economic activity, and a rapid narrowing of external deficits. In fact, we are already seeing improvements in exports, even though recent exchange rate changes have not had much opportunity yet to generate their effects. And as these adjustments take place, each of these countries will be embarking on a longer-term process of structural change that will strengthen their economies in fundamental ways—such as by restructuring their financial systems, increasing domestic competition, and otherwise improving the climate for productive investment and high, but sustainable, growth. That is why I believe that these economies will emerge from this period stronger and more dynamic than before.

What can you, as the business leaders of your countries, do to advance this process? The region has entered a period of slower growth, but with forceful action to tighten macroeconomic policies and forge ahead with financial sector restructuring and other structural measures, confidence can be restored sooner rather than later. One important way in which you can help shorten the period until stronger growth resumes is by helping to improve transparency—for example, by complying with "best practices" in accounting standards in the corporate sector, and by avoiding "connected lending" and other practices that raise doubts about the strength of corporate governance and the links between government, banks and industry. Such steps will help convince markets that your countries do indeed embrace reform and that they have the resolve to put current problems behind them.

TREATY BANNING LAND MINES
December 2–4, 1997

A worldwide movement to ban land mines reached fruition on December 2–4, when leaders from some 120 countries met in Ottawa to sign a treaty banning production, stockpiling, and use of the deadly weapons. The movement was spurred by a grassroots coalition organization, which won a Nobel Peace Prize for its work, and was carried forward by the Canadian government working outside the usual diplomatic channels. "For the first time the majority of nations of the world will agree to ban a weapon which has been in military use by almost every country in the world," Canadian prime minister Jean Chrétien said at the signing ceremony December 2. "For the first time, a global partnership of governments, international institutions and nongovernmental groups has come together—with remarkable speed and spirit—to draft the treat we will sign today."

The Convention on the Prohibition of the Use, Stockpiling, Production and Transfer of Anti-Personnel Mines and on their Destruction, as the treaty was formally called, banned all antipersonnel land mines and required existing stockpiles to be destroyed within four years after the treaty took effect. All existing minefields were to be cleared within ten years, and all signatories to the treaty committed financial and other assistance to the mine-clearing effort. The treaty was to take effect six months after forty countries had ratified it. Canadian foreign minister Lloyd Axworthy, who played a key role in winning approval for the treaty, said he thought that number would be reached within a year.

One signatory notably absent from the treaty was the United States. Although President Bill Clinton had called for the elimination of all land mines in a speech to the United Nations General Assembly in 1994, he subsequently deferred to his military advisers and refused to sign the treaty because it did not exempt the United States from using land mines in the demilitarized zone between North and South Korea. Other countries that did not sign the treaty included China and Russia.

An estimated 100 million land mines, some of them dating from World War II, were strewn through some sixty countries in Europe, Africa, Asia,

and Latin America. Laid during periods of war or civil strife, both in bat-
tlefields and in civilian areas, mines were used not only to stop the ad-
vances of the enemy but to terrorize local populations. Because they could
not be deactivated easily, land mines still killed long after the fighting
ceased. According to the American Red Cross, land mines killed 800 and
maimed 1,200 people every month; the vast majority of victims were civil-
ians, many of them children. "The problem with land mines is that wars
end, peace treaties are signed, armies march away, the guns grow silent—
but the land mines stay," Sen. Patrick J. Leahy, D-Vt., a leader in the fight
to ban the mines, told the Senate in June.

Banning their production and use was only the first step in the cam-
paign to rid the world of land mines. The far more difficult and expen-
sive task was likely to be clearing the millions of mines that had already
been deployed and often forgotten. A land mine cost between $3 and $30 a
piece to produce, but between $300 and $1,000 to deactivate, and the
process was potentially dangerous. About 100,000 mines were cleared each
year. (State Department report on land mines, Historic Documents of 1995,
p. 46)

A Grassroots Movement

Once started, the campaign to complete a land mine treaty moved re-
markably fast. It began in the fall of 1991 when the Vietnam Veterans of
America Foundation and Medico International, a German relief organiza-
tion, launched the International Campaign to Ban Landmines. The inter-
national coalition of nongovernmental organizations (NGOs) was coordi-
nated by Jody Williams, a longtime peace activist, who worked largely
through e-mail from her cabin in Putney, Vermont. Williams had worked
against official U.S. policy in Central America during the 1980s. Together
with other relief organizations that were providing prostheses for the vic-
tims of land mine explosions, these groups issued a joint call for an inter-
national ban on antipersonnel mines.

The coalition grew quickly. By 1993 it had attracted support from sev-
eral countries and from fifty international organizations, including the
International Red Cross and most mainstream religious organizations.
Eventually the coalition included about 1,000 organizations from about
sixty countries, including some 250 groups in the United States. It also at-
tracted support from high-profile figures, including Pope John Paul II and
South African president Nelson Mandela. Perhaps the most famous, how-
ever, was Diana, Princess of Wales; photographs of the princess with land
mine victims from Bosnia, Angola, and elsewhere appeared in tabloids and
photo magazines throughout the world, giving "a face to the victim," in
Jody Williams's words. (Diana's death, p. 647)

The campaign was successful in persuading some countries to stop
producing and exporting mines. But an initial effort to ban the mines
was not totally satisfactory. That occurred in the context of the 1994–1996
round of negotiations to strengthen the land mine protocol of the 1980 Con-
ventional Weapons Convention, which barred the use of inhuman weapons.

*With China, Russia, and other opponents of a ban involved in the talks, the
new protocol required only that all antipersonnel mines be detectable and
that certain of them be made capable of self-destructing. Producers had
nine years to comply with the new standards.*

*Frustrated that the new protocol did not go far enough and with the slug-
gish pace of the permanent United Nations Conference on Disarmament,
the forum in which the talks took place, Canada's Axworthy started a movement to ban the mines altogether. At a meeting of seventy-four governments
and numerous NGOs in Ottawa in October 1996, he invited all nations to
join with Canada to negotiate and sign a land mine ban treaty by the end
of 1997. Over the next few months, in what became known as the "Ottawa
Process," governments and the NGOs held regional meetings to solidify support for a treaty. In September representatives from nearly 100 countries
met in Oslo during a three-week period to negotiate the final language of a
treaty that had been drafted by the Austrian government. Their efforts were
boosted October 10 when the International Campaign to Ban Landmines
and Jody Williams were jointly awarded the Nobel Peace Prize for 1997.
The Nobel committee said its award was intended to influence the treaty
process. "This could be interpreted as a message to the great powers that we
hope they also will eventually choose to sign the treaty," the chairman of the
committee said.*

The U.S. Position

*Although the United States had been the leading producer of land mines,
it was one of the first major countries to promote a global ban. Senator
Leahy led the effort in Congress, successfully sponsoring legislation calling
for a one-year moratorium on the export of U.S. land mines. The moratorium was subsequently extended and then made permanent by President
Clinton on January 17, 1997. At the same time, the president said the nation would destroy most of its stockpile of "dumb" mines—those that do not
self-destruct.*

*Clinton, who in 1994 called for the "eventual elimination" of land mines,
refused to accept any international land mine ban unless it made two exceptions for the United States. On May 16, 1996, Clinton said he would
accept a treaty only if it allowed the United States to continue to deploy
"smart" mines, which self-destruct after a few hours or days, anywhere the
United States believed it was militarily necessary, and only if the United
States could continue to use both smart and dumb mines in the demilitarized zone between North and South Korea. "This initiative sets out a clear
path of a global ban on [antipersonnel land mines]," the administration
said, "but ensures that as the United States pursues a ban, essential U.S.
military requirements and commitments to our allies will be protected."*

*In January 1997, Clinton formally announced that the United States
would not participate in the Ottawa Process but would instead pursue a
treaty through the UN disarmament conference, which met in Geneva. The
reason the administration gave was because some countries, such as Rus-*

846

sia and China, that were major producers and suppliers of antipersonnel mines participated in the Geneva talks but not in the Ottawa Process. Critics of the administration said that in reality Clinton was stalling, knowing that Russia and China, among other countries, were unlikely to ever agree on a total ban on land mines; actions at the Geneva disarmament conference were adopted only when all participants agreed. In essence, critics said, Clinton was unwilling to oppose his senior military officials. In a letter dated July 10, 1997, sixteen four-star generals and admirals, including Gen. John M. Shalikashvili, chairman of the Joint Chiefs, wrote that continued reliance on antipersonnel land mines was necessary "to ensure maximum protection for our soldiers and Marines who carry out national security policy at grave personal risk."

When it became clear that the Ottawa Process was likely to produce a treaty totally banning land mines, the Clinton administration decided to make one last effort to win its exemptions. On August 18, the White House announced that it would join the Ottawa Process and send a delegation to Oslo for the final negotiations of the land mine treaty. But the administration's attempts to amend the treaty were rebuffed. "The poor countries won't give up 'dumb' mines if we don't give up 'smart' mines," said Caleb Rossiter, director of Demilitarization for Democracy, a pro-ban organization. The International Committee of the Red Cross, in an August 26 statement, said that "a total and immediate prohibition on the use of all antipersonnel mines is essential for the effectiveness and credibility of the treaty." That sentiment was echoed by many delegations during the Oslo meetings. At the conclusion of those meetings, the administration announced that it could not sign the treaty.

In an attempt to salvage some semblance of leadership on the issue, the administration on October 31 announced plans to increase its spending on demining activities to nearly $77 million in 1998 and to spearhead an effort to boost international spending on mine clearance by 500 percent to $1 billion a year. "This call for a concerted effort by the international community is based on the premise that the best way to protect civilians from land mines is to pull mines from the soil like the noxious weeds that they are," said Secretary of State Madeleine K. Albright.

The Signing Ceremony

Fittingly, Canada on December 3 was the first country to sign the treaty. It also was the first country to ratify the treaty, having done so the week before the treaty was even open for signing. By the end of the year, 123 countries had signed the treaty. Those, in addition to the United States, that did not sign included China, Russia, India, Pakistan, Israel, Egypt, and North and South Korea. In most of these areas, ongoing regional conflicts meant that continued use of land mines was likely. Although they did not sign the treaty, representatives from several of those countries attended the signing ceremonies in Ottawa and participated in round-table talks on clearing mines and providing aid to victims.

Clearing the already laid mine fields was likely to be the next big challenge for the land mine coalition. "The ban itself will provide little comfort to some 2,000 people whose lives will be forever shattered this month by the mines currently in the ground," said Cornelio Sommaruga, president of the International Committee of the Red Cross. Upon signing the treaty, several countries committed themselves to increased spending for mine removal. Canada said it would spend about $75 million over five years; Norway pledged $100 million.

Following are excerpts from the Convention of the Prohibition of the Use, Stockpiling, Production and Transfer of Anti-Personnel Mines and on their Destruction, which was opened for signing in Ottawa, Canada, on December 3–4, 1997:

Preamble

The States Parties,

Determined to put an end to the suffering and casualties caused by anti-personnel mines, that kill or maim hundreds of people every week, mostly innocent and defenceless civilians and especially children, obstruct economic development and reconstruction, inhibit the repatriation of refugees and internally displaced persons, and have other severe consequences for years after emplacement,

Believing it necessary to do their utmost to contribute in an efficient and coordinated manner to face the challenge of removing anti-personnel mines placed throughout the world, and to assure their destruction,

Wishing to do their utmost in providing assistance for the care and rehabilitation, including the social and economic reintegration of mine victims,

Recognizing that a total ban of anti-personnel mines would also be an important confidence-building measure,

Welcoming the adoption of the Protocol on Prohibitions or Restrictions on the Use of Mines, Booby-Traps and Other Devices, as amended on 3 May 1996, annexed to the Convention on Prohibitions or Restrictions on the Use of Certain Conventional Weapons Which May Be Deemed to Be Excessively Injurious or to Have Indiscriminate Effects, and calling for the early ratification of this Protocol by all States which have not yet done so,

Welcoming also United Nations General Assembly Resolution 51/45 S of 10 December 1996 urging all States to pursue vigorously an effective, legally-binding international agreement to ban the use, stockpiling, production and transfer of anti-personnel landmines,

Welcoming furthermore the measures taken over the past years, both unilaterally and multilaterally, aiming at prohibiting, restricting or suspending the use, stockpiling, production and transfer of anti-personnel mines,

Stressing the role of public conscience in furthering the principles of humanity as evidenced by the call for a total ban of anti-personnel mines and recognizing the efforts to that end undertaken by the International Red Cross and Red Crescent Movement, the International Campaign to Ban Landmines and numerous other non-governmental organizations around the world,

Recalling the Ottawa Declaration of 5 October 1996 and the Brussels Declaration of 27 June 1997 urging the international community to negotiate an international and legally binding agreement prohibiting the use, stockpiling, production and transfer of anti-personnel mines,

Emphasizing the desirability of attracting the adherence of all States to this Convention, and determined to work strenuously towards the promotion of its universalization in all relevant fora including, inter alia, the United Nations, the Conference on Disarmament, regional organizations, and groupings, and review conferences of the Convention on Prohibitions or Restrictions on the Use of Certain Conventional Weapons Which May Be Deemed to Be Excessively Injurious or to Have Indiscriminate Effects,

Basing themselves on the principle of international humanitarian law that the right of the parties to an armed conflict to choose methods or means of warfare is not unlimited, on the principle that prohibits the employment in armed conflicts of weapons, projectiles and materials and methods of warfare of a nature to cause superfluous injury or unnecessary suffering and on the principle that a distinction must be made between civilians and combatants,

Have agreed as follows:

Article 1

General obligations

1. Each State Party undertakes never under any circumstances:
   a) To use anti-personnel mines;
   b) To develop, produce, otherwise acquire, stockpile, retain or transfer to anyone, directly or indirectly, anti-personnel mines;
   c) To assist, encourage or induce, in any way, anyone to engage in any activity prohibited to a State Party under this Convention.
2. Each State Party undertakes to destroy or ensure the destruction of all anti-personnel mines in accordance with the provisions of this Convention.

Article 2

Definitions

1. "Anti-personnel mine" means a mine designed to be exploded by the presence, proximity or contact of a person and that will incapacitate, injure or kill one or more persons. Mines designed to be detonated by the presence, proximity or contact of a vehicle as opposed to a person, that are equipped with anti-handling devices, are not considered anti-personnel mines as a result of being so equipped.
2. "Mine" means a munition designed to be placed under, on or near the ground or other surface area and to be exploded by the presence, proximity or contact of a person or a vehicle.

3. "Anti-handling device" means a device intended to protect a mine and which is part of, linked to, attached to or placed under the mine and which activates when an attempt is made to tamper with or otherwise intentionally disturb the mine.

4. "Transfer" involves, in addition to the physical movement of anti-personnel mines into or from national territory, the transfer of title to and control over the mines, but does not involve the transfer of territory containing emplaced anti-personnel mines.

5. "Mined area" means an area which is dangerous due to the presence or suspected presence of mines.

Article 3

Exceptions

1. Notwithstanding the general obligations under Article 1, the retention or transfer of a number of anti-personnel mines for the development of and training in mine detection, mine clearance, or mine destruction techniques is permitted. The amount of such mines shall not exceed the minimum number absolutely necessary for the above-mentioned purposes.

2. The transfer of anti-personnel mines for the purpose of destruction is permitted.

Article 4

Destruction of stockpiled anti-personnel mines

Except as provided for in Article 3, each State Party undertakes to destroy or ensure the destruction of all stockpiled anti-personnel mines it owns or possesses, or that are under its jurisdiction or control, as soon as possible but not later than four years after the entry into force of this Convention for that State Party.

Article 5

Destruction of anti-personnel mines in mined areas

1. Each State Party undertakes to destroy or ensure the destruction of all anti-personnel mines in mined areas under its jurisdiction or control, as soon as possible but not later than ten years after the entry into force of this Convention for that State Party.

2. Each State Party shall make every effort to identify all areas under its jurisdiction or control in which anti-personnel mines are known or suspected to be emplaced and shall ensure as soon as possible that all anti-personnel mines in mined areas under its jurisdiction or control are perimeter-marked, monitored and protected by fencing or other means, to ensure the effective exclusion of civilians, until all anti-personnel mines contained therein have been destroyed. The marking shall at least be to the standards set out in the Protocol on Prohibitions or Restrictions on the Use of Mines, Booby-Traps and Other Devices, as amended on 3 May 1996, annexed to the Convention on Prohibitions or Restric-

tions on the Use of Certain Conventional Weapons Which May Be Deemed to Be Excessively Injurious or to Have Indiscriminate Effects.

3. If a State Party believes that it will be unable to destroy or ensure the destruction of all anti-personnel mines referred to in paragraph 1 within that time period, it may submit a request to a Meeting of the States Parties or a Review Conference for an extension of the deadline for completing the destruction of such anti-personnel mines, for a period of up to ten years.

4. Each request shall contain:
    a) The duration of the proposed extension;
    b) A detailed explanation of the reasons for the proposed extension, including:
        (i) The preparation and status of work conducted under national demining programs;
        (ii) The financial and technical means available to the State Party for the destruction of all the anti-personnel mines; and
        (iii) Circumstances which impede the ability of the State Party to destroy all the anti-personnel mines in mined areas;
    c) The humanitarian, social, economic, and environmental implications of the extension; and
    d) Any other information relevant to the request for the proposed extension.

5. The Meeting of the States Parties or the Review Conference shall, taking into consideration the factors contained in paragraph 4, assess the request and decide by a majority of votes of States Parties present and voting whether to grant the request for an extension period.

6. Such an extension may be renewed upon the submission of a new request in accordance with paragraphs 3, 4 and 5 of this Article. In requesting a further extension period a State Party shall submit relevant additional information on what has been undertaken in the previous extension period pursuant to this Article.

Article 6
International cooperation and assistance

1. In fulfilling its obligations under this Convention each State Party has the right to seek and receive assistance, where feasible, from other States Parties to the extent possible.

2. Each State Party undertakes to facilitate and shall have the right to participate in the fullest possible exchange of equipment, material and scientific and technological information concerning the implementation of this Convention. The States Parties shall not impose undue restrictions on the provision of mine clearance equipment and related technological information for humanitarian purposes.

3. Each State Party in a position to do so shall provide assistance for the care and rehabilitation, and social and economic reintegration, of mine

victims and for mine awareness programs. Such assistance may be provided, inter alia, through the United Nations system, international, regional or national organizations or institutions, the International Committee of the Red Cross, national Red Cross and Red Crescent societies and their International Federation, non-governmental organizations, or on a bilateral basis.

4. Each State Party in a position to do so shall provide assistance for mine clearance and related activities. Such assistance may be provided, inter alia, through the United Nations system, international or regional organizations or institutions, non-governmental organizations or institutions, or on a bilateral basis, or by contributing to the United Nations Voluntary Trust Fund for Assistance in Mine Clearance, or other regional funds that deal with demining.

5. Each State Party in a position to do so shall provide assistance for the destruction of stockpiled anti-personnel mines.

6. Each State Party undertakes to provide information to the database on mine clearance established within the United Nations system, especially information concerning various means and technologies of mine clearance, and lists of experts, expert agencies or national points of contact on mine clearance.

7. States Parties may request the United Nations, regional organizations, other States Parties or other competent intergovernmental or non-governmental fora to assist its authorities in the elaboration of a national demining program to determine, inter alia:

   a) The extent and scope of the anti-personnel mine problem;
   b) The financial, technological and human resources that are required for the implementation of the program;
   c) The estimated number of years necessary to destroy all anti-personnel mines in mined areas under the jurisdiction or control of the concerned State Party;
   d) Mine awareness activities to reduce the incidence of mine-related injuries or deaths;
   e) Assistance to mine victims;
   f) The relationship between the Government of the concerned State Party and the relevant governmental, inter-governmental or non-governmental entities that will work in the implementation of the program.

8. Each State Party giving and receiving assistance under the provisions of this Article shall cooperate with a view to ensuring the full and prompt implementation of agreed assistance programs.

Article 7

Transparency measures

1. Each State Party shall report to the Secretary-General of the United Nations as soon as practicable, and in any event not later than 180 days after the entry into force of this Convention for that State Party on:

a) The national implementation measures referred to in Article 9;

b) The total of all stockpiled anti-personnel mines owned or possessed by it, or under its jurisdiction or control, to include a breakdown of the type, quantity and, if possible, lot numbers of each type of anti-personnel mine stockpiled;

c) To the extent possible, the location of all mined areas that contain, or are suspected to contain, anti-personnel mines under its jurisdiction or control, to include as much detail as possible regarding the type and quantity of each type of anti-personnel mine in each mined area and when they were emplaced;

d) The types, quantities and, if possible, lot numbers of all anti-personnel mines retained or transferred for the development of and training in mine detection, mine clearance or mine destruction techniques, or transferred for the purpose of destruction, as well as the institutions authorized by a State Party to retain or transfer anti-personnel mines, in accordance with Article 3;

e) The status of programs for the conversion or de-commissioning of anti-personnel mine production facilities;

f) The status of programs for the destruction of anti-personnel mines in accordance with Articles 4 and 5, including details of the methods which will be used in destruction, the location of all destruction sites and the applicable safety and environmental standards to be observed;

g) The types and quantities of all anti-personnel mines destroyed after the entry into force of this Convention for that State Party, to include a breakdown of the quantity of each type of anti-personnel mine destroyed, in accordance with Articles 4 and 5, respectively, along with, if possible, the lot numbers of each type of anti-personnel mine in the case of destruction in accordance with Article 4;

h) The technical characteristics of each type of anti-personnel mine produced, to the extent known, and those currently owned or possessed by a State Party, giving, where reasonably possible, such categories of information as may facilitate identification and clearance of anti-personnel mines; at a minimum, this information shall include the dimensions, fusing, explosive content, metallic content, colour photographs and other information which may facilitate mine clearance; and

i) The measures taken to provide an immediate and effective warning to the population in relation to all areas identified under paragraph 2 of Article 5.

2. The information provided in accordance with this Article shall be updated by the States Parties annually, covering the last calendar year, and reported to the Secretary-General of the United Nations not later than 30 April of each year.

3. The Secretary-General of the United Nations shall transmit all such reports received to the States Parties.

Article 8
Facilitation and clarification of compliance

1. The States Parties agree to consult and cooperate with each other regarding the implementation of the provisions of this Convention, and to work together in a spirit of cooperation to facilitate compliance by States Parties with their obligations under this Convention.

2. If one or more States Parties wish to clarify and seek to resolve questions relating to compliance with the provisions of this Convention by another State Party, it may submit, through the Secretary-General of the United Nations, a Request for Clarification of that matter to that State Party. Such a request shall be accompanied by all appropriate information. Each State Party shall refrain from unfounded Requests for Clarification, care being taken to avoid abuse. A State Party that receives a Request for Clarification shall provide, through the Secretary-General of the United Nations, within 28 days to the requesting State Party all information which would assist in clarifying this matter.

3. If the requesting State Party does not receive a response through the Secretary-General of the United Nations within that time period, or deems the response to the Request for Clarification to be unsatisfactory, it may submit the matter through the Secretary-General of the United Nations to the next Meeting of the States Parties. The Secretary-General of the United Nations shall transmit the submission, accompanied by all appropriate information pertaining to the Request for Clarification, to all States Parties. All such information shall be presented to the requested State Party which shall have the right to respond.

4. Pending the convening of any meeting of the States Parties, any of the States Parties concerned may request the Secretary-General of the United Nations to exercise his or her good offices to facilitate the clarification requested.

5. The requesting State Party may propose through the Secretary-General of the United Nations the convening of a Special Meeting of the States Parties to consider the matter. The Secretary-General of the United Nations shall thereupon communicate this proposal and all information submitted by the States Parties concerned, to all States Parties with a request that they indicate whether they favour a Special Meeting of the States Parties, for the purpose of considering the matter. In the event that within 14 days from the date of such communication, at least one-third of the States Parties favours such a Special Meeting, the Secretary-General of the United Nations shall convene this Special Meeting of the States Parties within a further 14 days. A quorum for this Meeting shall consist of a majority of States Parties.

6. The Meeting of the States Parties or the Special Meeting of the States Parties, as the case may be, shall first determine whether to consider the matter further, taking into account all information submitted by

the States Parties concerned. The Meeting of the States Parties or the Special Meeting of the States Parties shall make every effort to reach a decision by consensus. If despite all efforts to that end no agreement has been reached, it shall take this decision by a majority of States Parties present and voting.

7. All States Parties shall cooperate fully with the Meeting of the States Parties or the Special Meeting of the States Parties in the fulfilment of its review of the matter, including any fact-finding missions that are authorized in accordance with paragraph 8.

8. If further clarification is required, the Meeting of the States Parties or the Special Meeting of the States Parties shall authorize a fact-finding mission and decide on its mandate by a majority of States Parties present and voting. At any time there quested State Party may invite a fact-finding mission to its territory. Such a mission shall take place without a decision by a Meeting of the States Parties or a Special Meeting of the States Parties to authorize such a mission. The mission, consisting of up to 9 experts, designated and approved in accordance with paragraphs 9 and 10, may collect additional information on the spot or in other places directly related to the alleged compliance issue under the jurisdiction or control of the requested State Party.

9. The Secretary-General of the United Nations shall prepare and update a list of the names, nationalities and other relevant data of qualified experts provided by States Parties and communicate it to all States Parties. Any expert included on this list shall be regarded as designated for all fact-finding missions unless a State Party declares its non-acceptance in writing. In the event of non-acceptance, the expert shall not participate in fact-finding missions on the territory or any other place under the jurisdiction or control of the objecting State Party, if the non-acceptance was declared prior to the appointment of the expert to such missions.

10. Upon receiving a request from the Meeting of the States Parties or a Special Meeting of the States Parties, the Secretary-General of the United Nations shall, after consultations with the requested State Party, appoint the members of the mission, including its leader. Nationals of States Parties requesting the fact-finding mission or directly affected by it shall not be appointed to the mission. The members of the fact-finding mission shall enjoy privileges and immunities under Article VI of the Convent ion on the Privileges and Immunities of the United Nations, adopted on 13 February 1946.

11. Upon at least 72 hours notice, the members of the fact-finding mission shall arrive in the territory of the requested State Party at the earliest opportunity. The requested State Party shall take the necessary administrative measures to receive, transport and accommodate the mission, and shall be responsible for ensuring the security of the mission to the maximum extent possible while they are on territory under its control.

12. Without prejudice to the sovereignty of the requested State Party, the fact-finding mission may bring into the territory of the requested State Party the necessary equipment which shall be used exclusively for gathering information on the alleged compliance issue. Prior to its arrival, the mission will advise the requested State Party of the equipment that it intends to utilize in the course of its fact-finding mission.

13. The requested State Party shall make all efforts to ensure that the fact-finding mission is given the opportunity to speak with all relevant persons who may be able to provide information related to the alleged compliance issue.

14. The requested State Party shall grant access for the fact-finding mission to all areas and installations under its control where facts relevant to the compliance issue could be expected to be collected. This shall be subject to any arrangements that the requested State Party considers necessary for:

   a) The protection of sensitive equipment, information and areas;

   b) The protection of any constitutional obligations the requested State Party may have with regard to proprietary rights, searches and seizures, or other constitutional rights; or

   c) The physical protection and safety of the members of the fact-finding mission.

   In the event that the requested State Party makes such arrangements, it shall make every reasonable effort to demonstrate through alternative means its compliance with this Convention.

15. The fact-finding mission may remain in the territory of the State Party concerned for no more than 14 days, and at any particular site no more than 7 days, unless otherwise agreed.

16. All information provided in confidence and not related to the subject matter of the fact-finding mission shall be treated on a confidential basis.

17. The fact-finding mission shall report, through the Secretary-General of the United Nations, to the Meeting of the States Parties or the Special Meeting of the States Parties the results of its findings.

18. The Meeting of the States Parties or the Special Meeting of the States Parties shall consider all relevant information, including the report submitted by the fact-finding mission, and may request the requested State Party to take measures to address the compliance issue within a specified period of time. The requested State Party shall report on all measures taken in response to this request.

19. The Meeting of the States Parties or the Special Meeting of the States Parties may suggest to the States Parties concerned ways and means to further clarify or resolve the matter under consideration, including the initiation of appropriate procedures in conformity with international law. In circumstances where the issue at hand is determined to be due to circumstances beyond the control of the requested State

Party, the Meeting of the States Parties or the Special Meeting of the States Parties may recommend appropriate measures, including the use of cooperative measures referred to in Article 6.

20. The Meeting of the States Parties or the Special Meeting of the States Parties shall make every effort to reach its decisions referred to in paragraphs 18 and 19 by consensus, otherwise by a two-thirds majority of States Parties present and voting.

Article 9

National implementation measures

Each State Party shall take all appropriate legal, administrative and other measures, including the imposition of penal sanctions, to prevent and suppress any activity prohibited to a State Party under this Convention undertaken by persons or on territory under its jurisdiction or control.

[Articles 10–14 omitted]

Article 15

Signature

This convention, done at Oslo, Norway, on 18 September 1997, shall be open for signature at Ottawa, Canada, by all States from 3 December 1997 until 4 December 1997, and at the United Nations Headquarters in New York from 5 December 1997 until its entry in to force.

Article 16

Ratification, acceptance, approval or accession

1. This Convention is subject to ratification, acceptance or approval of the Signatories.
2. It shall be open for accession by any State which has not signed the Convention.
3. The instruments of ratification, acceptance, approval or accession shall be deposited with the Depositary.

Article 17

Entry into force

1. This Convention shall enter into force on the first day of the sixth month after the month in which the 40th instrument of ratification, acceptance, approval or accession has been deposited.
2. For any State which deposits its instrument of ratification, acceptance, approval or accession after the date of the deposit of the 40th instrument of ratification, acceptance, approval or accession, this Convention shall enter into force on the first day of the sixth month after the date on which that State has deposited its instrument of ratification, acceptance, approval or accession.

Article 18

Provisional application

Any State may at the time of its ratification, acceptance, approval or accession, declare that it will apply provisionally paragraph 1 of Article 1 of this Convention pending its entry into force.

Article 19

Reservations

The Articles of this Convention shall not be subject to reservations.

Article 20

Duration and withdrawal

1. This Convention shall be of unlimited duration.
2. Each State Party shall, in exercising its national sovereignty, have the right to withdraw from this Convention. It shall give notice of such withdrawal to all other States Parties, to the Depositary and to the United Nations Security Council. Such instrument of withdrawal shall include a full explanation of the reasons motivating this withdrawal.
3. Such withdrawal shall only take effect six months after the receipt of the instrument of withdrawal by the Depositary. If, however, on the expiry of that six-month period, the withdrawing State Party is engaged in an armed conflict, the withdrawal shall not take effect before the end of the armed conflict.
4. The withdrawal of a State Party from this Convention shall not in any way affect the duty of States to continue fulfilling the obligations assumed under any relevant rules of international law.

[Articles 21–22 omitted]

UN TREATY ON GLOBAL WARMING
December 11, 1997

World leaders on December 11, 1997, reached agreement on a treaty that supporters said might save the Earth from environmental disaster—and that opponents predicted would cause economic hardship worldwide. If fully carried out, the United Nations treaty on climate change would represent a significant effort to curb man-made damage to the Earth's atmosphere, even though the actual extent of that damage was not clear.

In agreeing to the treaty, thirty-eight industrialized nations promised to curb their use of the major fossil fuels: coal, petroleum products, and natural gas. Burning fossil fuels produced carbon dioxide and other so-called greenhouse gases that, many scientists believed, were warming the Earth's climate.

Reducing reliance on those fuels would involve much more than changing energy sources: It would force a major transformation in modern industrial society by mandating more fuel-efficient automobiles, electrical generating plants, and industrial complexes. Developing nations were not required to take comparable steps, creating a likely conflict between the world's "have" and "have-not" nations that had the potential to undermine the treaty's effectiveness or even prevent it from ever becoming law.

In the United States, by far the leading producer of greenhouse gases, prospects for Senate ratification of the treaty appeared dim in the weeks after it was signed. A powerful coalition of treaty opponents included leading organizations representing the nation's manufacturers, farmers, and small businesses. President Bill Clinton, who had embraced the treaty, said he would delay asking the Senate to approve it until developing countries agreed to reduce their greenhouse gas emissions.

Global Warming Assumptions

For more than a decade numerous scientists had suggested that rapid increases in the production of greenhouse gases—resulting from factors such as world population growth, expanded industrial production, and eco-

nomic development in the Third World—would lead inevitably to a global warming of the planet. These gases trapped heat in the atmosphere, just as a greenhouse absorbs and contains heat from the sun.

These predictions became official doctrine of the United Nations in 1995 when the Intergovernmental Panel on Climate Change, a conference of some 2,000 scientists, concluded that global warming was underway. The panel predicted that the Earth's average temperature would rise by 1.8 to 6.3 degrees Fahrenheit by the year 2100, depending on a number of variables. Although the number of degrees of temperature might not seem large, scientists said the rate of change was the important factor. The Earth would heat up faster in 100 years than it had in the previous 10,000 years.

Among the panel's predictions: Sea levels would rise, possibly enough to flood low-lying coastal areas in the United States (such as those in Florida and Louisiana) and in other countries, especially Bangladesh. Some regions could see increased rainfall, while others would be plagued by prolonged drought. Humans might experience an upsurge in respiratory and heat-related illnesses. Some species of wildlife might become extinct because of changes in their habitat, while others would be able to adapt to those changes. Reductions in the moisture content of the soil in many areas (including the Great Plains of the United States) might curb agricultural production, but other areas might become more arable, permitting expanded agriculture. Forests would be decimated in many areas of the world.

Despite the 1995 consensus by the UN panel, a vocal minority of scientists derided these predictions and said they saw no evidence of serious climate change. One of the most prominent critics of the consensus was Richard S. Lindzen, the Alfred P. Sloan Professor of Meteorology at the Massachusetts Institute of Technology, who predicted that increases in carbon dioxide would not generate higher global temperatures.

Leading Up to Kyoto

At the 1992 "Earth Summit" in Rio de Janeiro, Brazil, delegates representing 160 nations approved a nonbinding treaty pledging to halt the global increase in greenhouse gas emissions. In the years after adoption of that treaty, the United States and most other industrialized nations fell short of its goals. The 1995 scientific consensus gave the impetus for an agreement in 1996 on the need for a legally binding treaty.

UN members held eight negotiating sessions leading up to the Kyoto conference, debating various proposals for stopping, and ultimately reversing, the growth of greenhouse gas emissions. Each of the proposals centered around the level of emissions to be allowed at benchmark points (the years 2000, 2010, and 2020) in comparison to the amount of gases actually generated in 1990. All those issues were still on the table when many of the world's leaders met for another Earth Summit at UN headquarters in 1997. (1992 Earth Summit, Historic Documents of 1992, p. 499; 1997 summit, p. 480)

As the eighth session was underway in Bonn in October, the two main opposing positions were announced on the same day, October 22. Speaking in Washington, Clinton announced the U.S. position calling for stabilizing emissions of greenhouse gases by the industrialized countries at the 1990 level by the year 2010. Emissions would then be reduced slightly by 2020. Clinton proposed a combination of tax credits and research subsidies to encourage U.S. industry to reduce greenhouse gas emissions. Clinton said his plan would confront the issue of climate change "with an environmentally sound and economically strong strategy." Clinton's plan disappointed environmentalists, who said it fell far short of what was needed to curb global warming.

A group of developing nations, calling themselves the Group of 77 Plus China, called for much sharper greenhouse gas reductions by the industrialized world on a faster schedule. As a first step, the developing nations demanded that the industrialized nations reduce their emissions by 7.5 percent below the 1990 levels by the year 2005. Further reductions would be required in the subsequent years so that by 2020 the emissions would be 35 percent below the 1990 levels.

Those sharply conflicting proposals illustrated the fundamental conflict in the negotiations. Representatives of developing nations said they would not curb their emissions until the industrialized nations took serious and measurable steps to curb their emissions. The developing nations argued that the United States, Great Britain, and other wealthy nations had built their economies for more than a century on industries that damaged the Earth's environment, and so they should lead any effort to reverse the damage.

Representatives of many industrialized nations acknowledged that history of environmental neglect and agreed to take the lead. But Clinton and others argued that developing nations should be required to limit emissions as well, so they would not repeat the mistakes of the past.

Kyoto Negotiations

Final negotiations toward a treaty began in Kyoto on December 1, with a great deal of pessimism on all sides about the prospects of a workable agreement. Negotiators representing 150 countries made virtually no progress at first, pending the arrival of the man considered the key to the U.S. position: Vice President Al Gore. An ardent environmentalist, Gore for years had studied and talked about global warming; it was generally assumed that Clinton relied heavily on him for advice on the issue.

Gore arrived in Kyoto on December 8 and told the 2,200 delegates that the United States was determined to reach an agreement and that he had instructed the U.S. delegation to "show increased negotiating flexibility." Three days later negotiators reached agreement on a treaty mandating deeper reductions than Clinton had proposed.

Under the agreed upon treaty, global emissions were to be reduced by 30 percent below the levels that had been projected for 2010. Each of the 38 industrialized nations would be assigned a target for reducing emissions, taking into account a variety of factors, including past emissions and economic production. For the United States, the treaty would require reducing emissions by 7 percent below the 1990 levels by 2012. That would mean significant reductions because U.S. emissions had been expected to be about 30 percent higher in 2010 than in 1990 if no steps were taken to curb the use of fossil fuels.

To meet the required reduction levels, industrial nations would have to produce more fuel-efficient automobiles and substantially reduce consumption of electricity by industry, business, and consumers at home. The burning of coal in electrical generating plants almost certainly would have to be phased out.

The agreement also included provisions encouraging international investment in environmentally sound projects in developing countries. Negotiators, however, left unresolved one of the central issues: the extent to which countries could sell or trade their permissible levels of emissions. The Clinton administration had called the issue crucial for U.S. ratification of the treaty, noting that the United States could meet its emissions-reduction target only by trading reductions with other countries. Negotiations on that issue were scheduled for late 1998, meaning that a Senate vote was not likely until 1999 at the earliest. In the meantime, the Clinton administration would make another attempt to persuade developing countries to accept emissions limits.

Reaction in the United States

Representatives of major business organizations denounced the agreement. "It is a terrible deal and the president should not sign it," was the response of William K. O'Keefe, president of the Global Climate Coalition, an industry association that long had opposed a global warming treaty. O'Keefe vowed an intense campaign against the treaty if it reached the Senate.

Even before the Kyoto negotiations, the Senate had laid down a marker, unanimously approving a resolution opposing any treaty that did not require emissions reductions by developing countries. Several senators who had observed the negotiations in Kyoto declared the Senate would not approve the treaty as written. They included John Kerry, D-Mass., who supported the treaty but said his colleagues would block it unless it applied to developing countries such as China and India. A harsh critic of the treaty, Frank H. Murkowski, R-Alaska, who chaired the Energy and Natural Resources Committee, called it "dead on arrival" at the Senate.

Following are excerpts from the Kyoto Protocol to the United Nations Framework Convention on Global Climate Change, adopted December 11, 1997, by a UN conference in Kyoto, Japan:

Article 2

1. Each Party included in Annex I in achieving its quantified emission limitation and reduction commitments under Article 3, in order to promote sustainable development, shall:

(a) Implement and/or further elaborate policies and measures in accordance with its national circumstances, such as:

(i) Enhancement of energy efficiency in relevant sectors of the national economy;

(ii) Protection and enhancement of sinks and reservoirs of greenhouse gases not controlled by the Montreal Protocol, taking into account its commitments under relevant international environmental agreements; promotion of sustainable forest management practices, afforestation and reforestation;

(iii) Promotion of sustainable forms of agriculture in light of climate change considerations;

(iv) Promotion, research, development and increased use of new and renewable forms of energy, of carbon dioxide sequestration technologies and of advanced and innovative environmentally sound technologies;

(v) Progressive reduction or phasing out of market imperfections, fiscal incentives, tax and duty exemptions and subsidies in all greenhouse gas emitting sectors that run counter to the objective of the Convention and apply market instruments;

(vi) Encouragement of appropriate reforms in relevant sectors aimed at promoting policies and measures which limit or reduce emissions of greenhouse gases not controlled by the Montreal Protocol;

(vii) Measures to limit and/or reduce emissions of greenhouse gases not controlled by the Montreal Protocol in the transport sector;

(viii) Limitation and/or reduction of methane through recovery and use in waste management, as well as in the production, transport and distribution of energy;

(b) Cooperate with other such Parties to enhance the individual and combined effectiveness of their policies and measures adopted under this Article, pursuant to Article 4, paragraph 2(e)(i), of the Convention. To this end, these Parties shall take steps to share their experience and exchange information on such policies and measures, including developing ways of improving their comparability, transparency and effectiveness. The Conference of the Parties serving as the meeting of the Parties to this Protocol shall, at its first session or as soon as practicable thereafter, consider ways to facilitate such cooperation, taking into account all relevant information.

2. The Parties included in Annex I shall pursue limitation or reduction of emissions of greenhouse gases not controlled by the Montreal Protocol from aviation and marine bunker fuels, working through the International Civil Aviation Organization and the International Maritime Organization, respectively.

3. The Parties included in Annex I shall strive to implement policies and measures under this Article in such a way as to minimize adverse effects, in-

cluding the adverse effects of climate change, effects on international trade, and social, environmental and economic impacts on other Parties, especially developing country Parties and in particular those identified in Article 4, paragraphs 8 and 9 of the Convention, taking into account Article 3 of the Convention. The Conference of the Parties serving as the meeting of the Parties to this Protocol may take further action, as appropriate, to promote the implementation of the provisions of this paragraph.

4. The Conference of the Parties serving as the meeting of the Parties to this Protocol, if it decides that it would be beneficial to coordinate any of the policies and measures in paragraph 1 (a) above, taking into account different national circumstances and potential effects, shall consider ways and means to elaborate the coordination of such policies and measures.

Article 3

1. The Parties included in Annex I shall, individually or jointly, ensure that their aggregate anthropogenic carbon dioxide equivalent emissions of the greenhouse gases listed in Annex A do not exceed their assigned amounts, calculated pursuant to their quantified emission limitation and reduction commitments inscribed in Annex B and in accordance with the provisions of this Article, with a view to reducing their overall emissions of such gases by at least 5 per cent below 1990 levels in the commitment period 2008 to 2012.

2. Each Party included in Annex I shall, by 2005, have made demonstrable progress in achieving its commitments under this Protocol.

3. The net changes in greenhouse gas emissions from sources and removals by sinks resulting from direct human-induced land use change and forestry activities, limited to afforestation, reforestation, and deforestation since 1990, measured as verifiable changes in stocks in each commitment period shall be used to meet the commitments in this Article of each Party included in Annex I. The greenhouse gas emissions from sources and removals by sinks associated with those activities shall be reported in a transparent and verifiable manner and reviewed in accordance with Articles 7 and 8.

4. Prior to the first session of the Conference of the Parties serving as the meeting of the Parties to this Protocol, each Party included in Annex I shall provide for consideration by the Subsidiary Body for Scientific and Technological Advice data to establish its level of carbon stocks in 1990 and to enable an estimate to be made of its changes in carbon stocks in subsequent years. The Conference of the Parties serving as the meeting of the Parties to this Protocol shall, at its first session or as soon as practicable thereafter, decide upon modalities, rules and guidelines as to how and which additional human-induced activities related to changes in greenhouse gas emissions and removals in the agricultural soil and land use change and forestry categories, shall be added to, or subtracted from, the assigned amount for Parties included in Annex I, taking into account uncertainties, transparency in reporting, verifiability, the methodological work of the Intergovernmental Panel on Climate Change, the advice provided by the Subsidiary Body for Scientific and Technological Advice in accordance with Article 5 and the decisions of the Con-

ference of the Parties. Such a decision shall apply in the second and subsequent commitment periods. A Party may choose to apply such a decision on these additional human-induced activities for its first commitment period, provided that these activities have taken place since 1990.

5. The Parties included in Annex I undergoing the process of transition to a market economy whose base year or period was established pursuant to decision 9/CP.2 of the Conference of the Parties at its second session, shall use that base year or period for the implementation of their commitments under this Article. Any other Party included in Annex I undergoing the process of transition to a market economy which has not yet submitted its first national communication under Article 12 of the Convention may also notify the Conference of the Parties serving as the meeting of the Parties to this Protocol that it intends to use a historical base year or period other than 1990 for the implementation of its commitments under this Article. The Conference of the Parties serving as the meeting of the Parties to this Protocol shall decide on the acceptance of such notification.

6. Taking into account Article 4, paragraph 6, of the Convention, in the implementation of their commitments under this Protocol other than those in this Article, a certain degree of flexibility shall be allowed by the Conference of the Parties serving as the meeting of the Parties to this Protocol to the Parties included in Annex I undergoing the process of transition to a market economy.

7. In the first quantified emission limitation and reduction commitment period, from 2008 to 2012, the assigned amount for each Party included in Annex I shall be equal to the percentage inscribed for it in Annex B of its aggregate anthropogenic carbon dioxide equivalent emissions of the greenhouse gases listed in Annex A in 1990, or the base year or period determined in accordance with paragraph 5 above, multiplied by five. Those Parties included in Annex I for whom land use change and forestry constituted a net source of greenhouse gas emissions in 1990 shall include in their 1990 emissions base year or period the aggregate anthropogenic carbon dioxide equivalent emissions minus removals in 1990 from land use change for the purposes of calculating their assigned amount.

8. Any Party included in Annex I may use 1995 as its base year for hydrofluorocarbons, perfluorocarbons and sulphur hexafluoride, for the purposes of the calculation referred to in paragraph 7 above.

9. Commitments for subsequent periods for Parties included in Annex I shall be established in amendments to Annex B to this Protocol, which shall be adopted in accordance with the provisions of Article 20, paragraph 7. The Conference of the Parties serving as the meeting of the Parties to this Protocol shall initiate the consideration of such commitments at least seven years before the end of the first commitment period mentioned in paragraph 7 above.

10. Any emission reduction units, or any part of an assigned amount, which a Party acquires from another Party in accordance with the provisions of Article 6 and of Article 16 shall be added to the assigned amount for that Party.

11. Any emission reduction units, or any part of an assigned amount, which a Party transfers to another Party in accordance with the provisions of Article 6 and of Article 16 shall be subtracted from the assigned amount for that Party.

12. Any certified emission reductions which a Party acquires from another Party in accordance with the provisions of Article 12 shall be added to the assigned amount for that Party.

13. If the emissions of a Party included in Annex I during a commitment period are less than its assigned amount under this Article, this difference shall, on request of that Party, be added to the assigned amount for that Party for subsequent commitment periods.

14. Each Party included in Annex I shall strive to implement the commitments mentioned in paragraph 1 above in such a way as to minimize adverse social, environmental and economic impacts on developing country Parties, particularly those identified in Article 4, paragraphs 8 and 9, of the Convention. In line with relevant decisions of the Conference of the Parties on the implementation of those paragraphs, the Conference of the Parties serving as the meeting of the Parties to this Protocol shall, at its first session, consider what actions are necessary to minimize the adverse effects of climate change and/or the impacts of response measures on Parties referred to in those paragraphs. Among the issues to be considered shall be the establishment of funding, insurance and transfer of technology.

Article 4

1. Any Parties included in Annex I that have agreed to jointly fulfil their commitments under Article 3 shall be deemed to have met those commitments provided that their total combined aggregate anthropogenic carbon dioxide equivalent emissions of the greenhouse gases listed in Annex A do not exceed their assigned amounts calculated pursuant to their quantified emission limitation and reduction commitments inscribed in Annex B and in accordance with the provisions of Article 3. The respective emission level allocated to each of the Parties to the agreement shall be set out in that agreement.

2. The Parties to any such agreement shall notify the secretariat of the terms of the agreement on the date of deposit of their instruments of ratification, acceptance, approval or accession. The secretariat shall in turn inform the Parties and signatories to the Convention of the terms of the agreement.

3. The agreement shall remain in operation for the duration of the commitment period specified in Article 3, paragraph 7.

4. If Parties acting jointly do so in the framework of, and together with, a regional economic integration organization, any alteration in the composition of the organization after adoption of this Protocol shall not affect existing commitments under this Protocol. Any alteration in the composition of the organization shall only apply for the purposes of those commitments under Article 3 that are adopted subsequent to that revision.

5. In the event of failure by the Parties to such an agreement to achieve their total combined level of emission reductions, each Party to such an agreement shall be responsible for its own level of emissions set out in the agreement.

6. If Parties acting jointly do so in the framework of, and together with, a regional economic integration organization which is itself a Party to this Protocol, each member State of that regional economic integration organization individually, and together with the regional economic integration organization acting in accordance with Article 23, shall, in the event of failure to achieve the total combined level of emission reductions, be responsible for its level of emissions as notified in accordance with this Article. . . .

Article 6

1. For the purpose of meeting its commitments under Article 3, any Party included in Annex I may transfer to, or acquire from, any other such Party emission reduction units resulting from projects aimed at reducing anthropogenic emissions by sources or enhancing anthropogenic removals by sinks of greenhouse gases in any sector of the economy, provided that:

(a) Any such project has the approval of the Parties involved;

(b) Any such project provides a reduction in emissions by sources, or an enhancement of removals by sinks, that is additional to any that would otherwise occur;

(c) It does not acquire any emission reduction units if it is not in compliance with its obligations under Articles 5 and 7; and

(d) The acquisition of emission reduction units shall be supplemental to domestic actions for the purposes of meeting commitments under Article 3.

2. The Conference of the Parties serving as the meeting of the Parties to this Protocol may, at its first session or as soon as practicable thereafter, further elaborate guidelines for the implementation of this Article, including for verification and reporting.

3. A Party included in Annex I may authorize legal entities to participate, under its responsibility, in actions leading to the generation, transfer or acquisition under this Article of emission reduction units.

4. If a question of implementation by a Party included in Annex I of the requirements referred to in this paragraph is identified in accordance with the relevant provisions of Article 8, transfers and acquisitions of emission reduction units may continue to be made after the question has been identified, provided that any such units may not be used by a Party to meet its commitments under Article 3 until any issue of compliance is resolved. . . .

Article 9

1. The Conference of the Parties serving as the meeting of the Parties to this Protocol shall periodically review this Protocol in the light of the best

available scientific information and assessments on climate change and its impacts, as well as relevant technical, social and economic information. Such reviews shall be coordinated with pertinent reviews under the Convention, in particular those required by Article 4, paragraph 2(d), and Article 7, paragraph 2(a), of the Convention. Based on these reviews, the Conference of the Parties serving as the meeting of the Parties to this Protocol shall take appropriate action.

2. The first review shall take place at the second session of the Conference of the Parties serving as the meeting of the Parties to this Protocol. Further reviews shall take place at regular intervals and in a timely manner.

Article 10

All Parties, taking into account their common but differentiated responsibilities and their specific national and regional development priorities, objectives and circumstances, without introducing any new commitments for Parties not included in Annex I, but reaffirming existing commitments in Article 4, paragraph 1, of the Convention, and continuing to advance the implementation of these commitments in order to achieve sustainable development, taking into account Article 4, paragraphs 3, 5 and 7, of the Convention, shall:

(a) Formulate, where relevant and to the extent possible, cost-effective national, and where appropriate regional programmes to improve the quality of local emission factors, activity data and/or models which reflect the socio-economic conditions of each Party for the preparation and periodic updating of national inventories of anthropogenic emissions by sources and removals by sinks of all greenhouse gases not controlled by the Montreal Protocol, using comparable methodologies to be agreed upon by the Conference of the Parties, and consistent with the guidelines for national communications adopted by the Conference of the Parties;

(b) Formulate, implement, publish and regularly update national and, where appropriate, regional programmes containing measures to mitigate climate change and measures to facilitate adequate adaptation to climate change:

    (i) Such programmes would, *inter alia*, concern the energy, transport and industry sectors as well as agriculture, forestry and waste management. Furthermore, adaptation technologies and methods for improving spatial planning would improve adaptation to climate change; and

    (ii) Parties included in Annex I shall submit information on action under this Protocol, including national programmes, according to the guidelines laid down in Article 8; and other Parties shall seek to include in their national communications, as appropriate, information on programmes which contain measures that the Party believes contribute to addressing climate change and its adverse impacts, including the abatement of increase in greenhouse gas emissions, and enhancement of and removals by sinks, capacity building and adaptation measures.

(c) Cooperate in the promotion of effective modalities for the development, application and diffusion of, and take all practicable steps to promote, facilitate and finance, as appropriate, the transfer of, or access to, environmentally sound technologies, know-how, practices and processes pertinent to climate change, in particular to developing countries, including the formulation of policies and programmes for the effective transfer of environmentally sound technologies that are publicly owned or in the public domain and the creation of an enabling environment for the private sector, to promote and enhance access to, and transfer of, environmentally sound technologies;

(d) Cooperate in scientific and technical research and promote the maintenance and the development of systematic observation systems and development of data archives to reduce uncertainties related to the climate system, the adverse impacts of climate change and the economic and social consequences of various response strategies, and promote the development and strengthening of endogenous capacities and capabilities to participate in international and intergovernmental efforts, programmes and networks on research and systematic observation, taking into account Article 5 of the Convention;

(e) Cooperate in and promote at the international level, and, where appropriate, using existing bodies, the development and implementation of education and training programmes, including the strengthening of national capacity building, in particular human and institutional capacities and the exchange or secondment of personnel to train experts in this field, in particular for developing countries, and facilitate at the national level public awareness and public access to information on climate change. Suitable modalities should be developed to implement these activities through the relevant bodies of the Convention taking into account Article 6 of the Convention;

(f) Include in their national communications information on programmes and activities undertaken pursuant to this Article in accordance with relevant decisions of the Conference of the Parties; and

(g) Give full consideration, in implementing the commitments in this Article, to Article 4, paragraph 8, of the Convention.

Article 11

1. In the implementation of Article 10, Parties shall take into account the provisions of Article 4, paragraphs 4, 5, 7, 8 and 9 of the Convention.

2. In the context of the implementation of Article 4, paragraph 1, of the Convention, in accordance with the provisions of Article 4, paragraph 3, and Article 11 of the Convention, and through the operating entity or entities of the financial mechanism of the Convention, the developed country Parties and other developed Parties included in Annex II to the Convention shall:

(a) Provide new and additional financial resources to meet the agreed full costs incurred by developing country Parties in advancing the implementation of existing commitments under Article 4, paragraph 1 (a), of the Convention that are covered in Article 10, subparagraph (a); and

(b) Also provide such financial resources, including for the transfer of technology, needed by the developing country Parties to meet the agreed full incremental costs of advancing the implementation of existing commitments in Article 4, paragraph 1, of the Convention that are covered by Article 10 and that are agreed between a developing country Party and the international entity or entities referred to in Article 11 of the Convention, in accordance with that Article.

The implementation of these existing commitments shall take into account the need for adequacy and predictability in the flow of funds and the importance of appropriate burden sharing among developed country Parties. The guidance to the financial mechanism of the Convention in relevant decisions of the Conference of the Parties, including those agreed before the adoption of this Protocol, shall apply *mutatis mutandis* to the provisions of this paragraph.

3. The developed country Parties and other developed Parties in Annex li to the Convention may also provide, and developing country Parties avail themselves of, financial resources for the implementation of Article 10, through bilateral, regional and other multilateral channels.

Article 12

1. A clean development mechanism is hereby defined.

2. The purpose of the clean development mechanism shall be to assist Parties not included in Annex I in achieving sustainable development and in contributing to the ultimate objective of the Convention, and to assist Parties included in Annex I in achieving compliance with their quantified emission limitation and reduction commitments under Article 3.

3. Under the clean development mechanism:

(a) Parties not included in Annex I will benefit from project activities resulting in certified emission reductions; and

(b) Parties included in Annex I may use the certified emission reductions accruing from such project activities to contribute to compliance with part of their quantified emission limitation and reduction commitments under Article 3, as determined by the Conference of the Parties serving as the meeting of the Parties to this Protocol.

4. The clean development mechanism shall be subject to the authority and guidance of the Conference of the Parties serving as the meeting of the Parties to this Protocol and be supervised by an executive board of the clean development mechanism.

5. Emission reductions resulting from each project activity shall be certified by operational entities to be designated by the Conference of the Parties serving as the meeting of the Parties to this Protocol, on the basis of:

(a) Voluntary participation approved by each Party involved;

(b) Real, measurable, and long-term benefits related to the mitigation of climate change; and

(c) Reductions in emissions that are additional to any that would occur in the absence of the certified project activity.

6. The clean development mechanism shall assist in arranging funding of certified project activities as necessary.

7. The Conference of the Parties serving as the meeting of the Parties to this Protocol shall, at its first session, elaborate modalities and procedures with the objective of ensuring transparency, efficiency and accountability through independent auditing and verification of project activities.

8. The Conference of the Parties serving as the meeting of the Parties to this Protocol shall ensure that a share of the proceeds from certified project activities is used to cover administrative expenses as well as to assist developing country Parties that are particularly vulnerable to the adverse effects of climate change to meet the costs of adaptation.

9. Participation under the clean development mechanism, including in activities mentioned in paragraph 3(a) above and acquisition of certified emission reductions, may involve private and/or public entities, and is to be subject to whatever guidance may be provided by the executive board of the clean development mechanism.

10. Certified emission reductions obtained during the period from the year 2000 up to the beginning of the first commitment period can be used to assist in achieving compliance in the first commitment period.

Article 13

1. The Conference of the Parties, the supreme body of the Convention, shall serve as the meeting of the Parties to this Protocol.

2. Parties to the Convention that are not Parties to this Protocol may participate as observers in the proceedings of any session of the Conference of the Parties serving as the meeting of the Parties to this Protocol. When the Conference of the Parties serves as the meeting of the Parties to this Protocol, decisions under this Protocol shall be taken only by those that are Parties to it.

3. When the Conference of the Parties serves as the meeting of the Parties to this Protocol, any member of the Bureau of the Conference of the Parties representing a Party to the Convention but, at that time, not a Party to this Protocol, shall be substituted by an additional member to be elected by and from amongst the Parties to this Protocol.

4. The Conference of the Parties serving as the meeting of the Parties to this Protocol shall keep under regular review the implementation of this Protocol and shall make, within its mandate, the decisions necessary to promote its effective implementation. It shall perform the functions assigned to it by this Protocol and shall:

(a) Assess, on the basis of all information made available to it in accordance with the provisions of this Protocol, the implementation of this Protocol by the Parties, the overall effects of the measures taken pursuant to this Protocol, in particular environmental, economic and social effects as well as their cumulative impacts and the extent to which progress towards the objective of the Convention is being achieved;

(b) Periodically examine the obligations of the Parties under this Protocol, giving due consideration to any reviews required by Article 4, paragraph 2(d), and Article 7, paragraph 2, of the Convention, in the light of the objective of the Convention, the experience gained in its implementation and the evolution of scientific and technological knowledge, and in this respect consider and adopt regular reports on the implementation of this Protocol;

(c) Promote and facilitate the exchange of information on measures adopted by the Parties to address climate change and its effects, taking into account the differing circumstances, responsibilities and capabilities of the Parties and their respective commitments under this Protocol;

(d) Facilitate, at the request of two or more Parties, the coordination of measures adopted by them to address climate change and its effects, taking into account the differing circumstances, responsibilities and capabilities of the Parties and their respective commitments under this Protocol;

(e) Promote and guide, in accordance with the objective of the Convention and the provisions of this Protocol, and taking fully into account the relevant decisions by the Conference of the Parties, the development and periodic refinement of comparable methodologies for the effective implementation of this Protocol, to be agreed on by the Conference of the Parties serving as the meeting of the Parties to this Protocol;

(f) Make recommendations on any matters necessary for the implementation of this Protocol;

(g) Seek to mobilize additional financial resources in accordance with Article 11, paragraph 2;

(h) Establish such subsidiary bodies as are deemed necessary for the implementation of this Protocol;

(i) Seek and utilize, where appropriate, the services and cooperation of, and information provided by, competent international organizations and intergovernmental and non-governmental bodies; and

(j) Exercise such other functions as may be required for the implementation of this Protocol, and consider any assignment resulting from a decision by the Conference of the Parties.

5. The rules of procedure of the Conference of the Parties and financial procedures of the Convention shall be applied *mutatis mutandis* under this Protocol, except as may be otherwise decided by consensus by the Conference of the Parties serving as the meeting of the Parties to this Protocol.

6. The first session of the Conference of the Parties serving as the meeting of the Parties to this Protocol shall be convened by the secretariat in conjunction with the first session of the Conference of the Parties that is scheduled after the date of the entry into force of this Protocol. Subsequent ordinary sessions of the Conference of the Parties serving as the meeting of the Parties to this Protocol shall be held every year and in conjunction with ordinary sessions of the Conference of the Parties unless otherwise decided by the Conference of the Parties serving as the meeting of the Parties to this Protocol.

7. Extraordinary sessions of the Conference of the Parties serving as the meeting of the Parties to this Protocol shall be held at such other times as may be deemed necessary by the Conference of the Parties serving as the meeting of the Parties to this Protocol, or at the written request of any Party, provided that, within six months of the request being communicated to the Parties by the secretariat, it is supported by at least one third of the Parties.

8. The United Nations, its specialized agencies and the International Atomic Energy Agency, as well as any State member thereof or observers thereto not party to the Convention, may be represented at sessions of the Conference of the Parties serving as the meeting of the Parties to this Protocol as observers. Any body or agency, whether national or international, governmental or non-governmental, which is qualified in matters covered by this Protocol and which has informed the secretariat of its wish to be represented at a session of the Conference of the Parties serving as the meeting of the Parties to this Protocol as an observer, may be so admitted unless at least one third of the Parties present object. The admission and participation of observers shall be subject to the rules of procedure, as referred to in paragraph 5 above. . . .

Article 18

The provisions of Article 14 of the Convention on settlement of disputes shall apply *mutatis mutandis* to this Protocol.

Article 19

1. Any Party may propose amendments to this Protocol.

2. Amendments to this Protocol shall be adopted at an ordinary session of the Conference of the Parties serving as the meeting of the Parties to this Protocol. The text of any proposed amendment to this Protocol shall be communicated to the Parties by the secretariat at least six months before the meeting at which it is proposed for adoption. The secretariat shall also communicate the text of any proposed amendments to the Parties and signatories to the Convention and, for information, to the Depositary.

3. The Parties shall make every effort to reach agreement on any proposed amendment to this Protocol by consensus. If all efforts at consensus have been exhausted, and no agreement reached, the amendment shall as a last resort be adopted by a three-fourths majority vote of the Parties present and

voting at the meeting. The adopted amendment shall be communicated by the secretariat to the Depositary, who shall circulate it to all Parties for their acceptance.

4. Instruments of acceptance in respect of an amendment shall be deposited with the Depositary. An amendment adopted in accordance with paragraph 3 above shall enter into force for those Parties having accepted it on the ninetieth day after the date of receipt by the Depositary of an instrument of acceptance by at least three fourths of the Parties to this Protocol.

5. The amendment shall enter into force for any other Party on the ninetieth day after the date on which that Party deposits with the Depositary its instrument of acceptance of the said amendment. . . .

Article 21

1. Each Party shall have one vote, except as provided for in paragraph 2 below.

2. Regional economic integration organizations, in matters within their competence, shall exercise their fight to vote with a number of votes equal to the number of their member States which are Parties to this Protocol. Such an organization shall not exercise its fight to vote if any of its member States exercises its fight, and vice versa.

Article 22

The Secretary-General of the United Nations shall be the Depositary of this Protocol.

Article 23

1. This Protocol shall be open for signature and subject to ratification, acceptance or approval by States and regional economic integration organizations which are Parties to the Convention. It shall be open for signature at United Nations Headquarters in New York from 16 March 1998 to 15 March 1999. This Protocol shall be open for accession from the day after the date on which it is closed for signature. Instruments of ratification, acceptance, approval or accession shall be deposited with the Depositary.

2. Any regional economic integration organization which becomes a Party to this Protocol without any of its member States being a Party shall be bound by all the obligations under this Protocol. In the case of such organizations, one or more of whose member States is a Party to this Protocol, the organization and its member States shall decide on their respective responsibilities for the performance of their obligations under this Protocol. In such cases, the organization and the member States shall not be entitled to exercise rights under this Protocol concurrently.

3. In their instruments of ratification, acceptance, approval or accession, regional economic integration organizations shall declare the extent of their competence with respect to the matters governed by this Protocol. These or-

ganizations shall also inform the Depositary, who shall in turn inform the Parties, of any substantial modification in the extent of their competence.

Article 24

1. This Protocol shall enter into force on the ninetieth day after the date on which not less than 55 Parties to the Convention, incorporating Parties included in Annex I which accounted in total for at least 55 per cent of the total carbon dioxide emissions for 1990 of the Parties included in Annex I, have deposited their instruments of ratification, acceptance, approval or accession.

2. For the purposes of this Article, "the total carbon dioxide emissions for 1990 of the Parties included in Annex I" means the amount communicated on or before the date of adoption of this Protocol by the Parties included in Annex I in their first national communications submitted in accordance with Article 12 of the Convention.

3. For each State or regional economic integration organization that ratifies, accepts or approves this Protocol or accedes thereto after the conditions set out in paragraph 1 above for the entry into force have been fulfilled, this Protocol shall enter into force on the ninetieth day following the date of deposit of its instrument of ratification, acceptance, approval or accession.

4. For the purposes of this Article, any instrument deposited by a regional economic integration organization shall not be counted as additional to those deposited by States members of the organization.

Article 25

No reservations may be made to this Protocol.

Article 26

1. At any time after three years from the date on which this Protocol has entered into force for a Party, that Party may withdraw from this Protocol by giving written notification to the Depositary.

2. Any such withdrawal shall take effect upon expiry of one year from the date of receipt by the Depositary of the notification of withdrawal, or on such later date as may be specified in the notification of withdrawal.

3. Any Party that withdraws from the Convention shall be considered as also having withdrawn from this Protocol.

Article 27

The original of this Protocol, of which the Arabic, Chinese, English, French, Russian and Spanish texts are equally authentic, shall be deposited with the Secretary-General of the United Nations.

Done at Kyoto this tenth day of December one thousand nine hundred and ninety-seven.

[Annex A omitted]

Annex B

Quantity emission limitation or reduction commitment

Party	(percentage of base year or period)
Australia	108
Austria	92
Belgium	92
Bulgaria[a]	92
Canada	94
Croatia[a]	95
Czech Republic[a]	92
Denmark	92
Estonia[a]	92
European Community	92
Finland	92
France	92
Germany	92
Greece	92
Hungary[a]	94
Iceland	110
Ireland	92
Italy	92
Japan	94
Latvia[a]	92
Liechtenstein	92
Lithuania[a]	92
Luxembourg	92
Monaco	92
Netherlands	92
New Zealand	100
Norway	101
Poland[a]	94
Portugal	92
Romania[a]	92
Russian Federation[a]	100
Slovakia[a]	92
Slovenia[a]	92
Spain	92
Sweden	92
Switzerland	92
Ukraine[a]	100
United Kingdom of Great Britain and Northern Ireland	92
United States of America	93

[a] Countries that are undergoing the process of transition to a market economy.

SECRETARY OF STATE ON NEW GOVERNMENT IN THE CONGO
December 12, 1997

President Mobutu Sese Seko of Zaire, one of the world's longest-reigning dictators, was toppled in May 1997 by a ragtag rebel army aided by some of his many local and regional enemies. After nearly thirty-two years in power, Mobutu was ousted with relative ease. His regime was so unpopular and corrupt that supporters barely made an effort to protect it.

Mobutu's place was taken by a little-known opponent, Laurent Kabila, who had led the victorious rebel forces only since October 1996. Kabila proclaimed himself president and promised democracy in the country he renamed the Democratic Republic of the Congo.

Kabila's initial steps toward democracy were not promising. He jailed many political opponents, including dozens of officials from the former Mobutu regime, and for more than two months he blocked a United Nations investigation into a massacre of Rwandan refugees and others allegedly committed by his forces. U.S. Secretary of State Madeleine K. Albright met with Kabila in the capital city, Kinshasa, on December 12 and pressed him to translate his promises on democracy and human rights into action.

The successful rebellion against Mobutu was one of two civil conflicts in African countries named after the Congo River. The Republic of the Congo, to the north and west of the former Zaire, was engulfed by factional fighting during the summer. Forces loyal to a former president, General Denis Sassou-Nguesso, captured much of the country from the government of President Pascal Lissouba. The fighting devastated the capital, Brazzaville, and made refugees of more than half its 900,000 residents.

In addition to humanitarian and diplomatic issues, the conflicts in the two Congolese nations were of interest worldwide because of the potential wealth of both countries. The Democratic Republic of the Congo (Zaire) possessed some of the greatest mineral riches, including copper, gold, magnesium, diamonds, and cobalt, of any country in Africa. The Republic of the Congo—along with Angola to the south—had jurisdiction over offshore oilfields in the Gulf of Guinea, which were said to have the potential to rival production in the Persian Gulf region.

Mobutu's Reign

Virtually no one outside of a handful of supporters mourned the departure of Mobutu—a leader who personified corruption and authoritarian rule in post-colonial Africa. Mobutu, then a colonel in the Congolese army, seized power in September 1960 from the government headed by leftist prime minister Patrice Lamumba. Congo was torn by a civil war at the time, with the eastern province of Katanga (now Shaba) attempting to secede. Many observers suggested that Mobutu was encouraged by the Central Intelligence Agency, which feared Lamumba's alleged ties to the Soviet Union. Regardless of the extent of the CIA role, the United States actively supported Mobutu with weapons and aid once he was in power. Mobutu stepped aside as leader in 1961 but again seized power in 1965 and did not relinquish it until driven from the country nearly thirty-two years later.

Mobutu renamed the country Zaire and in 1971 engineered his unopposed election as president. The Zairian constitution described him as "the embodiment of the nation." Along with a handful of trusted aides, Mobutu built a political and financial empire based on repression and corruption. Political dissent was repressed; foreign corporations doing business in Zaire were required to pay enormous commissions to the government treasury, which Mobutu looted for his own benefit and to pay for the cooperation of his military allies.

Mobutu amassed a personal fortune widely believed to amount to hundreds of millions of dollars and spent it lavishly on mansions along the French Riviera and in his home village of Gbadolite. Meanwhile the Zairian people remain mired in poverty despite the vast mineral wealth of their country. Battered by corruption and the decline of copper prices, Zaire's economy deteriorated in the 1980s, leaving a nation that should have been one of the richest in Africa just as impoverished as its neighbors.

Western governments diplomatically ignored Mobutu's excesses and supported him as an anticommunist bulwark in central Africa. Mobutu's intervention in one of Africa's cold war-era factional struggles planted the seeds of his eventual undoing. In 1975 he aided one of two rival factions attempting to take control of Angola following the withdrawal of the Belgian colonial regime. Mobutu sided with the faction also favored by the Ford administration, against a faction aided by the Soviet Union and Cuba. The latter faction prevailed at that time, and also a decade later when the Reagan administration called on Zaire for help in trying to oust the leftist Angolan regime. In 1997 the Angolan government won revenge by supporting Kabila's army as it marched against Mobutu.

Ousting Mobutu

The final assault on Mobutu's reign began in 1993 and 1994 when bloody civil wars in Burundi and Rwanda, to the east of Zaire, drove more than a million refugees into Zaire. Most of the refugees were Hutus, the majority ethnic faction in Rwanda that had been responsible for massacring hun-

dreds of thousands of minority Tutsis. In late 1996 the Tutsi-led Rwandan government, along with Uganda and Angola, provided weapons, soldiers, and logistical support for a small anti-Mobutu guerrilla force in eastern Zaire. Kabila, a one-time Marxist who for years had tried unsuccessfully to foment insurrection against Mobutu, emerged in October 1996 as spokesman for the guerrillas. (Rwandan massacres, Historic Documents of 1996, p. 809)

The Kabila forces, many of them Rwandan Tutsis led by Rwandan military officers, stormed through refugee camps in eastern Zaire—reportedly killing thousands of Hutus—and easily swept aside elements of Mobutu's faltering army. They won their key victory in March 1997 by taking over Kisangani, the most important city in eastern Zaire. Dying of prostate cancer, Mobutu returned from a hospital in Switzerland in a final effort to save his government but found little popular support and his military weakened by decades of corruption.

As Kabila's forces advanced on Kinshasa, Mobutu's former allies in Washington and Paris declared that he should seek a negotiated settlement. He followed that advice on April 29, agreeing to face-to-face talks with Kabila, moderated by South African president Nelson Mandela. Those talks led nowhere because Kabila had no reason to make concessions to a man his ragtag army was about to oust from power. The end came on May 17 when Mobutu, following the advice of his generals, yielded power and fled to his palace in Gbadolite. From there Mobutu quickly sought exile in Morocco, where he died in September.

Kabila Takes Over

As rebel forces stormed into Kinshasa the day after Mobutu capitulated, Kabila declared himself president of the Democratic Republic of Congo. Kabila said he was suspending Mobutu's constitution and would form a "national salvation government" to rule the country until a new constitution could be written and elections held.

Kabila inherited a country ravaged by war and Mobutu's thievery. But rather than reaching out to various segments of a troubled society, Kabila acted quickly to impose his will. He spurned other anti-Mobutu leaders, including former prime minister Etienne Tshisekedi, considered by many to have the broadest base of support in the country. Tshisekedi responded by refusing to recognize Kabila's government and going into opposition. According to estimates by diplomats, Kabila jailed several hundred officials of the former Mobutu regime, along with others who criticized the new government.

As evidence mounted that Kabila's forces had slaughtered thousands of Hutu refugees during their drive for power, Western governments demanded an accounting. Meeting early in June with UN Secretary General Kofi Annan and then with Bill Richardson, the U.S. ambassador to the United Nations, Kabila agreed to cooperate with a UN investigation of the alleged massacres. But Kabila threw numerous roadblocks in the way of the

UN investigation, leading Annan on October 1 to recall the leaders of the probe, as a sign of protest. Kabila later relented and allowed the investigations to proceed.

Amid the diplomatic skirmishing over whether Kabila would allow an investigation of his own forces, there were other indications that the post-Mobutu era might have some of the same features as the Mobutu era. Western companies that had negotiated mineral concessions with Kabila before he took power reported that his associates were demanding exorbitant payments, according to Newsweek *and other news organizations.*

Albright's Visit

Albright's one-day visit to Kinshasa on December 12 was part of a seven-nation trip to Africa, her first as secretary of state. Although she described her stop in Kinshasa as one of the most important of the trip, Albright spent just a few hours in the city. She had time for only two meetings: a breakfast with business and civic leaders, including several opposition figures, and a private session with Kabila. At the breakfast session, Albright said "no one expects the Congo to be transformed overnight" but added that she was "encouraged by President Kabila's expressed opposition to corruption and support for the rule of law."

After their meeting, Albright and Kabila held a joint news conference at which Albright read a statement praising Kabila for his promises to institute democracy and respect human rights and gentling chiding him for delays in keeping those promises. Albright said the administration in 1998 would ask Congress for $35 million in humanitarian aid for the Congo. State Department aides said Albright chose to support Kabila, despite reservations about the extent of his commitment to democracy and human rights, in hopes of encouraging him along those lines.

Following are excerpts from a joint news conference held by U.S. Secretary of State Madeleine K. Albright and President Laurent Kabila of the Democratic Republic of the Congo, in Kinshasa, December 12, 1997:

Secretary Albright: I am pleased to be here in Kinshasa and I thank President Kabila his hospitality, and for changing his schedule so that we could meet despite my late arrival yesterday.

I have come to the Democratic Republic of the Congo because there can be no doubt that what happens in this vast country will do much to shape the future of Central, Eastern and Southern Africa, and because we have an unprecedented opportunity to build a new relationship between our two nations.

Decades of misrule have left the Congo with grave economic and political problems. But today, the Congolese people are clearly ready and eager to end their country's long isolation and stagnation. We want to do all we can to help.

The new government, under President Kabila, has expressed a commitment to constitutional reform, democratic elections and economic recovery. There is a long way to go to reach these goals, but I am encouraged by a number of positive steps.

Today I congratulated President Kabila on the establishment of a Constitution Drafting Commission and a National Reconstruction Conference. If the work of these bodies is open and inclusive, they can be important tools in constructing government institutions that are representative, effective, and respected by the Congolese people.

Throughout the Great Lakes region, inter-ethnic violence has resulted both in great human tragedy and in new obstacles to political and social progress. As I discussed with President Kabila, it is vital that the region's leaders work together to end this violence, ensure respect for human rights, and build security and tolerance.

The United States supports the mission of the UN team here in the Congo and welcomes their deployment into the field with the support of the Congolese Government.

What has happened in the Congo was part of a lengthier tragedy, one for which the United States, the nations of the region, and the international community must share responsibility.

We believe it is also critical, however, that steps be taken to lay the foundation for long-term stability and progress.

Accordingly, I have encouraged President Kabila to move ahead with planned political reforms designed to permit broad-based and open dialogue among both official and nongovernmental representatives. And I expressed the hope that this would include an early end to restrictions on political party activities.

We also discussed the urgency of economic development and regional integration, to take advantage of Congo's tremendous natural and human resources, and make the country a regional force for growth. That requires a commitment to open markets, honest government and the rule of law. President Kabila has made a strong start toward these goals with his government's stabilization plan.

The United States is committed to supporting the people of the Congo as they seek to build the peace, freedom and growth they have been so long denied.

My government intends to expand our assistance to the Congo significantly. In the weeks ahead, we will be working with our Congress to prepare a package of $35–40 million dollars to assist the Congolese people and their government in building democratic institutions and governing capacity. That package will cover infrastructure programs in areas such as health, sanitation and finance.

To take just one concrete example where work will begin even sooner, we will fund the rebuilding of the Black River Bridge, a vital link between Kinshasa and eastern Congo that was destroyed by Mobutu's government last May.

Peace Corps volunteers will return to the Congo. Resource centers for civic education will be funded. And we will support Congolese projects to protect unique wildlife and rain forest.

The United States is also consulting with our Congress in order to contribute $10 million to the World Bank trust fund that the Friends of the Congo have pledged to establish. Through it, the international community will support projects that reflect Congolese priorities.

We also look forward to supporting debt relief for the Congo, once the government, working with the World Bank and the International Monetary Fund, has put an economic reform program in place.

Our meeting today was an important step toward building a strong relationship based on shared interests, mutual respect and a joint willingness to work together to resolve differences and solve problems. The relationship between the United States and the Congo is important for both countries. I look forward to building on it in my meetings with Congolese citizens, and in productive work with the people and government of this country in the weeks and months ahead.

Once again, I thank President Kabila for his hospitality.

Question: *(translated from French)* For the Secretary of State, you announced that you are working with Congress in order to prepare a package of $35 to $40 million. Could you tell us when this money will be available and what criteria do you use to establish the amount because the country needs billions of dollars, not millions?

Question for the President: Could you give us some details about the attack against the city of Bakavu and the murder of 200 Congolese in Rwanda?

Albright: Yes. Let me just say that I believe that the package that we have proposed is actually quite a generous package that has a number of aspects to it. But in terms of timing, let me say that our Congress is out of session at the moment. They will be back in January. We will be working with them as rapidly as possible to get the money. I can't give you an exact time but it is high on our priorities because clearly it is needed here.

And let me say that first of all there are a number of pieces, as I mentioned, in the amount itself; there is also the possibility of debt relief; there is the Peace Corps coming in here, the building of the bridge, the $10 million that was pledged at Brussels. And then the fact that we, through our membership in international financial institutions, also have a great deal of leverage in terms of how other countries distribute their funds and the assistance that they might give.

We have a catalytic or magnetic effect and we plan to use that. But let me also make an additional point, which is that I think that not just in the Congo but generally throughout the world, we are operating differently in terms of our bilateral assistance. We believe that rather than dispensing large sums of money for that kind of assistance, we should supplement our assistance with trade and investment and that in the long run is the kind of partnership/relationship we should be having with other countries and with Congo. And therefore, among the things that I was interested in talking about with the

President was the kind of environment that should be here in order to have that kind of investment possibility.

President Kabila: *(translated from French)* I am going to respond to the two questions. What happened in Bakavu first of all was actions taken by the rear guard of those who still have hopes against the republic. You've heard the details on the radio—I don't need to go into details here. What happened is they came; they tried; they failed. We pursued them. They are members of the ex-FAR, the former Rwandan Armed Forces, the Interhamwe and another group now called the Mi-Mis. The country is ready to defend itself however. Such events will happen but we'll be ready to oppose any incursions that may happen.

Second question of what happened in Rwanda. Killings of refugees were not 200—it was over 800 who were killed. One more time the international community and the United Nations should perhaps send an investigation team to examine the facts. What happens in Rwanda is very destabilizing; these are Interhamwe killers, they've killed 800 people. The international community is silent. However, if you had killed one of these assassins, the international community would of course name an investigative team.

Albright: Could I just add to that answer? I was in Rwanda yesterday, as many of you know, and we discussed the problems in the North. I have asked Ambassador David Scheffer, who was with me in Rwanda and is my Ambassador to deal with crimes against humanity, to return to Rwanda to try to assist in the investigation of this problem, because it seems that some of the same people who perpetrated genocide are continuing with this activity perhaps with the same intent. And therefore I would like to let you know, Mr. President, that I am asking David Scheffer to return there to see what we can find out.

Kabila: *(translated from French)* We of course are indebted and must thank the Secretary of State for this decision because this is really the first time that the international community reacts so quickly. Thank you, Madame Secretary.

Question: Laura Myers with the Associated Press: My question is for President Kabila. This morning there's a report that the United Nations team investigating the alleged massacres of Rwandan refugees was blocked this morning from working in Winjeck—I'm wondering what this does to your credibility as far as your pledge to allow free access to this team, and I'm wondering if you'll allow access in the future?

Kabila: *(translated from French)* I'll have to inform myself before I can answer your question. I'm not aware of what happened; I was not on the ground. I will ask my minister for rehabilitation to present a report to me about that and I need to be informed before I can voice any opinion.

All I know is that the commission is free to investigate anywhere it wants, but we must know what the exact facts are as it happened on the ground—and see whether what you are saying is really true.

Question: *(translated from French)* I have two questions for the Secretary and I work for a daily called the *(inaudible)*. Madame Secretary, I heard your assistant, Susan Rice, say that the U.S. Government regrets having created and supported Mobutu. However, while in Uganda you have made several compliments to President Museveni, almost indicating that he was the strong man of the region. Since Uganda is not a model of respect for human rights, don't you think you could be creating another Mobutu and you would regret that afterwards?

Second question is I would like for you to describe the feelings that you have as you travel throughout Africa—you are the U.S. foreign minister, like Mr. Visa Makata is our foreign minister. I would like for you to describe a little bit the way you feel.

Albright: Yes, thank you. First of all let me say that there are many who are responsible for the existence and the development of Mr. Mobutu and we take our share of the responsibility. I don't exactly know on what you are basing your comments about what I said about President Museveni. I made quite clear as I also did in Ethiopia with President Meles that Africa at this stage is fortunate to have a group of strong leaders who are interested in regional cooperation. And I also spoke to the same subject in Rwanda and I just finished with President Kabila making it clear that he is among those leaders for whom there—all of whom have a responsibility now to act together in support of economic development, democracy in this region of Africa.

I gave a speech at the OAU in Addis in which I outlined how I felt representing the United States at this stage in Africa. And I spoke about the importance of beginning a new chapter of our relations in which we worked as partners and in which I talked less and listened more. And I had a very good meeting with the foreign minister here today despite the fact that he is a man a little bit younger than I am. Just a little bit younger.

Question: This morning you paid tribute to the democratic opposition who had opposed Mobutu and supported democratic development and just now you said that you favor a freedom of association of the political opposition. Some of the political leaders you might have wanted to meet here are in jail or have been jailed in the past couple of weeks. Did you ask President Kabila to release anybody in jail now for political association? Has he given you any assurances that there will be genuine freedom of political association and is there any link between this U.S. aid to Congo and the freedom of political association?

Albright: Yes. President Kabila and I had a lengthy discussion about the importance of inclusiveness and about the importance of elections and the importance of dealing with numerous different political views. And in fact, I think that I can say that the bulk of our discussion was about the importance of building civil society, freedom of association, and generally the importance of building democratic institutions in a country that had been run in a dictatorial way with corruption for so many years.

And as you know, Congress is very interested in how Congo and President Kabila do in fact carry out obligations on issues of human rights and democracy. As of course do President Clinton and I.

And let me say that as part of this discussion with President Kabila, we established what I believe to be an excellent relationship and he and I decided that we would give each other our telephone numbers so that we could discuss problems when they come up. And I plan to use the phone fairly often and I hope he does also.

Kabila: *(translated from French)* With the lead from the Secretary of State, I would like to ask the journalist who asked the last question, if he could site the names of these political personalities because of their gains.

Question: The name I've heard is Zahidi Ngoma, in one of the leading publications. Is he now free or where is he?

Kabila: *(translated from French)* This gentleman is not a politician. Or do you call a politician those who have come off the street to incite people to kill each other, to divide people who will manufacture political pamphlets in foreign embassies with intent of dividing people. Do you call that a political leader? Do you let people like that free on the street?

I hope that you saw the pamphlet that was drafted by this gentleman. They will go to jail if they incite people to violence. Long live democracies.

FEDERAL APPEALS COURT ON CALIFORNIA TERM LIMITS
December 19, 1997

A federal appeals court on December 19 upheld a California law setting strict lifetime term limits on state legislators. The ruling was a significant victory for advocates of limiting the length of service of legislators at the state level. A move to impose term limits on members of Congress was blocked by the U.S. House of Representatives for the second time in two years, effectively killing the proposal for the time being.

Term limits had become popular in the late 1980s and early 1990s as a means of limiting the power of incumbents in elective offices. California voters in 1990 narrowly approved Proposition 140, limiting service in the state assembly to three two-year terms and in the state senate to two four-year terms. As of 1997 nineteen other states had enacted limits on the number of terms legislators could serve; most states for years had imposed limits on the number of terms for their governors.

The term limits had forced a rapid turnover in many state legislatures. By 1997, for example, California's assembly consisted entirely of members elected since 1990. The laws also had opened many legislative positions around the country to women and minorities. It was less clear, however, what kinds of qualitative changes the term limitation movement had produced. Numerous reports seemed to indicate that inexperienced legislators often lacked the skill or desire to craft the compromises necessary in political life. Such members, however, often were more willing than the career legislators they replaced to consider new ways of doing business. Critics of term limits said rapid turnover in legislatures was giving more power to lobbyists and staff members in the executive branches of state government.

A U.S. Supreme Court decision in 1995 had the effect of striking down twenty-two state laws that attempted to impose limits on the terms of members of Congress. The court said term limits at the federal level could be set only with a constitutional amendment. (Supreme Court ruling on term limits, Historic Documents of 1995, p. 259)

Turnover was taking place in Congress even without mandated term limits. The 1994 elections brought a host of new members to Congress— most of them Republicans—and the following years saw extraordinarily high rates of voluntary retirements. Many of those leaving Congress said they were discouraged by increasing partisanship and the continuing political stalemate in Washington.

The California Law

Proposition 140 was one of the most drastic of all state term limitation laws because it imposed a lifetime limit on service in any one office. For example, a legislator could serve up to six years in the assembly and could then run for the senate or some other office but could never again serve in the assembly. Term limitations in many other states imposed restrictions on consecutive service but allowed individuals to run again for an office after sitting out a term or two.

The California law had a dramatic effect in its early years, forcing the retirement by 1996 of the entire assembly. Among those forced out was the powerful Democratic speaker, Willie L. Brown, who chose in 1995 to run (successfully) for mayor of San Francisco. Many observers believed that forcing Brown out of office was one of the primary motivations of the sponsors of Proposition 140. In the four years after Brown left the assembly, four different members served as speaker, none of whom had significant experience in legislative leadership.

Tom Bates, an assembly member forced from office in 1996 by a term limit, filed suit in federal court against Proposition 140, challenging the law as discriminatory and as an unconstitutional infringement on the right of voters to choose their elected representatives. Bates won the first two rounds. On April 23 district court judge Claudia Wilken ruled that Proposition 140 was too broad in imposing a lifetime limit on legislative terms. A three-judge appeals court also struck down the law, but on different grounds; that panel said on October 7 that voters had not been adequately informed in 1990 that Proposition 140 would impose a lifetime limit.

The appellate ruling then went before the full eleven-judge panel of the Ninth U.S. Circuit Court of Appeals, based in San Francisco, for an expedited review. In its ruling December 19, that panel overturned the two lower court rulings and held that Proposition 140 was constitutional. The court acted on an 8–3 vote.

Writing for the majority, Judge David R. Thompson rejected Bates's contention that the law was discriminatory. "Proposition 140 makes no distinction on the basis of the content of protected expression, party affiliation or inherently arbitrary factors such as race, religion or gender," he wrote. The law's limitation on the rights of voters "is not severe," Thompson said, and was similar to such qualifications for office as a minimum age or residence in a particular district.

The full Appeals court also rejected the finding of the three-judge panel that California voters were not sufficiently informed in 1990 about the im-

pact of Proposition 140. Thompson noted that much of the debate before the 1990 vote concerned the fact that the proposition would impose a lifetime limit on legislative terms. The voters "had sufficient notice" of the intent of Proposition 140, Thompson's opinion said.

The court ruling meant that twenty-six California state legislators would be barred from seeking reelection in 1998. Among them were the speaker of the assembly and the majority leader of the senate. Opponents of Proposition 140 said they would appeal the ruling to the Supreme Court.

No Federal Term Limits

The drive for term limits on members of Congress suffered a serious defeat February 12 when the House of Representatives rejected eleven proposals for a constitutional amendment on the issue. One of the proposals—setting a flat twelve-year limit on service in the House or Senate—received a simple majority of 217–211 but fell 69 votes short of the necessary two-thirds majority necessary for a constitutional amendment. Perhaps more important in political terms, the proposal garnered ten fewer votes in 1997 than it had in 1995, when the House also rejected term limits.

House Republicans had made term limits a key part of their "Contract with America," a political manifesto that helped them wrest control of Congress from Democrats in the 1994 elections. But once the Republicans were in power their enthusiasm for term limits waned and they made only modest efforts on behalf of the issue in 1995 and 1997. (Contract With America, Historic Documents of 1994, p. 374)

The 1997 voting was affected by a controversial move by U.S. Term Limits, a lobbying group that was pressing for term limitations at the federal level. In the November 1996 elections U.S. Term Limits succeeded in nine states in winning ballot initiatives directing members of Congress from those states to vote only for one version of federal term limits. Members who refused to follow those directives would have a note placed next to their names on the ballots in the next election indicating that they had disregarded the voters' instructions. That strategy backfired when the matter came before the House, because the specific instructions given the members from the nine states caused them to split their votes among several different proposals.

Less than two weeks later, on February 25, the Supreme Court struck down one of the nine "instruct and inform" laws requiring members of Congress to vote a certain way on term limits. The court let stand a ruling by the Arkansas Supreme Court overturning a 1996 ballot initiative requiring members of Congress from that state to vote for term limits of twelve years each for the U.S. House and Senate.

The Arkansas Supreme Court in October 1996 had ruled the initiative was invalid because it attempted to skirt the requirement that all amendments to the U.S. Constitution originate in Congress or in the state legislatures. The U.S. Supreme Court upheld that state court ruling but made no comment on it.

Following are excerpts from the majority opinion written by Judge David R. Thompson in the case of Bates v. Jones, *issued December 19, 1997, in which the U.S. Court of Appeals for the Ninth Circuit upheld the constitutionality of California's Proposition 140 limiting the number of terms for members of the state legislature:*

Facts

In 1990, California voters approved Proposition 140, an initiative which imposed specific lifetime term limits for state legislators and certain state officers. The Proposition limited state senators to two terms, state assembly members to three terms, and the state governor to two terms.

The Proposition also limited to two terms the Lieutenant Governor, Attorney General, Controller, Secretary of State, Treasurer, Superintendent of Public Instruction, and the members of the Board of Equalization. The Proposition declared that the lack of term limits created "unfair incumbent advantages" which "discourage qualified candidates from seeking public office and create a class of career politicians, instead of the citizen representatives envisioned by the Founding Fathers." The Proposition stated the term limits were necessary "[t]o restore a free and democratic system of fair elections, and to encourage qualified candidates to seek public office. . . ."

In 1991, the state legislature and several individual legislators and constituents challenged before the California Supreme Court the constitutionality of Proposition 140's term limits. On a petition for a writ of mandate, the California Supreme Court concluded that Proposition 140's lifetime term limits did not violate the plaintiffs' federal constitutional rights.

Thereafter, in 1995, Tom Bates, a former member of the California Assembly, and a group of his constituents filed the present action, also alleging the lifetime term limits of Proposition 140 are unconstitutional. The district court agreed. The district court determined Proposition 140 imposed a severe burden on the plaintiffs' first and fourteenth amendment rights and was not narrowly tailored to advance a compelling state interest. The district court enjoined the enforcement of Proposition 140 but stayed its injunction pending appeal.

A panel of this court, with Judge Sneed dissenting, affirmed the judgment of the district court on other grounds and did not reach the issue whether the term limits are constitutional. This en banc review followed. . . .

Discussion

A. Res Judicata [omitted]
B. Notice

The three-judge panel did not resolve whether Proposition 140 violates the plaintiffs' first and fourteenth amendment rights. Instead, the panel determined Proposition 140 was invalid because the Proposition and the ballot materials did not provide California voters with sufficient notice that the Proposition imposed lifetime rather than consecutive term limits. *Bates*, 127 F.3d at 844. We disagree, and, consistent with the California Supreme Court, we hold that the relevant ballot materials and the surrounding context provided sufficient notice making it clear that Proposition 140 required lifetime bans.

The portion of the Proposition affecting legislators states: "No Senator may serve more than 2 terms" and "No member of the Assembly may serve more than 3 terms." Nowhere in the Proposition does it state that these bans are less than absolute. As Judge Sneed pointed out in his dissent from the three-judge panel decision, the twenty-second amendment to the Constitution uses similar language: "[n]o person shall be elected to the office of the President more than twice. . . ." There certainly is no confusion that this language imposes a lifetime ban on the office of the President—even though the amendment does not specifically use the term "lifetime."

The surrounding circumstances also clearly indicate the voters had sufficient notice that Proposition 140 imposed lifetime bans. The opposition materials to the Proposition, which were circulated to California voters, clearly state that elected state legislators will be "banned for life" and use "lifetime ban" or similar terminology no less than eleven times. Moreover, when Proposition 140 was submitted to the voters in 1990, there were two competing initiatives on the ballot imposing term limits. In contrast to Proposition 140's lifetime ban, Proposition 131 proposed consecutive term limits. The two propositions received extensive media attention, which was heightened after the California Supreme Court issued a decision five days before the election addressing which of two propositions would govern in the event both were approved.

Assuming, without deciding, that a federal court may determine whether a state has given adequate notice to its voters in connection with a statewide initiative ballot measure dealing with term limits on state officeholders, we hold that California's notice with regard to Proposition 140 was sufficient.

C. Constitutionality of Proposition 140's Lifetime Term Limits

In *Burdick*, the Supreme Court set forth the analysis we must apply to determine the constitutionality of Proposition 140. We

> must weigh "the character and magnitude of the asserted injury to the rights protected by the First and Fourteenth Amendments that the plaintiff seeks to vindicate" against "the precise interests put forward by the State as justifications for the burden imposed by its rule," taking into consideration "the extent to which those interests make it necessary to burden the plaintiff's rights."

If the measure in question severely burdens the plaintiffs' rights, we apply strict scrutiny review. If, however, the law "imposes only 'reasonable, nondiscriminatory restrictions' upon the First and Fourteenth Amendment rights of voters, 'the State's important regulatory interests are generally sufficient to justify' the restrictions."

The rights which the plaintiffs seek to vindicate in this case are the right to vote for the candidate of one's choice and the asserted right of an incumbent to again run for his or her office. Proposition 140's impact on these rights is not severe. As argued by the State, term limits on state officeholders is a neutral candidacy qualification, such as age or residence, which the State certainly has the right to impose. With regard to incumbents, they may enjoy the incumbency of a single office for a number of years, and, as pointed out by the California Supreme Court, they are not precluded from running for some other state office.

Most important, the lifetime term limits do not constitute a discriminatory restriction. Proposition 140 makes no distinction on the basis of the content of protected expression, party affiliation, or inherently arbitrary factors such as race, religion, or gender. Nor does the Proposition "limit[] political participation by an identifiable political group whose members share a particular viewpoint, associational preference, or economic status."

Proposition 140's minimal impact on the plaintiffs' rights is justified by the State's legitimate interests. As the Proposition itself states, a lack of term limits may create "unfair incumbent advantages." Long-term entrenched legislators may obtain excessive power which, in turn, may discourage other qualified candidates from running for office or may provide the incumbent with an unfair advantage in winning reelection. As the Supreme Court stated in *Thornton*,

> Term limits, like any other qualification for office, unquestionably restrict the ability of voters to vote for whom they wish. On the other hand, such limits may provide for the infusion of fresh ideas and new perspectives, and may decrease the likelihood that representatives will lose touch with their constituents.

California voters apparently perceived lifetime term limits for elected state officials as a means to promote democracy by opening up the political process and restoring competitive elections. This was their choice to make.

We hold that Proposition 140's lifetime term limits do not violate the plaintiffs' first and fourteenth amendment rights. The judgment of the district court invalidating Proposition 140 is reversed and its injunction enjoining enforcement of the Proposition is vacated. The stay pending appeal is vacated as moot.

Reversed.

KIM DAE-JUNG ON HIS ELECTION
AS PRESIDENT OF SOUTH KOREA
December 19, 1997

Kim Dae-jung, a longtime opposition leader who was once sentenced to death by the country's military regime, won election as president of South Korea on December 19. Kim's election came as a financial crisis threatened to undermine the results of nearly three decades of South Korean economic growth and prosperity. South Korea was one of several East Asian nations forced to appeal to the International Monetary Fund (IMF) for aid in the wake of a sudden collapse of their currencies and stock markets. (Asian financial crisis, p. 832)

Also in 1997, North Korea's de facto leader, Kim Jong Il, formally took over the top leadership post—general secretary of the Korean Workers Party—that had been vacant since the death of his father, Kim Il Sung, in 1994. North Korea was facing an economic and humanitarian crisis far more serious than the one confronting its richer rival in the south. Relief workers said millions of North Koreans were facing starvation due to a drought and the communist regime's chronic mismanagement of agricultural production.

The two Koreas, the United States, and China on December 9 opened four-way talks in Geneva intended to draft a peace agreement formally ending the Korean War. The fighting had stopped in 1953, but an armistice had never been translated into a peace treaty.

A Long Road to the Presidency

The election of Kim Dae-jung—the first opposition party candidate to win the presidency—may have completed the gradual transformation of South Korea into a working democracy. For most of its first five decades as an independent nation, South Korea was governed by authoritarian regimes closely allied with, and often run by, the military. Kim Dae-jung's predecessor, Kim Young Sam, was an opposition leader who was elected president in 1992 after he switched sides to join the ruling Grand National Party.

Despite his victory and his own personal popularity, Kim Dae-jung faced an enormous political hurdle upon taking office in February 1998:

The National Assembly remained under the control of the Grand National Party, which was considered likely to oppose many of his cabinet appointments and his policies. The next parliamentary elections were not scheduled until 2000. Moreover, Kim had no experience in government at any level, so it was unclear how well he would manage an entire nation facing one of its most difficult periods.

Kim Dae-jung was from the region of Cholla in southwest Korea. The region's largest city, Kwangju, was the site in 1980 of a massive student uprising against the government that was violently suppressed by the military. Kim was closely aligned with the Korean student and labor movements, and he was the country's most forceful and articulate spokesman for democracy and human rights. A succession of military governments considered him a dangerous radical and spread rumors that he was an agent of communist North Korea.

A successful businessman who began crusading in the late 1950s for democracy and the rights of the poor, Kim first sought the presidency in 1971, polishing oratorical skills that won him an immense following. According to many observers, he may have won more votes than the president, Park Chung Hee. Park was declared the victor, however, and a few months later Kim's car was rammed by a truck in what many people believed was an attempted assassination. The accident killed Kim's driver and wounded Kim, leaving him with a permanent limp.

The Korean Central Intelligence Agency kidnapped Kim from a Tokyo hotel room in 1973 and took him onto a ship in Japanese coastal waters, apparently intending to dump him overboard. Kim was saved by the intervention of the Japanese and U.S. governments, which had learned of the plot to kill him and demanded his release.

Yet another government attempt on Kim's life came in 1980, when President Chun Doo Hwan had him arrested, tried in a court-martial on charges of plotting the uprising in Kwangju, and sentenced to death by hanging. An enormous international protest—including a private intervention by U.S. president-elect Ronald Reagan—once again won Kim's reprieve. Chun commuted Kim's sentence to life imprisonment and, in an explicit quid pro quo, Chun was rewarded with a White House visit shortly after Reagan took office. In December 1982 the Korean government allowed Kim to go into exile in the United States.

Kim returned home to Korea in 1985 and was put under house arrest by the government. Two years later he ran again for president, but he split the opposition vote with Kim Young Sam, his long-time rival for leadership of opposition to the government. The presidency was won by Roh Tae Woo, a retired general who was Chun's hand-picked successor. Kim Dae-jung ran again for the presidency in 1992 but was defeated by Kim Young Sam, who had joined the ruling party. That defeat appeared to mark the end of Kim Dae-jung's political career, but he chose to run for president again—for the fourth time—in 1997.

Kim's election resulted from a lucky break and a shrewd calculation. His rival, Lee Hoi Chang, was embroiled in a scandal, leading another ruling *party candidate to join the race. Kim also promised the prime minister's post to a formerly bitter rival, Kim Jong Pil, who had arranged the military coup that brought Park Chung Hee to power in 1961. With the support from Kim Jong Pil's allies and with the ruling party's vote split, Kim Daejung won a 40.4 percent plurality.*

During his thirty-five year career in opposition to the government, Kim spent five-and-a-half years in prison, more than six years under house arrest or day-to-day surveillance by the intelligence service, and three years in exile. A succession of military regimes failed to break Kim's will, however, and their unrelenting persecution of him unwittingly enhanced his moral authority both at home and abroad.

One of Kim's first actions as president-elect gave him even greater moral authority and signaled his desire to move away from the bitter past. Kim asked for, and won, the release from prison of two of the presidents who had persecuted him, Chun Doo Hwan and Roh Tae Woo. Both had been convicted in 1996 on charges of corruption and plotting the 1979 coup in which President Park was assassinated; they had served two years in prison.

Economic Crisis

Kim's deep devotion to democracy may have boosted his political stature, but it did little to calm international investors who were more interested in economic stability and worried about his allegedly leftist leanings. As an opposition figure Kim had talked often of the need for social justice and the rights of labor unions, leading many critics to brand him a socialist. During the election campaign Kim had made ambiguous statements about the country's financial crisis, at first opposing, then supporting, an economic reform plan demanded by the IMF in exchange for $57 billion in loans from that agency, the World Bank, Japan, the United States, and other lenders.

Immediately after his election, Kim rushed to assure the international financial markets that he was committed to the IMF reform package. "We will diligently carry out the terms of the IMF," he said in his December 19 victory speech. "We shall practice market economics, fully and thoroughly, and we shall open our markets without hesitation." At least for the moment, Kim's words fell on deaf ears. The day after his election, the Korean currency, the won, dropped 9.5 percent against the U.S. dollar.

Kim later gave Koreans some unwelcome news. They would have to accept layoffs—previously unheard of in the country—and the likelihood that some Korean firms would be taken over by foreign investors, he said.

On December 24 the United States, Japan, Germany, and the IMF announced an emergency $10 billion loan package to prevent South Korea from defaulting on loan payments due by the end of the year. Private banks also agreed to defer payment on billions of loans and to consider converting much of Korea's short-term loans into longer-term debt. These actions, orchestrated by the Clinton administration, were intended to bolster international confidence in the Korean economy and slow the flight of overseas capital from Korean banks and companies.

Relations with the North

In his December 19 victory statements Kim called for a closer dialogue with North Korea and said he might ask for a summit meeting with Kim Jong Il. Kim Dae-jung for years had suggested the need for better relations between the two Koreas—a position that fostered the military's suspicions about his loyalty.

Kim's move came shortly after the first four-way talks involving the two Koreas, the United States, and China. The initial round of talks made no progress, but diplomats expressed pleasure that a dialogue had begun. The Korean peninsula remained one of the most heavily armed places on Earth and was perhaps the most dangerous remnant of the cold war.

Following are excerpts, provided by the South Korean Embassy in Washington, D.C., of a statement December 19, 1997, by Kim Dae-jung, following his election as president:

. . . I am proud of you, the people of this nation. At an historic juncture, ending the 20th century and ushering in the 21st, we have finally accomplished the great feat of changing the power of government between the ruling and the opposition parties for the first time in the 50 years of our Republic. As a democratic state which aspires to cherish, uphold, and further the cause of democracy, we can now stand proud and tall. . . .

As president, I shall eliminate all forms of discrimination; protect and ensure the legitimate rights of all component members of this state with fairness and equity so as to make certain that no discrimination or conflict can ever again flourish in our land. I shall emphatically end the era of regional conflict and friction and dedicate myself to the realization of national reconciliation and unity. Let's open a new age of democracy and economic progress. . . .

Up to this point in time, economic development has been of primary importance. As a people painfully rising again from the ashes of the Korean War, there indeed was a consensus that we should also enjoy material well-being. However, Democratic politics have been sacrificed too long because of authoritarian rule. The truth is that our political life has been an experience of the unending sacrifice of all other aspects of national life for economic development alone. As a consequence, there have been unhealthy distortions and irregularities in all facets of society. Thus there existed politico-economic collusion and paralyzing government control of the economy; and the irregularities and corruption could not be eliminated.

The sacrifice of medium and small businesses continues. The legitimate rights of the common folk were left unprotected, while the caring concern of the state towards the weak and powerless fell far too short. Without self-reflection, and deep in self-deception, the powers that be led the unwitting nation to the brink of a humiliating national bankruptcy, forcing upon themselves the burden of calling on the International Monetary Fund for an emergency rescue. Now with the advent of a new government in this land, we are about to open a new era in which democracy and economic development will go together shoulder to shoulder. . . .

Through thorough and systematic economic reforms, accomplished as soon as possible, the new government in Korea will endeavor to ensure future financial integrity so there is no need for an IMF bailout. I shall state once more, with utmost clarity and emphasis, that we shall cooperate with the IMF fully and completely. We shall also faithfully abide by the agreement between the IMF and the present government of this republic. For that, we shall try our best to legislate the necessary laws in the National Assembly. . . .

Politics

Politically, we will get ready for national reconciliation and the unification of our people. Only the united power of the people founded on genuine democracy can overcome our national crisis. We will establish a "participatory democracy"—a government in which the people are the masters and wherein the people participate together in the governance of the country. I will begin a direct dialogue with the people more than twice a year through the medium of television. Through this format, I will directly reflect their views and demands on running the country, and I shall make requests directly to the people, through the same format, about the tasks they will have to discharge for the national well-being. . . .

Decisive steps will be taken for administrative reforms of the government. However, any belt-tightening that is required will be done by the government first. The new government will be the engine and vehicle for overcoming the national crisis that faces us and for the necessary reforms. We will endeavor to bring forth a revitalized government that is trusted by the people and the world outside. Only then can we ask our people for cooperation; and only then can we have relations based on cooperation with the world community. . . .

Economy

In the area of economy, I emphasize that I will faithfully implement the agreement with the IMF. Painful as it may be, it is the road that we must take. Reform without pain is not possible. We will use the opportunity for implementing reforms so as to reinvigorate our economy. We will show the world that the "Miracle on the Han" is not finished at all.

We shall practice market economics—fully and thoroughly—and we shall open our market without hesitation. We will create a new environment for foreign investors to invest in Korea without fear or reservation—a paradise for business. In the 21st century, inducing foreign investment will be even more important than mere trade. The government will do its part in inviting foreign investment and will make sure that they will be treated the same as our own people. . . .

The greatest act of welfare for the people is to provide jobs for those who want to work. We shall provide the aged with opportunities for work and train the handicapped. The new government will place a high priority on the solution of the unemployment problem. . . .

Security

. . . We will preserve and maintain our alliance ties and close cooperation with the United States—the central factor in our national security. To maintain peace and stability on the Korean peninsula, we will do our best to elicit positive cooperation with the four major powers around us—the United States, Japan, China, and Russia. Since I became a presidential candidate in 1971, I consistently have advocated four power guarantees for a Korean peace. The need for such has increased today. I shall also pursue four party talks more effectively in the future. And we will do our part in the construction of the light water reactors through KEDO—without a hitch.

Through direct dialogue with the North, we shall search for a way to settle the problems between our two separated peoples. To do this, the implementation of the "Basic Agreement" between the two Koreans, signed in 1991, is most crucial. The Basic Agreement is an international agreement that the two sides ought to observe. I, therefore propose to North Korea a resumption of the inter-Korean dialogue on the basis of that agreement. For now, our goal is to secure peace and stability on the peninsula as well as exchanges and cooperation between the South and the North. National unification can be discussed and achieved later through progressive and gradual means. . . .

By faithfully and seriously adjusting ourselves to the spirit and substance of globalization (segyehwa), we shall strive to be a model to others. We shall faithfully abide by all the agreements and commitments we made with and to other nations. Our national reality is very serious, including the economic difficulties. We need positive cooperation from various countries of the world. We will exert our best efforts to promote friendly and cooperative relations with all nations. . . .

I shall ensure the transparency of my government. I shall sweep away corruption and sever the knot of politico-economic collusion completely. I will emphasize once again that I shall make the people the main role players in "participatory democracy" and continue with the politics of dialogue with the people. To open a new age of greatness for our nation, I pledge to devote all of myself. I hope and pray for you cooperation and encouragement.

CUMULATIVE INDEX, 1993-1997

A

Abacha, Sani, **1995** 696–697

Abbaas, Mahmoud, Israeli-Palestinian peace accord, **1993** 747, 751, 761, 765

Abbas, Maldom Bada, human rights report, **1993** 560

Abington Township School District v. Schempp, **1995** 547

Abortion

Catholic teaching on, **1993** 843–850, **1995** 145–146, 149–151, 153–155, 157–158, 161

Democratic Party platform on, **1996** 623–624, 639

Dole position on, **1996** 496

Eastern Europe, **1994** 428

Foster nomination and, **1995** 61–62

Republican Party platform on, **1996** 496–497, 518–519

Supreme Court decisions

clinic blockades, **1993** 93–112, **1994** 311–326

protesters and RICO law, **1994** 26–33

UN population conference, **1994** 352–353, **1995** 583

Abraham Lincoln Opportunity Foundation (ALOF), **1997** 6–7

Abrams, Elliott

Iran-contra conviction, **1994** 12

Iran-contra testimony, **1994** 13, 18–19

Abrams, Kathryn, **1993** 941

Acquired immunodeficiency syndrome. *See* AIDS

Acupuncture, NIH panel on, **1997** 749–759

Adams, Gerry

Northern Ireland peace efforts, **1993** 925

visa for U.S. visit, **1994** 449, 454, **1995** 728

Adams v. Richardson, **1995** 245

Adarand Constructors v. Peña, **1995** 307–326, 371, 485–486, **1997** 190, 191, 193, 194

Administrative Procedures Act, **1993** 381–383

Adolescents. *See* Teenage pregnancy; Teenagers

Adoption, Jessica DeBoer case, **1993** 515–529

Advertising

of distilled spirits, on television, **1996** 770–775

of tobacco products, **1994** 172–184, **1996** 590–591, 596–598, **1997** 38, 332, 334, 336–337

Advertising Council, adult attitudes toward children survey, **1997** 424, 426

Advisory Commission on Intergovernmental Relations (ACIR), unfunded mandates legislation, **1995** 142–143

Advisory Committee on Human Radiation Experiments, radiation tests on citizens, **1994** 55, 60

Affirmative action

ban, federal appeals court panel on, **1997** 183–194

California legislation, **1996** 759–763

Clinton endorsement of, **1995** 483–496, 574–575, **1997** 315

Clinton presidential debate on, **1996** 728

Dole opposition to, **1995** 483–484, 574–575

federal government plans, **1995** 307–326

student success stories, **1997** 321

Afghanistan, land mine casualties, **1995** 47, 48

Africa

Central African refugee crisis, **1996** 809–815

Democratic Party platform, **1996** 645

economic development, **1997** 352–355

land mine problem, **1995** 47–49, 50–51

Republican Party platform, **1996** 543–544

U.S. defense policy, **1993** 712–713

African National Congress (ANC), **1993** 887–884, **1994** 247–248, **1996** 250

H

Habitat for Humanity, and rebuilding of churches, **1997** 304, 306, 311

Habyarimana, Juvenal, assassination of, **1994** 541

Hagel, Churck (R-Neb.), food safety system, **1997** 692

Hagelin, John, **1996** 707

Hague v. Committee for Industrial Organization, **1995** 334

Haines, Gerald K., Roswell incident, **1997** 397

Haiti

Aristide's return to, **1994** 436–444

elections in, and UN, **1995** 355

refugees from

political asylum, **1993** 371–383

returned to, **1993** 413–421

UN peacekeeping mission, **1997** 150, 151, 154, 155, 156

U.S. forces in, **1994** 433–434, 437–438, 529

Haitian Refugee Center v. Baker, **1993** 417

Haitian Refugee Center v. Gracey, **1993** 417

Hakim, Albert A., Iran-contra conviction, **1994** 12

Hall, James E.

air bag safety, **1997** 775

on airline safety, **1994** 535

on railroad safety, **1996** 189

TWA flight 800 crash, **1997** 781, 783–786

Hall, Tony P. (D-Ohio), abortion issue, **1996** 624

Hamilton, Joseph G., human radiation experiments, **1993** 989

Hamilton, Lee H. (D-Ind.)

government secrecy, **1997** 103

"October Surprise" report, **1993** 4

Hanford Nuclear Reservation (Washington), cleanup efforts, **1994** 340–341, **1995** 114–115, 117–118

Harkin, Tom (D-Iowa)

apparel industry sweatshops, **1997** 209

farm bill opponent, **1996** 200

nuclear testing fallout, **1997** 593

Harman, John, unsafe chemicals in food, **1994** 379–386

Harris, Teresa, **1993** 939–945

Harris v. Forklift Systems, Inc., **1993** 939–945

Hart, Doug, **1993** 974

Hartford Public Schools (Connecticut), privatization of, **1994** 409–414

Hartzler, Joseph H., **1997** 623

Harvard School of Public Health, survey on children, **1997** 424–425

Hasenfus, Eugene, American pilot shot down in Nicaragua, **1994** 13

Hashemi, Cyrus, death of, **1993** 15

Hashemi, Jamshid, **1993** 15

Hashimoto, Ryutaro

at economic summit (Denver), **1997** 342

on hostage crisis in Peru, **1997** 234–237

Hasson, Kevin J., **1995** 386

Hastings, Alcee L. (D-Fla.), **1993** 82–83

Hatch, Orrin G. (R-Utah)

affirmative action opponent, **1997** 185–186

baseball exemption from antitrust laws, **1994** 361–362

physician-assisted suicide, **1997** 462

religious freedom, **1997** 408–409

Sessions investigation, **1993** 610

Hate crimes

church arson cases, **1997** 301–313

extremists in U.S. Army, task force on, **1996** 178–185

FBI report, **1997** 686

racially motivated, **1993** 385

Havel, Vaclav, NATO membership for Czech Republic, **1997** 516

Hawaii, same-sex marriages, **1996** 689

Hawkins, Vernon, **1996** 784

Head Start program, federal support for program, **1993** 212, 217–218, **1997** 36, 73

Health. *See also* Diet; Health, public; Mental health; Nutrition; Occupational health

benefits of drinking, **1995** 3–4, 16

benefits for girls in sports, **1997** 158–171

connective tissue disease and breast implants, **1995** 520–521

in Eastern Europe, **1994** 415–430

marijuana for medical uses, **1996** 755–758

physical exercise, benefits of, **1996** 418–429

sedentary lifestyle, CDC report on, **1993** 625–628

Health and Human Services (HHS) Department

child abuse and neglect, **1996** 778

federal dietary guidelines, **1996** 3–16

medical records privacy, **1997** 580–587

Health care

acupuncture treatments, NIH panel on, **1997** 747–759

for black Americans, heart attack incidence and care, **1993** 671–675

consumers' bill of rights, **1997** 787–799

and deficit reduction, **1996** 67

Democratic Party platform, **1996** 631–632

in Eastern European nations, **1994** 415–430

end-of-life care, **1997** 325–330

mammograms and mastectomy, **1997** 38

mammograms controversy, **1997** 142–149

medical records security, **1997** 580–587

Republican Party platform, **1996** 529–530

for women, **1993** 653–658, **1997** 38

Health care costs

and family finances, **1993** 271–285

prescription drug prices, **1994** 87–94

Hussein ibn Talal (king of Jordan)
eulogy for Yitzhak Rabin, **1995** 691, 693–694
and Israeli peace agreement, **1994** 329–335
West Bank peace agreement, **1995** 622
Hussein, Saddam
chemical weapons policy, **1997** 198
human rights report, **1993** 568, 570
Iraqi troop buildup, **1994** 431–435
political situation report, **1996** 680–686
UN weapons inspections, **1997** 767
Hutchison, Kay Bailey, Kennedy assassination anniversary, **1993** 960, 961
Hyde, Henry J. (R-Ill.)
and antiterrorism bill, **1995** 179
church arson prevention, **1997** 306
October Surprise Task Force chairman, **1993** 4
physician-assisted suicide, **1997** 462
on Reno conflict of interest, **1997** 824

I

IBM
benefits for partners of homosexual employees, **1996** 689
chess victory of "Deep Blue" computer, **1997** 273–276
Idaho National Engineering Laboratory, nuclear waste cleanup, **1995** 118
ILO. *See* International Labor Organization
IMF. *See* International Monetary Fund
Immigration
aid to immigrants, **1996** 452–453, 455–456, **1997** 34
California, Proposition 187, **1994** 388–389, **1995** 563
Census Bureau report, **1997** 175–182
Cuban and Haitian refugee boatlifts, U.S. policy on, **1995** 203–207
Democratic Party platform, **1996** 636–637
foreign-born population, in United States, **1995** 563–569, **1997** 175–182
legal immigrants, number of, **1995** 564–656
reform, U.S. commission report, **1994** 387–400
Republican Party platform, **1996** 520–521
U.S. strength in diversity, **1997** 43
Immigration and Naturalization Act (1952), Haitian refugees issue, **1993** 414, 415–418
Immigration and Naturalization Service (INS)
abolition proposal, **1997** 175
political asylum, for women, new rules on, **1995** 276–280
Impeachment, Senate impeachment powers, **1993** 81–91
Inaugural addresses, Clinton, **1993** 129–134, **1997** 20–26

Income distribution
human development, UN report on, **1996** 438–444
inequality, CEA on, **1997** 52
inequality, Census Bureau on, **1996** 396–400
median income of foreign-born, **1997** 181
India, weapons of mass destruction proliferation, **1996** 213, 222–223
Individuals with Disabilities Education Act (IDEA), **1993** 399, 402–405
Indonesia, IMF aid package, **1997** 836
Infant mortality
in Eastern European nations, **1994** 425
worldwide, **1996** 306
Infectious diseases
World Health Organization report on, **1996** 302–311
worldwide prevention, **1997** 348–349
Infertility, health effects of toxic substances, **1994** 149–152
Inflation rate, **1996** 51, **1997** 50, 53
Information Technology Association of America (ITAA), technology worker shortage, **1997** 669, 670
Infrastructure, protecting, **1997** 711–720
Ingraham v. Wright, **1995** 348
Inkatha Freedom Party, **1995** 102
Inman, Bobby Ray, defense secretary nomination withdrawal, **1993** 695–696, **1994** 22–25
Inner cities, Eisenhower Foundation report on, **1993** 211–233
Inouye, Daniel K. (D-Hawaii), television violence, **1993** 489
Institute of Medicine (IOM)
end-of-life care report, **1997** 325, 327–328
thyroid cancer from radiation study, **1997** 592, 594, 598
Insurgent groups, and weapons development, **1996** 224–225
Intelligence community
expanding powers of, **1996** 796–797
Republican Party platform on, **1996** 547–548
Interagency Council on the Homeless, report, **1994** 252–263
Interest rates, **1997** 721
Interior Department (U.S.), on endangered species, **1995** 359
Internal Revenue Service (IRS)
impact of year 2000 computer conversion on, **1997** 535
mistakes and abuses, **1997** 661–668
reform bill, **1997** 663
and tax exempt organizations, **1997** 9–13, 15
International Atomic Energy Agency (IAEA), North Korean nuclear weapons sites inspections, **1994** 602, 606–609

J

on Schott suspension for racist remarks, **1993** 168

on Texaco executives racial slurs, **1996** 765, 766

Jackson, Thomas P., line-item veto, **1997** 612

Jackson v. Virginia, **1993** 148

Jacobson, Michael, **1993** 690, **1996** 5

Jaffee v. Redmond, **1996** 388–395

JAMA. *See Journal of the American Medical Association*

Jamison v. Texas, **1994** 296

Japan

economic situation, **1997** 835

Hosokawa resignation, **1994** 221–224

hostage crisis in Peru, **1997** 234–237

Liberal Democratic Party (LDP), **1994** 221–223

U.S. trade relations, **1993** 541, 543

World War II, apology for suffering, **1995** 302–306

J.E.B. v. Alabama, **1994** 223–236

Jeffords, James M. (R-Vt.), on financing higher education, **1993** 173

Jehovah's Witness, religious freedom issues, **1997** 407, 564, 572

Jerusalem, status of, U.S. policy on, **1995** 623

Jewell, Richard, Olympic Park bombing suspect case, **1996** 445, 446–447

Jews

French, apology for complicity with Nazis, **1995** 478–482

Nazi genocide of, Holocaust Museum, **1993** 307–313

Jiang Zemin

China-U.S. summit meeting, **1997** 728–739

on death of Deng Xiaoping, **1997** 94–100

Hong Kong transfer ceremony statement, **1997** 502, 505–506

Job creation

Democratic Party platform, **1996** 629, 632–633

Republican Party platform, **1996** 506–507

technology worker shortage, **1997** 669–678

Job discrimination. *See* Discrimination, job

John Paul II

female priests ban, **1994** 276–280

on *Gospel of Life* ("culture of death"), **1995** 145–161

on human rights, UN speech, **1995** 639–645

land mines ban, **1997** 845

moral theology, encyclical on, **1993** 843–850

sexually abusive priests, **1993** 407–411

Vatican-Israel Diplomatic Accord, **1993** 1033, 1035

visits to United States, **1993** 659–669

Johns Hopkins Sexual Disorders Clinic (Baltimore), **1997** 385

Johnson, Nancy L. (R-Conn.), **1995** 748

Johnson v. Mississippi, **1993** 149

Johnston, J. Bennett (D-La.), **1995** 114–115

Johnston, Lloyd D., drug use among adolescents, **1996** 571

Jones, Ben, **1995** 748, 750, **1996** 840

Jones, Paula Corbin, sexual harassment suit, **1997** 21, 290–298

Jordan, Israel peace agreement, **1994** 329–335

Jordan, Barbara (D-Texas), immigration reform, **1995** 565

Jordan, Larry R., on extremists in the military, **1996** 179

Journal of the American Medical Association (JAMA)

end-of-life care report, **1997** 325–330

physical activity report, **1996** 420

Juppé, Alain, French government programs, **1995** 229–230

Jury selection, gender motivated peremptory challenges, **1994** 225–236

Justice Department

Bureau of Justice Statistics, use of guns in crime report, **1995** 463–471

Clinton secretary nomination, **1993** 135–139

curfews for juveniles, **1996** 325–333

FBI crime laboratory, Office of the Inspector General (OIG) investigations, **1997** 221–228

race-based redistricting, **1995** 369–372, 378–379

reports on violent crime, **1993** 375–378

violence against women report, **1994** 62–72

Waco incident report, **1993** 819–821, 829–840

Juvenile justice system

curfew ordinances, **1996** 325–333

Democratic Party platform, **1996** 635

Republican Party platform, **1996** 522–523

rise in juvenile crime, **1995** 711

violent crime, **1996** 733

K

Kabila, Laurent, Zaire coup and new Congo leader, **1997** 877, 879–885

Kallstrom, James, TWA flight 800 crash, **1997** 781, 783–786

Kalugin, Oleg, **1993** 114

Kanka, Megan, sex offender victim, **1997** 384

Kansas, Sexually Violent Predator Act, **1997** 382–394

Kansas City (Missouri), school uniform policy, **1996** 90

Kansas v. Hendricks, **1997** 382–394

Kantor, Mickey, commerce secretary appointment, **1996** 204

Long, Huey, **1993** 586

Lopez, Alfonso, Jr., **1995** 183

Lorillard Tobacco Company, claims settlement, **1997** 331

Los Angeles (California)
  earthquake, **1994** 3–7
  police department, sentencing of convicted officers, **1993** 631–651
  riots (1992), **1993** 213, 214

Lott, Trent (R-Miss.)
  104th Congress, closing remarks, **1996** 701–703
  balanced budget agreement, **1997** 604
  campaign finance reform, **1997** 31, 827
  chemical weapons treaty, **1996** 742, **1997** 196–197
  election as Senate majority leader, **1996** 271
  health care reform, **1997** 791
  Jiang Zemin state visit, **1997** 730
  limits on gifts to members of Congress, **1995** 701
  liquor advertising, **1996** 772
  television rating system, **1997** 529

Lovell v. Griffin, **1994** 296

Loving v. U.S., **1997** 296

Loving v. Virginia, **1995** 313

Lowery, Joseph E., at March on Washington thirtieth anniversary, **1993** 678–679

Lucid, Shannon W., space flight, **1996** 691–694

Lugar, Richard G. (R-Ind.)
  Agriculture Department reorganization, **1994** 404
  chemical weapons treaty, **1996** 741
  NATO expansion, **1997** 517
  nuclear materials in former Soviet states, **1996** 141

Lundberg, George D., gunshot wound treatment, **1993** 872

Lundgren v. Superior Court (Ct. App. 1996), **1997** 189

Lurie, Nicole, health care for women, **1993** 653–658

Luthuli, Albert, Nobel Peace Prize recipient, **1993** 877–878, 880–881, 883

Luzhkov, Yuri, **1993** 772

Lynch v. Donnelly, **1995** 399

Lynn, Joanne, end-of-life care, **1997** 327, 328–330

M

McAndrew, James, Roswell incident, **1997** 396–405

McCaffrey, Barry R.
  cocaine penalties, sentencing for, **1997** 246
  drug control programs, **1996** 617
  drug czar appointment, **1996** 30
  drug use among teenagers, **1996** 571–572

marijuana law enforcement, **1996** 756, **1997** 462

McCain, John (R-Ariz.)
  campaign finance investigations, **1996** 840
  campaign finance reform, **1997** 31, 33, 826–827
  Inman nomination, **1994** 24
  line-item veto, **1997** 611
  on presidential credibility abroad, **1995** 720
  Republican Party convention nomination speech, **1996** 479
  television rating system, **1997** 529
  on U.S.-Vietnam relations, **1995** 472–473
  Vietnam trade embargo, **1994** 97–98

McCarthy, Colman, on moral theology, **1993** 845

McCollum v. Bd. of Education, **1993** 406

McConnell, Mitch (R-Ky.), limits on gifts to members of Congress, **1995** 701

McCullough, David, U.S. Capitol bicentennial, **1993** 893, 895, 899

McCurdy, Dave (D-Okla.), on anti-Clinton sentiments, **1994** 610

McCurry, Michael D.
  on outreach events, **1997** 761
  security clearance reform, **1995** 532

McDermott, Jim (D-Wash.), single-payer health insurance, **1993** 784

McDonald, Brian, **1994** 241

McDonald's, smoking ban, **1994** 206

McDonnell Douglas Corp. v. Green, **1993** 424–427, 429–430

McDowell, Barbara, gun control laws, **1995** 185

McEntee, George, W., **1995** 681

McFarland v. Scott, **1994** 162

McFarlane, Robert C.
  Iran-contra affair, conviction, **1994** 12
  Iran-contra affair, role in, **1994** 11, 13, 14, 16
  "October Surprise" report, **1993** 11

McGhan Medical Corp., **1993** 369

McGinty, Kate, logging policy, **1993** 498

McGovern, George S. (D-S.D.) (1957–1961; 1963–1981), presidential campaign, **1994** 239

McGowan, Daniel, health care, **1997** 791

McGrath, Mary, **1993** 369

McGuinness, Jeffrey C., **1995** 130

McGuinness, Martin, **1994** 449

McHugh, James T., **1995** 145–146

McKay, David S., **1996** 472, 474–476

McKennon, Keith, **1993** 368–369

McKinney, Cynthia A. (D-Ga.), **1995** 370

McKinney, Gene C., **1997** 656–657

McLaughlin v. Florida, **1995** 313

McLaury, Bruce K., **1996** 785

McMillan, John L., and DC home rule charter, **1995** 497

McPeak, Gen. Merrill A., women in combat, **1993** 333–334

Mladic, Ratko, **1995** 718
Mobutu Sese Seko, ousted from Zaire, **1997** 877–879
Modjeski, Leland William, **1995** 256
Molinari, Susan (R-N.Y.)
  Republican Party convention keynote speech, **1996** 479
  welfare reform, **1996** 462
Molitoris, Jolene, on railroad safety regulations, **1996** 190
Monaghan, Henry P., on commerce clause, **1995** 185
Money laundering, asset forfeiture case, **1993** 431–438
Monsanto, jobs for welfare recipients, **1997** 34, 622
Montt, Efrain Rios, **1996** 851
Moore, Charles B., Roswell incident, **1997** 400
Morris, Dick, Clinton campaign strategist resignation, **1996** 601
Morris, Stephen J., **1993** 114
Morrison, Toni, Nobel Prize for Literature, **1993** 977–985
Mortality rates
  cancer deaths, **1996** 790–793
  in Eastern European nations, **1994** 425
  worldwide, **1996** 305–305
Moyer, Bruce, on government personnel cuts, **1993** 720
Moynihan, Daniel Patrick (D-N.Y.)
  government secrecy, **1997** 103–104
  health care costs, **1993** 783
  welfare reform, **1996** 452
Mozambique, UN role in, **1995** 355
Mubarak, Hosni
  eulogy for Yitzhak Rabin, **1995** 691, 694–695
  West Bank peace agreement, **1995** 622
Mueller v. Allen, **1993** 401–403, 406
Muhammad, Abdul-Rasheed, first army Muslim chaplain, **1993** 973–975
Mulligan, Deirdre K., medical records privacy, **1997** 582
Mundy, Carl E., Jr.
  chemical weapons, **1997** 201
  on women in combat, **1993** 334
Munford, Sarah W., **1993** 610
Murayama, Tomichi, apology for World War II suffering, **1995** 302–306
Murdoch, Rupert, **1995** 749–759
Murkowski, Frank H. (R-Alaska)
  global warming, **1997** 862
  Hanford cleanup, **1995** 114–115
Murphy, Austin J. (D-Pa.), Puerto Rican statehood, **1993** 949
Murray, James E. (D-Mont.), national health insurance, **1993** 782
Muslims, army's first Muslim chaplain, **1993** 973–975
Myers, Lewis, Jr., **1993** 580

N

NAACP. *See* National Association for the Advancement of Colored People
Nader, Ralph, on NAFTA, **1993** 955
NAFTA. *See* North American Free Trade Agreement
Nakajima, Hiroshi, on infectious diseases, **1996** 302
Namibia, UN role in, **1995** 355
Nandan, Satya, **1995** 524, 526–527
Nation of Islam, **1993** 580, 974, **1995** 453, 455, 646, 657
National Academy of Sciences (NAS). *See also* Institute of Medicine
  Hubble telescope, **1994** 458–462
  human radiation experiments, **1993** 988
National Adult Literacy Survey, **1993** 737–746
National Aeronautics and Space Administration (NASA)
  age of the universe estimates, **1996** 265–269
  Galileo mission to Jupiter's moons, **1997** 202–205
  Hubble space telescope, birth of stars, **1995** 288–293
  life on Mars, **1996** 471–477
  Pathfinder mission to Mars, **1997** 509–513
  radiation exposure experiments, **1993** 988
National Air and Space Museum, *Enola Gay* exhibit, **1995** 55–58
National Archives
  Holocaust victims, **1993** 310
  Supreme Court audiotapes, public use of, **1993** 935–937
National Association for the Advancement of Colored People (NAACP)
  Chavis address, **1993** 579–584
  church arson prevention, **1997** 311
  Evers assassination retrial, **1994** 100–106
  Evers-Williams address, **1995** 453–462
  on race-based redistricting, **1995** 372
National Association for the Advancement of Colored People (NAACP) v. Claiborne Hardware Co., **1994** 316, 317
National Association of Evangelicals, **1997** 311
National Bioethics Advisory Commission, cloning of humans moratorium, **1997** 213–214
National Board for Professional Teaching Standards, **1997** 35
National Cancer Institute (NCI)
  breast cancer report, **1993** 905–922
  cancer deaths declining, **1996** 790–793
  gay gene, existence of, **1993** 599–608
  mammogram controversy, **1997** 142–149
  nuclear testing fallout, **1997** 591–601
National Center for Children in Poverty, child care quality, **1994** 117–118

National Center for Education Statistics
(NCES), adult literacy report, **1993**
737–746
National Center for Missing and Exploited
Children, sex offenders, **1997** 384
National Center for Tobacco-Free Kids, **1997**
335
National Church Arson Task Force (NCATF),
report, **1997** 301–313
National Coalition Against Sexual Assault,
1993 386
National Commission on AIDS, final report,
1993 447–457
National Commission Responsibilities for
Financing Postsecondary Education,
restructuring college aid, **1993** 171–179
National Conference of Catholic Bishops
physician-assisted suicide, opposition to,
1996 124
sexually abusive priests, **1993** 407–409
National Council of Chain Restaurants,
smoking ban, **1994** 206
National Council of Churches
church arson prevention, **1997** 304, 306,
311
religious freedom, **1997** 408
National Crime Victimization Survey (NCVS)
analysis of results, **1994** 64–72
use of guns in crime, **1995** 463–471
National Declassification Center, **1997** 105,
108–109
National Defense Panel, national security
needs, **1997** 811–821
National Economic Council (NEC), **1997** 62
National Education Goals Panel, **1996** 106
National Endowment for the Arts (NEA),
future of nonprofit arts, **1997** 699–710
National Highway Traffic Safety
Administration (NHTSA)
aggressive driving, **1997** 550–561
automobile air bag regulations, **1996**
801–806, **1997** 774–779
General Motors truck safety, **1994**
443–448
National Household Survey on Drug Abuse
(NHSDA), **1996** 570–579
National Institute of Child Health and
Human Development, **1997** 425
National Institutes of Health (NIH)
acupuncture, panel on, **1997** 749–759
AIDS research, **1996** 156–166, **1997** 38, 83
end-of-life care research, **1997** 327, 330
*National Labor Relations Board v. Jones
& Laughlin Steel Corp.,* **1995** 188,
191–192
*National Labor Relations Board v. Mackay
Radio and Telegraph,* **1995** 129
National League of Cities (NLC), residential
signs, **1994** 290
National Longitudinal Study of Adolescent
Health, **1997** 424

National Organization for Women (NOW),
abortion protesters and RICO law, **1994**
26–33
*National Organization for Women v.
Joseph Scheidler et al.,* **1994** 26–33
National Park Service (NPS)
GAO report on deteriorating conditions,
1996 580–588
GAO testimony on management of, **1995**
120–128
new parks, **1996** 581
National Performance Review (NPR), report,
1993 695, 717–735, **1995** 75, 83–85
National Research Council (NRC)
carcinogens in the diet, **1996** 71–79
medical records security, **1997** 581
National Rifle Association (NRA)
assault weapon ban repeal efforts, **1995**
464–465
Brady Bill signing, **1993** 965–969
Bush resignation from, **1995** 208–215
crime bill, opposition to, **1994** 576
guns in the home study, **1993** 872–873
National School Boards Association, **1995**
341
National security
clearances of government employees,
1995 532–545
computer security threats, **1996** 312–324,
1997 111–112
declassifying government secrets, **1994**
524–527, **1997** 105, 108–109
Democratic Party platform, **1996** 641–644
Dole Republican convention speech on,
1996 493
in federal buildings, **1995** 178–179
government secrecy report, **1997**
103–112
infrastructure protection, **1997** 711–720
"leaking" of information, **1997** 106
National Defense Panel needs report,
1997 811–821
Pennsylvania Avenue closing, **1995**
254–258
Pentagon needs review, **1993** 695–715
Pentagon Papers case, **1997** 104, 105–106
U.S. nuclear strategy, **1997** 811, 814
"Verona" project, **1997** 104
National Security Act, **1997** 811
National Security Council (NSC), creation of,
1997 811
*National Socialist Party of America v.
Skokie,* **1995** 331
National Transportation Safety Board
(NTSB)
commuter airline safety recommendations,
1994 535–540
railroad safety recommendations, **1996**
189, 191
TWA flight 800 crash, **1997** 780–786
ValuJet crash, **1996** 238

Q

R

S

Jiang Zemin visit to, **1997** 730
volatility, **1997** 721–727, 834
Stockman, Steve, **1994** 514
Stoddard, Thomas B., on military homosexual ban, **1993** 154–155
Stolz, Richard, Ames espionage case, **1994** 488
Strategic Arms Reduction Treaty (START I), Ukrainian ratification requirement, **1993** 19–20, 714
Strategic Arms Reduction Treaty (START II)
analysis of text, **1993** 28–61
Bush statements, **1993** 20–23, 60–61
congressional actions on, **1995** 234, 236
Eagleburger letter of submittal, **1993** 23–27
and U.S. security needs, **1993** 714–715
U.S.-Russian pact, **1993** 17–61
Yeltsin statement, **1993** 59–60
Strategic Defense Initiative (SDI)
national security needs review, **1993** 697
Republican Party platform on, **1996** 541
Striking workers
on federal contracts, **1995** 129–133
steelworkers strike, **1997** 291
UPS strike, **1997** 628–635
Stringer, Howard, **1993** 487–488
Stromberg v. California, **1995** 331
Studds, Gerry E. (D-Mass.), **1995** 360
Student achievement, sports participation and, **1997** 168
Student aid
Clinton program, **1995** 82
Community Service Incentive Program, **1993** 177
Pell Grant program, **1993** 172, 176
restructuring of programs for, **1993** 171–179
Student's Total Education Package (STEP), **1993** 172, 175–176
tax-related incentives, **1993** 178–179
tuition tax credit proposal, **1997** 30, 36
Students
deaf parochial student, **1993** 399–406
random drug testing of, **1995** 339–349
religious publications, **1995** 385–395
Study to Understand Prognoses and Preferences for Outcomes and Risks of Treatment (SUPPORT), **1997** 329, 330
Sudan, religious persecution, **1997** 564
Sullivan, Gordon, on women in combat, **1993** 334
Sulmasy, Daniel P., end-of-life care, **1997** 327, 328–330
Summers, Lawrence, economic summit (Tokyo), **1993** 543
Summit conferences
Economic Summit (Tokyo), **1993** 541–557
European Security Summit, **1994** 583–591
Summit of the Americas, **1994** 595–601
Summit of the Americas, Declaration of Principles, **1994** 595–601

Superfund
Clinton reforms, **1994** 40
enactment of, **1995** 113
Supreme Court
abortion
clinic blockades, **1993** 93–112, **1994** 311–326
protesters and RICO law, **1994** 26–33
affirmative action, federal government plans, **1995** 307–326, 484–485
appointments, **1993** 391–398
asset forfeiture
drug trafficking, **1993** 431–438
pornography seized, **1993** 431, 432, 433–438
church and state, deaf parochial student, **1993** 399–406
congressional term limits, **1995** 259–275
death penalty
appeals by death row prisoners, **1993** 141–152
renunciation of, **1994** 161–171
drug testing of students, **1995** 339–349
endangered species on private lands, **1995** 359–368
free speech
on the Internet, **1997** 444–458
residential signs, **1994** 289–297
use of school facilities by religious groups, **1993** 363–370
gay rights, **1995** 327–335, **1996** 284–295
gun-free school zones, **1995** 183–200
hate crimes, racially motivated assault, **1993** 385–389
immigration act, Haitian refugees returned, **1993** 413–421
impeachment, Senate's authority to remove judge, **1993** 81–91
job discrimination, against African-American, **1993** 423–430
jury selection, **1994** 225–236
legislative intent, **1993** 249–258
liability, punitive damages, **1996** 274–283
liquor advertising, **1996** 771–772
patient-therapist privilege, **1996** 388–395
physician-assisted suicide, **1997** 459–479
presidential immunity, **1997** 290–298
property rights, developers and public land, **1994** 298–310
public use of audiotaped court cases, **1993** 935–937
race-based redistricting, **1993** 459–481, **1995** 369–384
racial gerrymandering, **1993** 459–481, **1996** 368–387
religious symbols and publications, **1995** 385–404
residential signs, **1995** 289–297
sex offenders, confining, **1997** 382–394
sexual harassment, in the workplace, **1993** 439–945